First Canadian Edition

business and society

Ethics and Stakeholder Management

Len Karakowsky
York University

Archie B. Carroll
University of Georgia

Ann K. Buchholtz
University of Georgia

THOMSON

NELSON

Australia   Canada   Mexico   Singapore   Spain   United Kingdom   United States

THOMSON

NELSON

**Business and Society: Ethics and
Stakeholder Management,
First Canadian Edition**

by Len Karakowsky, Archie B. Carroll,
and Ann K. Buchholtz

Editorial Director and Publisher:
Evelyn Veitch

Acquisitions Editor:
Anthony Rezek

Marketing Manager:
Don Thompson

Senior Developmental Editor:
Karina Hope

Permissions Coordinator:
Cynthia Howard

Senior Production Editor:
Bob Kohlmeier

Copy Editor:
Valerie Adams

Proofreader:
Wayne Herrington

Indexer:
Dennis A. Mills

Production Coordinators:
Renate McCloy, Kathrine Pummell

Creative Director:
Angela Cluer

Interior Design:
Rachel Sloat

Cover Design:
Rachel Sloat

Cover Image:
Ryan McVay/Photodisc Green/Getty
Images

Compositors:
Rachel Sloat, Carol Magee

Printer:
Transcontinental

**National Library of Canada
Cataloguing in Publication**

Karakowsky, Len
Business and society : ethics and
stakeholder management / Len
Karakowsky, Archie B. Carroll, and
Ann K. Buchholtz. — 1st Canadian
ed.

Includes bibliographical references
and indexes.
ISBN 0-17-641651-X

1. Business ethics. 2. Social
responsibility of business—Canada.
I. Carroll, Archie B. II. Buchholtz,
Ann K. III. Title.

HF5387.K37 2004   658.4'08
C2004-901124-3

Contents

Preface

There is much to be proud of with regard to our Canadian business environment. A recent report produced by the Economist Intelligence Unit (EIU) indicated that Canada is expected to be the best country in the world in which to conduct business in the coming years. The report included rankings among the world's 60 largest countries based on the quality or attractiveness of the business environment and its key components. In the report, Canada jumped three places from its ranking in the 1998–2002 study, to achieve the top position for the first time, ahead of the Netherlands. Finland, the United Kingdom, and the United States rounded out the top five. Canada earned particularly high scores in the quality of its infrastructure, its approach to foreign trade and capital, favourable market opportunities, and political environment.[1]

Canada is indeed poised to earn a distinguished reputation on the world scene. At the same time, it is important to consider how we can maintain and strengthen such a reputation. Perhaps central among the factors to consider is the manner in which we conduct business in this country—the integrity of our business environment. Unfortunately, we have witnessed that Canada, like any other country, is not immune to scandal and corruption. In recent years, both the private and public sectors have been forced to confront a host of misdeeds that speak to the issue of corporate governance, social responsibility, and business ethics. The challenge for Canadian business leaders is to ensure that, along with our industrial development, comes an equally well-developed sense of corporate ethics and social responsibility.

Business and Society: Ethics and Stakeholder Management, First Canadian Edition, employs a stakeholder management framework, emphasizing business's social and ethical responsibilities to both external and internal stakeholder groups. A managerial perspective is embedded within the book's dual themes of business ethics and stakeholder management. The ethics dimension is central because it is becoming increasingly clear that ethical or moral considerations are woven into the fabric of the public issues that organizations face. Economic and legal issues are inevitably present, too. However, these aspects are typically treated thoroughly in other business administration courses.

The stakeholder management perspective is essential because it requires managers to (1) identify the various groups or individuals who have stakes in the firm or its actions, decisions, and practices, and (2) incorporate the stakeholders' concerns into the firm's strategic plans and operations. Stakeholder management is an approach that increases the likelihood that decision makers will integrate ethical wisdom with management wisdom in all that they do.

1. Press Release, "Economist Intelligence Unit Ranks Canada as Best Place to Do Business" (July 17, 2003), http://store.eiu.com/index.asp?layout=pr_story&press_id=1020000702&ref=pr_list.

Course Description

This text is appropriate for college and university courses that are variously titled Business and Society; Business and Its Environment; Business and Public Policy; Social Issues in Business; Business, Government, and Society; Stakeholder Management; and Business Ethics. This book is appropriate for either an elective or a required course seeking to meet requirements for coverage of perspectives that form the context for business: ethical and global issues; the influence of political, social, legal and regulatory, environmental, and technological issues; and the impact of diversity on organizations. This book can be used in an equally effective manner at both the under-graduate and graduate level.

Course Objectives

Depending on the placement of a course in the curriculum or the individual instruc-tor's philosophy, this book could be used for a variety of objectives. The courses for which it is intended include several essential objectives, such as the following:

1. Students should be made aware of the demands that emanate from stakehold-ers and are placed on business firms.
2. As prospective managers, students need to understand appropriate business responses and management approaches for dealing with social, political, envi-ronmental, technological, and global issues and stakeholders.
3. Students should gain an appreciation of ethical issues and the influence these issues have on management decision making, behaviour, policies, and practices in the Canadian business context.
4. The broad question of business's legitimacy as an institution in a global society is at stake and must be addressed from both a business and societal perspective.
5. The increasing extent to which social, ethical, public, and global issues must be considered from a strategic perspective is critical in such courses.

Features of This Text

Current Coverage and Canadian Context

In addition to offering frameworks and principles central to the study of business ethics, we have endeavoured to provide an interesting and up-to-date presentation of relevant research, laws, and cases. We have also made every effort to infuse this text with "real life" illustrations. References are made to major ethics stories from across the globe. However, we are particularly interested in the Canadian context. Consequently, we also address Canadian stories and give ample attention to current Canadian business policies and practices for the topics covered throughout this book. The end-of-text cases are drawn from both Canadian and global contexts.

"Ethics in Practice" Feature

Interspersed throughout the text, these features present actual ethical situations or dilemmas faced personally in the work experiences of our former students. These were originally written for class discussion and are real-life situations actually confronted by college and university students in their part-time and full-time work experiences. The students contributed these experiences on a voluntary basis, and we are pleased they gave us permission to use them. We would like to acknowledge them for their contributions to the book. Instructors may wish to use these as mini cases for class discussion on a daily basis when a lengthier case is not assigned.

"Search the Web" Feature

The "Search the Web" boxes in each chapter highlight an important and relevant Web page or pages that augment each chapter's text material. The "Search the Web" feature may highlight a pertinent organization and its activities or special topics covered in the chapter. These features permit students to explore topics in depth. Most of the Web sites have links to other related sites. The use of search engines to find other relevant materials is encouraged as the Web now catalogues a wealth of information relevant to the text topics and cases.

Structure of the Book

Part 1 provides an introductory coverage of pertinent business and society topics and issues. Because most courses for which this book is intended evolved from the issue of corporate social responsibility, this concept is treated early on. Part 1 documents and discusses how corporate social responsiveness evolved from social responsibility and how these two matured into a concern for corporate social performance and corporate citizenship. Also given early coverage is the stakeholder management concept.

Part 2 addresses strategic management for stakeholder responsiveness. The purpose of this part is to discuss management considerations for dealing with the issues discussed throughout the text. A strategic management perspective is useful because these issues have impacts on the total organization and have become intense for many upper-level managers. Special treatment is given to corporate public policy, issues and crisis management, and public affairs management. Some instructors may elect to cover Part 2 later in their courses. Part 2 could easily be covered after Part 4 or 5. This option would be most appropriate for those using the book for a business ethics course or who desire to spend less time on the management perspective.

Part 3 contains four chapters dedicated to business ethics topics. In real life, business ethics cannot be separated from the full range of external and internal stakeholder concerns. Part 3 focuses on business ethics fundamentals, personal and organizational ethics, business ethics and technology, and ethical issues in the global arena.

External stakeholder issues are the subject of Part 4. Vital topics here include business's relations with government, consumers, the environment, and the community.

The theme of Part 5 is internal stakeholder issues. In this part, we consider workplace issues and the key themes of employee rights, employment discrimination, and employment equity. Owner stakeholders are also treated in Part 5. The topic of corporate governance captures most owner stakeholder concerns.

Case Studies

The cases placed at the end of the book address a wide range of topics and decision situations. The cases are of varying length. All the cases are intended to provide instructors and students with real-life contexts within which to further analyze course issues and topics covered throughout the book. The cases have intentionally been placed at the end of the text material so that instructors will feel freer to use them with any text material they desire.

Many of the cases in this book carry ramifications that spill over into several areas. Almost all of them may be used for different chapters. Preceding the cases is a set of guidelines for case analysis that the instructor may wish to use in place of or in addition to the questions that appear at the end of each case. The *Instructor's Manual with Test Bank* provides suggestions regarding which cases to use with each chapter.

Support for the Instructor

Instructor's Manual with Test Bank

The *Instructor's Manual with Test Bank* includes learning objectives, teaching suggestions, complete chapter outlines, highlighted key terms, answers to discussion questions, case notes, and supplemental cases. The test bank for each chapter includes true/false and multiple-choice questions.

A computerized version of the test bank is also available electronically. ExamView®Pro, an easy-to-use test-generating program, enables instructors to create printed tests, Internet tests, and online (LAN-based) tests quickly. Instructors can enter their own questions, using the software provided, and customize the appearance of the tests they create. The QuickTest wizard permits test generators to use an existing bank of questions to create a test in minutes, using a step-by-step selection process.

PowerPoint Slides

Prepared by Joseph Amodeo of Sheridan College, the PowerPoint presentation is colourful and varied, designed to hold students' interest and reinforce each chapter's main points. The PowerPoint presentation is only available on the Web site (**www.karakowsky.nelson.com**).

Web Site

A book Web site found at **www.karakowksy.nelson.com** offers test questions, links to organizations associated with the topic, and links to magazines and journals dealing with business ethics (all prepared by Mark Schwartz of Schulich School of Business at York University). Instructors can download resources, including the *Instructor's Manual with Test Bank* and PowerPoint presentation slides.

Acknowledgments

There are many people to acknowledge for their contributions to and support of this book. First, we would like to express gratitude to those individuals at Nelson who were responsible for making this book a reality. This text would not have been possible without the guidance and expertise offered by Anthony Rezek, Acquisitions Editor, and Karina Hope, Senior Developmental Editor. Anthony deserves much credit for recognizing the need for a Canadian text addressing issues of corporate ethics, responsibility, and governance—a text that had been largely absent from Canadian universities. Karina merits our deep gratitude for her dedicated attention to and rigorous work on this text. Thanks must also go to Bob Kohlmeier, Senior Production Editor; Valerie Adams, Copy Editor; Rachel Sloat, Designer and Compositor; Don Thompson, Marketing Manager; Wayne Herrington, Proofreader; Carol Magee, Compositor; Dennis Mills, Indexer; Cynthia Howard, Permissions Coordinator; and Renate McCloy and Kathrine Pummell, Production Coordinators, for their invaluable contributions.

We would also like to express gratitude to all of the authors of the cases that appear in this text. We are grateful, as well, to our students, who not only have provided comments on a regular basis but who have also offered accounts of ethical dilemmas, which are highlighted in the "Ethics in Practice" features that accompany many of the chapters.

We wish to thank our colleagues for their insights and suggestions, including Professors Diane Jurkowski, Joanne Magee, Louise Ripley, Mark Schwartz, and Gary Spraakman. Thanks go also to the following reviewers: Joseph Amodeo, Sheridan College; Dr. A. Scott Carson, Wilfrid Laurier University; Mary Runte, University of Lethbridge; Peter Seidl, British Columbia Institute of Technology; and Andrew Stark, University of Toronto. Our thanks also go to Rosenda Brown, Ruth Davis, Dana Myers, Mordechai Rothman, and Billie West, whose input and assistance were much appreciated.

Finally, we wish to express appreciation to our family members for their patience, understanding, and support. We dedicate this book to you.

Len Karakowsky
Archie B. Carroll
Ann K. Buchholtz

About the Authors

Len Karakowsky is an associate professor of management at York University. He earned his Ph.D. from the Joseph L. Rotman School of Management at the University of Toronto, his M.B.A. from the Schulich School of Business at York University, and his Bachelor of Commerce from the University of Toronto. He has served on the faculty of York University since 1997.

Professor Karakowsky's research has been published in the *Journal of Applied Psychology, Administration and Society, Journal of Management Studies, Group and Organization Management, Small Group Research, Journal of Management Systems, International Business Review*, and many other publications. He has authored and co-authored award-winning papers for academic conferences hosted by the Academy of Management as well as for the Administrative Sciences Association of Canada (ASAC). He is also the author of *The Nature of Management and Organizations: Challenges in the Canadian Context*, published by Captus Press.

Professor Karakowsky's teaching, research, and consulting interests are in organizational development, business and society, diversity in the workplace, business ethics, and human resource management. In 2003, he received the best paper award from the Organizational Behaviour division of ASAC for his research that addressed the issue of managing demographic diversity in organizations. His most recent research efforts focus on how organizations, teams, and leaders can establish and build a culture of trust among their work force. In 2002 and 2003, Dr. Karakowsky received the York University Merit Award for achievements in research, teaching, and service to the university.

Archie B. Carroll is professor of management and holder of the Robert W. Scherer Chair of Management and Corporate Public Affairs in the Terry College of Business at the University of Georgia. He has served on the faculty of the University of Georgia since 1972. Dr. Carroll received his three academic degrees from the Florida State University in Tallahassee.

Professor Carroll has published numerous books and articles. His research has appeared in the *Academy of Management Journal, Academy of Management Review, Business and Society, Journal of Business Ethics, Business Ethics Quarterly*, and many others.

His teaching, research, and consulting interests are in business and society, business ethics, corporate social performance, global stakeholder management, and strategic management. He is currently serving on the editorial review boards of *Business and Society, Business Ethics Quarterly*, and the *Journal of Public Affairs*. He is former division chair of the Social Issues in Management (SIM) Division of the Academy of

Management and a founding board member of the International Association for Business and Society (IABS). He is a Fellow of the Southern Management Association.

In 1992, Dr. Carroll was awarded the Sumner Marcus Award for Distinguished Service by the SIM Division of the Academy of Management; and in 1993, he was awarded the Terry College of Business, University of Georgia, Distinguished Research Award for his 20 years of work in corporate social performance, business ethics, and strategic planning. From 1995 to 2000, he served as chairman of the Department of Management at the University of Georgia. In 1998–1999, he served as president of the Society for Business Ethics. In 2000, he was appointed director of the Nonprofit Management and Community Service Program in the Terry College of Business.

Ann K. Buchholtz is an associate professor of strategic management in the Terry College of Business at the University of Georgia. She has served on the faculty of the University of Georgia since 1997. Dr. Buchholtz received her Ph.D. from the Leonard N. Stern School of Business at New York University.

Professor Buchholtz's teaching, research, and consulting interests are in business ethics, social issues, strategic management, and corporate governance. Her work has been published in *Business and Society, Business Ethics Quarterly, Academy of Management Journal, Academy of Management Review, Organization Science, Journal of Management, Business Horizons, Journal of General Management,* and *Human Resource Management Review.* She has served as a reviewer for the *Academy of Management Journal, Academy of Management Review, Journal of Management, Journal of Management Inquiry, Academy of Management Executive,* and numerous national and international conferences. She serves on the board of the Social Issues in Management (SIM) Division of the Academy of Management. Prior to entering academe, Dr. Buchholtz's work focused on the educational, vocational, and residential needs of individuals with disabilities. She has worked in a variety of organizations, in both managerial and consultative capacities, and has consulted with numerous public and private firms.

Part One

Business, Society, and Stakeholders

Chapter 1

The Business and Society Relationship

Chapter Objectives

After studying this chapter, you should be able to:

1 Characterize business and society and their interrelationships.

2 Describe pluralism and identify its strengths and weaknesses.

3 Clarify how our pluralistic society has become a special-interest society.

4 Identify and discuss the factors leading up to business criticism.

5 Identify the major criticisms of business and characterize business's general response.

6 Identify the major themes of the book: managerial approach, ethics, and stakeholder management.

For many years now, news stories have brought to the attention of the public countless social and ethical issues that have framed the business and society relationship. Because the news media have a flair for the dramatic, it is not surprising that the reporting of these issues has been highlighted by criticisms of various actions, decisions, and practices on the part of business management. However, the growing reports of corporate misconduct cannot be entirely blamed on the press. In fact, in very recent times we have witnessed an astounding flood of corporate scandals and crimes that can only be blamed on corrupt business practices, not on the dramatic flair of the news media. If recent years are any indication of the health of the business and society relationship, then there is cause for grave concern. For many observers, the rapidly expanding list of corporate wrongdoers has all but caused a breach in society's trust for business leaders.

Anyone who has attended to recent news reports understands that Canadian business is no less immune to corporate scandal and wrongdoing than any other business sector in the world. Consider the following examples:

- In 2004, Canadian media mogul Conrad Black was fired as chairman of Hollinger International Inc., which, in turn, controls Hollinger newspaper assets such as London's *Daily Telegraph* and Chicago's *Sun-Times*. A US$200 million lawsuit directed at Black alleged that he was responsible for altering the company's financial records, and for diverting company funds to himself, to an associate, and to other companies that he controlled.[1]
- In 2002, Canada earned the distinction of being home to a company that became the first multinational corporation to be fined ($2.2 million) for bribing a government official involved in a World Bank–funded dam project designed to provide water to South Africa. Acres International, an Ontario-based engineering firm, was found guilty of paying a bribe of $266 000 to the former chief executive of the Lesotho Highlands Water Project in Africa as a means to obtain a $21.5 million technical assistance contract for a multi-dam construction program.
- The Montreal family-entertainment company, Cinar, paid a total of $25 million in lawsuits stemming from fraudulent business ventures in 2002.
- That same year, following a four-year investigation, the RCMP filed criminal charges against four former executives of Livent Inc., a well-known Toronto-based theatre-production company. The charges allege that the executives falsified accounting records and defrauded investors of approximately $500 million during the 1990s.
- In 2003, the Ontario Securities Commission passed down a series of fines and penalties on the former directors of the Canadian YBM Magnex International Inc. for a number of corporate misdeeds involving financial reporting. YBM Magnex had collapsed in 1998 with allegations that it had served as a front for the Russian mafia.
- In 2004, a managing director of equity investments at the CIBC unit Canadian Imperial Holdings Inc. was arrested and charged in an investigation into illegal U.S. mutual fund trading.
- In 2004, the Canadian government, together with a number of Canadian businesses, faced charges of corruption stemming from a government advertising and corporate sponsorship program managed by the federal Public Works Department. The federal auditor general's report indicated that $100 million was paid to a number of communications agencies in the form of fees and com-

missions, and the program was essentially designed to generate commissions for these companies rather than to produce any benefit for Canadians.

- In 2003, the Canadian Imperial Bank of Commerce agreed to pay a penalty of US$80 million to settle charges of aiding and abetting the Enron Corporation's accounting fraud.
- Finally, though a little further back in time, many Canadians still recall the Bre-X fiasco. The Calgary-based Bre-X Minerals Ltd. met its demise in 1997 after perpetrating the biggest gold-mining fraud in history. The illusion of a huge gold deposit was created by placing foreign gold in rock samples in the company's mine in Indonesia.

While many have grown accustomed to reading reports that highlight criticisms of the actions, decisions, and practices on the part of business management, no one was prepared for the onslaught of business scandals that we came to read about in recent years. Among the biggest headline grabbers was Enron—an organization that, in 15 years, grew from being an obscure entity to the seventh largest company in the United States. Sadly, Enron's success was largely the product of an elaborate scam of falsely reported profits and debts perpetrated by Enron management and its auditor, public accounting firm Arthur Andersen. Ultimately, this led to Enron's collapse in 2001 and the subsequent demise of Arthur Andersen. It appears that the Enron disaster heralded the arrival of a massive list of subsequent corporate misdeeds.

In 2001, WorldCom, the second-largest long-distance telephone company in the U.S., went into bankruptcy as a result of corporate corruption. WorldCom's chief executive Bernard J. Ebbers was among the participants of WorldCom's fraudulent activities, including falsely reporting the company's revenues in order to meet shareholder expectations. This fraud and the consequent bankruptcy, the largest in U.S. history, ultimately cost shareholders US$180 billion as a result of the drop in the stock's value.

Numerous other companies worldwide have recently been exposed for falsely reporting their financial status, including such well-known U.S. players as Tyco International, Conseco, Adelphia Cable, Global Crossing, Xerox, and HealthSouth. Elsewhere, recent allegations of fraudulent activities have been levelled at the Dutch food distributor and retailer Royal Ahold, France's Vivendi, Britain's Marconi, SK Corp. in South Korea, and Tokyo Electric Power in Japan.

In addition to these specific incidents of corporate wrongdoing, many common issues that carry social or ethical implications have arisen within the relationship between business and society. Some of these general issues have included corporate abuse of the environment, sweatshop conditions employed by multinational corporations, sexual harassment in the workplace, corporate power, toxic waste disposal, minority rights, drug testing, insider trading, whistle-blowing, product liability crises, and the use of political action committees by business to influence the outcome of legislation. Other ongoing issues include business's alleged lack of concern for the welfare of consumers, which is reflected in the growing criticism of fast-food companies that encourage the consumption of unhealthy products and lawsuits against the tobacco industry for manufacturing and marketing an inherently dangerous product. Questions continue to be raised about the safety of many products. The litany of such issues could go on and on, but these examples illustrate the continuing tensions between business and society.

These samples of both specific corporate incidents and general issues typify the kinds of stories about business and society that one finds today in newspapers, magazines, and on television. We offer these issues as illustrations of the widespread interactions between business and society that capture the headlines almost daily. Most of these corporate episodes are situations in which the public or some segment of the public believes that a firm has done wrong or treated some individual or group unfairly. In some cases, major laws have been broken. In virtually all of these episodes, questions of whether or not business firms have behaved properly have arisen—whether they have been socially responsible or ethical. Ethical questions are typically present in these kinds of situations. In today's socially aware environment, a business firm frequently finds itself on the defensive—that is, it finds itself being criticized for some action it has taken or failed to take. For example, the spate of corporate accounting scandals has put much greater onus on firms to report their financial status in a fair and accurate manner.

At a general level, we are discussing the role of business in society. Many debates on this issue have taken place. In this book we will address some of these concerns—the role of business versus government in our socioeconomic system, what a firm must do to be considered socially responsible, and what managers must do to be considered ethical. The issues we mentioned earlier are anything but abstract. They require immediate attention and definite courses of action, which quite often become the next subject of debate on the roles and responsibilities of business in society. Many economic, legal, ethical, and technological questions and issues about business and society are under debate. This period is turbulent in the sense that it has been characterized by significant changes in the economy, in society, in technology, and in global relationships. Against this continuing turbulence in the business/society relationship, we want to set forth and discuss some ideas that are fundamental to an understanding of where we are and how we got here.

Business and Society

This chapter will discuss some basic concepts that are important in the continuing business/society discussion. Among these concepts are pluralism, our special-interest society, business criticism, corporate power, and corporate social response. But let us first define and explain two key terms: business and society.

Business: Defined

Business may be defined as the collection of private, commercially oriented (profit-oriented) organizations, ranging in size from one-person proprietorships (such as Benny K's Surplus Store) to corporate giants (such as Nortel, Bombardier, Coca-Cola, and Canadian Tire). Between these extremes, of course, are many medium-sized proprietorships, partnerships, and corporations.

When we discuss business in this collective sense, we refer to businesses of all sizes and in all types of industries. But as we embark on our discussion of business and society, we will, for a variety of reasons, doubtless find ourselves speaking more of big business in selected industries. Why? For one thing, big business is highly visible. Its products and advertising are more widely known. Consequently, big business is more frequently in the critical public eye. In addition, people in our society often associate size with power, and the powerful are given closer scrutiny. Although it is well known that small businesses in our society far outnumber large ones, the impact, pervasiveness, power, and visibility of large firms keep them on the front page much more of the time.

With respect to different industries, some are simply more conducive to the creation of visible, controversial social problems than are others. For example, many manufacturing firms by their nature cause air and water pollution. Such firms, therefore, are more likely to be subject to criticism than a life insurance company, which emits no obvious pollution. The auto industry is a particular case in point. Much of the criticism against General Motors (GM) and the other automakers is raised because of their high visibility as manufacturers, the products they make (which are the largest single source of air pollution), and the popularity of their products (nearly every family owns one or more cars). In the case of the auto industry, we have not yet worked out an ideal solution to the product-disposal problem, so we see unsightly remnants of metal and plastic on many roadsides.

Some industries are highly visible because of the advertising-intensive nature of their products (e.g., Johnson & Johnson, Sony, Wal-Mart). Other industries (e.g., the cigarette, toy, and food products industries) are scrutinized because of the possible effects of their products on health or because of their roles in providing health-related products (such as pharmaceutical firms).

When we refer to business in its relationship with society, therefore, we may focus our attention too much on large businesses in particular industries. But we should not lose sight of the fact that small and medium-sized companies also are important. In fact, over the past decade, problems have arisen for small businesses because they have been subjected to many of the same regulations and demands as those imposed by government on large organizations. In many instances, however, smaller businesses do not have the resources to meet the requirements for increased accountability on many of the social fronts that we will discuss.

Society: Defined

Society may be defined as a community, a nation, or a broad grouping of people having common traditions, values, institutions, and collective activities and interests. As such, when we speak of business/society relationships, we may in fact mean business and the local community, business and Canada as a whole, or business and a specific group of people (consumers, minorities, shareholders).

When we refer to business and the entire society, we think of society as being composed of numerous interest groups, more or less formalized organizations, and a variety of institutions. Each of these groups, organizations, and institutions is a purposeful aggregation of people who have banded together because they represent a common cause or share a set of common beliefs about a particular issue. Examples of interest groups or purposeful organizations are numerous: Canadian Business for Social Responsibility, Ethics Practitioners Association of Canada, Canadian Chamber of Commerce, Friends of the Earth, People for the Ethical Treatment of Animals, and Consumers' Association of Canada.

Society as the Macroenvironment

The environment is a key concept in understanding business/society relationships. At its broadest level, the environment might be thought of in terms of a **macroenvironment**, which includes the total environment outside the firm. The macroenvironment is the total societal context in which the organization resides. In a sense, the idea of the macroenvironment is just another way of thinking about society. In fact, early courses on business and society in business schools were sometimes (and some still are) entitled "Business and Its Environment." The concept of the macroenvironment, however, evokes different images or ways of thinking about business/society relationships and is therefore useful in terms of framing or understanding the total business context.

The view of the macroenvironment as developed by Fahey and Narayanan is useful for our purposes. They see the macroenvironment as being composed of four segments: social, economic, political, and technological.[2]

The **social environment**, as one component, focuses on demographics, lifestyles, and social values of the society. Of particular interest here is the manner in which shifts in these factors affect the organization and its functioning. The **economic environment** focuses on the nature and direction of the economy in which business operates. Variables of interest might include such indices as gross national product, inflation, interest rates, unemployment rates, foreign-exchange fluctuations, global trade, and various other aspects of economic activity. In the past decade, the global economy has dominated the economic segment of the environment.

The **political environment** focuses on the processes by which laws get passed and officials get elected and all other aspects of the interaction between the firm, political processes, and government. Of particular interest to business in this segment are the regulatory process and the changes that occur over time in business regulation of various industries and various issues. Finally, the **technological environment** represents the total set of technology-based advancements or progress taking place in society. Pertinent aspects of this segment include new products, processes, and materials, as well as the states of knowledge and scientific advancement in both theoretical and applied senses. The process of technological change is of special importance here.[3] In recent years, computer technology has been driving this segment of environmental turbulence.

Thinking of business/society relationships in terms of a macroenvironment provides us with a different but useful way of understanding the kinds of issues that constitute the broad milieu in which business functions. Throughout this book we will see evidence of these environmental segments in a state of turbulence and will come to appreciate what challenges managers face as they strive to develop effective organizations. Each of the many specific groups and organizations that make up our pluralistic society can typically be traced to one of these four environmental segments; therefore, it is helpful to appreciate at a conceptual level what these segments are.

Our Pluralistic Society

Our society's pluralistic nature makes for business/society relationships that are more interesting and novel than those in some other societies. **Pluralism** is a condition in which there is diffusion of power among the society's many groups and organizations. Joseph W. McGuire's straightforward definition of a pluralistic society is useful for our purposes: "A pluralistic society is one in which there is wide decentralization and diversity of power concentration."[4]

The key descriptive terms in this definition are *decentralization* and *diversity*. In other words, power is dispersed. Power is not in the hands of any single institution (such as business, government, labour, or the military) or a small number of groups. Some of the virtues of a pluralistic society are summarized in Figure 1–1.

FIGURE 1–1

The Virtues of a Pluralistic Society

- Prevents power from being concentrated in the hands of a few.
- Maximizes freedom of expression and action and strikes a balance between *monism* (social organization into one institution) on the one hand and *anarchy* (social organization into an infinite number of persons) on the other.[a]
- Is one in which the allegiance of individuals to groups is dispersed.
- Creates a widely diversified set of loyalties to many organizations and minimizes the danger that a leader of any one organization will be left uncontrolled.[b]
- Provides a built-in set of checks and balances, in that groups can exert power over one another with no single organization (business, government) dominating and becoming overly influential.

Sources: [a]Keith Davis and Robert L. Blomstrom, *Business and Society: Environment and Responsibility*, 3d ed. (New York: McGraw-Hill, 1975), 63. [b]Joseph W. McGuire, *Business and Society* (New York: McGraw-Hill, 1963), 132.

Strengths and Weaknesses of Pluralism

All social systems have strengths and weaknesses, and pluralism is no exception. A pluralistic society prevents power from being concentrated in the hands of a few. It also maximizes freedom of expression and action. Pluralism provides for a built-in set of checks and balances so that no single group dominates. By contrast, a weakness in a pluralistic system is that it creates an environment in which the diverse institutions pursue their own self-interests, with the result that there is no central direction to unify individual pursuits. Another weakness is that groups and institutions proliferate to the extent that their goals tend to overlap, thus causing confusion as to which organizations best serve which functions. Pluralism forces conflict onto centre stage because of its emphasis on autonomous groups, each pursuing its own objectives. In light of these concerns, a pluralistic system does not appear to be very efficient.

History and experience have demonstrated, however, that the merits of pluralism are considerable and that most people in our society prefer the situation that has resulted from it. Indeed, pluralism has worked to achieve equilibrium in the balance of power of the dominant institutions that constitute our way of life.

Business and Multiple Publics, Systems, and Stakeholders

Knowing that society is composed of so many different semiautonomous and autonomous groups might cause one to question whether we can realistically speak of society in a broad sense that has any generally agreed-upon meaning. Nevertheless, we do speak in such terms, knowing that, unless we specify a particular societal subgroup or subsystem, we are referring to all those persons, groups, and institutions that constitute our society. This situation raises an important point: When we speak of business/society relationships, we usually refer either to particular segments or subgroups of society (consumerists, women, minorities, environmentalists, youth) or to business and some system in our society (politics, law, custom, religion, economics). These groups of people or systems may also be referred to in an institutional form (business and the courts, business and consumers, business and labour, business and the government regulators).

Figure 1–2 displays in graphic form the points of interface between business and some of these multiple publics, systems, or stakeholders, with which business has social relationships. Stakeholders are those groups or individuals with whom an

FIGURE 1–2

Business and Selected Stakeholder Relationships

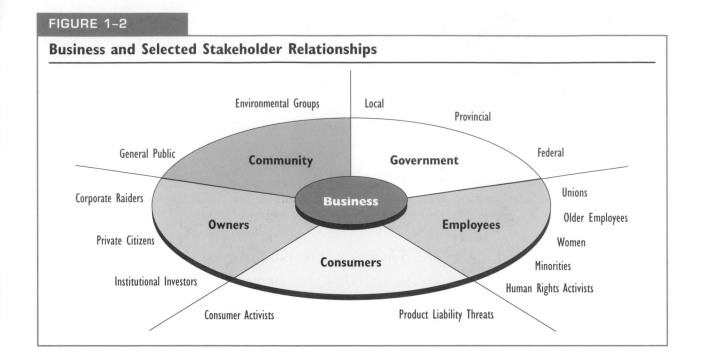

organization interacts or has interdependencies. We will develop the stakeholder concept further in Chapter 3. Note that each of the stakeholder groups may be further subdivided into more specific subgroups.

If sheer numbers of relationships are an indicator of complexity, we could easily argue that business's current relationships with different segments of society constitute a truly complex environment. If we had the capacity to draw a diagram similar to Figure 1–2 that noted all the detail composing each of those points of interface, it would be too overwhelming to comprehend. Today, business managers cannot sidestep this problem, because management must live with these interfaces on a daily basis.

Our Special-Interest Society

One could well argue that our pluralistic society has become a **special-interest society**. That is, we have carried the idea of pluralism to an extreme in which we have literally tens of thousands of special-interest groups, each pursuing its own limited agenda. General-purpose interest organizations, such as Democracy Watch and the Council of Canadians, still exist. However, the past two decades have been characterized by increasing specialization on the part of interest groups representing all sectors of society—consumers, employees, communities, the natural environment, government, and business itself. Special-interest groups not only have grown in number at an accelerated pace but also have become increasingly activist, intense, diverse, and focused on single issues. Such groups are increasingly committed to their causes.

The consequence of such specialization is that each of these groups has been able to attract a significant following that is dedicated to the group's goals. Increased memberships have meant increased revenues and a sharper focus as each of these groups has aggressively sought its narrow purposes. The likelihood of these groups working

Search the web www

Special-Interest Groups

One of the most interesting and demanding pressures on the business/society relationship is that exerted by special-interest groups. Many of these groups focus on specific topics. For example, the Canadian Community Reinvestment Coalition (**http://www.cancrc.org/**) is a coalition of over 100 anti-poverty, consumer, community economic development, labour, and small business groups representing over 3 million people across the country that advocates for bank accountability in Canada. For a sampling of other special-interest groups, you can check out Hillwatch.com, "The Web Advocacy Portal" (at **http://www.hillwatch.com/lobbylist/LobbyHome.htm**). Some of these notable organizations include:

- The Council of Canadians—A citizens' watchdog organization, composed of over 100 000 members and more than 70 chapters across the country. The Council lobbies Members of Parliament, conducts research, and runs national campaigns on issues including safeguarding our social programs, promoting economic justice, asserting Canadian sovereignty, and preserving the environment.

- Greenpeace Canada—An independently funded organization that works to protect the environment. They have confronted government and industry to halt harmful practices by negotiating solutions, conducting scientific research, and introducing clean alternatives.

- The Aboriginal Rights Coalition—A national organization formed via a partnership of community and social justice groups, churches, and First Nations. The Coalition is primarily concerned with achieving just solutions, preferably by negotiations to unresolved Aboriginal issues in Canada.

- Canadian Federation of Humane Societies—This group is focused on attempting to end the suffering of animals by working with the public, government, industry, the scientific community, educators, and the media on both the national and local levels toward this goal.

- MediaWatch—A national feminist organization dedicated to eliminating sexist and offensive portrayals of women and children in the media.

(continued)

at cross-purposes and with no unified set of goals has made life immensely more complex for the major institutions, such as business, that have to deal with them.

Business Criticism and Corporate Response

It is inevitable in a pluralistic, special-interest society that the major institutions that make up that society, such as business and government, will become the subjects of considerable criticism. Our purpose here is not so much to focus on the negative as to illustrate how the process of business criticism has shaped the major issues in the evolution of the business/society relationship today. Were it not for the fact that individuals and groups have been critical of business, we would not be dealing with this subject in a book or a course, and few changes would occur in the business/society relationship over time. But such changes have taken place, and it is helpful to see the role that business criticism has assumed. The concept of business response to criticism will be developed more completely in Chapter 2, where we present the complete business criticism/response cycle.

Figure 1–3 illustrates how certain factors that have arisen in the social environment have created an atmosphere in which business criticism has taken place and flourished. In this chapter, we see response on the part of business as entailing an increased concern for the social environment and a changed social contract (relationship) between business and society. Each of these factors merits special consideration.

Factors in the Social Environment

Many factors in the social environment have created a climate in which criticism of business has taken place and flourished. Some of these factors occur relatively independently, but some are interrelated with others. In other words, they occur and grow hand in hand.

Societal Beliefs Regarding Success in Business

The notion of business ethics has typically been viewed as an oxymoron. That is, many people believe that success in business cannot be achieved without bending if not breaking the rules. Certainly the recent spate of corporate scandals has reinforced this cynical view of business behaviour. The "profit-oriented" motive of business appears to run counter to any concern for societal values. Our disdain for business and our perception of the

(continued from page 11)

- The David Suzuki Foundation—An organization that is committed to promoting and revealing methods for society to better live in balance with nature. It supports the implementation of ecologically sustainable models—from habitat restoration to better frameworks for economic decisions. It seeks to educate business and society as a means to mobilize change efforts.

"greedy businessman" continues to be reinforced with every media report of the latest corporate scandal.

Even in the absence of reported corporate corruption, there is a pervasive belief that "material success" is typically derived from dishonesty of some kind. This almost-innate belief is evident in the media's depiction of "success" and how it is achieved. While TV's impact is discussed in more detail below, it is interesting to note the message we communicate about "success" from the stories that we tell on TV. For example, in recent years, television viewers witnessed a proliferation of so-called "reality" television shows with such names as *Survivor*, *The Mole*, *The Bachelor*, *Joe Millionaire*, and so on. Common among these shows is some kind of competition occurring among a group of individuals. What is interesting is the common thread that runs through these programs. All of them suggest that in order to succeed, you need to engage in some form of dishonesty, manipulation, or backstabbing. North American media has been feeding an audience appetite for programs that involve some form of deceit or treachery. This allegedly makes for good TV viewing. Moreover, perhaps it speaks to an implicit notion that we hold regarding success in North America—that to "get ahead," you need to step on other people. This belief reinforces our view of business—the only successful business-people are dishonest ones.

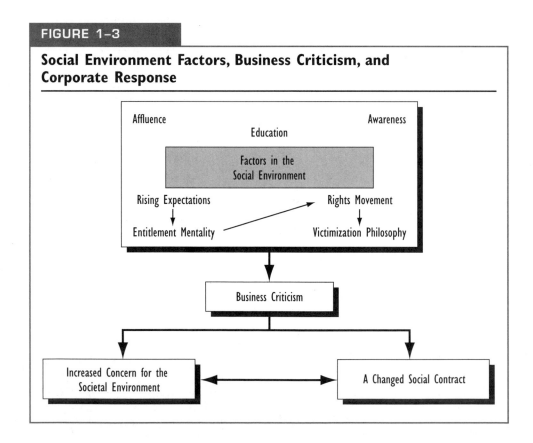

FIGURE 1–3

Social Environment Factors, Business Criticism, and Corporate Response

Affluence and Education   Two factors that have developed side by side are affluence and education. As a society becomes more affluent and better educated, higher expectations of its major institutions, such as business, naturally follow.

Affluence refers to the level of wealth, disposable income, and standard of living of the society. According to the Bank of Canada (http://www.bankofcanada.ca), a country's standard of living typically refers to the individual well-being of its citizens. In theory, our standard of living should reflect both economic welfare and social ("quality of life") elements (e.g., a clean environment, a low crime rate, etc). However, because the social elements are difficult to quantify, the focus is usually on measures of our *economic* well-being such as affluence.

The *Human Development Report 2003* published by the U.N. development program ranked Canada as the eighth best country in which to live. Canada was ranked third in the 2002 report, and was number one for eight years before that. As of 2003, Canada was ranked below Norway, Iceland, Sweden, Australia, the Netherlands, Belgium, and the United States, but just ahead of Japan and Switzerland. The index is based on life expectancy, education, health, income, poverty, and the environment.[5]

Over the years, alongside an increased standard of living has been a growth in the average formal **education** of the populace. The combination of affluence and education forms the underpinning for a climate in which societal criticism of major institutions, such as business, naturally arises. We are no longer mere servants to business, but intelligent critics who expect more than simply fulfilling our service to organizations and acting as passive recipients of the products that business churns out.

Awareness Through the Media   Closely related to formal education is the high and growing level of public awareness in our society. Although newspapers and magazines are still read by only a fraction of our population, a more powerful medium—television—is accessed by virtually our entire society. Through television, the citizenry gets a variety of information that contributes to a climate of business criticism.

First, let us establish the prevalence and power of TV. Several statistics document the extent to which our society is dependent on TV for information. According to data compiled by the A. C. Nielsen Company, the average daily time spent viewing television per household in 1950 was four-and-a-half hours. By 2001, Nielsen reports this figure grew to over seven-and-a-half hours. As one writer put it: "Think about it. A typical day ... now divides into three nearly equal parts: eight hours of sleep, seven hours of TV, and nine hours of work or school, including getting there and back."[6]

Straight News and Investigative News Programs.   There are at least three ways in which information that leads to criticism of business appears on television. First, there are straight news shows, such as the evening news on the major networks, and investigative news programs. It is debatable whether or not the major news programs are treating business fairly, but in one major study, an overwhelming 73 percent of the business executives surveyed indicated that business and financial coverage on TV news was prejudiced against business. TV pollster Lou Harris suggests that TV news has to deal with subjects too briefly and that, whenever a company makes the evening news, it is usually because the story is unfavourable.[7]

In another major study, chief executive officers of companies of all sizes reported overwhelmingly that newspapers and magazines report business and economic news with a negative bias. Of the total number of CEOs surveyed, 19 percent thought such coverage was very negative, 46 percent thought it was negative, 27 percent thought it was neutral, and only 7 percent thought it was positive.[8] This negativism in reporting both business news and political news led James Fallows to write a book titled *Breaking the News: How the Media Undermine American Democracy*. Fallows skewers what media writer Howard Kurtz calls "drive-by journalism," which tends to take down all institutions in its sights.[9] Fallows goes on to argue that the media favour sizzle over substance and that they have a mindless fixation on conflict rather than truth.

Although many business leaders believe that the news media are out to get them by exaggerating the facts and overplaying the issues, journalists see it differently. They counter that business executives try to avoid them, are evasive when questioned about major issues, and try to downplay problems that might reflect negatively on their companies. The consequence is an adversarial relationship that perhaps helps to explain some of the unfavourable coverage.

Business has to deal not only with the problems of straight news coverage but also with a growing number of investigative news programs, such as *Marketplace*, *The Fifth Estate*, *W-Five*, *60 Minutes*, *20/20*, *Dateline NBC*, and *Primetime Live*, that seem to thrive on exposés of business wrongdoings or questionable practices. These shows are enormously popular and influential, and many companies squirm when reporters show up on their premises complete with camera crews. Whether the targeted businesses indeed deserve to be exposed on national television is not the issue. In fact, such public displays of business corruption may actually be a public service. However, this does not change the fact that such news stories can certainly reflect poorly on the ethics of all related businesses.

Prime-Time Television Programs. The second way in which criticisms of business appear on TV is through prime-time television programs. Any redeeming social values that business and businesspeople may have rarely show up on prime-time television. Rather, businesspeople are cast as evil and greedy social parasites whose efforts to get more for themselves are justly condemned and usually thwarted.[10] There are many views as to why this portrayal has occurred. Some would argue that business is being characterized accurately. Others say that the television writers are dissatisfied with the direction our nation has taken and believe they have an important role in reforming society.[11]

When Hollywood is not depicting business in a bad light on TV, it may be doing it through the movies. Certainly, real-life cases of business corruption have made for rich fodder for movie scripts, including *A Civil Action* (1998), *The Insider* (1999), and *Erin Brockovich* (2000). Where such corrupt businesses do not take centre stage in the film, they typically make great cameos as the villain. Such action films as the James Bond series, including *Die Another Day* (2002), typically cast villains that are equal parts megalomaniac and savvy businessman. Other movies portray the hero seeking to save the world from "old-fashioned" business greed.[12]

Commercials. A third way in which television contributes to business criticism is through commercials. This may be business's own fault. To the extent that business does not honestly and fairly portray its products on TV, it undercuts its own credibility. Commercials are a double-edged sword. On the one hand, they may sell more products in the short run. On the other hand, they could damage business's long-term credibility if they promote products deceptively.

One major study hints at how this occurs. In an investigation of how television commercials were viewed by children, Harvard Business School researchers found considerable skepticism, tension, and anger among children because of misleading advertising. By age 11, the study concluded, "Most children have already become cynical—ready to believe that like advertising, business and other institutions are riddled with hypocrisy." About three-fourths of the 11- and 12-year-olds studied thought that advertising was sometimes designed to "trick" the consumer.[13]

Thus, we see three specific settings—news coverage, prime-time programming, and commercials—in which a strained environment is being created and fostered by this "awareness" factor made available through the power and pervasiveness of television. We should make it clear that the media are not to blame for business's problems. If it were not for the fact that the behaviour of some businesses is questionable, the media would not be able to create this kind of environment. The media, therefore, should be seen as only one major factor that contributes to the environment in which business now finds itself.

Revolution of Rising Expectations In addition to affluence, formal education, and awareness through television, there are other societal developments that have fostered the climate in which business criticism has occurred. Growing out of these factors has been a **revolution of rising expectations**. This might be defined as an attitude or a belief that each succeeding generation ought to have a standard of living higher than that of its predecessor and that its expectations of major institutions, such as business, should be greater also. Building on this line of thinking, one could argue that business is criticized today because society's expectations of its performance have outpaced business's ability to meet these growing expectations. To the extent that this has occurred over the past 20 to 30 years, business finds itself with a larger problem.[14]

A **social problem** has been described as a gap between society's expectations of social conditions and the present social realities.[15] From the viewpoint of a business firm, the social problem is the gap between society's expectations of the firm's social performance and its actual social performance. The nature of rising expectations is such that they typically outpace the responsiveness of institutions such as business, thus creating a constant predicament in that it is conducive to criticism. Figure 1–4 illustrates the larger "social problem" that business faces today.

Although the general trend of rising expectations continues, the revolution moderates at times when the economy is not as robust. Job situations, health, family lives,

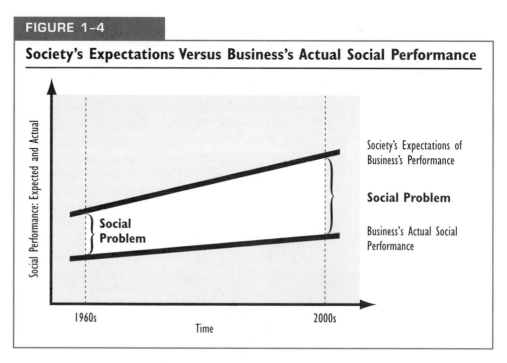

FIGURE 1–4

Society's Expectations Versus Business's Actual Social Performance

and overall quality of life continue to rise. The emergence or exacerbation of social problems such as crime, poverty, homelessness, environmental pollution, alcohol and drug abuse, and terrorism are always there to moderate rising expectations.[16]

Entitlement Mentality   One outgrowth of the revolution of rising expectations has been what has been called an **entitlement mentality**. Several years ago, the Public Relations Society conducted a study of public expectations, with particular focus on public attitudes toward the philosophy of entitlement. This philosophy is the general belief that someone is owed something (e.g., a job) just because she or he is a member of society. Respondents were asked to categorize items they thought people (1) were entitled to have and (2) have now. A significant gap existed between what people thought they were entitled to have and what they had—a steadily improving standard of living, a guaranteed job for all those willing and able to work, and products certified as safe and not hazardous to one's health.[17]

The current context of the workplace has contributed to making the issue of entitlement more salient. For example, while investigating why workers are absent from

Ethics In Practice

Drink Specials?

While working as a waitress in a busy restaurant/bar, I observed a practice that was very common but appeared questionable. Often, in busy places of business, it is all too easy for employees to bend the rules and get away with it. Managers have so much on their hands that they have to trust their employees and, sadly, not everyone is trustworthy. In our restaurant, servers and bartenders were given a daily "spill sheet" on which they were supposed to record any alcoholic (and, especially, expensive) drinks that were accidentally spilled in the course of business that day.

When an employee is moving fast and dodging customers, spills are a natural occurrence and the "spill sheet" was meant to take those accidents into account for the restaurant. When I began working there, I realized that at the end of the night not all of the spills on the list were genuine. Employees, typically bartenders because they had direct access, would serve free drinks to their friends all night and put the drinks on the spill sheet.

To accommodate large numbers of missing drinks, bartenders would serve their friends the same kind of beer all night and then claim a dropped case of that brand of beer. They could also claim a dropped liquor bottle and have enough to keep alcohol flowing for their friends. Other employees would also take responsibility for some of the spills to make the bartenders appear credible.

I was asked on several occasions to take responsibility for a fake "spill." In this way, employees used the spill sheet to their advantage instead of for its intended purpose. They would serve free drinks courtesy of "spilling" until the volume reached was just under the suspicious level. As long as a pattern was not formed, the managers never knew they were being deceived.

1. What type of ethical standards, if any, were the employees in the restaurant living by when they committed this common but questionable action? Is the "entitlement mentality" at work here?

2. If you were an employee and you saw this situation, would you feel it should be reported or would you keep your mouth shut and let the practice continue? If you were asked to participate and take a "spill" for the team, what would you do? Why?

3. If your manager ever confronted you about some excessive spilling, would you personally feel it was more ethical to protect the other employees or tell your manager the truth?

Contributed Anonymously

work in growing numbers, researchers concluded that the trend was part of an entitlement mentality—that workers think they are "due" more time off because they work so hard. The researchers concluded that this was part of a backlash triggered by the downsizings, mergers, and reorganizations that left millions of workers unemployed and shellshocked in the 1990s. The researchers call it part of the entitlement mentality because people now feel, "I deserve it. You owe me."[18]

Rights Movement   The revolution of rising expectations, the entitlement mentality, and all of the factors discussed so far have contributed somewhat to what might be termed the **rights movement** that is present today. Some of these rights, such as the right to privacy and the right to due process, have been perceived as generic for all citizens. However, in addition to these generalized rights, there has been activism for rights for particular groups in North American society. This modern movement began with the U.S. civil rights cases of the 1950s. Many groups in both the U.S. and Canada have been inspired by the success of blacks and have sought success by similar means. Thus, we have fortunately seen the protected status of certain groups increase, and with this increase comes an expectation of increased sensitivity toward all groups of our society. Such groups may have formerly been ignored or mistreated, including women, ethnic minorities, individuals with certain disabilities, and other groups.

Business, as one of society's major institutions, has been confronted with an expanding array of expectations as to how people want to be treated and dealt with, not only as employees but also as owners, consumers, and members of the community. The "rights" movement is interrelated with the special-interest society we discussed earlier and sometimes follows an "entitlement" mentality among some people and within some sectors of society.

In summary, affluence and education, awareness through the media, the revolution of rising expectations, entitlement beliefs, and the rights movement have formed a backdrop against which criticism of business has grown. To be sure, this list does not summarize all issues and trends that are present in the social environment. However, it does help to explain why we have an environment that is so conducive to criticism of business. In the next two subsections, we will see what some of the criticisms of business have been, and we will discuss some of the general results of such criticisms.

Criticisms: Use and Abuse of Power

Many criticisms have been levelled at business over the years: It's too big, it's too powerful, it pollutes the environment and exploits people for its own gain, it takes advantage of workers and consumers, it does not tell the truth, and so on. A catalogue of business criticisms would occupy too much space to be presented here. If one were to identify a common thread that seems to run through all the complaints, it seems to be business's use and abuse of power. This is an issue that will not go away. According to a 2003 poll by the Toronto-based Centre for Ethical Orientation, nine of ten Canadians believe that trust in both private business and government institutions is declining worldwide. The director of the survey suggested that a key reason Canadians are less trusting of companies and the government is that they feel mistreated and ignored as citizens and consumers.[19]

Some of the points of friction between business and the public, in which corporate power is identified as the culprit, include such topics as CEO pay, mounting anger and frustration over high gasoline and drug prices, poor airline service, faulty tires, in-your-face marketing, commercialism in schools, globalization, corporate bankrolling of politicians, sweatshops, urban sprawl, and wages.

What is **business power**? Business power refers to the ability or capacity to produce an effect or to bring influence to bear on a situation or people. Power, in and of itself, may be either positive or negative. In the context of business criticism, however, power typically is perceived as being abused. Business certainly does have enormous power, but whether it abuses power is an issue that needs to be carefully examined. We will not settle this issue here, but the allegation that business abuses power remains the central issue behind the details.

Levels of Power   To understand corporate power, one must recognize that it resides at and may be manifested at several different levels. Edwin M. Epstein identified four such levels: the macro level, the intermediate level, the micro level, and the individual level.[20] The *macro level* refers to the corporate system—the totality of business organizations. Power here emanates from the sheer size and dominance of the corporate system. The *intermediate level* refers to groups of corporations acting in concert in an effort to produce a desired effect—to raise prices, control markets, dominate purchasers, promote an issue, or pass or defeat legislation. Prime examples are the airlines, power companies, banks, OPEC, pharmaceutical companies, and defence contractors pursuing interests they have in common. The combined effect of companies acting in concert is significant. The *micro level* of power is the level of the individual firm. This might refer to the exertion of power or influence by any major corporation—Nortel, Bombardier, Microsoft, Wal-Mart, Procter & Gamble, or Nike, for example. The final level is the *individual level*. This refers to the individual corporate leader exerting power—Ted Rogers (Rogers Communications), Frank Stronach (Magna International), Carly Fiorina (Hewlett-Packard), Bill Gates (Microsoft), or Anita Roddick (The Body Shop).

The important point here is that as one analyzes corporate power, one should think in terms of the different levels at which that power is manifested. When this is done, it is not easy to conclude whether corporate power is excessive or has been abused. Specific levels of power need to be examined.

Spheres of Power   In addition to levels of power, there are also many different spheres or arenas in which this power may be manifested. Figure 1–5 depicts one way of looking at the levels Epstein identified and some of the spheres of power to which he was referring. *Economic power* and *political power* are two spheres that are referred to often, but business has other, more subtle forms of power as well. These other spheres include *social and cultural power*, *power over the individual*, *technological power*, and *environmental power*.

Is the power of business excessive? Does business abuse its power? Obviously, many people think so. To provide careful and fair answers to these questions, however, one must very carefully stipulate which level of power is being referred to and in which sphere the power is being employed. When this is done, it is not simple to arrive at generalizable answers.

Furthermore, the nature of power is such that it is sometimes wielded unintentionally. Sometimes it is consequential; that is, it is not wielded intentionally but nevertheless exerts its influence even though no attempt is made to exercise it.[21] An example of this might be a large firm such as IBM purchasing huge parcels of land in cities all across North America to keep in its real estate inventory for possible future

FIGURE 1-5

Levels and Spheres of Corporate Power

Levels / Spheres	Macro Level (the business system)	Intermediate Level (several firms)	Micro Level (single firm)	Individual Level (single executive)
Economic				
Social/Cultural				
Individual				
Technological				
Environmental				
Political				

use. Even if IBM comes right out and says that it has no definite plans to move into any of these cities—that is, even if it makes an attempt not to wield power—it still has enormous power with the various city councils and county commissions in the areas in which it has purchased land.

Balance of Power and Responsibility Whether or not business abuses its power or allows its use of power to get out of hand is a central issue that cuts through all the topics we will be discussing in this book. But power cannot be viewed in isolation from responsibility, and this power/responsibility relationship is the foundation of calls for corporate social responsibility. Davis and Blomstrom articulated this major concern in what they called the **Iron Law of Responsibility**: "In the long run, those who do not use power in a manner which society considers responsible will tend to lose it."[22] Stated another way, whenever power and responsibility become substantially out of balance, forces will be generated to bring them into closer balance.

When power gets out of balance, a variety of forces come to bear on business to be more responsible and more responsive to the criticisms being made against it. Some of these more obvious forces include governmental actions, such as increased regulations and new laws. The investigative news media become interested in what is going on, and a whole host of special-interest groups bring pressure to bear. In a *Business Week* cover story, the point was made that "it's this power imbalance that's helping to breed the current resentment against corporations."[23]

The tobacco industry is an excellent example of an industry that is feeling the brunt of efforts to address allegations of abuse of power. Complaints that the industry produces a dangerous, addictive product and markets that product to young people have been escalating for years. Tobacco firms in North America must submit to new regulations, and meet strict goals for reducing smoking. Although the industry continues to fight these measures, as it always has, it is expected that by the year 2022 tobacco's role in North American society will be forever reduced.[24]

Other industries have faced mounting criticism for their lack of concern for the consumers of their products and the misleading manner in which their products are marketed. For example, after increasing public pressure, the fast-food and junk-food industries have recently taken on more responsibility for their products. As the *Economist* magazine recently reported, "At last, in the face of mounting public outrage and the civic-minded efforts of America's trial lawyers, Big Food is coming out of denial …" The result is that such companies as Kraft Foods announced new "obesity initiatives," which are intended to dispense advice on food-marketing practices, labelling, and portion sizes.[25]

Business Response: Concern and Changing Social Contract

Growing out of criticisms of business and the idea of the power/responsibility equation has been an increased concern for the social environment on the part of business and a changed social contract. We previously indicated that the social environment was composed of such factors as demographics, lifestyles, and social values of the society. It may also be seen as a collection of conditions, events, and trends that reflect how people think and behave and what they value. As firms have sensed that the social environment and the expectations of business are changing, they have realized that they have to change, too. The **social contract** is that set of two-way understandings that characterizes the relationship between major institutions—in our case, business and society. The social contract is changing, and this change is a direct outgrowth of the increased importance of the social environment. The social contract has been changing to reflect society's expectations of business, especially in the social and ethical realms.

The social contract between business and society, as illustrated in Figure 1–6, is partially articulated through:

1. *Laws and regulations* that society has established as the framework within which business must operate
2. *Shared understandings* that evolve as to each group's expectations of the other

It is clear how laws and regulations spell out the "rules of the game" for business. Shared understandings, on the other hand, create more confusion and room for misunderstandings. In a sense, these shared understandings reflect mutual expectations regarding each other's roles, responsibilities, and ethics. These unspoken components of the social contract represent what Donaldson and Dunfee refer to as the normative

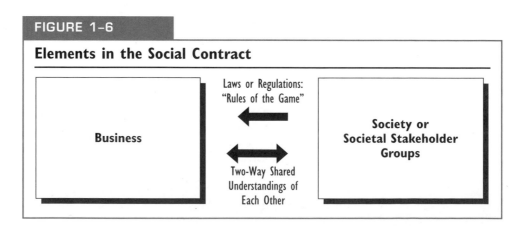

FIGURE 1-6

Elements in the Social Contract

Business

Laws or Regulations: "Rules of the Game"

Two-Way Shared Understandings of Each Other

Society or Societal Stakeholder Groups

perspective on the relationship (that is, what "ought" to be done by each party to the social contract).[26]

A parallel example to the business/society social contract may be seen in the relationship between a professor and the students in his or her class. University regulations and the syllabus for the course spell out the formal aspects of this relationship. The shared understandings address those expectations that are generally understood but not necessarily spelled out formally. An example might be "fairness." The student expects the professor to be "fair" in making assignments, in the level of work expected, in grading, and so on. Likewise, the professor expects the student to be fair in evaluating him or her on teaching evaluation forms, to be fair by not passing off someone else's work as his or her own, and so on.

An editorial from *Business Week* on the subject of the social contract summarizes well the modern era of business/society relationships:

> *Today it is clear that the terms of the contract between society and business are, in fact, changing in substantial and important ways. Business is being asked to assume broader responsibilities to society than ever before, and to serve a wider range of human values.... Inasmuch as business exists to serve society, its future will depend on the quality of management's response to the changing expectations of the public.*[27]

Such a statement suggests that we will continue to witness changes in the social contract between business and society.

Focus of the Book

This book takes a *managerial approach* to the business/society relationship. The managerial approach emphasizes two major themes that are important today: **business ethics** and **stakeholder management**. First, let us discuss the managerial focus.

Managerial Approach

Managers are practical, and they have begun to deal with social and ethical concerns in ways similar to those they have used to deal with traditional business functions—operations, marketing, finance, and so forth—in a rational, systematic, and administratively rigorous fashion. By viewing issues of social concern from a managerial frame of reference, managers have been able to reduce seemingly unmanageable social concerns to ones that can be dealt with in a rational and fair fashion. Yet, at the same time, managers have had to integrate traditional economic considerations with ethical or moral considerations.

A managerial approach to the business/society relationship confronts the individual manager continuously with questions such as:

- What changes are occurring or will occur in society's expectations of business that mandate business's taking the initiative with respect to particular societal or ethical problems?
- Did business in general, or our firm in particular, have a role in creating these problems?
- What impact is social change having on the organization, and how should we best respond to it?

- Can we reduce broad social problems to a size that can be effectively addressed from a managerial point of view?
- With which social and ethical problems can we act most effectively?
- What are the specific problems, alternatives for solving these problems, and implications for management's approach to dealing with social issues?
- How can we best plan and organize for responsiveness to socially related business problems?

From the standpoint of urgency in managerial response, management is concerned with two broad types or classes of social issues. First, there are those issues or crises that arise on the spur of the moment and for which management must formulate relatively quick responses. These may be either issues that management has never faced before or issues it has faced but does not have time to deal with, except on a short-term basis. A typical example might be a protest group that shows up on management's doorstep one day, arguing vehemently that the company should withdraw its sponsorship of a violent television show scheduled to air the next week.

Second, there are issues or problems that management has time to deal with on a more long-term basis. These issues include environmental pollution, employment discrimination, product safety, and occupational safety and health. In other words, these are enduring issues that will be of concern to society for a long time and for which management must develop a reasonably thoughtful organizational response. It is true that issues of this type could also appear in the form of ad hoc problems necessitating immediate responses, but they should suffice to illustrate areas that have matured somewhat. Management must thus be concerned with both short-term and long-term capabilities for dealing with social problems and the organization's social performance.

Our managerial approach, then, will be one that (1) clarifies the nature of the social or ethical issues that affect organizations and (2) suggests alternative managerial responses to these issues in a rational and ethical fashion. The test of success will

Ethics In Practice

The Boss

A few years ago, I worked for a health and fitness store in Calgary. We sold vitamins, weights, health food, exercise equipment, and clothing. I worked for a manager who showed a tendency to be lazy by always leaving work early. She would leave work early and ask the employees to cover for her if any of the upper managers called.

The manager was in charge of recording the hours we worked and always gave herself 40 hours. Most of the time she worked only about 30 hours a week and often left one of us in charge of the store. My hours were always set, so it did not matter if I stayed later, because I was credited only for the hours on her time sheet. The dilemma here

was that she was actually getting paid for time that she was spending away from the store. I was not sure if I was supposed to tell anyone or just look the other way, since she was my boss. I thought that her behaviour was wrong, especially for a manager, and that it was very unethical of her to ask us to lie in order to keep her out of trouble.

1. Are there any ethical issues involved in this case? What are they?

2. Should upper management be notified about the manager's actions? Why or why not?

3. What would you do if you were in my place?

Contributed by Terence O'Brien

be the extent to which we can improve an organization's social performance by taking a managerial approach rather than dealing with the issues on an ad hoc basis.

Ethics Theme

As hard as one might try to extricate business from the major ethical issues of the day, it just cannot be done. The managerial focus attempts to take a practical look at the social issues and expectations business faces, but ethical questions inevitably come into play. **Ethics** basically refers to issues of right, wrong, fairness, and justice, and business ethics focuses on ethical issues that arise in the commercial realm. Ethical threads run throughout our discussion because questions of right, wrong, fairness, and justice, no matter how slippery they are to deal with, permeate business's activities as it attempts to interact effectively with major stakeholder groups: employees, customers, owners, government, and the community.

The inevitable task of management is not only to deal with the various stakeholder groups in an ethical fashion but also to reconcile the conflicts of interest that occur between the organization and the stakeholder groups. Implicit in this challenge is the ethical dimension present in practically all business decision making where stakeholders are concerned. In addition to the challenge of treating fairly the groups with which business interacts, management faces the equally important task of creating an organizational climate in which all employees make decisions with the interests of the public, as well as those of the organization, in mind. At stake is not only the firm's reputation but also the reputation of the business community in general.

Stakeholder Management Theme

As we have indicated throughout this chapter, **stakeholders** are individuals or groups with which business interacts who have a "stake," or vested interest, in the firm. They could be called "publics," but this term may imply that they are outside the business sphere and should be dealt with as external players rather than as integral components of the business/society relationship. As a matter of fact, stakeholders actually constitute the most important elements of that broad grouping known as society.

We consider two broad groups of stakeholders in this book. First, we consider *external stakeholders*, which include government, consumers, and community members. We treat government first because it represents the public. It is helpful to understand the role and workings of government in order to best appreciate business's relationships with other groups. Consumers may be business's most important stakeholders. Members of the community are crucial, too, and they are concerned about a variety of issues. One of the most important is the natural environment. Two other major community issues include business giving (or corporate philanthropy) and plant closings (including downsizing). All these issues have direct effects on the community. Social activist groups representing external stakeholders also must be considered to be a part of this classification.

The second broad grouping of stakeholders is composed of *internal stakeholders*. Business owners and employees are the principal groups of internal stakeholders. We live in an organizational society, and many people think that their roles as employees are just as important as their roles as investors or owners. Both of these groups have legitimate claims on the organization, and management's task is to address their needs and balance these needs against those of the firm and of other stakeholder groups. We will develop the idea of stakeholder management more fully in Chapter 3.

Structure of the Book

The structure of this book is illustrated in Figure 1–7.

In Part 1, entitled "Business, Society, and Stakeholders," there are three chapters. Chapter 1 provides an overview of the business/society relationship. Chapter 2 covers corporate citizenship: social responsibility, responsiveness, and performance. Chapter 3 addresses the stakeholder management concept. These chapters provide a crucial basis for understanding all of the discussions that follow. They provide the context for the business/society relationship.

Part 2 is entitled "Strategic Management for Corporate Stakeholder Performance." Its two chapters address management-related topics. Chapter 4 covers strategic management and corporate public affairs. Chapter 5 deals with issues management and crisis management.

Part 3, "Business Ethics and Management," focuses exclusively on business ethics. Business ethics fundamentals are established in Chapter 6, and personal and organizational ethics are discussed in Chapter 7. Chapter 8 deals with business ethics and technology, and Chapter 9 treats business ethics in the global or international sphere. Although ethical issues cut through and permeate many of the discussions in this book, this significant treatment of business ethics is warranted by a need to explore in some detail what is meant by the ethical dimension in management.

Part 4, "External Stakeholder Issues," addresses the major external stakeholders of business. In Chapter 10, because government is such an active player in all the groups to follow, we consider business/government relationships and government regulations. Chapters 11 and 12 address consumer stakeholders. Chapter 13 addresses the natural environment as stakeholder. Chapter 14 addresses business and community stakeholder issues.

In Part 5, "Internal Stakeholder Issues," employees and owners are addressed. Chapter 15 considers employees and major workplace issues, and Chapter 16 looks carefully at the issues of employee privacy, safety, and health. In Chapter 17, we focus on the special case of employment discrimination. Chapter 18 concludes the text with a discussion of corporate governance and the management/shareholder relationship.

Depending on the emphasis desired in the course, Part 2 could be treated where it is currently located, or it could be postponed until after Part 5.

Taken as a whole, the book strives to take the reader through a building-block arrangement of basic concepts and ideas that are vital to the business/society relationship and to explore the nature of social and ethical issues and stakeholder groups with which management must interact. It considers the external and internal stakeholder groups in some depth.

FIGURE 1–7

The Structure and Flow of the Book

BUSINESS, SOCIETY, AND STAKEHOLDERS

PART ONE

1. The Business and Society Relationship
2. Corporate Citizenship: Social Responsibility, Responsiveness, and Performance
3. The Stakeholder Approach to Business, Society, and Ethics

STRATEGIC MANAGEMENT FOR CORPORATE STAKEHOLDER PERFORMANCE

PART TWO

4. Strategic Management and Corporate Public Affairs
5. Issues Management and Crisis Management

BUSINESS ETHICS AND MANAGEMENT

PART THREE

6. Business Ethics Fundamentals
7. Personal and Organizational Ethics
8. Business Ethics and Technology
9. Ethical Issues in the Global Arena

EXTERNAL STAKEHOLDER ISSUES

PART FOUR

10. Business, Government, and Regulation
11. Consumer Stakeholders: Information Issues and Responses
12. Consumer Stakeholders: Product and Service Issues
13. The Natural Environment as Stakeholder
14. Business and Community Stakeholders

INTERNAL STAKEHOLDER ISSUES

PART FIVE

15. Employee Stakeholders and Workplace Issues
16. Employee Stakeholders: Privacy, Safety, and Health
17. Employment Discrimination and Employment Equity
18. Owner Stakeholders and Corporate Governance

CASES

Summary

The pluralistic business system in Canada has several advantages and some disadvantages. Within this context, business firms must deal with a multitude of stakeholders and an increasingly special-interest society. A major force that shapes the public's view of business is the criticism that business receives from a variety of sources. Factors in the social environment that have contributed to an atmosphere in which business criticism thrives include affluence, education, public awareness developed through the media (especially TV), the revolution of rising expectations, a growing entitlement mentality, and the rights movement. In addition, actual questionable practices on the part of business have made it a natural target. Not all firms are guilty, but the guilty attract negative attention to the entire business community.

A major criticism of business is that it has abused its power. To understand power, you need to recognize that it may operate at four different levels: the level of the entire business system, groups of companies acting in concert, the level of the individual firm, and the level of the individual corporate executive. Moreover, business power may be manifested in several different spheres: economic, political, technological, environmental, social, and individual. It is difficult to assess whether business is actually abusing its power, but it is clear that business has enormous power and that it must exercise this power carefully. Power evokes responsibility, and this is the central reason that calls for corporate responsiveness have been prevalent in recent years. These concerns have led to a changing social environment for business and a changed social contract.

Key Terms

affluence (page 13)
business (page 6)
business ethics (page 21)
business power (page 18)
economic environment (page 8)
education (page 13)
entitlement mentality (page 16)
ethics (page 23)
Iron Law of Responsibility (page 19)
macroenvironment (page 7)
pluralism (page 8)

political environment (page 8)
revolution of rising expectations (page 15)
rights movement (page 17)
social contract (page 20)
social environment (page 8)
social problem (page 15)
society (page 7)
special-interest society (page 10)
stakeholder management (page 21)
stakeholders (page 23)
technological environment (page 8)

Discussion Questions

1. In discussions of business and society, why is there a tendency to focus on large rather than small or medium-sized firms?

2. What is the one greatest strength and the one greatest weakness of a pluralistic society? Do these characteristics work for or against business?

3. Identify and explain the major factors in the social environment that create an atmosphere in which business criticism takes place and prospers. How are the factors related to one another?

4. Give an example of each of the four levels of power discussed in this chapter. Also, give an example of each of the spheres of business power.

5. Explain in your own words the social contract. Give an example of a shared understanding between you as a consumer or an employee and a firm with which you do business or for which you work.

Endnotes

1. Theresa Tedesco and Barbara Shecter, "Black Heads to Court for Selloff Protection," *CanWest News Service* (January 20, 2004) http://www.canada.com/national/nationalpost/index.html; Theresa Tedesco and Barbara Shecter, "Conrad Black Sells Hollinger, Lashes Out," *CanWest News Service* (January 19, 2004).

2. Liam Fahey and V. K. Narayanan, *Macroenvironmental Analysis for Strategic Management* (St. Paul: West, 1986), 28–30.

3. *Ibid.*

4. Joseph W. McGuire, *Business and Society* (New York: McGraw-Hill, 1963), 130.

5. Human Development Reports, http://hdr.undp.org.

6. "Average American Family Watches TV 7 Hours Each Day," *Athens Banner Herald* (January 25, 1984), 23.

7. "Business Thinks TV Distorts Its Image," *Business Week* (October 18, 1982), 26.

8. "CEOs: Biz News Is Negative," *USA Today* (February 27, 1987), 1B.

9. James Fallows, *Breaking the News: How the Media Undermine American Democracy* (Pantheon Press, 1996). See also Howard Kurtz, *Hot Air: All Talk, All the Time* (Basic Books, 1997).

10. Linda S. Lichter, S. Robert Lichter, and Stanley Rothman, "How Show Business Shows Business," *Public Opinion* (November 1982), 10–12.

11. Nedra West, "Business and the Soaps," *Business Forum* (Spring 1983), 4.

12. Dan Seligman, "Tom Cruise Versus Corporate Evil," *Forbes* (September 4, 2000), 82.

13. Morton C. Paulson, "What Youngsters Learn on TV," *National Observer* (May 19, 1976), 10.

14. Robert J. Samuelson, *The Good Life and Its Discontents: The American Dream in the Age of Entitlement, 1945–1995* (Times Books, 1996).

15. Neil H. Jacoby, *Corporate Power and Social Responsibility* (New York: Macmillan, 1973), 186–188.

16. Linda DeStefano, "Looking Ahead to the Year 2000: No Utopia, But Most Expect a Better Life," *The Gallup Poll Monthly* (January 1990), 21.

17. Joseph Nolan, "Business Beware: Early Warning Signs for the Eighties," *Public Opinion* (April/May, 1981), 16.

18. Diane Lewis, "Today, Employees Who Play Hooky Think They're Entitled to, Expert Says," *The Boston Globe* (September 3, 2000), F8.

19. Kim Lunman, "Canadians Less than Trusting Now, Poll Finds," *National Post* (June 25, 2003), A8.

20. Edwin M. Epstein, "Dimensions of Corporate Power: Part I," *California Management Review* (Winter 1973), 11.

21. *Ibid.*

22. Keith Davis and Robert L. Blomstrom, *Business and Its Environment* (New York: McGraw-Hill, 1966), 174–175.

23. Aaron Bernstein, "Too Much Corporate Power?" *Business Week* (September 11, 2000), 146.

24. John Carey, "The Tobacco Deal: Not So Fast," *Business Week* (July 7, 1997), 34–37; Richard Lacayo, "Smoke Gets in Your Aye," *Time* (January 26, 1998), 50; Jeffrey H. Birnbaum, "Tobacco's Can of Worms," *Fortune* (July 21, 1997), 58–60; Dwight R. Lee, "Will Government's Crusade Against Tobacco Work?" (July 1997, Center for The Study of American Business).

25. "Thin Edge of the Wedge," *The Economist* (July 3, 2003), http://www.economist.com.

26. Thomas Donaldson and Thomas W. Dunfee, "Toward a Unified Conception of Business Ethics: Integrative Social Contracts Theory," *Academy of Management Review* (April 1994), 252–253.

27. "The New 'Social Contract,'" *Business Week* (July 3, 1971).

Chapter 2

Corporate Citizenship: Social Responsibility, Responsiveness, and Performance

Chapter Objectives

After studying this chapter, you should be able to:

1 Explain how corporate social responsibility (CSR) evolved and encompasses economic, legal, ethical, and philanthropic components.

2 Provide business examples of CSR and corporate citizenship.

3 Differentiate between social responsibility and responsiveness.

4 Elaborate on the concept of corporate social performance (CSP).

5 Provide an overview of studies relating social performance to financial performance.

6 Explain the socially conscious investing movement.

For the past 30 years, business has been undergoing the most intense scrutiny it has ever received from the public. As a result of the many allegations being levelled at it—charges that it has little concern for the consumer, cares nothing about the deteriorating social order, has no concept of acceptable ethical behaviour, and is indifferent to the problems of minorities and the environment—concern is continuing to be expressed as to what responsibilities business has to the society in which it resides. These concerns have generated an unprecedented number of pleas for corporate social responsibility (CSR), more recently included in the broad term *corporate citizenship*. Concepts that have evolved from CSR include corporate social responsiveness and corporate social performance. Today, many business executives prefer the term *corporate citizenship* as an inclusive reference to social responsibility issues.

The basic CSR issue can be framed in terms of two key questions: Does business have a social responsibility? If so, how much and what kinds? Although these questions seem simple and straightforward, responses to them must be phrased carefully. What is particularly paradoxical is that large numbers of businesspeople have enthusiastically embraced the concept of corporate social responsibility during the past three decades, but rather limited consensus has emerged about what corporate social responsibility really means.

In this chapter, we intend to explore several different facets of the CSR topic and to provide some insights into the previous questions. We are dedicating an entire chapter to the CSR issue and concepts that have emerged from it because it is a core idea that underlies most of our discussions in this book.

The Corporate Social Responsibility Concept

In Chapter 1, we traced how criticisms of business have led to increased concern for the social environment and a changed social contract. Out of these ideas has grown the notion of corporate social responsibility, or CSR. Before providing some historical perspective, let us impart an initial view of what corporate social responsibility means.

Raymond Bauer presented an early view of CSR as follows: "Corporate social responsibility is seriously considering the impact of the company's actions on society."[3] Another definition that may be helpful is "The idea of social responsibility ... requires the individual to consider his [or her] acts in terms of a whole social system, and holds him [or her] responsible for the effects of his [or her] acts anywhere in that system."[4]

Search the web WWW

Leading Corporate Citizen in 2003

In 2003, *Business Ethics* magazine presented its 100 best corporate citizens rankings. The top five companies for 2003, in rank order, are **General Mills**, **Cummins Inc.**, **Intel**, **Procter & Gamble**, and **IBM**. The list is drawn from the Russell 1000 (the 1000 largest public companies). According to the report, the leading-edge policies of these firms offer model business strategies in good corporate citizenship. The number one ranked company in 2003 was General Mills. One area in which General Mills was given particular accolades was in its concern for the community. The report noted that about 70 percent of General Mills' 21 000 U.S.-based employees volunteer in their communities. For example, the company actually helped an urban Minneapolis neighbourhood reduce crime by more than 30 percent and become a safer place for families. To review General Mills' policies on corporate citizenship, visit its Web site at **http://www.generalmills.com/corporate/commitment/**.[1]

Corporate Knights magazine posted its 2003 rankings of the top 50 Canadian corporate citizens, and among the top ten were the following:[2]

1. Alcan Inc.
2. Royal Bank of Canada
3. Suncor Energy Inc.
4. Nexen Inc.
5. Canadian Imperial Bank of Commerce
6. Bank of Nova Scotia
7. Domtar Inc.
8. MTS Inc.
9. Nova Chemicals Corp.
10. BMO Financial Group

To review Alcan's policies on corporate citizenship, visit its Web site at **http://www.alcan.com/**.

Both of these definitions provide preliminary insights into the idea of social responsibility that will help us appreciate some brief evolutionary history. Figure 2–1 illustrates the business criticism/social response cycle, depicting how the concept of CSR grew out of the ideas introduced in Chapter 1—business criticism and the increased concern for the social environment and the changed social contract. We see also in Figure 2–1 that the commitment to social responsibility by businesses has led to increased corporate responsiveness to stakeholders and improved social (stakeholder) performance—ideas that are developed more fully in this chapter.

As we will discuss later, some observers today prefer the language of "corporate citizenship" to collectively embrace the host of concepts related to CSR. However, for now, a useful summary of the themes or emphases of each of the chapter title concepts helps us see the flow of ideas accentuated as these concepts have developed:

Corporate Citizenship Concepts

Corporate social *responsibility*—emphasizes obligation, accountability

⬇

Corporate social *responsiveness*—emphasizes action, activity

⬇

Corporate social *performance*—emphasizes outcomes, results

The growth of these ideas has brought about a society more satisfied with business. However, this satisfaction, although it has reduced the number of factors leading to business criticism, has at the same time led to increased expectations that may result in more criticism; this double effect is indicated in Figure 2–1. The net result is that the overall levels of business performance and societal satisfaction should increase with time in spite of this interplay of positive and negative factors. Should business not be responsive to societal expectations, it could conceivably enter a downward spiral, resulting in significant changes in the business/society relationship.

Historical Perspective on CSR

The concept of business responsibility that prevailed in North America during most of our history was fashioned after the traditional, or classical, *economic model*. Adam Smith's concept of the "invisible hand" was its major point of departure. The classical view held that a society could best determine its needs and wants through the marketplace. If business is rewarded on the basis of its ability to respond to the demands of the market, the self-interested pursuit of that reward will result in society getting what it wants. Thus, the "invisible hand" of the market transforms self-interest into societal interest. Unfortunately, although the marketplace did a reasonably good job in deciding what goods and services should be produced, it did not fare as well in ensuring that business always acted fairly and ethically.

Years later, when laws constraining business behaviour began to proliferate, it might be said that a *legal model* prevailed. Society's expectations of business changed from being strictly economic in nature to encompassing issues that had been previously at business's discretion.

In practice, although business early subscribed to the economic emphasis and was willing to be subjected to an increasing number of laws imposed by society, the

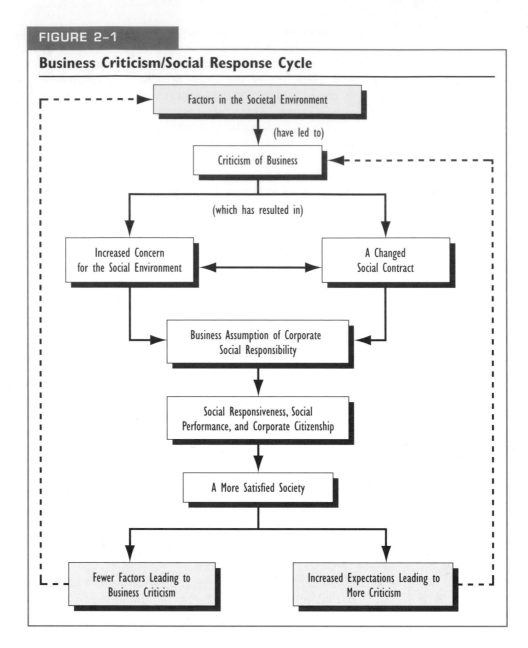

FIGURE 2-1

Business Criticism/Social Response Cycle

Factors in the Societal Environment

(have led to)

Criticism of Business

(which has resulted in)

Increased Concern for the Social Environment

A Changed Social Contract

Business Assumption of Corporate Social Responsibility

Social Responsiveness, Social Performance, and Corporate Citizenship

A More Satisfied Society

Fewer Factors Leading to Business Criticism

Increased Expectations Leading to More Criticism

business community later did not fully live by the tenets of even these early conceptions of business responsibility. As James W. McKie observed, "The business community never has adhered with perfect fidelity to an ideologically pure version of its responsibilities, drawn from the classical conception of the enterprise in economic society, though many businessmen have firmly believed in the main tenets of the creed."[5]

Modification of the Economic Model

A modification of the classical economic model was seen in practice in at least three areas: philanthropy, community obligations, and paternalism.[6] History shows that businesspeople did engage in **philanthropy**—contributions to charity and other worthy causes—even during periods characterized by the traditional economic view. Voluntary **community obligations** to improve, beautify, and uplift were evident. One early example of this, in the U.S., was the cooperative effort between the railroads and the YMCA immediately after the Civil War to provide community services in areas served by the railroads. Although these services economically benefited the railroads, they were at the same time philanthropic.[7]

During the latter part of the nineteenth century and even into the twentieth century, **paternalism** appeared in many forms. One of the most visible examples was the company town. Although business's motives for creating company towns (for example, Batawa) were mixed, business had to do a considerable amount of the work in governing them. Thus, the company accepted a form of paternalistic social responsibility.[8]

The emergence of large corporations during the late 1800s played a major role in hastening movement away from the classical economic view. As society grew from the economic structure of small, powerless firms governed primarily by the marketplace to large corporations in which power was more concentrated, questions of the responsibility of business to society surfaced.[9]

Although the idea of corporate social responsibility had not yet fully developed in the 1920s, managers even then had a more positive view of their role. Community service was in the forefront, whereby business leaders became involved with nongovernmental community groups for a common, nonbusiness purpose that necessitated their contribution of time and money to community welfare projects.[10] The social responsibility of business, then, had received a further broadening of its meaning.

The 1930s signalled a transition from a predominantly laissez-faire economy to a mixed economy in which business found itself one of the constituencies monitored by a more activist government. From this time well into the 1950s, business's social responsibilities grew to include employee welfare (pension and insurance plans), safety, medical care, retirement programs, and so on. McKie has suggested that these new developments were spurred both by governmental compulsion and by an enlarged concept of business responsibility.[11]

Neil J. Mitchell, in his book *The Generous Corporation*, presents an interesting thesis regarding how CSR evolved.[12] Mitchell's view is that the ideology of corporate social responsibility, particularly philanthropy, was developed by North American business leaders as a strategic response to the antibusiness fervour that was beginning in the late 1800s and early 1900s. The antibusiness reaction was the result of specific business actions, such as railroad price gouging, and public resentment of the emerging gigantic fortunes being made by late-nineteenth-century American moguls, such as Andrew Carnegie and John D. Rockefeller.[13]

As business leaders came to realize that the government had the power to intervene in the economy and, in fact, was being encouraged to do so by public opinion, there was a need for a philosophy that promoted large corporations as a force for social good. Thus, Mitchell argued, business leaders attempted to persuade those affected by business power that such power was being used appropriately. An example of this early progressive business ideology was reflected in Carnegie's 1889 essay, "The Gospel of Wealth," which asserted that business must pursue profits but that business wealth should be used for the benefit of the community. Philanthropy, therefore, became the most efficient means of using corporate wealth for public benefit. A prime example of this was American business mogul Andrew Carnegie's funding and building of more than 2500 libraries.

In a discussion of little-known history, Mitchell documents by way of specific examples how business developed this idea of the generous corporation and how it had distinct advantages: It helped business gain support from national and local governments, and it helped to achieve in North America a social stability that was unknown in Europe during that period. In Ronald Berenbeim's review of Mitchell's book, he argues that the main motive for corporate generosity in the early 1900s was essentially the same as it is in the present—to keep government at arm's length.[14]

Acceptance and Broadening of Meaning The period from the 1950s to the present may be considered part of the modern era in which the concept of corporate social responsibility gained considerable acceptance and broadening of meaning. During this time, the emphasis has moved from little more than a general awareness of social and moral concerns to a period in which specific issues, such as product safety, honesty in advertising, employee rights, environmental protection, and ethical behaviour, have been emphasized. The issue orientation eventually gave way to the more recent focus on social responsiveness and social performance, which we discuss later in this chapter. First, however, we can expand upon the modern view of CSR by examining various definitions or understandings of this term that have developed in recent years.

Corporate Social Responsibility: Evolving Viewpoints

Let's now return to the basic question: What does corporate social responsibility really mean? Up to this point, we have been operating with Bauer's definition of social responsibility:

> *Corporate social responsibility is seriously considering the impact of the company's actions on society.*

Although this definition has inherent ambiguities, we will find that most of the definitions presented by others also have limitations. Part of the difficulty in deriving a definition on which we might get consensus is the problem of determining, operationally, what the definition implies for management. This poses an almost insurmountable problem because organizations vary in size, in the types of products they produce, in their profitability and resources, in their impact on society and stakeholders, and so on. Because of this, the ways in which they embrace and practise social responsibility also vary.

One might ask: Why is this so? Are there not absolutes, areas in which all firms must be responsible? Yes, there are, and these are expressed by those expectations society has translated into legal components of the social contract. But as we will suggest here, CSR goes beyond simply "abiding by the law" (although abiding by the law is not always simple). In the realm of activities above and beyond abiding by the law, the variables (size of the firm, types of products produced, stakeholders affected, and so on) become more relevant.

A second definition is worth considering. Keith Davis and Robert Blomstrom defined corporate social responsibility as follows:

Search the web WWW

Canadian Business for Social Responsibility

Businesses are very interested in CSR. One organization that companies can join to learn more about CSR is Canadian Business for Social Responsibility (CBSR). This organization's goal is to support business in its effort to implement higher standards of social and environmental responsibility. CBSR's member companies include businesses that are committed to developing, sharing, and implementing corporate social responsibility best practices. To learn more about what business is doing in the realm of social responsibility, visit CBSR's Web site at **http://www.cbsr.ca**.

> *Social responsibility is the obligation of decision makers to take actions which protect and improve the welfare of society as a whole along with their own interests.*[15]

This definition is somewhat more pointed. It suggests two active aspects of social responsibility—*protecting* and *improving*. To protect the welfare of society implies the avoidance of negative impacts on society. To improve the welfare of society implies the creation of positive benefits for society. Like the first definition, this second characterization contains several words that are perhaps unavoidably vague. For example, words from these definitions that might permit managers wide latitude in interpretation include *seriously, considering, protect, improve,* and *welfare* (of society). The intention here is not to be critical of these good, general definitions but rather to illustrate how businesspeople and others become quite legitimately confused when they try to translate the concept of CSR into practice.

A third definition, by Joseph McGuire, is also quite general. But, unlike the previous two, it places social responsibilities in context vis-à-vis economic and legal objectives. McGuire asserts:

> *The idea of social responsibility supposes that the corporation has not only economic and legal obligations, but also certain responsibilities to society which extend beyond these obligations.*[16]

Although this statement is not fully operational either, its attractiveness is that it acknowledges the primacy of economic objectives side by side with legal obligations while also encompassing a broader conception of the firm's responsibilities.

A fourth definition, set forth by Edwin Epstein, relates CSR to business management's growing concern with stakeholders and ethics. He asserts:

> *Corporate social responsibility relates primarily to achieving outcomes from organizational decisions concerning specific issues or problems which (by some normative standard) have beneficial rather than adverse effects upon pertinent corporate stakeholders. The normative correctness of the products of corporate action have been the main focus of corporate social responsibility.*[17]

Epstein's definition is helpful because it concentrates on the outcomes, products, or results of corporate actions for stakeholders, which are only implicit in the other definitions. Over the decades, a number of different views on CSR have evolved.[18]

Carroll's Four-Part Definition of CSR

Each of the aforementioned definitions of corporate social responsibility has value. At this point, we would like to present Archie Carroll's four-part definition of CSR that focuses on the types of social responsibilities it might be argued that business has. Carroll's definition helps us to understand the component parts that make up CSR:

> *The social responsibility of business encompasses the economic, legal, ethical, and discretionary (philanthropic) expectations that society has of organizations at a given point in time.*[19]

Carroll's four-part definition attempts to place economic and legal expectations of business in context by relating them to more socially oriented concerns. These social concerns include ethical responsibilities and philanthropic (voluntary/discretionary) responsibilities. This definition, which includes four kinds of responsibilities, elaborates and builds upon the definition proposed by McGuire.

Economic Responsibilities   First, there are business's **economic responsibilities**. It may seem odd to call an economic responsibility a social responsibility, but, in effect, this is what it is. First and foremost, our social system calls for business to be an economic institution. That is, it should be an institution whose orientation is to produce goods and services that society wants and to sell them at fair prices—prices that society thinks represent the true values of the goods and services delivered and that provide business with profits adequate to ensure its perpetuation and growth and to reward its investors. While thinking about its economic responsibilities, business employs many management concepts that are directed toward financial effectiveness—attention to revenues, costs, strategic decision making, and the host of business concepts focused on maximizing the long-term financial performance of the organization.

Legal Responsibilities   Second, there are business's **legal responsibilities**. Just as society has sanctioned our economic system by permitting business to assume the productive role mentioned earlier, as a partial fulfillment of the social contract, it has also laid down the ground rules—the laws—under which business is expected to operate. Legal responsibilities reflect society's view of "codified ethics" in the sense that they embody basic notions of fair practices as established by our lawmakers. It is business's responsibility to society to comply with these laws. If business does not agree with laws that have been passed or are about to be passed, our society has provided a mechanism by which dissenters can be heard through the political process. In the past 30 years, our society has witnessed a proliferation of laws and regulations striving to control business behaviour. This aspect of the business and society relationship will be developed in more detail in later chapters.

As important as legal responsibilities are, legal responsibilities do not cover the full range of behaviours expected of business by society. The law is inadequate for at least three reasons. First, the law cannot possibly address all the topics, areas, or issues that business may face. New topics continually emerge such as Internet-based business (e-commerce) and genetically engineered foods. Second, the law often lags behind more recent concepts of what is considered appropriate behaviour. For example, as technology permits more exact measurements of environmental contamination, laws based on measures made by obsolete equipment become outdated but not frequently changed. Third, laws are made by lawmakers and may reflect the personal interests and political motivations of legislators rather than appropriate ethical justifications. A wise sage once said: "Never go to see how sausages or laws are made." It may not be a pretty picture.

Ethical Responsibilities   Because laws are important but not adequate, **ethical responsibilities** embrace those activities and practices that are expected or prohibited by societal members even though they are not codified into law. Ethical responsibilities embody the full scope of norms, standards, and expectations that reflect a belief of what consumers, employees, shareholders, and the community regard as fair, just, and in keeping with the respect for or protection of stakeholders' moral rights.[20]

Ethics In Practice

Feeling "Used"

While attending university, I spent a few years working at a used-textbook store. The majority of the books we sold were used books that we purchased from students, individuals, and used-book wholesalers. Sometimes when putting books out on the shelves I would encounter books with phrases like "Instructor's Copy" or "Sample Copy—Not for Resale" printed on the covers. When I asked my boss about these books, he told me that they were free copies given out to instructors, but it was perfectly legal for us to sell the books since we had purchased them from another person. This made sense to me and satisfied my curiosity.

Later in the day, my boss showed me a pile of these sample-copy books and said that we take coloured tape and cover up the areas that contain the phrases such as "Sample Copy." When I asked why we did this, he told me that although we are legally able to sell the books, the phrases sometimes discourage customers from buying these copies although the content is identical to the standard copies. I then asked how we got these books if they were instructor copies and were not supposed to be resold.

I was told that the publishing companies send free copies of books to professors to let them read and evaluate them with the hope that they will order the book as material for their classes. We get some of these books when professors sell their sample copies to us or a used-book wholesaler, but the majority come from individuals who go around college campuses (calling themselves book-buyers) buying these books from professors and then selling them to a used-book store or a used-book wholesaler. My boss also stated that since the content inside is the same, we really do not care if they are the standard copy or a sample copy and, therefore, we buy and sell these books for the same prices as the standard copies.

1. Is it a socially responsible practice for a bookstore to purchase and then resell these books that were given out as free copies?

2. Is it an ethical practice for the bookstore to conceal the fact that these books are, indeed, instructor's or sample copies?

3. Is it an ethical practice for book-buyers to roam the halls of university campuses and buy these free books from professors who no longer want them?

4. Is it an ethical practice for professors to sell books that were sent to them as free sample copies?

Contributed Anonymously

In one sense, changes in ethics or values precede the establishment of laws because they become the driving forces behind the initial creation of laws and regulations. For example, the civil rights, environmental, and consumer movements reflected basic alterations in societal values and thus may be seen as ethical bellwethers foreshadowing and leading to later legislation. In another sense, ethical responsibilities may be seen as embracing and reflecting newly emerging values and norms that society expects business to meet, even though they may reflect a higher standard of performance than that currently required by law. Ethical responsibilities in this sense are often ill defined or continually under public scrutiny and debate as to their legitimacy and, thus, are frequently difficult for business to agree upon. Regardless, business is expected to be responsive to newly emerging concepts of what constitutes ethical practices.

Superimposed on these ethical expectations emanating from societal and stakeholder groups are the implied levels of ethical performance suggested by a consideration of the great ethical principles of moral philosophy, such as justice, rights, and utilitarianism.[21]

Because ethical responsibilities are so important, we devote Part 3, composed of four chapters, to the subject. For the moment, however, let us think of ethical responsibilities as encompassing those areas in which society expects certain levels of moral or principled performance but for which it has not yet articulated or codified into law.

Philanthropic Responsibilities   Fourth, there are business's voluntary/discretionary or **philanthropic responsibilities**. These are viewed as responsibilities because they reflect current expectations of business by the public. These activities are voluntary, guided only by business's desire to engage in social activities that are not mandated, not required by law, and not generally expected of business in an ethical sense. Nevertheless, the public has an expectation that business will engage in philanthropy and thus this category has become a part of the social contract between business and society. Such activities might include corporate giving, product and service donations, volunteerism, partnerships with local government and other organizations, and any other kind of voluntary involvement of the organization and its employees with the community or other stakeholders. Examples of companies fulfilling their philanthropic responsibilities are many:

- CIBC sponsors such charitable events as Run for the Cure to raise funds for combating cancer.
- Microsoft Canada Inc. donates millions of dollars to areas such as youth, education, and community programs.
- Bell Canada has spent millions funding a partnership with universities and governments in Ontario and Quebec that supports student research in communications technology.
- Bombardier Inc. established the J. Armand Bombardier Foundation, which donates funds to such causes as shelters, food banks, and outreach programs.
- Nike Inc. donates large sums of cash and product to charitable causes. In 2003, Nike reported that it contributed US$30.7 million globally in cash, product, and in-kind services to more than 1500 nonprofit organizations and community partners.
- IBM gives away computers and computer training to schools around Canada and the U.S.
- UPS has committed US$2 million to a two-year program, the Volunteer Impact Initiative, designed to help nonprofit organizations develop innovative ways to recruit, train, and manage volunteers.
- Thousands of companies give away money, services, and volunteer time to education, youth, health organizations, arts and culture, neighbourhood improvement, minority affairs, and programs for the handicapped.

The distinction between ethical responsibilities and philanthropic responsibilities is that the latter typically are not expected in a moral or an ethical sense. Communities desire and expect business to contribute its money, facilities, and employee time to humanitarian programs or purposes, but they do not regard firms as unethical if they do not provide these services at the desired levels. Therefore, these responsibilities are more discretionary, or voluntary, on business's part, although the societal expectation that they be provided is always present. This category of responsibilities is often referred to as good "corporate citizenship."

In essence, then, our definition forms a four-part conceptualization of corporate social responsibility that encompasses the economic, legal, ethical, and philanthropic expectations placed on organizations by society at a given point in time. Figure 2–2 summarizes the four components, society's expectation regarding each component, and examples. The implication is that business has accountability for these areas of responsibility and performance. This four-part definition provides us with categories within which to place the various expectations that society has of business. With each of these categories considered as indispensable facets of the total social responsibility of business, we have a conceptual model that more completely describes the kinds of expectations that society expects of business. One advantage of this model is that it can accommodate those who have argued against CSR by characterizing an economic emphasis as separate from a social emphasis. This model offers these two facets along with others that collectively make up corporate social responsibility.

The Pyramid of Corporate Social Responsibility A helpful way of graphically depicting the four-part definition is envisioning a pyramid composed of four layers. This **Pyramid of Corporate Social Responsibility** is shown in Figure 2–3.[22]

The pyramid portrays the four components of CSR, beginning with the basic building block of economic performance, at the base. At the same time, business is expected to obey the law, because the law is society's codification of acceptable and unacceptable behaviour. Next is business's responsibility to be ethical. At its most basic level, this is the obligation to do what is right, just, and fair and to avoid or minimize harm to stakeholders (employees, consumers, the environment, and others). Finally, business is expected to be a good corporate citizen—to fulfill its voluntary/ discretionary or philanthropic responsibility to contribute financial and human resources to the community and to improve the quality of life.

No metaphor is perfect, and the Pyramid of CSR is no exception. It is intended to illustrate that the total social responsibility of business is composed of distinct components that, when taken together, make up the whole. Although the components

---

FIGURE 2-2

Understanding the Four Components of Corporate Social Responsibility

Type of Responsibility	Societal Expectation	Examples
Economic	*Required* of business by society	Be profitable. Maximize sales, minimize costs. Make sound strategic decisions. Be attentive to dividend policy.
Legal	*Required* of business by society	Obey all laws, adhere to all regulations. Environmental and consumer laws. Laws protecting employees. Obey the Criminal Code, the Income Tax Act, and the Corruption of Foreign Public Officials Act. Fulfill all contractual obligations. Honour warranties and guarantees.
Ethical	*Expected* of business by society	Avoid questionable practices. Respond to spirit as well as letter of law. Assume law is a floor on behaviour, operate above minimum required. Do what is right, fair, and just. Assert ethical leadership.
Philanthropic	*Desired/expected* of business by society	Be a good corporate citizen. Make corporate contributions. Provide programs supporting community—education, health/human services, culture and arts, civic. Provide for community betterment. Engage in volunteerism.

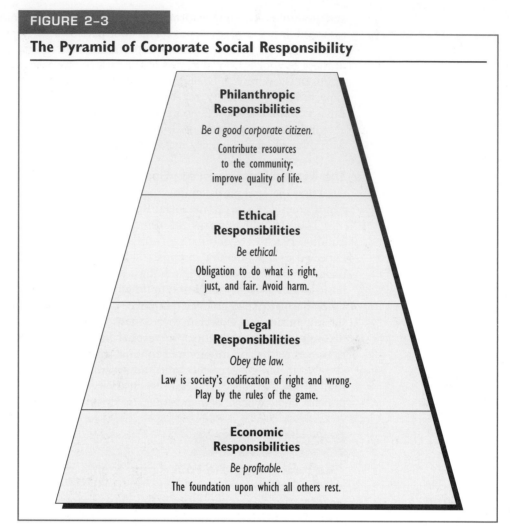

FIGURE 2-3

The Pyramid of Corporate Social Responsibility

Philanthropic Responsibilities

Be a good corporate citizen.

Contribute resources
to the community;
improve quality of life.

Ethical Responsibilities

Be ethical.

Obligation to do what is right,
just, and fair. Avoid harm.

Legal Responsibilities

Obey the law.

Law is society's codification of right and wrong.
Play by the rules of the game.

Economic Responsibilities

Be profitable.

The foundation upon which all others rest.

Source: Archie B. Carroll, "The Pyramid of Corporate Social Responsibility: Toward the Moral Management of Organizational Stakeholders," *Business Horizons* (July–August 1991), 42. Copyright © 1991 by the Trustees at Indiana University, Kelley School of Business.

have been treated as separate concepts for discussion purposes, they are not mutually exclusive and are not intended to juxtapose a firm's economic responsibilities with its other responsibilities. At the same time, a consideration of the separate components helps the manager to see that the different types or kinds of obligations are in constant and dynamic tension with one another.

The most critical tensions, of course, are those between economic and legal, economic and ethical, and economic and philanthropic. The traditionalist might see this as a conflict between a firm's "concern for profits" and its "concern for society," but it is suggested here that this is an oversimplification. A CSR or stakeholder perspective would recognize these tensions as organizational realities but would focus on the total pyramid as a unified whole and on how the firm might engage in decisions, actions, policies, and practices that simultaneously fulfill all its component parts. This pyramid should not be interpreted to mean that business is expected to fulfill its social responsibilities in some sequential fashion, starting at the base. Rather, business is expected to fulfill all its responsibilities simultaneously.

In summary, the total social responsibility of business entails the concurrent fulfillment of the firm's economic, legal, ethical, and philanthropic responsibilities. In equation form, this might be expressed as follows:

Economic Responsibilities + Legal Responsibilities + Ethical Responsibilities
+ Philanthropic Responsibilities
= Total Corporate Social Responsibility

Stated in more practical and managerial terms, the socially responsible firm should strive to:

- Make a profit.
- Obey the law.
- Be ethical.
- Be a good corporate citizen.

It is especially important to note that the four-part CSR definition and the Pyramid of CSR represent a stakeholder model. That is, each of the four components of responsibility addresses different stakeholders in terms of the varying priorities in which the stakeholders are affected. Economic responsibilities most dramatically impact owners and employees (because if the business is not financially successful, owners and employees will be directly affected). Legal responsibilities are certainly crucial with respect to owners, but in today's society the threat of litigation against businesses emanates frequently from employees and consumer stakeholders. Ethical responsibilities affect all stakeholder groups, but an examination of the ethical issues business faces today suggests that they involve consumers and employees most frequently. Finally, philanthropic responsibilities most affect the community, but it could be reasoned that employees are next affected because some research has suggested that a company's philanthropic performance significantly affects its employees' morale. Figure 2–4 presents this stakeholder view of CSR, along with a priority scheme in which the stakeholder groups are addressed/affected by the companies' actions in that realm. The numbers in the cells are not based on empirical evidence but are only suggestive. Other priority schemes could easily be argued.

FIGURE 2-4

A Stakeholder View of Corporate Social Responsibility

CSR Component	Stakeholder Group Addressed and Affected				
	Owners	Consumers	Employees	Community	Others
Economic	1	4	2	3	5
Legal	3	2	1	4	5
Ethical	4	1	2	3	5
Philanthropic	3	4	2	1	5

Note: Numbers in cells suggest the prioritization of stakeholders addressed and affected within each CSR component. Numbers are illustrative only.

As we study the evolution of business's major areas of social concern, as presented in various chapters in Parts 2 and 3, we will see how our model's four facets (economic, legal, ethical, and philanthropic) provide us with a useful framework for conceptualizing the issue of corporate social responsibility. The social contract between business and society is to a large extent formulated from mutual understandings that exist in each area of our basic model. But, it should be noted that the ethical and philanthropic categories, taken together, more nearly capture the essence of what people generally mean today when they speak of the social responsibility of business. Situating these two categories relative to the legal and economic obligations, however, keeps them in proper perspective.

Arguments Against and For Corporate Social Responsibility

In an effort to provide a balanced view of CSR, we will consider the arguments that traditionally have been raised against and for it. We should state clearly at the outset, however, that those who argue against corporate social responsibility are not using in their considerations the comprehensive CSR definition and model presented here. Rather, it appears that the critics are viewing CSR more narrowly—as only the efforts of the organization to pursue social, noneconomic/nonlegal goals (our ethical and philanthropic categories). Some critics equate CSR with only the philanthropic category. We should also state that only a very few businesspeople and academics continue to argue against the fundamental notion of CSR today. The debate among businesspeople more often centres on the kinds and degrees of CSR and on subtle ethical questions, rather than on the basic question of whether or not business should be socially responsible.

Arguments Against CSR

Let us first look at the arguments that have surfaced over the years from the anti-CSR school of thought. Most notable has been the classical economic argument. This traditional view holds that management has one responsibility: to maximize the profits of its owners or shareholders. This classical economic school, led by economist Milton Friedman, argues that social issues are not the concern of businesspeople and that these problems should be resolved by the unfettered workings of the free market system.[23] Further, this view holds that if the free market cannot solve the social problem, then it falls upon government and legislation to do the job. Friedman softens his argument somewhat by his assertion that management is "to make as much money as possible while conforming to the basic rules of society, both those embodied in the law and those embodied in ethical customs."[24] When Friedman's entire statement is considered, it appears that he accepts three of the four categories of the four-part model—economic, legal, and ethical. The only item not specifically embraced in his quote is the voluntary or philanthropic category. In any event, it is clear that the economic argument views corporate social responsibility more narrowly than we have in our conceptual model.

A second major objection to CSR has been that business is not equipped to handle social activities. This position holds that managers are oriented toward finance and operations and do not have the necessary expertise (social skills) to make social decisions.[25] Although this may have been true at one point in time, it is less true today.

Closely related to this argument is a third: If managers were to pursue corporate social responsibility vigorously, it would tend to dilute the business's primary purpose.[26] The objection here is that CSR would put business into fields not related, as F. A. Hayek has stated, to their "proper aim."[27]

A fourth argument against CSR is that business already has enough power—economic, environmental, and technological—and so why should we place in its hands the opportunity to wield additional power?[28] In reality, today, business has this social power regardless of the argument. Further, this view tends to ignore the potential use of business's social power for the public good.

One other argument that merits mention is that by encouraging business to assume social responsibilities we might be placing it in a deleterious position in terms of the international balance of payments. One consequence of being socially responsible is that business must internalize costs that it formerly passed on to society in the form of dirty air, unsafe products, consequences of discrimination, and so on. The increase in the costs of products caused by including social considerations in the price structure would necessitate raising the prices of products, making them less competitive in international markets. The net effect might be to dissipate the country's advantages gained previously through technological advances. This argument weakens somewhat when we consider the reality that social responsibility is quickly becoming a global concern, not one restricted to North American firms and operations.

The arguments presented here constitute the principal claims made by those who oppose the CSR concept, as it once was narrowly conceived. Many of the reasons given appear quite rational. Value choices as to the type of society the citizenry would like to have, at some point, become part of the total social responsibility question. Whereas some of these objections might have had validity at one point in time, it is doubtful that they carry much weight today.

Arguments for CSR

Thomas Petit's perspective is useful as our point of departure in discussing support of the CSR doctrine. He says that authorities have agreed upon two fundamental points: "(1) Industrial society faces serious human and social problems brought on largely by the rise of the large corporations, and (2) managers must conduct the affairs of the corporation in ways to solve or at least ameliorate these problems."[29]

This generalized justification of corporate social responsibility is appealing. It actually comes close to what we might suggest as a first argument for CSR—namely, that it is in business's long-range self-interest to be socially responsible. Petit's argument provides an additional dimension by suggesting that it was partially business's fault that many of today's social problems arose in the first place and, consequently, that business should assume a role in remedying these problems. It may be inferred from this that deterioration of the social condition must be halted if business is to survive and prosper in the future.

The long-range self-interest view holds that if business is to have a healthy climate in which to exist in the future, it must take actions now that will ensure its long-term viability. Perhaps the reasoning behind this view is that society's expectations are such that if business does not respond on its own, its role in society may be altered by the public—for example, through government regulation or, more dramatically, through alternative economic systems for the production and distribution of goods and services.

It is sometimes difficult for managers who have a short-term orientation to appreciate that their rights and roles in the economic system are determined by society. Business must be responsive to society's expectations over the long term if it is to survive in its current form or in a less restrained form.

One of the most practical reasons for business to be socially responsible is to ward off future government intervention and regulation. Today there are numerous areas in which government intrudes with an expensive, elaborate regulatory apparatus to fill a void left by business's inaction. To the extent that business polices itself with self-disciplined standards and guidelines, future government intervention can be somewhat forestalled. Later, we will discuss some areas in which business could have prevented intervention and simultaneously ensured greater freedom in decision making had it imposed higher standards of behaviour on itself.

Keith Davis has presented two additional supporting arguments that deserve mention together: "Business has the resources" and "Let business try."[30] These two views maintain that because business has a reservoir of management talent, functional expertise, and capital, and because so many others have tried and failed to solve general social problems, business should be given a chance. These arguments have some merit, because there are some social problems that can be handled, in the final analysis, only by business. Examples include a fair workplace, providing safe products, and engaging in fair advertising. Admittedly, government can and does assume a role in these areas, but business must make the final decisions.

Another argument is that "proacting is better than reacting." This position holds that proacting (anticipating and initiating) is more practical and less costly than simply reacting to problems once they have developed. Environmental pollution is a good example, particularly business's experience with attempting to clean up rivers, lakes, and other waterways that were neglected for years. In the long run, it would have been wiser to prevent the environmental deterioration from occurring in the first place. A final argument in favour of CSR is that the public strongly supports it. A 2003 poll sponsored by Environics International (discussed below) indicates that the public believes that companies should not only focus on profits for shareholders but that they should be responsible to their workers and communities, even if making things better for workers and communities requires companies to sacrifice some profits.

Assessing the State of Corporate Social Responsibility

The 2003 CSR Monitor survey sponsored by Environics International/GlobeScan assessed responses from over 21 000 consumers, shareholders, and corporate employees in 21 countries. This representative survey revealed that corporate social responsibility is critically important to the citizens of the world. The survey also indicated that more than eight in ten Canadians believe companies should contribute to more than the health of the economy.[31] The survey echoed the findings of the previous annual survey with regard to expectations that major companies should do more than make profits in the twenty-first century.[32]

According to a Conference Board of Canada survey, 77 percent of Canadians are most likely to invest in, and 79 percent to work for, companies they view as socially responsible.[33] In addition, a 2003 Ipsos-Reid poll showed that 55 percent of Canadians surveyed consciously decided to buy a product or service from one company over another because they felt the company was a good corporate citizen.[34] Another survey sponsored by Environics highlighted critical expectations held of corporate behaviour for the coming years. Major companies will be expected to do all the following:

- Demonstrate their commitment to society's values and their contribution to society's social, environmental, and economic goals through actions.
- Fully insulate society from the negative impacts of company operations and its products and services.
- Share the benefits of company activities with key stakeholders as well as with shareholders.
- Demonstrate that the company can make more money by doing the right thing, in some cases reinventing its business strategy. This "doing well by doing good" will reassure stakeholders that the new behaviour will outlast good intentions.[35]

Added together, these annual surveys strongly suggest that CSR is fast becoming a global expectation that requires a comprehensive strategic response. Ethics and CSR need to be made a core business value integrated into all aspects of the firm. However, what is striking in the 2003 survey is that significant proportions of respondents in most countries were unable to name a socially responsible company, despite the consistently high expectations for companies to be socially responsible.[36]

Corporate Social Responsiveness

We have discussed the evolution of corporate social responsibility, a model for viewing social responsibility, and the arguments for and against it. It is now important to address a concept that has arisen over the use of the terms *responsibility* and *responsiveness*. We will consider the views of several writers to develop the idea of **corporate social responsiveness**—the action-oriented variant of CSR.

Ackerman and Bauer's Action View

A general argument that has generated much discussion over the past several decades holds that the term *responsibility* is too suggestive of efforts to pinpoint accountability or obligation. Therefore, it is not dynamic enough to fully describe business's willingness and activity—apart from obligation—to respond to social demands. For example, Robert Ackerman and Raymond Bauer criticized the CSR term by stating, "The connotation of 'responsibility' is that of the process of assuming an obligation. It places an emphasis on motivation rather than on performance." They go on to say, "Responding to social demands is much more than deciding what to do. There remains the management task of doing what one has decided to do, and this task is far from trivial."[37] They argue that "social responsiveness" is a more apt description of what is essential in the social arena.

Their point was well made, especially when it was first set forth. *Responsibility*, taken quite literally, does imply more of a state or condition of having assumed an obligation, whereas *responsiveness* connotes a dynamic, action-oriented condition. We should not overlook, however, that much of what business has done and is doing has resulted from a particular motivation—an assumption of obligation—whether assigned by government, forced by special-interest groups, or voluntarily assumed.

Perhaps business, in some instances, has failed to accept and internalize the obligation, and thus it may seem odd to refer to it as a responsibility. Nevertheless, some motivation that led to social responsiveness had to be there, even though in some cases it was not articulated to be a responsibility or an obligation.

Sethi's Three-Stage Schema

S. Prakash Sethi takes a slightly different, but related, path in getting from social responsibility to social responsiveness. He proposes a three-stage schema for classifying corporate behaviour in responding to social or societal needs: social obligation, social responsibility, and social responsiveness.

Social obligation, Sethi argues, is corporate behaviour in response to market forces or legal constraints. Corporate legitimacy is very narrow here and is based on legal and economic criteria only. *Social responsibility*, Sethi suggests, "implies bringing corporate behavior up to a level where it is congruent with the prevailing social norms, values, and expectations."[38] He argues that whereas the concept of social obligation is proscriptive in nature, social responsibility is prescriptive in nature. *Social responsiveness*, the third stage in his schema, suggests that what is important is "not how corporations should respond to social pressure but what should be their long-run role in a dynamic social system."[39] He suggests that here business is expected to be "anticipatory" and "preventive." Note that his obligation and responsibility categories embody essentially the same message we were attempting to convey with our four-part conceptual definition of CSR.

Frederick's CSR_1, CSR_2, and CSR_3

William Frederick has distinguished between corporate social responsibility, which he calls CSR_1, and corporate social responsiveness, which he terms CSR_2, in the following way:

> *Corporate social responsiveness refers to the capacity of a corporation to respond to social pressures. The literal act of responding, or of achieving a generally responsive posture, to society is the focus.... One searches the organization for mechanisms, procedures, arrangements, and behavioral patterns that, taken collectively, would mark the organization as more or less capable of responding to social pressures.[40]*

Frederick further argued that advocates of social responsiveness (CSR_2) "have urged corporations to eschew philosophic questions of social responsibility and to concentrate on the more pragmatic matter of responding effectively to environmental pressures." He later articulated an idea known as CSR_3—corporate social rectitude—which addressed the moral correctness of actions taken and policies formulated.[41] However, we would argue that the moral dimension is implicit in CSR, as we included it in our basic four-part definition.

Epstein's Process View

Edwin Epstein discusses corporate social responsiveness within the context of a broader concept that he calls the corporate social policy process. In this context, Epstein emphasizes the *process* aspect of social responsiveness. He asserts that corporate social responsiveness focuses on the individual and organizational processes "for determining, implementing, and evaluating the firm's capacity to anticipate, respond to, and manage the issues and problems arising from the diverse claims and expectations of internal and external stakeholders."[42]

Other Views of Responsiveness

Several other writers have provided conceptual schemes that describe the responsiveness facet. Ian Wilson, for example, asserts that there are four possible business strategies: reaction, defence, accommodation, and proaction.[43] Terry McAdam has likewise described four social responsibility philosophies that mesh well with Wilson's and describe the managerial approach that would characterize the range of the responsiveness dimension: "Fight all the way," "Do only what is required," "Be progressive," and "Lead the industry."[44] Davis and Blomstrom describe alternative responses to societal pressures as follows: withdrawal, public relations approach, legal approach, bargaining, and problem solving.[45] Finally, James Post has articulated three major social responsiveness categories: adaptive, proactive, and interactive.[46]

Thus, the corporate social responsiveness dimension that has been discussed by some as an alternative focus to that of social responsibility is, in actuality, an action phase of management's response in the social sphere. In a sense, the responsiveness orientation enables organizations to rationalize and operationalize their social responsibilities without getting bogged down in the quagmire of definition problems, which can so easily occur if organizations try to get an exact determination of what their true responsibilities are before they take any action.

In an interesting study of social responsiveness among Canadian and Finnish forestry firms, researchers concluded that the social responsiveness of a corporation will proceed through a predictable series of phases and that managers will tend to respond to the most powerful stakeholders.[47] This study demonstrates that social responsiveness is a process and that stakeholder power, in addition to a sense of responsibility, may sometimes drive the process.

Corporate Social Performance

For the past few decades, there has been a trend toward making the concern for social and ethical issues more and more pragmatic. The responsiveness thrust that we just discussed was a part of this trend. It is possible to integrate some of the concerns into a model of corporate social performance (CSP). The performance focus is intended to suggest that what really matters is what companies are able to accomplish—the results of their acceptance of social responsibility and adoption of a responsiveness philosophy. In developing a conceptual framework for CSP, we not only have to specify the nature (economic, legal, ethical, philanthropic) of the responsibility, but we also need to identify a particular philosophy, pattern, or mode of responsiveness. Finally, we need to identify the stakeholder issues or topical areas to which these responsibilities are manifested. One need not ponder the stakeholder issues that have evolved under the rubric of social responsibility to recognize how they have changed over time. The issues, and especially the degree of organizational interest in the issues, are always in a state of flux. As the times change, so does the emphasis on the range of social issues that business must address. This will become especially clear in Chapter 8 where we address ethics and technology.

Also of interest is the fact that particular issues are of varying concern to businesses, depending on the industry in which they exist as well as other factors. A bank, for example, is not as pressed on environmental issues as a manufacturer. Likewise, a manufacturer is considerably more absorbed with the issue of environmental protection than is an insurance company.

Carroll's CSP Model

Figure 2–5 illustrates Carroll's **corporate social performance model**, which brings together the three major dimensions we have discussed:

1. Social responsibility categories—economic, legal, ethical, and discretionary (philanthropic)
2. Philosophy (or mode) of social responsiveness—e.g., reaction, defence, accommodation, and proaction
3. Social (or stakeholder) issues involved—consumerism, environment, discrimination, etc.[48]

One dimension of this model pertains to all that is included in our definition of social responsibility—the economic, legal, ethical, and discretionary (philanthropic) components. Second, there is a social responsiveness continuum. Although some writers have suggested that this is the preferable focus when one considers social responsibility, the model in Figure 2–5 suggests that responsiveness is but one additional aspect to be addressed if CSP is to be achieved. The third dimension concerns the scope of social or stakeholder issues (for example, consumerism, environment, and discrimination) that management must address.

Usefulness of the CSP Model to Academics and Managers

The corporate social performance model is intended to be useful to both academics and managers. For academics, the model is primarily a conceptual aid to perceiving the distinction among the concepts of corporate social responsibility that have appeared in the literature. What previously have been regarded as separate definitions of CSR are treated here as three separate aspects pertaining to CSP. The model's major use to the academic, therefore, is in helping to systematize the important concepts that must be taught and understood in an effort to clarify the CSR concept. The model is not the ultimate conceptualization. It is, rather, a modest but necessary step toward understanding the major facets of CSP.

The conceptual model can assist managers in understanding that social responsibility is not separate and distinct from economic performance. The model integrates economic concerns into a social performance framework. In addition, it places ethical and philanthropic expectations into a rational economic and legal framework. The model can help the manager systematically think through major stakeholder issues. Although it does not provide the answer to how far the organization should go, it does provide a conceptualization that could lead to better-managed social performance. Moreover, the model could be used as a planning tool and as a diagnostic problem-solving tool. The model can assist the manager by identifying categories within which the organization can be situated.

The following example may help show how an organization may position its actions using the CSP model (see the segments in Figure 2–5). The major pharmaceutical firm Merck & Co. discovered a drug (Mectizan) it later concluded could cure a disease known as "river blindness." Merck learned that this disease was common in tiny villages in Africa and in parts of the Middle East and Latin America. Initially,

---

FIGURE 2–5

Carroll's Corporate Social Performance Model

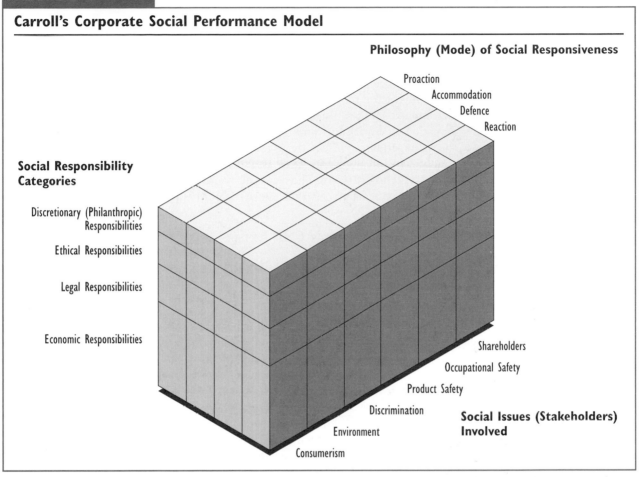

Philosophy (Mode) of Social Responsiveness

Proaction
Accommodation
Defence
Reaction

Social Responsibility Categories

Discretionary (Philanthropic) Responsibilities

Ethical Responsibilities

Legal Responsibilities

Economic Responsibilities

Shareholders
Occupational Safety
Product Safety
Discrimination
Environment
Consumerism

Social Issues (Stakeholders) Involved

Source: Archie B. Carroll, "A Three-Dimensional Conceptual Model of Corporate Social Performance," *Academy of Management Review* (Vol. 4, No. 4, 1979), 503. Reproduced with permission.

Merck wanted to market the drug at a profit. It learned, however, that there was no viable market for the drug because its potential customers were too poor, lived in isolated locations, and had no access to pharmacies or routine medical care. Merck then hoped a group like the World Health Organization (WHO) or a foundation would step forward to fund a distribution program for the drug, which could cost as much as US$20 million a year.

When no funding source came forward, Merck decided to supply Mectizan to everyone who needed it, indefinitely, and at no charge. By 1995, more than 6 million people in 21 countries had received at least one dose of Mectizan, and many others were receiving annual doses. Mectizan distribution received a significant boost in 1996 when the WHO and World Bank announced an ambitious 12-year project to wipe out river blindness. Former U.S. president Jimmy Carter agreed to coordinate the US$124 million project through the Carter Center in Atlanta.[49]

According to the social performance model in Figure 2–5, Merck saw itself moving from the economic category to the ethical or philanthropic one. On the social issues dimension, the firm initially focused on potential consumers who became consumer-recipients of the firm's socially responsible commitment. On the philosophy of social responsiveness continuum, Merck was at the proaction end. Given Merck's leadership on this issue, it is not surprising to note that the company was voted the "most admired" corporation from 1986–1992 in *Fortune* magazine's annual survey of corporate reputations. As recently as the late 1990s, Merck was still ranked as one of *Fortune*'s top ten most admired companies in the United States.[50]

The Merck example shows how a business's response can be positioned in the social performance model. The average business firm faces many such controversial issues and might use the model to analyze its stance on these issues and perhaps to help determine its motivations, actions, and response strategies. Managers would have a systematic framework for thinking through not only the social issues they face but also the managerial response patterns they should contemplate. The model could serve as a guide in formulating criteria to assist the organization in developing its posture on various stakeholder issues. The net result could be an increase in the amount of systematic attention being given to the entire realm of corporate social performance.

Wartick and Cochran's CSP Extensions

Before leaving our discussion of the CSP model, it is important to examine extensions of the model. The initial version of the model employed "social issues" as the third aspect or dimension, which embraced such issues as consumerism, environment, and discrimination. That dimension is now referred to as stakeholder issues, to place it within our current framework. While it was still being framed as social issues, however, Steven Wartick and Philip Cochran proposed that the dimension of social issues had, in fact, matured from simply an identification of the social issue categories in which companies must take action to a whole new management field, known as *social issues management*. Issues management, which we will treat more fully in Chapter 5, entails such activities as issues identification, issues analysis, and response development. Whether the third dimension is perceived as social issues or stakeholder issues, the issues management approach is useful.

Wartick and Cochran extended the social performance model even further by proposing that the three dimensions be thought of as depicting principles (corporate social responsibilities, reflecting a philosophical orientation), processes (corporate social responsiveness, reflecting an institutional orientation), and policies (social issues management, reflecting an organizational orientation). These extensions are useful because they help us to more fully appreciate complementary aspects that were neglected in the original model. Figure 2–6 summarizes Wartick and Cochran's extensions to the CSP model.[51]

Wood's Reformulated CSP Model

Donna Wood elaborated and reformulated Carroll's model and Wartick and Cochran's extensions and set forth a reformulated model. Using Wartick and Cochran's extensions, she produced a useful definition of corporate social performance:

> *A business organization's configuration of principles of social responsibility, processes of social responsiveness, and policies, programs, and other observable outcomes as they relate to the firm's societal relationships.*[52]

Wood's proposal is (1) to think of social responsiveness as a set of processes rather than as a single process and (2) to think of Wartick and Cochran's policies as entail-

FIGURE 2-6

Wartick and Cochran's Corporate Social Performance Model Extensions

Principles	Processes	Policies
Corporate Social Responsibilities	Corporate Social Responsiveness	Social Issues Management
(1) Economic	(1) Reactive	(1) Issues Identification
(2) Legal	(2) Defensive	(2) Issues Analysis
(3) Ethical	(3) Accommodative	(3) Response Development
(4) Discretionary	(4) Proactive	
Directed at:	**Directed at:**	**Directed at:**
(1) The Social Contract of Business	(1) The Capacity to Respond to Changing Societal Conditions	(1) Minimizing "Surprises"
(2) Business as a Moral Agent	(2) Managerial Approaches to Developing Responses	(2) Determining Effective Corporate Social Policies
Philosophical Orientation	**Institutional Orientation**	**Organizational Orientation**

Source: Steven L. Wartick and Philip L. Cochran, "The Evolution of the Corporate Social Performance Model," *Academy of Management Review* (Vol. 10, 1985), 767.

ing observable outcomes of corporate and managerial actions. Wood takes this definition further by proposing that each of the three components—principles, processes, and outcomes—is composed of specific elements.

These extensions and reformulations of Carroll's corporate social performance model add significantly to our appreciation of what is involved as we strive to think of CSP as a dynamic and multifaceted managerial concept.

After this discussion of CSP, one might ask whether people really care about CSP. In the next section, we will examine nonacademic research into CSP. We will close the current section, however, by reporting a study of whether U.S. consumers really care about CSP. In this study, Karen Paul and other researchers developed a scale to measure consumers' sensitivity to CSP. Among the researchers' findings were that CSP does matter, that women were more sensitive than men to CSP, and that those identifying themselves as Democrats were more sensitive to CSP than Republicans.[53]

Swanson's Reorientation of CSP

Swanson elaborated on the dynamic nature of the principles, processes, and outcomes reformulated by Wood. Relying on research on corporate culture, her reoriented model links corporate social performance to the personally held values and ethics of executive managers and other employees. Along these lines, Swanson proposes that the executive's sense of morality highly influences the policies and programs of environmental assessment, stakeholder management, and issues management carried out by employees.[54] According to her reorientation, these internal processes are means by which organizations can impact society through *economizing* (efficiently converting inputs into outputs) and *ecologizing* (forging community-minded collaborations).[55] Although Swanson's model casts corporate obligations broadly, it does not lose sight of the fact that responsibility translates into some particular mix of economic, legal, ethical, and discretionary obligations for any one firm.

By proposing that personally held values and ethics are bound up in the corporate decision processes that affect society, Swanson's model builds on the continuum of responsiveness in Carroll's model while elaborating on the philosophical and institutional extensions of Wartick and Cochran and Wood.

Nonacademic Research on Corporate Social Performance

Although there has been considerable academic research on the subject of corporate social performance over the past decade, we should stress that academics are not the only ones who are interested in this topic. Prominent organizations and periodicals that report on social performance include *Corporate Knights*, *Fortune* magazine, *Ethics in Action*, *Canadian Business for Social Responsibility*, and *Business Ethics* magazine.

Corporate Knights

In the summer of 2002, the inaugural issue of *Corporate Knights* magazine (http://www.corporateknights.ca/) named the "50 Best Canadian Corporate Citizens." The magazine noted that in the U.S. there has been a ranking of the Best 100 Corporate Citizens since 1996. However, practically no such rankings have existed in Canada, though the *Financial Post* attempted to do so in 1997. *Corporate Knights* uses a weighting schedule based on a stakeholder model (shareholders, nature, employees, customers, and citizens) that breaks down as follows:

- community: 7.5 percent
- employee relations/diversity: 15.0 percent
- environment: 17.5 percent
- product safety and business practices: 20.0 percent
- international: 17.5 percent
- corporate governance: 10.0 percent
- share performance (five-year): 12.5 percent

Among the leading companies in 2003 were Alcan Inc., the Royal Bank of Canada, Suncor Energy Inc., Nexen Inc., the Canadian Imperial Bank of Commerce, the Bank of Nova Scotia, and Domtar Inc.

Fortune

For many years now, *Fortune* magazine (http://www.fortune.com/fortune) has conducted rankings of "America's Most Admired Companies" and has included among their "Eight Key Attributes of Reputation" the category titled "Social Responsibility." The rankings are the result of a poll of more than 12 600 senior executives, outside directors, and financial analysts. In the social responsibility category, the most admired firms for 2003 were Wal-Mart, Southwest Airlines, Berkshire Hathaway, Dell Computer, General Electric, Johnson & Johnson, Microsoft, Federal Express, Starbucks, and Procter & Gamble.[56] It is not clear what impact, if any, the *Fortune* rankings have for these businesses, but surely they have some impact on the firms' general reputations. The important point to note here, however, is that the social responsibility category is one indicator of corporate social performance and that it was included as a criterion of admired companies by a major business magazine.

Ethics in Action

Ethics in Action (http://www.ethicsinaction.com/) was created in 1994 and its Ethics in Action Awards event was founded as a means to celebrate corporate social responsibility in a variety of businesses. This award recognizes organizations and individuals who reflect high standards of corporate citizenship and responsibility. The awards have attempted to generate greater awareness of the importance of corporate social responsibility in Canada.

Past award recipients include Husky Injection Molding Systems Ltd., Print Three, and Pfizer Canada Inc., which received recognition for its involvement in forming a national association of informal caregivers. One business leader who has been honoured is the president of Canadian Tire, who helped a nonprofit group collect and distribute sleeping bags to the homeless. The program also expanded to offer emergency disaster relief in Canada and abroad.

Canadian Business for Social Responsibility

Canadian Business for Social Responsibility (CBSR; http://www.cbsr.ca/) is a nonprofit membership network of businesses working to improve their social, environmental, and financial performance. CBSR's aim is to support Canadian business in implementing higher standards of social responsibility. CBSR produces a newsletter (*GoodCompany*) and sponsors events and workshops intended to encourage and educate the business community in areas of social responsibility. In addition, it released "The GoodCompany Guidelines," which are intended to serve as a corporate accountability tool in Canada by helping companies to assess, improve, and report on their social, environmental, and financial performance. The aim is to offer an accountability tool that assists companies in targeting their performance gaps, developing policies to address them, and reporting back to their stakeholders.

Business Ethics

For several years now, *Business Ethics* magazine (http://www.business-ethics.com/) has published its list of Annual Business Awards. Typically, award winners meet many (though not necessarily all) of the following criteria:

- Be a leader in their field, out ahead of the pack, showing the way ethically.
- Have programs or initiatives in social responsibility that demonstrate sincerity and ongoing vibrancy, and that reach deep into the company.
- Have a significant presence on the national or world scene, so their ethical behaviour sends a loud signal.
- Be a stand-out in at least one area of social responsibility, though recipients need not be exemplary in all areas.
- Have faced a recent challenge and overcome it with integrity, or taken other recent steps to show their ethical commitment is still very much alive.

Among recent award winners are the following businesses: Fastener Industries of Ohio, acknowledged for its "20-year commitment to democratic governance by employees"; White Dog Café in Philadelphia for being a model of business that is "locally rooted, human scale, stakeholder-owned, and life-serving"; and New Belgium Brewing Co. in Colorado, for its "dedication to environmental stewardship in every part of its brewing process."

Business Ethics magazine also publishes an annual volume in which it reports its "100 Best Corporate Citizens." Its goal is to "celebrate those companies that excel at serving multiple stakeholders well."[57] Among the criteria used by the panel of judges are firms:

- Having community-service programs that are employee-driven, not executive-driven
- Taking a rifle-shot rather than a shotgun approach to community service
- Encouraging employees to express their individuality
- Finding creative ways to relieve the pressures in employees' lives
- Taking a team-based approach to developing products and servicing customers
- Showing, in the end, that not even the best corporate citizens are perfect

The top five winners for 2003 were General Mills, Cummins Inc., Intel, Procter & Gamble, and IBM. Each of these companies scored high on its social performance with respect to community, minorities and women, employees, environment, non-U.S. stakeholders, and customers.

Corporate Citizenship

In recent years, business practitioners and academics alike have grown fond of the term "corporate citizenship" in reference to businesses' corporate social performance. But, what does **corporate citizenship** really mean? Does it have a distinct meaning apart from the concepts of corporate social responsibility, responsiveness, and performance discussed earlier? A careful look at the concept and its literature shows that although it is a useful and attractive term, it is not distinct from the terminology we have described earlier, except in the eyes of some writers who have attempted to give it a specific, narrow meaning. If one thinks about companies as "citizens" of the countries in which they reside, corporate citizenship just means that these companies have certain responsibilities that they must perform in order to be perceived as good corporate citizens. Altman and Vidaver-Cohen say that "corporate citizenship is not a new concept, but one whose time has come."[58]

Corporate citizenship has been described by some as a broad, encompassing term that basically embraces all that is implied in the concepts of social responsibility, responsiveness, and performance. Graves, Waddock, and Kelly, for example, define good corporate citizenship as "serving a variety of stakeholders well."[59] Fombrun also proposes a broad conception. He holds that corporate citizenship is composed of a three-part view that encompasses (1) a reflection of shared moral and ethical principles, (2) a vehicle for integrating individuals into the communities in which they work, and (3) a form of enlightened self-interest that balances all stakeholders' claims and enhances a company's long-term value.[60]

Davenport's research also resulted in a broad definition of corporate citizenship that includes a commitment to ethical business behaviour, and balancing the needs of stakeholders, while working to protect the environment.[61] Finally, Carroll has recast his four categories of corporate social responsibility as embracing the "four faces of corporate citizenship"—economic, legal, ethical, and philanthropic. Each face, aspect, or responsibility reveals an important facet that contributes to the whole. He poses that "just as private citizens are expected to fulfill these responsibilities, companies are as well."[62]

At the narrow end of the spectrum, Altman speaks of corporate citizenship in terms of corporate community relations. In this view, it embraces the functions through which business intentionally interacts with nonprofit organizations, citizen groups, and other stakeholders at the community level.[63] Other definitions of corporate citizenship fall in between these broad and narrow perspectives, and some refer to global corporate citizenship as well, as increasingly companies are expected to conduct themselves appropriately wherever they are doing business.

The benefits of good corporate citizenship to stakeholders are fairly apparent. But, what are the benefits of good corporate citizenship to business itself? A literature review of studies attempting to discern the benefits to companies of corporate citizenship, defined broadly, revealed empirical and anecdotal evidence supporting the following:[64]

- Improved employee relations (e.g., improves employee recruitment, retention, morale, loyalty, motivation, and productivity)
- Improved customer relationships (e.g., increases customer loyalty, acts as a tiebreaker for consumer purchasing, enhances brand image)
- Improved business performance (e.g., positively impacts bottom-line returns, increases competitive advantage, encourages cross-functional integration)
- Enhanced company's marketing efforts (e.g., helps create a positive company image, helps a company manage its reputation, supports higher prestige pricing, and enhances government affairs activities)

The terminology of corporate citizenship is especially attractive because it resonates so well with the business community's attempts to describe their own socially responsive activities and practices. Therefore, we can expect that this concept will be around for some years to come. Generally speaking, as we refer to CSR, social responsiveness, and social performance, we are also embracing activities that would typically fall under the purview of a firm's corporate citizenship.[65] Figure 2–7 suggests some of the characteristics of good corporate citizens or socially responsible companies.

Social Performance and Financial Performance

One issue that comes up frequently in considerations of corporate social performance is whether or not there is a demonstrable relationship between a firm's social responsibility or performance and its financial performance. Unfortunately, attempts to measure this relationship are typically hampered by measurement problems. The appropriate performance criteria for measuring financial performance and social responsibility are subject to debate. Furthermore, the measurement of social responsibility is fraught with definitional problems. Even if a definition of CSR could be agreed on, there still would remain the complex task of operationalizing the definition.

Over the years, studies on the social responsibility–financial performance relationship have produced varying results.[66] In one important study of this relationship, Preston and O'Bannon examined data from 67 large U.S. corporations covering the years 1982–1992. They concluded that "there is a positive association between social and financial performance in large U.S. corporations."[67] Research by Waddock and Graves has concluded that corporate social performance (CSP) was positively associated with prior financial performance (CFP) and future financial performance.[68] In a study of the chemical industry, Griffin and Mahon found that perceptual CSP measures are "somewhat related" to the financial information. Overall, however, they found contradictory results in studies they examined.[69] Finally, a study by Roman, Hayibor, and Agle, reanalyzing the Griffin and Mahon data, concluded that the "vast majority of studies support the idea that, at the very least, good social performance does not lead to poor financial performance." They go on to say that most of the studies they reviewed indicated a positive correlation between CSP and CFP.[70]

FIGURE 2-7

Good Corporate Citizens

- Makes products that are safe
- Does not pollute air or water
- Obeys the law in all aspects of business
- Promotes honest/ethical employee behaviour
- Commits to safe workplace ethics
- Does not use misleading/deceptive advertising
- Upholds stated policy banning discrimination
- Utilizes "environmentally friendly" packaging
- Protects employees against sexual harassment
- Recycles within company
- Shows no past record of questionable activity
- Responds quickly to customer problems
- Maintains waste reduction program
- Provides/pays portion of medical
- Promotes energy-conservation program
- Helps displaced workers with placement
- Gives money to charitable/educational causes
- Utilizes only biodegradable/recycling materials
- Employs friendly/courteous/responsive personnel
- Tries continually to improve quality

Source: WalkerInformation, 1994. Used with permission.

In qualifying the research, it is important to note that there have been at least three different views, hypotheses, or perspectives that have dominated these discussions and research. Perhaps the most popular view, which we will call *Perspective 1*, is built on the belief that socially responsible firms are more financially profitable. To those who advocate the concept of social performance, it is apparent why they would like to think that social performance is a driver of financial performance and, ultimately, a corporation's reputation. If it could be demonstrated that socially responsible firms, in general, are more financially successful and have better reputations, this would significantly bolster the CSP view, even in the eyes of its critics.

Perspective 1 has been studied extensively. Unfortunately, the findings of most of the studies that have sought to demonstrate this relationship have been either flawed in their methodology or inconclusive. Numerous studies have been done well, but even these have failed to produce conclusive results. In spite of this, some studies have claimed to have successfully established this linkage. For example, a study by Covenant Investment Management concluded that social concern pays. This study found that 200 companies ranking highest on Covenant's overall social responsibility scale had outperformed the Standard & Poor's 500-stock index during the five years (1988–1992) studied.[71] To be considered a valid finding, however, the Covenant research would have to be subjected to careful scrutiny. Part of the problem with Perspective 1 is that positive correlations may be found but causality is not clearly established.

Perspective 2, which has not been studied as extensively, argues that a firm's financial performance is a driver of its social performance. This perspective is built somewhat on the notion that social responsibility is a "fair-weather" concept; that is, when times are good and companies are enjoying financial success, we witness higher levels of social performance. In their study, Preston and O'Bannon found the strongest evidence that financial performance either precedes, or is contemporaneous with, social performance. This evidence supports the view that social–financial performance correlations are best explained by positive synergies or by "available funding."[72] The research of Waddock and Graves, cited earlier, is consistent with this finding.

Perspective 3 argues that there is an interactive relationship among social performance, financial performance, and corporate reputation. In this symbiotic view, the three major factors influence each other, and, because they are so interrelated, it is not easy to identify which factor is driving the process. Regardless of the perspective taken, each view advocates a significant role for CSP, and it is expected that researchers will continue to explore these perspectives for years to come. Figure 2–8 depicts the essentials of each of these views.

Finally, it should be mentioned that the "contingency" view of Husted suggests that CSP should be seen as a function of the fit between specific strategies and structures and the nature of the social issue. He argues that the social issue is determined by the expectational gaps of the firm and its stakeholders that occur within or between views of what is and/or what ought to be, and that high corporate social performance is achieved by closing these expectational gaps with the appropriate strategy and structure.[73]

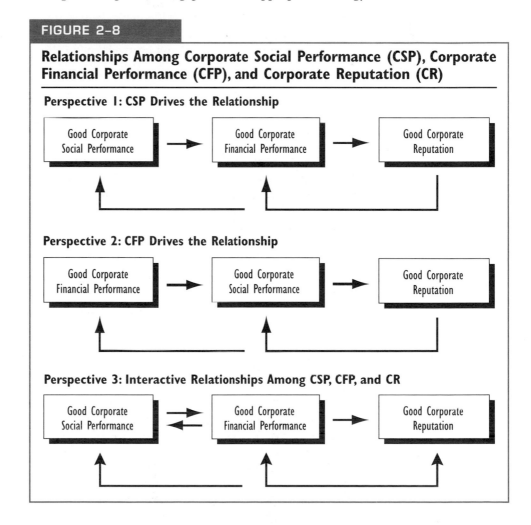

FIGURE 2–8

Relationships Among Corporate Social Performance (CSP), Corporate Financial Performance (CFP), and Corporate Reputation (CR)

Perspective 1: CSP Drives the Relationship

Good Corporate Social Performance → Good Corporate Financial Performance → Good Corporate Reputation

Perspective 2: CFP Drives the Relationship

Good Corporate Financial Performance → Good Corporate Social Performance → Good Corporate Reputation

Perspective 3: Interactive Relationships Among CSP, CFP, and CR

Good Corporate Social Performance ⇄ Good Corporate Financial Performance → Good Corporate Reputation

A Multiple Bottom-Line Perspective

A basic premise of all these perspectives is that there is only one "bottom line"—a corporate bottom line that addresses primarily the shareholders', or owners', investments in the firm. An alternative view is that the firm has "multiple bottom lines" that benefit from corporate social performance. This stakeholder-bottom-line perspective argues that the impacts or benefits of CSP cannot be fully measured or appreciated by considering only the impact of the firm's financial bottom line.

To truly operate with a stakeholder perspective, companies need to accept the multiple-bottom-line view. Thus, CSP cannot be fully comprehended unless we also consider that its impacts on stakeholders, such as consumers, employees, the community, and other stakeholder groups, are noted, measured, and considered. Research may never conclusively demonstrate a relationship between CSP and financial performance. If a stakeholder perspective is taken, however, it may be more straightforward to assess the impact of CSP on multiple stakeholders' bottom lines. This model of CSP and stakeholders' bottom lines might be depicted as shown in Figure 2–9.

Socially Conscious or Ethical Investing

Special-interest groups, the media, and academics are not alone in their interest in business's social performance. Investors are also interested. The **socially conscious or ethical investing** movement arrived on the scene in the 1970s and has continued to grow and prosper. By the early 2000s, social investing had matured into a comprehensive investing approach complete with social and environmental screens, shareholder activism, and community investment.[74] According to Michael Jantzi, ethical investing

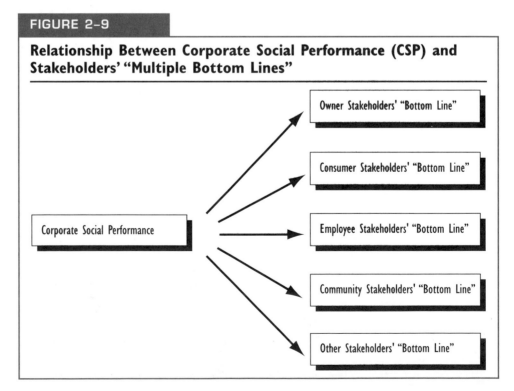

FIGURE 2–9

Relationship Between Corporate Social Performance (CSP) and Stakeholders' "Multiple Bottom Lines"

has a history in Canada of more than 25 years, represents about $50 billion in assets, and is the fastest-growing segment in the Canadian investment market.[75]

In North America, social responsibility investing can be traced back to the early 1900s, when church endowments refused to buy "sin" stocks—then defined as shares in tobacco, alcohol, and gambling companies. During the Vietnam War era of the 1960s and early 1970s, antiwar investors refused to invest in defence contracting firms. In the early 1980s, universities, municipalities, and foundations sold off their shares of companies that had operations in South Africa to protest apartheid. By the 1990s, self-styled socially responsible investing came into its own.[76] By the early 2000s, social investing was celebrating the fact that social or ethical investing was now part of the mainstream.

Socially conscious investments in pension funds, mutual funds, and municipal and private portfolios now exceed US$2.2 trillion in North America. However, managers of socially conscious funds do not use only ethical or social responsibility criteria to decide which companies to invest in. They typically consider a company's financial health before all else. Moreover, a growing corps of brokers, financial planners, and portfolio managers are available to help people evaluate investments for their social impacts.[77]

The concept of "social screening" is the backbone of the socially conscious investing movement. Investors seeking to put their money into socially responsible firms want to screen out those firms they consider to be socially irresponsible or to actively invest in those firms they think of as being socially responsible. Thus, there are negative social screens and positive social screens. Some of the negative social screens that have been used in recent years include the avoidance of investing in tobacco manufacturers, gambling casino operators, defence or weapons contractors, and firms doing business in South Africa.[78] In 1994, however, with the elimination of the official system of apartheid in South Africa, this was eliminated as a negative screen by many.

It is more difficult, and thus more challenging, to implement positive social screens, because they require the potential investor to make judgment calls as to what constitutes an acceptable or a good level of social performance on social investment criteria. Criteria that may be used as either positive or negative screens, depending on the firm's performance, might include the firm's record on issues such as equal employment opportunity, environmental protection, treatment of employees, corporate citizenship (broadly defined), and treatment of animals.

The financial performance of socially conscious funds shows that investors do not have to sacrifice profitability for principles. Recent evidence suggests that investors expect and receive competitive returns from social investments.[79]

It should be added, however, that there is no clear and consistent evidence that returns from socially conscious funds will equal or exceed the returns from funds that are not so carefully screened. Therefore, socially conscious funds are valued most highly by those investors who really care about the social performance of companies in their portfolios and are willing to put their money at some risk. A recent study concluded that there is no penalty for improved CSP in terms of institutional ownership and that high CSP tends in fact to lead to an increase in the number of institutional investors holding a given stock.[80]

The Council on Economic Priorities has suggested that there are at least three reasons why there has been an upsurge in social or ethical investing:[81]

1. There is more reliable and sophisticated research on CSP than in the past.
2. Investment firms using social criteria have established a solid track record, and investors do not have to sacrifice gains for principles.
3. The socially conscious 1960s generation is now making investment decisions.

In recent years, people have become much more sophisticated about making investment decisions than in the past. More people are seeing social investments as a way in which they can exert their priorities concerning the balance of financial and social concerns. Whether it be called social investing, ethical investing, or socially conscious investing, it is clear that social investing has "arrived" on the scene and become a part of the mainstream.

Among the numerous publications available on the topic, *Corporate Knights* and *Business Ethics* now give annual social investing awards to mutual funds or investment firms that combine great financial returns with strong social impact. Social investors can also receive up-to-date guidelines and data on social investing on the Web. For example, the Social Investment Forum has its own Web site (see http://www.socialinvest.org) dedicated to the topic, with insights into social and financial performance data. Also see http://www.socialfunds.com.[82] *Corporate Knights* has its report on socially responsible investing at http://www.corporateknights.ca/downloads/sri_table.pdf.

Socially conscious funds will continue to be debated in the investment community. The fact that they exist, have grown, and have prospered, however, provides evidence that the idea is a serious one and that there truly are investors in the real world who take the social performance issue quite seriously.

Summary

Important and related concepts include those of corporate citizenship, corporate social responsibility, responsiveness, and performance. The corporate social responsibility concept has a rich history. It has grown out of many diverse views and even today does not enjoy a consensus of definition. A four-part conceptualization was presented that broadly conceives CSR as encompassing economic, legal, ethical, and philanthropic components. The four parts were presented as part of the Pyramid of CSR.

The concern for corporate social responsibility has been expanded to include a concern for social responsiveness. The responsiveness focus suggests more of an action-oriented theme by which firms not only must address their basic obligations but also must decide on basic modes of responding to these obligations. A CSP model was presented that brought the responsibility and responsiveness dimensions together into a framework that also identified realms of social or stakeholder issues that must be considered. The identification of social issues has blossomed into a field now called "issues management" or "stakeholder management."

The interest in corporate social responsibility extends beyond the academic community. For example, on an annual basis, *Fortune* magazine polls executives on various dimensions of corporate performance; one major dimension is called "Social Responsibility." In addition, the term "corporate citizenship" has arrived on the scene to embrace a whole host of socially conscious activities and practices on the part of businesses. This term has become quite popular in the business community.

Finally, the socially conscious or ethical investing movement seems to be flourishing. This indicates that there is a growing body of investors who are sensitive to business's social and ethical (as well as financial) performance. Studies of the relationship between social responsibility and economic performance do not yield consistent results, but social efforts are nevertheless expected and are of value to both the firm and the business community. In the final analysis, sound corporate social (stakeholder) performance is associated with a "multiple-bottom-line effect" in which a number of different stakeholder groups experience enhanced bottom lines.

Key Terms

community obligations (page 33)

corporate citizenship (page 54)

corporate social performance model (page 48)

corporate social responsiveness (page 45)

economic responsibilities (page 36)

ethical responsibilities (page 36)

legal responsibilities (page 36)

paternalism (page 33)

philanthropic responsibilities (page 38)

philanthropy (page 32)

Pyramid of CSR (page 39)

socially conscious or ethical investing (page 58)

Discussion Questions

1. Identify and explain the Pyramid of Corporate Social Responsibility. Provide several examples of each "layer" of the pyramid. Identify and discuss some of the tensions among the layers or components.

2. In your view, what is the single strongest argument *against* the idea of corporate social responsibility? What is the single strongest argument *for* corporate social responsibility? Briefly explain.

3. Differentiate corporate social responsibility from corporate social responsiveness. Give an example of each.

4. Discuss the interrelationships among the concepts of corporate social performance (CSP), corporate financial performance (CFP), and corporate reputation (CR). Which perspective on these relationships seems most valid to you? Explain why.

5. Does socially conscious or ethical investing seem to you to be a legitimate way in which the average citizen might demonstrate her or his concern for CSR? Discuss.

Endnotes

1. "100 Best Corporate Citizens," *Business Ethics* (2003), http://www.business-ethics.com/100best.htm.
2. http://www.corporateknights.ca/best50/intro.asp.
3. Quoted in John L. Paluszek, *Business and Society: 1976–2000* (New York: AMACOM, 1976), 1.
4. Keith Davis, "Understanding the Social Responsibility Puzzle," *Business Horizon* (Winter 1967), 45–50.
5. James W. McKie, "Changing Views," in *Social Responsibility and the Business Predicament* (Washington, DC: The Brookings Institution, 1974), 22.
6. *Ibid.*
7. See Morrell Heald, *The Social Responsibilities of Business: Company and Community, 1900–1960* (Cleveland: Case Western Reserve University Press, 1970), 12–14.
8. McKie, 23.
9. *Ibid.*, 25.
10. Heald, 119.
11. McKie, 27–28.
12. Neil J. Mitchell, *The Generous Corporation: A Political Analysis of Economic Power* (New Haven, CT: Yale University Press, 1989).
13. Ronald E. Berenbeim, "When the Corporate Conscience Was Born" [A review of Mitchell's book], *Across the Board* (October 1989), 60–62.
14. *Ibid.*, 62.
15. Keith Davis and Robert L. Blomstrom, *Business and Society: Environment and Responsibility*, 3d ed. (New York: McGraw-Hill, 1975), 39.
16. Joseph W. McGuire, *Business and Society* (New York: McGraw-Hill, 1963), 144.
17. Edwin M. Epstein, "The Corporate Social Policy Process: Beyond Business Ethics, Corporate Social Responsibility and Corporate Social Responsiveness," *California Management Review* (Vol. XXIX, No. 3, 1987), 104.
18. For a more complete history of the CSR concept, see Archie B. Carroll, "Corporate Social Responsibility: Evolution of a Definitional Construct," *Business and Society* (Vol. 38, No. 3, September 1999), 268–295.
19. Archie B. Carroll, "A Three-Dimensional Conceptual Model of Corporate Social Performance," *Academy of Management Review* (Vol. 4, No. 4, 1979), 497–505.

20. Archie B. Carroll, "The Pyramid of Corporate Social Responsibility: Toward the Moral Management of Organizational Stakeholders," *Business Horizons* (July–August 1991), 39–48. Also see Archie B. Carroll, "The Four Faces of Corporate Citizenship," *Business and Society Review* (Vol. 100–101, 1998), 1–7.

21. *Ibid*.

22. *Ibid*.

23. Milton Friedman, "The Social Responsibility of Business Is to Increase Its Profits," *New York Times* (September 1962), 126.

24. *Ibid.*, 33.

25. Christopher D. Stone, *Where the Law Ends* (New York: Harper Colophon Books, 1975), 77.

26. Keith Davis, "The Case For and Against Business Assumption of Social Responsibilities," *Academy of Management Journal* (June 1973), 312–322.

27. F. A. Hayek, "The Corporation in a Democratic Society: In Whose Interest Ought It and Will It Be Run?" in H. Ansoff (ed.), *Business Strategy* (Middlesex: Penguin, 1969), 225.

28. Davis, 320.

29. Thomas A. Petit, *The Moral Crisis in Management* (New York: McGraw-Hill, 1967), 58.

30. Davis, 316.

31. http://www.globescan.com.

32. The Millennium Poll on Corporate Social Responsibility (Environics, Intl., Ltd., Prince of Wales Business Leaders Forum, The Conference Board, 1999), http://www.Environics.net.

33. Conference Board of Canada, http://www.conference board.ca/GCSR.

34. "Poll Rates Corporate Canada on CSR," P. 26, http://www.ipsos-reid.com.

35. The Millennium Poll on Corporate Social Responsibility (Environics, Intl., Ltd., Prince of Wales Business Forum, The Conference Board, 1999), http://www.Environics.net.

36. Conference Board of Canada, http://www.conference board.ca.

37. Robert Ackerman and Raymond Bauer, *Corporate Social Responsiveness: The Modern Dilemma* (Reston, VA: Reston Publishing Company, 1976), 6.

38. S. Prakash Sethi, "Dimensions of Corporate Social Performance: An Analytical Framework," *California Management Review* (Spring 1975), 58–64.

39. *Ibid.*, 62–63.

40. William C. Frederick, "From CSR1 to CSR2: The Maturing of Business-and-Society Thought," Working Paper No. 279 (Graduate School of Business, University of Pittsburgh, 1978), 6. See also *Business and Society* (Vol. 33, No. 2, August 1994), 150–164.

41. William C. Frederick, "Toward CSR3: Why Ethical Analysis Is Indispensable and Unavoidable in Corporate Affairs," *California Management Review* (Winter 1986), 131.

42. Epstein, 107.

43. Ian Wilson, "What One Company Is Doing About Today's Demands on Business," in G. A. Steiner (ed.), *Changing Business-Society Interrelationships* (UCLA, 1975).

44. T. W. McAdam, "How to Put Corporate Responsibility into Practice," *Business and Society Review/Innovation* (Summer 1973), 8–16.

45. Davis and Blomstrom, 85–86.

46. James E. Post, *Corporate Behavior and Social Change* (Reston, VA: Reston Publishing Co., 1978), 39.

47. Juha Näsi, Salme Näsi, Nelson Phillips, and Stelios Zyglidopoulos, "The Evolution of Corporate Responsiveness," *Business and Society* (Vol. 36, No. 3, September 1997), 296–321.

48. Carroll, 1979, 502–504.

49. David Bollier and the Business Enterprise Trust, *Aiming Higher* (New York: AMACOM, 1996), 280–293.

50. "America's Most Admired Companies," *Fortune* (March 2, 1998), 70.

51. Steven L. Wartick and Philip L. Cochran, "The Evolution of the Corporate Social Performance Model," *Academy of Management Review* (Vol. 10, 1985), 765–766.

52. Donna J. Wood, "Corporate Social Performance Revisited," *Academy of Management Review* (October 1991), 691–718.

53. Karen Paul, Lori Zalka, Meredith Downes, Susan Perry, and Shawnta Perry, "U.S. Consumer Sensitivity to Corporate Social Performance," *Business and Society* (Vol. 36, No. 4, December 1997), 408–418.

54. D. L. Swanson, "Addressing a Theoretical Problem by Reorienting the Corporate Social Performance Model," *Academy of Management Review* (Vol. 20, No. 1, 1995), 43–64; D. L. Swanson, "Toward an Integrative Theory of Business and Society: A Research Strategy for Corporate Social Performance," *Academy of Management Review* (Vol. 24, No. 3, 1999), 596–521.

55. W. C. Frederick, *Values, Nature, and Culture in the American Corporation* (New York: Oxford Press, 1995).

56. http://www.fortune.com/fortune/mostadmired.

57. Tom Klusmann, "The 100 Best Corporate Citizens," *Business Ethics* (March/April 2000), 12–16.

58. See special issue on "Corporate Citizenship," *Business and Society Review*, 105:1 (Spring 2000), edited by Barbara W. Altman and Deborah Vidaver-Cohen.

59. Samuel P. Graves, Sandra Waddock, and Marjorie Kelly, "How Do You Measure Corporate Citizenship?" *Business Ethics* (March/April 2001), 17.

60. Charles J. Fombrum, "Three Pillars of Corporate Citizenship," in Noel Tichy, Andrew McGill, and Lynda St. Clair (eds.), *Corporate Global Citizenship* (San Francisco: The New Lexington Press), 27–61.

61. Kimberly S. Davenport, "Corporate Citizenship: A Stakeholder Approach for Defining Corporate Social Performance and Identifying Measures for Assessing It,"

doctoral dissertation, The Fielding Institute, Santa Barbara, CA.

62. Archie B. Carroll, "The Four Faces of Corporate Citizenship," *Business and Society Review*, 100/101 (1998), 1–7.

63. Barbara W. Altman, *Corporate Community Relations in the 1990s: A Study in Transformation*, Unpublished doctoral dissertation, Boston University.

64. Archie B. Carroll, Kim Davenport, and Doug Grisaffe, "Appraising the Business Value of Corporate Citizenship: What Does the Literature Say?" Proceedings of the International Association for Business and Society, Essex Junction, VT, 2000.

65. For more on corporate citizenship, see the special issue "Corporate Citizenship," *Business and Society Review*, 105:1 (Spring 2000), edited by Barbara W. Altman and Deborah Vidaver-Cohen; also see Jorg Andriof and Malcolm McIntosh (eds.), *Perspectives on Corporate Citizenship* (London: Greenleaf Publishing, 2001). Also see Isabelle Maignan, O. C. Ferrell, and G. Tomas M. Hult, "Corporate Citizenship: Cultural Antecedents and Business Benefits," *Journal of the Academy of Marketing Science* (Vol. 27, No. 4, Fall 1999), 455–469. Also see Malcolm McIntosh, Deborah Leipziger, Keith Jones, and Gill Coleman, *Corporate Citizenship: Successful Strategies for Responsible Companies* (London: Financial Times/Pitman Publishing), 1998.

66. See, for example, Mark Starik and Archie B. Carroll, "In Search of Beneficence: Reflections on the Connections Between Firm Social and Financial Performance," in Karen Paul (ed.), *Contemporary Issues in Business and Society in the United States and Abroad* (Lewiston, NY: The Edwin Mellen Press, 1991), 79–108; and I. M. Herremans, P. Akathaporn, and M. McInnes, "An Investigation of Corporate Social Responsibility, Reputation, and Economic Performance," *Accounting, Organizations, and Society* (Vol. 18, No. 7/8, 1993), 587–604.

67. Lee E. Preston and Douglas P. O'Bannon, "The Corporate Social-Financial Performance Relationship: A Typology and Analysis," *Business and Society* (Vol. 36, No. 4, December 1997), 419–429.

68. Sandra Waddock and Samuel Graves, "The Corporate Social Performance–Financial Performance Link," *Strategic Management Journal* (Vol. 18, No, 4, 1997), 303–319.

69. Jennifer Griffin and John Mahon, "The Corporate Social Performance and Corporate Financial Performance Debate," *Business and Society* (Vol. 36, No. 1, March 1997), 5–31.

70. Ronald Roman, Sefa Hayıbor, and Bradley Agle, "The Relationship Between Social and Financial Performance," *Business and Society* (Vol. 38, No. 1, March 1999), 121. For a reply to this study, see John Mahon and Jennifer Griffin, "Painting a Portrait: A Reply," *Business and Society* (Vol. 38, No. 1, March 1999), 126–133.

71. *Chicago Tribune*, "Social Concern Pays, Study Suggests," *The Atlanta Journal* (June 7, 1993), E4.

72. Preston and O'Bannon, 428.

73. Bryan Husted, "A Contingency Theory of Corporate Social Performance," *Business and Society* (Vol. 39, No. 1, March 2000), 24–48; 41.

74. Philip Johansson, "Social Investing Turns 30," *Business Ethics* (January–February 2001), 12–16.

75. http://www.corporateknights.ca/sri/nuts_and_bolts.asp.

76. See, for example, Lawrence A. Armour, "Who Says Virtue Is Its Own Reward?" *Fortune* (February 16, 1998), 186–189; Thomas D. Saler, "Money & Morals," *Mutual Funds* (August 1997), 55–60; and Keith H. Hammonds, "A Portfolio with a Heart Still Needs a Brain," *Business Week* (January 26, 1998), 100.

77. See Jack A. Brill and Alan Reder, *Investing from the Heart* (New York: Crown Publishers, 1992); and Patrick McVeigh, "The Best Socially Screened Mutual Funds for 1998," *Business Ethics* (January–February 1998), 15–21.

78. William A. Sodeman, "Social Investing: The Role of Corporate Social Performance in Investment Decisions," Unpublished Ph.D. dissertation, University of Georgia, 1993. See also William A. Sodeman and Archie B. Carroll, "Social Investment Firms: Their Purposes, Principles, and Investment Criteria," in *International Association for Business and Society 1994 Proceedings*, edited by Steven Wartick and Denis Collins, 339–344.

79. "Good Works and Great Profits," *Business Week* (February 16, 1998), 8.

80. Samuel B. Graves and Sandra A. Waddock, "Institutional Owners and Corporate Social Performance," *Academy of Management Journal* (Vol. 37, No. 4, August 1994), 1034–1046.

81. *Ibid*.

82. The Social Investment Forum's Web address is http://www.socialinvest.org.

Chapter 3

The Stakeholder Approach to Business, Society, and Ethics

Chapter Objectives

After studying this chapter, you should be able to:

1 Define *stake* and *stakeholder* and describe the origins of these concepts.

2 Differentiate among the production, managerial, and stakeholder views of the firm.

3 Differentiate among the three values of the stakeholder model.

4 Discuss the concept of stakeholder management.

5 Identify and discuss the five major questions that capture the essence of stakeholder management.

6 Identify and discuss the concept of stakeholder management capability (SMC).

Life in business organizations was once simpler. First, there were the investors who put up the money to get the business started. This was in the precorporate period, so there was only one person, or a few at most, financing the business. Next, the owners needed employees to do the productive work of the firm. Because the owners themselves were frequently the managers, another group—the employees—was needed to get the business going. Then the owners needed suppliers to make raw materials available for production and customers to purchase the products or services they were providing. All in all, it was a less complex period, with minimal and understood expectations among the various parties.

It would take many books to describe how and why we got from that relatively simple period to the complex state of affairs we face in today's society. Many of the factors we discussed in the first two chapters were driving forces behind this societal transformation. The principal factor, however, has been the recognition by the public, or society, that the business organization has evolved to the point where it is no longer the sole property or interest of the founder, the founder's family, or even a group of owner-investors.

The business organization today, especially the modern corporation, is the institutional centrepiece of a complex society. Our society today consists of many people with a multitude of interests, expectations, and demands as to what major organizations ought to provide to accommodate people's lifestyles. We have seen business respond to the many expectations placed on it. We have seen an ever-changing social contract. We have seen many assorted legal, ethical, and philanthropic expectations and demands being met by organizations willing to change as long as the economic incentive was still present. What was once viewed as a specialized means of providing profit through the manufacture and distribution of goods and services has become a multipurpose social institution that many people and groups depend on for their livelihood, prosperity, and fulfillment.

In a society conscious of an always-improving lifestyle, with more groups every day laying claims to their pieces of the good life, business organizations today need to be responsive to individuals and groups they once viewed as powerless and unable to make such claims on them. We call these individuals and groups *stakeholders*.

The growing importance of the stakeholder concept to business was highlighted by several important conferences on stakeholder theory and thinking in the 1990s. The late Max Clarkson of the University of Toronto convened two conferences in 1993 and 1994 on stakeholder theory.[1] In 1994, Juha Näsi convened a conference on stakeholder thinking in Finland.[2] These conferences were predicated on the basic notion that the stakeholder approach to management was an idea poised for further development, especially in the business-and-society arena. In the academic community, advances in stakeholder theory have illustrated the crucial development of the stakeholder concept.[3]

The stakeholder view was advanced even further in 1996 when Britain's then Labour Party Leader Tony Blair called for an economy characterized by stakeholder capitalism as opposed to traditional shareholder capitalism. All over the world, people began re-discussing an age-old question: Who do companies belong to and in whose interests should they be run? These discussions sharply contrasted the traditional North American and British view, wherein a public company has the overriding goal of maximizing shareholder returns, with the view held by the Japanese and much of continental Europe, wherein firms accept broader obligations that seek to balance the interests of shareholders with those of other stakeholders, notably employees, suppliers, customers, and the wider "community."[4]

Within the context of stakeholder capitalism, David Wheeler and Maria Sillanpää have proposed a model for the "stakeholder corporation," which is discussed later in this chapter. For now, it suffices to summarize that Wheeler and Sillanpää believe "stakeholder inclusion" to be the key to company success in the twenty-first century.[5] More recently (2001), Steven Walker and Jeffrey Marr have published a book titled *Stakeholder Power*. Their book presents what they consider to be a "winning plan for building stakeholder commitment and driving corporate growth."[6]

An outgrowth of these discussions is that it is becoming apparent that business organizations must address the legitimate needs and expectations of stakeholders if they want to be successful in the long run.[7] Business must also address stakeholders because it is the ethical course of action to take. Stakeholders have claims, rights, and expectations that should be honoured, and the stakeholder approach encourages that pursuit. It is for these reasons that the stakeholder concept and orientation have become an essential part of the vocabulary and thinking in the arena of business, society, and ethics.

Origins of the Stakeholder Concept

The stakeholder concept has become a central idea in understanding business and society relationships. The term "stakeholder" is a variant of the more familiar and traditional idea of *stockholders* or *shareholders*—the investors in or owners of businesses. Just as a private individual might own his or her house, automobile, or video recorder, a shareholder owns a portion or a share of one or more businesses. Thus, a shareholder is also called a stakeholder. However, shareholders are just one group of many legitimate stakeholders that business and organizations must address today to be effective.

What Is a Stake?

To appreciate the concept of stakeholders, it helps to understand the idea of a stake. A **stake** is an interest or a share in an undertaking. If a group is planning to go out to dinner and a show for the evening, each person in the group has a stake, or interest, in the group's decision. No money has yet been spent, but each member sees his or her interest (preference, taste, priority) in the decision. A stake is also a claim. A claim is an assertion to a title or a right to something. A claim is a demand for something due or believed to be due. We can see clearly that an owner or a shareholder has an interest in and an ownership of a share of a business.

The idea of a stake, therefore, can range from simply an interest in an undertaking at one extreme to a legal claim of ownership at the other extreme. In between these two extremes is a "right" to something. This right might be a legal right to certain treatment rather than a legal claim of ownership, such as that of a shareholder. Legal rights might include the right to fair treatment (e.g., not to be discriminated against) or the right to privacy (not to have one's privacy invaded or abridged). The right might be thought of as a moral right, such as that expressed by an employee: "I've got a right not to be fired because I've worked here 30 years, and I've given this firm the best years of my life." Or a consumer might say, "I've got a right to a safe product after all I've paid for this."

As we have seen, there are several different types of stakes. Figure 3–1 summarizes various categories or types of stakes.

FIGURE 3-1

Types of Stakes

An Interest	A Right	Ownership
When a person or group will be affected by a decision, it has an interest in that decision.	Legal Right: When a person or group has a legal claim to be treated in a certain way or to have a particular right protected.	When a person or group has a legal title to an asset or a property.
Examples: This plant closing will affect the community. This TV commercial demeans women, and I'm a woman.	Examples: Employees expect due process, privacy; customers or creditors have certain legal rights.	Examples: "This company is mine, I founded it, and I own it," or, "I own 1000 shares of this corporation."
	Moral Right: When a person or group thinks it has a moral right to be treated in a certain way or to have a particular right protected.	
	Examples: Fairness, justice, equity.	

What Is a Stakeholder?

A **stakeholder**, then, is an individual or a group that has one or more of the various kinds of stakes in a business. Just as stakeholders may be affected by the actions, decisions, policies, or practices of the business firm, these stakeholders also may affect the organization's actions, decisions, policies, or practices. With stakeholders, therefore, there is a potential two-way interaction or exchange of influence. In short, a stakeholder may be thought of as "any individual or group who can affect or is affected by the actions, decisions, policies, practices, or goals of the organization."[8]

Who Are Business's Stakeholders?

In today's competitive, global business environment, there are many individuals and groups who are business's stakeholders. From the business point of view, there are certain individuals and groups that have legitimacy in the eyes of management. That is, they have a legitimate interest in, or claim on, the operations of the firm. The most obvious of these groups are shareholders, employees, and customers. From the point of view of a highly pluralistic society, stakeholders include not only these groups, but other groups as well. These other groups include competitors, suppliers, the community, special-interest groups, the media, and society or the public at large. It has also been strongly argued by Mark Starik that the natural environment, nonhuman species, and future generations should be considered among business's important stakeholders.[9]

Production → Managerial → Stakeholder Views

The evolution and progress of the stakeholder concept parallels the evolution of the business enterprise. In what has been termed the traditional **production view of the**

firm, owners thought of stakeholders as only those individuals or groups that supplied resources or bought products or services.[10] As time passed and we witnessed the growth of corporations and the resulting separation of ownership from control, business firms began to see the need for interaction with major constituent groups if they were to be managed successfully. Thus, we witnessed the evolution of the **managerial view of the firm**. Finally, as major internal and external changes occurred in business, managers were required to undergo a revolutionary conceptual shift in how they perceived the firm and its multilateral relationships with constituent or stakeholder groups. The result was the **stakeholder view of the firm**.[11] In actual practice, however, some managers have not yet come to appreciate the need for the stakeholder view. Figure 3–2 depicts the evolution from the production view to the managerial view of the firm, and Figure 3–3 illustrates the stakeholder view of the firm.

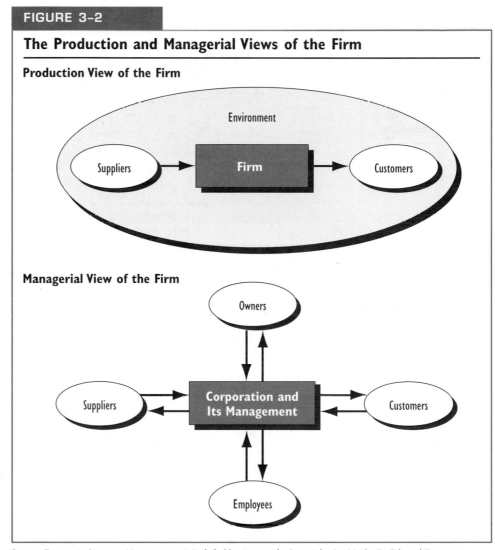

FIGURE 3–2

The Production and Managerial Views of the Firm

Production View of the Firm

Managerial View of the Firm

Source: Freeman's *Strategic Management: A Stakeholder Approach*, Copyright © 1984 by R. Edward Freeman. Reprinted with permission from Pitman Publishing Company.

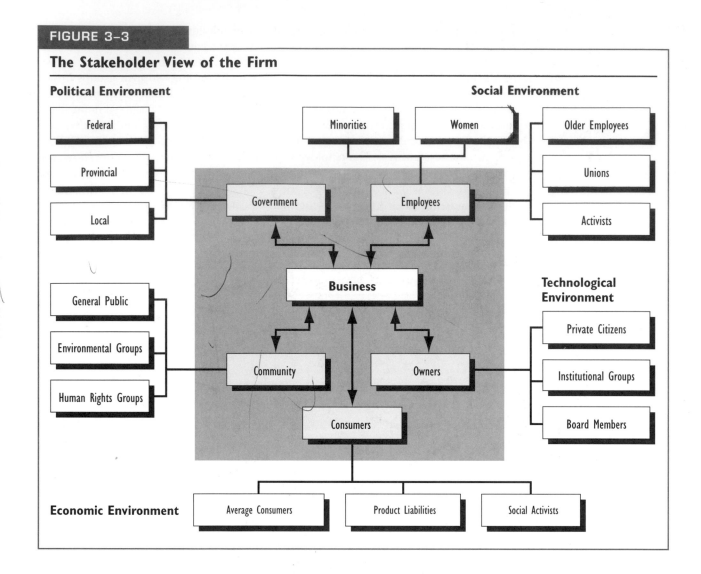

FIGURE 3-3

The Stakeholder View of the Firm

In the stakeholder view of the firm, management must perceive its stakeholders as not only those groups that management thinks have some stake in the firm but also as those groups that themselves think or perceive they have a stake in the firm. This must be the perspective that management takes at the outset, at least until it has had a chance to weigh very carefully the legitimacy of the claims and the power of the various stakeholders. We should note here that each stakeholder group is composed of subgroups. For example, the government stakeholder group includes federal, provincial, and municipal government stakeholders.

Primary and Secondary Stakeholders

Wheeler and Sillanpää have presented a useful way to categorize stakeholders. Using such categories as primary and secondary and social and nonsocial, they propose defining stakeholders as follows:[12]

Primary social stakeholders include:

- Shareholders and investors
- Employees and managers
- Customers
- Local communities
- Suppliers and other business partners

Secondary social stakeholders include:

- Government and regulators
- Civic institutions
- Social pressure groups
- Media and academic commentators
- Trade bodies
- Competitors

Primary social stakeholders have a direct stake in the organization and its success and, therefore, are influential. Secondary social stakeholders may be extremely influential as well, especially in affecting reputation and public standing, but their stake in the organization is more representational of public or special interests than direct. Therefore, the level of accountability to a secondary stakeholder tends to be lower, but these groups may wield significant power and quite often represent legitimate public concerns.[13]

Primary nonsocial stakeholders include:

- The natural environment
- Future generations
- Nonhuman species

Secondary nonsocial stakeholders include:

- Environmental pressure groups
- Animal welfare organizations

It should be kept in mind that secondary stakeholders can quickly become primary ones. This often occurs with the media or special-interest groups when the urgency of a claim (as in a boycott or demonstration) takes precedence over the legitimacy of that claim. In today's business environment, the media have the power to instantaneously transform a stakeholder's status with coverage on the evening news. Thus, it may be useful to think of primary and secondary classes of stakeholders for discussion purposes, but we should understand how easily and quickly those categories can shift.

Core, Strategic, and Environmental Stakeholders

There are other ways to categorize stakeholders. At the Second Toronto Conference on Stakeholder Theory, for example, a working group came up with an alternative scheme for classifying stakeholders. In this scheme, stakeholders were thought of as being core, strategic, or environmental. **Core stakeholders** are a specific subset of strategic stakeholders that are essential for the survival of the organization. **Strategic stakeholders** are those stakeholder groups that are vital to the organization and the particular set of threats and opportunities it faces at a particular point in time. **Environmental stakeholders** are all others in the organization's environment that are not core or strategic. One could conceptualize the relationship among these three groups of stakeholders by thinking of a series of concentric circles with core stakeholders in the middle and with strategic and environmental stakeholders moving out from the middle.[14]

The working group went on to assert that whether stakeholders were core, strategic, or environmental would depend on their characteristics or attributes, such as legitimacy, power, or urgency. Thus, stakeholders could move from category to category in a dynamic, fluid, and time-dependent fashion. It was thought that this set of terms for describing stakeholders would be useful because it captured, to some degree, the contingencies and dynamics that must be considered in an actual situation.

Legitimacy, Power, Urgency: A Typology of Stakeholder Attributes

Expanding on the idea that stakeholders have such attributes as legitimacy, power, and urgency, Mitchell, Agle, and Wood generated a typology of stakeholders based on these three attributes.[15] When these three attributes are superimposed, as depicted in Figure 3–4, seven stakeholder categories result.

A brief look at the three attributes of legitimacy, power, and urgency helps us to see how stakeholders may be thought of and analyzed in these key terms. **Legitimacy** refers to the perceived validity or appropriateness of a stakeholder's claim to a stake. Therefore, owners, employees, and customers represent a high degree of legitimacy due to their explicit, formal, and direct relationships with a company. Stakeholders that are more distant from the firm, such as social activist groups, competitors, or the media, might be thought to have less legitimacy.

Power refers to the ability or capacity to produce an effect—to get something done that otherwise may not be done. Therefore, whether one has legitimacy or not, power means that the stakeholder could affect the business. For example, with the help of the media, a large, vocal, social activist group such as People for the Ethical Treatment of Animals (PETA) could wield extraordinary power over a business firm.

Urgency refers to the degree to which the stakeholder claim on the business calls for the business's immediate attention or response. Urgency may imply that something is critical—it really needs to get done. Or, it may imply that something needs to be done immediately, or on a timely basis. A management group may perceive a union strike, a consumer boycott, or a social activist group picketing outside headquarters as urgent.

An interesting example of a stakeholder action that illustrates both power and urgency occurred recently in several dozen Home Depot stores in the United States. In each of the stores, strange announcements began blaring from the intercom systems: "Attention shoppers, on aisle seven you'll find mahogany ripped from the heart of the Amazon." Shocked store managers raced through the aisles trying to apprehend the environmental activists who were behind the stunt. The activists had apparently gotten the access codes to the intercoms. After months of similar antics, Home Depot bowed to the demands of the environmental group and announced that it would stop selling wood chopped from endangered forests and, instead, stock wood products certified by a new organization called the Forest Stewardship Council (FSC).[16] This newly founded group wasn't even on Home Depot's radar screen and then, all of a sudden, it had to capitulate to selling only wood certified by the FSC.

Mitchell, Agle, and Wood take the position that managers must attend to stakeholders based on their assessment of the extent to which competing stakeholder claims

FIGURE 3–4

Stakeholder Typology: One, Two, or Three Attributes Present

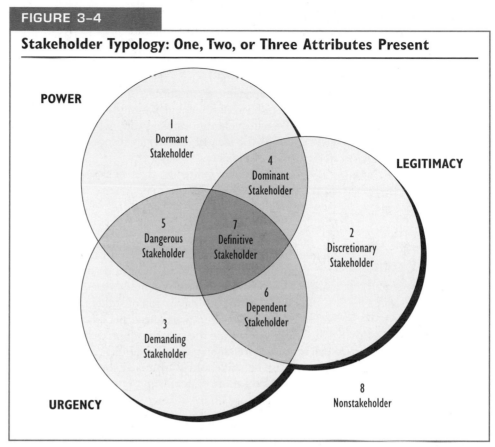

Reprinted with permission of Academy of Management, PO Box 3020, Briar Cliff Manor, NY 10510–8020. "Stakeholder Typology: One, Two, or Three Attributes Present" (Figure), R. K. Mitchell, R. K. Agle, and D. J. Wood, *Academy of Management Review*, October 1997. Reproduced by permission of the publisher via Copyright Clearance Center, Inc.

are characterized by legitimacy, power, and urgency. Using the categories in Figure 3–4, therefore, the stakeholder groups represented by overlapping circles (for example, those with two or three attributes, such as Categories 4, 5, 6, and 7) are highly "salient" to management and would likely receive priority attention.

Strategic, Multifiduciary, and Synthesis Views

One challenge embedded in the stakeholder approach is to determine whether it should be perceived primarily as a way to *manage better* those groups known as stakeholders or as a way to *treat more ethically* those groups known as stakeholders. Kenneth Goodpaster has addressed this issue by distinguishing among the strategic approach, the multifiduciary approach, and the stakeholder synthesis approach.[17] Goodpaster uses the term "strategic" in a sense slightly different from that in which it was used in the previous discussion.

The *strategic approach* views stakeholders primarily as factors to be taken into consideration and managed while the firm is pursuing profits for its shareholders. In this view, managers might take stakeholders into account because offended stakeholders might resist or retaliate (for example, through political action, protest, or boycott). This approach sees stakeholders as instruments that may facilitate or impede the firm's pursuit of its strategic objectives. Thus, it is an instrumental view.

The *multifiduciary approach* views stakeholders as more than just individuals or groups who can wield economic or legal power. This view holds that management has a fiduciary responsibility to stakeholders just as it has this responsibility to shareholders. Here, management's traditional fiduciary, or trust, duty is expanded to embrace stakeholders on roughly equal footing with shareholders. Thus, shareholders are no longer of exclusive importance as they would be under the strategic approach. This view expands the idea of a fiduciary responsibility to include shareholders and other important stakeholders.

Goodpaster recommends that business organizations take neither of these extreme postures but rather pursue a new *stakeholder synthesis approach*. This new view holds that business does have moral responsibilities to stakeholders but that they should not be seen as part of a fiduciary obligation. Thus, management's basic fiduciary responsibility to shareholders is kept intact, but it is also expected to be implemented within a context of ethical responsibility. This ethical responsibility is its duty not to harm, coerce, lie, cheat, steal, and so on.[18] Thus, the result is the same in the multifiduciary and stakeholder synthesis views. However, the reasoning is different.

As we continue our discussion of stakeholder management, it should be clear that we are pursuing it from a balanced perspective. This balanced perspective suggests that we are integrating the strategic approach with the stakeholder synthesis approach such that they are compatible. We should be managing strategically and morally at the same time. The stakeholder approach should not be just a better way to manage, it also should be a more ethical way to manage.

Three Values of the Stakeholder Model

As an alternative to Goodpaster's strategic, multifiduciary, and stakeholder synthesis views, Donaldson and Preston have articulated three aspects or values of the stakeholder model of the firm. These three aspects, although interrelated, are distinct. They differentiate among the descriptive, instrumental, and normative aspects of stakeholder theory or the stakeholder model.[19]

First, the stakeholder model is *descriptive*. That is, it provides language and concepts to effectively describe the corporation or organization. The corporation is a constellation of cooperative and competitive interests possessing both instrumental and intrinsic value. Understanding organizations in this way allows us to have a fuller description or explanation of how they function. The language and terms used in stakeholder theory are useful in helping us to understand organizations.

Second, the stakeholder model is *instrumental*. It is useful in establishing the connections between the practice of stakeholder management and the resulting achievement of corporate performance goals. The fundamental premise here is that practising effective stakeholder management should lead to the achievement of traditional goals, such as profitability, stability, and growth.

Third, the stakeholder model is *normative*. In the normative perspective, stakeholders are identified by their interest in the organization whether or not the organization has any corresponding interest in them. Thus, the interests of all stakeholders are of intrinsic value. Stakeholders are seen as possessing value irrespective of their instrumental use to management. The normative view is often thought of as the moral or ethical view because it emphasizes how stakeholders *should* be regarded.

In summarizing, Donaldson and Preston assert that stakeholder theory is *managerial* in the broad sense of the term. It is managerial in the sense that it does not simply describe or predict but also recommends attitudes, structures, and practices that constitute stakeholder management. Such management necessitates the simultaneous attention to the legitimate interests of all appropriate stakeholders in the creation of organizational structures and policies.[20]

Key Questions in Stakeholder Management

The managers of a business firm have the responsibility of establishing the firm's overall direction (its strategies, goals, and policies) and seeing to it that these plans are carried out. As a consequence, managers have some long-term responsibilities and many that are of more immediate concern. Before the stakeholder environment became as turbulent and rapidly changing as it now is, the managerial task was relatively straightforward and the external environment was stable. As we have evolved to the stakeholder view of the firm, however, we see the managerial task as an inevitable consequence of the trends and developments we described in our first two chapters.

Stakeholder management has become important as managers have discovered the many groups that have to be relatively satisfied for the firm to meet its objectives. Without question, we still recognize the significance and necessity of profits as a return on the shareholders' investments, but we also see the growing claims of other stakeholder groups and the success they have had in getting what they want.

The challenge of stakeholder management, therefore, is to see to it that the firm's primary stakeholders achieve their objectives and that other stakeholders are dealt with ethically and are also satisfied. At the same time, the firm is expected to be profitable. This is the classic "win-win" situation. It does not always occur, but it is a legitimate goal for management to pursue to protect its long-term best interests. Management's second-best alternative is to meet the goals of its primary stakeholders, keeping in mind the important role of its owner-investors. Without economic viability, all other stakeholders' interests are lost.

With these perspectives in mind, let us approach stakeholder management with the idea that managers can become successful stewards of their stakeholders' resources by gaining knowledge about stakeholders and using this knowledge to predict and deal with their behaviour and actions. Ultimately, we should manage the situation in such a way that we achieve our objectives ethically and effectively. Thus, the important functions of stakeholder management are to describe, to understand, to analyze, and, finally, to manage.

The quest for stakeholder management embraces social, ethical, and economic considerations. Normative as well as instrumental objectives and perspectives are essential. Five major questions must be asked if we are to capture the essential information we need for stakeholder management:

1. *Who* are our stakeholders?
2. What are our stakeholders' *stakes*?
3. What *opportunities and challenges* do our stakeholders present to the firm?
4. What *responsibilities* (economic, legal, ethical, and philanthropic) does the firm have to its stakeholders?
5. What *strategies* or *actions* should the firm take to best handle stakeholder challenges and opportunities?[21]

Who Are Our Stakeholders?

To this point, we have described the likely primary and secondary stakeholder groups of a business organization. To manage them effectively, each firm and its management group must ask and answer this question for itself: Who are our stakeholders? To answer this question fully, management must identify not only generic stakeholder groups but also the specific subgroups. A generic stakeholder group is simply a broad grouping, such as employees, shareholders, environmental groups, or consumers. Within each of these generic categories there may be a few or many specific subgroups. Figure 3–5 illustrates some of the generic and specific stakeholder subgroups of a very large organization.

To illustrate the process of stakeholder identification, we will consider some events in the life of the McDonald's Corporation that resulted in their broadening significantly who were considered their stakeholders. The case study starts in the fall of 1999 when the social-activist group PETA (People for the Ethical Treatment of Animals), which claims 700 000 members, decided it was dissatisfied with some of McDonald's practices and decided it would launch a billboard and bumper-sticker campaign against the hamburger giant.[22] PETA felt McDonald's was dragging its feet on animal welfare issues, and so PETA went on the attack. PETA announced it would

---

FIGURE 3–5

Some Generic and Specific Stakeholders of a Large Firm

Owners	Employees	Governments	Customers
Trusts	Young employees	Federal	Business purchasers
Foundations	Middle-aged employees	Provincial	Government purchasers
Mutual funds	Older employees	Municipal	Educational institutions
Board members	Women	Special-interest groups	
Management owners	Minority groups		
Employee pension funds	Special needs		
Individual owners	Special-interest groups		
	Unions		

Community	Competitors	Social Activist Groups
General fund-raising	Firm A	Greenpeace
Charities	Firm B	National Citizens' Coalition
Schools	Firm C	Council of Canadians
Hospitals		Friends of the Earth
Residents who live close by		Mothers Against Drunk Driving (MADD)
All other residents		Animal Alliance of Canada
Neighbourhood associations		Consumer's Association of Canada
Local media		Canadian Civil Liberties Association
		People for the Ethical Treatment of Animals (PETA)

put up billboards saying "The animals deserve a break today" and "McDonald's: Cruelty to Go" in Norfolk, Virginia, PETA's home city. The ad campaign was announced when talks broke down between PETA and McDonald's on the subject of ways the company might foster animal-rights issues within the fast-food industry. Using concepts introduced earlier, PETA was a secondary social or nonsocial stakeholder and, therefore, had low legitimacy. However, its power and urgency were high as it was threatening the company with a highly visible, potentially destructive campaign that was being favourably reported by a cooperative media.

It's not clear what all took place over the ensuing year, but it is evident that PETA's pressure tactics continued and escalated. In the fall of 2000, McDonald's announced significant changes in the demands it began placing on its chicken and egg suppliers. McDonald's announced that its egg suppliers must now improve the living conditions of its chickens. Specifically, McDonald's is now insisting that its suppliers no longer cage its chickens wing-tip to wing-tip. Suppliers must now increase the space allotted to each hen from 48 square inches to 72 square inches (approximately 310 square centimetres to 456 square centimetres) per hen. Suppliers will also be required to stop "forced molting," a process that increases egg production by denying hens food and water for up to two weeks.[23]

It came out that during the ensuing year, PETA escalated its pressure tactics against the firm. PETA began distributing "unhappy meals" at restaurant playgrounds and outside the company's shareholder meeting. The kits, which came in boxes similar to McDonald's Happy Meals that it sells to children, were covered with pictures of slaughtered animals. It also depicted a bloody, knife-wielding "Son of Ron" doll that resembled the Ronald McDonald clown, as well as toy farm animals with slashed throats. One image featured a bloody cow's head and the familiar fast-food phrase "Do you want fries with that?"[24]

As a result of this example, we can see how the set of stakeholders that McDonald's had to deal with grew significantly from its traditional stakeholders to include powerful groups such as PETA. With the aid of the media, especially major newspapers and magazines, PETA moved from being a secondary stakeholder to a primary stakeholder in McDonald's life.

In 2001, members of PETA and the Animal Rights Foundation of Florida (ARFF) began an attack on Burger King, similar to the attack on McDonald's. They greeted Burger King's new CEO with signs and banners reading "Burger King: King of Cruelty," while showing a video documenting the abuses that PETA hopes Burger King will put a stop to. The organizations also planned a full-page ad in *The Miami Herald* asking the new CEO to take action to reduce the suffering of chickens, pigs, and other animals on farms that supply the company's meat and eggs. This is the latest volley in PETA's "Murder King" campaign, in which hundreds of demonstrations against Burger King have taken place in more than a dozen countries and in every U.S. state.[25]

The purpose of this discussion has been to illustrate the evolving nature of the question, "Who are our stakeholders?" In actuality, stakeholder identification is an unfolding process. However, by recognizing early the potential of failure if one does not think in stakeholder terms, the value and usefulness of stakeholder thinking can be readily seen. Had McDonald's perceived PETA as a stakeholder earlier on, perhaps it could have dealt with this situation more effectively.

Many businesses do not carefully identify their generic stakeholder groups, much less their specific stakeholder groups. This must be done, however, if management is to be in a position to answer the second major question, "What are our stakeholders' stakes?"

What Are Our Stakeholders' Stakes?

Once stakeholders have been identified, the next step is to answer the question: What are our stakeholder's stakes? Even groups in the same generic category frequently have different specific interests, concerns, perceptions of rights, and expectations. Management's challenge here is to identify the nature and legitimacy of a group's stake(s) and the group's power to affect the organization. As we discussed earlier, urgency is another critical factor.

Identifying the Nature/Legitimacy of a Group's Stakes Let's consider an example of stakeholders who possess varying stakes. Assume that we are considering corporate owners as a generic group of stakeholders and that the corporation is large, with several million shares of stock outstanding. Among the ownership population are these more specific subgroups:

1. Institutional owners (trusts, foundations, churches, universities)
2. Large mutual fund organizations
3. Board of director members who own shares
4. Members of management who own shares
5. Tens of thousands of small, individual shareholders

For all these groups, the nature of stakeholder claims on this corporation is ownership. All these groups have legitimate claims—they are all owners.

Identifying the Power of a Group's Stakes When we examine power, we see significant differences. Which of the groups in the previous list are the most powerful? Certainly not the thousands of small, individual investors, unless they have found a way to organize and thus wield considerable power. The powerful stakeholders in this case are (1) the institutional owners and mutual fund organizations, because of the sheer magnitude of their investments, and (2) the board and management shareholders, because of their dual roles of ownership and management (control).

However, if the individual shareholders could somehow form a coalition based on some interest they have in common, they could exert significant influence on management decisions. This is the day and age of dissident shareholder groups filing stockholder suits and proposing shareholder resolutions. These shareholder resolutions address issues ranging from complaints of excessive executive compensation to demands that firms improve their environmental protection policies or cease making illegal campaign contributions.

Identifying Specific Groups Within a Generic Group Let us now look at a manufacturing firm in an industry in Vancouver that is faced with a generic group of environmental stakeholders. Within the generic group of environmental stakeholders might be the following specific groups:

1. Residents who live within a 25-kilometre radius of the plant
2. Other residents in the city
3. Residents who live in the path of the jet stream hundreds of kilometres away who are being impacted by acid rain
4. Environment Canada (federal government)
5. Provincial Ministry of the Environment (provincial government)
6. Friends of the Earth (social activist group)
7. The Wilderness Society (social activist group)
8. Pollution Probe (social activist group)

It would require some degree of care to identify the nature, legitimacy, power, and urgency of each of these specific groups. However, it could and should be done if the firm wants to get a handle on its environmental stakeholders. Furthermore, we should stress that companies have an ethical responsibility to be sensitive to legitimate stakeholder claims even if the stakeholders have no power or leverage with management.

If we return for a moment to the McDonald's example, we would have to conclude that PETA, as a special-interest, animal-welfare group, did not have much legitimacy vis-à-vis McDonald's. PETA did claim animal rights and treatment as a moral issue, however, and thus had some general legitimacy through the concerns it represented. Unfortunately for PETA, not all of the public shares its concerns or degree of concern with these issues. However, PETA had tremendous power and urgency. It was this power, wielded in the form of adverse publicity and media attention, that doubtless played a significant role in bringing about changes in McDonald's policies.

What Opportunities and Challenges Do Our Stakeholders Present to the Firm?

In many respects, opportunities and challenges represent opposite sides of the coin when it comes to stakeholders. Essentially, the opportunities are to build good, productive working relationships with the stakeholders. Challenges, on the other hand, usually present themselves in such a way that the firm must handle the stakeholders well or be hurt in some way—financially (short term or long term) or in terms of its public image or reputation in the community. Therefore, it is understandable why our emphasis is on challenges rather than on opportunities posed by stakeholders.

These challenges typically take the form of varying degrees of expectations or demands. In most instances, they arise because stakeholders think or believe that their needs are not being met adequately. The challenges also arise when stakeholder groups think that any crisis that occurs is the responsibility of the firm or that the firm caused the crisis in some way. Examples of some stakeholder crises from the 1990s and early 2000s include:[26]

- *Citigroup.* During morning rush hour in Manhattan, commuters in 2001 were greeted with the sight of two activists unfurling a 6-metre banner from flag poles outside of Citigroup's (Citi) headquarters reading, "Hey, Citi, not with my money!" The climbers were drawing attention to the growing controversy surrounding Citi's leading alleged role in financing environmentally and socially destructive projects around the globe. This event followed a recent student-led boycott against Citi credit cards and protests in more than 80 cities in 12 countries.
- *Coca-Cola.* In 1999, Coke faced a major crisis when reports came in that their world-famous product was causing illnesses among consumers in Europe. Dozens of consumers who drank the soft drinks became sick. The governments of France, Belgium, Luxembourg, and The Netherlands ordered Coca-Cola products off their shelves as a result of the reports. Coke executives later pinpointed the problem along two points in its bottling system controlled by Coca-Cola Enterprises in Belgium. The crisis occurred at a time when Coke products were already suffering declining sales in some regions. The biggest recall in Coke's history hurt its reputation in European markets.
- *Home Depot.* In 1998–1999, under pressure from social activist groups such as Rainforest Action Network and staged "Days of Action" by protestors, the

Atlanta-based chain agreed to stop selling products made from old-growth wood. The environmentalists threatened to follow up with newspaper ads, frequent pickets, and civil disobedience if the company did not agree.

- *Texaco.* Taped evidence of executive-level discrimination set off protests against the company in the late 1990s. A lawsuit settlement for US$176 million was one result. This created a crisis for Texaco that took years to overcome.
- *Enron and other corporate scandals (2001–2003).* The fraudulent accounting practices of such high-profile companies as Enron, WorldCom, and numerous others resulted in a crisis of confidence among shareholders in both the U.S. and Canada in the period following 2001. Alarm was raised regarding issues of disclosure, auditor independence, corporate governance, and ethics. This crisis of confidence in the business sector demanded changes in numerous accounting and reporting practices across many industries.

If one looks at the business experiences of the past couple of decades, including the crises mentioned here, it is evident that there is a need to think in stakeholder terms to fully understand the potential threats that businesses of all kinds face on a daily basis.

Opportunities and challenges might also be viewed in terms of potential for cooperation and potential for threat. Savage and his colleagues have argued that such assessments of cooperation and threat are necessary so that managers might identify strategies for dealing with stakeholders.[27] In terms of potential for threat, Savage et al. assert that managers need to consider the stakeholder's relative power and its relevance to a particular issue confronting the organization. In terms of potential for cooperation, the firm needs to be sensitive to the possibility of joining forces with other stakeholders for the advantage of all parties involved.

Savage et al. cite how Ross Laboratories, a division of Abbott Laboratories, was able to develop a cooperative relationship with some critics of its sales of infant formula in Third World countries. Ross and Abbott convinced these stakeholder groups (UNICEF and the World Health Organization) to join them in a program to promote infant health. Other firms, such as Nestlé, did not develop the potential to cooperate and suffered from consumer boycotts.[28] For example, among the numerous organizations targeting Nestlé, Baby Milk Action's Web site includes the following information about Nestlé:

- The company provides information to mothers that promotes artificial infant feeding and discourages breast-feeding.
- It donates free samples and supplies to health facilities to encourage artificial infant feeding.
- It gives inducements to health workers for promoting its products.
- It does not provide clear warnings on labels of the benefits of breast-feeding and dangers of artificial feeding. In some cases, the labels are in a language that the mothers are unlikely to understand.[29]

In 2003, numerous organizations in the U.S. called for a boycott of GlaxoSmithKline products. This occurred in response to the giant pharmaceutical company's ban on Canadian Internet sales of prescription drugs to U.S. customers; that is, the company announced its refusal to sell its supplies to Canadian drug stores that, in turn, sell to Americans. This outraged U.S. consumers who were benefiting from the significant savings by purchasing their pharmaceuticals from Canadian companies via the Internet.[30]

Figure 3–6 presents a list of the factors that Savage and his colleagues claim will increase or decrease a stakeholder's potential for threat or cooperation. By carefully analyzing these factors, managers should be able to better assess such potentials.

What Responsibilities Does the Firm Have to Its Stakeholders?

Once threats and opportunities of stakeholders have been identified and understood, the next logical question is, "What responsibilities does the firm have in its relationships with all stakeholders?" Responsibilities here could be thought of in terms of the concepts presented in Chapter 2. What economic, legal, ethical, and philanthropic responsibilities does management have to each stakeholder? Because most of the firm's economic responsibilities are principally to itself, the analysis really begins to focus on legal, ethical, and philanthropic questions. The most pressing threats present themselves as legal and ethical questions.

We should stress, however, that the firm itself has an economic stake in the legal and ethical issues it faces. For example, when Johnson & Johnson (J&J) was faced with the Tylenol poisoning incident, it had to decide what legal and ethical actions to take and what actions were in the firm's best economic interests. J&J probably judged that recalling the Tylenol products was not only the ethical action to take but also would ensure its reputation for being concerned about consumers' health and well-being. Figure 3–7 illustrates the stakeholder/responsibility matrix that management

FIGURE 3-6

Factors Affecting Potential for Stakeholder Threat and Cooperation

	Increases or Decreases Stakeholder's Potential for Threat?	Increases or Decreases Stakeholder's Potential for Cooperation?
Stakeholder controls key resources (needed by organization)	Increases	Increases
Stakeholder does not control key resources	Decreases	Either
Stakeholder more powerful than organization	Increases	Either
Stakeholder as powerful as organization	Either	Either
Stakeholder less powerful than organization	Decreases	Increases
Stakeholder likely to take action (supportive of the organization)	Decreases	Increases
Stakeholder likely to take nonsupportive action	Increases	Decreases
Stakeholder unlikely to take any action	Decreases	Decreases
Stakeholder likely to form coalition with other stakeholders	Increases	Either
Stakeholder likely to form coalition with organization	Decreases	Increases
Stakeholder unlikely to form any coalition	Decreases	Decreases

Source: Grant T. Savage, Timothy W. Nix, Carlton J. Whitehead, and John D. Blair, "Strategies for Assessing and Managing Organizational Stakeholders," *Academy of Management Executive* (Vol. V, No. 2, May 1991), 64. Reprinted with permission.

FIGURE 3–7

Stakeholder/Responsibility Matrix

Stakeholders	Types of Responsibilities			
	Economic	Legal	Ethical	Philanthropic
Owners				
Customers				
Employees				
Community				
Public at Large				
Social Activist Groups				
Others				

faces when assessing the firm's responsibilities to stakeholders. The matrix may be seen as a template that managers might use to systematically think through its array of responsibilities.

What Strategies or Actions Should Management Take?

Once responsibilities have been assessed, a business must contemplate strategies and actions for dealing with its stakeholders. In every decision situation, a multitude of alternative courses of action are available, and management must choose one or several that seem best. MacMillan and Jones suggest that management has before it a number of basic strategies or approaches in dealing with stakeholders. Important questions or decision choices include:

- Do we deal *directly* or *indirectly* with stakeholders?
- Do we take the *offence* or the *defence* in dealing with stakeholders?
- Do we *accommodate*, *negotiate*, *manipulate*, or *resist* stakeholder overtures?
- Do we employ a *combination of the above* strategies or pursue a *singular course* of action?[31]

Savage et al. argue that development of specific strategies may be based on a classification of stakeholders according to the classification of the potentials for cooperation and threat. If we use these two dimensions, four stakeholder types and resultant generic strategies emerge.[32] These stakeholder types and corresponding strategies are shown in Figure 3–8.

Stakeholder Type 1—the supportive stakeholder—is high on potential for cooperation and low on potential for threat. This is the ideal stakeholder. To a well-managed organization, supportive stakeholders might include its board, managers,

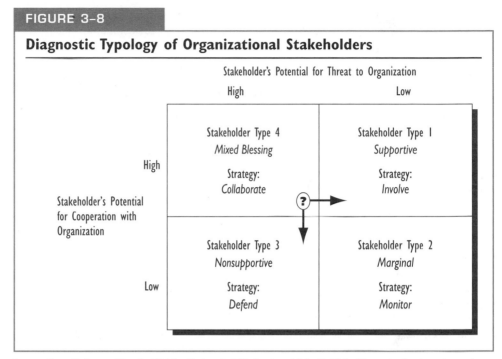

FIGURE 3–8

Diagnostic Typology of Organizational Stakeholders

Stakeholder's Potential for Threat to Organization

Stakeholder's Potential for Cooperation with Organization

	High	Low
High	Stakeholder Type 4 *Mixed Blessing* Strategy: *Collaborate*	Stakeholder Type 1 *Supportive* Strategy: *Involve*
Low	Stakeholder Type 3 *Nonsupportive* Strategy: *Defend*	Stakeholder Type 2 *Marginal* Strategy: *Monitor*

Source: Grant T. Savage, Timothy W. Nix, Carlton J. Whitehead, and John D. Blair, "Strategies for Assessing and Managing Organizational Stakeholders," *Academy of Management Executive* (Vol. V, No. 2, May 1991), 64. Reprinted with permission.

employees, and customers. Others might be suppliers and service providers. The strategy here is one of involvement. An example of this might be the strategy of involving employee stakeholders through participative management or decentralization of authority.

Stakeholder Type 2—the marginal stakeholder—is low on both potential for threat and potential for cooperation. For large organizations, these stakeholders might include professional associations of employees, consumer interest groups, or shareholders—especially those who are not organized. The strategy here is for the organization to monitor the marginal stakeholder. Monitoring is especially called for to make sure circumstances do not change. Careful monitoring could avert later problems.

Stakeholder Type 3—the nonsupportive stakeholder—is high on potential for threat but low on potential for cooperation. Examples of this group could include competing organizations, unions, federal or other levels of government, and the media. The authors' recommended strategy here is to defend against the nonsupportive stakeholder.

Stakeholder Type 4—the mixed blessing stakeholder—is high on both potential for threat and potential for cooperation. Examples of this group, in a well-managed organization, might include employees who are in short supply, clients, or customers. A mixed blessing stakeholder could become a supportive or a nonsupportive stakeholder. The recommended strategy here is to collaborate with the mixed blessing stakeholder. By maximizing collaboration, the likelihood is enhanced that this stakeholder will remain supportive.

The authors summarize their position regarding these four stakeholder types as follows:[33]

> *… managers should attempt to satisfy minimally the needs of marginal stakeholders and to satisfy maximally the needs of supportive and mixed blessing stakeholders, enhancing the latter's support for the organization.*

The four stakeholder types and recommended strategies illustrate what was referred to earlier in this chapter as the "strategic" view of stakeholders. But, it could be argued that by taking stakeholders' needs and concerns into consideration, we are improving our ethical treatment of them. We must go beyond just considering them, however. Management still has an ethical responsibility to stakeholders that extends beyond the strategic view. We will develop a fuller appreciation of what this ethical responsibility is in Chapters 6 through 9.

Effective Stakeholder Management

Effective stakeholder management requires the careful assessment of the five core questions we have posed. To deal successfully with those who assert claims on the organization, managers must understand these core questions at least at a basic level. It is tempting to wish that none of this was necessary. However, such wishing would require management to accept the production or managerial view of the firm, and these views are no longer tenable. Business today cannot turn back the clock to a simpler period. Business has been and will continue to be subjected to careful scrutiny of its actions, practices, policies, and ethics. This is the real world in which management lives, and management must accept it and deal with it. Criticisms of business and calls for better corporate citizenship have been the consequences of the changes in the business/society relationship, and the stakeholder approach to viewing the organization has become one needed response. To do less is to decline to accept the realities of business's plight in the modern world and to fail to see the kinds of adaptations that are essential if businesses are to prosper in the present and in the future.

In fairness, we should also note that there are criticisms and limitations of the stakeholder management approach. One major criticism relates to the complexity and time-consuming nature of identifying, assessing, and responding to stakeholder claims, which constitute an extremely difficult process. Also, the ranking of stakeholder claims is no easy task. Some managers continue to think in shareholder terms because this is easier. To think in stakeholder terms increases the complexity of decision making, and it is overly taxing for some managers to determine which stakeholders' claims take priority in a given situation. Despite its complexity, however, the stakeholder management view is most consistent with the environment that business faces today.

Stakeholder Management Capability

Another way of thinking about effective stakeholder management is in terms of the extent to which the organization has developed its **stakeholder management capability** (SMC).[34] Stakeholder management capability, as described by Freeman, may reside at one of three levels of increasing sophistication.

Level 1—the Rational Level

This simply entails the company identifying who their stakeholders are and what their stakes happen to be. This is the level of stakeholder maps. The **rational level** is descriptive and somewhat analytical, because the nature of stakes, the stakeholders' power, and urgency are identified. This actually represents a low level of SMC. Most organizations have at least identified who their stakeholders are, but not all have analyzed the nature of the stakes or the stakeholders' power. Mark Starik has referred to Freeman's first level as the component of familiarization and comprehensiveness, because management operating at Level 1 is seeking to become familiar with their stakeholders and to develop a comprehensive assessment as to their identification and stakes.[35]

Level 2—the Process Level

At the **process level**, organizations go a step further than Level 1 and actually develop and implement organizational processes (approaches, procedures, policies, practices) by which the firm may scan the environment and receive relevant information about stakeholders, which is then used for decision-making purposes. Typical approaches at this level include portfolio analysis processes, strategic review processes, and environmental scanning processes, which are used to assist managers in their strategic management processes.[36] Other approaches, such as issues management or crisis management (Chapter 5), might also be considered examples of Level 2 SMC. This second level has been described by Starik as planning integrativeness, because management does focus on planning processes for stakeholders and integrating a consideration for stakeholders into organizational decision making.[37]

Level 3—the Transactional Level

The **transactional level** is the highest and most developed of the three levels. This is the bottom line for stakeholder management—the extent to which managers actually engage in transactions (relationships) with stakeholders.[38] At this highest level of SMC, management must take the initiative in meeting stakeholders face to face and attempting to be responsive to their needs. Starik refers to this as the communication level, which is characterized by communication proactiveness, interactiveness, genuineness, frequency, satisfaction, and resource adequacy. Resource adequacy refers to management actually spending resources on stakeholder transactions.[39]

Steven F. Walker and Jeff Marr, in their book *Stakeholder Power: A Winning Plan for Building Stakeholder Commitment and Driving Corporate Growth*, argue that companies should compete on the basis of intangible assets—a company's priceless relationships with customers, employees, suppliers, and shareholders. Based on their own firm's 60-year history as a pioneer in corporate reputation and market research and from case studies of organizations as diverse as LensCrafters, DHL, and Edison International, the authors offer a practical model for hardwiring stakeholder management into company strategy and reaping the rewards through continuous innovation, learning, and profitable growth.[40] It appears that Walker and Marr would subscribe to the essential nature of Level 3—the transactional level—of stakeholder management capability.

An example of Level 3 is provided in the recent agreement between the Mitsubishi group and an environmentalist organization, the Rainforest Action Network (RAN), based in San Francisco. Mitsubishi agreed to curb its pollution and protect the rain forest in an agreement that was the result of five years of negotiations and meetings with RAN. The agreement would never have been possible if the two groups had not been willing to establish a relationship in which each side made certain concessions.[41]

The Stakeholder Corporation

Perhaps the ultimate form of the stakeholder approach or stakeholder management is the "stakeholder corporation," a concept argued persuasively by Wheeler and Sillanpää. The primary element of this concept is **stakeholder inclusiveness**. The authors argue this position as follows:[42]

> *In the future, development of loyal relationships with customers, employees, shareholders, and other stakeholders will become one of the most important determinants of commercial viability and business success. Increasing shareholder value will be best served if your company cultivates the support of all who may influence its importance.*

Advocates of the stakeholder corporation would doubtless believe in "**stakeholder symbiosis**," an idea that recognizes that all stakeholders depend on each other for their success and financial well-being.[43] Executives who have a problem with this concept would probably also have trouble becoming parts of stakeholder corporations.

Stakeholder Power: Four Gates of Engagement

Building upon these ideas, Steven Walker and Jeffrey Marr, in their book *Stakeholder Power*, have presented a practical framework for assessing the commitment level of each stakeholder group and moving them through a series of "gates."[44] It is the view of Walker and Marr that companies need to be proactive in their relationships with potential stakeholders such that these groups *desire* to be in relationships with the company. They hold that great stakeholder relationships evolve through different stages of development, and this knowledge helps management be proactive. They assert that every successful stakeholder relationship passes through four stages, which they refer to as the "four gates of engagement." These four gates include: Awareness, Knowledge, Admiration, and Action. The gates are generally sequential and each stage builds upon the previous stages.

Awareness is gate one. This means knowing that something or someone exists. This first gate seems fairly obvious. They argue, however, that there are often "hidden stakeholders" who may not be aware of the firm. These hidden stakeholders may include others, behind the scenes, who bear influence on decisions. How familiar are they with your firm? *Knowledge* is gate two. Developing knowledge among stakeholders addresses not only products and services but also knowledge about corporate character. This refers to the company's values, integrity, culture, and practices. At gate two, customers would see the "fit" for your product service; employees would know your values, mission, and strategies and what the firm stands for; the community would know what you do and how you do it.

Gate three is *Admiration*. Once a relationship has been established via awareness and knowledge, the potential for stakeholder admiration of the organization exists. To reach this stage, stakeholders must come to trust the firm. Loyalty and commitment are likely effects. Walker and Marr argue that this stage is an excellent time to "close" stakeholders—meaning to seal their trust in you by taking the next step of initiating or deepening the business relationship. This puts them into position for the final stage, which is action. *Action* is gate four. By taking steps to further collaboration, the company can build partnerships that benefit both of you. At this stage, you might get referrals from customers and employees, investors interested in recommending your stock or expanding their current positions, or suppliers entering into true collaboration and trust. The main implication of the "four gates" model is the need to effectively manage communications with stakeholders of all types. Management's responsibility in the model is to guide the stakeholders' progress through the gates so that strong, viable relationships may be established and maintained.[45]

Principles of Stakeholder Management

Based upon years of observation and research, a set of "**principles of stakeholder management**" has been developed. These principles, known as "The Clarkson Principles," were named after the late Max Clarkson, a dedicated researcher on the topic of stakeholder management. The principles are intended to provide managers with guiding precepts regarding how stakeholders should be treated. Figure 3–9 summarizes these principles. The key words in the principles suggest the kind of cooperative spirit that should be used in building stakeholder relationships: *acknowledge, monitor, listen, communicate, adopt, recognize, work, avoid, acknowledge conflicts.*

FIGURE 3–9

Principles of Stakeholder Management—"The Clarkson Principles"

Principle 1	Managers should **acknowledge** and actively **monitor** the concerns of all legitimate stakeholders, and should take their interests appropriately into account in decision making and operations.
Principle 2	Managers should **listen** to and openly **communicate** with stakeholders about their respective concerns and contributions, and about the risks that they assume because of their involvement with the corporation.
Principle 3	Managers should **adopt** processes and modes of behaviour that are sensitive to the concerns and capabilities of each stakeholder constituency.
Principle 4	Managers should **recognize the interdependence** of efforts and rewards among stakeholders, and should attempt to achieve a fair distribution of the benefits and burdens of corporate activity among them, taking into account their respective risks and vulnerabilities.
Principle 5	Managers should **work cooperatively** with other entities, both public and private, to insure that risks and harms arising from corporate activities are minimized and, where they cannot be avoided, appropriately compensated.
Principle 6	Managers should **avoid altogether** activities that might jeopardize inalienable human rights (e.g., the right to life) or give rise to risks that, if clearly understood, would be patently unacceptable to relevant stakeholders.
Principle 7	Managers should **acknowledge the potential conflicts** between (a) their own role as corporate stakeholders, and (b) their legal and moral responsibilities for the interests of stakeholders, and should address such conflicts through open communication, appropriate reporting, and incentive systems and, where necessary, third-party review.

Source: *Principles of Stakeholder Management*, Toronto: The Clarkson Centre for Business Ethics, Joseph L. Rotman School of Management, University of Toronto, 1999, 4.

Summary

A stakeholder is an individual or a group that claims to have one or more stakes in an organization. Stakeholders may affect the organization and, in turn, be affected by the organization's actions, policies, practices, and decisions. The stakeholder approach extends beyond the traditional production and managerial views of the firm and warrants a much broader conception of the parties involved in the organization's functioning and success. Both primary and secondary social and nonsocial stakeholders assume important roles in the eyes of management. A typology of stakeholders suggests that three attributes are especially important: legitimacy, power, and urgency.

Strategic, multifiduciary, and stakeholder synthesis views help us appreciate the perspectives that may be adopted with regard to stakeholders. The stakeholder synthesis perspective is recommended because it highlights the ethical responsibility business has to its stake-holders. The stakeholder model of the firm has three values: descriptive, instrumental, and normative.

Five key questions aid managers in stakeholder management: (1) Who are our stakeholders? (2) What are our stakeholders' stakes? (3) What challenges or opportunities are presented to our firm by our stakeholders? (4) What responsibilities does our firm have to its stakeholders? (5) What strategies or actions should our firm take with respect to our stakeholders? The concept of stakeholder management capability (SMC) illustrates how firms can grow and mature in their approach to stakeholder management. Seven principles of stakeholder management were set forth. Although the stakeholder management approach is quite complex and time-consuming, it is a way of managing that is in tune with the complex environment that business organizations face today. The stakeholder corporation is a model that represents stakeholder thinking in its most advanced form.

Key Terms

core stakeholders (page 71)

environmental stakeholders (page 71)

legitimacy (page 72)

managerial view of the firm (page 69)

power (page 72)

principles of stakeholder management (page 87)

process level (page 85)

production view of the firm (page 68)

rational level (page 84)

stake (page 67)

stakeholder (page 68)

stakeholder inclusiveness (page 86)

stakeholder management capability (SMC) (page 84)

stakeholder symbiosis (page 86)

stakeholder view of the firm (page 69)

strategic stakeholders (page 71)

transactional level (page 85)

urgency (page 72)

Discussion Questions

1. Explain the concepts of stake and stakeholder from your perspective as an individual. What kinds of stakes and stakeholders do you have? Discuss.

2. Differentiate between primary and secondary social and nonsocial stakeholders in a corporate situation.

3. Define the terms *core stakeholders*, *strategic stakeholders*, and *environmental stakeholders*. What

factors affect into which of these groups stakeholders are categorized?

4. Explain in your own words the differences among the production, managerial, and stakeholder views of the firm.

5. Choose any group of stakeholders listed in the stakeholder/responsibility matrix in Figure 3–7 (see

page 82) and identify the four types of responsibilities the firm has to that stakeholder group.

6. Is the stakeholder corporation a realistic model for business firms? Will stakeholder corporations become more prevalent in the twenty-first century? Why or why not?

Endnotes

1. For an overview of the first conference, see "The Toronto Conference: Reflections on Stakeholder Theory," *Business and Society* (Vol. 33, No. 1, April 1994), 82–131.

2. Juha Näsi, "A Scandinavian Approach to Stakeholder Thinking," presented at the Understanding Stakeholder Thinking Conference, Jyäskylä, Finland, June 21–23, 1994. Also see Archie B. Carroll and Juha Näsi, "Understanding Stakeholder Thinking: Themes from a Finnish Conference," *Business Ethics: A European Review* (Vol. 6, No. 1, January 1997), 46–51.

3. See, for example, Steven N. Brenner and Philip Cochran, "The Stakeholder Theory of the Firm: Implications for Business and Society Theory and Research," *International Association for Business and Society (IABS) 1991 Proceedings*, 449–467; Steven N. Brenner, "The Stakeholder Theory of the Firm and Organizational Decision Making," *International Association for Business and Society (IABS) 1993 Proceedings*, 205–210; Lee Preston and H. J. Sapienza, "Stakeholder Management and Corporate Performance," *The Journal of Behavioral Economics* (Vol. 19, No. 4, 1990), 361–375; Robert A. Phillips, "Stakeholder Theory and a Principle of Fairness," *Business Ethics Quarterly* (Vol. 7, No. 1, January 1997), 51–66; and Sandra A. Waddock and Samuel B. Graves, "Quality of Management and Quality of Stakeholder Relations," *Business and Society* (Vol. 36, No. 3, September 1997), 250–279.

4. "Stakeholder Capitalism," *The Economist* (February 10, 1996), 23–25. See also "Shareholder Values," *The Economist* (February 10, 1996), 15–16; and John Plender, *A Stake in the Future: The Stakeholding Society* (Nicholas Brealey, 1997).

5. David Wheeler and Maria Sillanpää, *The Stakeholder Corporation: A Blueprint for Maximizing Stakeholder Value* (London: Pitman Publishing, 1997).

6. Steven F. Walker and Jeffrey W. Marr, *Stakeholder Power: A Winning Plan for Building Stakeholder Commitment and Driving Corporate Growth* (Cambridge, MA: Perseus Publishing, 2001).

7. Jeanne M. Logsdon, Donna J. Wood, and Lee E. Benson, "Research in Stakeholder Theory, 1997–1998: The Sloan Foundation Minigrant Project" (Toronto: The Clarkson Centre for Business Ethics, 2000).

8. This definition is similar to that of R. Edward Freeman in *Strategic Management: A Stakeholder Approach* (Boston: Pitman, 1984), 25.

9. Mark Starik, "Is the Environment an Organizational Stakeholder? Naturally!" *International Association for Business and Society (IABS) 1993 Proceedings*, 466–471.

10. Freeman, 5.

11. *Ibid.*, 24–25.

12. Wheeler and Sillanpää (1997), 167.

13. *Ibid.*, 168.

14. Max B. E. Clarkson (ed.), *Proceedings of the Second Toronto Conference on Stakeholder Theory* (Toronto: The Centre for Corporate Social Performance and Ethics, University of Toronto, 1994).

15. Ronald K. Mitchell, Bradley R. Agle, and Donna J. Wood, "Toward a Theory of Stakeholder Identification and Salience: Defining the Principle of Who and What Really Counts," *Academy of Management Review* (October 1997), 853–886.

16. Jim Carlton, "How Home Depot and Activists Joined to Cut Logging Abuse," *The Wall Street Journal* (September 26, 2000), A1.

17. Kenneth E. Goodpaster, "Business Ethics and Stakeholder Analysis," *Business Ethics Quarterly* (Vol. 1, No. 1, January 1991), 53–73.

18. *Ibid.*

19. Thomas Donaldson and Lee Preston, "The Stakeholder Theory of the Corporation: Concepts, Evidence, Implications," *Academy of Management Review* (Vol. 20, No. 1, 1995), 65–91.

20. *Ibid.*

21. Similar questions are posed by Ian C. MacMillan and Patricia E. Jones, *Strategy Formulation: Power and Politics* (St. Paul, MN: West, 1986), 66.

22. "Animal Rights Group Aims Ad Attack at McDonald's," *The Wall Street Journal* (August 30, 1999), B7.

23. Marcia Yablon, "Happy Hen, Happy Meal: McDonald's Chick Fix," *U.S. News & World Report* (September 4, 2000), 46.

24. *Ibid.*, 46.

25. "News Release: Chicken and Friends Have Bone to Pick with New Burger King CEO." People for the Ethical Treatment of Animals (PETA) Web page: http://www.peta-online.org/news/0301/0301miamibk.html.

26. "Does It Pay to Be Ethical? *Business Ethics* (March/April 1997), 14. See also "Activists Hang Banner at CITIGROUP Headquarters: 'Hey Citi, Not with My Money,'" http://www.ran.org/news/newsitem.php?id=97&area=finance.

27. Grant T. Savage, Timothy W. Nix, Carlton J. Whitehead, and John D. Blair, "Strategies for Assessing and Managing Organizational Stakeholders," *Academy of Management Executive* (Vol. V, No. 2, May 1991), 61–75.

28. *Ibid.*, 64.

29. Baby Milk Action, http://www.babymilkaction.org/pages/boycott.html.

30. "Boycott Glaxo over Internet Medication: U.S. Seniors' Groups," *CBC Newsworld*, http://www.cbc.ca/storyview/CBC/2003/02/21/Consumers/Webdrugs_030221 (February 21, 2003); National Association of Socially Responsible Organizations Web page: http://www.global-equality.org/news/boycott_glaxo.shtml.

31. MacMillan and Jones, 66–70.

32. Savage, Nix, Whitehead, and Blair, 65.

33. *Ibid.*, 72.

34. Freeman, 53.

35. Mark Starik, "Stakeholder Management and Firm Performance: Reputation and Financial Relationships to U.S. Electric Utility Consumer-Related Strategies," Unpublished Ph.D. dissertation, University of Georgia, 1990, 34.

36. Freeman, 64.

37. Starik (1990), 36.

38. Freeman, 69–70.

39. Starik (1990), 36–42.

40. Steven F. Walker and Jeffrey Marr, *Stakeholder Power: A Winning Plan for Building Stakeholder Commitment and Driving Corporate Growth* (Perseus Books, 2001).

41. Charles McCoy, "Two Members of Mitsubishi Group and Environmental Activists Reach Pact," *The Wall Street Journal* (February 11, 1998), A8.

42. Wheeler and Sillanpää (1997), book cover.

43. "Stakeholder Symbiosis," *Fortune* (March 30, 1998), S2–S4, special advertising section.

44. Walker and Marr (2001), 56–65.

45. *Ibid.*

Part Two

Strategic Management for Corporate Stakeholder Performance

Chapter 4

Strategic Management and Corporate Public Affairs

Chapter Objectives

After studying this chapter, you should be able to:

1 Explain the concept of corporate public policy and relate it to strategic management.

2 Articulate the four major strategy levels and explain enterprise-level strategy.

3 Enumerate and briefly describe how a concern for social and ethical issues fits into the strategic management process.

4 Relate the notion of social audits to strategic control.

5 Identify and discuss four stages in environmental analysis.

6 Identify the major functions of public affairs departments.

7 Highlight trends with respect to the public affairs function.

8 Link public affairs with organizational characteristics.

9 Indicate how public affairs may be incorporated into every manager's job.

In this chapter and the next, we more closely examine how management has responded and should respond, in a managerial sense, to the kinds of social, ethical, and stakeholder issues developed in this book. In this chapter, we provide a broad overview of how social, ethical, and public issues fit into the general **strategic management processes** of the organization. We introduce the term *corporate public policy* to describe that component part of management decision making that embraces these issues. Finally, we discuss corporate public affairs, or public affairs management, as the formal organizational approach for dealing with these issues. The overriding goal of this chapter is to focus on planning for the turbulent social/ethical stakeholder environment, and this encompasses the strategic management process, environmental analysis, and public affairs management.

The Concept of Corporate Public Policy

The impact of the social-ethical-public-stakeholder environment on business organizations is becoming more pronounced each year. It is an understatement to suggest that this multifaceted environment has become tumultuous, and brief reminders of a few actual cases point out the validity of this claim quite dramatically. Firestone and its radial tire debacle, Ford Motor Company and its disastrous Pinto gas tank problem, and Johnson & Johnson and its tainted Tylenol capsules are *classic* reminders of how social issues can directly affect a firm's product offerings. In addition, there are many examples in which social issues have had major impacts on firms at the general management level. Exxon's catastrophic *Valdez* oil spill and the tobacco industry's battles with the government over the dangers of its product are all examples of the impacts of top-level decisions that entail ethical ramifications. Coca-Cola's disastrous and massive recall of soft drinks in Belgium and France and Bridgestone-Firestone's tire tread separations in a number of countries provide examples of ethical issues that have dramatic implications for top executive decision makers.

What started as an awareness of social issues and social responsibility matured into a focus on the management of social responsiveness and performance. Today, the trend reflects a preoccupation with ethics, stakeholders, and corporate citizenship as we navigate the first decade of the new millennium. The term *corporate public policy* is an outgrowth of an earlier term, *corporate social policy*, which had been in general usage for over 20 years. The two concepts have essentially the same meaning, but we will use "corporate public policy" because it is more in keeping with terminology more recently used in business. Much of what takes place under the banner of corporate public policy is also referred to as corporate citizenship by businesses today.

Corporate Public Policy Defined

What is meant by corporate public policy? **Corporate public policy** is a firm's posture, stance, strategy, or position regarding the public, social, and ethical aspects of stakeholders and corporate functioning. Later in the chapter we will discuss how businesses formalize this concern under the rubric of corporate public affairs, or public affairs management. Businesses encounter many situations in their daily operations that involve highly visible public and ethical issues. Some of these issues are subject to intensive public debate for specific periods of time before they become institutionalized. Examples of such issues include sexual harassment, employment equity, product safety, and employee privacy. Other issues are more basic, more enduring, and more philosophical. These issues might include the broad role of business in society, the corporate governance question, and the relative balance of business versus government direction that is best for our society.

The idea behind corporate public policy is that a firm must give specific attention to issues in which basic questions of right, wrong, justice, fairness, or public policy reside. The dynamic stakeholder environment of the past 40 years has necessitated that management apply a policy perspective to these issues. At one time, the social environment was thought to be a relatively constant backdrop against which the real work of business took place. Today these issues are centre stage, and managers at all levels must address them. Corporate public policy is the process by which management addresses these significant concerns.

Corporate Public Policy as Part of Strategic Management

Where does corporate public policy fit into strategic management? First, let us briefly discuss strategic management. **Strategic management** refers to the overall management process that focuses on positioning a firm relative to its environment. A basic way in which the firm relates to its environment is through the products and services it produces and the markets it chooses to address. Strategic management is also thought of as a kind of overall or comprehensive organizational management by the firm's top-level executives. In this sense, it represents the overall executive leadership function in which the sense of direction of the organization is decided upon and implemented.

Top management teams must address many issues as a firm is positioning itself relative to its environment. The more traditional issues involve product/market decisions—the principal decision thrust of most organizations. Other decisions relate to marketing, finance, accounting, information systems, human resources, operations, research and development, competition, and so on. Corporate public policy is that part of the overall strategic management of the organization that focuses specifically on the public, ethical, and stakeholder issues that are embedded in the functioning and decision processes of the firm. Therefore, just as a firm needs to develop policy on human resources, operations, marketing, or finance, it also must develop corporate public policy to proactively address the host of issues we have been discussing and will discuss throughout this book.

A company that concluded it needed a formal corporate public policy is Citizens Bank of Canada, a company that has been trying to build a strong reputation in the area of corporate social responsibility since it opened its doors in 1997. The bank's management concluded it needed more than the establishment of a few enlightened policies. It needed something that would set a systematic course and foundation for "doing well by doing good." Citizens' first step was the establishment of a document of guiding principles, called an ethical policy, that would steer the firm's practices toward its social and environmental commitments. To implement its policy and follow up on implementation, the bank created an "ethical policy compliance" unit. The initiatives of Citizens Bank illustrate the realization that companies come to regarding the need for formalized corporate public/ethics policy.[1]

Relationship of Ethics to Strategic Management

Although a consideration of ethics is implicit in corporate public policy discussions, it is useful to make this relationship more explicit. Over the years, a growing number of writers have stressed this point. Kenneth R. Andrews, for example, is well known for his emphasis on the moral component of corporate strategy. In particular, he highlights the leadership challenge of determining future strategy in the face of rising moral and ethical standards. He argues that coming to terms with the morality of choice may be the most strenuous undertaking in strategic decision making. This is particularly stressful in the inherently amoral corporation.[2]

The challenge of linking ethics and strategy was moved to centre stage by R. Edward Freeman and Daniel R. Gilbert, Jr., in their book *Corporate Strategy and the Search for Ethics*. The authors argued that if business ethics was to have any meaning beyond pompous moralizing, it must be linked to business strategy. Their view is that we can revitalize the concept of corporate strategy by linking ethics to strategy. This linkage permits the most pressing management issues of the day to be addressed in ethical terms. They suggest the concept of enterprise strategy as the idea that best links these two vital notions together, and we will examine this concept in more detail in the next section.[3]

The concept of corporate public policy and the linkage between ethics and strategy are better understood when we think about (1) the four key levels at which strategy decisions arise and (2) the steps in the strategic management process.

Four Key Strategy Levels

Because organizations are hierarchical, it is not surprising to find that strategic management is hierarchical, too. That is, there are several different levels in the firm at which strategic decisions are made or the strategy process occurs. These levels range from the broadest or highest levels (where missions, visions, goals, decisions, and policies entail higher risks and are characterized by longer time horizons, more subjective values, and greater uncertainty) to the lowest levels (where planning is done for specific functional areas, where time horizons are shorter, where information needs are less complex, and where there is less uncertainty). Four key strategy levels have been recognized and are important to consider: enterprise-level strategy, corporate-level strategy, business-level strategy, and functional-level strategy.

The Four Strategy Levels

The broadest level of strategic management is known as societal-level strategy or enterprise-level strategy, as it has come to be known. **Enterprise-level strategy** is the overarching strategy level that poses the basic questions, "What is the role of the organization in society?" and "What do we stand for?" Enterprise-level strategy, as we will discuss in more detail later, encompasses the development and articulation of corporate public policy. It may be considered the first and most important level at which ethics and strategy are linked. Until fairly recently, corporate-level strategy was thought to be the broadest strategy level. In a limited, traditional sense, this is true, because **corporate-level strategy** addresses what is often posed as the most defining question for a firm, "What business(es) are we in or should we be in?" It is easy to see how **business-level strategy** is a natural follow-on because this strategy level is concerned with the question, "How should we compete in a given business or industry?" Thus, a company whose products or services take it into many different businesses or industries might need a business-level strategy to define its competitive posture in each of them. A competitive strategy might be based on low cost or a differentiated product. Finally, **functional-level strategy** addresses the question, "How should a firm integrate its various subfunctional activities and how should these activities be related to changes taking place in the various functional areas (finance, marketing, operations)?"[4]

The purpose of identifying the four strategy levels is to clarify that corporate public policy is primarily a part of enterprise-level strategy, which, in turn, is but one level of strategic decision making that occurs in organizations. Figure 4–1 illustrates that enterprise-level strategy is the broadest level and that the other levels are narrower concepts that cascade from it.

Emphasis on Enterprise-Level Strategy

The terms *enterprise-level strategy* and *societal-level strategy* may be used interchangeably. Neither of these terms is used with any degree of regularity in the business community. Although many firms address the issues that enterprise-level strategy is concerned with, use of this terminology is restricted primarily to the academic community. This terminology arose in an attempt to describe the level of strategic thinking that an increasing number of observers believe is necessary if firms are to be fully responsive to today's complex and dynamic stakeholder environment. Many organizations today convey this enterprise or societal strategy in their missions, vision, or values statements. Others embed their enterprise strategies in codes of conduct.

Igor Ansoff visualized the enterprise strategy level as one in which the political legitimacy of the organization is addressed.[5] Ansoff later discussed this same concern for

FIGURE 4–1

The Hierarchy of Strategy Levels

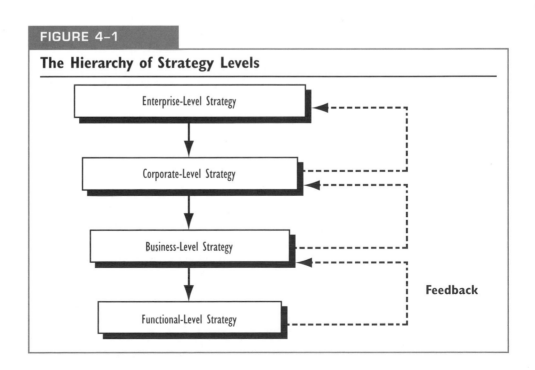

legitimacy using the phrase "Societal Strategy for the Business Firm."[6] Hofer and others have described the enterprise level as the societal level.

According to Ed Freeman, enterprise-level strategy needs to be thought of in such a way that it more closely aligns "social and ethical concerns" with traditional "business concerns."[7] In setting the direction for a firm, a manager needs to understand the impact of changes in business strategy on the underlying values of the firm and the new stakeholder relations that will emerge and take shape as a result. Freeman proposes that enterprise-level strategy needs to address the overriding question, "What do we stand for?"[8] Thus, at the enterprise level the task of setting strategic direction involves understanding the role in society of a particular firm as a whole and its relationships to other social institutions. Important questions then become:

- What is the role of our organization in society?
- How is our organization perceived by our stakeholders?
- What principles or values does our organization represent?
- What obligations do we have to society at large?
- What are the implications for our current mix of business and allocation of resources?

Many firms have addressed some of these questions—perhaps only in part, perhaps only in an ad hoc way. The point of enterprise-level strategy, however, is that the firm needs to address these questions intentionally, specifically, and cohesively in such a way that a corporate public policy is articulated.

How have business firms addressed these questions? What are the manifestations of enterprise-level thinking and corporate public policy? The manifestations show up in a variety of ways in different companies—for example, how a firm responds when faced with public crises. Does it respond to its stakeholders in a positive, constructive, and sensitive way or in a negative, defensive, and insensitive way? Corporate actions reveal the presence or absence of soundly developed enterprise-level strategy. Companies also demonstrate the degree of thinking that has gone into public issues by the presence or absence and use or nonuse of codes of ethics, codes of conduct, mission statements, values statements, corporate creeds, vision statements, or other such policy-oriented codes and statements.

One company that has addressed these concerns is the Canadian multinational corporation Nortel Networks. In a document entitled "Living the Values: A Guide to Ethical Business Practices at Nortel Networks," questions posed and then answered include:

- What kind of company are we anyway?
- What does Nortel stand for?
- What do we believe?

Figure 4–2 presents "The Integrity Value: Our Cornerstone," a portion of the larger document produced by Nortel that clearly manifests enterprise-level strategy and corporate public policy.

Another example of enterprise-level strategy is the corporate credo of Johnson & Johnson, shown in Figure 4–3. Note that the Johnson & Johnson credo focuses on statements of responsibility by enumerating its stakeholder groups in the following sequence:

- Doctors, nurses, patients, mothers and fathers (consumers)
- Employees
- Communities
- Stockholders

FIGURE 4-2

Nortel's Integrity Value

Integrity Means ...

We Strive to Do the Right Thing for Individuals, Organizations and Society in General.
Companies have obligations that extend well beyond the payment of taxes, employment of people, and provision of goods and services. As a global company, we face a special challenge: to uphold consistent corporate standards of ethical business conduct, while respecting the culture and varying business customs of every community and country in which we operate.

Our commitment means:

- **We consider communities in business decisions.**
  The long-term interests of the community influence such business decisions as the selection of sites for new facilities. We encourage the recruitment of qualified local personnel and local purchasing of materials and services where practical. We do not use forced labor or child labor.

- **We get involved.**
  Directly and through our employees, officers, and members of the board of directors, we contribute to the general well-being and improvement of the towns, cities, and regions where we operate. Many of our people are passionate about making a difference, and contribute time, financial resources, and experience to address the needs of their communities. In many locations, Nortel Networks provides support to community programs in such areas as social welfare, health, and education. For many years, we have focused our efforts on math, science, and technology education, with support given to universities, schools, students, and educators in communities across the globe. By sharing financial resources, equipment and expertise, Nortel Networks helps create innovative solutions to community challenges through the thoughtful application of communication technology.

- **We believe in environmental protection and enhancement.**
  Nortel Networks is committed to being environmentally responsible in all its endeavors. We take the initiative to develop innovative solutions to environmental issues before they arise. And we take responsibility for the environmental impacts of our products throughout their lifecycle—from design to final disposition. We work with customers, suppliers, industry associations, educational institutions, public interest groups, and governments throughout the world to promote the development and dissemination of innovative solutions to industry-related environmental impacts.

- **We support the international scientific community.**
  Where knowledge of product and manufacturing technology can be shared without harming our competitive position in the marketplace (or contravening national restrictions on the transfer of technology), we engage in technology cooperation projects with industry, institutions of higher education, and industry associations around the world.

- **We participate appropriately in the political process.**
  Nortel Networks does not use inappropriate measures to influence public issues—nor do we become involved in unethical or unlawful political activity. As a company, we express views on local and national issues that affect our business and our industry. We support and participate in the political process in accordance with applicable laws and regulations.

Source: Nortel Networks company document: "Living the Values: A Guide to Ethical Business Practices at Nortel Networks." Reproduced with the permission of Nortel Networks. Copyright © 2003 Nortel Networks. All rights reserved.

Alcan Inc. (which ranked number one among the top 50 most ethical companies in Canada in a ranking by *Corporate Knights*[9]) is a company with a strong global presence. It has approximately 53 000 employees in 41 countries and has been a leader in raw materials, primary metals, and fabricated products. These include products for the automotive and mass transportation markets, aluminum sheet for beverage cans, and specialty packaging for the food, pharmaceutical, and personal care industries worldwide. The "core values" at Alcan were identified and articulated in a recent "Corporate Sustainability" Statement, and include the following:[10]

FIGURE 4–3

Johnson & Johnson Credo

Our Credo

We believe our first responsibility is to the doctors, nurses and patients,
to mothers and fathers and all others who use our products and services.
In meeting their needs everything we do must be of high quality.
We must constantly strive to reduce our costs
in order to maintain reasonable prices.
Customers' orders must be serviced promptly and accurately.
Our suppliers and distributors must have an opportunity
to make a fair profit.

We are responsible to our employees,
the men and women who work with us throughout the world.
Everyone must be considered as an individual.
We must respect their dignity and recognize their merit.
They must have a sense of security in their jobs.
Compensation must be fair and adequate,
and working conditions clean, orderly and safe.
We must be mindful of ways to help our employees fulfill
their family responsibilities.
Employees must feel free to make suggestions and complaints.
There must be equal opportunity for employment, development
and advancement for those qualified.
We must provide competent management,
and their actions must be just and ethical.

We are responsible to the communities in which we live and work
and to the world community as well.
We must be good citizens—support good works and charities
and bear our fair share of taxes.
We must encourage civic improvements and better health and education.
We must maintain in good order
the property we are privileged to use,
protecting the environment and natural resources.

Our final responsibility is to our stockholders.
Business must make a sound profit.
We must experiment with new ideas.
Research must be carried on, innovative programs developed
and mistakes paid for.
New equipment must be purchased, new facilities provided
and new products launched.
Reserves must be created to provide for adverse times.
When we operate according to these principles,
the stockholders should realize a fair return.

Johnson & Johnson

Source: Reprinted with permission from Johnson & Johnson.

Integrity: We believe in operating with integrity in all our business deal-ings. We conduct ourselves in a responsible fashion as outlined in our Worldwide Code of Employee and Business Conduct, *which also applies to our contractors, consultants and suppliers.*

Accountability: We also strive to be openly accountable and willing to align decision-making power with responsibilities at all levels of our organization. For Alcan employees, accountability entails honoring commitments and accepting responsibility for our actions and behavior.

Teamwork: We believe in leveraging the abilities of our employees, suppliers, contractors, customers—our many stakeholders—through a cooperative team approach to problem solving and project implementation. Interaction with other group and team members is a vital part of everyone's job.

Trust and transparency: At the core of all ethical business dealings there must be trust. Trust that others will do as they say and trust that we will live up to our commitments. To accomplish this we must also be transparent in the way we communicate with others, providing timely and accurate information.

Another illustration of enterprise-level strategic thinking may be seen in the "Commitment to Integrity" statement articulated by The Boeing Company. This statement, presented in Figure 4–4, reflects the company's values and how these values are targeted toward a vision of full customer satisfaction. Merck & Co., Inc., the leading pharmaceutical firm, conveys its enterprise strategy in its values statement, which is part of its mission statement. Domtar Inc., with 12 000 employees across North America, manages 22 million acres of forestland in Canada and the United States, and produces lumber and other wood and paper products. It was ranked among the top 10 most ethical Canadian companies in a recent *Corporate Knights*

FIGURE 4–4

Commitment to Integrity

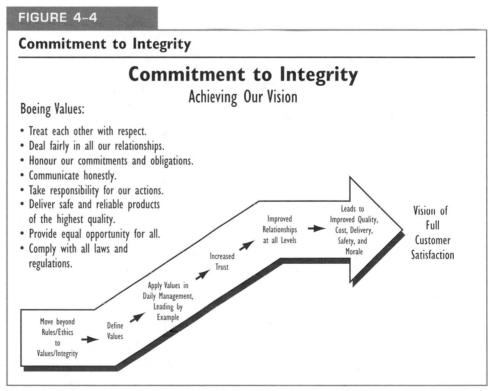

Source: Reprinted with permission from Boeing.

poll.[11] In the introduction to its clearly outlined ethics policy, Domtar Inc. provides a basic rationale for the purpose of such a policy:

> *The Code of Ethics (the "Code") of Domtar sets out the ground rules for maintaining and building our reputation as an ethical, fair-dealing corporate citizen concerned about our standing in the community. The Code applies to all Domtar employees, and to all Domtar subsidiaries, operating groups and locations.[12]*

Other manifestations of enterprise-level strategic thinking in corporations include the extent to which firms have established board or senior management committees. Such committees might include the following: public policy/issues committees, ethics committees, social audit committees, corporate philanthropy committees, and ad hoc committees to address specific public issues. The firm's public affairs function can also indicate enterprise-level thinking. Does the firm have an established public affairs office? To whom does the director of corporate public affairs report? What role does public affairs play in corporate-level decision making? Do public affairs managers play a formal role in the firm's strategic planning?

Another major indicator of enterprise-level strategic thinking is the extent to which the firm attempts to identify social or public issues, analyze them, and integrate them into its strategic management processes. We will now discuss how corporate public policy is integrated into the strategic management process.

The Strategic Management Process

To understand how corporate public policy is but one part of the larger system of management decision making, it is useful to provide an overview of the major steps that make up the strategic management process. There are several acceptable ways to conceptualize this process, but we will use the six-step process identified by Hofer and Schendel. These six steps are (1) goal formulation, (2) strategy formulation, (3) strategy evaluation, (4) strategy implementation, (5) strategic control, and (6) environmental analysis.[13] Figure 4–5 graphically portrays an expanded view of this process. Note that the environmental analysis component collects information on trends, events, and issues that are occurring in the stakeholder environment and that this information is then fed into the other steps of the process. Note also that, although the tasks or steps are discussed sequentially in this chapter, they are in fact interactive and do not always occur in a neatly ordered pattern or sequence. First, we will discuss the first five steps, and then consider environmental analysis, which links the stakeholder environment with the organizational environment.

Goal Formulation

The goal formulation process in an organization is a complex task. It involves both the establishment of goals and the setting of priorities among goals. Often a politically charged process, goal formulation integrates the personal values, perceptions, attitudes, and power of the managers and owners involved in the process. Economic or financial goals typically dominate the goal formulation process. It is being increasingly recognized, however, that goal setting as it pertains to the public, social, and ethical domains of the firm is in dire need of more attention.[14] Typical areas in which public

FIGURE 4–5

The Strategic Management Process and Corporate Public Policy

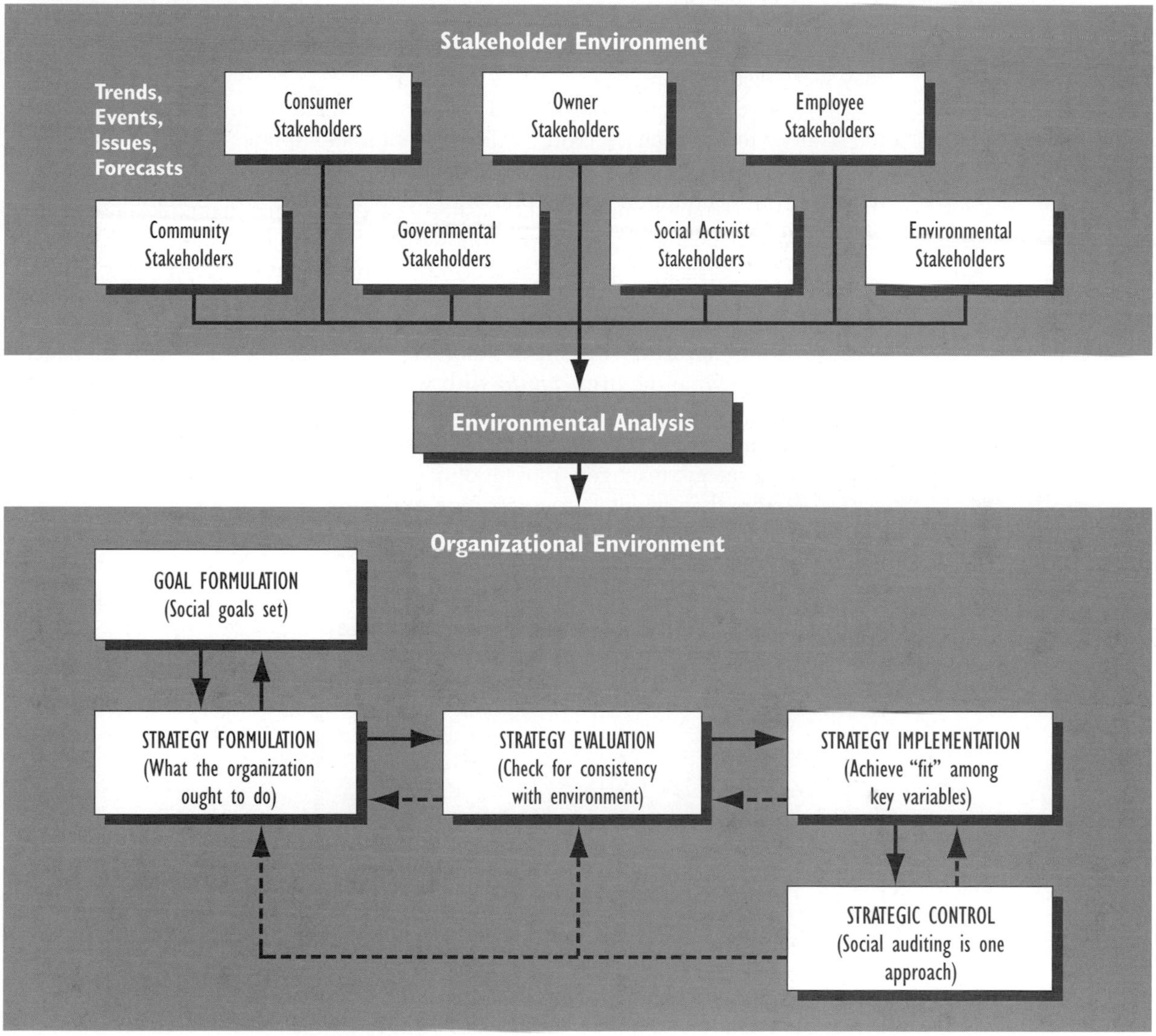

Stakeholder Environment

Trends,
Events,
Issues,
Forecasts

| Consumer Stakeholders | Owner Stakeholders | Employee Stakeholders |

| Community Stakeholders | Governmental Stakeholders | Social Activist Stakeholders | Environmental Stakeholders |

Environmental Analysis

Organizational Environment

GOAL FORMULATION
(Social goals set)

STRATEGY FORMULATION
(What the organization ought to do)

STRATEGY EVALUATION
(Check for consistency with environment)

STRATEGY IMPLEMENTATION
(Achieve "fit" among key variables)

STRATEGIC CONTROL
(Social auditing is one approach)

policy goals might be set include employment equity, consumer product safety, occupational safety and health, corporate philanthropy, and environmental protection. Furthermore, it has become clear that economic and social goals are not at odds with each other and that the two can be integrated in such a way that the firm's best interests, as well as the best interests of the stakeholders, are simultaneously served.[15]

The strategic management process entails a system of decisions in which goals are successively more refined—moving from broad to specific—just as we illustrated in Figure 4–1 (see page 97). The result is a cascading of goals that addresses the various levels that have been identified.

Strategy Formulation

Once goals have been established, the strategy formulation process becomes important. It is difficult to neatly factor out the formulation, evaluation, implementation, and control aspects of the process, because in real life they are intimately related and interdependent. For purposes of discussion, however, we will treat them as though they were distinct steps.

As shown in Figure 4–6, Andrews suggests that there are four major components of the strategy formulation decision: (1) identification and appraisal of the firm's *strengths and weaknesses*, (2) identification and appraisal of *opportunities and threats* in the environment, (3) identification and appraisal of *personal values and aspirations of management*, and (4) identification and appraisal of *acknowledged obligations* to society.[16]

Components 1 and 2 are the most basic, because they require a company to examine carefully its own capabilities—its strengths, weaknesses, and resources—and think in terms of matching those capabilities with the opportunities, threats, and risks present in the market environment. Another way of stating this is that management must compare what the firm *can do* with what it *might do*. An analysis of the company's strengths and weaknesses is compatible with the "resource-based view of the firm," which has become quite popular in strategic management theory. This view holds that strategic managers must look carefully at the firm's resources to identify critical factors that are likely to contribute to competitive advantage.[17]

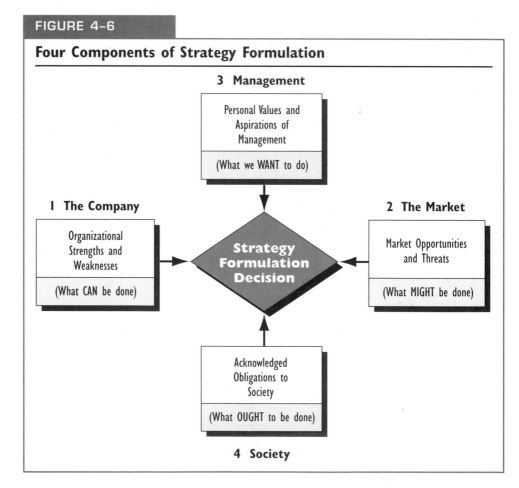

FIGURE 4–6

Four Components of Strategy Formulation

3 Management

Personal Values and
Aspirations of
Management

(What we WANT to do)

1 The Company

Organizational
Strengths and
Weaknesses

(What CAN be done)

**Strategy
Formulation
Decision**

2 The Market

Market Opportunities
and Threats

(What MIGHT be done)

Acknowledged
Obligations to
Society

(What OUGHT to be done)

4 Society

Components 3 and 4 are also vital. Realistically, attention needs to be paid to the personal values and aspirations of the management group. These subjective influences are real and must be factored into the strategy formulation process. Thus, Component 3—what management *wants to do*—is a key factor. Finally, strategic choice has a social or an ethical aspect that can no longer be ignored. Component 4—what the firm *ought to do* in terms of its acknowledged obligations to society—should be factored in as well.[18]

Component 4 is the corporate public policy component in strategy formulation. It is not the most strategic factor, because a firm that does not have an acceptable matching of organizational characteristics with market characteristics (Components 1 and 2) will not survive. However, in today's business environment, the successful firm blends these components in such a way that the needs or issues arising out of each are effectively addressed.

Part of the goal setting and strategy formulation stages is the creation of mission statements or vision statements. Many organizations today articulate their enterprise strategy by way of these statements. Several writers have argued that the most successful companies in the future will be those who state "a noble purpose." They point to some of the most admired companies today that are striving to be examples of greatness. Examples include Mary Kay, Inc., with its stated intention to "enrich women's lives"; Merck & Co., Inc., whose "business is preserving and improving human life"; and British Petroleum, which recently announced a brand-name change to "Beyond Petroleum," signalling its leadership role in moving civilization out of the fossil-fuel era.[19]

Strategy Evaluation

In some conceptualizations of the strategic management process, strategy evaluation occurs in conjunction with strategic control, after implementation has taken place. We are treating it as the third step in the strategic management process because, in an ongoing organization, it can also be viewed as an integrative process that takes place in conjunction with goal formulation and strategy formulation. In an ongoing organization that already has a strategy, strategy evaluation entails a continuing assessment of the firm's current goals and strategy relative to proposed goals and strategic alternatives.

Perhaps the most important evaluation criterion in terms of corporate public policy is the strategy's consistency with the environment. The stakeholder environment is complex and dynamic, and a strategy that was once successful may no longer be so. Careful attention to this criterion, then, should be the hallmark of successful public policy.

Strategy Implementation

No strategy design, however grand, will benefit an organization if it is left on the drawing board. In its simplest form, strategy implementation means putting the plans (goals, missions, strategies) that have been developed and evaluated into effect. It means working the plan with the aim of achieving the desired results. At a more complex level, implementation means that many different organizational processes must be activated and coordinated in such a way that the implementation is successful.

The McKinsey 7S framework is useful as a straightforward identification of seven key variables that must be skillfully coordinated in order for successful strategy implementation to occur. These seven variables are strategy, structure, systems, style, staff, skills, and shared values.[20]

The 7S framework was originally conceived as a way of broadly thinking about the problems of effective organizing, but it also provides an excellent vehicle for thinking about the elements that must be successfully coordinated in strategy implementation. Of particular note in terms of corporate public policy is the "shared values" element. Although these shared values did not refer to shared ethical or social responsiveness values in the original 7S framework, we can readily see how they should be expanded to embrace more than "corporate culture" as it has most typically been conceived. Much research, for example, has pointed to the significance of an organization's ethical culture.

The key to the successful use of the 7S framework is achieving "fit," or congruence, among all of the elements. Fit is a process, as well as a state, in which there is a dynamic quest that seeks to align an organization with its environment and to arrange internal resources in such a way that the alignment is supported. It is argued that a "minimal fit" is essential for survival in a competitive environment and that a "tight fit" is needed for long-term effectiveness.[21]

Strategic Control (via Social Auditing)

As a management function, strategic control seeks to ensure that the organization stays on track and achieves its goals, missions, and strategies. The first three elements we have discussed so far in this section—goal formulation, strategy formulation, and strategy evaluation—are parts of the overall planning that is essential if firms are to succeed. Planning is not complete without control, however, because control strives to keep management activities in conformance with plans.

Management control subsumes three essential steps: (1) *setting standards* against which performance may be compared, (2) *comparing* actual performance with what was planned (the standard), and (3) *taking corrective action* to bring the two into alignment, if needed.[22] It has been argued that a planning system will not achieve its full potential unless at the same time it monitors and assesses the firm's progress along key strategic dimensions. Furthermore, there is a need to monitor and control the "strategic momentum" by focusing on a particular strategic direction while at the same time coping with environmental turbulence and change.[23]

Development of the Social Audit   In the context of corporate social performance or corporate public policy, the idea of a **social audit**, or social performance report, as a technique for providing control has been experimented with for a number of years. Although the term *social audit* has been used to describe a wide variety of activities embracing various forms of social performance reporting, in this discussion we define it as follows:

> *The social audit is a systematic attempt to identify, measure, monitor, and evaluate an organization's performance with respect to its social efforts, goals, and programs.*

Implicit in this definition is the idea that some social performance planning has already taken place. And although we discuss the social audit here as a control process, it could just as easily be thought of as a planning/control system.[24]

In the context of strategic control, the social audit could assume a role much like that portrayed in Figure 4–7. This figure is similar to the diagram of the strategic management process and corporate public policy shown in Figure 4–5 (see page 103) but is modified somewhat to focus on social goals, corporate social performance, the social audit, and the first three steps in the strategic control process.

Although the corporate social audit is not in widespread use in Canadian or U.S. industry today, it is worth considering in more detail because of its potential for serving as a planning, control, and communication scheme. More and more today, various groups want companies to reveal their social performance results in such areas as environment, commitments to workplace conditions, fairness and honesty in dealings with suppliers, customer service standards, community and charitable involvement, and business practices in developing countries. The groups expecting this information range from social activist groups to investor groups such as mutual funds and institutional investors.

The components of the social audit include identification, measurement, monitoring, and evaluation. The identification function is included as a part of the definition because experience has shown that companies often are not completely aware of all

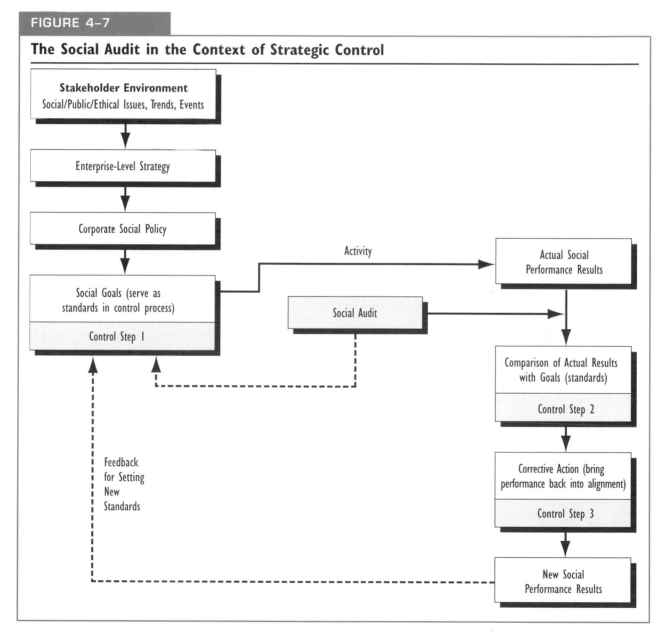

FIGURE 4–7

The Social Audit in the Context of Strategic Control

Stakeholder Environment
Social/Public/Ethical Issues, Trends, Events

Enterprise-Level Strategy

Corporate Social Policy

Social Goals (serve as standards in control process)

Control Step 1

Activity

Social Audit

Actual Social Performance Results

Comparison of Actual Results with Goals (standards)

Control Step 2

Corrective Action (bring performance back into alignment)

Control Step 3

New Social Performance Results

Feedback for Setting New Standards

that they are doing in the public, social, or ethics arena. Any serious effort to determine what a company is doing requires the development of measures by which performance can be reported, analyzed, and compared. Monitoring and evaluation stress that the effort is continuous and aimed at achieving certain standards or goals the company may have in mind. Increasingly, communicating the results of corporate social performance reports is also becoming an important issue. There is a desire today for companies to be "transparent" about their social records, and good arguments can be made for companies releasing such information on a regular basis.

The term *social audit* has been subjected to some criticism. The foremost objection has been that it implies an "independent attestation" to the company's social performance, whereas such an independent attestation typically does not exist. The term *audit*, as used by accountants, usually means a verification by some outside party that the firm's situation is as it has been reported. Because social audits are typically conducted by those within the organization, or consultants hired by the organization, it is obvious why this objection is raised. The criticism has also been made that there exist no generally accepted social accounting principles or standards, no professionally recognized independent auditors, and no generally agreed-on criteria against which to measure a firm's social performance.[25] Despite these concerns, the term *social audit* continues to be used. In addition, firms have been using "ethics audits" or "stakeholder audits" to describe efforts to review social, ethical, and stakeholder performance.

Another term, *social accounting*, is frequently used in reference to social auditing and has been defined as follows: "The measurement and reporting, internal or external, of information concerning the impact of an entity and its activities on society."[26] We can readily see that these definitions are quite similar. The only term for the function we have been describing that has not been criticized is "corporate social performance reporting." However, there is some evidence that this term is no longer in vogue. We will, nevertheless, use all these terms interchangeably and urge the reader to keep in mind the points we have made with respect to each. This is especially necessary in regard to social auditing, a term we will use frequently, because it is so much a part of the already existing literature on and experience of social performance measurement and reporting.

Evolution of Social Auditing   The social audit as a concept for monitoring, measuring, and appraising the social performance of business dates back over 60 years to at least 1940 in the United States.[27] In a 1940 publication of the Temporary National Economic Committee, Theodore J. Kreps presented a monograph entitled "Measurement of the Social Performance of Business."[28] Another landmark in the development of social audits came in 1953 in a book by Howard R. Bowen.[29] Bowen's concept of the social audit was that of a high-level, independent appraisal conducted about every five years by a group of disinterested auditors. The auditors' report would be an evaluation with recommendations intended for internal use by the directors and the management of the firm audited.

In Canada, the United Church of Canada engaged in the first social audits in the 1960s. Church audit teams attempted to assess the practices of companies in which the Church's pension and general funds were invested. This assessment typically involved interviewing corporate directors and surveying employees. This activity played a key role in raising corporate awareness of ethical issues and inspired the development of ethical codes of conduct in some Canadian businesses.[30]

The social audit, as it came of age in the 1970s, attempted to focus on such social performance categories as minority employment, pollution/environment, community

Search the web   WWW

The Body Shop and Social Auditing

The Body Shop's approach to social and ethical auditing encompasses three subject areas—social, environmental, and animal protection. The Body Shop reports that out of the 100 international company reports evaluated by Sustainability for the U.N. Environmental Programme (UNEP), its Values Report scored the highest rating for the second year running.

To review the UNEP's ratings, check out **http://www.sustainability.com/home.asp**. To review the social audits of The Body Shop, go to **http://www.bodyshop.com/usa/values/index.asp**. There you will find its Values Report and information on The Body Shop's Approach to Social and Ethical Auditing.

relations, consumer issues, and philanthropic contributions. Very few companies initially undertook social audits as control mechanisms. To use a device as a control mechanism implied that there were some goals or standards against which to compare actual performance. Initially, social audits were employed by companies to examine what the company was actually doing in selected areas, appraise or evaluate social performance, identify social programs that the company thought it ought to be pursuing, or just inject into the general thinking of managers a social point of view.[31]

Social auditing fell out of favour in the 1980s. In the 1990s and early 2000s, however, there was some resurgence in interest in social performance, ethics, and values audits and reports. The company that stands out as one of the leaders in social auditing is The Body Shop. This should not be surprising inasmuch as the company's founder, Anita Roddick, once said, "Auditing shouldn't just be for accounting. A company should open its heart as well as its books."[32]

Current Examples of Social Auditing One of the most comprehensive examples of social or ethical auditing is the process conducted by The Body Shop, the skin and hair products company. The Body Shop began its ethics audit process in the early 1990s, and the process yielded several major reports, the most complete of which was the *Values Report 1997*.[33]

This report detailed the goals, approach, and results of the company's ethical auditing process, including key components of the company's corporate public policy: mission statement, founder's statement, social and ecological milestones, approach to ethical auditing, performance reports with respect to key stakeholder groups, and other reports.[34] The Body Shop's "Framework for Social Auditing and Disclosure" involves continuous improvement via the implementation of a cyclical audit loop.

One of The Body Shop's units, The Body Shop in Australia, released its own social audit via the Internet in 2001. The social audit of the Australian unit utilized a methodology based upon opinions and relevant information being gathered from stakeholder groups via interviews, facilitated group discussions, and surveys. Participants included employees, customers, suppliers, and education outreach clients. The initial audit was conducted by a consultant. Then, community and academic leaders were invited to examine the report.[35] This approach appears to be permeating throughout the other units, with the announcement in 2003 that The Body Shop, globally, would be publishing individual stakeholder accounts relating to six key stakeholder groups: customers, employees, shareholders, franchisees, suppliers, and the environment. This information was made available via The Body Shop's global Web site and is subject to annual updates (see http://www.thebodyshop.com/web/tbsgl/index.jsp).

One additional indicator of the increasing popularity of social auditing recently is the appearance of consulting and research firms willing to help companies conduct audits. Smith OBrien Services, for example, offers as a core service the "Corporate Responsibility Audit.™" The company describes its audit as a "multidisciplinary methodology for identifying and eliminating often-overlooked negative effects of a company's operations on its stakeholders, and thus reducing legal exposure, production inefficiencies, and reputational risk."[36] The research firm WalkerInformation of

Indianapolis, which provides measurement services to companies that want to know more about their impact on key stakeholder groups, also deserves mention because its service is similar to social auditing.[37] WalkerInformation's "Reputation and Stakeholder Assessment" is a comprehensive tool for measuring and managing stakeholder relationships. Through its assessment process, Walker gathers information from multiple stakeholder groups and provides the company with a "scorecard" summary of how these groups perceive or evaluate the company's reputation. Among other measures, the scorecard shows a company's reputation relative to that of the competition and of world-class leaders in other industries.[38]

One of the most significant consulting initiatives in the realm of social auditing was undertaken in 1998–1999 by the consulting firm KPMG in London, England, which created a social auditing consulting unit. Major clients of KPMG have included The Body Shop, Royal Dutch Shell, and Cooperative Insurance, a niche player in the British market that promotes itself as an ethical investor. The model for KPMG's social auditing was patterned after the approach developed in the book that Wheeler and Sillanpää wrote, *The Stakeholder Corporation*, referred to earlier in Chapter 3. This book lays out a detailed approach by which companies might improve their social, environmental, and financial performance by a process of inclusion and dialogue with groups both inside and outside the organization. Wheeler agrees that social auditing is "an embryonic market at the moment," but he expects the demands for the company's services to increase in the future.[39]

Standard Setting Initiatives While organizations are increasingly reporting on their social, ethical, and environmental impacts, a major impediment to the advance of social auditing is the absence of standardized measures for social reporting. A recent article by Nicole Dando and Tracy Swift in *The Journal of Business Ethics* noted:

> *There is a growing realisation that the current upward trend in levels of disclosure of social, ethical and environmental performance by corporations and other organisations is not being accompanied by simultaneous greater levels of public trust ... a lack of consistency in assurance statements and their variable quality and content make reports impossible to compare and the organisations and their performance difficult to evaluate by, for example, the investment community and customers.... Low levels of confidence in the information communicated in public reporting is probably undermining the impetus for this disclosure ... there is need for a universal standard for the provision of assurance of social, ethical and environmental reporting, and indeed for the credibility of the assurance providers themselves.[40]*

This article went on to assert that the credibility gap could be narrowed through the use of third-party independent assurance via the use of standardization of reporting. Standardization is a challenge that was undertaken by a consortium of over 300 global organizations called the **Global Reporting Initiative (GRI)**. The GRI is an extension of the U.S.-based Coalition for Environmentally Responsible Economies (CERES), which developed many of the now-accepted environmental reporting guidelines. GRI hopes that all companies will adopt its guidelines. It is expected that many companies will use the standards as a kind of "best practices" document.[41] GRI's Web page states its purpose as follows:

The Global Reporting Initiative (GRI) is an international, multi-stakeholder effort to create a common framework for voluntary reporting of the economic, environmental, and social impact of organization-level activity. The GRI mission is to elevate the comparability and credibility of sustainability reporting practices worldwide.

To address the need for global reporting standards regarding social accounts and reports, as advocated by GRI, the Institute of Social and Ethical Accountability launched the AA1000 framework in 1999 to develop generally accepted standards for the assurance of social, ethical, and sustainability reporting. The Institute describes the fundamental assurance principles as follows:

Assurance Principles
The AA1000 Assurance Standard is based on assessment of reports against three Assurance Principles:
- *Materiality. Does the sustainability report provide an account covering all the areas of performance that stakeholders need to judge the organization's sustainability performance?*
- *Completeness. Is the information complete and accurate enough to assess and understand the organization's performance in all these areas?*
- *Responsiveness. Has the organization responded coherently and consistently to stakeholders' concerns and interests?*[42]

As firms develop enterprise-level strategies and corporate public policies, the potential for social and ethical audits remains high. Social auditing is best appreciated not as an isolated, periodic attempt to assess social performance but rather as an integral part of the overall strategic management process as it has been portrayed here. Because the need to improve planning and control will remain as long as management desires to evaluate its corporate social performance, the need for strategic control through approaches such as the social audit will likely be with us for some time, too. The net result of continued use and refinement should be improved corporate social performance and enhanced credibility of business in the eyes of its stakeholders and the public.

Environmental Analysis

To this point, we have described the strategic management process without dwelling on the sources of the information that management uses in its goal formulation, strategy formulation, and other processes. Now we should discuss environmental analysis, a process by which this information is gathered and assembled. Environmental analysis is the linking pin between the organization, which is the managerial setting for the strategic management process, and the stakeholder environment, from which information is gathered.

The Stakeholder Environment   Before we describe environmental analysis, let us briefly discuss the idea of the stakeholder environment as portrayed in Figure 4–5 (see page 103). One popular conception is to visualize the environment of business in terms of three levels: (1) the *task environment*, which is that set of customers, suppliers, competitors, and others with which a firm interacts on an almost daily basis;

(2) the *competitive or industry environment*, which comprises those firms functioning in the same markets or industry; and (3) the general environment, or *macroenvironment*, which includes everything else "out there" that influences the organization.[43]

Another way of thinking about the environment of business is in terms of its component subsystems, or segments, that compose it. The standard scheme here is that the environment is composed of social, economic, political, and technological components, or subenvironments. Because the macroenvironment is complex, these components are highly interdependent and often inseparable from one another. Although this scheme is useful, it overlooks important environmental segments such as the *natural environment*, which must also be considered. In addition, the environment is seen as having other dimensions that must be acknowledged and recognized. Some of these other dimensions are simplicity–complexity, homogeneity–heterogeneity, and stability–dynamism.[44]

In keeping with our general theme, we will refer to the environment of business, which possesses all of the attributes described here, as the **stakeholder environment**. As a basis or resource for information gathering, we should also observe that this environment is composed of trends, events, issues, expectations, and forecasts that may have a bearing on the strategic management process and the development of corporate public policy.

One further point needs to be made before we describe the environmental analysis process. In this chapter, we are striving to convey the idea that a concern for enterprise-level strategy and corporate public policy is just one part of the more comprehensive strategic management process. Therefore, we are concerned with all components of the business environment. In other words, we are just as interested in such economic and technological trends as interest rates, the balance of payments, global competitiveness, changes in computer technology, and trends in research-and-development expenditures as we are in ethical or other public issues. In the next chapter, however, we will focus on a set of management approaches that share a common heritage with environmental analysis but are more concerned with public, stakeholder, or ethical issues. These practices are known as *issues management* and *crisis management*.

Four Stages in Environmental Analysis   Narayanan and Fahey's conceptualization of the environmental analysis stage in the strategic management process is useful. They suggest that the process consists of four analytical stages:

1. *scanning* the environment to detect warning signals,
2. *monitoring* specific environmental trends,
3. *forecasting* the future directions of environmental changes, and
4. *assessing* current and future environmental changes for their organizational implications.[45]

Scanning the Environment.   The **environmental scanning stage** focuses on identification of precursors or indicators of potential environmental changes and issues. The purpose of this stage is to alert management to potentially significant events, issues, developments, or trends before they have fully formed or crystallized.[46] Early on, companies did their scanning in an informal, irregular, ad hoc manner. Executives simply read newspapers, magazines, institutional reports, polls, and surveys. As the environment became more turbulent, firms began engaging in periodic or continuous scanning rather than irregular scanning. As companies got more serious about scanning the environment, their techniques became more sophisticated, and a whole industry of research firms opened up to supply managers with professionally generated

Ethics In *Practice*

Not Much Range for This Manager

I used to work for a golf course at their driving range. The basic responsibility of my fellow employees and me was quite simple. We took money from customers, gave them a basket of golf balls to hit, made sure the supply of golf balls was adequate, and moved the tees on the driving range so there would be decent grass for the players to hit off. It was well known that everyone, including our manager, gave away free baskets of balls to family members and, occasionally, good friends. When the golf course acquired a new golf professional, the giving away of free baskets of balls was supposed to cease.

After the new golf pro had been working for a couple of months, he realized that all, or some, of the range personnel were still giving away free baskets of balls. Our manager at the time was still giving away free balls, along with all the employees, but the golf pro was not aware of this factor. The golf pro proceeded to talk to our manager and tell him that he needed to fire the employee who was continuing to give away free baskets of balls.

Since the job at the range did not require much work, everyone was laid back about the job and came in a little late almost every day. Our manager, who was regularly late at least 15 to 30 minutes, set this trend. Within a week of the golf pro telling our manager to fire the employee who was giving away the free baskets, I noticed that the employee who had been working there for the longest time had been fired. Once this employee was gone, our manager wrote up a new set of rules and posted them in the office. The first rule was NO FREE BASKETS OF BALLS. NO EXCEPTIONS! When I read this new rule, I assumed the fired employee got caught by the golf pro giving away free baskets of balls. After I spoke with the fired employee, he told me that our manager fired him due to excessive tardiness.

1. Who, if anyone, in this case acted in an unethical manner? If they did, how?
2. Should I have told the golf pro the whole story? If I did, how would it affect me and the other employees?
3. Does the employee who was fired have a legal recourse to pursue further action?

Contributed Anonymously

information. Examples include the Yankelovich "Corporate Priorities" service, and various newsletters and services provided by John Naisbitt, author of the book *Megatrends*.

Monitoring Environmental Trends. Whereas environmental scanning entails an open-ended viewing of the environment to identify early signals, the **environmental monitoring stage** focuses on the tracking of specific trends and events with an eye toward confirming or disconfirming trends or patterns. Monitoring often involves following up on indicators or signals that were detected during the scanning stage. The goal here is to gather and assemble sufficient data to discern patterns. Three outputs of scanning are useful: (1) specific descriptions of environmental patterns that may then be forecast, (2) the identification of other trends that need to be continually monitored, and (3) the identification of patterns that require future scanning.[47] We should note that many of the sources of information that are employed in scanning, such as the professional services mentioned, are also used in monitoring.

Forecasting Environmental Changes. Scanning and monitoring are restricted to the past and the present. Firms also need to obtain information concerning the likely future states of events, trends, or issues. The **environmental forecasting stage** is the future-oriented stage and is concerned with the development of plausible and realistic projections of the direction, scope, speed, and intensity of environmental change.[48]

Forecasts of the economic, technological, social, and political components of the environment are needed, and this information base then forms the premises on which goal formulation, strategy formulation, and other strategic planning activities are developed.

Economic forecasting is the most frequently addressed area in this process. Only in the past three decades or so have firms begun formal attempts to forecast the technological, social, and political environments. A technique known as **sociopolitical forecasting** emerged years ago at General Electric. Ian Wilson, an early proponent of this new technique, was one of the first to call to our attention the need to leave behind our two-sided approach to planning, which dwelt on economic and technological forecasts, and to adopt a "four-sided framework," which also included social and political forecasting.[49]

A whole industry focusing on futures research has evolved with the goal of identifying, studying, and forecasting emerging trends for use by businesses and government. More will be said about this in the next chapter when we examine issues management.

Assessment for Organizational Implications. Scanning, monitoring, and forecasting are done to enable current and projected environmental information and changes to be used for setting new goals and formulating strategies. The *assessment stage* of environmental analysis shifts the attention away from gathering and projecting and toward the task of understanding what the information means to management. The central question becomes, "What are the implications of our analysis of the environment for our organization?"[50] The key at this stage is to develop the ability to sift through all the information that has been generated and determine what is relevant to management. Relevance may be thought of in terms of two primary dimensions: (1) the probability that the event, trend, or forecast will occur and (2) the impact that the event, trend, or forecast will have on the organization. These two dimensions make it possible to create what is known as a *probability-impact matrix*. Such a matrix permits management to categorize issues according to priorities that then can be used as a framework for assessment, comparison, and discussion.

The strategic management process provides an excellent framework for thinking about stakeholder management. The processes of goal formulation, strategy formulation, strategy evaluation, strategy implementation, strategic control, and environmental analysis describe what managers must do in their leadership roles. The strategic management process provides a comprehensive context in which we can better appreciate how enterprise-level strategy and corporate public policy fit into the total array of managerial challenges and responsibilities. Only by seeing public and ethical issues emanating from the stakeholder environment and having to compete with economic, technological, and political factors can we fully appreciate what it means to be a manager in the business climate of the new millennium.

Corporate Public Affairs

Corporate public affairs and **public affairs management** are umbrella terms used by companies to describe the management processes that focus on the formalization and institutionalization of corporate public policy. The public affairs function is a logical and increasingly prevalent component of the overall strategic management process, which we discussed earlier. As an overall concept, public affairs management embraces corporate public policy, discussed earlier, along with **issues and crisis management**, which we consider in more detail in Chapter 5. Indeed, many issues management and crisis management programs are housed in public affairs departments or intimately involve public affairs professionals. Corporate public affairs also embraces the broad areas of governmental relations and corporate communications.

It is easy to get confused at this point by all the different terms that are used to describe management's efforts to address the stakeholder environment. Part of the confusion arises from the fact that companies use different titles for the same functions. For example, terms that are often used interchangeably by firms include "public affairs/external affairs," "public policy/corporate social responsibility," "corporate communications," and "public issues management/public affairs management." In addition, some companies create stand-alone public affairs departments without even addressing the strategic management issue or enterprise-level strategy.

Public Affairs as a Part of Strategic Management

In a comprehensive management system, which we have been describing in this chapter, the overall flow of activity would be as follows. A firm engages in strategic management, part of which includes the development of enterprise-level strategy, which poses the question, "What do we stand for?" The answers to this question should help the organization to form a corporate public policy, which is a more specific posture on the public, social, or stakeholder environment or specific issues within this environment. Some firms call this a **public affairs strategy**. Two important planning approaches in corporate public policy are issues management and, often, crisis management. These two planning aspects frequently derive from or are related to environmental analysis, which we discussed earlier. Some companies embrace these processes as part of the corporate public affairs function. These processes are typically housed, from a departmental perspective, in a **public affairs department**. Public affairs management is a term that often describes all these components. Figure 4–8 helps illustrate likely relationships among these processes.

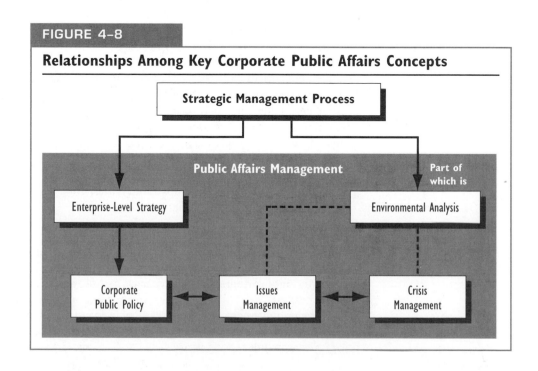

FIGURE 4–8

Relationships Among Key Corporate Public Affairs Concepts

We will now consider how the public affairs function has evolved in business firms, what issues public affairs departments currently face, and how public affairs thinking might be incorporated into the operating manager's job. This last issue is crucial, because public affairs management, to be most effective, is best thought of as an indispensable part of every manager's job, not as an isolated function or department that alone is responsible for the public issues and stakeholder environment of the firm.

Evolution of the Corporate Public Affairs Function

According to expert opinion, public affairs blossomed in both Canada and the United States in the 1960s because of four primary reasons: (1) the growing magnitude and impact of government; (2) the changing nature of the political system, especially its progression from a patronage orientation to an issues orientation; (3) the growing recognition by business that it was being outflanked by interests that were counter to its own on a number of policy matters; and (4) the need to be more active in politics outside the traditional community-related aspects.[51]

Thus, the public affairs function as we know it today was an outgrowth of the social activism begun decades ago. Just as significant federal laws were passed in the early 1970s to address such issues as discrimination, environmental protection, occupational health and safety, and consumer safety, corporations responded with a surge of public affairs activities and creation of public affairs departments. Corporate public affairs departments or units, therefore, are clearly a product of the past 30 years.

Public Affairs Activities/Functions

Public affairs as a management function progressed out of isolated company initiatives designed to handle such diverse activities as community relations, corporate philanthropy and contributions, governmental affairs, lobbying, grassroots programs, corporate responsibility, and public relations. In some firms, the public relations staff handled issues involving communication with external publics, so it is not surprising that public affairs often evolved from public relations. Part of the confusion between public relations and public affairs is traceable to the fact that some corporate public relations executives changed their titles, but not their functions, to public affairs.

Observers have noted the distinctions between **public relations (PR)** and **public affairs (PA)** in terms of their relative emphases, interests, and directions. The principal distinctions made are as follows: (1) whereas PR deals with government as one of many publics, PA professionals are experts on government, and (2) whereas PR has many communication responsibilities, PA deals with issues management and serves as a corporate conscience.[52] Though modern public affairs may have evolved from early public relations efforts and company activities, today public affairs embraces public relations as one of its many functions.

Modern Perspectives of Corporate Public Affairs

Corporate public affairs has been defined as follows:

> *The management function responsible for monitoring and interpreting the corporation's non-commercial environment and managing the company's response to those factors.*[53]

This definition is quite broad and encompasses a wide assortment of activities. To appreciate what specific activities are typically included in this definition, it is useful to consider the results of a survey on the state of public affairs. This survey asked corporate respondents to indicate whether they included certain activities as parts of their public affairs function. Figure 4–9 lists the activities they engaged in. Government relations—federal, provincial, and municipal—heads the list, along with community relations and corporate contributions philanthropy.[54]

James E. Post and Patricia C. Kelley provide an excellent perspective on the public affairs function in organizations today. They state:

> *The public affairs function serves as a window:* Looking out, *the organization can observe the changing environment.* Looking in, *the stakeholders in that environment can observe, try to understand, and interact with the organization.*[55]

When the public affairs function is viewed in this way, it is easy to understand how Post and Kelley concluded that the "product" of the public affairs department is the smoothing of relationships with external stakeholders and the management of company-specific issues.

Martin Meznar and Douglas Nigh have provided another important perspective on public affairs that is also useful. They suggest that corporate public affairs activities can be broken into two types: activities that "buffer" the organization from the social and political environment and activities that "bridge" with that environment. Meznar and Nigh found that as organizations experienced increased environmental uncertainty, buffering and bridging increased as well. They concluded that building bridges with external environmental uncertainty was positively related to top management's philosophy.[56] Bridging is a proactive stance that is most likely to be undertaken by companies with a stakeholder orientation.

A significant challenge today for public affairs professionals is to conduct their functions in an ethical fashion. There are many opportunities for questionable practices, especially in such arenas as political action, government relations, and communications. Therefore, it is encouraging to know that a code of conduct or set of ethical guidelines has been established for individuals working in public affairs. These ethical guidelines are set forth in Figure 4–10. They deserve scrutiny.

FIGURE 4–9

Current Public Affairs Activities

Government Relations	Educational Affairs/Outreach
Contributions/Philanthropy	Regulatory Affairs
Grassroots	Volunteer Program
Issues Management	Advertising
Media Relations	International Public Affairs
Political Action Committee	Environmental Affairs
Public Relations	Stockholder Relations
Employee Communications	Institutional Investor
Public Interest Group Relations	Consumer Affairs

Source: Based on James E. Post and Jennifer J. Griffin, *The State of Corporate Public Affairs,* Foundation for Public Affairs and Boston University School of Management, 1997, Figure 3.1.

FIGURE 4-10

Ethical Guidelines for Public Affairs Professionals

Public affairs professionals should:

1. Conduct their professional lives in a manner that does not conflict with the public interest and the dignity of the individual, with respect for the rights of the public as contained in the Constitution of Canada and the Charter of Rights and Freedoms.

2. Deal fairly and honestly with the communications media and the public. They shall neither propose nor act to improperly influence the communications media, government bodies or the legislative process. Improper influence may include conferring gifts, privileges or benefits to influence decisions

The public affairs professional:

1. Represents accurately his or her organization's policies on economic and political matters to government, employees, shareholders, community interests, and others.

2. Serves always as a source of reliable information, discussing the varied aspects of complex public issues within the context and constraints of the advocacy role.

3. Recognizes the diverse viewpoints within the public policy process, knowing that disagreement on issues is both inevitable and healthy.

The public affairs professional ...

... seeks to protect the integrity of the public policy process and the political system, and he or she therefore:

1. Publicly acknowledges his or her role as a legitimate participant in the public policy process and discloses whatever work-related information the law requires.

2. Knows, respects, and abides by laws that apply to lobbying and related public affairs activities.

3. Knows and respects the laws governing campaign finance and other political activities, and abides by the letter and intent of those laws.

The public affairs professional ...

... understands the interrelation of business interests with the larger public interests, and therefore:

1. Endeavours to ensure that responsible and diverse external interests and views concerning the needs of society are considered within the corporate decision-making process.

2. Bears the responsibility for management review of public policies that may bring corporate interests into conflict with other interests.

3. Acknowledges dual obligations—to advocate the interests of his or her employer, and to preserve the openness and integrity of the democratic process.

4. Presents to his or her employer an accurate assessment of the political and social realities that may affect corporate operations.

Sources: The Canadian Public Relations Society Inc. Web site: http://www.cprs.ca/AboutCPRS/e_code.htm; The Public Affairs Council (Washington, DC), *1998 Annual Report,* 32. Reprinted with permission.

International Public Affairs Continues to Grow

It is essential at this point to provide some specific comments on international public affairs. For at least the past 25 years, investigations into the field of public affairs have raised at least three key observations. First, it has become obvious that more and more significant public affairs challenges and problems are occurring in the global arena, with greater impacts on the company. Second, the number of firms with effective international PA capacities have been growing, albeit slowly. Third, there continue to be serious internal and external challenges that have often made an international PA program more difficult than a domestic program.[57]

International public affairs, to function properly, must balance externally and internally focused activities. Externally, the central challenge is to manage the com-

The Public Affairs Association of Canada (PAAC)

Founded in 1984, the Public Affairs Association of Canada (PAAC) is a national, not-for-profit organization of public affairs practitioners. It offers programs that focus on public affairs issues and management techniques and assists members in staying informed with regard to developments and trends affecting this field. Its membership includes both the private and public sectors: industrial and financial companies, Crown corporations, small business, government ministries and municipalities, government relations and PR counselling organizations, trade associations, educational institutions, law and chartered accountants' firms, and individual specialists and practitioners.

Some of the program topics the PAAC offers services in include the following:

- Public affairs management
- Government affairs
- Issues management
- Community relations
- Political action committees
- Corporate communications
- Grassroots
- Corporate philanthropy
- International affairs
- Other related fields

To learn more about the PAAC, visit its Web site at **http://www.publicaffairs.ca/**.

pany's relations with various host countries where business is conducted. Requirements here include understanding and meeting host-country needs and dealing with diverse local constituencies, audiences, cultures, and governments. Internally, international PA programs must establish and coordinate external programs, educate company officials on PA techniques, and assist wherever possible the company's efforts to improve operations, activities, and image.[58] According to Post and Griffin's survey of corporate public affairs, international public affairs was found to be one of the fastest-growing new areas of public affairs activities.[59]

More Research on Public Affairs

In terms of the activities being emphasized by public affairs departments of major corporations, research suggests that environmental affairs, education affairs, and grassroots activities are among the fastest-growing areas of new PA responsibility. Regarding involvement in political affairs, there is evidence that companies have concentrated on three specific forms of corporate political involvement: visits to political officials, use of political action committees (PACs), and meetings with political candidates.[60]

In addition, corporate communication with various stakeholders on public policy issues has grown in recent years. The growing importance of international public affairs has been documented, and many companies prefer to treat international public affairs as country-specific political matters that are best managed by local managers in the respective countries.[61]

As organizations have become more sensitive to their investments in and expenditures on public affairs activities, the evaluation and measurement of public affairs management have increased. In a comprehensive study of this topic, Craig S. Fleisher found quite different approaches to evaluation and measurement taking place. He concluded that in common use were three evaluation archetypes based primarily on three factors: (1) the nature of PA evaluation policies/systems, where evaluations ranged from none to highly formalized; (2) the nature of the evaluation methods used, with methods ranging from mostly intuitive to mostly analytical; and (3) the nature of the information utilized, with information ranging from mostly objective to mostly subjective. An increasing trend toward evaluation and measurement was disclosed.[62]

Out of the focus on evaluation and measurement of public affairs activities has arisen the concept of public affairs **benchmarking**. Fleisher defines this as "an ongoing, systematic approach by which a public affairs unit measures and compares itself with higher performing and world-class units in order to generate knowledge and action about public affairs roles, practices, processes, products, services, and strategic issues that will lead to improvement in performance."[63] The concept of benchmarking had its origins in the total quality management (TQM) movement.

Survey Findings and Trends To update what has been going on in the area of corporate public affairs, it is useful to look at some of the findings of a major survey of public affairs management. The researchers found that various forces, perhaps most notably restructuring and downsizing driven by competitive pressures, have produced important changes. They found that there is a sharpened and expanded use of benchmarking. The study found that nearly half the companies responding had undertaken benchmarking in the previous year. The rationales offered for this trend included mandates from the CEO and continuous self-improvement. The activities studied by way of benchmarking were most often public affairs operations, issues management processes, government office operations, and philanthropy.[64]

The study also revealed that a large number of public affairs officers had reorganized their departments, partially or across the board, in recent years. Key trends seem to be (1) changes in organizational relationships, often caused by retirement and non-replacement of previous senior public affairs staff; (2) new linkages to internal customers (e.g., in one company each business unit has a specific PA executive assigned to service all its public affairs needs; and (3) contradictory trends in consolidation versus "disaggregation" of external public affairs functions.[65]

Other trends include use of the profit-centre concept and increased attempts to measure the costs-benefits of PA efforts. PA has been seeking to contribute more to the "bottom line" by more deliberately and aggressively looking for marketing opportunities in government relations work (e.g., modifications in legislation or regulations that would increase the likelihood of government purchase of company products or services). Other trends in the use of technology include greater use of the Internet, using e-mail for company-wide alerts on breaking legislation, requiring lobbyists to use networked laptop computers, and using interactive computer systems to manage all aspects of public policy work.[66]

Craig S. Fleisher, an expert on corporate public affairs, proposed a "new public affairs model."[67] Fleisher describes a public affairs organization as one that:

1. Manages public affairs as an ongoing, year-round process, internally and externally
2. Cultivates and harvests the capability to build, develop, and maintain enduring stakeholder relationships
3. Recognizes the importance of managing the grassroots
4. Communicates in an integrated manner
5. Continuously aligns its values and strategies with the public's interests
6. Is systematically and proactively focused on helping the organization to compete

It is becoming clear that public affairs management professionals today are keenly interested in making sure that their function continues to add value to the bottom lines of corporations. In an era of corporate downsizings and reorganizations, staff functions such as PA are quite susceptible to budget cuts by higher executives who do not see clearly how PA's performance, effectiveness, and efficiency contribute to the company's profitability and success. Figure 4–11 depicts how a quality improvement program might be implemented in corporate public affairs.[68]

FIGURE 4–11

Initiating a Quality Improvement Program in Public Affairs

Competency Rating

Grade

B– Business linkage
C   Mission, strategy
A   Policy formulation...
B   Program orientation
D   Coordination...
C   Measurement...

Assess competencies from
perspective of:

• Internal clients
• External publics
• Self-evaluation

High

Investor Relations	Media Support
Annual Report	Community Program X

Relative Value

Low   High

Relative Cost

Assess value of major programs,
products, or services

Cross-Functional Team(s)

Improvement
Priorities

1. _____
2. _____
3. _____
4. _____
5. _____

Revised Process(es)

Program Plan

New/Revised Program(s)

New Partnerships
(Internal or External)

Mission

Revised Mandate/Role

Source: Peter Shafer, *Adding Value to the Public Affairs Function: Using Quality to Improve Performance* (Washington, DC: Public Affairs Council, 1994), 44.

Public Affairs Strategy

We will not discuss the issue of public affairs strategy extensively, but we want to report the findings of a major research project that was undertaken by Robert H. Miles and resulted in a book entitled *Managing the Corporate Social Environment: A Grounded Theory*. Because very little work has been done on public affairs strategy, Miles's work deserves reference even though we cannot do it complete justice here. Miles's study focused on the insurance industry, but many of his findings may be applicable to other businesses.[69]

Design of the Corporate External Affairs Function and Corporate Social Performance

Miles studied the external affairs strategies (also called public affairs strategies) of major insurance firms in an effort to see what relationships existed between the strategy and design of the corporate external affairs function and corporate social performance. He found that the companies that ranked best in corporate social performance had top management philosophies that were *institution oriented*. That is, top management saw the corporation as a social institution that had a duty to adapt to a changing society and thus needed a collaborative/problem-solving external affairs strategy. The **collaborative/problem-solving strategy** was one in which firms emphasized long-term relationships with a variety of external constituencies and broad problem-solving perspectives on the resolution of social issues affecting their businesses and industries.[70] Note how similar this is to the stakeholder management view and the bridge-building activity identified by Meznar and Nigh.

Miles also found that the companies with the worst social performance records employed top management philosophies based on operation of the company as an independent economic franchise. Such philosophies were in sharp contrast with the institution-oriented perspectives of the best social performers. In addition, Miles found that these worst social performers employed an **individual/adversarial external affairs strategy**. In this posture, the executives denied the legitimacy of social claims on their businesses and minimized the significance of challenges they received from external critics. Therefore, they tended to be adversarial and legalistic.[71]

Business Exposure and External Affairs Design

On the subject of the external affairs units within firms, Miles found that a contingency relationship existed between what he called business exposure to the social environment and four dimensions of the external affairs design: breadth, depth, influence, and integration. High business exposure to the social environment means that the firm produces products that move them into the public arena because of such issues as their availability, affordability, reliability, and safety. In general, consumer products tend to be more exposed to the social environment than do commercial or industrial products.[72]

Breadth, depth, influence, and integration refer to dimensions of the external affairs unit that provide a measure of sophistication versus simplicity. Units that are high on these dimensions are sophisticated, whereas units low on these dimensions are simple. Miles found that firms with high business exposure to the social environment require more sophisticated units, whereas firms with low business exposure to the social environment could manage reasonably well with simple units.[73]

It is tempting to overgeneralize Miles's study, but we must note it as a significant advance in the realm of public affairs strategy and organizational design research. The important conclusion seems to be that a firm's corporate social performance (as well as its industry legitimacy and viability and economic performance) is a function of business exposure, top management philosophy, external affairs strategy, and external affairs design. Figure 4–12 presents Miles's theory of corporate social performance.

Other initiatives in public relations strategy include integrating public affairs into corporate strategic planning, using strategic management audits for public affairs, building a balanced performance scorecard for public affairs, managing the corporation's reputation, and using core competencies to manage performance.[74]

Incorporate Public Affairs Thinking into Managers' Jobs

In today's highly specialized business world, it is easy for operating managers to let public affairs departments worry about government affairs, community relations, issues management, or any of the numerous other PA functions. David H. Blake has taken the position that organizations ought to incorporate public affairs, or what we would call *public affairs thinking*, into every operating manager's job. He argues that operating managers are vital to a successful PA function, especially if they can identify

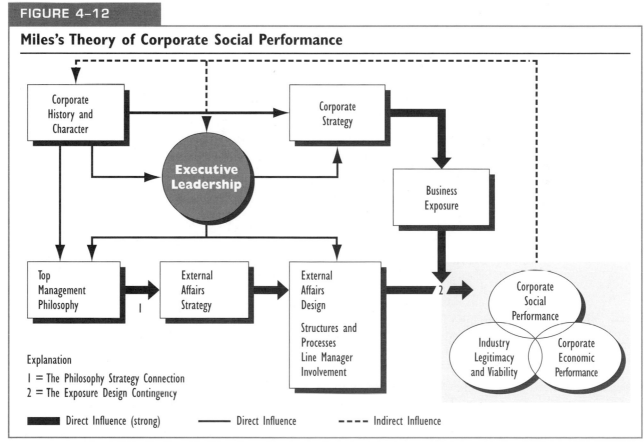

FIGURE 4–12

Miles's Theory of Corporate Social Performance

Explanation
1 = The Philosophy Strategy Connection
2 = The Exposure Design Contingency

Direct Influence (strong) ——— Direct Influence - - - - Indirect Influence

Source: Robert H. Miles, *Managing the Corporate Social Environment: A Grounded Theory* (Englewood Cliffs, NJ: Prentice-Hall Inc., 1987), 274.

the public affairs consequences of their actions, be sensitive to the concerns of external groups, act to defuse or avoid crisis situations, and know well in advance when to seek the help of the PA experts. There are no simple ways to achieve these goals, but Blake proposes four specific strategies that may be helpful: (1) make public affairs truly relevant, (2) develop a sense of ownership of success, (3) make it easy for operating managers, and (4) show how public affairs makes a difference.[75] Each of these strategies is discussed in the following sections.

Make Public Affairs Truly Relevant

Operating managers often need help in seeing how external stakeholder factors can and do affect them. A useful mechanism is analysis of the manager's job in terms of the likely or potential impacts that her or his decisions may have on the stakeholder environment and possible developments in the environment that may affect the company or the decision maker. One procedure for doing this might be to list the manager's various impacts, the interested or affected strategic stakeholder groups, the potential actions of the groups, and the effects of the groups on jobs or the company.

Another mechanism is linking achievement of the manager's goals to public affairs. A plant manager, for example, can be shown how failure to pay attention to community groups can hinder plant expansion, increased output, and product delivery. Failure to address the affected stakeholders can be shown to be related to extensive delays as these neglected groups seek media attention or pressure local officials.

A third way to make PA relevant is to use the language of the operating manager. Instead of using the jargon of public affairs, every effort should be made to employ language and terms with which the manager is familiar. Thus, terms such as *environment* to mean local community and *stakeholder* to mean employees and residents must be used cautiously, because operating managers may not be able to fully comprehend them.[76]

Still another way to make public affairs relevant is to demonstrate to operating managers that several operations areas are affected by public affairs issues. John E. Fleming has argued that some of these key areas include marketing, manufacturing, and human resources. Some of the specifics he identifies in the manufacturing arena are product safety and quality, energy conservation, water pollution, air pollution, transportation, and raw materials. Fleming goes on to suggest that public affairs should be linked with corporate planning.[77]

Help Managers Develop a Sense of Ownership

It is helpful for operating managers to have participated in planning and goal setting and thus to have had an opportunity to develop a sense of ownership of the public affairs endeavour. Operating managers may be formally or informally enlisted in these planning efforts. At PPG Industries, Inc., operating managers have been given the responsibility for coordinating all actions concerning specific issues. As issue managers, they are asked to see to it that issue and environmental monitoring occurs, that strategy is developed, and that actions are implemented at various governmental levels.[78]

At Kroger, Inc., regional public affairs executives have worked with the individual operating divisions as they have developed their business plans. A public affairs section has been included in each operating division's plan, and it is the division's plan, not the PA department's plan. As a result of these efforts, the divisions have begun to feel that they have "ownership" of the PA goals in their plans.[79] This approach seems to work much better than having PA executives simply impose goals or expectations on the operating units.

Make It Easy for Operating Managers

Operating managers have experience in meeting goals and timetables in their own realms. The PA area, however, can often appear nebulous, fuzzy, or inconclusive. Further, operating managers have neither the time for nor the interest in setting up systems or strategies for PA initiatives. This is where the PA professionals can assist them by making their tasks easier. Any procedures, data collection systems, or strategies that PA can supply should be used.

Training in public affairs can be helpful, too. Operating managers can better see the relevance and importance of PA work if carefully chosen topics are put on the agendas of their periodic training sessions. If PA effectiveness is to be monitored, measured, and made a part of performance evaluation systems, care must be taken to make sure that such systems are fair and straightforward, or at least understandable. If PA does not make a careful effort to ensure that its expectations are reasonably met, resistance, resentment, and failure will surely follow.

Show How Public Affairs Makes a Difference

Part of what professional PA staff members need to do is to keep track of public affairs successes in such a way that operating managers can see that their specific actions or efforts have led to identifiable successes for the company. A scorecard approach, whereby operating managers can see that their efforts have helped to avoid problems or prevent serious problems, is useful. The scorecard may be used to reinforce managers' efforts and to help other managers see the potential of the PA function. The scorecard should explicitly state the objectives that have been achieved, the problems that have been avoided, and the friends that have been made for the company.

Obviously, such a scorecard would be of a qualitative nature, but this is necessary in order to describe clearly what has been accomplished. Operating managers need to be shown that there are specific payoffs to be enjoyed from their public affairs efforts. It is up to the PA professionals to document these achievements. If no payoff is demonstrable from PA efforts, operating managers are likely to invest their time elsewhere.[80]

Public affairs is not just a specialized set of management functions to be performed by a designated staff. The nature of the tasks and challenges that characterize public affairs work is such that participation by operating managers is essential. It is likely that PA departments will continue to serve as the backbones of corporate organizations, but true effectiveness will require that operating managers be integrated into the accomplishment of these tasks. The mutual interdependence of these two groups—professionals and operating managers—will produce optimal results.

Summary

Corporate public policy is a firm's posture or stance regarding the public, social, or ethical aspects of stakeholders and corporate functioning. It is a part of strategic management, particularly enterprise-level strategy. Enterprise-level strategy is the broadest, overarching level of strategy, and its focus is on the role of the organization in society. The other strategy levels include the corporate, business, and functional levels.

The strategic management process entails six stages, and a concern for social, ethical, and public issues may be seen at each stage. The stage at which public issues are most addressed for planning purposes is the environmental analysis stage. Vital components of environmental analysis include scanning, monitoring, forecasting, and assessing. In the overall environmental analysis process, social, ethical, and public issues are considered along with economic, political, and technological factors.

Public affairs might be described as the management function that is responsible for monitoring and interpreting a corporation's noncommercial environment and managing its response to that environment. Public affairs is intimately linked to corporate public policy, environmental analysis, issues management, and crisis management. The major functions of public affairs departments today include government relations, political action, community involvement/responsibility, issues management, international public affairs, and corporate philanthropy. A major growth area is international public affairs.

In terms of public affairs strategy, a collaborative/problem-solving strategy has been shown to be more effective than one that is individualistic/adversarial. Research has shown that a firm's corporate social performance, as well as its industry legitimacy, viability, and economic performance, is a function of business exposure, top management's philosophy, external affairs strategy, and external affairs design. In addition to being viewed as a staff function, public affairs is important for operating managers. Four specific strategies for incorporating public affairs into operating managers' jobs include make it relevant, develop a sense of ownership, make it easy, and show how it can make a difference.

Key Terms

benchmarking (page 119)

business-level strategy (page 96)

collaborative/problem-solving strategy (page 122)

corporate-level strategy (page 96)

corporate public affairs (page 114)

corporate public policy (page 94)

enterprise-level strategy (page 96)

environmental forecasting stage (page 113)

environmental monitoring stage (page 113)

environmental scanning stage (page 112)

functional-level strategy (page 96)

Global Reporting Initiative (GRI) (page 110)

individual/adversarial external affairs strategy (page 122)

issues and crisis management (page 114)

public affairs (PA) (page 116)

public affairs department (page 115)

public affairs management (page 114)

public affairs strategy (page 115)

public relations (PR) (page 116)

social audit (page 106)

sociopolitical forecasting (page 114)

stakeholder environment (page 112)

strategic management (page 95)

strategic management processes (page 94)

Discussion Questions

1. Explain the relationship between corporate public policy and strategic management.

2. Which of the four strategy levels is most concerned with social, ethical, or public issues? Discuss the characteristics of this level.

3. Identify the steps involved in the strategic management process. In which step is a concern for social issues planning most evident? Explain.

4. What is a social audit? Describe how it may be seen as a tool for strategic control.

5. What are the four stages in environmental analysis? Briefly explain each stage.

6. What is the difference between public relations and public affairs? Why has there been confusion regarding these two concepts?

7. Why do you think international public affairs is a major growth area? Give specific reasons for your answer.

8. Differentiate between a collaborative/problem-solving strategy and an individual/adversarial strategy. Which seems to be more effective in corporate public affairs?

9. What are the major ways in which public affairs might be incorporated into every manager's job? Rank them in terms of what you think their impact might be.

Endnotes

1. Victoria Miles, "Auditing Promises: One Bank's Story," *CMA Management* (Vol. 74, No. 5, June 2000), 42–46.

2. Kenneth R. Andrews, *The Concept of Corporate Strategy*, 3d ed. (Homewood, IL: Irwin, 1987), 68–69.

3. R. Edward Freeman and Daniel R. Gilbert, Jr., *Corporate Strategy and the Search for Ethics* (Englewood Cliffs, NJ: Prentice-Hall, 1988), 20. Also see R. Edward Freeman, Daniel R. Gilbert, Jr., and Edwin Hartman, "Values and the Foundations of Strategic Management," *Journal of Business Ethics* (Vol. 7, 1988), 821–834; and Daniel R. Gilbert, Jr., "Strategy and Ethics," in *The Blackwell Encyclopedic Dictionary of Business Ethics* (Malden, MA: Blackwell Publishers Ltd., 1997), 609–611.

4. Charles W. Hofer, Edwin A. Murray, Jr., Ram Charan, and Robert A. Pitts, *Strategic Management: A Casebook in Policy and Planning*, 2d ed. (St. Paul, MN: West Publishing Co., 1984), 27–29. Also see Gary Hamel and C. K. Prahalad, *Competing for the Future* (Boston: Harvard Business School Press, 1994).

5. H. Igor Ansoff, "The Changing Shape of the Strategic Problem," Paper presented at a Special Conference on Business Policy and Planning Research: The State of the Art (Pittsburgh, May 1977).

6. H. Igor Ansoff, *Implanting Strategic Management* (Englewood Cliffs, NJ: Prentice-Hall, International, 1984), 129–151.

7. R. Edward Freeman, *Strategic Management: A Stakeholder Approach* (Boston: Pitman, 1984), 90.

8. *Ibid.*, 90–91. For further discussion, see Martin B. Meznar, James J. Chrisman, and Archie B. Carroll, "Social Responsibility and Strategic Management: Toward an Enterprise Strategy Classification," *Business & Professional Ethics Journal* (Vol. 10, No. 1, Spring 1991), 47–66. Also see William Q. Judge, Jr., and Hema Krishnan, "An Empirical Examination of the Scope of a Firm's Enterprise Strategy," *Business & Society* (Vol. 33, No. 2, August 1994), 167–190.

9. *Corporate Knights* Web site: http://www.corporate knights.ca/best50/2003best50.asp.

10. Alcan Web site: http://www.alcan.com/corporate/ AlcanCom.nsf/libweb/Shared+values.

11. *Corporate Knights* Web site: http://www.corporate knights.ca/best/50/2003best50.asp.

12. Domtar, http://www.domtar.com/corporate_section/ code_of_ethics/introduction.asp.

13. C. W. Hofer and D. E. Schendel, *Strategy Formulation: Analytical Concepts* (St. Paul: West, 1978), 52–55. Also see J. David Hunger and Thomas L. Wheelen, *Essentials of Strategic Management* (Reading, MA: Addison-Wesley, 2000).

14. Archie B. Carroll, "Setting Operational Goals for Corporate Social Responsibility," *Long Range Planning* (April 1978), 35. Also see Joseph A. Petrick and John F.

Quinn, *Management Ethics: Integrity at Work* (Thousand Oaks, CA: Sage Publications, 1997), 129–165.

15. James J. Chrisman and Archie B. Carroll, "Corporate Responsibility: Reconciling Economic and Social Goals," *Sloan Management Review* (Winter 1984), 59–65.

16. Kenneth R. Andrews, *The Concept of Corporate Strategy*, 3d ed. (Homewood, IL: Irwin, 1987), 18–20.

17. R. M. Grant, "The Resource-Based Theory of Competitive Advantage: Implications for Strategy Formulation," *California Management Review* (Spring 1991), 114–135.

18. Andrews, 18–20.

19. Art Kleiner, George Roth, and Nina Kruschwitz, "Should a Company Have a Noble Purpose?" *Across the Board* (January 2001), 18–24.

20. Robert H. Waterman, Jr., Thomas J. Peters, and Julien R. Phillips, "Structure Is Not Organization," *Business Horizons* (June 1980), 14–26.

21. R. Miles and C. Snow, *Environmental Strategy and Organization Structure* (New York: McGraw-Hill, 1978), 1. Also see Hamel and Prahalad, 160–161.

22. Archie B. Carroll, *Business and Society: Managing Corporate Social Performance* (Boston: Little, Brown, 1981), 381.

23. Peter Lorange, Michael F. Scott Morton, and Sumantra Ghoshal, *Strategic Control Systems* (St. Paul, MN: West, 1986), 1, 10. Also see Hunger and Wheelen, 161–162.

24. David H. Blake, William C. Frederick, and Mildred S. Myers, *Social Auditing: Evaluating the Impact of Corporate Programs* (New York: Praeger, 1976), 3. Also see Roger Spear, "Social Audit and Social Economy," August 8, 1998, http://www.ny.airnet.ne.jp/ccij/eng/public-e.htm.

25. *Ibid.*

26. Ralph Estes, *Corporate Social Accounting* (New York: John Wiley, 1976), 3.

27. Archie B. Carroll and George W. Beiler, "Landmarks in the Evolution of the Social Audit," *Academy of Management Journal* (September 1975), 589–599.

28. Theodore J. Kreps, *Measurement of the Social Performance of Business, Monograph No. 7*, "An Investigation of Concentration of Economic Power for the Temporary National Economic Committee" (Washington, DC: U.S. Government Printing Office, 1940).

29. Howard R. Bowen, *Social Responsibilities of the Businessman* (New York: Harper & Row, 1953).

30. Leonard Brooks, "Business Ethics in Canada," *Journal of Business Ethics* (1997), 591–604.

31. John J. Corson and George A. Steiner, *Measuring Business's Social Performance: The Corporate Social Audit* (New York: Committee for Economic Development, 1974), 33.

32. Quoted in Jackie Blondell, "Body Language," *Australian CPA* (Vol. 71, No. 2, March 2001), 28–29.

33. The Body Shop, *Values Report 1997* (October 1997). For more information, visit the Body Shop Internet Web site at http://www.the-body-shop.com.

34. *Ibid.*

35. Jackie Blondell, *ibid.*, 29.

36. SmithOBrien Services, August 22, 1998, http://www.smithobrien.com/1Frame.html.

37. WalkerInformation, "Reputation and Stakeholder Assessment" (Indianapolis: WalkerInformation, undated).

38. *Ibid.*, 2–3.

39. Tim Watts, "Social Auditing: the KPMG UK Experience," *Australian CPA* (Vol. 69, No. 8), 46–47.

40. Nicole Dando and Tracey Swift, *Journal of Business Ethics* (May 2003, Vol. 44, No. 2/3, Part 1/2), 195.

41. "Dow Social Reporting Raises Bar: Chemical Firm Voluntarily Releases a Lot of Negative Information," *Investor Relations Business* (March 6, 2000), 1: 12–23.

42. http://www.accountability.org.uk/default.asp.

43. Liam Fahey and V. K. Narayanan, *Macroenvironmental Analysis for Strategic Management* (St. Paul, MN: West, 1986), 25.

44. *Ibid.*, 28–30.

45. V. K. Narayanan and Liam Fahey, "Environmental Analysis for Strategy Formulation," in William R. King and David I. Cleland (eds.), *Strategic Planning and Management Handbook* (New York: Van Nostrand Reinhold, 1987), 156.

46. *Ibid.* Also see John D. Stoffels, *Strategic Issues Management: A Comprehensive Guide to Environmental Scanning* (New York: Pergamon Press, 1994).

47. *Ibid.*, 159–160. Also see Liam Fahey and Robert Randall (eds.), *Learning from the Future: Competitive Foresight Scenarios* (New York: Wiley, 1998).

48. *Ibid.*, 160.

49. Ian H. Wilson, "Socio-Political Forecasting: A New Dimension to Strategic Planning," in Archie B. Carroll (ed.), *Managing Corporate Social Responsibility* (Boston: Little, Brown, 1977), 159–169.

50. Narayanan and Fahey, 162. Also see Frank Vanclay and Daniel Bronstein (eds.), *Environmental and Social Impact Assessment* (Brisbane: Chichester, John Wiley, 1995).

51. Craig S. Fleisher, "Evaluating Your Existing Public Affairs Management System," in Craig S. Fleisher (ed.), *Assessing, Managing and Maximizing Public Affairs Performance* (Washington, DC: Public Affairs Council, 1997), 4.

52. Richard A. Armstrong, "Public Affairs vs. Public Relations," *Public Relations Quarterly* (Fall 1981), 26. Also see Craig S. Fleisher and Natasha M. Blair, "Tracing the Parallel Evolution of Public Affairs and Public Relations: An Examination of Practice, Scholarship, and Teaching" (Paper presented at The Fifth International Public Relations Research Symposium, Lake Bled, Slovenia, July 1998).

53. Public Affairs Council (Washington, DC: Public Affairs Council), 5.
54. James E. Post and Jennifer J. Griffin, *The State of Corporate Public Affairs: Final Report* (Washington, DC, and Boston: Foundation for Public Affairs, 1997), Figure 3.1.
55. James E. Post and Patricia C. Kelley, "Lessons from the Learning Curve: The Past, Present and Future of Issues Management," in Robert L. Heath and Associates, *Strategic Issues Management* (San Francisco: Jossey-Bass, 1988), 352.
56. Martin B. Meznar and Douglas Nigh, "Buffer or Bridge? Environmental and Organizational Determinants of Public Affairs Activities in American Firms," *Academy of Management Journal* (August 1995), 975–996.
57. The Public Affairs Council, "International Public Affairs: A Preliminary Report by a PAC Task Force" (Washington, DC: Public Affairs Council, April 1983), 2. For further perspectives on international public affairs, see D. Jeffrey Lenn, Steven N. Brenner, Lee Burke, Diane Dodd-McCue, Craig S. Fleisher, Lawrence J. Lad, David R. Palmer, Kathryn S. Rogers, Sandra S. Waddock, and Richard E. Wokutch, "Managing Corporate Public Affairs and Government Relations: U.S. Multinational Corporations in Europe," in James E. Post (ed.), *Research in Corporate Social Performance and Policy*, Vol. 14 (Greenwich, CT: JAI Press, 1993), 103–108.
58. The Public Affairs Council, "Effective Management of International Public Affairs," (Washington, DC: Public Affairs Council, April 1985), 1.
59. Post and Griffin, Figure 3.2.
60. James E. Post and the Foundation for Public Affairs, "The State of Corporate Public Affairs in the United States: Results of a National Survey," in James E. Post (ed.), *Research in Corporate Social Performance and Policy*, Vol. 14 (Greenwich, CT: JAI Press, 1993), 81–85.
61. *Ibid.*, 85–88.
62. Craig S. Fleisher, "Public Affairs Management Performance: An Empirical Analysis of Evaluation and Measurement," in James E. Post (ed.), *Research in*
Corporate Social Performance and Policy, Vol. 14 (Greenwich, CT: JAI Press, 1993), 139–163.
63. Quoted in Peter Shafer, "Benchmarking: Here's a Management Fad You Could Learn to Love," *Impact* (July/August 1994), 1–3. Also see Craig S. Fleisher, *Public Affairs Benchmarking: A Comprehensive Guide* (Washington, DC: Public Affairs Council, 1995).
64. Post and Griffin. Also see "Public Affairs: Its Origins, Its Present and Its Trends," http://www.pac.org/whatis/index.htm.
65. *Ibid.*
66. *Ibid.*
67. Craig S. Fleisher, "The New Public Affairs," *Impact* (July/August 1998), 1–3.
68. Fleisher, 1997.
69. Robert H. Miles, *Managing the Corporate Social Environment: A Grounded Theory* (Englewood Cliffs, NJ: Prentice-Hall, Inc., 1987).
70. *Ibid.*, 8.
71. *Ibid.*, 9–10, 111.
72. *Ibid.*, 2–3.
73. *Ibid.*, 11, 113.
74. Fleisher (ed.), 1997, 139–196.
75. David H. Blake, "How to Incorporate Public Affairs into the Operating Manager's Job," *Public Affairs Review* (1984), 35.
76. *Ibid.*, 36–38.
77. John E. Fleming, "Linking Public Affairs with Corporate Planning," *California Management Review* (Winter 1980), 42.
78. Blake, 38–39.
79. Jack W. Partridge, "Making Line Managers Part of the Public Affairs Team: Innovative Ideas at Kroger," in Wesley Pederson (ed.), *Cost-Effective Management for Today's Public Affairs* (Washington, DC: Public Affairs Council, 1987), 67. Also see Fleisher, 1997.
80. *Ibid.*, 40–41. Also see Craig Fleisher and Darren Mahaffy, "Building the Balanced Performance Scorecard for Public Affairs," in Fleisher, 1997, 152–156.

Chapter 5

Issues Management and Crisis Management

Chapter Objectives

After studying this chapter, you should be able to:

1 Distinguish between the conventional and strategic management approaches to issues management.

2 Identify and briefly explain the stages in the issues management process.

3 Describe the major components in the issues development process and some of the factors that have characterized issues management in actual practice.

4 Define a crisis and identify the four crisis stages.

5 List and discuss the major stages in managing business crises.

Throughout this book, we discuss major social and ethical issues that have become controversies in the public domain. Some have been serious events or crises that continue to serve as recognizable code words for business—Enron, Bre-X Minerals, Three Mile Island, the Tylenol poisonings, the Union Carbide Bhopal tragedy, the *Exxon Valdez* oil spill, the Coca-Cola soft drink recalls in Europe, and the Firestone/Ford tread separation controversy. In September 2001, the attacks on the Twin Towers of the World Trade Center in New York presented an unprecedented crisis not only for the businesses located there but for others as well.

Other issues—employee rights, sexual harassment, product safety, workplace safety, sweatshops, bribery and corruption, employment equity, deceptive advertising, and so on—have demanded increased attention on the part of business. To business, these are formidable social and ethical issues that have evolved over time and that must be addressed.

Managerial decision-making processes known as **issues management** and **crisis management** are two major ways by which business has responded to these situations. These two approaches symbolize the extent to which the environment has become turbulent and the public has become sensitized to business's responses to the issues that have emerged from this turbulence. In the ideal situation, issues management and crisis management might be seen as the natural and logical byproducts of a firm's development of enterprise-level strategy and overall corporate public policy, but this has not always been the case. Some firms have not thought seriously about public and ethical issues; for them, these approaches represent first attempts to come to grips with the practical reality of a threatening social environment.

Many of these firms have been fortunate that major crises have not materialized to stun them as they did in the Johnson & Johnson Tylenol poisonings, the Union Carbide Bhopal explosion, the Dow Corning breast implant probe, the crash of TWA Flight 800, or the attacks on the World Trade Center. Thus, they have seen what major business crises can do to companies without having experienced such crises themselves. Such firms should now be concerned with issues management and crisis management.

Like all planning processes, issues management and crisis management have many characteristics in common. They also have differences and we have chosen to treat them separately for discussion purposes. One common thread that should be mentioned at the outset is that both processes are focused on improving stakeholder management and enabling the organization to be more ethically responsive to stakeholders' expectations. Issues and crisis management, to be effective, must have as their ultimate objective an increase in the organization's social responsiveness to its stakeholders. They are also related to the extent that effective issues management may enable managers to engage in more effective crisis management. That is, some crises may be anticipated and avoided through a carefully implemented issues management initiative.

Issues Management

Issues management is a process by which organizations identify issues in the stakeholder environment, analyze and prioritize those issues in terms of their relevance to the organization, plan responses to the issues, and then evaluate and monitor the results. It is helpful to think of issues management in connection with concepts introduced in the preceding chapter, such as the strategic management process, enterprise-level strategy, corporate public policy, and environmental analysis. The process of strategic management and environmental analysis requires an overall way of managerial thinking that includes economic, technological, social, and political issues. Enterprise-level strategy and corporate public policy, on the other hand, focus on public or ethical issues. Issues management, then, devolves from these broader concepts.

Two Approaches to Issues Management

Thinking about the concepts mentioned here requires us to make some distinctions. A central consideration seems to be that issues management has been thought of in two major ways: (1) narrowly, in which public, or social, issues are the primary focus, and (2) broadly, in which strategic issues and the strategic management process are the focus of attention. Liam Fahey provides a useful distinction between these two approaches. He refers to (1) the conventional approach and (2) the strategic management approach.[1] The **conventional approach** (narrowly focused) **to issues management** has the following characteristics:[2]

- Issues fall within the domain of public policy or public affairs management.
- Issues typically have a public policy/public affairs orientation or flavour.
- An issue is any trend, event, controversy, or public policy development that might affect the corporation.
- Issues originate in social/political/regulatory/judicial environments.

The **strategic management approach** (broadly inclusive) **to issues management** has evolved in a small number of companies and is typified by the following:[3]

- Issues management is typically the responsibility of senior line management or strategic planning staff.
- Issues identification is more important than it is in the conventional approach.
- Issues management is seen as an approach to the anticipation and management of external and internal challenges to the company's strategies, plans, and assumptions.

The strategic approach to issues management has also been advocated by such authorities as H. Igor Ansoff[4] and William R. King.[5] Figure 5–1 portrays strategic issues management as depicted by Ansoff. Note the "strategic" characteristics—threats/opportunities and strengths/weaknesses—that we alluded to in the preceding chapter.

At the risk of oversimplification, we will consider the principal distinction between the two perspectives on issues management to be that the conventional approach focuses on public/social issues, whereas the strategic approach is broadly inclusive of all issues. In addition, the conventional approach can be used as a "stand-alone" decision-making process, whereas the strategic approach is intimately interconnected with the strategic management process as a whole. Another difference may be whether operating managers/strategic planners or public affairs staff members are implementing the system. Beyond these distinctions, the two approaches have much in common.

Our discussion in this chapter will emphasize the conventional approach, because this book focuses on public, social, and ethical stakeholder issues. We should point out, however, that our purpose in the preceding chapter was to convey the notion that social issues ought to be seen as just one part of the broader strategic management process. There we discussed environmental analysis as a broad phenomenon. Now we emphasize social or ethical issues, although it is obvious that a consideration of these issues is embedded in a larger, more strategically focused process, such as that depicted in Figure 5–1.

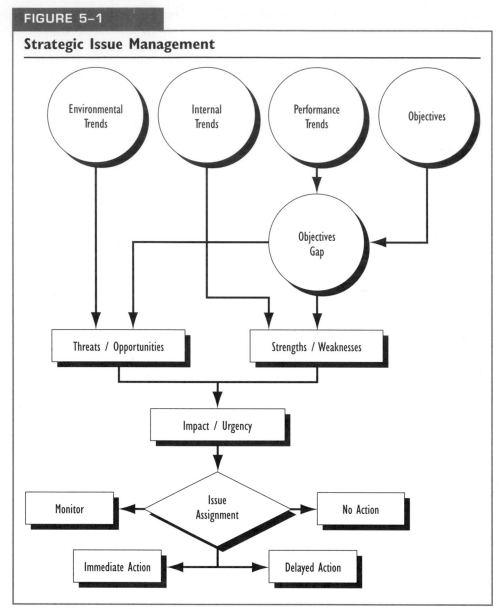

FIGURE 5–1

Strategic Issue Management

Source: H. Igor Ansoff, "Strategic Issue Management," *Strategic Management Journal* (Vol. I, 1980), 137. Reprinted by permission of John Wiley & Sons, Ltd.

Therefore, we are comfortable with both of these perspectives on issues management. We should point out that the conventional approach could be perceived as a subset of the strategic approach, although this is typically not the way companies see it. In a sense, the two approaches are highly inseparable, and it is difficult for organizations to operate effectively unless both are addressed in some way. For our purposes, however, the conventional perspective will be emphasized.

The Changing Issue Mix

The emergence in the past two decades of new "company issues management groups" and "issues managers" has been a direct outgrowth of the changing mix of issues that managers have had to handle. Economic and financial issues have always been an inherent part of the business process, although their complexity seems to have increased as international markets have broadened and competitiveness has become such an important issue. The growth of technology, especially the Internet, has presented business with other issues that need to be addressed. The most dramatic growth has been in social, ethical, and political issues—all public issues that have high visibility, media appeal, and interest among special-interest stakeholder groups. We should further observe that these issues become more interrelated over time.

For most firms, social, ethical, political, and technological issues are at the same time economic issues, because firms' success in handling them frequently has a direct bearing on their financial statuses and well-being. Over time, there is a changing mix of issues and an escalating challenge that management groups face as these issues create a cumulative effect.

Issue Definition and the Issues Management Process

Before describing the issues management process, we should briefly discuss what constitutes an issue and what assumptions we are making about issues management. An **issue** may be thought of as a matter that is in dispute between two or more parties. The dispute typically evokes debate, controversy, or differences of opinion that need to be resolved. At some point, the organization needs to make a decision on the unresolved matter, but such a decision does not mean that the issue is resolved. Once an issue becomes public and subject to public debate and high-profile media exposure, its resolution becomes increasingly difficult. One of the features of issues, particularly those arising in the social or ethical realm, is that they are ongoing and therefore require ongoing responses.

Joseph Coates et al., authors of *Issues Management*,[6] identify the following characteristics of an "**emerging issue**":

- The terms of the debate are not clearly defined.
- The issue deals with matters of conflicting values and interest.
- The issue does not lend itself to automatic resolution by expert knowledge.
- The issue is often stated in value-laden terms.
- Trade-offs are inherent.

John Mahon has described how complicated the question of issue definition can be in his observation about the multiple viewpoints that come into play when an issue is considered. He has noted that there are multiple stakeholders and motivations in any given management situation. Personal stakes frequently can be important factors but often are ignored or not taken into consideration. For example, some of the participants may be interested in the issue from a deep personal perspective and will not compromise or give up their positions even in the face of concrete evidence that clearly refutes them.[7] Thus, we can see that the resolution of issues in organizations is not easy.

What about the assumptions we make when we choose to use issues management? Coates et al. go on to say that the following assumptions are made:[8]

- Issues can be identified earlier, more completely, and more reliably than in the past.
- Early anticipation widens the organization's range of options.
- Early anticipation permits study and understanding of the full range of issues.
- Early anticipation permits the organization to develop a positive orientation toward the issue.
- The organization will have earlier identification of stakeholders.
- The organization will be able to supply information to influential publics earlier and more positively, thus allowing them to better understand the issue.

These are not only assumptions of issues management but also benefits to the extent that they make the organization more effective in its issues management process.

Model of the Issues Management Process   Like the strategic management process that entails a multitude of sequential and interrelated steps or stages, the issues management process has been conceptualized by many different authorities in a variety of ways. Conceptualizations of issues management have been developed by companies, academics, consultants, and associations. The issues management process we will discuss here has been extracted from many of the conceptualizations previously developed. This process represents the elements or stages that seem to be common to most of those conceptualizations and consistent with the stakeholder orientation we have been developing and using.

Figure 5–2 presents a model of the issues management process as we will discuss it. It contains planning aspects (identification, analysis, ranking/prioritization of issues, and formulation of responses) and implementation aspects (implementation of responses and evaluation, monitoring, and control of results). Although we will discuss the stages in the issues management process as though they were discrete, we should recognize that in reality they may be interrelated and overlap one another.

Identification of Issues   Many names have been given to the process of issue identification. At various times, the terms *social forecasting*, *futures research*, *environmental scanning*, and *public issues scanning* have been used. Similarly, many techniques have been employed. All of these approaches/techniques are similar, but each has its own unique characteristics. Common to all of them, however, is the need to scan the environment and to identify emerging issues or trends that might later be determined to have some relevance to or impact on the organization.

Issue identification, in its most rudimentary form, involves the assignment to some individual in the organization the tasks of continuously scanning a variety of publications—newspapers, magazines, specialty publications, the World Wide Web—and developing a comprehensive list of issues. Often this same person, or group, is instructed to review public documents, records of parliamentary hearings, and other such sources of information. One result of this scanning is an internal report or a newsletter that is circulated throughout the organization. The next step in this evolution may be for the company to subscribe to a trend information service or newsletter that is prepared and published by a private individual or consulting firm that specializes in environmental or issue scanning.[9]

Writer and consultant T. Graham Molitor proposed that there are five leading forces as predictors of social change:[10]

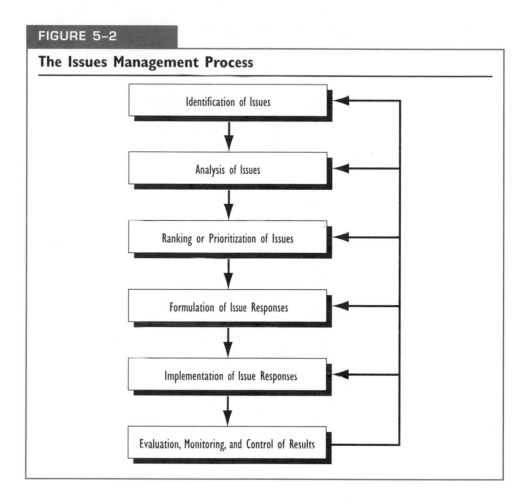

FIGURE 5–2

The Issues Management Process

- Identification of Issues
- Analysis of Issues
- Ranking or Prioritization of Issues
- Formulation of Issue Responses
- Implementation of Issue Responses
- Evaluation, Monitoring, and Control of Results

- Leading events
- Leading authorities/advocates
- Leading literature
- Leading organizations
- Leading political jurisdictions

If these five forces are monitored closely, impending social change can be identified and, in some cases, predicted. Figure 5–3 presents a number of Molitor's leading forces, as well as examples that might be thought to illustrate his points.

Molitor is president and founder of Public Policy Forecasting, Inc. He has assembled an amazing reservoir of knowledge as he has spent four decades advising hundreds of *Fortune* 500 companies and institutions on how the world might change the next day, the next decade, even the next millennium, and how to make the most of these changes.[11]

Companies vary considerably in their willingness to spend tens or hundreds of thousands of dollars for the kinds of professional services we have described, but some rely almost exclusively on these kinds of sources for issue identification. Others use less costly and more informal means.

FIGURE 5-3

Examples of Forces Leading Social Change

Leading Forces	Examples	Public Issue Realm
Events	Three Mile Island/Chernobyl nuclear plant explosions	Nuclear plant safety
	Bhopal explosion	Plant safety
	Earth Day	Environment
	Tylenol poisonings	Product tampering
	Love Canal	Toxic waste—environment
	Firestone Tires	Product safety
	Martha Stewart scandal	Insider trading abuses
	Thomas hearings	Sexual harassment
	Valdez oil spill	Environment
Authorities/Advocates	Ralph Nader	Consumerism
	David Suzuki	Environment
	Rev. Martin Luther King	Civil rights
	Craig Kielburger	Children's rights
Literature	*Silent Spring* (Rachel Carson)	Pesticides—environment
	Unsafe at Any Speed (Ralph Nader)	Automobile safety
	Boom, Bust & Echo (David K. Foot & Daniel Stoffman)	Issues identification
Organizations	Friends of the Earth	Environment
	Free the Children	Children's welfare
	Mothers Against Drunk Driving (MADD)	Highway safety/alcohol abuse

Analysis of Issues   The next two steps (analysis and ranking of issues) are closely related. To analyze an issue means to carefully study, dissect, break down, group, or engage in any specific process that helps you better understand the nature or characteristics of the issue. An analysis requires that you look beyond the obvious manifestations of the issue and strive to learn more of its history, development, current nature, and potential for future relevance to the organization. William King proposed a series of key questions that focus on stakeholder groups in attempting to analyze issues:[12]

- Who (which stakeholders) are affected by the issue?
- Who has an interest in the issue?
- Who is in a position to exert influence on the issue?
- Who has expressed opinions on the issue?
- Who ought to care about the issue?

In addition to these questions, a consulting firm—Human Resources Network—proposed the following key questions to help with issue analysis:[13]

- Who started the ball rolling? (Historical view)
- Who is now involved? (Contemporary view)
- Who will get involved? (Future view)

Answers to these questions place management in a better position to rank or prioritize the issues so that it will have a better sense of the urgency with which the issues need to be addressed.

Ranking or Prioritization of Issues Once issues have been carefully analyzed and are well understood, it is necessary to rank them in some form of a hierarchy of importance or relevance to the organization. We should note that some issues management systems place this step before analysis. This is done especially when it is desired to screen out those issues that are obviously not relevant and deserving of further analysis.

The prioritization stage may range from a simple grouping of issues into categories of urgency to a more elaborate or sophisticated scoring system. Two examples will serve to illustrate the grouping technique. Xerox has used a process of categorizing issues into three classifications: (1) *high priority* (issues on which management must be well informed), (2) *nice to know* (issues that are interesting but not critical or urgent), and (3) *questionable* (issues that may not be issues at all unless something else happens). PPG Industries has grouped issues into three priorities: *Priority A* (critical issues that warrant executive action and review), *Priority B* (issues that warrant surveillance by the division general manager or staff), and *Priority C* (issues that have only potential impact and warrant monitoring by the public affairs department).[14]

A somewhat more sophisticated approach uses a **probability-impact matrix** requiring management to assess the *probability of occurrence of an issue* (high, medium, or low) on one dimension and its *impact on the company* (high, medium, or low) on the other dimension. In using such an approach, management would place each issue in the appropriate cell of the matrix, and the completed matrix would then serve as an aid to prioritization. As a variation on this theme, management could rank issues by considering the mathematical product of each issue's impact (for example, on a scale from 1 to 10) and probability of occurrence (on a scale from 0 to 1).

William R. King has provided a somewhat more elaborate issues-ranking scheme. He recommends that issues be screened on five filter criteria: strategy, relevance, actionability, criticality, and urgency.[15] Once each issue has been scored on a 10-point scale on each criterion, issues are then ranked according to their resulting point totals. Figure 5–4 illustrates this filtering/ranking process. Other techniques that have been used in issues identification, analysis, and prioritization include polls/surveys, expert panels, content analysis, the Delphi technique, trend extrapolation, scenario building, and the use of precursor events or bellwethers.[16]

Earlier we described a simple issues identification process as involving an individual in the organization or a subscription to a newsletter or trend-spotting service. The analysis and ranking stages could be done by an individual, but more often the company has moved up to a next stage of formalization. This next stage involves assignment of the issues management function to a team, often as part of a public affairs department, which begins to specialize in the issues management function. This group of specialists can provide a wide range of issues management activities, depending on the commitment of the company to the process. A number of companies have created issues management units to alert management to emerging trends and controversies and to help mobilize the companies' resources to deal with them. Firms such as Monsanto and Sears are among those that have used such units. At Monsanto, an issues manager organized a committee of middle managers to help do the work.

Formulation and Implementation of Responses These two steps in the issues management process are combined here because we do not discuss them extensively. Also, we should observe that the formulation and implementation stages in the issues management process are quite similar to the corresponding stages we discussed in the preceding chapter, which pertained to the strategic management process as a whole.

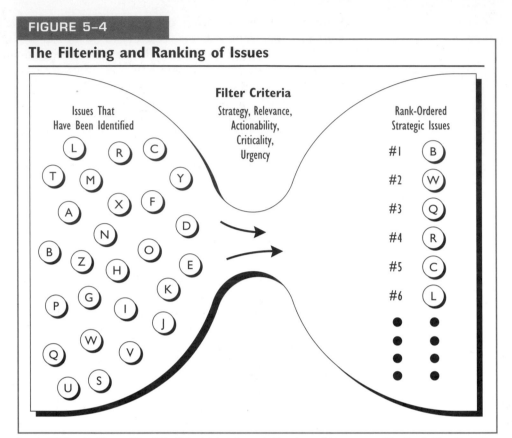

FIGURE 5-4

The Filtering and Ranking of Issues

Source: William R. King and David I. Cleland (eds.), *Strategic Planning and Management Handbook* (New York: Van Nostrand Reinhold, 1987), 257.

Formulation in this case refers to the response design process. Based on the analysis conducted, companies can then identify options that might be pursued in dealing with the issues, in making decisions, and in implementing those decisions. Strategy formulation refers not only to the formulation of the actions that the firm intends to take but also to the creation of the overall strategy, or degree of aggressiveness, employed in carrying out those actions. Options might include aggressive pursuit, gradual pursuit, or selective pursuit of goals, plans, processes, or programs.[17] All of these more detailed plans are part of the strategy formulation process.

Once plans for dealing with issues have been formulated, implementation becomes the focus. There are many organizational aspects that need to be addressed in the implementation process. Some of these include the clarity of the plan itself, resources needed to implement the plan, top management support, organizational structure, technical competence, and timing.[18] For additional implementation considerations, refer to our discussion of the McKinsey 7S framework in Chapter 4.

Evaluation, Monitoring, and Control These recognizable steps in the issues management process were also treated as steps in the strategic management process in Chapter 4. In the present context, they mean that companies should continually evaluate the results of their responses to the issues and ensure that these actions are kept on track. In particular, this stage requires careful monitoring of stakeholders' opinions. A form of stakeholder audit—something derivative of the social audit discussed in

Chapter 4—might be used. The information that is gathered during this final stage in the issues management process is then fed back to the earlier stages in the process so that changes or adjustments might be made as needed. Evaluation information may be useful at each stage in the process.

We have presented the issues management process as a complete system. In actual practice, companies apply the stages in various degrees of formality or informality as needed or desired. For example, because issues management is more important in some situations than in others, some stages of the process may be truncated to meet the needs of different firms in different industries. In addition, some firms are more committed to issues management than others. Those firms that are committed are probably members of the Issues Management Association. Today, this association has hundreds of member firms.

Issues Development Process

A vital attribute of issues management is that issues tend to develop according to an evolutionary pattern. This pattern might be thought of as a developmental or growth process or, as some have called it, a life cycle. It is important for managers to have some appreciation of this **issues development process** so that they can recognize when an event or trend is becoming an issue and also because it might affect the strategy that the firm employs in dealing with the issue. Companies may take a variety of courses of action depending on the stage of the issue in the process.

One view of the issues development process holds that issues tend to follow an eight-year curve, although it is very difficult to generalize about the time frame, especially in today's world of instantaneous global communications. For the first five years or so of this hypothetical period, a nascent issue emerges in local newspapers, is enunciated by public-interest organizations, and is detected through public-opinion polling. According to Margaret Stroup, former director of corporate responsibility at Monsanto, the issue is low-key and flexible at this stage.[19] During this time, the issue may reflect a felt need, receive media coverage, and attract interest-group development and growth. A typical firm may notice the issue but take no action at this stage. John Mahon's view is that more issues-oriented firms may become more active in their monitoring and in their attempts to shape or help "define the issue."[20] Active firms have the capacity to prevent issues from going any further, through either effective responses to the issues or effective lobbying.

In the fifth or sixth year of the cycle, national media attention and leading political jurisdictions (e.g., cities, provinces, countries) may address the issue. Quite often, federal government attention is generated in the form of studies and hearings; legislation, regulation, and litigation follow. Today, it would not be uncommon for issues to mature much more quickly than the eight-year model just described. Figure 5–5, however, presents a simplified view of what this issue development life cycle process might look like.

We should note that the stages in the process, especially the early stages, might occur in a different sequence or in an iterative pattern. Further, not all issues complete the process; some are resolved before they reach the stage of legislation or regulation. Thomas G. Marx takes the view that issues go from social expectations to political issues to legislation and finally to social control. Marx illustrates this evolution through two examples.

First, consider the issue of environmental protection. The social expectation was manifested in Rachel Carson's book *Silent Spring* (1963); it became a political issue

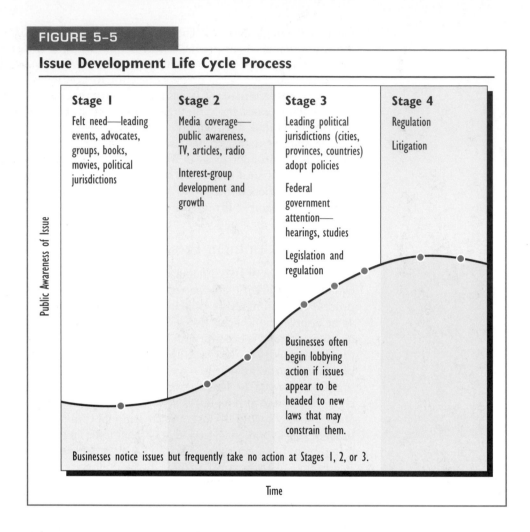

FIGURE 5-5

Issue Development Life Cycle Process

Stage 1

Felt need—leading events, advocates, groups, books, movies, political jurisdictions

Stage 2

Media coverage—public awareness, TV, articles, radio

Interest-group development and growth

Stage 3

Leading political jurisdictions (cities, provinces, countries) adopt policies

Federal government attention—hearings, studies

Legislation and regulation

Stage 4

Regulation

Litigation

Businesses often begin lobbying action if issues appear to be headed to new laws that may constrain them.

Businesses notice issues but frequently take no action at Stages 1, 2, or 3.

Public Awareness of Issue

Time

that inspired subsequent legislation in North America; and it was reflected in social control by emissions standards, pollution fines, product recalls, and environmental permits in later years. The second example involves product/consumer safety. The social expectation was manifested in Ralph Nader's book *Unsafe at Any Speed* (1964); it became a political issue that resulted in improved auto safety legislation in North America; and it was reflected in social control through the ordering of seat belts in all cars, defects litigation, product recalls, and driver fines.[21]

Finally, we are reminded by Bigelow, Fahey, and Mahon that "issues do not necessarily follow a linear, sequential path, but instead follow paths that reflect the intensity and diversity of the values and interests stakeholders bring to an issue and the complexity of the interaction among ..." all the variables.[22] This should serve as a warning not to oversimplify the issues development process.

Issues Management in Practice

Issues management in practice today has very much become a subset of activities performed by the public affairs departments of major corporations, as noted in the previous chapter. A survey of corporate public affairs officers of major corporations revealed that 67 percent engage in issues management functions. Furthermore, the survey revealed that there is now greater use of interdepartmental issues teams, with the public affairs department serving as coordinator and strategist but with appropriate line and staff executives charged with ultimate accountability for implementation. In practice, therefore, it can be seen that issues management does not function as a stand-alone activity but has been subsumed into a host of functions for which modern public affairs departments take responsibility.[23]

Issues management faces a serious challenge in business today. From the standpoint of the turbulence in the stakeholder environment, issues management may be needed. To become a permanent part of the organization, however, issues management will have to continuously prove itself. We can talk conceptually about the process with ease, but the field still remains somewhat nebulous even though it is struggling to become more scientific and legitimate. Managers in the real world want results, and if issues management cannot deliver those results, it will be destined to failure as a management process.

Some companies have claimed specific successes for their issues management programs. S. C. Johnson & Sons, the maker of floor waxes and other chemicals, claimed it removed environmentally chancy fluorocarbons from its aerosol sprays three years before U.S. federal action required the industry to do so. Sears claims it spotted the flammable-nightwear controversy early and got nonflammable goods into its stores before government action mandated it. Bank of America claimed it was alerted early by its issues managers about a practice known as "redlining" and took action to change its lending policies two years before the U.S. Congress required banks to disclose whether they were barring all loans in certain parts of a city. According to the bank, its early action reduced its eventual cost of compliance significantly and spared it "a lot of grief and antagonism from cities and public-interest groups."[24] In the final analysis, identifiable successes such as these will be needed to ensure the future of issues management.

Issues Management Is a Bridge to Crisis Management

Ideally, firms use issues management to assist them in planning for and preventing crises that then require crisis management. Issues management represents careful planning that may head off impending crises. This is because many crises are embedded in issues or erupt from issues that could have been anticipated and studied in carefully designed issues management processes. Issues management can be seen as a form of precrisis planning. It is intended to help organizations anticipate and plan for possible crisis eruptions. Not all crises can be planned for, of course, but many can be anticipated through effective issues management programs. It has been suggested by Kate Miller that one of the most effective ways for keeping a crisis plan "living" is issues management.[25] Thus, we can see how issues and crisis management are different, but related.

Crisis Management

Crisis management as a management term is largely a product of the past two decades. This has been the era of the mega-crisis: Union Carbide's Bhopal disaster, which killed over 2000 people in India; Johnson & Johnson's Tylenol poisonings, which resulted in numerous deaths; and Procter & Gamble's Rely tampon crisis, in which that product was associated with toxic shock syndrome; the terrifying attacks on the World

Trade Center in New York, which resulted in the deaths of approximately 3000 people. In Canada, the recent battle with SARS raised many concerns about the ability of hospitals to deal with such outbreaks and the ability of cities like Toronto to cope with the fallout of this illness. As *The Financial Post* reported:

> *Memories of the SARS crisis are already starting to fade in Canada and around the world, but the virulent respiratory disease is still giving some in the airline industry a lot to worry about. Merrill Lynch aerospace analyst Byron Callan issued a report on the industry yesterday, and said that SARS remains the number one threat to the commercial airline industry. The spread of the SARS virus has been halted for now, and researchers are trying to develop treatments for the illness that claimed 44 lives in Ontario alone this year. But information about how the SARS situation has been handled in China has been scarce, and many worry that the illness could erupt again.*[26]

Another significant blow to Canada and Canadian business in recent years was mad cow disease. In May 2003 Canada's cattle industry was shaken by the discovery of bovine spongiform encephalopathy (BSE) in a northern Alberta Black Angus breeder cow. Subsequently, over 30 countries closed their borders to Canadian beef at that time. By October 2003, the crisis had cost Canadian exporters alone more than $1 billion in lost revenue. Producers were also hard hit after the price of animals collapsed and the market largely dried up at that time.[27]

Prior to these more recent disasters, those living in Walkerton, Ontario, were also forced to cope with life-and-death situations. Seven people died and 2300 others became severely ill after this small town's water system was besieged with the E. coli bacteria in May of 2000. Upon investigation of the source for this tragedy, it was uncovered that individual incompetence and fraudulent behaviour played a central role. Stan and Frank Koebel, who worked for the Walkerton Public Utilities, failed to maintain the water system in a satisfactory manner, including ensuring adequate levels of chlorination, and they consistently reported false chlorination levels. Ultimately, had the Koebel brothers admitted to their incompetence and deception earlier, the tragedy may have been averted.

Other significant crises have included the following:

- Schwan's ice cream company was charged as the responsible party in a salmonella outbreak in 39 states in the U.S.
- Star-Kist Foods was charged with shipping rancid and decomposing tuna.
- Dow Corning was targeted in a silicone breast implant probe. By 1999 the company had paid out approximately $40 million in damages to Canadian women. In 2001, a number of class action lawsuits were directed at Health Canada for their failure to recall implants from the market, despite having evidence they were harmful.
- Sudafed capsules were tainted with cyanide, leading to two deaths.
- Perrier Water's benzene incident led to product recalls.
- Intel's distribution of flawed Pentium chips in computers created a nightmare for the company.
- Coca-Cola experienced a crisis when its soft drinks were associated with illnesses in Belgium and France.
- Firestone and Ford were implicated in massive tire recalls due to faulty tires causing tread separations and deaths.

Search the web www

Myths in Crisis Management

The Institute for Crisis Management (ICM) has compiled a database that contains information about 60 000 specific crises that organizations have experienced over the past decade. By content analyzing the types of crises, the ICM has been able to conclude that there are several myths regarding crisis management.

One myth is the stereotype of business crises being industrial accidents, oil spills, and bizarre crimes like terrorist bombings or the Tylenol incident. ICM's analysis of business crises indicates that these "no warning" crises are actually in the minority. The majority of crises are smouldering crises where management knows about them before they go public. Another myth is that most crises are caused by employee errors or natural disasters.

According to ICM's analysis, over 60 percent of business crises have their origins in management. During one recent year, the primary categories of business crises were mismanagement, white-collar crime, and labour disputes.

To learn more about crisis management and some of these myths, check out the ICM's Web site at **http:// www.crisisexperts.com**.

It has been said by a number of observers, including Ian Mitroff, author of *Managing Crises Before They Happen*, that the Tylenol poisonings in 1982 was the case that put crisis management "on the map." That is, it was the case that marked the beginning of the new corporate discipline known as crisis management because Johnson & Johnson's voluntary recall of some 31 million bottles of Tylenol was the first important example of an organization assuming responsibility for its products without being forced to do so.[28] Thus, the field of crisis management is just over 20 years old.

It should be apparent from this list of crises that there is a major distinction between issues management, discussed in the preceding section, and crisis management, the subject of this section. Issues typically evolve gradually over a period of time. Issues management is a process of identifying and preparing to respond to potential issues. Crises, on the other hand, occur abruptly. They cannot always be anticipated or forecast. Some crises occur within an issue category considered; many do not. Issues and crisis management are related, however, in that they both are concerned about organizations becoming prepared for uncertainty in the stakeholder environment.

The Nature of Crises

There are many kinds of crises. Those we have just mentioned have all been associated with major stakeholder groups and have achieved high-visibility status. Hurt or killed customers, hurt employees, injured stockholders, and unfair practices are the concerns of modern crisis management. Not all crises involve such public or ethical issues, but these kinds of crises almost always ensure front-page status. Major companies can be seriously damaged by such episodes, especially if the episodes are poorly handled.

What is a crisis? Dictionaries state that a crisis is a "turning point for better or worse," an "emotionally significant event," or a "decisive moment." We all think of crises as being emotion charged, but we do not always think of them as turning points for better or for worse. The implication here is that a crisis is a decisive moment that, if managed one way, could make things worse but, if managed another way, could make things better. Choice is present, and how the crisis is managed can make a difference.

From a managerial point of view, a line needs to be drawn between a problem and a crisis. Problems, of course, are common in business. A crisis, however, is not as common. A useful way to think about a **crisis** is with a definition set forth by Laurence Barton:

A crisis is a major, unpredictable event that has potentially negative results. The event and its aftermath may significantly damage an organization and its employees, products, services, financial condition, and reputation.[29]

Another definition set forth by Pearson and Clair is also helpful in understanding the critical aspects of a crisis:

> *An organizational crisis is a low-probability, high-impact event that threatens the viability of the organization and is characterized by ambiguity of cause, effect, and means of resolution, as well as by a belief that decisions must be made swiftly.*[30]

Consider, for a moment, the case referred to earlier wherein Star-Kist Foods, a subsidiary of H. J. Heinz Co., faced a management crisis. Gerald Clay was appointed general manager of the Canadian subsidiary and was given the mandate to develop a five-year business strategy for the firm. Just after his arrival in Canada, the crisis hit: The Canadian Broadcasting Corporation accused his company of shipping 1 million cans of rancid and decomposing tuna. Dubbed "Tunagate" by the media, the crisis dragged on for weeks. With guidance from Heinz, Clay chose to keep quiet, even as Prime Minister Mulroney ordered the tuna seized. The silence cost plenty. According to Clay's boss, "We were massacred in the press." The company, which used to have half the Canadian tuna market, watched revenues plunge by 90 percent. At one point, Clay's boss observed that the company's future was in doubt.[31] In the recent Firestone tire tread separation tragedy, many observers have wondered out loud whether the tire brand can be saved after the company has been ravaged by this crisis. Ford, for its part, has been fighting to save its Explorer SUV, which has been implicated in the tread separation controversy.

Being prepared for crises has become a primary activity in a growing number of companies. Part of being prepared entails knowing something about the nature of crises. Steven Fink conducted a major survey of *Fortune* 500 firms on the subject and wrote one of the first books on crisis management. Fink's survey disclosed that a staggering 89 percent of those who responded agreed that "a crisis in business today is as inevitable as death and taxes," but 50 percent of the executive respondents admitted that they did not have prepared crisis plans.[32] Today, more companies may be prepared for crises, but their degree of preparedness varies widely.

Types of Crises Situations in which the executives surveyed by Fink felt they were vulnerable to crises included industrial accidents, environmental problems, union problems/strikes, product recalls, investor relations, hostile takeovers, proxy fights, rumours/media leaks, government regulatory problems, acts of terrorism, and embezzlement.[33] Other common crises include product tampering, executive kidnapping, work-related homicides, malicious rumours, and natural disasters that destroy corporate offices or information bases.[34] Since September 11, 2001, we have had to add terrorism to this list.

Search the web

Crisis Management

An article in *Time* magazine called crisis management the "new corporate discipline." Every company today, large or small, runs the risk of a crisis. Forward-looking companies practise crisis management and either develop their own in-house crisis management programs or avail themselves of the many consulting firms that provide crisis management consulting. One consulting firm that specializes in crisis management is Lexicon Communications Corporation. Among its many services Lexicon provides crisis management training seminars, workshops, and full-blown crisis simulations to help executives hone the skills they may need to serve on crisis management teams or to respond to the media in a crisis-filled atmosphere. To learn more about which topics might be covered in such seminars, check out the Lexicon Web site at **http://www.crisismanagement.com**.

Another major consulting firm that specializes in crisis management is The Wilson Group. Whether it's a chemical spill, a plant explosion, a plant closing, or another crisis, The Wilson Group offers personalized crisis management and media training workshops, crisis communication plans, community relations programs, and on-the-scene counsel. Part of the group's intense training includes on-camera media training for executives in a mock disaster context. To learn more about crisis management, visit The Wilson Group Web site at **http://www.wilson-group.com**.

Mitroff and Anagnos (2001) have suggested that crises may be categorized according to the following types of crises:[35]

- *Economic*—labour strikes, market crashes, major declines in earnings
- *Informational*—loss of proprietary information, false information, tampering with computer records
- *Human resource*—loss of key executives, personnel or workplace violence
- *Reputational*—slander, tampering with corporate logos
- *Psychopathic*—product tampering, kidnapping, hostage taking
- *Natural*—earthquakes, fire, tornadoes

Of the major crises that have recently occurred, the majority of the companies reported the following outcomes: The crises escalated in intensity, were subjected to media and government scrutiny, interfered with normal business operations, and damaged the company's bottom line. As a result of the horrific attacks on the World Trade Center, companies have experienced major power shifts among executives as some bosses fumbled with their responsibilities and didn't handle the crisis well. Those bosses who handled the crisis well have garnered more responsibility while others have lost responsibilities.[36]

Four Crisis Stages

There are a number of ways we could categorize the stages through which a crisis may progress. According to Steven Fink, a crisis may consist of as many as four distinct stages: (1) a **prodromal crisis stage**, (2) an **acute crisis stage**, (3) a **chronic crisis stage**, and (4) a **crisis resolution stage**.[37]

Prodromal Crisis Stage   This is the warning stage. ("Prodromal" is a medical term that refers to a previous notice or warning.) This warning stage could also be thought of as a symptom stage. Although it could be called a "precrisis" stage, this presupposes that one knows that a crisis is coming. According to Mitroff and Anagnos, crises "send out a repeated trail of early warning signals" that managers can learn to recognize.[38] Perhaps management should adopt this perspective: Watch each situation with the thought that it could be a crisis in the making. Early symptoms may be quite obvious, such as in the case where a social activist group tells management it will boycott the company if a certain problem is not addressed. On the other hand, symptoms may be more subtle, as in the case where defect rates for a particular product a company makes start edging up over time.

Acute Crisis Stage   This is the stage at which the crisis actually occurs. There is no turning back; the incident has occurred. Damage has been done at this point, and it is now up to management to handle or contain the damage. If the prodromal stage is the precrisis stage, the acute stage is the actual crisis stage. The crucial decision point at which things may get worse or better has been reached.

Chronic Crisis Stage   This is the lingering period. It may be the period of investigations, audits, or in-depth news stories. Management may see it as a period of recovery, self-analysis, or self-doubt. In Fink's survey of major companies, he found that crises tended to linger as much as two and a half times longer in firms without crisis management plans than in firms with such plans.

Crisis Resolution Stage This is the final stage—the goal of all crisis management efforts. Fink argues that when an early warning sign of a crisis is noted, the manager should seize control swiftly and determine the most direct and expedient route to resolution. If the warning signs are missed in the first stage, the goal is to speed up all phases and reach the final stage as soon as possible.

Figure 5–6 presents one way in which these four stages might be depicted. It should be noted that the phases may overlap and that each phase varies in intensity and duration. It is hoped that management will learn from the crisis and thus will be better prepared for, and better able to handle, any future crisis.

Other views of crises and crisis management may be taken. Gerald C. Meyers, former chairman of American Motors Corporation and a consultant on crisis management, and others lay out the scenario for a *poorly managed crisis*, which typically follows a predictable pattern.[39] The pattern is as follows:

- Early indications that trouble is brewing occur.
- Warnings are ignored/played down.
- Warnings build to a climax.
- Pressure mounts.
- Executives are often overwhelmed or can't cope effectively.
- Quick-fix alternatives look appealing. Hasty moves create trouble.
- Clamming-up versus opening-up options present themselves.
- Most firms choose the former.
- A siege mentality prevails.

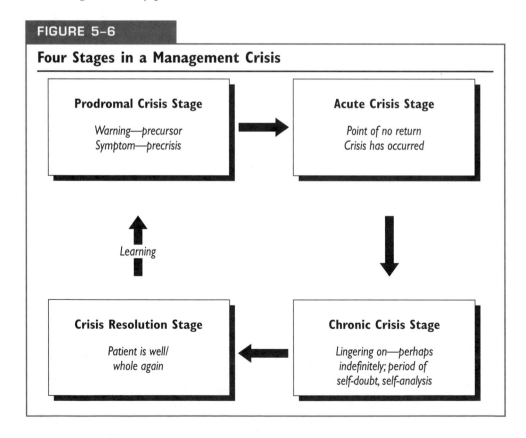

FIGURE 5–6

Four Stages in a Management Crisis

Prodromal Crisis Stage

Warning—precursor
Symptom—precrisis

Acute Crisis Stage

Point of no return
Crisis has occurred

Learning

Crisis Resolution Stage

*Patient is well/
whole again*

Chronic Crisis Stage

*Lingering on—perhaps
indefinitely; period of
self-doubt, self-analysis*

Visualizing the attributes or pattern of a poorly managed crisis is valuable because it illustrates how not to do it—a lesson that many managers may find quite valuable.

Managing Business Crises

Fink's Three-Stage Model There are many suggestions for managing a crisis, although they cannot be reduced to a cookbook recipe. Steven Fink presents a simple model by arguing that there are three vital stages in crisis management:

1. *identifying* the crisis,
2. *isolating* the crisis, and
3. *managing* the crisis. All should be done quickly.[40]

Business Week's Five Practical Steps in Managing Crises A more complete view of crisis management holds that a series of five steps must be taken. These five steps, synthesized by *Business Week* magazine from the actual experiences of companies experiencing crises, are discussed next and are summarized in Figure 5–7.[41]

First: Identifying Areas of Vulnerability. In this first step, some areas of vulnerability are obvious, such as potential chemical spills, whereas others are more subtle. The key seems to be in developing a greater consciousness of how things can go wrong and get out of hand. At Heinz, after the "Tunagate" incident, a vice president set up brainstorming sessions. He said, "We're brainstorming about how we would be affected by everything from a competitor who had a serious quality problem to a scandal involving a Heinz executive."[42]

Second: Developing a Plan for Dealing with Threats. A plan for dealing with the most serious crisis threats is a logical next step. One of the most crucial issues is communications planning. After a Dow Chemical railroad car derailed near Toronto, forcing the evacuation of 250 000 people, Dow Canada prepared information kits on the hazards of its products so that executives would be knowledgeable enough to respond properly if a similar crisis were to arise in the future. Dow Canada also

---

FIGURE 5–7

Steps in Crisis Management

1. Identifying areas of vulnerability
   A. Obvious areas
   B. Subtle areas
2. Developing a plan for dealing with threats
   A. Communications planning is vital
   B. Training executives in product dangers and dealing with media
3. Forming crisis teams
   A. Vital to successful crisis management
   B. Identifying executives who can work well under stress
4. Simulating crisis drills
   A. Experience/practice is helpful
   B. "War rooms" serve as gathering places for team members
5. Learning from experience
   A. Assess effectiveness of crisis strategies
   B. Move from reaction to proaction

trained executives in interviewing techniques. This effort paid off several years later when an accident caused a chemical spill into a river that supplied drinking water for several nearby towns. The company's emergency response team arrived at the site almost immediately and established a press centre that distributed information about the chemicals. In addition, the company recruited a neutral expert to speak on the hazards and how to deal with them. Officials praised Dow for its handling of this crisis.[43]

Richard J. Mahoney, former CEO of Monsanto Company, has offered the following *ten "Rs" for the effective handling of public policy crises*. He recommends these steps as part of an overall crisis plan:[44]

- Respond early.
- Recruit a credible spokesperson.
- Reply truthfully.
- Respect the opposition's concerns.
- Revisit the issue with follow-up.
- Retreat early if it's a loser.
- Redouble efforts early if it's a critical company issue.
- Reply with visible top management.
- Refuse to press for what is not good public policy.
- Repeat the prior statement regularly.

Some of these steps may not apply to every crisis situation, but many may be useful as part of a crisis management plan. Mahoney notes that getting an entire organization trained to deal with crises is difficult and expensive, but he paraphrases what a car repairman said in a TV commercial: "You can pay now or pay a lot more later." Mahoney thinks that now is infinitely better for everyone.[45]

Third: Forming Crisis Teams. Another step that can be taken as part of an overall planning effort is the formation of **crisis teams**. Such teams have played key roles in many well-managed disasters. A good example is the team formed at Procter & Gamble when its Rely tampon products were linked with the dreaded disease toxic shock syndrome. The team was quickly assembled, a vice president was appointed to head it, and after one week the decision was made to remove Rely from marketplace shelves. The quick action earned the firm praise, and it paid off for P&G in the long run.

Another task in assembling crisis teams is identifying managers who can cope effectively with stress. Not every executive can handle the fast-moving, high-pressured, ambiguous decision environment that is created by a crisis, and early identification of executives who can is important. We should also note that it is not always the CEO who can best perform in such a crisis atmosphere.

Despite the careful use of crisis teams, crises can often overwhelm a carefully constructed plan. When ValuJet's Flight 592 crashed in the Florida Everglades in 1996, for example, ValuJet flawlessly executed a three-pronged, team-based crisis management plan calling for the company to (1) show compassion, (2) take responsibility, and (3) demonstrate that the airline learned from the crisis. Experts have said that the company handled the crisis well. However, a close look at the tragedy revealed that a series of complicating factors turned the crisis into something even more difficult than a well-scripted, perfectly executed crisis management plan could handle.[46]

Fourth: Simulating Crisis Drills. Some companies have gone so far as to run crisis drills in which highly stressful situations are simulated so that managers can "practise" what they might do in a real crisis. As a basis for conducting crisis drills and experiential exercises, a number of companies have adopted a software package known as Crisis Plan wRiter (CPR). This software allows companies to centralize and maintain up-to-date crisis management information and allows company leaders to assign responsibilities to their crisis team, target key audiences, identify and monitor potential issues, and create crisis-response processes.[47]

Fifth: Learning from Experience. The final stage in crisis management is learning from experience. At this point, managers need to ask themselves exactly what they have learned from past crises and how that knowledge can be used to advantage in the future. Part of this stage entails an assessment of the effectiveness of the firm's crisis-handling strategies and identification of areas where improvements in capabilities need to be made. Without a crisis management system of some kind in place, the organization will find itself reacting to crises after they have occurred. If learning and preparation for the future are occurring, however, the firm may engage in more proactive behaviour.[48]

Augustine's Six Stages of Crisis Management As an alternative to the previous steps in crisis management, Norman Augustine, former president of Lockheed Martin Corporation, distinguished among six stages of crisis management. To some extent, these overlap and embrace the steps, but it is useful to see an alternative conceptualization of the steps that should be taken in crisis management. Augustine's list begins with the idea that the crisis should be avoided:[49]

Stage 1: Avoiding the Crisis

Stage 2: Preparing to Manage the Crisis

Stage 3: Recognizing the Crisis

Stage 4: Containing the Crisis

Stage 5: Resolving the Crisis

Stage 6: Profiting from the Crisis

We should note that Pearson and Mitroff have accurately observed that effective crisis management requires a program that is tailored to a firm's specific industry, business environment, and crisis management experience. Effective crisis managers will understand that there are major crisis management factors that may vary from situation to situation, such as the type of crisis (e.g., natural disaster or human induced), the phase of the crisis, the systems affected (e.g., humans, technology, culture), and the stakeholders affected. Managers cannot eliminate crises. However, they can become keenly aware of their vulnerabilities and make concerted efforts to understand and reduce these vulnerabilities through continuous crisis management programs.[50]

Crisis Communications

An illustration of crisis management without effective communications occurred during the Jack in the Box hamburger disaster of 1993. There was an outbreak of E. coli bacteria in the Pacific Northwest area, resulting in the deaths of four children. Following this crisis, the parent company, San Diego–based Foodmaker, entered a downward spiral after lawsuits by the families of victims enraged the public and franchisees. Foodmaker did most of the right things and did them quickly. The company immediately suspended hamburger sales, recalled suspect meat from its distribution system, increased cooking time for all foods, pledged to pay for all the medical costs related to the disaster, and hired a food safety expert to design a new food-handling system. But, it forgot to do one thing: communicate with the public, including its own employees.[51]

The company's **crisis communications** efforts were inept. It waited a week before accepting any responsibility for the tragedy, preferring to point fingers at its meat supplier and even the Washington state health officials for not explaining the state's new guidelines for cooking hamburgers at higher temperatures. The media pounced on the company. The company was blasted for years even though within the company it was taking the proper steps to correct the problem. The company suffered severe financial losses, and it took at least six years before the company really felt it was on the road to recovery. "The crisis," as it is still called around company headquarters, taught the firm an important lesson. CEO Robert Nugent was quoted as saying in 1999, "Nobody wants to deal with their worst nightmare, but we should have recognized you've got to communicate."[52]

Virtually all crisis management plans call for effective crisis communications. There are a number of different stakeholder groups with whom effective communications are critical, especially the media and those immediately affected by the crisis. Many companies have failed to successfully manage their crises because of inadequate or failed communications with key stakeholder groups. Successful communications efforts are crucial to effective crisis management. It is axiomatic that *prepared* communications will be more helpful than *reactive* communications. Jonathan L. Bernstein has offered **ten steps of crisis communication** that are worth summarizing:[53]

1. Identify your crisis communications team.
2. Identify key spokespersons who will be authorized to speak for the organization.
3. Train your spokespersons.
4. Establish communications protocols.
5. Identify and know your audience.
6. Anticipate crises.
7. Assess the crisis situation.
8. Identify key messages you will communicate to key groups.
9. Decide on communications methods.
10. Be prepared to ride out the storm.

A brief elaboration on the importance of identifying key messages that will be communicated to key groups is useful (point 8). It is important that you communicate with your *internal stakeholders* first because rumours are often started there, and uninformed employees can do great damage to a successful crisis management effort. Internal stakeholders are your best advocates and can be supportive during a crisis. Prepare news releases that contain as much information as possible and get this information out to all *media outlets* at the same time. Communicate with *others in the community* who have a need to know, such as public officials, disaster coordinators, stakeholders, and others. *Uniformity of response* is of vital importance during a crisis. Finally, have a designated "release authority" for information (point 2). The first 24 hours of a crisis can make or break the organization, and how these key spokespersons work is of vital importance to handling the crisis.[54]

Mitroff and Anagnos have stressed the importance of "telling the truth" in effective crisis communications. They argue that there are no secrets in today's society and

Ethics In Practice

The Slackest of Them All

During my final two years of university, I worked in a retail clothing store. There was one general manager, Chrissy, one operations manager, and five merchandise managers. Chrissy was a strict manager who followed every corporate policy and even created her own stricter rules for the store. Each merchandise manager is responsible for a department of the store, such as women's, men's, kids, babies, and accessories.

For each department, the managers must keep the displays updated, plan for biweekly shipments, and redo the "look" once a month to match the suggested layout sent from the corporate offices. The only male among the six merchandise managers was Jamie. He also happens to be the slackest of the managers. Many of the other managers and employees say the only reason he has this job is because he and Chrissy were childhood friends.

There were many strict policies to follow at this store that ranged from customer service to loss prevention. Yet, Jamie managed to break all of the policies. Here are some examples: Every night that he closed the store, he would turn off the lights at closing time to hurry the customers out of the store. When he would encounter a shoplifter, he would tell them to return the merchandise to its place while he turned his back. He would stand by the registers his entire shift instead of circulating

the floor helping customers, work in his department, or perform other managerial duties. Jamie would also make the employees leave early at night even when the store was not straightened up so he could go out drinking.

Jamie engaged in all these activities on a daily basis. They were in direct violation of policies and all the employees were well aware of it. Yet nothing was ever done about it. I often wanted to say something to Chrissy to see if she ever noticed his behaviour. However, I did not because of the constant rumours that Chrissy knows about his behaviour, but ignores it since their friendship dates back to childhood. I could not believe Chrissy would allow this kind of behaviour from a manager. She fired employees for similar actions.

1. Is it an ethical practice to allow Jamie to slack off and not take action? Should others be allowed to slack off?

2. Should the other managers confront Chrissy for an explanation of why she tolerates this behaviour from Jamie, but would fire anyone else who tried it?

3. What, if anything, would you do in this situation? Why?

Contributed by Tiffany Kemph

that eventually the truth will get out. Therefore, from a practical point of view, the question is not whether the truth will be revealed but rather when that truth will become public and under what circumstances.[55] From both an ethical and a practical perspective, truth-telling is an important facet of crisis communications.

Successful Crisis Management

It is informative to conclude this chapter with an illustration of a successful crisis management case study. This case study started with the kind of phone call every company dreads—"Your product is injuring people; we're announcing it at a press conference today." Schwan's Sales Enterprises, Inc., got the call from the Minnesota Department of Health at about noon on October 7, 1994. The Health Department reported that it had found a statistical link between Schwan's ice cream and confirmed cases of salmonella. Thousands of people in at least 39 U.S. states became ill with salmonella after eating tainted Schwan's ice cream, potentially setting the company up for a decade's worth of litigation. Instead, in a little more than a year after the outbreak, the vast majority of claims had been handled outside the legal system through direct settlements or as part of a class action in Minneapolis.[56]

Schwan's knew that its image of the smiling man in the sunshine-yellow Schwan's truck (with a Swan on the side) busily hand-delivering ice cream to grateful consumers was one of its major assets. Before the company was sure of the Health Department's findings, it halted sales and production, shut down, and invited the state health department, the Department of Agriculture, and the U.S. Food and Drug Administration into the plant to investigate. It also notified all its sales offices nationwide. Also, within the first 24 hours of the crisis, the company set up a hotline to answer consumer questions, contacted employees and managers to staff the hotline, prepared for a product recall, and began working with its insurer.[57]

By placing consumer safety as its number one priority, Schwan's was able to resolve the crisis much more quickly than ever would have been possible without a carefully designed crisis management plan. Whether by coincidence or preparedness, the manager of public affairs and the company's general counsel had completed a review and rewriting of the company's crisis management manual just two months before the outbreak. One vital component of the plan was a crisis management team, which went to work immediately when the news came. The crisis management team quickly set up a process for handling consumers who had been affected. The team, working with its insurance company, quickly helped customers get medical treatment and get their bills paid. Settlements to customers who suffered from salmonella symptoms included financial damages, medical expenses, and other costs, such as reimbursement for workdays missed.[58]

How did the ice cream get contaminated with salmonella? After a month's investigation that kept the Marshall, Minnesota, plant closed, it was determined that the ice cream mix supplied by a few vendors was the culprit. The mix of cream, sugar, and milk had been shipped in a tanker truck that had previously held raw, unpasteurized eggs that had the bacteria. Schwan's quietly sought and received legal damages from the suppliers but stayed focused on its customers throughout the crisis.

What did Schwan's learn from this crisis? Previously, Schwan's did not repasteurize its ice cream mix once the mix arrived at the Marshall plant. Within a few weeks of the outbreak, however, the company had broken ground to build its own repasteurization plant. The company also leased a dedicated fleet of tanker trucks to deliver the ice cream mix from the suppliers to the plant, set up a system for testing each shipment, and delayed shipping the final product until the test results were known. In summary, Schwan's planning, quick response, and customer-oriented strategy combined to retain customer loyalty and minimize the company's legal exposure.[59] It was a case of good crisis management.

Summary

Issues management and crisis management are two key approaches by which companies may plan for the turbulent stakeholder environment. Both these approaches are frequently found housed in a company's department of public affairs. Issues management is a process by which an organization identifies issues in the stakeholder environment, analyzes and prioritizes those issues in terms of their relevance to the organization, plans responses to the issues, and then evaluates and monitors the results. There are two approaches to issues management: the conventional approach and the strategic management approach. Issues management requires a knowledge of the changing mix of issues, the issues management process, the issues development process, and how companies might implement issues management in practice. Issues management serves as a bridge to crisis management.

Crisis management, like issues management, is not a panacea for organizations. In spite of well-intended efforts by management, not all crises will be resolved in the company's favour. Nevertheless, being prepared for the inevitable makes sense, especially in today's world of instantaneous global communications and obsessive media coverage. Whether we are thinking about the long term, the intermediate term, or the short term, managers

need to be prepared to handle crises. A crisis has a number of different stages, and managing crises requires a number of key steps in the process. These steps include identifying areas of vulnerability, developing a plan for dealing with threats, forming crisis teams, using crisis drills, and learning from experience. Crisis communications is critical for successful crisis management. When used in tandem, issues and crisis management can help managers fulfill their economic, legal, ethical, and philanthropic responsibilities to stakeholders.

Key Terms

acute crisis stage (page 147)

chronic crisis stage (page 147)

conventional approach to issues management (page 133)

crisis (page 145)

crisis communications (page 152)

crisis management (page 132)

crisis resolution stage (page 147)

crisis teams (page 150)

emerging issue (page 135)

issue (page 135)

issues development process (page 141)

issues management (page 132)

probability-impact matrix (page 139)

prodromal crisis stage (page 147)

strategic management approach to issues management (page 133)

ten steps of crisis communication (page 152)

Discussion Questions

1. Which of the major stages in the issues management process do you think is the most important? Why?

2. Identify one example, other than those listed in Figure 5–3 (page 138), of each of the leading force categories: events, authorities/advocates, literature, organizations, and political jurisdictions.

3. Identify a crisis that has occurred in your life or in the life of someone you know, and briefly explain it

in terms of the four crisis stages: prodromal, acute, chronic, and resolution.

4. Do research on the impacts on business organizations of the attacks on the World Trade Center in New York. What have been successful and unsuccessful examples of crisis management that have come out of this research? Is terrorism a likely crisis for which business may prepare?

Endnotes

1. Liam Fahey, "Issues Management: Two Approaches," *Strategic Planning Management* (November 1986), 81, 85–96.

2. *Ibid.*, 81.

3. *Ibid.*, 86.

4. H. Igor Ansoff, "Strategic Issue Management," *Strategic Management Journal* (Vol. I, 1980), 131–148.

5. William R. King, "Strategic Issue Management," in William R. King and David I. Cleland (eds.), *Strategic*

Planning and Management Handbook (New York: Van Nostrand Reinhold, 1987), 252–264.

6. Joseph F. Coates, Vary T. Coates, Jennifer Jarratt, and Lisa Heinz, *Issues Management* (Mt. Airy, MD: Lomond Publications, 1986), 19–20.

7. John Mahon, "Issues Management: The Issue of Definition," *Strategic Planning Management* (November 1986), 81–82. For further discussion on what constitutes an issue, see Steven L. Wartick and John F. Mahon,

"Toward a Substantive Definition of the Corporate Issue Construct," *Business & Society* (Vol. 33, No. 3, December 1994), 293–311.

8. Coates et al., 18.

9. *Ibid.*, 32.

10. T. Graham Molitor, "How to Anticipate Public Policy Changes," *SAM Advanced Management Journal* (Vol. 42, No. 3, Summer 1977), 4.

11. Aimee Welch, "The New Futurists," *Insight* (January 15–22, 2001), 10–13.

12. King, 259.

13. James K. Brown, *This Business of Issues: Coping with the Company's Environment* (New York: The Conference Board, 1979), 45.

14. *Ibid.*, 33.

15. King, 257.

16. Coates et al., 46.

17. I. C. MacMillan and P. E. Jones, "Designing Organizations to Compete," *Journal of Business Strategy* (Vol. 4, No. 4, Spring 1984), 13.

18. Roy Wernham, "Implementation: The Things That Matter," in King and Cleland, 453.

19. Earl C. Gottschalk, Jr., "Firms Hiring New Type of Manager to Study Issues, Emerging Troubles," *The Wall Street Journal* (June 10, 1982), 3.

20. Mahon, 81–82.

21. Thomas G. Marx, "Integrating Public Affairs and Strategic Planning," *California Management Review* (Fall 1986), 145.

22. Barbara Bigelow, Liam Fahey, and John Mahon, "A Typology of Issue Evolution," *Business & Society* (Spring 1993), 28. For another useful perspective, see John F. Mahon and Sandra A. Waddock, "Strategic Issues Management: An Integration of Issue Life Cycle Perspectives," *Business & Society* (Spring 1992), 19–32. Also see Steven L. Wartick and Robert E. Rude, "Issues Management: Fad or Function," *California Management Review* (Fall 1986), 134–140.

23. Public Affairs Council, "Public Affairs: Its Origins, Its Present, and Its Trends," http://www.pac.org/whatis/index.htm; 2001.

24. Gottschalk, 21.

25. Kate Miller, "Issues Management: The Link Between Organization Reality and Public Perception," *Public Relations Quarterly* (Vol. 44, No. 2, Summer 1999), 5–11.

26. Steve Maich, *Financial Post* (October 8, 2003), http://www.nationalpost.com/financialpost/index.html.

27. Canadian Press, "Cattle Ban Not likely to Be Lifted," *Globe & Mail* (October 21, 2003), http://www.globeandmail.ca/.

28. Ian Mitroff, with Gus Anagnos, *Managing Crises Before They Happen: What Every Executive and Manager Needs to Know about Crisis Management* (New York: Amacom, 2001), Chapter 2.

29. Laurence Barton, *Crisis in Organizations: Managing and Communicating in the Heat of Chaos* (Cincinnati: South-Western Publishing Co., 1993), 2.

30. Christine M. Pearson and Judith Clair, "Reframing Crisis Management," *Academy of Management Review* (Vol. 23, No. 1, 1998), 60.

31. "How Companies Are Learning to Prepare for the Worst," *Business Week* (December 23, 1985), 74.

32. Steven Fink, *Crisis Management: Planning for the Inevitable* (New York: Amacom, 1986).

33. *Ibid.*, 68. For further discussion of types of crises, see Ian Mitroff, "Crisis Management and Environmentalism: A Natural Fit," *California Management Review* (Winter 1994), 101–113.

34. Pearson and Clair, 60.

35. Mitroff and Anagnos, 2001, Chapter 3.

36. Fink, 69. Also see Sharon H. Garrison, *The Financial Impact of Corporate Events on Corporate Stakeholders* (New York: Quorem Books, 1990); and Joe Marconi, *Crisis Marketing: When Bad Things Happen to Good Companies* (Chicago: NTC Business Books, 1997). See also Carol Hymowitz, "Companies Experience Major Power Shifts as Crises Continue," *The Wall Street Journal* (October 9, 2001), B1; and Sue Shellenbarger, "Some Bosses, Fumbling in Crisis, Have Bruised Loyalty of Employees," *The Wall Street Journal* (October 17, 2001), B1.

37. Fink, 20.

38. Mitroff and Anagnos, 2001.

39. "How Companies Are Learning to Prepare for the Worst," *Business Week* (December 23, 1985), 74–75.

40. Fink, 70.

41. "How Companies Are Learning to Prepare for the Worst," *Business Week* (December 23, 1985), 76.

42. *Ibid.*

43. *Ibid.*

44. Richard J. Mahoney, "The Anatomy of a Public Policy Crisis," *The CEO Series*, Center for the Study of American Business (May 1996), 7.

45. *Ibid.*

46. Greg Jaffe, "How Florida Crash Overwhelmed ValuJet's Skillful Crisis Control," *The Wall Street Journal* (June 5, 1996), S1.

47. Melissa Master, "Keyword: Crisis," *Across the Board* (September 1998), 62.

48. Ian Mitroff, Paul Shrivastava, and Firdaus Udwadia, "Effective Crisis Management," *Academy of Management Executive* (November 1987), 285.

49. Norman R. Augustine, "Managing the Crisis You Tried to Prevent," *Harvard Business Review* (November–December 1995), 147–158.

50. Christine M. Pearson and Ian I. Mitroff, "From Crisis Prone to Crisis Prepared: A Framework for Crisis Management," *Academy of Management Executive* (Vol. VII, No. 1, February 1993), 58–59. Also see Ian Mitroff, Christine M. Pearson, and L. Katherine Harrington, *The Essential Guide to Managing Corporate Crises* (New York: Oxford University Press, 1996).

51. Robert Goff, "Coming Clean," *Forbes* (May 17, 1999), 156–160.

52. *Ibid.*

53. Johnathan L. Bernstein, "The Ten Steps of Crisis Communications" (June 4, 2001), http://www.crisis navigator.org.

54. Richard Wm. Brundage, "Crisis Management— An Outline for Survival" (June 4, 2001), http://www. crisisnavigator.org.

55. Mitroff and Anagnos, 2001.

56. Bruce Rubenstein, "Salmonella-Tainted Ice Cream: How Schwan's Recovered," Corporate Legal Times Corp., Untitled Web page, June 1998.

57. *Ibid.*

58. *Ibid.*

59. *Ibid.*

Part Three

Business Ethics and Management

Chapter 6

Business Ethics Fundamentals

Chapter Objectives

After studying this chapter, you should be able to:

1 Describe how the public regards business ethics.

2 Define business ethics and appreciate the complexities of making ethical judgments.

3 Explain the conventional approach to business ethics.

4 Analyze economic, legal, and ethical aspects by using a Venn model.

5 Enumerate and discuss the four important ethics questions.

6 Identify and explain three models of management ethics.

7 Describe Kohlberg's three levels of developing moral judgment.

8 Identify and discuss the elements of moral judgment.

In regard to public interest in business ethics during the modern business period—approximately the past 30 to 40 years—two conclusions may be drawn. First, interest in business ethics has heightened during each of the past four decades. Second, the interest in business ethics seems to have been spurred by major headline-grabbing scandals, particularly within the last several years. Certainly, there has been an ebb and flow of interest on society's part, but lately this interest has grown to a preoccupation or, as some might say, an obsession. Both the media's reporting of business "behaving badly" and the fact that the scope and number of business scandals appear to have proliferated in recent years contribute to a perception of a deterioration in the state of North American business ethics.

During the first decade of the 2000s, business ethics scandals continue in the headlines. Archer Daniels Midland pleaded guilty to a price-fixing conspiracy that cost consumers millions in higher prices for soft drinks and detergents. ADM agreed to pay a US$100 million fine. Royal Dutch Shell scrapped its plans for sinking a North Sea oil rig that environmentalists said was contaminated. They were later accused of colluding with the Nigerian government in the oppression of the Ogoni people and for failing to speak out against the execution of one of their leaders. In 2001, Bridgestone/Firestone and the Ford Motor Company apologized to consumers for a pattern of deadly tire failures, while blaming each other for the debacle. Almost every year, it seems, some major corporation is enveloped in an ethics scandal that generates a new tremor of public distrust of large corporations.[1]

Corruption and scandal have rocked countless corporate boardrooms in recent years. Among those companies devastated by scandal was telecom giant WorldCom Inc. with a US$11 billion fraud, one of the biggest in corporate history. Leading drug maker Pfizer Inc. was forced to pay US$49 million to settle charges of overcharging the U.S. government health insurance program for its cholesterol drug Lipitor. The famous auctioneer Sotheby's was fined US$30 million over its seven-year price-fixing conspiracy with rival Christie's. Video game maker Nintendo was fined US$147 million for engaging in price collusion with its distributors over a seven-year period.

As of October 2003, 11 former Enron executives were facing criminal charges. In addition, several of North America's most important financial institutions, including Merrill Lynch and J. P. Morgan, admitted to helping enable the Enron fraud. Three Merrill Lynch bankers were indicted, while Citi and J. P. Morgan settled their cases with the U.S. government, along with an agreement to change the way they do business.[2] Arthur Andersen, Tyco, Global Crossing, and Xerox were other companies tainted by scandal. Some of the largest accounting scandals in recent years occurred at HealthSouth Corp., Xerox Corp., and Waste Management Inc. In these cases, the auditors allegedly were aware of the potential frauds but failed to thoroughly investigate. Consequently, numerous media reports have raised the question of whether increased demands should be placed on public accounting firms to detect and report fraudulent activities while conducting their audits.[3]

Corruption and scandal have not been the sole domain of big business. In fact, the media themselves have had their share of scandal. For example, in 2003, the executive and managing editors of *The New York Times* were forced to resign following the revelation that one of the newspaper's reporters, Jayson Blair, had committed journalistic fraud by fabricating parts of his reports and plagiarizing material for many of his stories. An earlier case of fraudulent reporting occurred in 1993, when the NBC news program *Dateline NBC* aired a supposed exposé of exploding gas tanks in GM trucks. NBC officials later admitted that toy rocket engines had been used as "igniters" to ensure that the staged crashes resulted in explosions for TV purposes. NBC, a unit of General Electric Co., eventually apologized for the misrepresentation and agreed to reimburse GM the roughly US$2 million it had incurred investigating the NBC report. In exchange, GM agreed to drop its defamation suit against NBC.[4]

We continue to read reports of individuals caught up in webs of lies and deceit. A particular case of interest was the contaminated water supply in Walkerton, Ontario, in May 2000. Seven people died and 2300 others became severely ill after the town's water system was besieged with E. coli bacteria. Upon investigation of the source for this tragedy, it was uncovered that individual incompetence and fraudulent behaviour played a central role. Stan and Frank Koebel, who worked for the Walkerton Public Utilities, failed to maintain the water system in a satisfactory manner and consistently reported false chlorination levels, leading to widespread contamination.

Notoriety gained through unethical behaviour can be observed in other press reports in recent years. For example, in 2001 one of Canada's most prestigious law schools was shaken with the revelation that law students had lied to prospective employers about the academic grades achieved in their first year of law school. An inquiry launched by the Dean of the University of Toronto's Law School indicated that approximately 30 of the 170 students were guilty of this offence. All those accused readily admitted that they had lied to prospective employers about grades earned for the purpose of gaining a potential advantage in securing employment. The shock of this offence is reflected in the words of the Dean's legal advisor David Scott: "They are enrolled in a program whose underpinnings depend on scrupulous honesty since, as lawyers, they will be expected to uphold the integrity of our system of justice by their own personal conduct. Honesty, in this context, involves acceptance of responsibility for one's acts."[5] This Canadian story, while frightening in its implications, has been vastly overshadowed in more recent times by other instances of individual deceit and scandal perpetrated by higher-profile individuals.

More recently, former Tyco CEO Dennis Kozlowski and former CFO Mark Swartz faced charges of allegedly looting the company. Individuals who faced charges associated with the WorldCom scandal, the largest alleged fraud in history, included former CEO Bernard Ebbers (an Edmonton native) and former CFO Scott Sullivan. In 2004, Toronto native Daniel Duic agreed to pay back $1.9 million in ill-gotten gains for his role in a large insider trading scandal stemming from his involvement with a friend and former RBC Dominion Securities executive, Andrew Rankin.

In 2003, the internationally renowned celebrity and business icon Martha Stewart, president of Martha Stewart Living Omnimedia, was indicted on criminal charges of securities fraud relating to the sale of her shares in a biotechnology firm, ImClone Systems. Stewart was accused of obtaining insider information regarding ImClone shares through a close friend that had managed the company. While this story gained huge press attention because of the celebrity status of its main actor, many "non-celebrity" businesspeople across corporate North America have gained celebrity status through either questionable or downright corrupt business activity.

During the last decade or so, many of the ethical scandals found in business involved massive charges of racial discrimination and sexual harassment. Among the well-known companies that experienced such allegations were Home Depot, Mitsubishi, Coca-Cola, and Texaco. The Texaco case involved a US$196 million settlement in a class-action race discrimination lawsuit brought by employees fighting for equal pay and a chance for promotions. Bari-Ellen Roberts, lead plaintiff in the case against the oil company, revealed a dark side of corporate America in her 1998 book, *Roberts vs. Texaco: A True Story of Race and Corporate America.*[6]

Another industry that attracted widespread criticism in the late 1990s was the tobacco industry. In the U.S., the Food and Drug Administration's (FDA's) crackdown on tobacco, along with the U.S. Congress's 1998 attempts to draft and pass landmark tobacco legislation, caused tobacco executives to begin thinking in settlement terms that would have been unthinkable in years past.[7] This issue continues today.

Sadly enough, business ethics scandals gained momentum in the closing moments of the twentieth century and continue to thrive in the new century. Perhaps this has been a major reason why ethics, morals, and values have come to characterize the general public debate concerning business in North America. Examples of this elevated discussion include the 2003 *Forbes* story "Criminalizing Capitalism"[8] and the 2003 article in *Newsweek* entitled "Capitalism Must Develop More of a Conscience."[9] Other recent articles that reflect a similar distress over corporate ethics include the *Maclean's* article "Crooks in the Boardroom"[10] and a *Newsweek* piece entitled "Corruption: A Spectator Sport."[11]

Recent public opinion polls reveal widespread concern about ethics in society and the workplace. According to a poll by *Maclean's* magazine in partnership with Global Television, Canadians have little faith in the ethics of corporate boardrooms across Canada. Forty-five percent of the respondents indicated that their view of the business community had become more negative within the past year. Respondents also felt that the current cases of corporate wrongdoing are reflective of a widespread problem within the business community. Finally, 43 percent of the respondents felt that the ethics and morality of business leaders are among the highest concerns regarding business (overshadowing concerns regarding the health of the economy).[12]

A recent study conducted in the U.S. among human resource practitioners suggests that ethical behaviour is not rewarded in the workplace. The 2003 study conducted by the Society for Human Resource Management and the Ethics Resource Center discovered the following:

- Twenty-four percent of the respondents felt pressured to compromise ethics standards (up from 13 percent in a similar poll in 1997).
- Major causes of ethics violations included the need to follow a boss's orders, meeting overly aggressive business objectives, and helping an organization survive.
- Misconduct most often cited included falsely reporting number of hours worked, employees lying to supervisors, and managers lying to employees, customers, vendors, and the general public.[13]

It appears that North American society is clamouring for a renewed emphasis on values, morals, and ethics and that the business ethics debate of this period is but a subset of this larger societal concern. Whether the business community will be able to respond and ratchet its reputation to a new plateau remains to be seen. One thing is sure: There is a growing interest in business ethics, and the proliferation of business ethics courses in colleges and universities, along with the revitalized interest on the part of the business community, paints an encouraging picture for the "ethics industry" of the future.

To gain an appreciation of the kinds of issues that are important under the rubric of business ethics, Figure 6–1 presents an inventory of business ethics issues. Here we see business ethics issues categorized on the basis of stakeholder relationships. Against this backdrop, we plan to discuss business ethics, specifically, in this chapter and the next three. In this chapter, we will introduce fundamental business ethics background

FIGURE 6–1

Inventory of Ethical Issues in Business

This checklist is designed to stimulate thought and discussion on important ethical concerns in your company and the larger business community.

For each of the following issues indicate whether ethical problems are:
5 = Very serious; 4 = Serious; 3 = Not very serious; 2 = Not a problem; 1 = No opinion.

Column I = In the business world in general   **Column II** = In your company

Employee–Employer Relations

1. Work ethic—giving a full day's work for a full day's pay
2. Petty theft (i.e., supplies, telephone, photocopying, etc.)
3. Cheating on expense accounts
4. Employee acceptance of gifts or favours from vendors
5. Distortion or falsification of internal reports
6 Cheating or overreaching on benefits (sick days, insurance, etc.)

Employer–Employee Relations

7. Sexual or racial discrimination in hiring, promotion, or pay
8. Sexual harassment
9. Invasions of employee privacy
10. Unsafe or unhealthy working conditions
11. Discouragement of internal criticism re: unfair, illegal, or improper activities
12. Unfair or insensitive handling of assignment changes or major reorganizations
13. Improper dealing with persons with disabilities
14. Failure to give honest, fair, and timely work appraisals
15. Recruiting for employee's replacement without telling employee being replaced
16. Using strategies or technical justifications to deny employees earned benefits
17. Dealing peremptorily or unfairly with employee complaints
18. Misleading employees about the likelihood of layoffs, terminations, or job changes
19. Inadequate training or supervision to ensure employee's success
20. Inadequate participation by qualified staff in major policy decisions
21. Unfair demands on or expectations of paid staff
22. Inadequate compensation
23. Inadequate recognition, appreciation, or other psychic rewards to staff
24. Inappropriate blame-shifting or credit-taking to protect or advance personal careers
25. Unhealthy competition among employees about "turf," assignments, budget, etc.
26. Inadequate communication among departments and divisions for the wrong reasons
27. Inadequate mutual support and teamwork; individuals focus primarily on their own narrow jobs

Company–Customer Relations

28. Unfair product pricing
29. Deceptive marketing/advertising
30. Unsafe or unhealthy products
31. Unfair and/or legalistic handling of customer complaints
32. Discourtesy or arrogance toward customers

(continued)

FIGURE 6-1

Inventory of Ethical Issues in Business *(continued)*

Company—Shareholder Relations

_____ _____ 33. Excessive compensation for top management
_____ _____ 34. Self-protective management policies (golden parachutes, poison pills, etc.)
_____ _____ 35. Mismanagement of corporate assets or opportunities
_____ _____ 36. Public reports and/or financial statements that distort actual performance

Company—Community/Public Interest

_____ _____ 37. Injury to the environment
_____ _____ 38. Undue influence on the political process through lobbying, etc.
_____ _____ 39. Payoffs, "grease," or bribes to union or public officials
_____ _____ 40. Payoffs, "grease," or bribes in foreign countries
_____ _____ 41. Doing business in countries with inhumane policies
_____ _____ 42. Inadequate corporate philanthropy
_____ _____ 43. Inadequate community involvement

Source: Reprinted with permission. Copyright © Josephson Institute of Ethics, *Ethics: Easier Said Than Done*, Vol. 2, No. 1, 1989.

and concepts. In Chapter 7, we will consider personal and organizational ethics. Chapter 8 addresses newly emerging technology and business ethics. Finally, in Chapter 9 our attention will turn to the international sphere as we discuss ethical issues in the global arena.

The Public's Opinion of Business Ethics

The public's view of business ethics has never been very high. Anecdotal evidence suggests that many citizens see business ethics as essentially a contradiction in terms, an oxymoron, and think that there is only a fine line between a business executive and a crook. It is useful for our discussion here, however, to look at the most recent results of the Gallup Poll, which surveys the public's assessment of the ethics of major groups in our society. This poll has been repeated annually for a number of years.

The Gallup Poll Ranks Business Ethics

Perhaps the most reliable expression of public attitudes on business ethics may be found in the Gallup Poll, which regularly surveys public opinion of social and political issues. Gallup periodically quizzes the public on its perceptions about the ethics of business executives and other professionals. Survey data from the fall 2002 Gallup Poll on Honesty/Ethics in the Professions, the latest data available as of this writing, reveals that the honesty and ethics of business executives are not thought to be "high" among many respondents. Over the past decade, this percentage has fluctuated between a low of 17 percent in 1996 and a high of 22 percent in 2000. Specific groups of businesspeople rank even lower than the general category of business executives. Among those specific groups are real estate agents, stockbrokers, advertising practitioners, insurance salespeople, and car salespeople. In the 2002 poll, nurses again were among the most highly rated profession, while telemarketers and car salesmen were at the bottom of the honesty and ethics scale.

It is useful to compare the public's perception of business executives' ethics with its perception of the ethics of other professionals. Such a comparison finds that business ranks about in the middle of the pack of those considered. Although business executives do not achieve the high rankings of such professionals as pharmacists, clergy, doctors, professors, and dentists, they do rank higher than politicians![14]

It is difficult to pinpoint the exact public sentiment on business ethics today. In general, however, it is safe to conclude that the public thinks business ethics is at least somewhat suspect and that it would like to see improvements. There is the opinion that business is only one of the major institutions that have questionable ethics today; however, business is the focus of our attention here.

If we were to make judgments about the current state of business ethics by reading the daily newspapers or news magazines or watching investigative TV programs such as *The Fifth Estate*, *60 Minutes*, or *20/20*, we might quickly reach the conclusion that business is not highly regarded and that behind every business door an evil-minded individual is lurking. To help us understand the public sentiment, it is useful to ask three intriguing questions: (1) Has business ethics really deteriorated? (2) Are the media reporting ethical problems more frequently and vigorously? (3) Is it actually society that is changing so that once-accepted practices are now considered unacceptable by the public?

Has Business Ethics Really Deteriorated?

Unfortunately, there is no scientific way to determine whether or not business ethics has really deteriorated. Max Ways's description of a statistical analysis (modern society's favourite kind of investigation) aimed at answering the question "How widespread is corporate misconduct?" is enlightening. He says that to describe such a project would demonstrate its impossibility. He argues that the researcher would have to count the transgressions publicly exposed in a certain period of time. Then the total number of known misdeeds would have to be correlated with the trillions and trillions of business transactions that occur daily. He concludes:

If we assume (recklessly) that a believable estimate of total transactions could be made, then the sum of the publicly known malfeasances almost certainly would be a minute fraction of the whole. At this point the investigator would have to abandon the conclusion that the incidence of business misconduct is so low as to be insignificant.[15]

In fact, no such study has ever been attempted. Public opinion polls might be our best way to gather data about the current state of business ethics, but such polls are hardly definitive. The polls do not indicate that business ethics has deteriorated significantly in recent years, but we must consider some other factors that affect the public's opinions, such as media reporting and society's expectations of business's ethics.

Search the web

Ethics Practitioners' Association of Canada

What is going on in the world of business ethics? One way to find out is to check out what the Ethics Practitioners' Association of Canada (EPAC) is doing. The EPAC Web site is located at **http://www.epac-apec.ca/**. The EPAC is the professional association of managers of corporate ethics and compliance programs. The EPAC Web site has a wealth of information about what the professional practitioners of business ethics are doing. You may find out about their mission, vision, and values. It also has links to other useful business ethics Web sites.

Are the Media Reporting Ethics More Vigorously?

There is no doubt that the media are reporting ethical problems more frequently and fervently. Spurred on by the Watergate events in 1974 and the post-Watergate moral climate, the media have found business ethics and, indeed, ethics questions among all institutions to be subjects of growing and sustaining interest during the past three decades.

Of particular interest in recent years has been the in-depth investigative reporting of business ethics on such TV shows as *The Fifth Estate*, *Marketplace*, *60 Minutes*, *20/20*, *Dateline NBC*, and *Primetime Live*. Such investigations keep business ethics in the public eye and make it difficult to assess whether public opinion polls are reflecting the actual business ethics of the day or simply the reactions to the latest scandals covered on a weekly basis. In addition, the Internet contributes to a wealth of insights on and scrutiny of the ethics of business. For example, *Straight Goods* (http://www.straightgoods.com/) is a Canadian-based Internet magazine that offers a critical look at corporate behaviour and misbehaviour.

Is It Society That Is Actually Changing?

We would definitely make this argument here, as we did in Chapter 1. Many business managers subscribe to this belief. W. Michael Blumenthal, former U.S. Secretary of the Treasury and chief executive officer of the Bendix Corporation, has been one of the leading advocates of this view. He argued:

> *It seems to me that the root causes of the questionable and illegal corporate activities that have come to light recently ... can be traced to the sweeping changes that have taken place in our society and throughout the world and to the unwillingness of many in business to adjust to these changes.*[16]

He goes on to say, "People in business have not suddenly become immoral. What has changed are the contexts in which corporate decisions are made, the demands that are being made on business, and the nature of what is considered proper corporate conduct."[17]

Although it would be difficult to prove Blumenthal's thesis, it is an intuitively attractive one. You do not have to make a lengthy investigation of some of today's business practices to realize that a good number of what are now called unethical practices were at one time considered acceptable. Or, it may be that the practices never really were acceptable to the public but that, because they were not known, they were tolerated, thus causing no moral dilemma in the mind of the public. For the first time, in 2002, Canada's prime minister made public recognition of the worrisome effects that business scandals and corruption could have on both the Canadian and U.S. economies.

Figure 6–2 illustrates how the magnitude of the ethics problem may be more detectable today than it once was, as a result of the public's expectations of business's ethical behaviour rising more rapidly than actual business ethics. Note in the figure that actual business ethics is assumed to be improving but not at the same pace as public expectations are rising. The magnitude of the current ethics problem, therefore, is seen here partially to be a function of rapidly rising societal expectations about business behaviour.

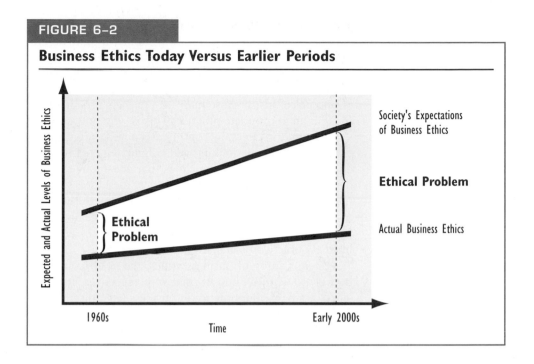

FIGURE 6-2

Business Ethics Today Versus Earlier Periods

Business Ethics: What Does It Really Mean?

In Chapter 2, we discussed the ethical responsibilities of business in an introductory way. We contrasted ethics with economics, law, and philanthropy. To be sure, we all have a general idea of what business ethics means, but here we would like to probe the topic more deeply. To understand business ethics, it is useful to comment on the relationship between ethics and morality.

Ethics is the discipline that deals with what is good and bad and with moral duty and obligation. Ethics can also be regarded as a set of moral principles or values. Morality is a doctrine or system of moral conduct. Moral conduct refers to that which relates to principles of right and wrong in behaviour. For the most part, then, we can think of ethics and morality as being so similar to one another that we may use the terms interchangeably to refer to the study of fairness, justice, and right and wrong behaviour in business.

Business ethics, therefore, is concerned with good and bad or right and wrong behaviour and practices that take place within a business context. Concepts of right and wrong are increasingly being interpreted today to include the more difficult and subtle questions of fairness, justice, and equity.

Two key branches of moral philosophy, or ethics, are descriptive ethics and normative ethics. It is important to distinguish between the two because they each take a different perspective. **Descriptive ethics** is concerned with describing, characterizing, and studying the morality of a people, a culture, or a society. It also compares and contrasts different moral codes, systems, practices, beliefs, and values.[18] In descriptive business ethics, therefore, our focus is on learning what is occurring in the realm of behaviour, actions, decisions, policies, and practices of business firms, managers, or, perhaps, specific industries. The public opinion polls cited earlier give us glimpses of descriptive ethics—what people believe to be going on based on their perceptions and understandings. Descriptive ethics focuses on "what is" the prevailing set of ethical standards in the business community, specific organizations, or on the part of specific managers. A real danger in limiting our attention to descriptive ethics is that some people may adopt the view that "if everyone is doing it," it must be acceptable. For example, if a survey reveals that 70 percent of employees are padding their expense accounts, this describes what is taking place but it does not describe what *should* be taking place. Just because many are participating in this questionable activity doesn't make it an appropriate practice. This is why normative ethics is important.

Normative ethics, by contrast, is concerned with supplying and justifying a coherent moral system of thinking and judging. Normative ethics seeks to uncover, develop, and justify basic moral principles that are intended to guide behaviour, actions, and decisions.[19] Normative business ethics, therefore, seeks to propose some principle or principles for distinguishing ethical from unethical in the business context. It deals more with "what ought to be" or "what ought not to be" in terms of business practices. Normative ethics is concerned with establishing norms or standards by which business practices might be guided or judged.

In our study of business ethics, we need to be ever mindful of this distinction between descriptive and normative perspectives. It is tempting to observe the prevalence of a particular practice in business (e.g., discrimination or deceptive advertising) and conclude that because so many are doing it (descriptive ethics), it must be acceptable behaviour. Normative ethics would insist that a practice be justified on the basis of some ethical principle, argument, or rationale before being considered acceptable. Normative ethics demands a more meaningful moral anchor than just "everyone is doing it." Normative ethics is our primary frame of reference in this discussion, though we will frequently compare "what ought to be" with "what is (going on in the real world)."

In this chapter and continuing into Chapter 7, we will introduce three major approaches to thinking about business ethics:

1. Conventional approach (Chapter 6)
2. Principles approach (Chapter 7)
3. Ethical tests approach (Chapter 7)

We will discuss the conventional approach to business ethics in this chapter and the other two approaches in Chapter 7.

The Conventional Approach to Business Ethics

The **conventional approach to business ethics** is essentially an approach whereby we compare a decision or practice with prevailing norms of acceptability. We call it the conventional approach because it is believed that this is the way that conventional or general society thinks. The major challenge of this approach is answering the questions "Whose norms do we use?" in making the judgment, and "What norms are prevailing?" This approach may be depicted by highlighting the major variables to be compared with one another:

Decision or Practice ⟷ Prevailing Norms of Acceptability

There is considerable room for variability on both of these issues. With respect to whose norms are used as the basis for ethical judgments, the conventional approach would consider as legitimate those norms emanating from family, friends, religious beliefs, the local community, one's employer, law, the profession, and so on. In addition, one's conscience, or the individual, would be seen by many as a legitimate source of ethical norms.

Figure 6–3 illustrates some of the sources of norms that come to bear on the individual and that might be used in various circumstances, and over time, under the conventional approach. These sources compete in their influence on what constitutes the "prevailing norms of acceptability" for today.

In many circumstances, the conventional approach to ethics may be useful and applicable. What does a person do, however, if norms from one source conflict with norms from another source? Also, how can we be sure that societal norms are really appropriate or defensible? Our society's culture sends us many and often conflicting messages about what is appropriate behaviour. We get these messages from television, movies, music, and other sources in the culture. There is little doubt that media representations of what is acceptable behaviour have changed dramatically over the last two decades.

Another example of the conflicting messages people get today from society occurs in the realm of sexual harassment in the workplace. On the one hand, today's television, movies, advertisements, and music are replete with sexual innuendo and the treatment of women and men as sex objects. This would suggest that such behaviour is normal, acceptable, even desired. On the other hand, the law and the courts are stringently prohibiting sexual gestures or innuendo in the workplace. As we will see in a later chapter, it does not take much sexual innuendo to constitute a "hostile work environment" and a sex discrimination charge. In this example, we see a norm arising from culture and society clashing with a norm evolving from employment law and business ethics.

Ethics and the Law

We have made various references to ethics and the law. In Chapter 2, we said that ethical behaviour is typically thought to reside above behaviour required by the law. This

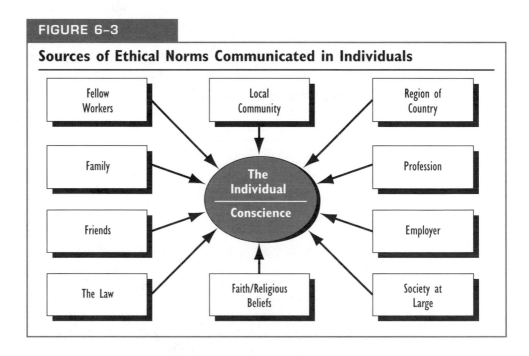

FIGURE 6-3

Sources of Ethical Norms Communicated in Individuals

Fellow Workers

Local Community

Region of Country

Family

Profession

The Individual

Conscience

Friends

Employer

The Law

Faith/Religious Beliefs

Society at Large

is the generally accepted view of ethics. We should make it clear, however, that in many respects the law and ethics overlap. To appreciate this, you need to recognize that the law embodies notions of ethics. That is, the law may be seen as a reflection of what society thinks are minimal standards of conduct and behaviour. Both law and ethics have to do with what is deemed appropriate or acceptable, but law reflects society's *codified* ethics. Therefore, if a person breaks a law or violates a regulation, she or he is also behaving unethically. In spite of this overlap, we continue to talk about desirable ethical behaviour as behaviour that extends beyond what is required by law. Viewed from the standpoint of minimums, we would certainly say that obedience to the law is generally regarded to be a minimum standard of behaviour.

In addition, we should make note of the fact that the law does not address all realms in which ethical questions might be raised. Thus, there are clear roles for both law and ethics to play. It should be noted that research on illegal corporate behaviour has been conducted for some time. Illegal corporate behaviour, of course, comprises business practices that are in direct defiance of law or public policy. Research has focused on two dominant questions: (1) Why do firms behave illegally (or what leads them to engage in illegal activities), and (2) what are the consequences of behaving illegally?[20] We will not deal with these studies of law-breaking in this discussion; however, we should view this body of studies and investigations as being closely aligned with our interest in business ethics.

Making Ethical Judgments

When a decision is made about what is ethical (right, just, fair) using the conventional approach, there is room for variability on several counts (see Figure 6–4). Three key elements compose such a decision. First, we observe the *decision, action,* or *practice* that has been committed. Second, we *compare the practice with prevailing norms of acceptability*—that is, society's or some other standard of what is acceptable or unacceptable. Third, *we must recognize that value judgments are being made* by someone as to what really occurred (the actual behaviour) and what the prevailing norms of acceptability really are. This means that two different people could look at the same behaviour, compare it with their concepts of what the prevailing norms are, and reach different conclusions as to whether the behaviour was ethical or not. This becomes

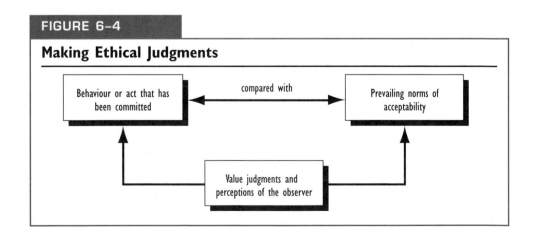

FIGURE 6–4

Making Ethical Judgments

Behaviour or act that has been committed   *compared with*   Prevailing norms of acceptability

Value judgments and perceptions of the observer

quite complex as perceptions of what is ethical inevitably lead to the difficult task of ranking different values against one another.

If we can put aside for a moment the fact that perceptual differences about an incident do exist, and the fact that we differ among ourselves because of our personal values and philosophies of right and wrong, we are still left with the problematic task of determining society's prevailing norms of acceptability of business behaviour. As a whole, members of society generally agree at a very high level of abstraction that certain behaviours are wrong. However, the consensus tends to disintegrate as we move from the general to specific situations.

Let us illustrate with a business example. We might all agree with the general dictum that "You should not steal someone else's property." At a high level of abstraction (as a general precept), we probably would have consensus on this. But as we look at specific situations, our consensus may tend to disappear. Is it acceptable to take home from work such things as pencils, pens, paper clips, paper, staplers, computer discs, adding machines, and calculators? Is it acceptable to use the company telephone for personal long-distance calls? Is it acceptable to use company gasoline for private use or to pad expense accounts? What if everyone else is doing it?

What is interesting in this example is that we are more likely to reach consensus in principle than in practice. Some people who would say these practices are not acceptable might privately engage in them. Furthermore, a person who would not think of shoplifting even the smallest item from a local store might take pencils and paper home from work on a regular basis. A comic strip depicting the "Born Loser" illustrates this point. In the first panel, the father admonishes his son in the following way: "You know how I feel about stealing. Now tomorrow I want you to return every one of those pencils to school." In the second panel, father says to son, "I'll bring you all the pencils you need from work." This is an example of the classic double standard, and it illustrates how actions may be perceived differently by the observer or the participant.

Thus, in the conventional approach to business ethics, determinations of what is ethical and what is not require judgments to be made on at least three counts:

1. What is the *true nature* of the practice, behaviour, or decision that occurred?
2. What are society's (or business's) *prevailing norms* of acceptability?
3. What *value judgments* are being made by someone about the practice or behaviour, and what are that person's *perceptions* of applicable norms?

The human factor in the situation thus introduces the problem of perception and values.

The conventional approach to business ethics can be valuable, because we all need to be aware of and sensitive to the total environment in which we exist. We need to be aware of how society regards ethical issues. It has limitations, however, and we need to be cognizant of these as well. The most serious danger is that of falling into an **ethical relativism** where we pick and choose which source of norms we wish to use based on what will justify our current actions or maximize our freedom. A recent comic strip is relevant. In a courtroom, while swearing in, the witness stated, "I swear to tell the truth ... *as I see it*."

In the next chapter, we will argue that a principles approach is needed to augment the conventional approach. The principles approach looks at general guides to ethical decision making that come from moral philosophy. We will also present the ethical tests approach, which is more of a practical approach, in the next chapter.

Ethics, Economics, and Law: A Venn Model

When we focus on ethics and ethical decision making, it is useful to consider the primary forces that come into tension while making ethical judgments. In Chapter 2, these were introduced as part of the four-part definition of corporate social responsibility, and they were depicted in the Pyramid of CSR. When we are discussing a firm's CSR, philanthropy definitely enters the discussion. This is because philanthropic initiatives are the primary way many companies display their CSR in the community—through good and charitable works. In ethical decision making, however, we tend to set aside philanthropic expectations and focus on ethical expectations and, especially, those forces that primarily come into tension with ethics—economics (the quest for profits) and law. Thus, in most decision-making situations, ethics, economics, and law become the central expectations that must be considered and balanced against each other in the quest to make wise decisions.

A firm's economic, legal, and ethical responsibilities can be depicted in a Venn diagram model illustrating how certain actions, decisions, or policies fulfill one, two, or three of these responsibility categories. Figure 6–5 presents this Venn diagram model, illustrating the overlapping potential of these responsibility categories.

In Area 1, where the decision, action, or practice fulfills all three responsibilities, the management prescription is to "go for it." That is, the action is profitable, in com-

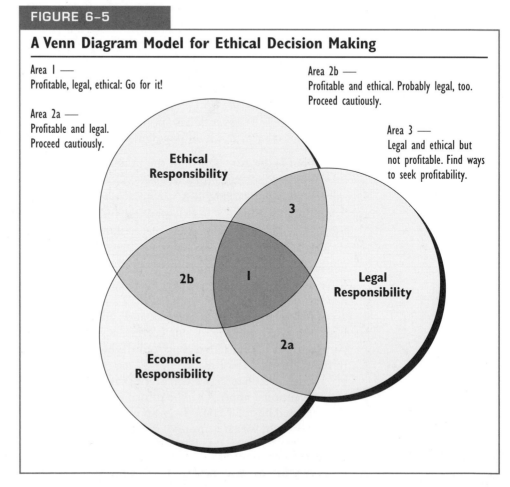

FIGURE 6-5

A Venn Diagram Model for Ethical Decision Making

Area 1 —
Profitable, legal, ethical: Go for it!

Area 2a —
Profitable and legal.
Proceed cautiously.

Area 2b —
Profitable and ethical. Probably legal, too.
Proceed cautiously.

Area 3 —
Legal and ethical but not profitable. Find ways to seek profitability.

Ethical Responsibility

Legal Responsibility

Economic Responsibility

3

2b

1

2a

pliance with the law, and represents ethical behaviour. In Area 2a, the action under consideration is profitable and legal, but its ethical status may be uncertain. The guideline here is to "proceed cautiously." In these kinds of situations, the ethics of the action needs to be carefully considered. In Area 2b, the action is profitable and ethical, but perhaps the law does not clearly address the issue or is ambiguous. If it is ethical, there is a good chance it is also legal, but the guideline again is to proceed cautiously. In Area 3, the action is legal and ethical but not profitable. Therefore, the strategy here would be to avoid this action or find ways to make it profitable. However, there may be a compelling case to take the action if it is legal and ethical and, thus, represents the right thing to do. Mark Schwartz has agreed that the four-part CSR model can appropriately be recast into a Venn model, especially for ethical analysis.[21]

By taking philanthropy out of the picture, the ethics Venn model serves as a useful template for thinking about the more immediate expectations that society has on business in a situation in which the ethical dimension plays an important role.

Four Important Ethics Questions

It is also useful to provide some additional "big picture" perspectives that could legitimately be asked of ethics, in general, or of business ethics, in particular. Philosophers have concepts and terminology that are more academic, but let us approach this broad perspective, as Otto Bremer has done,[22] by starting with four apparently simple but really different kinds of questions:

1. What is?
2. What ought to be?
3. How do we get from what is to what ought to be?
4. What is our motivation in all this?

These four questions capture the core of what ethics is all about. They force an examination of *what really is* (descriptive ethics) going on in a business situation, *what ought to be* (normative ethics), how we *close the gap* between what is and what ought to be (practical question), and what our *motivation* is for doing all this.

Before we discuss each question briefly, let us suggest that these four questions may be asked at five different levels: the level of the individual (the personal level), the level of the organization, the level of the industry or profession, the societal level, and the global or international level. By asking and then answering these questions, a greater understanding of a business ethics dilemma may be achieved.

What Is?

The "what is?" question forces us to face the reality of what is actually going on in an ethical sense in business or in a specific decision or practice. Ideally it is a factual, scientific, or descriptive question. Its purpose is to help us understand the reality of the ethical behaviour we find before us in the business environment. As we discussed earlier when we were describing the nature of making ethical judgments, it is not always simple to state exactly what the "real" situation is. This is because we are humans and thus make mistakes when we "sense" what is happening. Also, we are conditioned by our personal beliefs, values, and biases, and these factors affect what we see or sense. Or, we may perceive real conditions for what they are but fail to think in terms of alternatives or in terms of "what ought to be." Think of the difficulty you might have in attempting to describe "what is" with respect to business ethics at the personal,

Ethics In Practice

To Steal or Not to Steal, That Is the Question

A very good friend of mine worked for a large department store in a nearby large city. The store is known for its quality and name-brand products. A position with the inventory staff became available and my friend suggested that I apply. I did and later received the job.

As part of the inventory staff, I was placed in the back of the store, where inventory came to be checked in. The inventory staff members were left pretty much on their own to do their own jobs, because the supervisors were very busy with various other duties. The system of inventory was set up so that it was difficult for the store to know exactly what it had ordered before it was stocked. This was readily apparent to my colleagues. On several occasions, I noticed thefts by my co-workers and, unfortunately, thefts by my close friend. This activity didn't sit well with me, so I asked my

friend about it. He dismissed my concern in a joking fashion and even bragged about his great employee "five-finger discount." I did not want to be a part of this type of activity, and I had only worked for the store for a few days. I decided that staying too long in that environment would not be the best idea, and so I left the store without notice.

1. Is this an example of deteriorating ethics in society, or has this kind of behaviour gone on all along in business?
2. What would the conventional approach to business ethics say about this practice of employees helping themselves?
3. Was quitting the correct course of action, or should I have done something different?

Contributed by David W. Jeffrey

---

organizational, industry/professional, societal, or global levels. The questions then become:

- What are your personal ethics?
- What are your organization's ethics?
- What are the ethics of your industry or profession?
- What are society's ethics?
- What are global ethics?

What Ought to Be?

This second question is quite different from the first question. It is normative rather than descriptive. It is certainly not a scientific question. The "what ought to be?" question seldom gets answered directly, particularly in a managerial setting. Managers are used to identifying alternatives and choosing the best one, but seldom is this done with questions that entail moral content or the "rightness, fairness, or justice" of a decision. The "ought to be" question is often viewed in terms of what management *should* do (in an ethical sense) in a given situation. Examples of this question in a business setting might be:

- How *ought* we treat our aging employees whose productivity is declining?
- How safe *ought* we make this product, knowing full well we cannot pass all the costs on to the consumer?
- How clean an environment *should* we aim for?
- How *should* we treat long-time employees when the company is downsizing or moving the plant to a foreign country?

At a corporate planning seminar several years ago, the leader suggested that if you are the president of a large corporation the place to start planning is with a vision of society, not with where you want to be five or ten years into the future. What kind of world do you want to have? How does your industry or your firm fit into that world? An executive cannot just walk into the office one day and say, "I had a vision last night," and expect many adherents.[23] But this does not make the question or the vision invalid. It simply suggests that we must approach the "what ought to be?" questions at a more practical level. There are plenty of issues to which this question can be applied in the everyday life of a manager. Therefore, such lofty, visionary exercises are not necessary.

How Do We Get from What Is to What Ought to Be?

This third question represents the challenge of bridging the gap between where we are and where we ought to be with respect to ethical practices. Therefore, it represents an action dimension. We may discuss endlessly where we "ought" to be in terms of our own personal ethics or the ethics of our firm, of our industry, or of society. As we move further away from the individual level, we have less control or influence over the "ought to be" question.

When faced with these ideas as depicted by our "ought to be" questions, we may find that from a practical point of view we cannot achieve our ideals. This does not mean we should not have asked the question in the first place. Our "ought to be" questions become goals or objectives for our ethical practices. They form the normative core of business ethics. They become moral benchmarks that help us to measure progress.

In all managerial situations, we are faced with this challenge of balancing what we ought to do with what we must or can do. This is also the stage at which managerial decision making and strategy come into play. The first step in managerial problem solving is identifying the problem (what "is"). Next comes identifying where we want to be (the "ought" question). Then comes the managerial challenge of closing the gap. "Gap analysis" sets the stage for concrete business action.

What Is Our Motivation?

Pragmatic businesspeople do not like to dwell on this fourth question, which addresses the motivation for being ethical, because sometimes it reveals some manipulative or self-centred motive. At one level, is it perhaps not desirable to discuss motivation, because isn't it really actions that count? If someone makes a $100 contribution to a charitable cause, is it fair to ask whether the person did it (1) because she or he really believes in the cause (altruistic motivation) or (2) because she or he just wanted a tax deduction or wanted to "look" benevolent in the eyes of others (selfish motive)? Most of us would agree that it is better for a person to make a contribution rather than not make it, regardless of the motive.

Ideally, we would hope that people would be ethical because they intrinsically see that being ethical is a better way to live or manage. What kind of world (or organization) would most people prefer: one in which people behave ethically because they have selfish or instrumental reasons for doing so, or one in which they behave ethically because they really believe in what they are doing? We will accept the former, but the latter is more desirable. We will be better off in the long run if "right" managerial practices are motivated by the knowledge that there is inherent value in ethical behaviour.

This can be compared to the organizational situation in which managers are attempting to motivate their workers. If a manager is interested only in greater productivity and sees that being "concerned" about employees' welfare will achieve this goal, she or he had better be prepared for the fact that employees may see through the "game playing" and eventually rebel against the manager's effort. On the other hand, employees can see when management is genuinely concerned about their welfare, and they will be responsive to such well-motivated efforts. This is borne out in practice. You can examine two companies that on the surface appear to have identical human resource policies. In one company, the employees know and feel they are being manipulated; in the other company, there is confidence that management really does care.[24]

Although we would like to believe that managers are appropriately motivated in their quest for ethical business behaviour and that motivations are important, we must continue to understand and accept Andrew Stark's observation that we live in a "messy world of mixed motives." Therefore, managers do not typically have the luxury of making abstract distinctions between altruism and self-interest but must get on with the task of designing structures, systems, incentives, and processes that accommodate the "whole" employee, regardless of motivations.[25]

Three Models of Management Ethics

In attempting to understand the basic concepts of business ethics, it is useful to think in terms of key ethical models that might describe different types of management ethics found in the organizational world.[26] These models should provide some useful base points for discussion and comparison. The media have focused so much on immoral or unethical business behaviour that it is easy to forget or not think about the possibility of other ethical styles or types. For example, scant attention has been given to the distinction that may be made between those activities that are *immoral* and those that are *amoral*; similarly, little attention has been given to contrasting these two forms of behaviour with ethical or *moral* management.

Believing that there is value in developing descriptive models for purposes of clearer understanding, here we will describe, compare, and contrast three models or types of ethical management:

1. Immoral management
2. Moral management
3. Amoral management

A major goal is to develop a clearer understanding of the gamut of management approaches in which ethics or morality is a defining characteristic. By seeing these approaches come to life through description and example, managers can be in an improved position to assess their own ethical approaches and those of other organizational members (supervisors, subordinates, and peers).

Another central objective is to identify more completely the amoral management model, which often is overlooked in the human rush to classify things as good or bad, moral or immoral. In a later section, we will discuss the elements of moral judgment that must be developed if the transition to moral management is to succeed. Figure 6–6 depicts these three models of management ethics. A more detailed development of each management model is valuable in coming to understand the range of ethics that leaders may intentionally or unintentionally display. Let us consider the two extremes first—immoral and moral management—and then amoral management.

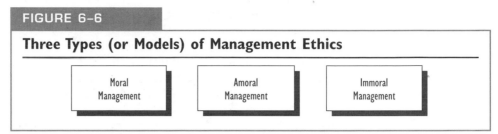

Immoral Management

Using *immoral* and *unethical* as synonyms, **immoral management** is defined as a posture that not only is devoid of ethical principles or precepts but also implies a positive and active opposition to what is ethical. Immoral management decisions, behaviours, actions, and practices are discordant with ethical principles. This model holds that management's motives are selfish and that it cares only or principally about its own or its company's gains. If management's activity is actively opposed to what is regarded as ethical, this suggests that management knows right from wrong and yet chooses to do wrong. Thus, its motives are deemed greedy or selfish. According to this model, management's goals are profitability and organizational success at virtually any price. Management does not care about others' claims to be treated fairly or justly.

What about management's orientation toward the law, considering that law is often regarded as an embodiment of minimal ethics? Immoral management regards legal standards as barriers that management must avoid or overcome in order to accomplish what it wants. Immoral management would just as soon engage in illegal activity as in immoral or unethical activity.

Operating Strategy The operating strategy of immoral management is focused on exploiting opportunities for corporate or personal gain. An active opposition to what is moral would suggest that managers cut corners anywhere and everywhere it appears useful. Thus, the key operating question guiding immoral management is, "Can we make money with this action, decision, or behaviour, *regardless of what it takes?*" Implicit in this question is that nothing else matters, at least not very much.

Illustrative Cases of Immoral Management Examples of immoral management abound. American prosecutors unravelled a long-running fraud scheme in which a group of U.S. Honda Motor Co. executives had pocketed in excess of US$10 million in bribes and kickbacks paid them by car dealers. In exchange, the executives gave dealers permission to open lucrative dealerships, and they also received Honda automobiles, which were in short supply at the time. Eight executives pleaded guilty, and many others were indicted. American Honda, the parent company, maintained that it was a victim in the case and had plans to sue the guilty executives.[27]

In 2001, Procter & Gamble (P&G) admitted to corporate espionage in that some of its employees had rummaged through the trash cans outside the Chicago offices of Unilever, the British-Dutch Company that makes Lipton tea, Dove soap, and several brands of shampoo. Agents of P&G retrieved about 80 pages of Unilever's confidential plans. In its defence, P&G said its agents did not violate the law, but did violate the company's own ethics policies, which prohibit rummaging through garbage to acquire information on competitors. P&G agreed to pay Unilever US$10 million in the spying case and agreed to an unusual third-party audit to monitor the product development and marketing plans of the company. P&G's chairman pledged that he had taken steps to ensure that the acquired material would not be used by his company.[28]

Among the most striking examples of immoral management is the case documented in the book *IBM and the Holocaust* by Edwin Black. Black offers compelling evidence that IBM played an important role in some of the most horrific events of the 1930s and 1940s in Europe. Specifically, IBM's production of hundreds of Hollerith machines, the precursor to the computer, played a central role in the first racial censuses conducted by the Nazis. Beginning in 1933, the Hollerith machine was used by the German government to identify its intended targets. As Black comments in his book:

> *Nearly every Nazi concentration camp operated a Hollerith Department ... in some camps ... as many as two dozen IBM sorters, tabulators and printers were installed ... [I]t did not matter whether IBM did or did not know exactly which machine was used at which death camp. All that mattered was that the money would be waiting—once the smoke cleared.*

The author suggests that IBM's involvement with Nazi Germany helps explain one mystery of the Holocaust—how so many people were killed in so little time. With the knowledge of top IBM management in the United States, IBM's European subsidiaries actually perfected the means for the Nazis to quickly collect census data for its murderous plans. Hitler awarded IBM chairman Thomas Watson a medal for his company's work.[29]

All of these are examples of immoral management where executives' decisions or actions were self-centred, actively opposed to what is right, focused on achieving organizational success at whatever the cost, and cutting corners where it was useful. These decisions were made without regard to the possible consequences.

Moral Management

At the opposite extreme from immoral management is **moral management**. Moral management conforms to the highest standards of ethical behaviour or professional standards of conduct. Although it is not always crystal clear what level of ethical standards prevail, moral management strives to be ethical in terms of its focus on high ethical norms and professional standards of conduct, motives, goals, orientation toward the law, and general operating strategy.

In contrast to the selfish motives in immoral management, moral management aspires to succeed, but only within the confines of sound ethical precepts—that is, standards predicated on such norms as fairness, justice, respect for rights, and due process. Moral management's motives, therefore, likely would be termed fair, balanced, or unselfish. Organizational goals continue to stress profitability, but only within the confines of legal obedience and sensitivity to and responsiveness to ethical standards. Moral management pursues its objectives of profitability, legality, and ethics as both required and desirable. Moral management would not pursue profits at the expense of the law and sound ethics. Indeed, the focus here would be not only on the letter of the law but on the spirit of the law as well. The law would be viewed as a minimal standard of ethical behaviour, because moral management strives to operate at a level above what the law mandates.

Operating Strategy of Moral Management The operating strategy of moral management is to live by sound ethical standards, seeking out only those economic opportunities that the organization or management can pursue within the confines of ethical behaviour. The organization assumes a leadership position when ethical dilemmas arise. The central question guiding moral management's actions, decisions, and behaviours is, "Will this action, decision, behaviour, or practice be fair to all stakeholders involved as well as to the organization?"

Lynn Sharp Paine has set forth what she calls an "integrity strategy" that closely resembles the moral management model.[30] The **integrity strategy** is characterized by a conception of ethics as the driving force of an organization. Ethical values shape management's search for opportunities, the design of organizational systems, and the decision-making process. Ethical values in the integrity strategy provide a common frame of reference and serve to unify different functions, lines of business, and employee groups. Organizational ethics, in this view, helps to define what an organization is and what it stands for. Some common features of an integrity strategy include the following,[31] which are all consistent with the moral management model:

- Guiding values and commitments make sense and are clearly communicated.
- Company leaders are personally committed, credible, and willing to take action on the values they espouse.
- Espoused values are integrated into the normal channels of management decision making.
- The organization's systems and structures support and reinforce its values.
- All managers have the skills, knowledge, and competencies to make ethically sound decisions on a daily basis.

Corporate Knights magazine annually presents awards for Canada's 50 Best Corporate Citizens. Considering the criteria for these awards is useful, because these criteria are representative of moral management as we have been describing it. *Corporate Knights'* award criteria include characteristics of an ethically "well-run" corporation. Here are some of the issues they consider in identifying "well-run" corporations:[32]

- A well-run corporation can be a place where its workers not only make a living wage, but a place where they build their self-worth.
- A well-run corporation can transfer know-how, capital, and culture to Third-world nations and assist the impoverished.
- A well-run corporation strives to minimize environmental harm and develop ways of doing things that are environmentally sound.
- A well-run corporation provides products that meet the highest safety and quality standards, even if it costs a little more in the short term.
- A well-run corporation allows all its shareholders to propose resolutions by providing transparency on the Triple-Bottom Line (financial, social, and environmental).
- A well-run corporation rewards prudence by guiding itself in a legitimate way to create long-term value.

Corporate Knights does not expect companies to be perfect in all their actions. Likewise, the moral management model acknowledges that a firm may exhibit moral management by overcoming a challenge with integrity.

Related to moral management is moral leadership. Carroll has set forth what he refers to as the "Seven Habits of Highly Moral Leaders."[33] Borrowing from the language used by Stephen Covey in his best-selling book *The Seven Habits of Highly Effective People*,[34] these qualities would need to be so prevalent and present in the leader's approach that they become habitual as a leadership approach. Helping to further flesh out what constitutes a moral manager, the seven habits of highly moral leaders have been set forth as follows:

- They have a passion to do right.
- They are morally proactive.
- They consider all stakeholders.
- They have a strong ethical character.
- They have an obsession with fairness.
- They undertake principled decision making.
- They integrate ethics wisdom with management wisdom.[35]

Illustrative Cases of Moral Management

3M Company. An excellent example of moral management was provided by the 3M Company in an action it took in mid-2000. While conducting some blood scans of its factory workers, 3M discovered that the tests were revealing trace amounts of a chemical that 3M had made for nearly 40 years. They also found evidence that the chemical was showing up in people's bloodstreams in various parts of the United States. The chemical was perfluorooctane sulfonate (PFO). How the PFOs got into people's bloodstreams, whether it could pose a health risk, and what should be done about it were all questions the company had to face. Although they could not come up with answers to these questions, company executives decided to take action anyway.

On its own, 3M decided to phase out PFOs and products containing related chemicals. The most important product to be affected was Scotchgard, the company's fabric protector. Because there is no replacement chemical yet available, the company faces a potential loss of US$500 million in annual sales. Given that 3M was under no mandate to act, it makes the company's actions especially noteworthy. In complimenting 3M, Carol Browner, administrator of the U.S. Environmental Protection Agency, said that "3M deserves great credit for identifying this problem and coming forward voluntarily."[36]

McCullough. Another excellent example of moral management taking the initiative in displaying ethical leadership was provided by McCulloch Corporation, a manufacturer of chain saws. Chain saws are notoriously dangerous. The U.S. Consumer Product Safety Commission one year estimated that there were 123 000 medically attended injuries involving chain saws, up from 71 000 five years earlier. In spite of these statistics, the Chain Saw Manufacturers Association fought mandatory safety standards. The association claimed that the accident statistics were inflated and did not offer any justification for mandatory regulations. Manufacturers support voluntary standards, although some of them say that when chain brakes—major safety devices—are offered as an option, they do not sell. Apparently, consumers do not have adequate knowledge of the risks inherent in using chain saws.

McCulloch became dissatisfied with the Chain Saw Manufacturers Association's refusal to support higher standards of safety and withdrew from it. Chain brakes have been standard on McCulloch saws since 1975 and are mandatory for most saws produced in Finland, Britain, and Australia. A Swedish company, Husqvarna, Inc., now installs chain brakes on saws it sells in the United States. Statistics from the Quebec Logging Association and from Sweden demonstrate that kickback-related accidents were reduced by about 80 percent after the mandatory installation of safety standards, including chain brakes.[37]

Ethics In Practice

A Taxing Job

While in university, I worked part-time for a prominent tax preparation service. I prepared customers' taxes along with about 20 other employees at different local offices. Bill had been working with the service for about three seasons, but this was my first tax season. Bill was very good at tax preparation and had a pretty good reputation. He was respected by management and did what he was asked to do.

On a few occasions, I had customers come in and ask to see Bill. When I explained that Bill was not at the office that day and asked if I could assist them with any questions, they would want to wait for Bill before continuing any further. This seemed odd to me because all of the files are located in the office as well as on the hard drives of the computers. Any employee can assist any customer, no matter who did the actual return.

Later, when I asked Bill about the customers, he told me that he did a few on his own time for people that couldn't afford the office fees. This was bothersome to me because there is no telling how many times Bill had done this and how many customers he took away from the business.

1. What are the ethical issues in this case? Who are the stakeholders and what are their stakes?

2. Was Bill engaging in an unethical practice by doing the taxes on his own time, or on company time using a different software program?

3. Should I have told the manager the little bit of information I knew about this situation? What is my ethical responsibility in this case?

Contributed Anonymously

McCulloch is an example of moral management. After attempting and failing to persuade its association to adopt a higher ethical standard that would greatly reduce injuries, it took a courageous action and withdrew from the association. This is a prime example of moral leadership.

Merck. Another well-known case of moral management occurred when Merck & Co., the pharmaceutical firm, invested millions of dollars to develop a drug for treating "river blindness," a Third World disease that was affecting almost 18 million people. Seeing that no government or aid organization was agreeing to buy the drug, Merck pledged to supply the drug for free forever. Merck's recognition that no effective mechanism existed to distribute the drug led to its decision to go far beyond industry practice and organize a committee to oversee the drug's distribution.[38]

We should stress at this time that not all organizations now engaging in moral management have done so all along. These companies sometimes arrived at this posture after years or decades of rising consumer expectations, increased government regulations, lawsuits, and pressure from social and consumer activists. We must think of moral management, therefore, as a desirable posture that in many instances has evolved over periods of several years. If we hold management to an idealistic, 100 percent historical moral purity test, no management will fill the bill. Rather, we should consider moral those managements that now see the enlightened self-interest of responding in accordance with the moral management model rather than alternatives.

Amoral Management

Amoral management is not just a middle position on a continuum between immoral and moral management. Conceptually it has been positioned between the other two, but it is different in kind from both. There are two kinds of **amoral management**. First, there is **intentional amoral management**. Amoral managers of this type do not factor ethical considerations into their decisions, actions, and behaviours because they believe business activity resides outside the sphere to which moral judgments apply. These managers are neither moral nor immoral. They simply think that different rules apply in business than in other realms of life. Intentionally amoral managers are in a distinct minority today. At one time, however, as managers first began to think about reconciling business practices with sound ethics, some managers adopted this stance. A few intentionally amoral managers are still around, but they are a vanishing breed in today's ethically conscious world.

Second, there is **unintentional amoral management**. Like intentionally amoral managers, unintentionally amoral managers do not think about business activity in ethical terms. These managers are simply casual about, careless about, or inattentive to the fact that their decisions and actions may have negative or deleterious effects on others. These managers lack ethical perception and moral awareness; that is, they blithely go through their organizational lives not thinking that what they are doing has an ethical dimension or facet. These managers are well intentioned but are either too insensitive or too self-absorbed to consider the effects of their behaviour on others.

Amoral management pursues profitability as its goal but does not cognitively attend to moral issues that may be intertwined with that pursuit. If there is an ethical guide to amoral management, it would be the marketplace as constrained by law—the letter of the law, not the spirit. The amoral manager sees the law as the parameters within which business pursuits take place.

Operating Strategy of Amoral Management   The operating strategy of amoral management is not to bridle managers with excessive ethical structure but to permit free rein within the unspoken but understood tenets of the free enterprise system. Personal ethics may periodically or unintentionally enter into managerial decisions, but it does not preoccupy management. Furthermore, the impact of decisions on others is an after-thought, if it ever gets considered at all. Amoral management represents a model of decision making in which the managers' ethical mental gears, to the extent that they are present, are stuck in neutral. The key management question guiding decision making is, "Can we make money with this action, decision, or behaviour?" Note that the question does not imply an active or implicit intent to be either moral or immoral.

Paine has articulated a "compliance strategy" that is consistent with amoral management. The **compliance strategy**, as contrasted with her integrity strategy, is more focused on obedience to the law as its driving force. The compliance strategy is lawyer driven and is oriented not toward ethics or integrity but more toward compliance with existing regulatory and criminal law. The compliance approach uses deterrence as its underlying assumption. This approach envisions managers as rational maximizers of self-interest, responsive to the personal costs and benefits of their choices, yet indifferent to the moral legitimacy of those choices.[39]

Figure 6–7 provides a summary of the major characteristics of amoral management and the other two models that have been identified and discussed.

Illustrative Cases of Amoral Management   There are perhaps more examples of unintentionally amoral management than any other kind. When police departments stipulated that recruits must be at least 5' 10" (1.8 metres) and weigh at least 180 pounds (82 kg), they were making an amoral decision, because they were not considering the harmful exclusion this would impose on women and other ethnic groups who do not, on average, attain that height and weight. When companies decided to

FIGURE 6-7

Three Approaches to Management Ethics

Organizational Characteristics		Immoral Management	Amoral Management	Moral Management
	Ethical Norms	Management decisions, actions, and behaviour imply a positive and active opposition to what is moral (ethical). Decisions are discordant with accepted ethical principles. An active negation of what is moral is implied.	Management is neither moral nor immoral, but decisions lie outside the sphere to which moral judgments apply. Management activity is outside or beyond the moral order of a particular code. May imply a lack of ethical perception and moral awareness.	Management activity conforms to a standard of ethical, or right, behaviour. Conforms to accepted professional standards of conduct. Ethical leadership is commonplace on the part of management.
	Motives	Selfish. Management cares only about its or the company's gains.	Well-intentioned but selfish in the sense that impact on others is not considered.	Good. Management wants to succeed but only within the confines of sound ethical precepts (fairness, justice, due process).
	Goals	Profitability and organizational success at any price.	Profitability. Other goals are not considered.	Profitability within the confines of legal obedience and ethical standards.
	Orientation Toward Law	Legal standards are barriers that management must overcome to accomplish what it wants.	Law is the ethical guide, preferably the letter of the law. The central question is what we can do legally.	Obedience toward letter and spirit of the law. Law is a minimal ethical behavior. Prefer to operate well above what law mandates.
	Strategy	Exploit opportunities for corporate gain. Cut corners when it appears useful.	Give managers free rein. Personal ethics may apply but only if managers choose. Respond to legal mandates if caught and required to do so.	Live by sound ethical standards. Assume leadership position when ethical dilemmas arise. Enlightened self-interest.

Source: Archie B. Carroll, "In Search of the Moral Manager," *Business Horizons* (March/April, 1987), 8. Copyright © 1987 by the Trustees at Indiana University, Kelley School of Business.

use scantily clad young women to advertise autos, men's cologne, and other products, these companies were not thinking of the degrading and demeaning characterization that would result from what they thought was an ethically neutral decision. When firms decided to do business in South Africa years ago, their decisions were neither moral nor immoral, but a major, unanticipated consequence of these decisions was the appearance of approval of apartheid.

Nestlé. Nestlé's initial decision to market infant formula in Third World countries (see Chapter 3) could have initially been an amoral decision. Nestlé may not have considered the detrimental effects such a seemingly innocent business decision would have on mothers and babies in a land of impure water, poverty, and illiteracy.

Video-Game Industry. It could be argued that the video-game industry has been unintentionally amoral because it has developed games that glorify extreme violence, sexism, and aggression without paying much attention to how these games impact the young people who become addicted to them. In *Mortal Kombat*, for example, players rip out an opponent's still-beating heart or bloody spinal cord. In *Night Trap*, Ninja-like vampires stalk minimally dressed, cowering co-eds and drill through their necks with power tools. These "games" have changed significantly since Atari introduced the popular video game *Pong* in 1972, a digital version of Ping-Pong consisting of a square ball and two rectangular paddles.[40]

Today's video games have plenty of critics—educators, psychologists, politicians—who worry about the multitude of themes that are bloodthirsty and sexist and have foul language. About the only response from the game makers has been to introduce an age-based rating system similar to that now used in the movie industry. The game makers' view seems to be that their games are legal and harmless and that little else is left to say.

Sears. A final useful illustration of unintentionally amoral management involves the case of Sears Roebuck and Co. and its automotive service business, which spanned much of the 1990s. Paine describes how consumers and attorneys general in 40 U.S. states accused the company of misleading consumers and selling them unneeded parts and services.[41] In the face of declining revenues and a shrinking market share, Sears' executives put into place new goals, quotas, and incentives for auto-centre service personnel. Service employees were told to meet product-specific and service-specific quotas—sell so many brake jobs, batteries, and front-end alignments—or face consequences such as reduced working hours or transfers. Some employees spoke of the "pressure" they felt to generate business. Although Sears' executives did not set out to defraud customers, they put into place a commission system that led to Sears' employees feeling pressure to sell products and services that consumers did not need. Soon after the complaints against Sears occurred, CEO Edward Brennan acknowledged that management had created an environment in which mistakes were made, although no intent to deceive consumers had existed. Fortunately, Sears eliminated its quota system as a partial remedy to the problem.[42]

The Sears case is a classic example of unintentionally amoral management—a well-intentioned company drifting into questionable practices because it just did not think ethically. The company simply did not think through the impacts that its strategic decisions would have on important stakeholders.

Two Hypotheses Regarding the Moral Management Models

There are numerous other examples of amoral management, but the ones presented here should suffice to illustrate the point. A thorough study has not been conducted to ascertain precisely what proportions of managers each model represents in the total management population. However, two possible hypotheses regarding the moral management models may be set forth.

Population Hypothesis. One hypothesis is that the distribution of the three models might approximate a normal curve, with the amoral group occupying the large middle part of the curve and the moral and immoral categories occupying the smaller tails of the curve. It is difficult to research this question. If you asked managers what they thought they were or what others thought they were, a self-serving bias would likely enter in and you would not get an accurate picture. Another approach would be to observe management actions. This would be nearly impossible because it is not possible to observe all management actions for any sustained period of time. Therefore, the supposition remains a hypothesis based on one person's judgment of what is going on in the management community.

Individual Hypothesis. Equally disturbing as the belief that the amoral management style is common among managers today is an alternative hypothesis that, within the average manager, these three models may operate at various times and under various circumstances. That is, the average manager may be amoral most of the time but may slip into a moral or an immoral mode on occasion, based on a variety of impinging factors. Like the population hypothesis, this view cannot be empirically supported at this time, but it does provide an interesting perspective for managers to ponder. This perspective would be somewhat similar to the situational ethics argument that has been around for some time.

Amoral Management as a Serious Organizational Problem The more serious social problem in organizations today seems to be the group of well-intended managers who for one reason or another subscribe to or live out the amoral ethic. These are managers who are driven primarily by the profitability or bottom-line ethos, which regards economic success as the exclusive barometer of organizational and personal achievement. They are basically good people, but they essentially see the competitive business world as ethically neutral. Until this group of managers moves toward the moral ethic, we will continue to see North American business and other organizations criticized as they have been in the past two decades.

To connect the three models of management morality with concepts introduced earlier, we show in Figure 6–8 how the components of corporate social responsibility (Chapter 2) would likely be viewed by managers using each of the three models of management morality. We illustrate in Figure 6–9 how managers using the three models would probably embrace or reject the stakeholder concept or stakeholder thinking (Chapter 3). It is hoped that these depictions of the interrelationships among these concepts will make them easier to understand and appreciate.

FIGURE 6–8

Three Models of Management Morality and Emphases on CSR

Models of Management Morality	Components of the CSR Definition			
	Economic Responsibility	Legal Responsibility	Ethical Responsibility	Philanthropic Responsibility
Immoral Management	✓✓✓	✓		✓
Amoral Management	✓✓✓	✓✓	✓	✓
Moral Management	✓✓✓	✓✓✓	✓✓✓	✓✓✓

Weighing Code:
✓ = token consideration (appearances only)
✓✓ = moderate consideration
✓✓✓ = significant consideration

FIGURE 6-9

The Moral Management Models and Acceptance of Stakeholder Thinking (SHT)

Moral Management Model	Acceptance of Stakeholder Thinking (SHT)	Stakeholder Thinking Posture Embraced
Immoral Management	SHT rejected: management is self-absorbed.	SHT rejected, not deemed useful. Accepts profit maximization model but does not really pursue it.
Amoral Management	SHT accepted: narrow view (minimum number of stakeholders considered).	Instrumental view of SHT prevails. How will it help management?
Moral Management	SHT enthusiastically embraced: wider view (maximum number of stakeholders considered).	Normative view of SHT prevails. SHT is fully embraced in all decision making.

Making Moral Management Actionable

The characteristics of immoral, moral, and amoral management discussed in this chapter should provide some useful benchmarks for managerial self-analysis, because self-analysis and introspection will ultimately be the way in which managers will recognize the need to move from the immoral or amoral ethic to the moral ethic. Numerous others have suggested management training for business ethics; therefore, this prescription will not be further developed here, although it has great potential. However, until senior management fully embraces the concepts of moral management, the transformation in organizational culture that is so essential for moral management to blossom, thrive, and flourish will not take place. Ultimately, senior management has the leadership responsibility to show the way to an ethical organizational climate by leading the transition from amoral to moral management, whether this is done by business ethics training and workshops, codes of conduct, mission/vision statements, ethics officers, tighter financial controls, more ethically sensitive decision-making processes, or leadership by example.

Underlying all these efforts, however, needs to be the fundamental recognition that amoral management exists and that it is an undesirable condition that can be certainly, if not easily, remedied. Most notably, organizational leaders must acknowledge that amoral management is a morally vacuous condition that can be quite easily disguised as just an innocent, practical, bottom-line philosophy—something to take pride in. Amoral management is, however, and will continue to be, the bane of management until it is recognized for what it really is and until managers take steps to overcome it. North American managers are not all "bad guys," as they so frequently are portrayed, but the idea that managerial decision making can be ethically neutral is bankrupt and no longer tenable in the society of the new millennium.[43]

Developing Moral Judgment

It is helpful to know something about how individuals, whether they are managers or employees, develop moral (or ethical) judgment. Perhaps if we knew more about this process, we could better understand our own behaviour and the behaviour of those around us and those we manage. Further, we may be able to better design reward systems for encouraging ethical behaviour if we knew more about how employees think about ethics. A good starting point is to come to appreciate what psychologists have to say about how we as individuals develop morally. The major research on this point is **Kohlberg's levels of moral development**.[44] After this discussion, we will consider other sources of a manager's values, especially those emanating from both societal sources and from within the organization itself.

Levels of Moral Development

An American psychologist, Lawrence Kohlberg, has done extensive research into the topic of **moral development**. He has concluded, on the basis of over 20 years of research, that there is a general sequence of three levels (each with two stages) through which individuals evolve in learning to think or develop morally. Although his theory is not universally accepted, there is widespread practical usage of his levels of moral development, and this suggests a broad if not unanimous consensus. Figure 6–10 illustrates Kohlberg's three levels and six stages.

Level 1: Preconventional Level At the preconventional level of moral development, which is typically descriptive of how people behave as infants and children, the focus is mainly on *self*. As an infant starts to grow, his or her main behavioural reactions are in response to punishments and rewards. Stage 1 is the *reaction-to-punishment stage*. If you want a child to do something (such as stay out of the street) at a very early age, spanking or scolding is typically needed. The orientation at this stage is toward avoidance of pain.

As the child gets a bit older, rewards start working. Stage 2 is the *seeking-of-rewards stage*. The child begins to see some connection between being "good" (that is, doing what Mom or Dad wants the child to do) and some reward that may be forthcoming. The reward may be parental praise or something tangible, such as candy,

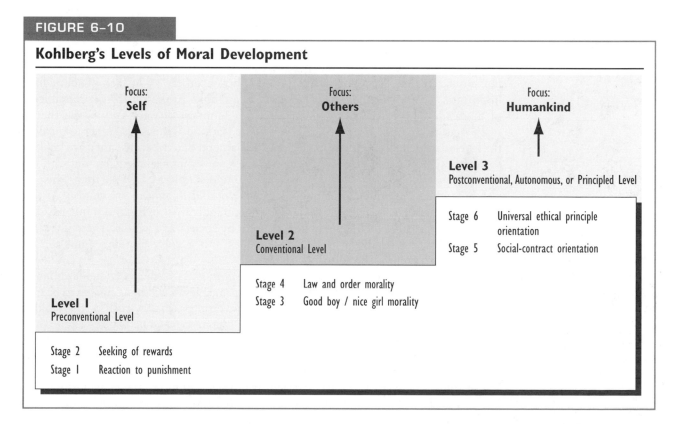

FIGURE 6–10

Kohlberg's Levels of Moral Development

Focus:
Self

Focus:
Others

Focus:
Humankind

Level 3
Postconventional, Autonomous, or Principled Level

| Stage 6 | Universal ethical principle orientation |
| Stage 5 | Social-contract orientation |

Level 2
Conventional Level

| Stage 4 | Law and order morality |
| Stage 3 | Good boy / nice girl morality |

Level 1
Preconventional Level

| Stage 2 | Seeking of rewards |
| Stage 1 | Reaction to punishment |

extra TV time, or a trip to the movies. At this preconventional level, children do not really understand the moral idea of "right" and "wrong" but rather learn to behave according to the consequences—punishment or reward—that are likely to follow. Like children, adults frequently learn to behave in appropriate ways in response to threats of punishment or promises of reward.

Level 2: Conventional Level   As the child gets older, she or he learns that there are others whose ideas or welfare ought to be considered. Initially, these others include family and friends. At the conventional level of moral development, the individual learns the importance of *conforming* to the conventional norms of society.

The conventional level is composed of two stages. Stage 3 has been called the *"good boy/nice girl" morality stage.* The young person learns that there are some rewards (such as feelings of acceptance, trust, loyalty, or warmth) for living up to what is expected by family and peers, so the individual begins to conform to what is generally expected of a good son, daughter, sister, brother, friend, and so on.

Stage 4 is the *law-and-order morality stage.* Not only does the individual learn to respond to family, friends, the school, and religious institutions, as in Stage 3, but the individual now recognizes that there are certain norms in society (in school, in the theatre, in the mall, in stores, in the car) that are expected or needed if society is to function in an orderly fashion. Thus, the individual becomes socialized or acculturated into what being a good citizen means. These rules for living include not only the actual laws (don't run a red light, don't walk until the "Walk" light comes on) but also other, less official norms (don't break into line, be sure to tip the server, turn your cell phone off in the library). At Stage 4 the individual sees that she or he is part of a larger social system and that to function in and be accepted by this social system requires a considerable degree of acceptance of and conformity to the norms and standards of society.

Level 3: Postconventional, Autonomous, or Principled Level   At this third level, which Kohlberg argues few people reach (and those who do reach it have trouble staying there), the focus moves beyond those "others" who are of immediate importance to the individual to *humankind* as a whole. At the postconventional level of moral development, the individual develops a notion of right and wrong that is more mature than the conventionally articulated notion. Thus, it is sometimes called the level at which moral principles become self-accepted, not because they are held by society but because the individual now perceives and embraces them as "right."

Kohlberg's third level seems to be easier to understand as a whole than when its two individual stages are considered. Stage 5 is the *social-contract orientation.* At this stage, right action is thought of in terms of general individual rights and standards that have been critically examined and agreed upon by society as a whole. There is a clear awareness of the relativism of personal values and a corresponding emphasis on processes for reaching consensus.

Stage 6 is the *universal-ethical-principle orientation.* Here the individual uses his or her conscience in accord with self-chosen ethical principles that are anticipated to be universal, comprehensive, and consistent. These universal principles (such as the Golden Rule) might be focused on such ideals as justice, human rights, and social welfare.

Kohlberg suggests that at Level 3 the individual is able to rise above the conventional level where "rightness" and "wrongness" are defined by societal institutions and that she or he is able to defend or justify her or his actions on some higher basis. For example, in our society the law tells us we should not discriminate against minorities. A Level 2 manager might not discriminate because to do so is to violate the law.

A Level 3 manager would not discriminate but might offer a different reason—for example, it is wrong to discriminate because it violates universal principles of human justice. Part of the difference between Levels 2 and 3, therefore, is traceable to our motivation for the course of action we take. This takes us back to our earlier discussion of motivation as one of the important ethics questions.

Our discussion to this point may have suggested that we are at Level 1 as infants, at Level 2 as youths, and, finally, at Level 3 as adults. There is some approximate correspondence between chronological age and Levels 1 and 2, but the important point should be made that Kohlberg thinks many of us as adults never get beyond Level 2. The idea of getting to Level 3 as managers is desirable, because it would require us to think about people, products, and markets at a level higher than that generally attained by conventional society. However, even if we never get there, Level 3 urges us to continually ask "What ought to be?" The first two levels tell us a lot about moral development that should be useful to us as managers. There are not many managers who consistently operate according to Level 3 principles. Sometimes a manager may dip into Level 3 on a certain issue or for a certain period of time. Sustaining that level, however, is quite challenging.

If we state the issue in terms of the question, "Why do managers behave ethically?" we might infer conclusions from Kohlberg that look like those in Figure 6–11.

Feminist Views of Kohlberg's Research One of the major criticisms of Kohlberg's research was set forth by Carol Gilligan. Gilligan argued that Kohlberg's conclusions may accurately depict the stages of moral development among men, whom he used as his research subjects, but that his findings are not generalizable to women.[45] According to Gilligan's view, men tend to deal with moral issues in terms that are impersonal, impartial, and abstract. Examples might include the principles of justice and rights that Kohlberg argues are relevant at the postconventional level. Women, on the other hand, perceive themselves to be part of a network of relationships with family and friends and thus are more focused on relationship maintenance

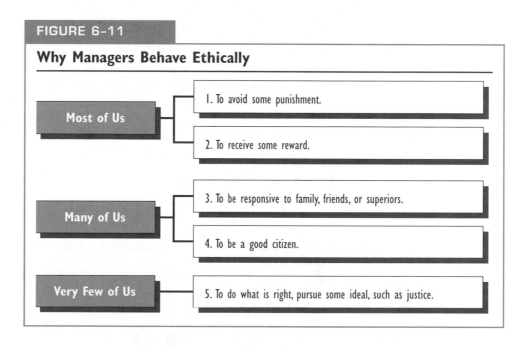

FIGURE 6–11

Why Managers Behave Ethically

Most of Us
- 1. To avoid some punishment.
- 2. To receive some reward.

Many of Us
- 3. To be responsive to family, friends, or superiors.
- 4. To be a good citizen.

Very Few of Us
- 5. To do what is right, pursue some ideal, such as justice.

and hurt avoidance when they confront moral issues. For women, then, morality is more a matter of caring and showing responsibility toward those involved in their relationships than in adhering to abstract or impersonal principles, such as justice.

According to Gilligan, women move in and out of three moral levels.[46] At the first level, the self is the sole object of concern. At the second level, the chief desire is to establish connections and participate in social life. In other words, maintaining relationships or directing one's thoughts toward others becomes dominant. Gilligan says that this is the conventional notion of women. At the third level, women recognize their own needs and the needs of others—those with whom they have relationships. Gilligan goes on to say that women never settle completely at one level. As they attain moral maturity, they do more of their thinking and make more of their decisions at the third level. This level requires care for others as well as care for oneself. In this view, morality moves away from the legalistic, self-centred approach that feminists say characterizes traditional ethics.

Some recent research does not show that moral development varies by gender in the fashion described by Gilligan. However, it does support Gilligan's claim that a different perspective toward moral issues is sometimes used. Apparently, both men and women sometimes employ an impartial or impersonal moral-rules perspective and sometimes they employ a care-and-responsibility perspective. This "care perspective" is still at an early stage of research, but it is useful to know that perspectives other than those found by Kohlberg are being considered.[47] More will be said about feminist theory in the next chapter.

Sources of a Manager's Values

In addition to considering the levels of moral development as an explanation of how and why people behave ethically, it is also useful to look at the *sources of a manager's values*. Ethics and values are intimately related. We referred earlier to ethics as the rightness or wrongness of behaviour. Ethics is also seen as the set of moral principles or values that drives behaviour. Thus, the rightness or wrongness of behaviour really turns out to be a manifestation of the ethical beliefs held by the individual. *Values*, on the other hand, are the individual's concepts of the relative worth, utility, or importance of certain ideas. Values reflect what the individual considers important in the larger scheme of things. One's values, therefore, shape one's ethics. Because this is so, it is important to understand the many different value-shaping forces that influence employees and managers.

The increasing pluralism of the society in which we live has exposed managers to a large number of values of many different kinds, and this has resulted in ethical diversity. One way to examine the sources of a manager's values is by considering both forces that originate from outside the organization to shape or influence the manager and those that emanate from within the organization. This, unfortunately, is not done as simply as we would like, because some sources are difficult to pinpoint. It should lend some order to our discussion, however.

Sources External to the Organization: The Web of Values The external sources of a manager's values refers to those broad sociocultural values that have evolved in society over a long period of time. Although current events (kickbacks, fraud, bribery cases) seem to affect these historic values by bringing specific ones into clearer focus at a given time, these values are rather enduring and change slowly. Quite often they emanate from major institutions or institutional themes in society.

George Steiner once stated that "every executive is at the center of a web of values" and that there are five principal repositories of values influencing businesspeople. These five include religious, philosophical, cultural, legal, and professional values.[48]

Religious Values. Religion has long been a basic source of morality in North American society, as in most societies. Religion and morality are so intertwined that William Barclay relates them for definitional purposes: "Ethics is the bit of religion that tells us how we ought to behave."[49] The biblical tradition of Judeo-Christian theology forms the core for much of what North Americans believe today about the importance of work, the concept of fairness, and the dignity of the individual. Other religious traditions likewise inform management behaviour and action.

Philosophical Values. Philosophy and various philosophical systems are also external sources of the manager's values. Beginning with preachments of the ancient Greeks, philosophers have claimed to demonstrate that reason can provide us with principles or morals in the same way it gives us the principles of mathematics. John Locke argued that morals are mathematically demonstrable, although he never explained how.[50] Aristotle with his Golden Rule and his doctrine of the mean, Kant with his categorical imperative, Bentham with his pain and pleasure calculus, and modern-day existentialists have shown us time and again the influence of various kinds of reasons for ethical choice.

Cultural Values. Culture, that broad synthesis of societal norms and values emanating from everyday living, has also had an impact on the manager's thinking. Modern examples of culture include music, movies, and television. Canadian culture is a potpourri of norms, customs, and rules that defy summarization. In recent years, it has become difficult to summarize what messages the culture is sending managers about ethics. In a recent book, *Moral Freedom: The Search for Virtue in a World of Choice*, by Alan Wolfe, the author argues that Western nations are undergoing a radical revolution in morals.[51] Wolfe thinks the traditional values that our culture has looked upon with authority (churches, families, neighbourhoods, civic leaders) have lost the ability to influence people.

He goes on to say that as more and more areas of North American life have become democratized and open to consumer "choice," people have come to assume that they have the right to determine for themselves what it means to lead a good and virtuous life. Wolfe says that a key element in this new moral universe is nonjudgmentalism, which pushes society to suspend judgment on much immoral behaviour or interpret immoral behaviour as not the fault of the perpetrator. Thus, although many North Americans may uphold the old virtues, in principle, they turn them into personal "options" in practice.[52] This clearly is a departure from the past, and it is probably impacting the way managers perceive the world of business.

Legal Values. The legal system has been and continues to be one of the most powerful forces defining what is ethical and what is not for managers. This is true even though ethical behaviour generally is that which occurs over and above legal dictates. As stated earlier, the law represents the codification of what the society considers right and wrong. Although we as members of society do not completely agree with every law in existence, there is typically more consensus for law than for ethics. Law, then, "mirrors the ideas of the entire society."[53] Law represents a minimum ethic of behaviour but does not encompass all the ethical standards of behaviour. Law addresses only the grossest violations of society's sense of right and wrong and thus is not adequate to describe completely all that is acceptable or unacceptable. Because it represents our official consensus ethic, however, its influence is pervasive and widely accepted.

In recent years, it has become an understatement to observe that we live in a litigious society. This trend toward suing someone to bring about justice is clearly having an impact on management decision making. Whereas the threat of litigation may make managers more careful in their treatment of stakeholders, the threat of losing millions of dollars has distorted decision making and caused many managers and companies to be running scared—never knowing what exactly is the best or fairest course of action to pursue.

Professional Values. These include those emanating, for the most part, from professional organizations and societies that represent various jobs and positions. As such, they presumably articulate the ethical consensus of the leaders of those professions. For example, the Canadian Public Relations Society has a code of ethics that public relations executives have imposed on themselves as their own guide to behaviour. The Real Estate Council of Alberta has been responsible for regulation of the real estate industry in that province, even though it is not a government agency. It is an independent industry-funded regulatory body. Professional values thus exert a more particularized impact on the manager than the four broader values discussed earlier.

In sum, several sources of values that are external to the organization come to bear on the manager. In addition to those mentioned, the manager is influenced by family, friends, acquaintances, and social events and currents of the day. The manager thus comes to the workplace with a personal philosophy that is truly a composite of numerous interacting values that have shaped her or his views of the world, of life, and of business.

Sources Internal to the Organization The external forces constitute the broad background or milieu against which a manager or an employee behaves or acts. They affect a person's personal views of the world and of business and help the person to formulate what is acceptable and unacceptable. There are, in addition, a number of less remote and more immediate factors that help to channel the individual's values and behaviour; these grow out of the specific organizational experience itself. These internal sources of a manager's values (within the business organization) constitute more immediate and direct influences on one's behaviour and decisions.

When an individual goes to work for an organization, a socialization process takes place in which the individual comes to assume the predominant values of that organization. The individual learns rather quickly that, to survive and to succeed, certain norms must be perpetuated and revered. There are several norms that are prevalent in business organizations, including:

- respect for the authority structure
- loyalty
- conformity
- performance
- results

Each of these norms may assume a major role in a person who subordinates her or his own standard of ethics to those of the organization. In fact, research suggests that these internal sources play a much more significant role in shaping business ethics than do the host of external sources we considered first.

Respect for the authority structure, loyalty, conformity, performance, and *results* have been historically almost synonymous with survival and success in business. When these influences are operating together, they form a composite business ethic that is remarkably persuasive in its impact on individual and group behaviour. These values form the central motif of organizational activity and direction.

Underlying the first three norms is the focus on performance and results. Carl Madden referred to this as the "calculus of the bottom line."[54] One does not need to study business organizations for long to recognize that the bottom line—profits—is the sacred instrumental value that seems to take precedence over all others. "Profits now" rather than later seems to be the orientation that spells success for managers and employees alike. Respect for authority, loyalty, and conformity become means to an end, although one could certainly find organizations and people who see these as legitimate ends in themselves. We will examine these internal sources in more detail in the next chapter.

Elements of Moral Judgment

For growth in moral judgment to take place, it is useful to appreciate the key elements involved in making moral judgments. This is a notion central to the transition from the amoral management state to the moral management state. Charles Powers and David Vogel suggest that there are six major elements or capacities that are essential to making moral judgments: (1) moral imagination, (2) moral identification and ordering, (3) moral evaluation, (4) tolerance of moral disagreement and ambiguity, (5) integration of managerial and moral competence, and (6) a sense of moral obligation.[55] Each reveals an essential ingredient in developing moral judgment.

Moral Imagination

Moral imagination refers to the ability to perceive that a web of competing economic relationships is, at the same time, a web of moral or ethical relationships. Developing moral imagination means not only becoming sensitive to ethical issues in business decision making but also developing the perspective of searching out subtle places where people are likely to be detrimentally affected by decision making or behaviours of managers. This is a necessary first step but is extremely challenging because of prevailing methods of evaluating managers on bottom-line results. It is essential before anything else can happen, however.

Moral Identification and Ordering

Moral identification and ordering refers to the ability to discern the relevance or non-relevance of moral factors that are introduced into a decision-making situation. Are the moral issues real or just rhetorical? The ability to see moral issues as issues that can be dealt with is at stake here. Once moral issues have been identified, they must be ranked, or ordered, just as economic or technological issues are prioritized during the decision-making process. A manager must not only develop this skill through experience but also finely hone it through repetition. It is only through repetition that this skill can be developed.

Moral Evaluation

Once issues have been identified and ordered, evaluations must be made. *Moral evaluation* is the practical phase of moral judgment and entails essential skills, such as coherence and consistency, that have proved to be effective principles in other contexts. What managers need to do here is to understand the importance of clear principles, develop processes for weighing ethical factors, and develop the ability to identify what the likely moral as well as economic outcomes of a decision will be.

The real challenge in moral evaluation is to integrate the concern for others into organizational goals, purposes, and legitimacy. In the final analysis, though, the manager may not know the "right" answer or solution, although moral sensitivity has been introduced into the process. The important point is that amorality has not prevailed or driven the decision process.

Tolerance of Moral Disagreement and Ambiguity

An objection managers often have to ethics discussions is the amount of disagreement generated and the volume of ambiguity that must be tolerated in thinking ethically. This must be accepted, however, because it is a natural part of ethics discussions. To be sure, managers need closure and precision in their decisions. But the situation is seldom clear in moral discussions, just as it is in many traditional and more familiar decision contexts of managers, such as introducing a new product based on limited test marketing, choosing a new executive for a key position, deciding which of a number of excellent computer systems to install, or making a strategic decision based on instincts. All of these are precarious decisions, but managers have become accustomed to making them in spite of the disagreements and ambiguity that prevail among those involved in the decision or within the individual.

In a real sense, the *tolerance of moral disagreement and ambiguity* is simply an extension of a managerial talent or facility that is present in practically all decision-making situations managers face. But managers are more unfamiliar with this special kind of decision making because of a lack of practice.

Integration of Managerial and Moral Competence

The *integration of managerial and moral competence* underlies all that we have been discussing. Moral issues in management do not arise in isolation from traditional business decision making but right smack in the middle of it. The scandals that major corporations face today did not occur independently of the companies' economic activities but were embedded in a series of decisions that were made at various points in time and culminated from those earlier decisions. Therefore, moral competence is an integral part of managerial competence. Managers are learning—some the hard way—that there is a significant corporate, and in many instances personal, price to pay for their amorality. The amoral manager sees ethical decisions as isolated and independent of managerial decisions and competence, but the moral manager sees every evolving decision as one in which an ethical perspective must be integrated. This kind of future-looking view is an essential executive skill.

A Sense of Moral Obligation

The foundation for all the capacities we have discussed is a *sense of moral obligation* and integrity. This sense is the key to the process but is the most difficult to acquire. This sense requires the intuitive or learned understanding that moral fibres—a concern for fairness, justice, and due process to people, groups, and communities—are woven into the fabric of managerial decision making and are the integral components that hold systems together.

These qualities are perfectly consistent with, and indeed are essential prerequisites to, the free-enterprise system as we know it today. One can go back in history to Adam Smith and the foundation tenets of the free-enterprise system and not find references to immoral or unethical practices as being elements that are needed for the system to work. Milton Friedman, our modern-day Adam Smith, even alluded to the importance of ethics when he stated that the purpose of business is "to make as much money as possible while conforming to the basic rules of society, both those embodied in the law and *those embodied in ethical custom.*"[56] The moral manager, then, has a sense of moral obligation and integrity that is the glue that holds together the decision-making process in which human welfare is inevitably at stake.

Figure 6–12 summarizes the six elements of moral judgment identified by Powers and Vogel as they might be perceived by amoral and moral managers.

FIGURE 6-12

Elements of Moral Judgment in Amoral and Moral Managers

Amoral Managers	Moral Managers
Moral Imagination	
See a web of competing economic claims as just that and nothing more.	Perceive that a web of competing economic claims is simultaneously a web of moral relationships.
Are insensitive to and unaware of the hidden dimensions of where people are likely to get hurt.	Are sensitive to and hunt out the hidden dimensions of where people are likely to get hurt.
Moral Identification and Ordering	
See moral claims as squishy and not definite enough to order into hierarchies with other claims.	See which moral claims being made are relevant or irrelevant; order moral factors just as economic factors are ordered.
Moral Evaluation	
Are erratic in their application of ethics if it gets applied at all.	Are coherent and consistent in their normative reasoning.
Tolerance of Moral Disagreement and Ambiguity	
Cite ethical disagreement and ambiguity as reasons for forgetting ethics altogether.	Tolerate ethical disagreement and ambiguity while honestly acknowledging that decisions are not precise like mathematics but must finally be made nevertheless.
Integration of Managerial and Moral Competence	
See ethical decisions as isolated and independent of managerial decisions and managerial competence.	See every evolving decision as one in which a moral perspective must be integrated with a managerial one.
A Sense of Moral Obligation	
Have no sense of moral obligation and integrity that extends beyond managerial responsibility.	Have a sense of moral obligation and integrity that holds together the decision-making process in which human welfare is at stake.

Source: Archie B. Carroll, "In Search of the Moral Manager," *Business Horizons* (March/April, 1987), 15. Copyright © 1987 by the Trustees at Indiana University, Kelley School of Business.

Summary

Business ethics has become a serious challenge for the business community over the past several decades. Polls indicate that the public does not have a high regard for the ethics of managers. It is not easy to say whether business's ethics have declined or just seem to have done so because of increased media coverage and rising public expectations. Business ethics concerns the rightness, wrongness, and fairness of managerial behaviour, and these are not easy judgments to make. Multiple norms compete to determine which standards business behaviour should be compared with. The conventional approach to business ethics was introduced as an initial way in which managers might think about ethical judgments. One major problem with this approach is that it is not clear which standards or norms should be used, and thus the conventional approach is susceptible to ethical relativism. A Venn diagram model was presented as an aide to making decisions when economics, law, and ethics expectations compete with each other. Four important ethics questions are (1) What is? (2) What ought to be? (3) How can we get from what is to what ought to be? and (4) What is our motivation in this transition?

Three models of management ethics are (1) immoral management, (2) moral management, and (3) amoral management. Amoral management is further classified into intentional and unintentional categories. There are two hypotheses about the presence of these three moral types in the management population and in individuals. A generally accepted view is that moral judgment develops according to the pattern described by Lawrence Kohlberg. His three levels of moral development are (1) preconventional, (2) conventional, and (3) postconventional, autonomous, or principled. Some research, however, suggests that there are gender differences between the perspectives taken by men and by women as they perceive and deal with moral issues. Managers' ethics are affected by sources of values originating external to the organization and sources from within the organization. The latter category includes respect for the authority structure, loyalty, conformity, and a concern for financial performance and results. Finally, six elements in developing moral judgment were presented. If the moral management model is to be realized, these six elements need to be developed.

Key Terms

amoral management (page 183)

business ethics (page 169)

compliance strategy (page 184)

conventional approach to business ethics (page 170)

descriptive ethics (page 169)

ethical relativism (page 173)

ethics (page 169)

immoral management (page 179)

integrity strategy (page 181)

intentional amoral management (page 184)

Kohlberg's levels of moral development (page 188)

moral development (page 189)

moral management (page 180)

normative ethics (page 170)

unintentional amoral management (page 184)

Discussion Questions

1. Give a definition of ethical business behaviour, explain the components involved in making ethical decisions, and give an example from your personal experience of the difficulties involved in making these determinations.

2. To demonstrate that you understand the three models of management ethics—moral, immoral, and amoral—give an example, from your personal

experience, of each type. Do you agree that amorality is a serious problem? Explain.

3. Give examples, from your personal experience, of Kohlberg's Levels 1, 2, and 3. If you do not think you have ever gotten to Level 3, give an example of what it might be like.

4. Compare your motivations to behave ethically with those listed in Figure 6–11 (page 191). Do the rea-

sons given in that figure agree with your personal assessment? Discuss the similarities and differences between Figure 6–11 and your personal assessment.

5. From your personal experience, give an example of a situation you have faced that would require one of the six elements of moral judgment.

Endnotes

1. Amy Zipkin, "Management: Getting Religion on Corporate Ethics: A Scourge of Scandals Leaves Its Mark," *The New York Times* (October 18, 2000).
2. "Partners in Crime," *Fortune Magazine* (October 27, 2003).
3. Cassell Bryan-Low, "Accounting Firms Aim to Dispel Cloud of Corporate Fraud," *Wall Street Journal* (May 27, 2003).
4. "Tale of the Tape: How GM One-Upped an Embarrassed NBC on Staged News Event," *The Wall Street Journal* (February 11, 1993), A1.
5. *Globe and Mail* (May 16, 2001).
6. Bari-Ellen Roberts, with Jack E. White, *Roberts vs. Texaco: A True Story of Race and Corporate America* (New York: Avon Books, 1998).
7. Matthew Cooper, "Tobacco: Turning Up the Heat," *Newsweek* (April 13, 1998), 50–51.
8. Neil Weinburg, "Criminalizing Capitalism," *Forbes* (May 12, 2003) 74–80.
9. Klaus Schwab, "Capitalism Must Develop More of a Conscience," *Newsweek* (February 24, 2003), 10–12.
10. Katherine Macklem, "Crooks in the Boardroom," *Maclean's* (December 30, 2002), 30–32.
11. David Gates, "Corruption: A Spectator Sport," *Newsweek* (February 25, 2002), 46–47.
12. "*Maclean's* Annual Poll," *Maclean's* (Dec. 30, 2002).
13. Society for Human Resources Management, http://www.shrm.org/hrresources/surveys_published.
14. The Gallup Organization, "Honesty/Ethics in Professions," http://www.gallup.com/poll/topics/hnsty_ethics.asp.
15. Max Ways, "A Plea for Perspective," in Clarence C. Walton (ed.), *The Ethics of Corporate Conduct* (Englewood Cliffs, NJ: Prentice Hall, 1977), 108.
16. Michael Blumenthal, "Business Morality Has Not Deteriorated—Society Has Changed," *The New York Times* (January 9, 1977).
17. *Ibid.*
18. Richard T. DeGeorge, *Business Ethics*, 4th ed. (New York: Prentice Hall, 1995), 20–21; see also Rogene A. Buchholz and Sandra B. Rosenthal, *Business Ethics* (Upper Saddle River, NJ: Prentice Hall, 1998), 3.
19. DeGeorge, 15.
20. See, for example, Melissa Baucus and Janet Near, "Can Illegal Corporate Behavior Be Predicted? An Event History Analysis," *Academy of Management Journal* (Vol. 34, No. 1, 1991), 9–36; and P. L. Cochran and D. Nigh, "Illegal Corporate Behavior and the Question of Moral Agency," in William C. Frederick (ed.), *Research in Corporate Social Performance and Policy*, Vol. 9 (Greenwich, CT: JAI Press, 1987), 73–91.
21. For examples that may fit in the various portions of the model, see Mark Schwartz, "Developing Portraits of Corporate Social Responsibility," 1995, unpublished manuscript; see also Mark Schwartz, "Carroll's Pyramid of Corporate Social Responsibility: A New Approach," IABS Proceedings, 1997, 236–241.
22. Otto A. Bremer, "An Approach to Questions of Ethics in Business," *Audenshaw Document No. 116* (North Hinksey, Oxford: The Hinksey Centre, Westminster College, 1983), 1–12.
23. *Ibid.*, 7.
24. *Ibid.*, 10–11.
25. Andrew Stark, "What's the Matter with Business Ethics?" *Harvard Business Review* (May–June, 1993), 7.
26. Most of the material in this section comes from Archie B. Carroll, "In Search of the Moral Manager," *Business Horizons* (March/April 1987), 7–15; see also Archie B. Carroll, "Models of Management Morality for the New Millennium," *Business Ethics Quarterly* (Vol. 11, Issue 2, April 2001), 365–371.
27. "Honda Bribery Case Brings Guilty Pleas," *The Atlanta Journal* (March 15, 1994), D5.
28. Julian E. Barnes, "P&G Said to Agree to Pay Unilever $10 Million in Spying Case," *The New York Times* (September 7, 2001).
29. Edwin Black, *IBM and the Holocaust: The Strategic Alliance between Nazi Germany and America's Most Powerful Corporation* (New York: Crown Publishers, 2001), 375.
30. Lynn Sharp Paine, "Managing for Organizational Integrity," *Harvard Business Review* (March–April, 1994), 106–117.
31. *Ibid.*, 111–112.
32. *Corporate Knights* Web site: http://www.corporate knights.ca/.
33. Archie B. Carroll, "The Moral Leader: Essential for Successful Corporate Citizenship," in Jorg Andriof and Malcolum McIntosh (eds.), *Perspectives on Corporate Citizenship* (Sheffield, UK: Greenleaf Publishing Co., 2001), 139–151.
34. Stephen Covey, *The Seven Habits of Highly Effective People* (New York: Simon & Schuster, 1989).
35. Carroll (2001), 145–150.
36. Joseph Weber, "3M's Big Cleanup," *Business Week* (June 5, 2000), 96–98.

37. Ray Vicker, "Rise in Chain-Saw Injuries Spurs Demand for Safety Standards, But Industry Resists," *The Wall Street Journal* (August 23, 1982), 17.

38. Business Enterprise Trust, 1994, "The Business Enterprise Trust Awards—1991 Recipients," unpublished announcement.

39. Paine, 109–113.

40. "Video-Game Systems," *Consumer Reports* (December 1996), 38–41.

41. Paine, 107–108.

42. *Ibid.*

43. Carroll (1987), 7–15.

44. Lawrence Kohlberg, "The Claim to Moral Adequacy of a Highest Stage of Moral Judgment," *The Journal of Philosophy* (Vol. LXX, 1973), 630–646.

45. Carol Gilligan, *In a Different Voice: Psychological Theory and Women's Development* (Cambridge, MA: Harvard University Press, 1982).

46. Manuel G. Velasquez, *Business Ethics*, 3d ed. (Englewood Cliffs, NJ: Prentice Hall, 1992), 30; see also Brian K. Burton and Craig P. Dunn, "Feminist Ethics as Moral Grounding for Stakeholder Theory," *Business Ethics Quarterly* (Vol. 6, No. 2, 1996), 136–137.

47. See, for example, Robbin Derry, "Moral Reasoning in Work Related Conflicts," in William C. Frederick (ed.), *Research in Corporate Social Performance and Policy*, Vol. 9 (Greenwich, CT: JAI Press, 1987), 25–49. See also Velasquez, 30–31.

48. George A. Steiner, *Business and Society* (New York: Random House, 1975), 226.

49. William Barclay, *Ethics in a Permissive Society* (New York: Harper & Row, 1971), 13.

50. Marvin Fox, "The Theistic Bases of Ethics," in Robert Bartels (ed.), *Ethics in Business* (Columbus, OH: Bureau of Business Research, Ohio State University, 1963), 86–87.

51. Alan Wolfe, *Moral Freedom: The Search for Virtue in a World of Choice* (New York: W. W. Norton & Co., 2001).

52. John Leo, "My Morals, Myself," *U.S. News & World Report* (August 13, 2001), 10.

53. Carl D. Fulda, "The Legal Basis of Ethics," in Bartels, 43–50.

54. Carl Madden, "Forces Which Influence Ethical Behavior," in Clarence C. Walton (ed.), *The Ethics of Corporate Conduct* (Englewood Cliffs, NJ: Prentice Hall, 1977), 31–78.

55. Charles W. Powers and David Vogel, *Ethics in the Education of Business Managers* (Hastings-on-Hudson, NY: The Hastings Center, 1980), 40–45. Also see Patricia H. Werhane, *Moral Imagination and Management Decision Making* (New York: Oxford University Press, 1999).

56. Milton Friedman, "The Social Responsibility of Business Is to Increase Its Profits," *The New York Times* (September, 1962), 126 (italics added).

Chapter 7

Personal and Organizational Ethics

Chapter Objectives

After studying this chapter, you should be able to:

1 Understand the different levels at which business ethics may be addressed.

2 Enumerate and discuss principles of personal ethical decision making and ethical tests.

3 Identify the factors affecting an organization's moral climate and provide examples of these factors at work.

4 Describe and explain actions or strategies that management may take to improve an organization's ethical climate.

The ethical issues on which managers must make decisions are numerous and varied. The news media tend to focus on the major ethical scandals involving well-known corporate names. Therefore, Nortel, Texaco, Dow Corning, Nike, IBM, Coca-Cola, Wal-Mart, McDonald's, and other such high-visibility firms attract considerable attention. The consequence of this is that many of the everyday, routine ethical dilemmas that managers face in medium-sized and small organizations are often overlooked.

A 2003 PriceWaterhouseCoopers survey involving over 3600 interviews in 50 countries with chief executive officers, chief financial officers, and those responsible for detecting and preventing economic crime, revealed that Canada and the U.S. reported the second-highest levels of economic crime, ranking only behind Africa. Moreover, it was found that in Canada, one fifth of fraud cases are uncovered by chance or accident.[1]

Managers can encounter day-to-day ethical dilemmas in such arenas as conflicts of interest, sexual harassment, inappropriate gifts to corporate personnel, unauthorized payments, customer dealings, evaluation of personnel, and pressure to compromise personal standards. Employees at all levels invariably face decisions with some kind of ethical dimension. The decision to compromise personal ethics for the sake of organizational objectives can bring devastating results. Consider the case of Betty Vinson:

> *Betty Vinson has always kept her life well ordered. She posts one list on the refrigerator of what she needs to buy at Wal-Mart and another for the grocery store. She keeps a list of the clothes she wears to work so she doesn't repeat outfits too often. The daughter of the former owner of a small typewriter shop, she is known among her friends for her spicy Texas chili.*
>
> *In 1996, she took a job as a midlevel accountant at a small long-distance company. Five years later, her solid career took a sudden turn in a very sorry direction. Today Ms. Vinson, 47 years old, is awaiting sentencing on conspiracy and securities-fraud charges. She has begun to prepare her 12-year-old daughter for the possibility that she will go to jail.*
>
> *The long-distance company grew up to be telecom giant WorldCom Inc., which melted down [in 2002] in an [US]$11 billion fraud, the biggest in corporate history. Asked by her bosses there to make false accounting entries, Ms. Vinson balked—and then caved. Over the course of six quarters she continued to make the illegal entries to bolster WorldCom's profits at the request of her superiors. Each time she worried. Each time she hoped it was the last time. At the end of 18 months she had helped falsify at least [US]$3.7 billion in profits.[2]*

Unfortunately, many managers face ethical quandaries on a daily basis but have no background or training in business ethics or ethical decision making to help them. A recent training program conducted by one of the authors illustrates this point well. The training session was in a continuing-education program, and the topic was business ethics. The 62 managers in attendance were asked how many of them had had formal business ethics training before—in college or in a company-sponsored program. Not one hand went up.

The ethics problem in business is, indeed, a serious one, but what is a manager to do? While the need for integrity in business has been repeatedly stressed in the popular press, many find it an elusive concept in the workplace. How does one get personal integrity and, as a manager, how do you instill it in your organization and create an ethical organizational climate? These are significant challenges. How, for example, do you keep your own personal ethics focused in such a way that you avoid immorality and amorality? What principles or guidelines are available to help you to be ethical? What specific strategies or approaches might be emphasized to bring about an ethical culture in your company or organization?

Levels at Which Ethical Issues May Be Addressed

As individuals and as managers, we experience ethical pressures or dilemmas in a variety of settings. These pressures or dilemmas occur on different levels. These levels include the individual or personal level, the organizational level, the industry level, the societal level, and the international level. These levels cascade out from the individual to the global.

Personal Level

First, we all experience *personal level* ethical challenges. These include situations we face in our personal lives that are generally outside the work context. Questions or dilemmas that we might face at the personal level include:

- Should I cheat on my income tax return?
- Should I return this extra pair of socks that the department store sent me by accident?
- Should I notify my bank that it credited someone else's $500 to my chequing account?
- Should I tell the cashier that she gave me change for a $20 bill when all I gave her was a $10 bill?

Wanda Johnson of Savannah, Georgia, faced a personal level ethical dilemma in September 2001. Johnson, a 34-year-old single mother of five, found temptation knocking in the form of a bagful of money that contained US$120 000. Johnson, a US$7.88-an-hour custodian at a local hospital, was on her lunch break when she witnessed a bag of money falling off an armoured truck. Johnson could have surely used the money. She was behind in her bills and had recently pawned her television set, trying to come up with enough cash to keep the bill collectors at bay. The bag contained small bills and nobody saw her find the bag. What should she do?

Johnson later admitted that she knew she had to turn it in. After consulting with her pastor, Johnson turned in the money to the police. Johnson said that her religious upbringing had taught her what was the right thing to do. Johnson was later rewarded when SunTrust bank promised her a reward of US$5000, and she received a promise of an unspecified sum by EM Armored Car Company.[3]

Organizational Level

People also confront ethical issues at the *organizational level* in their roles as managers or employees. Certainly, many of these issues are similar to those we face personally. However, these issues may carry consequences for the company's reputation and success in the community and also for the kind of ethical environment or culture that will prevail on a day-to-day basis at the office. Some of the issues posed at the organizational level might include:

- Should I set high production goals for my subordinates to benefit the organization, even though I know it may cause them to cut corners to achieve such goals?
- Should I overlook the wrongdoings of my colleagues and subordinates in the interest of harmony in the company?
- Should I authorize a subordinate to violate company policy so that we can close the deal and both be rewarded?
- Should I make this product safer than I'm required to by law, because I know the legal standard is grossly inadequate?
- Should I accept this gift or bribe that is being given to me to close a big deal for the firm?

In August 2001, it was revealed that months before people began dying in 1998, managers at a Sara Lee Corp.–owned plant in Michigan knew they were shipping tainted hot dogs and deli meats. This was an organization-level ethical dilemma. The 1998–1999 outbreak of listeriosis killed 15, caused six miscarriages, and sickened 101 people. Employees of the Bil Mar plant later came forward and revealed that several employees, as well as management, were aware of the contaminated meat but shipped it anyway. According to a report, a U.S. Department of Agriculture (USDA) worker had told a Bil Mar employee at the time that the plant was running a risk of getting into trouble if it shipped contaminated foods, but the worker said "they would never know it was our product since [listeria] has about a 2-week incubation period." Before these latest revelations, the company had pleaded guilty to a misdemeanour charge, paid a US$200 000 fine, and made a US$3 million grant to Michigan State University for food safety research.[4]

Industry Level

A third level at which a manager or organization might influence business ethics is the *industry level*. The industry might be stock brokerage, real estate, insurance, manufactured homes, financial services, telemarketing, automobiles, or a host of others. Related to the industry might be the profession of which an individual is a member—accounting, engineering, pharmacy, medicine, or law. Examples of questions that might pose ethical dilemmas at this level include the following:

- As accountants, are we providing completely fair and objective audited financial statements for our clients?
- Is this practice that we stockbrokers have been using for years with prospective clients really fair and in their best interests?
- Is this safety standard we electrical engineers have passed really adequate for protecting the consumer in this age of do-it-yourselfers?
- Is this standard contract we mobile home sellers have adopted really in keeping with the financial disclosure laws that have recently been strengthened?

In the summer of 2001, an industry-level group of 14 U.S. investment firms endorsed a set of ethical practices for the industry covering broad areas such as analysts' compensation, personal ownership of stocks by analysts, and the objectivity of reports. The action was taken by major firms such as Goldman Sachs, Merrill Lynch, and Morgan Stanley Dean Witter to counter the growing belief among many investors that Wall Street research is biased, obfuscating, or untrustworthy. The move was designed to shore up the ethical and professional standards of their investment analysts and other employees.[5] This action illustrates an industry-level problem that was addressed by the group of leading firms.

Societal and International Levels

At the *societal and international levels*, it becomes very difficult for the individual manager to have any direct effect on business ethics. However, managers acting in concert through their companies and trade and professional associations can definitely bring about high standards and constructive changes. Because the industry, societal, and international levels are quite removed from the actual practising manager, we will focus our attention in this chapter primarily on the personal and organizational levels. The manager's greatest impact can be felt through what he or she does personally or as a member of the management team.

We should also note that managers have an important role to play as ethical role models for society. To the extent that they successfully convey to the general public that they believe in the importance of integrity in business and throughout society, managers may have a significant impact on society's general level of ethics and on the future course of the free enterprise system. In Chapter 9, we will deal with global ethics—a crucial topic that is increasing in importance with each passing year.

Personal and Managerial Ethics

The point of departure for discussing personal and managerial ethics is the assumption that the individual wants to behave ethically or to improve his or her ethical behaviour in personal or managerial situations. Keep in mind that each individual is a stakeholder of someone else. Someone else—a friend, a family member, an associate, or a businessperson—has a stake in your behaviour; therefore, your ethics are important to them also. What we discuss here is aimed at those who desire to be ethical and are looking for help in doing so. All the difficulties with making ethical judgments that we discussed in the previous chapter are applicable in this discussion as well.

Personal and managerial ethics, for the most part, entails making decisions. Decision situations typically confront the individual with a conflict-of-interest situation. A conflict of interest is usually present when the individual has to choose between her or his interests and the interests of someone else or some other group (stakeholders). What it boils down to in the final analysis is answering the question, "What shall I do in this situation?"

In answering this question, more often than not it seems that individuals think about the situation briefly and then go with their instincts. There are, however, guides to ethical decision making that one could turn to if she or he really wanted to make the best ethical decisions. What are some of these guides?

In Chapter 6 we indicated that there are three major approaches to ethics or ethical decision making we would like to discuss: (1) the conventional approach, (2) the principles approach, and (3) the ethical tests approach. In Chapter 6, we discussed the conventional approach, which entailed a comparison of a decision or a practice with prevailing norms of acceptability. We discussed some of the challenges inherent in that approach. In this chapter, we discuss the other two approaches and other ethical principles and concepts as well.

Principles Approach to Ethics

The principles approach to ethics or ethical decision making is based on the idea that managers may desire to anchor their decisions on a more solid foundation than the conventional approach to ethics. Several principles of ethics have evolved over the centuries as moral philosophers and ethicists have attempted to organize and codify their thinking. This raises the question of what constitutes a principle of business ethics and how it might be applied. A principle of business ethics is a concept, guideline, or rule that, if applied when you are faced with an ethical dilemma, will assist you in making an ethical decision.[6]

There are many different principles of ethics, but we must limit our discussion to those that have been deemed most useful in business settings. Therefore, we will concentrate on three major principles: utilitarianism, rights, and justice. In addition, we will consider the ethics of care, virtue ethics, and servant leadership—views that are gaining popularity today—as well as a few other key ethical principles. The basic idea behind the principles approach is that managers may improve their ethical decision making if they factor into their proposed actions, decisions, behaviours, and practices a consideration of certain principles or concepts of ethics. We will conclude this section with a brief consideration of how we might reconcile ethical conflicts that might arise in the use of these principles.

Principle of Utilitarianism

Many have held that the rightness or fairness of an action can be determined by looking at its results or consequences. If the consequences are good, the action or decision is considered good. If the consequences are bad, the action or decision is considered wrong. The **principle of utilitarianism** is, therefore, a *consequential* principle. In its simplest form, **utilitarianism** asserts that "we should always act so as to produce the greatest ratio of good to evil for everyone."[7] Another way of stating utilitarianism is to say that one should take that course of action that represents the "greatest good for the greatest number." Two of the most influential philosophers who advocated this consequential view were Jeremy Bentham (1748–1832) and John Stuart Mill (1806–1873).

The attractiveness of utilitarianism is that it forces us to think about the general welfare. It proposes a standard outside of self-interest by which to judge the value of a course of action. It also forces us to think in stakeholder terms: What would produce the greatest good in our decision, considering stakeholders such as owners, employees, customers, and others, as well as ourselves? Finally, it provides for latitude in decision making in that it does not recognize specific actions as inherently good or bad but rather allows us to fit our personal decisions to the complexities of the situation.

A weakness of utilitarianism is that it ignores actions that may be inherently wrong. By focusing on the ends (consequences) of a decision or an action, the means (the decision or action itself) may be ignored. Thus, we have the problematic situation where one may argue that the end justifies the means, using utilitarian reasoning. Therefore, the action or decision is considered objectionable only if it leads to a lesser ratio of good to evil. Another problem with the principle of utilitarianism is that it may come into conflict with the idea of justice. Critics of utilitarianism say that the mere increase in total good is not good in and of itself because it ignores the distribution of good, which is also an important issue. Another stated weakness is that, when using this principle, it is very difficult to formulate satisfactory rules for decision making. Therefore, utilitarianism, like most ethical principles, has its advantages and disadvantages.[8]

Principle of Rights

One major problem with utilitarianism is that it does not handle the issue of **rights** very well. That is, utilitarianism implies that certain actions are morally right (i.e., they represent the greatest good for the greatest number) when in fact they may violate another person's rights.[9] **Moral rights** are important, justifiable claims or entitlements. The right to life or the right not to be killed by others is a justifiable claim in our society. The Declaration of Independence referred to the rights to life, liberty, and the pursuit of happiness. John Locke earlier had spoken of the right to property. Today we speak of human rights. Some of these are **legal rights** and some are moral rights.

The basic idea undergirding the **principle of rights** is that rights cannot simply be overridden by utility. A right can be overridden only by another, more basic or important right. Let us consider the problem if we apply the utilitarian principle. For example, if we accept the basic right to human life, we are precluded from considering whether killing someone might produce the greatest good for the greatest number. To use a business example, if a person has a right to equal treatment (not to be discriminated against), we could not argue for discriminating against that person so as to produce more good for others.[10] However, some people would say that this is precisely what we do when we advocate affirmative action.

The rights principle expresses morality from the point of view of the individual or group of individuals, whereas the utilitarian principle expresses morality in terms of the group or society as a whole. The rights view forces us in our decision making to ask what is due each individual and to promote individual welfare. The rights view also limits the validity of appeals to numbers and to society's aggregate benefit.[11] However, a central question that is not always easy to answer is: "What constitutes a legitimate right that should be honoured, and what rights or whose rights take precedence over others?"

Figure 7–1 provides an overview of some of the types of rights that are being claimed in our society today. Some of these rights are legally protected, whereas others are claimed as moral rights but are not legally protected. Managers are expected

---

FIGURE 7–1

A Variety of Legal Rights and Claimed Moral Rights in Society Today

Human rights	Right to life
Minorities' rights	Criminals' rights
Women's rights	Children's rights
Disabled people's rights	Fetal rights
Older people's rights	Embryo rights
Religious affiliation rights	Animals' rights
Employee rights	Right of due process
Consumer rights	Gay rights
Shareholder rights	Victims' rights
Privacy rights	

to be attentive to both legal and moral rights, but there are no clear guidelines available to help one sort out which claimed moral rights should be protected, to what extent they should be protected, and which rights should take precedence over others.

Principle of Justice   Just as the utilitarian principle does not handle well the idea of rights, it does not deal effectively with justice either. One way to think about the **principle of justice** is to say that it involves the fair treatment of each person. But how do you decide what is fair to each person? How do you decide what each person is due? People might be given what they are due according to their type of work, their effort expended, their merit, their need, and so on. Each of these criteria might be appropriate in different situations. At one time, the view prevailed that married heads of households ought to be paid more than single males or women. Today, however, the social structure is different. Women have entered the work force in significant numbers, some families are structured differently, and a revised concept of what is due people has evolved. The just action now is to pay everyone more on the basis of merit than needs.[12]

To use the principle of justice, we must ask, "What do we mean by justice?" There are several kinds of justice. **Distributive justice** refers to the distribution of benefits and burdens. **Compensatory justice** involves compensating someone for a past injustice. **Procedural justice** refers to fair decision-making procedures, practices, or agreements.[13]

John Rawls provides what some have referred to as a comprehensive principle of justice.[14] His theory is based on the idea that what we need first is a fair method by which we may choose the principles through which conflicts will be resolved. The two principles of justice that underlie his theory are as follows:[15]

1. Each person has an equal right to the most extensive basic liberties compatible with similar liberties for all others.
2. Social and economic inequalities are arranged so that they are both (a) reasonably expected to be to everyone's advantage and (b) attached to positions and offices open to all.

Under Rawls's first principle, each person is to be treated equally. The second principle is more controversial. It is criticized by both those who argue that the principle is too strong and those who think the principle is too weak. The former think that, as long as we have equal opportunity, there is no injustice when some people benefit from their own work, skill, ingenuity, or assumed risks. Therefore, such people deserve more and should not be required to produce benefits for the least advantaged. The latter group thinks that the inequalities that may result may be so great as to be clearly unjust. Therefore, the rich get richer and the poor get only a little less poor.[16]

Supporters of the principle of justice claim that it preserves the basic values—freedom, equality of opportunity, and a concern for the disadvantaged—that have become embedded in our moral beliefs. Critics object to various parts of the theory and would not subscribe to Rawls's principles at all. Utilitarians, for example, think the greatest good for the greatest number should reign supreme.

Principle of Caring

It is useful to introduce the ethics of care or **principle of caring** right after our discussion of utilitarianism, rights, and justice, because the theory, frequently referred to as "feminist theory," is critical of these traditional views. These views, it has been argued, embrace a masculine approach to perceiving the world. The feminist or "care" perspective builds on the work of Carol Gilligan, whose criticisms of Kohlberg's theory of moral development were discussed in the previous chapter.

The care perspective holds that traditional ethics like the principles of utilitarianism and rights focus too much on the individual self and on cognitive thought processes. In the traditional view, "others" may be seen as threats, so rights become important. Resulting moral theories then tend to be legalistic or contractual.

Feminist theory is founded on wholly different assumptions. Feminist philosophers, for example, view the person as essentially relational, not individualistic. These philosophers do not deny the existence of the self but hold that the self has relationships that cannot be separated from the self's existence. This view emphasizes the relationships' moral worth and, by extension, the responsibilities inherent in those relationships, rather than in rights, as in traditional ethics.[17]

Feminist moral theory, therefore, emphasizes caring as opposed to justice or rights. Several writers have argued that this is consistent with stakeholder theory, or the stakeholder approach, in that the focus is on a more cooperative, caring type of relationship. In this view, firms should seek to make decisions that satisfy stakeholders, leading to situations in which all parties in the relationship gain.

Jeanne Liedtka has questioned whether organizations can care in the sense in which feminist moral theory proposes. Liedtka contends that to care in this sense, an organization would have to care in a way that is:

- Focused entirely on people, not quality, profits, or other such ideas that today use "care talk"
- Undertaken with caring as an end, not merely as a means to an end (such as quality or profits)
- Essentially personal, in that the caring reflects caring for other individuals
- Growth enhancing for the cared-for, in that the caring moves the cared-for toward the development and use of their capacities

Liedtka takes the position that caring people could lead to a caring organization that offers new possibilities for simultaneously enhancing the effectiveness and the moral quality of organizations.[18] The principle of caring offers a different perspective to guide ethical decision making—a perspective that clearly is thought-provoking and valuable.

Virtue Ethics   The major principles just discussed have been more action oriented. That is, they were designed to guide our actions and decisions. Another ethical tradition, often referred to as **virtue ethics**, merits consideration even though it is not a principle per se. Virtue ethics, rooted in the thinking of Plato and Aristotle, focuses on the individual becoming imbued with virtues (e.g., honesty, fairness, truthfulness, benevolence, nonmalfeasance).[19]

Virtue ethics is a system of thought that is centred in the heart of the person—in our case, the manager. This is in contrast to the principles we have discussed, which see the heart of ethics in actions or duties. Action-oriented principles focus on *doing*. Virtue ethics emphasizes *being*. The assumption, of course, is that the actions of a virtuous person will also be virtuous. Traditional ethical principles such as utilitarianism, rights, and justice focus on the question, "What should I do?" Virtue ethics focuses on the question, "What sort of person should I be or become?"[20]

Programs that have developed from the notion of virtue ethics have sometimes been called *character education*, because this particular theory emphasizes character

Ethics In Practice

Whose Rights Are *Right*?

In 1990, the Recording Industry Association of America (RIAA) voluntarily decided to add warning labels to musical albums containing explicit lyrics. According to the RIAA, "The Parental Advisory is a notice to parents that recordings identified by this logo may contain strong language or depictions of violence, sex or substance abuse. Parental discretion is advised."

Recently, while I was working for a small record store, Aftermath Entertainment and Interscope Records released an album by Marshall Mathers (whose stage name is Eminem) titled, "The Marshall Mathers LP." It contained the advisory on the front left corner in compliance with the self-adopted guidelines of the RIAA.

Upon the release of the album, many groups, including those representing gay, lesbian, and women's rights, immediately cried for a recall of the album because of the slurs and messages contained within some of the songs. Women's rights groups were upset because of the extremely violent episodes describing the beatings, rapes, and murders of Mr. Mathers's wife and mother. Gay and lesbian rights groups were equally outraged at the slurs of antigay messages contained in just about every song.

Marshall Mathers has stated that messages in his albums are not to be taken seriously; they are purely for entertainment purposes. Further, he claimed the slurs contained in his album that gay and lesbian rights groups find offensive are not meant in a manner offensive only to homosexuals, but rather are slang words that degrade anyone. This argument by Mr. Mathers was defended by a description contained in the RIAA code describing which albums should be labelled with the advisory: "Lyrics are often susceptible to varying interpretations. Words can have different meanings. Also, words cannot be viewed in isolation from the music that accompanies them. Lyrics when accompanied by loud and raucous music can be perceived differently than the same lyrics when accompanied by soft and soothing music."

This only argues for a very minor part of the issue though. The main concern arose when it became public that Interscope Records refused to release the album until certain lyrics about the shootings in 1999 at Columbine High School in Littleton, Colorado, were removed. This censoring of some of the lyrics and not others led the rights groups to believe that Interscope Records was fully aware of the impact that the lyrics would have and, in fact, chose which lyrics could be financially capitalized on, and left those on the album. The financial gains turned out to be larger than anyone expected and Eminem has built his career on this type of notoriety.

All of this considered, the most intriguing issue that arises from this case is where the line between the artist's freedom of expression and a record company's social responsibility should lie.

1. Whose rights are more important than another's rights in a business situation such as this? How is this decision made and by whom?

2. How much responsibility concerning what is and is not appropriate for an artist to say should be decided by the recording company? By consumer demand?

3. What do you think is the record company's reasoning or logic behind protecting the rights of those associated with the Columbine shootings versus the other groups protesting in the case?

4. How do the principles of rights, justice, and utilitarianism apply in this case?

Contributed by Steve Minster

development. Many observers think that one reason we have moral decline in business and society today is because we have failed to teach our young people universal principles of good character.

Esther Schaeffer, executive director of the Character Education Partnership, has argued that character education is needed not only in schools, but in corporations as well. She holds that corporate well-being demands character and that business leaders are a vital and necessary force for putting character back into education.[21] In recent times, the common perception has been that there is a lack of such character in business. This dim perception of business is best expressed in the following quotation from Marianne M. Jennings:

> *There is a perplexing disdain among these business students for business and a cynical attitude about their decision to pursue it as a career. Feeling very much as if they have sold their souls by going into business in the first place, they are resigned to, and comfortable with, myriad forms of immoral conduct as a routine part of business. It's as if they have concluded: If you are going to rob a Seven-Eleven convenience store, what difference does it make if you get a speeding ticket during the getaway? ... A recent survey of MBAs found that 73 percent would hire a competitor's employee to obtain trade secrets. The same survey found that only 60 percent of convicts would. One student's response when asked if he would leave a note if he hit a parked car in a parking lot was, "You mean a note with my name?" ... They have the yearnings of the liberal heart.... That businesses cheat is a given for them and they are cynically resigned to participation. Such is the result of this generation's students schooled amidst a curriculum and academy aligned against the evils of capitalism and comfortable avoiding the judgmentalism of right versus wrong.*[22]

Virtue ethicists have brought back to the public debate the idea that virtues are important whether they be in the education of the young or in management training programs. Virtues such as honesty, integrity, loyalty, promise keeping, fairness, and respect for others are completely compatible with the major principles we have been discussing. The principles, combined with the virtues, form the foundation for effective ethical action and decision making. Whether the virtues are seen as character traits or as principles of decision making is not our major concern at this point. That they be used, whatever the motivation, is our central concern here. Business ethicists Oliver Williams and Patrick Murphy have strongly argued that the ethics of virtue in business is an idea whose time has arrived.[23]

The Golden Rule   The **Golden Rule** merits discussion because of its popularity as a basic and strong principle of ethical living and decision making. A number of studies have found it to be the most powerful and useful to managers.[24] The Golden Rule— "Do unto others as you would have them do unto you"—is a fairly straightforward, easy-to-understand principle. Further, it guides the individual decision maker to behaviour, actions, or decisions that she or he should be able to express as acceptable or not based on some direct comparisons with what she or he would consider ethical or fair.

The Golden Rule simply argues that, if you want to be treated fairly, treat others fairly; if you want your privacy protected, respect the privacy of others. The key is impartiality. According to this principle, we are not to make an exception of ourselves. In essence, the Golden Rule personalizes business relations and brings the ideal of fairness into business deliberations.[25]

Perhaps the reason the Golden Rule is so popular is that it is rooted in history and religious tradition and is among the oldest of the principles of living. Further, it is universal in the sense that it requires no specific religious belief or faith. Almost since time began, religious leaders and philosophers have advocated the Golden Rule in one form or another. It is easy to see, therefore, why Martin Luther could say that the Golden Rule is a part of the "natural law," because it is a moral rule that anyone can recognize and embrace without any particular religious teaching. In three different studies, when managers or respondents were asked to rank ethical principles according to their value to them, the Golden Rule was ranked first.[26]

In addition to the ethical principles and theories that we have chosen to discuss in some detail, Figure 7–2 provides a brief sketch of several ethical principles that have evolved over the years.

There is no single principle that is recommended to be always used. As one gets into each principle, one encounters a number of problems with definitions, with measurement, and with generalizability. The more one gets into each principle, the more one realizes how difficult it would be for a person to use each principle consistently as a guide to decision making. On the other hand, to say that an ethical principle is imperfect is not to say that it has not raised important issues that must be addressed in personal or business decision making. The major principles and approaches we have discussed have raised to our consciousness the importance of the collective good, individual rights, caring, character, and fairness.

Reconciling Ethical Conflicts   What does a manager do when using some of the ethical principles and guidelines we have been discussing and she or he finds that there are conflicts between and among the principles? For example, what if the manager perceives that one employee's right to safety conflicts with another's right to privacy? How should this conflict be resolved? There is no unqualified way to reconcile ethical principles; however, some brief discussion may be helpful. Shaw and Barry have argued, following the ideas introduced by V. R. Ruggiero, that three common concerns must be addressed in conflict situations: obligations, ideals, and effects.[27] We will tie these concepts into our current discussion.

First, we enter into *obligations* as a part of our daily organizational lives. An example might be a verbal or written contract to which we have agreed. Principles of justice, rights, and virtue would hold that we should honour obligations. Second, as managers we might hold certain *ideals*. Such an ideal may be some morally important goal, principle, virtue, or notion of excellence worth striving for. A quest for justice, protection of rights, and balancing of individual versus group goals might be examples. Third, we are interested in the *effects*, or consequences, on stakeholders of our decisions or actions.[28] Hopefully, we can see how obligations, goals, and effects are all aspects of the ethical principles we have been discussing.

The question now arises as to how we might handle a situation wherein our obligations, goals, and effects conflict or produce mixed effects. Three rough guidelines have been proposed by Shaw and Barry:[29]

1. When two or more moral obligations conflict, *choose the stronger one.*
2. When two or more ideals conflict, or when ideals conflict with obligations, *honour the more important one.*
3. When the effects are mixed, *choose the action that produces the greater good or less harm.*

These guidelines are rough because they do not precisely answer the question of which obligations or ideals should take precedence over others. However, they do give us a general approach or process for raising the issue of how such conflicts might be

---

FIGURE 7–2

A Brief Sketch of Ethical Principles

- **The Categorical Imperative:** Act only according to that maxim by which you can at the same time "will" that it should become a universal law. In other words, one should not adopt principles of action unless they can, without inconsistency, be adopted by everyone else.

- **The Conventionalist Ethic:** Individuals should act to further their self-interests so long as they do not violate the law. It is allowed, under this principle, to bluff (lie) and to take advantage of all legal opportunities and widespread practices and customs.

- **The Disclosure Rule:** If the full glare of examination by associates, friends, family, newspapers, television, etc., were to focus on your decision, would you remain comfortable with it? If you think you would, it probably is the right decision.

- **The Golden Rule:** Do unto others as you would have them do unto you. It includes not knowingly doing harm to others.

- **The Hedonistic Ethic:** Virtue is embodied in what each individual finds meaningful. There are no universal or absolute moral principles. If it feels good, do it.

- **The Intuition Ethic:** People are endowed with a kind of moral sense with which they can apprehend right and wrong. The solution to moral problems lies simply in what you feel or understand to be right in a given situation. You have a "gut feeling" and "fly by the seat of your pants."

- **The Market Ethic:** Selfish actions in the marketplace are virtuous because they contribute to efficient operation of the economy. Decision makers may take selfish actions and be motivated by personal gain in their business dealings. They should ask whether their actions in the market further financial self-interest. If so, the actions are ethical.

- **The Means-Ends Ethic:** Worthwhile ends justify efficient means—i.e., when ends are of overriding importance or virtue, unscrupulous means may be employed to reach them.

- **The Might-Equals-Right Ethic:** Justice is defined as the interest of the stronger. What is ethical is what an individual has the strength and power to accomplish. Seize what advantage you are strong enough to take without respect to ordinary social conventions and laws.

- **The Organization Ethic:** The wills and needs of individuals should be subordinated to the greater good of the organization (be it church, state, business, military, or university). An individual should ask whether actions are consistent with organizational goals and what is good for the organization.

- **The Professional Ethic:** You should do only that which can be explained before a committee of your peers.

- **The Proportionality Principle:** I am responsible for whatever I "will" as a means or an end. If both the means and the end are good in and of themselves, I may ethically permit or risk the foreseen but unwilled side effects if, and only if, I have a proportionate reason for doing so.

- **The Revelation Ethic:** Through prayer or other appeal to transcendent beings and forces, answers are given to individual minds. The decision makers pray, meditate, or otherwise commune with a superior force or being. They are then apprised of which actions are just and unjust.

- **The Utilitarian Ethic:** The greatest good for the greatest number. Determine whether the harm in an action is outweighed by the good. If the action maximizes benefit, it is the optimum course to take among alternatives that provide less benefit.

Source: T. K. Das, "Ethical Preferences Among Business Students: A Comparative Study of Fourteen Ethical Principles," *Southern Management Association* (November 13–16, 1985), 11–12. For further discussion, see T. K. Das, "Ethical Principles in Business: An Empirical Study of Preferential Rankings," *International Journal of Management* (Vol. 9, No. 4, December, 1992), 462–472.

resolved. In the final analysis, the manager will need to consider carefully which values or obligations are more important than others.

In summary, the principles approach to ethics focuses on guidelines, ideas, or concepts that have been created to help people and organizations make wise, ethical decisions. In our discussion, we have treated the following as important components of the principles-based approach: utilitarianism, rights, justice, caring, virtue, and the

Ethics In Practice

Promise Versus Lie

During the spring, I worked in the billing department of a large organization as a student worker. All of the secretaries who worked in the billing department were close and would talk to each other about almost anything. One of the topics we enjoyed talking about the most was the office manager of the billing department and how much we would like to find another job to get away from her, because we did not like working with her. While I was working in the department, I became very close friends with the senior secretary, who worked with me in the front office.

During the same spring, my friend was offered a very prestigious job at the company. She told a few of us about having applied for the job, but she did not want us to let the office manager know that she was applying for it in case she did not get it. I was her friend, so I was not going to say anything about the situation. After a few weeks of waiting to find out if she got the job or not, she was offered the job and took it immediately. After she knew she had the new job, she told the office manager that she had been offered another job and was giving her two weeks' notice. All was well until the office manager came up to me one day and asked me if I had known anything about the secretary planning to leave. I was not sure what to say. I did not want to lie to the office manager, but I also did not want to break a promise I made to a good friend. What was I to do?

1. Is this ethical dilemma at the personal level or the organizational level?

2. What ethical principles are at stake in this situation?

3. What should the person who faces this ethical situation do?

Contributed by Erika Carlson-Durham

Golden Rule. Such principles, or principle-based approaches, ought to cause us to think deeply and to reflect carefully on the ethical decisions we face in our personal and organizational lives. For the most part, these principles are rooted in moral philosophy and religion. On a more pragmatic level, we turn now to a series of ethical tests that constitute our third major approach to ethics.

Ethical Tests Approach

In addition to the ethical principles approach to guiding personal and managerial decision making, a number of practical **ethical tests** might be set forth, too. Whereas the principles have almost exclusively been generated by philosophers, the ethical tests we discuss here are more practical in orientation and do not require the depth of moral thinking that the principles do. No single test is recommended as a universal answer to the question, "What action or decision should I take in this situation?" However, each person may find one or more tests that will be useful in helping to clarify the appropriate course of action in a decision situation. To most students, the notion of a test invokes the thought of questions posed that need to be answered. Indeed, each of these tests for personal ethical decision making requires the thoughtful deliberation of a central question that gets to the heart of the matter.

Test of Common Sense With this first test, the individual simply asks, "Does the action I am getting ready to take really make sense?" When you think of behaviour that might have ethical implications, it is logical to consider the practical consequences. If, for example, you would surely get caught engaging in a questionable practice, the action does not pass this test. Many unethical practices have come to light where one is led to ask whether a person really used her or his common sense at all. This test has severe limitations. For example, if you conclude that you would not get caught engaging in a questionable practice, this test might lead you to think that the questionable practice is an acceptable course of action, when in fact it is not. In addition, there may be other common-sense aspects of the situation that you have overlooked.

Test of One's Best Self   Each person has a self-concept. Most people could construct a scenario of themselves at their best. This test requires the individual to pose the question, "Is this action or decision I'm getting ready to take compatible with my concept of myself at my best?" This test addresses the notion of the esteem in which we hold ourselves and the kind of person we want to be known as. Naturally, this test would not be of much value to those who do not hold themselves in high esteem.

Test of Making Something Public   This is one of the most powerful tests.[30] It is similar to the disclosure rule defined in Figure 7–2 (page 213). If you are about to engage in a questionable practice or action, you might pose the following questions: "How would I feel if others knew I was doing this? How would I feel if I knew that my decisions or actions were going to be featured on the national evening news tonight for all the world to see?" This test addresses the issue of whether your action or decision can withstand public disclosure and scrutiny. How would you feel if all your friends, family, and colleagues knew you were engaging in this action? If you feel comfortable with this thought, you are probably on solid footing. If you feel uncomfortable with this thought, you ought to rethink your position.

The concept of public exposure is quite powerful. Several years ago, a poll asked managers what would stop bribes abroad. Most managers thought that public exposure would be most effective. "If the public knew we were accepting bribes, this knowledge would have the best chance of being effective," they replied.

Test of Ventilation   The idea of ventilation is to expose your proposed action to others and get their thoughts on it. This test works best if you get opinions from people who you know might not see things your way. The important point here is that you do not isolate yourself with your dilemma but seek others' views. After you have subjected your proposed course of action to other opinions, you may find that you have not been thinking clearly.

Test of the Purified Idea   An idea or action may be thought to be "purified"—that is, made right—when a person with authority says it is appropriate. Such a person might be a supervisor, an accountant, or a lawyer. The central question here is, "Am I thinking this action or decision is right just because someone with appropriate authority or knowledge says it is right?" If you look hard enough, you can find a lawyer or an accountant to endorse almost any idea if it is phrased right.[31] However, neither of them is the final arbiter of what is right or wrong. Similarly, just because a superior says an action or a decision is ethical does not make it so. The decision or course of action may still be questionable or wrong even though someone else has sanctioned it with her or his approval. This is one of the most common ethical errors people make, and they must constantly be reminded that they themselves ultimately will be held accountable if the action is indefensible.

Gag Test   This test was provided by a U.S. judge on the Louisiana Court of Appeals. He argued that a manager's clearest signal that a dubious decision or action is going too far is when you simply gag at the prospect of carrying it out.[32] Admittedly, this test can only capture the grossest of unethical behaviours, but there are some managers who may need such a general kind of test. Actually, this test is intended to be more humorous than serious, but a few might be helped by it.

None of the previously mentioned tests alone offers a perfect way to question whether a decision or an act is ethical. If several tests are used together, especially the more powerful ones, they do provide a means of examining proposed actions before engaging in them. To repeat, this assumes that the individual really wants to do what is right and is looking for assistance. To the fundamentally unethical person, however, these tests would not be of much value.

Phillip V. Lewis conducted a five-year study of ethical principles and ethical tests. Based on his findings, he asserted that there is high agreement on how a decision maker should behave when faced with a moral choice. He concludes:

> *In fact, there is almost a step-by-step sequence. Notice: One should (1) look at the problem from the position of the other person(s) affected by a decision; (2) try to determine what virtuous response is expected; (3) ask (a) how it would feel for the decision to be disclosed to a wide audience and (b) whether the decision is consistent with organizational goals; and (4) act in a way that is (a) right and just for any other person in a similar situation and (b) good for the organization.*[33]

Implicit in Lewis's conclusion is evidence of the Golden Rule, the disclosure rule, and Rawls's principle of justice.

Managing Organizational Ethics

To this point, our discussion has centred on principles and approaches to personal or managerial decision making. Clearly, ethical decision making is at the heart of business ethics, and we cannot stress enough the need to sharpen decision-making skills if amorality is to be prevented and moral management is to be achieved. Now we shift our attention more to the *organizational level*, where we find the context in which decision making occurs. Actions and practices that take place within the organization's culture, or climate, are just as vital as decision making in bringing about ethical business practices and results.

To manage ethics in an organization, a manager must appreciate that the organization's ethical climate is just one part of its overall corporate culture. When McNeil Laboratories, a subsidiary of Johnson & Johnson, voluntarily withdrew Tylenol from the market immediately after the reports of tainted, poisoned products, some people wondered why they made this decision as they did. An often-cited response was, "It's the J&J way."[34] This statement conveys a significant message about the firm's ethical climate. It also raises the question of how organizations and managers should deal with, understand, and shape business ethics through actions taken, policies established, and examples set. The organization's moral climate is a complex entity, and we can discuss only some facets of it in this section.[35]

Figure 7–3 illustrates several levels of moral climate and some of the key factors that may come to bear on the manager as she or he makes decisions. Our focus in this section is on the organization's moral climate. Two major questions that need to be considered are (1) What factors contribute to ethical or unethical behaviour in the

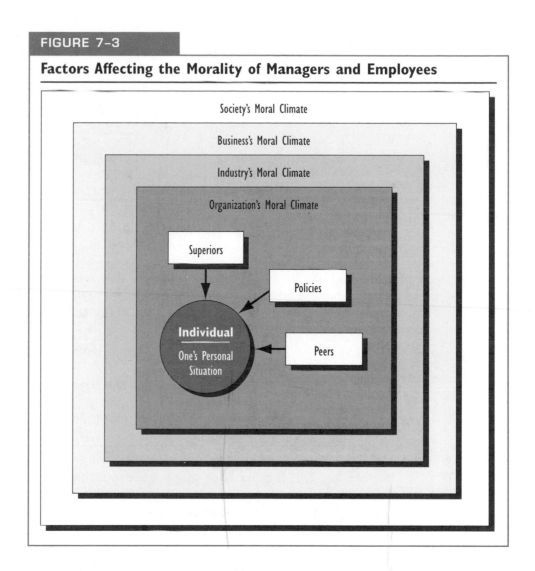

FIGURE 7–3

Factors Affecting the Morality of Managers and Employees

Society's Moral Climate

Business's Moral Climate

Industry's Moral Climate

Organization's Moral Climate

Superiors

Policies

Individual
One's Personal Situation

Peers

organization? and (2) What actions or strategies might management employ to improve the organization's ethical climate?

Factors Affecting the Organization's Moral Climate

For managers to be in a position to create an ethical climate, they must first understand the factors at work in the organization that influence whether or not other managers or employees behave ethically. In a 2003 survey conducted by the U.S.-based Society for Human Resources Management, more than half of the 462 Human Resource professionals surveyed reported that they had been pressured to act unethically in the last year, and 52 percent said they felt at least some pressure to compromise their organization's ethical standards (up from 47 percent in a similar poll conducted six years earlier). The most commonly cited sources for acting unethically included a need to follow the boss's orders (49 percent), pressure to meet overly aggressive business objectives (48 percent), and helping the organization survive (40 percent).[36]

More than a few studies have been conducted that have sought to identify and to rank the sources of ethical behaviour in organizations. Baumhart conducted one of the earliest studies, in which he surveyed over 1500 *Harvard Business Review* readers (executives, managers).[37] One of the questions asked was to rank several factors that the managers thought influenced or contributed to unethical behaviours or actions. The factors found in his study, in descending order of frequency of mention, were:

1. Behaviour of superiors
2. The ethical practices of one's industry or profession
3. Behaviour of one's peers in the organization
4. Formal organizational policy (or lack thereof)
5. Personal financial need

Brenner and Molander later replicated the Baumhart study using over 1200 *Harvard Business Review* readers. They added one additional factor to the list: society's moral climate.[38] Posner and Schmidt surveyed over 1400 managers, again asking them to rank the list of six factors in terms of their influence or contribution to unethical behaviour.[39] Figure 7–4 presents the findings of these three landmark studies.

Although there is some variation in the rankings of the three studies, several findings are worthy of note:

1. *Behaviour of superiors* was ranked as the number one influence on unethical behaviour in all three studies.
2. *Behaviour of one's peers* was ranked high in two of the three studies.

FIGURE 7–4

Factors Influencing Unethical Behaviour Question: "Listed below are the factors that many believe influence unethical behaviour. Rank them in order of their influence or contribution to unethical behaviours or actions by managers."[a]

Factor	Posner & Schmidt Study[b] (N = 1443)	Brenner & Molander Study[c] (N = 1227)	Baumhart Study[d] (N = 1531)
Behaviour of superiors	2.17(1)	2.15(1)	1.9(1)
Behaviour of one's organizational peer	3.30(2)	3.37(4)	3.1(3)
Ethical practices of one's industry or profession	3.57(3)	3.34(3)	2.6(2)
Society's moral climate	3.79(4)	4.22(5)	e
Formal organizational policy (or lack thereof)	3.84(5)	3.27(2)	3.3(4)
Personal financial need	4.09(6)	4.46(6)	4.1(5)

[a] Ranking is based on a scale of 1 (most influential) to 6 (least influential).

[b] Barry Z. Posner and Warren H. Schmidt, "Values and the American Manager: An Update," *California Management Review* (Spring 1984), 202–216.

[c] Steve Brenner and Earl Molander, "Is the Ethics of Business Changing?" *Harvard Business Review* (January/February 1977).

[d] Raymond C. Baumhart, "How Ethical Are Businessmen?" *Harvard Business Review* (July/August 1961), 6ff.

[e] This item not included in 1961 study.

3. *Industry or professional ethical practices* ranked in the upper half in all three studies.
4. *Personal financial need* ranked last in all three studies.

What stands out in these studies from an organizational perspective is the influence of the behaviour of one's superiors and peers. Also notable about these findings is that quite often it is assumed that society's moral climate has a lot to do with managers' morality, but this factor was ranked low in the two studies in which it was considered. Apparently, society's moral climate serves as a background factor that does not have a direct and immediate bearing on organizational ethics. Furthermore, it is enlightening to know that personal financial need ranked so low.

Pressures Exerted on Subordinates by Superiors One major consequence of the behaviour of superiors and peers is that pressure is placed on subordinates and/or other organizational members. In a study conducted by one of the authors of this text, managers were asked to what extent they agreed with the following proposition: "Managers today feel under pressure to compromise personal standards to achieve company goals."[40] It is insightful to consider the management levels of the 64.4 percent of the respondents who agreed with the proposition. The results were:

Top management: 50 percent agreed
Middle management: 65 percent agreed
Lower management: 85 percent agreed

This study revealed that the perceived pressure to compromise seems to be felt most by those in lower management, followed by those in middle management. In their subsequent study, Posner and Schmidt also asked managers whether they sometimes had to compromise their personal principles to conform to organizational expectations.[41] Twenty percent of the top executives agreed, 27 percent of the middle managers agreed, and 41 percent of the lower managers agreed. In other words, the same pattern prevailed in this second study.

This co-author's study posed another proposition: "I can conceive of a situation where you have sound ethics running from top to bottom, but because of pressures from the top to achieve results, the person down the line compromises." The pattern of findings on this proposition was similar to that of the other two findings.[42]

What is particularly troublesome about these findings is the pattern of response. It seems that the lower a manager is in the hierarchy, the more that manager perceives pressures toward unethical conduct. Although there are several plausible explanations for this phenomenon, one explanation seems particularly attractive because of its agreement with conversations this co-author has had with various managers. This interpretation is that top-level managers do not know how strongly their subordinates perceive pressures to go along with their bosses. These varying perceptions at different levels in the managerial hierarchy suggest that higher-level managers may not be tuned in to how pressure is perceived at lower levels. There seems to be a gap in the understanding of higher managers and lower managers regarding the pressures toward unethical behaviour that exist, especially in the lower echelons. This breakdown in understanding, or lack of sensitivity by top management to how far subordinates will go to please them, can be conducive to lower-level subordinates behaving unethically out of a real or perceived fear of reprisal, a misguided sense of loyalty, or a distorted concept of their jobs.

Search the web   WWW

"Acting with Integrity" at Nortel

Nortel Networks has posted its ethics policies on the Web for all to see. Visit Nortel Network's Web site at **http://www.nortelnetworks.com** and follow the path through corporate information and corporate citizenship to review the company's code of business conduct titled "Acting with Integrity." As the Nortel CEO has stated on the company Web site, "A reputation for integrity is a significant corporate asset. We know that acting with integrity builds credibility." You may also review their "Ethical Business Practices" on this Web site.

In a glass container plant in Gulfport, Mississippi, for example, the plant manager began to fear that top management might close the aging facility because its output was falling behind those of other plants. So, the plant manager secretly started altering records and eventually inflated the value of the plant's production by 33 percent. Top management learned of this when a janitor acquired documents and reported this bogus information to company auditors. The plant manager was fired. He was not willing to discuss the matter, but his wife said her husband was under "constant pressure" to raise the plant's production and that he believed he and the other employees would have jobs as long as he was able to do so. The company's president said he had no intention of firing the plant manager for failing to meet the production goal.[43]

Another interesting case involved a big Chevrolet truck plant in Flint, Michigan. Here, three plant managers installed a secret control box in a supervisor's office so that they could override the control panel that governed the speed of the assembly line. The plant managers claimed they felt pressure to do this because top management did not understand that high absenteeism, conveyor breakdowns, and other problems were preventing them from reaching their goals. Once they began using the hidden controls, they began meeting their production goals and winning praise from their superiors. The plant managers claimed they thought top management knew that the plant managers were speeding up the line and that what the plant managers were doing was unethical. However, top management never said anything and, therefore, it was thought that the practice was accepted. The executives denied any knowledge of the secret box. The speed-up was in violation of GM's contract with the United Auto Workers' union. Once it was exposed, the company had to pay US$1 million in back pay to the affected UAW members.[44]

The motive behind managers putting pressure on subordinates to perform, even at the sacrifice of their ethical standards, seems to be driven by the *"bottom-line" mentality* that places economic success above all other goals. Employees frequently find themselves making compromises as a result of the pressure coupled with the socialization process that emphasizes compliance with the authority structure, the need to conform to their superiors' wishes, and the expectation of loyalty.

Other Behaviours of Superiors and/or Peers   Other behaviours of one's superiors and/or peers that create a questionable organizational atmosphere include:

1. *Amoral decision making.* This includes managers who themselves fail to factor ethical considerations into their actions, decisions, and behaviours. The result of this is a vacuous leadership environment.
2. *Unethical acts, behaviours, or practices.* Some managers simply are not ethical themselves, and this influence wears off on others. Employees watch their superiors' behaviour carefully and take cues from them as to what is acceptable.
3. *Acceptance of legality as a standard of behaviour.* Some managers think that if they are strictly abiding by the law they are doing the most they ought to do.
4. *"Bottom-line" mentality and expectations of loyalty and conformity.* This focus places little value on doing what is right and on being sensitive to other stakeholders.

5. *Absence of ethical leadership.* This is a global indicator of sorts that includes some of the other points already mentioned. In addition, management never steps out ahead of the pack and assumes a leadership role in doing what is right. This reflects an absence of moral management.
6. *Objectives and evaluation systems that overemphasize profits.* If management sets unrealistic goals or does not take ethics into consideration in evaluating employees, it is creating a potentially destructive environment.
7. *Insensitivity toward how subordinates perceive pressure to meet goals.* This is related to several of the previous points. Management must be constantly vigilant of the directives and expectations it is making on employees. The manager might always ask, "How might this goal, directive, or expectation be misread or misunderstood in terms of how far I want people to go to achieve it?"
8. *Inadequate formal ethics policies.* Problems here might include inadequate management controls for monitoring and compliance, unreasonable reimbursement/expense policies, and the absence of a clear code of conduct.

Improving the Organization's Ethical Climate

Because the behaviour of managers has been identified as the most important influence on the ethical behaviour of organization members, it should come as no surprise that most actions and strategies for improving the organization's ethical climate must emanate from top management and other management levels as well. The process by which these kinds of initiatives have taken place is often referred to as "institutionalizing ethics" into the organization.[45] In this section, we will consider some of the best practices that managers have taken to improve their organizations' ethical climate. Figure 7–5 depicts a number of best practices for creating an ethical organization climate or culture. Top management leadership is at the hub of these initiatives, actions, or practices.

FIGURE 7–5

Best Practices for Improving an Organization's Ethical Climate or Culture

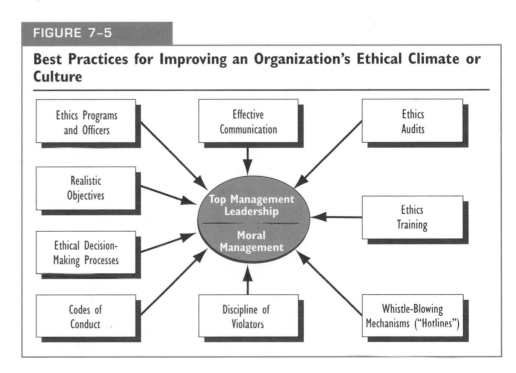

Top Management Leadership (Moral Management)   It has become a cliché, but this premise must be established at the outset: *The moral tone of an organization is set by top management.* This is because all managers and employees look to their bosses at the highest level for their cues as to what is acceptable practice. A former chairman of a major steel company stated it well: "Starting at the top, management has to set an example for all the others to follow."[46]

Top management, through its capacity to set a personal example and to shape policy, is in the ideal position to provide a highly visible role model. The authority and ability to shape policy, both formal and implied, forms one of the vital aspects of the job of any leader in any organization. Trevino, Hartman, and Brown have referred to this aspect of becoming a moral manager as "role modelling through visible action." They continue by saying that effective moral managers recognize that they live in a fishbowl and that employees are watching them for cues about what's important.[47]

Weak Ethical Leadership.   An example of weak ethical leadership (or role modelling) and one of strong ethical leadership make these points clear. In one of his consulting experiences, one of the authors encountered a situation in a small company where a long-time employee was identified as having embezzled about $20 000 over a 15-year period. When the employee was approached and questioned as to why she had done this, she explained that she thought it was all right because the president had led her to believe it was by his actions. She further explained that any time during the fall, when the leaves had fallen in his yard and he needed them raked, he would simply take company personnel off their jobs and have them do it. When the president needed cash, he would take it out of the company's petty cash box or get the key to the soft drink machine and raid its coin box. When he needed stamps to mail his personal Christmas cards, he would take them out of the company stamp box. The woman's perception was that it was all right for her to take the money because the president did it frequently. Therefore, she thought it was an acceptable practice for her as well.

Strong Ethical Leadership.   An example of positive ethical leadership may be seen in the case of a firm that was manufacturing vacuum tubes. One day the plant manager called a hurried meeting to announce that a sample of the tubes had failed a critical safety test. This meant that the batch of 10 000 tubes was of highly questionable safety and performance. The plant manager wondered out loud, "What are we going to do now?" Ethical leadership was shown by the vice president for technical operations, who looked around the room at each person and then declared in a low voice, "Scrap them!" According to a person who worked for this vice president, that act set the tone for the corporation for years, because every person present knew of situations in which faulty products had been shipped under pressures of time and budget.[48]

Each of these cases provides a vivid example of how a leader's actions and behaviour communicated important messages to others in the organization. In the absence of knowing what to do, most employees look to the behaviour of leaders for their cues as to what conduct is acceptable. In the second case, another crucial point is illustrated. When we speak of management providing ethical leadership, it is not just restricted to top management. Vice presidents, plant managers, and, indeed, all managerial personnel carry the responsibility for ethical leadership.

It has been argued by Trevino, Hartman, and Brown that a manager's reputation for ethical leadership is founded on two pillars: perceptions of the manager as both a moral person *and* as a moral manager. Being a moral person is composed of three major attributes: traits, behaviours, and decision making. Important traits are stable personal attributes such as integrity, honesty, and trustworthiness. Critical behaviours—what you do, not what you say—include doing the right thing, concern shown for people, being open, and being personally moral. Decision making of the moral person needs to reflect a solid set of ethical values and principles. In this activity, the manager would hold to values, be objective/fair, demonstrate concern for society, and follow ethical decision rules.[49]

The second pillar is being a moral manager, a concept we developed in the previous chapter. According to these researchers, moral managers recognize the importance of proactively putting ethics at the forefront of their ethical agenda. This involves three major activities. First, the moral manager must engage in *role modelling* through visible action. An emphasis is placed on visible action—action that can be witnessed by others. Second, the moral manager *communicates about ethics and values*. This is not to be done in a sermonizing way, but in a way that explains the values that guide important actions. Third, the moral manager needs to *use rewards and discipline effectively*. This is a powerful way to send signals about desirable and undesirable conduct.[50]

In a period in which the importance of a sound corporate culture has been strongly advocated, ethical leaders must stress the primacy of integrity and morality as vital components of the organization's culture. There are many different ways and situations in which management needs to do this. In general, management needs to create a climate of moral consciousness. In everything it does, it must stress the importance of sound ethical principles and practices. A former president and chief operating officer for Caterpillar Tractor Company suggested four specific actions for accomplishing this:[51]

1. Create clear and concise policies that define the company's business ethics and conduct.
2. Select for employment only those people and firms whose characters and ethics appear to be in keeping with corporate standards.
3. Promote people on the basis of performance and ethical conduct and beliefs.
4. Company employees must feel the obligation and the opportunity to report perceived irregularities in ethics or in accounting transactions.

We should conclude by noting that the leader must infuse the organization's climate with values and ethical consciousness, not just run a one-person show. This point is made vividly clear by Steven Brenner, who observed: "Ethics programs which are seen as part of one manager's management system, and not as a part of the general organizational process, will be less likely to have a lasting role in the organization."[52]

Effective Communication   Management also carries a heavy burden in terms of providing ethical leadership in the area of effective communication. We have seen the importance of communicating through acts, principles, and organizational climate. We will discuss further the communication aspects of setting realistic objectives, codes of conduct, and the decision-making process. Here, however, we want to stress the importance of communication principles, techniques, and practices.

Conveying the importance of ethics through communication includes both written and verbal forms of communication. In each of these settings, management should operate according to certain key ethical principles. Candour is one very important principle. *Candour* requires that a manager be forthright, sincere, and honest in communication transactions. In addition, it requires the manager to be fair and free from prejudice and malice in the communication. Related to this is the principle of fidelity.

Fidelity in communication means that the communicator should be faithful to detail, should be accurate, and should avoid deception or exaggeration. *Confidentiality* is a final principle that ought to be stressed. The ethical manager must exercise care in deciding what information she or he discloses to others. Trust can be easily shattered if the manager does not have a keen sense of what is confidential in a communication.

Ethics Programs and Ethics Officers   In recent years, many companies have begun creating ethics programs. These programs are often headed up by an ethics officer who is in charge of implementing the array of ethics initiatives of the organization. In some cases, the creation of ethics programs and designation of ethics officers have helped reduce penalties to those companies with ethics programs that were found guilty of ethics violations.[53] Other companies started ethics programs as an effort to centralize the coordination of ethics initiatives in those companies. Typical initiatives of companies include codes of conduct (or ethics), ethics hotlines, ethics training, and ethics audits, which we will discuss later.

An illustration of an ethics program is the one created over a decade ago by NYNEX, the US$18 billion Baby Bell, which was one of the U.S.'s most impressive ethics programs. At NYNEX, chairman and CEO William Ferguson initiated the program partially in anticipation of stiffer government penalties for white-collar crime and partially in response to a troubling pattern of ethical problems the company had faced in prior years. Historically, the company had decades of culture building and a durable set of corporate values. When AT&T broke up in 1984, however, the new company was thrown into chaos and, in the late 1980s, allegations of illegal gifts to suppliers and other questionable transactions led to federal investigators probing into company activities. This was when Ferguson tapped a 30-year executive to head up the new ethics program and to provide new leadership. The program at NYNEX eventually included ethics training initiatives, a company code of conduct, and an Ethics Policy Committee. An ethics hotline was also installed whereby company employees could phone in their ethics questions and concerns.[54]

Numerous other major companies have adopted some kind of ethics program, including Bell Canada, General Motors, Nortel, Texas Instruments, Xerox, and Sears.

Setting Realistic Objectives   Closely related to all ethics initiatives and programs being implemented by top management is the necessity that managers at all levels set realistic objectives or goals. A manager may quite innocently and inadvertently create a condition leading to unethical behaviour on a subordinate's part. Take the case of a marketing manager setting a sales goal of a 25 percent increase for the next year when a 15 percent increase is all that could be realistically expected, even with outstanding performance. In the absence of clearly established and communicated ethical norms, it is easy to see how a subordinate might believe that she or he should go to any lengths to achieve the 25 percent goal. With the goal having been set too high, the salesperson faces a situation that is conducive to unethical behaviour in order to please the superior.

Fred T. Allen, a former executive, reinforces this point:

> *Top management must establish sales and profit goals that are realistic— goals that can be achieved with current business practices. Under the pressure of unrealistic goals, otherwise responsible subordinates will often take the attitude that "anything goes" in order to comply with the chief executive's target.[55]*

The point here is that there are ethical implications to even the most routine managerial decisions, such as goal setting. Managers must be keenly sensitive to the possibility of innocently creating situations in which others may perceive a need or an incentive to do the wrong thing.

Ethical Decision-Making Processes Decision making is at the heart of the management process. If there is any practice or process that is synonymous with management, it is decision making. Decision making usually entails a process of stating the problem, analyzing the problem, identifying the possible courses of action that might be taken, evaluating these courses of action, deciding on the best alternative, and then implementing the chosen course of action.

Decision making at best is a challenge for management. Many decisions management faces turn out to be ethical decisions or to have ethical implications or consequences. Once we leave the realm of relatively ethics-free decisions (such as which production method to use for a particular product), decisions quickly become complex, and many carry with them an ethical dimension.

According to LaRue Hosmer, five important points should be made about the character and nature of ethics and decision making:[56]

1. Most ethical decisions have extended consequences. First level consequences are followed by a multitude of effects having impacts both within and outside the organization that should be considered when decisions are made.
2. Most ethical decisions have multiple alternatives. Such decisions do not present themselves in simple yes-or-no form, such as "Do we pay a bribe or not?" The simple dichotomy makes for sharp contrasts but does not always capture the real complex alternatives presented.
3. Most ethical decisions have mixed outcomes. Like alternatives, outcomes are mixed and complex rather than occurring in any clear, unambiguous fashion.
4. Most ethical decisions have uncertain consequences. Some consequences may occur that were not anticipated. Thus, it is not always clear what consequences will follow a decision.
5. Most ethical decisions have personal implications. The ethical issues that management faces are not all impersonal but often have very real individual benefits and costs for the decision makers.

Ethical decision making is not a simple process but rather a multifaceted process that is complicated by the characteristics just described. It would be nice if a set of ethical principles were readily available for the manager to "plug in" and walk away from, with a decision to be forthcoming. However, such was not the case when we discussed principles that help personal decision making, and it is not the case when we think of organizational decision making. The ethical principles we discussed earlier are useful here, but there are no simple formulas.

Although it is difficult to portray graphically the process of ethical decision making, it is possible as long as we recognize that such an effort cannot totally capture reality. Figure 7–6 presents one conception of the ethical decision-making process. In this model, the individual is asked to identify the action, decision, or behaviour that is being considered and then to articulate all dimensions of the proposed course of action. Next, the individual is asked to subject the course of action to what we call an *ethics screen*. An ethics screen consists of several select standards against which the proposed course of action is to be compared. In the illustrated ethics screen, we reference our earlier discussion of the conventional approach (embodying standards/

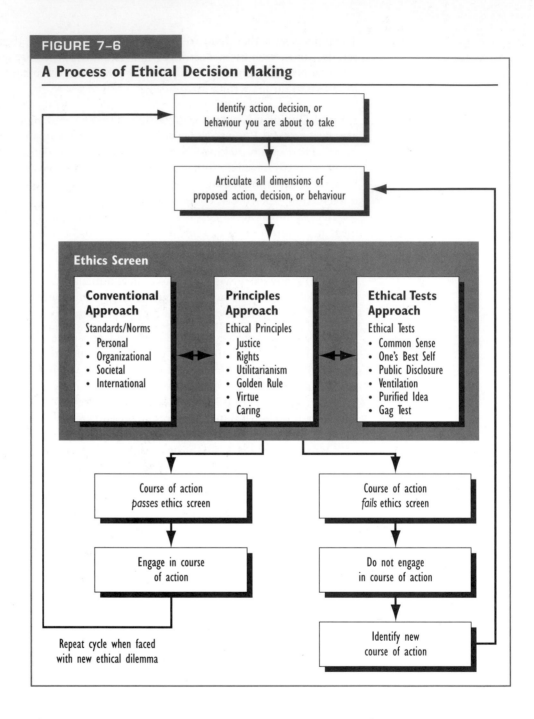

FIGURE 7–6

A Process of Ethical Decision Making

Identify action, decision, or behaviour you are about to take

Articulate all dimensions of proposed action, decision, or behaviour

Ethics Screen

Conventional Approach

Standards/Norms
- Personal
- Organizational
- Societal
- International

Principles Approach

Ethical Principles
- Justice
- Rights
- Utilitarianism
- Golden Rule
- Virtue
- Caring

Ethical Tests Approach

Ethical Tests
- Common Sense
- One's Best Self
- Public Disclosure
- Ventilation
- Purified Idea
- Gag Test

Course of action *passes* ethics screen

Course of action *fails* ethics screen

Engage in course of action

Do not engage in course of action

Identify new course of action

Repeat cycle when faced with new ethical dilemma

norms), the principles approach, and the ethical tests approach to ethical decision making.

In this model, it is left up to the individual to determine what mix of guidelines to use as the ethics screen. Normally, some combination of the guidelines contained in the screen would be helpful to the manager who truly is attempting to make an ethical decision. If the proposed course of action fails the ethics screen, the decision maker should not engage in the course of action but should consider a new decision, behaviour, or action and submit it to this same process. If the proposed course of action passes the screen (the decision maker has determined it to be an ethical course of action), she or he should engage in the action, decision, or behaviour and then repeat the cycle only when faced with a new ethical dilemma.

Another useful approach to making ethical decisions is to systematically ask and answer a series of simple questions. It should quickly be realized that this approach is similar to the ethical tests approach presented earlier in the chapter.

Ethics Check. One well-known set of questions merits mention here because of its popularity in the book *The Power of Ethical Management.*[57] Kenneth Blanchard and Norman Vincent Peale proposed the "ethics check" questions as follows:

1. *Is it legal?* Will I be violating either civil law or company policy?
2. *Is it balanced?* Is it fair to all concerned in the short term as well as the long term? Does it promote win-win relationships?
3. *How will it make me feel about myself?* Will it make me proud? Would I feel good if my decision was published in the newspaper? Would I feel good if my family knew about it?

Ethics Quick Test. Using a brief set of questions to make ethical decisions has become popular in business. For example, Texas Instruments has printed its seven-part "Ethics Quick Test" on a wallet card its employees may carry. The test's seven questions and reminders are as follows:[58]

- Is the action legal?
- Does it comply with our values?
- If you do it, will you feel bad?
- How will it look in the newspaper?
- If you know it's wrong, don't do it.
- If you're not sure, ask.
- Keep asking until you get an answer.

Sears' Guidelines. In its Code of Business Conduct, Sears, Roebuck and Co. presents its five "Guidelines for Making Ethical Decisions," which are:[59]

1. Is it legal?
2. Is it within Sears' shared beliefs and policies?
3. Is it right/fair/appropriate?
4. Would I want everyone to know about this?
5. How will I feel about myself?

The sets of practical questions posed here are intended to produce a process of ethical inquiry that is of immediate use and understanding to a group of employees and managers. Note that many of the items are similar or identical to points raised earlier in the ethical tests approach. These questions help ensure that ethical due process takes place. They cannot tell us whether our decisions are ethical or not, but they can help us be sure that we are raising the appropriate issues and genuinely attempting to be ethical.

Codes of Conduct Top management has the responsibility for establishing standards of behaviour and for effectively communicating those standards to all managers and employees in the organization. One of the classic ways by which companies and ethics officers have fulfilled this responsibility is through the use of codes of ethics, or **codes of conduct. Codes of ethics** are a phenomenon of the past 20 years. Over 95 percent of all major corporations have them today, and the central questions in their usefulness or effectiveness revolve around the managerial policies and attitudes associated with their use.[60] There are a number of potential values or benefits that business organizations receive as a result of their codes of ethics, including the following:[61]

1. Legal protection for the company
2. Increased company pride and loyalty
3. Increased consumer/public goodwill
4. Improved loss prevention
5. Reduced bribery and kickbacks
6. Improved product quality
7. Increased productivity

Among the most common topics addressed in corporate codes are:[62]

1. Conflicts of interest
2. Receiving gifts, gratuities, entertainment
3. Protecting company proprietary information
4. Giving gifts, gratuities, entertainment
5. Discrimination
6. Sexual harassment
7. Kickbacks
8. General conduct
9. Employee theft
10. Proper use of company assets

There have been both successes and failures reported with organizational codes of ethics, but the acid test seems to be whether or not such codes actually become "living documents," not just platitudinous public relations statements that are put into a file drawer upon dissemination. Codes may not be a panacea for management, but, when properly developed and administered, they serve to raise the level of ethical behaviour in the organization by clarifying what is meant by ethical conduct and encouraging moral behaviour.

A major study of the effectiveness of corporate codes found that there is a relationship between corporate codes and employee behaviour in the workplace, particularly to the degree that employees perceive the codes to be implemented strongly and embedded in the organizational culture. Therefore, when codes are implemented forcefully and embedded strongly in the culture, reports of unethical employee behaviour tend to be lower.[63]

A major study of corporate codes by Mark Schwartz revealed that there are a number of different ways in which employees perceive or understand codes of conduct.[64] Schwartz's research yielded eight themes or metaphors that helped to explain how codes influence behaviour within organizations:

1. As a *rule book*, the code acts to clarify what behaviour is expected of employees.
2. As a *signpost*, the code can lead employees to consult other individuals or corporate policies to determine the appropriateness of behaviour.
3. As a *mirror*, the code provides employees with a chance to confirm whether their behaviour is acceptable to the company.
4. As a *magnifying glass*, the code suggests a note of caution to be more careful or engage in greater reflection before acting.

5. As a *shield*, the code acts in a manner that allows employees to better challenge and resist unethical requests.
6. As a *smoke detector*, the code leads employees to try to convince others and warn them of their inappropriate behaviour.
7. As a *fire alarm*, the code leads employees to contact the appropriate authority and report violations.
8. As a *club*, the potential enforcement of the code causes employees to comply with the code's provisions.[65]

In summary, the code metaphors provide insights into a number of ways in which codes are perceived or viewed by organizational members.

Disciplining Violators of Ethics Standards To bring about an ethical climate that all organizational members will believe in, management must discipline violators of its accepted ethical norms. A major reason the general public, and even employees in many organizations, have questioned business's sincerity in desiring a more ethical environment has been business's unwillingness to discipline violators. There are numerous cases of top management officers who behaved unethically and yet were retained in their positions. At lower levels, there have been cases of top management overlooking or failing to penalize unethical behaviour of subordinates. These evidences of inaction on management's or the board's part represent implicit approval of the individual's behaviour.

Fred Allen has argued that an organization should respond forcefully to the individual who is guilty of deliberately or flagrantly violating its code of ethics: "From the pinnacle of the corporate pyramid to its base, there can only be one course of action: dismissal. And should actual criminality be involved, there should be total cooperation with law enforcement authorities."[66]

Based on their research, Trevino, Hartman, and Brown have argued: "The moral manager consistently rewards ethical conduct and disciplines unethical conduct at all levels in the organization, and these actions serve to uphold the standards and rules."[67] The effort on the part of management has to be complete in communicating to all, by way of disciplining offenders, that unethical behaviour will not be tolerated in the organization. It is management's tacit approval of violations that has seriously undermined efforts to bring about a more ethical climate in many organizational situations.

Whistle-Blowing Mechanisms and "Hotlines" One problem that frequently leads to the covering up of unethical acts by people in an organization is that they do not know how to react when they observe a questionable practice. An effective ethical climate is contingent on employees having a mechanism for (and top management support of) "blowing the whistle" on or reporting violators. Allen has summarized this point as follows: "Employees must know exactly what is expected of them in the moral arena and how to respond to warped ethics."[68]

In a 2003 survey conducted by PricewaterhouseCoopers involving over 3600 interviews in 50 countries, it was found that 40 percent of Canadian companies surveyed have implemented whistle-blowing systems, compared to 28 percent of companies globally.[69]

The whistle-blowing mechanism in most common use today is the ethics "hotline." At both NYNEX and Northrop, for example, hotlines are used whereby employees may phone in their inquiries about the company's ethics code or report suspected wrongdoing. In one recent year, Northrop reported that about 5 percent of the company's 32 000 employees used its hotline. NYNEX also receives thousands of calls per year. At NYNEX, it was estimated that half the callers were seeking information or clarification about the corporate code, whereas only about 10 percent of the callers made allegations of wrongdoing. Ethics officers see this as a positive indication that employees are proacting and trying to head off potential problems before they occur.[70]

Hotlines can have a downside risk, however. Ethicist Barbara Ley Toffler argues that the hotlines may do harm. She suspects that many of the reported wrongdoings are false accusations and that if the company does not handle these issues carefully, it may do a lot of damage to morale.[71]

Xerox Corporation has a complaint resolution process to handle reported wrong-doings. Xerox employs a four-step process.[72] First, the company receives and examines a complaint. The complaint, or allegation, may come from its hotline; from outside sources such as vendors, customers, or former employees; from whistle-blowers; or from law enforcement agencies. Second, the company conducts an investigation. This is completed by a team—a senior manager, legal counsel, and a human resources executive. Third, there is a management review of the team's report. Finally, step four involves the resolution. Part of the resolution is an attempt to determine why and how the reported incident occurred in the first place. Xerox thinks that the essential elements of the ethics investigation include adherence to a plan, good management communications, and a dedicated interest in ensuring a fair and impartial investigation.

In addition to hotlines for reporting wrongdoing, some companies employ toll-free numbers wherein employees may simply inquire about ethics matters. For example, the Sears Office of Ethics and Business Policy employs an "Ethics Assist" program in which employees may call about such topics as:[73]

- Interpretation of or guidance on company policy
- General ethics questions
- Code of conduct issues
- Workplace harassment/discrimination
- Selling practices
- Theft

Given the recent spate of corporate scandals, and the now-famous accounts of whistle-blowers like Sherron Watkins of Enron or Cynthia Cooper of WorldCom, there has been increasing pressure for governments to bolster legislation that protects whistle-blowers from the consequences of their decision to "go public."

Business Ethics Training   For several years, there has been debate and controversy about whether managerial ethics can and should be taught. One school of thought assumes that ethics is personal, already embedded within the employee or manager and, hence, not alterable or teachable. A growing school of thought, on the other hand, argues that instruction in business ethics should be made a part of business school education, management training, executive development programs, and seminars.

Professor Kirk Hanson has been teaching business ethics for many years. Whereas he agrees with some critics who say it is tough to infuse values in university students, he also thinks that there is a legitimate role for business ethics courses. Hanson believes that we can most help the fundamentally decent, well-intentioned student. He says:

> *If we teach techniques and strategies for handling a wide variety of business decisions, we can do the same for predictable ethical decisions or challenges. Among those situations are finding a match between a person's values and those of his or her employer; managing the pushback point where one's values are tested by peers, subordinates, or superiors; handling an unethical directive from one's boss; and coping with a performance system that gives strong incentives to cut ethical corners.[74]*

In addition, in numerous organizations in Canada and the United States today, management training in business ethics is taking place. What might be the purposes or objectives of such ethics training? Several purposes have been suggested:

1. To increase the manager's sensitivity to ethical problems
2. To encourage critical evaluation of value priorities
3. To increase awareness of organizational realities
4. To increase awareness of societal realities
5. To improve understanding of the importance of public image and public/society relations[75]

To this list we might add some other desirable goals:

6. To examine the ethical facets of business decision making
7. To bring about a greater degree of fairness and honesty in the workplace
8. To respond more completely to the organization's social responsibilities

In terms of the effectiveness of ethics training, Thomas Jones discovered in his research that exposure to lengthy programs (e.g., 10 weeks) resulted in significant improvements in moral development. Brief exposures to business ethics, however, yielded less encouraging results.[76] Questions remain, therefore, as to the ultimate and lasting value of superficial ethics education.

Ethics Audits and Self-Assessments   In increasing numbers, companies today are beginning to appreciate the need to follow up on their ethics initiatives and programs. **Ethics audits** are mechanisms or approaches by which a company may assess or evaluate its ethical climate or programs. Ethical audits are intended to carefully review such ethics initiatives as ethics programs, codes of conduct, hotlines, and ethics training programs. Ethics audits are similar to social audits discussed in Chapter 4. In addition, they are intended to examine other management activities that may add to or subtract from the company's initiatives. This might include management's sincerity, communication efforts, incentive and reward systems, and other management activities. Ethics audits may employ written instruments, committees, and employee interviews.[77]

More and more companies will assess and attempt to improve their organizations' ethical climates as instruments, methods, and services are made available for conducting such programs. An example of the resources now available include the services offered by EthicScan, a Canadian ethics consultancy, established by David Nitkin. In addition to the research this firm conducts, it offers such tools as ethics audits, ethical assurance programs, and ethics empowerment and assurance programs.[78] Figure 7–7 summarizes what major companies have been doing in order to improve their organizations' ethical climates.

Although we have not touched on all that can be done at the organizational level to improve or manage business ethics, the actions suggested represent best practices

FIGURE 7-7

Improving the Organization's Ethical Climate

Executives and managers seeking to improve the ethical climate of their organizations should consider the following conclusions from the present survey report:

Companies that see their ethics monitoring and enforcement methods as very effective share these characteristics:

- Written codes, policies, or guidelines;
- Distribution of policies to all employees, not just management;
- Reinforcement through communications, including videotapes, articles, posters, and public talks by company executives;
- Additional training geared toward application of policies to everyday work situations;
- Sources of information and advice, such as ombudspersons and hotlines; and
- Monitoring and enforcement through a Corporate Ethics Office and a Board of Directors Ethics Committee.

If companies' perceptions correlate with actual effectiveness, then companies that do not have the above elements are risking greater amounts of unethical conduct than companies that do.

Source: *Ethics Policies and Programs in American Business* (Washington, DC: Ethics Resource Center and Behavior Research Center, 1990). Used with permission.

that can move management a long way toward improving the organization's ethical climate. If management takes specific steps as suggested, many behaviours or decisions that might otherwise have been questionable have a greater chance of being in line with leadership's ethical standards. Thus, ethics can be positively supervised, and managers do not have to treat value concerns as matters totally out of their influence or control. On the contrary, managers can intercede and improve the organization's ethical climate.[79]

From Moral Decisions to Moral Organizations

In the last two chapters, we have discussed ethical or moral acts, decisions, practices, managers, and organizations. Though the goal of ethics initiatives is to develop moral organizations, sometimes all we get are isolated ethical acts, decisions or practices, or, if we are fortunate, isolated moral managers. Achieving the status of moral standing is a goal, whatever the level on which it may be achieved. Sometimes all we can do is bring about ethical acts, decisions, or practices. A larger goal is to create moral managers, in the sense in which they were discussed in Chapter 6. Finally, the highest-level goal for managers may be to create moral organizations.

The important point here is to state that the goal is to create moral decisions, moral managers, and ultimately, moral organizations while recognizing that what we frequently observe in business is the achievement of moral standing at only one of these levels. The ideal is to create a moral organization that is fully populated by moral managers making moral decisions (and practices, policies, and behaviours), but this is seldom achieved. Figure 7–8 depicts the essential characteristics of each of these levels.

From Moral Decisions to Moral Organizations

Moral Decision(s)

Single or isolated moral acts, behaviours, policies, practices, or decisions made by a manager or managers of an organization. These are the simplest and most basic form of achieving moral status.

Moral Manager(s)

A manager or managers who have adopted the characteristics of moral management and this approach dominates all their decision making. These managers manifest ethical leadership and are always occupying the moral high ground.

Moral Organization(s)

An organization that is dominated by the presence of moral managers making moral decisions. Moral management has become an integral part of the culture. Moral management permeates all the organization's decisions, policies, and practices. The organization uses the best practices for achieving a moral management culture.

Summary

The subject of business ethics may be addressed at several different levels: personal, organizational, industry, societal, and international. This chapter focuses on the personal and organizational levels.

A number of different ethical principles serve as guides to personal decision making. Major philosophical principles include utilitarianism, rights, and justice. The Golden Rule was singled out as a particularly powerful ethical principle among various groups studied. Virtue ethics was identified as an increasingly popular concept. A general method for reconciling ethical conflicts was introduced. Six practical tests were proposed to assist the individual in making ethical decisions: the test of common sense, the test of one's best self, the test of making something public, the test of ventilation, the test of the purified idea, and the gag test.

At the organizational level, factors were discussed that affect the organization's moral climate. It was argued that the behaviour of one's superiors and peers and industry ethical practices were the most important influences on a firm's ethical climate. Society's moral climate and personal needs were considered to be less important. Best practices for improving the firm's ethical climate include providing leadership from management, ethics programs and ethics officers, setting realistic objectives, infusing the decision-making process with ethical considerations, employing codes of conduct, disciplining violators, creating whistle-blowing mechanisms or hotlines, training managers in business ethics, and using ethics audits.

The goal of ethics initiatives is to achieve a status that may be characterized not just by isolated moral decisions, but by the presence of moral managers and the ultimate achievement of a moral organization.

Key Terms

codes of conduct (page 227)

codes of ethics (page 227)

compensatory justice (page 208)

distributive justice (page 208)

ethical tests (page 214)

ethics audits (page 231)

Golden Rule (page 211)

legal rights (page 207)

moral rights (page 207)

principle of caring (page 208)

principle of justice (page 208)

principle of rights (page 207)

principle of utilitarianism (page 206)

procedural justice (page 208)

rights (page 207)

utilitarianism (page 206)

virtue ethics (page 209)

Discussion Questions

1. From your personal experience, give two examples of ethical dilemmas in your personal life. Give two examples of ethical dilemmas you have experienced as a member of an organization.

2. Using the examples you provided for Question 1, identify one or more of the guides to personal decision making or ethical tests that you think would have helped you resolve your dilemmas. Describe how it would have helped.

3. Assume that you are in your first real managerial position. Identify five ways in which you might provide ethical leadership. Rank them in terms of importance, and be prepared to explain your ranking.

4. What do you think about the idea of codes of conduct? Give three reasons why an organization ought to have a code of conduct, and give three reasons why an organization should not have a code of conduct. On balance, how do you regard codes of conduct?

5. A lively debate is going on today concerning whether business ethics can or should be taught in business schools. Do you think business ethics can and should be taught? Be prepared to explain your reasons carefully.

Endnotes

1. PricewaterhouseCoopers, http://www.pwc.com/ca/crime survey.

2. Susan Pulliam, "Over the Line: A Staffer Ordered to Commit Fraud Balked, Then Caved—Pushed by WorldCom Bosses, Accountant Betty Vinson Helped Cook the Books—A Confession at the Marriott," *Wall Street Journal* (June 23, 2003), A1.

3. Dan Chapman, "Woman Rewarded for Act of Honesty," *The Atlanta Journal-Constitution* (September 8, 2001).

4. Jennifer Dixon, "Bosses Knew Shipped Meat Was Tainted, Workers Say," *Chicago Tribune* (August 30, 2001).

5. Gretchen Morgenson, "Wall Street Firms Endorse Ethics Standards for Analysts," *The New York Times* (June 13, 2001).

6. Archie B. Carroll, "Principles of Business Ethics: Their Role in Decision Making and an Initial Consensus," *Management Decision* (Vol. 28, No. 28, 1990), 20–24.

7. Vincent Barry, *Moral Issues in Business* (Belmont, CA: Wadsworth, 1979), 43.

8. *Ibid.*, 45–46.

9. Manuel C. Velasquez, *Business Ethics: Concepts and Cases*, 3d ed. (Englewood Cliffs, NJ: Prentice Hall, 1992), 72–73.

10. Richard T. DeGeorge, *Business Ethics*, 5th ed. (Upper Saddle River, NJ: Prentice Hall, 1999), 69–72.

11. Velasquez, 73.

12. DeGeorge, 69–72.

13. *Ibid.*

14. John Rawls, *A Theory of Justice* (Cambridge, MA: Harvard University Press, 1971).

15. DeGeorge, 69–72.

16. *Ibid.*, 72.

17. Brian K. Burton and Craig P. Dunn, "Feminist Ethics as Moral Grounding for Stakeholder Theory," *Business*

Ethics Quarterly (Vol. 6, No. 2, 1996), 133–147; see also A. C. Wicks, D. R. Gilbert, and R. E. Freeman, "A Feminist Reinterpretation of the Stakeholder Concept," *Business Ethics Quarterly* (Vol. 4, 1994), 475–497.

18. Jeanne M. Liedtka, "Feminist Morality and Competitive Reality: A Role for an Ethic of Care?" *Business Ethics Quarterly* (Vol. 6, 1996), 179–200. See also John Dobson and Judith White, "Toward the Feminine Firm," *Business Ethics Quarterly* (Vol. 5, 1995), 463–478.

19. Alasdair MacIntyre, *After Virtue* (University of Notre Dame Press, 1981). See also Louis P. Pojman, *Ethics: Discovering Right and Wrong*, 2d ed. (Belmont, CA: Wadsworth, 1995), 160–185.

20. Pojman, 161. See also Bill Shaw, "Sources of Virtue: The Market and the Community," *Business Ethics Quarterly* (Vol. 7, 1997), 33–50; and Dennis Moberg, "Virtuous Peers in Work Organizations," *Business Ethics Quarterly* (Vol. 7, 1997), 67–85.

21. Esther F. Schaeffer, "Character Education: A Prerequisite for Corporate Ethics," *Ethics Today* (Summer 1997), 5.

22. Marianne M. Jennings, "What's Happening in Business Schools?" *Public Interest* (Vol. 137, Fall 1999), 25–32.

23. Oliver F. Williams and Patrick E. Murphy, "The Ethics of Virtue: A Moral Theory for Business," in Oliver F. Williams and John W. Houck (eds.), *A Virtuous Life in Business* (Lanham, MD: Rowman & Littlefield Publishers, Inc., 1992), 9–27.

24. Carroll, 22.

25. Barry, 50–51.

26. Carroll, 22.

27. William Shaw and Vincent Barry, *Moral Issues in Business* (Belmont, CA: Wadsworth, 1989), 77–78; and Vincent R. Ruggiero, *The Moral Imperative* (Port Washington, NY: Alfred Publishers, 1973).

28. Shaw and Barry, 77.

29. *Ibid.*, 78.

30. Gordon L. Lippett, *The Leader Looks at Ethics*, 12–13.

31. "Stiffer Rules for Business Ethics," *Business Week* (March 30, 1974), 88.

32. Frederick Andrews, "Corporate Ethics: Talks with a Trace of Robber Baron," *The New York Times* (April 18, 1977), C49–52.

33. Phillip V. Lewis, "Ethical Principles for Decision Makers: A Longitudinal Study," *Journal of Business Ethics* (Vol. 8, 1989), 275.

34. Cited in John B. Cullen, Bart Victor, and Carroll Stephens, "An Ethical Weather Report: Assessing the Organization's Ethical Climate," *Organizational Dynamics* (Autumn 1989), 50.

35. For an excellent discussion, see Deborah Vidaver Cohen, "Creating and Maintaining Ethical Work Climates: Anomie in the Workplace and Implications for Managing Change," *Business Ethics Quarterly* (Vol. 3, No. 4, October 1993), 343–355. See also B. Victor and J. Cullen,

"The Organizational Bases of Ethical Work Climates," *Administrative Science Quarterly* (Vol. 33, 1988), 101–125; and H. R. Smith and A. B. Carroll, "Organizational Ethics: A Stacked Deck," *Journal of Business Ethics* (Vol. 3, 1984), 95–100.

36. Society for Human Resource Management, http://www.shrm.org/.

37. Raymond C. Baumhart, "How Ethical Are Businessmen?" *Harvard Business Review* (July/August, 1961), 6ff.

38. Steve Brenner and Earl Molander, "Is the Ethics of Business Changing?" *Harvard Business Review* (January/February 1977).

39. Barry Z. Posner and Warren H. Schmidt, "Values and the American Manager: An Update," *California Management Review* (Spring 1984), 202–216.

40. Archie B. Carroll, "Managerial Ethics: A Post-Watergate View," *Business Horizons* (April 1975), 75–80.

41. Posner and Schmidt, 211.

42. Carroll, 75–80.

43. George Getschow, "Some Middle Managers Cut Corners to Achieve High Corporate Goals," *The Wall Street Journal* (November 8, 1979), 1, 34.

44. *Ibid.*, 34.

45. T. V. Purcell and James Weber, *Institutionalizing Corporate Ethics: A Case History, Special Study No. 71* (New York: The President's Association, American Management Association, 1979). See also James Weber, "Institutionalizing Ethics into Business Organizations: A Model and Research Agenda," *Business Ethics Quarterly* (Vol. 3, No. 4, October, 1993), 419–436.

46. L. W. Foy, "Business Ethics: A Reappraisal," Distinguished Lecture Series, Columbia Graduate School of Business (January 30, 1975), 2.

47. Linda Klebe Trevino, Laura Pincus Hartman, and Michael Brown, "Moral Person and Moral Manager: How Executives Develop a Reputation for Ethical Leadership," *California Management Review* (Vol. 42, No. 4, Summer 2000), 134.

48. Harvey Gittler, "Listen to the Whistle-Blowers Before It's Too Late," *The Wall Street Journal* (March 10, 1986), 16.

49. Trevino, Hartman, and Brown, 128–142.

50. *Ibid.*, 133–136.

51. Lee L. Morgan, "Business Ethics Starts with the Individual," *Management Accounting* (March 1977), 14, 60.

52. Steven N. Brenner, "Influences on Corporate Ethics Programs" (San Diego, CA: International Association for Business and Society, March 16–18, 1990), 7.

53. Susan Gaines, "Handing Out Halos," *Business Ethics* (March/April 1994), 20–24.

54. *Ibid.*, 20–24; see also Stephen J. Garone (ed.), *Business Ethics: Generating Trust in the 1990s and Beyond* (New York: The Conference Board, 1994).

55. Fred T. Allen, "Corporate Morality: Is the Price Too High?" *The Wall Street Journal* (October 17, 1975), 16.

56. LaRue T. Hosmer, *The Ethics of Management* (Homewood, IL: Richard D. Irwin, 1987), 12–14.

57. Kenneth Blanchard and Norman Vincent Peale, *The Power of Ethical Management* (New York: Fawcett Crest, 1988), 20.

58. Texas Instruments, "Ethics Quick Test" (Texas Instruments Ethics Office), wallet card.

59. Sears, Roebuck and Co., *Code of Business Conduct* (1997), 2.

60. Gary Edwards, "And the Survey Said ...," in Garone (1994), 25.

61. *Creating a Workable Company Code of Ethics* (Washington, DC: Ethics Resource Center, 1990), VIII–1.

62. *Ethics Policies and Programs in American Business* (Washington, DC: Ethics Resource Center, 1990), 23–24; see also W. F. Edmondson, *A Code of Ethics: Do Corporate Executives and Employees Need It?* (Itawamba Community College Press, 1990).

63. Donald L. McCabe, Linda Klebe Trevino, and Kenneth D. Butterfield, "The Influence of Collegiate and Corporate Codes of Conduct on Ethics-Related Behavior in the Workplace," *Business Ethics Quarterly* (Vol. 6, October 1996), 473.

64. Mark Schwartz, "The Nature of the Relationship Between Corporate Codes of Ethics and Behavior," *Journal of Business Ethics* (Vol. 32, 2001), 247.

65. *Ibid.*, 255.

66. Allen, 16.

67. Trevino, Hartman, and Brown, 136.

68. Allen, 16.

69. PricewaterhouseCoopers, http://www.pwc.com/ca/crime survey.

70. Cited in Gaines, 22.

71. *Ibid.*, 22–23.

72. Brian R. Hollstein, "From Complaint to Resolution," in Garone (1994), 21–22.

73. Sears *Code of Business Conduct*, 1997.

74. Kirk O. Hanson, "What Good Are Ethics Courses?" *Across the Board* (September 1987), 10–11.

75. Ron Zemke, "Ethics Training: Can We Really Teach People Right from Wrong?" *Training HRD* (May 1977), 39.

76. Thomas M. Jones, "Can Business Ethics Be Taught? Empirical Evidence," *Business & Professional Ethics Journal* (Vol. 8, 1989), 86.

77. Michael Metzger, Dan R. Dalton, and John W. Hill, "The Organization of Ethics and the Ethics of Organizations: The Case for Expanded Organizational Ethics Audits," *Business Ethics Quarterly* (Vol. 3, No. 1, January, 1993), 27–43. Also see S. Andrew Ostapski, "The Moral Audit," *Business and Economic Review* (Vol. 38, No. 2, January–March 1992), 17–20; and Thomas Petzinger, Jr., "This Auditing Team Wants You to Create a Moral Organization," *The Wall Street Journal* (January 19, 1996), B1.

78. EthicScan Canada Ltd., http://www.ethicscan.ca/index.html.

79. W. Edward Stead, Dan L. Worrell, and Jean Garner Stead, "An Integrative Model for Understanding and Managing Ethical Behavior in Business Organizations," *Journal of Business Ethics* (Vol. 9, 1990), 223–242. See also Robert D. Gatewood and Archie B. Carroll, "Assessment of Ethical Performance of Organization Members: A Conceptual Framework," *Academy of Management Review* (Vol. 16, No. 4, 1991), 667–690.

Chapter 8

Business Ethics and Technology

Chapter Objectives

After studying this chapter, you should be able to:

1 Identify the role that technology plays in our business lives.

2 Gain an understanding of the technological environment and the characteristics of technology that influence business ethics and stakeholders.

3 Identify the benefits and side effects of technology in business.

4 Gain an appreciation of society's intoxication with technology and the consequences of this intoxication.

5 Learn to differentiate between information technology and biotechnology and their ethical implications for the management of enterprises.

We live in an age characterized by advancing technology. Each new generation experiences technological advances that were not seen by previous generations; technology is how we sustain life and make it comfortable. Technology is the core of many businesses, whether it is used to pursue new products or processes or as a means to achieve other worthwhile ends. But, technology, as many have observed, is a two-edged sword. Many positive benefits flow from technological advances. By the same token, however, many new problems or challenges are posed by advancing technology. Futurist John Naisbitt, for example, has questioned whether advancing technology has the potential to be a "liberating" or "destructive" force in society. He has said that at best, technology supports and improves human life, and at its worst it alienates, isolates, distorts, and destroys.[1]

In either case, technology has become such a central part of doing business in the twenty-first century that it cannot be ignored. Moreover, ethical issues for business and for society have arisen as a result of technological advances. Many would argue that technology has developed at a speed that significantly outstrips the capacity of society, government, or business to grasp its consequences or ethics. In this chapter, we will explore some of these issues, knowing full well that other aspects will be mentioned in ensuing chapters as specific stakeholder groups are discussed.

From genetically modified foods to technological surveillance, understanding the ethical implications of technology will no doubt generate an ever-increasing source of controversy in the coming years. Consider the case of businesses using "Big Brother" tactics to collect customer information. Several bars in Edmonton and Calgary recently came under close scrutiny for their use of technology to collect information on bar patrons. The ID scanning device installed in a number of bars scans the government ID cards of people as they enter and allows bar owners to maintain a customer database and alert owners to any "problematic" customers. Any customers who are "red flagged" would then be banned from bars linked together in Edmonton, Calgary, and Vancouver. However, critics have argued that such a system could easily be used for marketing and for tracking the movement of people, and Alberta's privacy commissioner and the Alberta Civil Liberties Association ruled that such a scanning system was excessive and an invasion of privacy.[2]

Consider also the application of surveillance technology that was used at the 2001 Super Bowl held in Tampa, Florida. Unbeknownst to people entering Raymond James Stadium, they were unwitting participants in what might be called an "electronic police lineup." Cameras located at each entrance "taped" every face that entered the stadium. We are all familiar with camera technology, of course, so what is the big deal? Coupled with sophisticated face-recognition software, these cameras facilitated the instant measurement of the dimensions of the human face (such as the distance between eyes) and reduced each face to a numerical code. That code was then matched against the codes of known criminals and suspected terrorists that were stored in a law-enforcement database.[3]

According to the president of Viisage Technology, the developer of the face-recognition software, his company was able to match 19 faces from the Super Bowl crowd to faces in the database of people with criminal records. As it turns out, no arrests were made because none of those 19 people were wanted by the police at the time, even though they all had criminal records. Was this an ethical usage of technology? The American Civil Liberties Union (ACLU) dubbed this application "Snooper Bowl." The ACLU holds that this application is just one more example of the kinds of issues that arise in the ongoing debate about the power of technology to shrink our privacy. This application may not seem too intrusive because it was done in a public place

Search the web

Is Technology Good or Evil?

The two founders of the Institute for Business, Technology and Ethics (IBTE) come at the issue of technology from two different sides. One says that technology is good and one says that technology is evil. The two friends since the 1970s came together to create this unique, nonprofit organization that features ethics conversations regarding technology issues.

An example of the questions raised includes: "What are the primary ethical challenges we must face up to in the bioethics realm?" Web visitors are given the chance to share their opinions.

Visit **http://www.ethix.org** for an interesting exploration of business and technology ethics.

where expectations of privacy are low. The head of the Florida ACLU thinks that an application like this, however, is just one more step toward broad and permanent surveillance of society's members. His position was that we should first discuss a technology such as this one before using it. Further, he noted that there had been no announcement to people entering the stadium that they would be checked out in this technologically advanced way.[4]

Though you were likely unaware of it, technological surveillance could be as close as the car you drive. As of 2003, millions of North American automobiles have event data recorders, a scaled-down version of the "black boxes" that monitor cockpit activity in airplanes, which are closely examined following an accident. Carmakers like General Motors Corp. have been using recording-capable devices, called Sensing and Diagnostic Modules, since the 1990s as a means to improve safety and collect statistics. While the devices' central purpose is to monitor various sensors and decide whether to fire air bags, other, more recent features include the ability to store data from a few seconds before a crash, including information on speed, seat-belt use, physical forces, brakes and other factors. GM and Ford Motor Co. permit outside parties (mainly accident reconstructionists, law enforcement, and insurance companies) to access the data by buying a US$2500 reader built by Santa Barbara, California–based Vetronix Corp.

The black box devices have been used as evidence in legal cases and consequently have led critics to suggest that recorders are an invasion of privacy and should not have been allowed without adequate public knowledge or approval. Recently, and for the first time, evidence from a black box was permitted in a Quebec court. Eric Gauthier, 20, was found guilty of dangerous driving causing death. While there were no witnesses to the crash, the black box in Gauthier's car was used to determine the speed. Another example of monitoring technology occurred when an individual rented a vehicle from Acme Rent-a-Car in New Haven, Connecticut, only to find out later that he was the unwitting victim of a global-positioning-system device planted in the minivan he leased. The surveillance device recorded him speeding in three states at rates from 78 to 83 m.p.h. (approximately 125 to 134 km/h), and each violation, digitally recorded, automatically added a US$150 charge to his bill.[5]

In this chapter, we intend to explore the subject of technology and business ethics. Technology has become such an integral aspect of our work lives and consumer lives that special treatment of these topics is warranted. First, we will consider what technology means and some of its benefits and challenges. Second, we will briefly discuss the subject of ethics and technology. Finally, we will consider ethical issues connected with two major realms of technology: computers and information technology, and biotechnology.

Technology and the Technological Environment

Technology means many things to many people. In this chapter, **technology** will refer to the "totality of the means employed to provide objects necessary for human sustenance and comfort." It is also seen as a scientific method used in achieving a practical purpose.[6] Technology refers to all the ways people use their inventions and discoveries to satisfy their needs and desires. Since time began, people have invented and developed tools, techniques, machines, and materials to sustain life and to improve the quality of life. Sources of power have also been discovered and developed. Taken together, these technological advances have made work easier and more productive.[7] It is little surprise, therefore, that businesses have embraced and used technology as much or more than any other sector of society.

In Chapter 1, we discussed the macroenvironment of business and how this total environment was composed of a number of significant and interrelated segments such as the social, economic, political, and technological. The **technological environment,** our current topic of concern, represents the total set of technology-based advancements or progress taking place in society. Pertinent aspects of this segment include new products, processes, materials, states of knowledge, and scientific advancement in both theoretical and applied senses. The rate of change and complexity of the technological environment have made it of special interest to business today. Consider the following examples. An electronic greeting card that today plays "Happy Birthday" holds more computing power than existed in the world before 1950. Home video cameras wield more processing power than the old IBM 360, the wonder machine that launched the age of mainframe computers. Computers are being used to aid scientists in comprehending the secrets of matter at the atomic level and to create amazing new materials.[8] In both information technology and the burgeoning field of biotechnology, the shape of how we are living, what products we are using, and what processes we are being exposed to are changing at an accelerating pace.

Characteristics of Technology

We have moved from a world characterized by industrial technology to one dominated by **information technology** and **biotechnology**. Whatever the technological level of advancement, there are general benefits of technology, undesirable side effects of technology, and challenges inherent in technological advancement. A brief consideration of each is useful.

Benefits of Technology

Few would dispute that we as a society have benefited greatly from technology and innovation. We live better lives today as employees, consumers, and members of the community due to technology. Technology has helped us gain control over nature and to build for ourselves a civilized life. Through the ages, technology has benefited society in four main ways.[9] First, it has increased society's production of goods and services, a benefit attributable chiefly to the business sector. In the mid-1800s, people and animals were the main source of power on farms in North America. In the early 1900s, tractors and other machines powered by gasoline and electricity became commonplace. Today, machines do virtually all the work on farms. These same kinds of results have been achieved in manufacturing, mining, and other industries; the number of products available for sale and consumption have increased significantly.

Second, technology has reduced the amount of labour needed to produce goods and services. Not only has production increased, but productivity has also increased. This has resulted in more leisure time, which has significantly affected lifestyles. Third, technology has not only enabled greater production with a lesser amount of human labour, but it has also made labour easier and safer. Fourth, higher standards of living have been a direct result of labour-saving technology. Today in economies that have been able to take advantage of technology, people are better fed, clothed, and housed, and they enjoy more health and comfort than any other people in history. Even life expectancy has increased as a result of these other factors.[10]

Side Effects and Challenges of Technology

Technologies have benefited people in many ways. There have also been some unanticipated side effects of technology—problems or effects not anticipated before technologies were implemented. One major reason for this is that technologies were sometimes implemented before much thought was given to possible side effects or downside risks of the technologies. The automobile is a classic example. From the late 1800s to early 1900s, it was believed that automobiles would be quieter and less smelly than horses. As more autos came into use, however, it quickly became obvious that roaring traffic noise exceeded the clatter of horse hoofs. Automobile exhaust became more toxic than the smell of horse manure. Fumes polluted the air with carbon monoxide and other impurities that threatened human health.[11] In addition, we experienced traffic jams, shortages of gasoline, and automobile accidents—some aided by cell phone users and "road rage."

Four categories of undesirable side effects of technology merit mention. First, there is *environmental pollution*. This ranks as one of the most undesirable side effects of technology. In spite of efforts to address this problem, most industrial nations today face significant air, water, soil, solid waste, and noise pollution. Global warming is an inevitable topic of concern today, due to technology. Second, there is *depletion of natural resources*. The rapid advance of technology continually threatens the supply of natural resources. Fuel shortages and power shortages have become a way of life. Third, there is the issue of *technological unemployment*. The most common form of technological unemployment occurs when machines take the place of humans, as we experienced in the automation phase of industrial development. At an aggregate level, this has not been as much of a problem as was once anticipated. In the short run, and to specific individuals locked into certain jobs with limited skills, however, it remains a real threat. Fourth, there has been a *creation of unsatisfying jobs* due to technology. Many jobs in the technological world fail to give the workers a sense of accomplishment. As jobs are broken down into smaller component parts, each individual worker is further removed from the finished product that might provide a greater sense of fulfillment and pride. Monotony and boredom can easily set in when jobs are significantly shaped by certain technological processes.[12]

New technologies present many challenges to managers, organizations, and society. Foremost among the challenges is anticipating and avoiding the unwanted side effects. Some side effects cannot be forecast or overcome, of course, but much more could be done than is currently being done. Overcoming the technological determinism that seems to be driving society today would be a step in the right direction. For example, one of the most important issues today in the realm of biotechnology is that of human cloning. It is difficult to get the scientists and researchers to slow down and talk about the possible consequences (practical and ethical) of human cloning. Many of them seem driven by the technological capacities for achieving this instead of asking the important questions concerning ethics and side effects. Another challenge lies in spreading the benefits of technology. Currently, the benefits of technology are rather restricted to the developed world. The developing nations enjoy few of the benefits of technology enjoyed in North America.[13] It is anticipated that as multinational corporations increasingly move to developing countries for production or exploration for resources, the opportunities for technology transfer will be greatly enhanced. The challenge, however, is to move technologies into these countries in socially responsible ways.

Ethics and Technology

To be sure, technology has many benefits for humankind. Our perspective at this juncture, however, is to raise the ethical questions that may be related to business development and use of technology. To do so does not mean that one is against technology. It simply means that one is concerned about the ethical use of and implications of technology. Like management decision making and globalization of business, the actions of the business community with respect to technology have ethical implications that should be discussed. Management's goal should certainly be to avoid immoral and amoral practices with respect to technology and to move toward a moral management posture with respect to this potent business resource.

Applying business ethics to questions involving technology is but an extension of our discussions of business ethics up to this point. The goal of managers and businesses striving to be ethical should be to do what is right, what is fair, and to avoid harm. In making ethical judgments, the prevailing norms of acceptability regarding technology must be tested by the principles of fairness and justice, protection of rights, and utilitarianism. The goal should be to reconcile and build bridges over the gap between "what is" and "what ought to be."

With respect to the three models of management ethics, the mission should be to avoid immoral technological practices in products, processes, and applications. There is much room for abuse and misinterpretation. Technology is such a gift for humankind that it is easy to overlook or fail to discern the ethical dimensions of decision making and application. Managers should strive to adhere to high standards of ethical behaviour and policies, pay careful attention to what is legal (both that which conforms to the spirit as well as the letter of the law), and display ethical leadership in anticipating and responding to ethical dilemmas.

To emphasize the ethical dimension of technology, it is useful to note how society has become obsessed with technology and its power over our lives. Only by fully understanding the magnitude of this love affair we have with technology can we focus on the ethical aspects of it and the actions that should be taken. One way to appreciate what technology is doing to us is to consider the thoughts of John Naisbitt, Nana Naisbitt, and Douglas Phillips, who recently wrote the book *High Tech/High Touch*. In this book, they outlined our current obsession with technology and described the symptoms of this obsession.[14]

Symptoms of Society's Intoxication with Technology

In *High Tech/High Touch*, Naisbitt calls upon all members of society to understand and question the place of technology in our lives. He and his colleagues argue that our world has changed from a "technologically comfortable place" into a "technologically intoxicated zone." As Naisbitt analyzes the world, he concludes that there are six symptoms of society's intoxication with technology.[15] Some of these touch upon how we are as a people, and some touch upon the ethical issues business faces with technology. The six symptoms are as follows:

1. *We favour the quick fix.* This is true whether it relates to nutrition or religion. As we perceive a recurring void, we search for something and we want it quickly. Ironically, he says that technology promises to detoxify us—to simplify our complex lives, relieve our stress, and calm our nerves. However, this Band-Aid culture of the quick fix is ultimately an empty one. We are seduced by the promise of technology.

2. *We fear and worship technology.* Our behaviour moves us from the extremes of worship one moment to fear the next. We accept technology, fearing that we will fall behind our competitors or co-workers. We embrace technology but then feel frustrated and annoyed when it fails to deliver.

3. *We blur the distinction between what is real and what is fake.* When technology can transform nature, we frequently ask "Is that real, or is that fake?" Is it authentic or simulated?

4. *We accept violence as normal.* Technology has made it possible for us to package violence in the form of merchandise, often spin-offs from television or movies. This violent material is often targeted at children.

5. *We love technology as a toy.* As affluence finances play, leisure tends toward diversion—something to fill the time. We live in a culture dominated by consumer technology, where leisure is often passively received. Electronic distractions busy us as we can't find anything worthwhile to do. The problem is that real leisure is not based on the desire to consume. It requires tranquility, patience, and attentiveness. Technology seldom delivers.

6. *We live our lives distanced and distracted.* The Internet, cell phones, and wireless technologies promise to connect us to the world, but when is it appropriate and when is it a distraction? Technology's bells and whistles are seductive, and they distance us and distract us.

Naisbitt's solution to this intoxication with technology is to find the right balance. That is, we need to embrace technology that preserves our humanity and reject technology that intrudes upon it. We need to know when we should push back on technology, in our work and our lives, and to affirm our humanity. We need to understand that technology zealots are as short-sighted as technology bashers. We need to question the place of technology in our lives.[16]

There is significant evidence that society is becoming concerned with the ethics of technology and the intoxication with technology that Naisbitt has so aptly described. This information should be useful for individuals as well as businesses desiring to use technology in a more ethical manner. Following are three examples of this increased societal concern. First, books are being published on the topic of ethics and technology. One example is *Practical Ethics for a Technological World* by Paul Alcorn.[17] It is encouraging to see books of this nature that attempt to bridge the gap between ethics and technology and to discuss where we are now and where we need to go. Second, special encyclopedias are being developed, such as *The Concise Encyclopedia of the Ethics of New Technologies.*[18] This encyclopedia, which is devoted to applied ethics, is one of a number that has come out in the past decade. Third, there are developing new organizations concerned about ethics and technology. One example is the non-profit Institute for Business, Technology, and Ethics (IBTE), a unique organization dedicated to exploring the mix of business, technology, and ethics. One of the major concerns of one of IBTE's founders is the unintended consequences of technology on people and how these consequences often lead to "damage control" ethics.[19]

There are a number of arenas in which specific issues of business ethics and technology might be explored. Research over the past couple of years reveals two broad categories of issues that now merit our consideration. Each is broad and deep, so we can only consider them in an introductory way in this chapter. Each, however, significantly touches business, either directly or indirectly. The two areas are computer-based information technology and biotechnology. Within each, there are dozens of technologies that raise ethical questions. Our quest, therefore, will be to focus on the major ones that give us the best representation of ethical issues with technology.

Information Technology

Computer-based information technology, or information technology (IT), as it is most often called, touches practically all businesses and stakeholders involved in those businesses. Businesses and people are either affected by technology or are directly involved in pursuits that are based on technology. We will consider them both. There are two broad areas we will discuss in this section: electronic commerce, or Web-based marketing, and computer technology in the workplace, including telecommunications. These areas overlap significantly and are interdependent, so our separation is to lend some order to the discussion.

Electronic Commerce as an Emerging Technology

Electronic commerce, often referred to as *e-commerce, e-business,* or *Web-based marketing,* is one of the most significant technological phenomena of our day. It primarily affects consumer stakeholders and competitors of the e-commerce firm. Most experts today are convinced that the Internet is rapidly reshaping the way business will be conducted around the world. Part of this is firms selling products and services online. Beyond this, companies are integrating the Internet into every aspect of their businesses. According to a recent Conference Board of Canada survey, Canadians are second only to the U.S. in the use of information and communication technologies. More Canadians are browsing, learning, and buying online every year, and businesses have been using technology to reduce transaction costs and increase customer interaction.[20]

According to Forrester Research, while Canadians have been slow to adopt online shopping, predictions are that Canadian e-commerce sales will grow from $2.8 billion in 2003 to $12.2 billion in 2008. It is estimated that, by 2006, global online trade will expand to $12.8 trillion.[21] Home Depot, with 99 stores across Canada, launched its online shopping site in 2003. While acknowledging the challenges of online retailing, Home Depot spokespersons have noted that this move was designed more to promote Home Depot's products and services overall rather than solely as a means to generate e-sales. This reflects the reality that online selling so far is only a small part of the overall retailing sector in Canada.[22] Many observers agree that while e-commerce has yet to really take off, the lure of e-business will likely continue to strengthen in the coming years.[23] That is, despite the slow adoption of this industry, electronic commerce remains a burgeoning business. As this industry grows, so too will we witness increased growth in the opportunities for questionable practices.

Along with the growth of electronic commerce, business ethics problems have arisen as well. One major category of problems is online scams. Internet Fraud Watch (http://www.fraud.org/ifw.htm) is an organization that maintains a large database of fraud resources and allows for both online and telephone incident reporting from

Canada and the United States. This organization has noted that con artists are taking advantage of the Internet's growth in popularity to bilk the unwary. Top frauds over the Internet have included online auctions, general merchandise sales, Internet access services, work-at-home offers, and advance fee loans. Other scams were credit card fraud, travel and vacation scams, pyramid schemes, and bogus investment opportunities. It is estimated that millions of dollars are lost annually in consumer scams.[24]

Invasion of Privacy via Electronic Commerce

The average person encounters two forms of Internet electronic commerce: business-to-consumer transactions and business-to-business transactions. Most of us are quite familiar with business-to-consumer transactions when we do personal business on the Internet—buying products, arranging credit cards, accessing travel Web sites, and doing financial business. Employees also encounter business-to-business transactions; this is anticipated to be the greatest area of e-commerce growth over the coming years. In terms of Web-based marketing to consumers, consumer stakeholders are primarily affected by such issues as database sharing, identity theft, and invasion of privacy. Invasion of privacy is a legitimate concern in all business transactions; however, the special case of electronic commerce or Web-based marketing deserves particular attention because of the ease with which data can be stored and transmitted in electronic form.

One illustration of a potential invasion of privacy was that of DoubleClick, Inc., a New York–based Internet advertising company that planned to share customer information with an offline marketing firm. Consumer advocates were up in arms that DoubleClick would betray such confidential information. Another example occurred when Toysmart.com, Inc., went out of business and offered its online customer list for sale, thus violating privacy agreements or understandings previously made with customers. Questions that arise from such situations include "What limits should there be on how online businesses use the information they gather about their customers?" and "What responsibility do companies have to publicly disclose such practices?"[25]

The number one ethical issue with respect to doing business over the Internet is the question of possible invasions of consumer privacy. This is a hot topic for business executives today.[26] The general, consuming public is concerned as well.[27] Figure 8–1 summarizes some of the concerns that privacy advocates and law enforcement experts have about the Internet's threat to privacy.

Some of the technological means by which companies invade consumers' privacy include the use of cookies and spam. *Cookies* are those little identification tags that Web sites drop on our personal computer hard drives so they can recognize repeat visitors the next time we visit their Web sites. Surveys show that some consumers don't know what cookies are; others are aware of them but don't take the time to block them. According to recent surveys, only 10 percent of users set their browsers to block cookies. Part of this is due to the fact that 56 percent of Internet users didn't know what a cookie was.[28]

Some consumers interpret the receipt of *spam* as an invasion of their privacy. Opening our e-mail mailboxes only to find a few dozen unsolicited ads is aggravating, at the least, and an invasion of privacy to many. Too, some companies experiment with pulsing background ads that never go away. Interestingly, dozens of companies make programs that protect our e-mail privacy, block cookies, and filter spam and porn, but very few consumers bother to use them.[29]

Probably the most serious invasion of privacy issue with respect to electronic commerce is the collection and use of personal information. Though non-Internet companies have engaged in this practice for years, everything seems magnified in the e-world

FIGURE 8-1

Ways in Which the Internet's Threat to Privacy is the Greatest

Identity theft	Someone might use the Internet to steal your identity.
Unintentionally revealing information	You may be unintentionally revealing information about yourself as you move through cyberspace.
Lost/stolen personal information	That personal information you just provided to a Web site might be sold or stolen.
Fake Web sites	That Web site on which you just entered your credit card number and personal information may be a fake.
Government distribution	The government may be giving out your home address, social insurance number, and other personal information online.
Broadcasting information	Companies and people who do not like you may be broadcasting your private information on the Internet.
Victim of spying—employer or spouse	Your employer or spouse may be using your computer to spy on you.
Victim of spying—strangers	Someone you do not know may be using your computer to spy on you (e.g., hackers).
Cyberstalker	You may have a cyberstalker harassing you.

Source: Summarized from "Internet Insecurity," *Time* (July 2, 2001), 46–50.

in which we now live. None of us really know how much personal information is collected, saved, swapped, or sold in e-commerce. Thousands of retailers, from department stores to catalogue companies, collect and store personal information, from asking customers for their postal codes to collecting names, addresses, household income, and purchasing patterns through a store credit card. Retailers also share, exchange, and even sell their customer databases to other companies. In short, the average consumer has very little control over what is done with his or her personal data once it is collected.[30] An extreme concern is identity theft or tampering with one's financial accounts. Less serious is the inundation of marketing attempts, both online and offline, that consumers are subjected to as a result of information being distributed.

Government's Involvement in Privacy Protection   Canadians are protected by two federal privacy laws, the Privacy Act (effective July 1, 1983) and the Personal Information Protection and Electronic Documents Act *(PIPEDA)* (effective January 1, 2001). The Privacy Act imposes obligations on approximately 150 federal government departments and agencies to respect the privacy rights of Canadians by restricting the collection, use, and disclosure of personal information. The PIPEDA establishes rules for how private-sector organizations can collect, use, and disclose personal information in conducting business. As of January 1, 2004, the PIPEDA will cover the collection, use, and disclosure of personal information in any commercial activities within a province. Any challenges or oversights found within both acts are dealt with by the Privacy Commissioner of Canada, who is also authorized to receive and investigate complaints.[31]

Since 2001, federally regulated companies like banks, insurers, and telecommunications and transportation companies had been subject to the act. However, as of 2004, the act covers all commercial activity, and it prohibits businesses collecting, using, or disclosing personal information without consent. PIPEDA also dictates that every company designate a privacy officer who is responsible for conducting personal information audits—assessing what personal information is being collected and determining how it is used. This act prohibits newspapers and general interest magazines from selling names and home addresses of subscribers to third parties without the consent of subscribers.[32]

Business Initiatives There are a number of different ways companies might strive to protect the privacy of their customers in electronic commerce.

Ethical Leadership. First, business needs to recognize the potential ethical issues involved in electronic commerce and be committed to treating customers and all affected stakeholders in an ethical fashion. This commitment and ethical leadership undergird all other initiatives.

Privacy Policies. Companies may take the initiative with their own carefully crafted privacy policies designed to protect customers. An example of this might be a company deciding to do more than the law requires. FleetBoston Financial Corporation decided to resolve concerns regarding its use of customer financial data by adopting a new privacy policy requiring a customer's affirmative approval (an "opt in" policy) prior to the company sharing nonpublic personal information with third parties for marketing purposes. Fleet's new privacy policy was a response to the New York attorney general's concern about Fleet sharing customer account information without providing full disclosure to its customers. Under Fleet's new policy, the bank will not share customers' personal information without their informed, voluntary, specific, and documented consent.[33]

Canadian financial institutions have also been increasing efforts to ensure online consumer transactions are protected. To help its customers better protect their privacy when surfing the Internet, RBC Royal Bank, for example, provides them with security software tools. The tools, from Zero-Knowledge Systems (a Montreal-based manufacturer of security and privacy software), give consumers greater control over how they share personal information when online. Such tools alert consumers to any unauthorized attempts to access their computers, prevent cookies from being stored, and send personal information only when it's the consumer's choice. These tools are in addition to the previously existing security for the actual online bank offering.[34] For virtual-banking to succeed, it is critical for banks to ensure that customers' privacy is guaranteed with online banking.

Chief Privacy Officers. An innovative approach to protecting consumers' privacy is through the appointment of a **chief privacy officer (CPO)**. CPOs are joining the executive ranks at major technology-related companies, such as American Express, Sony Corporation, Citigroup, and IBM.[35] In other companies, these responsibilities are falling under the responsibility of a chief technology officer.

It is the primary responsibility of the chief privacy officer to keep a company out of trouble, whether in a court of law or the court of public opinion. This includes developing Internet policies, helping their companies avoid consumer litigation, creating methods of handling and resolving consumer complaints, and assessing the risk of privacy invasion of company activities and practices. Because the position is so new at most companies, these newly appointed individuals are still trying to figure out what they need to be doing. The job is a challenging one. CPOs must balance their customers' right to privacy with the employer's need for information for profit purposes.[36]

Questionable Businesses and Practices Several questionable businesses and practices have been made possible by electronic commerce and the use of the Internet. Three business categories that are viewed as questionable by some include Web-based pornography, Internet gambling, and Web-based music services such as Napster, MusicNet, Pressplay, and others that raise the question of the protection of intellectual property.[37] According to Robert Kuttner, the Internet has created situations not anticipated by previous laws for thoughtful public policy defining the public interest as well as individuals' private interests in protecting intellectual property.[38]

Two practices that have raised questions include companies paying Internet search engine providers to ensure that their Web page appears early when consumers do Internet searches and the use of monitoring technology to watch consumers as they use the company's products. In the U.S., Commercial Alert, a group founded by consumer activist Ralph Nader, asked the U.S. Federal Trade Commission (FTC) to investigate online search engine companies that are concealing the impact that special fees have on Internet searches. The group asked the FTC to investigate whether eight of the Web's largest search engines (e.g., AltaVista, Lycos, AOL Time Warner, LookSmart) are violating laws against deceptive advertising. The group charged that some of these search engines have abandoned their traditional, objective formulas to determine the order of the results they list and have sold the top spots to the highest bidders, without making adequate disclosures to Internet users. Apparently, to boost revenues, search engine companies have been accepting payments from businesses interested in receiving a higher ranking in certain search categories.[39] This raises an interesting question of Internet ethics: Is this an unfair advertising practice, or is this just the free-enterprise system at work?

Obviously, these business types and practices will have adherents as well as critics. However, their existence points to the kinds of controversial ethical issues that arise in connection with electronic commerce.

The Workplace and Computer Technology

Computers now have an overwhelming presence in the Canadian workplace. In 1990 only three out of ten workers regularly used a computer on the job. By the end of the 1990s, 70 percent of Canadian workplaces (accounting for 90 percent of employment) had at least one computer user. Moreover, six out of ten workers regularly used a computer on the job.[40]

Whereas computer-based information technology creates ethical issues for consumer stakeholders with respect to electronic commerce and Web-based marketing, employee stakeholders also are significantly affected by technology in the workplace. We will discuss some of these issues, especially employee privacy, in Chapter 16. At this juncture, however, some brief coverage of the types of activities, technologies, and issues that arise merit consideration.

Is work affected by the introduction of computers? A study by Human Resources Development Canada indicated that 39 percent of workers reported that their work has been greatly affected, another 21 percent said that their work has been somewhat affected, while the remaining 40 percent felt that their work has been hardly or not at all affected.[41] In addition, employees generally have a positive impression of the impact of technology in the workplace, and typically positive attitudes are reflected in the following areas:[42]

- Expands job-related knowledge
- Increases productivity during normal work hours
- Improves communication with clients and customers
- Relieves job stress

Other benefits of technology in the workplace include improved time management, expanded professional networks, development of a competitive edge, balance of work and family needs, and increased productivity during commuting time.[43] Have computers made work more or less interesting? In the Human Resources Development Canada study cited above, of those who felt that their work has been affected, nearly six out of ten felt that their work has become more interesting.[44]

What are some of the technologies that are currently being used in the workplace? Following is a list that is representative of the most popular technologies being used:[45]

- Desktop computers
- Fax machine
- Answering machine
- Voice mail
- Cellular phone
- Internet
- CD-rom/DVD
- E-mail
- Intranet/network
- Laptop computers
- Palm computer
- Videoconferencing
- Personal electronic organizer
- Robotics

How do ethical issues arise when companies use technology in the workplace? In a word—surveillance. **Surveillance** involves companies electronically watching, monitoring, or checking up on their employees. The major ethical issue, of course, is the question of invasion of privacy. Employees are increasingly concerned about the extent to which their employers are monitoring their work-related activities and possibly their personal lives. Surveillance creates stress. Stress, in turn, may have a detrimental impact on performance or productivity. Thus, surveillance comes with attendant problems. It is useful to consider some of the technologies or ways that companies observe and monitor what their employees are doing on the job.

Monitoring E-Mail and Internet Usage   The most intensely checked activities of employees are their e-mail and use of the Internet. It is little wonder why employers do this. There is evidence that employees are spending more and more of their time online in such pursuits as personal e-mail, shopping, and visiting entertainment sites. Companies are taking these concerns seriously. They do this by checking their employees' use of these technologies. In 1996, only 35 percent of companies engaged in e-mail monitoring. By 2001, 47 percent of large companies monitored e-mail use on the job. In addition, checking up on the Web site connections employees visited grew significantly.[46]

One major reason employers check up on their employees is that inexpensive technologies are now available that enable them to do so. Most companies today do not monitor telephone calls or postal mail because it is too time-consuming and expensive to do so. However, companies can get software that monitors Internet usage for less than $10 per employee. Consequently, employee monitoring has been increasing at almost twice the rate of employees getting Net access. According to Andrew Schulman, "It's an example of the technology cart driving the policy horse."[47]

An example of the kind of e-mail abuse that plagues companies occurred when a young click-happy financial executive started using his e-mail in a way that eventually led to his dismissal, and this was not even a result of company monitoring. A 24-year-old Princeton graduate moved to Seoul, South Korea, to begin his new assignment for his employer. After being there only a few days, he began to send e-mails to his friends back home in the United States, boasting of tawdry exploits and his lavish lifestyle. He sent this message to 11 of his buddies in his former New York office. The message ended up being forwarded to thousands of people on Wall Street and eventually was forwarded to his bosses at his new employer. The young executive was given the option of resigning or being dismissed.[48]

An example of a company monitoring employee e-mail illustrates the kinds of ethical issues that may arise as a consequence of monitoring:

> *Man goes to Doctor for a checkup and a battery of tests. Doctor gets results and sends them via e-mail: Man has a life-threatening disease. Meanwhile, Man's company monitors his e-mail simply to ensure he uses it only for work. Technology officer reads Man's e-mail and blabs to coworkers about Man's diagnosis. Human resources gets involved. CEO gets called in, sees very expensive lawsuit looming. Health insurance company finds out about Man's problem, considers dropping coverage. Big problems for Man. Big problems for Company.[49]*

According to Joe Murphy, managing director of Interactive Integrity, the Internet has introduced enormous compliance risk and ethical issues for companies. There is the potential for sexual harassment, improper contact with competitors, people using chat rooms, pornography, and employees sending out proprietary information over the Net. Technology, therefore, has shifted the burden onto companies to monitor the workplace.[50]

In spite of the potential invasion of privacy issues, companies are monitoring employees' e-mail and Internet usage as never before. Some of the ways in which this is being done include:[51]

- Developing policies prohibiting the Internet for personal use
- Using monitoring software
- Restricting Web site access
- Restricting hours of access

Other Technology Issues in the Workplace

Surveillance extends beyond companies monitoring e-mail and Internet usage. In addition to these activities, other forms of surveillance include monitoring faxes, using video cameras in the workplace, drug testing, doing online background checks, logging photocopies, and recording phone calls. Each of these poses privacy implications that must be considered from an ethical perspective.

The world of security via computers and technology entered a new era on September 11, 2001, as a result of the terrorist attacks on the World Trade Center in New York and the Pentagon in Washington, DC. People's attitudes about privacy changed somewhat as they realized that heightened security checks are needed to guard against terrorist attacks. These added security measures have begun in public institutions (airports, government buildings, large entertainment venues), and they are spilling over into the employment arena as companies become more cautious about their own security. There is already evidence that some use of facial-recognition technology, "active" badges that track where you are, and other such technology-driven security measures have landed squarely in the workplace.

Ethical Implications of Cell Phone Use   Although e-mail and the Internet most often create ethical problems in the workplace, the use of cell phones by employees rep-

resents one of the fastest-growing technologies with significant ethical and legal implications. To many, use of a cell phone is a private matter, and most seem to want to keep
it that way. As companies now make cell phones available to their employees, however,
this issue spills over into the business arena and becomes a business ethics topic.

A case occurred in March 2000 that dramatically illustrated this point. As
reported in *The Wall Street Journal*, Jane Wagner, a San Francisco–based lawyer, was
toting up billable hours on her cell phone for her employer while driving to a scheduled 10 P.M. meeting with a client. This was typical for Ms. Wagner—continuing to
make business calls on her cell phone while driving home. As she talked, her Mercedes
swerved and struck a 15-year-old girl who was walking on the shoulder of the road,
throwing her fatally injured body down an embankment. Ms. Wagner later said she
didn't even realize she had hit someone. She said it wasn't until morning when she was
watching the news while dressing for work that she realized what she had done. She
turned herself in and pleaded guilty to hit and run—a felony. The victim's family was
seeking US$30 million in damages from Ms. Wagner's employer.[52]

In another major U.S. court case, a New York investment-banking firm was sued
for damages by the family of a motorcyclist killed when one of its brokers, using a car
phone, ran a red light and struck him. Plaintiffs claimed that employer pressure to contact clients after hours contributed to the tragedy, and the company settled the suit for
US$500 000. They did not admit any wrongdoing, but wanted to avoid a jury trial.[53]

A trend with huge implications for employers is the growing number of employees—salespeople, consultants, lawyers, ad executives, and others—who are using cell
phones while driving and chalking up sales or billable hours. Sixty-eight percent of the
general population say they use a cell phone while driving,[54] and, surely, the percentage is higher among employees. Plaintiffs are increasingly claiming that the employer
is partly to blame because it presses employees to work long hours from distant locations, often encouraging them to use cell phones without setting safety guidelines.

Cases such as the two described above—both linked to technology, the cell
phone—should raise red flags for employers. Few companies have policies on cell
phone use at this time. In addition to cell phones, as wireless or mobile Net access
gains in popularity, the same applies to this use of technology. It appears that as high-
tech tools extend the workplace into every nook and corner of life, companies have
been leaving the responsibility entirely up to the employees. These cases are tragic
examples of what can happen when employees, using technology, become too distracted, pressured, or overfocused on their work.[55] These applications of technology
in the workplace raise significant ethical issues for business now and in the future.

Unethical Activities by Employees Related to Technology In most of the
instances described to this point, the employer has had responsibility for the use of
technology and its implications. There is a final area that should be mentioned: questionable activities that are the responsibility of the employee. These activities have
been aided by computer technologies. In a major study of workers, the following per-
centages of workers surveyed said they had engaged in this unethical activity during
the previous year:[56]

- Created a potentially dangerous situation by using new technology while driving—19 percent
- Wrongly blamed an error the employee made on a technological glitch—14 percent
- Copied the company's software for home use—13 percent

- Used office equipment to shop on the Internet for personal reasons—13 percent
- Used office equipment to network/search for another job—11 percent
- Accessed private computer files without permission—6 percent
- Used new technologies to intrude on co-workers' privacy—6 percent
- Visited porn Web sites using office equipment—5 percent

Company Actions   Companies have many options for addressing the kinds of ethical issues described to this point. A major survey of *Fortune* 500 nonmanagement employees revealed that management should define ethical computer use for employees. Options for doing this include company management making these decisions, using the Information Systems Society's code of ethics, and involving employees and users in a collaborative attempt to decide computer ethics. Only about one-half of those surveyed indicated that company guidelines were written and well known.[57]

The technology we have discussed to this point is computer-driven. Therefore, guidelines for employee computer use would help in many of the arenas described. Several professional societies also offer guidelines for computer use. As more workplaces expand online access to employees, the importance of having a clear Internet and e-mail use policy is obvious. Organizations such as the Computer Ethics Institute have suggested the communication of a set of principles that should govern employees' use of office computers. Other organizations like Carswell Publishers have taken their own measures to avoid employee misuse of office technology. Figure 8–2 outlines some steps taken by Carswell, a publisher based in Toronto, that implemented a clear usage policy after giving almost all of its nearly 600 employees access to the Internet at work. The company's HR department developed a policy that has been effective in preventing the abuse of corporate assets. The first step in setting up the policy was to meet with the company's lawyer to ensure employee privacy was honoured. It took about five weeks to implement the policy until the completed draft was ready to present to employees.[58]

Biotechnology

The twentieth century's revolution in information technology is merging with the twenty-first century's revolution in biotechnology. Indeed, Walter Isaacson has labelled the 2000s as the "biotech century."[59] The seeds for this revolution were spawned in 1953 when James Watson blurted out to Francis Crick how four nucleic acids could pair to form the self-copying code of a DNA molecule. Now, we are poised for the most significant breakthrough of all time—deciphering the human genome, the 100 000 genes encoded by 3 billion chemical pairs in our DNA. Among other achievements, this accomplishment will lead to the next medical revolution, which will not only increase the natural life span of healthy human beings but will also help to conquer cancer, grow new blood vessels, block the growth of blood vessels in tumours, create new organs from stem cells, and certainly much more.[60]

The field of biotechnology carries with it significant implications for business and for business ethics. In fact, it is spawning a new industry—the biotechnology industry. Biotechnology involves "using biology to discover, develop, manufacture, market, and sell products and services."[61] The biotech industry today consists of a number of small entrepreneurial start-up companies funded largely by venture capitalists, along with larger, more established companies. Most of the applications of biotechnology will be in health care, the pharmaceutical industry, and agriculture.[62]

FIGURE 8-2

What Carswell Does to Regulate Computer Use and Abuse

Monitoring Internet Use

Carswell uses software that blocks employees from accessing prohibited Web sites. The software has a list of prohibited sites, continually updated, that employees cannot access.

E-Mail Use Rules

Eventually, Carswell decided to block inappropriate external e-mail from coming in by using filtering software but chose not to monitor e-mail being sent by employees around and outside the company. Instead, they came up with a written policy that sets out clearly what employees can and can't use e-mail for.

Communicating the Policy to Employees

Even the best policy is ineffective if employees aren't clearly aware of what the policy is and what the ramifications are for breaking the rules. The policy is also communicated to new employees who are required to sign a business conduct policy that includes e-mail and Internet use.

Source: Adapted from Todd Humber, "Developing an Internet Use Policy Is Painless—and Crucial," *Canadian HR Reporter* (Vol. 15, No. 19, November 4, 2002), G4.

Bioethics

A field called **bioethics** has emerged that deals with the ethical issues that are embedded in the use of biotechnology. As new biotech products are developed, thorny ethical issues will undoubtedly arise. In the medical field, for example, you may soon be able to determine the genetic makeup of your baby well before birth. Does this mean that those who control the technology have power over the population? Does it mean that people who can spend the money on customizing their baby's genetic makeup will in turn create an underclass of the genetically less fortunate?[63] These are just some of the ethical issues that arise as we think about their implications in the commercial sphere.

Bioethics is a hotly debated topic and has received special attention by the Canadian government. In October 2003, the House of Commons passed a reproductive technology bill that would ban human cloning and allow limited stem cell research on human embryos. The question of the government's role in funding stem-cell research has also been addressed in the United States. One of the actions U.S. President Bush took was to appoint a bioethicist, Dr. Leon Kass, to chair a presidential council on bioethics. Dr. Kass was trained both as a doctor and a biochemist before entering the field of bioethics.[64] Kass has been quoted as saying, "Where you have technologies that touch so deeply on the nature of our humanity, [decisions about their use] shouldn't be left to a kind of technological fatalism and free markets.... The task is to clarify the issues, to lift the public understanding of the human and moral significance of doing what we're doing."[65]

Some biotechnology companies have adopted the idea of bioethics to guide them in their decision making. A question is being continually raised, however, of whether bioethical decision making is really taking place or whether the companies are using the bioethicists for public relations purposes. Companies such as Geron have pioneered the idea of a corporate bioethics advisory board. When the Jones Institute for Reproductive Medicine began its research on human embryos, it talked up the idea of panels of bioethicists. It has been observed that many companies are savvy enough to know that the greatest single obstacle to utilizing their new technologies is the potential for public backlash.[66]

According to William Saletan, who has written extensively about bioethics, the primary tool bioethicists use is *proceduralism*. This involves elaborate protocols being established that ensure that certain classical worries, such as informed consent, are not violated. The focus, in other words, is being sure that appropriate procedures are being followed—rather than on the actual ethical content of the decisions. The worry continues, however, over whether corporate executives and scientists are deceiving their own consciences by focusing on the *how* rather than the why, on the *means* rather than the end.[67]

Both critics and supporters say that the use of bioethicists lends companies an air of credibility. The real question is this: Can they really be objective if they are on a company's payroll? Supporters say "yes," that they function like a newspaper ombudsperson who gets paid by the paper to criticize coverage and prevent potential conflicts. Detractors say "no," there's no way around at least the appearance of a conflict of interest if money is changing hands. A real danger is that the participation of bioethicists may be interpreted as a stamp of approval.[68]

Charles Colson has observed that "the biotech revolution has surged forward as the defining issue of this new century. On the one hand, it holds out great promise for medical advances enhancing life and health for all humankind. On the other, it raises unprecedented ethical issues." He goes on to conclude that "the biotech revolution is moving like a steamroller, fueled by huge potential profits, crushing everything—including moral restraint—in its path."[69] We may be too early into the biotechnology revolution to know whether this will turn out to be the case; however, it is important to raise the question of the balance between costs and benefits early on.

It is useful to consider two broad realms of biotechnology to appreciate what each represents in terms of challenges in business ethics: **genetic engineering** and **genetically modified foods (GMFs)**. Genetic engineering, primarily of humans, and genetic engineering of agricultural and food products are both part of genetic science. For discussion, however, we will separate them out from one another.

Figure 8–3 summarizes a list of several nonprofit bioethics organizations that may be found on the Web.

Genetic Engineering

Two major areas of genetic engineering, or genetic science, seem to capture the public's imagination today. One is stem cell research, and the second is cloning. Both pose huge and interesting challenges for business and business ethics.

Stem Cell Research **Embryonic stem cells**, the basic building blocks that are the progenitors of all other cells, were isolated in 1998 by scientists at the University of Wisconsin. Stem cells are the raw materials upon which a human body is built. Since their isolation, stem cell research has been proliferating around the world. Though the United States has historically been the world leader in biotechnology, some experts say the United States has fallen behind other countries as debate over ethical implications has slowed progress.[70]

Stem cells come from embryos, and they may be obtained in three ways: frozen embryos, fresh embryos, or cloned embryos. Spare frozen embryos may come from fertility clinics, having been donated by infertile couples who no longer need them for

FIGURE 8–3

Nonprofit Bioethics Organizations on the Web

Bioethics is such an expansive topic that there are many different organizations, especially public action organizations, that provide information regarding specific topics via the World Wide Web. Some of these include the following:

Canadian Bioethics Society (http://www.bioethics.ca/english/)

This organization was founded in 1988 by the amalgamation of the Canadian Society of Bioethics and the Canadian Society for Medical Bioethics. Currently, it has approximately 600 members, composed of health-care administrators, lawyers, nurses, philosophers, physicians, theologians, and others concerned with the ethical and humane dimensions of health care. The aim of the society is (1) to encourage collaboration among persons and organizations involved in bioethics; (2) to offer a forum for the exchange of views and ideas; (3) to help solve the problems of daily practice; and (4) to generate long-term solutions to broader social questions. The society strives to unite professions, disciplines, and individuals in this common cause.

Joint Centre for Bioethics (http://www.utoronto.ca/jcb/)

This organization was formed in 1995, as a partnership between the University of Toronto and affiliated hospitals. It maintains a network of over 160 members, approximately 20 of whom work full-time in bioethics, and represents the largest multi-disciplinary group of in-hospital bioethicists in Canada. As of 2003, it trained more than 70 students through its two bioethics graduate programs and produced more than 500 articles on the subject, along with the attainment of $20 million in research grants for pursuing this topic.

Council of Canadians (http://www.canadians.org/)

Founded in 1985, this watchdog organization is composed of approximately 100 000 members and more than 70 chapters across Canada. It lobbies Members of Parliament, conducts research, and runs national campaigns aimed at drawing attention to many important issues affecting Canadians. Its "Biotech Campaign" includes raising awareness of the ethical and health concerns of new technologies and practices. For example, it initiated a campaign to stop the introduction of genetically engineered (GE) wheat in Canada. In addition, the council has aimed to raise attention toward the ethics of genetic engineering. Their critical view of this area is reflected in a comment posted on the organization's Web site: "More importantly, the biotech industry's ability to patent life forms has given way to the commodification of life, allowing them to sell, buy, or trade the very basic building blocks of life for a sizeable profit."[71]

American Society for Bioethics and Humanities (http://www.asbh.org)

The American Society for Bioethics and Humanities (ASBH) is a professional society of more than 1500 individuals, organizations, and institutions interested in bioethics and humanities. This Web site, established in January 1998, is intended initially to serve as a source of information about ASBH for members and prospective members. It also will serve as a resource for anyone interested in bioethics and humanities by providing a group of additional online resources and links to aid in finding other related information through the Internet.

The Council for Responsible Genetics (http://www.gene-watch.org)

The council fosters debate on social, ethical, and environmental implications of new genetic technologies. It publishes GeneWATCH, a national bulletin on the implications of biotechnology. The site contains testimony presented to the U.S. Congress, position papers, and a legislative clearinghouse.

Bioethics.net (http://www.bioethics.net)

This Web page is quite extensive. It hosts the *American Journal of Bioethics Online* and the Center for Bioethics at the University of Pennsylvania. It has a special section on bioethics for beginners as well as a special section on cloning and genetics.

National Human Genome Research Institute (http://www.nhgri.nih.gov)

This Web site describes the Ethical, Legal, and Social Implications (ELSI) Research program. This program supports basic and applied research that identifies and analyzes the ethical, legal, and social issues surrounding human genetics research. The ELSI Research program currently is the largest U.S. federal supporter of bioethics research, with an annual budget of over US$12 million.

pregnancy. Most ethical guidelines recommend research only on these. Fresh embryos are those that have been specially created for research, usually in a fertility clinic. Embryos can also be created by cloning human cells. In fact, in an example of how stem cell research is outrunning public policy, a Massachusetts company recently used cloning technology to create human embryos that would yield the cells that might give rise to tissues that would be perfect matches for patients. This technique, known as **therapeutic cloning**, has been the subject of intense debate in the U.S. Congress, which has been considering legislation to ban such research.[72] The value of stem cells is that they offer hope for developing treatments for diseases such as cancer, Alzheimer's, Parkinson's disease, and juvenile diabetes.[73] Further, stem cells may be grown into tissues for transplanting into patients who need them for nerve cells, bone cells, or muscle cells.[74]

The stem cell controversy has been particularly salient in many parts of the world in recent years. U.S. President Bush considered the arguments for and against the federal government funding research using stem cells. After much debate, the president decided to proceed, but cautiously. His announced decision was to allow federal government funding for research only on stem cells that have already been harvested. By allowing federally sponsored research only on existing stem cell lines, where "the life-and-death decision had already been made," the president was able to draw a line on stem cell research that most of the public supported.[75]

In Canada in 2003, the House of Commons gave their approval to a bill that would allow human embryos to be used for stem cell research, but ban human cloning. However, the legislation, entitled the Assisted Human Reproduction Bill, has not yet passed through the Senate, as of the writing of this textbook. The law, as originally proposed, would allow embryos remaining from in vitro fertilization treatments at fertility clinics to be used for research. For example, scientists assert that stem cells in human embryos can be used to replace tissues destroyed by spinal cord injuries, diabetes, muscular dystrophy, Parkinson's, and Alzheimer's disease. Advocates of this research argue that failure to use "surplus" embryos from in vitro fertilization amounts to forfeiting the opportunity for advancing knowledge in these areas. On the other hand, others argue that the concept of "surplus" embryos is in itself offensive and that these organisms, however reproduced, are "innocent living human beings" deserving the same protection. Based on this view, stem cell research is "killing" because it destroys the embryo. Moreover, the use of embryos for research has been compared to the murder of hundreds of thousands of disabled people in Nazi Germany.

While the details of the legislation remain much debated, there is agreement for the need to maintain control over reproductive technologies, and generate regulations to ensure that technology is used safely and beneficially. Although the Assisted Human Reproduction Bill did not receive final approval in 2003, the Canadian Institutes of Health Research warned that regardless of the outcome of the bill, they would begin funding embryonic stem cell research without waiting for the law to pass. In addition, some Canadian researchers feel that they need to advance this research to compete with U.S. researchers who are operating without legislative restrictions.

Most of the ethical debate over stem cell research has occurred in the public arena, not business. One gets the distinct impression that businesses are ready to move forward once the societal debate begins to show some clarity. A real danger in the debate over the use of embryonic stem cells is the almost irresistible tendency to treat them as "property" ripe for commercial exploitation. The interested parties are not isolated individuals. The beneficiaries are not just the sick, the aged, or the prematurely infirm. Research universities seeking funding and prestige will benefit; pharmaceutical companies seeking new products and investors will benefit; and governments have a stake as nations race against each other to market therapies for degenerative diseases.[76]

Cloning Stem cell research is well underway. Now, **cloning** is forcing itself into the news. Some scientists say human cloning is a distant project; however, according to some reports, people are already lining up to freeze the DNA of their dead loved ones, including pets and racehorses. Several different groups have claimed they are attempting to clone a human being. In March 2001, a group of controversial scientists—an Italian fertility specialist, an American fertility researcher, and an Israeli biotechnologist—started to tinker with cells in the laboratory and claimed they would soon produce a human clone.[77] Also in 2001, the U.S. Food and Drug Administration cracked down on a group in the United States who had a secret lab where they were trying to clone a human being. Other groups have also stated they are trying to clone human beings.[78] In 2002, Clonaid, a company linked to the Raelians, a bizarre Quebec-based religious group, claimed to have produced the world's first human clone, but they have yet to produce any evidence.[79]

There are at least two debates surrounding cloning and genetic science. First, there is the issue of cloning human beings. Second, there is the issue of cloning animals and plants and using genetics to identify and fight diseases. This second quest is currently the primary focus of science. But, it is the fascination with duplicating human beings that arouses the most debate and fear. Surveys in the United States have shown that as many as 90 percent of Americans are against human cloning; in 22 other countries around the world and four U.S. states, human cloning has been declared illegal. In Japan, legislation banning human cloning became effective in June 2001.[80]

Canadians appear to be a little more optimistic about genetic testing and cloning, though cautiously optimistic. For example, a PricewaterhouseCoopers poll found that over 90 percent of respondents believe that it's acceptable to use genetic testing to diagnose diseases or to predict a person's future risk of an illness. Seventy-one percent of the respondents indicated that genetic engineering prior to birth is acceptable if it's done to cure an inherited medical condition. Eighty-one percent supported using the technology to decrease the risk of disease in an unborn child. While most of the Canadians surveyed were opposed to human cloning, many thought cloning was acceptable when limited to human organs under specific medical circumstances.[81]

A variation of cloning, known as *therapeutic cloning*, has also raised ethical issues. In a technique similar to the one that produced Dolly, the cloned sheep, Dr. Michael West of Advanced Cell Technology (ACT) in Worcester, Massachusetts, produced the world's first-ever cloned human embryo—a microscopic, 100-cell version of an already-living person. The company claims it will not use the cloned embryo to create identical humans. Rather, it plans to extract the stem cells, a process that destroys the embryos, and then turn these specialized cells into human tissues that could help treat a host of diseases. To Dr. West and others, the cloning experiment is a gateway to great new cures, lucrative patents, and, perhaps, a measure of immortality.[82] However, to others, this work seems to be creating more potential harm than good. In fact, to some observers, the scenario unfolding at ACT is drawn from a horror film—nascent human lives, created by cloning, used as fodder for high-tech tissue factories.

Where does cloning lead? For many, the difficulties arise when biotechnologists leap from stopping diseases to adding advantages—enhancing the genes that make you more intelligent or more musical. According to William Galston, "The species should be how we *are*, not how we *might be*." In *Remaking Eden*, Lee Silver, a Princeton biologist, foresees the possibility of a two-class system, with the rich, genetically enhanced

"GenRich" class lording it over the poorer, inferior "Naturals."[83] The ethical implications of such potential futures for business are mind-boggling.

Genetic Testing and Profiling   One of the most significant areas of potential questionable application of biotechnology is **genetic testing**. Genetic testing flows from genetic profiling. It is said that someday each of us will have a DNA chip that contains all our genetic information. Genetic information is useful to people including:

- doctors and health-care providers
- medical researchers—to investigate the cause of certain health conditions
- forensic scientists—to help investigate crimes
- insurance companies—to predict health risks
- employers who provide health-care benefits—to predict employees' future health[84]

There are positives associated with this. It will help each person manage his or her own personal health risks. It will also help a physician predict how well a patient will respond to various therapies. Future drugs will be developed using genetic information so that the therapy will be coupled with the DNA information. However, **genetic profiling** also provides a perfect means for identifying a person and thus raises questions of privacy and possible discrimination based on genetic factors.[85] Genetic testing information is controversial for a number of reasons:

- It can yield information not only about yourself, but also about your relatives, given that your genetic makeup is similar to that of your family.
- Genetic information could be used in a way other than initially intended. Further, the information could be used in a range of personal matters where discrimination or preferential treatment may occur. (For example, people predisposed to a particular illness might have problems when arranging life insurance.)
- Every cell in a person's body (except sex cells and red blood cells) contains all their genes. One cell can therefore be analyzed to provide the entire genetic code of a person, which can be used for a variety of purposes.
- Genetic information gives insights into a person's predisposition to illness and disease.[86]

In May 2001, the U.S. Equal Employment Opportunity Commission (EEOC) settled its first court action challenging the use of workplace genetic testing under the Americans with Disabilities Act of 1990 (ADA). The EEOC had sought an injunction against Burlington Northern Santa Fe Railway (BNSF) to end genetic testing of employees who filed claims for work-related injuries based on carpal tunnel syndrome. According to the EEOC, the company's genetic testing program was carried out without the knowledge or consent of its employees, and at least one worker was threatened with termination for failing to submit a blood sample for a genetic test.[87] Under the settlement, BNSF also agreed that it would not analyze blood it had previously obtained, nor would it retaliate against employees who opposed the testing. According to the EEOC, "Our swift action in this case allows Burlington Northern employees to continue to work free of retaliation and future invasions of privacy."[88] In Canada, genetic testing has typically occurred within a clinical research setting. Consequently, there are currently no government-approved guidelines on genetic testing. However, the Canadian College of Medical Geneticists (CCMG) has presented policy statements and guidelines related to various aspects of genetic testing, screening, and services.

Genetically Modified Foods

Another major category of biotechnology that carries important ethical implications for business is the topic of genetically modified foods. This is especially the case for the multibillion-dollar agribusiness industry. Many wholesalers and retailers, however, are also involved in the distribution of genetically modified foods. Genetically modified foods (GMFs) are also commonly referred to as *genetically engineered foods (GEFs)*. Extreme critics call them "Frankenfoods," calling attention to the parallels with the mythical character Frankenstein. The world today seems to be divided into those who favour GMFs and those who fear them. Also, there are a significant number of consumers who are simply not informed enough to know but are quick to offer their gut-reaction opinions, usually based on fear rather than facts. Because no one seems to have been "hurt" by GMFs, there is a lot of wild speculation as well as apathy or indifference at work in judging the ethics and implications of GMFs.

Little information is available to the public as to the actual safety or lack of safety of these products because field-testing is continuing. According to L. Val Giddings, vice president for food and agriculture at the Biotechnology Industry Organization, "There is still not so much as a single, solitary sniffle or headache positively linked to their consumption."[89] Therefore, the debate seems to hinge on whether the pros or cons of GMFs will win out as the arguments are presented. Beyond that, many people have opinions concerning whether the products or ingredients produced by genetically engineering agricultural products are dangerous or should be more strenuously regulated. In the absence of convincing evidence as to their safety, the major debate seems to be on the degree to which products that contain genetically modified ingredients should be labelled.

Two events have called the public's attention to the topic of genetically modified foods. The first was the discovery in September 2000 that genetically engineered animal corn—*potentially* harmful to humans—was found in Taco Bell taco shells. Later it showed up in Safeway Inc.'s house-brand taco shells. The genetically engineered corn, called *Starlink*, is a product that was altered to make it resistant to pests. It contains a foreign protein that is probably safe for human consumption but has some of the chemical characteristics of a human allergen, a term for substances that can trigger anything from a mild allergic reaction to a fatal case of shock. Animal feed, of course, is not supposed to get into the human food supply whether it is genetically modified or not. The event apparently happened by accident, but it represents a case where special tracking of biotech crops might have allowed the industry to identify the corn and remove it.[90]

The second event is the publicity on the almost universal objection to GMFs in Europe, especially in the European Union (EU). Vocal European objections to GMFs have been around for several years. For the past few years, the European Union has banned new bioengineered seeds and crops while it writes laws to govern the sale and distribution of biotech products. A major consequence for North American corn growers is that they have been shut out of markets worth about US$200 million a year. The EU is in the process of enacting strict new controls on the sale of GMFs. This action could have significant implications for agribusiness firms and could possibly lead to a serious setback for the booming biotech industry. In Europe, polls show that a majority of people believe that products made from genetically modified organisms (GMOs) are hazardous to their health.[91]

An estimated 70 percent of groceries contain genetically modified ingredients. Some estimates suggest that as many as 30 000 different products on grocery store shelves are "modified" largely because many processed foods contain soy. And about one half of North America's soy crop is genetically engineered. North Americans have been growing and consuming genetically modified foods for years, especially foods such as herbicide-tolerant soybeans and pest-repellent corn. Ongoing investigations continue to examine claims that such consumption has generated allergic reactions.[92] Companies such as Nestlé U.K. and Unilever U.K. have dropped genetically modified ingredients from their products; however, their North American counterparts, as of 2003, continue to permit these ingredients.

In May 2003, North American scientists, consumer groups, and businesses attempted to forge an alliance as a means to generate a set of industry-wide safety standards for genetically modified foods. Led by the University of Minnesota, the Safety First Initiative's goals include the establishment of a set of standards for building human and environmental safety into the development process for two classes of GMFs: fish modified for increased production in fish farms and plants modified to produce pharmaceuticals.[93]

Labelling   One of the most frequently discussed issues with respect to GMFs is the topic of labelling. Many consumer activists think that, at a minimum, foods that contain genetically engineered contents ought to be labelled as such. Proponents of mandatory labelling argue that the consumer has a right to full disclosure about product contents and that the consumers' right to safety argues that such knowledge should be available to them. Opponents of mandatory labelling for GMFs argue that there is no evidence that the products have any health hazards and that being required to carry a "genetically engineered" label would stigmatize the food products and raise issues of safety where none exist. They support their argument by pointing to the fact that both the U.S. Food and Drug Administration and Health Canada have largely concluded that GMFs are "substantially similar" to conventional foods.

In Canada, food must be labelled if it is pasteurized, irradiated, or contains possible allergens; however, a 2001 vote in Parliament defeated a bill that would have required mandatory labelling of genetically altered foods. Health Canada has held the view that GMFs are just as safe as traditional foods, given that to date there have been virtually no actual reports of specific health risks of GMFs to consumers. Consequently, while at least 36 countries have mandatory GMF labelling laws, Canada has yet to develop clear voluntary standards.

The Council of Canadians has accused Canada's food distributors of failing to move forward the development of a system for labelling genetically modified foods. Consumer groups believe that people want to know about these ingredients, and labelling would provide them with this information in order to make their own decisions. Both Greenpeace and the Council of Canadians have argued that GMFs are a health risk and such groups are concerned that no long-term studies have addressed the effects of modified foods on human health. In addition, these groups have demanded that the food industry become more transparent in its creation and testing of GMFs.[94]

Canadian Food Inspection Agency (CFIA) officials claim that it's difficult to generate enforceable rules because of the complicated food growing processes in Canada.

Farmers can grow different varieties of corn or wheat, with some modified while others are not. Even where farmers grow GMF crops in separate fields, there is no guarantee that the different crops won't become mixed at some stage in the process. In addition, according to the Canadian Federation of Agriculture, the industry will face huge losses if mandatory labelling is imposed. At best, the labels will increase the price of foods produced and processed in Canada. And at worst, according to the federation, consumers will view these labels as a warning and avoid these foods entirely.[95]

One of the hottest trends in food marketing in the United States is the *non-GMO label*, which stands for "non-genetically modified organisms." Just a few years ago, this was unknown in the United States. Now, however, it is popping up frequently as companies attempt to take strategic advantage of their products that do not contain GMOs. The non-GMO label is now being seen on hundreds of products ranging from pasta, produce, and breakfast cereals to frozen entrees, condiments, and beverages. Industry executives believe this is a fast-growing market segment, and though labels are not mandatory, some consumer segments are attracted to this product feature. The Council of Canadians has pointed out the irony that although Canadian producers are not required to label GMOs, if an organic producer wants to label a product GMO-free, most major food retailers won't allow it.[96] For example, in 2001, a company that wished to publicize its "unmodified" ingredients was precluded from doing so by a government agency. The Quebec brewery, Unibrouc, wanted to use a recent certification from the Canadian Food Inspection Agency (CFIA) as part of its advertising campaign. The CFIA had certified the brewery's beer as GMO-free to help the firm's export business in Europe. However, the agency denied the brewery the right to use this certification in the promotion of their products.[97] Greenpeace Canada has released its own consumers' list of GMO-free foods.[98]

The issues of safety and labelling of GMFs are not likely to go away. Special-interest groups on both sides of the debate continue to be active in advocating their points of view. The agribusiness industry continues to argue that the foods are safe and that mandatory testing and labelling are not necessary. Consumer activists, however, have brought together environmentalists, organic farmers, chefs, and religious leaders, and they continue to make the case for rigorous safety testing and labelling. To be sure, all consumer stakeholders are potentially affected by the outcome of these debates, so it is likely that they will continue into the near future.

Summary

Business use of technology today is so dramatic that the topic merits a separate chapter. In this chapter, basic concepts such as technology and the technological environment were introduced and defined. The benefits and side effects or hazards of technology were discussed. The symptoms of society's intoxication with technology were outlined. Questions regarding the ethics of technology were raised in two broad domains: information technology and biotechnology.

In the realm of information technology, the category with the most widespread current impact in business, topics included electronic commerce, invasion of privacy via e-commerce, government's involvement in Internet privacy invasion, and business initiatives. Questionable practices and uses of technology were raised, including particular industries such as the porn industry, Internet gambling, and Web-based music services. Computer technology in the workplace, one of the most significant areas of application, has been used for monitoring e-mail and Internet usage and other forms of surveillance. Questions regarding the ethics of new technologies such as cell phones were also raised.

The field of biotechnology was discussed with respect to social and ethical implications. A key topic in this sphere included the new field of bioethics. Two arenas of biotechnology were identified and discussed—that of genetic engineering, to include a discussion of stem cell research, cloning, and genetic testing and profiling; and the general domain of genetically modified foods. It is anticipated that the debate over food safety and labelling will continue for years as different interest groups raise questions about the appropriateness of genetically modified foods.

Key Terms

bioethics (page 253)
biotechnology (page 240)
chief privacy officer (CPO) (page 247)
cloning (page 257)
electronic commerce (page 244)
embryonic stem cells (page 254)
genetic engineering (page 254)
genetic profiling (page 258)

genetic testing (page 258)
genetically modified foods (GMFs) (page 254)
information technology (page 240)
surveillance (page 249)
technological environment (page 240)
technology (page 239)
therapeutic cloning (page 256)

Discussion Questions

1. Are there any benefits or negative side effects of technology in business that have not been mentioned in this chapter? Discuss.

2. Do you agree that society is intoxicated with technology? Does this pose special problems for business with respect to the ethics of technology? Will such intoxication blind people to ethical considerations?

3. Do you think business is abusing its power with respect to invasion of privacy of both consumers and employees? What about surveillance? Which particular practice do you think is the most questionable?

4. Is it an exaggeration to question the ethical implications for business of cell phone use? Discuss both sides of this issue.

5. Do you think genetically modified foods raise a legitimate safety hazard? Should Health Canada take action to require safety testing? What about warning labels? Do you think warning labels would unfairly stigmatize GMFs and make consumers question their safety? Is this fair to the GMF industry?

Endnotes

1. John Naisbitt, Nana Naisbitt, and Douglas Phillips, *High Tech/High Touch: Technology and our Search for Meaning* (Nicholas Brealey Publishing Co, 1999).
2. "Invasion of Privacy at Issue as Computers Used to Track Bar Patrons," http://www.cbc.ca.
3. Jay Bookman, "Technology in Your Face," *Atlanta Journal-Constitution,*" D1.
4. *Ibid.*
5. John Bowman, "Event Data Recorder or 'Black Box,'" CBC News Online (October 23, 2003), http://www.cbc.ca/consumers/market.
6. *Webster's Ninth New Collegiate Dictionary* (Springfield, MA: Merriam-Webster, Inc., 1983), 1211.
7. "Technology," *The World Book Encyclopedia* (Chicago: World Book, Inc., 1988), 76.
8. Richard L. Daft, *Management*, 5th ed. (New York: The Dryden Press, 2000), 75.
9. "Technology," *The World Book Encyclopedia*, 77–78.
10. *Ibid.*, 78–79.
11. *Ibid.*, 79.
12. *Ibid.*, 80.
13. *Ibid.* 80–81.

14. Naisbitt, Naisbitt, and Phillips (1999).

15. John Naisbitt, "High Tech, High Touch," *Executive Excellence* (Vol. 16, No. 12, December 1999), 5ff.

16. *Ibid.* Also see, Stephen Goode, "Naisbitt Questions the Future of Technology," *Insight* (June 11, 2001), 37–38.

17. Paul A. Alcorn, *Practical Ethics for a Technological World* (Upper Saddle River, NJ: Prentice Hall, 2001).

18. Ruth Chadwick (ed.), *The Concise Encyclopedia of the Ethics of New Technologies* (Academic Press, 2001).

19. Sandy Reed, "The Ethics of Technology: This Group Looks at Issues for the Next Millennium," *Infoworld* (Vol. 21, Issue 42, October 18, 1999), 79ff.

20. "Pursuing Excellence Through Connectedness: Canada's Quest for Global Best," Conference Board of Canada (2002), http://www.conferenceboard.ca.

21. Forrester Research, http://www.foresters.com/home/.

22. Marina Strauss, "Home Depot Moves On-Line," *Globe and Mail* (October 22, 2003), http://www.theglobeandmail.com/business/.

23. "E-Biz: Down But Hardly Out," *Business Week* (March 26, 2001), 126–130. See also Internet Fraud Watch, http://www.fraud.org/internet.

24. ITWorldCanada.com, http://www.itworldcanada.com.

25. "Putting the Ethics in E-Business," *Computerworld* (Vol. 34, No. 45, November 6, 2000), 81ff.

26. "Executives Note Hot Business Topics," *USA Today* (July 26, 2001), 1B.

27. "Exposure in Cyberspace," *The Wall Street Journal* (March 21, 2001), B1.

28. "Privacy Options Are a Blur," *USA Today* (April 10, 2001), 3D.

29. *Ibid.*

30. Donna De Marco, "What's in a Name?" *Insight* (July 30, 2001), 30–31.

31. Privacy Commissioner of Canada, http://www.privcom.gc.ca/index_e.asp.

32. Paul Lim, "Small Firms Grapple with New Privacy Law," *Financial Post* (October 20, 2003), http://www.nationalpost.com/home/index.html.

33. "Privacy Win," *Multinational Monitor* (March 2001), 29.

34. Jim Middlemiss, "RBC Pilots Online Privacy Tools Program," *Bank Systems & Technology* (Vol. 38, Issue 12, December 2001), 11.

35. Michelle Kessler, "Position of Privacy Officer Coming into Public Eye," *USA Today* (November 30, 2000), 1B.

36. Jared Sandberg, "The Privacy Officer," *The Wall Street Journal* (July 16, 2001), R10.

37. Timothy Egan, "Technology Sent Wall Street into Market for Pornography," *The Wall Street Journal* (October 23, 2000), A1, A20; Jefferson Graham, "As Napster Shuts, Others Carry the Tune," *USA Today* (July 12, 2001), 3D.

38. Robert Kuttner, "Sorry, But the New Economy Demands New Regulations," *Business Week* (July 30, 2001), 23.

39. "Consumer Group Says Search Engines Use Deceptive Advertising," *The Wall Street Journal* (July 17, 2001), B7. See also Margaret Mannix, "Search Me, Please," *U.S. News & World Report* (July 30, 2001), 37.

40. "Working Smarter: The Skill of Bias of Computer Technologies," Human Resources Development Canada (May 2002), http://www.hrdc-drhc.gc.ca; "Working with Computers in Canada: An Empirical Analysis of Incidence, Frequency and Purpose," Human Resources Development Canada (April 2003), http://www.hrdc-drhc.gc.ca.

41. "The Effects of Computers on Workplace Stress, Job Security and Work Interest in Canada," Human Resources Development Canada (December 2002), http://www.hrdc-drhc.gc.ca.

42. Darryl Haralson and Sam Ward, "Technology's Positive Impact," *USA Today* (October 22, 2001), 1B.

43. Amanda Mujica, Edward Petry, and Dianne Vickery, "A Future of Technology and Ethics," *Business and Society Review* (Vol. 104, No. 3, 1999), 279–290.

44. "The Effect of Computers on Workplace Stress, Job Security and Work Interest in Canada," Human Resources Development Canada (December 2002), http://www.hrdc-drhc.gc.ca.

45. Mujica, 280.

46. "Big Bro Is Eye-ing Your E-Mail," *Business Week* (June 4, 2001), 30.

47. Janet Kornblum, "The Boss Is Tracking Moves of a Third of Online Workers," *USA Today* (July 10, 2001), 3D.

48. Andrew Ross Sorkin, "An E-Mail Boast to Friends Puts Executive Out of Work," *The New York Times* (May 22, 2001).

49. John Galvin, "The New Business Ethics: Cheating, Lying, Stealing—Technology Makes It Easy, Get Used to It," *Smartbusinessmag.com* (June 2000), 86.

50. *Ibid.*, 88.

51. "Keeping Tabs on Employees Online," *Business Week* (February 19, 2001), 16.

52. Sue Shellenbargar, "Should Employers Play a Role in Safe Use of Cellphones in Cars?" *The Wall Street Journal* (July 18, 2001), B1.

53. *Ibid.*

54. "Driving and Dialing," *Business Week* (July 23, 2001), 16.

55. Shellenbarger, B1.

56. Mujica, Petry, and Vickery, 286.

57. Thomas Hilton, "Information System Ethics: A Practitioner Survey," *Journal of Business Ethics* (December 2000), 279–284.

58. Todd Humber, "Developing an Internet Use Policy Is Painless—and Crucial," *Canadian HR Reporter* (Vol. 15, No. 19, November 4, 2002), G4.

59. Walter Isaacson, "The Biotech Century," *Time* (January 11, 1999), 42–43.

60. *Ibid.*

61. Alison Taunton-Rigby, "Bioethics: The New Frontier" (Waltham, MA: The Sears Lectureship in Business Ethics, Center for Business Ethics, Bentley College, April 19, 2000), 7.

62. *Ibid.*, 7–8.

63. Maggie Biggs, "In Implementing Emerging Technology, We May Face Thorny Ethical Problems," *Infoworld* (October 16, 2000), 106.

64. "Leon Kass, Philosopher-Politician: The President's Choice for Bioethicist-in-Chief," *The Economist* (August 18, 2001), 25.

65. Bret Stephens, "… And the President's New Ethicist," *The Wall Street Journal* (August 14, 2001), A14.

66. "Bioethics: Wanna Buy a Bioethicist?" *Christianity Today* (October 1, 2001), 32–33.

67. *Ibid.*

68. Nell Boyce, "And Now, Ethics for Sale," *U.S. News & World Report* (July 30, 2001), 18–19.

69. Charles Colson, "The New Tyranny: Biotechnology Threatens to Turn Humanity into Raw Material," *Christianity Today* (October 1, 2001), 128.

70. Kerry Capell, "At Risk: A Golden Opportunity in Biotech," *Business Week* (September 10, 2001), 85–87.

71. Council of Canadians, http://www.canadians.org.

72. Sheryl Gay Stolberg, "Company Using Cloning to Yield Stem Cells," *The New York Times* (July 13, 2001).

73. Tim Friend, "The Stem Cell Hard Sell," *USA Today* (July 17, 2001), 6D.

74. Rick Weiss, "Which Life Matters More?" *Washington Post National Weekly Edition* (July 23–29, 2001), 31.

75. Nancy Gibbs and Michael Duffy, "We Must Proceed with Great Care," *Time* (August 20, 2001), 12–23.

76. Kenneth Woodward, "A Question of Life or Death," *Newsweek* (July 9, 2001), 31.

77. "Science and Technology: Cloning Around," *The Economist* (March 17, 2001), 79–80.

78. Nell Boyce and David Kaplan, "The God Game No More," *U.S. News & World Reports* (July 9/July 16, 2001), 20–21.

79. "Critics Doubt Group Has Cloned a Human," *CBC News Online* (December 28, 2002), http://www.cbc.ca.

80. "After Darwin, Ethics Again," *Far East Economic Review* (March 22, 2001), 40–41.

81. "Canadians Give Conditional Support to Cloning Survey," *CBC News Online* (June 16, 2000), http://www.cbc.ca.

82. Antonio Regalado, "Experiments in Controversy," *The Wall Street Journal* (July 13, 2001), B1.

83. "America's Next Ethical War," *The Economist* (April 14, 2001), 2122.

84. Arthur, Allens, Robinson, http://www.aar.com.au/privacy/ind/hea/gen.htm.

85. Taunton-Rigby, 18–19.

86. Arthur, Allens, Robinson, http://www.aar.com.au/privacy/ind/hea/gen.htm.

87. "Genetic Discrimination," *Multinational Monitor* (May 2001), 30.

88. "EEOC Settles Genetics Suit with Burlington Northern," *The Wall Street Journal* (April 19, 2001), B10.

89. L. Val Giddings, "No: These Crops Pass Multiple Tests Before Approval and Are a Boon to the World's Hungry," *Insight* (August 6, 2001), 43.

90. Paul Raeburn, "After Taco Bell: Can Biotech Learn Its Lesson?" *Business Week* (November 6, 2000), 54.

91. William Drozdiak, "Look for the European Union Label," *The Washington Post National Weekly Edition* (April 16–22, 2001), 20.

92. *Ibid.*

93. June Chua, "Genetically Modified Foods: A Primer," *CBC Online* (June 2001), http://www.cbc.ca/index.html.

94. "Group Says Canada Too Slow on GMO Labeling," *CBC Online* (June 13, 2001), http://www.cbc.ca/index.html.

95. Chua (2001).

96. "Group Says Canada Too Slow…" (2001).

97. "Brewer Fights for GMO-Free Labelling in Canada," *CBC Online* (June 7, 2001), http://www.cbc.ca/index.html.

98. Greenpeace Canada, http://www.greenpeace.ca/e/.

Chapter 9

Ethical Issues in the Global Arena

Chapter Objectives

After studying this chapter, you should be able to:

1 Identify and describe the concepts of internationalization and globalization of business.

2 Summarize the arguments for and against globalization.

3 Explain the evolving role of and problems with multinational corporations in the global environment.

4 Recognize the major ethical challenges of operating in the multinational environment.

5 Describe ISCT and the concepts of hypernorms and moral free space.

6 Discuss strategies for improving global ethics.

7 Enumerate seven moral guidelines for improving multinational corporations' operations in the global sphere.

The rise of international business as a critical element in the world economy is one of the most significant developments of the past 50 years. This period has been characterized by the rapid growth of direct investment in foreign lands by Canada and the U.S., by countries in Western Europe, by Japan, and by other industrialized countries as well. We have also seen the rise of direct foreign investment in Canada, with an increasing presence of U.S.-owned multinationals in many sectors of the Canadian economy. Domestic issues have been made immensely more complex by the escalating international trend. At the same time, the internationalization of business has created unique problems of its own. It no longer appears that international markets can be seen as opportunities that may or may not be pursued. Rather, international markets now are seen as natural extensions of an ever-expanding marketplace that must be pursued if firms are to remain competitive. Only recently has there been evidence of a backlash against global business. The attacks on the World Trade Center on September 11, 2001, the most shocking development to date, have been seen by many as an attack on global capitalism, especially that practised by the United States. This event likely will modify in yet unseen ways the practice of global business and its ramifications for business ethics.

Peter Drucker has termed the expanded marketplace the **transnational economy**. He goes on to say that, if business expects to establish and maintain leadership in one country, it must also strive to hold a leadership position in all developed markets worldwide. This apparent need helps explain the worldwide boom in transnational investments.[1] One early definition of this transnational or global economy was as follows: trade in goods, a much smaller trade in services, the international movement of labour, and international flows of capital and information.[2]

The complexity introduced by the transnational economy and the internationalization of business is seen clearly in cases in which ethical issues arise. At best, business ethics is difficult when we are dealing with one culture. Once we bring two or possibly more cultures into consideration, it gets extremely problematic. Managers have to deal not only with differing customs, protocol, and ways of operating but also with differing concepts of law and notions of what is acceptable or unacceptable behaviour in an ethical sense. All of this is then exacerbated by the fact that world political issues become intertwined. For example, what might be intended as a corporate attempt to simply bribe an official of a foreign government, in keeping with local custom, could explode into major international political tension between two countries.

The New, New World of International Business

We have traversed through several different eras in the internationalization of business since the post–World War II decade (1945–1955). There have been the Growth Years (1955–1970), the Troubled Years (1970–1980), and the New International Order (1980–present), according to one international business expert.[3] The New, New World of international business and business ethics can be said to have begun in the fall of 1999. At that time, the World Trade Organization (WTO) was meeting in Seattle, and there were massive demonstrations and protests outpouring into the streets. The WTO talks collapsed as 50 000 protestors rioted, expressing extreme hostility and violence toward the idea of global business.[4] This backlash against globalism continued with massive demonstrations in Washington, DC, in April 2000, Prague in the fall of 2000, Quebec in April 2001, and Genoa during the summer of 2001.

First, it is helpful to consider again what global business really means. Second, it is useful to briefly consider some of the sentiments behind the massive protests against globalism, for this new reality of world attitudes and questions being raised about global capitalism cannot be ignored.

Concepts of Global Business

There are a number of different terms to describe the trends in global business over the past several decades. Some of the more prominent ones include internationalization, globalization, globalism, and global capitalism. Countless businesses today have become internationalized but not necessarily globalized. **Internationalization** may be thought of as a "process by which firms increase their awareness of the influence of international activities on their future and establish and conduct transactions with firms from other countries."[5] Some of the characteristics of internationalization include exporting, acting as licensor to a foreign company, establishing joint ventures outside the home country with foreign companies, and establishing or acquiring wholly owned businesses outside the home country.[6]

In contrast, the terms **globalism** or **globalization** suggest the economic integration of the globe. Globalization refers to "global economic integration of many formerly national economies into one global economy."[7] This is made possible by free trade, especially by free capital mobility, and by easy or uncontrolled migration. Whereas internationalization simply recognizes that nations increasingly rely on understandings among one another, globalization is the "effective erasure of national boundaries for economic purposes."[8] Though these are technical distinctions that are helpful to be aware of, it is not always clear when people talk about globalization whether they are just using it as another term for internationalization of business or seeing it as global economic integration. Sometimes observers are just referring to global capitalism, which is the system of free movement of resources around the world. Obviously, true globalization is an extreme status that has not yet been achieved, but one that many hold as an ultimate aspiration.

According to *Business Week*, globalization today is a term that has come to encompass everything from "expanded trade" and "factories shifting around the world" to the "international bodies that set the rules for the global economy" (i.e., World Trade Organization, International Monetary Fund, and the World Bank).[9] For our purposes, *Business Week*'s broad concept of globalism or globalization probably fits best. It encompasses both internationalization and trends toward globalization. We should remember, however, that we often need to probe deeply to figure out how someone is using these terms, for they may mean different things to different people.

Backlash Against Globalization

We stated earlier that there has been an evident backlash against globalization that has been most apparent since the protests in Seattle in fall 1999 against the activities of the World Trade Organization (WTO). The protestors at the Seattle meeting have been described in various ways. They have been identified as a peculiar meld of extreme leftists and rightists, trade unionists, radical environmentalists, and self-appointed representatives of civil society insisting on saving the poor people of developing countries from economic development.[10] They have also been described as a visible coalition between labour and environmentalists—"teamsters and turtles"—as one sign said, as well as other key constituencies, such as human rights activists.[11] In short, they are special interest groups committed to halting the expansion of global capitalism and trade.

The backlash against globalization that began in Seattle has been perpetuated at a number of important global meetings since then. After Seattle came the meeting of the IMF and the World Bank in Washington, DC, in April 2000. These organizations were accused by environmental and anti-poverty groups of inflicting misery and poverty on developing nations. Next, came the European meeting of the IMF and World Bank in Prague in the fall of 2000, and a meeting of the heads of state of 34 nations in Quebec City in April 2001 to discuss a hemispheric free-trade zone.

The height of protest and destruction came in Genoa, Italy, in the summer of 2001 at the G8 Summit meeting of the eight wealthiest countries in the world. There were at least two days of violent riots that resulted in death and destruction. The violence at the G8 Summit shocked the world. One positive outcome of the Genoa meetings was an exposure of and split within the antiglobalization ranks between those who want to peacefully reform global capitalism and the anarchists who want to destroy it.

Other protest meetings were planned for Washington, DC, in September 2001, but these meetings were postponed in the aftermath of the terrorist attacks on the World Trade Center and the Pentagon. Protestors promised to continue their opposition at future meetings, saying that the attacks in New York and Washington were a direct result of U.S. foreign policy and that only an end to global capitalism would ensure safety for all.[12] Surely, there was more behind the terrorism than opposition to global business, but this is how it was seen by many. In any case, the New, New World of globalization is one in which the pros and cons of globalization are now back on the table for consideration and discussion.

Many studies have been conducted to investigate the nature and consequences of globalization. A myriad of reports have been generated on the pros and cons of globalization. Numerous reports have observed that on one side we see the "globalists," who strongly advocate open markets with private firms moving freely across the globe. They believe that investors, consumers, employees, and environmentalists are better off due to globalization. On the other side are the "antiglobalists," who have taken to the streets to protest the expansion and greed of corporate global enterprises. They believe that globalization is responsible for the destruction of local environments and emerging economies, abuses of human rights, the undermining of local cultures, and the sovereignty of nation-states. The antiglobalists also decry the power of international bodies, notably the World Trade Organization, the International Monetary Fund, and the World Bank.[13] These opposing views were succinctly stated by Nicholas Stern in an article in the *Ivey Business Journal*:

> *Is globalization making the rich, richer and the poor, poorer? ...*
> *Corporations are a driving force and important beneficiaries of global economic integration. They are also the ultimate targets of anti-globalization demonstrators, who blame multinational corporations for ills ranging from deforestation to child labor. If development efforts have failed and globalization is further impoverishing the world's poorest people, then corporations surely deserve part of the blame. If, on the other hand, global poverty is declining and global integration is helping people to escape poverty, then corporations are presumably part of the solution.[14]*

Figure 9–1 summarizes some of these two groups' opposing views on globalization as it affects consumers, workers, the environment, developing nations, and human rights. It should be clear from these pros and cons that globalization has significant ethical issues embedded in it for stakeholders.

FIGURE 9–1

The Pros and Cons of Globalization

Impact On:		Globalists	Antiglobalists
	Consumers	Open markets allow for free trade of goods and services, lower costs, greater efficiency. Lower prices, greater variety of goods and services, rising living standards.	Benefits the wealthy and further impoverishes the poor. Widening wealth gap worldwide. Harmful to low-income consumers.
	Employees	Faster economic growth; higher wages; more employment; improved working conditions.	Globalism places profits above people—depressing wages, displacing workers, undermining workers' rights.
	Environment	Global capitalism means rapid economic growth, resources necessary to clean up environments, development of more efficient CO_2-reducing technologies, protection of ecosystems; pollution reduction.	Results in exploitation and destruction of ecosystems in name of corporate greed. Ignores adverse impacts on environments. More pollution, especially carbon dioxide. Exacerbated global warming.
	Developing Nations	Open markets, cross-border investments are keys to national economic development. Higher standards of living, better working conditions, cleaner environments.	Global capitalism, world trade bodies, world financial institutions conspire to keep developing nations in debt, destroys local economies, further impoverishes peoples.
	Human Rights	Free and open markets create cultures/institutions supporting rule of law and free expression. Spreads economic/political freedom to far corners of world (e.g., Taiwan and South Korea).	In blind pursuit of profits, global corporations ignore abuses of human rights, including political and religious oppression, false imprisonment, torture, free speech, and abuses of workers, especially women and children.

Source: Summarized from Robert Batterson and Murray Weidenbaum, *The Pros and Cons of Globalization* (St. Louis: Center for the Study of American Business, January 2001), 3–12.

Against this backdrop of the New, New World of business we now find ourselves in, we can now consider some of the conventional ethical challenges faced by multinational corporations (MNCs) as they do business in the global sphere.

MNCs and the Global Environment

A global business is a business that engages directly in some form of international business activity, including such activities as exporting, importing, or international production. A business that has direct investments (whether in the form of marketing or manufacturing facilities) in at least two different countries is specifically referred to as a **multinational corporation** (**MNC**). In other words, multinational organizations, or MNCs, are business enterprises that control assets, factories, and so on, operated either as branch offices or affiliates in two or more countries. An MNC generates products or services through its affiliates in several countries, and it maintains control over the operations of those affiliates, and manages from a global perspective. MNCs may also be referred to as global companies when they operate in many countries around the world.

Typically, MNCs are very large organizations and, in terms of their relative role in the world setting, it has been estimated that the 600 largest MNCs account for about one-quarter of the activity in the world's economies. Most MNCs have head-quarters in developed countries—the home country. More specifically, over half of the MNCs have headquarters in the United States. France, Germany, the United Kingdom, and Japan are among the other countries that are home to headquarters for most of the remaining MNCs. MNCs maintain branch plants or subsidiaries in two or more foreign countries—these are the host countries, and they are either developed, developing, or Third World countries.

Among Canada's well-known MNCs is Bata Corp., which operates footwear manufacturing and distribution facilities in about 60 countries. Bombardier Inc. is also very much a part of the global market. This company has operations that include transportation equipment and aircraft production. While its head office is in Montreal, nearly 90 percent of its sales are made in markets outside of Canada. It has production facilities in Canada, the United States, France, and Austria, and it markets products on five different continents.

Not all problems of operating in a global business environment are attributable to MNCs. However, MNCs have become the symbolic heart of the problem because they represent the archetypal international business form. Given their pervasiveness (in the Canadian context and abroad), we will focus on U.S.-based MNCs. However, we should remember that the MNCs of Canada and other countries experience these same challenges. In fact, the presence of MNCs from multiple countries makes for a complex operating environment for all firms.

Changed Scope and Nature of U.S.-Based MNCs

Over the years, both the scope and the nature of U.S.-based MNCs have changed. In the early 1900s, the United Fruit Company was growing bananas in Central America and achieving a degree of notoriety for its "invasion" of Honduras. Another wave of MNCs was in the extractive industries (oil, gas, gems). Today, financial institutions, chemical companies, pharmaceutical companies, manufacturers, and service firms represent the kinds of enterprises that may be found operating in the global business environment.

The investment of U.S.-based MNCs has been phenomenal over the past three decades or more, growing to well into the hundreds of billions of dollars. We should also note that the most challenging situation for MNCs is when they are operating in so-called emerging nations, developing countries, or **less-developed countries** (**LDCs**), where charges of exploitation and abuse of power seem more plausible. These situations are ripe for charges of American imperialism in struggling economies, and they are often cited by the antiglobalists.

Underlying Challenges of Operating in a Multinational Environment

It has been argued that there are at least two underlying and related challenges or problems as firms attempt to operate in a multinational environment. One problem is *corporate legitimacy* as the MNC seeks a role in a foreign society. The other problem is the fundamentally *differing philosophies* that may exist between the firm's home country and the host country in which it seeks to operate.[15] These two challenges set the stage for understanding how ethical problems arise in the global environment.

Corporate Legitimacy   For an MNC to be perceived as legitimate in the eyes of a host country, it must fulfill its social responsibilities. As we discussed earlier, these include economic, legal, ethical, and philanthropic responsibilities. Larger firms, in particular, are seen as outsiders, and the expectations on them are greater than on smaller, less visible firms. Further, the similarities and differences between the cultures of the two countries affect the perceived legitimacy. For example, an American firm operating in Canada is not likely to experience major problems. An American or a Western firm operating in Iran, however, could be perceived as quite alien.[16] Differences between the values and lifestyles of managers who live in the two countries could pose serious legitimacy problems. If a host country finds the lifestyles or values repugnant—as many LDCs may well find the materialistic lifestyles and values of American managers—legitimacy may be difficult to achieve.

Another, perhaps more basic, barrier to achieving legitimacy is the inherent conflict that may exist between the interests of the MNC and those of the host country. The MNC is seeking to *optimize globally*, while host governments are seeking to *optimize locally*. This may pose little difficulty for an MNC operating in a developed country, where macroeconomic or regulatory policies are sophisticated and appropriate. But it may pose serious problems in the LDCs, where there is often the perception that MNCs are beyond the control of local governments. In these latter situations, especially, it is not uncommon to see the local government impose various control devices, such as indigenization laws requiring majority ownership by locals, exclusion of foreign firms from certain industries, restrictions on foreign personnel, or even expropriation.[17]

Part of the reason MNCs have difficulty achieving legitimacy is a reaction to the real or perceived conflicts between the interests of the firm and those of the host country or government that place the MNC in a "no-win" situation. If the MNC tries to bring in the latest labour-saving technology, this may conflict with the perceived need for labour-creating technology in high-unemployment-prone LDCs. If the MNC repatriates large parts of its profits, this may be seen as depriving the local economy of new wealth. If the MNC reinvests the profits locally, this may be perceived as furthering its control over the economy. If the MNC pays market rate wages, this may be seen as exploiting labour with low wage rates. If the MNC pays a premium for labour, this may be seen as skimming the cream of the local labour supply and thus hurting local businesses that cannot afford to pay a premium. Consequently, whatever it does, the MNC is a convenient target for criticism from some faction or stakeholders. In this sometimes hostile environment, legitimacy can be both elusive and fleeting—difficult to get and even harder to keep.[18]

Differing Philosophies Between MNCs and Host Countries   Closely related to the legitimacy issue is the dilemma of MNCs that have quite different philosophical perspectives from those of their host countries. The philosophy of Western industrialized nations, and thus their MNCs, focuses on economic growth, efficiency, specialization, free trade, and comparative advantage. By contrast, LDCs, for example, have quite different priorities. Other important objectives for them might include a more equitable income distribution or increased economic self-determination. In this context, the industrialized nations may appear to be inherently exploitative in that their presence may perpetuate the dependency of the poorer nation.[19]

These philosophical differences build in an environment of tension that sometimes results in stringent actions being unilaterally taken by the host country. During the 1970s, for example, the environment for MNCs investing in LDCs became much more harsh. Some of these harsh actions initiated by the host countries included outright expropriation (as occurred in the oil industry) and creeping expropriation (as occurred in the manufacturing industries when foreign subsidiaries were required to take on some local partners). Other restrictions included limits on profits repatriation.[20] As a result of the dilemmas that the MNCs face, it is easy to understand why philosopher Richard DeGeorge has argued that "First World MNCs are both the hope of the Third World and the scourge of the Third World."[21]

Thus, MNCs increasingly find themselves in situations where their very legitimacy is in question and their philosophical perspective is radically different from that of their host countries. Added to this are the normal problems of operating in a foreign culture with different types of governments, different languages, different legal systems, diverse stakeholders, and different social values. One could well argue that ethical problems are built into this environment. MNCs are attempting to bridge the cultural gaps between two peoples; yet, as they attempt to adapt to local customs and business practices, they are assailed at home for not adhering to the standards, practices, laws, or ethics of their home country. Indeed, these pose ethical dilemmas for MNCs. Figure 9–2 portrays the dilemma of MNCs caught between the characteristics and expectations of their home country and those of one or more host countries.

MNC–Host Country Challenges

Globalization is "one of the most powerful and pervasive influences on nations, businesses, workplaces, communities, and lives at the end of the 20th century," according to Rosabeth Moss Kanter, in *World Class: Thriving Locally in a Global Economy*.[22] Recent research suggests that global issues are at the forefront of CEOs' agendas. According to Richard Cavanagh, president and CEO of The Conference Board, a hot topic has been "navigating the management maze of globalization."[23] As part of this, challenges facing business have been significant in the social values and ethics arenas.

There are so many issues characterizing the challenges between MNCs and host countries that it is almost impossible to draw limits on them. However, we must limit our focus in this chapter. Before discussing a few select ethical issues in the next section, we will first attempt at least to identify what some of these broader challenges are. The issues we will touch on include the cultural aspects of global business, business/government interactions in global operations, management and control of resources in global operations, and, finally, exploration of global markets.[24]

Facing Cultural Differences   It has been argued that the most significant reason why MNC managers fail is their inability to cope with the foreign cultural environ-

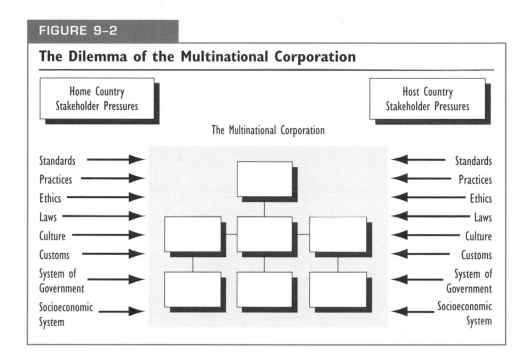

FIGURE 9-2

The Dilemma of the Multinational Corporation

ment. Managers and companies experience culture shock when they are faced with cultures and languages that are significantly different from their own. Culture becomes one of the most critical make-or-break factors in successful multinational corporate operations. Culture, customs, language, attitudes, and institutions vary from country to country, and these differences pose sometimes-insurmountable obstacles to success for MNCs.

Business and Government Differences   Beyond the differences that stem from cultural variables, the interaction of the business and government sectors poses challenges for MNC executives. Depending on the region of the world and industry under consideration, the extent of the business/government interactions may vary widely. In worldwide financial services, for example, heavy regulation was typical until the 1980s, when deregulation began in the United States and Canada and spread to other countries as well. Deregulation came fast to world banking, yet now some re-regulation is occurring.

Government continues to be very important in some countries. "Japan, Inc.," for example, refers to the close-knit relationship between the Japanese government and the private sector. By contrast, government and business are more at arm's length in Canada and the United States. In Korea, government has always been influential, and only in recent years has the banking sector been privatized. In Europe, government has been intimately involved in business and banking from time to time. Many key industries have been nationalized in Great Britain, depending on which political party is in power.[25]

It is not uncommon for conflicts to arise between host country governments and MNCs. These conflicts typically relate to control over operations in the host country and the division of profits that accrue from the operations. Host governments are also typically interested in such issues as the regulation of technology transfer and transfer prices used by MNCs for conducting intrafirm trade.[26]

Management and Control of Global Operations Two issues are worthy of mention here. One issue is *organizational structure and design*, and the other issue is *human resource management*. MNCs must employ a multiplicity of organizational approaches in their markets. This is in significant part due to host government regulations. MNC management becomes complex when the firm licenses in Country A, has joint ventures in Country B, and countertrades in Country C. In each environment, the firm faces different organizational challenges. A second major topic that needs to be mentioned is the proper use of human resources. In the arena of staffing, a question arises concerning the tactical use of home versus host country nationals. Use of each implies different costs and benefits for the firm. Other critical human resource issues include selection and training.[27]

Exploration of Global Markets A final topic in this section is the exploration of global markets as a vital MNC–host country challenge. Although U.S. MNCs dominated world markets for a period of time, this is no longer the case. Today, we have a world of intense competition among firms all over the globe. In the past 20 years, there has been a remarkable resurgence, not only from Japan and the European economies but from some other countries as well (e.g., China, Korea, Latin America). One major issue in this general topic is the question of strategic alternatives that may be used by MNCs considering expansion into new foreign markets. Various strategies involving products and promotions are possible. Relevant factors in such strategic planning include the product function or need satisfied, conditions of product use, consumers' ability to buy, and communications strategy.[28]

Another major issue surrounds the pursuit of developing Third World markets. Marketing concepts for Asia, Africa, and some countries in Latin America may differ markedly from those we have become accustomed to in North America. This category of issue is quite important in connection with our discussion of global ethics, because less-developed countries pose significant temptations to MNCs to exploit and cut corners. International expert Richard D. Robinson suggests that we need to be sensitive to the long-run national interests of such countries. He advocates three levels of sensitivity. First, management of MNCs should be sensitive to the need to *modify or redesign products* so that they will be appropriate for their intended markets. An example of this was a truck manufacturer that modified its truck design to accommodate the rough roads, extreme heat, and high elevations found in Turkey. Second, management must be sensitive to the *impacts of products*, especially in terms of their impacts on the long-term interests of non-Western markets. For example, luxury products and those of a fundamentally labour-saving nature would not necessarily be appealing under all circumstances to a development-conscious foreign government. Third, MNC managers should be sensitive to the extent to which their *products are politically vulnerable*. Products that are politically vulnerable may lead to labour agitation, public regulation (e.g., price fixing and allocation quotas), nationalization, or political debates. Examples of products that in the past have led to political debates and action include sugar, salt, kerosene, gasoline, tires, and medicines.[29]

The need to be sensitive to marketing in other countries provides an appropriate transition to our discussion of ethical issues in the global business environment. It should be clear from this discussion that ethical issues or conflicts might easily arise from cultural conditions that are not anticipated by the MNCs. Further, even though we will examine in more detail such visible issues as marketing practices, plant safety, questionable payments, and sweatshops in cheap-labour factories in developing countries, we should be ever vigilant of the fact that ethical dilemmas can also arise in such realms as operations management, financial management, labour relations, and global strategic management.

Ethical Issues in the Global Business Environment

For many companies, most of the ethical problems that arise in the international environment are in the same categories as those that arise in their domestic environments. These ethical issues reside in all of the functional areas of business: production/operations, marketing, finance, and management. These issues concern the fair treatment of stakeholders—employees, customers, the community, and competitors. These issues involve product safety, plant safety, advertising practices, human resource management, environmental problems, and so on.

The ethical problems seem to be somewhat fewer in developed countries, but they exist there as well. The ethical difficulties seem to be worse in underdeveloped

Ethics In Practice

An Innocent Revelation?

For a couple of years, I worked as an assistant manager at a gas station in my hometown of Randers, Denmark. The location of the station was perfect, and this was proven every day by long lines and big sales. The way the job was scheduled was that the person on duty would always manage the station single-handedly, standing behind the desk, running the cash register. Every day, several thousand dollars was secured in the gas station's safe. Six people worked the gas station—all around the age of 18. The key to the safe was hidden in the back, and only the employees and the manager knew the hiding place. The manager would take the money stored in the safe and deposit it at the local bank every third day, but one week this action was postponed a couple of days because of a holiday. Therefore, a large sum of money was accumulating at the station. One employee was aware of this fact and revealed it to her friends. At the same time, she agreed to tell about the hiding place for the key, and within a few days her friends broke into the station, found the key, and stole $17 000 to $19 000.

The employee and her friends had figured that the insurance company would pay for my manager's loss and therefore all parties would be satisfied, except for the insurance company, whom, they thought, would not really be affected by the loss. They claimed, "Everybody knows how rich these insurance companies are."

The bottom line of this story was that the insurance company did not pay, because the key was hidden in the same room where the safe was kept.

The ethical question in this story is this: If you knew that no one would discover the employee's irresponsible decision to tell about the hidden key, and that the insurance company would reimburse the manager, would you also have done the same thing if you had received a fairly big portion of the money? In this case, I assume that the insurance company could easily afford the reimbursement, which means that all parties should be satisfied (and you would get a little richer).

1. What is the ethical dilemma in this story? Is it a situation unique to business in Denmark?

2. If the employee's decision to tell about the hidden key was never discovered, can her action somehow be justified as just an innocent revelation? Why or why not? Identify the ethical principles involved here.

3. Imagine that the employee's revelation was never discovered. Would you have chosen to do as she did if we assume that the manager got reimbursed? Many of us pay a lot of money in insurance premiums, so why not get a little back?

Contributed by Anders Braad

countries, LDCs, or developing countries because these countries are at earlier stages of economic development. This situation creates an environment in which there is a temptation to adhere to lower standards, or perhaps no standards, because few government regulations or activist groups exist to protect the stakeholders' interests. In the LDCs, the opportunities for business exploitation and the engagement in questionable (by developed countries' standards) practices are abundant.

We will illustrate some prominent examples of ethical problems in the multinational sphere to provide some appreciation of the development of these kinds of issues for business. We will discuss two classic ethical issues that have arisen with regard to questionable marketing and safety practices. Next, will discuss the issue of "sweatshops" (the use of cheap labour in developing countries)—a topic that has dominated international business in the decade of the 1990s and carries forward into the new millennium. Then, we will consider the special problems of bribery, corruption, and questionable payments, which have been ethical issues in North America for over 30 years. From these examples, we should be able to develop an appreciation of the ethical challenges that confront MNCs and others doing business globally.

Questionable Marketing and Plant Safety Practices

A classic example of a questionable marketing practice is the now-infamous infant formula controversy that spanned most of the 1970s, continued into the 1980s and 1990s, and remains an issue today. The plant safety issue is best illustrated by examining the Union Carbide Bhopal crisis that began in late 1984 and continued into the 1990s and is not completely resolved today.

Questionable Marketing: The Infant Formula Controversy   The infant formula controversy is a classic in illustrating the ethical questions that can arise while doing business abroad. We will briefly refer to James Post's observations about this now-classic case.[30] For decades, physicians working in tropical lands (many of which were LDCs) realized that there were severe health risks posed to infants from bottle-feeding as opposed to breast-feeding. Such countries typically had neither refrigeration nor sanitary conditions. Water supplies were not pure, and, therefore, infant formula mixed with this water contained bacteria that would likely lead to disease and diarrhea in the bottle-fed infant. Because these LDCs are typically poor, this condition encourages mothers to overdilute powdered formula, thus diminishing significantly the amount of nutrition the infant receives. Once a mother begins bottle-feeding, her capacity for breast-feeding quickly diminishes. Poverty also leads the mother to put in the bottle less expensive substitute products. These products, such as powdered whole milk and cornstarch, are not acceptable substitutes. They are nutritionally inadequate and unsatisfactory for the baby's digestive system.

By the late 1960s, it was apparent that in the LDCs there was increased bottle-feeding, decreased breast-feeding, and a dramatic increase in the numbers of malnourished and sick babies. Bottle-feeding was cited as one of the major reasons. The ethical debate began when it was noted that several of the infant formula companies, aware of the environment just described, were promoting their products and, therefore, promoting bottle-feeding in an intense way. Such marketing practices as mass advertising, billboards, radio jingles, and free samples became commonplace. These promotional devices typically portrayed the infants who used their products as healthy and robust, in sharp contrast with the reality that was brought about by the conditions mentioned.

One of the worst marketing practices entailed the use of "milk nurses"—women dressed in nurses' uniforms who walked the halls of maternity wards urging mothers to get their babies started on formula. In reality, these women were sales representatives employed by the companies on a commission basis. Once the infants began bottle-feeding, the mothers' capacity to breast-feed diminished.[31]

Although several companies were engaging in these questionable marketing practices, the Swiss conglomerate Nestlé was singled out by a Swiss social activist group in an article published in 1974 entitled "Nestlé Kills Babies." At about the same time, an article appeared in Great Britain entitled "The Baby Killers."[32] From this point on, a protracted controversy developed with Nestlé and other infant formula manufacturers on one side and a host of organizations on the other side filing shareholder resolutions and lawsuits against the company. Among the groups that were actively involved in the controversy were church groups such as the National Council of Churches and its Interfaith Center on Corporate Responsibility (ICCR), UNICEF, the World Health Organization (WHO), and the Infant Formula Action Coalition (INFACT). Nestlé was singled out because it had the largest share of the world market and because it aggressively pushed sales of its infant formula in developing countries, even after the World Health Organization developed a sales code to the contrary.[33]

In 1977, INFACT and ICCR organized and led a boycott against Nestlé that continued for almost seven years. More than 70 American organizations representing churches, doctors, nurses, teachers, and other professionals participated in the boycott. These groups mounted an international campaign aimed at changing these objectionable marketing practices in the LDCs.[34] In 1984, after spending tens of millions of dollars resisting the boycott, Nestlé finally reached an accord with the protesters. The company agreed to four changes in its business practices:

1. It would restrict the distribution of free samples.
2. It would use Nestlé labels to identify the benefits of breast-feeding and the hazards of bottle-feeding.
3. It promised to help ensure that hospitals would use its products in accordance with the WHO code.
4. It agreed to drop its policy of giving gifts to health professionals to encourage them to promote infant formula.

The protesters, in return, agreed to end their boycott but to continue monitoring Nestlé's performance.[35]

The infant formula controversy continued through the 1980s and well into the 1990s. In 1991, Nestlé (which controlled more than 40 percent of the worldwide market) and American Home Products (which controlled about 15 percent of the worldwide market) announced that after decades of boycotts and controversy, they planned to discontinue the practice of providing free and low-cost formula to developing countries.

With this action—its most aggressive ever—Nestlé attempted to quell the protracted criticism that it had defied WHO's marketing restrictions by dumping huge quantities of baby formula on Third World hospitals. The distribution of supply had been a lingering concern in the infant formula controversy. Until this announcement, Nestlé had supplied formula on a request basis but over the next several years planned to distribute formula only on a request basis to children "in need," as outlined in the WHO guidelines. The pledges by Nestlé and American Home Products, the world's two biggest infant formula makers, were regarded as a watershed in the bitter infant formula controversy.[36]

The infant formula controversy has been rich with examples of the actions and power of social activist groups and governments and the various strategies that might be employed by MNCs. For our purposes, however, it illustrates the character of questionable business practices by firms pursuing what might be called normal practices were it not for the fact that they were being pursued in foreign countries where local circumstances made them questionable.[37] The infant formula controversy also illustrates the endurance of certain ethical issues, particularly in the global arena.

A recent survey shows numerous Web sites that are still devoted to the infant formula controversy and that document how the Nestlé boycott continues still today (http://www.infactcanada.ca, http://www.wfn.org, http://www.essential.org/monitor).

Plant Safety and the Bhopal Tragedy   The Union Carbide **Bhopal tragedy** in late 1984 brings into sharp focus the dilemma of multinationals operating in a foreign, particularly less-developed, environment. At this writing, the legal issues surrounding this event have not been totally resolved and may not be for years to come. On December 3, 1984, a leak of methyl isocyanate gas caused what many have termed the "worst industrial accident in history." The gas leak killed more than 2000 people and injured 200 000 others. The tragedy has raised numerous legal, ethical, social, and technical questions for MNCs.[38] Observers who have studied this tragedy say the death toll and destruction are many times greater than the "official" numbers indicate.

Interviews with experts just after the accident revealed a belief that the responsibility for the accident had to be shared by the company and the Indian government. According to Union Carbide's own inspector, the Bhopal plant did not meet U.S. standards and had not been inspected in over two years. The Indian government allowed thousands of people to live very near the plant, and there were no evacuation procedures.[39]

Many different questions have been raised by the Bhopal disaster. Among the more important of these issues are:[40]

1. To what extent should MNCs maintain identical standards at home and abroad regardless of how lax laws are in the host country?
2. How advisable is it to locate a complex and dangerous plant in an area where the entire work force is basically unskilled and where the populace is ignorant of the inherent risks posed by such plants?
3. How wise are laws that require plants to be staffed entirely by local employees?
4. What is the responsibility of corporations and governments in allowing the use of otherwise safe products that become dangerous because of local conditions? (This question applies to the infant formula controversy also.)
5. After reviewing all the problems, should certain kinds of plants be located in developing nations?

At the heart of these issues is the question of differing standards in different parts of the world. This dilemma arose in the 1970s, when U.S. firms continued to export drugs and pesticides that had been restricted in the United States. Pesticides, such as DDT and others that had been associated with cancer, were shipped to and used in LDCs by farmers who did not understand the dangers or the cautions that were needed in the use of these products. Not surprisingly, poisonings occurred. In 1972, hundreds to thousands of Iraqis died from mercury-treated grain from the United States. In 1975, Egyptian farmers were killed and many made ill by a U.S.-made pesticide. Asbestos and pesticide manufacturing plants that violated American standards were built in several countries. These companies typically broke no laws in the host countries, but many experts are now saying that the Bhopal tragedy has taught us that companies have a moral responsibility to enforce high standards, especially in developing countries not yet ready or able to regulate these firms.[41]

One major problem that some observers say contributed to the Bhopal explosion and, indeed, applies to MNCs generally is the requirement that firms be significantly owned by investors in the host country. Union Carbide owned only 50.9 percent of the Bhopal, India, subsidiary. It has been observed that this situation may have reduced Union Carbide's motivation and/or capacity to ensure adequate industrial and environmental safety at its Bhopal plant, mainly by diluting the degree of parent control and reducing the flow of technical expertise into that plant. If developing countries continue to insist on a dilution of MNC control over manufacturing plants, this may also diminish the MNC's motivation and incentive to transfer environmental management and safety competence.

Another major problem highlighted by the Bhopal explosion was the fact that the people of developing countries are often unaware of the dangers of new technology. As one expert observed, countries such as India have not "internalized the technological culture."[42] On the one hand, the LDCs want technology because they see it as critical to their economic development, but their ability to understand and manage the new technology is in serious doubt.

The complexity and tragedy of the Bhopal explosion case for its victims, the Indian government, and Union Carbide are attested to by the fact that this issue is still unresolved even today. In 1989, Union Carbide extricated itself from relief efforts by agreeing to pay the Indian government US$470 million to be divided among victims and their families. By 1993, courts had only distributed US$3.1 million of this sum. The overburdened government relief programs in India have been mired in mismanagement and corruption. It has been observed that virtually every level of the relief bureaucracy in India is rife with corruption. Government officials demanded bribes from illiterate victims trying to obtain documents required for the relief money. Doctors have taken bribes from victims to testify in their court cases, and unscrupulous agents have fished for bribes by claiming they could get victims' cases expedited on the crowded docket. Claims courts that would determine final compensation for victims were not set up until 1992—eight years after the gas leak. Lawyers and officials say it could be another 20 years before this case is settled.[43]

According to more recent information put out by Dow Chemical, the gas that leaked from the plant was formed when a disgruntled employee, apparently bent on spoiling a batch of the gas, added water to a storage tank. The company said it took moral responsibility for the incident despite its being an act of sabotage. Union Carbide subsequently sold its 50.9 percent interest in Union Carbide India Limited and donated the proceeds from the sale to a trust to build a hospital in Bhopal.[44]

Current Web pages (http://www.bhopal.org, http://www.bhopal.net, http://www.bhopal.com) show that the Bhopal tragedy continues to be of deep concern, even in the first decade of the twenty-first century.

The lessons from the Bhopal disaster are many and will continue to be debated. In companies around the globe, the Bhopal disaster has sparked continued enthusiasm in the debate about operating abroad. To be sure, ethical and legal issues are central to the discussions. What is at stake, however, is not just the practices of businesses abroad but also the very question of the presence of businesses abroad. Depending on the final outcome of the Union Carbide debacle, MNCs may decide that the risk of doing business abroad is too great.

Sweatshops and Labour Abuses

No issue has been more prominent since the early 1990s in the global business ethics debate than MNCs' use and abuse of women and children in cheap-labour factories in developing countries. The major players in this controversy, large corporations, have highly recognizable names—Nike, Wal-Mart, Kmart, Reebok, J. C. Penney, and Disney—to name a few. The countries and regions of the world that have been involved are also recognizable—Southeast Asia, Pakistan, Indonesia, Honduras, Dominican Republic, Thailand, the Philippines, and Vietnam. Sweatshops have not been eliminated in the United States or Canada either.[45]

Though **sweatshops**, characterized by child labour, low pay, poor working conditions, worker abuse, and health and safety violations, have existed for decades, they have grown in number in the past few years as global competition has heated up and corporations have gone to the far reaches of the world to lower their costs and increase their productivity. A landmark event that brought the sweatshop issue into sharp focus was the 1996 revelation by labour rights activists that part of Wal-Mart's Kathie Lee Collection, a line of clothes endorsed by prominent U.S. talk-show host Kathie Lee Gifford, was made in Honduras by seamstresses slaving 20 hours a day for 31 cents an hour. The revelation helped turn Gifford, who was unaware of where the clothes were being made or under what conditions, into an anti-sweatshop activist.[46] The Nike Corporation has also become a lightning rod for social activists concerned about overseas manufacturing conditions, standards, and ethics. A major reason for this is the company's high visibility, extensive advertising, and expensive shoes, as well as the stark contrast between the tens of millions of dollars Nike icon Michael Jordan earned and the $2.23 daily wage rate the company's subcontractors paid their Indonesian workers.[47]

Former U.S. ambassador to the United Nations Andrew Young calls the recent debate over child labour "the world's next moral crusade."[48] Young likens the sweatshop issue with the civil rights movement, a crusade for freedom against the injustices done to helpless children and poor women. To support his argument, Young invoked a 1997 UNICEF publication, "The State of the World's Children 1997," which documented the high level of suffering that millions of child labourers are forced to endure. Referring to India, the UNICEF report disclosed:

Thousands of children in the carpet industry are kidnapped or lured away or pledged by their parents for paltry sums of money. Most of them are kept in captivity, tortured, and made to work for 20 hours a day without a break. Little children are made to crouch on their toes, from dawn to dusk every day, severely stunting their growth during formative years.[49]

The International Labor Organization (ILO) reported that there are an unprecedented number of child labourers in the world—some 250 million. The ILO estimate, which is double previous estimates, documents almost 153 million child labourers in Asia, 80 million in Africa, and 17.5 million in Latin America. All these children are between ages five and fourteen, and nearly half work full-time.

Search the web WWW

United Students Against Sweatshops

USAS is an international student movement of campuses and individual students fighting for sweatshop-free labour conditions and workers' rights. USAS believes that university standards should be brought in line with those of its students who demand that their school's logo be emblazoned on clothing made in decent working conditions. There are currently over 180 student chapters of USAS in Canada and the United States. For more information about USAS's goals and activities and about sweatshops generally, visit its Web site at **http://www.usasnet.org** and the Canadian affiliate, Students Against Sweatshops, at **http://opirg.sa.utoronto.ca/groups/sweatshops/sas-c.html**.

Critics of MNC labour practices, including social activist groups and grassroots organizations, have been speaking out, criticizing business abusers and raising public awareness. These critics claim certain businesses are exploiting children and women by paying them poverty wages, working them to exhaustion, punishing them for minor violations, violating health and safety standards with them, and tearing apart their families. Many of these companies counter that they offer the children and women workers a superior alternative. They say that, although their wage rates are embarrassing by developed-world standards, those rates frequently equal or exceed local legal minimum wages, or average wages. They further say that, because so many workers in LDCs work in agriculture and farming, where they make less than the average wage, the low but legal minimums in many countries put sweatshop workers among the higher-paid workers in their areas.[50]

The sweatshop issue has been so prominent in the past few years that, to improve their situations or images, many criticized companies have begun working to improve working conditions, further joint initiatives, establish codes of conduct or standards for themselves and their subcontractors, conduct social or ethical audits, or take other steps. In 1996, U.S. President Clinton, with Kathie Lee Gifford, was instrumental in helping to establish the Fair Labor Association (FLA), an organization of clothing firms, unions, and human-rights groups focused on the worldwide elimination of sweatshops. Its members, which include L. L. Bean, Nike, Liz Claiborne, Nicole Miller, and Reebok, were encouraged by a survey showing that three-quarters of shoppers would pay higher prices for clothes and shoes bearing "No Sweat" labels.

The U.S. is spearheading a proposal to help eliminate sweatshops. This proposal calls for clothing firms and their contractors to impose a code of conduct that would prohibit child labour, forced labour, and worker abuse; establish health and safety regulations; recognize workers' right to join a union; limit the workweek to 60 hours (except in exceptional business circumstances); and insist that workers be paid at least the legal minimum wage (or the "prevailing industry wage") in every country in which garments are made. Under this proposal, the garment industry would also create an association to police the agreement.[51]

This proposal has some drawbacks, however. For example, the legal minimum wage in many developing countries is below the poverty line. In addition, the "prevailing industry wage" could prove to be a convenient escape clause. Some groups are also concerned that the task force has, in effect, sanctioned 60-hour working weeks and that it will still allow 14-year-olds to work if local laws do. Another big issue will be monitoring the agreement abroad. For example, Liz Claiborne alone has 200 contractors in over 25 countries. Furthermore, in some countries, like the Philippines, Malaysia, Thailand, and Vietnam, sweatshops go to great lengths to hide their business dealings by "fronting" businesses using false documents to "prove" they pay minimum wages and by intimidating workers to keep quiet.[52]

In Canada, the Ethical Trading Action Group (ETAG) is an anti-sweatshop coalition, combining the forces of such parties as the Canadian Auto Workers, the Steelworkers' Humanity Fund, the church-based Kairos coalition, Oxfam Canada, and Students Against Sweatshops. A central focus is to lobby for stricter corporate codes of conduct in the apparel industry. ETAG has fought to establish a code that would require a company and its contractors to treat workers fairly by paying a living wage that meets workers' basic needs, stopping forced overtime, ensuring that workers have the right to form trade unions without harassment or firings and can engage in collective bargaining, and committing to not using child labour or prison labour.[53]

The labour movement is a major force behind the growing anti-sweatshop movement in Canada. For example, UNITE—the Union of Needletrades, Industrial and Textile Employees—has played a major role in fighting sweatshops, a central part of its mission which is described as follows:

> *Our mission is to strengthen and improve working conditions for all UNITE members and to give a voice to the concerns of working people, particularly low-wage workers, women and immigrant workers whose voices are under-represented … to mobilize for a workers' agenda and to fight sweatshops through international solidarity.*[54]

The Toronto-based Maquila Solidarity Network (MSN) is a major player in Canada's anti-sweatshop movement. Its members include such organizations as the B.C. Teachers Federation, Canadian Auto Workers, Canadian Catholic Organization for Development and Peace, the Communications, Energy and Paperworkers Union, the Canadian Labour Congress, and the Canadian Union of Public Employees. MSN facilitates communication with anti-sweatshop groups in Mexico, Central America, and Asia. This network targets specific companies such as Disney and Nike, lobbies for government intervention, and tries to educate the public. MSN has been pressuring the government to force companies to disclose where their clothes are made, using provisions under the Textile Labelling Act. The aim is to make companies accountable for the employee abuses that occur in the process of producing the merchandise that they distribute. In the absence of such information, the potential for poor working conditions increases. However, most companies have refused to provide such disclosure.[55] ETAG persuaded several universities and municipalities across Canada to adopt "no sweat" buying policies, which require companies that sell to those organizations to provide evidence that their clothing is not made in sweatshops.[56]

Another initiative to improve sweatshop conditions has been organized by the Council on Economic Priorities (CEP), a U.S.-based public-interest group. The CEP, with a group of influential companies, introduced a new scheme called Social Accountability 8000, or SA8000, which is designed to piggyback on the ISO8000 quality-auditing system of the International Standards Organization (ISO), now used in 80 countries.[57] The SA8000 initiative, launched in fall 1997, involved a broad spectrum of companies, such as Avon, Sainsbury, Toys 'R' Us, Otto Versand (which owns Eddie Bauer), KPMG-Peat Marwick, and SGS-ICS, plus a number of labour and human rights groups. The group approved an initial set of labour standards, which would then be monitored. The initial labour standards were as follows:[58]

- Do not use child or forced labour.
- Provide a safe working environment.
- Respect workers' right to unionize.
- Do not regularly require more than 48-hour workweeks.
- Pay wages sufficient to meet workers' basic needs.

Companies that want to comply with SA8000 standards can apply for certification by an outside auditor. CEP has set up an agency to accredit the auditors, and most are likely to be accounting firms. Companies like Avon and Toys 'R' Us expect to get their plants certified and will expect that their suppliers get their plants certified. Skeptics of the CEP initiative include human rights and labour groups that think real change in sweatshops will not occur. Skeptics fear that companies will use the CEP monitoring process as a cover and that real changes will not take place. For its part, the CEP thinks the system will work and that millions of consumers will eventually insist on SA8000-approved products.[59]

Sweatshops and labour abuses sharply contrast the "haves" and the "have-nots" of the world's nations. Consumers in developed countries have benefited greatly by the lower prices made possible by cheap labour. It remains to be seen how supportive those consumers will be if prices rise because MNCs improve wage rates and conditions in LDCs. The MNCs face a new and volatile ethical issue that is not likely to go away. Their profits, public image, and reputations may hinge on how well they respond. The MNCs must handle a new dimension in their age-old quest to balance shareholder profits with the desires of expanded, global stakeholders who want better corporate social performance.

Recently, the Maquila Solidarity Network awarded the infamous title of "Sweatshop Retailer of the Year" to the Hudson's Bay Company and Wal-Mart. The Bay received this unwelcome award for its alleged acceptance of sweatshop abuses in three Lesotho factories. Wal-Mart was targeted for its alleged unethical treatment of its North American employees, such as illegal intimidation and harassment of employees seeking union representation. In addition, Wal-Mart was cited for its use of over 20 factories in Lesotho, where poverty wages and employee abuse are rampant.[60]

Corruption, Bribery, and Questionable Payments

Corruption, **bribes**, and questionable payments occurred for decades prior to the 1970s. It was in the mid-1970s, however, that evidence of widespread questionable corporate payments to foreign government officials, political parties, and other influential persons became widely known. Such major corporations as Lockheed, Gulf Oil, Northrop, Carnation, and Goodyear were among those firms admitting to such payments. Huge sums of money were involved. Gulf, for example, admitted paying US$4.2 million to the political party of Korean President Park. Gulf also created a subsidiary in the Bahamas that was then used as a conduit for unlawful political contributions. Lockheed acknowledged payments of US$22 million, mostly to officials in the Middle East.[61]

One of the most notorious cases was that of Lockheed giving US$12.5 million in bribes and commissions in connection with the sale of US$430 million worth of Tri-Star airplanes to All Nippon Airways. The president of Lockheed defended the payments, claiming that it was common practice and it was expected to give bribes in Japan. The news of the payments rocked Japan more than it did the United States, because Prime Minister Kakuei Tanaka and four others were forced to resign and stand trial. Another important point made about this case was that Lockheed did not offer a bribe, but rather the Japanese negotiator demanded it. This point raises the continuing question in matters of this kind: "Are those who accede to bribery equal in guilt to those who demand bribes?"[62]

In recent times, Canada has endured the embarrassing spotlight as home to a company convicted of bribing a government official in South Africa. In 2002, the Canadian engineering company Acres International was fined $15 million for the bribery of Masupho Sole, the former chief executive of the Lesotho Highlands Development Authority, in order to secure a contract on the construction of the Katse Dam. Sole was sentenced to 18 years in prison. In delivering his verdict, the judge said, "Corruption is of growing international and regional concern. Corruption has a particularly devastating impact on development and good governance in developing countries in Africa, because it undermines economic growth, discourages foreign

Ethics In Practice

I Love My Job, Just Don't Ask How I Got It!

Last spring, one of my very close friends graduated with an MBA. She interviewed with many companies during her last semester at school. However, there was no job. After graduating, she decided to apply to other companies. At one of the companies, she got preselected and then selected for the final round of interviews. After the final interview was conducted, she was informed that a decision would be mailed to her within the next six weeks.

My friend's father happened to know the general manager of this company. When there was no reply for almost five weeks, my friend's father decided to speak with the general manager. The general manager checked with the human resources department and informed my friend's father that his daughter had not been short-listed and, therefore, was not being considered in the final list of applicants for a position.

About five days later, my friend's father called the general manager again, but this time for something else. He had decided to offer a bribe to his friend the general manager in order to get his daughter the job. Bribing high-ranking managers to secure employment is an accepted practice in my country. A sum of money was mutually agreed upon and my friend's father personally delivered the cash to the general manager. Within the next four weeks, she was offered the management trainee position.

After working there for a month, my friend told me this whole story and how glad she was that her father had done all this for her. She loved her job and said that she couldn't have been happier anywhere else. She also told me not to mention this to anyone, as it would harm her family's reputation. Bribing is an accepted practice in my country, but not out in the open.

1. Is it ethical to give or take bribes just because everybody does it and it is an accepted practice in one's country?

2. If bribery is an accepted practice, why did the friend want to keep this quiet?

3. Should employees be hired on the basis of merit or according to how much they can bribe to secure a job?

4. If you were in my friend's place, would you have accepted the job?

Contributed by Radhika Sadanah

investment and reduces the optimal utilisation of limited resources available for infrastructure, public services and antipoverty programmes."[63]

Corruption in international business continues to be a major problem. It starts with outright bribery of government officials and the giving of questionable political contributions. Beyond these there are many other activities that are corrupt: the misuse of company assets for political favours, kickbacks and protection money for police, free junkets for government officials, secret price-fixing agreements, and insider dealing, just to mention a few. All of these activities have one thing in common. They are attempts to influence the outcomes of decisions wherein the nature and extent of the influence are not made public. In essence, these activities are abuses of power.[64] Bribes, more than any other form of corruption, have been the subject of continuing debate, and they merit closer examination.

Arguments For and Against Bribery   Arguments typically given in favour of permitting bribery include the following: (1) they are necessary for profits in order to do business; (2) everybody does it—it will happen anyway; (3) it is accepted practice in many countries—it is normal and expected; and (4) bribes are forms of commissions, taxes, or compensation for conducting business between cultures.

Arguments frequently cited against giving bribes include (1) bribes are inherently wrong and cannot be accepted under any circumstances; (2) bribes are illegal in North America and, therefore, unfair elsewhere; (3) one should not compromise her or his own beliefs; (4) managers should not deal with corrupt governments; (5) such demands, once started, never stop; (6) one should take a stand for honesty, morality, and ethics; (7) those receiving bribes are the only ones who benefit; (8) bribes create dependence on corrupt individuals and countries; and (9) bribes deceive shareholders and pass on costs to customers.[65]

The costs of bribes and other forms of corruption are seldom fully understood or described. Several studies suggest the economic costs of such corrupt activities. When government officials accept "speed" money or "grease payments" to issue licences, the economic cost is 3 to 10 percent above the licensing fee. When tax collectors permit underreporting of income in exchange for a bribe, income tax revenues may be reduced by up to 50 percent. When government officials take kickbacks, goods and services may be priced 20 to 100 percent higher to them. In addition to these direct economic costs, there are many indirect costs—demoralization and cynicism and moral revulsion against politicians and the political system. Due to bribery and corruption, politicians have been swept from office in Brazil, Italy, Japan, and Korea.[66]

Legislation The United States was among the first countries to aggressively pursue antibribery legislation for MNCs. Many of the payments and bribes made by U.S.-based MNCs were not illegal prior to the passage of the 1977 Foreign Corrupt Practices Act (FCPA). Even so, firms could have been engaging in illegal activities depending on whether and how the payments were reported to the Internal Revenue Service. With the passage of the FCPA, however, it became a criminal offence for a representative of an American corporation to offer or give payments to the officials of other governments for the purpose of getting or maintaining business. The FCPA specifies a series of fines and prison terms that can result if a company or management is found guilty of a violation.[67] The legislation was passed not only for ethical reasons but also out of a concern for the image of the United States internationally.

Over its history, the FCPA has been controversial. The law does not prohibit so-called **grease payments**, or minor, facilitating payments to officials, for the primary purpose of getting them to do whatever they are supposed to do anyway. Such payments are commonplace in many countries. The real problem is that some forms of payments are prohibited (e.g., bribes), but other payments (e.g., grease payments) are not prohibited. The law is sometimes ambiguous on the distinctions between the two.[68] To violate the FCPA, payments (other than grease payments) must be made corruptly to obtain business. This suggests some kind of *quid pro quo*. The idea of a corrupt *quid pro quo* payment to a foreign official may seem clear in the abstract, but the circumstances of the payment may easily blur the distinction between what is acceptable "grease" (e.g., payments to expedite mail pickup or delivery, to obtain a work permit, to process paperwork) and what is illegal bribery. The safest strategy for managers to take is to be careful and to seek a legal opinion when questions arise.

With all its flaws, the U.S. legislation at the very least encouraged other countries to follow suit with similar attempts to control foreign practices. Under U.S. pressure, the Organization for Economic Cooperation and Development introduced an antibribery convention in late 1997, since ratified by 35 signatories. Those countries promised to adopt national legislation making it a crime to bribe foreign officials.

One such country influenced by the U.S. example was Canada. Since 1892, bribery of public officers has been an offence under Canada's criminal law. However, until recently, the bribery of a foreign public official was not given comparable treatment in Canadian criminal law. U.S. pressure encouraged numerous international organizations to study the effects of corruption and reduce its impact on business. Consequently, Canada passed Bill S-21, the Corruption of Foreign Public Officials Act (CFPOA), on December 7, 1998, and it came into effect in 1999 with the purpose of reducing bribery abroad. Under the CFPOA, persons found guilty of bribing such officials can be imprisoned for up to five years.[69] Figure 9–3 summarizes some of the key features of the antibribery provisions of the CFPOA. Figure 9–4 presents a basic distinction with examples between bribes (which are prohibited) and grease (or facilitating) payments (which are not prohibited) based on the FCPA and the CFPOA.

Bribery Trends: The Growing Anticorruption Movement Corruption and bribery in international business continue to be popular topics. With significant increases in global competition, free markets, and democracy over the past decade, this comes as no surprise. Two developments in the past decade are worthy of mention. Both have contributed to what some have called a growing **anticorruption movement**.

Transparency International. First, a new special-interest group was founded in Berlin in 1993—Transparency International (TI)—modelled after the human rights group Amnesty International. TI has established itself as the world's foremost anticorruption lobby. It maintains over 70 national chapters run by local activists and compiles an annual corruption rating using surveys of businesspeople, political analysts, and the general public. Using various colour shades to represent labels varying from "least corrupt" to "most corrupt" on a map of the world, TI's "Corruption Perception Index" depicts countries in various ways. In the Corruption Perception Index of 2002, the least corrupt countries were identified as Finland, Denmark, New Zealand, Iceland, Singapore, and Sweden. Out of the 133 countries ranked, Canada was ranked 11th least corrupt and the United States was ranked 18th least corrupt. Among the most cor-

---

FIGURE 9–3

Key Features of the Bribery Provisions of the Corruption of Foreign Public Officials Act

- Section 3 of the new Act prohibits the bribery of a foreign public official (representing a foreign state or public international organization) to obtain or retain an advantage in the course of business.

- This offence is punishable on indictment. The law sets no maximum limit for fines, which judges could order corporations to pay. Individuals could be sentenced to a maximum of five years of imprisonment.

- It is also a crime to conspire or attempt to bribe a foreign public official. Corporations and individuals could also be prosecuted for aiding and abetting in committing the offence.

- Under the new law, "facilitation payments," or payments made to expedite routine service provided by a foreign public official, are not bribes and therefore are not subject to prosecution. It is not an offence if the benefit that was given is lawful in the foreign public official's country or public international organization. Reasonable expenses incurred in good faith and directly related to the promotion, demonstration, or explanation of products and services or to carrying out a contract with the foreign state, could also be argued as a defence.

- Section 4 of the new Act makes it illegal to possess property or proceeds of property obtained or derived from the offence of bribing a foreign public official or from laundering that property or those proceeds.

Source: Department of Justice Backgrounder *Highlights of the Corruption of Foreign Public Officials* (Justice Canada Internet site), Department of Justice Canada, 1999. Reproduced with the permission of the Minister of Public Works and Government Services, 2004.

FIGURE 9–4

Bribes versus Grease Payments

Definitions	Examples
Grease Payments	
Relatively small sums of money given for the purpose of getting minor officials to: • Do what they are supposed to be doing • Do what they are supposed to be doing faster or sooner • Do what they are supposed to be doing better than they would otherwise.	Money given to minor officials (clerks, attendants, customs inspectors) for the purpose of expediting. This form of payment helps get goods or services through red tape or administrative bureaucracies.
Bribes	
Relatively large amounts of money given for the purpose of influencing officials to make decisions or take actions that they otherwise might not take. If the officials considered the merits of the situation only, they might take some other action.	Money given, often to high-ranking officials. Purpose is often to get these people to purchase goods or services from the bribing firm. May also be used to avoid taxes, forestall unfavourable government intervention, secure favourable treatment, and so on.

rupt nations, according to the CPI, were Bangladesh, Nigeria, Haiti, Paraguay, Angola, Kenya, and Libya.[70] Undoubtedly, TI hopes and expects that public exposure to its corruption ratings will bring pressure to bear on countries and companies.

OECD Antibribery Initiatives. A second development in the growing anticorruption movement is a new antibribery treaty and initiatives that the 29 industrialized nations of the Organization for Economic Cooperation and Development (OECD) and five other countries agreed to in late 1997.[71] The OECD member nations agreed to ban international bribery and to ask each member to introduce laws patterned after the U.S. FCPA in its country. The main thrust of the treaty was to criminalize bribes to foreign officials who have sway over everything from government procurement contracts and infrastructure projects to privatization tenders.

The OECD Convention to combat bribery went into effect on February 15, 1999. The Convention makes it a crime to offer, promise, or give a bribe to a foreign public official in order to obtain or retain international business deals. A related text effectively puts an end to the practice of according tax deductibility for bribe payments made to foreign officials. The Convention commits 34 signatory countries, including all the world's biggest economies, to adopt common rules to punish companies and individuals who engage in bribery transactions. Twenty-one countries have been subjected to close monitoring to determine the adequacy of their implementing legislation.[72] It may be some years to come before the Antibribery Convention is fully implemented. However, the OECD represents a significant initiative in the global battle to eliminate corruption from commercial transactions.

In addition to OECD antibribery initiatives, some individual countries have begun antibribery campaigns on their own. A case in point is the efforts recently initiated in Mexico under the leadership of President Vicente Fox. Fox appointed a new anticorruption czar. The first such czar, Francisco Barrio, a former governor of Chihuahua state in northern Mexico, is responsible for unearthing corruption and federal spending irregularities in a country with a long history of both. In a pilot undercover program started in 2001, Barrio's office discovered that public servants in seven

Mexican cities were charging and pocketing the equivalent of US$100 apiece, in addition to regular fees, to issue driver's licences. Barrio stated that corruption cannot be eradicated in Fox's six-year term, but the government can lay the foundation for reducing it on all levels.[73]

The best way to deal with bribes seems to be to stem the practice before it starts. A major paradox is that the very people who often benefit from illicit payments—the politicians—are the ones who must pass the laws and set the standards against bribes and corruption in the first place. Another factor is that bribes and corruption, whenever possible, need to be exposed. Public exposure, more than anything else, has the potential to bring questionable payments under control. This means that practices and channels of accountability need to be made public.[74] The new Corruption Perception Index should help in this regard. Beyond these steps, managers need to be able to see that such activities are no longer in their best interests. Not only do bribes corrupt the economic system, but they corrupt business relationships as well and cause business decisions to be made on the basis of factors that ultimately destroy all the institutions involved. In a sense, the new OECD treaty indicates that member nations now understand this important point. It will not eliminate bribery, but it does represent a significant step toward reducing bribery and bringing it under control.

We have by no means covered all the areas in which ethical problems reside in the global business environment. The topics treated have been major ones subjected to extensive public discussion. Examples of other issues that have become important recently and will probably increase in importance include the issues of international competitiveness, protectionism, industrial policy, political risk analysis, and antiterrorism. These issues are of paramount significance in discussions of business's relations with international stakeholders. Other issues that include an ethical dimension are national security versus profit interests, the use of internal transfer prices to evade high taxes in a country, mining of the ocean floor, and harbouring of terrorists. Space does not permit us to discuss these issues in detail.

Improving Global Business Ethics

The most obvious conclusion to extract from the discussion up to this point is that business ethics is more complex at the global level than at the domestic level. The complexity arises from the fact that a wide variety of value systems, stakeholders, cultures, forms of government, socioeconomic conditions, and standards of ethical behaviour exists throughout the world. Recognition of diverse standards of ethical behaviour is important, but if we assume that North American firms should operate in closer accordance with North American standards than with foreign standards, the strategy of ethical leadership in the world is indeed a challenging one. MNCs have a heavy responsibility, particularly in underdeveloped countries and LDCs. The power-responsibility equation also argues that MNCs have a serious ethical responsibility in global markets. That is, the larger sense of ethical behaviour and social responsiveness that should exist derives from the enormous amount of power that MNCs possess.

In this section, we will first discuss the challenge of honouring and balancing the ethical traditions of a business's home country with those of its host country. We will do this primarily through a discussion of Enderle's four global types and an application of Donaldson and Dunfee's Integrative Social Contract Theory (ISCT). Next, we will discuss Laczniak and Naor's four recommended courses of action for conducting business in foreign environments: (1) Develop worldwide codes of conduct, (2) factor ethics into global strategy, (3) suspend activities when faced with unbridgeable ethical gaps, and (4) develop periodic "ethical impact statements."[75]

In addition, Donaldson has set forth ten fundamental international rights that are based on the principle of rights discussed in Chapter 7. These are worthy of consideration, as are Richard DeGeorge's seven "moral guidelines" that provide guidance for MNCs.

Balancing and Reconciling the Business Ethics Traditions of Home and Host Countries

Perhaps one of the greatest challenges that face businesses operating in foreign countries is achieving some kind of reconciliation and balance in honouring both the cultural and moral standards of their home and host countries. Should a business adhere to its home country's ethical standards for business practices or to the host country's ethical standards? There is no simple answer to this question. The diagram presented in Figure 9–5 frames the extreme decision choices businesses face when they consider operating globally.

At one extreme is a position some might call "ethical imperialism." This position argues that the MNC should continue to follow its home country's ethical standards even while operating in another country. Because North American standards for treating employees, consumers, and the natural environment are quite high relative to the standards in many other less-developed countries, it is easy to see how managers might find this posture appealing.

As reliance on foreign factories has soared in recent years and harsh conditions have been documented by the media, an increasing number of companies, such as Levi Strauss, Nordstrom, Wal-Mart, and Reebok, have espoused higher standards for foreign factories that cover such issues as wages, safety, and workers' rights to organize.[76] These standards more nearly approximate North American views on how such stakeholders ought to be treated than some host countries' views. Such higher standards could be seen by foreign countries, however, as North America and particularly the United States attempting to impose its standards on the host country—thus the name "ethical imperialism" for one end of the continuum.

At the other extreme in Figure 9–5 is a position often called "cultural relativism." This position is characterized by foreign direct investors such as MNCs following the host country's ethical standards. This is the posture reflected in the well-known saying, "When in Rome, do as the Romans." This position would argue that the investing MNC should set aside its home country's ethical standards and adopt the ethical standards of the host country. For example, if Saudi Arabia holds that it is illegal to hire women for most managerial positions, the investing MNC would accept and adopt this standard, even if it counters its home country's standards. Or, if the host country has no environmental protection laws, this position would argue that the MNC need not be sensitive to environmental standards.

As Tom Donaldson has argued, cultural relativism holds that no culture's ethics are better than any other's and that there are, therefore, no international rights or wrongs. If Thailand tolerates the bribery of government officials, then Thai tolerance is no worse than Japanese or German intolerance. If Switzerland does not find insider trading morally repugnant, then Swiss liberality is no worse than American restrictiveness.[77] Most ethicists find cultural relativism to be a case of moral or ethical relativism and, therefore, an unacceptable posture for MNCs to take.

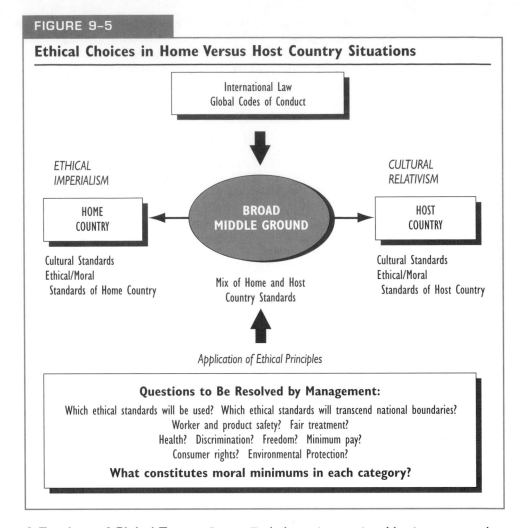

FIGURE 9–5

Ethical Choices in Home Versus Host Country Situations

International Law
Global Codes of Conduct

ETHICAL IMPERIALISM

CULTURAL RELATIVISM

HOME COUNTRY

BROAD MIDDLE GROUND

HOST COUNTRY

Cultural Standards
Ethical/Moral
Standards of Home Country

Mix of Home and Host
Country Standards

Cultural Standards
Ethical/Moral
Standards of Host Country

Application of Ethical Principles

Questions to Be Resolved by Management:

Which ethical standards will be used? Which ethical standards will transcend national boundaries?
Worker and product safety? Fair treatment?
Health? Discrimination? Freedom? Minimum pay?
Consumer rights? Environmental Protection?

What constitutes moral minimums in each category?

A Typology of Global Types George Enderle, an international business expert, has observed and categorized at least four different types of global firms with respect to their use of home versus host country ethical standards:[78]

- Foreign country type
- Empire type
- Interconnection type
- Global type

Foreign Country Type. This type of firm conforms to local customs and ethics, assuming that the ethical standards of the host country are adequate and appropriate. This approach represents moral or cultural relativism.

Empire Type. This type of company applies its domestic or home country standards without making any serious adaptations to the host country. These companies export their values in a wholesale fashion, often disregarding the consequences. An example would be Great Britain in India and elsewhere prior to 1947. This approach represents moral imperialism.

Interconnection Type. These companies regard the international sphere as differing significantly from the domestic sphere in that their interconnectedness transcends national identities. An example of this would be states engaging in commercial business in the European Union or NAFTA. In this type, the entire concept of national interests is blurred. Companies don't try to project a national identity.

Global Type. This type of business firm abstracts from all regional differences. These firms view the domestic or home standards as not relevant or applicable. With this type, the nation-state may be seen as vanishing as only global citizenry applies.

The purpose of identifying each of these types is to illustrate the various mixtures or combinations of home and host country standards that a business operating in the global sphere might adopt.

Integrative Social Contract Theory (ISCT) Donaldson and Dunfee (1999) have presented Integrative Social Contract Theory (ISCT) as an approach to navigating cross-national cultural differences.[79] Two key concepts in their theory are the notions of *hypernorms* and *moral free space*. They explain these two concepts by depicting a series of concentric circles representing the core norms held by corporations, industries, or economic cultures. At the centre are **hypernorms**, which are transcultural values. They include, for example, fundamental human rights or basic prescriptions common to most major religions. The values they represent are by definition acceptable to all cultures and all organizations.

Moving out from the centre of the concentric circles, next would be **consistent norms**. These values are more culturally specific than those in the centre, but are consistent with hypernorms and other legitimate norms. The next circle is **moral free space**. Here, one finds norms that are inconsistent with at least some other legitimate norms existing in other economic cultures. These norms could be in mild tension with hypernorms, though they may be compatible with them. These are strongly held cultural beliefs in particular countries. Finally, in the outer circle are **illegitimate norms**. These are norms that are incompatible with hypernorms. An example of this might be the practice of exposing workers to unacceptable levels of carcinogens.

Donaldson and Dunfee then use these different levels of norms to comment on Enderle's four types of corporations. Regarding the foreign country type, they say that nothing limits the free moral space of the host country. Thus, if a host country accepts government corruption and environmental degradation, then so much the worse for honest people and environmental integrity. Both the global and empire types succeed in avoiding the fierce relativism of the foreign country type, but may fall pr the opposite problem. Because each of these ha set blueprint of right and wrong, each ma host country's moral free space and legitimate local norms. The emp of moral imperialism; the home country morality o its version of a global mor

According to Donaldson and Dunfee, only the interconnection type satisfies ISCT by acknowledging both universal moral limits (hypernorms) and the ability of communities to set moral standards of their own (moral free space). This type balances better than the others a need to retain local identity with the acknowledgment of values that transcend individual communities; thus, it manages to balance moral principles with moral free space in a more convincing way than in the other three models.[81]

In summary, ISCT uses the principles of moral free space and adherence to hypernorms as a balanced approach to navigating global international waters. While honouring hypernorms, companies do not have to simply adopt a "do in Rome as the Romans do" philosophy. But, they do need to be sensitive to the transcultural value implications of their actions. In turn, the concept of moral free space makes them ever vigilant of the need to precede judgment with an attempt to understand the local host country culture. The result, of course, is the very real probability that moral tension will be an everyday part of doing business in the global sphere.[82]

It may sound like a simplistic solution to say that the MNC needs to operate in some broad middle ground where a mix of home and host country ethical standards may be used. The challenge for managers will be to determine what mix of ethical standards should be used and how this decision should be made. Managers will need to ask themselves which moral standards are applicable in the situations they face. Use of ethical principles such as those articulated in the previous chapters—rights, justice, utilitarianism, and the Golden Rule—still apply. Managers will need to decide which ethical standards should transcend national boundaries and thus represent hypernorms: safety? health? discrimination? freedom? Managers will need to decide what will represent their moral minimums with respect to these and other issues. It would be nice to think that international laws and global codes of conduct will make these decisions easier. Though some are available, it is doubtful that such guidelines will be easily applicable. In the interim, managers will need to be guided by the ethical concepts at their disposal, possibly with help from some of the approaches to which we now turn.

Four Actions for Improving International Business Ethics

Laczniak and Naor have set forth four actions that would help MNCs conduct international business while maintaining an ethical sensitivity in their practices and decision making. We will now discuss these and use them to help organize suggested actions that have been made by a number of experts.

Global Codes of Conduct   There are two ways of thinking about global codes of conduct. First, there are specific corporate global codes that individual companies have developed. Second, there are global codes or guidelines that have been developed by various international organizations. Each of these deserves some consideration.

   Corporate Global Codes. In Chapter 7, we discussed codes of conduct, and that discussion applies in the global sphere as well. While operating in the global sphere, MNCs have been severely criticized for operating with divergent ethical standards in different countries, thus giving the impression that they are attempting to exploit local circumstances. A growing number of MNCs, such as Caterpillar Tractor, Allis Chalmers, Johnson's Wax, and Rexnord, have developed and used codes geared to worldwide operations.[83]

   One of the first and most well known of the codes is that of Caterpillar Tractor Company, issued by the chairman of the board, entitled "A Code of Worldwide

Business Conduct." The code goes into considerable detail and has major sections that cover the following vital areas: ownership and investment, corporate facilities, relationships with employees, product quality, sharing of technology, accounting and financial records, different business practices, competitive conduct, observance of local laws, business ethics, relationships with public officials, and international business. The purpose of the code is clearly set forth in its introduction:

> This revised "Code of Worldwide Business Conduct" is offered under the several headings that follow. Its purpose continues to be to guide us, in a broad and ethical sense, in all aspects of our worldwide business activities. Of course, this code isn't an attempt to prescribe actions for every business encounter. It is an attempt to capture basic, general principles to be observed by Caterpillar people everywhere.[84]

Other companies do not have comprehensive codes addressing their international operations but rather codes containing sections that address foreign practices. For example, in its "General Dynamics Standards of Business Ethics and Conduct," General Dynamics has a section entitled "International Business." One excerpt from this section is encouraging and illustrates the point we have been developing:

> Our policy is to comply with all laws which apply in the countries where we do business. In countries where common practices might indicate acceptance of standards of conduct lower than those to which we aspire, we will follow our own Standards as outlined in this booklet.[85]

An example of a global code of conduct aimed at improving workplace standards and workers' standards of living was implemented the late 1990s by Mattel, Inc., the US$4.5 billion toy manufacturer. According to Jill E. Barad, then Mattel chairman and CEO, "We are as concerned with the safety and fair treatment of the men and women who manufacture our products as we are with the safety and quality of the products themselves, and our new Global Manufacturing Principles demonstrate our strong commitment to that philosophy."[86]

With offices in 36 countries and products being marketed in 150 nations around the world, Mattel is a classic example of the kind of MNC that needs, and can benefit from, a global code of conduct.

Global Codes and Standards Set by International Organizations. In addition to individual corporate codes, there are a number of international organizations that have developed global codes or standards that they aspire companies to adopt and follow. Some of these codes focus on one specific issue; many provide standards across a number of issue areas. Figure 9–6 summarizes brief information about some of the more prominent of these external standards.

Ethics and Global Strategy The major recommendation here is that the ethical dimensions of multinational corporate activity should be considered as significant inputs into top-level strategy formulation and implementation.[87] Carroll, Hoy, and Hall have argued even more broadly that corporate social policy should be integrated into strategic management.[88] At the top level of decision making in the firm, corporate strategy is established. At this level, commitments are made that will define the underlying character and identity that the organization will have. The overall moral tone of the organization and all decision making and behaviours are set at the strategic level,

FIGURE 9-6

Global Standards or Codes of Conduct Developed by International Organizations

		Brief Description
Code, Standard, Guideline	Caux Principles	Issued in 1994 by the Caux Round Table, comprised of senior business leaders from Europe, Japan, and North America. An aspirational set of recommendations for corporate behaviour that seeks to express a worldwide standard for ethical and responsible corporate behaviour. Principles address the social impact of company operations on the local community and respect for rules and ethics.
	Global Reporting Initiative	Established in 1997 by the Coalition for Environmentally Responsible Economies (CERES), the GRI became independent in 2002. GRI promotes an international reporting standard for voluntary use by organizations reporting on the economic, environmental, and social dimensions of their activities, products, and services.
	Norms on the Responsibilities of Transnational Corporations and Other Business Enterprises with Regard to Human Rights	Proposed by the U.N. Human Rights Commission in 2003, it departs from the voluntary initiative contained in the Global Compact (below). This proposal is intended to hold companies accountable for implementing a code of conduct that matches the human rights principles defined in this initiative. This code also aims to subject companies to U.N. monitoring and to liability for any violation of the code.
	OECD Guidelines for Multinational Enterprises	Revised in 2000, the guidelines are recommendations addressed by governments to MNEs and are voluntary principles and standards. Governments adhering to the guidelines encourage the companies operating within the countries to observe the guidelines wherever they operate. The 2000 revisions strengthen the guidelines in human rights and environmental issues.
	Principles for Global Corporate Responsibility Benchmarks	Established in 1993 (and revised in 1998) by the Taskforce on the Churches and Corporate Responsibility [Canada], along with U.S.- and U.K.-based interfaith organizations. The Principles for assessing corporate policies and practices are based on social, environmental, and business performance criteria drawn from an internationally recognized body of human rights, labour, and environmental standards.
	U.N. Global Compact	Issued in 1999 by the United Nations and formally launched in 2000. A set of nine principles that includes specific standards that endorsing companies would commit to enact.

Source: Summarized from *Comparison of Selected CSR Standards* (San Francisco: Business for Social Responsibility, November 2000), 10–11. Additional table material and background taken from the following: Andrew James Samet, "Voluntary Guidelines May Be Mandatory," *Journal of Commerce* (October 20, 2003), 1, http://www.globalreporting. org/about/brief.asp; http://www.web.net/~tccr/benchmarks/.

and management needs to ensure that social and ethical factors do not get lost in the preoccupation with market opportunities and competitive factors.

If ethics does not get factored in at the strategic formulation level, it is doubtful that ethics will be considered at the level of operations where strategy is being implemented. Unfortunately, much current practice has tended to treat ethics and social responsibility as residual factors. A more proactive stance is needed for dealing with ethical issues at the global level. Strategic decisions that may be influenced by ethical considerations in the global sphere include, but are not limited to, product/service decisions, plant location, manufacturing policy, marketing policy and practices, and human resources management policies.

A useful illustration of ethics being factored into strategic decision making is provided by Levi Strauss & Co. Because Levi Strauss operates in many countries and diverse cultures, it reasoned that it must take special care in selecting its contractors and the countries where its goods are produced in order to ensure that its products are being made in a manner consistent with its values and reputation. In the early 1990s, therefore, the company developed a set of *global sourcing guidelines* that established standards its contractors must meet. As examples, their guidelines banned the use of child and prison labour. They stipulated certain environmental standards. Wages must, at minimum, comply with the law and match prevailing local practice. By factoring these ethical considerations into its strategic decisions, Levi argued that it receives important short- and long-term commercial benefits.[89]

Another example of a company integrating ethical concerns into its corporate strategies is that of Starbucks Coffee Co., the Seattle-based firm. In an innovative pilot program announced in 1998, Starbucks plans to pay a premium above-market price for coffee, with the bonus going to improve the lives of coffee workers. The initial payments would be made to farms and mills in Guatemala and Costa Rica, which would cofund health-care centres, farm schools, and scholarships for farm workers' children. Starbucks' incentive program was part of a larger "Framework for Action," its plan for implementing its code of conduct, created in 1995.[90]

Suspension of Activities   An MNC may sometimes encounter unbridgeable gaps between the ethical values of its home country and those of its host country. When this occurs, and reconciliation does not appear to be in sight, the MNC should consider suspending activities in the host country. For example, years ago IBM and Coca-Cola suspended their activities in India because of that country's position on the extent of national ownership and control.[91]

Also, Levi Strauss undertook a phased withdrawal from China, largely in response to human rights concerns, and suspended sourcing in Peru because of concerns about employee safety. It later lifted the suspension because conditions had improved.[92] More recently, companies have pulled out of Burma (Myanmar) due to human rights violations.

Numerous Canadian MNCs have also faced the question of whether they should be conducting business with countries that have questionable human rights practices. Such was the case faced by Talisman Energy Inc., one of Canada's largest independent oil and gas producers. The company had operations in Sudan since 1998 and, with a 25 percent stake, was the lead partner in the Greater Nile Oil Project. The Sudanese government received about $1 million a day from Talisman and part of these funds were being used to fund a war effort against antigovernment rebels. Critics argued that the company was helping to finance a war that included slavery, scorched earth, and depopulation campaigns. Consequently, Talisman's business activity was heavily criticized by human rights groups and members of the investment community. In 2001, a U.S. human rights group filed a $1 billion lawsuit against Talisman claiming that its operations in Sudan contributed to an ethnic cleansing campaign against civilians. After mounting public pressure, Talisman sold its 25 percent stake in the Greater Nile

Petroleum Operating Company to India's state-owned Oil and Natural Gas Corp. for $1.2 billion in 2002.[93] This case underscores the need for multinationals to consider the role they play in the host country and their impact on all stakeholders.

Suspension of business in a foreign country is not a decision that can or should be taken precipitously, but it must be regarded as a viable option for those firms that desire to travel on the higher moral road. Each country is at liberty to have its own standards, but this does not mean that North American firms must do business in that country. What does ethical leadership mean if it is not backed up by a willingness and an ability to take a moral stand when the occasion merits?

Ethical Impact Statements   MNCs should be constantly aware of the impacts they are having on society, particularly foreign societies. One way to do this is to periodically assess the company's impacts. Companies have a variety of impacts on foreign cultures, and ethical impacts represent only a few of these. The impact statement idea probably derived, in part, from the practice of environmental impact statements that environmental protection legislation pioneered in the1970s and 1980s. These statements are similar to the corporate social audit, a concept discussed in Chapter 4. *Social auditing* is "a systematic attempt to identify, analyze, measure (if possible), evaluate, and monitor the effect of an organization's operations on society (that is, specific social groups) and on the public well-being."[94] **Ethical impact statements** would be an attempt to assess the underlying moral justifications for corporate actions and the consequent results of those actions. The information derived from these actions would permit the MNCs to modify or change their business practices if the impact statement suggested that such changes would be necessary or desirable.

One form of ethical impact assessment is some firms' attempts to monitor their compliance with their companies' global ethics codes. For example, Mattel developed an independent audit and monitoring system for its code. Mattel's monitoring program is headed by an independent panel of commissioners who select a percentage of the company's manufacturing facilities for annual audits. In one audit, for example, Mattel terminated its relationship with three contractor facilities—one in Indonesia for its inability to confirm the age of its employees and two in China for refusing to meet company-mandated safety procedures.[95] Such audits conducted for monitoring compliance are not as comprehensive as ethical impact statements, but they serve similar purposes.

Fundamental International Rights

One major approach to doing business ethically in the global sphere has been for companies to adhere to various sets of international rights or moral guidelines. Thomas Donaldson set forth ten fundamental international rights that he argues should be honoured and respected by all international actors, including nation-states, individuals, and corporations. He argues that these rights serve to establish a "moral minimum" for the behaviour of all international economic agents. Donaldson's ten fundamental rights are as follows:[96]

1. The right to freedom of physical movement
2. The right to ownership of property
3. The right to freedom from torture
4. The right to a fair trial
5. The right to nondiscriminatory treatment (freedom from discrimination on the basis of such characteristics as race and gender)

6. The right to physical security
7. The right to freedom of speech and association
8. The right to minimal education
9. The right to political participation
10. The right to subsistence

Such a list of rights is somewhat general and still leaves considerable room for interpretation. However, the list serves to establish a beginning point for MNCs as they contemplate what responsibilities they have in international markets. These rights are similar to hypernorms in our earlier discussion.

Seven Moral Guidelines

Another way of looking at what MNCs should be doing in the global sphere is the recommendation that they follow certain moral guidelines in their operations. According to Richard DeGeorge, MNCs should apply seven moral guidelines in their international operations.[97] Some of these are rather straightforward and general, but they do summarize a useful perspective that might well improve MNC operations in the global sphere. Like the principles of rights stated earlier, these moral guidelines are similar to the hypernorms discussed earlier:

- MNCs should do no intentional, direct harm.
- MNCs should produce more good than bad for the host country.
- MNCs should contribute by their activities to the host country's development.
- MNCs should respect the human rights of their employees.
- MNCs should pay their fair share of taxes.
- To the extent that local culture does not violate moral norms, MNCs should respect the local culture and work with it, not against it.
- MNCs should cooperate with the local government in the development and enforcement of just background institutions (e.g., the tax system and health and safety standards).

DeGeorge does not present these seven guidelines as a panacea. He does suggest that if they were brought to bear on the dilemmas that MNCs face, the companies could avoid the moral stings of their critics. The spirit of these seven guidelines, if adopted, would go a long way toward improving MNC–host country relations.

Like the other lists presented, these guidelines can serve only as general principles for managers who are aspiring to make ethical decisions in the global arena. They do, however, provide the consensus thinking of a host of stakeholder representatives as to the responsibilities of international corporations.

Summary

Ethical dilemmas pose difficulties, in general, for businesses, and those arising in connection with doing business in foreign lands are among the most complex. The current period is characterized by an increasing antiglobalism sentiment, and the attacks on the World Trade Center have contributed to an unstable global environment. A cursory examination of major issues that have arisen in global business ethics over the past several decades shows that they rank right up there with the most well-known news stories. The infant formula controversy, the Bhopal tragedy, corruption and bribery, concern about sweatshops, and the exploits of MNCs in Third World countries have all provided an opportunity for business critics to assail corporate ethics in the international sphere. These problems arise for a multiplicity of reasons, but differing cultures, value systems, forms of government, socioeconomic systems, and underhanded and ill-motivated business exploits have all been contributing factors.

The balancing of home and host country standards using Integrative Social Contract Theory, global codes of conduct, the integration of ethical considerations into corporate strategy, the option of suspending activities, the use of ethical impact statements, and the adherence to international rights and moral guidelines offer some

hope that global business can be better managed. Despite any resistance, current trends point to a growth in business activity in the transnational economy, and though there is some evidence of a backlash against globalization, these issues will become more rather than less important in the future. Indeed, it could easily be argued that business's greatest ethical challenges in the future will be at the global level.

Key Terms

anticorruption movement (page 286)

Bhopal tragedy (page 278)

bribes (page 283)

consistent norms (page 291)

ethical impact statements (page 296)

globalization, globalism (page 267)

grease payments (page 285)

hypernorms (page 291)

illegitimate norms (page 291)

infant formula controversy (page 276)

internationalization (page 267)

less-developed countries (LDCs) (page 270)

moral free space (page 291)

multinational corporation (MNC) (page 270)

sweatshops (page 280)

transnational economy (page 266)

Discussion Questions

1. Drawing on the notions of moral, amoral, and immoral management introduced in Chapter 6, categorize your impressions of (a) Nestlé, in the infant formula controversy and (b) Union Carbide in the Bhopal tragedy.

2. As an MNC seeks to balance and honour the ethical standards of both the home and host countries, conflicts inevitably will arise. What criteria do you think managers should consider as they try to decide whether to use home or host country ethical standards?

3. Explain ISCT and the concepts of hypernorms and moral free space. What difficulties would a manager encounter in applying these concepts?

4. Differentiate between a bribe and a grease payment. Give an example of each.

5. Using Donaldson's fundamental international rights, rank what you consider to be the top five of the ten rights. Explain your ranking.

6. Of DeGeorge's seven moral guidelines, identify which single guideline you think is of most practical value for an MNC. Give a brief explanation of your choice.

Endnotes

1. Peter F. Drucker, "The Transnational Economy," *The Wall Street Journal* (August 25, 1987), 38. See also T. S. Pinkston and Archie B. Carroll, "Corporate Citizenship Perspectives and Foreign Direct Investment in the U.S.," *Journal of Business Ethics* (Vol. 13, 1994), 157–169.

2. Paul Krugman, cited in Alan Farnham, "Global—Or Just Globaloney?" *Fortune* (June 27, 1994), 97–98.

3. Richard D. Robinson, "Background Concepts and Philosophy of International Business from World War II to the Present," in William A. Dymsza and Robert G. Vambery (eds.), *International Business Knowledge: Managing International Functions in the 1990s* (New York: Praeger, 1987), 3–4.

4. "The Meaning of Seattle," *Multinational Monitor* (December 1999), 5. See also Ernesto Zedillo, "Globaphobia," *Forbes*, March 19, 2001, 49.

5. Paul Beamish, Allen Morrison, Philip Rosenzweig, and Andrew Inkpen, *International Management: Text and Cases* (Boston: Irwin McGraw Hill, 2000), 3.

6. *Ibid*, 3.

7. Herman E. Daly, "Globalization and Its Discontents," *Philosophy & Public Policy Quarterly* (Vol. 21, No. 2/3, Spring/Summer 2001), 17.

8. *Ibid.*, 17.

9. "Backlash Behind the Anxiety over Globalization," *Business Week* (April 24, 2000), 38.

10. Ernesto Zedillo, "Globaphobia," *Forbes* (March 19, 2001), 49.

11. *Ibid.*; "The Meaning of Seattle" (1999), 5.

12. Michael Elliott, "Death in Genoa," *Time* (July 30, 2001), 22–23; "After the Genoa Summit: Picking Up the Pieces," *The Economist* (July 28, 2001), 50; "Confronting Anti-Globalism," *Business Week* (August 6, 2001); Yaroslav Trofimov, "Antiglobalization Campaigners Vow to Carry Out Protests This Month," *The Wall Street Journal* (September 14, 2001), A8.

13. Robert Batterson and Murray Weidenbaum, *The Pros and Cons of Globalization* (St. Louis: Center for the Study of American Business, January 2001), i.

14. Nicholas Stern, "Businesses Are Helping to Overcome Global Poverty," *Ivey Business Journal* (Vol. 66, No. 1, September/October 2001), 9–13.

15. John Garland and Richard N. Farmer, *International Dimensions of Business Policy and Strategy* (Boston: Kent Publishing Company, 1986), 166–173.

16. *Ibid.*, 167–168.

17. *Ibid.*, 169.

18. *Ibid.*, 170–171.

19. *Ibid.*, 172.

20. *Ibid.*

21. "Ethical Dilemmas of the Multinational Enterprise," *Business Ethics Report*, Highlights of Bentley College's Sixth National Conference of Business Ethics (Waltham, MA: The Center for Business Ethics at Bentley College, October 10 and 11, 1985), 3. See also Richard T. DeGeorge, *Competing with Integrity in International Business* (New York: Oxford University Press, 1993).

22. Rosabeth Moss Kanter, *World Class: Thriving Locally in the Global Economy* (New York: Simon & Schuster, 1995).

23. Michael L. Wheeler, "Global Diversity: Reality, Opportunity, and Challenge," *Business Week* (December 1, 1997), special section.

24. James C. Baker, John C. Ryans, Jr., and Donald G. Howard, *International Business Classics* (Lexington, MA: Lexington Books, 1988), 73–367.

25. *Ibid.*, 127–138.

26. Alan M. Rugman, Donald J. Lecraw, and Laurence D. Booth, *International Business: Firm and Environment* (New York: McGraw-Hill, 1985), 293.

27. Baker, Ryans, and Howard, 245–246.

28. *Ibid.*, 314–315.

29. Richard D. Robinson, "The Challenge of the Underdeveloped National Market," in Baker, Ryans, and Howard, 347–356.

30. James E. Post, "Assessing the Nestlé Boycott: Corporate Accountability and Human Rights," *California Management Review* (Winter 1985), 115–116.

31. *Ibid.*, 116–117.

32. Rogene A. Buchholz, William D. Evans, and Robert Q. Wagley, *Management Response to Public Issues* (Englewood Cliffs, NJ: Prentice Hall, 1985), 80.

33. *Ibid.*, 81–82.

34. Oliver Williams, "Who Cast the First Stone?" *Harvard Business Review* (September–October, 1984), 155.

35. "Nestlé's Costly Accord," *Newsweek* (February 6, 1984), 52.

36. Alix M. Freedman, "Nestlé to Restrict Low-Cost Supplies of Baby Food to Developing Nations" and "American Home Infant-Formula Giveaway to End," *The Wall Street Journal* (February 4, 1991), B1.

37. For further discussion, see S. Prakash Sethi, *Multinational Corporations and the Impact of Public Advocacy on Corporate Strategy: Nestlé and the Infant Formula Case* (Boston: Kluwer Academic, 1994).

38. Stuart Diamond, "The Disaster in Bhopal: Lessons for the Future," *The New York Times* (February 5, 1985), 1. See also Russell Mokhiber, "Bhopal," *Corporate Crime and Violence* (San Francisco: Sierra Club Books, 1988), 86–96.

39. Stuart Diamond, "Disaster in India Sharpens Debate on Doing Business in Third World," *The New York Times* (December 16, 1984), 1.

40. *Ibid.*, 1.

41. *Ibid.*

42. Thomas M. Gladwin and Ingo Walter, "Bhopal and the Multinational," *The Wall Street Journal* (January 16, 1985), 1.

43. Molly Moore, "In Bhopal, A Relentless Cloud of Despair," *The Washington Post National Weekly Edition* (October 4–10, 1993), 17.

44. "The Bhopal Tragedy," *Around Dow: Special Commemorative Issue*, 41 (undated).

45. Mark Clifford, Michael Shari, and Linda Himelstein, "Pangs of Conscience: Sweatshops Haunt U.S. Consumers," *Business Week* (July 29, 1996), 46–47. See also Keith B. Richburg and Anne Swardson, "Sweatshops or Economic Development?" *The Washington Post National Weekly Edition* (August 5–11, 1996), 19; *Unite Magazine* (Summer 1999), http://www.uniteunion.org/magazine/sum99/canada.html.

46. "Stamping Out Sweatshops," *The Economist* (April 19, 1997), 28–29.

47. Clifford, Shari, and Himelstein, 46.

48. Andrew Young, "A Debate over Child Labor: The World's Next Moral Crusade," *The Atlanta Journal* (March 9, 1997), R2.

49. *Ibid.*

50. *Ibid.*

51. *The Economist* (April 19, 1997), 28.

52. *Ibid.*
53. Maquila Solidarity Network, http://www.web.net/~msn/3codehistory.htm; Murray MacAdam, *The CCPA Monitor* (March 2003); Canadian Centre for Policy Alternatives, http://www.policyalternatives.ca.
54. UNITE Canada, http://www.unite-svti.org/En/en.html.
55. Maquila Solidarity Network, http://www.maquilasolidarity.org/.
56. "Clothing label Info May Not Help Battle Sweatshops: Conference Board," *CBC Online* (June 3, 2003), http://www.cbc.ca/.
57. Aaron Bernstein, "Sweatshop Police: Business Backs an Initiative on Global Working Conditions," *Business Week* (October 20, 1997), 39.
58. *Ibid.*
59. *Ibid.*
60. Maquila Solidarity Network, http://www.maquilasolidarity.org/.
61. Dwight R. Ladd, "The Bribery Business," in Tom L. Beauchamp (ed.), *Case Studies in Business, Society and Ethics* (Englewood Cliffs, NJ: Prentice Hall, 1983), 251.
62. Richard T. DeGeorge, *Business Ethics* (New York: Macmillan, 1982), 53.
63. Neil Ford, "Turning Water into Money," *African Business* (Issue 291, October 2003), 48.
64. Bruce Lloyd, "Bribery, Corruption and Accountability," *Insights on Global Ethics* (Vol. 4, No. 8, September 1994), 5.
65. Ian I. Mitroff and Ralph H. Kilmann, "Teaching Managers to Do Policy Analysis: The Case of Corporate Bribery," *California Management Review* (Fall 1977), 50–52.
66. "The Destructive Costs of Greasing Palms," *Business Week* (December 6, 1993), 133–138; see also Henry W. Lane and Donald G. Simpson, "Bribery in International Business: Whose Problem Is It?" (Reading 12) in H. W. Lane, J. J. DiStefano, and M. L. Maznevski (eds.), *International Management Behavior*, 4th ed., (Oxford: Blackwell Publishers, 2000), 469–487.
67. Ladd, 256.
68. Garland and Farmer, 183.
69. Peter M. German, "To Bribe or Not to Bribe—A Less than Ethical Dilemma, Resolved?" *Journal of Financial Crime* (Vol. 9, No. 3, February 2002), 249–259.
70. Transparency International, "2002 Corruption Perception Index," http://www.transparency.org.
71. Paul Deveney, "34 Nations Sign Accord to End Bribery in Deals," *The Wall Street Journal* (December 18, 1997), A16.
72. "Welcome to the OECD Anti-Corruption Division," http://www1.oecd.org/daf/nocorruption/index.htm. See also Neil King, Jr., "Bribery Ban Is Approved by OECD,"

The Wall Street Journal (November 24, 1997), A14; and William M. Davey, "The Battle Against Bribery," *The Wall Street Journal* (December 17, 1997), A22.
73. Susan Ferriss, "Chihuahua Watchdog: Anti-Corruption Czar in Mexico Has Hands Full," *Atlanta Journal-Constitution* (September 23, 2001), B6.
74. Lloyd, 5.
75. Gene R. Laczniak and Jacob Naor, "Global Ethics: Wrestling with the Corporate Conscience," *Business* (July–September 1985), 3–10.
76. G. Pascal Zachary, "Levi Tries to Make Sure Contract Plants in Asia Treat People Well," *The Wall Street Journal* (July 28, 1994), A1.
77. Tom Donaldson, "Global Business Must Mind Its Morals," *The New York Times* (February 13, 1994), F-11. See also Tom Donaldson, "Ethics Away from Home," *Harvard Business Review* (September–October, 1996).
78. George Enderle, "What Is International? A Typology of International Spheres and Its Relevance for Business Ethics," paper presented at annual meeting of International Association for Business and Society, Vienna, Austria, 1995, as quoted and described in Tom Donaldson and Thomas W. Dunfee, "When Ethics Travel: The Promise and Peril of Global Business Ethics," *California Management Review* (Vol. 41, No. 4, Summer 1999), 48–49.
79. Donaldson and Dunfee, *op. cit.*
80. *Ibid.*
81. *Ibid.*
82. *Ibid.*
83. Laczniak and Naor, 7.
84. "A Code of Worldwide Business Conduct," in Frederick D. Sturdivant (ed.), *The Corporate Social Challenge: Cases and Commentaries* (Homewood, IL: Richard D. Irwin, 1985), 159–169.
85. "General Dynamics Standards of Business Ethics and Conduct" (August 1985), 17.
86. "Mattel, Inc. Launches Global Code of Conduct," unpublished press release, November 20, 1997; see also "Global Manufacturing Principles" (1997), 1–11.
87. Laczniak and Naor, 7–8.
88. Archie B. Carroll, Frank Hoy, and John Hall, "The Integration of Corporate Social Policy into Strategic Management," in S. Prakash Sethi and Cecilia M. Falbe (eds.), *Business and Society: Dimensions of Conflict and Cooperation* (Lexington, MA: Lexington Books, 1987), 449–470.
89. Robert D. Haas, "Ethics in the Trenches," *Across the Board* (May 1994), 12–13.
90. "Starbucks Pays Premium Price to Benefit Workers," *Business Ethics* (March/April 1998), 9.
91. Laczniak and Naor, 8.

92. Haas, 12.

93. Toby Heaps, "After Talisman's Exit from Sudan, Other Canadian Resource Companies in Focus," *Corporate Knights*, http://www.corporateknights.ca/index.asp.

94. David H. Blake, William C. Frederick, and Mildred S. Myers, *Social Auditing: Evaluating the Impact of Corporate Programs* (New York: Praeger, 1976), 3.

95. Mattel press release, November 20, 1997.

96. Thomas Donaldson, *The Ethics of International Business* (New York: Oxford University Press, 1989), 81.

97. Richard T. DeGeorge, "Ethical Dilemmas for Multinational Enterprise: A Philosophical Overview," in Hoffman, Lange, and Fedo (eds.), 39–46; see also Richard T. DeGeorge, *Business Ethics*, 5th ed. (Englewood Cliffs, NJ: Prentice Hall, 1999), Chapters 18–20; and Richard T. DeGeorge, *Competing with Integrity in International Business* (New York: Oxford University Press, 1993).

Part Four

External Stakeholder Issues

Business, Government, and Regulation

After studying this chapter, you should be able to:

1 Articulate a brief history of government's role in its relationship with business.

2 Appreciate the complex interactions among business, government, and the public.

3 Identify and describe government's nonregulatory influences, especially the concepts of industrial policy and privatization.

4 Explain government regulation and identify the major reasons for regulation, the types of regulation, and issues arising out of regulation.

5 Provide a perspective on regulation versus deregulation along with accompanying trends.

Over the past 40 years, the depth, scope, and direction of government's involvement in business has made the business/government relationship one of the most hotly debated issues of modern times. Government's role, particularly in the regulation of business, has ensured its place among the major stakeholders with which business must establish an effective working relationship if it is to survive and prosper.

Business has never been fond of government's having an activist role in establishing the ground rules under which it operates. In contrast, public interest has been cyclical, going through periods when it has thought that the federal government had too much power and other periods when it has thought that government should be more activist.

The traditional relationship between government and business is clearly undergoing change across the world. Canada, like many other countries, has experienced a marked shift toward reduced government involvement in the business sector, reflected in such trends as deregulation and privatization. It has been suggested that what we are witnessing is a significant decrease in government involvement as public preferences shift toward a more purely private market system. It seems that many observers view the decrease in the level of government influence in business as a positive change. However, some believe that there is good reason for advocating a continued—and, perhaps, increased—role for government in business. What kind of role should government play in the business sector?

The question of government involvement in business has been debated for years. Certainly, the trend toward reduced government in terms of deregulation, privatization, and elimination of tariff barriers seems to reflect the ideology that "less government is better." However, scholars such as Michael Porter suggest that the government still has a critical role to play in the health and well-being of business. For some, the answer lies in the government's ability to work with industry in order to develop a long-term industrial strategy to lead the country out of its current problems and ensure a more secure future for working Canadians. Consequently, rather than simply taking a "hands-off" approach, it may be argued that what is required is a clear rethinking of the different types of roles that government can play, or how it may play its current roles in a different manner.

In this chapter, we will examine the relationship between business and government, although the general public will assume an important role in the discussion as well. A central concern in this chapter is the government's role in influencing business. Exploring this relationship carefully will provide an appreciation of the complexity of the issues surrounding business/government interactions. From the prospective manager's standpoint, one needs a rudimentary understanding of the forces and factors that are involved in these issues before one can begin to talk intelligently about strategies for dealing with them. Unfortunately, more is known about the nature of the problem than about the nature of solutions, as is common when dealing with complex social issues.

A Brief History of Government's Role

Historically, government has played a critical role in the Canadian economy. From our very beginning as a nation, the government has taken responsibility for the success of business. It is useful to briefly consider the nature of our economic or business enterprise system, within which all business operates. The Canadian economic system has been described as a mixed system. This refers to the notion that while we possess a capitalist economy, government nonetheless plays an important role.

All developed countries have some sort of economic or business enterprise system that essentially determines (1) what goods and services are produced and distributed to society, and (2) how the goods and services are produced and distributed to society. What kind of business enterprise system we have determines how or by whom these decisions are made. For example, the two decisions above might be made purely by business, or they might be determined by government, or perhaps by a combination of the two. To understand the basis of our Canadian business enterprise system, it is necessary to understand the nature of capitalist economic systems.

Capitalism is a type of economic system that is based on a number of fundamental principles:

1. *Rights of the individual.* The notion of capitalism is based on the view that it is the individual who takes precedence in society, as opposed to institutions, or the overall society. This implies that the individual has every right to pursue his or her own self-interest, which includes seeking to make profits from business enterprises. The notion of the individual as the most important element of society is not entirely representative of the ideology present in Canadian society. There are limits placed on individuals' right to pursue their self-interest. Government regulations enforce rules that affect how business owners conduct their affairs. For example, government guidelines regarding job candidate selection criteria may affect who is hired for a job, and place emphasis on certain groups in society over others.

2. *Rights of private property.* As opposed to state ownership, capitalism asserts that individuals have the right to own land, labour, and capital. In Canada, certainly, individuals are permitted to own their means of production, whether it is land, labour, or capital. However, because there has been an uneven distribution of wealth in society, the government has intervened in a number of ways. For example, taxation is one approach that can be partly aimed at redistributing wealth among members of society. Much of the natural resources in Canada have still been retained by federal or provincial governments. The government may also decide that where a product or service is of a national interest, this product or service should be nationalized (e.g., government control of health care).

3. *Competition.* Capitalism advocates competition. The belief is that sufficient competition among business enterprises will ensure that business provides the goods and services required by society at a fair cost. Competition is the "invisible hand" (in the words of economist Adam Smith) that ensures the market works in this manner. In Canada, the notion of "perfect competition" does not exist in practice—there is no guarantee that an adequate supply of competitors exists across all industries.

4. *The role of government.* The view of government is reflected in the French term *laissez faire*, which means, "let people do as they choose." This suggests minimal government interference in the business enterprise system.

This notion of capitalism has also been referred to as the "free enterprise system," reflecting the notion of the right to private ownership of property, competition, and restricted government involvement.

Of course, the polar extreme of capitalism is another economic system referred to as *communism.* Whereas the capitalist system allows individuals or businesses the responsibility for the allocation of resources, the communist system, on the other hand, places the responsibility for the allocation of society's resources into the hands of the government.

There really are no societies today that are purely capitalist or communist. Canada has been referred to as a "mixed economy" because, while it is primarily a capitalist-based economy, government does play a role in the business enterprise system. In Canada, government does intervene in the affairs of business. Business is not left entirely to conduct its own affairs. When Canada first came into existence as a country, the federal government was granted the power to "regulate trade and commerce." And the fact is, throughout our history, the government has played a major role in fostering industrial development, and continues to provide significant support to the business sector.

Just as the areas in which government has chosen to initiate legislation have changed, the multiplicity of roles that government has assumed has increased the complexity of its relationship with business. Several of the varied roles that government has assumed in its relationship with business are worth looking at because they suggest the influence, interrelationships, and complexities that are present.[1] These roles indicate that government:

1. Prescribes the rules of the game for business
2. Is a major purchaser of business's products and services
3. Uses its contracting power to get business to do things it wants
4. Is a major promoter and subsidizer of business
5. Is the owner of vast quantities of productive equipment and wealth
6. Is an architect of economic growth
7. Is a financier
8. Is the protector of various interests in society against business exploitation
9. Directly manages large areas of private business
10. Is the repository of the social conscience and redistributes resources to meet social objectives

After examining and assessing these various roles, one can perhaps begin to appreciate the crucial interconnectedness between business and government and the difficulty both business and the public have in fully understanding (much less prescribing) what government's role ought to be in relation to business.

The Roles of Government and Business

We do not intend to philosophize in this chapter on the ideal role of government in relation to business, because this is outside our stakeholder frame of reference. However, we will strive for an understanding of current major issues as they pertain to this vital relationship. For effective management, government, as a stakeholder, must be understood.

The fundamental question underlying our entire discussion of business/government relationships is, "What should be the respective roles of business and government in our socioeconomic system?" This question is far easier to ask than to answer, but as we explore it, some important basic understandings begin to emerge.

The issue could be stated in a different fashion: Given all the tasks that must be accomplished to make our society work, which of these tasks should be handled by government and which should be handled by business? This poses the issue clearly, but there are other questions that remain to be answered. If we decide, for example, that it is best to let business handle the production and distribution roles in our society, the next question becomes "How much autonomy are we willing to allow business?" If our goals were simply the production and distribution of goods and services, we would not have to constrain business severely. In modern times, however, other goals have been added to the production and distribution functions: for example, a safe working environment for those engaging in production, equal employment opportunities, fair pay, clean air, safe products, employee rights, and so on. When these goals are superimposed on the basic economic goals, the task of business becomes much more complex and challenging.

Because these latter, more socially oriented goals are not automatically factored into business decision making and processes, it often falls on government to ensure that those goals that reflect concerns of the public interest be achieved. Thus, whereas the marketplace dictates economic production decisions, government becomes one of the citizenry's designated representatives charged with articulating and protecting the public interest.

A Clash of Ethical Belief Systems

A clash of emphases partially forms the crux of the antagonistic relationship that has evolved between business and government over the years. This problem has been termed "a clash of ethical systems." The two ethical systems (systems of belief) are the **individualistic ethic of business** and the **collectivistic ethic of government**. Figure 10–1 summarizes the characteristics of these two philosophies.[2]

The clash of these two ethical systems partially explains why the current business/government relationship is adversarial in nature. In elaborating on the adversarial nature of the business/government relationship, Jacoby offered the following comments:

> *Officials of government characteristically look upon themselves as probers, inspectors, taxers, regulators, and punishers of business transgressions. Businesspeople typically view government agencies as obstacles, constraints, delayers, and impediments to economic progress, having much power to stop and little to start.[3]*

FIGURE 10–1

The Clash of Ethical Systems Between Business and Government

Business Beliefs	Government Beliefs
• Individualistic ethic	• Collectivistic ethic
• Maximum concession to self-interest	• Subordination of individual goals and self-interest to group goals and group interests
• Minimizing the load of obligations society imposes on the individual (personal freedom)	• Maximizing the obligations assumed by the individual and discouraging self-interest
• Emphasizes inequalities of individuals	• Emphasizes equality of individuals

The business/government relationship not only has become adversarial but also has been deteriorating. The goals and values of our pluralistic society have become more complex, more numerous, more interrelated, and, consequently, more difficult to reconcile. The result has been increasing conflicts among diverse interest groups, with trade-off decisions becoming harder to make. In this process, it has become more difficult to establish social priorities, and consensus has in many cases become impossible to achieve.[4]

Social, Technological, and Value Changes

As we attempt to understand why all this has happened, it is only natural to look to changes in the social and technological environments for some explanations. According to Daniel Bell, since World War II four major changes have had profound impacts on North American society in general and on the business/government relationship in particular. First, out of local and regional societies a truly national one has arisen.[5] Second, we have seen a "communal society" arise, characterized by a great emphasis on public goods and the internalization of external costs. Third, the revolution of rising expectations has brought with it the demand for "entitlements"—good jobs, excellent housing, and other amenities. Fourth, a rising concern has emerged for an improved "quality of life."[6] In addition to these, other societal value changes have shaped the course of business/government relations, including: the youth movement, the consumer protection movement, the ecology movement, the human rights movement, and the women's liberation movement.[7]

The value changes that have taken place "have multiplied the number of political decisions that have to be made relative to the number of decisions made in markets."[8] To the extent that these political decisions affect business—and they do to a great extent—we can understand the basic conflict arising once again in a clash between individualist and collectivist belief systems. Government's responses to changes taking place in society have put it in direct opposition to business in terms of both philosophy and mode of operation. Although one might argue that this clash of belief systems is not as severe today as it once was, the basic differences still serve to frame the positions of the two groups.

Interaction of Business, Government, and the Public

This section offers a brief overview of the influence relationships among business, government, and the public. This should be helpful in understanding both the nature of the process by which public policy decisions are made and the current problems that characterize the business/government relationship. Figure 10–2 illustrates the pattern of these influence relationships.

One might rightly ask at this point, "Why include the public? Isn't the public represented by government?" In an ideal world, perhaps this would be true. To help us appreciate that government functions somewhat apart from the public, it has been depicted separately in the diagram. In addition, the public has its methods of influence that need to be singled out.

Government/Business Relationship

Government influences business through regulation, taxation, and other forms of persuasion that we will consider in more detail in the next section.

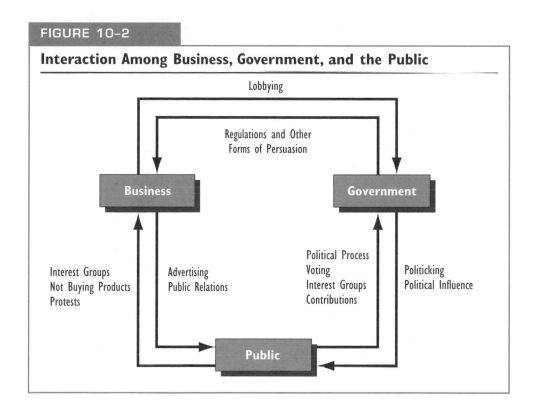

FIGURE 10-2

Interaction Among Business, Government, and the Public

Public/Government Relationship

The public uses the political processes of voting and electing officials (or removing them from office) to influence government. It also exerts its influence by forming special-interest groups (farmers, small business owners, educators, senior citizens, truckers, manufacturers, etc.) to wield more targeted influence. Government, in turn, uses politicking, public policy formation, and other political influences to have an impact on the public.

Business/Public Relationship

Business influences the public through advertising, public relations, and other forms of communication. The public influences business through the marketplace or by forming special-interest or advocacy groups (e.g., Greenpeace, Aboriginal Rights Coalition, Canadian Federation of Humane Societies).

Earlier we raised the question of whether government really represents the public. This question may be stated another way: "Who determines what is in the public interest?" In our society, determining the public interest is not a simple matter. Whereas government may be the official representative of the public, we should not assume that representation occurs in a straightforward fashion. As we saw in Figure 10–2, the public takes its own initiatives both with business and with government. The three major groups, therefore, are involved in a dynamic interplay of influence processes that determine what is currently considered to be in the public interest.

Our central concern in this chapter is with government's role in influencing business, and we now turn our attention to that topic. Here we will begin to see more clearly how government is a major stakeholder of business. Government's official priority is in representing the public interest as it sees and interprets the public's wishes. But, like all large bureaucratic organizations, government also takes on a life of its own with its own goals and agenda.

Government's Nonregulatory Influence on Business

Given its magnitude, it is not difficult to appreciate the significant effect government actions have on all institutions in society. We will limit our treatment to the federal government's influence on business, but we must remain mindful of the presence and influence of provincial and local governments as well.

Broadly speaking, we may categorize the kinds of influence government has on business as *nonregulatory* and *regulatory*. In the next major section, we will focus on government regulation, but in this section let us consider the wide range of nonregulatory influences that government has on business.

Two major issues merit consideration before we examine some of the specific policy tools or mechanisms government uses to influence business. These two major issues are (1) industrial policy and (2) privatization. Industrial policy is concerned with the role that our government plays in the world of international trade, and privatization zeroes in on the question of whether current public functions (e.g., public education, public transit, health care, social security, fire service) should be turned over to the private (business) sector. Both of these issues have important implications for the business/government relationship. They are both important, because they seem to come into and out of popularity on a fairly regular basis.

Industrial Policy

Important initial questions include: "What does industrial policy mean, and why has it become such a hotly debated issue?" An **industrial policy** may be defined as follows: "Any selective government measure that prevents or promotes changes in the structure of an economy."[9]

This very broad definition by itself does not give us enough focus to understand the concept. Let us elaborate. One school of thought thinks of industrial policy as some variation of the British model, wherein government provides help for older, declining industries. Therefore, when steel company executives in Canada argue for tax breaks and tariffs that would enable them to survive and compete with foreign competition, they are asking for an industrial policy.[10]

Another school of thought is exemplified by Robert Reich in his book *The Next American Frontier*, wherein he argues for a national industrial policy that attempts to identify winning (or sunrise) industries and foster their growth. As for losing (or sunset) industries, industrial policy would have as its goal redirecting resources into growth fields.[11]

Search the web   WWW

Think Tanks

There are a number of excellent sources for insights, critiques, and explanations of the impact of government on business and society. Among the popular "think-tank" Web sites that offer such insights into government policy issues are:

- Canadian Policy Research Networks (**http://www.cprn.org/**). This private, nonpartisan, nonprofit organization specializes in reporting on social and economic policy research and public engagement.
- C. D. Howe Institute (**http://www.cdhowe.org/**). Since its formation in 1973, the C. D. Howe Institute has functioned as an independent, nonprofit, economic and social policy research institution. The organization and its Web site offer analyses of issues of national interest to business, government, and society.
- Fraser Institute (**http://www.fraserinstitute.ca/**). This organization describes itself as an independent public policy organization, focusing on the role competitive markets play in providing for the economic and social well-being of all Canadians.

Variations on these themes could yield a variety of industrial policy schools of thought. Five schools of thought that give us insights into industrial policy include the following: the accelerationists, the adjusters, the targeters, the central planners, and the bankers.[12] The **accelerationists** would try to pinpoint industries that promise to become strong international competitors and position them to move rapidly into world markets. Their goal would be to accelerate changes already signalled by the marketplace. The **adjusters** would offer adjustment assistance to declining industries in return for commitments that they would slim down, modernize, and help their employees relocate and train for new skills and jobs.

The **targeters** would target a select group of sectors or industries (e.g., high tech, agriculture, energy, finance, health-care equipment) to be turned into engines for growth. The **central planners** would advocate growth-oriented macroeconomic policies that would come close to comprehensive planning. Finally, the **bankers** would advocate a federally backed industrial development bank that would provide "patient capital"— money that could be sunk into a high risk venture for five to ten years or longer.

Arguments for Industrial Policy   Proponents of an industrial policy (more active role of government in the business sector) cite a variety of reasons for supporting it. First, of course, is the threatened competitiveness of Canada in world markets. A second argument is the use of industrial policy by other world governments, including Germany, Britain, France, and Italy. A third major argument is that Canada does not have a comprehensive industrial policy, but rather operates based on the haphazard results of unplanned taxes, tariffs, regulatory policies, and research and development policies. Our current system has been called an ad hoc industrial policy because the government has, in fact, intervened in many specific industries as emergencies have arisen.

In Canada, though the relationship has not been shaped by a clear industrial policy, we have a long history of government involvement in business in the sense of promoting and protecting our industries. For example, tariff and nontariff barriers on imported goods were designed to protect our domestic business by making foreign goods more expensive relative to Canadian goods. In fact, it can be argued that a large portion of Canada's industrial development is due to protectionism through tariffs first imposed in 1879 by Sir John A. Macdonald's National Policy. Eventually, the government also offered direct incentives for industrial and resource development.

The pervasiveness of globalization has demanded that governments reconsider the extent to which they feel obligated to maintain a relationship with the private business sector. Thomas Friedman, in his book *The Lexus and the Olive Tree*, asserts that globalization is, in fact, increasing the importance of government while changing the roles that it plays:

> *The ability of an economy to withstand the inevitable ups and downs depends in large part on the quality of its legal system, financial system and economic management—all matters still under the control of governments and bureaucrats. Chile, Taiwan, Hong Kong, and Singapore all survived the economic crises of the 1990s so much better than their neighbours because they had better-quality states running better-quality software and operating systems.*

Consequently, while governments may find their role increasingly challenged by the onslaught of multinationals, globalization may dictate a greater need for government involvement.

In the following sections, the roles governments play in the global business scene are discussed.

1. Nurturing Young Industries. The notion that government must play a role in nurturing domestic industry was raised earlier in this chapter. The infant-industry argument asserts that the government should help a young industry to grow and develop by ensuring that the industry maintains a dominant share of the domestic market until it is mature enough to compete against foreign competition. Consequently, this philosophy is still applied, particularly, among developing countries. The rationale is that the infant industry may be less competitive, particularly because of initially high output costs; however, with maturity, the production will become more efficient, and protection will no longer be necessary.

2. Encouraging Direct Foreign Investment. The action of reducing foreign imports may result in the foreign business directly investing in the target country instead. That is, a foreign company can decide to set up business in the target country if it wishes to gain access to this country's consumer market and it is unable to achieve that with imports. Of course, from the domestic country's viewpoint, this foreign investment may be desirable if it increases job opportunities, contributes to the growth of industry, and adds to the amount of capital.

3. Maintaining Favourable Balance of Trade. Government may seek to influence the relative status of exports and imports to avoid running a trade deficit. Trade surpluses come about when a country's exports exceed its imports and, consequently, more money is entering the country (from foreign consumers buying these exports) than is leaving the country (from domestic consumers buying foreign imports). A trade deficit is the reverse—when a country imports more than it exports. Traditionally, governments intervened to ensure a trade surplus by imposing tariffs or quotas or by banning outright some foreign-imported commodities. Typically, the governments would also subsidize domestic industries in order to encourage growth in their exports.

4. Protecting Domestic Business from Unfair Competition. There is a concern among some businesses that foreign competitors will offer their products at extremely low prices as a means of monopolizing their share of the target country's market. The ultimate consequence would be that domestic producers could potentially be driven out of business and replaced by the foreign imports. A foreign competitor who manages to export the products at such low prices may be accused of dumping—which is pricing the product below cost or below the cost in the target country. In other words, a foreign supplier who sells a product at a loss or for less than the price of the seller's domestic market would be considered guilty of dumping.

Steel companies have been among the most avid users of antidumping legislation in Canada and the United States. Hamilton-based Dofasco Inc. lodged a dumping complaint against steel mills in Asia and South America. The aim was to seek government assistance, which in this case resulted in a decision by the Canadian government to place antidumping tariffs on low-cost imported steel from these foreign suppliers. In total, these antidumping tariffs were aimed at blocking the dumping of steel shipments from nine countries. This echoes similar action taken in the United States. Steel producers in both the United States and Canada have blamed increasing foreign imports of steel for reducing demand for their product domestically and, consequently, reducing product prices and revenue.

5. Maintaining Adequate Levels of Domestic Employment. A government knows that society holds it responsible for ensuring the unemployment rates are not high. Imports that come to dominate an industry bring the threat of causing domestic industries to go bankrupt. Consequently, where businesses claim they are under threat of bankruptcy due to foreign competition, the government is forced to consider what action it can take to combat this threat. In the past, the government protected Canadian business and employment from the risk of foreign competition via the implementation of tariffs. Clearly, such an option is complicated by the fact that reducing imports is not necessarily feasible. Protectionist policies are not compatible with the sentiments of free trade, and thus governments are sometimes placed in the unenviable position of balancing the needs of the domestic economy with the need to honour the rules governing global business. A case in point is the issue of government subsidies.

6. Offering Subsidies to Compete Globally. Whether it is for the purpose of maintaining employment levels or of assisting businesses in the global marketplace, the issue of government subsidies to business has become much more controversial in the context of globalization. Whether it is cash payments, low-interest loans, or tax breaks, such financial assistance is referred to as a subsidy. And in the case of the global context, such subsidies are intended to help domestic industry deal with global competition.

Arguments Against Industrial Policy   Critics of industrial policy also have significant reasons for their views. Critics say that government interference reduces the market's efficiency. How do you keep politics out of what ought to be economic decisions? Some politicians, as well as experts, think Canada should focus on rescuing flagging or "sunset" industries. Others argue we ought to promote emerging "sunrise" industries, such as breakthrough products in high technology.

Those who oppose industrial policy say that foreign success with it has been highly variable. Japan, for example, has had as many failures as successes with its government's development agency, Ministry of International Trade and Industry (MITI). MITI is generally credited with helping to build Japan's computer, semiconductor, and steel industries, but efforts to promote the aluminum-refining, petrochemical, shipping, and commercial aircraft industries were viewed as failures.[13] One economist, Gary Saxonhouse, reports that Japanese support for research and development is less than that in North America. He says that less than 2 percent of nondefence business research and development is financed by government in Japan, compared with 22 percent in the United States.[14] Further, Japan's favourable industrial policies (*keiretsu*), combined with lifetime employment, are ill suited to surviving economic recessions: The Japanese business system has produced too few entrepreneurial risk-takers.[15]

Finally, attempts at forming an industrial policy have been criticized as being irrational and uncoordinated and composed largely of "voluntary" restrictions on imports, occasional bailouts for near-bankruptcy companies, and a wide array of subsidies, loan guarantees, and special tax benefits for particular firms and industries. Thus, such efforts have constituted an industrial policy by default.[16] One could argue that Canada is incapable of developing a successful and planned industrial policy, given its experience and the composition of the public policy process that has characterized past decision making. Moreover, many critics would suggest that business must learn to survive on its own without looking to government involvement whenever it is in need. Based on that sentiment, any kind of industrial policy that requires government to come to the aid of business in order to help it compete internationally is problematic.

Government interventions in the international context may be viewed as another form of undesirable protectionism. For example, while Canadian steel producers welcomed government intervention to restrict access to cheaper foreign competitors' imports, other domestic players were not happy with the implementation of antidumping tariffs. These tariffs effectively raised the price of the foreign-produced goods. Many

Canadian steel businesses argued that they would lose access to cheaper foreign sources and be forced to rely on costlier steel sources in Ontario. The argument of these businesses is that they feel that they should have access to the lowest-cost sources of steel, whether these sources are from Canada or from foreign producers. In this regard, they are opposed to the government's protectionist policy of imposing antidumping tariffs.

Government assistance to business in the form of subsidies has significant implications in the global business context. Subsidies have been identified as either cash payments, low-interest loans, or potentially reduced taxes. Specifically, subsidies in the global context are intended to assist domestic industry to compete against foreign businesses, whether in the home country or through exports. One central argument against subsidies, whether in the domestic or global context, is that businesses should be required to manage their costs without external help, or "handouts," from the government. This is part of the requirement of fair competition, according to the critics. In addition, it is argued that consumers essentially pay for these subsidies. The government collects revenues through income and sales taxes, and it is these funds, collected from the general public, that are used to help some businesses. The question is: Are subsidies to business an unfair drain on public funds? There is no clear resolution to this ongoing debate.

From the global perspective, there is a second central criticism aimed at companies that receive subsidies from their local government. The criticism asserts that subsidies are not merely harmless forms of assistance to businesses; rather, they constitute a form of trade barrier, just like tariffs, and they create unfair competition. According to some critics, the Canada–U.S. softwood lumber dispute was an example of the difficulty in establishing the degree to which government should aid business in the global context. The U.S. lumber industry accused the Canadian government of unfairly subsidizing the Canadian softwood lumber industry.

In recent years, the WTO has been involved in many international disputes regarding whether a local government has given its domestic industry an unfair advantage through some form of subsidy. Consider the recurring controversy regarding government support of research and development programs. Disputes arose regarding government subsidies to Canada's aerospace giant Bombardier and its main competitor in the jet market, Embraer SA (Empresa Brasileira de Aeronautica SA) of Brazil. In 2001, the Canadian government offered low-interest loans worth up to $1.7 billion to assist Bombardier in winning a $2.35 billion contract to construct regional jets for Air Wisconsin Inc. Officials said that they had proof that the Brazilian government was offering their businesses high subsidies, and this measure allegedly was intended to maintain a "level playing field."[17]

There is an ebb and flow of interest in the concept of industrial policy depending on the current health of business and what is happening in the external environment. Many of the problems that initially started the current debate are still with us. New problems have arisen to add further complexity to the issue. Industrial policy is a powerful nonregulating approach by government to influence business that is certain to be a topic of debate for years to come.

Privatization

Privatization, generally speaking, refers to the process of "turning over to" the private sector (business) some function or service that was previously handled by some government body.[18] More than US$700 billion in assets have been privatized worldwide, with emerging economies accounting for almost 40 percent of that.[19] Privatization is an integral part of the twenty-first century strategies of both developed and developing countries, with the intent being to capture both the discipline of the free market and a spirit of entrepreneurial risk-taking.[20]

To understand privatization, we need to differentiate two functions government might perform: (1) producing a service and (2) providing a service.[21]

Producing Versus Providing a Service

A city government would be *providing* a service if it employed a private security firm to work at the coliseum during the local basketball playoffs. This same city government would be *producing* a service if its own police force provided security at the same basketball tournament. The terminology can be confusing, but the distinction must be made, because sometimes government provides a service (has a program for and actually pays for a service) and at other times it also produces a service (has its own employees who do it).[22]

The Privatization Debate

Proponents of privatization suggest that the functions of entire bureaucracies need to be contracted out to the private sector. They maintain that government at all levels is involved in thousands of businesses in which it has no real comparative advantage and no basic reason for being involved. They also argue that publicly owned enterprises are less efficient and less flexible than competitive private firms.[23] Opponents of privatization contend that there are certain activities that cannot be safely or effectively handled by the private sector. For example, in the U.S., following the September 11 terrorist attacks, there were many calls for **federalization** of airport security (the return of airport security to the government sector).

Traditionally, Canada embraced the need for Crown corporations. Such public enterprises are organizations accountable, through a minister, to Parliament for its operations. Crown corporations may be federal (e.g., Canada Post, the Canadian Broadcasting Corporation, the Canadian Wheat Board) or provincial (e.g., the Liquor Control Board of Ontario). Governments establish Crown corporations for a number of possible reasons:

- *To implement public policy that includes protecting or safeguarding national interests.* For example, federal Crown corporations, such as Air Canada and Petro-Canada, helped facilitate government policy in the area of cross-Canada transportation and Canadian ownership in the domestic oil industry.
- *To protect industries deemed to be vital to the economy.* The Canadian Radio Broadcasting Commission was established by the Canadian government in 1932 to administer a national broadcasting service in order to prevent Canadian broadcasting from becoming inundated with material originating in the United States. Similarly, this was a reason for taking control of the Canadian National Railways (CNR). The CNR originated in 1919 in order to safeguard the government's large investment in the railways and to protect Canada's image in foreign capital markets. While few municipal governments have traditionally held significant corporate holdings, they have been owners of public transit systems, recreational centres, and other facilities that are intended to enhance the quality of life in society.
- *To provide special services that could not otherwise be made available by private business.* For example, Trans Canada Airlines (Air Canada) was established in the 1930s, after it was observed that no private business was willing or able to provide domestic air services. Consider also the Bank of Canada. The Bank of Canada, created in 1935, was established to serve first as a control agent for the chartered banks—for example, requiring the banks to report

regularly on their operations and to hold deposit reserves with the Bank of Canada. Second, the Bank of Canada is responsible for developing monetary policy and regulating monetary operations in Canada.

- *To nationalize or federalize industries that were considered to be "natural monopolies," including the generation and distribution of electricity.* It is not hard to imagine that in the early days of Canadian society the private sector was too small to undertake the creation of a national electricity supply grid. On the other hand, government was capable of raising the necessary capital and, consequently, it took on the establishment of public utilities, including things like water supply, sewage treatment plants, and electricity generating plants, in addition to road construction and the like. In some cases, there were companies capable of building their own private utilities, which then became subject to government regulation, as we will discuss further below.

Each Crown corporation is a legally distinct entity wholly owned by the Crown, and each is managed by a board of directors. The range of Crown corporations has been relatively diverse, with corporations operating in a variety of areas of the economy. Naturally, the corporations differ with regard to their public policy purpose, as well as in their size and in their relative need for government financial support.

Privatization efforts are always undertaken with the hope that they will lead to improvements in efficiency and overall performance. In some cases, these hopes are realized but in many they are not. On average, a privatized firm's performance improves, but there is considerable variance in post-privatization performance among individual firms.[24] This variance is likely to be caused by differences in the ways that firms implement privatization programs. The nature of top management, the functioning of the board, and the strategic actions the firms undertake will all contribute to the likelihood of a privatization strategy's success.[25]

These two issues—industrial policy and privatization—are largely unresolved. As a result, they continue to be discussed and debated. As we have seen, the success of these efforts is largely dependent on their context—both the environments in which they are adopted and the ways in which they are implemented. It is clear that both industrial policy and privatization will have significant implications for the business/government relationship for years to come.

We now return to our discussion of the ways in which government uses various policies and mechanisms for influencing business.

Other Nonregulatory Governmental Influences on Business

Government has a significant impact on business by virtue of the fact that it has a large payroll and is a *major employer* itself. At all levels, government employs thousands of people who, as a consequence of being government employees, see things from the government's perspective.

Government is one of the largest *purchasers* of goods and services produced in the private sector. Some key industries, such as aerospace, electronics, and shipbuilding, are very dependent on government purchasing. Government can exert significant influence over the private sector by its insistence that minorities be hired, depressed areas be favoured, small businesses be favoured, and so on. Changes in government policy can dramatically change a firm's business environment.[26] For some firms in narrow markets, such as defence, the government dominates and controls whether or not those firms have a good year—indeed, whether or not they survive at all.[27]

Government influences the behaviour of business through the use of *subsidies* in a variety of ways. Generous subsidies are made available to industries such as agriculture, fishing, transportation, nuclear energy, and housing and to groups in special categories, such as minority-owned enterprises and businesses in depressed areas. Quite often these subsidies have special qualifications attached. Incentive programs were established to encourage managers to conduct business in a manner desired by the government. For example, it may be desirable for managers to invest in a new product development, or engage in greater export activities, or locate in an underdeveloped region. Consequently, incentives will be offered to engage in such activities. Receiving government financial support or reward for such activities would influence decisions to engage in these activities. For example, provincial and municipal governments can encourage new employment opportunities by offering incentives to industry for locating in their areas. The municipal government might offer property tax incentives to attract industry to its jurisdiction, and the provincial government might even offer an outright grant to attract large-scale industry.

Government loans and *loan guarantees* are sources of influence as well. Government lends money directly to small businesses, housing providers, farmers, and energy companies. Often such loans are made at lower interest rates than those of private competitors. Loan guarantee programs are another way in which government's influence is felt.[28] Governments at all levels have provided both direct and indirect assistance for businesses, in the form of grants, loans, information, consulting advice, and so on. Among the better-known and largest forms of government assistance to a business occurred in the 1980s, when both the Canadian and U.S. governments provided a loan guarantee to banks of over US$1 billion in an effort to prevent the Chrysler corporation from bankruptcy. Why the high level of assistance? If Chrysler had collapsed, hundreds of thousands of jobs would have been lost in both Canada and the United States.

The government has also tried to offer assistance to those industries deemed to be of particular importance. Industries with leading-edge technology, or those providing highly skilled jobs, or oriented toward exports, might be among the more likely recipients of government aid. The federal and provincial governments have also provided financial incentives in an effort to dissuade companies from moving their operations outside of Canada. For example, Pratt & Whitney Canada Corp. was given an $11.7 million interest-free loan from the Quebec and federal governments to encourage them to retain the development of a new aircraft component within Canada.

Government bailouts may involve a one-time financial assistance to combat significant financial troubles that a business may be experiencing. This financial assistance could also take the form of a loan or loan guarantee, for example. Bailouts were relatively common in the 1980s, involving such companies as Dome Petroleum, Chrysler Canada, and Massey Ferguson. By the 1990s, while complete bailouts became rare, the government nevertheless did not refuse to offer some assistance in a bailout arrangement, as evidenced in the 1992 bailout of Algoma Steel, which involved government loan guarantees. In 2001, after the attack on the World Trade Center, the crippled North American airline industry requested bailouts of about US$24 billion.[29] Other affected industries soon made requests as well. There is a long history of government stepping in to rescue industries in distress.

Taxation, through Revenue Canada, is another example of a government influence. Tax deductibility, tax incentives, depreciation policies, and tax credits are tools that are all at the disposal of the government.

Finally, *moral suasion* is a tool of government.[30] This refers to the government's attempts to "persuade" business to act in the public interest by taking or not taking a particular course of action. These public-interest appeals might include a request to roll back a price hike, show restraint on wage and salary increases, or exercise "voluntary" restraints of one kind or another.

Government's Regulatory Influences on Business

For more than two decades, government regulation has been the most controversial issue in the business/government relationship. Government regulation has affected virtually every aspect of how business functions. It has affected the terms and conditions under which firms have competed in their respective industries. It has touched almost every business decision ranging from the production of goods and services to packaging, distribution, marketing, and service. Most people agree that some degree of regulation has been necessary to ensure that consumers and employees are treated fairly and are not exposed to unreasonable hazards and that the environment is protected. However, they also think that government regulation has often been too extensive in scope, too costly, and inevitably burdensome in terms of paperwork requirements and red tape.

Regulation: What Does It Mean?

Generally, **regulation** refers to the act of governing, directing according to rule, or bringing under the control of law or constituted authority. Although there is no universally agreed-upon definition of federal regulation, we can look to the definition provided by the Economic Council of Canada as "the imposition of constraints, backed by the authority of a government, that are intended to modify economic behaviour in the private sector significantly."

There has been a relatively wide scope for government regulation in business activity: for example, regulation focused on consumer protection, regulation aimed at environmental protection, and regulation regarding the nature of competition. One obvious set of regulations exists fundamentally to protect the consumer, and the Canadian government has initiated a number of programs designed for consumer protection, many of which are administered by Health Canada. Among the numerous regulations, there is the Food and Drugs Act, which was designed to protect the public from potential risks to health as well as from fraud or deception as it relates to food, drugs, cosmetics, and the like. Similarly, the Hazardous Products Act serves to protect public safety by either banning products because they are deemed dangerous or requiring warning labels on products that might be considered hazardous. Ecological regulations are designed to protect the environment, and include legislation such as the Environmental Contaminants Act, which creates regulations to limit any dangerous byproducts of industrial production that could be harmful to people's health.

Reasons for Regulation

Why does the government need to intervene in the functioning of the business enterprise system? Regulations have come about over the years for a variety of reasons. There are several legitimate reasons why government regulation has evolved, although many businesspeople may not entirely agree with them. For the most part, however, government regulation has arisen because some kind of **market failure** (failure of the free-enterprise system) has occurred and government, intending to represent the public interest, has chosen to take corrective action. In addition, regulations can be encouraged through the efforts of special-interest groups that have lobbied successfully for them.

Four major reasons or justifications for regulation are typically offered: (1) controlling natural monopolies, (2) controlling negative externalities, (3) achieving social goals, and (4) other reasons.

Controlling Natural Monopolies One of the earliest circumstances in which government felt a need to regulate occurred when a natural monopoly existed. A **natural monopoly** exists in a market where the economics of scale are so great that the largest firm has the lowest costs and thus is able to drive out its competitors. Such a firm can supply the entire market more efficiently and cheaply than several smaller firms. Local telephone service is a good example, because parallel sets of telephone wires would involve waste and duplication that would be much more costly.

Monopolies such as this may seem "natural," but when left to their own devices could restrict output and raise prices. This potential abuse justifies the regulation of monopolies. As a consequence, we have seen telephone service providers (e.g., Bell Canada) subject to government regulators like the Canadian Radio-television and Telecommunications Commission (CRTC). Among other issues, such government regulators would determine the rates that the company may charge its customers.[31]

National regulators include the Canadian Transport Commission, which judges route and rate applications for commercial air and railway companies. In terms of provincial regulatory bodies, like the provincial liquor boards, provincial boards or commissions will assess and judge proposals from private business. Liquor boards, for example, are responsible for approving any price changes proposed by breweries within their province. The CRTC, under the auspices of the Department of Communications, regulates the telecommunications industry and its carriers, such as Bell Canada, and its traditional responsibilities have included accepting or refusing requests for rate increases among these carriers. We have also seen government regulation in the area of public utilities, such as an electric power company or a telephone company. The government has traditionally regulated these industries because of an absence of competition. Consequently, public utility boards or commissions monitor the performance of companies, as well as assess requests for rate increases and changes in the types of services provided.

Related to the control of natural monopolies is the government's desire to intervene when it thinks companies have engaged in anticompetitive practices. A famous, recent example of this was the U.S. Justice Department's investigation of the Microsoft Corporation case in which the company was accused of anticompetitive trade practices. The U.S. Court of Appeals in a mixed ruling overturned an initial court ruling, recommending that Microsoft be split in two. The appeals court reprimanded the judge for publicly criticizing Microsoft but upheld the finding of fact that the Windows operating system constitutes a monopoly in the PC market and that Microsoft violated the Sherman Antitrust Act with its marketing tactics. Microsoft would bundle new features into their Windows operating system as a way of breaking into new markets. They then designed their operating system so that it worked more smoothly with Microsoft products than with others—giving it a clear and, according to the courts, unfair marketing advantage.[32] A *Business Week* editorial opined, "The courts should insist that Windows is a common carrier that must be open to all competitors, much like phone lines and cable . . . Microsoft must accept the legal finding that it is a monopoly. As such, it has an obligation to open its operating system to competitors. If it does, it should be able to do the very thing it says is essential to its future—bundle new features into Windows that consumers want."[33]

Controlling Negative Externalities   Another important rationale for government regulation is that of controlling the **negative externalities** (or spillover effects) that result when the manufacture or use of a product gives rise to unplanned or unintended side effects on others (other than the producer or the consumer). Examples of these negative externalities are air pollution, water pollution, and improper disposal of toxic wastes. The consequence of such negative externalities is that neither the producer nor the consumer of the product directly "pays" for all the "costs" that are created by the manufacture of the product. The "costs" that must be borne by the public include an unpleasant or a foul atmosphere, illness, and the resulting health-care costs. Some have called these **social costs**, because they are absorbed by society rather than incorporated into the cost of making the product.

Preventing negative externalities is enormously expensive, and few firms are willing to pay for these added costs voluntarily. This is especially true in an industry that produces an essentially undifferentiated product, such as steel, where the millions of dollars needed to protect the environment would only add to the cost of the product and provide no benefit to the purchaser. In such situations, therefore, government regulation is seen as reasonable, and even welcomed, because it requires all firms competing in a given industry to operate according to the same rules. By forcing all firms to incur the costs, regulations level the competitive playing field.

Just as companies do not voluntarily take on huge expenditures for environmental protection, individuals often behave in the same fashion. For example, automobile emissions are one of the principal forms of air pollution. But how many private individuals would voluntarily request an emissions control system if it were offered as optional equipment? In situations such as this, a government standard that requires everyone to adhere to the regulation is much more likely to address the public's concern for air pollution.[34]

Achieving Social Goals   Government not only employs regulations to address market failures and negative externalities but also seeks to use regulations to help achieve certain **social goals** it deems to be in the public interest. Some of these social goals are related to negative externalities in the sense that government is attempting to correct problems that might also be viewed as negative externalities by particular groups. An example of this might be the harmful effects of a dangerous product or the unfair treatment of minorities resulting from employment discrimination. These externalities are not as obvious as air pollution, but they are just as real.

Another important social goal of government is to keep people informed. One could argue that inadequate information is a serious problem and that government should use its regulatory powers to require firms to reveal certain kinds of information to consumers. Thus, Health Canada's Product Safety Programme requires firms to warn consumers of potential product hazards through labelling requirements. Other regulatory mandates that address the issue of inadequate information include grading standards, weight and size information, truth-in-advertising requirements, product safety standards, and so on. A prime example of recent labelling requirements can be seen on canned goods and other products at the grocery store. Most canned goods now carry a "Nutrition Facts" label that provides consumer information on calories, fat content, and quantities of sodium, cholesterol, carbohydrates, proteins, and vitamins.

Other important social goals that have been addressed include preservation of national security (deregulation of oil prices to lessen dependence on imports), considerations of fairness or equity (employment discrimination laws), protection of those who provide essential services (farmers), allocation of scarce resources (gasoline rationing), and protection of consumers from excessively high price increases (natural gas regulation).[35]

Finally, the issue of protecting or preserving Canadian culture has been an issue of concern to the government and one that has been reflected in the rationale for some types of government regulation. For example, the media has often been viewed as an instrument to promote Canadian culture and consequently the government has at times been called upon to consider whether any regulations would help or harm the media's impact on Canadian culture. The notion of preserving national identity or culture has been an argument for regulating the extent of foreign ownership in Canadian businesses involved in cultural activities, such as television and publishing.

One such example was the recent controversy with dual-run U.S. publications in Canada. The controversy centres on split-run magazines, which are essentially U.S.-produced magazines like *Time* or *Sports Illustrated*, whose Canadian edition carries Canadian advertising, but little in the way of Canadian editorial content. Because split-run magazines have no additional editorial or design costs, the publishers can offer advertising at a rate well below the price required by Canadian-produced publications. The World Trade Organization initially ruled that it would be unfair for Canada to ban outright these split-run magazines. In June 1999, a compromise deal between Canada and the United States was reached that gave U.S. split-run magazines limited access to the Canadian advertising market. (American publishers will eventually be able to sell up to 18 percent of their ads to Canadian advertisers.) The United States threatened $3 billion in trade sanctions if Ottawa went ahead with proposed magazine legislation designed to keep split-run magazines out of Canada. Canadian publishers of such magazines as *Maclean's* and *Canadian Business*, among many others, have argued that this will create an unfair advantage for U.S. publishers, who can offer much lower advertising rates because they are producing split-run editions in much larger quantities. Consequently, these U.S. competitors will take away critical advertising revenues and could, in fact, threaten the survival of Canadian publishers. The threat is that eventually Canadian advertisers would stop advertising in Canadian magazines in favour of the cheaper advertising rates offer by these U.S. split-run magazines. Opponents argue that the U.S. publishers simply want to exploit the Canadian market for advertising profits, and are not interested in investing in Canadian versions of their magazines. Canadian publishers have continued to demand that these magazines be banned. The U.S. magazine industry requested a threshold as high as 40 percent of Canadian advertisements before they would be required to include Canadian content.

It has been estimated that more than 80 percent of newsstand sales of magazines in English Canada are U.S.-owned publications. Should the Canadian government impose restrictions on U.S. split-run publications? Should the power of competition and consumer demand dictate which businesses survive? Should the Canadian government protect Canadian business? This case suggests that another critical question is: Must the government intervene because the businesses involved here are connected to Canadian culture and identity? The argument is that the government needs to consider the impact of U.S.-owned businesses taking over an industry that reports about the nature of Canada and tells stories that involve Canadian heritage.

It is not uncommon for governments to restrict trade in goods and services as a means to achieve cultural objectives, including preservation of national identity. The earlier discussion of globalization suggested that international business and trade brings with it a mingling of different cultures. This can create a sense of attack on a domestic culture. Many countries have, for example, enacted laws to protect their media programming to help preserve national culture.

Other Reasons   There are several other reasons for government regulation. One is to control **excess profits**. The claim for regulation here would be aimed at transferring income for the purposes of economic fairness. For example, as a result of the Arab oil embargo between 1973 and 1980, oil stocks went up suddenly by a factor of 10. One argument is that the extra profits collected by these producers are somehow undeserved and the result of plain luck, not wise investment decisions. So, in situations such as this in which profits are drastically, suddenly, and perhaps undeservedly increased, an argument has been made for government regulation.[36]

Another commonly advanced rationale for regulation is to deal with **excessive competition**. The basic idea behind this rationale is that excessive competition will lead to prices being set at unprofitably low levels. This action will force firms out of business and ultimately will result in products that are too costly because the remaining firm will raise its prices to excessive levels, leaving the public worse off than before.[37]

Types of Regulation

Broadly speaking, government regulations have been used for two central purposes: achieving certain economic goals and achieving certain social goals. Therefore, it has become customary to identify two different types of regulation: economic regulation and social regulation.

Economic Regulation   **Economic regulation** is best exemplified by such regulatory bodies as Transport Canada or the CRTC. These regulatory bodies typically operate along industry lines and were created for the purpose of regulating business behaviour through the control of or influence over economic or market variables such as prices (maximum and minimum), entry to and exit from markets, and types of services that can be offered.

The railway industry was among the very first to have regulations applied, with the deal made in 1895 between Prime Minister Wilfrid Laurier and the Canadian Pacific Railway (CPR). Essentially, the government promised the CPR the financing it needed to complete a transcontinental line if the CPR would carry wheat produced by western farmers for shipping on a regular basis at a negotiated rate. Many years later, the National Transportation Act created the Canadian Transport Commission (in 1970), whose job it was to regulate and control the various means of transportation in Canada, including motor, air, water transport, and railways. National regulators include Transport Canada, which develops and administers policies, regulations, and programs for a safe, efficient, and environmentally friendly transportation system.[38]

The Canadian Radio-television and Telecommunications Commission (CRTC), under the auspices of the Department of Communications, regulates the telecommunications industry. The CRTC is responsible for issuing broadcasting licences, and can require companies seeking such a licence to conform with standards regarding type or content of programming. The CRTC's responsibilities extend far beyond broadcasting, and also govern the nature of competition in the telecommunications and media industries. For example, in the telecommunications industry, there are regulations regarding the permissible amount of foreign ownership. Specifically, non-Canadians have been restricted in the voting shares that they can hold in telecommunications and media companies. In 2001, the government's Broadband Task Force released a report recommending that the government change foreign ownership rules to permit greater foreign investment and, consequently, increase competition in that industry.

The government has also established a competition policy to control the nature of competition in the business sector. Earlier, we identified the importance of competition in our economy, given its ability to encourage the production and distribution of goods and services at the lowest possible cost. Consequently, the competition policy, set out in the Competition Act, is intended to stimulate open competition and eliminate any restrictive business practices with the aim of encouraging maximum production, distribution, and employment opportunities. While it is not specific to any one industry, the Competition Bureau's aim is in many ways reflective of the notion of economic regulation.

Competition policy is aimed at creating equity in the marketplace among all the different and potentially competing interests, including consumers and producers; wholesalers and retailers; dominant players and minor players; and the public interest and the private interest. The Competition Bureau (under the auspices of Industry Canada) is responsible for enforcing and administering the Competition Act, and it has four main functions:

1. The Bureau informs companies of what they can and cannot do under competition law. It also informs consumers with regard to their rights.
2. It takes on an advocacy role in promoting greater competition in the business sector. For example, the Bureau has been actively involved in the deregulation process of the telecommunications sector, including its numerous appearances before the CRTC to urge regulators to take the least restrictive action possible so as to minimize the level of regulation, and therefore maximize potential competition.
3. The Bureau closely reviews mergers prior to their occurrence in order to ensure that they do not lead to undue concentration that would limit competition.
4. It seeks to rectify anticompetitive activities, including the use of suasion (warning letters, visits, interviews, etc.); enforcing compliance by obtaining injunctions, consent orders, adoption of voluntary codes; or prosecuting for violations of the Competition Act.[39]

Social Regulation   The 1960s ushered in a new form of regulation that for all practical purposes has become what regulation means to modern-day business managers. This new form of regulation has come to be known as **social regulation**, because it has had as its major thrust the furtherance of societal objectives quite different from the earlier focus on markets and economic variables. Whereas the older form of economic regulation focused on markets, the new social regulation focuses on business's impacts on people. The emphasis on people essentially addresses the needs of people in their roles as employees, consumers, and citizens.

Two major examples of social regulations having specific impacts on people as employees were Employment Equity regulations and Occupational Safety and Health regulations. The 1950s and 1960s ushered in new employment statutes in most Canadian jurisdictions prohibiting racial and religious discrimination and prescribing equal pay for men and women. The first Canadian Bill of Rights was introduced in 1960. Equal opportunity became one of the first concepts commonly used to define equality in employment for all Canadians. Finally, in 1986 the Employment Equity Act was passed with its purpose to "achieve equality in the workplace so that no person shall be denied employment opportunities or benefits for reasons unrelated to ability and, in the fulfillment of the goals, to correct the conditions of disadvantage in employment experienced by women, Aboriginal peoples, persons with disabilities, and visible minority people ..."

The goal of occupational health and safety regulation is to ensure that the nation's workplaces are safe and healthful. Health and safety legislation regulates the standards of workplace safety with the objective of preventing workplace accidents and injury. Typically, this legislation requires that the employer take all reasonable actions to protect the health and safety of employees. This includes, but is not limited to, offering appropriate training for handling potentially dangerous equipment or material, informing employees of potential dangers in the workplace, and establishing safe work practices. Employees have the right to refuse work that is unsafe. Regulations cover a variety of issues, including the bases for refusal to work (because of unsafe conditions), workers' compensation, substance abuse in the workplace, violence in the workplace, and employees working alone. Often Workers Compensation Boards act as insurance boards responsible for compensating workers for costs and lost income relating to workplace injury or illness. These boards protect employers from being sued by employees and ensure that employees do not suffer income loss if they are injured at work. Some Workers Compensation Boards provide ongoing training and awareness campaigns for the public about occupational health and safety. The Canadian Centre for Occupational Health and Safety (CCOHS), established in 1978, is a Canadian federal government agency based in Hamilton, Ontario, which serves to support the aim of eliminating all Canadian work-related illnesses and injuries. The CCOHS provides information and advice for promoting safe and healthy working environments. It collaborates with organizations from Canada and around the world to improve the quality and quantity of health and safety resources and programs. Its comprehensive Web site can be found at http://www.ccohs.ca.

A key body governing regulation in both the areas of occupational health and safety and employment equity is the Ministry of Labour. It was created in 1919 to develop and enforce labour legislation, and advance safe, fair, and harmonious workplace practices that are essential to the social and economic well-being of Canadian citizens.[40] Among the central areas of concern are occupational health and safety, employment rights and responsibilities, labour relations, and internal administration. While the ministry is responsible for establishing, communicating, and enforcing workplace standards, there are a host of commissions and agencies that assist the Ministry of Labour with this mandate. The Canadian Human Rights Commission, for example, is one instrument for helping to reduce barriers to equality in employment and access to services.

Whereas the older form of economic regulation was aimed primarily at companies competing in specific industries, the newer form of social regulation addresses business practices affecting all industries. Figure 10–3 summarizes the nature of economic versus social regulations along with pertinent examples.

The new wave of government regulation brought about in the past 30 years through use of the social regulatory model has had sweeping effects on society. It has signalled a new and seemingly increasing role for government in the affairs of business. As a consequence, no manager today, whether she or he operates a small neigh-

FIGURE 10–3

Comparison of Economic and Social Regulations

	Economic Regulations	Social Regulations
Focus	Market conditions, economic variables (entry, exit, prices, services)	People in their roles as employees, consumers, and citizens
Industries Affected	Often industry specific (e.g., breweries, transportation, telecommunications)	Virtually all industries
Examples	Transport Canada	Human Rights Commission
Current Trend	From regulation to deregulation; however, problems with deregulation could reverse that trend	Stable—No significant increase or decrease in agencies

bourhood grocery store or manages a *Fortune* 500 firm, is exempt from the many and varied standards, guidelines, and restrictions that the government imposes. Close attention must be paid to these issues, just as close attention needs to be paid to making traditional managerial decisions. Figure 10–4 summarizes the major areas of government regulation in Canada. To better appreciate the impact that government regulation is having on business, it is helpful to consider some of the issues that have arisen as a direct outgrowth of government regulations.

Issues Related to Regulation

It is important to consider some of the issues that have arisen out of the increased governmental role in regulating business. In general, managers have been concerned with what might be called "regulatory unreasonableness."[41] We could expect that business would just as soon not have to deal with these regulatory bodies. Therefore, some of business's reactions are simply related to the nuisance factor of having to deal with a complex array of restrictions. Other legitimate issues that have arisen over the past few years also need to be addressed.

To be certain, there are benefits of government regulation. Employees are treated more fairly and have safer work environments. Consumers are able to purchase safer products and receive more information about them. Citizens in all walks of life have cleaner air to breathe and cleaner water in lakes and rivers where they go for recreational purposes. These benefits are real, but their exact magnitudes are difficult to measure.

In addition to the **direct costs of regulation**, there are **indirect costs** such as forms, reports, and questionnaires that business must complete to satisfy the requirements of the regulatory agencies. These costs of government regulation get passed on to the consumer in the form of higher prices. Lastly, there are **induced costs**. The induced effects of regulation are diffuse and elusive, but they constitute some of the most powerful consequences of the regulatory process. In a real sense, then, these induced effects have to be thought of as costs. Three effects are worthy of elaboration:[42]

1. *Innovation is affected.* When corporate budgets must focus on "defensive research," certain types of innovation do not take place. To the extent that firms must devote more of their scientific resources to meeting government requirements, fewer resources are available to dedicate to new product and process research and development and innovation. One industry affected in this

FIGURE 10–4

The Scope of Regulation in Canada

Communications

Broadcasting
- radio (AM, FM)
- television

Telecommunications
- telephone
- cable TV
- satellite

Cultural and Recreational
- Language (bilingualism)
- Sports
- Canadian Content in Broadcasting

Energy
- Hydro-electric
- Natural Gas

Health and Safety
- Building Codes
- Animal Health
- Plant Health
- Occupational Health and Safety

Environmental Protection

Pollution Control
- air
- water

Resource Development
- minerals
- forestry

Land Use
- planning/zoning
- development approval

Consumer Protection
- Disclosure (product content)
- Packaging and Labelling
- Weights and Measures

Human Rights
- Anti-discrimination Legislation
- Proctection of Privacy

Food Production and Distribution

Agricultural Products Marketing
- pricing
- grading
- distribution
- entry
- quotas

Labour
- Hours of Work
- Minimum Wage Laws
- Collective Bargaining

Others
- Rent Control
- General Wage and Price Controls

Liquor
- Alcohol Content
- Distribution and Sale

Financial Markets and Institutions
- Banks
- Trust Companies
- Pension Funds
- Insurance

Framework Laws
- Competition Policy
- Bankruptcy Laws
- Intellectual Property Law

Transportation
- Airlines
- Taxis
- Trucking
- Urban Public Transit

Occupational Licensure
- Certification/Licensure
- Apprenticeship

Source: Economic Council of Canada, *Responsible Regulation: An Interim Report* (Ottawa: Ministry of Supply and Services, 1979), p. 11. Reproduced with the permission of the Minister of Public Works and Government Services, 2004.

Ethics In Practice

To Comply or Not to Comply with the Government Regulation?

Every summer and Christmas vacation for the past four years I have worked in the maintenance department of Gilman Paper Company. Working there to help finance my college education, I have been exposed to many questionable practices. One of the most prominent problems is the adherence to safety regulations.

Occupational Health and Safety standards require that a vessel-confined-space entry permit be filled out before a person enters the confined area, and that a "sniffer" (a device used to detect oxygen deficiencies and other harmful or combustible gases) be present and operational whenever a person is inside. A confined space is defined as any area without proper air ventilation and/or an area more than five feet deep. For example, tanks and pits are confined spaces.

Anytime a person enters or leaves a confined space, the person is required to place her or his initials on the entry permit. This is for the physical protection of the worker and the liability protection of the company. If workers are seen violating this policy, they can be reprimanded or fired on the spot.

In my many experiences with these confined spaces, I have observed on numerous occasions that these policies are not broken by the workers, but by the supervisors. It is their responsibility to obtain these permits and sign them, as well as obtain the use of a sniffer. Sometimes the supervisors and the workers will forget that we are working in a confined space, and thus forget the permit and sniffer. When someone has realized that we are in a confined space, however, the supervisors have often asked us to initialize the permit at various places as if the permit had been there all along.

When we are working for extended periods of time in these areas, the sniffer's batteries often go dead as well. Instead of following regulations and leaving the area until a new sniffer is obtained, the supervisors often tell employees to stay, declaring, "The air is fine. You don't need a sniffer!"

My problem is this: Should I sign these permits when I know it is dishonest, or should I do the "right" thing and let the Workplace Safety and Insurance Board (WSIB) know that this regulation is being broken time and time again? After all, I'm not even a full-time employee, so who am I to cause trouble?

1. Who are the stakeholders in this case, and what are their stakes?

2. What should I have done in this situation? Is this regulation important, or is this just more government "red tape"? Should I have just "gone along to get along" with the supervisors?

Contributed by Dale Dyals

way is the drug industry. Economists estimate that stringent FDA regulations in the U.S., as well as Health Canada regulations, seriously hinder innovation in the drug industry. The consequences are a slowed pace and a decreased number of new drugs arriving on the marketplace for consumer use.

2. *New investments in plant and equipment are affected.* To the extent that corporate funds must be used for regulatory compliance purposes, these funds are diverted from more productive uses. One estimate is that environmental and job safety requirements diminish by one-fourth the potential annual increase in productivity. It should also be pointed out that uncertainty about future regulations has an adverse effect on the introduction of new products and processes.[43]

3. *Small business is adversely affected.* Although it is not intentional, most federal regulations have a disproportionately adverse effect on small firms. Large firms have more personnel and resources and are therefore better able to get the work of government done than are small firms. More than any other group, small business seems to feel keenly affected by government regulation.

Deregulation

Quite frequently, trends and countertrends overlap with one another. Such is the case with regulation and its counterpart, **deregulation**. There are many reasons for this overlapping, but typically they include both the economic and the political. From an economic perspective, there is a continual striving for the balance of freedom and control for business that will be best for society. From a political perspective, there is an ongoing interplay of different societal goals and means for achieving those goals. The outcome is a mix of economic and political decisions that seem to be in a constant state of flux. Thus, in the economy at any point in time, trends that appear counter to one another can coexist simultaneously. These trends are the natural result of competing forces seeking some sort of balance or equilibrium.

This is how we can explain the trend toward deregulation that evolved in a highly regulated environment. Deregulation represents a counterforce aimed at keeping the economy in balance. It also represents a political philosophy that was prevailing during the period of its origin and growth.

Deregulation may be thought of as one kind of regulatory reform. But, because it is unique and quite unlike the regulatory reform measures discussed earlier, we will treat it separately. Deregulation has taken place primarily with respect to economic regulations, and this, too, helps to explain its separate treatment.

Purpose of Deregulation

The basic idea behind deregulation has been to remove certain industries from the old-line economic regulations of the past. The purpose of this deregulation, or at least a reduced level of regulation, has been to increase competition with the expected benefits of greater efficiency, lower prices, and enhanced innovation. These goals have not been uniformly received, and it is still undecided whether deregulation works as a method of maximizing society's best interests.

Trend Toward Deregulation

When the trend toward deregulation began in the 1980s, most notably exemplified in the financial industry, the telecommunications industry, and the transportation (trucking, airline, railroad) industry, it represented business's first major redirection in 50 years.[44] The result seemed to be a mixed bag of benefits and problems. On the benefits side, prices fell in many industries, and better service appeared in some industries along with increased numbers of competitors and innovative products and services.

Several problems arose also. Although prices fell and many competitors entered some of those industries, more and more of those competitors were unable to compete with the dominant firms. They were failing, going bankrupt, or being absorbed by the larger firms. Entry barriers into some industries were enormous and had been greatly underestimated. This has been shown to be the case in airline, trucking, railroad, and long-distance telephone service.[45]

Dilemma with Deregulation

The intent of deregulation was to deregulate the industries, thus allowing for freer competition. The intent was not to deregulate health and safety requirements. The dilemma with deregulation is how to enhance the competitive nature of the affected industries without sacrificing the applicable social regulations. This is the second major problem with deregulation that needs to be discussed. Unfortunately, the potential competition unleashed by economic deregulation can force many companies to cut corners in ways that endanger the health and/or safety of their customers. This pattern, which seems to occur in any deregulated industry, was apparent in the trucking and airline industries.[46]

Trucking Industry   On January 1, 1988, the new National Transportation Act came into effect, and brought with it a new era of deregulation. This act brought with it the passage of the new Motor Vehicle Transport Act. Prior to that time, anyone wanting to enter the trucking business was required to appear before the provincial licensing board and prove there was a public need for their service in order to get a licence to operate a truck. However, under the new act the prospective trucker must simply present proof that he or she is insurable and can pass some minimal safety criteria. A major benefit of the reduction in requirements for new entrants was increased competition: more truckers entered the industry. Shippers gained from a wider choice of trucking services and more competitive rates.

Following the passage of this act, shippers could negotiate the level of service and price of any domestic movement with any carrier. Consequently, consumers benefited in terms of reduced costs arising from increased competition in highway carriers. In fact, a central aim of this deregulation was to encourage greater efficiency in Canada's over $2 billion transportation market. In a more recent report of the trucking industry in Canada, the following observation was made: What has emerged is a new breed of Canadian trucker—one that is more efficient, value-priced, eager to customize to shippers' needs, and adept at filling specialized niches in a North American market dominated by huge and efficient American carriers.[47]

In the related railway shipping industry, recent reports have indicated that shipper rates dropped by 35 percent since deregulation, and were considered lowest in the world—60 percent below the international average.[48] However, there has been a downside for some. With increased competition, some trucking companies have been unable to compete effectively and have gone bankrupt, resulting in the loss of hundreds of jobs. In fact, in 1990 about 130 trucking companies declared bankruptcy— over twice as many as those in the previous year. A major threat has come from U.S. trucking companies, which have lower labour, equipment, and tax costs, and consequently, lower operating costs.

During the years following deregulation, the Canadian carriers admitted that they were slow to adapt to new technologies such as electronic data interchange, bar coding, and satellite tracking of trailers. For example, by 1997 almost all U.S. truckload tractors were equipped for satellite tracking, while only 50 percent of Canadian tractors were equipped.[49]

To survive in a deregulated industry, many truckers delayed essential maintenance and spent too many hours behind the wheel. This was an issue in both Canada and the U.S. According to some U.S. industry experts, as many as one-third of the long-haul drivers turned to illegal drugs to help them cope with the gruelling hours on the road. Others turned to alcohol. Statistics showed a sharp increase in the number of truck accidents from 1980 to 1986, and roadside inspections in one year turned up serious problems in 30 to 40 percent of the trucks inspected.[50]

Banking Industry   In the financial services industry, deregulation permitted banks to enter the brokerage business and allowed them to sell insurance. This has not yet received widespread approval. A case was made for deregulating the insurance industry to allow banks to enter.[51] The banks have long served as an example of an industry with inadequate competition and that, consequently, requires rigorous government regulation. In fact, the pressure exerted on the government by banks to allow them to merge was faced with a public fear of the creation of a greater monopoly situation and the negative consequences of such a situation. Interestingly, on the other hand, there has been an opposite sentiment with regard to allowing banks to expand their services into the insurance industry through their branch networks.

Critics have asserted that the insurance industry and, specifically, the traditional insurance distribution system failed to meet the requirements of the Canadian consumer. Relatively lower sales and a distinct lack of insurance availability have suggested the need for more competition within the insurance industry. The argument was that allowing banks to enter the insurance industry would be a great service, particularly to lower-income Canadians, who currently cannot afford proper insurance coverage. Deregulation offers the banks entry into the insurance field. However, as with the general notion of deregulation, permitting the banks to enter the insurance industry would, allegedly, result in less costly, more comprehensive insurance service for Canadians, and create a more competitive, stronger, financial services industry. In addition, advocates of deregulation in this industry offer examples of similar practices in other countries. For example, allowing integration of insurance services has occurred in France, where banks are allowed to sell insurance policies in their branches.

The average expense ratio for bank insurance policies was under 5 percent, compared with almost 14 percent for other companies selling insurance. The lower cost structure contributes to lower policy costs for consumers of insurance obtained through the banks. Combining banking and insurance services for French consumers allows banks to offer small, standardized policies for low-income persons that under normal circumstances would not generate sufficient commissions for a typical insurance agent. The advantages of permitting banks to enter the insurance industry are also evident in New Zealand, where there is evidence that competition from the insurance subsidiaries of banks led to falling prices for term life insurance.

Electric Utilities The last decade has seen a great interest in deregulation in the energy sector, specifically energy supply, with Britain and Scandinavia largely initiating this practice in the early 1990s. Traditionally, electricity costs have been higher in Europe than in North America. After a number of European governments privatized their public utilities, the cost of electricity dropped in those regions. Deregulation also welcomed much more competition, and this competition forced the power companies to become more efficient and improve customer service.

It seems that the Canadian government, drawing on the European experience, decided to initiate privatization and deregulation in the energy sector in Canada, beginning with Alberta in 1995. Unfortunately, the reaction to this transition has been mixed, with some observers criticizing the deregulation process in Alberta, and others adding that the purchase of electricity has become more complicated with the advent of deregulation.

Ontario has followed Alberta's lead in electricity deregulation, although Ontario proceeded somewhat more slowly. By 2001, Ontario Power Generation (the government-owned utility, formerly part of Ontario Hydro) provided 85 percent of the province's electricity, while the aim was to sell off much of its generating capacity to private enterprise. In January 2001, the government of New Brunswick announced its plans to deregulate its electricity system.

While advocates of deregulation feel that the benefits of increased competition will ultimately prevail, opponents believe that public ownership should continue to exist for essential services in order to ensure that all members of society will be guaranteed access to the same service at a reasonable price.

Summary

Business cannot be discussed without considering the paramount role played by government. Although the two institutions have opposing systems of belief, they are intertwined in terms of their functioning in our socioeconomic system. In addition, the public assumes a major role in a complex pattern of interactions among business, government, and the public. Government exerts a host of nonregulatory influences on business. Two influences with a macro orientation include industrial policy and privatization. A more specific influence is the fact that government is a major employer, subsidizer, financier, taxation agent, and persuader. These roles permit government to affect business significantly.

One of government's most controversial interventions in business is direct regulation. Government regulates business for several legitimate reasons, and in the past two decades social regulation has been more dominant than economic regulation. There are many benefits and various costs of government regulation. A response to the problems with regulation has been deregulation. However, bad experiences in key industries have caused many to wonder whether the government has gone too far in that direction.

Key Terms

accelerationists (page 313)

adjusters (page 313)

bankers (page 313)

capitalism (page 307)

central planners (page 313)

collectivistic ethic of government (page 309)

deregulation (page 330)

direct costs of regulation (page 327)

economic regulation (page 324)

excess profits (page 324)

excessive competition (page 324)

federalization (page 317)

indirect costs (page 327)

individualistic ethic of business (page 309)

induced costs (page 327)

industrial policy (page 312)

market failure (page 321)

natural monopoly (page 321)

negative externalities (page 322)

privatization (page 316)

regulation (page 320)

social costs (page 322)

social goals (page 322)

social regulation (page 325)

targeters (page 313)

Discussion Questions

1. Briefly explain how business and government represent a clash of ethical systems (belief systems). With which do you find yourself identifying most? Explain. With which would most business students identify? Explain.

2. Explain why the public is treated as a separate group in the interactions among business, government, and the public. Doesn't government represent the public's interests? How should the public's interests be manifested?

3. What is regulation? Why does government see a need to regulate? Differentiate between economic and social regulation. What social regulations do you think are most important, and why? What social regulations ought to be eliminated? Explain.

4. Outline the major benefits and costs of government regulation. In general, do you think the benefits of government regulation exceed the costs? In what areas, if any, do you think the costs exceed the benefits?

5. Electricity regulation in Alberta was cited as an example of a problem resulting from deregulation. What is the current mood of Canada regarding deregulation? What evidence can you present to substantiate your opinion?

Endnotes

1. George A. Steiner, *Business and Society*, 2d ed. (New York: Random House, 1975), 359–361.

2. L. Earle Birdsell, "Business and Government: The Walls Between," in Neil H. Jacoby (ed.), *The Business–Government Relationship: A Reassessment* (Santa Monica, CA: Goodyear, 1975), 32–34.

3. Jacoby, 167.

4. *Ibid.*, 168.

5. For a view somewhat counter to this, see Kevin Phillips, "The Balkanization of America," *Harper's* (May 1978), 37–47.

6. Daniel Bell, "Too Much, Too Late: Reactions to Changing Social Values," in Jacoby, 17–19.

7. Alfred L. Seelye, "Societal Change and Business–Government Relationships," *MSU Business Topics* (Autumn 1975), 7–8.

8. Jacoby, 168.

9. Arthur T. Denzau, "Will an 'Industrial Policy' Work for the United States?" (St. Louis: Center for the Study of American Business, Washington University, September 1983), 1.

10. *Ibid.*, 2.

11. Robert B. Reich, *The Next American Frontier* (New York: Penguin Books, 1983).

12. "Industrial Policy: Is It the Answer?" *Business Week* (July 4, 1983), 55–56.

13. Monroe W. Karmin, "Industrial Policy: What Is It? Do We Need One?" *U.S. News & World Report* (October 3, 1983), 47.

14. Robert J. Samuelson, "The New (Old) Industrial Policy," *Newsweek* (May 23, 1994), 53.

15. Hiroyuki Tezuka, "Success as the Source of Failure? Competition and Cooperation in the Japanese Economy," *Sloan Management Review* (Vol. 38, No. 2, March 1997), 83–93.

16. Ira C. Magaziner and Robert B. Reich, *Minding America's Business: The Decline and Rise of the American Economy* (New York: Vintage Books, 1983), 255.

17. Heather Scoffield, "WTO Ruling Seen As Win-Win," *The Globe and Mail* (June 23, 2001), B2.

18. Ted Kolderie, "What Do We Mean by Privatization?" (St. Louis: Center for the Study of American Business, Washington University, May 1986), 2–5.

19. Ravi Ramamurty, "A Multilevel Model of Privatization in Emerging Economies," *Academy of Management Review* (July 2000), 525–550.

20. Shaker A. Zahra, R. Duane Ireland, Isabel Gutierrez, and Michael A. Hitt, "Privatization and Entrepreneurial Transformation: Emerging Issues and a Future Research Agenda," *Academy of Management Review* (July 2000), 509–524.

21. Kolderie, 2–5.

22. *Ibid.*, 3–5.

23. Steve Coll, "Retooling Europe," *The Washington Post National Weekly Edition* (August 22–28, 1994), 6–7.

24. Alvaro Cuervo and Bélen Villalonga, "Explaining the Variance in the Performance Effects of Privatization," *Academy of Management Review* (July 2000), 581–590.

25. *Ibid.*, 581–590.

26. Richard Reed, David J. Lemak, and W. Andrew Hesser, "Cleaning Up After the Cold War: Management and Social Issues," *Academy of Management Review* (Vol. 22, No. 3, July 1997), 614–642.

27. Murray L. Weidenbaum, *Business, Government and the Public*, 3d ed. (Englewood Cliffs, NJ: Prentice Hall, 1986), 5–6.

28. *Ibid.*, 6, 8.

29. Paul Magnusson, "Suddenly, Washington's Wallet Is Open," *Business Week* (October 1, 2001), 34; http://www.cnn.com.

30. Alan Keyes, "Why 'Good Government' Isn't Enough," *Imprimis* (Vol. 21, No. 10, October 1992), 2, 10–11.

31. *Congressional Quarterly's Federal Regulatory Directory*, 5th ed. (1985–1986), 9.

32. "Microsoft: Time to Change," *Business Week* (July 16, 2001), 100.

33. *Ibid.*, 100.

34. *Congressional Quarterly's Federal Regulatory Directory*, 5th ed. (1985–1986), 10–11.

35. *Ibid.*, 12.

36. Stephen Breyer, *Regulation and Its Reform* (Cambridge, MA: Harvard University Press, 1982), 21–22.

37. *Ibid.*, 31–32.

38. Transport Canada, http://www.tc.gc.ca/aboutus/whatwedo.htm.

39. Based on statement by Konrad von Finckenstein, Q.C. Commissioner of Competition Bureau to the "Meet the Competition Bureau," Forum Insight Conference, Toronto, May 3, 1999.

40. http://www.gov.on.ca/LAB/english/about.

41. Graham K. Wilson, *Business and Politics: A Comparative Introduction* (Chatham, NJ: Chatham House, 1985), 39.

42. Murray L. Weidenbaum, *Costs of Regulation and Benefits of Reform* (St. Louis: Center for the Study of American Business, Washington University, November 1980), 12–14. See also Murray Weidenbaum and Melinda Warren, *It's Time to Cut Government Regulations* (St. Louis: Center for the Study of American Business, Washington University, February 1995).

43. *Ibid.*, 12.

44. "Deregulating America," *Business Week* (November 28, 1983), 80–89.

45. "Is Deregulation Working?" *Business Week* (December 22, 1986), 50–55.

46. Frederick C. Thayer, "The Emerging Dangers of Deregulation," *The New York Times* (February 23, 1986), 3.

47. W. Garret, "A New World for Canadian Truckers," *World Trade* (Vol. 10, No. 2, 1998), 48–50.

48. "Deregulations Real Winner: The Consumer," *Railway Age* (1999), 18–20.

49. Garret, 48–50.

50. Kenneth Labich, "The Scandal of Killer Trucks," *Fortune* (March 30, 1987), 85–87.

51. Jordy Barnes, "Let Banks Fill the Low Income Insurance Gap," *National Post* (June 28, 2001).

Chapter 11

Consumer Stakeholders: Information Issues and Responses

Chapter Objectives

After studying this chapter, you should be able to:

1 Identify the fundamental expectations of consumers.

2 Identify the major abuses of advertising and discuss specific controversial advertising issues.

3 Enumerate and discuss other product information issues that present problems for consumer stakeholders.

4 Describe the role and functions of the Competition Bureau.

5 Discuss the strengths and weaknesses of regulation and self-regulation of advertising.

How important are consumers as stakeholders? According to management expert Peter Drucker, there is only one valid definition of business purpose: to create a customer.[1] Of course, retaining that customer is essential, too. In *The Loyalty Effect*, Frederick Reichheld showed that small increases in customer retention rates can lead to dramatic increases in profits.[2] Clearly, businesses must create and retain customers if they are to succeed in today's competitive marketplace. It is not surprising, therefore, that **customer relationship management (CRM)** has become the mantra of marketing.[3] Customer relationship management is "the ability of an organization to effectively identify, acquire, foster, and retain loyal profitable customers."[4] With CRM guiding businesses in their customer relations, one would expect consumers to be pleased, or at least satisfied, with the way they have been treated. Unfortunately, that hasn't been the case. The consumer is still "often ignored"[5] and, in practice, CRM has been said to be "an awful lot of bland talk and not a lot of action."[6]

The issue of business and the consumer stakeholder is at the forefront of discussions about business and its relationships with and responsibility to the society in which it exists. Products and services are the most visible manifestations of business in society. For this reason, the whole issue of business and its consumer stakeholders deserves a careful examination. We devote two chapters to it. In this chapter, we focus on the evolution and maturity of the consumer movement and product information issues—most notably, advertising. In Chapter 12, we consider product issues, especially product safety and liability, and business's response to its consumer stakeholders.

The Paradox of the Customer Revolution

If one studies the history of business in North America, one sees how business has evolved through different eras in the evolution of marketing. Basically, the focus shifted from problems of production to problems of marketing. The product business can make became less important than the product the consumer wants business to make. Putting the customer first became the motto of business.

In her new book, *The Customer Revolution*, Patricia Seybold argues that putting the customer first is no longer sufficient.[7] Now businesses must relinquish control to the customer. In fact, she contends that the relinquishing isn't really optional—customers are already in control and that, like most revolutions, the customer revolution cannot be stopped. "We can't turn our backs on it," says Seybold. "We have no choice but to surrender gracefully."[8]

Technological advances have enabled consumers not only to demand what they want but also to expect to get it. Consumers have a wide range of choices and a great deal of information available to them. Mass customization, which allows companies to customize products or services to customers' needs, has evolved as a way for companies to serve customers on a one-to-one basis. Companies in industries as diverse as clothing, computers, software, and hotels have implemented the mass customization concept.[9] Paul Saffo, a director at the Institute for the Future, says that mass customization has brought new meaning to "the customer is king" nature of business:

> The thing about yesterday's kings is they were very remote and they didn't bother you very often. Now I think the customer is an ever-more demanding partner. And, if you just blindly follow the old "customer is king" idea, you are going to miss opportunities.[10]

According to Glover T. Ferguson, chief scientist at Accenture:

> *Yes, the customer is still king. But now it's not just a king who says,*
> *"Bring me my costly raiments and a horse to ride." It's a king who says,*
> *"I want my raiments in this color, and I want them to fit. And this is the*
> *kind of horse I want. This is the saddle I want. This is the bridle I want.*
> *And here's where I want to go."*[11]

The paradox of the consumer revolution is that in a period when many marketing theorists and practitioners proclaim the importance of the consumer and technological advances have given the consumer greater power, we continue to see consumers exclaiming that business does not care enough about them and treats them badly. The consumer movement has arisen as a response to this general level of dissatisfaction.

The Consumer Movement

In North America, much credit for the birth of the modern consumer movement has been given to U.S. President John F. Kennedy. The basic expectations of the consumer movement can be found in the "**consumer's Magna Carta**," or the four basic consumer rights spelled out by Kennedy in his "Special Message on Protecting the Consumer Interest."[12] Those rights included the right to safety, the right to be informed, the right to choose, and the right to be heard.

The **right to safety** is concerned with the fact that many products (insecticides, foods, drugs, automobiles, appliances) are dangerous. The **right to be informed** is intimately related to the marketing and advertising function. Here the consumer's right is to know what a product really is, how it is to be used, and what cautions must be exercised in using it. This right includes the whole array of marketing: advertising, warranties, labelling, and packaging. The **right to choose**, although perhaps not as great a concern today as the first two rights, refers to the assurance that competition is working effectively. The fourth right, the **right to be heard**, was proposed because of the belief of many consumers that they could not effectively communicate to business their desires and, especially, their grievances.[13]

Although these four basic rights do not embody all the responsibilities that business owes to consumer stakeholders, they do capture the fundamentals of business's social responsibilities to consumers. Consumers today want "fair value" for money spent, a product that will meet "reasonable" expectations, full disclosure of the product's (or service's) specifications, a product/service that has been truthfully advertised, and a product that is safe and has been subjected to appropriate product safety testing. Consumers also expect that if a product is too dangerous it will be removed from the market or some other appropriate action will be taken.

For decades, there have been outcries that business has failed in these responsibilities to consumers, leaving them often neglected or mistreated.[14] The roots of consumer activism date back to 1906, when Upton Sinclair published *The Jungle*, his famous exposé of unsanitary conditions in the U.S. meat-packing industry.[15] The contemporary wave of consumer activism, however, started to build in the late 1950s, took form in the 1960s, matured in the 1970s, and continues even today, although in a different form. The following definition of **consumerism** captures the essential nature of the consumer movement:

> *Consumerism is a social movement seeking to augment the rights and*
> *powers of buyers in relation to sellers.*[16]

Henry Assael elaborates by saying that consumerism is a "set of activities of independent consumer organizations and consumer activists designed to protect the consumer. Consumerism is concerned primarily with ensuring that the consumer's rights in the process of exchange are protected." He also clarifies that it is somewhat misleading to use the term *consumer movement* unless we understand it to mean the conglomeration of the efforts of many groups rather than the efforts of any single unified organization of consumers.[17]

Although the consumer movement is often said to have begun with the publication of Ralph Nader's criticism of General Motors in *Unsafe at Any Speed*,[18] the impetus for the movement was actually a complex combination of circumstances. With respect to consumerism, Philip Kotler asserted:

> *The phenomenon was not due to any single cause. Consumerism was reborn because all of the conditions that normally combine to produce a successful social movement were present. These conditions are structural conduciveness, structural strains, growth of a generalized belief, precipitating factors, mobilization for action, and social control.*[19]

Ralph Nader's Consumerism

We cannot overstate the contribution that Ralph Nader made to the birth, growth, and nurturance of the consumer movement in North America. It is now about 40 years since Nader arrived on the scene, but he is still the acknowledged father of the consumer movement. Figure 11–1 summarizes some interesting information on Nader.

Consumer complaints did not disappear with the advent of Ralph Nader's activism. On the contrary: They intensified. Someone once said that Nader made consumer complaints respectable. Indeed, consumer complaints about business proliferated. It is impossible to catalogue them all, but Figure 11–2 lists examples of the major problems consumers worry about in terms of business's products and services. Nader and the consumer movement were the impetus for consumer legislation being passed

FIGURE 11–1

Ralph Nader: Father of the Consumer Movement

In 1965, Ralph Nader published his auto safety exposé, *Unsafe at Any Speed*. If any book ever created a "movement," this one did—the consumer movement. His book not only gave rise to auto safety regulations and devices (safety belts, padded dashboards, stronger door latches, head restraints, air bags, and so on) but also created a new era—that of the consumer. Nader, personally, was thrust into national prominence.

Unsafe at Any Speed criticized the auto industry generally and General Motors specifically. Nader objected to the safety of the GM Corvair in particular. GM could not figure out what motivated Nader, so in 1966 it hired a couple of detectives to trail and discredit him. Later, GM apologized to Nader at a congressional hearing and paid him US$480 000 for invasion of his privacy.

Nader put his money to work and built an enormous and far-reaching consumer protection empire. His legions of zealous activists became known as "Nader's Raiders." Today, Nader-operated nonprofit groups include the Public Interest Research Group, Center for Study of Responsive Law, and Public Citizen. He initiated public interest research groups (PIRGs) in over 26 U.S. states, and he inspired numerous public action groups.

Source: UPI, "Raiders Gather to Honor Nader 20 Years After Car Safety Exposé," *The Atlanta Constitution* (November 21, 1985).

FIGURE 11-2

Examples of Consumer Problems with Business

- The high prices of many products
- The poor quality of many products
- The failure of many companies to live up to claims made in their advertising
- The poor quality of after-sales service
- Too many products breaking or going wrong after you bring them home
- Misleading packaging or labelling
- The feeling that it is a waste of time to complain about consumer problems because nothing substantial will be achieved
- Inadequate guarantees and warranties
- Failure of companies to handle complaints properly
- Too many products that are dangerous
- The absence of reliable information about various products and services
- Not knowing what to do if something is wrong with a product you have bought

---

in the 1970s in both the U.S. and Canada. In recent years Nader continued to voice opinions on a variety of consumer-oriented concerns.

Consumerism in the Twenty-First Century

Many groups make up the loose confederation known as the consumer movement. For example, the Consumers Council of Canada is an independent, not-for-profit organization designed to provide a voice for consumer concerns. Its members work with the federal and provincial governments, industry, and consumers in order to help manage current consumer issues. The Consumers' Association of Canada (CAC), established in 1947, is similarly aimed at ensuring that consumers have a role in government and industry decisions that substantially affect the public. This organization also offers information and advice to consumers on marketplace rights and responsibilities. The CAC has successfully represented consumers in government decisions resulting in mandatory seat belts, safety standards for children's car seats, a voluntary code for advertising directed at children, a hazardous products symbol program, and a ban on DDT and other hazardous pesticides.

Although organized groups are not being recognized as effective lobbyists, the grassroots activism of consumers has never been stronger. In England, a relatively small group of disgruntled consumers brought the country to a halt by protesting the price of gas. They set up blockades that emptied roads, closed schools, and caused panic buying in supermarkets. The Internet has made it easier for consumer groups to respond to issues more quickly and more forcefully. It makes it possible to not only inform consumers of concerns that have arisen but also to rally the troops to take action. This is of special concern for global companies whose interests are far-flung. According to Cordelia Brabbs of *Marketing* magazine, "Global companies find themselves under the watchful eye of their customers. If they fail to behave impeccably at all times, they risk finding their misdemeanors broadcast on a high-speed information network."[20]

Before we consider more closely the corporate response to the consumer movement and the consumer stakeholder, it is fruitful to look in more detail at some of the issues that have become prominent in the business/consumer relationship and the role that the major federal regulatory bodies have assumed in addressing these issues. Broadly, we may classify the major kinds of issues into two groups: **product information** and the product itself. As stated earlier, in this chapter we focus on product information issues such as advertising, warranties, packaging, and labelling. The next chapter will focus on the product itself. Throughout our discussion of products, the reader should keep in mind that we are referring to services also.

Product Information Issues

Why have questions been raised about business's social and ethical responsibilities in the area of product information? Most consumers know the answer. Companies understandably want to portray their products in the most flattering light. However, efforts to paint a positive portrait of a product can easily cross the line into misinformation regarding the product's attributes. Consumers Union (CU), an independent, nonprofit testing and information organization, exists to protect consumer's interests. They conduct independent tests of products and report their findings in their print and online editions of *Consumer Reports*.[21] "Selling It" is a segment of *Consumer Reports* that is designed to "memorialize the excesses in the world of marketing." The following are but a few of the items recently reported:

- Blue Crab Bay's "Crab Cake Kit" has a logo that proudly proclaims "tastes and traditions of the Chesapeake." The label encourages customers to "treat yourself to this Chesapeake Bay delicacy." Under the listing of ingredients, there is an asterisk after the ingredient "handpicked white crabmeat." An alert consumer who goes to the asterisk will find the following disclaimer: "Crabmeat is a product of Thailand."[22]
- The package label says "Havarti Spread" in large red letters. Under the large title, in much smaller print, the product is said to be "pasteurized process cheese spread havarti-type flavor." The customer must go to the back label to learn that the cheese in the product is not havarti—it's cheddar.[23]
- The front of the package for Philips 85 Watt Recessed Flood Lights says that the product "replaces 100 Watt Indoor Flood." However, an asterisk leads to the following note: "Provides 23% less output than the 100 watt bulb it replaces." Using that line of reasoning, *Consumer Reports* wondered, "Why couldn't a 60 watt bulb replace a 200 watt bulb?"[24]

In addition to *Consumer Reports*, there are a host of Canadian watchdog organizations whose job includes assessing the validity of product information claims. For example, in 2003, the Canadian Food Inspection Agency launched an investigation into nutritional supplements such as power drinks, energy bars, and weight-loss preparations. A report by federal inspectors questioned the safety of energy bars and power drinks, saying they contain ingredients not stated on the label and consequently those products could jeopardize the health of people who are allergic to certain ingredients.

Search the web WWW

The Better Business Bureau (BBB) maintains a Web site that provides useful information for both business and individual consumers (**http://www.bbb.org**). This site links the user to specific BBB sites in both Canada and the U.S. Funded by member businesses, the purpose of the BBB is to "promote and foster the highest ethical relationship between businesses and the public." To further that goal, the BBB's Web site provides a variety of helpful resources, such as business and consumer alerts, consumer buying guidelines, and business publications. Web site visitors can file complaints online, obtain reports on businesses or charities, or locate the BBB serving their local communities. Although the BBB is best known for its work as a watchdog organization, it also acknowledges organizations that exemplify the best in marketplace ethics. Information about past and present BBB Torch Award winners is available on the BBB Web site.

The report also asserts that those products make health and performance claims that can't be substantiated.[25]

These cases are actual examples of the questionable use of product information. It is not clear whether the firms that created the aforementioned communications were intending to deceive, but one might reasonably conclude that some effort to mislead might have been present. Whether the motive was there or not, business has a legal responsibility, and an ethical responsibility, to fairly and accurately provide information on its products or services.

In Canada, the Competition Act, enforced by the Competition Bureau, is intended to prohibit false or misleading advertising. Any company that employs false or misleading advertising can face fines or be punished under the act. Of course, what constitutes misleading advertising is not always easily identifiable, and consumers consequently need to remain vigilant in their attention to product or service promotions.

The primary issue with product or service information falls in the realm of advertising. Other information-related areas include warranties or guarantees, packaging, labelling, instructions for use, and the sales techniques used by direct sellers.

Advertising Issues

The debate over the role of advertising in society has been going on for decades. Most observers have concentrated on the economic function of advertising in our market system, but opinions are diverse as to whether advertising is beneficial or detrimental as a business function. Critics charge that it is a wasteful and inefficient tool of business and that our current standard of living would be even higher if we could be freed from the negative influence of advertising. These critics argue that advertising raises the prices of products and services because it is an unnecessary business cost whose main effect is to circulate superfluous information that could better and more cheaply be provided on product information labels or by salespeople in stores. The result is that significant amounts of money are spent that produce no net consumer benefit.[26] In response, others have claimed that advertising is a beneficial component of the market system and that the increases in the standard of living and consumer satisfaction may be attributed to it. They argue that, in general, advertising is an efficient means of distributing information because there is such an enormous and ever-changing array of products about which consumers need to know. Advertising is an effective and relatively inexpensive way to inform consumers of new and improved products.[27]

It has been argued that even uninformative advertising still tells consumers a lot. Advertising heavily, even if vaguely, helps attract shoppers to retail stores through a kind of they-must-be-doing-something-right logic. The increased traffic then enables the retailer to offer a wider selection of goods, raising the incentive to invest in cost-reduction technologies such as computerized inventory, modern warehouses, and quantity discounts, thus further lowering marginal costs. The advertising can promote efficiency, even if it provides no hard information, by signalling to consumers where the big-company, low-price, high-variety stores are. Economists have argued that retail

Ethics In Practice

Where Are My Slippers?

For the past six months I have been working as a telesales accounts manager for a manufacturer of bedroom slippers. The firm had recently opened the telesales department, on a trial basis, to reach smaller retailers whose sales volumes were not large enough to attract the attention of the regional field representatives. Traditionally, the busiest time for the firm is the period from September to December, when retailers are ordering the inventories they want to have on hand for the holiday shopping season. Last year, the number of orders coming in was unexpectedly heavy and the lead-time needed to ship the orders was nearly a month. Unless the order was placed by the end of November, it was unlikely that the customer would have the merchandise on its shelves by the holidays.

However, the department manager encouraged us to take the late orders and promise delivery by December, even though we knew that the merchandise wouldn't be delivered until early January. Most likely, the retailers wouldn't have wanted the merchandise if they had known the actual delivery date. Our manager's reasoning for this practice was that we needed to boost our department's sales revenue to ensure that upper management saw our department as a success at the end of the trial period. In other words, our jobs could be on the line. Also, each order that we may have lost meant a smaller commission cheque.

1. How would you characterize the practice our firm engaged in?

2. Were the jobs of all the people associated with the telesales department more important than ethical principles?

3. Should I have followed my manager's orders and gone along with what I thought was a deceptive marketing practice? Is the practice all that bad if there is some chance we could deliver on time?

Contributed by David Alan Ostendorff

juggernauts such as Wal-Mart and Home Depot have taken advantage of this phenomenon. Viewed in this way, advertising is seen as a net plus for society because it tends to lower prices and increase variety.[28]

The debate over whether advertising is a productive or wasteful business practice will undoubtedly continue. As a practical matter, however, advertising has become the lifeblood of the free-enterprise system. It stimulates competition and makes available information that consumers can use in comparison buying. It also provides competitors with information with which to respond in a competitive way and contains a mechanism for immediate feedback in the form of sales response. So, despite its criticisms, advertising does provide social and economic benefits to consumers.

With the thousands of products and their increasing complexity, the consumer today has a real need for information that is clear, accurate, and adequate. **Clear information** is that which is direct and straightforward and on which neither deception nor manipulation relies. **Accurate information** communicates truths, not half-truths. It avoids gross exaggeration and innuendo. **Adequate information** provides potential purchasers with enough information to make the best choice among the options available.[29]

Whereas providing information is one legitimate purpose of advertising in our society, another legitimate purpose is persuasion. Most consumers today expect that business advertises for the purpose of persuading them to buy their products or services, and they accept this as a part of the commercial system. Indeed, many people enjoy companies' attempts to come up with yet another interesting way to sell their products. It is commonplace for people to talk with one another about the latest interesting or clever advertisement they have seen. Thus, awards for outstanding or interesting advertisements have appeared on the scene. Awards for bad advertisements have become popular also.

Ethical issues in advertising usually arise as companies attempt to inform and persuade consumer stakeholders. The frequently heard phrase "the seamy side of advertising" alludes to the economic and social costs that derive from advertising abuses, such as those mentioned earlier in the chapter, and of which the reader is probably able to supply ample personal examples.

Advertising Abuses   William Shaw and Vincent Barry have identified four types of advertising abuses in which ethical issues reside. These include situations in which advertisers are ambiguous, conceal facts, exaggerate, or employ psychological appeals.[30] These four types cover most of the general criticisms levelled at advertising.

Ambiguous Advertising.   One of the more gentle ways that companies deceive is through **ambiguous advertising,** in which something about the product or service is not made clear because it is stated in a way that may mean several different things.

There are several ways in which an ad can be made ambiguous. One way is to make a statement that leaves to the viewer the opportunity to infer the message by using **weasel words.** These are words that are inherently vague and for which the company could always claim it was not misleading the consumer. An example of a weasel word is "help." Once an advertiser uses the qualifier "help," almost anything could follow, and the company could claim that it was not intending to deceive. We see ads that claim to "help us keep young," "help prevent cavities," or "help keep our houses germ-free." Think how many times you have seen expressions in advertising such as "helps stop," "helps prevent," "helps fight," "helps you feel," "helps you look," or "helps you become."[31] Other weasel words include "like," "virtually," and "up to" (e.g., stops pain "up to" eight hours). The use of such words makes ads clearly ambiguous. Other vague terms that are ambiguous include "big" savings, "low" prices, "mild" cigarettes, and "sporty" cars.

Another way to make an ad ambiguous is through use of legalese, or other excessively complex and ambiguous terminology. In "Selling It," *Consumer Reports* provides the following paragraph that was included in a department store's advertising:

> *Items indicated on sale or referencing a comparative former or future price represent reductions from former or future offering prices (with or without actual sales) at Kohl's or at a competitor of the item or of comparable merchandise. Intermediate markdowns may have been taken. Clearance merchandise is excluded from entire stock categories herein.*[32]

Concealed Facts.   A type of advertising abuse called **concealed facts** refers to the practice of not telling the whole truth or deliberately not communicating information the consumer ought to have access to in making an informed choice. Another way of stating this is to say "a fact is concealed when its availability would probably make the desire, purchase, or use of the product less likely than its absence."[33] This is a difficult area, for few would argue that an advertiser is obligated to tell "everything," even if that were humanly possible. For example, a pain reliever company might claim the effectiveness of its product in superlative terms without stating that there are dozens of other products on the market that are just as effective. Or, an insurance company might promote all the forms of protection that a given policy would provide without enumerating all the situations for which the policy does not provide coverage.

Few of us honestly expect business to inform us of all the facts in all situations. As consumers, it is up to us to be informed about factors such as competitors' products, prices, and so on. Ethical issues arise when a firm, through its advertisements, presents facts in such a selective way that a false belief is created. Of course, judgment is required in determining which ads have and have not created false beliefs. This makes the entire realm of deceptive advertising a challenge. In a humorous vein, a burrito restaurant in a college town ran a newspaper ad with "FREE BEER" in large block letters; underneath in small letters were the words "will not be served." No one accused this company of unlawful deception; however, not all instances of concealed facts are considered benign.

In 2002, an individual from British Columbia filed a class action lawsuit against Shell Canada. The suit alleged that Shell didn't do enough to notify consumers about a problem with its gasoline. Shell subsequently admitted that an additive in its gas was responsible for causing damage to fuel gauges or pumps in certain cars. The lawsuit also claimed that Shell continued to sell the product even though it was aware of the problem. A Shell representative issued a news release that offered a "sincere apology for any inconvenience this problem may have caused." Shell also had discretely compensated consumers for months by offering Air Miles or free gas. In response to Shell's behaviour, a representative of the Automobile Protection Association, a consumer advocacy group, commented: "It's a longstanding principle that when you put out something that's defective, you put the word out. It would appear the company sort of ducked when they had a decision to make."[34]

The airline travel industry has also been forced to reconsider its treatment of consumers with regard to misleading information. In a 2003 report responding to air traveller concerns, the Air Travel Complaints Commissioner stated that commercial airline passengers have the right to know the true cost of an airplane ticket. In a letter to the Transport Minister, the commissioner outlined a series of recommendations that address air travel consumers, including the need to avoid misleading advertising. According to the commissioner, "Some carriers have been advertising fares each way when actual tickets can only be purchased on a round-trip basis. They show the equivalent of half the round-trip, thus leading customers to believe they can actually get a cheap one-way fare when they cannot." Second, the commissioner emphasized the need to prominently display the limits of liability. The commissioner noted that limits of liability with respect to baggage used to be printed on the ticket, but this was discontinued with the newer electronic tickets.[35]

Another recent concern has been the way in which some search engines incorporate advertising into their Web sites. Commercial Alert filed a formal complaint with the U.S. Federal Trade Commission, naming Alta Vista, AOL Time Warner, Direct Hit Technologies, iWon Inc., LookSmart Ltd., Microsoft Corporation, and Terra Lycos S.A. The complaint addressed two forms of Web advertising in search engines: paid placement and paid inclusion. With paid placement, ads are outside the editorial content in another box or a sidebar. With paid inclusion, advertising is within the actual search results. Commercial Alert charged that the practice of allowing companies to pay to have their products and services listed "high" is not disclosed to the consumer by these companies. In contrast, Google clearly labels its paid placements as "sponsored links" (and has no paid placements); therefore, Google was not included in the complaint.

Exaggerated Claims. Companies can also mislead consumers by exaggerating the benefits of their products and services. **Exaggerated claims** are claims that simply cannot be substantiated by any kind of evidence. An example of this would be a claim that a pain reliever is "50 percent stronger than aspirin" or "superior to any other on the market."

One kind of exaggeration is known as **puffery**, a euphemism for hyperbole or exaggeration that usually refers to the use of general superlatives. Is Budweiser really the "King of Beers"? Is Wheaties the "Breakfast of Champions"? Normally, a claim of general superiority fits squarely into puffery and is allowable. However, companies walk a fine line when engaging in puffery. They need to be certain no direct comparison is being made. According to attorney D. Reed Freedman, "... it is no longer enough to take comfort in making the same kinds of claims that have been made in an industry for some time. Those (marketers) making aggressive claims need to consider ways a reasonable consumer will interpret those claims, and marketers need to be able to prove every interpretation that is reasonable."[36]

Sears Canada engaged in a form of puffery by making exaggerated claims regarding its "sale" prices. In 2003, the Competition Bureau ruled that Sears Canada practised "deceptive marketing" in 1999 by advertising false sale prices on five lines of automobile tires. The bureau's commissioner said Sears intentionally deceived consumers by pretending to offer them special prices on major lines of all-season tires, while having little intention of selling substantial quantities of the tires at the regular prices.[37]

Most people are not too put off by puffery, because the claims are so general and so frequent that any consumer would know that the firm is exaggerating and simply doing what many do by claiming their product is the best. It has been argued, however, that such exaggerated product claims (1) induce people to buy things that do them no good, (2) result in loss of advertising efficiency as companies are forced to match puffery with puffery, (3) drive out good advertising, and (4) generally result in consumers losing faith in the system because they get so used to companies making claims that exceed their products' capabilities.[38]

Psychological Appeals. In advertising, **psychological appeals** are those designed to persuade on the basis of human emotions and emotional needs rather than reason. There is perhaps as much reason to be concerned about ethics in this category as in any other category. One reason is that the products can seldom deliver what the ads promise (i.e., power, prestige, masculinity, femininity, approval, acceptance, and other such psychological satisfactions).[39] Another reason is that psychological appeals can stir emotions in a way that is manipulative and appears designed to take advantage of difficult situations.

After the tragic events of September 11, 2001, some companies with regular print contracts put messages of condolence where their ads would have run. When U.S. President Bush and New York Mayor Rudy Giuliani urged Americans to get back to work and to life as normal, businesses used the opportunity to suggest to customers that buying their product or using their service was the patriotic thing to do. A plastic surgery practice announced, "In keeping with the spirit of President Bush's message to return to business, we are continuing our monthly seminars." Former U.S. Labor Secretary, Robert Reich, called this practice "market patriotism" and said it was "a strange kind of sacrifice: Continue the binge we've been on for years."[40]

After September 11, many advertising campaigns were reworked with psychological appeals that sounded a patriotic theme. General Motors adopted "Keep America Rolling" as its new slogan for selling cars. Flags were emblazoned across the chests of Ralph Lauren models and in department store displays. Many questioned the appropriateness of using patriotism to sell products. "It's just gross to sell your products on the graves of these victims and their families," said Bob Garfield of *Advertising Age*.

"[These are] heinous marketing programs built around the nation's emotions in this tragedy."[41] Opinions about the appropriateness of such ads will always vary, but one thing is clear: Advertisers walk a fine line when using psychological appeals, particularly at a time of tragedy.

Specific Controversial Advertising Issues We have considered four major kinds of deceptive advertising—ambiguous advertising, concealed facts, exaggerated claims, and psychological appeals. There are many other variations on these themes, but these are sufficient to make our point. Later in this chapter we will discuss government attempts to keep advertising honest. But even there we will see that the whole issue of what constitutes deceptive advertising is an evolving and amorphous concept, particularly when it comes to the task of proving deception and recommending appropriate remedial action. This is why the role of business responsibility is so crucial as business sincerely attempts to deal with its consumer stakeholders in a fair and honest manner.

Let us now consider seven specific advertising issues that have become particularly controversial in recent years: comparative advertising, exploitive advertising, advertising to children, advertising of alcoholic beverages, cigarette advertising, health and environmental claims, and ad creep.

Comparative Advertising. One advertising technique that has become controversial and threatens to affect advertising negatively, in general, is **comparative advertising**. This refers to the practice of directly comparing a firm's product with the product of a competitor. Some examples are AT&T long-distance service versus Bell or Sprint, Coke versus Pepsi, Whopper versus Big Mac, Sprite versus 7-Up, and Avis versus Hertz. A recent example is the fierce battle raging between Pizza Hut and Papa John's as they attack and counterattack each other. When Pizza Hut ran an ad daring the customer to find a better pizza, Papa John's ran taste tests. When Papa John's ran ads claiming to have the freshest sauce, Pizza Hut ran a full-page ad describing Papa John's sauce as cooked, concentrated, and canned and extolling the popularity of its own pan pizza. When Pizza Hut sent its employees punching bags with a Papa John's logo, Papa John's ran TV commercials ridiculing the move. In a particularly stunning move, Papa John's brought out Frank Carney, one of the founders of Pizza Hut but a current owner of 53 Papa John's franchises, to declare he found a better pizza at Papa John's.[42]

At one time, the idea of naming your competitor or competitor's product in an ad was taboo in North America. For years, the television networks did not allow it, so companies had to be content with referring to their competition as "the other leading brand" or "Brand X." In about 1972, the U.S. Federal Trade Commission began to accept the direct comparison approach, because it thought this approach would provide more and better information to the consumer. The networks cooperated by lifting their ban. Thus, the United States entered the new era of comparative advertising and Canada soon followed suit. Due to the supportive attitude of the European Union, companies in Western Europe have also been warming to the practice.[43]

Whether out of pride or general business interest, more and more companies are fighting back when they think the competition has gone too far. Companies may take their adversaries to court, before the Competition Bureau, or before voluntary associations, such as the Council of Better Business Bureaus, that attempt to resolve these kinds of disputes.

It is unclear what the future of comparative advertising will be. However, it has become one of a few controversial advertising issues that have the potential for more detrimental effects. The pizza wars sparked a three-year legal battle and ran up lawyers' fees in the millions. In 2001, it finally ended up in the U.S. Supreme Court where the Pizza Hut petition was denied and Papa John's was allowed to continue its "better ingredients, better pizza" slogan. Along the way, customers of both chains learned some unappetizing truths about how the pizzas are made.[44] Managers should carefully examine any practice that is likely to evoke consumer and competitor criticism to determine if it is a legitimate practice that should be used in the future.

Bruce Buchanan suggests that there are several questions that should be asked by both those who are victims of comparative ads and those who are contemplating using them. For example, were consumers actually asked to compare one brand with another? Was the sample of consumers representative of product users? Could the consumers in the study really discriminate between the products being compared?[45] Questions such as these are essential if companies are to develop sound research methods on which to base comparative ads. To do otherwise is to invite criticism from the public and competitors alike.

Exploitive Advertising. Attracting consumer attention has always been a challenge for advertisers. Consequently, many advertisers, for years, have resorted to a variety of controversial methods to ensure that their ads do not go unnoticed. The use of provocative or "shock" advertising appears to have risen dramatically in recent years. As John Heinzl, marketing reporter for *The Globe and Mail*, commented:

> *There's a lot of noise out there. It is getting harder and harder to stand out. Everywhere you look, there's an ad—on the movie screen, in the washroom of a bar, on a banana, being pulled around downtown on flatbed trucks, on private cars and public buses ... The challenge for advertisers is: how do you stand out? For many, the answer is you shock people, and in some cases you upset them.*[46]

While the tendency to "shock" may be on the rise, the notion of employing controversial or even offensive images in advertisements has been around for many years. Benetton, the garment retailer, became famous for its placement of controversial advertisements, running ads that have employed such themes as AIDS, violence, terrorism, and death-row inmates. While Benetton has claimed their ads feature social issues, critics view these ads as blatantly exploitive and generated solely for the purpose of attracting attention to the Benetton name. Calvin Klein's continual efforts to remain at the leading edge of the youth trend in advertising typically resulted in provocative images in its advertising campaigns. While the company no longer appears to arouse much controversy, in a 1995 campaign for Calvin Klein Jeans, the images of pubescent models in provocative poses triggered much debate regarding whether these advertisements had crossed the line between fashion and pornography.[47]

Does "shock" advertising really shock us anymore? The continued use of exploitive or provocative images in advertising by companies like Calvin Klein and Benetton no longer seems to raise the ire of the public. In fact, sexual references and innuendos in North American advertising have become commonplace, and consumers arguably "... have become more accustomed to promiscuity in the media, largely because they've become deadened to it," says consumer behaviour professor Bruce Stern. "We're moving into an arena that we are becoming numb to things that would have offended us a few years ago."[48] As one observer recently commented:

> *Advertising is a mirror. In a culture where extreme snarkiness, even crudeness, has become a dominant tone (Eminem, Maxim, Tom Green,*

the Farrelly Brothers), it's no surprise that admakers listen, and reflect what they hear. Like it or not, they wouldn't be doing their jobs if they didn't.[49]

Many observers have suggested that very little offends us anymore as a society. One can't help but wonder how advertisers can be held to some kind of ethical yardstick in the images they present to us, when our society offers little in the way of a measure for judging their ethics.

Advertising to Children. A hotly debated issue over the past several decades has been advertising to children, specifically on television. A typical weekday afternoon or Saturday morning in North America finds millions of kids sprawled on the floor, glued to the TV. It is estimated that children aged six to eleven watch an average of 27 hours of TV a week, or a total of 1400 hours a year. Preschoolers watch more.[50] One study estimated that, on average, children are exposed to about 20 000 commercials per year, mostly for toys, cereals, candies, and fast-food restaurants. The report goes on to say that children under eight years old have great difficulty in differentiating between commercials and programs.[51]

Television is one of the most powerful media influences in children's lives. According to a recent survey, almost 80 percent of Canadian kids watch at least one hour of TV each day.[52] Children are the consumers of the future, and so companies are eager to get their foot in the door and develop some brand loyalty. This was taken to a new level when merchandisers began to instill brand loyalty in the adults children would eventually become. "Cool Shopping Barbie" has her own personal toy MasterCard, with a cash register that has the MasterCard logo and a terminal through which Barbie can swipe her card to make a purchase. According to William F. Keenan of Creative Solutions, an advertising and marketing agency, "One of the smartest places to plant marketing seeds in the consumer consciousness is with kids."[53]

Canadian broadcasters are required to adhere to the Broadcast Code for Advertising to Children published by the Canadian Association of Broadcasters together with Advertising Standards Canada. The Broadcast Code is administered by the Canadian Advertising Foundation (CAF) and was created by advertisers and broadcasters in 1971. This code acts as a guide to advertisers in the development of commercials that recognize the special characteristics of children. However, given the nature and amount of television advertising aimed at children, one questions the effectiveness of any rules that have attempted to regulate such activities.

According to a number of sources, the bulk of food advertising on children's TV shows is for fast foods, soft drinks, candy, and pre-sweetened cereals, while commercials for healthy food make up only 4 percent of those shown.[54] Much of the $3 billion in advertising spent annually by the fast-food industry is directed at children. In fact, fast-food restaurants offer attractions such as playgrounds, contests, free toys, and other merchandise related to movies and TV shows. In addition, the Internet has become a new way for firms to advertise to children. More than two-thirds of the Internet sites directed at children and teens rely on advertising for their revenue. Banner ads were not successful in reaching children, and so these Internet sites have employed games, e-mail, and wireless technology in creative ways. For example, Nabisco's Candystand.com boasts a very popular golf game with Lifesaver holes.[55]

The cross-promotion trend has employed familiar children's TV faces and used them to sell products to children. For example, in 1999, PBS licensed *Teletubbies* merchandise to Burger King and McDonald's. What are the consequences of this aggressive marketing campaign directed at children? According to some observers, children have been enticed to adopt an unhealthy lifestyle that has resulted in a generation of overweight children.[56]

The Media Awareness Network, founded in 1996, is a Canadian-based nonprofit organization that offers wonderful insights, advice, and guidance regarding ethical issues and the media. Working in partnership with Canadian and international organizations, MNET promotes media and Internet education by producing online programs and resources, and speaking to audiences across Canada and around the world. Among other issues, MNET discusses the ethics of marketing toys to children. They note the questionable but common industry practice of marketing toys to young children that are based on restricted movies and mature-rated video games. For example, toy action figures aimed at kids four years old and up invite them to "join in the blood bath," and are based on M-rated Nintendo games (for ages 17 and up). Similarly, a company marketing World Wrestling Federation action figures to children four years old and up encourages them to use their play sets to "bash and dump opponents senseless with an array of street fighting accessories."[57]

In addition to the controversial marketing of violence in toys, MNET also notes the use of marketing ploys to seduce kids to spend exorbitant sums on "fad toys." While in days long gone, children might have collected such things as marbles, stamps, or coins, much has changed. Today, toy "collectibles" are a huge industry. Starting with the Cabbage Patch doll craze of the 1980s, marketers have attempted to create a cult-like status around their toys—from Crazy Bones, to Beanie Babies, to Barbies, to Pokémon cards, to Bay Blades, to Mighty Beanz, and so on. The template is often the same: create a variety of characters and then launch a marketing campaign that entices the child to "collect 'em all!" This was the simple marketing strategy behind Pokémon, which involved over 100 cheaply made and overpriced figures.[58] This manipulative strategy that seduces children into creating a buying frenzy has proven its effectiveness.

Advertising Standards Canada (ASC) is the not-for-profit industry body that aims to maintain community confidence in advertising by encouraging the integrity of advertising through industry self-regulation. The Standards Division of the ASC administers the industry's central self-regulatory code, the *Canadian Code of Advertising Standards*, and it handles complaints from consumers and special interest groups regarding advertising. The Broadcast Code for Advertising to Children is intended to enhance the general principles for ethical advertising as outlined in the Canadian Code of Advertising Standards. Both codes are supplementary to all federal and provincial laws and regulations governing advertising, and generated by such bodies as the Canadian Radio-television and Telecommunications Commission (CRTC), the Department of Consumer and Corporate Affairs, and Health and Welfare Canada.

The aim of the Canadian Code of Advertising Standards is to serve as a guide to those creating commercial messages and to ensure that such advertisers recognize the special characteristics of the audience.[59] The function of the guidelines is to delineate those areas that need particular attention to help avoid deceptive advertising messages to children. Figure 11–3 summarizes the basic principles from those guidelines.

Advertising of Alcoholic Beverages. Special issues about advertising to adults also exist. One that has become quite controversial in recent years is advertising of alcoholic beverages on television. In 1996, Seagram & Sons broke a 48-year voluntary ban on advertising hard liquor on television. The company argued that a standard serving of hard liquor contained the same amount of alcohol as beer or wine, and advertising is allowed for those products.[60] Although networks and cable TV moved quickly to ban the ads, the Seagram decision created a groundswell for change in all possible directions. Beer and wine sellers tried to distance themselves from the

FIGURE 11-3

Principles of Advertising to Children

A number of basic principles underlie the Broadcast Code for Advertising to Children, as presented by Advertising Standards Canada and the Canadian Association of Broadcasters:

1. Advertisers need to consider and abide by requirements regarding the avoidance of sex-role stereotyping and violence consistent with the principles of industry broadcast self-regulatory codes such as those endorsed by the Canadian Association of Broadcasters (CAB), Advertising Standards Canada (ASC), and the Canadian Broadcasting Corporation (CBC).

2. Children, especially the very young, live in a world that is part imaginary, part real, and sometimes do not distinguish clearly between the two. Children's advertising should respect and not abuse the power of the child's imagination.

3. Products and content which are inappropriate for use by children should not be advertised or promoted directly to children.

4. Advertisers should communicate information in a truthful and accurate manner and in language understandable to young children.

5. Children's advertising must not encourage or portray a range of values that are inconsistent with the moral, ethical, or legal standards of contemporary Canadian society.

6. It is recognized, of course, that it remains the primary responsibility of parents "to instruct a child in the way that he/she should go." The code and the guidelines that are issued from time to time are designed to help advertisers avoid making that task more difficult.

Source: Advertising Standards Canada, http://www.adstandards.com/en/Clearance/childrencode.asp2003.

distilled-spirits industry in the hope of returning to the old arrangement where they were free to advertise but makers of spirits were not. Advertisers positioned themselves between the two industries, hoping simply to avoid a ban.[61]

In 1996, the CRTC revised the regulations governing the advertising of alcoholic beverages in Canada. The CRTC's revised Code for Broadcast Advertising of Alcoholic Beverages contains 17 guidelines for commercial messages for alcoholic beverages, including the following:

- Advertisements should not be directed at persons under the legal drinking age.
- Advertisements should not attempt to influence nondrinkers of any age to drink or to purchase alcoholic beverages.
- Advertisements should not imply directly or indirectly that the presence or consumption of alcohol is, in any way, essential to the enjoyment of an activity or an event.
- Advertisements should not imply that social acceptance, personal success, or business or athletic achievement may be acquired through consumption of the product.
- Advertisements should not attempt to establish the product as a status symbol, a necessity for the enjoyment of life, or an escape from life's problems, or attempt to establish that consumption of the product should take precedence over other activities.
- Advertisements should not contain scenes in which any such product is consumed, or that give the impression, visually or in sound, that it is being or has been consumed.[62]

Given the above list of "don'ts" and considering the wealth of beer commercials on Canadian television, it's hard to imagine that these principles are really followed in practice. Advertising Standards Canada reviews alcohol advertisements before they are broadcast and decides if they have complied with the CRTC's code.

Of course, television is no longer the only option now available. The hard liquor industry is now increasingly turning to the Internet, using games, videos, and chat rooms to attract consumers. In 2000 and 2001, hundreds of liquor industry Web sites were opened. In one of the more elaborate sites, Absolut Vodka of Sweden allows customers to make their own films, view ads, and even peel orange rind off a bottle to reveal Absolut Mandrin.[63] Hard liquor is not the only concern. Ralph Nader's "Commercial Alert" organization has targeted Anheuser-Busch for its use of a variety of cartoon characters in its campaigns. They cite a KidCom market study that shows that the Budweiser frogs were American children's favourite ads, just as the tobacco-smoking "Joe Camel" had been their favourite ad some years ago.[64]

Cigarette Advertising. No industry has been under greater attack than the cigarette industry for its products and its marketing and advertising practices. As a *Time* magazine article concluded, cigarette makers are "under fire from all sides."[65] Two particularly important issues dominate the current debate about cigarette advertising. First, there is the general opposition to promotion of a dangerous product. The second issue concerns the ethics of the tobacco industry's advertising to young people and to less-educated consumer markets.

An example of the latter concern was when R. J. Reynolds (RJR) was publicly taken to task by several consumer groups for its Joe Camel campaign. One frequently cited study appeared in the *Journal of the American Medical Association*. In this study, it was found that more than half the children age three to six were able to match the Joe Camel logo with a photograph of a cigarette. Six-year-olds were almost as familiar with Joe Camel as they were with a Mickey Mouse logo.[66] Perhaps one of the strongest indicators of the success of the Joe Camel ad campaign was the statistic of smoking among the youth market. Since the Joe Camel mascot was introduced in 1987, Camel's share of the under-18 market soared from 0.5 to 33 percent, according to data supplied by a coalition of health groups. The market share among smokers age 18 to 24 increased from 4.4 to 7.9 percent. In 1997, the U.S. Federal Trade Commission ruled that the Joe Camel ads violated the law by targeting children under 18, and asked RJR to remove the cartoon from any venue where a child might see it. RJR cancelled the ad campaign.[67] Shortly after that, the U.S. government asked Philip Morris to retire the Marlboro man.[68]

In Canada, tobacco companies must abide by the Tobacco Act, established in 1997, which regulates the manufacture, sale, labelling, and promotion of tobacco products. Among the central regulations of the act are the following:

- Retailers must post signs that inform the public that the sale or giving of a tobacco product to a young person is prohibited by law.
- Manufacturers or retailers may not sell a tobacco product unless the package containing it displays information about the product and its emissions, and about the health hazards and health effects arising from the use of the product or from its emissions.
- Tobacco products or tobacco product-related brand elements may not be promoted, except as authorized by the Tobacco Act.

In 1998, the Tobacco Act was amended to include the eventual banning of cigarette company sponsorship promotions.[69]

Health and Environmental Claims. Always under criticism are an assortment of advertising and labelling practices that entail product claims related to health and environmental safety. One major reason that these issues have come to the forefront is the renewed enforcement activities of Health Canada and Canada's Competition

Bureau in cracking down on misleading claims. In the U.S., the Federal Trade Commission is engaged in similar pursuits. Since the health- and environmentally conscious 1990s, these issues have taken on major importance. Given consumers' desires for products that are healthy and protect the environment, it is not too surprising that these issues have gained so much attention.

Because health and environmental claims attract customers, marketers are tempted to tout claims that aren't really there. Nutrition bars have a US$1 billion yearly market that has attracted a variety of companies. However, there are concerns that such products do not live up to their claims. Consumerlab.com tested 30 nutrition bars for levels of fat, sodium, and carbohydrates, among other ingredients. According to the lab, 18 of the bars were found to underreport those things that dieters try to avoid; only 12 bars reported accurately. Seven bars contained two to three times the amount of sodium they reported; four bars contained more saturated fat. Half of the products tested contained more carbohydrates than their label indicated.[70]

Diet products are often offenders in this category. In April 2000, marketers of the Enforma System settled charges of deceptive advertising by agreeing to pay US$10 million in consumer redress. They were accused of making false claims about their products, "Fat Trapper" and "Exercise in a Bottle." The product had been promoted through infomercials that featured former baseball player Steve Garvey. The claims made included, "Lose weight without dieting," "Eat anything that you want," and "Permanently blocks fat so it can't be absorbed by your body." In addition to the payout, the final order set stipulations about the company's future activities.[71]

Typically, food labels are designed to offer the impression of healthy, nutritious food elements. While Canadian manufacturers are required to list their ingredients in order of quantity, few labels are genuinely informative with regard to the nutritional value of the product. For example, Smucker's Simply Fruit advertises "spreadable fruit," suggesting that the product is purely or largely strawberries. However, the first (and therefore largest) ingredient listed is grape juice, used as a sweetener. Similarly, Lipton's Chicken Soup is equally misleading in that the only chicken it contains is in the form of chicken fat and it's the sixth ingredient listed in the product. Multi-Grain Cheerios claims it has just a "touch of sweetness," even though it contains more sugar than it does barley, rice, or wheat. In addition, it contains seven times more sugar per serving than regular Cheerios. Health Valley Organic Wheat Crackers with Vegetables connotes a very nutritional product, with its emphasis on the boldly printed "vegetables." Yet, it contains more honey, malt, and grape juice sweeteners than it does vegetables.[72]

Among the major controversial advertising practices are companies claiming that their products and/or their product packages are environmentally friendly or safe. Consumers are concerned about the environmental effects of materials that are being used in the products and services that they buy. Regulations, set out in the Consumer Packaging and Labelling Act and the Competition Act, reflect the following fundamental principles:

- Those making environmental claims are responsible for ensuring that any claims and/or representations are accurate, and in compliance with the relevant legislation.
- Consumers are responsible, to the extent possible, for appropriately using the information made available to them in labelling and advertising, thereby enhancing their role in the marketplace.
- Environmental claims and/or representations that are ambiguous, vague, incomplete, misleading, or irrelevant, and that cannot be substantiated through credible information and/or test methods should not be used.

- Claims and/or representations should indicate whether they are related to the product or the packaging materials.[73]

In 2000, DuraLube agreed to pay US$2 million in consumer redress for what were found, among other things, to be unsubstantiated claims of being environmentally friendly. In the U.S., the Federal Trade Commission (FTC) had previously charged a half dozen other motor oil additive manufacturers, including STP and Valvoline. Along with the performance claims, the FTC found DuraLube's environmental claims regarding emission reduction and lack of chlorinated compounds to be unsubstantiated. In addition, DuraLube had claimed inaccurately that the product was tested by the U.S. Environmental Protection Agency. In addition to the US$2 million settlement, DuraLube was required to visit their distributors to notify them of the FTC order and replace all labels and packaging.[74]

Ad Creep. **Ad creep** refers to the way that advertising can increasingly be found everywhere one looks. It is generally estimated that people see about 3000 ads each day. According to Jim Twitchell, author of *Twenty Ads That Shook the World*, the problem of ad creep is only going to get worse. He believes that the average person is exposed to about 5000 ads each day, and the last time one could go an entire day without seeing an ad was probably about 1915. "That's nothing compared to what you'll see in the next 10 years," says Twitchell. "We're already putting them on the floor tiles in grocery stores, on worksheets in home economics classes, on video screens in shopping carts. Eventually, we could see ads on stoplights or in drinks with bubbles that will bring you a message from their sponsor."[75]

A variety of factors contribute to ad creep. A declining network TV audience and increased dispersion from cable and Internet outlets combine with soaring network television rates to make it difficult to blanket the population with an advertising message. Furthermore, ad creep just generates more ad creep because people become numb to messages in traditional places and so unique new venues are sought—just to get the consumer's attention.[76] An example of the lengths advertisers go to get a person's attention can be found in bathrooms. Zoom Media, a company that places advertising in club and restaurant bathrooms, had difficulty when they launched at the beginning of the 1990s because companies didn't want their products associated with toilets. However, it didn't take long for the companies to realize that toilets held targeted, and captive, audiences. The company's revenues went from US$40 000 in 1991 to over US$12 million by 2000. The company began with posters, but it has now gone high-tech with CD-Roms and audio pitches.

Ads have also gone to places that once were not considered acceptable for advertisements. School buses, textbooks, doctor's offices, and historical monuments have all been festooned with advertisements. The traditional term for advertising that is located in nontraditional places is *ambient*, but *ad creep* reflects both the way the ads have grown and the way people often feel about its creators.[77]

These seven controversial advertising methods are simply the tip of the iceberg. Issues have been raised about the marketing of pharmaceutical drugs directly to patients through magazine and television ads. These ads encourage patients to ask their doctor for the prescription drug, to the frustration of doctors everywhere. Critics also charge that product placements, a practice in which companies place their products into scenes in movies and television shows for a fee, is deceptive in that it isn't clear to the public that they're seeing an advertisement. Further on the topic of movies, audiences everywhere have bemoaned the inclusion of commercials in the preview clips as they are captive audiences, unable to change the channel. There is no end to the list of concerns about the advertising practices undertaken today. Astute businesspeople must tread carefully to make certain they don't cross the line where their customers become more angry at their practices than attracted to their products.

Warranties

With the rise of e-commerce, **warranties** have become an important issue. Companies find that warranties or guarantees are essential when marketing by mail. The internationalization of commerce that has resulted from the Internet has presented new challenges. International e-commerce has been largely unregulated, but Scott Nathan, a lawyer who specializes in e-commerce law, warns that those days are soon over. Although warranties present challenges whenever international commerce occurs, Nathan explains that the "speed 'n' ease" factor heightens the warranty problems. "Because of the lack of international law governing warranties," says Nathan, "be prepared to defend the performance of your polka dot widgets in a foreign court."[78]

Of course, if companies simply offer complete satisfaction, with no fine print, the warranty problem is not such a problem. Few companies accomplish this, but one prime example is L. L. Bean, whose guarantee says, "Our products are guaranteed to give 100 percent satisfaction in every way. Return anything purchased from us at any

---

Ethics In Practice

The "Lifetime" of a Backpack

For the past few years, I have been working at a sporting goods store that sells high-quality backpacks. One day I was working at the customer counter, ringing up sales and responding to queries. A man came in with a backpack that had obviously seen a great deal of life. It was torn and worn from years of heavy use. He gave it to me and said that he was returning it so that we could make good on the backpack's "Lifetime Guarantee." The backpack is of high quality and the well-known manufacturer prominently displays the guarantee in its advertising materials.

I explained to the customer that the "lifetime guarantee" does not mean that he can return the backpack after any amount of use. The guarantee is not for *his* lifetime but, instead, it is for the *lifetime of the backpack*. I then explained that, according to the manufacturer, the lifetime of a backpack is considered to be about four years.

The customer became irate. He said that the wording of the guarantee was purposely deceptive and that one shouldn't have to read the fine print, or visit the company's Web site, to determine what the guarantee really means. Then he threw the backpack in my face and stormed out, leaving his backpack behind. I thought he was being incredibly rude

so I followed him out to the parking lot to tell him so. We talked about the situation and I explained that the information has always been available on the Web site. He questioned why he should be expected to double-check a company's Web site before buying a product. We parted cordially.

After he left, I thought about his upset and his argument. Was the customer right? Did the wording of the guarantee deceive him? If it is a four-year warranty—why not say that? If it is deception, to what extent am I complicit? Should I warn customers about the meaning of the guarantee even if that information is likely to steer them to other products, and perhaps other stores? To whom am I most responsible?

1. Is the "lifetime guarantee" deceptive advertising?

2. Does an employee of the store have a responsibility to warn customers?

3. Does the store have a responsibility to clarify the guarantee?

4. If you were in this position, what would you do?

Contributed Anonymously

time if it proves otherwise. We will replace it, refund your purchase price or credit your credit card, as you wish. We do not want you to have anything from L. L. Bean that is not completely satisfactory."[79]

The Competition Bureau

Both the federal and provincial governments have responsibilities in dealing with marketplace issues. The federal government oversees national marketplace standards in an effort to ensure a fair, efficient, and competitive marketplace for producers, traders, and consumers. Current federal consumer statutes govern issues of product safety (except electrical equipment), competition, labelling, and weights and measures. On the other hand, the provincial government enforces provincial statutes over such issues as the conditions of sale, guarantees, and licensing. Typically, services are regulated by the provinces or, in some cases, by municipalities. Most provinces have a statute to regulate unfair business practices. Though provincial acts can vary from province to province, the nature of consumer protection is similar across the country.[80]

We have already discussed issues regarding product information. The Competition Bureau along with other government bodies such as Health Canada and Environment Canada are actively involved in these issues. It is important now to look more closely at the federal government's major instrument, the Competition Bureau, for ensuring that business lives up to its responsibilities in these areas. Actually, the Competition Bureau has broad and sweeping powers, and it delves into several other areas that we will refer to throughout the book.

Two major activities of the Competition Bureau are (1) to maintain free and fair competition in the economy and (2) to protect consumers from unfair or misleading practices. The Competition Bureau is responsible for administration and enforcement of the Competition Act, the Consumer Packaging and Labelling Act, the Textile Labelling Act, and the Precious Metals Marking Act. Its role is to promote and maintain fair competition so that Canadians can gain from lower prices, product choice, and quality services.[81]

Competition policy is aimed at creating equity in the marketplace among all the different and potentially competing interests, including consumers and producers, wholesalers and retailers, dominant players and minor players, the public interest and the private interest. In its responsibilities to enforce and administer the Competition Act, the Competition Bureau's duties include:

- Informing companies of what they can and cannot do under competition law. It also informs consumers with regard to their rights.
- Taking on an advocacy role in promoting greater competition in the business sector. For example, the Competition Bureau has been actively involved in the deregulation process of the telecommunications sector, including its numerous appearances before the CRTC to urge regulators to take the least restrictive action possible so as to minimize the level of regulation, and therefore maximize potential competition.
- Reviewing mergers prior to their occurrence in order to ensure that they do not lead to undue concentration that would limit competition.
- Seeking to rectify anticompetitive activities, including the use of suasion (warning letters, visits, interviews, etc.), enforcing compliance by obtaining injunctions, consent orders, adoption of voluntary codes, or prosecuting for violations of the Competition Act.[82]

The Competition Bureau may issue cease and desist orders against companies it believes to be engaging in unlawful practices. In the arena of possible deceptive advertising practices, the Competition Bureau monitors advertising and may ask advertisers for proof of their claims. If it decides an ad is false or misleading, it may order the advertiser to withdraw the ad or run "corrective" advertising to inform the public that the former ads were deceptive. Advertisers also may be fined for violating an order.

Over the years, the government has given the Competition Bureau enforcement responsibility in a variety of consumer-related fields. It was given broad powers out of fear that any specification of a list of prohibitions might lead business to reason that it could do anything not on the list. The Competition Bureau is part of the federal department of Industry Canada and is headed by the Commissioner of Competition. The Bureau is organized into separate branches, dealing with civil matters, criminal matters, mergers, and fair business practices. There are two coordinating branches—the Compliance and Operations Branch and the Competition Policy Branch.[83] Figure 11–4 presents an overview statement of the vision, mission, and goals of the Competition Bureau.

Self-Regulation in Advertising

Cases of deceptive or unfair advertising are handled through such government regulatory bodies as the Competition Bureau. In addition to this regulatory approach, however, self-regulation of advertising has become an important business response, primarily in the past two decades. Under the regulatory approach, advertising behav-

---

FIGURE 11–4

Role of the Competition Bureau

Vision, Mission, and Goals

The Competition Bureau (CB) enforces a variety of laws. It seeks to ensure that the nation's markets function competitively and efficiently, and are free of undue restrictions. The CB also works to enhance the smooth operation of the marketplace by eliminating acts or practices that are unfair or deceptive. In general, the CB's efforts are directed toward stopping actions that threaten consumers' opportunities to exercise informed choice. Competition policy is aimed at creating equity in the marketplace among all the different and potentially competing interests, including consumers and producers; wholesalers and retailers; dominant players and minor players; the public interest and the private interest. The Competition Bureau (Industry Canada) is responsible for enforcing and administering the Competition Act.

The basic operating assumption of the Competition Bureau is that competition is good for both business and consumers.

Fair competition:

- makes the economy work more efficiently;
- strengthens businesses' ability to adapt and compete in global markets;
- gives small and medium businesses an equitable chance to compete and participate in the economy;
- provides consumers with competitive prices, product choices and the information they need to make informed purchasing decisions; and
- balances the interests of consumers and producers, wholesalers and retailers, dominant players and minor players, the public interest and the private interest.

Source: The Competition Bureau, http://cb-bc.gc.ca/epic/internet/incb-bc.nsf/vwGeneratedInterE/ct01254e.html.

iour is controlled through various governmental rules that are backed by the use of penalties. **Self-regulation**, on the other hand, refers to the control of business conduct and performance by business itself rather than by government or by market forces.[84]

Types of Self-Regulation

Business self-regulation of advertising may take on various forms. One is **self-discipline**, where the firm itself controls its own advertising. Another is **pure self-regulation**, where the industry (one's peers) controls advertising. A third type is **co-opted self-regulation**, where the industry, of its own volition, involves nonindustry people (e.g., consumer or public representatives) in the development, application, and enforcement of norms. A fourth type is **negotiated self-regulation**, where the industry voluntarily negotiates the development, use, and enforcement of norms with some outside body (e.g., a government department or a consumer association). Finally, a fifth type is **mandated self-regulation** (which may sound like a contradiction of terms), where the industry is ordered or designated by the government to develop, use, and enforce norms, whether alone or in concert with other bodies.[85]

The most prominent instance of self-regulation in the advertising industry is the program sponsored by Advertising Standards Canada (ASC). ASC (formerly the Canadian Advertising Foundation) is an industry body committed to establishing and maintaining community confidence in advertising. ASC administers the Canadian Code of Advertising Standards, the main instrument of advertising self-regulation.

The Canadian Code of Advertising Standards, designed in 1963 and continually revised, was developed to promote the professional practice of advertising. It provides criteria for acceptable advertising and establishes the basis upon which advertising is assessed in response to consumer, trade, or special-interest group complaints. The code's provisions deal with a variety of issues related to responsible advertising practices, including:

- accuracy and clarity
- disguised advertising techniques
- price claims
- safety, advertising aimed at children and minors
- unacceptable depictions and portrayals

The code has been widely endorsed by advertisers, advertising agencies, media that exhibit advertising, and suppliers to the advertising process. Consumer complaints to Advertising Standards Canada about alleged violations of advertising standards are reviewed and adjudicated by the English national and regional Consumer Response Councils and by their counterpart in Montreal, le Conseil des normes. These autonomous bodies are composed of senior industry and public representatives and are independent from ASC.

Trade complaints regarding violations of advertising standards are separately administered under ASC's Trade Dispute Procedure, and complaints from special-interest groups are separately administered under ASC's Special Interest Group Complaint Procedure.[86]

It is useful to conclude this chapter by providing insights into how the three types of moral manager models, as introduced in Chapter 4, would view consumer stakeholders. Therefore, Figure 11–5 presents a brief statement as to the likely orientations of immoral, amoral, and moral managers to this vital stakeholder group.

FIGURE 11–5	

Three Moral Management Models and Their Orientations Toward Consumer Stakeholders

Model of Management Morality	Orientation to Consumer Stakeholders
Immoral Management	Customers are viewed as opportunities to be exploited for personal or organizational gain. Ethical standards in dealings do not prevail; indeed, an active intent to cheat, deceive, and/or mislead is present. In all marketing decisions—advertising, pricing, packaging, distribution—the customer is taken advantage of to the fullest extent.
Amoral Management	Management does not think through the ethical consequences of its decisions and actions. It simply makes decisions with profitability within the letter of the law as a guide. Management is not focused on what is fair from the perspective of the customer. The focus is on management's rights. No consideration is given to ethical implications of interactions with customers.
Moral Management	Customers are viewed as equal partners in transactions. The customer brings needs/expectations to the exchange transaction and is treated fairly. Managerial focus is on giving the customer fair value, full information, fair guarantee, and satisfaction. Consumer rights are liberally interpreted and honoured.

Summary

Among stakeholder groups, consumers rank at the top. In a consumption-driven society, business must be especially attentive to the issues that arise in its relationships with consumers. It is a paradox that consumerism arose during the very period that the business community discovered the centrality of the marketing concept to business success. The consumer's rights include the right to safety, to be informed, to choose, and to be heard. Consumers expect more than this, however, and thus the consumer movement, or consumerism, was born. Ralph Nader was the father of this movement and made consumer complaining respectable.

Product information issues compose a major area in the business/consumer stakeholder relationship. Foremost among these is advertising. Many issues have arisen because of perceived advertising abuses, such as ambiguity, concealed facts, exaggerations, and psychological appeals. Specific controversial spheres have included, but are not limited to, comparative advertising, exploitive advertising, advertising to children, advertising of alcoholic beverages, advertising of cigarettes, health and environmental claims, and ad creep. Among the major bodies regulating product information issues has been the Competition Bureau. On its own behalf, however, business has initiated a variety of forms of self-regulation.

Key Terms

accurate information (page 344)

ad creep (page 355)

adequate information (page 344)

ambiguous advertising (page 345)

clear information (page 344)

comparative advertising (page 348)

concealed facts (page 345)

consumerism (page 339)

consumer's Magna Carta (page 339)

co-opted self-regulation (page 359)

customer relationship management (CRM) (page 338)

exaggerated claims (page 346)

mandated self-regulation (page 359)

negotiated self-regulation (page 359)

product information (page 342)

psychological appeals (page 347)

puffery (page 347)

pure self-regulation (page 359)

right to be heard (page 339)

right to be informed (page 339)

right to choose (page 339)

right to safety (page 339)

self-discipline (page 359)

self-regulation (page 359)

warranties (page 356)

weasel words (page 345)

Discussion Questions

1. In addition to the basic consumer rights expressed in the consumer's Magna Carta, what other expectations do you think consumer stakeholders have of business?

2. What is your opinion of the consumerism movement? Is it "alive and well" or is it dead? Provide evidence for your observations.

3. Give an example of a major abuse of advertising from your own observations and experiences. How do you feel about this as a consumer?

4. With which of the kinds of controversial advertising issues are you most concerned? Explain.

Endnotes

1. Peter F. Drucker, *Management: Tasks, Responsibilities, Practices* (New York: Harper & Row, 1973), 61.

2. Frederick F. Reichheld, *The Loyalty Effect* (Cambridge, MA: Harvard Business School Press, 1996).

3. Russell S. Winer, "A Framework for Customer Relationship Management," *California Management Review* (Summer 2001), 89–105.

4. "The Customer Is Often Ignored," *Marketing Week* (September 27, 2001), 3.

5. Camilla Ballesteros, "Don't Talk About CRM; Do It," *Marketing Week* (September 27, 2001), 49.

6. *Ibid.*

7. Patricia Seybold, Ronni T. Marshak, and Jeffrey M. Lewis, *The Customer Revolution: How to Thrive When Customers Are in Control* (New York: Crown Publishing Group, 2001).

8. "Patricia Seybold Wants You to Surrender to Your Customers," *Across the Board* (May–June 2001), 19–20.

9. "The Customer Is King," *Chief Executive* (1998 CEO Brief Supplement), 8–9. For a comprehensive study of mass customization, see Suresh Kotha, "Mass Customization: Implementing the Emerging Paradigm for Competitive Advantage," *Strategic Management Journal* (Summer 1995), 21–42, special issue.

10. *Ibid.*

11. *Ibid.*

12. Robert J. Holloway and Robert S. Hancock, *Marketing in a Changing Environment*, 2d ed. (New York: John Wiley & Sons, 1973), 558–565.

13. *Ibid.*, 565–566.

14. Robert O. Herrmann, "Consumerism: Its Goals, Organizations, and Future," *Journal of Marketing* (October 1970), 55–60.

15. Ruth Simon, "You're Losing Your Consumer Rights," *Money* (Vol. 25, No. 3, 1996), 100–111.

16. Philip Kotler, "What Consumerism Means for Marketers," *Harvard Business Review* (May–June 1972), 48–57.

17. Henry Assael, *Consumer Behavior and Marketing Action*, 3d ed. (Boston: Kent, 1987), 667.

18. Ralph Nader, *Unsafe at Any Speed* (New York: Grossman Publishers, 1965).

19. Kotler, 50. Kotler states that these conditions were proposed by Neil J. Smelser, *Theory of Collective Behavior* (New York: The Free Press, 1963).

20. Cordelia Brabbs, "Web Fuels Consumer Activism," *Marketing* (September 21, 2000), 23.

21. *Consumer Reports*, http://www.consumerreports.org.

22. "Selling It," *Consumer Reports* (October 2001), 63.

23. *Ibid.*

24. "Selling It," *Consumer Reports* (November 2001), 67.

25. "Food Inspectors Probing Nutritional Supplements," *CBC Online* (November 17, 2003), http://www.cbc.ca.

26. William Leiss, Stephen Kline, and Sut Jhally, *Social Communication in Advertising* (Toronto: Methuen, 1986), 13.

27. *Ibid.*

28. Rob Norton, "How Uninformative Advertising Tells Consumers Quite a Bit," *Fortune* (December 26, 1994), 37.

29. William Shaw and Vincent Barry, *Moral Issues in Business*, 4th ed. (Belmont, CA: Wadsworth, 1989), 389–414.

30. *Ibid.*, 403.

31. *Ibid.*, 404.

32. "Selling It," *Consumer Reports* (October 2001), 63.

33. Shaw and Barry, 389–414.

34. "Car Owner Sues Shell for Bad Gas," http://www.cbc.ca, July 8, 2002.

35. "Air Travel Complaints Boss Cites Misleading Advertising," *CBC Online* (January 31, 2003), http://www.cbc.ca.

36. James Heckman, "Puffery Claims No Longer So Easy To Make," *Marketing News* (February 14, 2000), 6.

37. Simon Tuck, "Tribunal Hears First Allegations of 'Deceptive Marketing' by Sears," *Globe and Mail* (October 28, 2003), http://www.globeandmail.com.

38. Eli P. Cox, "Deflating the Puffer," *MSU Business Topics* (Summer 1973), 29.

39. Shaw and Barry, 406–407.

40. Ann Gerhart, "The Patriotic Pitch: Buy, America, Buy," *The Washington Post* (October 11, 2001), C1.

41. *Ibid.*

42. Dennis Berman and Robert McNatt, "Louisville's Pizza Sluggers," *Business Week* (May 4, 1998), 6.

43. Robert Gray, "Fighting Talk," *Marketing* (September 20, 2001), 26–27.

44. Jim Edwards, "Sour Dough: Pizza Hut vs. Papa John's," *Brandweek* (May 21, 2001), 26–30.

45. Bruce Buchanan, "Can You Pass the Comparative Ad Challenge?" *Harvard Business Review* (July–August 1985), 106.

46. Leslie C. Smith, "In Your Face!" Retail Council of Canada, 2003, http://www.retailcouncil.org.

47. Calvin Klein: A Case Study, 2003, http://www.media-awareness.ca/english/index.cfm.

48. Hillary Chura, "Spirited Sex," *Advertising Age* (July 9, 2001), 1.

49. Rogier van Bakel, "Do the Taste Test," (May 18, 2001), http://creative.fastchannel.com/news/01-05-18/cre-test.asp.

50. Claudia Mills, "Children's Television," *Report from the Center for Philosophy and Public Policy* (College Park, MD: University of Maryland, 1986), 11. See also David Walsh, *Selling Out America's Children* (Minneapolis: Deaconess Press, 1994).

51. Marie Winn, *The Plug-in-Drug*, 2d ed. (Middlesex: Penguin, 1985).

52. "Young Canadians in a Wired World Survey," Mnet (2001), http://www.media-awareness.ca.

53. "Barbie Gets Her First Credit Card," *Credit Card Management* (January 1998), 6–8.

54. Canadian Paediatric Society, http://www.cps.ca.

55. Ellen Neuborne, "For Kids on the Web, It's an Ad, Ad, Ad, Ad World," *Business Week* (August 13, 2001), 108–109.

56. Heart and Stroke Foundation of Canada, http://www.heartandstroke.ca.

57. Media Awareness Network, http://www.media-awareness.ca.

58. *Ibid.*

59. Advertising Standards Canada, http://www.adstandards.com.

60. Kirk Davidson, "Look for Abundance of Opposition to TV Ads," *Marketing News* (January 6, 1997), 26–28.

61. Alicia Mundy, "The Bar Will Soon Open," *Mediaweek* (January 27, 1997), 26–28.

62. CRTC, http://www.crtc.gc.ca/eng/general/rodes/alcohol.htm.

63. Hillary Chura, "Drinking in the Internet," *Advertising Age* (September 3, 2001), 16.

64. Commercial Alert, http://www.commercialalert.org.

65. Gallagher, 41. See also "Tobacco: Does It Have a Future?" *Business Week* (July 4, 1994), 24–29.

66. Eben Shapiro, "FTC Staff Recommends Ban of Joe Camel Campaign," *The Wall Street Journal* (August 11, 1993), B1.

67. Ira Teinowitz, "FTC's Camel Case Hinges on Ad's Power Over Kids," *Advertising Age* (June 2, 1997), 4, 45.

68. Judann Pollack and Ira Teinowitz, "With Joe Camel Out, Government Wants the Marlboro Man Down," *Advertising Age* (July 14, 1997), 3, 34.

69. Health Canada, http://www.hc-sc.gc.ca/hecs-sesc/tobacco/legislation/tobacco_act.html.

70. Benedict Carey, "Nutritional Analysis of Bars Reveals Discrepancies," *Los Angeles Times* (November 5, 2001), S2.

71. Federal Trade Commission, http://www.ftc.gov.

72. http://www.cbc.ca/consumers/market/files/food/labels.html.

73. Industry Canada, Competition Bureau, http://www.cb.bc.gc.ca/internet/incb-bc.nsf.vwGeneratedInterE/cp01026e.html.

74. "DuraLube, Motor-Up Settle FTC Charges," *FTC Press Release* (March 29, 2000), http://www.ftc.gov.

75. Charles Pappas, "Ad Nauseum," *Advertising Age* (July 10, 2000), 16–18.

76. Carrie McLaren, "Ad Creep," *Print* (November/December 2000), 102–107.

77. *Ibid.*

78. Amy Zuckerman, "Order in the Courts?" *World Trade* (September 2001), 26–28.

79. L. L. Bean, http://www.llbean.com.

80. http://strategis.ic.gc.ca/epic/internet/inoca-bc.nsf/vwGeneratedInterE/ca00179e.html.

81. http://cb-bc.ca/epic/internet/incb-bc.nsf/vwGenerated InternetE/home.

82. Based on Statement by Konrad von Finckenstein, Q.C. Commissioner of Competition Bureau to the "Meet the Competition Bureau," Forum Insight Conference, Toronto (May 3, 1999).

83. http://cb-bc.gc.ca/epic/internet/incb-bc.nsf/vwGenerated InterE/ct02035e.html.

84. J. F. Pickering and D. C. Cousins, *The Economic Implications of Codes of Practice* (Manchester, England: University of Manchester Institute of Science and Technology, Department of Management Sciences, 1980), 17. Also see J. J. Boddewyn, "Advertising Self-Regulation: Private Government and Agent of Public Policy," *Journal of Public Policy and Marketing* (1985), 129.

85. *Ibid.*, 135.

86. Advertising Standards Canada, http://www.adstandards.com/en/Standards/adstandards.asp#self.

Chapter 12

Consumer Stakeholders: Product and Service Issues

Chapter Objectives

After studying this chapter, you should be able to:

1 Describe and discuss the two major product issues: quality and safety.

2 Explain the role and functions of Health Canada.

3 Enumerate and discuss the reasons for the growing concern about product liability and differentiate strict liability, absolute liability, and market share liability.

4 Outline business's responses to consumer stakeholders to include consumer affairs offices, product safety offices, total quality management (TQM) programs, and Six Sigma.

Although product information is a pivotal issue between business and consumer stakeholders, product and service issues such as quality and safety occupy centre stage. The quest to improve product and service quality has been driven by the demands of a competitive marketplace and an increasingly sophisticated consumer base. With product safety, an additional driving force has been the threat of product liability lawsuits and the damage they can wreak to both the balance sheet and the reputation.

The Ford Motor Company provides a notable example of the havoc that can result from product quality and safety problems. On October 30, 2001, Ford CEO Jacques Nasser departed the post after two years in the position. His tenure had been tumultuous. Product quality problems had plagued the launches of new products, even before the problems with Firestone-brand tires hit the news in August 2000. The tire problems were eventually traced to production problems at a Bridgestone/Firestone plant, but the tire maker's accusations against Ford, coupled with the high number of Ford recalls on other vehicles, made the Ford image easier to tarnish.[1] According to J. D. Power and Associates, the company went from the best in car quality, among Detroit automakers, to the worst in just three years. Ford's profits plunged 11 percent, double the decline of the other U.S. automakers.[2] Of course, the decline was not only due to product quality and safety: Unsuccessful diversification attempts were a factor as well. However, for a company that once boasted "Quality Is Job One," the decline in the J. D. Power ranking must have been a bitter pill to swallow. The fall of 2001 was a difficult time for all car companies, but the host of problems Ford faced, beyond the falling economy, made it even more difficult for them to weather the storm. As *Newsweek* commented, "This hasn't been easy for Ford, which just 2 years ago was revered as America's best automaker."[3]

In this chapter, we will limit our discussion to product quality and safety issues. In connection with safety, we consider the product liability issue. Various related responsibilities housed within Health Canada are also discussed. Finally, we will discuss business's response to consumer stakeholders regarding the issues introduced both in Chapter 11 and in this chapter.

Two Central Issues: Quality and Safety

The two central issues we are concerned with in this chapter represent the overwhelming attention that has been given to product and service issues over the past decade: quality and safety. Of course, quality and safety are not separate concepts—safety is one aspect of quality. Its importance, however, merits separate attention.

The Issue of Quality

There are several particularly important reasons for the current obsession with product quality. First, a concern for quality has been driven by the fact that the average consumer household has experienced a rise in family income and consequently demands more. With both adults often working outside the home, consumers become more demanding of a higher lifestyle. In addition, no one has surplus time to hang around repair shops or wait at home all day for service representatives to show up. This results in a need for products to work as they should, to be durable and long lasting, and to be easy to maintain and fix. The Internet has also made it possible for customers to communicate with other customers about their satisfaction, or dissatisfaction, with a product. A *Time*/CNN survey showed that consumers were less interested in technical innovation and attractive designs than they were in the product's ability to function as promised, its durability, and its ease of maintenance and repair.[4] A survey of households by Walker Research found that quality ranked first, price ranked second, and service ranked third among a list of factors consumers felt impacted a firm's reputation and their own purchasing decisions.[5]

Closely related to rising household expectations is the global competitiveness issue. Businesses now compete in a hypercompetitive landscape in which multinational strategies have given way to global strategies, and the solutions that once worked, no longer will.[6] As firms jockey for position in these hypercompetitive markets, they vie to attract customers by increasing the value of the product or service. Value is quality divided by price: A Sears Craftsman spark-plug wrench that sells for $8.95 is expected to be of proportionally higher quality than a spark-plug wrench sold at Wal-Mart for $3.95. To increase value, firms try to provide higher quality than their competitors for the same price, offer the same quality at a lower price, or some combination of the two. Each time a competitor raises the quality and/or lowers the price, other competitors scramble to catch up and the bar is raised.[7] The greater the competition, the more firms will be jockeying for position and the more often the bar will be raised. Firms that aren't continually improving their quality are certain to be left behind. The aforementioned story about Ford shows how quickly, in this highly competitive atmosphere, a well-respected company can derail.

It should be emphasized that our discussion of quality here includes service as well as products. We have clearly become a service economy in North America, and poor quality of service has become one of the great consumer frustrations of all time. In spite of the importance of maintaining service quality, most companies seem to be receiving a failing report card. Typically, both the popular press and industry surveys have reported a fairly bleak view of customer service in North America.[8] On the front line of the new economy, service—bold, fast, imaginative, and customized—is now the ultimate strategic business imperative. This is little surprise when it is considered that service-producing industries contribute ever-increasing shares of our gross national product compared to goods-producing industries.

Consumers today seem to swap horror stories about poor service as a kind of ritualistic, cathartic exercise. Consider the following examples: repeated trips to the car dealer; poor installation of refrigerator ice makers, resulting in several visits from repair people; returned food to the supermarket, resulting in brusque treatment; fouled-up travel reservations; poorly installed carpeting; no clerk at the shoe department of your favourite department store—and on and on. Shoddy service comes at a price. In a recent study, 54 percent of the people interviewed indicated that they would lose all loyalty to a company that had rude or unhelpful staff. One in ten said they would walk away if a company did not seem to listen.[9]

The rising clamour about service quality suggests that there has been something fundamentally wrong in the North American service sector. Sloppy service has the potential to become more than just a consumer annoyance. Some economists warn that diminishing quality standards could cost North American industry more of its international competitive standing in services and thus worsen existing trade problems.[10]

With respect to quality, it is not clear whether North American business has fully appreciated the spectrum of meanings that quality takes on for the consumer stakeholder. As David Garvin has expressed, there are at least eight critical dimensions of product or service quality that must be understood if business is to respond strategically to this factor.[11] These eight dimensions include (1) performance, (2) features,

(3) reliability, (4) conformance, (5) durability, (6) serviceability, (7) aesthetics, and (8) perceived quality.

Performance refers to a product's primary operating characteristics. For an automobile, this would include such factors as handling, steering, and comfort. *Features* are the "bells and whistles" of products that supplement their basic functioning. *Reliability* reflects the probability of a product malfunctioning or failing. *Conformance* is the extent to which the product or service meets established standards. *Durability* is a measure of product life. *Serviceability* refers to the speed, courtesy, competence, and ease of repair. *Aesthetics* is a subjective factor that refers to how the product looks, feels, tastes, and so on. Finally, *perceived quality* is a subjective inference that the consumer makes on the basis of a variety of tangible and intangible product characteristics. To address the issue of product or service quality, a manager must be astute enough to appreciate these different dimensions of quality and the subtle and dynamic interplays among them.

An important question is whether quality is a social or an ethical issue or just a competitive factor that business needs to emphasize to be successful in the marketplace. Manuel Velasquez proposes three ethical theories based on the concept of duty that informs our understanding of the ethical dimensions of quality: (1) **contractual theory**, (2) **due care theory**, and (3) **social costs view**. The contractual theory focuses on the contract between the firm and the customer. Firms have a responsibility to comply with the terms of the sale, inform the customer about the nature of the product, avoid misrepresentation of any kind, and not coerce the customer in any way. The due care theory focuses on the relative vulnerability of the customer, who has less information and expertise than the firm, and the ethical responsibility that places on the firm. Customers must depend on the firm providing the product or service to live up to the claims about it and to exercise due care to avoid customer injury. The third view, social costs, extends beyond contractual theory and due care theory to suggest that, if a product causes harm, the firm should pay the costs of any injury even if the firm had met the terms of the contract, exercised all due care, and taken all reasonable precautions. This perspective serves as the underpinning of strict liability and its extension into absolute liability, which we will discuss shortly.[12]

The Issue of Safety

Business clearly has a duty to consumer stakeholders to sell them safe products and services. The concept of safety, in a definitional sense, means "free from harm or risk" or "secure from threat of danger, harm, or loss." In reality, however, the use of virtually any consumer product or service entails some degree of risk or some chance that the consumer may be harmed by the product or service.

In the 1800s, the legal view that prevailed was *caveat emptor* ("let the buyer beware"). The basic idea behind this concept was that the buyer had as much knowledge of what she or he wanted as the seller and, in any event, the marketplace would punish any violators. In the 1900s, *caveat emptor* gradually lost its favour and rationale, because it was frequently impossible for the consumer to have complete knowledge about manufactured goods.[13] Today, manufacturers are held responsible for all products placed on the market. We have a weak version of *caveat vendor*—"let the seller take care."[14]

Through a series of legal developments as well as changing societal values, business has become significantly responsible for product safety. Court cases and legal doctrine now hold companies financially liable for harm to consumers. Yet this still does not answer the difficult question, "How safe are manufacturers obligated to make

Ethics In *Practice*

To Check or Not to Check the Chicken?

Over the winter holiday break of 2003/2004, I went back to work at a fast-food restaurant where I had been working since high school. The restaurant sold lots of chicken sandwiches. We were supposed to measure the temperature of the chicken every hour to make sure that it was below 40°F (I assume in response to the incident in which a few people died as a result of bacteria formed in warm meat). That responsibility was assigned to whoever was battering the chicken at the time. All that the person had to do was stick a thermometer in the chicken, measuring the bottom, middle, and top until the digital read stayed at a single temperature for about 10 to 15 seconds. The whole process took a few minutes at most. This information was then sent to the restaurant's home office every day.

Unfortunately, not everyone would keep up with taking the temperatures. As an assistant manager, I was responsible for making sure the temperatures were checked, but it was difficult when I had other things to do. For instance, if I were at the register, I could not leave the customers to go back and make sure the batterer was taking the temper-

atures. At the end of the shift, I would sometimes see a sheet of paper with few or no temperatures noted on it. The store manager would have been upset had he known that I was making up temperatures I did not know to be true, but he would have been even more upset if there had been no temperatures on the sheet at all. He would just make up the numbers himself before he sent them off to the home office, with all the temperatures, of course, below 40°F. I have even seen the store manager make up temperatures when he was battering chicken and had forgotten to check the temperatures on the hour.

1. What is the ethical issue in this case? Is it product quality, product safety, or deceptive practices?

2. What responsibilities does the restaurant have to consumers in this situation?

3. As an assistant manager, what should I have done about this situation?

Contributed by Jason Greene

products?" It is not possible to make products totally "risk free"; experience has shown that consumers seem to have an uncanny ability to injure themselves in novel and creative ways, many of which cannot be anticipated. The challenge to management, therefore, is to make products as safe as possible while at the same time making them affordable and useful to consumers. Successfully meeting such a challenge is critical to establishing and maintaining consumer confidence and trust in business. The importance of building consumer trust is highlighted in Industry Canada's discussion of "the Consumer Connection":

> *Consumer confidence and participation are critical to the performance of the national economy, to the efficient functioning of Canadian markets, and to our ability to compete in other countries' markets. Consumer expenditures contribute about 60% to Canada's gross national product, and traditionally have been the leading force in "kick-starting" the economy out of a recession.... Because of the consumer's importance to the Canadian economy, relatively small improvements to the consumer framework could provide important dividends to our overall economic well-being.[15]*

Today the public is concerned about a variety of hazards, such as the rise in genetically modified food (see Figure 12–1 for an example), the dangers of living near toxic

FIGURE 12-1

Questioning the Safety of Our Food

Greenpeace Canada ran the following recent campaign to protest the trend toward genetically modified food:

Our Wheat Is in Danger

Monsanto is trying to introduce genetically engineered wheat in Canada.

Monsanto and other big biotech companies are tinkering with a mainstay of Canadian farming and a staple food for many people around the world—wheat. Monsanto, in collaboration with the government of Canada, is developing genetically engineered (GE) wheat that is designed to resist its "Roundup Ready" herbicide when applied to a farmer's field to kill weeds. The company plans to bring it to market by 2005 or so.

Take Action

Help Greenpeace stop the introduction of GE wheat in Canada: Send a free fax to your Member of Parliament, sign our petition against GE wheat and let people know that GE wheat is a risk to Canadians.

Why Is GE Wheat Risky?

Greenpeace is opposed to the environmental release of genetically engineered organisms due to the harm, possibly irreversible, they may cause to the environment.

What Can the Food Industry Do?

Health and scientific authorities have identified possible health risks associated with GE food. These possible health risks might be exacerbated with the introduction of GE wheat into the food supply, since wheat is so widely consumed globally, often in a minimally processed form. So we think the food industry has a special responsibility to protect consumers and the environment from the introduction of GE wheat.

We are asking companies such as Loblaws to use their influence in Ottawa to oppose the introduction of GE wheat, and to stop using other GE ingredients in their products. In the interim, all GE food should be labelled so that consumers concerned about impacts to human and environmental health can choose to avoid food produced with GE ingredients. But the food companies need to hear this from you, the consumer. Please let your grocery store and favourite food manufacturers know that you do not want them to use GE ingredients. Ask them to publicly state their opposition to GE wheat and to use their influence in Ottawa to stop its introduction.

Source: Greenpeace Canada, http://www.greenpeace.ca/e/campaign/gmo/depth/wheat/index.php. Reprinted by permission.

waste dumps or nuclear plants, and so on. Food scares, both real and imagined, have occupied much of the public's attention. Although they occur everywhere, consumers in the European Union have been especially hard hit. The discovery of cancer-causing dioxin in Belgian food products caused many countries to temporarily halt imports from Belgium. Then, Coca-Cola recalled 2.5 million bottles of soft drinks that originated in two Belgian factories after children who drank it complained of stomachaches, nausea, and headaches.

In recent years, a variety of health threats connected with food products have shaken consumer confidence in a number of industries. Bovine spongiform ecephalopathy (BSE), or mad cow disease, precipitated a crisis for beef farmers throughout Europe. Beef consumption dropped by 27 percent in the 15 member states of the European Union, with Greece reporting a 50 percent drop.[16] In Canada, the beef industry was shaken in the summer of 2003 when it was announced that a single breeder cow in northern Alberta tested positive for mad cow disease. Following the discovery, prices collapsed, costing 90 000 producers across the country more than $11 million a day.[17] Because of reduced consumption, including a U.S. ban on Canadian beef imports, production was reduced, with consequent job losses and damages to many businesses in Alberta and Saskatchewan and other related Canadian businesses.[18]

Manufactured products create hazards not only because of unsafe product design but also as a result of consumers being given inadequate information regarding the hazards associated with using the products. Consequently, it is not surprising in product liability claims to find that the charges are based on one or more of several allegations. First, it may be charged that the product was improperly manufactured. Here the producer failed to exercise due care in the product's production, and this failure contributed directly to the accident or injury. Second, if the product was manufactured properly, its design could have been defective in that alternative designs or devices, if used at the time of manufacture, may have prevented the accident. Third, it may be charged that the producer failed to provide satisfactory instructions and/or warnings and that the accident or injury could have been prevented if such information had been provided. Fourth, it may be charged that the producer failed to foresee a reasonable and anticipated misuse of the product and warn against such misuse.[19] To appreciate the "big picture" of dangerous products, consider the following list of categories of consumer products that are most frequently associated with hospital-treated injuries:[20]

1. Sports and recreational activities and equipment
2. Home structures and construction materials
3. Home furnishings and fixtures
4. Housewares
5. Personal use items
6. Home workshop apparatus, tools, and attachments
7. Packaging and containers for household products
8. Toys

According to Safe Kids Canada, the national injury prevention program of Toronto's Hospital for Sick Children, the following products are considered high risk to children and toddlers:

1. *Products specifically identified as hazardous that have been used in prior years.* For example, baby walkers may be passed on from family to family. While some parents mistakenly believe that baby walkers help children learn to walk, these walkers have been responsible for hundreds of injuries resulting from toddlers trying to climb down stairs in their walkers. In addition, older cribs, strollers, playpens, and other products don't meet current safety standards. And some outdated models have been known to cause serious injury and death (e.g., cribs made before 1986).
2. *Products used incorrectly can be dangerous.* For example, baby gates that fasten to the wall should be used at the top of stairs, rather than gates that fit into place with pressure, which could be easily dislodged with movement from a child. Misuse of car seats and baby seats can also result in serious injury or death. These items need to be kept off raised surfaces such as tables since they can fall or be knocked off.
3. *Some products may provide a false sense of security.* For example, child-resistant caps on medicine containers or cleaning products may not be sufficient to stop a child from opening these items.
4. *Some safety products lose their effectiveness over time.* This presents a danger for individuals who may obtain used products such as car seats or bike helmets. These types of products lose their safety protection over time, because the plastics begin to deteriorate.[21]

Whether we are dealing with consumer products, where there is potential for harm as a result of accidents or misuse, or with food products, where not-so-visible threats to human health may exist, the field of product safety is a significant responsibility and a growing challenge for the business community. It seems that no matter how careful business is with respect to these issues, the threat of product liability lawsuits has become an industry unto itself and becomes intimately linked with discussions of product safety. Therefore, we will now turn our attention to this vital topic.

Product Liability   Product liability has become a monumental consumer issue, particularly due to the sheer number of cases where products have resulted in illness, harm, or death. In addition, more and more consumers are resorting to legal action against the alleged offender when faced with situations about which they are unhappy. While the U.S. has traditionally been among the most litigious societies, Canada has also experienced a growing trend in litigation.

Closely paralleling the rise in the number of lawsuits in North America has been the growing size of the financial awards given by the courts. A path-breaking award in the product liability category was obtained in the United States in 1978. The US$128.5 million award was granted in the case of a 19-year-old who at age 13 was severely injured. He was riding with a friend in a Ford Pinto that was struck from behind. The Pinto's gas tank ruptured, and the passenger compartment was filled with flames that killed his friend and severely burned him over 90 percent of his body. The badly scarred teenager underwent more than 50 operations. Ford was required by the jury to pay US$666 280 to the dead driver's family and to pay the survivor US$2.8 million in compensatory damages and US$125 million in punitive damages.[22] The Pinto case was the beginning, but the awards have grown since then. The largest judgment in a personal injury case since then was the US$4.9 billion a jury awarded to six people in 1999. Six years earlier they had been seriously burned in a collision that allegedly caused the gas tank in their 1970 Malibu to explode. The average jury award went from US$520 000 in 1993 to US$1 million in 1999, an increase of 93 percent. Also from 1993 to 1999, jury awards rose 79 percent for medical malpractice cases, 128 percent in business negligence cases, and 410 percent in cases involving product liability.[23]

Since the Pinto case, multimillion-dollar lawsuits have become commonplace in North America, particularly in the U.S. Some major North American companies have been hit so hard by lawsuits that they have filed for bankruptcy protection. One famous example of this is the Johns Manville Corporation, which faced an avalanche of asbestos-related lawsuits that totalled 16 500 suits demanding over US$12 billion.[24] Another well-known case is that of A. H. Robins, which filed for protection after facing over 5000 product liability lawsuits in which women charged that its Dalkon Shield, an intrauterine contraceptive device, had injured them.[25] Dow Chemical, the principal manufacturer of silicone breast implants, entered bankruptcy protection in 1995.[26] The strategy continues today. In April 2001, W. R. Grace & Co. filed for bankruptcy protection to shield it from asbestos-related claims.[27] Other companies encountering large lawsuits have included Union Carbide, with its poison gas explosion in Bhopal, India; Dow Chemical, with its Agent Orange defoliant; and Bridgestone/Firestone, with its defective tires.

It is useful to point out that, according to some critics, one major source of the relatively greater presence of consumer-related lawsuits in the U.S. compared to Canada may be partly a result of legal differences in the conceptions of product liability. In the U.S., product liability has been reinforced by the doctrine of **strict liability** and the expansion of this concept in the courts. As we mentioned previously, the social costs view of product quality underlies the concept of strict liability and its extensions. In its most general form, the doctrine of strict liability holds that anyone in the value chain of a product is liable for harm caused to the user if the product as sold was unreasonably dangerous because of its defective condition. This applies to anyone involved in the design, manufacture, or sale of a defective product. Beyond manufacturing, courts have ruled against plaintiffs from a broad array of functions, such as selling, advertising, promotion, and distribution.[28] For example, the U.S. Department of Transportation holds warehouses liable for violations of hazardous materials regulations even when the warehouse relied on information provided by the customer (the depositor) when documenting the shipment.[29] In other words, there is no legal defence for placing on the market a product that is dangerous to a consumer because of a known or knowable defect.

Canada's legal view of product liability differs somewhat from the U.S. notion of strict liability. Canada did not adopt the doctrine of strict liability for defective products. Instead, product liability in Canada is governed by contract law and basic negligence law. That means that in addition to proving what the doctrine of strict liability requires, the plaintiff must also prove that the product's defect arose due to the defendant's negligence. In this sense, Canadian law is "fault-based," whereas U.S. law holds companies accountable for preventing defects, not simply for taking all reasonable steps to prevent them (hence, the notion of strict liability).

Which system is better for the consumer? While some critics view the U.S. system as more protective of the consumer, others see the systems as essentially producing similar results. As Bruce Feldthusen points out, "In negligence, we employ a doctrine in Canadian law called *res ipsa loquitur* (the thing speaks for itself) that permits the jury to infer negligence from the accident itself, which in practice brings us close to strict liability. There are few cases in Canadian law reports where the plaintiff has succeeded on all the elements of the action including proof of defect, but lost on the issue of negligence."[30] In practice then, the Canadian context may in fact be enforcing the spirit of the strict liability doctrine. Given the importance of this concept to both the U.S. and Canada, it is useful to consider that the law in both countries may eventually lead to even higher corporate standards of diligence toward consumer safety concerns.

Toward Absolute Liability. Certain countries and parts of the U.S. have established a standard that is much more demanding than even the standard U.S. concept of strict liability. This concept is called **absolute liability**. The ruling that established this new concept was handed down by the New Jersey Supreme Court in *Beshada v. Johns Manville Corporation* (1982). The plaintiffs in the Beshada case were employees of Johns Manville and other companies who had developed asbestos-related diseases as a result of exposure in the workplace.[31] The court ruled in this case that a manufacturer could be held strictly liable for failure to warn of a product hazard, even if the hazard was scientifically unknowable at the time of manufacture and sale. Therefore, a company cannot use as its defence the assurance that it did its best according to the state of the art in the industry at that time. Under this ruling, the manufacturer is liable for damages even if it had no way of knowing that the product might cause a problem later. Similarly, in 2000, the Supreme Court of India upheld the absolute liability of a common carrier, in this case Patel Roadways Ltd., for goods destroyed by fire. The court ruled that, in the case of damage or loss, it is not necessary for the plaintiff to establish negligence.[32]

The absolute-liability rule frequently involves cases involving chemicals or drugs. For example, a drug producer might put a drug on the market (with government approval) thinking that it is safe based on current knowledge. Under the doctrine of absolute liability, the firm could be held liable for side effects or health problems that develop years, or even decades, later. The result is that a large amount of uncertainty is injected into the production process.[33]

Another extension of strict liability is known as **market share liability**. This concept evolved from **delayed manifestation cases**—situations in which delayed reactions to such products appear years later after consumption of, or exposure to, the product.[34] Market share liability was derived from a California case in which a group of women with birth defects claimed that the defects had been caused by the drug DES, which their mothers had taken while pregnant years earlier. The women could not name the company that had made the pills their mothers had taken. But in 1980 the California Supreme Court upheld a ruling that the six drug firms that made DES would be held responsible in proportion to their market shares of DES sales unless they could prove that they had not made the actual doses the women had taken.[35] When this verdict was reached, the business press expressed alarm about the potential impact of the decision. Their concern, however, was premature. With very few exceptions, market share liability has been rejected in subsequent non-DES cases and in second-generation DES cases. DES was uniquely suited to that defence because it was a generic product, the entire industry used the same formula, and it was marketed and promoted generically by all industry members. Efforts to apply the concept to cases involving asbestos products, blood products, breast implants, DPT vaccines, polio vaccines, multipiece tire rims, lead-based paints, and benzene all failed.[36]

Product Tampering and Product Extortion   Two other concerns that have contributed to the product liability discussion are *product tampering* and *product extortion*. The most well-known cases involved Tylenol in the 1980s—first in 1982, when seven Chicago people died from taking tainted Extra Strength Tylenol capsules, and again in 1986, when cyanide-laced bottles of Tylenol were found in New York and one woman died. James Burke, chairman of Johnson & Johnson, characterized the case as "terrorism, pure and simple."[37] In response to these and other incidents, firms began to employ tamper-evident packaging. Although improvements in packaging have slowed the rate of pharmaceutical product tampering, they have not stopped it. In 2000, two Australian pharmaceutical manufacturers received extortion threats. The extortionists are believed to have bought over-the-counter analgesics, poisoned them with strychnine, and returned them to the shelves. Four people were hospitalized, and nationwide product recalls cost the firms millions of dollars.[38]

Tampering may also involve product information. For example, consumers often rely on the "best before" dates on many kinds of food products. Following an investigation by CBC's *Marketplace*, the Canadian Food Inspection Agency confirmed tampering had occurred on the "best before" dates of products sold by Santa Maria Foods. This large Canadian distributor of food products was charged for this offence as well as for the misuse of government inspection stamps.[39] Other Canadian businesses have been found guilty of similar offences, including a small food store in Dorchester, Ontario, that was fined for switching the dates on meat products sold at the meat counter, in an effort to "squeeze a few extra days out of the product."[40]

In 2001, cancer patients in the U.S. sued pharmaceutical giant Eli Lilly & Co. for failing to alert authorities to indications that a pharmacist was diluting its best-selling chemotherapy drug when filling prescriptions. The pharmacist, Robert Courtney, was indicted on 20 counts of product tampering and drug misbranding, which he allegedly engaged in to boost his profits.[41]

Consumer Demands and Product Liability The need to keep up with a changing environment and changing consumer demands provides an incentive to continually revisit the appropriateness of consumer protection laws.

The system of consumer law and policy in Canada has been viewed as a "patchwork" rather than a framework for governing business activity. The system evolved incrementally within the social, economic, and political systems present in Canada about 30 years ago. Responsibilities for consumer law are shared between the federal and provincial governments. This shared responsibility distinguishes the consumer system from most of the other marketplace laws within Industry Canada (competition law, insolvency law, intellectual property statutes), which are largely within the federal domain. In addition, with the government reorganization of 1993, federal responsibilities for implementing federal consumer laws were transferred to different federal agencies, including Industry Canada, Health Canada, Agriculture and Agrifood, Natural Resources, and Fisheries and Oceans. Prior to 1993, the Department of Consumer and Corporate Affairs had central responsibility for most federal consumer statutes and took a leadership role in establishing consumer policy within the government of Canada.[42]

We now consider Health Canada's role in establishing and enforcing standards of product safety.

Health Canada

Health Canada is a federal government department that acts in cooperation with provincial bodies to protect the health of Canadians. Figure 12–2 offers an organizational chart of the branches of Health Canada. As you can see, Health Canada is the umbrella department for a wide-ranging body of government responsibilities, but here we will only focus on several of these branches that have high relevance for consumer safety concerns.

Among its numerous responsibilities, Health Canada administers the Food and Drugs Act and releases advisories and warnings on foods, drugs, medical devices, natural health products, and consumer products. More recent responsibilities have come to include providing information and policies on genetically modified foods, nutrition labelling, and biotechnology products such as blood, tissues, and reproductive technologies in the Canadian marketplace and health system. Health Canada also monitors health and safety risks related to the sale and use of drug products, natural health products, medical devices, pesticides, radiation-emitting devices, and certain other consumer products.[43]

Through its Healthy Environments and Consumer Safety Branch (HECS), Health Canada also administers the Product Safety Programme (PSP). This program is aimed at protecting the health of Canadians by researching, assessing, and collaborating in the management of the health risks and safety hazards associated with consumer products, cosmetics, new chemical substances, products of biotechnology, workplace chemicals, radiation-emitting devices, environmental noise, and solar UV radiation. The PSP mandate is governed by a variety of legislation, including the Hazardous Products Act, Radiation Emitting Devices Act, Canadian Environmental Protection Act, New Substances Notification Regulations, Canada Labour Code, Treasury Board Regulations (Health and Safety), and Food and Drugs Act (including the Cosmetics Regulations).[44]

The consumer products portion of the PSP, referred to as Consumer Product Safety (CPS), is aimed at protecting consumers from product-related hazards and promoting

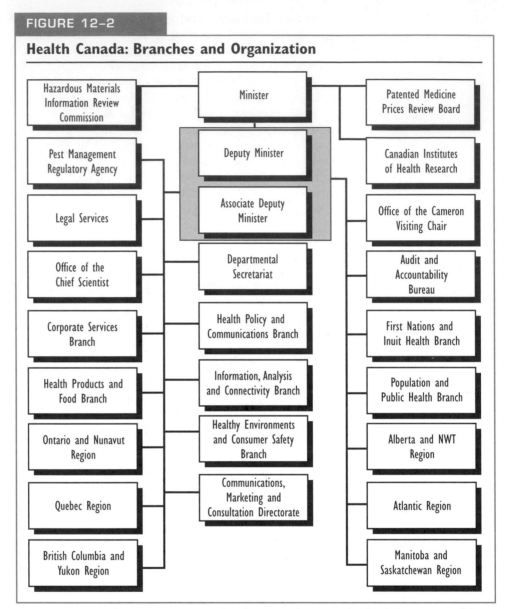

FIGURE 12-2

Health Canada: Branches and Organization

Source: Health Canada, http://www.hc-sc.gc.ca/english/about/org.html#9a. Reproduced with the permission of the Minister of Public Works and Government Services Canada, 2004.

the safe use of products through raising consumer awareness. CPS also encourages the design of safer products for the Canadian market by providing importers and manufacturers with hazard and product technical information, including the following:

- *Chemical hazards.* Consumer chemical products such as detergents, paints, solvents, and glues are assessed for potential hazards or harm from their use.
- *Flammability hazards.* Textile products including children's sleepwear, clothing, tents, bedding, and mattresses are assessed.
- *Mechanical hazards.* Possible hazards such as strangulation are assessed in children's products including toys, cribs, and bunk beds, and in products intended for household or recreational use.[45]

Figure 12–3 provides a description of other central areas of responsibility covered within the Product Safety Programme.

Another responsibility of the PSP is fulfilled by the Product Safety Laboratory (PSL), which focuses on research and developmental work pertaining to consumer products covered by the Hazardous Products Act (HPA). These responsibilities include the following:

- Testing and evaluating products for compliance and enforcement purposes with regulations under the Hazardous Products Act.
- Developing methods to measure, analyze, and assess product hazards in support of current and new regulations or to provide scientific advice when the need for new regulations has been determined.
- Developing performance criteria to address hazards posed by new products.
- Identifying and assessing chemical, flammable, or mechanical hazards associated with consumer products.
- Conducting safety-related investigations to evaluate the state of the Canadian market.
- Transferring scientific and technical knowledge to inspectors, the medical profession, consumer interest groups, other government agencies, and industry.
- Providing advice for the application or development of test procedures to private laboratories.

FIGURE 12-3

The Product Safety Programme: Other Features

In addition to consumer product safety, the Product Safety Programme (PSP) also conducts work in the following areas:

Cosmetics

The PSP is responsible for managing the health risks associated with the use of cosmetics and personal-care products marketed in Canada. Manufacturers and importers must notify Health Canada of their intention to market a cosmetic product and provide ingredient and labelling information for review to ensure that the product is free of restricted or prohibited ingredients and that no inappropriate health claims are being made.

Workplace Hazardous Materials

The Workplace Hazardous Materials Information System (WHMIS) is Canada's national workplace hazard communication system and serves to protect Canadian workers from the adverse effects of exposure to hazardous materials by providing information through labelling, the availability of material safety data sheets, and worker education and training programs.

Consumer and Clinical Radiation Protection

Consumer and Clinical Radiation Protection (CCRP) assesses, monitors, and assists in the reduction of the health and safety risks associated with radiation-emitting devices and other sources of radiation. CCRP conducts research into the biological effects of radiation; develops guidelines, standards, and safety codes; and provides radiation safety inspections of facilities containing radiation-emitting devices and the devices themselves, as well as training on the proper operation of the devices.

New Substances and Products of Biotechnology

The New Substances Assessment Control Bureau conducts the pre-market assessment of the potential health risk to the general population associated with new chemical substances (e.g., fabric dyes and fuel additives), as well as products of biotechnology (e.g., the micro-organisms used in reclaiming land after an oil spill). For new substances covered by the *Food and Drugs Act*, both the environmental impact and risks to human health through environmental exposure to these substances are assessed. Should a risk be identified, measures are taken to reduce the risk by controlling or even banning the substance or product.

Source: Health Canada, http://www.hc-sc.gc.ca/hecs-sesc/hecs/psp.htm.

- Participating in the development of voluntary standards at national and international levels, and representing the PSP in standards writing organizations such as the Canadian Standards Association (CSA).
- Contributing to the development of standards and product safety regulations that are enforced by product safety officers in the provinces or regions who oversee investigations, seizures, recalls, and prosecutions.[46]

Food and Drug Safety Administration in Canada

The Minister of Health is responsible for a number of activities related to consumer safety, including establishing policies and safety standards for food sold in Canada; administering those provisions of the Food and Drugs Act that relate to public health, safety, and nutrition; and assessing the effectiveness of various government agencies in regard to food safety.

We will now consider the two branches of Health Canada that are particularly pertinent to food and drug safety administration in Canada: the Healthy Environments and Consumer Safety Branch (HECS) and the Health Products and Food Branch (HPFB). In addition, we briefly look at the role of the Canadian Food Inspection Agency (CFIA).

Healthy Environments and Consumer Safety Branch (HECS)

The objectives of the HECS are broader than simply product safety concerns. This branch of Health Canada aims to do the following:

- Promote safe living, working, and recreational environments, with a special emphasis on health in the work environment and delivering occupational health and safety services.
- Assess and reduce health risks posed by environmental factors.
- Promote initiatives to reduce and prevent the harm caused by tobacco and the abuse of alcohol and other controlled substances.
- Regulate tobacco and controlled substances, and provide drug analytical services.
- Regulate the safety of industrial and consumer products in the Canadian marketplace, and promote their safe use.[47]

HECS's principal programs include the following:

- Drug Strategy and Controlled Substances
- Product Safety
- Safe Environments
- Sustainable Development
- Tobacco Control
- Workplace Health and Public Safety

Health Products and Food Branch (HPFB)

Another branch of Health Canada with responsibilities for consumer health and safety is the HPFB. Its main objectives include:

- Minimizing health risk factors to Canadians while maximizing the safety provided by the regulatory system for health products and food.
- Promoting conditions that enable Canadians to make healthy choices and providing information so that they can make informed decisions about their health.[48]

The major programs operated through HFPB are focused on the following areas:

- Therapeutic products (medical devices and drugs)
- Food, including all Health Canada nutrition activities
- Natural health products
- Biologics and genetics (e.g., blood and blood products, viral and bacterial vaccines, genetic therapies and diagnostics, tissues, organs, and reproductive technologies)

Canadian Food Inspection Agency (CFIA)

Another instrument through which the Canadian government can maintain product safety is the **Canadian Food Inspection Agency (CFIA)**, established in April 1997. This body consolidated the delivery of all federal food, animal, and plant health inspection programs previously provided through the activities of four federal government departments (Agriculture and Agri-Food Canada, Fisheries and Oceans Canada, Health Canada, and Industry Canada).

The CFIA aims to protect consumers by contributing to food safety, the protection of plants, and the health of animals in Canada. Among the central responsibilities of the CFIA is the enforcement of food safety and nutritional quality standards established by Health Canada. Specific activities include inspecting federally registered meat-processing facilities, inspecting borders for foreign pests and diseases, enforcing practices related to fraudulent labelling, conducting food investigations and recalls, and performing laboratory testing and environmental assessments of seeds, plants, feeds, and fertilizers.[49] Figure 12–4 outlines the responsibilities of the CFIA.

FIGURE 12–4

The Work of the Canadian Food Inspection Agency (CFIA)

- CFIA veterinarians and inspectors conduct rigorous inspections in some 1800 meat- and fish-processing establishments across Canada.
- CFIA inspectors check shipments from abroad—examining plants, animals, foods, and even packaging materials that can harbour diseases and pests, such as beetles or moths.
- CFIA agricultural officers inspect potato fields and greenhouses, hatcheries, feed mills, and live-stock premises.
- CFIA laboratory scientists analyze food samples for impurities, drug residues, or disease-causing agents.
- CFIA regulators evaluate the safety of the newest kinds of seeds, feeds, fertilizers, and animal health products, such as vaccines, for use in Canada.
- CFIA officers review food labels for honesty and accuracy, investigate complaints, and prosecute offenders.

Source: Canadian Food Inspection Agency, http://www.inspection.gc.ca/english/toce.shtml.

The U.S. Food and Drug Administration (FDA)

Given the increasing integration of activities between Canadian and U.S. business and consumers, Health Canada and its branches often work together with the U.S. **Food and Drug Administration (FDA)**. In 2003, Health Canada and the FDA signed a Memorandum of Understanding (MOU) that "builds on existing collaborative efforts between Health Canada and the U.S. FDA. In general, it will better enable the two regulatory authorities to share information on the post-market safety of therapeutic products, information related to the review and evaluation of new product submissions and information on product investigations and enforcement activities."[50]

The FDA's goals are largely the same as Health Canada, and as it describes on its Web site, its mission includes the following:[51]

1. To promote the public health by promptly and efficiently reviewing clinical research and taking appropriate action on the marketing of regulated products in a timely manner.

2. With respect to such products, protect the public health by ensuring that foods are safe, wholesome, sanitary, and properly labelled; human and veterinary drugs are safe and effective; there is reasonable assurance of the safety and effectiveness of devices intended for human use; cosmetics are safe and properly labelled; public health and safety are protected from electronic product radiation.

3. Participate through appropriate processes with representatives of other countries to reduce the burden of regulation, harmonize regulatory requirements, and achieve appropriate reciprocal arrangements.

4. As determined to be appropriate by the Secretary, carry out paragraphs (1) through (3) in consultation with experts in science, medicine, and public health, and in cooperation with consumers, users, manufacturers, importers, packers, distributors, and retailers of regulated products.

Ethics In Practice

Pushing Products

I worked for a children's store in Toronto and among the items sold were strollers and baby car seats. The manager informed us of financial bonuses attached to the sale of specific items. Those items that the manager wished to "unload first" received the highest sales bonus. This presented some disturbing situations. Young couples with a newborn would come and ask for my advice as an "expert" salesperson. While I would pretend to offer "genuine" advice regarding store purchases, my job was really to "push" those items that the manager had indicated would give me the highest bonus. Consequently, customers often were not given the most suitable advice for their baby/toddler products. While this did not result in faulty or unsafe products being sold, it often meant that customers bought items that were not necessarily most suitable to their needs. For example, a couple with a newborn might be persuaded to purchase a specific car seat or stroller simply because it was on the list of "products to push" rather than being best suited to their needs and budget. This store has a strong reputation for customer service and product knowledge—if only customers knew that our knowledge rarely benefited the customer.

1. Do businesses owe customers anything beyond selling a safe product? What exactly do businesses owe consumers?

2. What actions, if any, should employees take with regard to this practice?

3. How often do you think this practice occurs? As consumers, what protection do we have against this type of behaviour?

Contributed Anonymously

Business's Response to Consumer Stakeholders

Business's response to consumerism and consumer stakeholders has varied over the years. It has ranged from poorly conceived public relations ploys at one extreme to well-designed and implemented departments of consumer affairs and product safety and programs like total quality management (TQM) and Six Sigma at the other. The history of business's response to consumers parallels its perceptions of the seriousness, pervasiveness, effectiveness, and longevity of the consumer movement. When the consumer movement first began, business's response was casual, perhaps symbolic, and hardly effective. Today, the consumer movement has matured, and formal interactions with consumer stakeholders have become more and more institutionalized. Business has realized that consumers today are more persistent than in the past, more assertive, and more likely to use or exhaust all appeal channels before being satisfied. Armed with considerable power, consumer activists have been a major stimulus to more sincere responses on behalf of business. These responses have included the creation of toll-free hotlines, user-friendly Web sites, consumer service representatives, the designation of specific consumer affairs officers, and the creation of specific company departments to handle consumer affairs.

Early attempts to be responsive to consumer stakeholders involved the creation of organizational units such as consumer affairs offices and product safety offices. Today, these kinds of responses have become an institutionalized part of business's response to consumers. Programs like Six Sigma and total quality management have become the strategic responses. These responses merit brief consideration.

Consumer Affairs Offices

There are various ways of organizing the corporate response to consumers. A company might appoint a consumer affairs officer or create a consumer affairs task force or committee, but a more sophisticated way is to establish a consumer affairs office or department. To be sure, the establishment of such a formalized unit is not a substitute for a consumer-stakeholder focus on the part of all members of the organization. But it does provide a hub around which a dedicated consumer-stakeholder thrust might be built.

Basic Mission The basic mission of a consumer affairs office is to heighten management responsiveness to consumer stakeholders. In accomplishing this mission, consumer affairs professionals have to execute two key roles: one is the role of consumer advocate in the company, and the other is the role of consumer specialist making managerial recommendations about corporate practices that mesh well with the needs of both consumers and the company. Some companies take one or the other of these two postures, whereas other companies use both approaches and/or additional approaches. There are potential conflicts between the two roles, but they need not create conflicts if consumer affairs professionals and management have a sympathetic understanding of each other's goals.[52]

Essential Functions Consumer affairs practitioners have suggested that there are at least four essential functions of an effective consumer affairs office:

- *Establish a comprehensive, complete, and accurate database* that assesses the levels of consumer satisfaction and dissatisfaction with the company's products and services in all important areas involving consumers, such as billing and collection practices, repair services, guarantee policy and practice, handling of complaints, quality of products and services, and pricing.

- *Audit the company's programs* to determine how adequate they are in responding to consumer complaints and interests. Use company records, special task forces, outside consultants, and consumer groups.
- *Recommend specific consumer programs, policies, and practices* in all areas where needed.
- *Establish programs to ensure effective communication* between the company and consumers to build public confidence and understanding of company policy and practice.[53]

In addition, consumer affairs experts argue that there are at least four principal factors that determine the success or failure of consumer affairs offices. These factors, which are essential if the office is to be able to accomplish its two central objectives of raising consumer satisfaction and improving long-term company profitability, are as follows:

- The office should be located close to that of the chief executive of the company.
- The office should have access to all relevant information in the company about consumers and must be given authority to create effective mechanisms to get it.
- Information about consumers should be quantified to the extent feasible. This is necessary to make intelligent decisions/trade-offs.
- These managers should be skilled in designing effective performance measurement tools with which to evaluate what people throughout the company are doing. (Cliché: People will do what is inspected, not expected.)[54]

In general, the appropriate response of a company to consumer stakeholders is to ensure an understanding of the consumer movement throughout the organization, especially at top management levels, where it is easy for executives to get isolated from company activities.

Product Safety Offices

Obviously, a consumer affairs office could be divided into units, one of which might focus on product safety. In a growing number of firms, however, product safety offices are being established independently. This is quite logical, given what we documented earlier as the product safety and product liability problems.

Three particular factors contribute to the need for greater organization in handling the product safety issue. First, there is the complexity of most current products. Products today may be made of exotic materials and incorporate complex and sensitive control devices. They are often built up from subsystems that themselves are quite complex. Second, there is the subtlety of the hazards that can be generated during product use. People often use products in novel and strange ways, not for their intended purposes. Complexity contributes to an impatience with reading the instructions, and this can lead to additional hazards, too. Third, there are coordination problems in large, multidivision manufacturing organizations that can inhibit communications among departments, and structures are sometimes set up wherein top management is insulated from safety problems. The net effect of these three factors working together is to create a need for some sort of product safety organization.[55]

Levels at Which to Locate Product Safety Offices The most important locations for product safety offices in organizations, according to a study by George Eads and Peter Reuter, are the divisional level and the corporate level. The division responsible for the product is a logical location, because the interactions among processes such as manufacturing, quality control, and packaging can best be monitored at this level. The division is also likely to know the most about the product's basic technology and conditions for use. Finally, the division's financial performance might be directly linked to the product's success, and, therefore, the division has the strongest incentive to ensure the product's safety.

Whereas a product safety office at the divisional level would have the greatest operational responsibility, one at the corporate level could also be critical. At the corporate level, the product safety officer would most likely serve in a liaison role with the divisions. Activities that the product safety officer might perform include supervision of safety education and training, auditing of corporate design and safety policies, transmitting and reinforcing top management's commitment to safety, and acting as a court of appeals when safety issues arise. A corporate-level product safety officer has greater organizational access to key decision makers, and this is an important factor, also.[56]

Other Functions of a Product Safety Office Other important functions of a product safety office include the following:

- Setting the tone for the firm's product safety effort
- Structuring and helping to enforce financial and nonfinancial rewards and penalties
- Developing links to other safety- and quality-related activities in the firm
- Helping with product safety litigation
- Helping with regulatory liaison[57]
- Setting up product safety committees
- Performing periodic safety audits and tests
- Designing a contingency plan for product recalls[58]

Of all the product issues management faces, product safety has become one of the most important. Some companies produce high-hazard products and might need to incorporate all the ideas we have discussed, plus more. Other companies produce products in which the hazards are much lower. In any event, the product safety issue has become a "front burner" consumer issue, and there is no sign of it abating. Because human health and safety are involved, product safety is justified as a central concern on its own merit. Trends in litigation, jury awards, and insurance premiums offer other practical reasons why the consumer stakeholder must be carefully considered when management is planning its responsiveness efforts.

Total Quality Management Programs

Total quality management (TQM) has many different characteristics, but it essentially means that all of the functions of the business are blended into a holistic, integrated philosophy built around the concepts of quality, teamwork, productivity, and customer understanding and satisfaction.[59] Figure 12–5 depicts one useful view of the principles, practices, and techniques of TQM. It should be noted that the customer, or consumer stakeholder, is the focus of the process.

A vital assumption and premise of TQM is that the customer is the final judge of quality. Therefore, the first part of the TQM process is to define quality in terms of customer expectations and requirements. Figure 12–6 presents several different popular definitions of quality and their strengths and weaknesses.

FIGURE 12-5

Principles, Practices, and Techniques of Total Quality Management

	Customer Focus	Continuous Improvement	Teamwork
Principles	• Paramount importance of customers • Providing products and services that fulfill customer needs; requires organization-wide focus on customers	• Consistent customer satisfaction can be attained only through relentless improvement of processes that create products and services	• Customer focus and continuous improvement are best achieved by collaboration throughout an organization as well as with customers and suppliers
Practices	• Direct customer contact • Collecting information about customer needs • Using information to design and deliver products and services	• Process analysis • Re-engineering • Problem solving • Plan/do/check/act	• Search for arrangements that benefit all units involved in a process • Formation of various types of teams • Group skills training
Techniques	• Customer surveys and focus groups • Quality function deployment (translates customer information into product specifications)	• Flowcharts • Pareto analysis • Statistical process control • Fishbone diagrams	• Organizational development methods, such as the nominal group technique • Team-building methods (e.g., role clarification and group feedback)

Source: James W. Dean, Jr., and David E. Bowen, "Management Theory and Total Quality: Improving Research and Practice Through Theory Development," *Academy of Management Review* (Vol. 19, No. 3, July 1994), 395.

Customer expectations and requirements are then converted to standards and specifications. Finally, the entire organization is realigned to ensure that both conformance quality (adherence to standards and specifications) and perceived quality (meeting or exceeding customer expectations) are achieved.[60] It is clear in TQM that "delighted customers" is the overarching goal of management's efforts.[61]

Opportunities for recognition have helped to propel quality efforts. In North America and the rest of the industrialized world, the Malcolm Baldrige Award, ISO 9000, and the Deming Quality Award have enhanced the reputations of firms that undertake quality initiatives and complete them successfully. However, TQM became the buzzword of the 1980s, and many of its slogans, such as "Getting it right the first time," became viewed as clichés. It is against that backdrop that other tools developed, such as just in time (JIT) and business process re-engineering (BPR). Many were concerned about a TQM shortcoming, as described by Phil Crosby, a leading TQM consultant: "TQM never did anything to define quality, which is conformance to standards."[62] The need for a more rigorous definition of quality was part of the appeal of Six Sigma, which we will describe briefly.

Six Sigma

Six Sigma is a development in total quality management that has become a way of life for many corporations. Basically, Six Sigma is a heading under which are grouped a body of methodologies and techniques. Scarcely a week goes by without a major cor-

FIGURE 12-6

FIGURE 12-6

Strengths and Weaknesses of Quality Definitions

Definition	Strengths	Weaknesses
Excellence	• Strong marketing and human resource benefits • Universally recognizable—mark of uncompromising standards and high achievement	• Provides little practical guidance to practitioners • Measurement difficulties • Attributes of excellence may change dramatically and rapidly • Sufficient number of customers must be willing to pay for excellence
Value	• Concept of value incorporates multiple attributes • Focuses attention on a firm's internal efficiency and external effectiveness • Allows for comparisons across disparate objects and experiences	• Difficulty extracting individual components of value judgment • Questionable inclusiveness • Quality and value are different constructs
Conformance to Specifications	• Facilitates precise measurement • Leads to increased efficiency • Necessary for global strategy • Should force disaggregation of consumer needs • Most parsimonious and appropriate definition for some customers	• Consumers do not know or care about internal specifications • Inappropriate for services • Potentially reduces organizational adaptability • Specifications may quickly become obsolete in rapidly changing markets • Internally focused
Meeting and/or Exceeding Expectations	• Evaluates from customer's perspective • Applicable across industries • Responsive to market changes • All-encompassing definition	• Most complex definition • Difficult to measure • Customers may not know expectations • Idiosyncratic reactions • Prepurchase attitudes affect subsequent judgments • Short-term and long-term evaluations may differ • Confusion between customer service and customer satisfaction

Source: Carol A. Reeves and David A. Bednar, "Defining Quality: Alternatives and Implications," *Academy of Management Review* (Vol. 19, No. 3, July 1994), 437.

poration adopting Six Sigma as a way of improving quality and reducing costs.[63] Dow, DuPont, Sony, Honeywell, Nokia, GlaxoSmithKline, and Raytheon are but a few of the major corporations relying on the Six Sigma methodology. According to Jack Welch, former CEO of GE, "[Six Sigma—the Breakthrough Strategy] is the most important initiative GE has ever taken … it is part of the genetic code of our future leadership."[64] Although some deride Six Sigma as "TQM on steroids," it has brought new commitment and energy to the quest for quality in the new millennium. It is even said to have brought "more prominence to the quality world than it has enjoyed since the glory days of the mid-1980s."[65]

Motorola first developed Six Sigma, and Allied Signal later experimented with it, but most observers believe that GE perfected it. *Sigma* is a statistical measure of variation from the mean; higher values of sigma mean fewer defects. The six sigma level of operation is 3.4 defects per million. Most companies operate around the four sigma level (i.e., 6000 defects per million). Corporations adopting the program must develop "black belts"—people specifically trained to fill sponsorship roles, provide assistance, and see the program through. They must also find "champions" at senior levels of management who are committed to shepherding the program when needed.[66]

One of Six Sigma's strengths has been the clarity of the process and the steps companies must take to adopt it. However, Six Sigma is more than a toolbox with clear instructions. The program also represents a philosophy that stresses the importance of customers as well as careful measurement. Six Sigma practitioners look for facts rather than opinions, and they believe in fixing the process rather than the product.[67] Of course, these underlying principles are the foundation of TQM and most other quality efforts. The basis for all of these is the satisfaction of the consumer. Figure 12–7 outlines a consumer-stakeholder satisfaction model.

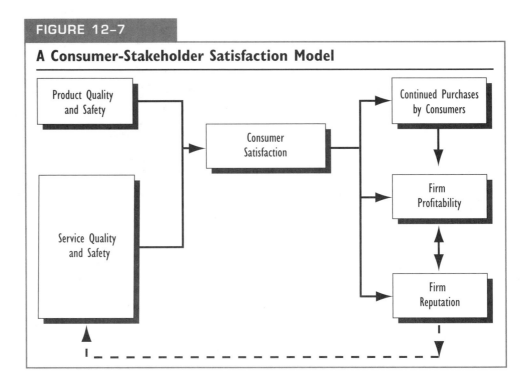

FIGURE 12–7

A Consumer-Stakeholder Satisfaction Model

Summary

Consumer stakeholders have become concerned with product quality and safety, largely because businesses have failed to meet their needs reliably on these two fronts. The situation has been the same with both manufacturing and services. One major challenge has been to identify and understand all the different dimensions of the quality issue. Today, quality may mean performance, features, reliability, conformance, durability, serviceability, aesthetics, perceived quality, or some combination of these dimensions.

An extremely important legal and ethical issue has been the consumer's right to safety. Product safety has become one of the most crucial consumer issues for firms. The product liability crisis has been an outgrowth of business's lack of attention to this issue. Other factors contributing to the product liability crisis have been the sheer number of harmful-product cases, our increasingly litigious society, the growing size of financial awards given by the courts, and rising insurance rates. Product tampering and product extortion have also become safety-related issues. In recent years, the health and safety issues related to foods, drugs, and medical devices have propelled the various branches in Health Canada and the Canadian Food Inspection Agency into prominent roles.

Quality improvement initiatives like TQM and Six Sigma have not solved all the problems. However, they and other techniques have the potential for addressing the problems in a significant way if they are properly formulated and implemented. In addition to these specific responses, a consumer focus and orientation needs to permeate management decision making if the concerns of consumers are to be handled effectively. In today's business environment, consumers have many choices. Consequently, companies have no alternative but to internalize the consumer focus if they are to succeed.

Key Terms

absolute liability (page 373)

Canadian Food Inspection Agency (CFIA) (page 379)

contractual theory (page 368)

delayed manifestation cases (page 374)

due care theory (page 368)

Food and Drug Administration (FDA) (page 380)

Health Canada (page 375)

market share liability (page 374)

Six Sigma (page 384)

social costs view (page 368)

strict liability (page 372)

total quality management (TQM) (page 383)

Discussion Questions

1. Identify the dimensions of quality. Give an example of a product or service in which each of these characteristics is important.

2. What ethical theories can help us to better understand the issue of quality? Discuss.

3. Identify the principal reasons why we have a product liability crisis. Have any reasons been omitted? Discuss.

4. Differentiate the doctrine of strict liability from the doctrines of absolute liability and market share liability. What implications do these views have for the business community and for future products and services that might be offered?

5. Given the current business and consumer climate, do you anticipate business becoming more responsive to consumer expectations? What role does politics play in your answer?

Endnotes

1. Terril Yue Jones, "Ford Board Deposes CEO Nasser," *Los Angeles Times* (October 30, 2001), part 3, page 1.

2. Keith Naughton, "Ford's Perfect Storm," *Newsweek* (September 17, 2001), 48.

3. *Ibid.*

4. Janice Castro, "Making It Better," *Time* (November 13, 1989), 78–80. See also "Quality: How to Make It Pay," *Business Week* (August 8, 1994), 54ff.

5. Walker Research, "Reputation and Social Performance Assessment Study" (Indianapolis: Walker Research, August 1994), 17.

6. Michael Harvey, Milorad M. Novicevic, and Timothy Kiessling, "Hypercompetition and the Future of Global Management in the Twenty-First Century," *Thunderbird International Review* (September/October 2001), 599–616.

7. Rajaram Veliyath and Elizabeth Fitzgerald, "Firm Capabilities, Business Strategies, Customer Preferences, and Hypercompetitive Arenas," *Competitiveness Review* (Vol. 10, 2000), 56–82.

8. Robert Trigaux, "Customer Satisfaction Down," *Chicago Sun-Times* (May 30, 2001), 64.

9. "Customers Turned Off by Poor Service Levels," *Marketing Week* (March 5, 1998), 11.

10. Stephen Koepp, "Pul-eese! Will Somebody Help Me?" *Time* (February 1987), 50.

11. David A. Garvin, "Competing on the Eight Dimensions of Quality," *Harvard Business Review* (November–December 1987), 101–109.

12. Manuel G. Velasquez, *Business Ethics: Concepts and Cases* (Upper Saddle River, NJ: Prentice Hall, 2002), 335–344.

13. Yair Aharoni, *The No Risk Society* (Chatham, NJ: Chatham House Publishers, 1981), 62–63.

14. Velasquez, 348.

15. Industry Canada, http://strategis.ic.gc.ca/epic/internet/inoca-bc.nsf/vwGeneratedInterE/ca00321e.html.

16. Douglas Herbert, "Food Frights Mount in Europe," *CNN.com* (March 13, 2001).

17. CNEWS, http://cnews.canoe.ca/CNEWS/Canada/Canadiana/2003/06/26/120540-cp.html.

18. *The National Post*, http://www.nationalpost.com/home/index.html

19. E. Patrick McGuire, "Product Liability: Evolution and Reform" (New York: The Conference Board, 1989), 6.

20. "2000 Report of the Consumer Products Safety Commission to the United States Congress," http://www.cpsc.gov.

21. Safe Kids Canada, http://www.safekidscanada.ca/ENGLISH/home.html.

22. "Ford's $128.5 Million Headache," *Time* (February 10, 1978), 65.

23. Robert P. Hartwig, "Whatever Happened to Tort Reform?" *National Underwriter* (November 20, 2000), 31–33.

24. Andrew Hacker, "The Asbestos Nightmare," *Fortune* (January 20, 1986), 121.

25. Francine Schwadel, "Robins and Plaintiffs Face Uncertain Future," *The Wall Street Journal* (August 23, 1985), 4.

26. David J. Morrow, "Implant Maker Reaches Accord on Damage Suits," *The New York Times* (July 9, 1998), A1.

27. Kristine Henry, "Chapter 11 Fails to Hurt Grace Much," *The Sun* (July 26, 2001), 2C.

28. Fred W. Morgan and Karl A. Boedecker, "A Historical View of Strict Liability for Product-Related Injuries," *Journal of Macromarketing* (Spring 1996), 103–117.

29. Ann Christopher, "Avoiding a Hazardous Violation," *Warehousing Management* (August 2001), 20.

30. Bruce Feldthusen, "Civil Liability in Canada: No Tip, No Iceberg," http://oldfraser.lexi.net/publications/books/laws_markets/civil_liability_in_canada_no_tip.html.

31. Terry Morehead Dworkin and Mary Jane Sheffet, "Product Liability in the 1980s," *Journal of Public Policy and Marketing* (1985), 71.

32. "Business Line: India Supreme Court Ruling on Damage Liability of Common Carrier," *Businessline* (June 30, 2000), 1.

33. Roger Leroy Miller, "Drawing Limits on Liability," *The Wall Street Journal* (April 4, 1984), 28.

34. Dworkin and Sheffet, 69.

35. Clemens P. Work, "Product Safety: A New Hot Potato for Congress," *U.S. News & World Report* (June 14, 1982), 62.

36. Edward J. Schoen, Margaret M. Hogan, and Joseph S. Falcheck, "An Examination of the Legal and Ethical Public Policy Consideration Underlying DES Market

Share Liability," *Journal of Business Ethics* (Vol. 24, 2000), 141–163.

37. "Tampering with Buyers' Confidence," *U.S. News & World Report* (March 3, 1986), 46.

38. Damien Thomlinson, "Drug Extortion Highlights Risks," *Business Insurance* (June 26, 2000), 33–37.

39. http://www.cbc.ca/consumers/market/files/food/best before/.

40. http://www.cbc.ca/consumers/market/files/food/bestbefore/inspection.html?8@@.ee91bdb).

41. http://www.cbc.ca/storyview/CBC/2001/08/27/cancer 010827.

42. Industry Canada, http://strategis.ic.gc.ca/epic/internet/inoca-bc.nsf/vwGeneratedInterE/ca00321e.html.

43. Health Canada, http://www.hc-sc.gc.ca/english/protection/index.html.

44. Health Canada, http://www.hc-sc.gc.ca/hecs-sesc/psp/index.htm.

45. Health Canada, http://www.hc-sc.gc.ca/hecs-sesc/cps/index.htm.

46. Health Canada, http://www.hc-sc.gc.ca/hecs-sesc/cps/laboratory.htm.

47. Health Canada, http://www.hc-sc.gc.ca/english/about/org.html#13.

48. Health Canada, http://www.hc-sc.gc.ca/hpfb-dgpsa/index_e.html.

49. Canadian Food Inspection Agency, http://www.inspection.gc.ca/english/corpaffr/publications/prog/agence.shtml.

50. Health Canada, http://www.hc-sc.gc.ca/english/media/index.html.

51. Food and Drug Administration, http://www.fda.gov.

52. Mary Gardner Jones, "The Consumer Affairs Office: Essential Element in Corporate Policy and Planning," *California Management Review* (Summer 1978), 63.

53. *Ibid.*, 64–69.

54. *Ibid.*, 70–72.

55. George Eads and Peter Reuter, "Designing Safer Products: Corporate Response to Product Liability Law and Regulation," *Journal of Products Liability* (Vol. 7, 1984), 265–267.

56. *Ibid.*, 268–271.

57. *Ibid.*, 285–289.

58. Rajan Chandran and Robert Linneman, "Planning to Minimize Product Liability," *Sloan Management Review* (Fall 1978), 36.

59. K. Ishikawa, *What Is Total Quality Control?* (Milwaukee, WI: Quality Press, 1985).

60. Lawrence A. Crosby, "Measuring Customer Satisfaction," in E. E. Scheuing and W. F. Christopher (eds.), *The Service Quality Handbook* (New York: AMACOM, 1993), 392.

61. A. Blanton Godfrey and E. G. Kammerer, "Service Quality vs. Manufacturing Quality: Five Myths Exploded," *The Service Quality Handbook*, 5.

62. Ron Basu, "Six Sigma to Fit Sigma," *IIE Solutions* (July 2001), 28–33.

63. Michael Hammer and Jeff Godling, "Putting Six Sigma in Perspective," *Quality* (October 2001), 58–62.

64. The Six Sigma Academy Website (http://www.6-sigma.com).

65. Hammer and Godling, 58.

66. Basu, 28–33.

67. *Ibid*.

Chapter 13

The Natural Environment as Stakeholder

Chapter Objectives

After studying this chapter, you should be able to:

1. Discuss why natural environment issues are complex.
2. Describe eight major natural environment issues.
3. Describe the NIMBY environmental problem.
4. Discuss the roles that business and government play in environmental issues.
5. Explain the concept of environmental ethics.

This chapter was co-authored by Mark Starik of George Washington University, Ann K. Buchholtz of the University of Georgia, and Len Karakowsky of York University.

Ask folks what they value about nature and most would probably be quick to mention aesthetic and spiritual properties like beauty, serenity and peace. We hold these values dear to our hearts because they resonate with strong emotional ties. But there are other, even more pragmatic, reasons to value nature—reasons even a hard-headed economist can't deny.... Without the rest of nature propping us up, we could not survive—a fact so obvious that it seems silly to point it out. The problem is, we don't behave as though this were obvious. We behave as though the economy is completely separate from the world in which we live. Industrialized society is geared entirely towards output—how many Playstations, SUVs and cans of Pepsi we can create, sell and consume. What aren't factored into the equation are the natural services needed to support this output. Why? Because nature's services are considered free.[1]

—Award-winning scientist, environmentalist, and Canadian broadcaster David Suzuki

A Brief Introduction to the Natural Environment

Similar to other broad terms, **environment** means many things to many people—trees in the backyard, a family's favourite vacation spot, a mare and her colt in a pasture, a trout stream in the mountains, earth and the other planets and space objects in our solar system. This chapter focuses on the natural environment—specifically, what it is, why it is important, how it has become a major concern, and what businesses and other organizations have done both to and for it. This chapter identifies what we mean when we use the term *environment* and why it has become one of the most significant societal issues of our time. We will also describe the variety of responses human organizations, including businesses, have developed to address this issue. Throughout the chapter, we will emphasize two themes: that humans are a part of their natural environment and that the environment itself, as well as the issues and human responses related to it, are extremely complex, defying simple analyses.

To assist you in making business environmental decisions in the future, we will present facts and figures, some of which will be technical and scientific, related to environmental issues and responses. These facts and figures are included to help you understand the complexities involved in the business and public environmental issues of today. Because of the influence of business, government, and environmental interest groups and individuals, these and many other technical terms and concepts are discussed in the media and, increasingly, in business and society texts. Environmental literacy, whether for wise business, government, or individual decision making, requires, at minimum, some rudimentary knowledge. Without at least some basic technical information, would-be stakeholder managers abdicate their responsibility to make prudent choices potentially crucial to the survival of their organizations, as well as to the survival of humans and other species in the natural environment. We call your attention to Figure 13–1, which presents definitions of a few of the most important environmental terms that might be helpful to you now and in the future.

The Impact of Business upon the Natural Environment

Unfortunately, businesses have played a major role in contributing to natural environment pollution and depletion. Virtually every sector of business in every country is

FIGURE 13–1

Glossary of Important and Helpful Environmental Terms

Environment	Broadly, anything that is external or internal to an entity. For humans, the environment can include external living, working, and playing spaces and natural resources, as well as internal physical, mental, and emotional states.
Carrying Capacity	The volume of and intensity of use by organisms that can be sustained in a particular place and at a particular time without degrading the environment's future suitability for that use. A resource's carrying capacity has limits that need to be respected for continued use.
Entropy	A measure of disorder of energy, indicating its unavailability for recycling for the same use. Energy tends to break down into lower quality with each use. For instance, a kilowatt of electricity, once it is produced and consumed, can never be used as electricity again, and, if stored, will allow far less than 1 kilowatt to be consumed.
Ecosystem	All living and nonliving substances present in a particular place, often interacting with others.
Greenhouse Effect	A warming of the Earth's surface and lower atmosphere that tends to intensify with an increase in atmospheric carbon dioxide.
Niche	The role an organism plays in its natural community, including what it eats and the conditions it requires for survival. Habitats and niches are interrelated concepts.
Cycle	The continuous looplike movement of water, air, and various nutrients, such as nitrogen, phosphorous, and sulfur, through the environment. Such cycles can be impaired in performing their evolutionary roles, such as purification and sustenance, by excessive human-caused pollution and depletion.
Threshold	The point at which a particular phenomenon, previously suppressed, suddenly begins to be activated. For instance, when a population's carrying capacity threshold is exceeded, the population tends to decrease or even crash as a result of increased morbidity and mortality.
Pollution	The existence of material or energy that has gone through a transformation process and is perceived as unwanted or devalued in a particular place at a particular time.
Irreversibility	The inability of humans and nature to restore environmental conditions to a previous state within relevant timeframes. Human environment-related actions that appear irreversible are the destruction of a rainforest or wilderness area and the extinction of a species.
Sustainability	The characteristic of an entity, such as an economic or environmental system, that is related to its ability to exist and flourish over an acceptably long period of time.

responsible for consuming significant amounts of materials and energy and causing waste accumulation and resource degradation. For instance, forestry firms and companies that process raw materials, such as uranium, coal, and oil, have caused major air, water, and land pollution problems in their extraction, transportation, and processing stages. Manufacturing firms, such as those in steel, petrochemicals, and paper products, have long been identified as major sources of air and water pollution. However, most major industry sectors contribute significant levels of pollution.

According to a recent assessment conducted by the Commission for Environmental Cooperation, U.S.-based companies actually show greater success in controlling emissions of hazardous pollutants compared to Canadian companies. According to the report, air pollutants released by Canadian industries increased by 7 percent from 1998 to 2000, while they decreased by 8 percent in the United States.

About half the increase in Canada was caused by one facility, the Ontario government's large, coal-fired Nanticoke power station on Lake Erie, which increased emissions by almost 3000 tonnes. In addition, the report ranked Ontario third in North America (only after Texas and Ohio), in terms of the amount of pollutants its businesses created. The 2003 report was based on the latest figures available from 1998–2000 and noted a disturbing increase in the output of hazardous materials by 15 000 medium-sized and small factories on both sides of the border. These facilities released about 100 tonnes a year each of chemicals that cause cancer or birth defects, or poison wildlife. And Canadian businesses reported a 66 percent increase in emissions over that period, which was more than twice the percentage increase in the United States.[2]

Why does Canada lag significantly behind the U.S.? Environmentalists have attributed the differences between the two countries to greater regulation in the United States. In addition, observers have noted that the U.S. does not allow hazardous wastes to be put in dumps. Canada, traditionally, has permitted this practice and it has not effectively forced Canadian companies to maintain long-term responsibility for their hazardous wastes.[3]

Figure 13–2 reports the differences among Canadian provinces in terms of the relative harm they bring to the environment via pollutants.

Although manufacturing and operations processes are the most visible contributors to air, water, and land pollution, virtually every other department within a business potentially plays some role in affecting the natural environment. Research labs and engineering departments, for instance, could be producing their own non-negligible amounts of environmental contaminants and often forwarding to their manufacturing departments products they have designed that are toxic and nonrecyclable. Finance departments, using inadequate accounting department data, could be recommending decisions based on short-term criteria that have not incorporated the full costs to the environment of potentially damaging projects. Human resources departments could be neglecting to incorporate environmental concerns in their personnel recruitment,

FIGURE 13–2

Ranking Provinces by Total Reported Pollutants (2001)

Rank	Province/Territory	Total Reported Releases and Transfers of Pollutants (kg)	Percentage
1	Ontario	129 934 059	28.92%
2	Alberta	118 314 158	26.33%
3	British Columbia	114 201 424	25.42%
4	Quebec	54 358 031	12.10%
5	Manitoba	10 501 184	2.34%
6	New Brunswick	8 606 831	1.92%
7	Nova Scotia	6 760 512	1.50%
8	Saskatchewan	4 861 926	1.08%
9	Newfoundland	1 260 182	0.28%
10	Prince Edward Island	504 190	0.11%
11	Northwest Territories	23 733	—
12	Nunavut	16 721	—

Source: Pollution Watch, http://www.pollutionwatch.org/home.do (2003). Reprinted by permission.

selection, and development decisions, potentially advancing individuals within the organization who do not share the organization's environmental values. Finally, marketing departments could be advertising and selling environmentally dubious products and services, with or without their customers' knowledge of this fact.

Of course, every coin has two sides. The power and productivity of business, which have been the source of so much environmental damage, can also be used to support the environment and mitigate the harm that was previously caused. Later in this chapter, we will introduce you to businesses that are good stewards of the environment. First, however, we will go into more detail about the range of issues facing the natural environment.

Natural Environment Issues

The latest wave of environmentalism has paralleled a growing public perception that global environmental problems are severe and worsening with time.[4] The following are eight key global natural environment problems:

- Ozone depletion
- Global warming
- Solid and hazardous wastes
- Fresh water quantity and quality
- Degradation of marine environments
- Deforestation
- Land degradation
- Endangerment of biological diversity

We will discuss each of these environmental problems briefly to give the reader a sense of the complexity and urgency with which these issues are increasingly viewed.

Ozone Depletion

Ozone is an oxygen-related gas that is harmful to life near the earth's surface but is vital in the stratosphere in blocking dangerous ultraviolet radiation from the sun. In 1985, NASA scientists observed a huge decrease in ozone over Antarctica. They then discovered a "hole" in the ozone layer that had grown as large as the North American continent. Their measurements showed that the flow of ultraviolet light had increased directly under the ozone hole. This phenomenon was attributed to human-produced chemicals—chlorofluorocarbons (CFCs), used in refrigeration, and halons, used in fire extinguisher systems, as well as other ozone-depleting chemicals. In 1987, the international community enacted strict controls on the use of these gasses through the United Nations Montreal Protocol. Recently, scientists reported that the joint effort may be succeeding—and that the ozone hole may repair itself over the next 50 years. Charles Kolb, an atmospheric research specialist and president of Aerodyne, noted, "We're all feeling very proud of the fact that we identified the problem and then the international community responded."[5]

Global Warming

According to a number of reputable sources, the earth's atmosphere is in danger of heating up. The **greenhouse effect**—that is, the prevention of solar heat absorbed by

Search the web

To interact effectively with environmental stakeholders, managers must educate themselves about environmental movement issues. Hundreds of organizations and Web sites deal with the natural environment. One particularly valuable Web site is EnviroLink Network, a grassroots environmental community located at **http://www.envirolink.org**. EnviroLink is a nonprofit organization that unites hundreds of organizations and volunteers around the world with millions of people in more than 150 countries. EnviroLink states that it "is dedicated to providing you with the most comprehensive, up-to-date environmental resources available." To learn more about EnviroLink's purposes, news, library, services, and awards, and such topics as sustainable business, animal rights, the green marketplace, and green living, visit this interesting and comprehensive Web site.

our atmosphere from returning to space—is expected to precipitate a rate of warming that is unprecedented in the last 10 000 years.[6] The burning of fossil fuels bears the primary responsibility (75 percent) for this phenomenon, with changes in land use, such as deforestation, accounting for the rest. In 2001, U.N. scientists predicted that temperatures would rise from 1.4°C to 5.8°C.[7] These recent temperature increases are about half of the entire warming of the earth that has occurred in the last 10 000 years. Some atmospheric prediction models indicate that, with continued global warming of from 2 to 9° Fahrenheit by the middle of the next century, coastal flooding from glacial melting might result and that forests, farm belts, wildlife habitats, and deserts might shift significantly. Both the severity and the effects of these shifts are unknown, as is the adaptability of ecosystems and living species, including humans, to these effects.[8,9] We do not yet know if we have crossed a threshold beyond which many of these projected effects will begin to be more substantially, perhaps threateningly, realized.

Canada has been accused of being among the higher contributors of greenhouse gas emissions in the industrialized world.[10] Greenhouse gas emissions dropped for the first time in a decade in 2001. However, emissions in 2001 were still about 19 percent higher than in 1990.[11] Figure 13–3 shows how provinces compared between 1990 and 2001 in terms of greenhouse gas emissions.

Solid and Hazardous Wastes

According to the Organization for Economic Cooperation and Development (OECD), the composition of municipal waste in Canada includes paper, cardboard, food, garden refuse, plastics, glass, metals, and textiles.[12] Recently the Conference Board of Canada noted Canada's poor performance in the OECD rankings among member nations. Canada ranked relatively poorly in terms of water quality, waste generation and disposal, and recycling.[13]

About 90 percent of the global wastes considered hazardous—that is, those requiring special handling to protect humans and the environment—is produced in industrialized countries.[14] These hazardous wastes include pesticides, petrochemicals, other organic chemicals such as dioxin and PCBs, and heavy metals. Unfortunately, many of these substances were not identified as hazardous until the 1970s and, consequently, their disposal up to that point is cause for great concern today: Many of these older disposal sites are unlined and are located within leaching distance of various bodies of water, especially underground aquifers.[15] In addition, as a result of tightening site controls in some areas, hazardous wastes are being transported away from their sources with greater frequency in recent years, both within countries and between countries, often to sites with weaker controls.

Approximately 6 million tonnes of hazardous waste are generated annually in Canada. Just over half this amount is destined for recycling, while about 5 percent of this amount is exported out of Canada. The responsibility for controlling hazardous waste and recyclable material in Canada is shared by the different levels of govern-

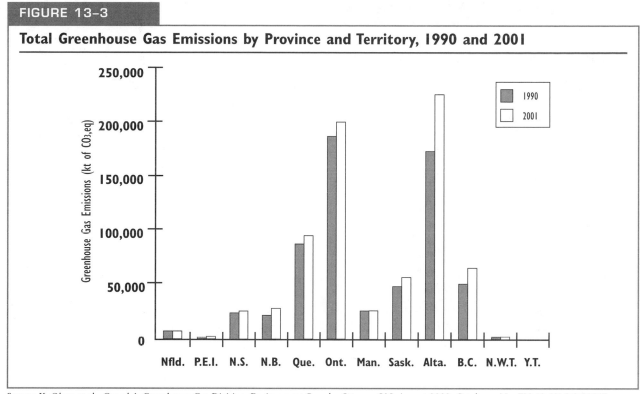

FIGURE 13–3

Total Greenhouse Gas Emissions by Province and Territory, 1990 and 2001

Source: K. Olsen et al., Canada's Greenhouse Gas Division, Environment Canada, Ottawa, ON, August 2003, Catalogue No. EN-49-5/5-9-2-2001E.

ment. The federal government regulates international and interprovincial movements of waste, while the provincial and territorial governments regulate intraprovincial movements of hazardous waste and recyclable material.[16]

Figure 13–4 shows changes in the importing and exporting of hazardous waste in Canada. In 2002, Canada decreased the import of hazardous wastes and hazardous recyclable material from the previous two years, totalling 423 067 tonnes, down from 500 000 tonnes in 2001. Imports of hazardous waste for landfilling decreased to 65 500 tonnes, a drop of 38 percent from 2001 levels (106 000 tonnes) and down by a total of 72 percent from 1999. About 97 percent of Canadian imports came from the United States in 2002, with a significant portion of the remainder coming from Germany.[17]

Fresh Water Quality and Quantity

Municipal sewage, industrial wastes, urban runoff, agricultural runoff, atmospheric fallout, and overharvesting all contribute to the degradation of the world's oceans and waterways. So too do dam sedimentation, deforestation, overgrazing, and overirrigation. Although water pollution is a global issue, consider just the effects of businesses and cities in Canada. For example, press reports in 2003 noted that the level of agricultural pollution in the Lake Champlain area is so significant that Missisquoi Bay, one of the largest bodies of water in Quebec, has been considered unsafe for swimming for many years. In addition, hundreds of notices advising citizens to boil their water are issued across Canada annually.[18]

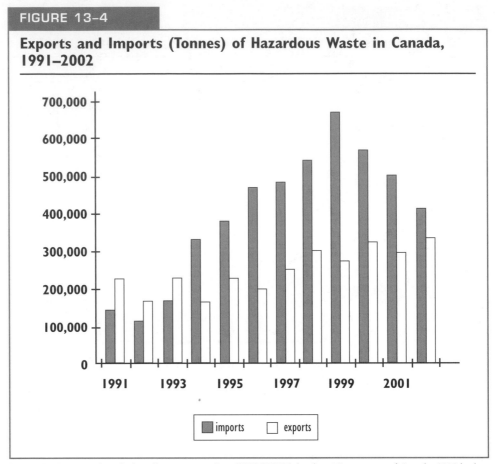

FIGURE 13–4

Exports and Imports (Tonnes) of Hazardous Waste in Canada, 1991–2002

Source: Environment Canada, http://www.ec.gc.ca/Press/2003/030820_b_e.htm (Government of Canada, 2003 backgrounder).

In a 2002 report by the North American Commission for Environmental Cooperation, it was noted that industrial pollution dumped into U.S. and Canadian lakes, rivers, and streams rose 26 percent from 1995 to 1999.[19] In 2003, it was reported that the largest water polluter in Canada was the city of Calgary's Bonnybrook Wastewater Treatment Plant, discharging 7.6 million kg of contaminants in the treated sewage it releases into the Bow River. The company's pollutants included 7.5 million kg of nitrate, which reduces the ability of blood to carry oxygen, and 107 200 kg of ammonia, a substance that has been declared toxic by the Canadian government.[20] Figure 13–5 ranks the provinces and territories in terms of water pollution.

Because global fresh water is unequally distributed, supplies are already over-taxed in shortage areas, reducing the quality of fresh water available for necessary human purposes. The associated results have been drought, desertification, and water-borne diseases in the developing world, as well as river, lake, bay, and accessible groundwater contamination on a large scale in developed countries. These water-shortage areas include rapidly shrinking water tables in China, the loss of two-thirds of the Aral Sea in the former Soviet Union, and the overappropriation of about half the rivers in the American West.[21] By the year 2025, two-thirds of the world's population may be living in countries under water stress conditions.[22]

FIGURE 13-5

Provinces Ranked by Water Pollution (2001)

Rank	Province/Territory	Water Releases (kg)	Percentage
1	Ontario	19 011 736	36.84%
2	Alberta	12 492 752	24.21%
3	British Columbia	11 814 118	22.90%
4	Manitoba	3 143 283	6.09%
5	Quebec	2 113 555	4.10%
6	New Brunswick	1 554 141	3.01%
7	Saskatchewan	1 057 101	2.05%
8	Prince Edward Island	209 965	0.41%
9	Nova Scotia	122 379	0.24%
10	Newfoundland	65 084	0.13%
11	Northwest Territories	13 805	0.03%
12	Nunavut	2 896	—

Source: Pollution Watch, http://www.pollutionwatch.org/rank.do. Reprinted by permission.

Degradation of Marine Environments

Many of the same factors that affect fresh water have an impact on the marine environments. Each year, trillions of litres of sewage and industrial waste are dumped into marine waters. These and other pollutants, such as oil and plastics, have been associated with significant damage to a number of coastal ecosystems, including salt marshes, mangrove swamps, estuaries, and coral reefs. The result has been local and regional shellfish bed closures, declining fish populations, seafood-related illnesses, and reduced shoreline protection from floods and storms.[23] Toxic and nutrient runoffs are resulting in algae blooms; trawling is destroying the sea floor; and climate change is warming the waters, causing coral reefs to die. Add to this the fact that fleets are currently 40 percent larger than the ocean can sustain, and it is no surprise that about one-third of the major commercial fish are in decline.[24]

Deforestation

Although humans depend on forests for building materials, fuel, medicines, chemicals, food, employment, and recreation, the world's forests can be quickly depleted by a variety of human factors. **Deforestation** adds to soil erosion problems and is a major cause of the greenhouse effect. Forests are major receptacles or "sinks" of carbon. Carbon is absorbed from the atmosphere and stored in forests (in living or dead biomass, soils, or in forest products). Scientists have indicated that increases in the amount of carbon stored in forests (i.e., creating "carbon sinks") can potentially help mitigate climate change. On the other hand, deforestation on a global level contributes to climate change due to the permanent loss of stored carbon that occurs when the trees are removed. Approximately one-third of all human-caused emissions of greenhouse gases (GHGs) over the previous 150 years have been due to changes in land use, largely from deforestation and forest degradation.[25]

In addition, while felled trees can no longer absorb carbon dioxide, those that are burned for land clearing and charcoal actually release carbon dioxide. Moisture and nutrient ecosystem cycles can also be severely damaged in deforesting activities, negatively affecting adjacent land and water ecosystems.

Canada has experienced less deforestation than the global average, but loss of forests remains as a significant GHG contributor. In terms of deforestation in Canada, the best estimates indicate that between 54 000 and 80 500 hectares of forests are lost per year. A major cause of deforestation in Canada involves the conversion for agriculture and forestry operations, mining and petroleum exploration, and urban conversion.[26]

Deforestation is a problem for developed and developing countries alike. Tropical deforestation is also the main reason that 25 percent of the world's primates could disappear by 2030.[27] Fortunately, there is some good news on this front. The Food and Agriculture Organization (FAO) of the United Nations reported that there are strong indications of a slowdown in the rate of deforestation. From 1980 to 1990, deforestation took place at an estimated loss of 15.5 million hectares per year. A 2000 report, however, indicated a reason for hope. Since the 1990s, there has been a 10 percent slowdown in the rate of tropical deforestation. "These preliminary results do not mean that the battle against deforestation is over.... It does show, however, that the long-term efforts of FAO and others to build awareness of and capacity for sustainable forest management are worthwhile and should be reinforced."[28]

Land Degradation

Another disturbing environmental issue that human populations face is the continuing and increasing problem of **soil erosion** and spoilage. Productive, nutrient-rich soil is blown away by winds and carried away by rains when unprotected. Deforestation, acid rain, ozone depletion, and overgrazing all contributed to a loss of 260 billion tonnes of topsoil in the 1980s.[29] World grain production has fallen 14 percent since 1984, and famine, drought, and overpopulation and distribution inequities have annually been responsible for 40 to 60 million human deaths from hunger and hunger-related disease.[30] Although many of these land degradation problems are regionalized in Third World countries, developed nations, too, have experienced land productivity difficulties. As the population of the world continues to grow, the problems created by the loss of productive soil will only increase.

While Canada's total supply of farmland has remained constant at approximately 68 million hectares, over the past 30 years significant changes have occurred in how this land is used. Recent reports by Statistics Canada using information available between 1901 and 1996 indicated that Canada's cultivated land areas expanded fivefold over that period. However, the availability of dependable agricultural land diminished by about 16 percent over that period because of conversion to urban and other nonagricultural uses. By the 1980s, land under cultivation surpassed the supply of dependable land. This striking contrast reflects the fact that agricultural production in Canada is increasingly reliant on marginal land, which could have negative consequences for productivity, soil quality, wildlife habitat, and other environmental issues.[31]

Endangerment of Biological Diversity

Throughout most of time, species lived an average of one million years, with species dying out at the rate of about one species per million years. The current rate of species extinction is about 100 to 1000 times greater than that.[32] Furthermore, not only is the extinction rate soaring, but the birthrate of new species is also declining.[33] In addition to the depletion of large mammal species, such as the elephants and black rhinos of

Africa, and birds such as the California condor and mosquito-catcher, there are some 20 000 endangered species of animals around the world, many of which are in trouble because of overhunting and poaching. Ecosystem and habitat destruction through agricultural and urban development activities and, of course, pollution have put at risk not only wildlife, but many species of very beneficial plants as well. Up to half of all human medicines are derived from plants, and yet, in especially productive areas such as the world's rain forests, excesses in individual and organizational activities are responsible for significant and tragic ecosystem and species degradation.

Other Environmental Issues

In addition to these eight major environmental issues, other concerns have arisen around the world that appear to threaten human health and other aspects of the natural environment. **Air pollution**, both outdoors and indoors, often rates high in concern according to public opinion polls. An estimated 50 million children in developing countries suffer from chronic coughing because of smog.[34] Figure 13–6 identifies six leading air pollutants and their associated human health concerns.

In addition to causing human health problems, ambient air pollution is also responsible for a condition called **acid rain**, which has caused a variety of significant negative impacts on the natural environments of several countries. Figure 13–7 defines this condition and lists some of its causes. The damage from this fossil fuel–caused problem has been blamed for sterilizing up to 80 percent of the lakes and streams in Norway, damaging 64 percent of British forests, and destroying more than 40 percent of the coniferous forests in central Switzerland.[35] Acid rain has caused significant deterioration of both the natural environment and human structures in other areas of the world, including Pennsylvania; Nova Scotia; Agra, India; Tokyo; Central Africa; and Sao Paulo, Brazil.[36]

Approximately 142 000 Canadian lakes have been damaged by acid rain since the 1970s.[37] Acid rain has been particularly problematic for eastern Canada because many of the water and soil systems in this region lack natural alkalinity (i.e., a lime base) and consequently cannot neutralize acid naturally. The provinces most affected by acid rain are Ontario, Quebec, New Brunswick, and Nova Scotia. The water and soil systems of these regions cannot battle the damaging consequences of acid rain. Unfortunately,

---

FIGURE 13–6

Health Effects of Several Air Pollutants

Pollutants	Health Concerns
Ozone	Respiratory tract problems such as difficult breathing and reduced lung function. Asthma, eye irritation, nasal congestion, reduced resistance to infection, and possible premature aging of lung tissue.
Particulates	Eye and throat irritation, bronchitis, lung damage, and impaired vision.
Carbon Monoxide	Impairment of the blood's ability to carry oxygen and effects on cardiovascular, nervous, and pulmonary systems.
Sulfur Dioxide	Respiratory tract problems, permanent harm to lung tissue.
Lead	Retardation and brain damage, especially in children.
Nitrogen Dioxide	Respiratory illness and lung damage.

Source: Environmental Protection Agency, *Meeting the Environmental Challenge* (Washington, DC: USGPO, December 1990), 10.

FIGURE 13–7

Definition and Sources of Acid Rain

Acid rain is rain, snow, or fog that is polluted by acid in the atmosphere and damages the environment. Two common air pollutants acidify rain: sulfur dioxide (SO_2) and nitrogen oxide (NO_X). When these substances are released into the atmosphere, they can be carried over long distances by prevailing winds before returning to earth as acidic rain, snow, fog, or dust. When the environment cannot neutralize the acid being deposited, damage occurs.

Sulfur dioxide (SO_2) is generally a byproduct of industrial processes and burning of fossil fuels. Ore smelting, coal-fired power generators, and natural gas processing are the main contributors. In 1998, for instance, U.S. SO_2 emissions were measured at 17.7 million tonnes—more than six times greater than Canada's 2.7 million total tonnes. But the sources of SO_2 emissions from the two countries are quite different. While 74 percent of Canada's emissions come directly from industrial sources, 67 percent of the U.S.'s emissions are from electric utilities.

Canada cannot win the fight against acid rain on its own. Only reducing acidic emissions in both Canada and the U.S. will stop acid rain. More than half of the acid deposition in eastern Canada originates from emissions in the United States.

Source: Environment Canada (2003), http://www.ec.gc.ca/acidrain/acidfact.html.

more than half of Canada includes areas consisting of susceptible hard rock (i.e., granite) and therefore cannot neutralize the effects of acid rain. The water and soil systems are more alkaline-based in western Canada and consequently are more capable of neutralizing or "buffering" against acid rain naturally in that region.[38]

Indoor air pollution is another environmental problem that is becoming an increasing concern, primarily in industrialized countries. Asbestos was used as an insulator in schools and other buildings in Canada for many years but has been identified as causing asbestosis, an incurable lung disease afflicting those who inhale asbestos fibres. Other serious indoor air pollutants include radon, tobacco smoke, formaldehyde, pesticide residues, and perchloroethylene (associated with dry cleaning). Certain construction materials and other household products, such as some paints, carpeting, and gas furnaces, are primarily responsible for these contaminants, which are associated with a variety of human health problems from nausea to cancer.[39]

A third environmental problem is **energy inefficiency**, or the wasting of precious nonrenewable sources of energy. Nonrenewable energy sources, such as coal, oil, and natural gas, were formed millions of years ago under unique conditions of temperature, pressure, and biological phenomena (hence the term *fossil fuels*). Once these are depleted, they will apparently be gone forever. In addition, because these fuels are not equally distributed around the world, they are the cause of significant power imbalances worldwide, with associated armed conflicts that are typically disastrous for both humans and the natural environment in general.[40]

Part of the answer to the nonrenewability problem is to use as little as possible of these energy sources through implementation of sound energy conservation practices. In addition, shifting to renewable energy sources, such as solar, wind, hydroelectric, and biomass forms of energy, is an increasingly attractive option for both industrial and agricultural societies. Several technologies for tapping these renewable, low-polluting energy sources are becoming economically competitive with nonrenewable sources.[41,42] However, even though proponents argue that solar and wind power are ready for mass utilization, much of Canada's electricity has come from nonrenewable and highly polluting coal.

The importance of considering alternate energy sources has been emphasized by such scholars as David Suzuki, who has criticized large crude oil producers such as ESSO of denying the need to act on the detrimental impact of its products on the environment:

We now consume petroleum products, which slowly accumulated over millions of years, at a tremendous rate. The combustion of fuel in our cars, factories and power plants has pumped billions of tonnes of microscopic particles and greenhouse gases into our atmosphere, fundamentally changing its composition. Switching from fossil fuels to clean, renewable energy sources is vital to protect our atmosphere and climate. While much of the oil and gas sector opposes action on climate change, some fossil fuel companies now recognize it as a reality. Re-shaping themselves as energy suppliers, rather than just than oil and gas companies, they are making investments in renewable energy.[43]

Another environmental problem, which is interconnected with those mentioned earlier, deserves special attention because of its potential for harm: the production of **toxic substances**, whether as constituents of intended end-products or as unwanted byproducts. Toxic substances, defined by Health Canada and Environment Canada as chemicals or mixtures that may present unreasonable risks of injury to health or to the environment, can include pesticides, herbicides, solvents, fuels, radioactive substances, and many other potential candidates.[44] Whether or not they are considered waste materials, toxic substances can have significant negative impacts on humans and on the natural environment in general. The problem with materials such as benzyl chloride, hydrogen cyanide, and methyl isocyanate is that very small amounts are incompatible with living tissue, destroy cell functions, and eventually cause total system shutdown.[45]

Although extreme care may be exercised if society decides it needs to manufacture such substances, which is a questionable prospect, two problems remain. First, we are not always aware of the effects, especially the long-term and interactive effects, of exposure to the thousands of chemicals that are produced each year. Even in those instances where the toxicity of a chemical is known and the chemical is banned for sale in one country (such as the pesticide DDT in Canada), the substance can still be manufactured in that country and exported, only to return when products that have been exposed to these substances are imported.

Second, toxic substances can be associated with industrial accidents, causing unforeseen widespread biological damage. The 1984 Bhopal, India, chemical plant leak; the 1986 Chernobyl nuclear power plant meltdown in the former Soviet Union; and the 1989 *Exxon Valdez* oil spill in Alaska are three well known environmental disasters involving toxic substances. Not so well known are the 14 000 oil spills that are reported each year.[46] Although the *Exxon Valdez* spill covered 2000 kilometres of Alaskan shoreline and was as wide as three football fields, that spill was only 53rd in the rankings of worldwide oil spills.[47]

Canada also has its share of environmental scandals that go largely unnoticed. For example, Uniroyal Chemical Company was fined a total of $125 000 after pleading guilty to two charges under the Environmental Protection Act. The company was convicted of discharging pollutants into the environment as a result of a spill at the company's operations in Elmira, Ontario, in 2000. The company was also charged for failing to notify the regional municipality of the spill.[48] The world seems awash in toxic substances, and this and the other environmental issues mentioned in this section lead us to ask about the core causes of this perceived crisis.

Three types of pollution that recently have received less attention than they once did are *radon*, *noise pollution*, and *aesthetic pollution*. Radon is a radioactive gas that has been found in an increasing number of residential structures resulting from the natural radioactive decay of certain substances either found in the soil or used in construction materials. Radon has been identified as a cause of lung cancer.[49] Noise pollution can exist anywhere unwanted sounds are heard, but it most often results from operation of heavy machinery within limited areas. Factories, construction sites, and airports are frequently identified as noise pollution areas. Severe noise pollution can cause hearing impairment in humans and habitat disruption for other species. Aesthetic pollution occurs when visual tastes are violated and typically centre around construction, signage, and land appearance. Commercial building facades, outdoor billboards, and litter were significant local issues in the past. We mention these pollution sources to illustrate that environmental issues change with time and can vary from place to place, arguing for a flexible approach to environmental management.

Responsibility for Environmental Issues

Problems such as smog, toxic waste, and acid rain can be described as "wicked problems"—that is, problems with characteristics such as interconnectedness, complexity, uncertainty, ambiguity, conflict, and societal constraints.[50] Affixing responsibility for such messy situations is problematic, because solutions to wicked problems are seldom complete and final and, therefore, credit for these solutions is seldom given or taken. *Chlorofluorocarbons*, or *CFCs*, for example, were once thought to be safe alternatives to other, more toxic refrigerants, which is why these ozone destroyers are so ubiquitous in our society's technologies.

The NIMBY Problem

One example of this question of responsibility is the **NIMBY**, or "Not In My Back Yard," phenomenon. This acronym, which can be found on bumper stickers and conference agendas and in newspaper articles, college courses, and many other communication vehicles, is the human denial of responsibility for the misuse of the environment. One example of NIMBY is the community that uses ever-increasing amounts of electricity but decides it does not want a power plant that produces electricity to locate nearby. Another is a company that generates increasing amounts of waste but is unwilling to pay the full cost of proper disposal. Essentially, NIMBY is an attitude/behaviour set based on avoidance or denial of responsibility. When applied to the field of environmental management, NIMBY spells big trouble.

The obvious difficulty with the NIMBY syndrome is that the entities (human individuals, organizations, or both) causing environmental pollution or degradation are not identified as the sources of the problem, and therefore no action is taken to reduce the problem. The NIMBY phenomenon avoids or denies the root cause of the damage and addresses only the symptoms with an attitude of nonresponsibility characterized by an approach of "I'll create an environmental problem, but I want to have as little as possible to do with solving it." One popular cartoon characterizing the NIMBY problem pictures a stream of polluting, honking cars passing along a highway in front of a huge billboard that reads "Honk if you love the environment!"

Environmental Ethics

What does human environmental sensitivity mean? Humans must consume at least some plants and water to survive. If humans and their organizations need to pollute

Ethics In Practice

Going Down the Drain

I worked at a small business that used cars in their daily deliveries. To save money, the brothers who owned the business would conduct most of their own maintenance on the vehicles. As a result, they would periodically be involved in doing tune-ups, changing oil, and other such activities. One day I noticed that the brothers would pour the old motor oil down the drain rather than take it for recycling. This troubled me because I know how greatly old oil can add to the degradation of the environment. I brought up the subject with them and they laughed it off. They told me that, as a small business, they did not have the time nor the money to be concerned with the "niceties" of life. We discussed it several times and they made it clear they would not change their ways.

I didn't know what to do. I liked this job. The location was perfect and the people were nice (in every other way). I wanted to keep working there until I finished school. However, I felt that I shared in the responsibility for the damage caused by the oil if I knew it was happening and did nothing about it. If I reported it to someone, I knew they'd know the report came from me. What could I do?

1. Is NIMBY involved here? If so, in what way?

2. Do you share in the responsibility for negative action when you know it is happening and say nothing?

3. What would you do if you were in that position?

Contributed Anonymously

and destroy at least some of nature for their survival, what is the relative level of degradation that is ethical? Do nonhuman species have any "rights," and, if so, what are they, and how can they be reconciled with human rights? Concerning human rights and the environment, how do we assess the claims of indigenous cultures to the use of their respective environments? Is there any connection between the domination of humans by humans (e.g., the domination of one nation, race, or gender by another) and the domination of nature by humans? This latter question is especially central to several schools of environmental ethical thought, including social ecology and environmental justice.

Whose standards will determine what is or is not ethical? Numerous public opinion surveys have indicated that most citizens in many countries (such as Canada and the United States) support the concept of environmental protection,[51] but how much the public will do itself or insist that governments and businesses do to protect the environment is still an unanswered question. How clean do the air and water need to be, and how much is the public willing to pay to meet these standards? As in our earlier discussion of business ethics, values play a major role and can be highly variable in breadth and depth across perspectives, situations, and time.

What are some environmental values (or **green values**)? According to one source associated with the "green" movement, many environmentalists hold four beliefs as fundamental values: (1) life on earth should continue; (2) human life on earth should continue; (3) natural justice should be done; and (4) nonmaterial qualities of life are worth pursuing.[52] These four principles underlie the twelve points of the *Green Manifesto*, identified in Figure 13–8. They are summed up in the statement: "Overall, the Green goal is to allow everyone the opportunity to live a fulfilling life, caring and sharing with each other, future generations and other species, while living sustainably within the capacities of a limited world."[53]

FIGURE 13–8

One Listing of "Green" Values

Put earth first: respect nature's life support systems.

Live within limits: unlimited expansion is self-defeating.

Think in terms of sufficiency: "enough" must replace "more."

Tread lightly: seek productive coexistence, not domination.

Defend diversity: promote variety of environment and culture.

Respect our descendants' rights: save for future generations.

Design with nature: respect long-term, stable patterns.

Keep things in proportion: human scale for human-made systems.

Balance rights and responsibilities: society has value.

Decentralize and democratize: localism and participation.

Tread carefully: technology can have unforeseen results.

Bad means produce bad ends: how is as important as what.

Source: S. Irvine and A. Pouton, *A Green Manifesto* (London: Optima, 1988), 14–16.

Following the ethical models discussed in Chapters 6 and 7, other environmental issues can be added to develop a better idea of what environmental ethics is and how it can be practised. Kohlberg's model of moral development, for instance, can be used to identify environment-related attitudes and behaviours by developmental level. At the preconventional (infant) level in environmental ethics, humans and human organizations can be perceived as being concerned only with self or with their own species and habitats. A conventional (adolescent) level might entail some appreciation of nature, but only when and where such appreciation is commonplace or "in." A post-conventional (adult) environmental ethic might include more mature attitudes and behaviours that are more universal (including all species and habitats), of greater duration (including unborn generations), and more consistent (if we humans have a right to survive as a species, why don't all species have that right?). Similarly, the moral principle of utilitarianism—the greatest good for the greatest number—could be expanded in environmental ethics to the greatest good for the greatest numbers of species and ecosystems. The Golden Rule could read, "Do unto other species as you would have them do unto you." Finally, the "Best Self" ethical test could include the question, "Is this action or decision related to the natural environment compatible not only with my concept of myself at my best but also with my concept of myself as a human representing my species at its best?"

Environmental ethics is an important and intriguing subtopic of business ethics and is gaining attention in both academics and business. However, the prudent business environmentalist is advised to guard against becoming self-righteous in terms of either personal or organizational environmental ethics. The concept of "ecological correctness" is a very slippery issue (because both nature and humans and their technology are so varied around the planet and are constantly changing). It can even be an obstacle to those who might wish to become more environmentally sensitive but are put off by a "more-ecological-than-thou" attitude.

To return to the question of who sets environmental norms, the answer may be similar to the question of who sets society's norms—We all do, in part. This analysis implies that, as in ethical questions in general, the best approach to environmental ethics may be to practise tolerance, to see the world through others' perspectives, and to continue to question one's own environmental values as well as those of others.

The Role of Governments in Environmental Issues

As we mentioned earlier, governments have played major roles in environmental issues since the inception of such issues. Governments have procured, distributed, and developed habitable lands and other resources; protected, taxed, and zoned natural environment–based areas; and, more recently, exercised regulatory control over how those environments could be used. In this section, we'll look at how governments in Canada have dealt with environmental challenges and then identify what has been done in several other countries and at the international level.

Responses of Governments in Canada

At the federal level two government bodies, Health Canada and Environment Canada, have a key focus on environmental issues. In 1988, the **Canadian Environmental Protection Act (CEPA)** was passed as federal environmental law, stating that "the protection of the environment is essential to the well-being of Canada."[54]

The new (1999) Canadian Environmental Protection Act is aimed at:

contributing to sustainable development through pollution prevention and to protect the environment, human life and health from the risks associated with toxic substances. CEPA also recognizes the contribution of pollution prevention and the management and control of toxic substances and hazardous waste to reducing threats to Canada's ecosystems and biological diversity. It acknowledges for the first time the need to virtually eliminate the most persistent toxic substances that remain in the environment for extended periods of time before breaking down and bioaccumulative toxic substances that accumulate within living organisms. Health Canada works in partnership with Environment Canada to assess potentially toxic substances and to develop regulations to control toxic substances.[55]

Air Quality Legislation Provincial governments have the central responsibility for many areas of air pollution control, though the federal government is also involved. The CEPA is the main federal legislation for the regulation of environmental contaminants. The CEPA permits the federal government to regulate and control substances through national quality guidelines and standards. Specifically, the federal government can assess air pollutants and control their consequences through the establishment of the National Ambient Air Quality Objectives (NAAQOs) and Canada-Wide Standards (CWSs) under CEPA.[56] NAAQOs play a key role in air quality management by identifying benchmark levels of protection for

Search the *web*   W W W

Within Health Canada, Healthy Environments and Consumer Safety (HECS) is organized into five programs, each with responsibilities for a vast array of policies, programs, and services, which are planned, coordinated, and delivered by more than 1000 staff located in every region of the country. One of these programs, Safe Environments, is involved with the following areas:

- Radiation protection
- Environmental contaminants
  - Health and air quality
  - Existing substances
  - Toxics management
  - Indoor air quality
- Water quality and health
- Health impacts
  - Environmental health assessment services
  - Climate change and health office
  - Toxic substances research initiative
  - Children's environmental health

For a review of the latest information on regulations, proposed rules, and current legislation, visit HECS's Web site at **http://www.hc-sc.gc.ca/hecs-sesc/hecs/sep/index.htm**.

people and the environment. CWSs offer achievable targets on air pollutant reduction in order to reduce health and environmental risks within a specific time frame.[57]

One type of air pollution that is increasing in importance is *indoor air pollution*. It has been estimated that indoor levels of air pollutants may be two to five times, and occasionally, more than 100 times, higher than outdoor levels. This is of special concern because it is estimated that most people spend as much as 90 percent of their time indoors.[58] Tobacco smoke, paints, fumes, furnace exhaust, and out-gassing products of many kinds have been identified as potential indoor air pollutants, causing business employees and housing residents to complain about a variety of health problems.

There is no single organization in Canada that has sole responsibility for investigating and regulating the potential health impact of residential indoor air pollutants. Consequently, business largely governs its own behaviour in this regard. However, there are a number of national agencies in Canada that can play in this area, including:

- Health Canada
- Environment Canada
- Public Works and Government Services Canada
- Natural Resources Canada
- Agriculture and Agri-Foods Canada
- Canada Mortgage and Housing Corporation
- National Research Council Canada, Division of Building Research
- Housing and Urban Development Association of Canada
- Canadian General Standards Board[59]

Water Quality Legislation   Environment Canada is the federal government's central source regarding water-related legislation, including the Canada Water Act (1970), the Canadian Environmental Protection Act (1999), the Fisheries Act, the Navigable Waters Protection Act, the Yukon Waters Act, the Northwest Territories Waters Act, the Arctic Waters Pollution Prevention Act, the Canada Shipping Act, and the Dominion Water Power Act.[60]

The Canada Water Act authorizes the Minister of the Environment to establish consultative arrangements with provinces on water resource issues, including planning and implementation programs in any waters where there is a significant national interest in water resource management. It also permits the minister to conclude agreements with provinces for the joint designation of water quality management areas for federal waters or any other waters where water quality management has become a matter of urgent national concern. The Canada Water Act also contains regulations regarding the concentration of nutrients in cleaning agents and water conditioners.[61]

According to Environment Canada, the government's federal water policy is intended to:

- encourage the use of fresh water in an efficient and equitable manner consistent with the social, economic, and environmental needs of present and future generations;
- protect and enhance the quality of the water resource; and,
- promote the wise and efficient management and use of water.[62]

Land-Related Legislation   Land pollution and degradation issues differ from air and water quality issues, because land by definition is far less fluid and therefore somewhat more visible than air and water and is more amenable to local or regional problem-solving approaches.

The Canadian Environmental Protection Act (CEPA) focuses on pollution prevention and protection of the environment, human life, and health from the risks associated with toxic substances. To be determined toxic under CEPA, "substances must enter the environment in amounts that have or may have an immediate or long-term harmful effect on the environment or human health."[63] Approximately 23 000 chemicals and other substances were already in use in Canada when the CEPA was first passed in 1988.[64] Even small releases of certain chemicals or substances (such as PCBs and DDT) to the environment can cause problems that are harmful, costly, or impossible to correct.

CEPA-toxic substances considered to pose the greatest threat are those that accumulate in living tissue, remain in the environment for a long time without breaking down, and are the result of human activity. If an existing substance is found to be CEPA-toxic, Health Canada and Environment Canada will aim to establish appropriate controls on the manufacture, import, use, release into the environment, and/or disposal of the substance. The governmental controls may involve generating restrictions, guidelines, or codes of practice. These controls may also be used to govern the entire life cycle of a substance, including where and how it is produced and used, and the amount that can be produced and used in a given time period.[65] The 1995 Toxic Substances Management Policy represents a preventive approach to deal with toxic substances through "virtual elimination" and "life cycle management."

Existing substances that meet the criteria of CEPA-toxic, such as dioxins and PCBs, are slated by the government for "virtual elimination" from the environment. Virtual elimination refers to the reduction in toxic substance releases to the point where they can no longer be measured. Given that the existence of social, economic, or technical factors may make it impossible to reach virtual elimination immediately, the government can establish a phased approach with ever-decreasing limits until the desired minimum level is reached. CEPA requires companies to prepare "virtual elimination plans" to achieve the regulatory release limit. Life cycle management involves preventive or control measures regarding the generation of toxic substances. Manufacturing and importing of new substances found to be toxic can be prohibited or subjected to conditions pointed out by the government. For existing substances (such as those on the Domestic Substances List) found to be toxic, the Minister of the Environment must develop preventive or control measures within a two-year period, which can include voluntary arrangements, economic instruments, and requirements for pollution prevention planning.

There is little doubt that all individuals are highly concerned with the control of toxic substances in the environment. And certainly it is obvious that government legislation to ensure a safe environment is critical. Yet, many observers note the incongruity between societal concerns and the actual conditions under which we eat, breathe, and live—conditions that seem to be increasingly filled with unwanted and harmful substances. Consider David Suzuki's striking comments:

> *Having safe water and reducing our exposure to toxic substances are*
> *also national security concerns. The tragedy in Walkerton, Ontario, that*
> *resulted in seven deaths, and the hundreds of boil-water advisories across*
> *the country have made Canadians acutely aware of the connection*
> *between ecosystem health and human health. Medical professionals are*
> *all too aware of this connection. The Canadian Institute of Child Health,*
> *for example, says that exposure to toxic substances in the environment*
> *has likely contributed to a 25 percent increase in childhood cancer over*

the past 25 years.... Public safety ultimately depends as much on a healthy environment as on secure borders and airports.[66]

International Government Environmental Responses

The global nature of many natural environment issues has meant that international institutions have played important roles. Certainly, one international institution that has led the way in identifying global environmental problems and in working toward their resolution has been the United Nations Environment Programme (UNEP). Since its creation in 1972, this agency has been at the forefront in each of eight major environmental areas mentioned earlier in this chapter. As early as 1977, UNEP was studying the ozone problem and began to lay the groundwork for the 1987 **Montreal Protocol**, in which most of the CFC (chlorofluorocarbon) producing and consuming nations around the world agreed to a quick phase-out of these ozone-destroying substances. As a result, the worldwide consumption of ozone-depleting substances declined nearly 75 percent from 1994–2001. The UNEP reports that an estimated 1.5 million cases of melanoma will have been averted by the year 2060, thanks to the Montreal Protocol.[67]

UNEP is also funding research and assisting in information exchange on the protection and more sustainable use of international waters. The Global Waters Assessment will examine the problems surrounding shared transboundary waters, develop scenarios on the future condition of the world's water, and analyze various policy options. UNEP is also the driving force behind efforts to initiate global sound management of hazardous chemicals. They were an integral part of the Rotterdam Convention, which requires that countries give explicit informed consent before hazardous chemicals cross their borders. UNEP also works to protect the world's biological diversity. Through their efforts, the elephant has been brought back from the brink of extinction.[68]

The **Kyoto Protocol** is an international treaty aimed at reducing greenhouse gas emissions that cause global warming. It is legally binding and requires member countries to reduce their greenhouse gas emissions to an average of 5 to 6 percent below 1990 levels by 2010.

On December 17, 2002, Canada signed the Kyoto Protocol, and thereby agreed to reduce greenhouse gas emissions (to 6 percent below 1990 levels) between 2008 and 2012. In response, the federal government has established commissions, task forces, written reports, and Web sites as a means to help facilitate this goal. In their article written for *Corporate Knights*, George Greene and Desiree McGraw also noted the central role of Canadian business in achieving the Kyoto objectives:

> *[W]e need corporate leadership and demonstrated corporate responsibility. In each of the key sectors both affected by and contributing to rising greenhouse-gas emissions, there are companies which have identified climate change as both a risk and a strategic driver for their businesses in the future. Companies in oil and gas, utilities, mining, manufacturing and forest products, among others, have used their public sustainability reports to show shareholders and communities that they are serious about global warming. And many have for years been laying the technological and investment foundations to respond to this challenge. It is now time for these corporate leaders to fully step forward.*[69]

Other Environmental Stakeholders

Environmental Interest Groups

Perhaps no force in today's society is more responsible for the "greening" of nations around the world than the many environmental interest groups making up what has come to be known as "the environmental movement." This collection of nonprofit membership and think-tank organizations has been credited with moving the world's governments and businesses, as well as publics, in the direction of environmental responsibility through a host of activities, including demonstrations, boycotts, public education, lobbying, and research.

The history of the environmental movement is instructive. Whereas a few North American groups (the National Audubon Society, the Izaak Walton League, and the Sierra Club) were formed in the early 1900s during the first green wave of the last century, many of the largest international environmental groups, such as the Environmental Defense Fund (now called Environmental Defense) and Greenpeace were created during the second environmental wave in North America, during the late 1960s and early 1970s. Since that time, all of these groups and hundreds of other smaller, more locally focused environmental organizations have grown in size and clout. It was the twentieth century's third wave of environmentalism, beginning in the late 1980s, however, that gave many of these groups the power and legitimacy to become credible players in environmental policy making around the globe.

Environmental interest groups have been instrumental in significantly influencing business environmental policy in this third wave. For example, Environmental Defense co-researched and co-planned a comprehensive waste reduction plan with McDonald's Corporation, with the ultimate goal of reducing corporate waste by 80 percent. Other outcomes of relationships between environmental interest groups and business stakeholders have included corporate selection of environmental group representatives for corporate boards and top management positions, mutual participation in environmental "cleanup" projects, and corporate donations of time and money to environmental groups for their environmental conservation programs. This trend toward cooperation between otherwise adversarial groups is a characteristic of the third environmental or green wave that sets this wave apart from the two previous environmental eras. The former chairman of the Sierra Club identified three types of major North American environmental organizations based on this criterion of cooperation with business. He labelled groups characterized by confrontational behaviours as "radicals" (e.g., Greenpeace, Friends of the Earth), groups that seek pragmatic reform through a combination of confrontation and cooperation as "mainstreamers" (e.g., Sierra Club), and groups that avoid confrontation and are more trusting of corporations as "accommodators" (e.g., the World Wildlife Fund).[70] Figure 13–9 offers a brief description of the purpose of the Sierra Club of Canada.

Whatever the exact levels of support and resources the environmental movement will command, businesses and governments should consider that decisions to avoid engaging in cooperative negotiations with environmental groups can lead to involvement in unproductive adversarial relationships with these organizations and their dedicated constituencies. Toxic and hazardous waste producers, such as the nuclear power and petrochemical industries, respectively, appear especially vulnerable to "direct action" and other potentially embarrassing and costly situations, as do mineral and forest products companies and waste management firms. Managers in these

FIGURE 13-9

The Sierra Club of Canada

The Sierra Club of Canada's mission is to develop a diverse, well-trained grassroots network working to protect the integrity of our global ecosystems. The Sierra Club mission focuses on five overriding threats: loss of animal and plant species, deterioration of the planet's oceans and atmosphere, the ever-growing presence of toxic chemicals in all living things, destruction of our remaining wilderness, and spiralling population growth and over consumption.

In Canada, the Sierra Club functions locally, provincially, nationally and internationally. Through the Sierra Club of Canada's National Office in Ottawa, we run a number of major national campaigns:

- promoting energy efficiency to fight climate change
- protecting Canada's forests from unrestricted clear-cut logging
- conserving our biological diversity (the range of wildlife and plant species)
- exposing the risks of pesticides working for wilderness preservation from coast to coast to coast
- following up global commitments made in Rio at the Earth Summit
- exposing the economic causes of global environmental decline
- advocating the phase-out of nuclear power in Canada and challenging the federal government's sale of CANDU reactors abroad.

Through our British Columbia, Prairie, Eastern Canada and Atlantic Canada chapters, Sierra Club of Canada pursues issues from toxic clean-up of the Great Lakes and Sydney Tar Ponds in Nova Scotia to protecting the remaining ancient rain-forests of Vancouver Island and B.C.'s mainland coast.

Across the country, Club chapters and their local groups are pursuing a variety of campaigns. Volunteers are the backbone of our campaigns—organizing locally, raising awareness, and holding elected representatives responsible for their actions.

Source: Sierra Club of Canada, http://www.sierraclub.ca/backgrounder.html. Reprinted by permission.

high-environmental-exposure firms should consider improving their stakeholder relationships with environmental organizations and working on ways to move toward more environmentally friendly operations.

Green Consumers, Employees, and Investors

In addition to environmental groups, businesses are paying more attention to the latest green wave because of at least three other stakeholder groups: green consumers, green employees, and green investors. So-called green consumers are actual and potential customers of retail firms, usually in the industrialized countries, who express preferences for products, services, and companies that are perceived to be more environmentally friendly than other competitive products, services, and firms. Marketing research firms in these countries have identified a range of green consumerism on the basis of the strengths of these preferences and reported consumer purchases. Some observers have referred to "light green" consumers as those who are more likely to support the environment through purchases rather than volunteer action.[71] They are a sought-after segment of the market—young, well-paid, highly educated, Internet savvy, predominately female, and mostly professional or white-collar employees.[72] Experts expect an increase in green consumers over the next 15 to 25 years as Generation Y (those born between 1977 and 1994) assume positions of responsibility.[73] Nearly 100 percent of the Y generation received environmental education in school, as opposed to 19 percent of the adults in general. As a result, they have been shown to be much more likely to spend money for environmentally friendly products than their parents were.[74]

A second stakeholder group with which most businesses are concerned is green employees. Although the popular press has not focused as much attention on green employees as it has on green consumers, there is evidence that employees are playing a major role in promoting environmentalism at work. In addition to union and general employee environmental concerns with plant, warehouse, and office safety and health, employees in many companies have assisted management in going beyond these traditional concerns into areas such as pollution prevention, recycling, energy and environmental audits, and community environmental projects. Successful "Green Teams" have been operating at such diverse businesses as Goldman Sachs, Eastman Kodak, and Apple Computer.[75] Green employees want their workplaces to reflect their environmental values. According to Jon Whiteman of Vishay Siliconix, "There's pressure from everyone from the janitor to the CEO to make sure that we're doing our part. It's almost like running for office—you've got to make sure you're doing something for everyone."[76]

Another important business stakeholder involved in environmental issues is the green investor. Similar to investors interested in advancing social causes, individuals and organizations sometimes want to "put their money where their environmental values are" by identifying and utilizing financial instruments that are associated with environmentally oriented companies. A growing number of mutual funds, stock and bond offerings, money market funds, and other financial instruments have included environmental components in recent years. In her book *Vanishing Borders*, Hilary French argues that companies with strong environmental management are likely to outperform those companies that have environmental liabilities. According to French, new communications technologies enable groups of investors to mount coordinated campaigns against companies with questionable practices. She calls for an increase in the quality and quantity of environmental reporting by companies.[77] Companies are increasingly taking note of the desire for this type of reporting. For example, Petro-Canada's "Report to the Community," first published in 2001, offers readers information on its environmental programs and performance. However, in 2002, Ethical Funds Inc. raised investors' concerns regarding Petro-Canada's weak efforts on behalf of the company's climate change challenge. Ethical Funds Inc. asserted that Petro-Canada should more fully disclose the financial risks related to their greenhouse gas emissions and urged Petro-Canada to reduce these risks through greater investments in renewable energy. The vice president of Ethical Funds Inc. stated: "While Petro-Canada has taken progressive steps to reduce greenhouse gas emissions and invest in alternative energy sources, company officials have, in recent months, made alarming statements about the impact of Kyoto Protocol ratification…. But in its 2002 disclosure documents, we see little in the way of a discussion of Kyoto and no detailed, rigorous assessments of how the company is positioning itself with regard to reducing greenhouse gas emissions. Regardless of the fate of Kyoto, Petro-Canada needs an action plan for a carbon-constrained future."[78]

After the *Exxon Valdez* oil spill, several environmental, labour, and social investor groups formed an organization called CERES and developed a preamble and a set of ten policy statements called the Valdez Principles (later renamed the **CERES Principles**). These principles have been advanced as models for businesses to express and practise environmental sensitivity. Excerpts from these principles are listed in Figure 13–10. Companies that have endorsed the principles include Coca-Cola, American Airlines, General Motors, Polaroid Corporation, and Sunoco.[79]

FIGURE 13-10

CERES Principles

By adopting these Principles, we publicly affirm our belief that corporations have a responsibility for the environment by operating in a manner that protects the earth. We believe that corporations must not compromise the ability of future generations to sustain themselves. We will update our practices constantly in light of advances in technology and new understandings in health and environmental science. In collaboration with CERES, we will promote a dynamic process to ensure that the Principles are interpreted in a way that accommodates changing technologies and environmental realities. We intend to make consistent, measurable progress in implementing these Principles and to apply them to all aspects of our operations throughout the world.

1. Protection of the Biosphere: We will reduce and make continual progress toward eliminating the release of any substance that may cause environmental damage to the air, water, or earth or its inhabitants. We will safeguard all habitats affected by our operations and will protect open spaces and wilderness, while preserving biodiversity.

2. Sustainable Use of Natural Resources: We will make sustainable use of renewable natural resources, such as water, soils, and forests. We will conserve nonrenewable natural resources through efficient use and careful planning.

3. Reduction and Disposal of Waste: We will reduce and where possible eliminate waste, through source reduction and recycling. All waste will be handled and disposed of through safe and responsible methods.

4. Energy Conservation: We will conserve energy and improve the energy efficiency of our internal operations and of the goods and services we sell. We will make every effort to use environmentally safe and sustainable energy sources.

5. Risk Reduction: We will strive to minimize the environmental, health, and safety risks to our employees and the communities in which we operate through safe technologies, facilities, and operating procedures, and by being prepared for emergencies.

6. Safe Products and Services: We will reduce and where possible eliminate the use, manufacture, or sale of products and services that cause environmental damage or health or safety hazards. We will inform our customers of the environmental impacts of our products or services and try to correct unsafe use.

7. Environmental Restoration: We will promptly and responsibly correct conditions we have caused that endanger health, safety, or the environment. To the extent feasible, we will redress injuries we have caused to persons or damage we have caused to the environment and will restore the environment.

8. Informing the Public: We will inform in a timely manner everyone who may be affected by conditions caused by our company that might endanger health, safety, or the environment. We will regularly seek advice and counsel through dialogue with persons in communities near our facilities. We will not take any action against employees for reporting dangerous incidents or conditions to management or to appropriate authorities.

9. Management Commitment: We will implement these Principles and sustain a process that ensures that the Board of Directors and Chief Executive Officer are fully informed about pertinent environmental issues and are fully responsible for environmental policy. In selecting our Board of Directors, we will consider demonstrated environmental commitment as a factor.

10. Audits and Reports: We will conduct an annual self-evaluation of our progress in implementing these Principles. We will support the timely creation of generally accepted environmental audit procedures. We will annually complete the CERES Report, which will be made available to the public.

Source: CERES, *CERES Principles* (Boston: The Social Investment Forum, 1992). Reprinted with permission.

Business Environmentalism

The 3M Company is one of the best-known multinational companies to have adopted a comprehensive, beyond-compliance, environmental policy and program. Begun in 1975, 3M's Pollution Prevention Pays program was a multiproduct, multiprocess approach to manufacturing. In its first year alone, through product reformulation, process modification, equipment redesign, and waste recycling, 3M prevented 66 000 tonnes of air emissions and 2500 tonnes of sludge. They also saved more than US$700 million for the company by reducing various pollutants at their sources. The company gives the credit (and financial rewards) for these environmental successes to its employees, who have developed more than 4500 subprojects under this program.[80] 3M scientists received the Heroes of Chemistry Award in 1997 for developing 3M HFEs as a CFC replacement. By the year 2000, 3M had cut its volatile organic air emissions by 85 percent, its releases to water by 80 percent, its solid wastes by 20 percent, and its waste generation by 35 percent.[81]

DuPont Canada Inc. was among the highest-ranked corporations in *Corporate Knights* magazine's recent assessment of environmental efforts in business. DuPont Canada, makers of numerous household items, scored high points for maintaining rigorous environmental performance indicators, including emissions, incidents, recycling, and waste. The company also closely adheres to the Canadian Chemical Producers' Association Responsible Care Program. Among their environmental accomplishments were reducing total emissions (excluding CO_2) by 85 percent from 1990 to 2000 and reducing energy use per unit of production by 25 percent from 1990 to 1999. They have also aimed to eliminate packaging waste from raw materials and products. In addition, they stopped producing chlorofluorocarbons (CFCs) three years ahead of the goal of the Montreal Protocol.[82]

Husky Injection Molding Systems Ltd., producers of injection mouldings systems for the plastics industry, was also lauded for their environmental efforts by *Corporate Knights* magazine. Husky maintains an environmental, health, and safety policy for integrating environmental considerations in such areas of business as design of its products and facilities, and in its operational practices. The company has strived to manufacture products that are less noisy, and that require less energy and less material. Among Husky's environmental accomplishments are a successful waste-minimization program, a program to reduce the use of ozone-depleting substances, and the elimination of the use of herbicides, pesticides, and chemical fertilizers by converting 60 000 square metres of grass to a naturalized landscape.[83]

TELUS Inc., Suncor Energy Inc., Alcan Inc., Dofasco Inc., Shell Canada Ltd., and Nova Chemicals Corp. were among other organizations receiving high praise for their environmental policies in *Corporate Knights'* 2003 rankings. Canada's RBC Financial Group was noted for putting into place an energy-saving retrofitting program to help generate more efficient lighting and building automation systems. RBC also requires that newly constructed facilities implement state-of-the-art energy efficiency systems where possible. RBC's actions were intended to save about 660 000 kilowatt hours each year, potentially eliminating approximately 1000 tonnes of carbon dioxide generated by fossil fuel–powered generating stations.[84]

Small businesses, too, are promoting green products and services. Smaller companies can serve as excellent incubators for new environmentally friendly processes because their size makes them more manageable. The Tunweni Brewery in Tsumeb, Namibia, was the site of the first commercial application of the Zero Emissions Research Initiative (ZERI). They recovered fibres from the spent gain through the cultivation of mushrooms, used earthworms to feed on the leftover protein, and used "waste" streams to farm fish as part of the initiative.[85] Ecotech Autoworks was one of the first green auto repair shops in North America. Ecotech recycled all car fluids, especially CFC-containing air-conditioning fluid, and used recycled auto parts at customer request. This innovative service used recycled–tire shop floor mats and carbon monoxide–absorbing hanging spider plants, and offered a full range of environmental magazines in the customer waiting room.[86]

The greening of business is a global phenomenon. Toyota campaigned to produce a solar-powered car, while Mitsubishi pursued its Malaysian rain forest reforestation effort—the environmental credit card of the Daiei Supermarket Group. This program, which was designed by two well-known Japanese environmental groups, allowed grocery consumers who use these cards to direct 0.5 percent of their grocery bills to any of 20 different environmental causes.[87] PlanetBound, a Tokyo-based firm specializing in Internet-based environmental communication, established the Eco500 project. In it they studied the Web sites of the world's largest corporations in an effort to gauge the importance that companies in diverse industry sectors and markets place on communicating a commitment to environmental responsibility and conservation. On the top of the list was the electronics giant, NEC: It was the only firm to be accorded a full 100 points for its Web site. Multiple firms, however, received a score of zero.[88]

Business environmentalism is also blossoming on the European continent. Europe is deeply divided on the environmental front. The Nordic countries, Germany, and the Netherlands have stringent regulations and a strong concern for the environment. At the opposite extreme are the former Soviet Union and Eastern Bloc countries, which are facing severe environmental damage from years of neglect and little money with which to effect a solution. Other European countries lie somewhere in between. In an effort to address this problem, Western environmental ministers are being paired with their Eastern counterparts and are working together to address the challenge of Eastern Bloc pollution. The 1997 Treaty for Europe stressed the importance of sustainable development. Moreover, the treaty gives the European Parliament the power to legislate environmental policy. With the Greens gaining political momentum and Western European consumers willing to pay a premium for green products and services, environmental issues are certain to occupy Europe's businesses for many years to come.[89]

Environmental and Financial Performance

The prudent future business manager will likely ask, "Although protecting the earth may be a good reason to practise environmental management, will it pay off on the bottom line?" There are many anecdotes about firms making money from their environmental programs. One example is the experience of Lightolier, Inc., a lighting fixture manufacturer, which retrofitted its gas boiler to use 90 000 litres of its otherwise-wasted hydraulic oil, saving US$40 000, which paid for the investment in less than one year.[90] In her book *Lean and Green: Profit for Your Workplace*, Pamela Gordon describes 20 situations in which corporations enhanced their profits through sound environmental management. Savings came not only from cost reduction but also through avoiding litigation and liability, while enhancing reputation and sales.[91] In the semiconductor industry, environmentally proactive firms such as Intel Corp. and Advanced Micro Devices have been shown to outperform competitors who are not as environmentally oriented. In another study, Miles and Covin showed that being a good environmental steward enhances a firm's reputation, which benefits a firm's marketing and its subsequent financial performance.[92]

Systematic Business Responses to the Environmental Challenge

Various management tools are available for use in selecting or constructing an environmental strategy. These include several management approaches that were discussed in more general terms in earlier chapters and a few that are specific to natural environment issues. In the first group are crisis management, issues management, and stakeholder management. Because these topics were addressed more fully in Chapters 4 and 5, only their applicability to environmental management will be discussed here. In the second group of decision-making tools are cost-benefit analysis, risk management, and strategic environmental management, which will be discussed more fully in this chapter.

Generic Management Decision-Making Tools   Managers can use crisis management in the environmental area by focusing on two factors: prevention and contingency plans. As can be seen in the *Exxon Valdez* case, Exxon, Alyeska, and governments apparently did not pay enough attention to preventing the 1989 Alaskan oil spill disaster or to implementing the inadequate contingency plan to recover the oil once it had been spilled. Although some attention had been paid to the vulnerability of the Alaskan natural environment to a small oil spill, this appears to have been understated and generally ignored. That either Exxon or Alyeska assessed its own vulnerability to a spill of any size appears doubtful. Finally, the lack of coordination between the two companies in immediately addressing the spill indicated a response plan that was only a paper tiger, never really put into practice. Had the businesses and governments followed basic crisis management principles, including vulnerability assessments and simulation drills, the outcome may have been different for both of these organizations and for Prince William Sound.

Issues management can be employed to track public interest in natural environment issues and to develop and implement plans to attempt to ensure that the scope of environmental problems is minimized and that the firm develops effective responses at each stage in the life cycles of environmental issues. Environmental issues can be developed as part of the environmental impact statement process or as part of the strategic-planning macroenvironmental analysis process.

Similarly, stakeholder management applies to environmental management in that environmental stakeholders and their stakes can be identified, including the environmental public, environmental regulators, environmental groups, and various entities (human and nonhuman) across the entire natural environment. The follow-up stages of stakeholder management—that is, planning for and interacting with stakeholders—can then be conducted, so that each important environmental stakeholder is given adequate attention after it is identified.

Although crisis management, issues management, and stakeholder management can be used as generic approaches to environmental management, there are other, more traditional management approaches that have been used in the past specifically to decide natural environment issues. Two of these approaches are cost-benefit analysis and risk management.

Cost-Benefit Analysis   Although **cost-benefit analysis** has been used in other areas, especially those related to public and private capital budgeting and investment, it has also received an extraordinary amount of attention in natural environmental policy decisions. For instance, most environmental impact assessments performed by companies have one or more cost-benefit analyses as the basis for many of the environmental decisions resulting from these studies. The idea behind cost-benefit analysis is that, in a rational planning situation, an organization wants to ensure that an environmental project is worth the investment. Costs are totalled and compared with overall benefits. If benefits are sufficiently greater than costs, the project is given the go-ahead; if not, it is shelved, revised, or scrapped. Decision makers in many dam projects, other water reclamation projects, and land development projects have utilized cost-benefit analysis to determine the value of these environment-oriented projects.

Although cost-benefit analysis sounds straightforward, several problems have been identified with this environmental decision-making approach. First, measuring all costs and all benefits of a proposed action is often very difficult. What will the costs be to an ecosystem if a species is pressured into extinction? What is the benefit or value of a wilderness area? Second, comparing costs and benefits can be problematic, because these factors are not always measured in the same units. How does one compare the advantages of a commercial or light industrial development project with the loss of scenic beauty and wildlife habitats? Finally, costs can accrue to one party, whereas another party receives the benefits. For instance, a real estate firm wishing to develop residential property may be prevented from earning profits (an opportunity cost) while an ecosystem and its species accrue the benefit of continued existence. One typical way to handle this generic inequality has been through side payments to correct the balance. However, humans have not yet developed a consensus on whether, how, and how much to "pay back" the natural environment for problems they have caused.

Given these significant weaknesses, how can the prudent manager use cost-benefit analysis as a tool in addressing the environmental challenge? First, attempting to identify and measure costs and benefits can be helpful in using other decision methodologies (e.g., stakeholder management). In such cases, costs and benefits can be thought of as negative and positive stakes. Second, if any costs and benefits can be compared, the trade-offs between them can in some cases serve to simplify the often complex decisions involved in environmental management. However, the shortcomings of cost-benefit analysis appear to warrant continuous attention and require the use of additional environmental decision-making methods.

Risk Management **Risk management** is a second managerial decision-making tool currently being employed by organizations attempting to address the environmental challenge. This approach is similar to cost-benefit analysis in that quantified trade-offs are evaluated in deciding whether or not an environmental project or program is worth developing and implementing. The difference with this method, however, is that the risk of environmental damage (to ecosystems, nonhuman species, or humans) is substituted for either costs or benefits. In this scheme, the relevant decision-making factor is either the amount that should be invested to reduce the risk of environmental damage resulting from the business activity or the amount of environmental risk that is acceptable in relation to the benefits of the economic development activity. The difficulties of this technique are similar to those of cost-benefit analyses—that is, how can risks (especially long-term risks) be measured, and how can they be appropriately compared with costs or benefits? For instance, even if the risk of a nuclear meltdown could be measured and found to be statistically insignificant, would this assessment of the risk be convincing to community residents who would be neighbours of the proposed nuclear power plant? Again, it is suggested that the disadvantages of using this method in environmental decisions be kept in mind and that additional criteria be incorporated into decision-making frameworks involving the natural environment.

Because they are quantification-oriented methodologies, both cost-benefit analysis and risk management appear to be inappropriate for many environmental decisions. Science often lacks the quantified data that would allow us to estimate carrying capacities, thresholds, and cyclical and long-term effects to work into our cost-benefit or risk calculations. Wicked problems, such as the effects of global warming or the adequacy of nuclear waste storage, often require qualitative data from a wide spectrum of perspectives for their "resolution." Exclusive reliance on either approach, quantitative or qualitative, appears unwise in environmental decision making.

Strategic Environmental Management The final managerial approach to addressing the business environmental challenge presented here is a well-known organization effectiveness tool that has been adapted by the authors to assist managers in developing and implementing overall approaches to natural environment issues. This model is called **Strategic Environmental Management (SEM)** and is presented as one way in which organizations can readily respond to their environmental challenges and integrate a wide range of responses for environmental effectiveness.

As can be seen in Figure 13–11, this method uses the McKinsey 7S framework, in which seven typical organizational components necessary for success are identified and integrated, and several green suggestions are given for each "S." Businesses can build environmental components into their superordinate goals, strategies, structures, and so on, in order to develop an overall organizational environmental response. Superordinate goals can include an emphasis on environmental protection in a company's mission statement, for instance, whereas one of its strategies can be developing or acquiring environmentally sensitive businesses. The key to using this model is for managers to identify opportunities for developing environmental responses in each of the S categories and to ensure that each of these responses is compatible with the others.

Using this approach, the environmental manager can incorporate concern for the environment and take environmentally sensitive actions in all organization departments and at all organizational levels. For instance, the shared value of waste minimization can translate into the low-cost strategy, enhanced by environmental quality circle structures, energy-conservation systems in manufacturing facilities, and environmentally skilled staff personnel who are motivated by incentives for meeting personal environmental objectives and by managers exhibiting an environmentally sensitive style. As mentioned in the previous chapters, each organizational department can play a role in the organization's interaction with the natural environment. Research and development departments can work with manufacturing personnel to alter their products and processes to limit pollution and depletion. Finance and accounting personnel can develop effective environmental auditing systems and cost out the potential for environmentally damaging projects, with the aim of reducing this cost as much as possible. Human resources managers can begin to incorporate environmental concerns in their recruitment and training programs, attempting to build an "environmental culture" in the organization. Marketers can identify their customers' "real needs," as opposed to their frivolous (and potentially environmentally damaging) desires for products and services, and adjust their distribution systems in transportation, packaging, and labelling so as to promote environmental sensitivity. This strategic environmental management approach is similar to both the concept of industrial ecology, which "requires that an industrial system be viewed not in isolation from its surrounding systems, but in concert with them,"[93] and the international environmental management standard called **ISO 14000**, which includes organizational environmental objectives, issues, policies, systems, and documentation aimed at "continued improvement of the environmental management process, leading to improvement in environmental performance."[94]

The limitations of the SEM approach are similar to those of the McKinsey 7S model itself, including a decidedly internal orientation (nonorganization stakeholders and forces are not explicitly emphasized) and a potential for much complexity. The prudent manager, once again, is advised to remember these weaknesses and to supplement this method with others mentioned in this section. The stakeholder management

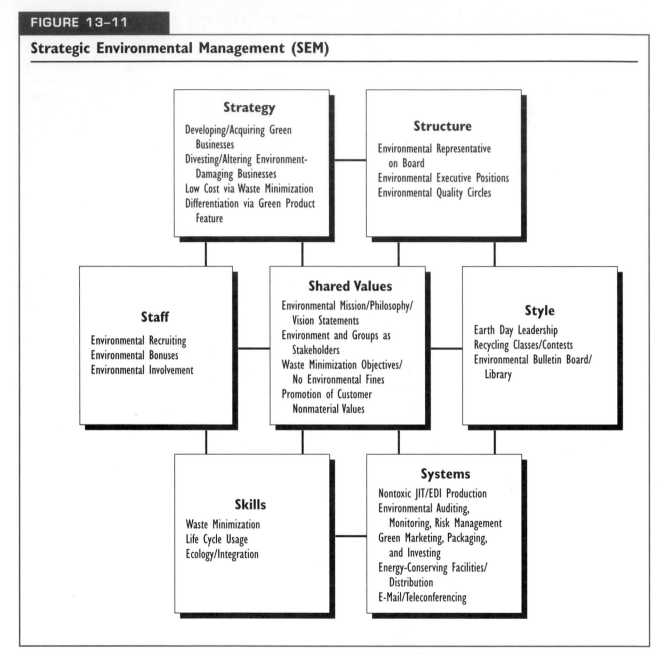

FIGURE 13–11

Strategic Environmental Management (SEM)

Strategy
Developing/Acquiring Green
  Businesses
Divesting/Altering Environment-
  Damaging Businesses
Low Cost via Waste Minimization
Differentiation via Green Product
  Feature

Structure
Environmental Representative
  on Board
Environmental Executive Positions
Environmental Quality Circles

Staff
Environmental Recruiting
Environmental Bonuses
Environmental Involvement

Shared Values
Environmental Mission/Philosophy/
  Vision Statements
Environment and Groups as
  Stakeholders
Waste Minimization Objectives/
  No Environmental Fines
Promotion of Customer
  Nonmaterial Values

Style
Earth Day Leadership
Recycling Classes/Contests
Environmental Bulletin Board/
  Library

Skills
Waste Minimization
Life Cycle Usage
Ecology/Integration

Systems
Nontoxic JIT/EDI Production
Environmental Auditing,
  Monitoring, Risk Management
Green Marketing, Packaging,
  and Investing
Energy-Conserving Facilities/
  Distribution
E-Mail/Teleconferencing

Source: M. Starik and A. B. Carroll, "Strategic Environmental Management Business as if the Earth Really Mattered," *Proceedings of 1991 International Association for Business and Society*, Sundance, UT (March 22–24, 1991), 28.

approach, with its external focus, might be a good match for the more internal SEM focus. Indeed, an eighth "S" that could be added to this model is "stakeholders," which could include environmentally oriented suppliers, customers, investors, and regulators, as well as the natural environment itself.

The Future of Business: Greening and/or Growing?

The salient environmental question we all may need to address in the future is: "How much is enough?" A common business and, indeed, public policy goal in most human societies has been economic growth. Typically, businesses and societies have needed increasing amounts of either materials or energy, or both, to achieve that economic growth. Limits on growth, similar to limits on human reproduction, at either the macro or micro level, have not been widely popular. One potential problem with unrestrained economic growth worldwide is that, unless technology or people change significantly within a generation, environmental problems can change in degree from significant to severe.

World population is projected to continue to increase, potentially requiring greater demands on food and fuel resources. Both industrialized and less-industrialized nations may contribute to this dilemma. The West and Japan continue to use increasing amounts of materials and energy to maintain highly consumptive lifestyles, whereas the rest of the world continues to use these developed nations as models for their own development. Two pressing questions are: (1) Can the earth support a high-consumption Western lifestyle for an increasing world population? and, if not, (2) What are the implications for business and how should business managers respond?

David Suzuki offers the following insights and advice:

> *The industrial revolution was exactly that—revolutionary—driven by technological changes that the world had never before seen. The move to a sustainable use of world resources requires a shift in values and a deeper understanding of the interconnectedness of life on Earth. These sorts of changes are evolutionary. They take time and are on-going. There will never be a point when we can sit back and say, "There, we've solved all our environmental problems!" Living in balance with the Earth's capacity to maintain all its natural services will always be a challenge. If you want to help make the world a better place this year, resolve not to fall into despair, but embrace this challenge that, ultimately, we all must meet.[95]*

Summary

We have explored a variety of environmental challenges and several actual and potential responses to these challenges. What themes appear to be woven throughout this chapter that can be especially helpful to prospective managers? First, many scientists, policy makers, public-interest groups, individuals, and businesses recognize that the natural environment is crucial for human survival and that a number of complex and interconnected human-induced activities may be threatening this environment. Problems such as human deforestation, pollu-

tion, and expanding populations are potentially endangering nonhuman species and ecosystems and reducing the quality of human life. Individuals and their organizations, including businesses, have been found to be directly or indirectly responsible for this situation.

Second, there are significant differences of opinion on how these problems will develop in the future and, of course, what should be done to resolve them. The facts that nature continues to evolve and human knowledge and actions regarding nature also continuously change argue against an "ecological correctness" approach. Instead, individuals and organizations, including businesses, concerned about reducing environmental degradation might adopt a flexible and prudent approach to keeping themselves informed and taking actions, no matter how small, in the direction of "walking lightly on the earth." A minimum baseline of not increasing human-caused pollution and depletion may be a potential starting point for consensus building and environmental consciousness.

Key Terms

acid rain (page 401)

air pollution (page 401)

Canadian Environmental Protection Act (CEPA) (page 407)

CERES Principles (page 413)

cost-benefit analysis (page 417)

deforestation (page 399)

energy inefficiency (page 402)

environment (page 392)

green values (page 405)

greenhouse effect (page 395)

ISO 14000 (page 419)

Kyoto Protocol (page 410)

Montreal Protocol (page 410)

NIMBY (page 404)

ozone (page 395)

risk management (page 418)

soil erosion (page 400)

Strategic Environmental Management (SEM) (page 419)

toxic substances (page 403)

Discussion Questions

1. What is the natural environment?

2. What are several of the most important environmental issues now receiving worldwide attention?

3. What are some of the causes of environmental pollution and depletion?

4. What is the future outlook for the natural environment?

5. Who has responsibility for addressing environmental issues?

6. How can ethics be applied in response to environmental issues?

7. What are some examples of business environmentalism and decision models for addressing environmental concerns?

8. Should businesses and societies continue to focus on unlimited economic growth?

Endnotes

1. "Conserving Nature Is Like Money in the Bank " (Aug. 30, 2002), http://www.davidsuzuki.org/About_us/Dr_David_Suzuki/Article_Archives/weekly08300201.asp.

2. Commission for Environmental Cooperation, http://www.cec.org/home/index.cfm.

3. Martin Mittelstaedt, "Canadian Polluters Worse Than in U.S., Report Says," (April 17, 2003, Globe and Mail), A4; http://www.ec.gc.ca/international/regorgs/cec_e.htm.

4. UNEP Profile (Nairobi, Kenya: United Nations Environment Programme, 1990), 2.

5. R. Cooke, "Scientists Report Gains in Protecting Ozone Layer May Be Paying Off," Seattle Times (March 4, 2001), A13.

6. N. Wilkes, "Global Warming Will Be Greater Says U.N.," Professional Engineering (January 31, 2001).

7. Ibid.

8. *UNEP Profile*, 6, 7.
9. W. H. Corson (ed.), *The Global Ecology Handbook* (Boston: Beacon Press, 1990), 231–233.
10. Environment Canada, *Clean Air* (2003), http://www.cleanair.ca/science_facts.html.
11. Environment Canada (2003), http://www.ec.gc.ca/pdb/ghg/1990_01_report/executive_e.cfm#i1.
12. http://www.oecd.org.
13. http://www.oecd.org; http://www.conferenceboard.ca/.
14. Corson, 247.
15. *UNEP Profile*, 8.
16. Government of Canada, http://www.ec.gc.ca/Press/2003/030820_b_e.htm.
17. Government of Canada (2003), http://www.ec.gc.ca/Press/2003/030820_b_e.htm.
18. Marccl Cote, "We Are the Environment," *CA Magazine* (Vol. 136, No. 4, May 2003), 64.
19. Commission for Environmental Cooperation, http://www.cec.org.
20. "Canadian Polluters Increased Chemical Releases by 20% from 1995 to 2001," *Canada NewsWire* (June 19, 2003), 1.
21. S. Postel, "Saving Water for Agriculture" in L. R. Brown et al., *State of the World, 1990* (New York: Norton, 1990), 49.
22. "Commission on Sustainable Development Holds First of Four Dialogues," Press release from the United Nations (April 24, 2000).
23. Corson, 137.
24. E. Linden, "Condition Critical," *Time—Special Edition on How to Save the Earth* (Spring 2000), 18–24.
25. Intergovernmental Panel on Climate Change. 2000. *Land Use, Land-use Change and Forestry: A Special Report of the IPCC* (Cambridge University Press, 2000), 4; Climatechangesolutions.com, http://www.climatechangesolutions.com/index.asp.
26. Climatechangesolutions.com, http://www.climatechangesolutions.com/index.asp.
27. E. Check, "The Silence of the Woods," *Newsweek* (November 13, 2000), 65.
28. "FAO: Strong Indications for Slowdown in Deforestation," Press release from the United Nations (August 8, 2000), 1.
29. Postel, 60.
30. Corson, 68.
31. Government of Canada (2003), http://www.agr.gc.ca/policy/environment/soil_e.phtml.
32. E. Wilson, "Vanishing Before Our Eyes," *Time—Special Edition on How to Save the Earth* (Spring 2000), 29–34.
33. *Ibid.*
34. "The Battle for Planet Earth," *Newsweek* (April 24, 2000), 51–53.

35. J. Seager (ed.), *The State of the Earth Atlas* (New York: Simon & Schuster, 1990), 110.
36. J. Naar, *Design for a Livable Planet* (New York: Harper & Row, 1990), 101.
37. Clean Air (2003), http://www.cleanair.ca/science_facts.html.
38. Environment Canada (2003), http://www.ec.gc.ca/acidrain/acidfact.html.
39. Environmental Protection Agency, *Meeting the Environmental Challenge* (Washington, DC: USGPO, December 1990), 11.
40. J. Mathews, "Acts of War and the Environment," *The Washington Post* (April 8, 1991), A17.
41. T. W. Lippman, "Future of Wind Power Gets a Lift," *The Washington Post* (November 17, 1991), H1.
42. T. Coffin (ed.), "A Look at Alternative Energy," *The Washington Spectator* (Vol. 16, No. 18, 1991), 1–3.
43. David Suzuki, "Fossil Fuels," The David Suzuki Foundation, http://www.davidsuzuki.org/climate_change/science/fossil_fuels.asp.
44. Environment Canada, http://www.ec.gc.ca/CEPARegistry/gene_info/cepa_toxic.cfm; Health Canada, http://www.hc-sc.gc.ca/hecs-sesc/tsri/.
45. Naar, 38.
46. "Responding to Oil Spills" (2001), http://www.epa.gov.
47. "Ten Years After the Spill," *Newsweek* (March 29, 1999).
48. Ministry of Environment (November 6, 2002), http://www.ene.gov.on.ca/envision/news/2002/110601.htm.
49. Environmental Protection Agency (1990), 10.
50. R. O. Mason and I. I. Mitroff, *Challenging Strategic Planning Assumptions* (New York: Wiley, 1981), 12–13.
51. R. E. Dunlap, "Public Opinion in the 1980s: Clear Consensus, Ambiguous Commitment," *Environment* (Vol. 33, No. 8, 1991), 10–15, 32–37.
52. S. Irvine and A. Pouton, *A Green Manifesto* (London: Optima, 1988), 14–16.
53. *Ibid.*, 16.
54. Environment Canada, http://www.ec.gc.ca/ceparegistry/.
55. Environment Canada, http://www.ec.gc.ca/EnviroRegs/.
56. Health Canada, http://www.hc-sc.gc.ca/hecs-sesc/air_quality/regulations.htm.
57. Health Canada, http://www.hc-sc.gc.ca/hecs-sesc/air_quality/cws.htm.
58. EPA Indoor Air Quality Division (2001), http://www.epa.gov/iaq.
59. Health Canada, http://www.hc-sc.gc.ca/ehp/ehd/bch/air_quality/indoor_air.htm.
60. Environment Canada, http://www.ec.gc.ca/water/en/policy/legreg/e_legis.htm.
61. Environment Canada, http://www.ec.gc.ca/EnviroRegs.
62. Environment Canada, http://www.ec.gc.ca/water/en/policy/pol/e_pol.htm.

63. Environment Canada (2003), http://www.ec.gc.ca/CEPARegistry/the_act/guide/part5.cfm#anchor1.

64. Health Canada, http://www.hc-sc.gc.ca/english/iyh/environment/assessing.html.

65. Health Canada, http://www.hc-sc.gc.ca/english/iyh/environment/assessing.html.

66. David Suzuki, "Green Budget Would Boost National Security," (Nov. 9, 2001), http://www.davidsuzuki.org/about_us/dr_david_suzuki/article_archives/weekly11090101.asp.

67. UNEP Achievements (2001), http://www.unep.org.

68. *Ibid.*

69. George Greene and Désirée McGraw, "Beyond Kyoto," *Corporate Knights*, http://www.corporateknights.ca/stories/beyond_kyoto.asp.

70. M. E. Kriz, "Shades of Green," *National Journal* (July 28, 1990).

71. R. Gardyn, "Saving the Earth, One Click at a Time," *American Demographic* (January 2001), 30–33.

72. *Ibid.*

73. *Ibid.*

74. *Ibid.*

75. J. Makower, "Green Teams," *The Green Business Letter* (November 6, 1991), 1.

76. B. Mueller, "Distributors Help with Green Efforts," *Purchasing* (December 22, 2000), 73–76.

77. H. French, *Vanishing Borders* (New York: W. W. Norton & Co., 2000).

78. "Cut Greenhouse Gas Emissions, Investors Tell Petro-Canada" (December 12, 2002), http://www.ethicalfunds.com/do_the_right_thing/about_ef/newsroom/2002_articles/12_12_02.asp.

79. CERES (2001), http://www.ceres.org.

80. *3M's Pollution Prevention Pays: An Initiative for a Cleaner Tomorrow* (St. Paul, MN: 3M Company, 1991).

81. 3M, CEO's Message (2001), http://www.3M.com.

82. *Corporate Knights* (2003), http://www.corporateknights.ca/best50/medalists_environment.asp

83. *Ibid.*

84. *Ibid.*

85. European Eco-Efficiency Initiative (EEE) (2001), http://www.wbcsd.org.

86. J. Saddler, "Going for the Green," *The Wall Street Journal* (November 22, 1991), R13.

87. D. Porter, "A Greening Corporate Image—Japan Business Survey," Advertising supplement to *The Wall Street Journal* (September 23, 1991), B12.

88. Eco500 (2001), http://www.eco500.com.

89. A. Sains, "Seeing Green," *Europe* (February 2001), 16–24.

90. M. M. Hamilton, "Generating Profit from the Waste Up," *The Washington Post* (April 12, 1995), F1.

91. P. Gordon, *Lean and Green: Profit for Your Workplace* (San Francisco: Berrett Koehler, 2001).

92. M. Miles and J. Covin, "Environmental Marketing: A Source of Reputational, Competitive, and Financial Advantage," *Journal of Business Ethics* (February 2000), 299–311.

93. T. E. Graedel and B. R. Allenby, *Industrial Ecology* (Englewood Cliffs, NJ: Prentice Hall, 1995), 9.

94. J. B. Charm, "Joel Charm on ISO 14000," *Environment Today* (Vol. 6, No. 1, 1995), 22.

95. David Suzuki, "Making Our Resolutions Count" (January 19, 2001), http://www.davidsuzuki.org/about_us/dr_david_suzuki/article_archives/weekly01190101.asp.

Business and Community Stakeholders

Chapter Objectives

After studying this chapter, you should be able to:

1 Discuss reasons for community involvement, various types of community projects, and management of community stakeholders.

2 Explain the pros and cons of corporate philanthropy and explain why and to whom companies give.

3 Differentiate between strategic philanthropy, cause-related marketing, and cause branding.

4 Characterize the nature of, magnitude of, and reasons for business and plant closings.

5 Address steps that a business might take before a decision to close is made.

6 Identify strategies that a business might employ after a decision to close has been made.

When we speak of a community, we usually mean the immediate locale—the town, city, or province—in which a business resides. In our modern age of global business, instantaneous communication, and speedy travel, however, the region, the nation, or even the world can become the relevant community. Businesses are affected by events throughout the world. Traditional geographic boundaries have been eclipsed by communications technology and high-speed travel. The business community now encompasses the entire world.

When we think of business and its community stakeholders, two major kinds of relationships come to mind. One is the positive contribution business can make to the community. Examples of these positive contributions include volunteerism, company contributions, and support of programs in education, culture, urban development, the arts, civic activities, and other health and welfare endeavours. On the other hand, business can also cause harm to community stakeholders. It can pollute the environment, put people out of work by closing a plant, abuse its power, and exploit consumers and employees.

In this chapter, we will concentrate on community involvement and corporate philanthropy as community stakeholder issues. In addition, we will discuss the topic of business or plant closings as community stakeholder concerns. This discussion should provide us with an opportunity to explore both the positive and the detrimental effects that characterize business/community relationships. We will begin with the positive.

In addition to being profitable, obeying the law, and being ethical, a company may create a positive impact in the community by giving in basically two ways: (1) donating the time and talents of its managers and employees and (2) making financial contributions. The first category manifests itself in a wide array of voluntary activities in the community. The second category involves corporate philanthropy or business giving. We should note that there is significant overlap between these two categories, because companies quite frequently donate their time and talents and give financial aid to the same general projects. First, we will discuss community involvement and the various ways in which companies enhance the quality of life in their communities.

Community Involvement

There are a variety of Canadian-based organizations that encourage corporations to increase their commitment to their communities. For example, the Canadian Centre for Philanthropy focuses on increasing corporate funding of Canadian charities. In 1988, it launched the Imagine campaign, whose goals include encouraging companies to increase their charitable donations and to increase their support for employee volunteering.

Deloitte & Touche is a respected professional services firm that employs more than 6600 people in 46 locations across Canada. The Canadian Centre for Philanthropy's Imagine program recently lauded Deloitte & Touche for their strong community involvement.[1] Perhaps one of the most compelling arguments for increased **community involvement** was offered by the chairman and chief executive officer of Deloitte & Touche:

> *We have an absolutely enormous stake in the communities where our*
> *people live and work. If we have good educational systems, good safety,*
> *and good activity programs for young people, we're going to be much*
> *more effective in attracting and retaining quality people.*[2]

Therefore, business must—not only for a healthier society, but also for its own well-being—be willing to give the same serious consideration to human needs that it gives to its own needs for production and profits. Robert Cushman, former president of the Norton Company, enumerates six reasons for business involvement in the community:[3]

1. Businesspeople are efficient problem solvers.
2. Employees gain satisfaction and improved morale from involvement in community programs.
3. A positive image in the community facilitates hiring.
4. Often a company gains prestige and greater acceptance in a community when it gets actively involved.
5. Social responsibility in business is the alternative to government regulation.
6. Business helps itself by supporting those institutions that are essential to the continuation of business.

Business involvement in the community can be enlightened self-interest. Businesses are in a position to help themselves in the process of helping others. This dual objective of business clearly illustrates that making profits and addressing social concerns are not mutually exclusive endeavours. Other rationales for business involvement in community affairs provide moral justification, beyond that of enlightened self-interest. For example, utilitarianism has been used to support corporate giving, with arguments that improvement of the social fabric creates the greatest good for the greatest number. This need not contradict the mandates of self-interest, because the corporation is a community member that will benefit.[4] Although justifications for corporate involvement in the community can be made from various perspectives, one thing is clear: Business has a public responsibility to build a relationship with the community and to be sensitive to its impacts on the world around it.

This point is driven home in Petro-Canada's *2003 Community Report*:

> *Petro-Canada's success as an energy company depends on the support of Canadians, so we work hard to invest and participate in the communities where we work and live across the country.*[5] *... Petro-Canada has played an active role in Canadian communities for 27 years. We know that we must continually earn Canadians' support, so we work hard to invest and participate in the communities where we work and live across the country.*[6]

Contributing to Communities

Volunteer Programs   One of the most pervasive examples of business involvement in communities is a volunteer program. Corporate volunteer programs reflect the resourcefulness and responsiveness of business to communities in need of increasing services. Canadian businesses are increasingly giving attention to volunteerism. From the period 1997 to 2000, the number of employed volunteers who reported receiving approval from their employer to modify their work hours in order to volunteer increased from 22 percent to 27 percent. In addition, more employed volunteers indicated that they received recognition from their employer for their volunteer work (from 14 percent in 1997 to 22 percent in 2000).[7] The activities used by companies to encourage employee volunteerism include:

- Recognition through articles, awards, and commendations
- Publicity about community volunteer opportunities

- Board membership (encouraging executives to serve on boards)
- Company-sponsored projects involving multiple volunteers
- Ongoing endorsement of programs by CEOs

There are numerous examples of corporations making a difference in communities through volunteer activities. CIBC, Canadian National, Hewlett-Packard (Canada) Ltd., Suncor Energy Inc., and TransCanada PipeLines Ltd. joined together in 2002 to establish a project called "Taking Pulse." This private-sector effort is aimed at increasing the participation of Aboriginal people in the Canadian work force. In the words of Rick George, the president of Suncor Energy Inc., "This is an excellent opportunity for involvement in creating a long-term strategy that will benefit Aboriginal people and indeed the greater economy…. We are committed to corporate social responsibility and strongly believe our workforce should be reflective of the communities in which we work."[8] Microsoft Canada engaged in a partnership with the nonprofit organization Boys and Girls Club of Canada to increase computer accessibility for children who lacked the opportunity. Microsoft Canada received high accolades for its contributions to the community, including its financial donations in the millions of dollars, software, resources, online support, and training by employee volunteers.[9] Miller Brewing holds a "day of caring" during which the entire company gives up its time for community projects in Milwaukee. Philip Morris/Kraft employees can champion the charity of their choice and, after employees give 50 hours of service, the company contributes US$1000 to that charity. American Express employees are also encouraged to champion the charity they choose: The company's Global Volunteer Action Fund then provides grants of up to US$1000 for individuals and US$2500 for teams.[10]

The potential results of these efforts are limitless. By joining with a community-based effort, General Electric helped convert a closed high school in East Harlem to a centre for science and mathematics. In addition to providing enrichments that made the school comparable to the best schools in the United States, GE arranged for its employees to become mentors and tutors to the students. The rate of college-bound students at the school became one of the highest in the city and that program became the starting point of GE's award-winning College Bound initiative.[11]

Communities obviously benefit from such volunteer programs, but how do companies benefit from employee volunteerism? Among the variety of benefits that company executives have indicated are as follows:[12]

- *Indirect community benefits*
  Creation of "healthier" communities
  Improved corporate public image
  Enhanced impact of monetary contributions
- *Employee benefits*
  Building of teamwork skills
  Improved morale
  Attraction of better employees
- *Bottom-line benefits*
  Facilitation of attainment of strategic corporate goals
  Increased employee productivity
  Positive impacts on company productivity

How might involvement in volunteer activities make employees more productive? Kristin Smith, the director of corporate relations for Volunteer Canada, has offered insights into the potential value of employer-supported volunteer initiatives. Smith has observed that volunteerism can enhance interpersonal skills, improve communication abilities, strengthen organizational and management/leadership capacities, and offer new skills that directly apply to the employee's paid job. In addition, such involvement can improve morale by making employees feel good about working for an association that supports them in their interests.[13]

Figure 14–1 presents a sample of corporate community contributions and illustrates the range of activities in which companies can and have become involved.

Resource-Based Giving The increasingly competitive global environment has heightened pressure for efficiency in all areas, including community service. A key goal of corporate community service is to get the most good possible from each dollar spent on giving. Companies often find that they can achieve the greatest good by providing services that fit their resources and competencies. For example, LensCrafters can provide vision care more efficiently and effectively than can a business that does not specialize in eye care. TELUS uses its high-tech expertise to help educators exploit the benefits of computer and Internet-based education. CN is obviously an expert for the promotion of rail safety.

Resource-based giving involves assessing a firm's resources and competencies and determining where sharing those resources and competencies would accomplish the most good. In the aftermath of the attack on New York's World Trade Center, rescue workers were using cell phones around the clock in a situation where they couldn't afford to have a dead battery but didn't have the time or electricity to recharge phones. Electric Fuel Corporation donated 500 Instant Power cell phone chargers and batteries to keep the phones working. With their head office located in lower Manhattan, only a 10-minute walk from the scene of the tragedy, they were able to hand over their entire inventory to the rescue effort.[14] Information technology (IT) firms have found their capabilities to be in great demand. Because many nonprofits are technologically

FIGURE 14–1

Examples of Corporate Commitments to Communities

Company	Community Service Commitment
CN	Established the CN Safe Community Fund which offers an annual $25 000 incentive award to encourage communities across the country to incorporate rail safety initiatives and campaigns with local school participation.
Sears	Sears works together with the Boys and Girls Clubs of Canada to offer support and funding for youth-focused programs such as *I Can Swim* and the *Sears Ontario Drama Festival. Sears Young Futures* initiative has contributed over $3 million to youth groups across Canada
TELUS	Working in cooperation with the Alberta School Boards, TELUS provides a portion of the funding, office space, and the technology to help teachers and educators develop the necessary skills to effectively use the Internet as a teaching tool and to develop online educational materials.
Petro-Canada	Provides financial support, and assists the Canadian Association of Food Banks with business planning and marketing communications directed at providing food to those in need and raising public awareness about hunger in Canada.
Home Depot Canada	Provides funding and materials to community-based organizations for the development and building of safe community playgrounds across Canada (in 2002 provided $1 million for this cause).

behind, the skills and resources of technology-based firms can make significant differences in nonprofit operations. For example, Hewlett-Packard (Canada) Co. has supported the nonprofit group Computers for Schools since 1996 with donations of used PCs and equipment.

Drug companies have also found they can accomplish more by drawing on their specific resources. In conjunction with the World Health Organization (WHO), SmithKline Beecham has launched a 20-year, US$1.7 billion program to eradicate elephantiasis, a disease that affects about 120 million people in Asia, South America, and Africa. The plan is to give annual doses of albendazole to the 1.1 billion people worldwide who are at risk of infection by the disease. To accomplish its goal, SmithKline will donate several billion doses of the drug, as well as technical assistance and health-education support. Similarly, Merck has worked with WHO to provide free ivermectin to treat patients with river blindness in Africa, and it will help support the elephantiasis project by donating ivermectin for clinical trials to determine the drug's ability to treat elephantiasis when used jointly with albendazole.[15]

Managing Community Involvement

For discussion purposes, we are separating our treatment of managing community involvement from that of managing corporate philanthropy. It should be kept in mind, however, that in reality this separation is impossible to achieve. There are significant overlaps between these two areas. Corporate philanthropy involves primarily the giving of financial resources. Community involvement focuses on other issues in the business/community relationship, especially the contribution of managerial and employee time and talent. This section addresses these broader community issues; a later section of this chapter deals with the more specific issue of managing corporate philanthropy.

Business Stake in the Community When one speaks with corporate executives in the fields of community and civic affairs and examines community affairs manuals and other corporate publications, one sees a broad array of reasons why companies need to keep abreast of the issues, problems, and changes expressed as community needs. One central reason is directly related to self-interest and self-preservation. For example, companies usually have a significant physical presence in the community and want to protect that investment. Issues of interest to them are zoning regulations, the threat of neighbourhood deterioration, corporate property taxes, the community tax base, and the availability of an adequately trained work force.[16]

A second major reason companies need to stay abreast of community needs and problems is that certain issues involve direct or indirect benefits to them. Examples of such issues include health services, social services, community services, the physical environment, the appearance of the community, and the overall quality of life. A third reason has to do with the company's reputation and image in the community. For example, companies want to be thought of as responsible corporate citizens by residents, employees, and competitors. Companies may have expertise that can help solve community problems, and they want to build a reserve of community goodwill.[17]

Development of a Community Action Program The motivation for developing a **community action program** is evident when one considers the stake a firm has in the community. Likewise, the community represents a major stakeholder of business. Therefore, business has an added incentive to be systematic about its relationship with the community. The four steps in developing a community action program, as articulated by the Norton Company, provide a useful framework for approaching the community from a managerial frame of reference.[18] These four steps are:

1. Knowing the community
2. Knowing the company's resources
3. Selecting projects
4. Monitoring projects

These steps may be beneficial whether the company is considering specific community projects or is attempting to build a strong, long-term relationship with community stakeholders.

Knowing the Community. A key to developing worthwhile community involvement programs is knowing the community in which the business resides. This is a research step that requires management to assess the characteristics of the local area. Every locale has particular characteristics that can help shape social programs of involvement. Who lives in the community? What is its ethnic composition? What is its unemployment level? Are there inner-city problems or pockets of poverty? What are other organizations doing? What are the really pressing social needs of the area? What is the community's morale?

Knowledge of community leadership is another factor. Is the leadership progressive? Is the leadership cohesive and unified, or is it fragmented? If it is fragmented, the company may have to make difficult choices about the groups with which it wants to work. If the community's current approach to social issues is well led, "jumping on the bandwagon" may be all that is necessary. If the community's leadership is not well organized, the company may want to provide an impetus and an agenda for restructuring or revitalizing the leadership. Figure 14–2 presents a checklist of items that companies might include in conducting an assessment of a community's needs.

Knowing the Company's Resources. Effective addressing of various community needs requires an inventory and assessment of the company's resources and competencies. What are the variety, mix, and range of resources—personnel, money, meeting space, equipment, and supplies? Many companies are willing to give employees time to engage in and support community projects. This involvement may be in the form of managerial assistance, technical assistance, or personnel. Wide spectra of abilities, skills, interests, potentials, and experience exist in most organizations. To put any of these resources to work, however, it is necessary to know what is available, to what extent it is available, on what terms it is available, and over what period of time it is available.

Selecting Projects. The selection of community projects for company involvement grows out of the matching of community stakeholders' needs with company resources. Frequently, because there are many such matches, the company must be selective in choosing among them. Sometimes companies develop and refine policies or guidelines to help in the selection process. These policies are extremely useful, because they further delineate areas in which the company may be involved and provide perspective for channelling the organization's energies. Frank Koch has spelled out guidelines for developing a strategy for community involvement.[19] The following list summarizes some of these guidelines:

- Community involvement must be planned and organized with the same care and energy that are devoted to other parts of the business.
- Community projects should meet the same measure of cost-effectiveness as that applied to investments in research, marketing, production, or administration.

FIGURE 14–2

A Checklist of Items Companies Might Include in a Community Needs Assessment

Demographics
- Basic descriptions (sex, level of education)
- Racial mix
- Poverty and unemployment
- Neighbourhood characteristics

Environment and Land Use
- Housing stock (including restoration and preservation)
- Commercial and industrial space
- Open space planning; recreation
- Quality of water, air, and land

Infrastructure and Physical Services
- Condition of roads and bridges
- Traffic patterns and parking space
- Utilities
- Sanitation
- Communications

Leadership
- Business
- Government
- Civic groups
- Community groups

Leisure
- Parks and indoor recreational facilities
- Cultural and art facilities (museums, libraries, galleries)
- Shopping facilities
- Restaurants

Local Economy
- Tax base and rates
- Cost of living
- Economic development plans and agenda
- Employment and labour-force characteristics
- Aid to small business

Local Education
- Primary and secondary
- Vocational
- Colleges and universities

Local Government
- Structure (e.g., mayor or city manager)
- Municipal finance
- Crime and safety capabilities

Local Health and Human Services
- Social- and family-service capabilities
- Hospitals, ambulance service, emergency care facilities
- Degree of community problems relating to above (e.g., alcohol and drug abuse)

Source: Kathryn Troy, *Studying and Addressing Community Needs: A Corporate Case Book* (New York: The Conference Board, 1985), 8. Reprinted with permission.

- The corporation should capitalize on its talents and resources. Those responsible should get involved in things they understand. The company should look at social problems that affect its realm of operations.

- Employees should be involved in community programs. The programs should focus on some of the things that affect and interest those employees.
- The corporation should get involved in the communities it knows, the people it knows best, and the needs that have the best chance of being fulfilled and are important goals of the community.
- Corporate policy should allow continuing support of established causes while new initiatives are being sought.
- The best kind of support is that which helps others help themselves.

Policies and guidelines can go a long way toward rationalizing and systematizing business involvement in the community. Such policy statements should be developed and articulated throughout the organization to help provide a unified focus for company efforts.

An excellent example of a community project that was carefully chosen and is likely to meet most of the guidelines discussed here is the Ronald McDonald House sponsored by McDonald's Corporation. These houses, which annually provide shelter and solace for half a million people whose children are seriously ill, were begun in 1974. By 2003, there were over 250 such houses across the world. McDonald's employs the same pattern in all the communities in which the houses are located. Each is operated by a nonprofit corporation and is staffed by volunteers, except for a paid manager. Each house is located near a hospital that treats children, and families are charged a nominal amount if they can afford it and nothing if they cannot. The families may remain for as long as their children are undergoing treatment.[20] Among the many contributions was a recent donation of $50 000 to the Children's Hospital of Western Ontario as a means to establish the Ronald McDonald Family Room, a facility in the hospital that will allow parents to stay close to their sick child during the day.[21]

Monitoring Projects. Monitoring company projects involves review and control. Follow-up is necessary to ensure that the projects are being executed according to plans and on schedule. Feedback from the various steps in the process provides the information management needs to monitor progress. In later chapters, we will elaborate on the managerial approach to dealing with various social issues. The guidelines previously listed, however, provide some insights into the development of business/community stakeholder relationships. As we stated earlier, community involvement is a discretionary or philanthropic activity in our corporate social performance model. The costs are significant but the potential returns, for both the corporation and the community, are great. Just as other business functions, it should be carefully managed.

Community Involvement of Foreign-Based Firms

Foreign direct investing in Canada and its communities is a growing phenomenon. Some observers have questioned the social consequences of foreign direct investment. It is not surprising, therefore, that researchers have sought to ascertain the extent to which these firms are becoming good "corporate citizens." Why might foreign-owned companies want to contribute to the welfare of local communities? In terms of their motivations for community involvement, surveys conducted among foreign direct investors have shown that they gave reasons very similar to those of domestic executives[22]—namely:

- They felt a moral obligation to be involved.
- They were responding to community expectations.

- They felt that community involvement strengthened their corporate image.
- They felt they were acting in enlightened self-interest.

In interviews, these executives stated that if community involvement was done well, it allowed the business to become an accepted and valued member of society, which was good for its image with customers, employees, governments, and the wider community. Although their involvement was dominated by cash giving, the foreign-based companies had initiated other community programs, such as employee volunteerism and sponsorship (e.g., arts or sports events).[23]

In another study of the "corporate citizenship" practices and viewpoints of foreign direct investors, Pinkston and Carroll reported that these investors had "corporate citizenship orientations" that were quite similar to those of North American firms. Foreign direct investors want to "fit in," and they perceive involvement with community stakeholders as a vital and integral part of that process.[24]

So should communities be concerned that more and more Canadian companies are subject to foreign takeovers? While the answer to that question is unclear, Alison Azer offers a very insightful summary report on foreign ownership and corporate philanthropy in Canada. Her report, *The Changing Corporate Landscape and Its Effect on Charitable Giving*,[25] includes the following observations:

- In a foreign takeover of a Canadian firm, the major determinant of continued philanthropy is the location of corporate decision makers. That is, local community involvement/donations will likely continue if the acquired company maintains relative autonomy from its foreign head office. On the other hand, if the acquired company becomes a "branch plant" with little decision-making power, community initiatives will likely decrease.
- To maintain goodwill with stakeholders, foreign acquirers tend to honour the charitable commitments made by the Canadian company prior to acquisition.
- Whether foreign or domestically owned, Canadian citizens expect companies to contribute to the communities in which they are located.
- Foreign-owned companies, particularly those that are U.S.-owned, are focusing on funding strategic partnerships with the charitable sector that enhance corporate objectives.
- Foreign-owned companies tend to make large charitable donations to high-profile causes and campaigns within the first year of entry into Canada ("rapid response giving") as a means of showing their commitment to the community.
- Foreign-owned companies have shown greatest preference for charities involved in youth, education, and health. They have shown less interest in charities operating in the arts, amateur sports, the environment, addictions, homelessness, and domestic abuse.
- Many observers perceive a decrease in the value of corporate donations because of the increase in foreign-ownership via acquisitions, mergers, and relocations.
- U.S.-owned companies tend to be as supportive of employee volunteerism and employee giving (to such causes as the United Way) as their Canadian counterparts.

Corporate Philanthropy or Business Giving

The dictionary defines **philanthropy** as "a desire to help mankind as indicated by acts of charity; love of mankind."[26] Robert Payton, an expert on philanthropy, argues that

Search the web

The Canadian Centre for Philanthropy (CCP) is a national charitable organization that focuses on advancing the interests of the voluntary sector for the benefit of Canadian communities. With a membership of 1200 voluntary organizations, corporations, and foundations, the CCP plays a leadership role in public affairs, research, and information resources for charitable and nonprofit organizations. CCP established the Imagine program to promote public and corporate giving, volunteering, and support to the community. The program encourages partnerships between the corporate and charitable sectors. Check out CCP's Web site at **http://www.ccp.ca/**.

philanthropy is defined as three related activities: voluntary service, voluntary association, and voluntary giving for public purposes.[27] He goes on to state that it includes "acts of community to enhance the quality of life and to ensure a better future."[28] These definitions of philanthropy suggest a broad range of activities.

One more restricted contemporary usage of the word "philanthropy" is "business giving." In this section, we will concentrate on the voluntary giving of financial resources by business. One problem with the dictionary definition is that the motive for the giving is characterized as charitable, benevolent, or generous. In actual practice, it is difficult to assess the true motives behind businesses'—or anyone's—giving of themselves or their financial resources.

The findings of a survey conducted by the Muttart Foundation and the Canadian Centre for Philanthropy underscored the value Canadians place on the charitable sector, with 90 percent of the 4000 Canadians polled indicating that they perceive charities to be increasingly important. On the other hand, about 60 percent felt that charities do not have enough money to do their work.[29] According to recent Statistics Canada estimates, the Canadian voluntary or nonprofit sector consists of an estimated 180 000 nonprofit organizations, of which 80 000 are registered as charities. There exist hundreds of thousands of additional volunteer groups that are not incorporated. In 2000, 6.5 million Canadians were contributing some of their time to a voluntary sector organization. That same year, 22 million people donated a total of $5.0 billion to this sector. Canadian charitable donations rose to $5.51 billion in 2001, continuing a decade-long trend of growth in charitable donations.[30]

In 2003, *Business Week* featured its first ranking of corporate philanthropists. General Mills figured prominently in this ranking because of its tradition of corporate generosity that dates back to the late 1800s, and which includes its effort to reduce crime in U.S. communities, its support of food backs, and its generous donation of US$65 million to a variety of charitable causes in 2002. In addition, *Business Week*'s poll of companies in the Standard & Poor's 500-stock index revealed that only four out of 218 respondents agreed with the notion that the sole responsibility of business is to make profits. That is, corporations appear to see increasing value in philanthropy. Among the highest ranked corporate donors in 2002 were Wal-Mart Stores Inc. (US$156 million), Ford Motor (US$131 million), Altria Group (US$113.4 million), SBC Communications (US$100 million), Exxon Mobil (US$97.2 million), and General Mills (US$65 million).[31]

Although Canada's charitable sector receives financial support from business, it is a relatively small portion of the total funding currently received. Individual donations make up a larger source of revenue for the nonprofit and voluntary sector than corporate donations. With recent estimates indicating that corporate donors account for only 1 percent of total sector revenues, it is fair to say that, traditionally, the corporate sector in Canada has not been a generous donor to charitable causes.[32]

Giving to the "Third Sector"—The Nonprofits

According to philanthropist John D. Rockefeller III, business giving is necessary to support what has been called the **third sector**—the nonprofit sector. The first two sectors—

Ethics In Practice

Tugging the Heart or Twisting the Arm?

While working for a large corporation, I received numerous e-mails telling me of the large charitable contribution fund in which the company participates. All employees were highly encouraged to attend a town-hall meeting where other employees and managers spoke of how the fund had affected their lives and showed videos of the good work the fund had done. Top executives travelled to the town-hall meetings to promote the campaign and encourage 100 percent employee participation. They told us to ask our fellow employees if they had contributed yet. They wanted to reach a goal of $1 million and believed that everyone should be able to contribute. Furthermore, all managers were expected to contribute. There was even documentation on the company's intranet Web site with guidelines for how much to give. Although the company claims all donations (or lack thereof) are anonymous and have no effect on promotions or job performance ratings, many wondered if that was entirely true. This was not the first company

to strongly encourage me to contribute to its fund drive and I doubt it will be the last.

1. Why do companies participate in charitable fund programs? Is it for societal recognition, to aid a worthy cause, or is it some combination? If different firms differ in their motivation—why might that be so?

2. Is it ethical for a company to solicit voluntary charitable contributions from employees? Can they be truly voluntary? If so, how should these campaigns be designed and implemented? Where would you draw the line?

3. If companies no longer participate in charitable fund campaigns, what would be the repercussion for the charities? Does that affect your answer?

4. If you worked in this company, what would you do? Why? If you chose to contribute, what would be your driving motivation?

Contributed by Melissa S. Magoon

business and government—receive support through profits and taxes. The third sector (which includes thousands of churches, museums, hospitals, libraries, private colleges and universities, and performing arts groups) depends on philanthropy for support. Philanthropy gives these institutions the crucial margin that assures them of their most precious asset—their independence.[33]

Philanthropy can take a variety of forms and so it is difficult to measure. In the past decade, business giving has increased, but not at the same rate as corporate profits. The volunteer programs previously discussed are not included in calculations of philanthropy dollars. In addition, cause-related marketing, such as Walt Disney's multimillion-dollar merchandising agreements with the American Society for the Prevention of Cruelty to Animals (ASPCA), is generally deemed a marketing expense and so does not necessarily contribute to the official tally of a company's charitable giving.[34]

Why Do Companies Give?   Perhaps it would be more worthwhile to know why companies give to charitable causes rather than to know how much they give. There are several ways to approach this question. We get initial insights when we consider five categories of corporate contributions programs as shown in Figure 14–3.[35] The motivations that are reflected in these categories range from pure self-interest to a desire to practise good corporate citizenship by supporting both traditional and innovative programs in the community.

Saiia, Carroll, and Buchholtz found that corporate giving managers believe their firms are becoming more strategic in their giving and that top managers are requiring

FIGURE 14–3

Categories of Corporate Contributions Programs

1. *The Nondonor*—This is a firm for which no evidence of charitable giving was found.
2. *The "What's in It for Us" Donor*—With this firm, most contributions relate to the company's direct interest or to the welfare of its employees.
3. *The "Company President Believes in Art Support" Donor*—With this firm, most contributions relate to the company's direct interest, employees' welfare, or management's interest.
4. *The "We Are a Good Citizen" Donor*—Here a substantial portion of the company's giving provides support for traditional nonprofit institutions.
5. *The "We Care" Donor*—Here some funds go to newer organizations and established organizations that deal with nontraditional issues.

greater strategic accountability in their corporate giving programs. They also found that firms that are more "exposed" to the environment (i.e., more open and vulnerable to the environment) are more likely to engage in strategic philanthropy.[36] In another study, Fry, Keim, and Meiners found that corporate contributions are motivated by profit considerations that influence both advertising expenditures and corporate giving. They concluded that corporate giving is a complement to advertising and is, therefore, a profit-motivated expense.[37]

As economic pressures and increased international competitiveness force companies to be more careful with their earnings, we should not be surprised to see the profit motive co-existing with loftier goals in corporate contributions programs. Indeed, in a subsequent section of this chapter, we show that philanthropy can be "strategic," which means that corporate giving can be aligned with the firm's economic or profitability objectives.

The authors of *Business Week*'s 2003 special report on corporate philanthropy made the following observations:

> *Many big companies are upfront about their desire to use philanthropy to polish their image. In an age of social activism and instant communication, when a Web log can energize a mass boycott overnight, some say it's essential to build a public narrative about your company as a good global citizen. Thus, we found pharmaceutical companies Merck and Pfizer working to stem the spread of infectious diseases; network-equipment maker Cisco providing voice mail to the homeless; and bank Washington Mutual building affordable housing near its branches....*
> *Of course, just because a company gives lots of its shareholders' money away doesn't mean that it has a heart of gold. Enron Corp. donated heavily to board member John Mendelson's cancer research center. And L. Dennis Kozlowski, the former CEO of Tyco International Ltd. who is now in court fighting charges that he looted the company, allegedly used more than [US]$40 million of Tyco funds to make charitable contributions that either benefited him or that he represented as his personal donations.[38]*

To Whom Do Companies Give?   During the course of any budget year, companies receive numerous requests for contributions from a wide variety of applicants. Companies must then weigh both quantitative and qualitative factors to arrive at decisions regarding the recipients of their gifts. By looking at the beneficiaries of corporate contributions, we can estimate the value business places on various societal needs in the community.

Data on corporate contributions show that business giving is distributed among five major categories of recipients in the following order of emphasis: (1) education, (2) health and human services, (3) community activities, (4) culture and the arts, and (5) other or unspecified. These areas have traditionally received consistent attention from corporations. A brief discussion of the first four categories will help explain the nature of business's involvement in philanthropy.

Education. Most of the corporate contributions in this category have gone to higher education—colleges and universities. The major educational recipients have been capital grants (including endowments), unrestricted operating grants, departmental and research grants, scholarships and fellowships, and employee matching gifts. Also included in this category are contributions to educational groups (e.g., literacy organizations) and to primary and secondary schools.

As we noted earlier, business's most frequently reported reason for supporting higher education has been to increase the pool of trained personnel. This has obvious credibility, because higher education institutions do, indeed, form the resource base from which business fills its managerial and professional positions.

Although contributions to educational institutions rank high in business giving, companies do not always give blindly and expect nothing in return. Over the years, there has been some controversy about whether business should give to educational institutions that do not support the free enterprise values so important to business. The basic issue has been whether support of education should be "with strings attached" or "without strings attached."

Those who argue that business should give to education without strings attached think that attempts to dictate to educational institutions will create conflict between the institutions and industry. Louis W. Cabot, former chairman of the board of Cabot Corporation, argued that it is neither wise nor advantageous for business to limit its gifts to institutions that support free enterprise. His belief is that the corporate self-interest criterion is both illusory and dangerous. It is illusory in that it calls for sweeping generalizations about faculty members; it is dangerous because it tends to discourage all educational giving. He believes, in addition, that if a company genuinely wants to help education function with maximum effectiveness, it should support schools as a whole rather than try to control the use of its funds. Cabot summarized his view as follows: "It is in the corporate community's self-interest to step up its level of financial support. At the same time, it is not in the corporate interest to dilute this effort by burdening it with uncalled-for constraints."[39]

On the other side of the issue have been those who think business ought to be more selective in its giving. Robert H. Malott, former chairman of the board of FMC Corporation, argued that corporate self-interest ought to serve as a guide for business giving to education. Malott is especially concerned about corporations giving financial support to schools and colleges that teach the views of radical economists and others who want government to grow at the expense of free enterprise.[40]

Irving Kristol also argues forcefully that business has a responsibility to be discerning in its corporate contributions. He maintains that although universities believe they have a right to business's money, "they have no such right." His position is that if educational institutions want money from a particular segment of the population, they must earn the good opinion of that segment. If educational institutions are indifferent to that good opinion, they also will have to learn to be indifferent to the money.

Kristol has argued against business giving money to support educational organizations whose views are "inimical to corporate survival." He summarizes his feelings as follows: "Your philanthropy must serve the longer-term interests of the corporation. Corporate philanthropy should not be, cannot be, disinterested."[41]

Unfortunately, there is no data to tell us which of these extreme positions is the most effective; they represent opposite philosophical postures. A philosophy tempered with the belief that managers should exercise some discretion over their corporate giving to education and at the same time serve the company's self-interest would achieve economic and social goals simultaneously.

Health and Human Services. The major reason that health and welfare is one of the largest categories of business giving is the huge amount donated to such federated drives as the United Way. Business has traditionally cooperated with federated giving mechanisms. Money given to federated drives usually goes directly to assist various agencies in a local community. Great public pressure is placed on businesses to support actively such federated campaigns, and so it is not surprising that this category is one of the largest beneficiaries. Business hopes, just as the community does, that such consolidated efforts will lend some order to the requests of major recipients in the community that business has chosen to support.[42]

In addition to federated drives, major recipients in this category include hospitals, youth agencies, and other local health and welfare agencies. Hospitals represent an obviously important need in most communities. They receive financial support for capital investments (new buildings and equipment), operating funds, and matching employee gifts. Youth agencies include such groups as the YMCA, YWCA, Boy Scouts, Girl Guides, and Boys and Girls Clubs. CanWest Global Foundation, the philanthropic arm of CanWest Global Communications Corp., has worked with literacy organizations to contribute to the Raise a Reader Campaign, which is designed to create awareness of children's literacy and to raise funds and resources for children's literacy programs and organizations.[43] Dreyer's Grand Ice Cream, Inc., focuses its philanthropic activities on youth to enable those youth to "develop individual initiative and talent in order for them to become contributing members of their communities and caretakers of the communities' values for the next generation."[44]

Community Activities. This category of business giving represents a wide variety of philanthropic activities in the community. The dominant contributions in this category are those given in support of community improvement activities, environment and ecology, nonacademic research organizations, and neighbourhood renewal.

Eli Lilly and Company's education-oriented programs exemplify civic involvement with youth as the focus. For example, in Lilly's Junior Achievement programs, employees serve as business consultants to the local schools. Subjects such as applied economics, global learning, and personal economics are learned by children from kindergarten through twelfth grade. Lilly's "Partners in Education" is a mentoring program that pairs employees with children with special needs. The Minority Engineering Program exposes minority students to career opportunities in engineering and computer science through mentoring, hands-on exercises, computer presentations, and field trips. In other Eli Lilly programs, employees promote interest in and awareness of science careers.[45]

The Canadian clothes retailer Roots unveiled a new line of sports apparel in 2003. The line was inspired by, and a portion of each sale was designated for contributions to, the humanitarian organization Right to Play. Right to Play is dedicated to improving the lives of disadvantaged children and their communities through sport. Roots co-founder Michael Budman commented on the logic of his contributions:

"Opportunities for sport and play are scarce for millions of children. Through its programs, Right To Play is changing this. Roots new line of sports wear will give Canadians the opportunity to play their part in supporting every child's right to play." The Right to Play president observed that Roots' involvement "… is a great initiative not only because it will help raise money for our programs, but because it will help raise awareness of the need for these programs."[46]

Culture and the Arts. Support for culture and the arts has been a favourite and prestigious outlet for business philanthropy for decades. Of the various cultural beneficiaries of business support, museums tend to be the most frequent, followed in order by radio and television (especially public broadcasting), music (symphony orchestras, for example), arts funds and councils, and theatres. But as the data show, culture and the arts rank behind health and welfare, civic and community activities, and education in total business giving.

One of the most prominent organized efforts on the part of Canadian business to support the arts is the Council for Business and Arts in Canada (CBAC). Formed in 1974 by business leaders from such organizations as duMaurier Arts Ltd., Great West Life & London Life, Imperial Oil Limited, and the Royal Bank of Canada, the CBAC is an association of arts sponsors, patrons, and volunteers. The broad aim of this organization is to increase private sector support of the arts and to encourage business to develop partnerships with arts organizations. According to the CBAC, prior to its creation Canadian businesses allocated about 3 percent of their donations budgets to the arts. Through the CBAC's efforts, arts organizations now receive an average of about 10 percent of Canadian corporate community investment budgets.[47] Its current membership includes such organizations as AGF Management Ltd., the Bank of Montreal, the Bank of Nova Scotia, Bell Canada, the Canadian Imperial Bank of Commerce, CanWest, FirstEnergy Capital Corp., Four Seasons Hotels and Resorts, Hudson's Bay Company, Imperial Oil Limited, National Post, Onex Corporation, and the Royal Bank of Canada.[48]

In the late 1990s, philanthropy began to place new emphasis on concrete results, leading to less interest in funding the arts as philanthropy is directed toward environmental, educational, and technological causes.[49] Despite this move away from funding the arts, substantial art donations continue. Sara Lee donated about 40 pieces of Impressionist and early modern work, worth an estimated US$100 million, to 20 U.S. art museums. This record-setting donation came from paintings that had once hung in the corporation's main offices.[50]

In 2002, Canadian media mogul Ken Thomson of the Thomson Corporation pledged $70 million to help fund the Art Gallery of Ontario's expansion. Thomson also donated his estimated $300 million art collection, much of which had been maintained in a gallery housed by the Hudson's Bay Company, one of Thomson's businesses.[51]

It is interesting to consider why business gives to the arts. Companies seem to gain none of the direct benefits that they receive from their donations to education. As with other philanthropic categories, businesses claim various motives for their giving. There are those who argue altruistically that the reason for business's largesse is that it recognizes that art contributes to the kinds of vitality and creativity that are important to society. On the other hand, there are business executives who say openly that their support for the arts has been at least in part a reflection of self-interest. Paul H. Eliker, former president of SCM Corporation, argues that companies should give to the arts in order to gain recognition or visibility and for general image building.[52] He claims that the great patrons of the Renaissance—the Medicis and Pope Julius II—supported culture and the arts for much the same reason: to associate themselves with the grandeur of the times.

Eliker told the story of a reporter who once asked the vice chairman of Philip Morris why his company supported such exhibitions as Folk Art. The vice chairman is reported to have responded, "It's a lot cheaper than taking out ads saying how great we think we are."[53]

Although no one can peer into the minds of business executives to find out why business really gives to the arts, at least one sociologist suggests that the motive is really self-interest, not altruism and social responsibility. This may not sound very startling, given the public admission of some executives that it is true. But M. David Ermann sees the giving efforts as part of an extremely selfish scenario. Citing gifts from major corporations totalling US$12 million per year to the Public Broadcasting System (PBS), Ermann argues that such contributions are intended to create a less hostile social climate and thus mute the critics of business. In his words, the purpose of the corporate charity was to favourably "influence the social milieu ... to ensure rewards and reduce penalties and uncertainty for the company."[54]

Recipients of business donations to the arts are not likely to turn down such contributions because the givers' motives may not be purely altruistic. Business giving, whatever the intent, does benefit the giver and the receiver, as well as the general public.

Managing Corporate Philanthropy

As performance pressures on business have continued and intensified, companies more and more have had to turn their attention to managing corporate philanthropy. Early on, managers did not subject their contributions to the same kinds of rigorous analysis given to expenditures for plants and equipment, inventory, product development, marketing, and a host of other budgetary items. This began to change in the 1980s because cutbacks in federal spending on charitable causes created an increasing need for contributions by business. At the same time, however, the economy was struggling through a severe recession. Recessions are generally accompanied by a decline in donations, and the money given to the relief funds may cannibalize the contributions that companies would have given to other causes.[55]

By the 1990s, demands for business to become more competitive became the authoritative view on corporate survival. It became increasingly clear that business had to reconcile its economic and social goals, both of which were essential.[56]

Today, many observers have suggested that although competition continues to be fierce, Canadian business continues to play a respectable role in support of the arts. As James Fleck commented:

> *As in many areas, Canada is somewhere between our neighbours to the south and Europe in funding for the arts. In Europe, massive (by our standards) government but not private support for the arts is a long-established and widely accepted tradition. In the United States, the ratio is reversed and the preponderant support is from the private sector. In Canada, we have more public funds than the United States and more private support than Europe. That presents an opportunity to develop a uniquely Canadian approach.*[57]

According to the CBAC, Canadian business can be proud of its many supporters of the arts. The Business in the Arts Awards, a program organized by the CBAC and the

National Post, recognizes outstanding partnerships between business and the arts with these national awards. Figure 14–4 includes profiles of three such recent award recipients.

Public Purpose Partnerships   A report by the Voluntary Sector Initiative (VSI) indicated that there has been a significant shift in the nature of corporate giving to the nonprofit sector:

> *The larger trend … has been the pervasive shift away from corporate donations to corporate sponsorships. Marketing departments are now in control of "philanthropic" budgets. Corporations very carefully seek out potential nonprofit and voluntary sector partners to form strategic relationships that will deliver defined benefits, value and return for their investments in the form of heightened community profile and increased customer loyalty. There are fewer and fewer sources of unrestricted donations or funds. Rather, decisions are taken to maximize positive corporate exposure.*[58]

As a broad response to this growing need to reconcile financial and social goals, both of which were deemed by business to be desirable and necessary, the concept of public purpose partnerships evolved.[59] A public purpose partnership occurs when a

---

FIGURE 14–4

National Post Awards for Business in the Arts

Best Arts/Entrepreneur Partnership: EPCOR

To underscore its commitment to the Calgary market, Edmonton-based utility EPCOR bought the naming rights to the Centre for the Performing Arts for $4 million dollars, payable into its endowment, over 10 years. The decision to partner with the arts centre provides the electricity marketer with high visibility in the province's largest business market, while providing the facility with known fixed costs for its utilities over the next decade. But the Epcor/Centre partnership goes beyond cash and kind to include the provision of marketing expertise, not just to the Centre itself, but to support all the performing arts in Calgary. In addition, the two have undertaken the challenge of making the Centre a model of energy-efficiency in its use of electricity, water, and gas.

Award of Distinction: TELUS

In British Columbia TELUS has long been known as a supporter of arts programs aimed at youth, a techno-savvy market that the communications company understands well. It has now extended the reach of this effective corporate program nationwide through its strategic partnership with the National Arts Centre's Youth and Education Trust. TELUS provided the lead funding to enable the creation of ArtsAlive.ca, a bilingual Web site that allows children, youth, and teachers the opportunity to interact in real time with NAC artists. Beyond the Web site, TELUS also undertook to help the NAC launch a multifaceted strategy to encourage young people to explore the performing arts.

Award of Distinction Profile: Lexus of Oakville

Oakville Galleries has developed an enviable reputation for its contemporary exhibitions—and with that has come a dedicated following of art collectors who appreciate quality design. Eight years ago a Lexus car dealer saw a great opportunity to reach the town's market for luxury vehicles by sponsoring the Oakville Galleries. What began as a single exhibit sponsorship has extended into an $80 000, eight-year cross-promotional partnership between the Galleries and Lexus, which has helped the Galleries to produce excellent exhibitions. It has also helped Lexus to broaden its customer base in the community to the point that, in 2001, the company built one of only six Canadian dealerships in Oakville.

Source: National Post Awards for Business in the Arts, Winners' Profiles (2003), http://www.businessforarts.org/awards/np-a.asp#epcor.

for-profit business enters into a cooperative arrangement with a nonprofit organization for their mutual advantage. Businesses see in public purpose partnerships the opportunity for simultaneous achievement of economic and philanthropic objectives. An example of a public purpose partnership is the one between 3M Company and the University of Minnesota. The 3M Company gave US$1 million to the MBA program at Minnesota. Rather than just give the money and run, 3M officials formed a committee with university officials to discuss how the two organizations could work together. This was seen as a smart move on 3M's part, because about 15 percent of its employees are alumni of the university.[60]

Nortel Networks has developed collaborative relationships with a number of universities across Canada, including the University of Toronto, Carleton University, and the University of Calgary. Nortel provides funding for university chairs, new faculty positions, and cooperative education programs across Canada. This obviously helps universities in attracting high-calibre faculty and enhancing curricula. For example, with Nortel's support, the University of Toronto established a new Master's of Engineering Degree in Telecommunications (MET) and created a comprehensive summer school program focused on advanced telecommunications topics. Nortel's collaborative efforts will also benefit the company itself. Nortel's involvement generates a closer network of highly qualified recruits that may look first to Nortel when they are considering the job market.[61]

McDonald's Corporation has also entered into multimillion-dollar sponsorships with universities. In one such case, the arrangement called for McDonald's to give the Georgia Institute of Technology US$5.5 million to complete the financing of its US$12.5 million renovation. As part of the agreement, the building was named the McDonald's Center. McDonald's representatives said they thought this investment could lead to other interactions and arrangements in academic and research-related activities.[62]

Public purpose sponsorship, particularly in the university setting, has attracted both controversy and criticism. One common question raised is: Does private sector funding of university programs and research generate any constraints or threats to academic freedom and integrity? A commentary in the Canadian Association of University Teachers (CAUT) bulletin entitled "Canada's Universities Mean Business" referred to this criticism of public purpose sponsorship in an academic setting:

> *Increased corporate funding poses serious threats to the quality and integrity of the university. Nowhere has this been more apparent than in research. There are a growing number of examples of corporate interests infringing on research practices and ethics. University of Toronto clinician, Dr. Nancy Olivieri, received widespread attention recently when her research at the Hospital for Sick Children led her to believe that a new drug treatment posed serious dangers to some patients. The corporate co-sponsor of the research objected to her findings, threatened legal action should she publish her results, and had her removed as the study's principal investigator. Dr. Olivieri was only reinstated after the intervention of the Canadian Association of University Teachers and the University of Toronto Faculty Association.[63]*

This sentiment was shared in a recent report on public-private partnerships (PPPs) in universities in Ontario conducted by the Canadian Centre for Policy Alternatives.[64] The report suggests that public purpose partnerships between the universities and the private sector are adversely affecting the quality of education and appropriate research practices. The report alleges that academic programs favoured by Canadian industry will prosper, while those not considered valuable will be ignored and suffer from underfunding. Specifically, according to this report, this form of university funding (facilitated by both the private sector as well as such government initiatives as SuperBuild and the Ontario Challenge Research and Development Fund) tends to overemphasize support for science and technology disciplines and underemphasize support for the liberal arts programs. These concerns led one of the authors of this report to argue that "these vehicles of PPPs have begun to transform public-serving universities into contracted-out centres for private-sector R & D initiatives, particularly as the public funding for research is often tied to securing private funding."[65]

Public purpose partnerships can take on many different forms. Two of the most important are strategic philanthropy and cause-related marketing. Other partnership options include sponsorships, vendor relationships, licensing agreements, and in-kind donations.[66] We will consider strategic philanthropy and cause-related marketing in detail.

Strategic Philanthropy   **Strategic philanthropy** is an approach by which corporate giving and other philanthropic endeavours of a firm are designed in a way that best fits with the firm's overall mission, goals, or objectives. This implies that the firm has some idea of what its overall strategy is and that it is able to articulate its missions, goals, or objectives. One goal of all firms is profitability. Therefore, one requirement of strategic philanthropy is to make as direct a contribution as possible to the financial goals of the firm. Philanthropy has long been thought to be in the long-range economic interest of the firm. Strategic philanthropy simply presses for a more direct or immediate contribution of philanthropy to the firm's economic success.

An important way in which philanthropy can be made strategic is to bring contribution programs into sharper alignment with business endeavours. This means that each firm should pursue those social programs that have a direct rather than an indirect bearing on its success. Thus, a local bank should logically pursue people-oriented projects in the community in which it resides; a manufacturer might pursue programs having to do with environmental protection or technological advancement.

A third way to make philanthropy strategic is to ensure that it is well planned and managed rather than handled haphazardly and without direction. When a program is planned, this implies that it has clearly delineated goals, is properly organized and staffed, and is administered in accordance with certain established policies. Figure 14–5 presents one company's views on what constitutes an effective strategic corporate contributions program.

Timothy Mescon and Donn Tilson elaborate on the need for managing the philanthropic function:

> *A professionally run contributions program requires a set of strategic plans, goals, and objectives which are reviewed regularly; a set of guidelines for determining how much money will be allocated to it; criteria for making and evaluating grants; and either an in-house staff or access to competent consultants.*[67]

An example of a firm that turned its philanthropic program around by making it more strategic is Burger King. For years, Burger King was an average corporate good citizen, quietly dribbling out US$200 000 to the United Way along with small contributions to

> ### FIGURE 14–5
>
> ## Characteristics of an Effective Strategic Corporate Contributions Program
>
> An effective strategic corporate contributions program will have most of the following characteristics:
>
> 1. It will be based on the longer-term, strategic self-interest of the company.
> 2. It will have a clearly stated strategy, agreed to by top management.
> 3. It will have clear, well-defined guidelines.
> 4. By definition, it will be planned. (But not all planned giving programs are necessarily strategic.)
> 5. It will be based on objective criteria understood by all concerned.
> 6. It will be actively managed and evaluated for results.
> 7. It will focus on programs, not on capital or endowments. (Strategies change.)
> 8. It will be recognized as another function or tool in the entire public affairs process—not simply as a measure of corporate conscience.

Sources: Gerald S. Gendell, Manager, Public Affairs Division, Procter & Gamble. Excerpted from his talk at the Public Affairs Council's conference on strategic uses of philanthropy in public affairs. Diane R. Shayon, "Strategic Philanthropy Beginning to Take Hold," *Impact* (October 1984), 2. Reprinted with permission.

arts organizations and a scattering of other causes. At the same time, McDonald's, its major competitor, was gaining a reputation for strong social programs through its strategically focused Ronald McDonald Houses for children with terminal cancer. Then, suddenly, Burger King woke up and turned its corporate image around with a contributions strategy that sought to make a social statement. This Pillsbury subsidiary began pumping US$4 million a year into highly focused programs to help students, teachers, and schools. Much of Burger King's philanthropy began to consist of scholarships to its own teen work force, designed to reduce the high turnover rate among those workers. As one direct result of the firm's education focus, its turnover rate dropped by more than half during the first six months of its national effort.[68]

Another example of strategic philanthropy was the decision of *People* magazine to promote charities that have particular significance to its readers. Thus, in one year, the magazine planned to give up more than US$3 million worth of advertising space to charities that represent such causes as women with ovarian cancer, children with AIDS, and homeless children. The magazine planned to go even further. It decided to experiment with a program whereby it would eliminate many of the usual "perks" offered to its best advertisers—golf outings, expensive dinners, Broadway theatre tickets—and, instead, invite these companies' executives to engage in charitable activities themselves.[69]

In recent years, popular social causes adopted by corporations have included hunger, community and economic development, literacy, school reform, and environmentalism.[70] In his book titled *Corporate Social Investing*, Curt Weeden details the importance of selecting the right corporate giving manager to oversee philanthropic activities. First, the giving manager should be no more than one executive away from the CEO or chief operating officer (COO), with both a title and a level of compensation that reflect her or his position in the hierarchy. That person should have basic business skills as well as a solid knowledge of the profit-and-loss activities of the company. In addition, the giving manager should be aware of and interested in the nonprofit sector. Last, the giving manager must have the respect of fellow executives and the ability to be an effective company representative.[71]

Craig Smith goes on to identify six steps companies and their executives can take to implement strategic philanthropy.[72] These steps, which are listed here, help companies institutionalize strategic philanthropy:

1. Appoint and empower a philanthropy leader.
2. Support the leader's efforts to find the company's "natural" causes.
3. Promote and oversee a feisty dialogue between business functions and philanthropy.
4. Decentralize the philanthropic function.
5. Make the parts add up to more than the whole.
6. Continue research, testing, evaluation, and revision of corporate philanthropy.

All of these recommendations have one purpose in common—professionalizing the corporate contributions function so that it is more effective and more efficient. As giving managers become more professionalized, firms become more strategic in their philanthropy.[73]

Now let us turn our attention to a special kind of strategic philanthropy that has become quite prevalent in recent years: cause-related marketing.

Cause-Related Marketing There is some debate as to whether or not cause-related marketing is really philanthropy, but it does represent the closest of linkages between a firm's financial objectives and corporate contributions. Therefore, we will treat it here as one form of strategic philanthropy. Cause-related marketing represents a unique joining of business and charity with the potential for great benefit to each. Stated in its simplest form, cause-related marketing is the direct linking of a business's product or service to a specified charity. Each time a consumer uses the service or buys the product, a donation is given to the charity by the business.[74] Cause-related marketing has, therefore, sometimes been referred to as "quid pro quo strategic philanthropy."

The term **cause-related marketing** was coined by the American Express Company to describe a program it began in 1983 in which it agreed to contribute a penny to the restoration of the Statue of Liberty every time one of its credit cards was used to make a purchase. The project generated US$1.7 million for the statue restoration and a substantial increase in usage of the American Express card.[75] Since that time, companies have employed this same approach to raise millions of dollars for a wide variety of causes.

Cause-related marketing has been used by business to achieve a variety of objectives. Listed here are four different, but related, purposes to which the approach has been directed:[76]

- *Global marketing.* Avon, Inc., promotes various causes in its several international markets. These causes include efforts to combat violence against women in Malaysia, child malnourishment in China, and AIDS in Thailand.
- *Short-term promotion.* American Express offered to give 2 cents per transaction to the antihunger organization Share Our Strength. The campaign raised US$5 million.
- *Image building.* Coors Brewing Co. pledged to spend US$40 million over five years for funding literacy organizations and causes.
- *Marketing to women.* Midas courted women drivers with its Project Baby Safe program. Every driver who bought a $42 car seat got a certificate worth that amount in Midas services.

When the Canadian beef industry suffered through the mad-cow scare in the summer of 2003 and was harmed by sanctions, McDonald's and Burger King tried to come to their aid by hosting cause-related marketing initiatives. McDonald's Canada announced that it was purchasing 100 percent of its beef in Canada and offered a two-for-one hamburger promotion in a bid to help the beef industry. Burger King held a $1 Whopper Day to offer its help and it introduced its "I Support Canadian Beef" sticker/coupon campaign.[77]

Recently, cause-related marketing has given way to a new concept, **cause branding**. Cause branding represents a longer-term commitment than cause marketing. It also is more directly related to the firm's line of business and their target audience. Avon Products, Inc., is a recognized leader in cause branding. Their target audience is women, and so they have developed an array of programs to raise awareness of breast cancer, a disease that mostly affects women. The company raises money for programs that provide low-income women with education and free screening. Avon sells products featuring the pink ribbon that is worn for breast cancer awareness and then donates proceeds from these products to nonprofit and university programs.[78]

The move to cause branding is likely to be successful as a marketing tool. A report entitled *Cause-Related Trends Report: Evolution of Cause Branding* showed that 61 percent of consumers felt companies should make cause branding part of their regular business.[79] Studies also suggests that most consumers feel more positively disposed toward companies that support a cause about which they care, and consumers are more likely to select the more socially responsible brand when price and quality are equal. The benefits do not apply only to consumers: Employees react to cause branding as well. In companies with cause programs, 87 percent of employees indicate they feel strong loyalty, while only 67 percent feel strong loyalty in firms that do not have cause programs.[80]

Proponents of cause-related marketing argue that everyone involved in it comes out a winner. Business enhances its public image by being associated with a worthy cause and increases its sales at the same time. Nonprofit organizations get cash for their programs as well as enhanced marketing and public visibility made possible by business's expertise.

Critics of cause-related marketing suggest that there are issues that make the approach controversial. For nonprofit organizations that participate, one issue is the "taint of commercialism" that cause-related marketing may bring. The direct link between the nonprofit organization and the product being marketed may appear to be a promotional effort on the part of the nonprofit organization, and some may see this as compromising the organization's altruistic image. Other critics fear that if cause-related marketing becomes widespread, it could undermine the very basis of philanthropy. Still others fear that some corporations may use cause-related marketing as a substitute for, rather than a supplement to, regular corporate contributions. The consequence of this would be a zero net increase in the amount of funds available.[81]

Global Philanthropy Formal international philanthropy efforts are now part of global business strategies. Companies among the top ten global contributors state that their contributions go where they have operations as well as a strong presence. In general, giving programs tend to focus on infrastructure needs, education, the environment, and health care. Some companies, such as IBM and Merck & Co., donate large quantities of product, especially to undeveloped countries.[82]

One recent example of global philanthropy involves firms that do business in sub-Saharan Africa, a region where AIDS has killed 17 million people and infected

25 million more. These companies have seen the disease take a devastating toll on their employees. They often must train two people for the same job so that they will be prepared if the employee or a family member becomes ill. Frequent absences, caused by the disease, are the norm. In response, companies such as Chevron, Coca-Cola, and the Ford Motor Company have undertaken sweeping initiatives to address the problem.[83]

Chevron provides AIDS education, psychological counselling, and free medical facilities for its employees. Although employees do not have access to retroviral treatments, they have had success using available antibiotics to treat the opportunistic infections so common with AIDS. Coca-Cola also sponsors two-day AIDS seminars, provides condoms in all restrooms, and makes health coverage available for all employees. It provides AIDS benefits based on reasonable and customary allowances. The Ford Motor Company also promotes education and prevention while providing health coverage. It takes a three-pronged approach that includes programs for the employees, joint efforts with other employers, and a community outreach program.[84]

Executives claim several advantages of global contributions programs,[85] including:

- An improved corporate image
- A boost in market penetration
- Improved personal relations
- Improved government relations

Executives also note, however, that it can be difficult to administer programs in some cultures that do not place a high priority on voluntary activity. In addition, getting information about the impacts of their programs is difficult.

It is expected that global philanthropy will continue to be an integral and growing part of corporate contributions programs. As long as companies continue to generate revenues and profits abroad, involvement in these countries and their communities will continue.[86]

Business and Plant Closings

We now shift our focus to business and plant closings. In the preceding sections, we considered the ways in which business firms might have positive, constructive, and creative impacts on community stakeholders. Firms can also have detrimental impacts on communities. We see a most pervasive example of such negative effects when a business or plant closes and its management does not carefully consider the community stakeholders affected.

In the remainder of this chapter, we will examine the nature of the business or plant closing problem, identify some reasons for these occurrences, and consider some actions and strategies that businesses might employ to minimize their negative impacts on community stakeholders. We will also consider the status of plant-closing legislation and the role of public action groups and researchers in helping us to understand this problem.

Reasons for Closings

There is no single reason why so many businesses and plants close. The recession in the 1980s provided a major catalyst for these shutdowns. Some of the affected companies were in declining industries; some had outdated facilities or technology; some moved to less unionized areas; some sought access to new markets; some were victims of the merger/acquisition frenzy; and many were victims of global competition. Plant closings continued in the 1990s. As we entered the new millennium, the sharp decline in the technology sector resulted in the sudden closing of dot-coms and other technology-based firms. It is clear that closings will continue to occur and to profoundly impact employees and the community. Therefore, it is important to understand why they happen.

In the mid-1980s, when plant closings became rampant in North America, a major survey was conducted among public affairs executives to ascertain why they thought business closings were occurring. Figure 14–6 summarizes the reasons that were cited. The major reasons included economic recession, consolidation of company operations, outmoded technology/facilities, changes in corporate strategy, and unmet corporate objectives.[87] In later years, foreign competition became a vital factor. It is clear from these findings and other studies that the primary reasons for companies deciding to close down plants have been related to economics.[88]

What Should Business Do?

Although the right to close a business or plant has long been regarded as a management prerogative, the business shutdowns of the past two decades—especially their dramatic effects—have called attention to the question of what place rights and responsibilities business has in relation to employee and community stakeholders. The

---

FIGURE 14–6

Reasons Cited for Business/Plant Closings

Reason	Frequency of Mention	Percent
Economic recession	67	48.9
Consolidation of company operations	64	46.7
Outmoded technology/facilities	41	29.9
Changes in corporate strategy	39	28.5
Unmet corporate objectives	39	28.5
Firms in declining industry	32	23.4
Foreign competition	31	22.6
Domestic competition	20	14.6
Search for lower labour costs	18	13.1
Local attitudes toward business	11	8.0
Costly regulations	10	7.3
Other	8	5.8
Automation	6	4.4
Poor long-term planning	5	3.6
Inadequate capital investment	4	2.9
Quality of life	1	0.7

Note: This survey was answered by executives of 137 firms that had experienced shutdowns in the preceding five years. Frequency of mention indicates the number of times the reason was cited as one of the top four factors. It also includes instances in which multiple reasons were cited.

Source: Archie B. Carroll, Elizabeth I. Gatewood, and James J. Chrisman, "Plant Closings: PAOs Respond to a Survey on an Increasingly Troublesome Issue," *Public Affairs Review*, Copyright © 1984, Public Affairs Council, 64. Reprinted with permission.

literature of business social responsibility and policy has documented corporate concern with the detrimental impact of its actions. Indeed, business's social response patterns over the past 20 years have borne this out. Management expert Peter Drucker has suggested the following business position regarding social impacts of management decisions:

> *Because one is responsible for one's impacts, one minimizes them. The fewer impacts an institution has outside of its own specific purpose and mission, the better does it conduct itself, the more responsibly does it act, and the more acceptable a citizen, neighbor, and contributor it is.*[89]

The question is raised, therefore, whether business's responsibilities in the realm of plant closings and their impacts on employees and communities are any different from the host of responsibilities that have already been assumed in areas such as employment discrimination, employee privacy and safety, honesty in advertising, product safety, and concern for the environment. From the perspective of the employees affected, their role in plant and business closings might be considered an extension of the numerous employee rights issues.

Of the executives who have spoken out on this issue, several have indicated that there is an obligation to employees and to the community when a business opens or decides to close. As one observer noted:

> *A corporation has a responsibility not only to its employees but to the community involved. It's a simple question of corporate citizenship. Just as an individual must conduct himself [or herself] in a way relating to the community, so must a corporation. As a matter of fact, a corporation has an even larger responsibility since it has been afforded even greater advantages than the individual. Just as a golfer must replace divots, a corporation must be prepared at all times to deal with hardships it may create when it moves or closes down.*[90]

Others have also argued that there is a moral obligation at stake in the business-closing issue. In an extensive consideration of plant closings, philosopher John Kavanagh has asserted that companies are not morally free to ignore the impact of a closing on employees and the community. His argument is similar to those that have been given on many other social issues—namely, that business should minimize the negative externalities (unintended side effects) of its actions.[91]

Business essentially has two opportunities to be responsive to employee and community stakeholders in shutdown situations. It can take certain actions before the decision to close is made and other actions after the decision to close has been made.

Before the Decision to Close Is Made Before a company makes a decision to close down, it has a responsibility to itself, its employees, and its community to thoroughly and diligently study whether the closing is the only option available. A decision to leave should be preceded by critical and realistic investigations of economic alternatives.

After a careful study has been made, it may be concluded that finding new ownership for the plant or business is the only feasible alternative. Two basic options exist at this point: (1) find a new owner or (2) explore the possibility of employee ownership.[92]

New Ownership. Malcolm Baldrige argued that the first obligation a company has to its employees and the community is to try to sell the business as a going unit instead of shutting down. This is often not possible, but it is an avenue that should be explored.[93] Quite often, the most promising new buyers of a firm are residents of the region who have a long-term stake in the community and are willing to make a strong commitment.

For example, when Viner Brothers, an American shoe manufacturer, filed for bankruptcy, its three plants presented an attractive investment opportunity for area shoe companies. Within several weeks, Wolverine, the maker of Hush Puppies, was the new owner. Part of the multimillion-dollar sale agreement was that Wolverine hire at least 60 percent of the laid-off workers. About 90 percent of the 900 workers who were laid off were eventually rehired.[94]

Employee Ownership. The idea of a company selling a plant to the employees as a way of avoiding a closedown is appealing at first glance. Hundreds of North American companies with at least ten workers are **employee owned**. Most of these arrangements are the results of last-ditch efforts to stay in business. Such firms as General Motors, Algoma Steel, Spruce Falls Power and Paper Co. Ltd., Spruce Falls/Tembec, Great Western Brewery, Creo, and Pacific Regeneration Technologies have sold plants to employees—typically plants that otherwise would have been closed.

Algoma Steel in Sault Ste. Marie, Ontario, remains one of the most prominent examples of an employee buyout in Canada. Confronted by huge losses due to poor economic conditions, outdated production processes, and low productivity, the steel maker was taken over by Dofasco Steel in 1989. Because the losses continued, Dofasco decided that, in the absence of prospective purchasers, it would shut down the business. Faced with pending job losses, the United Steel Workers union, with support from the Ontario government, facilitated an employee buyout of the company in 1992, acquiring 60 percent of the voting shares. In addition, procedures for employee involvement in decision making were established, including employee representation on the board of directors. Following the buyout, the company also gained in strength due to a renewed demand for the company's product, along with productivity improvements.[95]

According to researchers such as Dr. Carol Beatty, director of the School of Industrial Relations at Queen's University, there is a great strength in employee ownership evidenced by some Canadian success stories. With reference to several such stories, Dr. Beatty made the following comments:

> *One of the stories I really love is Pacific Regeneration Technologies. Here was a bunch of civil servants—who everybody looks down upon because "they are not living in the real world"—who bought the company and made it into a hugely successful corporation. Now they are taking over other operations all across Canada and they are going to go into the States.... I also really love the Spruce Falls/Tembec story because here is a turn-around of an old economy company that was really sinking. It is a Canadian story too because the American owners wanted to get rid of their Canadian assets and here you had the whole town of Kapuskasing completely dependent on this mill. Employee ownership saved the mill, they got their investment back in spades and they continued to have their jobs. It is a real happy ending.[96]*

Of course, not all employee buyouts result in happy endings. While the buyout of Algoma Steel and other such companies in distress saved jobs, the longer-term experiences of many of these firms have not been extremely favourable.[97] In numerous cases, employees have been forced to take significant wage and benefit reductions to make the business profitable. In other cases, morale and working conditions have not been satisfactory under the new method of ownership and management.

One such case in point is the U.S.-based Weirton Steel. Negotiators worked out an agreement whereby the employees of the National Steel's Weirton, West Virginia, mill would purchase the mill. The new company, Weirton Steel, became what was then the U.S.'s largest employee-owned enterprise, as well as its eighth-largest producer of steel. Experts gave the mill a surprisingly good chance of succeeding, although Weirton's workers had to take a pay cut of about 32 percent. The mill's union president argued, "32 percent less of $25 an hour is a whole lot better than 100 percent of nothing."[98] In 1990, however, as demand sank for the steel sheet it produced, Weirton Steel found itself in the unenviable position of actually having to lay off some of its employee-owners. By 1991, Weirton had eliminated 1000 of its 8200 jobs, had furloughed another 200 workers, and had plans to cut 700 more jobs. After a decade as owners of the company, Weirton employees became extremely frustrated and angry that employee ownership did not guarantee them that they would not lose their jobs. One employee posed the question many were asking: "How can we be laid off if we own the company?" The reality of the situation, however, is that even an employee-owned company must take whatever actions are necessary if it is to remain solvent and profitable. One of the major pitfalls of worker ownership is that it does not rewrite the laws of capitalism—the bottom line is still the bottom line.[99]

In 2001, United Airlines found themselves in a similar situation. In 1994, United Airlines became North America's largest employee-owned corporation. In one of the nastiest and most prolonged corporate battles ever, shareholders of UAL Corp., the parent of United Airlines, awarded employee groups 55 percent of the company's stock in exchange for a US$4.9 billion bundle of wage and productivity concessions. U.S. labour leaders hailed this new arrangement in worker control as a model alternative to the way companies usually battle to control costs. U.S. Labor Secretary Robert Reich, whose department facilitated the deal, asserted: "If United is successful, this will be a major landmark in American business history." But the success of the new firm was by no means ensured, because the airline has been buffeted for over a decade by infighting among employee groups, repeated forays by outside potential buyers, and takeover attempts.[100] From the beginning, there were problems with workers who resented taking pay cuts in exchange for loans to buy 55 percent of United's common stock and flight attendants whose union opted not to join because of concerns about the pay cuts involved and other policies. Problems began in 2000, when the airline pilots conducted a slowdown during contract negotiations. Then the machinists' union threatened to strike, and United took them to court.[101] By 2001, when the attack on the World Trade Center shook the airline industry, United was in no better position than firms without employee owners.

According to Suzanne Cohen of Cornell University, United Airlines failed as an employee-owned enterprise because workers thought employee ownership would mean they no longer needed to be concerned about labour–management issues. Research has shown that employee ownership can provide a firm with competitive advantage; for employee ownership to work, however, it is critical that employees believe they have a part to play in leading the company. A positive ownership culture provides employees with access to information, the power to exert influence, a sense of fairness, and a feeling of ownership and entrepreneurship.[102]

After the Decision to Close Is Made   There are a multitude of actions that a business can take once the decision has been made that a closedown or relocation is unavoidable. The overriding concern should be that the company seriously attempt to mitigate the social and economic impacts of its actions on employees and the community. Regardless of the circumstances of the move, some basic planning can help alleviate the disruptions felt by those affected. There are several possible actions that management can take,[103] including:

* Conducting a community-impact analysis
* Providing advance notice to the employees/community
* Providing transfer, relocation, and outplacement benefits
* Phasing out the business gradually
* Helping the community attract replacement industry

Community-Impact Analysis. If management is responsible for its impacts on employees and the community, as Drucker stated, a thorough community-impact analysis of a decision to close down or move is in order. The initial action should be to identify realistically those aspects of the community that would be affected by the company's plans. This would entail asking several questions,[104] such as:

* What groups will be affected?
* How will they be affected?
* What is the timing of initial and later effects?
* What is the magnitude of the effect?
* What is the duration of the impact?
* To what extent will the impact be diffused in the community?

Once these questions have been answered, management is better equipped to modify its plans so that negative impacts can be minimized and favourable impacts, if any, can be maximized.

Advance Notice. One of the most often discussed responsibilities in business- or plant-closing situations is the provision of advance notice to workers and communities. The Employment Standards Act (ESA) establishes the minimum notice required to terminate an employee. Additional requirements are dependent on the situation. In the U.S., the Worker Adjustment and Retraining Notification Act (WARN) came into effect in 1989. WARN requires those firms employing 100 or more workers to provide 60 days' advance notice to employees before shutting down or conducting substantial layoffs. With WARN, the United States joined many other nations, including Canada, in mandating advance notice of shutdowns. Great Britain requires 60 to 90 days, depending on the case, and Japan requires "sufficient advance notice."[105]

The advantages of advance notice accrue primarily to the affected employees and their communities. Workers are given time to prepare for the shutdown both emotionally and financially. Advance notice makes it easier for employees to find new jobs, because research has shown that employees have an improved chance at re-employment while they are still employed. Advance notice is motivational in that, once one joins the ranks of the unemployed, there is a tendency to coast until benefits start to be exhausted. Also, the company is in a better position to provide references, retraining, or counselling during the advance-notice period.[106]

The disadvantages of advance notice—particularly long-term advance notice—accrue principally to the business firm. Once word leaks out in the community, financial institutions may be reluctant to grant credit, customers may become worried about items purchased or promised, and the overall level of business activity may decline rapidly. One of the major disadvantages of a lengthy notice is the task of motivating workers who know they are going to lose their jobs. Declines in employee morale, pride in work, and productivity can be expected. Absenteeism may increase as workers begin to seek other employment. In addition, there is the likelihood of vandalism, pilferage, and neglect of property as employees lose interest or attempt to strike back against the employer.[107]

Transfer, Relocation, and Outplacement Benefits. Enlightened companies are increasingly recognizing that the provision of separation or outplacement benefits is in the long-range best interest of all parties concerned. Everyone is better off if disruptions are minimized in the lives of the firm's management, the displaced workers, and the community. Outplacement benefits have been used for years as companies have attempted to remove redundant or marginal personnel with minimum disruption and cost to the company and maximum benefit to the individuals involved. Increasingly these same benefits are beginning to be used in business and plant closings.

Gradual Phase-Outs. Another management action that can significantly ameliorate the effects of a business shutdown is the gradual phasing out of the business. A gradual phase-out buys time for employees and the community to adjust to the new situation and to solve some of their problems.

The American Hospital Supply (AHS) Company provides a useful model of a socially responsive firm. One year, AHS announced its intent to sell its medical manufacturing company of about 275 employees.[108] A meeting of all employees was held to explain the rationale for the decision. Although AHS received numerous inquiries from outside firms, the business did not sell. In preparing for this possible outcome, department heads prepared termination lists specifying those employees essential to the phase-out. Two months later, another all-employee meeting was held, and it was announced that the business would be gradually phased out. A retention/outplacement program was prepared and explained in detail immediately following the meeting.

At AHS, terminated employees with no specific skills or with unique situations (such as illnesses) were identified early so that special outplacement support could be provided. The first group of terminated employees included the entire sales department, half of research and development, all of marketing, and various others not crucial to the wind-down. The outplacement activities resembled those of a college placement office. Over 25 firms visited to conduct on-site interviews. Résumés were drafted by the employees, reviewed and proofed by the personnel department, and typed on the company's word-processing equipment. The volume of outplacement correspondence was so high that additional word-processing capability and clerical support had to be acquired. Final survey results showed that one-fourth of the outplaced employees received "similar" compensation packages and another 65 percent received "superior" compensation packages as compared with those of their previous positions.

In addition, severance pay was offered, and a benefits plan was created for the employees. The benefits plan provided for 100 percent vesting in the company incentive program, retirement and profit-sharing plans, three months' basic benefit coverage (medical, dental, life insurance) beyond the date of termination, and various other extensions (maternity, orthodontia) as considered necessary.[109]

Helping to Attract Replacement Industry. The principal responsibility for attracting new industry falls on the community, but the management of the closing firm can provide cooperation and assistance. The closing company can help by providing inside information on building and equipment characteristics and capabilities, transportation options based on its experience, and contacts with other firms in its industry that may be seeking facilities. Helping the community attract replacement industry has the overwhelming advantage of rapidly replacing large numbers of lost jobs. Also, because attracted businesses tend to be smaller than those that closed, this strategy enables the community to diversify its economic base while regaining jobs.[110]

Decision Factors in a Plant-Closing Situation Several factors may go into a business's decision regarding the extent to which it should assist displaced employees and the community. These factors include:

- The general size of the negative impact the closedown is creating
- The extent of commitment to the firm displayed over the years by its employees and the community
- How large an employer the firm was in relation to the total economic base
- The length of time the firm was in the community
- The length of time employees had worked for the firm
- The economic options available to the firm for use in providing assistance
- The firm's overall sense of corporate responsibility or corporate social policy

Any one or several of these factors, along with other issues, may assume a major role in dictating the responses of management and the firm.

One recent example of a socially responsible firm undertaking massive layoffs shows the influence of these factors. Levi Strauss & Co. began to close 11 North American plants, eliminating 6395 manufacturing positions and more than one-third of its North American manufacturing capacity. Long recognized as a leader in employee/community relations, Levi took several measures to lessen the impact of the closures. First, it announced that no jobs would be moving overseas.[111] It also announced an unprecedented US$200 million employee benefits plan to help laid-off workers make successful transitions back into the work force. Three weeks of severance pay for each year of service was given to each laid-off worker, even if that worker immediately found another job. In addition, eight months' pay from the date of the announcement and outplacement and career counselling services were provided to everyone. The company also paid up to 18 months of health-care benefits and up to US$6000 in education, job training, or moving expenses for each worker. For the communities affected, the Levi Strauss foundation provided up to US$8 million in grants to ease the impact of the plant closings.[112]

Community Lawsuits

To this point we have been focusing on socially responsible actions a company might take before or after a decision to close a plant has been made. One of the most recent trends in the business-closings arena is for communities to file lawsuits against companies that are not being as responsible as the communities believe they should be.

One landmark case occurred in 1993 when General Motors announced it was planning to close its plant in Ypsilanti, Michigan, and shift production to Arlington, Texas. In that case, Michigan Circuit Court Judge Donald Shelton enjoined GM from moving its operation. Judge Shelton wrote:

There would have been a gross inequity and patent unfairness if General Motors, having lulled the people of Ypsilanti into giving up millions of dollars which they so desperately need to educate their children and provide basic governmental services, is allowed to simply decide that it will desert 4,500 workers and their families because it thinks it can make these same cars a little cheaper somewhere else.[113]

Judge Shelton's ruling was overturned by a higher court, and the plant did close soon thereafter.[114]

Communities today expect more of businesses than they once did, and they are not likely to settle for what they perceive to be unfair plant closings. This is all the more reason why it is in a company's best long-term interest to arrange for an equitable departure.

We are only just beginning to define the stakes and stakeholders involved in the plant-closing issue, the impacts that business closings have on employees and communities, the public's reaction to the problem, and types of corresponding actions that management might take. From observations of other social issues that have received the kind and degree of attention that business closings have, it seems to be necessary for businesses to take positive steps if they are to be responsive to their employees and communities. It appears that business closings and their adverse consequences is an issue that business will be well advised to address in the future.

Summary

Community stakeholders are extremely important to companies. Companies may have positive impacts on their communities in two basic ways: donating the time and talents of managers and employees (volunteerism) and making financial contributions. Because business has a vital stake in the community, it engages in a variety of community projects. Examples include literacy programs. Community action programs are a key part of managing community involvement. Important components of such efforts include knowing the company's resources, selecting projects to pursue, and monitoring corporate efforts.

Business also contributes to community stakeholders through philanthropy. The third sector, or nonprofit sector, depends on business's support. Companies give for a variety of reasons—some altruistic, some self-interested. Major recipients of business giving include education, health and welfare, community activities, and culture and the arts. As companies have attempted to manage their philanthropy, two major types of public purpose partnerships have been emphasized: (1) strategic philanthropy, which seeks to improve the overall fit between corporate needs and charitable programs, and (2) cause-related marketing, which tightens the linkage between a firm's profits and its contribu-

tions. Cause-related marketing represents a unique joining of business and charity with the potential for great benefit to each. Global philanthropy has recently become an important trend.

Just as firms have beneficial effects on community stakeholders, they can have detrimental effects as well. Business or plant closings are a prime example of these detrimental effects. Plant closings have a pervasive influence in the sense that a multitude of community stakeholders—employees, local government, other businesses, and the general citizenry—are affected. There is no single reason why these closings have occurred, but among the major reasons are economic conditions, consolidation of company operations, outmoded technology or facilities, changes in corporate strategy, and international competition.

Before management makes the decision to close a facility, it has a responsibility to itself, its employees, and the community to study thoroughly whether closing is the only or the best option. Finding a new owner for the business and pursuing the possibility of employee ownership are reasonable and desirable alternatives. After the decision to close has been made, possible actions include community-impact analysis; giving advance notice; providing transfer, relocation, or outplacement benefits; phasing out operations gradually; and helping the community attract replacement industry. Companies have an added incentive to be responsive to the business-closing issue, because the government may be watching the manner in which firms are handling this problem. Companies that are sensitive to community stakeholders will want to fashion socially responsive postures in dealing with their stakeholders.

Key Terms

cause branding (page 447)

cause-related marketing (page 446)

community action program (page 430)

community involvement (page 426)

employee owned (page 451)

philanthropy (page 434)

resource-based giving (page 429)

strategic philanthropy (page 444)

third sector (page 435)

Discussion Questions

1. Outline the essential steps involved in developing a community action program.

2. Explain the pros and cons of community involvement and corporate philanthropy, and explain why and to whom companies give.

3. Differentiate among public purpose partnerships, strategic philanthropy, cause-related marketing, and cause branding. Provide an example of each that is not discussed in the text.

4. In your opinion, why does a business have a responsibility to community stakeholders in a business-closing decision? Enumerate what you think are the major reasons.

5. Identify and discuss briefly what you think are the major trade-offs that firms face as they think about possible plant closings or substantial layoffs and their responsibility to their employees and their communities.

6. Describe what you think are a firm's social responsibilities in a plant- or business-closing situation and what factors influence the degree of those responsibilities.

Endnotes

1. Imagine, http://www.imagine.ca/.
2. Carole Schweitzer, "Corporate Assets," *Association Management* (January 1998), 30–37.
3. *Community Action Manual* (Worcester, MA: Norton Company, April 1978), 1–2.
4. Bill Shaw and Frederick Post, "A Moral Basis for Corporate Philanthropy," *Journal of Business Ethics* (October 1993), 745–751.
5. Petro-Canada, http://www.petro-canada.ca/eng/about/environment/7087.htm.
6. Petro-Canada, http://www.petro-canada.ca/eng/about/environment/7088.htm.
7. National Survey of Giving Volunteering and Participating, http://www.nsgvp.org/.
8. National Aboriginal Achievement Foundation, http://www.naaf.ca/news_releases/Release17.html.
9. Imagine, http://www.imagine.ca/content/awards&recognition/partnership_awards_2003_Microsoft.asp?section=awards.
10. Jeff Barbian, "The Charitable Worker," *Training* (July 2001), 50–55.
11. Paul Ostergard and Benjamin R. Barber, "Should Corporations Be Praised for Their Philanthropic Efforts," *Across the Board* (May/June 2001), 44–53.
12. Cathleen Wild, *Corporate Volunteer Programs: Benefits to Business* (New York: The Conference Board, 1993), 37.
13. *Association Magazine*, http://www.associationmagazine.com/client/csae/AM.nsf/0/C119FFA8A7F3264D85256B5F007895FF?OpenDocument.
14. "Electric Fuel Donates 500 Instant Power™ Chargers & Batteries to Keep New York Rescue Workers' Cellphones Working," *PR Newswire* (September 17, 2001).
15. Clive Cookson, "Drug Group in Bid to Wipe Out Elephantiasis," *Financial Times* (January 27, 1998), 5.
16. Kathryn Troy, *Studying and Addressing Community Needs: A Corporate Case Book* (New York: The Conference Board, 1985), 1.
17. *Ibid.*

18. *Community Action Manual*, 1–2.

19. Frank Koch, "A Strategy for Corporate Giving and Community Involvement," *Management Review* (December 1977), 7–13.

20. Ronald McDonald House (2001), http://www.rmhc.com/about/programs/education/rmh.

21. Ronald McDonald House, http://www.ronaldmcdonaldhouse.ca/press.asp?process=view&houseID=6&articleID=2.

22. David Logan, *Community Involvement of Foreign-Owned Companies* (New York: The Conference Board, 1994), 16.

23. *Ibid.*, 15.

24. Tammie S. Pinkston and Archie B. Carroll, "Corporate Citizenship Perspectives and Foreign Direct Investment in the U.S.," *Journal of Business Ethics* (Vol. 13, 1994), 168–169.

25. Alison Azer, "The Changing Corporate Landscape and Its Effect on Charitable Giving," Canadian Centre for Social Entrepreneurship (2003), http://www.bus.ualberta.ca/ccse/Publications/.

26. *Webster's New World Dictionary* (Cleveland: World Publishing Company, 1964), 1098.

27. Robert L. Payton, *Philanthropy: Voluntary Action for the Public Good* (New York: Macmillan, 1988), 32.

28. Robert L. Payton, "Philanthropy in Action," in Robert L. Payton, Michael Novak, Brian O'Connell, and Peter Dobkin Hall, *Philanthropy: Four Views* (New Brunswick: Transaction Books, Inc.), 1.

29. The Muttart Foundation, http://www.muttart.org/public.htm.

30. Statistics Canada, http://www.statcan.ca/english/freepub/89F0123XIE/00002/volunteer.htm; http://www.statcan.ca/english/sdds/4106.htm.

31. Michelle Conlin and Jessi Hempel, Joshua Tanzer and David Polek, "The Corporate Donors," *Businesss Week* (December 1, 2003), http://www.businessweek.com/magazine/content/03_48/b3860616.htm.

32. Voluntary Sector Initiative, http://www.vsi-isbc.ca/eng/funding/fundingmatters/02.cfm.

33. John D. Rockfeller III, "In Defense of Philanthropy," *Business and Society Review* (Spring 1978), 26–29.

34. Curt Weeden, *Corporate Social Investing* (San Francisco: Berret Koehler, Inc., 1998), 4–6.

35. Sam Sternberg, *National Directory of Corporate Charity* (San Francisco: Regional Young Adult Project, 1984), 14.

36. David Saiia, Archie Carroll, and Ann Buchholtz, "Does Philanthropy Begin at Home? The Strategic Motivation Underlying Corporate Giving Programs," Presented at the 2001 Academy of Management Conference, Washington, DC.

37. Louis W. Fry, Gerald D. Keim, and Roger E. Meiners, "Corporate Contributions: Altruistic or For-Profit?" *Academy of Management Journal* (March 1982), 94–106.

38. Conlin et al., "The Corporate Donors."

39. Louis W. Cabot, "Corporate Support of Education: No Strings Attached," *Harvard Business Review* (July–August 1978), 139–144.

40. Robert H. Malott, "Corporate Support of Education: Some Strings Attached," *Harvard Business Review* (July–August 1978), 133–138.

41. Irving Kristol, "On Corporate Philanthropy," *The Wall Street Journal* (March 21, 1977), 18.

42. For an interesting study of workplace giving, see Melissa A. Berman, *The Future of Workplace Giving* (New York: The Conference Board, 1994).

43. Raise-a-Reader, http://www.canada.com/national/features/raiseareader/index.html.

44. Dreyer's Philanthropy Mission Statement, http://www.dreyersinc.com.

45. Lilly 1998 Corporate Citizenship Report, http://www.lilly.com/about/.

46. "Roots and Right to Play Launch Special Line of Apparel That Lets Canadians Give" (February 19, 2003), http://www.community-online.com/community articlepf.cfm?ArticleID=648.

47. CBAC (2003), http://www.businessforarts.org/about_us/default.asp.

48. CBAC, http://www.businessforarts.org/default.asp.

49. "The Glories of Philanthropy," *Business Week* (October 6, 1997), 182.

50. "Sara Lee Makes Huge Art Donation," *Fund Raising Management* (July 1998), 10.

51. CBAC, http://www.businessforarts.org/news_events/default.asp.

52. Paul H. Eliker, "Why Corporations Give Money to the Arts," *The Wall Street Journal* (March 31, 1978), 15.

53. *Ibid.*

54. Cited in Robert Toth, "PBS Corporate Gifts Selfish?" *The Atlanta Journal* (September 11, 1977), F–7.

55. Louis Lavelle, "Giving as Never Before," *Business Week* (October 1, 2001), 10.

56. James J. Chrisman and Archie B. Carroll, "Corporate Responsibility: Reconciling Economic and Social Goals," *Sloan Management Review* (Winter 1984), 59–65.

57. James D. Fleck, "Don't Look to the Arts for Tax Fixes," *National Post* (October 27, 2003), http://www.canada.com/national/nationalpost/index.html.

58. "Funding Matters: The Impact of Canada's New Funding Regime on Nonprofit and Voluntary Organizations" (2003), http://www.vsi-isbc.ca/eng/funding/fundingmatters/02.cfm.

59. Public purpose partnerships are discussed in Richard Steckel and Robin Simons, *Doing Best by Doing Good* (New York: Dutton Publishers, 1992).

60. Andrew E. Serwer, "Company Givers Get Smart," *Fortune* (August 22, 1994), 16.

61. NSERC, http://www.nserc.ca/synergy/articles/98nortel_e.htm.

62. "Happy Deal for Tech: McDonald's Sponsorship to Finance Coliseum Facelift," *The Atlanta Journal* (January 19, 1995), C1–C2.

63. "Canada's Universities Mean Business," CAUT Commentary (Vol. 1, No. 1, May–June 1999), http://www.caut.ca/english/publications/commentary/199905_business.asp.

64. "For Cash and Future Considerations: Ontario Universities and Public-Private Partnerships" (2003), http://www.policyalternatives.ca/.

65. *Ibid.*

66. Steckel and Simons.

67. Timothy S. Mescon and Donn J. Tilson, "Corporate Philanthropy: A Strategic Approach to the Bottom Line," *California Management Review* (Winter 1987), 50.

68. Avery Hunt, "Strategic Philanthropy," *Across the Board* (July/August 1986), 27.

69. Deirdre Carmody, "For *People* Magazine, a New Charity Program May Be Good Business Too," *The New York Times* (February 14, 1994), C6.

70. Craig Smith, "The New Corporate Philanthropy," *Harvard Business Review* (May–June 1994), 106; *Business Week* (December 1, 2003), http://www.businessweek.com/magazine/toc/03_48/B38600348giving.htm.

71. Weeden (1998), 202–205.

72. Richard J. Morris and Daniel A. Biederman, "How to Give Away Money Intelligently," *Harvard Business Review* (November–December 1985), 151–159.

73. Saiia, Carroll, and Buchholtz (2001).

74. Patricia Caesar, "Cause-Related Marketing: The New Face of Corporate Philanthropy," *Business and Society Review* (Fall 1986), 16.

75. Martin Gottlieb, "Cashing in on a Higher Cause," *The New York Times* (July 6, 1986), 6F.

76. Geoffrey Smith and Ron Stodghill, "Are Good Causes Good Marketing?" *Business Week* (March 21, 1994), 64.

77. Michelle Warren, "Standing Shoulder to Shoulder," *Marketing Magazine* (Vol. 108, No. 34, October 6–13, 2003), 22.

78. Michelle Wirth Fellman, "Cause Marketing Takes a Strategic Turn," *Marketing News* (April 26, 1999), 4–8.

79. Peggy Bernstein, "Philanthropy, Reputation Go Hand in Hand," *PR News* (January 17, 2000), 1–8.

80. *1999 Cone/Roper Cause-Related Trends Report.*

81. Caesar, 17–18. Also see Richard Steckel and Robin Simons, *Doing Best by Doing Good* (New York: Dutton Publishers, 1992), Chapter 6, "Cause-Related Marketing."

82. Anne Klepper, *Global Contributions of U.S. Corporations* (New York: The Conference Board, 1993), 6–7.

83. Judy Greenwald, "Employers Confront AIDS in Africa," *Business Insurance* (July 23, 2001), 15–22.

84. *Ibid.*

85. Klepper (1993), 6–7.

86. *Ibid.*

87. Archie B. Carroll, Elizabeth J. Gatewood, and James J. Chrisman, "Plant Closings: PAOs Respond to a Survey on an Increasingly Troublesome Issue," *Public Affairs Review* (1984), 64.

88. Cooper and Lybrand, *Closing Plants: Planning and Implementing Strategies* (Morristown, NJ: Financial Executives Research Foundation, 1986), 2.

89. Peter F. Drucker, *Management: Tasks, Responsibilities, Practices* (New York: Harper & Row, 1974), 327–328.

90. Quoted in "A Firm's Obligations: To Employees, Community," *The Atlanta Journal* (September 19, 1977), 4–C.

91. John P. Kavanagh, "Ethical Issues in Plant Relocation," *Business and Professional Ethics Journal* (Winter 1982), 21–33.

92. Archie B. Carroll, "When Business Closes Down: Social Responsibilities and Management Actions," *California Management Review* (Winter 1984), 131.

93. Quoted in *The Atlanta Journal* (September 19, 1977), 4–C.

94. Jeff Strout, "Viner Shoe Expected to Be in Full Swing Soon," *Bangor News* (January 21, 1981), 9.

95. Richard Long, "Employee Buyouts: The Canadian Experience," *Canadian Business Economics* (1995), http://www.cabe.ca/cbe/vol3_4/34-long.pdf.

96. David Creelman, Interview with Dr. Carol Beatty on Employee Ownership, for *HR.com* http://startribune.hr.com/HRcom/index.cfm/WeeklyMag/825C5B69-090D-4CF7-B48F9E902E3D59EF?ost=wmFeature.

97. Terri Minsky, "Gripes of Rath: Workers Who Bought Iowa Slaughterhouse Regret That They Did," *The Wall Street Journal* (December 2, 1981), 1.

98. "A Steel Town's Fight for Life," *Newsweek* (March 28, 1983), 49.

99. Maria Mallary, "How Can We Be Laid Off If We Own the Company?" *Business Week* (September 9, 1991), 66.

100. Kenneth Labich, "Will United Fly?" *Fortune* (August 22, 1994), 70–78.

101. Suzanne Cohen, "United Airlines ESOP Woes," *Risk Management* (June 2001), 9.

102. *Ibid.*

103. Carroll, 132.

104. Grover Starling, *The Changing Environment of Business* (Boston: Kent, 1980), 319–320.

105. Paul D. Staudohar, "New Plant Closing Law Aids Workers in Transition," *Personnel Journal* (January 1989), 87–90.

106. Robert B. McKersie, "Advance Notice," *The Wall Street Journal* (February 25, 1980), 20.

107. *Ibid.*

108. Philip D. Johnston, "Personnel Planning for a Plant Shutdown," *Personnel Administrator* (August 1981), 53–57.

109. *Ibid.*

110. *Cornell University Workshop Report*, 28–30.

111. Kathleen DesMarteau, "Levi Closes 11 U.S. Plants," *Bobbin* (January 1998), 14–16.

112. Mike Verespej, "How to Manage Diversity," *Industry Week* (January 19, 1998), 24.

113. David Moberg, "Flight Cancelled: A Michigan Judge Halts GM from Fleeing Ypsilanti," *In These Times* (March 8, 1993), 8.

114. Benjamin Weiser, "When the Plant Closes," *The Washington Post Weekly Edition* (January 10–16, 1994), 6.

Part Five

Internal Stakeholder Issues

Chapter 15
Employee Stakeholders and Workplace Issues

Chapter 16
Employee Stakeholders: Privacy, Safety, and Health

Chapter 17
Employment Discrimination and Employment Equity

Chapter 18
Owner Stakeholders and Corporate Governance

Employee Stakeholders and Workplace Issues

Chapter Objectives

After studying this chapter, you should be able to:

1 Identify the major changes that are occurring in the work force today.

2 Outline the characteristics of the new social contract between employers and employees.

3 Explain the employee rights movement and its underlying principles.

4 Describe and discuss the notion of just cause.

5 Discuss the right to due process and fair treatment.

6 Describe the actions companies are taking to make the workplace friendlier.

7 Elaborate on the freedom-of-speech issue and whistle-blowing.

Society's changing values are having a great impact on the workplace. Although external stakeholders such as government, consumers, the environment, and the community continue to be major facets of business's concern for the social environment, considerable attention is now being given to employee stakeholders—their status, their treatment, their rights, and their satisfaction. This should come as no surprise when it is considered that most adults spend the bulk of their daytime hours at work.

The development of employee stakeholder rights has been a direct outgrowth of the kinds of social changes that have brought other societal issues into focus. The history of work has been one of steadily improving conditions for employees. Today's issues are quite unlike the old bread-and-butter concerns of higher pay, shorter hours, more job security, and better working conditions. These expectations still exist, but they have given way to other, more complex workplace trends and issues.

In the new millennium, two major themes or trends seem to be characterizing the modern relationship between employees and their employers. First, we will discuss the dramatic changes that have been occurring in the workplace. Prominent here will be our discussion of a newly evolving social contract between organizations and workers that is quite different from any such contract of the past. This new social contract is being driven by global competition. Second, we will consider a continuation of a trend toward more expansive employee rights. These two trends are interrelated, and we will describe how the changes in the workplace have precipitated a renewal in the employee rights movement.

Because these topics are so extensive, we dedicate two chapters to employee stakeholders and workplace issues. In this chapter, we discuss some of the workplace changes that have been taking place, the emerging social contract, and the employee rights movement. Three employee rights issues, in particular, are treated here: the right to not be fired without just cause, the right to due process and fair treatment, and the right to freedom of speech in the workplace. In Chapter 16, we will continue our discussion of employee rights by examining the related issues of the rights of employees to privacy, safety, and health. These two chapters should be considered a continuous discussion of employee stakeholders wherein economic, legal, and ethical responsibilities are all involved in the treatment.

The New Social Contract

Thirty years ago, employees stayed in the same job at the same company for years, and those companies rewarded that loyalty by offering job stability, a decent wage, and good benefits.[1] Today's typical worker has had nine jobs by the age of 30.[2] The work force of today is more mobile, less loyal, and more diverse. Their trust in their employers has eroded over the past 20 years. Recent studies indicate that fewer and fewer employees feel that their employer is committed to them.[3] A 2003 survey conducted by the Centre for Ethical Orientation (CEO) indicated that nine of ten Canadians view trust as declining worldwide, and most feel that they are losing trust in private businesses and government institutions.[4] The CEO's director, Jim Allen, commented, "Generally, in today's society it takes more to earn people's trust than it used to. The thing that is most troubling is Canada appears to be moving from a high-trust society to a low-trust society." In addition, Mr. Allen speculated that Canadians are becoming less trusting of companies and have "lost faith in the system" partly as a consequence of feeling mistreated and ignored.[5]

Today's employees aren't looking for a promise of lifetime employment. Instead, they are seeking competitive pay and benefits coupled with opportunities for professional growth. They want employers who provide them with opportunities, recognize their accomplishments, and communicate openly and honestly.[6] These work force changes have contributed to a newly emerging social contract between employers and employees. This new **social contract**—or set of reciprocal understandings and expectations regarding each party's role and responsibilities—represents a "revolution" in the workplace.[7] The revolution is basically this: The get-along-to-get-ahead culture of the past has been displaced by a high-risk environment in which North Americans are being asked to give up the employment security they once took for granted for opportunities that are no longer clearly defined or guaranteed.[8]

As *Business Week* appropriately observed, there are "no villains at work, just the inexorable forces of economic and technological change." But if there are no villains, there are certainly victims. Workers have been impacted as companies have had to reorganize, slim down, "re-engineer," and "reinvent" themselves. Downsizing and restructuring have significantly altered pay compensation systems. Pay based on longevity and status has been replaced with rewards based on performance, contributions, and value added.[9]

What is driving the collapse of the old social contract and the emergence of the new? Chilton and Weidenbaum, in their discussions of the new social contract, pinpoint three sweeping forces that began in the 1970s, grew in salience in the 1980s, and became dominant drivers in the 1990s.[10] These three forces are:

1. Global competition
2. Technology advances (especially in computers and telecommunications)
3. Deregulation (especially of transportation and telecommunications)

As a result of these forces and others in the workplace, we have witnessed the destabilization of organizations and their old social contract. The old social contract between companies and workers was clearer than the new social contract will be. The old, traditional arrangement was predicated on a security-loyalty-paternalism pact. Attributes of the old social contract included lifetime employment, steady advancement, and loyalty.[11] It is easy to see how this arrangement engendered an entitlement mentality on the part of employees.

The new social contract places on employees more responsibility for their own success and prosperity in the employment relationship. Job security, compensation, and advancement depend more on what the employee is contributing to the organization's mission. The notion of "adding value" to the organization has become a crucial factor. In exchange, companies are expected to provide learning opportunities, meaningful work, and honest communication.[12] Figure 15–1 presents some of the characteristics of the old and new social contracts. An outline of the features of the new social contract between employers and employees has been provided by Chilton and Weidenbaum. This outline is presented in Figure 15–2.

It is challenging to say whether the new social contract will be bad or good. More than anything else, it represents an adaptation to the changing world and changing business circumstances. In some respects, workers may prefer the new model. Whatever turns out to be the case, it is clear that employee stakeholders' expectations of fair treatment will continue to rise. We will continue to see the employee rights movement that has characterized business for decades, but it will grow in the new environment. Employee rights will be moderated by employer expectations that are being driven by uncontrollable economic, social, and technological forces.

FIGURE 15–1

The Changing Social Contract Between Employers and Employees

Old Social Contract	New Social Contract
Job security, long, stable career and employment relationships	Few tenure arrangements; jobs constantly "at risk"; employment as long as you "add value" to the organization.
Life careers with one employer	Fewer life careers; employer changes common; careers more dynamic
Stable positions/job assignments	Temporary project assignments
Loyalty to employer; identification with employer	Loyalty to self and profession; diminished identification with employer
Paternalism; family-type relationships	Relationships far less warm and familiar; no more parent–child relationships
Employee sense of entitlement	Personal responsibility for one's own career/job future
Stable, rising income	Pay that reflects contributions; pay for "value added"
Job-related skills training	Learning opportunities; employees in charge of their own education and updating
Focus on individual job accomplishments	Focus on team building and projects

FIGURE 15–2

One View of the New Social Contract Between Employers and Employees

Outline for a New Social Contract

Employer Expectations of Employees	Employee Expectations of Employers
• Performance to the best of one's ability	• "Fair" pay and benefits proportionate to contribution to company success
• Commitment to the objectives of the firm	• Security tied to fortunes of the company and ability to perform
• Participation (suggestions)	• Respect, recognition, and participation
• Willingness to take training to improve	• Opportunities for growth productivity
• Ethical and honest behaviour	• Access to timely information and openness by candid leaders
	• Safe and healthy workplace

Joint Expectations

- Partnering replaces paternalism
- Employees are value-adding resources, not merely costs to be cut
- Employee and employer must focus on customer needs and desires

Source: Kenneth Chilton and Murray Weidenbaum, *A New Social Contract for the American Workplace: From Paternalism to Partnering* (St. Louis: Center for the Study of American Business, Washington University, 1994), 43. Used with permission.

The Employee Rights Movement

To appreciate the background of employee rights issues (especially the rights of freedom of speech and due process), it is useful to consider the underlying public sector/private sector dichotomy that organizations in society face. The public sector is subject to constitutional control of its power. The private sector generally has not been subject to government control because of the concept of **private property**. The private property notion holds that individuals and private organizations are free to use their property as they desire. As a result, private corporations historically and traditionally have not had to recognize employee rights because society honoured the corporation's private property rights. The underlying issues then become why and to what extent the private property rights of business should be changed or diluted.

The Meaning of Employee Rights

Before we consider specific employee rights issues, it is useful to discuss briefly what the term **employee rights** means. A lawyer might look at employee rights as claims that may be enforced in a court of law. To many economists as well, rights are only creations of the law. More generally, however, employee rights might refer to legitimate and enforceable claims or privileges obtained by workers through group membership

Ethics In Practice

Manager's Makeshift Rules

It is Holland Flowers' mission to deliver fresh and innovative floral designs. To achieve this, Holland Flowers hires creative university students from the local area. The company feels it is important to make every possible attempt to work around the students' schedules.

John Smith was a delivery driver for Holland Flowers and a university student. Before accepting the position with Holland Flowers in August 2003, John requested several days off the week prior to the winter holiday season. December is a very busy time at Holland Flowers. To accommodate the increase in business, Holland Flowers hires seasonal employees. That year, the owner's son, Bob, was one of the seasonal employees. Bob was to work with John and the other drivers. The week prior to the holidays, the owner informed John that Bob was sick and unable to work. Subsequently, the owner told John he was to work that week, even though, before John was hired, they had agreed that John would be off. Reluctantly, John agreed to work.

The following night, John was downtown when he saw Bob with a drink in his hand and appearing quite healthy. John approached Bob, questioning his sickness and absence from work. Bob denied his illness, acting as if being the owner's son meant he could be off when he wanted.

John was furious, because the owner had previously stressed that Holland Flowers was built on honest working relationships. John felt that this incident went against the principles on which the company was founded. John no longer felt respect for the owner or Holland Flowers; instead, he felt lied to and betrayed. John called the owner that night and informed him of his feelings. Because the owner offered no defence, John felt he could no longer work for Holland Flowers, and he resigned.

1. Did the management of Holland Flowers behave unethically with respect to employee treatment in this case?

2. Was John right in questioning the owner's employee practices?

3. If you were John, what action would you have taken in this dilemma?

Contributed by Christopher Lockett

that entitle or protect them in specific ways from the prevailing system of governance. This latter perspective is the meaning that we adopt here. That is, employee rights represent guarantees of fair treatment in the workplace granted by the courts, legislatures, or by employers.[13] In this light, employee rights are seen as individuals' legitimate and enforceable claims to some desired treatment, situation, or resource.[14] Richard Edwards has argued that employee or workplace rights serve to provide workers with either (1) desired outcomes or (2) protection from unwanted outcomes.

In Canada, two central employee rights are statutory rights and employer promises or contractual rights. Rights provided by law are called **statutory rights**. These rights include, for example, protection from discrimination on the basis of age, sex, and race under employment equity legislation. Pay equity legislation is aimed at addressing inequities in the compensation between men and women. Occupational health and safety legislation focuses on protecting employee rights for a safe and healthful work environment. These rights will be discussed in more detail in the following two chapters. The right to form and belong to unions and to negotiate for improvements in working conditions are rights provided by labour relations legislation.

Contractual rights are rights that derive from contracts that can be based on oral or written statements. Such contracts are legally binding statements. Formal, written contracts are not typically arranged between employers and full-time employees; rather, the "unwritten employment contract" governs much of this arrangement. An **implied contract** involves an employer's promise of some kind of job security. The legal system tends to judge both explicit and implicit promises of job security as binding.

The importance of employer promises is reflected in the case of *Wallace v. United Grain Growers*. This case involved the claim of an implicit contract or employer promise regarding job security. The claimant (Wallace) left his present employer in order to join a Winnipeg printing firm owned by United Grain Growers with a promise of job security. However, shortly after being hired, Wallace was dismissed by his new employer. The Supreme Court of Canada awarded Wallace damages after finding the employer acted in bad faith. The court based the salary and benefits award on what they felt would constitute a reasonable notice for dismissal (24 months) and the ruling also asserted that it is the responsibility of employers to ensure that the information about a job is accurate. This case and others caution employers to avoid making unsupportable claims of job security.[15]

According to human resource management expert Monica Belcourt, employers should take the necessary precautions to reduce the risk of implied contract lawsuits, including the following:

1. Train supervisors and managers to conduct hiring procedures properly. This includes ensuring that recruiters/managers do not imply contract benefits in conversations with new or current employees.
2. Insert clear statements in employment offers that make explicit the expectations regarding employment and termination conditions. For example, organizations might include a statement that the employee may voluntarily terminate employment with proper notice, and that the employee may be dismissed by the employer at any time and for a justified reason (just cause).
3. Provide further documentation regarding the nature of the employment relationship in materials such as employee handbooks, employment applications, and letters of employment.
4. Obtain written confirmation that employees have read all the documents regarding the employment relationship.[16]

How employers treat their employees might extend beyond rights that are governed purely by law. Rights afforded to employees beyond the "letter of the law" may be justified on the basis of customs and practices that are necessary for the firm to remain competitive (and thus are economically justified). In addition, these rights are sometimes afforded on the basis of some normative ethical principle or reasoning (e.g., "This is the way workers ought to be treated"). In this situation, the ethical principles of justice, rights, and utilitarianism, as well as notions of virtue and ethics, may be employed as rationales.

In this connection, management may provide the employee rights as part of an effort to display moral management, as discussed in Chapter 6. To illustrate this point further, Figure 15–3 characterizes how moral managers, as well as amoral and immoral managers, might view employee stakeholders.

To summarize, employee rights may be afforded on the basis of economic, legal, or ethical sources of justification. In a limited number of cases, companies even use philanthropic arguments as the bases for providing employee rights or benefits. For example, some companies have justified daycare rights and benefits to employees on philanthropic grounds. For purposes of our discussion here, however, we will concentrate on legal and ethical bases for considering employee rights. In all these discussions, moreover, we take the perspective of organizations blending ethical wisdom with management wisdom.

The job-related rights that are mentioned often enough to merit further discussion here include (1) the *right not to be fired without just cause*; (2) the *right to due process and fair treatment*; and (3) the *right to freedom*, particularly *freedom of expression* and *freedom of speech*. In Chapter 16, we will consider the rights to privacy, safety, and health in the workplace.

FIGURE 15–3

Three Models of Management Morality and Their Orientations Toward Employee Stakeholders

Model of Management Morality	Orientation Toward Employee Stakeholders
Moral Management	Employees are a human resource that must be treated with dignity and respect. Employees' rights to due process, privacy, freedom of speech, and safety are maximally considered in all decisions. Management seeks fair dealings with employees. The goal is to use a leadership style, such as consultative/participative, that will result in mutual confidence and trust. Commitment is a recurring theme.
Amoral Management	Employees are treated as the law requires. Attempts to motivate focus on increasing productivity rather than satisfying employees' growing maturity needs. Employees are still seen as factors of production, but a remunerative approach is used. The organization sees self-interest in treating employees with minimal respect. Organization structure, pay incentives, and rewards are all geared toward short- and medium-term productivity.
Immoral Management	Employees are viewed as factors of production to be used, exploited, and manipulated for gain of individual manager or company. No concern is shown for employees' needs/rights/expectations. Short-term focus. Coercive, controlling, alienating environment.

The Right Not to Be Fired Without Cause

In the U.S., the employment-at-will doctrine was a traditional, common-law principle asserting that the relationship between employer and employee is a voluntary one and can be terminated at any time by either party. Just as employees are free to quit a company any time they choose, this doctrine holds that employers can discharge employees for any reason, or no reason, as long as they do not violate federal discrimination laws, state laws, or union contracts. What this doctrine means is that if you are not protected by a union contract (the vast majority of the work force is not) or by one of the discrimination laws, your employer is free to let you go anytime, for any reason. This is not the case in Canada. There is no concept of at-will employment in Canada. The employment relationship in Canada is contractual in nature (oral or written). The terms of this relationship are implied by Canadian law and drawn from custom in the industry and the conduct between employer and employee during the employment relationship.

The employment-at-will doctrine assumes that employer (and employee) have a right to terminate the employment relationship at any time, for any reason and without notice.[17] Consequently, employees work "at the will" of the employer when the employment relationship exists for an unspecified period of time. In contrast, in Canada, in the absence of a formal contract specifying the duration of employment, the employment relationship is construed as ongoing. Thus, even when employment is not necessarily considered to be permanent, the employer must provide reasonable notice as well as grounds for termination.

It appears that the U.S. system is moving closer to the Canadian system, given that the employment-at-will doctrine is being eroded by U.S. court decisions. The courts have ruled with increasing frequency that employers have responsibilities to employees that, from the standpoint of fairness, restrict management's former prerogative to fire at will.

Although Canadian employees may have reason to view their jobs as an established right, the law does not guarantee permanent or continuous employment. Employers weigh employee rights against the employer's responsibility to provide a safe workplace for all employees, and safe goods and services of high quality to consumers. Consequently, there may be grounds for terminating an individual's employment under the notion of **just cause**.

As lawyer Janice Payne observes, there are many activities that can constitute just cause for dismissal, and each case depends on numerous factors. However, in broad terms, the following are activities that *may* constitute just cause, depending on the specifics of the situation:[18]

1. *Serious misconduct.* Activities that may be included in this category are theft, dishonesty, and assault. On the other hand, absenteeism, lateness, and poor performance might only be considered serious misconduct if there has been some form of progressive discipline.
2. *Habitual neglect of duty or incompetence.* This involves failure to improve over a period of time, even though the job requirements are reasonable, the employee understands them, and has been given some assistance to correct the problems that were brought to the employee's attention.
3. *Conduct incompatible with the employee's responsibilities.* This may include activities that interfere with employment obligations or that compete with the employer's business.
4. *Willful disobedience.* This may involve an employee challenging or disobeying a manager's instructions.

When employers aim to terminate on the basis of just cause, it is their responsibility to prove the existence of just cause "beyond the balance of probabilities." For example, actual misconduct must exist rather than concern for a potential misconduct. If the employer cannot demonstrate the existence of just cause, the employee would be entitled to damages for wrongful dismissal.[19]

It is interesting to note that there appears to be a rise in employee lawsuits against former employers for "wrongful or unjust dismissal." A recent review of such lawsuits indicated the highest success rate (65 percent) for employers in such lawsuits involved claims of incompatible conduct/conflicts of interest on the part of the employee. In cases involving claims of employee disobedience or insubordination, employers were successful 54 percent the time. Employers had a 40 percent success rate when charges involved employee dishonesty, theft, substance abuse, or abusive behaviour. Employers were least likely to be successful (25 percent) for claims of poor employee performance.[20]

Employers must take great caution before they terminate an employee for just cause. In the case of *Di Vito v. Macdonald Dettwiler & Associates,* two former employees of the high-tech company Macdonald Dettwiler & Associates (MDA) sued their former employer for wrongful dismissal. The two male employees had been fired for circulating a vulgar and degrading e-mail message regarding a female co-worker. The employer attempted to prove the existence of just cause by arguing that the two employees had engaged in malicious conduct toward another employee, which had negatively affected the work environment. In addition, the company claimed that the two employees had been dishonest in their discussions with management during the investigation. While the B.C. Supreme Court agreed that the e-mail and hard copy messages were hurtful to the co-worker, the court did not view this as sufficient grounds for dismissal and recommended a severe reprimand instead.[21]

Other recent cases, like the one illustrated in Figure 15–4, underscore the challenges inherent in terminations for just cause. According to human resources consultant Julie McAlpine, managers should take the following precautions to minimize their risk of wrongful dismissal lawsuits:

1. *Do not make promises of permanent employment.* Like the case cited earlier, employers who promise someone permanent employment and instead dismiss the employee shortly thereafter are very likely to be found guilty of wrongful dismissal.
2. *Document disciplinary actions.* If an employee is a poor performer, the onus is on the employer to handle this employee properly. Given the difficulties of proving just cause for dismissal based upon poor performance, employers must maintain a clear and detailed "paper trail" of all employee performance problems. Such documentation must demonstrate that the employer:
   - established a standard of performance for the employee
   - informed the employee that he or she was failing to meet the standard
   - offered the employee an opportunity to meet the standard
   - provided the employee with assistance to meet the standard
   - explained the consequence of failing to meet the standard
3. *Conduct an investigation.* Prior to any termination, the employer must conduct a thorough investigation of the alleged problems during which time the employee must be given an opportunity to respond to any allegations.
4. *Provide a termination letter and settlement offer.* Termination letters should indicate that the employee is being dismissed, and should state the effective date of dismissal. The reasons for the dismissal should be clearly set out.

5. *Conduct a termination meeting.* At least two members of management should conduct a termination meeting that informs the employee of the termination, the reasons for the termination, and what he or she is required to do next. The employee should not be forced to sign a settlement offer during the meeting but rather should be permitted some time in order to review the offer and seek legal advice.[22]

In addition to unfair dismissal, some employers have been found guilty of engaging in **constructive dismissal**. Constructive dismissal occurs when an employer, without the consent of the employee, changes the fundamental terms of employment in a manner that adversely impacts the employee. Specifically it involves altering the employee's working conditions in a way that reduces compensation, status, or prestige. Such actions result in the employee quitting the job because of the employer's wrongful actions. Claims for constructive dismissal most often result when an employer changes the employee's working conditions, job description and responsibilities (including a demotion), salary and benefits, or location of work (e.g., a transfer to another city).

Of course, changes can occur in many of the areas of the employment relationship without amounting to constructive dismissal. According to the Supreme Court of Canada (SCC), in order for these changes to constitute constructive dismissal they must be seen by the court to be "fundamental, severe, serious, unilateral, and substantial so as to result in the employee performing a different job." This was illustrated in a 1997 ruling that set the standard for constructive dismissal in Canada.

FIGURE 15–4

Is Employee Dishonesty Just Cause for Dismissal?

Does a dishonest employee deserve to be fired? That was the question posed in a 2001 case before the Supreme Court of Canada (SCC).

Martin McKinley had worked as Controller, Treasurer & Assistant Secretary for BC Tel company. In 1994, after about 17 years of service, he was fired while he was on sick leave for high blood pressure. Subsequently, he sued BC Tel for unjust dismissal.

At the trial, BC Tel claimed that Mr. McKinley was fired for just cause because he was dishonest about his medical condition and the treatments that were available for it. Specifically, it was alleged that Mr. McKinley did not disclose to BC Tel that he was medically able to resume work and, if necessary, he could have used beta blockers to control his blood pressure.

What was the verdict? The SCC acknowledged that Mr. McKinley may not have provided full disclosure of all significant facts concerning his medical condition to BC Tel. However, the SCC upheld the ruling of the lower court: BC Tel did not have just cause to terminate Mr. McKinley's employment. The British Columbia jury awarded Mr. McKinley 22 months' notice of termination, plus four additional months' notice for bad-faith termination.

So when is dishonesty just cause for dismissal? According to the SCC, just cause for termination exists where dishonesty violates the essential condition of the employment contract, breaches the faith inherent in the work relationship, or is fundamentally or directly inconsistent with the employee's obligations to his or her employer.

Whether or not an act of dishonesty amounts to just cause requires an analysis of the specific circumstances, its level of seriousness, and the degree to which it affected the employment relationship.

Employers can insert a specific penalty clause in a written employment contract. For example, if an employer considers dishonesty in connection with sick leave to warrant termination, it can include a clause in the standard employment contract which states that the employee agrees that if he or she claims sick leave when he or she is not sick, then the employer has just cause to terminate his or her employment without notice.

Source: Doug MacLeod, barrister & solicitor and employment law expert, Fulcrum Search Sciences Inc., http://www.fulcrumsearchscience.com/Client/Articles/JustCauseTerminations.htm.

Ethics In Practice

Rowdy Recruiting

Last summer, I interned for a large company. The economy was strong and so a large part of the company's time and money were put toward recruiting. The overwhelming majority of the company's employees were under the age of 30 and so young, energetic employees, who had recently been through the hiring process, did most of the recruiting. One Thursday night, I was asked to join a group of our employees and a young prospect for dinner. The idea was to take the recruit out for a night on the town and entertain him on his first night in our city. The next morning he was scheduled to meet with a partner at 8 A.M. for the first of many interviews.

At 7 P.M. sharp, we met the recruit, Mike, in the lobby of the hotel where he was staying. My first impression was that Mike was very nervous about dining with such a large group of our workers. When we arrived at the restaurant, the waiter handed us a wine list. As usual, we ordered a few bottles of wine for the table. When Mike refused our offer of a drink, my manager assured him it was okay. He consented and started in for a long night of alcohol consumption. We hopped from the restaurant to several bars in an upscale area of the city. Eventually, it was way past our bedtime and we had all surpassed our limit. So we walked Mike back to his hotel and reminded him that we would be back to meet him bright and early in the morning.

Early Friday morning, my manager and I pushed our way through the revolving door of the hotel that we had just exited a few hours earlier. Though we were both feeling a bit hung over, we put on a smile and acted very professional. After a few minutes, the elevator door opened and Mike stumbled out. As he approached us, we noticed the lack of colour in his face and wondered what kind of impression he would make in his interviews. As I reached out my hand to shake his, Mike turned his head and vomited on the floor of the hotel. After getting himself together, Mike began apologizing profusely. At that point my manager informed Mike that he would no longer be interviewing with our company. I was shocked! All of us stayed out too late and had too much fun. Why would my manager punish Mike for something we had all done and even encouraged him to do?

1. Did the manager behave unethically with respect to treatment of the recruit? Does the fact that the recruit initially turned down the wine and the manager encouraged him to drink it affect your answer?

2. Do the rights of recruits differ from the rights of employees? If so, how?

3. If you were the manager, what action would you have taken in this situation? How would you handle Mike? Would you do anything to lessen the likelihood of this happening again?

Contributed Anonymously

Employers restructuring their operations may have to consider altering the terms of employment for certain employees. If these changes are sufficiently significant, employees may be in a position to claim damages for constructive dismissal.

The SCC ruled on a case of constructive dismissal for the first time in 1997, in *Farber v. Royal Trust Company*. The SCC was asked to rule on a previous lower court's judgment. In 1983, Mr. Farber worked as regional manager for Western Quebec, and supervised 400 real estate agents working out of 21 offices. His earnings were $150 000, of which $48 800 was a base salary. In 1984, Western Quebec underwent a restructuring that involved the elimination of most of its regional manager positions, including Mr. Farber's position. Mr. Farber was offered a position as a branch manager in another office, which was one of the least profitable in the province and from which he had been promoted eight years earlier. Mr. Farber would no longer receive a guaranteed base salary and he estimated that this compensation package would reduce his income by half its former amount. While Mr. Farber tried to persuade his employer either to reassign him to a more profitable branch, or to be given a guaranteed base salary for three years, the employer refused. Consequently, Mr. Farber quit and sued for constructive dismissal.

The lower courts ruled against Mr. Farber and so he appealed to the SCC. The SCC ruled that the employer had unilaterally substantially altered the fundamental terms of the employment contract. Interestingly, it was unnecessary to prove that the employer had intended to force the employee to leave or that it was acting in bad faith. In fact, the SCC found that in Mr. Farber's case, the employer was acting in good faith in attempting to restructure its operations. Nonetheless, the employer was found guilty of constructive dismissal. Consequently, the SCC overturned the lower court rulings and awarded Farber compensation based on one year's notice with interest from 1984, or approximately $350 000.[23]

Management's Response to Employees' Job Claims

With respect to employees' job claims, management needs to be aware of two important points: (1) It is now appropriate stakeholder management policy to treat workers fairly and to dismiss them only for justifiable cause, and (2) the law today increasingly protects workers who do not get fair treatment. Therefore, management has an added incentive not to get embroiled in complex legal entanglements over wrongful discharges. Four specific actions that management might consider in dealing with this issue[24] include the following:

1. *Stay on the right side of the law.* It is management's responsibility to know the law and to obey it. This is the clearest, best, and most effective position to take. The company that conducts itself honestly and legally has the least to fear from disgruntled employees.

2. *Investigate any complaints fully and in good faith.* Well-motivated complainers in organizations are likely to report problems or concerns to someone within the company first. Therefore, employee complaints about company activities should be checked out. If there is substance to the problem, management has time to make corrections internally, with a minimum of adverse publicity.

3. *Deal in good faith with your employees.* Honour commitments, including those made in writing and those that employees have a reasonable right to expect as matters of normal policy, behaviour, and good faith. Employees continue to win court cases when it is determined that their companies have acted in bad faith.

4. *When you fire someone, make sure it is for a good reason.* This is the best advice possible. Also make sure that the reason is supported by sound records and documentation. Effective performance appraisals, disciplinary procedures, dispute-handling procedures, and employee communications are all keys to justifiable discharges. Management needs to be attentive to abusive or retaliatory firings that are supported by thin technicalities. If the need arises to fire someone, it should not be difficult to document sound reasons for doing so.

Before an employee is terminated, wisdom suggests that management should ask the supervisor, "If you had to appear before a jury, why would you say the employee should be discharged?" Management should also ask the supervisor if the action being taken is consistent with other actions and whether the employee was aware that certain conduct would result in discharge. Finally, management should assume that litigation might result from the firing and that the supervisor making the decision to fire might not be with the company when the case goes to court. Therefore, documentation for each event leading to the termination should be assembled immediately.[25]

Effective stakeholder management suggests that organizations seriously consider their obligations to employee stakeholders and their rights and expectations with respect to their jobs. Not only are the courts increasingly affording employees greater job protection, but evolving notions of ethical treatment are increasingly expanding employees' job rights as well. Companies that are aspiring to emulate the tenets of the moral management model will need to re-examine continuously their attitudes, perceptions, practices, and policies with respect to this issue.

Reasonable Notice Versus Just Cause

When an employer has grounds for dismissal (just cause), the employee can be fired without notice, and the termination can take effect immediately. However, in most cases, employers are required to provide "reasonable notice" to the employee for a termination. Why? Largely because "just cause" exists typically in relatively restricted situations. Recall that dismissals for cause require that an employee has engaged in significant misconduct in some way. As discussed above, it is difficult to claim just cause and, consequently, organizations seeking to dismiss an employee for any variety of reasons will more commonly employ reasonable notice.

The Labour Standards Code, which governs employment relationships within provincial jurisdictions, and the Canada Labour Code, which is applied in the federal jurisdiction, indicate the minimal notice periods and standards that must be provided (in the absence of just cause). There are also common-law standards regarding reasonable notice. Before terminating an employee, an employer should determine what constitutes reasonable notice, given that reasonable notice can depend on a number of factors. For example, length of employment, performance record, age of the employee, and the time the employee will require to become re-employed are among the factors that may need to be taken into account.

While some employers retain the employee during the notice period, more commonly, employers will pay a salary or compensation to the employee instead of providing reasonable notice. Why is this typically done? Employers view this compensation approach or "severance package" as preferable because of the belief that office morale or performance may be adversely affected during the notice period.[26]

The Right to Due Process and Fair Treatment

One of the most frequently proclaimed employee rights issues of the past decade has been the right to due process. Basically, **due process** is the right to receive an impartial review of one's complaints and to be dealt with fairly. In the context of the workplace, due process is thought to be the right of employees to have decisions that adversely affect them be reviewed by objective, impartial third parties.

Due process is consistent with the democratic ideal that undergirds the universal right to fair treatment. It could be argued that, without due process, employees do not receive fair treatment in the workplace.

Patricia Werhane, a leading business ethicist, contends that, procedurally, due process extends beyond simple fair treatment and should state, "Every employee has a right to a public hearing, peer evaluation, outside arbitration, or some other open and mutually agreed-upon grievance procedure before being demoted, unwillingly transferred, or fired."[27] Thus, we see due process ranging from the expectation that employees be treated fairly to the position that employees deserve a fair system of decision making.

Sometimes the employee is treated unfairly in such a subtle way that it is difficult to know that unfair treatment has taken place. What do you do, for example, if your supervisor refuses to recommend you for promotion or permit you to transfer because she or he considers you to be exceptionally good at your job and doesn't want to lose you? How do you prove that a manager has given you a low performance appraisal because you resisted improper advances? The issues over which due-process questions may arise can be quite difficult and subtle.

Only in the past 30 years have some leading companies given special consideration to employees' rights to due process. Historically, managers have had almost unlimited freedom to deal with employees as they wished. In many cases, unfair treatment was not intentional but was the result of inept or distracted supervisors inflicting needless harm on subordinates.[28] It can also be easily seen how amoral managers may have failed to provide employees with acceptable due process and fair treatment. By failing to institute alternative ways to resolve disputes, the managers lost an opportunity to avoid the time, energy, and money that is often lost in protracted administrative and judicial processes.[29]

A Due Process System

David Ewing, an authority on the question of employee rights, has argued that employee due process should be regarded as but one part of **employee constitutionalism**. He suggests that employee constitutionalism "consists of a set of clearly defined rights, and a means of protecting employees from discharge, demotion, or other penalties imposed when they assert their rights." He goes on to enumerate the main requirements of a due-process system in an organization:[30]

1. It must be a procedure; it must follow rules. It must not be arbitrary.
2. It must be sufficiently visible and well known that potential violators of employee rights and victims of abuse are aware of it.
3. It must be predictably effective.
4. It must be institutionalized—a relatively permanent fixture in the organization.
5. It must be perceived as equitable.
6. It must be easy to use.
7. It must apply to all employees.

Ewing has gone on to define corporate due process in the following way:

> *A fair hearing procedure by a power mediator, investigator, or board with the complaining employee having the right to be represented by another employee, to present evidence, to rebut the other side's charges, to have an objective and impartial hearing, to have the wrong corrected if proved, to be free from retaliation for using the procedure, to enjoy reasonable confidentiality, to be heard reasonably soon after lodging the complaint, to get a timely decision, and so forth.*[31]

Ewing's concept of corporate due process represents a formal ideal, and it is doubtful that many corporate due-process systems meet all his requirements. However, there are many due-process systems or mechanisms in use by companies today that strive to treat employees fairly. In the next section we will briefly discuss some of these approaches.

Alternative Dispute Resolution

In unionized organizations, the grievance procedures are typically stated in the collective agreement. In nonunionized workplaces, **alternative dispute resolution (ADR)** procedures are becoming more and more common. There are several ways companies can and do provide due process for their employees. The approaches described here represent some of the ADR methods that have been employed over the past 30 years.

Common Approaches   One of the most often-used mechanisms is the **open-door policy**. This approach typically relies on a senior-level executive who asserts that her or his "door is always open" for those who think they have been treated unfairly. Another approach has been to assign to a human resources department executive the responsibility for investigating employee grievances and either handling them or reporting them to higher management. Closely related to this technique is the assignment of this same responsibility to an assistant to the president.[32] From the employee's standpoint, the major problems with these approaches are that (1) the process is closed, (2) one person is reviewing what happened, and (3) there is a tendency in organizations for one manager to support another manager's decisions. The process is opened up somewhat by companies that use a **hearing procedure**, which permits employees to be represented by a lawyer or another person, with a neutral company executive deciding the outcome based on the evidence. Similar to this approach is the use of a management *grievance committee*, which may involve multiple executives in the decision process.

The Ombudsperson   An innovative due-process mechanism that has become popular in the past decade for dealing with employee problems is the use of a corporate **ombudsperson**. "Ombudsman," the word from which ombudsperson is derived, is a Swedish word that refers to one who investigates reported complaints and helps to achieve equitable settlements. The ombudsperson approach has been used in Sweden since 1809 to curb abuses by government against individuals. In North America, the corporate version of the ombudsperson was first experimented with in 1972, when the Xerox Corporation named an ombudsperson for its largest division. General Electric and the Boeing Vertol division of Boeing were quick to follow.[33] The ombudsperson is also known as a "troubleshooter."[34]

The operation of the ombudsperson program at Xerox is generally representative of ombudsperson programs. The ombudsperson began as an employee relations manager on the organization chart in Xerox's Information Technology Group (ITG). Everyone soon knew that the ombudsperson's function was to ensure fair treatment of employees. This person reported directly to the ITG president, who was the only one who could reverse the ombudsperson's decisions. During the early years of the program, none of the ombudsperson's decisions was overturned—a point signifying the power and effectiveness of the one holding the job.

Under the Xerox system, the employee was expected to try to solve her or his problem through an immediate supervisor or the personnel department before submitting a complaint to the ombudsperson. At this point, the ombudsperson studied the complaint and the company file on the case. Then the ombudsperson discussed both items with a personnel department representative and then with the employee. Subsequently, the ombudsperson's recommended solution was passed on to the personnel department, which presented it as its own idea to the manager involved. Only if the manager declined to go along did the ombudsperson reveal her or his identity and put her or his authority behind the recommendation.[35]

A recent example of the use of the ombudsperson is provided by Sony Electronics, Inc. Sony named an ombudsperson to function as a clearinghouse for employee concerns. The position was intended especially to handle matters regarding illegal or unethical behaviour observed within the company. The goal was early identification of legal or ethical violations. The ombudsperson at Sony also acts as a neutral third party in resolving employee complaints and as one who listens to and handles employee and manager complaints and concerns. As an independent third party, the ombudsperson functions as a reporting link between employees and management. The ombudsperson serves as a confidential assistant, counsellor, mediator, fact finder, and upward-feedback facilitator. He or she endeavours to protect the rights of all employees and managers involved in any matter under consideration. In addition, the ombudsperson plays a key role in all business ethics matters, including the company's business ethics committee, ethics training, and implementation of the company's code of conduct.[36]

The ombudsperson approach to ensuring due process is not without problems. Managers may feel threatened when employees go to the ombudsperson, who must be willing to anger executives in order to get the job done. There is also the fear that employees might experience retribution for going to the ombudsperson in the first place. Despite these potential problems, once in place and understood, the system has worked. A positive and unexpected result of the Xerox experience was that even supervisors went to the ombudsperson for advice on personnel problems. Thus, in some cases, issues were referred to the ombudsperson even before managerial decisions were made.[37] A recent study showed that large firms are more likely to have an ombudsperson on board.[38] This is undoubtedly due to the larger pool of resources from which large firms can draw.

The Peer Review Panel   The **peer review panel** is another due-process mechanism currently under use at several large companies. Control Data Corporation (CDC) was one of the pioneers in the use of the peer review process. Over 30 years ago, Control Data was one of the first nonunion companies in North America to introduce an employee grievance system. It was a system whereby an aggrieved employee could appeal all the way up the chain of authority through six management levels. The company tried to make the system work, but many times the grievance either died because of the cumbersome process or was "kicked upstairs" for some higher level of management to handle. Rulings in favour of the worker were rare. The company determined that this approach was not fair, and in 1983 it added a peer review process to the system.[39]

The peer review process at CDC required the same initial steps as had the traditional grievance system. The employee was to talk first with her or his manager, then to the human resources manager, and then to one higher executive in the management chain. If the employee was still not satisfied that due process had prevailed, she or he was entitled to request a peer review board. The central feature of a peer review board is a panel of two randomly chosen "peers" of the aggrieved employee, along with one

The ADR Institute of Canada

The ADR Institute of Canada (ADR Canada) is a national, nonprofit organization that supports the development and promotion of dispute resolution services in Canada. The aim of this organization is to represent and support professionals who provide dispute resolution services and the individuals and organizations that use those services. ADR Canada also serves as a national clearinghouse for information and skill building in ADR. It offers a broad range of tools and services for practitioners and users of ADR services, including assistance with the creation of national standards and a code of ethics for ADR training and trainers.

Among its numerous corporate members are Alberta Energy Company Ltd., the Bank of Montreal, BP Canada Energy Company, Canadian Forest Oil Ltd., Canadian National, Canadian Pacific Railway Company, Chevron Canada Resources, DuPont Canada Inc., Enbridge Inc., IBM Canada Ltd., Imperial Oil Ltd., Insurance Council of Canada, Mobil Oil Canada, Nortel Networks Corporation, NOVA Corporation, PricewaterhouseCoopers, Shell Canada Ltd., Sun Microsystems of Canada Inc., and Suncor. For more information on ADR Canada, check their Web site at **http://www.adr canada.ca/index.html**.

disinterested executive from a different division. Peers were defined as fellow workers in the same job family at a grade level equal to or higher than that of the grievant.[40]

Managers on the losing side sometimes complain because they think that outsiders are deciding on local issues about which they are not intimately knowledgeable. The company's position is that a manager not only has to convince herself or himself and local superiors that a personnel action is right but also must have it deemed as right against a company-wide policy. The success of the system depends on (1) its having the clear support of top management for fair treatment of employees and (2) its being seen as a permanent fixture. The people who operate the peer review system must have sufficient respect and stature to make the process credible in the eyes of even the most authoritarian line manager.[41] This is especially important because peer review has no professional community to provide standards or procedural guidelines.[42]

The trend toward using ADR is growing. This growth is spurred partly by the time and money saved by avoiding costly litigation. Numerous companies have indicated that their legal fees have dropped significantly since employing ADR, and many cases can be settled in a much shorter period of time. Further, the proportion of adverse settlements and the size of the judgments are no different from when they went through the court system.[43] A recent survey conducted by Cornell University, the Foundation for the Prevention and Resolution of Conflict, and Price Waterhouse, LLP, showed that most *Fortune* 1000 corporations have used some form of ADR. Of these, 81 percent found ADR to be "a more satisfactory process" than litigation, while 59 percent indicated that ADR "preserves good relationships."[44]

As one expert indicated, "Due process is a way of fighting institutionalized indifference to the individual—the indifference that says that productivity and efficiency are the goals of the organization, and any person who stands in the way must be sacrificed."[45] In a recent study, Marc Lampe found that alternative dispute resolution is preferable to the adversarial strategies that preceded it.[46] Increasingly, companies are learning they must acknowledge due process to be not only an employee right but also a sound and ethical management practice in keeping with the wishes and expectations of employees.

Freedom of Expression in the Workplace

Employees may sometimes find themselves in a balancing act—balancing obligations of loyalty to the employer with the right to free expression of opinions. How much weight should be placed on loyalty versus freedom of expression has been subject to much debate.

Imagine a situation where unionized employees choose to go and strike and picket their employer. Prior to 2002, the picketers were restricted in terms of where they could picket their employer. Traditionally, this activity was limited to the employer's premises. However, on January 24, 2002, the Supreme Court of Canada (SCC) ruled that individuals involved in a labour dispute may legally picket not only outside the employer's premises, but at other locations as well ("secondary picketing"). Consequently, this could include picketing a company that sells the product of the company involved in the dispute.

Prior to this ruling, this activity was considered illegal. The SCC based this judgment on the view that secondary picketing is an element of the fundamental right to freedom of expression, and it must be protected in a democratic society. This ruling was the result of a dispute between Pepsi-Cola Canada in Saskatchewan and its unionized workers. In 1997, Pepsi workers picketed retail outlets carrying Pepsi products, and encouraged staff not to accept deliveries from the company. A lower court ruled that workers could only picket at Pepsi's main building. The workers appealed this decision to the SCC because they claimed their rights to freedom of expression were restricted by not being allowed to picket at other Pepsi locations.[47]

In other situations, employees may find themselves caught between preserving the reputation of their employer, protecting their own job security, and exposing improper conduct in the workplace. One such famous Canadian example involves Dr. Nancy Olivieri and research work conducted in cooperation with a drug company.

In the late 1990s, among Dr. Olivieri's numerous research activities was work aimed at developing new drugs to treat thalassaemia, an often-fatal blood disorder most common in children. This research was funded by the drug company Apotex. While initial tests results with a drug called L-1 looked promising, Olivieri subsequently discovered that this drug could be harmful to children.

Apotex argued that Olivieri's findings, which cast serious doubt on the drug, were incomplete and inaccurate. While Olivieri wanted to publish her findings to protect children who might be taking the experimental drug, Apotex threatened to sue if Olivieri went public with this negative information. In addition, Olivieri failed to gain the support of her senior administrators at Toronto's Hospital for Sick Children and supervisors at the University of Toronto. Though her job was threatened, Olivieri decided to publicize the findings of her research. Following publication of her findings, Olivieri was sued by Apotex. She told her story to the press, which led to a number of inquiries. Apotex then withdrew its legal action, and Olivieri returned to her work.[48]

A famous U.S. case with some similarities to the Olivieri case occurred around the same time. Henry Boisvert was a testing supervisor at FMC Corp., makers of the Bradley Fighting Vehicle. The Bradley was designed to transport soldiers around battlefields and, when necessary, "swim" through rivers and lakes. When Boisvert tested the Bradley's ability to move through a pond, he found it filled quickly with water. He wrote the U.S. Army a report of his findings but was told by FMC supervisors that the report would never be sent. When Boisvert refused to sign a falsified report of his test results, he was fired.[49]

About the same time that Boisvert was discovering the Bradley's inability to swim, U.S. Air Force Lieutenant Colonel James Burton found additional problems with the fighting machine. When hit by enemy fire, the Bradley's aluminum armour melted and filled the inside of the vehicle with poisonous fumes. After 17 years of development and US$14 billion for research and prototypes, the Bradley was unfit for warfare. Burton uncovered tests of the Bradley that were rigged by filling the gas tanks with water and the ammunition with noncombustible sand, making it impossible for the Bradley to explode. He also fought an attempt to transfer him to Alaska. After persevering to successfully force changes in the Bradley, Burton was forced to take early retirement as the officers who tried to stop his investigation were promoted.[50]

For most whistle-blowers, the story ends here, but Boisvert and Burton prevailed in their fights to fix the Bradley. In 1998, after a 12-year legal battle, Boisvert received one of the largest damage awards ever seen in a U.S. federal case, well over US$300 million. During the trial, evidence emerged about employees using putty to fix cracks in the machine while vehicles to be selected for random inspection were marked with "X"s and worked on more carefully than the rest.[51] Burton's story also ends happily. The U.S. Congress mandated that the Bradley be tested under the supervision of the National Academy of Sciences, using conditions that resembled true battlefield combat. As a result of these tests, the Bradley was redesigned and used successfully during the Persian Gulf War. Burton wrote a successful book about his experiences, *The Pentagon Wars*.[52] It is impossible to estimate how many soldiers' lives were saved by the courage and persistence of these two men.

Unfortunately for employees who believe they have a legitimate right to speak out against a company engaging in an illegal or unethical practice, most whistle-blowers' stories lack happy endings. Studies of whistle-blowers have found that as many as 90 percent experience negative outcomes, and more than half lose their jobs. Many end up taking prescription medicine to ease the stress, while others even contemplate suicide.[53] Nevertheless, the willingness to challenge management by speaking out is typical of a growing number of employees today, and these individuals are receiving increasing amounts of protection from the courts.

Whistle-Blowing

In its December 30, 2002, edition, *Time* magazine chose as its "persons of the year" three whistle-blowers: Sherron Watkins of Enron, Coleen Rowley of the FBI, and Cynthia Cooper of WorldCom. Though all these individuals worked for diverse organizations, all three share one thing in common: They helped bring to public attention some of the worst corporate misdeeds in recent years:

> Sherron Watkins is the Enron vice president who wrote a letter to chairman Kenneth Lay in the summer of 2001 warning him that the company's methods of accounting were improper. In January, when a congressional subcommittee investigating Enron's collapse released that letter, Watkins became a reluctant public figure, and the Year of the Whistle-Blower began. Coleen Rowley is the FBI staff attorney who caused a sensation in May with a memo to FBI Director Robert Mueller about how the bureau brushed off pleas from her Minneapolis, Minnesota, field office that Zacarias Moussaoui, who is now indicted as a September 11 co-conspirator, was a man who must be investigated. One month later Cynthia Cooper exploded the bubble that was WorldCom when she informed its board that the company had covered up [US]$3.8 billion in losses through the prestidigitations of phony bookkeeping.
>
> ... Their lives may not have been at stake, but Watkins, Rowley and Cooper put pretty much everything else on the line. Their jobs, their health, their privacy, their sanity—they risked all of them to bring us badly needed word of trouble inside crucial institutions.[54]

We appear to be witnessing an increasing trend in employee whistle-blowing. Regardless of whether this is due to a rise in corporate corruption, increased employee

Search the web   W W W

Help for Whistle-Blowers

Though no equivalent Canadian site exists yet, the U.S.-based National Whistleblower Center (**http://www.whistle blowers.org**) offers a wealth of information regarding issues of concern to both Americans and Canadians. It is a "nonprofit educational and advocacy organization committed to environmental protection, nuclear safety, civil rights, government accountability and protecting the rights of employee whistleblowers." The centre has successfully established many of the most important precedents protecting employee whistle-blowers throughout the United States and has revolutionized the protection afforded them.

The Web site has a wide variety of resources related to whistle-blowing. Included among them are a whistle-blower law library, a list of whistle-blower resources, model whistle-blower laws, and sources of whistle-blower protection. In addition to educating the public, they provide counselling to whistle-blowers and support for precedent-setting litigation.

vigilance toward corporate behaviour, or simply less trust in and more scrutiny of "the boss," we have seen an unprecedented number of employees blowing the whistle on their employers.

A **whistle-blower** has been called a "muckraker from within, who exposes what he [or she] considers the unconscionable practices of his [or her] own organization."[55] What constitutes whistle-blowing? For our purposes, we define a whistle-blower as "an individual who reports to some outside party [e.g., media, government agency] some wrongdoing [illegal or unethical act] that he or she knows or suspects his or her employer of committing." An alternative but similar definition of whistle-blowing is provided by Miceli and Near, two experts on the subject, who characterize it as "the disclosure by organization members [former or current] of illegal, immoral, or illegitimate practices under the control of their employers, to persons or organizations that may be able to effect action."[56]

Thus, there are four key elements in the whistle-blowing process: the whistle-blower, the act or complaint the whistle-blower is concerned about, the party to whom the complaint or report is made, and the organization against which the complaint is made.[57] Although our definition indicates that whistle-blowing is done to some outside party, there have been many cases where "internal whistle-blowers" have simply reported their concerns to members of management and yet have been treated as though they had gone to outside parties.

What is at stake is the employee's right to speak out in cases where she or he thinks the company or management is engaging in an unacceptable practice. Whistle-blowing is contrary to our cultural tradition that an employee does not question a superior's decisions and acts, especially not in public. The traditional view holds that loyalty, obedience, and confidentiality are owed solely to the corporate employer. The emerging view of employee responsibility holds that the employee has a duty not only to the employer but also to the public and to her or his own conscience. Whistle-blowing, in this latter situation, becomes a viable option for the employee should management not be responsive to expressed concerns. Figure 15–5 depicts these two views of employee responsibility.

Most whistle-blowers seem to be engaging in these acts out of a genuine or legitimate belief that the actions of their organizations are wrong and that they are doing the right thing by reporting them. They may have learned of the wrongful acts by being requested or coerced to participate in them, or they may have gained knowledge of them through observation or examination of company records. The genuinely concerned employee may initially express concern to a superior or to someone else within the organization.[58] Other potential whistle-blowers may be planning to make their reports for the purpose of striking out or retaliating against the company or a specific manager for some reason. This motive is illegitimate. One recent survey of 233 whistle-blowers disclosed that the average whistle-blower is not an oddball, "loose cannon," or disgruntled employee. The average whistle-blower turns out to be a family man, in his mid-40s, who was motivated by conscience, or what might be termed "universal moral values."[59]

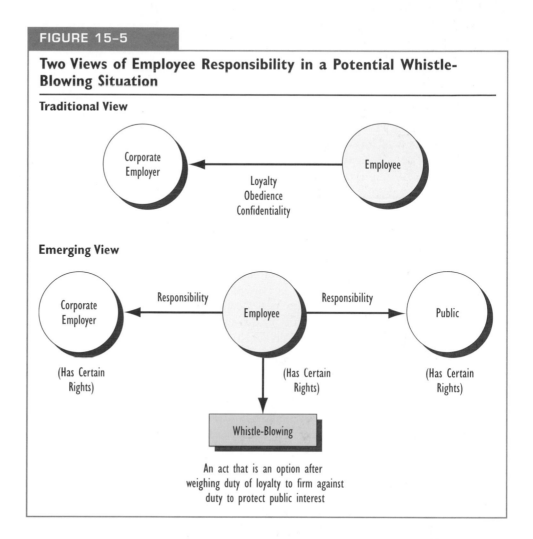

FIGURE 15–5

Two Views of Employee Responsibility in a Potential Whistle-Blowing Situation

Consequences of Whistle-Blowing

What happens to employees after they blow the whistle? Unfortunately, whistle-blowers are seldom rewarded for their perceived contributions to the public interest. Although they are now more likely to get some form of protection from the courts, whistle-blowers in general have paid dearly for their lack of company loyalty. Short of firings, various types of corporate retaliation have been taken against whistle-blowers,[60] including:

- More stringent criticism of work
- Less desirable work assignments
- Pressure to drop charges against the company
- Heavier workloads
- Lost perquisites (e.g., telephone and parking privileges)
- Exclusion from meetings previously attended

One example of what can happen to whistle-blowers as a consequence of their actions is the case of Charles Atchison. At age 40, Atchison stood up before regulators and told them about numerous safety violations at the Commanche Peak Nuclear

Plant in Glen Rose, Texas. Atchison was a quality control inspector for Brown & Root, the construction company that built the plant for the Texas Utilities Electric Company. Atchison claimed he couldn't get anyone to fix the problems. Atchison lost his job and ended up in debt. Although Atchison was proud of the stance he had taken, he indicated that he often felt psychological scars from the experience. "The whistle-blower today is probably the most discriminated against individual in the country," Atchison exclaimed.[61]

Another example is the case of Anne Livengood, a 51-year-old medical office worker who claimed she was fired from a physical therapy clinic in Fremont, California, after she had notified management that its accounting system was billing insurance companies for services that had not been performed. Livengood was escorted out of her building by the company accountant. Her response to the experience was, "You feel so alone and intimidated."[62]

Famous cases of whistle-blowing include Ernest Fitzgerald, the U.S. Air Force employee who blew the whistle on billions of dollars in cost overruns at Lockheed, and the Morton Thiokol engineers who tried to halt the launch of the space shuttle *Challenger* because of frozen O-rings. All of these whistle-blowers were fired.[63]

Figure 15–6 identifies a pattern that Donald Soeken refers to as the seven stages of life of a typical whistle-blower.

Although whistle-blowers frequently do get fired, as public policy increasingly sides with them and their courageous stances, other corporate actions are becoming possible. One encouraging episode is the case of Mark Jorgensen, who was employed at Prudential Insurance Co.[64] Jorgensen was a manager of real estate funds for Prudential. He thought he was just being an honest guy when he exposed fraud he saw occurring in his company. His world then began to fall apart. He was abandoned by his boss, who had once been his friend. His colleagues at work began to shun him. Company lawyers accused him of breaking the law. Jorgensen, who was once a powerful and respected executive in the firm, began to hide out at the local library because he had been forbidden to return to his office. His long and successful career appeared to be dwindling to a pathetic end. Finally, he was fired.

FIGURE 15–6

The Seven Stages of Life of a Typical Whistle-Blower

After extensive research into the life experiences of whistle-blowers, Donald Soeken identified a pattern that he calls the "seven stages of life" of a typical whistle-blower. The seven stages are as follows:

1. Discovery of the organizational abuse
2. Reflection on what action to take
3. Confrontation with superiors
4. Retaliation (against the whistle-blower)
5. Long haul of legal action
6. Termination of the case
7. Going on to a new life

In terms of personal effects, Soeken found in a survey of 233 whistle-blowers that 90 percent of them had lost their jobs or been demoted, 26 percent had sought psychiatric and medical care, 15 percent had divorced in the aftermath of the episode, 10 percent had attempted suicide, and 8 percent had gone bankrupt.

Source: Cited in Ana Radelat, "When Blowing the Whistle Ruins Your Life," *Public Citizen* (September/October 1991), 18–19.

Unlike most whistle-blowers, however, Jorgensen received a phone call from the company chairman, Robert Winters, who wanted to meet with Jorgensen to tell him some startling news: The company now believed him and wanted to reinstate him. Further, the company wanted to force out the boss he had accused of falsely inflating the values of funds that he managed. The turnabout was attributed to Jorgensen's persistence in fighting all odds in his quest to justify his convictions. Coming to the realization that Jorgensen had been right in his allegations all along, Prudential found itself in an unusual situation in business today—siding with the whistle-blower it had fought for months and eventually had fired. The company offered to reinstate Jorgensen in his job, but he elected instead to move on to another company. Prudential paid him a sizable amount to settle his lawsuit.[65] Although we do not read about many stories that end this way, it is encouraging to know that there are some stories that have good endings.

Government's Protection of Whistle-Blowers

Consistent with the illustrations cited earlier, Peter Bowal, Law Professor at the University of Calgary, commented on the risks that employee whistle-blowing entails:

> *Historically, blowing the whistle about something to others has been risky. Despite the increasing emphasis at work on equality, employee rights, workplace democracy, and quality of life issues, the whistleblower can be seen as disloyal or a snitch. The implied common law duty of the employee of fidelity to the employer can get one fired or cause one to suffer other retaliation for blowing the whistle at work. Unwanted whistleblowing is still likely to be seen today as sanctionable worksite misconduct. It can render one's job less secure or hurt one's chances of promotion.*[66]

Given the huge risks involved, how can an employee who observes corporate wrongdoing feel comfortable blowing the whistle? Clearly, one potentially powerful source of support for whistle-blowers derives from government legislation. Unfortunately, to date, Canada appears to lag significantly behind the U.S. in terms of government legislation aimed at protecting the rights of the whistle-blower.

Portions of legislation at the federal level exist in specific sections of the Environmental Protection Act, Labour Code, Competition Law, and Human Rights Code. Provincial laws have also taken a piecemeal approach to whistle-blower protection with some support for whistle-blower rights and protection afforded in laws such as the Occupation Health and Safety Act, Human Rights Act, and Environment Act. However, there is no comprehensive protection plan for whistle-blowers in Canada, especially in the private sector.

Democracy Watch, a well-known Canadian nonprofit organization "advocating democratic reform, government accountability and corporate responsibility,"[67] has consistently called for more comprehensive whistle-blower protection in Canada. In a recent media release, it drew attention to the lack of whistle-blower legislation where it may matter most:

> *While the right to blow the whistle and be protected from retaliation already exists under the* Canadian Environmental Protection Act, *the* Canadian Human Rights Act, *the* Canada Labour Code, *and the*

Competition Act, *it does not exist under the* Canada Business
Corporations Act *(under which 155,000 corporations are set up, including half of the 500 largest corporations in Canada) nor in the* Bank Act
or other financial institution laws.[68]

Reports in the Canadian press indicate that even public sector employees in
Canada feel unprotected when it comes to reporting employer misdeeds. In 2003 a
public sector scandal emerged with the discovery that a federal privacy commissioner,
George Radwanski, enjoyed extravagant meals and trips at taxpayers' expense, spending almost $500 000 over two years. Employees were aware of wrongdoing but failed
to report it out of fear of reprisal. Only after the scandal was exposed did employees
come forward to denounce Radwanski, who subsequently resigned.[69]

A 2003 survey conducted by Environics Research Group for the Public Service
Alliance of Canada found that 89 percent of Canadians want legislation that would
better protect whistle-blowers who expose government corruption.[70] In a survey conducted by the Government and General Employees Union, results indicated that more
than one quarter of Nova Scotia civil servants had witnessed mistakes, corruption,
ethical misconduct, or unsafe conditions at work that should be exposed, but they
were too afraid to report this. The survey also found that 27 percent of 400 union
members surveyed had seen something serious enough to report but did not speak up
for fear of retaliation.[71]

The lack of sufficient protection for whistle-blowers in Canada, particularly in
the private sector, is reflected in the critical comments made recently by Larry Brown,
secretary treasurer of the National Union of Public and General Employees:

> *Whistleblowing is often thought of as a public sector issue. It is a public
> sector issue, of course. Public sector workers are employed by the gov-
> ernment of the day, but they work for the people of the country or their
> province. They owe a higher duty to the public than to the government
> of the day. That being said, whistleblowing is also a private sector
> issue…. It would be rare to find a private company where the public had
> no interest in the environmental practices of the organization, or where
> the public had no legitimate interest in whether the company practiced or
> encouraged corruption. There are hundreds of examples of public safety
> issues arising from private corporations. Consider the cost of silence in
> the case of Union Carbide in India where 3,800 people were killed by a
> gas leak. Think of the Clapham Rail Crash, in the United Kingdom, with
> 35 killed, 500 injured. Think of the oil rigs, the tankers, the transport
> trucks, the manufacturing processes that the public has every right to be
> worried about.*[72]

The relatively weak Canadian whistle-blower laws stand in stark contrast to the
post-Enron U.S. environment. Largely in response to the myriad of corporate scandals
in recent years, the U.S. government strengthened its whistle-blower legislation.
Traditionally, most U.S. federal and state whistle-blower laws only protected employees who exposed certain types of public health, safety, or health-care fraud issues.
However, following the Enron scandal and a host of other cases, the U.S. Congress
aimed to afford whistle-blowers of corporate fraud and accounting abuses the same
kind of special protection provided for those other issues. In 2002, Congress passed
the Sarbanes-Oxley Act, which significantly improved the protection provided to cor-

porate whistle-blowers. The Sarbanes-Oxley legislation, built on extensive provisions, including the Whistleblowers Protection Act (passed in 1978 and strengthened in 1989 and 1994), aims to protect employees who reveal corrupt and harmful activities.

Among the coverage provided, the Sarbanes-Oxley legislation permits an employee of a publicly traded company to sue the company if the employee suffers retaliation as a result of providing information regarding corporate violations of any federal securities laws, rules, or regulations, or actions that constitute securities fraud. The legislation also includes the Corporate and Criminal Fraud Accountability Act, which protects corporate whistle-blowers against retaliation by their employers. The aim is to protect employees who face retaliation for filing, testifying, or assisting in an investigation relating either to violations of any federal securities laws, rules, and regulations, or to securities fraud.[73]

Twelve U.S. states give comprehensive blanket protection for whistle-blowers that expose any violation of state or federal laws or regulations. A number of states also offer protection for whistle-blowers who report violations of codes of conduct or ethics. Several states even include a reward for those who report corporate wrongdoing. For example, in California, whistle-blowers earn 10 percent of what they save a corporation or taxpayers by exposing the misdeeds.

In Canada, traditionally New Brunswick has been the only province that offers specific protection of the rights of whistle-blowers in the private sector. Since 1989, New Brunswick's Employment Standards Act has provided general protection to all private (as well as public) sector employees who report violations of any provincial or federal law or regulation. Specifically, Section 28 of that province's Employment Standards Act, Chapter E-7.2, indicates the following:

> *Notwithstanding anything in this Act an employer shall not dismiss, suspend, lay off, penalize, discipline or discriminate against an employee if the reason therefor is related in any way to:*
>
> *(b) the making of a complaint or the giving of information or evidence by the employee against the employer with respect to any matter covered by this act; or*
>
> *(c) the giving of information or evidence by the employee against the employer with respect to the alleged violation of any Provincial or federal Act or regulation by the employer while carrying on the employer's business; or if the dismissal, suspension, layoff, penalty, discipline or discrimination constitutes in any way an attempt by the employer to evade any responsibility imposed upon him under this Act or any other Provincial or federal Act or regulation or to prevent or inhibit an employee from taking advantage of any right or benefit granted to him under this Act.*[74]

According to Wes Cragg, director of the Ethics Program at the Schulich School of Business at York University in Toronto, "We should be moving more quickly to protect people who want to bring unethical behaviour to the attention of their organizations, but who are afraid to do so for fear of censure, for fear of losing their jobs."[75] Is Canada doing anything about its relatively weak protection of whistle-blowers?

While it may not be moving fast enough for many critics, Canada is attempting to bolster its legislation aimed at protecting whistle-blowers. In fact, recent government efforts appear to be following the lead of many U.S. states as well as New

Brunswick in an attempt to create a comprehensive protection for anyone who reports violations of any law, regulation, or code. For example, in 2003, with pressure from the Government Ethics Coalition and Corporate Responsibility Coalition, Canada's Senate Finance Committee considered adding whistle-blower protection to Bill C-25, the public service reform bill (along with Bills C-34, C-45, and C-46). The aim is to create a complete whistle-blower protection system that would protect anyone in Canada who reports any violation of a law, regulation, policy, guideline, or code by government institutions or corporations.

Democracy Watch suggested that such government efforts should include the following provisions for ensuring whistle-blower protection:[76]

- Allow whistle-blowers to report anonymously if they so desire.
- Establish completely independent enforcement agencies with full investigative powers to examine the reports of whistle-blowers.
- Empower the enforcement agencies to fully protect whistle-blowers from any form of retaliation.
- Permit the right to appeal any enforcement agency's decisions to court (to ensure accountability of the agency).
- Reward whistle-blowers accordingly if their allegations are proven true (whistle-blowers typically suffer financial and other losses even when protected from retaliation).

On a final note, the urgency of establishing specific legislation is perhaps best communicated in the comments of Larry Brown of the National Union of Public and General Employees:

Whistleblower protection would add to our collective integrity as a nation. The lack of whistleblower protection in Canada means we are condoning silence, in fact condoning the silencing of employees by employers. We are allowing employees to be forced to lie by their silence. It is time for the laws to allow us all to speak the truth.[77]

Although we see more and more cases of employees wanting the right to question management and to speak out, David Ewing[78] argues that there are some forms of speech that should not be protected:

- Employees should not have the right to make personal accusations or slurs that are irrelevant to questions about policies and actions that seem illegal or irresponsible.
- Employees should not be entitled to disrupt an organization or damage its morale by making accusations that do not reflect a conviction that wrong is being done.
- Employees should not be entitled to rail against the competence of a manager to make everyday work decisions that have nothing to do with the legality, morality, or responsibility of management actions.
- Employees should not be entitled to object to discharge, transfer, or demotion, no matter what they have said about the organization or how they have said it, if management can demonstrate that unsatisfactory performance or violation of a code of conduct was the reason for its actions.

In the final analysis, an employee should have a right to dissent, but this right may be constrained or limited by the kinds of reasons just given, and perhaps others as well.

Management Responsiveness to Potential Whistle-Blowing Situations

How can an organization work with its employees to reduce their need to blow the whistle? Kenneth Walters[79] has suggested five considerations that might be kept in mind:

1. The company should assure employees that the organization will not interfere with their basic political freedoms.
2. The organization's grievance procedures should be streamlined so that employees can obtain direct and sympathetic hearings for issues on which they are likely to blow the whistle if their complaints are not heard quickly and fairly.
3. The organization's concept of social responsibility should be reviewed to make sure that it is not being construed merely as corporate giving to charity.
4. The organization should formally recognize and communicate respect for the individual consciences of employees.
5. The organization should realize that dealing harshly with a whistle-blowing employee could result in needless adverse public reaction.

Companies are learning that whistle-blowing can be averted if visible efforts are made on the part of management to listen and be responsive to employees' concerns. One specific approach is the use of an ombudsperson, which we discussed earlier, as a due-process mechanism. The ombudsperson can also be used to deal with employee grievances against the company. The Corporate Ombudsman Association, which includes such firms as Anheuser-Busch, Control Data, McDonald's, and Upjohn, even goes so far as to prepare training materials that include likely whistle-blowing scenarios. According to one report, the grapevine among corporate ombudspersons is constantly buzzing with rumours of front-page scandals that they have averted. The companies that have put money into such programs say they are well worth the investment.[80]

Whether or not an ombudsperson is used, management should respond in a positive way to employee objectors and dissenters. At a minimum, companies that want to be responsive to such employees[81] should engage in the following four actions:

1. *Listen.* Management must listen very carefully to the employee's concern. Be particularly attentive to the employee's valid points, and acknowledge them and show that you have a genuine respect for the employee's concerns. It is recommended that you attempt to "draw out the objector's personal concerns."
2. *Delve into why the employee is pursuing the complaint or issue.* Determining the objector's motives may give you important insights into the legitimacy of the complaint and how it should best be handled.
3. *Look for solutions that will address the interests of both the objector and the company.*
4. *Attempt to establish an equitable means of judging future actions.* Objective tests or criteria that are agreeable to both sides are superior to perseverance or negotiation as a means of resolving an impasse.

In a related set of recommendations, *Business Week* and The Conference Board have set forth four key components of a model whistle-blower policy.[82] These four recommended actions are as follows:

1. *Shout it from the rooftops.* The company should aggressively publicize a reporting policy that encourages employees to bring forward valid complaints of wrongdoing.

2. *Face the fear factor.* Employee fear may be defused by directing complaints to someone outside the whistle-blower's chain of command.
3. *Get right on it.* The complaint should be investigated immediately by an independent group, either within or outside the company.
4. *Go public.* The outcomes of investigations should be publicized whenever possible so that employees can see that complaints are taken seriously.

The desire of employees to speak out is increasingly becoming a right in their eyes and in the eyes of the courts as well, and it is likely that whistle-blowers and employees' rights to free expression will increasingly be protected in the future. This being the case, management needs to assess carefully where it stands on this vital issue. It is becoming more and more apparent that respecting an employee's right to publicly differ with management may indeed serve the longer-term interests of the organization. We should also remember, however, that companies need and deserve protection from employees who do not perform as they should.

Summary

Employee stakeholders today are more sensitive about employee rights issues for a variety of reasons. Underlying this new concern are changes in the social contract between employers and employees. Central among the growing employee rights issues that are treated in this chapter are the right not to be fired without just cause, the right to due process and fair treatment, and the right to freedom of expression. Society's concept of what represents fair treatment to employees is also changing.

The right to due process is concerned primarily with fair treatment. Common approaches for management responding to this concern include the open-door policy, human resource specialists, grievance committees, and hearing procedures. The ombudsperson approach is becoming more prevalent, and recently the peer review panel seems to have become a popular due-process mechanism. A special case in which due process is needed is the employee who chooses to speak out against management or blow the whistle on unethical or illegal actions. These individuals often face severe reprisals for taking actions against their employers. Managers should be genuinely attentive to employees' rights in this realm if they wish to avert major scandals and prolonged litigation. A stakeholder approach that emphasizes ethical relationships with employees would ordain this attention and concern.

Key Terms

alternative dispute resolution (ADR) (page 477)

constructive dismissal (page 472)

contractual rights (page 468)

due process (page 475)

employee constitutionalism (page 476)

employee rights (page 467)

hearing procedure (page 477)

implied contract (page 468)

just cause (page 470)

ombudsperson (page 477)

open-door policy (page 477)

peer review panel (page 478)

private property (page 467)

social contract (page 465)

statutory rights (page 468)

whistle-blower (page 482)

Discussion Questions

1. Rank the various changes that are occurring in the workplace in terms of their importance to the growth of the employee rights movement. Briefly explain your ranking.

2. Do you think that the criteria for just cause are fair and reasonable? Explain.

3. In your own words, explain the right to due process. What are some of the major ways management is attempting to ensure due process in the workplace?

4. If you could choose only one, which form of alternative dispute resolution would be your choice as the most effective approach to employee due process? Explain.

5. How do you feel about whistle-blowing now that you have read about it? Are you now more sympathetic or less sympathetic to whistle-blowers? Explain.

Endnotes

1. Diane Lewis, "Out in the Field: Workplace Want Loyal Workers? Then Help Them Grow," *Boston Globe* (July 15, 2001), H2.
2. Michelle Conlin, "Job Security, No. Tall Latte, Yes," *Business Week* (April 2, 2001), 62–64.
3. Lewis, H2.
4. Centre for Ethical Orientation, "Aiming High: Renewing Trust in a Time of Suspicion" (May 2003), http://www.ceo-ethics.com/aiminghigh.pdf.
5. Kim Lunman, "Canadians Less Trusting Now, Poll Finds," *National Post* (June 25, 2003), A8.
6. Lewis, H2.
7. "Revolution in America's Workplace," *Business Week* (October 17, 1994), 252.
8. *Ibid.*
9. *Ibid.*
10. Kenneth Chilton and Murray Weidenbaum, *A New Social Contract for the American Workplace: From Paternalism to Partnering* (St. Louis: Center for the Study of American Business, Washington University, November 1994), 2.
11. John Wyatt, "The New Deal: What Companies and Employees Owe One Another," *Fortune* (June 13, 1994), 44–52.
12. Hal Lancaster, "A New Social Contract to Benefit Employer and Employee," *The Wall Street Journal* (November 29, 1994), B1.
13. Alfred G. Felio, *Primer on Individual Employee Rights* (Washington, DC: Bureau of National Affairs, 1996).
14. Richard Edwards, *Rights at Work* (Washington, DC: The Brookings Institution, 1993), 25–26.
15. K. Makin, "Insensitive Firings Not Tolerated: Supreme Court Decision Will Aid Future Victims of Wrongful Dismissal, Lawyers Say," *The Globe and Mail* (October 31, 1997), A4; D. Johnston, "Promises, Promises: the Case of Queen versus Cognos," *Law Now* (Vol. 22, No. 3, December 1997/January 1998), 16–18.

16. Monica Belcourt, George W. Bohlander, Scott A. Snell, and Arthur W. Sherman, *Managing Human Resources*, 4th Canadian ed. (Toronto: Nelson Canada, 2004).
17. Christopher Bouvier, "Why At-Will Employment Is Dying," *Personnel Journal* (Vol. 75, No. 5, May 1996), 123–128. See also Marvin J. Levine, "The Erosion of the Employment-at-Will Doctrine: Recent Developments," *Labor Law Journal* (Vol. 45, No. 2, February 1994), 79–89.
18. Janice B. Payne, "Termination for Cause Update: A Briefing for Human Resource Professionals," http://www.nelligan.ca/e/PDF/terminationforcause.pdf2001.
19. *Ibid.*
20. T. Wagar, "Wrongful Dismissal: Perception vs. Reality," *Human Resources Professional* (Vol. 8, No. 10, 1996).
21. Payne.
22. Julie McAlpine, "10 Steps for Reducing Exposure to Wrongful Dismissal," *Canadian HR Reporter* (Vol. 15, No. 9, May 6, 2002), 8.
23. Emond Harnden, "Labour and Employment Law," http://www.emond-harnden.com/farber.html.
24. T. J. Condon, "Fire Me and I'll Sue: A Manager's Guide to Employee Rights" (Alexander Hamilton Institute, 1984–1985), 12.
25. Andrew M. Kramer, "The Hazards of Firing at Will," *The Wall Street Journal* (March 9, 1987), 22.
26. Kathryn A. Raymond, Boyne Clarke Law Practice (2003), http://www.boyneclarke.ns.ca/Law_Letters/fired.html.
27. Patricia H. Werhane, *Persons, Rights and Corporations* (Englewood Cliffs, NJ: Prentice Hall, 1985), 110.
28. David W. Ewing, *Freedom Inside the Organization: Bringing Civil Liberties to the Workplace* (New York: McGraw-Hill, 1977), 10.
29. Kay O. Wilburn, "Employment Disputes: Solving Them Out of Court," *Management Review* (March 1998), 17–21. See also Marc Lampe, "Mediation as an Ethical

Adjunct of Stakeholder Theory," *Journal of Business Ethics* (May 2001), 165–173.

30. Ewing, *Freedom Inside the Organization* (1977), 11.

31. David W. Ewing, *Justice on the Job: Resolving Grievances in the Nonunion Workplace* (Boston: Harvard Business School Press, 1989), 324.

32. Ewing, *Harvard Business Review* (1977).

33. "Where Ombudsmen Work Out," *Business Week* (May 3, 1976), 114–116.

34. John T. Ziegenfuss, Jr., *Organizational Troubleshooters: Resolving Problems with Customers and Employees* (San Francisco: Jossey-Bass Publishers, 1988).

35. "How the Xerox Ombudsman Helps Xerox," *Business Week* (May 12, 1973), 188–190.

36. "Pathway to Excellence: A Guide to Ethical Business Conduct" (Sony Electronics, April 1994), Company handouts.

37. *Ibid.*, 190.

38. Alan K. Reichert, Marion S. Webb, and Edward G. Thomas, "Corporate Support of Ethical and Environmental Policies: A Financial Management Perspective," *Journal of Business Ethics* (May 2000).

39. Fred C. Olson, "How Peer Review Works at Control Data," *Harvard Business Review* (November–December 1984), 58.

40. *Ibid.*, 58–59.

41. *Ibid.*, 58, 64.

42. Cynthia F. Cohen, "Justice and Peer Review Systems: A Framework for Analysis," *Journal of Collective Negotiations in the Public Sector* (1999), 83–92.

43. Wilburn, 17–21.

44. Elaine McShulski, "ADR Gains Overwhelming Acceptance," *HR Magazine* (November 1997), 22.

45. Ewing, *Freedom Inside the Organization* (1977), 172–173.

46. Lampe, 165–173.

47. "Court Okays Picketing of Employers' Clients," *Canadian HR Reporter* (Vol. 15, No. 4 February 25, 2002), 1–2.

48. Andrew Mitrovica, "Whistle Blower Doctor: Winner of the Open Television Category, CTV," *Media* (Vol. 6, No. 2, Summer 1999), 20.

49. Lee Gomes, "A Whistle-Blower Finds Jackpot at the End of His Quest," *The Wall Street Journal* (April 27, 1998), B1.

50. Robert P. Lawrence, "Go Ahead, Laugh at Army's Expense," *The San Diego Union-Tribune* (February 27, 1998), E12.

51. Gomes, B1.

52. Lawrence, E12.

53. Marcy Mason, "The Curse of Whistleblowing," *The Wall Street Journal* (March 14, 1994), A14.

54. Richard Lacayo and Amanda Ripley, "Persons of the Year," *Time* (Vol. 160, No. 27, December 30, 2002/January 6, 2003), 32.

55. Charles Peters and Taylor Branch (eds.), *Blowing the Whistle: Dissent in the Public Interest* (New York: Praeger, 1972), 4.

56. Marcia P. Miceli and Janet P. Near, *Blowing the Whistle: The Organizational and Legal Implications for Companies and Employees* (New York: Lexington Books, 1992), 15.

57. Janet P. Near and Marcia P. Miceli, *The Whistle-Blowing Process and Its Outcomes: A Preliminary Model* (Columbus, OH: The Ohio State University, College of Administrative Science, Working Paper Series 83–55, September, 1983), 2. See also Miceli and Near, 1992.

58. Nancy R. Hauserman, "Whistle-Blowing: Individual Morality in a Corporate Society," *Business Horizons* (March–April 1986), 5.

59. Ana Radelat, "When Blowing the Whistle Ruins Your Life," *Public Citizen* (September/October 1991), 16–20.

60. Janet P. Near, Marcia P. Miceli, and Tamila C. Jensen, "Variables Associated with the Whistle-Blowing Process" (Columbus, OH: The Ohio State University, College of Administrative Science, Working Paper Series 83–11, March 1983), 5.

61. N. R. Kleinfield, "The Whistle-Blower's Morning After," *The New York Times* (November 9, 1986), 1–F.

62. Joan Hamilton, "Blowing the Whistle Without Paying the Piper," *Business Week* (June 3, 1991), 139.

63. *Ibid.*, 138.

64. Kurt Eichenwald, "He Told. He Suffered. Now He's a Hero," *The New York Times* (May 29, 1994), 1–F.

65. *Ibid.*

66. Peter Bowal, "Whistleblowers: All Truth Is Good, but Not All Truth Is Good to Say," *Law Now* (Vol. 27, No. 6, June/July 2003), 55–59.

67. Democracy Watch, http://www.dwatch.ca/.

68. Democracy Watch, Media Release, "Whistleblower Protection Needed Not Just in Bill C-25, but Also in Bills C-34, C-45, etc." (September 8, 2003), http://www.dwatch.ca/camp/RelsSep0803.html.

69. "Public Sector Wants Whistleblower Protection After Radwanski Case," *Canadian Press NewsWire* (September 2, 2003).

70. Luma Muhtadie, "Canadians Want Whistle-Blowers Protected," *Globe and Mail* (October 28, 2003), http://www.globeandmail.com/.

71. Clare Mellor, "Whistle stop, Canada Lacks Protection for Employees Who Blow the Whistle on Misdeeds," *Halifax Herald* (November 9, 2003), http://www.herald.ns.ca/stories/2003/11/09/fBusiness102.raw.html.

72. Larry Brown, "The Case for Whistleblowing Legislation in Canada" (November 5, 2003), http://www.nupge.ca/news_2003/n06no03a.htm.

73. Veronica Greenbaum, "Laws Exist to Protect Whistleblowers from Revenge," *Boston Business Journal* (November 18, 2002), http://www.bizjournals.com/boston/stories/2002/11/18/focus5.html.

74. Employment Standards Act, http://www.gnb.ca/acts/acts/e-07-2.htm.

75. Kate MacNamara, "Blowing Whistle Risky for Canadians: Employment Experts," *National Post* (November 1, 2003), FP06.

76. Democracy Watch, Media Release, "Whistleblower Protection Needed Not Just in Bill C-25, but Also in Bills C-34, C-45, etc." (September 8, 2003), http://www.dwatch.ca/camp/RelsSep0803.html.

77. Brown, *op cit.*

78. Ewing, *Freedom Inside the Organization* (1977), 109–110.

79. Kenneth D. Walters, "Your Employees' Right to Blow the Whistle," *Harvard Business Review* (July–August 1975), 161–162.

80. Michael Brody, "Listen to Your Whistle-Blower," *Fortune* (November 24, 1986), 77–78.

81. David W. Ewing, "How to Negotiate with Employee Objectors," *Harvard Business Review* (January–February 1983), 104.

82. Lisa Driscoll, "A Better Way to Handle Whistle-Blowers: Let Them Speak," *Business Week* (July 27, 1992), 36.

Chapter 16

Employee Stakeholders: Privacy, Safety, and Health

Chapter Objectives

After studying this chapter, you should be able to:

1 Articulate the concerns surrounding the employee's right to privacy in the workplace.

2 Identify the implications of employee information collection, employee testing, and workplace surveillance with regard to employee rights to privacy.

3 Identify the role of government and the key elements of government legislation with regard to occupational safety and health.

4 Discuss the role of employer and employee with regard to workplace health and safety.

5 Elaborate on actions that management can take to create a safer and healthier work environment.

Employee stakeholders are concerned not only with the issues we discussed in the preceding chapter but also with several other issues. These other issues should be thought of as extensions of the concept of employee rights developed in Chapter 15. In this chapter, we are concerned with the employee's rights to privacy, safety, and a healthy work environment.

The right to privacy primarily addresses the psychological dimension, whereas the rights to health and safety primarily address the physical dimension. While recent legislation is directly addressing workplace privacy issues, the status of an employee's right to privacy in the workplace today continues to be tested. Technology has made the issue of privacy much more complex. Technological surveillance via the computer or cameras has been an increasingly controversial issue. Hence, there is a genuine need for management groups to impose ethical thinking and standards in this increasingly important area.

Employee rights to safety and health are issues of rising intensity, too. In today's workplace, whether it be a manufacturing facility or an office complex, workers are exposed to hazards or risks of accidents or occupational diseases. If the normal hazards of work were not enough, the phenomenon of violence in the workplace should cause management to pay serious attention to this threat to workplace peace and stability.[1]

Let us continue our consideration of social and ethical issues that have become important to employee stakeholders in recent years. If managers are to be successful in dealing with employees' needs and treating them fairly as stakeholders, they must address these concerns now and in the future.

Right to Privacy in the Workplace

Big brother is watching you where you least expect it. In the 2001 Super Bowl, hidden cameras scanned the faces of spectators as they arrived, and police used facial recognition software to compare the arriving patrons' faces with their database of terrorists and other serious criminals.[2] Technological developments such as this have made it simpler and less expensive to conduct various types of surveillance—not only in public but also in the workplace. In turn, workplace monitoring has grown and with it come new ethical considerations. According to human resource expert Ellen Bayer, "**Privacy in the workplace** is largely illusory."[3] An increasing number of class-action privacy-related lawsuits have been filed in North America in recent years.[4] As such, privacy has become a "hot button" issue for businesses.[5]

Most experts say that privacy means the right to keep personal affairs to oneself and to know how information about one is being used.[6] Patricia Werhane, a business ethicist, opts for a broader definition. She says that privacy includes (1) the right to be left alone, (2) the related right to autonomy, and (3) the claim of individuals and groups to determine for themselves when, how, and to what extent information about them is communicated to others.[7]

Defining privacy in this way, however, does not settle the issue. In today's world, achieving these ideals is extremely difficult and fraught with judgment calls about our own privacy rights versus other people's rights. This problem is exacerbated by the increasingly computerized, technological world in which we live. We gain great efficiencies from computers and new technologies, but we also pay a price. Part of the price we pay is that information about us is stored in dozens of places, including federal agencies (e.g., Revenue Canada), provincial agencies (e.g., courts and motor vehicle departments), and many local departments and businesses (e.g., school systems, credit bureaus, banks, life insurance companies, and direct-mail companies).

In 1984, Canada joined with 22 other industrialized nations in adopting the OECD Guidelines for the Protection of Privacy and Transborder Flows of Personal Data. The guidelines were aimed at harmonizing privacy laws and practices among OECD member countries by creating minimum standards for handling personal information. While the guidelines applied to both the public and private sectors, they were only a voluntary code of conduct.

Currently, Canadians are protected by two federal privacy laws, the Privacy Act (effective July 1, 1983) and the Personal Information Protection and Electronic Documents Act (effective January 1, 2001). The Privacy Act applies to about 150 federal government departments and agencies with regard to the privacy rights of Canadians by placing limits on the collection, use, and disclosure of personal information. The Privacy Act also permits Canadians to have the right to access and correct personal information about them held by these federal government organizations.[8]

The **Personal Information Protection and Electronic Documents Act (PIPEDA)** has applied to the commercial activities and employment relationships of all federally regulated employers like banks, telecommunications companies, and airlines since 2001. On January 1, 2004, the PIPEDA extended its application to almost all other Canadian organizations and the commercial activity in provinces where no substantially similar legislation has been passed. As of 2004, only Quebec was exempt from the PIPEDA. Other provinces, such as British Columbia, Alberta, and Ontario, had proposed draft legislation for discussion and review. The implications of this act will be discussed in more detail below.

While legislation is much needed and will help support employee privacy rights, there is little doubt that legislation alone will not guarantee fairness in the treatment of employees. Both employers and employees will need to mutually define acceptable boundaries of privacy and both parties will need to consider how technology can create new challenges to privacy at work. As human resource expert Yosie Saint-Cyr points out:

> *Workplace privacy is a controversial subject. Employers, on the one hand, believe that they are entitled to gather certain kinds of personal information about job applicants and to monitor their employees to ensure that the highest possible level of productivity is maintained. Job applicants and employees, on the other hand, believe that they are entitled to a degree of privacy. Differing attitudes toward privacy, and confusion over what sorts of monitoring are legally acceptable, can undermine the trust that employees place in their employers and possibly result in lawsuits by employees seeking compensation for invasion of privacy.[9]*

In the realm of employee privacy, which is our central concern here, the following three important issues stand out as representative of the major workplace privacy issues of the past decade:

1. *Collection and use of employee information in personnel files.* What information can employers gather about their workers? What methods can the boss use to gain access to personal information? How is employee information to be maintained and communicated? These are among the central ethical questions facing organizations in the area of workplace privacy.

2. *Testing of employees.* Employers naturally want to ensure that their organization is made up of productive and trustworthy members. What steps can organizations take to assess the quality of their employees? Specifically, we can consider the use of a variety of employee tests, including polygraph testing, integrity testing, and drug testing.

3. *Monitoring of employee work and conversations by electronic means.* Technology affords employers the opportunity to maintain tight control over assessments of worker productivity. How might this assessment address or violate expectations of privacy in the workplace?

There are other issues that involve protection or invasion of privacy, but the three listed here account for the majority of today's concerns. Therefore, they merit separate consideration.

Collection and Use of Employee Information by Employers

What is personal information? According to the Privacy Commissioner of Canada, personal information includes any factual or subjective information about an individual, including such information as age, name, ID numbers, income, ethnic origin, or blood type; opinions, evaluations, comments, social status, or disciplinary actions; and employee files, credit records, loan records, and medical records.[10] Controlling a person's personal information means controlling the collection, use, and disclosure of that information.

The Personal Information Protection and Electronic Documents ACT (PIPEDA) is directly aimed at controlling employers' behaviour with regard to the collection, use, and disclosure of personal information. Indeed the central purpose of the PIPEDA is:

> to provide Canadians with a right of privacy with respect to their personal information that is collected, used or disclosed by an organization in the private sector in an era in which technology increasingly facilitates the collection and free flow of information.[11]

The PIPEDA establishes the ground rules regarding the manner in which private sector organizations can collect, use, or disclose personal information in the course of their commercial activities. The act aims to balance the individual's right to privacy with the need of organizations to collect, use, or disclose personal information for legitimate business purposes.[12]

Among the fundamental requirements of the PIPEDA are the following:

- Companies that wish to collect, use, or disclose personal information about individuals must obtain their consent, except in a few specific and limited circumstances.
- Companies can use or disclose people's personal information only for the purpose for which they gave consent.
- Even with consent, companies must limit collection, use, and disclosure of personal information to purposes that a reasonable person would consider appropriate under the circumstances.
- Individuals have a right to access the personal information that their company holds about them, and to correct any inaccuracies.
- Roles of the Privacy Commissioner of Canada include ensuring that businesses conform to the law and upholding the rights of individuals.[13]

Arguably, the most significant legal principle with regard to information collection and privacy law is the notion of consent. According to the PIPEDA, companies are required to obtain informed, prior consent before collecting or disseminating personal information. Before providing any personal information, the individual must be made fully aware of such issues as:

- the fact that the company is seeking personal information
- the reason or purpose behind the data collection
- the recipients of the personal information
- the nature of the privacy controls surrounding the data collection

The PIPEDA is based on the Canadian Standards Association's Model Code for the Protection of Personal Information. The code lists ten principles for business to follow in order to ensure conformity with fair information practices. These principles are summarized in Figure 16–1.

Given the relatively new demands of the PIPEDA, many businesses are currently grappling with the development of internal policies for privacy protection. In their report on the recent changes to privacy law in Canada, the law firm of Osler, Hoskin & Harcourt LLP recently outlined recommended steps for companies to develop a privacy policy for employee and customer protection that ensures conformance with the

---

FIGURE 16–1

Ten Principles of Fair Information Practices

The Canadian Standards Association's Model Code for the Protection of Personal Information includes the following principles of fair information practices for business.

1. **Accountability:** An organization is responsible for personal information under its control and shall designate an individual or individuals who are accountable for the organization's compliance with the following principles.

2. **Identifying Purposes:** The purposes for which personal information is collected shall be identified by the organization at or before the time the information is collected.

3. **Consent:** The knowledge and consent of the individual are required for the collection, use, or disclosure of personal information, except when inappropriate.

4. **Limiting Collection:** The collection of personal information shall be limited to that which is necessary for the purposes identified by the organization. Information shall be collected by fair and lawful means.

5. **Limiting Use, Disclosure, and Retention:** Personal information shall not be used or disclosed for purposes other than those for which it was collected, except with the consent of the individual or as required by the law. Personal information shall be retained only as long as necessary for fulfillment of those purposes.

6. **Accuracy:** Personal information shall be as accurate, complete, and up-to-date as is necessary for the purposes for which it is to be used.

7. **Safeguards:** Personal information shall be protected by security safeguards appropriate to the sensitivity of the information.

8. **Openness:** An organization shall make readily available to individuals specific information about its policies and practices relating to the management of personal information.

9. **Individual Access:** Upon request, an individual shall be informed of the existence, use, and disclosure of his or her personal information and shall be given access to that information. An individual shall be able to challenge the accuracy and completeness of the information and have it amended as appropriate.

10. **Challenging Compliance:** An individual shall be able to address a challenge concerning compliance with the above principles to the designated individual or individuals for the organization's compliance.

Source: Department of Justice Canada, http://canada.justice.gc.ca/en/news/nr/1998/attback2.html.

expectations of the PIPEDA. The following steps were suggested as part of the development of such a system:[14]

1. *Appoint a compliance team.* Designate a team of individuals who will be responsible for ensuring compliance. Members should include marketing, human resources, and legal representatives.
2. *Assess existing privacy policies.* Ensure existing policies are in compliance with PIPEDA.
3. *Adopt a privacy code or policy.* Your privacy code/policy becomes your organization's public statement about its privacy standards and it will help in developing a privacy compliance plan.
4. *Conduct a personal information practices audit.* Identify what personal information is collected about employees and customers, how it is used, how long it's kept, and to whom it's disclosed.
5. *Assess purposes for use and disclosure.* Ensure personal information is collected for "reasonable use"—PIPEDA requires that organizations use personal information only for purposes that "a reasonable person" would consider appropriate in the circumstances.
6. *Assess existing information on file.* Individuals have the right to access their personal information, and so it must be kept accurate.
7. *Identify when, where, and what kinds of consents are required.* This task involves identifying all areas where personal information is collected about either customers or employees and where it is used. Instruments for obtaining consent must be designed. Keep in mind the sensitivity of the personal information being collected and the form of consent required (e.g., express consent, opt-out, or implied consent).
8. *Assess collateral collection and uses of personal information.* If your organization desires to collect information on such items as age or telephone number for marketing purposes or wishes to verify customers' identities by checking addresses or birthdates, you are required to ensure these uses are reasonable and strictly necessary to achieve the purpose. You also need to make consent for these uses optional.
9. *Implement organizational protocols.* Develop and communicate policies and procedures to oversee continued accountability, requirements, and approvals for all information collection, use or disclosure of information, security of customer and employee data, and other factors.
10. *Plan for regular compliance audits.* To maintain adequate compliance with policies, it is necessary to assess how your organization is conforming on a regular basis.

The overriding principle that should guide corporate decision making in regard to the collection and use of employee information is that companies should only collect that information from employees that is absolutely necessary and only use it in ways that are appropriate. Companies should be careful not to misuse this information by employing it for purposes for which it was not intended. Another important principle is that the employer should understand that information collected from employees is not a commodity to be exchanged, sold, or released in the marketplace.[15] Thus, the release of information to a landlord, credit grantor, or any other third party without the employee's consent may be seen as an invasion of privacy.[16] A final important principle pertains to employees' access to information about themselves in company personnel files or other record-keeping systems. Employees should have some way of knowing what information is being stored about them, and they should have the opportunity to correct or amend inaccurate information.[17]

Testing of Employees

Employers can use a myriad of tests to assess the nature of their work force. Among the most controversial forms of employee testing are integrity testing and drug testing.

Ethics In Practice

Does Honesty Pay?

My last two years of high school were spent working part-time at a country club as a cart boy. One day I was told that $10 000 had been stolen from the golf shop the previous day and that all the employees would be subject to intense scrutiny and interviews. Being one of the few employees with keys to the shop and knowledge of the alarm code, I felt I would be a natural target for scrutiny.

I decided to prove my innocence by telling the truth. During the interview, after answering a few simple questions, I expected to be asked one question about the missing money. Instead, I was asked if I had ever stolen anything in my life, if I had ever done drugs on the job, and if I had stolen anything from the country club. I admitted that I had taken soft drinks from the beverage cart and discarded golf balls off the used cart—actions that many people do not consider stealing.

As a result, I was called into the Head Pro's office and rebuked for taking club property—I nearly lost my job. Should I have lied? It turns out the thief was never caught.

1. What are the ethical issues in this situation?

2. Did the club have the right to pose questions that were unrelated to the issue at hand?

3. What would you have done if you were in this position? Why?

Contributed by Shaun M. Bank

Ethics In Practice

Give Me What I Want or I'll Tell the President!

Place yourself in the role of a personnel director for a bank. It is company policy that neither personnel files nor copies of files are to leave the personnel office. The director of accounting and computer services is due to give his employees their yearly employee evaluations and has sent a memo to your secretary requesting copies of his employees' evaluations from the previous year. Your secretary shows you the memo. You are upset that the director would send such a memo to your secretary, because he should be aware of the policy concerning employee files.

So, you decide to call the director and inform him that he is welcome to read the evaluations of his employees from the previous year in the personnel office. He tells you that he does not have the time to come to personnel and read the files and that he will speak to the president of the bank about this issue. The working relationship between you and the director has been addressed by the president before, and she has informed the two of you that you need to be able to work out problems such as this between yourselves.

The dilemma is whether you should go against company policy in an effort to avoid another lecture from the president, and let the director take the copies of the evaluations to his office, or adhere to the bank's policy on protection of employee privacy.

1. What are the main ethical dilemmas in this situation?

2. Should you report the director's threat to step over you to the president?

3. What would you do in this situation?

Contributed by Leah Herrin

Integrity Testing   As criticism grew concerning the use of lie detectors, many companies anticipated an eventual elimination of lie detector use and began experimenting with paper-and-pencil **integrity tests** (also known as *honesty tests* or *personality tests*). David Nye dubbed this type of test the "son of the polygraph."[18] There is a certain irony in this title, because integrity tests are already being subjected to the same kinds of criticisms that led to severe restriction of lie detector testing.

The findings of a study included in a report entitled *Truth and Honesty Testing* suggested that it is not possible to determine the validity of integrity tests in accurately predicting dishonesty. However, the report[19] did suggest four reasons why employers were using integrity tests:

1. To stem employee theft
2. To avoid "negligent hiring" suits
3. To screen employees cost-effectively
4. To replace polygraphs

An integrity test typically poses 80 to 90 statements with which the employee or applicant is asked to agree or disagree. Some test questions are framed as yes-or-no and multiple-choice options. Examples include, "Would you tell your boss if you knew of another employee stealing from the company?" and "What percent of employee thieves are never caught?" and "What is the dollar value of cash or merchandise you have stolen from past employers?"[20]

Integrity tests are inexpensive, quick to administer, and easy to grade. This compares favourably with lie detector tests, which are costly to administer. Perhaps integrity tests have attracted less attention than polygraphs because they seem less intrusive or intimidating than lie detector tests, in which the examinee is hooked up to wires and sensors. The integrity test comes across more as a red-tape item or a job application to be filled out than as an interrogation.[21]

In a recent survey, 22 percent of the organizations indicated that they had used personality tests (i.e., integrity tests) in the past year.[22] Faced with the elimination of the polygraph, companies wanted to find a substitute, and integrity tests seemed to be a convenient alternative. Critics of integrity tests claim they are intrusive and invade privacy by the nature of their inquiries. Critics also say that they are unreliable and that employers use them as the sole measure of the fitness of an applicant. Even when these tests are properly administered, opponents charge that employers end up rejecting many honest applicants in their efforts to screen out the dishonest ones. Management and testing companies claim the tests are very useful in weeding out potentially dishonest applicants. They claim that each question asked has a specific purpose.

Psychologists disagree widely on the validity and effectiveness of integrity tests. The American Psychological Association issued a report accepting the concept of integrity testing as superior to most other pre-employment tests but noting that test publishers' accountability and documentation needed serious improvement.[23] The test publishers themselves have done much of the research. The future of integrity tests is uncertain, but it is anticipated that they will face the same kinds of legal and ethical hurdles that affected polygraph and drug tests.[24]

Drug Testing   "Drug testing" is an umbrella term intended to embrace drug and alcohol testing and employer testing for any suspected substance abuse. The issue of drug testing in the workplace has many of the same characteristics as the lie detector and integrity test issues. Companies say they need to do such testing to protect themselves and the public, but opponents claim that drug tests are not accurate and invade the employee's privacy.

As opposed to the U.S., Canadian businesses have been much more reluctant to conduct testing of workers or job applicants for drug abuse.[25] Reported reasons for the reluctance of business to conduct drug testing[26] include the following:

- Moral issue/privacy
- Inaccuracy of tests
- Negative impact on employee morale
- Tests show use, not abuse
- High cost
- Management, employee, and union opposition

In Canada, much of the opposition to drug testing has gained strong legal support. The blanket drug testing of employees, according to Canadian law, would constitute an unwarranted invasion of a person's private life. In addition, opposition to drug testing has come from human rights commissions. Traditionally, many human rights commissions have viewed drug and alcohol problems as dependencies. Consequently, attempts to test for such dependencies may be deemed to be a form of discrimination. In 2002, the Canadian Human Rights Commission implemented a new policy banning all drug testing on employees, though random alcohol testing is still allowed. Commenting on the ban, Catherine Barrett, the spokesperson for the commission, stated the following intended impact on Canadian employees:

> *Hopefully it gives them an increased awareness of what their rights are. Employers are not supposed to administer random drug tests of their staff whether they are in safety or non-safety-sensitive positions. Many employees are not aware of that.*[27]

It is important to note that while Canadian employers have largely avoided the use of such tests, the problem of drug abuse does appear to be adversely affecting the Canadian workplace. The consequences of employee drug abuse have been estimated to cost Canadian employers approximately $4.1 billion a year for alcohol, $6.8 billion for tobacco, and $823.1 million for illicit drugs—for a total of $11.8 billion in productivity losses.[28] According to research, employees that are substance abusers create higher financial burdens for the employer in such areas as sick leave, workers' compensation claims, accidents on the job, and negligence in their work.[29]

Added to the productivity issue is a legal issue. An employer may find itself in trouble with other employees if it fails to maintain a workplace that is free of such abuse. That is, an employer's failure to maintain a safe and drug-free workplace can result in liability claims if any injuries arise due to the negligence of an employee.[30]

Consequently, while we can applaud Canadian business for not embracing a widespread, blanket-approach to drug testing, we cannot help but wonder how the issue of substance abuse in the workplace should be treated. The issue of employee drug abuse is a real one, and it is an issue that many Canadian businesses will likely need to grapple with in the future. Because of these ramifications, some Canadian companies, including Imperial Oil Ltd. and the Toronto Dominion Bank, have been fighting in court for the right to test freely.[31]

Arguments for Drug Testing. Proponents of drug testing argue that the costs of drug abuse on the job are staggering. The consequences range from accidents and injuries to theft, bad decisions, and ruined lives. The greatest concern is in industries where mistakes can cost lives—for example, the railroad, airline, aerospace, nuclear power, and hazardous equipment and chemicals industries. Edwin Weihenmayer, vice president at Kidder, Peabody, a New York–based investment banking firm, believes that drug testing is essential in his industry, "where the financial security of billions of dollars is entrusted to us by clients."[32] Thus, the primary ethical argument for employers conducting drug tests is the responsibility they have to their own employees and to the general public to provide safe workplaces, secure asset protection, and safe places in which to transact business.

Arguments Against Drug Testing. Opponents of drug testing see it as both a due-process issue and an invasion-of-privacy issue. The due-process issue relates to the questionable accuracy of drug tests. Although one test manufacturer claims a 95 percent accuracy rate, some doctors disagree. For example, some medical experts have indicated that "false positives can range up to 25 percent or higher. The test is essentially worthless."[33] In addition, some legal experts argue that, even if the tests were foolproof, they would still be an invasion of employee privacy. They claim that tests represent an unconstitutional attempt on the part of companies to control employees' behaviour at home, because the tests can yield positive results days and even weeks after at-home drug use.[34]

Many legitimate questions arise in the drug-testing issue. Do employers have a right to know if their employees use drugs? Are employees performing on the job satisfactorily? Obviously, some delicate balance is needed, because employers and employees alike have legitimate interests that must be protected. This issue is a fairly new one for business, but it is apparent that it will not go away. Therefore, if companies are going to engage in some form of drug testing, they should think carefully about developing policies that not only will achieve their intended goals but also will be fair to the employees and minimize invasions of privacy. Such a balance will not be easy to achieve but must be sought. To do otherwise will guarantee decreased employee morale, more and more lawsuits, and new government regulations.

Guidelines for Drug Testing. If management perceives the need to conduct a drug-testing program to protect other stakeholders, it should carefully design and structure the program so that it will be minimally intrusive of employees' privacy rights. The following guidelines[35] may be helpful:

- Management should not discipline or fire someone for refusing to take a drug test because the results of such tests are inconclusive.
- Drug tests should typically be used only when there is legitimate suspicion of abuse by an employee or work group.
- The focus of testing should be on-the-job performance rather than off-the-job conduct.
- Employees should be informed of methods used and results obtained and given the chance to rebut the test findings.
- If an employee's status is going to be affected by the outcome of a drug test, a confirmatory test should be conducted.
- All tests should be conducted in such a way that the dignity and privacy of the employee are respected and honoured.

Obviously, there are exceptions to these guidelines, and there are other guidelines that might be used. The major point is that management needs to think through its policies and their consequences very carefully when designing and conducting drug-testing programs.

The ethics of employee testing will continue to be debated. Should employees be subject to any type of tests of their ability, character, or health in employment contexts?

Critics such Julien Delisle, former executive director of the office of the Privacy Commissioner of Canada, made the following blanket condemnations of employee tests:

> *Tests may soon be available to identify people with an increased genetic risk of high blood pressure, heart disease, manic-depressive illness or schizophrenia. I stress that most of these tests will indicate only an increased risk, not a certainty of developing the condition. Other related medical tests are being developed to identify very early signs of cancer. How many employers will want to hire as a senior executive someone with even a slightly increased genetic risk of schizophrenia, or Alzheimer's? How many employers will want to hire someone with a genetically heightened sensitivity to harm from workplace chemicals? Why hire someone who may have an increased genetic risk—if one exists—for drug dependency or alcoholism? How many people would want to hire a person whose blood tests show early signs of cancer? Why not simply hire a genetically superior worker and leave the rest to the fate that Darwin predicted for them—languishing in the background while only the fittest survive and prosper?*[36]

Monitoring Employees on the Job

In the old days, supervisors monitored employees' work activities by peeking over their shoulders and judging how things were going. Next came cameras and listening devices whereby management could keep track of what was going on from remote locations. With the advent of computers, workers and civil liberties activists are concerned about the use of technology to gather information about workers on the job.[37] These concerns are well founded. In a recent survey, the American Management Association (AMA) found that 82 percent of mid- to large-sized firms participate in some type of **employee monitoring**. In some cases, the method is passive, such as video cameras in a lobby. However the vast majority, 78 percent, used more active means of monitoring their workers, such as recording their phone calls or voice mail, reading their computer files, or videotaping them.[38] Clearly, employer monitoring of employees has become the norm in businesses today. The consequence is that millions of workers are labouring under the relentless gaze of electronic supervision.

What Can Be Monitored?   According to the AMA survey, 63 percent of companies monitor their employees' Internet connections; 47 percent store and then review their employees' e-mail. Nearly one in four firms use keyword searches to review their employees' e-mail. The most commonly used search was for words with explicit sexual content or scatological language (70.2 percent). Firms also search the e-mail using names of current employees (18.3 percent), names of clients (16.3 percent), names of vendors and suppliers (14.4 percent), and names of former employees (13.5 percent). Of the firms surveyed, 43 percent monitor telephone numbers called and time spent on the phone; 38 percent use video surveillance. According to Eric Rolfe Greenberg, director of management studies for the AMA, "It's not just a matter of corporate curiosity, but very real worries about productivity and liability that push these policies."[39]

In addition to monitoring those at computer terminals, there is increasing surveillance by management of employees in other work settings. Monitoring of telephone conversations is a significant arena for electronic eavesdropping. Workers in telecommunications, mail-order houses, airline reservations, and brokerage firms are especially hard hit. Not only do supervisors frequently listen in on their conversations, but computers also gather and analyze data about their work habits.

Effects of Being Monitored Invasion of privacy is one major consequence of employee monitoring. Another is unfair treatment. Employees working under such systems complain about stress and tension resulting from their being expected and pressured to be more productive now that their efforts can be measured. The pressure of being constantly monitored is also producing low morale and a sense of job insecurity in many places. Employees have good reason to be concerned. According to the AMA survey, 27 percent of the firms fired employees who misused office e-mail or Internet connections; 65 percent administered some sort of punishment for those offences.[40]

While employers that use electronic surveillance do run the risk of being sued for invasion of privacy, the courts have held that to win damages, the employee must prove that the reasonable expectation of privacy outweighed the organization's reason for surveillance.[41] Employers are allowed to monitor employees via electronic surveillance provided they do so for compelling business reasons and provided that the employees have been told that they will be monitored.[42] For example, some businesses have implemented electronic surveillance in response to concerns about theft, which has been estimated to cost Canadian retailers about $2 million a day and which represents about one-third of all losses.[43]

In response to alleged employee crimes, companies like General Electric installed tiny fish-eye lenses behind pinholes in walls and ceilings to observe suspected employees. Similarly, DuPont has used long-distance cameras to monitor its loading docks. With the use of legally admissible video evidence, one company terminated an employee after videotaping him sleeping on the job.[44]

One of the most common means of electronic surveillance has traditionally been telephone surveillance. This is often conducted to assess the competence of customer service employees. Of course, with the advent of the "wired workplace," other forms of surveillance have become equally popular across many types of jobs, including monitoring the use of company computers, monitoring Internet activity, and monitoring e-mail usage. While employees might assume that they are working in privacy, the reality may in fact be quite different.

Currently, there is little legislation governing e-mail or voice mail monitoring, and laws have traditionally permitted employers to monitor employee materials created, received, or sent for business-related reasons.[45] This emphasizes an urgent need for employers to develop and communicate clear policies and guidelines regarding the proper usage of the Internet, e-mail, and voice mail. Employers should also communicate to employees the conditions under which they can be monitored.[46] At present, only about 5 percent of Canadian companies have established such policies, compared with about 40 percent of U.S. firms.[47]

Policy Guidelines on the Issue of Privacy

As we have discussed various privacy issues, we have indicated steps that management might consider taking in an attempt to be responsive to employee stakeholders. As a final recommendation, we set forth four policy guidelines that touch on several of the issues we have discussed. Robert Goldstein and Richard Nolan[48] assert that organizations should do the following:

1. *Prepare a "**privacy impact statement.**"* This would require the firm to analyze the potential privacy implications to which all systems (especially computerized ones) should be subjected.
2. *Construct a comprehensive privacy plan.* The purpose of such planning would be to ensure that the necessary privacy controls are integrated into the design of a system at the very beginning.
3. *Train employees who handle personal information.* Be sure they are aware of the importance of protecting privacy and the specific procedures and policies to be followed.
4. *Make privacy a part of social responsibility programs.* Companies need to acknowledge that they have an internal responsibility to their employees and not fail to consider this when designing and implementing corporate social efforts.

Business's concern for protection of the privacy of its employees, customers, and other stakeholders is a growing business. It is not surprising, therefore, that a new form of corporate executive has come on the horizon. **Chief privacy officers (CPOs)** are high-ranking executives responsible for monitoring and protecting the private information held by firms. While currently there are few CPOs working in Canadian and U.S. corporations, the number is expected to grow as concerns for privacy continue to be raised.[49]

Workplace Health and Safety

There is little doubt that workplace health and safety ranks as a major concern for employee stakeholders and their employers. It has been estimated that annually, approximately 375 000 workers are injured on the job, and nearly 1000 Canadian workers die.[50] In addition, one in seven young workers is injured on the job. After auto accidents, the leading causes of death among young people are machine injuries and electrocutions.[51] Clearly, employers have a legal and moral obligation to ensure the safety and health of their employees.

An **occupational injury** is defined as any cut, fracture, sprain, or amputation resulting from a workplace accident. The worker's involvement in the accident can be direct, or indirect, as is the case of a worker injured as a result of being in the proximity of an accident. An **occupational illness** is defined as any condition or disorder (other than one resulting from an occupational injury) caused by the work environment. The scope of an occupational illness can vary from acute to chronic; it can result from inhaling, absorbing, ingesting, or directly contacting an illness-causing agent.

Beyond the countless injuries and illnesses occurring across the corporate world, the need for greater attention to workplace health and safety is blatantly illustrated in the aftermath of some very memorable workplace disasters. In addition, several illustrations show the extent to which management can be held accountable for workplace safety. The issue of management liability is perhaps most strikingly illustrated in a U.S.-based lawsuit that occurred in the 1980s, and which became a landmark case on job safety.

In Elk Grove Village, Illinois, Film Recovery Systems operated out of a single plant that extracted silver from used hospital X-ray and photographic film. To extract the silver, the employees first had to dump the film into open vats of sodium cyanide and then transfer the leached remnants to another tank. On February 10, 1983, employee Stefan Golab staggered outside and collapsed, unconscious. Efforts to revive him failed, and he was soon pronounced dead from what the local medical examiner labelled "acute cyanide toxicity."[52]

An intensive investigation by lawyers in Cook County, Illinois, revealed a long list of incriminating details: (1) Film Recovery workers seldom wore even the most rudimentary safety equipment, (2) workers were labouring in what amounted to an industrial gas chamber, and (3) company executives played down the dangers of cyanide poisoning and removed labelling that identified it as poisonous. The prosecutors took action under an Illinois homicide statute that targets anyone who knowingly commits acts that "create a strong probability of death or serious bodily harm." Three executives at Film Recovery Systems—the president, the plant manager, and the foreman—were convicted of the murder of Stefan Golab and sentenced to 25 years in prison. Their convictions marked the first time in U.S. history that managers had been convicted of homicide in a corporate matter such as an industrial accident.[53] The Film Recovery Systems case marked a new era in managerial responsibility for job safety. A variety of other prosecutions of managers have followed the Film Recovery Systems case. What this clearly signals is not only that employees have a moral right to a safe working environment but also that managers face prosecution if they do not ensure that employees are protected.

Another event was the dramatic and catastrophic poisonous gas leak at the Union Carbide plant in Bhopal, India, in 1984. The death toll topped 2000, and tens of thousands more were injured. People around the globe were startled and shocked at what the results of one major industrial accident could be. Lawsuits sought damages that quickly exceeded the net worth of the company.[54] In 1991, India's Supreme Court upheld a US$470 million settlement that Union Carbide had already paid, and it lifted the immunity from criminal prosecution that it had granted the company in 1989. The name "Union Carbide" became inextricably linked with the Bhopal disaster. In 2001, Union Carbide became a wholly owned subsidiary of Dow Chemical.

Both cases, however tragic, illustrate the level of accountability to which organizations can be held for workplace safety. Ironically, according to some observers, this level of accountability has been lacking in the Canadian legal system. Consider the case of the Westray mine disaster in Nova Scotia.

The Westray mine disaster occurred in 1992. The mine suffered an underground explosion in which 26 miners were killed. This tragedy occurred despite repeated safety warnings to the mine's owners and managers. Following the disaster, a public inquiry found evidence of a number of managerial defects in the operation of the mine and in the application of basic safety measures. While the families of the victims fought a legal battle for years, charges against the corporate leaders were dropped in 1998. According to many observers, the case appeared to show clear elements of criminal negligence and yet neither the corporation nor any of its managerial officers were ever found guilty of any crime. One such observer, Chantal Plamandon, made the following indictment of the Canadian legal system: "Canada's regime of corporate criminal liability bears an important share of the blame with regard to the difficulty the Crown faced in prosecuting both the corporation and its officers."[55]

Of course, not all hazards can be anticipated. The 2001 attack on the World Trade Center in New York was a shock and surprise to the world. Shortly after the tragedy occurred, many were wondering what the impact would be on Morgan Stanley, one of the world's biggest brokerages and investment firms. The company was the largest tenant in the World Trade Center, with about 3700 employees in two of the towers. Amazingly, fewer than ten of their employees were among the missing, and only about 50 reported being injured. Company officials credit the evacuation procedures that Morgan Stanley developed after the 1993 bombing of the World Trade Center with saving so many of their employees' lives. The security staff used megaphones to keep people moving despite announcements over the building's public address system that instructed people to return to work. They moved their employees down the smoke-filled stairs (some more than 70 flights) and away from the twin towers. The earlier 1993 incident had alerted them to their vulnerability, and they took the steps necessary to protect the health and safety of as many of their employees as possible.[56]

The Role of Government

The Canadian Centre for Occupational Health and Safety summarizes the government's role in workplace health and safety as follows:[57]

- Enforcing occupational health and safety legislation
- Conducting workplace inspections
- Disseminating health and safety information
- Promoting training, education, and research in the area of health and safety
- Resolving workplace disputes regarding occupational health and safety

The federal, provincial, and territorial governments regulate occupational health and safety. While efforts have been made to harmonize differences, regulations and standards vary from jurisdiction to jurisdiction. It is important that employers and employees understand their legal obligations regarding the protection of workplace health and safety. Figure 16–2 outlines the variety of bodies and regulations based on jurisdiction.

Established in 1978, the Canadian Centre for Occupational Health and Safety (CCOHS) is a federal department corporation based in Hamilton, Ontario, which is aimed at enhancing workplace health and safety through supporting efforts to eliminate work-related illnesses and injuries. CCOHS is governed by a council representing three central stakeholder groups: government (federal, provincial, and territorial), employers, and workers.

CCOHS provides Canadians with information and advice that promotes safe and healthy working environments. Globally, CCOHS collaborates with agencies and organizations from around the world to generate resources and programs, as well as expand the breadth of usage of occupational health and safety information to many different societies. As presented on its Web site, CCOHS defines its missions as follows:

> *It is our mission to be the Canadian Centre of Excellence for work-related injury and illness prevention initiatives and occupational health and safety information,*
>
> *To promote health and safety in the workplace in Canada to:*
> - *Facilitate*
>   - *Consultation and cooperation among federal, provincial and territorial jurisdictions*
>   - *Participation by labour and management*
> - *Assist in the development and maintenance of policies and programs*
> - *Serve as a national centre for information relating to occupational health and safety.*[58]

FIGURE 16-2

Occupational Health and Safety in Canada

Jurisdiction	Legislation	Enforcement
Canada	Canada Labour Code, Regulations	Labour Canada
Alberta	Occupational Health and Safety Act	Department of Labour
British Columbia	Regulations under Workers' Compensation Act	Workers' Compensation Board
Manitoba	Workplace Safety and Health Act	Department of Environment and Workplace Health and Safety
New Brunswick	Occupational Health and Safety	Occupational Health and Safety Commission
Newfoundland	Occupational Health and Safety Act	Department of Labour
Nova Scotia	Occupational Health and Safety Act	Department of Labour
Ontario	Workplace Safety and Insurance Act	Ministry of Labour
Prince Edward Island	Occupational Health and Safety Act	Department of Fisheries and Labour
Quebec	Act Respecting Occupational Health and Safety	Commission de la Santé et de la Sécurité du Travail
Saskatchewan	Occupational Health and Safety Act	Department of Labour
Northwest Territories	Safety Act	Commissioner NWT
Yukon	Occupational Health and Safety Act	Commissioner of the Yukon Territories; administered by the Workers' Compensation Board
Nunavut	Safety Act	For information only; not an official act

Source: Monica Belcourt, George W. Bohlander, Scott A. Snell, and Arthur W. Sherman, *Managing Human Resources*, Fourth Canadian Edition (Toronto: Nelson Canada, 2004). Copyright © 2004 Thomson Nelson. Reprinted with permission of Nelson, a division of Thomson Learning: www.thomsonrights.com. Fax 1-800-730-2215.

If anything positive arose from the Westray mine disaster, it was increased pressure on the Canadian government to legislate stricter laws of safety accountability. Consequently, in 2003, the Minister of Justice introduced Bill C-45, an act to amend the Criminal Code. This law imposes criminal liability on corporations and organizations that fail to take reasonable measures to protect employee and public safety. Specifically, under this law, an organization can be held criminally liable:

- as a consequence of actions by senior officers who oversee day-to-day operations but who may not be directors or executives
- when officers with executive or operational authority intentionally commit, or direct employees to commit, crimes in order to benefit the organization
- when officers with executive or operational authority are aware of offences committed by other employees but do not take action to stop them
- when the actions of those with authority and other employees show a lack of care that constitutes criminal negligence

The legislation also imposes a legal obligation on all those who direct work, including employers, to take reasonable measures to protect employee and public safety. Negligence toward this duty that causes death or bodily harm would result in a charge of criminal negligence.[59] Essentially, the law is intended to hold organizations criminally liable for actions by "senior" members even if they aren't directors or executives.

The law also permits a court to place a company on "probation" and effectively dictate that certain policies or procedures be established.

Patrick Healy, a professor of criminal law at Montreal's McGill University, said Bill C-45 "brings into the criminal law a much wider basis on which to prosecute corporations for failure to take appropriate measures to ensure the safety of their employees and others who work for them." Bill Trudell of the Canadian Council of Criminal Defence Lawyers commented that the new law "is changing the whole world of corporate criminal liability as we know it…. Organizations are going to have to put in all kinds of layers of due diligence to be able to protect themselves.[60]

The Role of the Employer

The Canadian Centre for Occupational Health and Safety summarizes the employer's role in workplace health and safety as follows:[61]

- Establishing a joint health and safety committee.
- Taking appropriate precautions to ensure the workplace is safe.
- Training employees to deal with potential hazards and emergencies; as well as how to use, handle, store, and dispose of hazardous substances.
- Supplying personal protective equipment and training in the use of this equipment.
- Reporting all critical injuries to the proper government department.
- Appointing a supervisor for setting standards and ensuring safe working conditions are observed.

As the list illustrates, simple compliance with the regulations is not enough. Employers must engage in such activities as communicating to their employees the health and safety requirements. In addition, employers must maintain records, document an annual summary of work-related injuries and illnesses, and ensure that supervisors are properly trained to deal with work hazards. Employers are required to offer safety training and enforce employee compliance with safety rules.

Occupational health and safety acts demand that supervisors inform employees of potential workplace hazards; enforce the appropriate use of safety equipment, devices, or clothing; offer written guidance where applicable; and ensure all reasonable precautions are taken to protect the safety of workers. Most jurisdictions require that health and safety committees be established, with both union and management representation, in order to build a safe and healthy workplace. Depending on its size, the organization may even require the presence of a health and safety officer.

Regardless of the jurisdiction, employers must report any work-related injuries or illnesses to the Workers' Compensation Board. Should any cases arise, employers are increasingly being required to prove due diligence in their treatment of safety issues. Proving due diligence would require proof that the company maintained a comprehensive occupational health and safety management system; provided competent supervision, training, and instruction; and took every reasonable precaution to safeguard the well-being of its employees.

Added to these basic responsibilities is the obligation to compensate employees for illnesses or injuries that arise from sources in the workplace. Where employers are held responsible for violating occupational health and safety regulations, they can face a variety of penalties depending on the jurisdiction. For example, many health and safety acts have established fines of up to $500 000, and offenders can face imprisonment. Following an accident that resulted in an employee's death, General Motors was fined $375 000 for failing to ensure that a machine was properly maintained.[62]

Based on the policy of workers' compensation, employees who are injured at work can receive benefits in the form of a cash payout (if the disability is permanent) or wage loss payments (if the worker can no longer earn the same amount of money). Other compensation may include unlimited medical support and vocational rehabilitation (including physical, social, and psychological services). Often the central aim is to assist the employee in resuming his or her job as soon as possible. Sun Life of Canada has encouraged employers to create programs that help employees return to work by offering premium credits to employers that allow injured workers to change jobs in order to return to work. Canadian Pacific Railway and Weyerhaeuser Canada Ltd. are among the organizations attempting to assist injured employees by offering supportive return-to-work programs.[63]

The Role and Rights of Employees

Just as employers are required to abide by the relevant regulations, it is also expected that employees will comply with the regulations governing workplace health and safety. The Canadian Centre for Occupational Health and Safety summarizes the employee's responsibilities in workplace health and safety as follows:[64]

- Duty to work in compliance with occupational health and safety acts and regulations
- Duty to use personal protective equipment and clothing as directed by the employer
- Duty to report workplace hazards and dangers, including any unsafe conditions or defective equipment
- Duty to work in a manner as required by the employer and using the prescribed safety equipment

The Occupational Health and Safety Act outlines three fundamental rights of all employees to a healthy and safe workplace:[65]

- The right to refuse unsafe or hazardous work, without fear of reprisal
- The right to participate in the workplace health and safety activities through a Joint Health and Safety Committee (JHSC) or as a worker health and safety representative
- The right to know, or the right to be informed about, workplace safety and health conditions, including any actual and potential dangers in the workplace

Right to Refuse   The right to refuse hazardous work may not be strictly related to potential physical harm. For example, recently such accidents or injuries have come to include industrial diseases and stress. An industrial disease is a disease or illness that is the consequence of exposure to a substance derived from a particular process, trade, or occupation in industry. Stress-related illnesses have typically been classified into three categories: physical injuries leading to mental disabilities (e.g., depression following an injury); mental stress resulting in a physical disability (e.g., emotional stress leading to migraines); and mental stress resulting in a mental condition (e.g., work-related anxiety causing depression).

The need for organizations to acknowledge stress-related illnesses is strikingly illustrated in a recent case involving an employee with the Bank of Montreal. Susanne Zorn-Smith, who suffered a breakdown after working days, nights, and weekends for the Bank of Montreal, was awarded $15 000 for mental suffering by the Ontario

Superior Court. In the ruling, the judge noted that the bank was aware of Zorn-Smith's long hours, and "This callous disregard for the health of an employee was flagrant and outrageous."

Zorn-Smith had started work for the Bank of Montreal on a part-time basis when she was 15 years old. Eventually, she climbed the ranks, working at numerous branches around Ontario. Prior to the breakdown, she was working as the financial services manager at a branch in Smiths Falls, earning about $43 000 annually. Because the branch was busy and understaffed, Zorn-Smith often worked long hours. Following her daily work hours, she would return to work again in the evenings once her children were in bed, and continued to work from 9 P.M. to midnight or 1 A.M., two or three nights a week. Occasionally, she would visit the office on Sunday night to prepare for the coming workweek. In addition, the bank encouraged Zorn-Smith to complete, on her own time, several courses to maintain her skills, knowledge, and qualifications.

As a consequence of the increasing amount of work and stress, her marriage suffered. In 2000, she took a disability leave and returned to a lesser position. However, she was soon given additional work and increased responsibilities. According to the court, on February 20, 2001, Zorn-Smith essentially stopped functioning as a result of work stresses. She informed a company nurse that she had not slept more than two or three hours nightly for several months. On June 28, the company doctor deemed her fit to resume part-time work. After refusing to return to work at that time, she was fired and was offered no severance pay. The judge's ruling also required the Bank of Montreal to pay Zorn-Smith 16-months' severance in addition to the damages for mental suffering.[66]

Right to Know Prompted by the Union Carbide tragedy in Bhopal and other industrial accidents, workers have demanded to know more about the thousands of chemicals and hazardous substances they are being exposed to in the workplace. Experts argue that employers have a duty to provide employees with information on the hazards of workplace chemicals and to make sure that workers understand what the information means in practical terms.

In Canada, recent changes to the Canadian Occupational Health and Safety legislation provide workers' with the "right to know" about the hazards they may encounter on the job. The central right-to-know law is called the **Workplace Hazardous Materials Information System (WHMIS)**, which is Canada's hazard communication standard. WHMIS is implemented through federal, provincial, and territorial legislation.

WHMIS is a nationwide system that provides a standardized classification system for the control, safe handling, storage, and disposal procedures of hazardous materials in the workplace. According to WHMIS, employers are required to do the following:[67]

1. *Label containers of hazardous materials.* The Hazardous Products Act and associated Controlled Products Regulations indicate the requirements for supplier labelling. In addition, the Controlled Products Regulations set out a national standard for the classification of hazardous workplace materials. The regulations list criteria for biohazards, chemical and acute hazards, chronic health hazards (including mutagenicity and carcinogenicity), embryo and reproductive toxicity, and respiratory tract and skin sensitization.
2. *Provide material safety data sheets (MSDSs) with additional information.* The MSDS is a document that contains information about potential hazards of a

material, including health, fire, and interactions between chemicals. The document also provides advice on how to work safely with the material and is used to develop procedures, such as the type of ventilation or other hazard controls required, the protective equipment needed in handling the product, and how to clean up a spill.

3. *Provide education and training so that employees understand the hazards of the substances that they may handle.*

In Canada, all employers must provide WHMIS instructions to all employees who work in contact with, or in proximity to, any materials defined as "hazardous." Numerous materials and products may be hazardous to a worker's health if they are not handled properly, including cleaning products, solvents, paints, glues, and toners.

Search the web www

The Canadian Centre for Occupational Health and Safety (CCOHS) has a Web site that serves as a clearinghouse for information about employee safety and health on the job (**http://www.canoshweb.org/en/**). The site describes its aims as follows:

> The purpose of this site is to enable Canadians to easily and independently locate Canadian occupational safety and health (OSH) information for the purpose of legal compliance, improving workplace health and safety practices and ultimately to facilitate the acquisition of information required for reduction in workplace fatalities, injuries and illnesses. It is designed to provide Canadians with a convenient and efficient way to access the health and safety information provided by the federal, provincial and territorial government agencies responsible for OSH, Workers' Compensation Boards and the Canadian Centre for Occupational Health and Safety (CCOHS).

On this site are links to legislation, manuals, continually updated statistics and inspection data, hazard information bulletins, directives, and a library of resources.

Workplace Violence

Unfortunately, the Canadian workplace is not immune to **workplace violence**. In 2002, 481 employees were assaulted at work (compared to 281 in 1996). The largest occupational group that experienced workplace violence are nurses and other health-care providers. In addition, according to estimates from the Workers' Compensation Board, hospitals ranked number one in workplace violence in 2002.[68] In that same year, the Ontario Workplace Safety and Insurance Board received 1747 claims for lost-time injuries—injuries that forced the employee to take at least one day off work. These injuries resulted from assaults and violent acts in the workplace.[69] While Canada has failed to maintain systematic and timely records of the occurrence of workplace violence, the little data that does exist is disturbing. For example, according to a 1998 report on workplace violence by the International Labour Organization:[70]

- Canada ranked fourth out of 32 countries for the number of women assaulted in the workplace.
- Canada ranked fifth for the number of men assaulted in the workplace.
- Canadian women reported the fourth highest incidence of sexual harassment in the workplace.

"Top Security Threats," a recent survey of *Fortune* 1000 companies, shows the seriousness of the problem, with corporate security managers rating workplace violence as their number one concern. The U.S.-based Workplace Violence Research Institute reports that each workday, in the United States, an estimated 16 400 threats are made, 723 workers are attacked, and 43 800 are harassed. As one writer astutely observed, "Violence has crept from city to suburb, from dim alley to sunny schoolyard. It was only a matter of time before its malevolent shadow darkened the workplace."[71] Another observer concluded, "Workplace violence is the new poison of corporate America."[72]

According to Manon Blanc of Queen's University and Kevin Kelloway of St. Mary's University, a number of job characteristics may trigger a higher risk of workplace aggression and violence, including making decisions that influence other people's lives (e.g., terminating an employee or assigning a failing grade); denying the public a service or request; supervising and/or disciplining others; working nights or working alone; and caring for the physical or emotional needs of others.[73]

Companies Respond   How are companies responding to this new kind of workplace hazard? Experts on workplace violence emphasize the importance of anticipating these crises and formulating specific procedures through which employees can report potential trouble so companies can respond. Some firms have decided to fold workplace violence into an already existing department that oversees other personnel matters. Others have decided to take a more proactive strategy. The U.S. Postal Service, for example, has trained a nine-person intervention team to be deployed to post offices if tensions get high. It is also striving to screen potential employees more carefully and encourage existing employees to use a hotline to report hot-tempered workers they perceive to be dangerous.[74] DuPont's Personal Safety Program is a comprehensive workplace protection program that includes counsellors, workshops, and a 24-hour hotline. Both DuPont and the U.S. Postal Service claim success with their programs.[75]

Increased government legislation in Canada also reflects the concern for workplace violence. For example, recent changes to the Occupational Health and Safety Code require employers to investigate cases of workplace violence and write a report on the incident. The report must describe what corrective action will be taken and what changes will be made in the workplace to prevent future violence. These reports may also be subject to scrutiny of provincial officials during random inspections of a workplace.[76]

Effective stakeholder management necessitates that companies address the growing problem of workplace violence. Companies have only recently started to put safety measures into place, but such measures will become more important in the future. Programs that deal with crises, and long-range efforts to bring about safer workplace environments, will be essential.

Promoting Health and Safety in the Workplace

A recent survey conducted by the Canadian Labour and Business Centre (CLBC) assessed over 1100 business and labour leaders from the public and private sectors in terms of healthy workplace practices and overall organizational health.[77] Respondents were asked about the presence of ten specific health and safety practices:

- joint health and safety committees
- lifestyle information
- flexible working hours
- employee involvement initiatives
- active lifestyle programs
- monitoring of safety/health/wellness impacts
- joint wellness committees
- work–life balance initiatives
- wellness needs assessments
- self-directed work teams

Sixty-four percent of the respondents (from the private sector) cited joint health and safety committees as the most common practice in their organization. There does appear to be a growing recognition of the importance of employee health and wellness programs.

While many managerial (private sector) respondents indicated an overall improvement in their organization's health in the past two years, the union perception differed. Over 50 percent of private sector labour leaders indicated that health and safety issues had worsened over the past two years. Those claiming overall improvements in organizational health were also asked to identify which programs had the most positive impact. While wellness programs were not a significant factor in improving workplace health, improved communication and increased employee training were cited as having the greatest impact.[78]

Safety Programs The expression, "an ounce of prevention is worth a pound of cure" applies to this area. Both employers and employees have come to recognize that efforts made to avoid workplace injuries and illnesses are far superior to any focus on compensation that results from work-related accidents or disease.

Organizations with formal safety programs typically maintain an employee–management safety committee that includes representatives from management, each department or manufacturing/service unit, and employee representatives. Committees may be involved in such activities as investigating accidents and helping to publicize the importance of safety rules and their enforcement. The majority of organizations have established some type of safety awareness program, ranging from safety lectures, to commercially produced films, to other media such as pamphlets. All are aimed at teaching and motivating employees to follow safe work procedures.

Collaboration between management and employees in the design of a safety program usually leads to higher motivation to conform with the safety rules. Consequently, it is a good idea for management to encourage employees to participate

Ethics In Practice

The Inspector's Surprise Visit

During the summers, Mark Price worked at a chemical plant in Quebec. One hot and busy July day, Willie Truit and Mark received a call from the plant manager's secretary authorizing them to dispose of a batch of monomers, which are a type of hazardous waste. The order was to remove them from the inspector's sight. Willie and Mark bagged them up and threw them in the dumpster, but Mark kept asking why they were doing this. Improper disposal of hazardous materials usually results in heavy fines. This violation would have resulted in a fine of about $20 000.

Mark asked Willie what he thought would happen if they decided not to do what they were told. Willie said that failure to do what they were authorized to do would definitely result in termination. The health and safety inspector asked Mark if he had been trained in handling hazardous waste. He also asked if Mark had been told to do things that he normally didn't engage in while working. Not wearing the proper clothing and disposing of the material improperly could result in danger to both Willie and Mark. It could also endanger whoever comes into contact with the material not disposed of properly.

1. If Mark chose not to perform the task he was told, how could he have protected his job?

2. What would you have done if caught in this ethical dilemma?

3. How would you have responded to the inspector's questions?

Contributed by Mystro Whatley

in establishing the organization's safety program. Employee involvement can include (1) collaboration with management on the setting of safety standards, (2) participation in safety training, (3) assistance with the design and implementation of special safety training programs, (4) involvement in establishing safety incentives and rewards, and (5) participation in accident investigations.[79]

Motivation to abide by safety rules should also include penalties for violations. Typically, employee handbooks will contain information regarding penalties for violation of safety rules. For many organizations, the penalties imposed on violators are identical to those for violations of other rules. Disciplinary actions for safety violations would usually include an oral or written warning for the first violation, suspension for repeated violations, and, as a last resort, dismissal. Of course, more serious violations, such as smoking around volatile substances, may be cause for termination even if committed as a first offence.

Employee Assistance Programs What should organizations do about employees who have an addiction or other health-related concerns? Is testing intended to simply be a punitive measure or do organizations have an obligation to help employees in need? In addition to improving the safety of working conditions, many employers provide services and programs that facilitate improvements in employee health and well-being.

In a recent study conducted by the Warren Shepell Research Group, it was found that Canadian retail and hospitality employees experience greater stress and depression symptoms than employees in other industries. Both retail and hospitality employees reported higher incidences of domestic violence (a three-year average of 1.01 percent compared to a national average of 0.52 percent). Employees in both industries also experience higher frequencies of alcohol consumption, smoking, and anxiety compared to other industries. In addition, hospitality employees reported a higher proportion of substance abuse with alcohol and smoking. Given the potential link between the stresses of the industry and substance abuse, should organizations offer some assistance to the affected employees?[80]

One of the most significant strategies undertaken by North American companies to deal with the growing alcohol- and drug-abuse problem in the workplace has been **Employee Assistance Programs (EAPs)**. EAPs originated, for the most part, in the 1940s, 1950s, and 1960s to deal with alcoholism on the job.[81] By the 1990s, EAPs had extended into other employee problem areas as well, such as job stress, financial stress, emotional stress, marital difficulties, aging, legal problems, and other psychological, emotional, and social difficulties. The term **"broad brush EAP"** was created to describe this more comprehensive model.[82]

According to the Canadian Centre for Occupational Health and Safety, EAPs should be part of a comprehensive company plan "to promote wellness that involves written policies, supervisor and employee training, and, where appropriate, an approved drug testing program."[83] EAPs represent a positive and proactive step companies can take to deal with these serious problems.

EAPs are designed to be confidential and nonpunitive, and they affirm three important propositions: (1) Employees are valuable members of the organization, (2) it is better to help troubled employees than to discipline or discharge them, and (3) recovered employees are better employees. It is encouraging that in an era when employees are increasingly exerting their workplace rights, enlightened companies are offering EAPs in an effort to help solve their mutual problems. More information on EAPs can be found at the Employee Assistance Program Association Web site at http://www.eap-association.org.[84]

In Canada, organizations such as the National Quality Institute, working in cooperation with the Canadian government, are endeavouring to arouse greater corporate attention to and interest in EAPs. Created in 1992, the National Quality Institute (NQI) is a Canadian not-for-profit organization that promotes high standards in healthy workplace practices. NQI organizes and administers the Nationwide Healthy Workplace Week, which according to Dan Corbett, president and CEO of NQI, is intended to:

> remind Canadian businesses annually about the increasing urgency to address workplace health, the positive effect a healthy workplace can have on employees, productivity and profitability and the wealth of resources available to incorporate comprehensive healthy workplace practices into their business strategies.[85]

More information about NQI and their work can be found at their Web site (http://www.nqi.ca/).

The Family-Friendly Workplace   One of the rationales that companies have given in recent years for having become more family friendly is that they are looking out for the mental and psychological health of their employees. Whether it be for altruistic or business reasons, workplaces today are becoming more **family friendly**. By using this term, we are repeating a catch-all phrase that refers to a whole host of policies and programs that today's companies have been putting into place.

A special report in *The Wall Street Journal* suggested that corporations are sending out positive messages to the public, including the following message:

> We are attuned to your families. The evidence is everywhere. Corporate child care centers are popping up around the country. "Work-family managers" appear on organization charts, and "flextime" has become a buzzword.[86]

Although not everyone thinks that companies are becoming as family friendly as they are espousing to be, it is clear that workers are talking more and more about the importance of family-friendly policies, and many leading companies are responding. With the growth in the numbers of women, single parents, and two-paycheque couples in the work force, it seems that corporate support for families, many of whom are stressed out from their busy lives, is on the growth curve. New issues are being raised: Family-support programs may be developing resentment among childless couples, family feuds at work are occurring more frequently, men want to be sure they are treated as well as women, and corporate cultures are changing. Into the vocabulary of managers have emerged new terms for dealing with employee stakeholders: *employee assistance, parenting workshops, dependent-care spending accounts, flexible scheduling, family-care leave*, and so on.[87]

Summary

Critical employee stakeholder issues include the rights to privacy, safety, and health. These issues should be seen as extensions of the issues and rights outlined in Chapter 15.

With the development of new technologies, workplace privacy has increasingly become a serious issue. The level of concern surrounding workplace privacy is evidenced by the frequency with which it has been a topic in the print and broadcast media. We have been inundated with reports of "Big Brother" at work, and we are familiar with the fact that e-mail and voice mail can be monitored, even after messages are deleted. The wealth of available technology presents new challenges for companies as they weigh the importance of knowing their workers' activities against the importance of maintaining trust and morale.

Of equal, if not more, importance to employee stakeholders are the issues of workplace safety and health. Legislation has been passed in recent years to provide employees with an added measure of protection, especially against harmful effects of exposure to chemicals and toxic substances. However, existing laws and regulations only deal with known problems. As the world changes, so do the threats to worker health and safety. Different kinds of threats to worker health and safety are certain to occur and will represent new challenges for managers.

Key Terms

broad brush EAP (page 517)

chief privacy officers (CPOs) (page 507)

drug testing (page 502)

Employee Assistance Programs (EAPs) (page 517)

employee monitoring (page 505)

family-friendly workplace (page 518)

integrity tests (page 502)

occupational illness (page 507)

occupational injury (page 507)

Personal Information Protection and Electronic Documents Act (PIPEDA) (page 497)

privacy impact statement (page 507)

privacy in the workplace (page 496)

Workplace Hazardous Materials Information System (WHMIS) (page 513)

workplace violence (page 514)

Discussion Questions

1. In your own words, describe what privacy means and what privacy protection companies should give employees.

2. Enumerate the strengths and weaknesses of the polygraph as a management tool for decision making. What polygraph uses are legitimate? What uses of the polygraph are illegitimate?

3. What are the two major arguments for and against integrity testing by employers? Under what circumstances could management most legitimately argue that integrity testing is necessary?

4. How has technology affected workplace privacy? What are the implications for the social contract between firms and their employees?

5. How has the World Trade Center tragedy affected workplace privacy? What are the long-term implications of that?

6. Which two of the four guidelines on the issue of privacy presented in this chapter do you think are the most important? Why?

Endnotes

1. Asra Q. Nomani, "Murder in Workplace Is a Major Part of the Latest Death-on-the-Job Statistics," *The Wall Street Journal* (August 11, 1994), A4.

2. Michael A. Gips, "Face Off over Facial Recognition," *Security Management* (May 2001), 12–14.

3. A. Scott, "No Privacy in the Workplace," *The Internal Auditor* (June 2001), 15–16.

4. Suzanne Cohen, "Chief Privacy Officers," *Risk Management* (July 2001), 9.

5. "Privacy: The New Minefield," *HR Focus* (April 2001), 1–13.

6. "Big Brother, Inc., May Be Closer Than You Think," *Business Week* (February 9, 1987), 84.

7. Patricia H. Werhane, *Persons, Rights, and Corporations* (Englewood Cliffs, NJ: Prentice Hall, 1985), 118.

8. Privacy Commissioner of Canada, http://www.privcom.gc.ca/fs-fi/02_05_d_15_e.asp.

9. Yosie Saint-Cyr, "Workplace Privacy," Hrinfodesk (December 2000), http://www.hrinfodesk.com/Articles/workplaceprivacy.htm.

10. Privacy Commissioner of Canada, http://www.privcom.gc.ca/fs-fi/02_05_d_16_e.asp.

11. Department of Justice Canada, http://canada.justice.gc.ca/en/news/nr/1998/attback2.html.

12. Privacy Commissioner of Canada, http://www.privcom.gc.ca/fs-fi/02_05_d_16_e.asp.

13. Privacy Commissioner of Canada, http://www.privcom.gc.ca/fs-fi/02_05_d_16_e.asp.

14. Osler, Hoskin & Harcourt LLP, http://www.osler.com/index.asp?navid=1086&layid=1124&csid=7&csid1=1342.

15. Jolie Solomon, "As Firms' Personnel Files Grow, Worker Privacy Falls," *The Wall Street Journal* (April 19, 1989), B1.

16. Joseph R. DesJardins, "Privacy in Employment," in Gertrude Ezorsky (ed.), Moral Rights in the Workplace (Albany, NY: State University of New York Press, 1987), 133.

17. Solomon, B1.

18. David Nye, "Son of the Polygraph," *Across the Board* (June 1989), 21.

19. Alfred G. Feliu, *Primer on Individual Employee Rights* (Washington, DC: The Bureau of National Affairs, 1992), 211–212.

20. *Ibid.*

21. Ed Bean, "More Firms Use Attitude Tests to Keep Thieves off the Payroll," *The Wall Street Journal* (January 27, 1987), 41.

22. Matthew Budman, "The Honesty Business," *Across the Board* (November/December 1993), 34–37.

23. *Ibid.*, 36.

24. Elizabeth M. Cosin, "Tests to Spot the Pinocchios May Fail the Honest Abes," *Insight* (July 30, 1990), 42–43.

25. G. H. Siejts, "Canadians More Opposed to Workplace Drug Testing Than U.S Counterparts," *HR Professional* (April/May 2003), 10–12; B. Butler, "Alcohol and Drug Testing in Canada: Do You Have a Right To Test? Do You Have a Right Not To?" *Occupational Health and Safety* (Vol. 13, No. 1, January–February 1997), 28–31.

26. "Why Firms Don't Test for Drugs," *USA Today* (February 18, 1987), 7B.

27. Ontario Human Rights Commission, "Policy on Drug and Alcohol Testing," http://www.ohrc.onc.ca/english/publications/drug_alcohol_testing_eng.html; "Canada Says No to Drug Testing" (July 11, 2002), http://calgary.cbc.ca/regional/servlet/View?filename=ts_07112002.

28. Canadian Centre on Substance Abuse, Substance Abuse and the Workplace: Canadian Profile 1999, http://www.ccsa.ca/cp1999work.html.

29. *Drug-Free Workplace: Back on Track* (Virginia Beach, VA: Coastal Human Resources, 1993.

30. Edward J. Miller, "Investigating in a Drug-Free Workplace," *HRMagazine* (Vol. 36, No. 5, May 1991), 48–51.

31. "Marijuana: Taking Another Look," http://www.tv.cbc.ca/newsinreview/apr98/marjuana/corport.htm.

32. Michael Waldholz, "Drug Testing in the Workplace: Whose Rights Take Precedence?" *The Wall Street Journal* (November 11, 1986), 39.

33. "The Many Tests for Drug Abuse," *The New York Times* (February 24, 1985), F17.

34. *Ibid.*

35. Curtis J. Sitomer, "Privacy and Personal Freedom: Balancing the Trade-Offs," *The Christian Science Monitor* (December 3, 1986), 33.

36. Julien Delisle, Executive Director, Office of the Privacy Commissioner, "Privacy: A New Human Right" (October 24, 1994), http://www.stthomasu.ca/~ahrc/conferences/privacy.html.

37. Laura Pincus Hartman, "The Rights and Wrongs of Workplace Snooping," *Journal of Business Strategy* (May/June 1998), 16.

38. A. Scott, "No Privacy in the Workplace," *The Internal Auditor* (June 2001), 15–16.

39. *Ibid.*

40. *Ibid.*

41. Ann K. Bradley, "An Employer's Perception on Monitoring Telemarketing Calls: Invasion of Privacy or Legitimate Business Practice?" *Labor Law Journal* (Vol. 42, No. 5, May 1991), 259–73.

42. Jennifer J. Laabs, "Surveillance: Tool or Trap?" *Personnel Journal* (Vol. 71, No. 6, June 1992), 102.

43. J. Towler, "Dealing with Employees Who Steal," *Canadian HR Reporter* (Vol. 15, No. 16, September 23, 2002), 4.

44. Peter Carlisle, "Videotape Can Be Used as Evidence in Civil Court," *Financial Post* (May 27, 1997).

45. Don A. Cozzetto and Thomas B. Pedeliski, "Privacy and the Workplace," *Public Personnel Administration* (Vol. 16, No. 2, Spring 1996), 21–31. See also Donald H. Seifman and Craig W. Trepanier, "Evolution of the Paperless Office: Legal Issues Arising Out of Technology in the Workplace," *Employee Relations Law Journal* (Vol. 21, No. 3, Winter 1995–96), 5–15.

46. Robert L. Brady, "Electronic Mail: Drafting a Policy," *HRFocus* (Vol. 72, No. 10, October 1995), 19.

47. G. Arnaut, "Electronic Big Brother Is on the Job," *The Globe and Mail* (October 22, 1996), C1.

48. Robert C. Goldstein and Richard L. Nolan, "Personal Privacy Versus the Corporate Computer," *Harvard Business Review* (March–April 1975), 62–70.

49. Cohen, 9.

50. Association of Workers Compensation Boards of Canada, Table 1, http://www.awcbc.org.

51. Canadian Centre for Occupational Health and Safety, http://www.ccohs.ca/youngworkers/tips.html.

52. Joseph P. Kahn, "When Bad Management Becomes Criminal," *Inc.* (March 1987), 47.

53. David R. Spiegel, "Enforcing Safety Laws Locally," *The New York Times* (March 23, 1986), 11F.

54. "Union Carbide Fights for Its Life," *Business Week* (December 24, 1984), 52–56.

55. Chantal Plamondon, "Dealing with Corporate Crimes in Canada," http://www.ethicscentre.ca/html/resources/spring2001.html.

56. "By the Numbers Operation at Morgan Stanley Finds Its Human Side," *The New York Times* (September 16, 2001), section 3, page 8; "War on Terrorism: The Victims—Snapshot of the Briton Who Became an American Hero, Seconds Before Death," *The Independent* (September 27, 2001), 3.

57. Canadian Centre for Occupational Health and Safety, http://www.ccohs.ca/oshanswers/legisl/responsi.html.

58. Canadian Centre for Occupational Health and Safety, http://www.ccohs.ca/ccohs.html.

59. Department of Justice, http://canada.justice.gc.ca/en/news/nr/2003/doc_31024.html.

60. Colin Perkel, "Law Arising from Westray Mine Disaster Casts Wide Criminal Net for Companies" (November 3, 2003), http://cnews.canoe.ca/CNEWS/Law/2003/11/03/245813-cp.html.

61. Canadian Centre for Occupational Health and Safety, http://www.ccohs.ca/oshanswers/legisl/responsi.html.

62. Joel Murray, "GM Fined for Disabled Limit Switches," *Occupational Health and Safety* (Vol. 16, No. 6, Summer 2000), 13, 14.

63. M. Basch Scott, "Insures, Support Services Focus on Enabling Return to Work from Disability," *Employee Benefits Plan Review* (Vol. 54, No. 9, March 2000), 16–21; V. Galt and K. Harding, "No Safety in the Numbers," *The Globe and Mail* (June 18, 2003), C1.

64. Canadian Centre for Occupational Health and Safety, http://www.ccohs.ca/oshanswers/legisl/responsi.html.

65. Canadian Centre for Occupational Health and Safety, http://www.ccohs.ca/oshanswers/legisl/responsi.html.

66. "Bank Ordered to Pay Employee $15,000 for Mental Suffering," *hrreporter.com* (December 3, 2003), http://www.hrreporter.com/loginarea/members/viewing.asp?ArticleNo=2848&subscriptionType=PRINT).

67. Health Canada, http://www.hc-sc.gc.ca/hecs-sesc/whmis/index.htm; Virtual WHMIS, http://www.virtualwhmis.com/index.php?view=WhyWhmis; Health Canada, Canadian Health Network, http://testeditchn.globalx.net/faq-faq/workplace_health-sante_en_milieu_de_travail/4e.html.

68. John Cotter, "Alta. Employers Responsible for Workplace Violence" (November 13, 2003), http://cnews.canoe.ca/CNEWS/Canada/2003/11/13/256770-cp.html.

69. Workopolis, http://www.workopolis.com/servlet/Content/torontostar/20031202/officeviolence?section=TORSTAR.

70. International Labour Organization, http://www.ilo.org/.

71. Tom Dunkel, "Hazardous Duty," *The Atlanta Journal* (October 2, 1994), Q1, Q3.

72. *Ibid.*, Q1.

73. Kevin Kelloway, "Predictors and Outcomes of Workplace Violence," *HR Professional* (Vol. 20, No. 1, February/March 2003), 50.

74. Dunkel, Q3.

75. *Ibid.*, Q3.

76. Cotter, *op cit.*

77. Viewpoints 2002: Healthy Workplace Practices, CLBC Web site, http://www.clbc.ca.

78. *Ibid.*

79. Monica Belcourt, George W. Bohlander, Scott A. Snell, and Arthur W. Sherman, *Managing Human Resources*, 4th Canadian ed. (Toronto: Nelson, 2004).

80. Jack Kapica, "Study: Christmas Sressful to Workers" *Globe and Mail* (December 12, 2003), http://www.globeandmail.com/servlet/story/RTGAM.20031212.wstress12/BNStory/National/; http://www.warrenshepell.com/index.asp.

81. Sarah F. Mulladay, "The Champion Paper Company EAP and Major Issues for Employee Assistance Programs in the 1990s—Managed Care and Aging," *Employee Assistance Quarterly* (Vol. 6, No. 3, 1991), 37–50.

82. Eileen Smith, "How to Choose the Right EAP for Your Employee," *Employee Benefit News* (November 1, 2000).

83. Canadian Centre for Occupational Health and Safety, http://www.ccohs.ca/oshanswers/hsprograms/eap.html.

84. Smith, *op cit.*

85. National Quality Institute, http://www.nqi.ca/newsevents/details.aspx?ID=422.

86. Sue Shellenbarger, "Work and Family: So Much Talk, So Little Action," *The Wall Street Journal* (June 21, 1993), R1.

87. Robert L. Rose, "Small Steps," *The Wall Street Journal* (June 21, 1993), R10.

Chapter 17

Employment Discrimination and Employment Equity

Chapter Objectives

After studying this chapter, you should be able to:

1 Understand the challenges faced by certain groups in the labour force.

2 Discuss the notion of discrimination and the legal bases for protection against discrimination in Canada.

3 Provide two different meanings of discrimination and give examples of how each might be committed.

4 Explain the purpose and functions of employment equity.

5 Define the key elements of pay equity and its relationship to employee equity.

6 Elaborate on issues in employment discrimination and equity.

Canadian business operates within a diverse society. The Canadian population reflects a multitude of cultures and demographic backgrounds. For example, recent census figures provided by Statistics Canada show that over 5 million Canadian citizens were foreign-born, comprising nearly 20 percent of the total population.[1] This diversity is increasingly reflected in the Canadian labour pool. Immigrants who came to Canada in the 1990s have accounted for approximately 70 percent of the total growth of the labour force in recent years. Women also comprise a significant component of the Canadian labour force and account for about half of both the employed work force and all union members. Visible minorities and people with disabilities, together with women, make up over 60 percent of Canada's labour force.[2]

Diversity in our work force is also reflected in the growing presence of older workers. At the start of the twenty-first century, Canadians 37–55 years old made up about 47 percent of the labour force, and by 2011, half of these workers will be 55 or over.[3] Given the existence of an aging society and forecast labour shortages in almost every sector across Canada, recruiting workers from all groups of society is critical. Consequently, it is clear that organizations must attend to the rights of a diverse group of individuals.

In the previous two chapters, we considered employee rights issues that affect virtually everyone in the workplace. In this chapter, we concentrate on that group of stakeholders whose rights are protected by discrimination laws. In general, these groups include minorities, Native people, women, and people with disabilities that might affect their conditions of employment. Many of the issues we treat in this chapter have grown out of the general notion that employees have certain workplace rights that ought to be protected. Employment discrimination is clearly an issue with both legal and ethical implications. We will consider the issue of discrimination and the obligations that employers have with regard to ensuring workplace equity for all groups.

Challenges in the Labour Pool

A significant portion of our valued labour pool is derived from members of **designated groups** whose participation in the workplace contributes to the success of an organization. With regard to past discrimination, there are four groups in Canada that traditionally have not received equitable treatment in employment: women, Aboriginal peoples, visible minorities, and people with disabilities. Figure 17–1 identifies their relative presence in the population and the labour pool. Ironically, while these groups represent 60 percent of the total work force, they have historically been denied fair treatment at work. These designated groups have faced significant obstacles related to their status in the labour force, including high unemployment, occupational segregation, pay inequities, and limited opportunities for career advancement. We have come to expect that organizations will help address the challenges faced by these groups.

The Four Designated Groups

Women Traditionally, women have been segregated in occupations that are accorded both lower status and lower pay. According to a 2003 report by Statistics Canada (based on 2001 census data), while women represented 44.8 percent of the total work force, they were clearly not equally represented across occupations. For example, women have been underrepresented in such areas as semiprofessional occu-

FIGURE 17–1

Representation of Designated Groups in the Labour Force

	Representation in the Canadian Population	Representation in the Work Force
Women	50.85%	44.8%
Aboriginal people	3.3	1.6
People with disabilities	12.4	2.3
Members of visible minorities	13.4	11.7

Source: Statistics Canada, http://www.statcan.ca/english/Pgdb/labor20a.htm, table 282-0002.

pations, management and board positions, supervisors in crafts and trades, and sales and service personnel.[4] The failure of women to achieve higher-level corporate positions has been attributed to a variety of sources, including lack of mentoring opportunities, lack of female role models, stereotyping and preconceptions of women's roles and abilities, exclusion from informal networks of communication, and failure of senior leaders to assume accountability for women's advancement.[5]

In a report recently commissioned by the Women's Executive Network (WEN) in Canada, the majority of women executives surveyed believe they have to work twice as hard as men to achieve success. Respondents also indicated that they continuously find themselves hitting the "glass ceiling," and are not accepted into the executive-level culture, which includes participation in "the boys club." The findings also revealed a concern that women continue to face more barriers to career advancement than men with the same qualifications, and are often presented with fewer opportunities. Among the greatest career barriers identified was the "the lack of comfort on the part of men in dealing with women on a professional level." Gender-based stereotyping was also indicated as a career barrier. In addition, many respondents felt that they are paid less than men with similar qualifications and they receive less credit and recognition for accomplishments.[6]

Aboriginal or First Nations People Aboriginals make up about 3.3 percent of the population. They represent one of the fastest growing populations in Canada but remain vastly underrepresented in the work force, with their unemployment rate hovering at the 20 percent range. Researchers have estimated that the Aboriginal population "baby boom" will result in 350 000 Native people reaching working age by the next few years, and this underscores the growing need for Canada to absorb more Native people into its work force. However, as researcher Stelios Loizedes of the Conference Board of Canada observed:

> *A major difficulty in achieving this goal is that most of this large cohort of Native Canadians coming of working age will have insufficient education and limited job experience, restricting their ability to compete for jobs…. Native communities and the private and public sectors will have to implement creative solutions to narrow the education and employment gaps.*[7]

The educational challenge has proven to be a significant barrier with Aboriginal populations experiencing a high-school drop-out rate of 70 percent.[8] In addition, the lack of job experience and language and cultural barriers have made the plight of this group often appear bleak.

Another barrier to improved employment is the geographical distribution of the Native community. Employment opportunities on or near the Aboriginal reserves are limited. In addition, while over half the Aboriginal population lives in the four western provinces, these provinces account for a relatively small percentage of the total jobs in Canada, compared to Quebec and Ontario.[9] Sadly, in many urban contexts, Aboriginal workers have typically been largely segregated in low-wage, unstable employment.

Among the biggest barriers faced by the Aboriginal community may be perception—with many Aboriginal Canadians feeling that they do not "fit" with the corporate environment. As David Brown observed:

That's a problem for both the First Nations community and corporate Canada to address. Aboriginal Canadians have been prevented from playing a part in the modern corporate world for so long that many now feel that exclusion is normal.[10]

Individuals with Disabilities Individuals with disabilities have faced a variety of employment obstacles. Typically, this group has experienced a higher unemployment rate compared to the national average. Among the challenges faced are attitudinal barriers in the workplace, physical demands unrelated to the job requirements, and inadequate access to the technical and human support systems.

The Canadian Health Network, a national, nonprofit, Web-based health information service, clearly notes the importance of acknowledging this segment of the population and of the labour pool:

In the coming decades, people with a disability will comprise a larger percentage of the population in Canada than ever before. The math is pretty straightforward. As the baby boom generation grows older, the overall age of the population will increase. And because the incidence of disabilities is strongly correlated to age, these numbers will rise together. The degree of accessibility available to this aging population will play a key role in determining their level of health or of hardship, just as it plays a critical role in the daily lives of the more than four million people currently living with a disability in Canada.[11]

A major challenge faced by persons with disabilities is the issue of accessibility. This can entail a variety of obstacles. While physical barriers may be the most visible obstacle to full accessibility, economic barriers, social discrimination, and obstacles to communication can all prevent someone from having equal access to a building, a service, or a job.[12]

Visible Minorities This group makes up a growing segment of the population. In the last decade, almost 70 percent of the growth in the labour force was accounted for by newcomers who arrived in the 1990s. In addition, as the baby boom generation retires, immigrant workers will play a greater role in the labour pool. It is estimated that by 2011, new immigrants will comprise most of the labour force growth.[13]

Workplace obstacles faced by visible minorities include culturally biased aptitude tests, lack of recognition of foreign credentials, and excessively high language requirements. Recent statistics indicate that while visible minorities are well educated, they experience the highest unemployment rates, with recent estimates at roughly twice as high as that for the Canadian-born population.[14]

A study released by the Canadian Race Relations Foundation indicated that desirable jobs and promotions elude many visible minorities and Aboriginal people, who believe that subtle forms of racism permeate the workplace. The report, prepared by Jean Lock Kunz, Anne Milan, and Sylvain Schetagne from the Canadian Council on Social Development (CCSD), examined the experiences of visible minorities and Aboriginal peoples in cities across Canada. Among the findings, were the following:

- Aboriginal peoples, visible minorities, and immigrants to Canada encounter more challenges in finding employment in all regions in Canada.
- Foreign-born visible minorities experience the greatest difficulty finding desirable work, and only half of those with a university education have high-skill jobs.
- Compared to white Canadians, visible minorities and Aboriginals who possess a university education are less likely to hold managerial and professional jobs. Among those visible minorities who do hold managerial jobs, over 50 percent are self-employed, compared with only 30 percent of white Canadians.
- Higher education appears to yield fewer benefits for minorities and Aboriginals in terms of employment and income. Given the same level of education, white Canadians (both foreign-born and Canadian-born) are three times as likely as Aboriginals and about twice as likely as foreign-born visible minorities to rank among the top 20 percent of income earners.[15]

Search the web WWW

The Web site for the Council of Canadians with Disabilities (CCD) (**http://www.pcs.mb.ca/~ccd/**) states:

CCD's membership includes both cross-disability organizations and national advocacy organizations, all controlled by people with disabilities. CCD believes in:

- *Citizenship.* Persons with disabilities hold the same rights and responsibilities as other Canadians. Barriers to our participation discriminate against us and must be removed.
- *Self-determination.* As full citizens, we assert our right to direct our own lives and make our own decisions.
- *Equality.* The Charter of Rights and Freedoms guarantees equal benefit and protection of the law and prohibits discrimination based on physical or mental disability. All other legislation must be brought into line with the Charter.

The Web site for the National Institute of Disability Management and Research (**http://www.nidmar.ca/**) states:

As an education, training and research organization, NIDMAR's primary focus is the implementation of workplace-based reintegration programs which international research has proven is the most effective way of restoring and maintaining workers' abilities, while reducing the costs of disability for workers, employers, government and insurance carriers.

The National Institute's success is the result of collaborative initiatives undertaken by leaders in labour, business, government, education, insurance and rehabilitation.

Discrimination

Legal Protection

The Department of Justice defines discrimination as occurring "when a law, program or policy—expressly or by effect—creates a distinction between groups of individuals which disadvantages one group based on shared personal characteristics of members of that group in a manner inconsistent with human dignity."[16]

There are a number of legal sources aimed at protecting individuals against discrimination, including the Charter of Rights and Freedoms and the federal Canadian Human Rights Act. In this section we will also consider employment equity legislation.

Canadian Charter of Rights and Freedoms A central principle behind human rights legislation in Canada is to balance individual and collective rights. Consequently, courts have traditionally upheld restrictions to individual rights in order to protect vulnerable groups in society. For example, while individuals have a right to free speech, there are also laws that place limits on this freedom if such speech threatens other groups.

The Constitution Act of 1982, which contains the Canadian Charter of Rights and Freedoms, is the central legislation governing human rights in Canada. It protects the fundamental rights of all Canadians, including:

- Fundamental freedoms that comprise the standard rights of freedom of speech, press, assembly, association, and religion
- Democratic rights
- Mobility rights regarding the right to move freely from province to province for the purposes of residence or employment
- Legal rights, which provide standard procedural rights in criminal proceedings
- Equality rights, which guarantee no discrimination by law on grounds of race, ethnic origin, colour, religion, sex, age, or mental and physical ability
- Language rights[17]

The Charter only applies to activities and institutions controlled by the government and, consequently, it does not protect individual rights against private businesses or individuals. Therefore, rights are additionally protected via other federal and provincial human rights legislation, as discussed below. With the increasing number of cases of alleged human rights violations perpetrated by employers, it is critical that management understand their responsibilities under the legislation, and consider that damages can be awarded for bad faith if there is noncompliance with the law.

The Canadian Human Rights Act In 1977, Parliament passed the Canadian Human Rights Act. This act is aimed at ensuring equality of opportunity and freedom from discrimination in the federal jurisdiction. The spirit of the act reflects the view that individuals should not be disadvantaged or discriminated against simply because of their membership in any of the following categories:

- Race
- Colour
- National or ethnic origin
- Religion
- Age

- Sex (including pregnancy and childbearing)
- Marital status
- Family status
- Physical or mental disability (including dependence on alcohol or drugs)
- Pardoned criminal conviction
- Sexual orientation

The act protects the rights of Canadians but applies to a specific class of organizations: all federal government departments and agencies; Crown corporations; and other businesses and industries under federal jurisdiction, such as banks, airlines, railway companies, and insurance and communications companies. An organization that doesn't fall into one of these categories will be governed by one or more of the provincial or territorial human rights acts or codes. Therefore, organizations not covered under the federal jurisdiction will be covered under provincial human rights laws. For example, if a company has offices in Nova Scotia and Alberta, then the codes from both of those provinces will apply.

The Canadian Human Rights Act and each of the provincial human rights codes govern human rights issues and provide detailed procedures for investigation and resolution. Provincial laws are similar to federal laws, and the provisions of most provincial codes are largely identical. For example, each provincial jurisdiction or territory has a human rights act or code. In addition, all codes contain a blanket provision that outlaws discrimination based on disability and provisions that specifically relate to discrimination in employment.

The Canadian Human Rights Commission   At the federal level, the Canadian Human Rights Commission (CHRC) is granted authority under the Canadian Human Rights Act to prohibit employment discrimination in federally regulated businesses, including such areas as race, religion, sex, age, national or ethnic origin, physical handicap, and marital status. Each of the provincial human rights codes also enforces fundamental freedoms and governs human rights issues.

The role of the CHRC is to examine allegations of discrimination (addressed by the Canadian Human Rights Act) and to assist in the establishment of greater equality of opportunity. The CHRC describes its mandate as follows:

- To provide effective and timely means for resolving individual complaints.
- To promote knowledge of human rights in Canada and to encourage people to follow principles of equality.
- To help reduce barriers to equality in employment and access to services.[18]

Individuals have a right to file a complaint if they feel they have been the target of discrimination. The complainant is first required to complete a written report describing the discriminatory action. A CHRC representative assesses the facts and determines whether the claim is legitimate. After a complaint has been accepted by the CHRC, an investigator is assigned the task of gathering more facts, and a report is subsequently submitted to the CHRC recommending a finding of either substantiation or nonsubstantiation of the allegation. Once a claim is substantiated, the parties may choose to attempt to settle the matter in the course of the investigation. However, if the parties cannot reach an agreement, a human rights tribunal may be appointed to further investigate. The tribunal has the power to seek damages for the victim, in the event that the accused is found guilty of a discriminatory practice. The enforcement of human rights through commissions can occur at both the federal and provincial levels.

Discrimination Resources

1. The Canadian Human Rights Commission (**www.chrc -ccdp.ca/**). The CHRC's Web site covers rights regarding Aboriginal peoples, disability, employment equity, harassment, sex discrimination, race, and religion.

2. The Human Rights Research and Education Centre (**www.cdp-hrc.uottawa.ca/**). The Human Rights Research and Education Centre has been delivering an active and extensive program out of the University of Ottawa since May 1981. Its purpose includes:

   - Furthering the discussion of the linkages between human rights, governance, legal reform, and development.
   - Supporting national human rights institutions in Canada and abroad.
   - Evaluating and working to improve domestic social justice institutions and programs.
   - Engaging in multidisciplinary research and education in the above areas.

   Its website contains a Virtual Human Rights Research Library with a wealth of links to Canadian and international human rights—related Web sites.

3. The Canadian Union of Public Employees (**www.cupe.ca/**). The Canadian Union of Public Employees (CUPE) is Canada's largest union, with over half a million members across Canada. CUPE represents workers in health care, education, municipalities, libraries, universities, social services, public utilities, transportation, emergency services, and airlines. CUPE members are service-providers, white-collar workers, technicians, labourers, skilled tradespeople, and professionals. More than half of CUPE members are women. About one-third are part-time workers.

   CUPE's Web site offers labour's perspective on workplace controversies regarding such topics as gender, disability, Aboriginal issues, and racism.

In a recent article in the *Canadian HR Reporter*, Natalie McDonald made the following observation:

With the growing number of cases alleging human rights violations in the courts, it is critical that all employees at the management level understand the legislation under which they are governed and the duty to comply with the legislation, particularly given the damages which can be awarded for bad faith if there is non-compliance.[19]

Expanded Meanings of Discrimination

Over time, it has become apparent that two specific kinds of discrimination have been identified. These two kinds can be viewed as (1) direct discrimination or disparate treatment and (2) indirect discrimination, also referred to as adverse effect or disparate impact.

Direct Discrimination or Disparate Treatment

Initially, the word *discrimination* meant the use of race, colour, sex, and so on, as a basis for treating people differently or unequally. This direct form of discrimination became known as unequal treatment, or **disparate treatment**. The Department of Justice defines direct discrimination as involving "a law, rule or practice which on its face creates harmful differential treatment on the basis of particular group characteristics."[20]

Examples of direct discrimination or disparate treatment might include refusing to consider Aboriginals for a job, paying women less than men for the same work, or supporting any decision rule with a racial or sexual premise or cause.[21] A famous example of direct discrimination involved the U.S.-based Texaco corporation. In 1994, six Texaco employees filed a class-action lawsuit charging racial discrimination in hiring practices and workplace treatment. In 1996, when a tape of Texaco executives surfaced containing racial slurs directed at employees, as well as evidence that the executives were planning to shred incriminating documents and withhold information from the plaintiff's lawyers, they settled the suit for US$115 million.[22] When news of the tape became public, an activist friend called New York State Comptroller Carl McCall, the first African-American to be elected to statewide office in New York, and asked him to join a picket line at the company's headquarters. McCall replied, "When you own 1 million shares of stock, you don't have to picket." McCall oversaw a public pension fund that is one of the largest in the United States and one of the few that is managed by an individual rather than by a committee. He simply called Texaco Chairman Peter Bijur to express his concern. Since then, Bijur has continued to update McCall regularly on the progress of Texaco's diversity plan.[23]

Indirect Discrimination: Adverse Effect or Disparate Impact As discussed above, disparate treatment may include such direct discrimination as including in a job posting the statement that "no women need apply" or "foreigners not allowed." One method to combat such direct discrimination was to permit the employer to impose any employment criteria so long as they were imposed on all groups alike.[24] This view of discrimination equated nondiscrimination with colour-blind decision making. In other words, to avoid this kind of discrimination it meant that all groups or individuals had to be treated equally, without regard for colour, sex, or other characteristics.[25]

However, more subtle forms of discrimination also exist. For example, an individual may believe that he or she has somehow been treated differently, such as failing to be hired for a job simply because of that person's age, race, gender, and so on. Sometimes, the only feasible way to determine if discrimination exists in such cases is to assess the effects at an aggregate or group level. How many women who work in that company have high-level positions? Does the company hire any Aboriginals who have applied for jobs there? If a company appears to be treating members of such groups in certain ways, we can question whether the reasons are legitimate or discriminatory.

The government's intent in prohibiting discrimination was to eliminate practices that contributed to economic inequality. What it found was that, although companies could adhere to the disparate treatment definition of discrimination, this did not eliminate all of the economic inequalities it was intended to address. For example, a company could use two neutral criteria for selection, whereby men and women could be treated the same under the criteria. However, a problem can arise when it becomes apparent that the policy of equal treatment results in unequal consequences for men and women.

According to the Department of Justice, adverse effect discrimination "occurs when the application of an apparently neutral law or policy has a disproportionate and harmful impact on individuals on the basis of particular group characteristics. It is also referred to as 'indirect' discrimination or 'disparate (unequal) impact' discrimination."[26]

In the United States, the case of *Griggs v. Duke Power Company* was among the first cases to draw attention to the issue of adverse effect or disparate impact discrimination. The U.S. Supreme Court had to decide whether an action was discriminatory if it resulted in unequal consequences in the *Griggs v. Duke Power Company* case.[27] In this case, the court concluded that it was the consequences of an employer's actions, not the employer's intentions, that determined whether discrimination had taken place. If any employment practice or test had an adverse or differential effect on minorities, then it was a discriminatory practice.

An adverse effect or disparate impact, as this new kind of discrimination came to be known, simply meant that fewer minorities were included in the outcome of the test or the hiring or promotion practice than would be expected by their numerical proportion. The court also held that a policy or procedure with a disparate impact would be permissible if the employer could demonstrate that it was a business- or job-related necessity. In the *Duke Power* case, for example, a high school diploma and good scores on a general intelligence test were not shown to have a clearly demonstrable relationship to successful performance on the job under consideration.[28]

Employers may be justified in maintaining such discriminatory policies or practices if they are based on a bona fide occupational qualification (BFOQ) or BFOR (bona fide occupational requirement). Any policy or practice viewed as discriminatory must pass three criteria in order to support the claim that it is a bona fide occupational requirement:[29]

- It must be rationally related to the requirements of job performance.
- It must be created in good faith.
- It must be reasonably necessary in order to accomplish a valid purpose. That is, no other standard could be employed that it could not use a different standard without undue hardship, such as compromising safety.

In other words, a BFOQ or BFOR is permissible if the employer can prove that this "discrimination" is necessary for business operations (e.g., for safety or effectiveness reasons). In other words, disparate treatment and disparate impact are not discrimination if there is a legitimate or justifiable reason (this was not proven in the *Duke Power* case). In Canada, this issue was clearly brought to the public's attention in a Supreme Court decision regarding a female firefighter who lost her job following an employment test.

In 1994, a 33-year-old woman, Tawney Meiorin, was dismissed by her employer, the B.C. Ministry of Forests, because she took 49.4 seconds too long to complete a 2.5-kilometre run, a component of the provincial firefighting test. Because the test standards did not account for the differing physiology of men and women, the test largely excluded women (i.e., 65 to 70 percent of men who took the test passed on their initial attempt, but only 35 percent of female applicants passed on their initial attempt). This was a form of indirect discrimination—the test standards resulted in a disparate impact. Consequently, when the case appeared before the Supreme Court, it was necessary for the employer to prove that the test standards were based on a bona fide occupational qualification (BFOQ) or BFOR (bona fide occupational requirement).

The employer (B.C. Ministry of Forests) proved two of the three requirements necessary to support the claim that the testing was a bona fide occupational requirement (the test was rationally related to the job and it was created in good faith). However, the court deemed that the employer failed to show that the additional difficulty of the standard for women was necessary in order to achieve the standard's purpose—the physical tests for British Columbia forest firefighters were not considered to be bone fide occupational requirements. Consequently, the test's adverse effect on women could not be justified as a BFOQ/BFOR.

In 1999, five years after Meiorin lost her job, the Supreme Court of Canada reinstated the woman's position as a firefighter and ordered the B.C. Ministry of Forests to compensate her for lost wages and benefits.[30]

Cases such as this one underscore the obligations of employers to assess whether their workplace rules and standards exclude any individuals—and, if so, the employer must be prepared to justify such exclusion. Prior to this case, a policy or test that had a disparate impact simply required that employers find a way to accommodate the individual facing adverse discrimination. However, subsequent to this case, any discriminatory effect must be scrutinized as to whether or not it is a bona fide occupational requirement. The rationale behind this change is: Why maintain any rule with discriminatory effects if it is not required by the workplace?

Systemic Discrimination   The potential for indirect discrimination exists in many organizational policies and processes and, consequently, a lack of scrutiny on the part of the employer may unwittingly contribute to the development of systemic discrimination. According to the Department of Justice, systemic discrimination "occurs when problems of discrimination are embedded in institutional policies and practices. Although the institution's policies or practices might apply to everyone, they create a distinction between groups of individuals which disadvantage one group based on shared personal characteristics of members of that group in a manner inconsistent with human dignity."[31]

A recent U.S. lawsuit faced by Coca-Cola Co. underscores the need for vigilance against systemic discrimination. The class-action racial discrimination lawsuit alleged that Coke's pay policies, promotions, and performance evaluations discriminated against black employees. The company was forced to compensate 2000 black employees and former employees (between 1995 and 2000) an average of US$40 000 each. The company also agreed to pay out an estimated US$43.5 million over ten years in order to eliminate pay disparities between white and black employees. An additional US$36 million was to be spent in order to implement an employment equity plan that will ensure that most of the company's personnel policies and practices (i.e., pay, promotions, and performance evaluation) be reviewed by an independent committee.[32]

The threat of systemic discrimination demands that organizations closely examine their employment policies and practices in such areas as job classifications and descriptions, recruitment processes, training and development, performance evaluation systems, promotions, compensation, termination policies, discipline procedures, and facilities (e.g., building design, barrier-free access). The traditional test for assessing whether organizational policies harbour systemic barriers includes the following criteria:

- Is it job-related?
- Is it valid? (i.e., does it have a direct relationship to job performance?)
- Is it consistently applied?
- Does it have a disparate impact? (i.e., does it impact members of certain groups more than those of other groups?)
- Is it a business requirement?
- Does it conform to human rights and employment standards legislation?[33]

The concepts of systemic discrimination and disparate impact are quite significant because they run counter to so many traditional employment practices. There are many examples. The minimum height and weight requirements of some police departments have unequal impact and have been struck down by courts because they tend to disproportionately screen out women and certain ethnic groups.[34]

Systemic discrimination is also reflected in the perpetuation of a homogeneous workplace due to recruitment strategies that are unintentionally exclusive. Imagine a company that recruits new employees by posting job vacancies only within the company or by word of mouth among the employees. This recruitment strategy may be deemed to be discriminatory given that it encourages only those candidates similar to those in the current work force to apply, to the exclusion of other groups of potential candidates from the broader labour pool.

Other examples of indirect and systemic discrimination can include the following:

- A workplace environment that does not expressly discourage sexual or racial harassment.
- Job descriptions and job evaluation systems that undervalue the work of positions traditionally held by women.

- Physical access that restricts those who are mobility impaired (e.g., no ramps, heavy doors, narrow passageways).[35]

With at least two different ways in which to commit discrimination, managers have to be extremely careful, because many actions they take could possibly have discriminatory effects. Figure 17–2 summarizes the characteristics of indirect and direct discrimination.

Issues in Workplace Discrimination

Sex Discrimination

Statistics show that women are flooding the job market, boosting economic growth, and helping to reshape the economy dramatically. A study released in 2004 by Catalyst, an independent, nonprofit organization supporting the advancement of women in business, suggests that companies with a higher representation of women in senior management positions financially outperform companies with proportionally fewer women at the top. According to the authors of the study, the findings offer support for facilitating greater representation of women in leadership roles—companies that recruit, retain, and advance women may have a competitive advantage in the global marketplace.[36] However, observations still reveal that women face extreme challenges in the workplace, including getting into professional and managerial positions (and out of traditional female-dominated positions) and dealing with sexual harassment.

Moving into Professional/Managerial Positions   A recent study conducted by Catalyst found that while women are making progress in moving into the top ranks of Canadian companies, they are still vastly underrepresented in corporate leadership positions. In their review of Canada's 500 largest companies in 2002, only 14 percent of corporate officers were women (compared to 12 percent in 1999), filling only 752 out of 5631 top corporate officer positions in Canada. Women held only 6.7 percent of the highest corporate titles in 2002 (compared to 3.4 percent in 1999). Both Canada and the U.S. had relatively few female CEOs (13 among the 500 largest

FIGURE 17-2	
Two Kinds of Employment Discrimination	
Definition 1 Direct Discrimination	Definition 2 Indirect Discrimination
Disparate treatment	Adverse effect/disparate impact
Unequal treatment	Unequal consequences or results
Decision rules with a racial/sexual premise or cause	Decision rules with racial/sexual consequences or results
Intentional discrimination	Unintentional discrimination
Prejudiced actions	Neutral, colour-blind actions
Different standards for different groups	Same standards, but different consequences for different groups

Sources: James Ledvinka and Vida G. Scarpello, *Federal Regulation of Personnel and Human Resources Management*, 2d ed. (Boston: PWS-Kent, 1991), 48; Department of Justice Canada, 2003.

Canadian companies and only six female CEOs among the U.S.'s *Fortune* 500 companies). The study also indicated that Canada has a smaller percentage of female corporate officers compared to U.S. companies—85.6 percent of *Fortune* 500 companies had at least one female corporate officer, compared with only 62.5 percent of the top 500 Canadian companies.[37] The results of a 2003 Catalyst census of women board directors among *Fortune* 500 companies are presented in Figure 17–3, and Figure 17–4 lists several award-winning organizations in the realm of support for women in the workplace.

Another recent study asked *Fortune* 1000 male CEOs and senior-level female executives for their views on why glass ceilings exist. Their views differed. The male CEOs blamed the glass ceiling on women's lack of experience and time "in the pipeline." The female executives disagreed sharply, citing an exclusionary corporate culture as the reason for women's lack of advancement to senior positions. They described a corporate playing field that was not level due to negative preconceptions and stereotypes. Despite their differences about the causes of the glass ceiling, the male CEOs and female executives agreed that both individuals and the organization are responsible for creating positive organizational changes.[38]

Sexual Harassment A recent U.S.-based survey showed that four out of every ten employees have seen ethical or legal problems at work. The most common problem was sexual harassment; 19 percent of the respondents reported that they had seen it in the past two years.[39] In Canada, according to one study, only four of every ten women who endure sexual harassment at work actually take any formal action, and

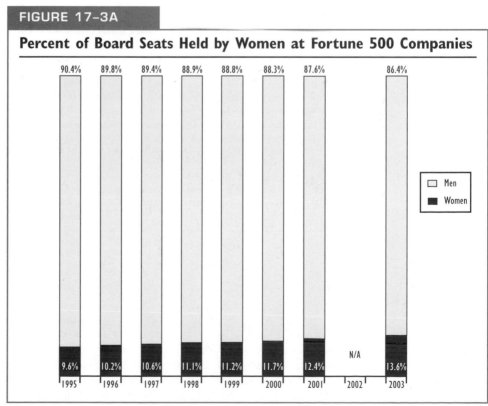

FIGURE 17–3A

Percent of Board Seats Held by Women at Fortune 500 Companies

	1995	1996	1997	1998	1999	2000	2001	2002	2003
Men	90.4%	89.8%	89.4%	88.9%	88.8%	88.3%	87.6%	N/A	86.4%
Women	9.6%	10.2%	10.6%	11.1%	11.2%	11.7%	12.4%		13.6%

Source: 2003 Catalyst Census of Women Board Directors. Reprinted by permission.

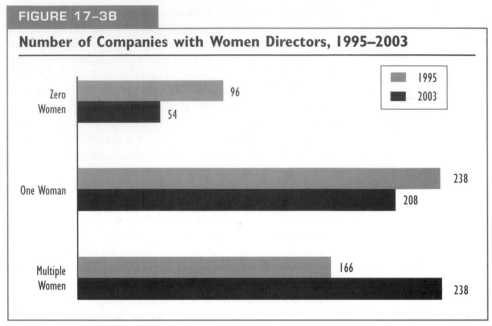

FIGURE 17-3B

Number of Companies with Women Directors, 1995–2003

Legend: 1995, 2003

Zero Women: 96 (1995), 54 (2003)

One Woman: 238 (1995), 208 (2003)

Multiple Women: 166 (1995), 238 (2003)

Source: 2003 Catalyst Census of Women Board Directors, http://www.catalystwomen.org/press_room/factsheets/WBD_03_ff.pdf. Reprinted by permission.

FIGURE 17-4

2004 Catalyst Award Winners for Innovative, Effective, and Measurable Initiatives to Advance Women

General Electric's initiative, *Developing Women Leaders: Synergistic Forces Driving Change,* aligns the goals of the company's performance management and succession planning system with those of the General Electric Women's Network to provide women the information, tools, and experiences to become leaders.

Harley-Davidson's program, *Optimizing Talent: A Culture of Empowerment,* encourages the development and promotion of diverse talent through a flattened organizational structure, intensive employee development and empowerment to make business decisions, and a performance management process that ensures the visibility of talent across functional boundaries.

Shell's initiative, *Valuing and Leveraging Diversity to Become a Model of Inclusiveness,* focuses on developing and advancing women and people of colour. This is a comprehensive effort based on the organization's business principles and includes tools to assess the current state, map future goals, and provide specific direction for diversity management.

Source: Catalyst, news release, http://www.catalystwomen.org/2004award.htm.

only one out of every two women believes that a complaint would be seriously addressed in their workplace.[40]

It is difficult to document fully the extent to which sexual harassment has become a major issue in North American business today. With the increasing number of women in the work force, however, it is understandable why sexual harassment has become a much-debated issue. Sexual harassment has been a high-profile issue ever since 1991, when U.S. Supreme Court nominee Clarence Thomas was accused of sexual harassment by Anita Hill, a former employee of the U.S. Equal Employment Opportunity Commission. People witnessed days of televised hearings over the issue, and the event created a springboard for many women to come forward and publicly claim that they had been sexually harassed by co-workers in the past. Opinion was divided as to whether Hill had actually been sexually harassed by Thomas ten years earlier, and Thomas was eventually confirmed to a seat on the highest court. The Thomas hearings were a watershed event for sexual harassment. The hearings catapulted sexual harassment into the limelight, just as the explosion at the Union Carbide plant in Bhopal, India, and the massive oil spill from the Exxon *Valdez* made workplace safety and environmental issues, respectively, major concerns.

Implicit in this definition are two broad types of sexual harassment. First is what has been called *quid pro quo* harassment. This is a situation where something is given or received for something else. For example, a boss may make it explicit or implicit that a sexual favour is expected if the employee wants a pay raise or a promotion. Second is what has been referred to as *hostile work environment* harassment. In this type, nothing is given or received, but the employee perceives a hostile or offensive work environment by virtue of uninvited sexually oriented behaviours or materials being present in the workplace. Examples of this might include sexual teasing or jokes or sexual materials, such as pictures or cartoons, being present in the workplace.

Figure 17–5 lists the kinds of experiences women are typically talking about when they say they have been sexually harassed.

Corporate Responses to Sexual Harassment. It is clear that sexual harassment is legally and ethically wrong. Most major companies have already begun taking steps to raise the corporate consciousness about sexual harassment. These efforts include, but are not limited to, letters from the CEO, workshops and training as to what constitutes sexual harassment, policies highlighted in company handbooks, worker orientation programs, films, and role-playing exercises.[41] Other companies are employing sexual harassment audits, which pose a series of questions designed to root out discriminatory practices.[42] Following are some other suggested guidelines:[43]

- Educate employees as to prohibited conduct.
- Re-examine, revise, and reissue written policy statements on the subject.
- Make employees aware of how to obtain redress if harassed.
- Introduce, or update, training programs.
- Make certain that environmental harassment ("hostile environment") is absent from the workplace.
- Get input from women employees and union leaders.

FIGURE 17–5

Examples of Sexual Harassment Complaints

- Being subjected to sexually suggestive remarks and propositions
- Being subjected to sexual innuendo and joking
- Being touched by a boss while working
- Co-workers' "remarks" about a person sexually cooperating with the boss
- Suggestive looks and gestures
- Deliberate touching and "cornering"
- Suggestive body movements
- Sexually oriented materials being circulated around the office
- Pressure for dates and sexual favours

Note: It should be noted that these are "complaints." Whether each item turns out to be sexual harassment or not in the eyes of the law is determined in an official hearing or trial.

Ethics In Practice

Matters of the Heart?

I had been working as a staff accountant for a well-known Canadian public accounting firm for six months. One evening, my manager approached me and asked if I would be interested in going to dinner with him one weekend. I declined. Following this incident, I noticed that my performance appraisals seemed less positive and I did not receive as many interesting work allocations from my manager.

1. Has sexual harassment taken place in this case?

2. What would you have done in this situation?
   a. Continued this job without confronting the manager about the work situation.
   b. Quit and acted as if nothing had happened.
   c. Confronted the manager to see if anything changed following the incident.
   d. Other. (Describe.)

Contributed Anonymously

In 1998, Mitsubishi Motors agreed to make a record US$34 million payment to settle a sexual harassment case involving female factory workers at a plant in Illinois. In 1997, Mitsubishi made a reported US$9.5 million payment to settle a separate lawsuit with similar charges.[44] It is not surprising, therefore, that a 1998 survey by the National Association of Independent Insurers found that insurers offering sexual harassment coverage have begun writing more policies and seeing more claims.[45] Clearly, companies are taking a two-pronged approach to sexual harassment, adopting policies that discourage harassment while protecting themselves from the financial costs that can result from sexual harassment lawsuits.

The huge surge in sexual harassment claims that took place in the early 1990s has slowed, but the number of claims remains high: with thousands of cases filed each year in North America.[46] Clearly, employers must develop comprehensive programs to protect their employees from harassment as well as to support the advancement of women in the workplace.

Age and Religious Discrimination

Issues surrounding discrimination on the basis of age or religion are increasing with each year. In the case of age discrimination, the aging of millions of North American baby boomers caused a rise in the cost of age discrimination lawsuits.[47] However, the awards for age discrimination are not obtained easily. One typical type of age discrimination involves older workers, some only in their 40s, being laid off to save money because younger workers can be paid less. Many companies get around this issue by requiring workers to sign waivers of their right to sue in order to receive severance packages. One employment lawyer is quoted as saying that his firm is agreeing to take fewer age bias cases, not because there is less bias occurring but because age discrimination cases are notoriously hard to win.[48] After a review of age discrimination in the workplace, Sheldon Steinhauser concluded:

> … firms can no longer afford to tolerate cultures of negativity toward older workers…. This number will increase drastically as the baby boomer generation ages. Further, trends in pension benefits, potential

changes in Social Security, better health and fitness, and higher education levels will keep many of these people working longer. And they will all be covered by workplace laws banning age discrimination. Employers that fail to wake up to age discrimination and age bias in the workplace could collectively spend millions, perhaps even billions, of dollars in court-imposed fines, punitive damages, and legal fees. Executives need to take action now to minimize wrongful termination complaints and lawsuits in the future.[49]

The issue of age discrimination was clearly illustrated in the case of *Galbraith v. Acres International Limited*. David Galbraith was hired in 1988 as controller of Acres International with responsibility for the financial services group, including treasury, accounting, commercial, financial analysis, and management information services. He subsequently received a series of promotions until 1997. In 1997, management consultants were hired to assess Acres' financial performance and their report recommended that "fresh younger members be introduced to the management team." Consequently, the president proposed that a financial officer be hired to take over the accounting responsibilities from Galbraith.

Galbraith would essentially be demoted and his salary would be frozen except for increases in the cost of living. Galbraith, insulted that his role was reduced, brought an action for wrongful dismissal. The court agreed with his claim that the change in job duties constituted a constructive dismissal. In addition, the court believed that the central factor in the employer's decision to change employment duties was the employee's age—a prohibited ground of discrimination.[50]

With regard to avoiding religious discrimination, companies should pay particular note to the notion of reasonable accommodation. **Reasonable accommodation** involves adapting employment policies and practices so that no individual is denied benefits, disadvantaged with respect to employment opportunities, or precluded from carrying out the central components of a job because of race, colour, sex, or disability. This can include reallocating tasks, redesigning job duties, revising work schedules, providing technical, financial, and human support services, and upgrading facilities.

Human rights tribunals across Canada require employers to demonstrate flexibility in accommodating the reasonable needs of employees. Employers may be required to revise their current policy or practice in order to meet the needs of their employees, provided this does not cause "undue hardship to the employer." Undue hardship may entail safety or efficiency issues.

A case presented before the Ontario Human Rights Commission illustrates the responsibilities of employers to prove undue hardship where reasonable accommodation is not given to employees with specific needs. Two employees of the Ford Motor Company of Canada, in Oakville, Ontario, refused to work on Friday nights because it conflicted with their religious day-of-rest observance required by the Worldwide Church of God. Ford argued that they were not obliged to accommodate these employees because of undue hardship. Specifically, Ford offered evidence of the practical difficulties of providing the two employees with alternate work schedules, including the fact that the plant was currently battling high levels of absenteeism on Friday evenings for reasons unrelated to religious observance, the alternative work schedule would interfere with seniority arrangements under the collective bargaining agreement, and replacement workers were reluctant to work the Friday evening shift. In sum, the court agreed that Ford would face undue hardship and consequently was not obliged to accommodate the religious observance of these two employees.[51]

While Ford's unique circumstances did not require them to accommodate their employees, employers are nevertheless well advised to consider how they can better meet the diverse needs of an increasingly diverse work force. It is clear from our discussion that workers rights need to be respected, and employers who consider ways of accommodating such diversity will gain in both employee morale and reputation. Future lawsuits are certain to break new ground as companies and the courts determine how to deal with religious discrimination in the workplace.[52]

Employment Equity

The Department of Justice Canada defines equity as focusing on "treating people fairly by recognizing that different individuals and groups require different measures to ensure fair and comparable results."[53] In layperson's terms, the notion of equity is equated with fairness and impartiality. **Employment equity** refers to the treatment of employees in a fair and nonbiased manner. This term was developed by Judge Rosalie Silberman Abella, Commissioner of the Royal Commission on Equality in Employment (1984), to reflect a distinct Canadian process for achieving equality in all areas of employment. In addition, the term was intended to distinguish the process from the U.S. notion of "affirmative action," as well as to move beyond the "equal opportunity" measures that were available in Canada at that time.

Under the authority of the Commission, a process was developed to deal with systemic discrimination in the workplace. According to the Commission, "systemic discrimination" was responsible for most of the inequality found in employment.

Ethics In Practice

Is Religion Allowed in the Workplace?

For six months I worked as a receptionist at a local doctor's office that employed about 30 people. The owner and head practitioner was a member of a religious cult. During business hours, everything seemed normal for a doctor's office of this size, but during the two-hour lunch break, all of the employees had to go upstairs and go "on course." These mandatory courses encompassed everything from communication skills to office efficiency. They were all designed by a man who founded the religious cult of which my boss was a member. Granted that they were business teachings, other staff members and I felt that these teachings were heavily weighted with religious undertones.

For example, one of the most important keys to these lessons was that you had to understand every word. After every exercise we were individually tested to make sure that we knew all of the words. Most of the words that I didn't understand could not be found in the dictionary, because they came straight from the man's religious teachings. Whenever I questioned my boss about a word, it usually led to a long discussion about the cult leader's works and I would have to read paragraphs out of the religious teachings to "fully understand" the meaning. To me, it felt as though I was being brainwashed, and from then on I scheduled my university classes during this course time.

My dilemma was this: Did the doctor have the right to insist that we submit to such "teachings," which made us uncomfortable?

1. Is any form of discrimination or harassment taking place in this case?

2. What ethical issues arise in this case?

3. If you were faced with this dilemma, what action would you take?

Contributed by Allison Grice

Employment equity was designed as an ongoing planning process used by an employer to accomplish a number of objectives, including:

- Eliminating employment barriers for the four designated groups identified in the Employment Equity Act—women, persons with disabilities, Aboriginal people, and members of visible minorities.
- Redressing past discrimination in employment opportunities and preventing future barriers.
- Improving access for the designated groups and increasing their distribution throughout all occupations and at all levels.
- Fostering a climate of equity in the organization.
- Implementing positive policies and practices to ensure the effects of systemic barriers are eliminated.[54]

Employment equity is an issue for all individuals regardless of their sex, religion, age, national origin, colour, or position in an organization. Consequently, managers must understand the issue of fairness and how personal biases can influence the employee–employer relationship. They should also be aware that both direct discrimination and indirect discrimination are forbidden by employment law.

Employment equity is a desirable aim beyond the ethical and legal reasons. By extending the base of qualified individuals for employment, training, and promotions, it can help organizations improve effectiveness. By ensuring fair treatment across the board, it reduces the risk of losing valued members due to discontent with the work environment. It can also help build employee moral and commitment by sending out a clear message that the company cares about the treatment of its employees. In addition, such treatment can reflect positively on the organization's image and reputation.[55]

The Legal Basis of the Employment Equity Act

The notion of employment equity is derived from the wording of federal and provincial employment standards legislation, human rights codes, and the Canadian Charter of Rights and Freedoms. Employment equity encompasses a number of activities, including identifying and removing systemic barriers to employment opportunities that adversely affect the four designated groups and implementing special measures to remove any barriers and provide reasonable accommodation.

The Employment Equity Act was passed in 1986. Its purpose includes the following mandate:

> ... to achieve equality in the workplace so that no person shall be denied employment opportunities or benefits for reasons unrelated to ability and, in the fulfillment of the goals, to correct the conditions of disadvantage in employment experienced by women, Aboriginal peoples, persons with disabilities, and visible minority people by giving effect to the principle that employment equity means more than treating persons in the same way but also requires special measures and the accommodation of differences.[56]

The second Employment Equity Act received royal assent in 1995 and came into force on October 24, 1996. It built upon the earlier legislation and clarifies and enforces employer obligations as outlined in the act. The act governs private sector employers under federal jurisdiction as well as almost all employees of the federal government.[57]

Figure 17–6 offers a brief outline of the history leading up to the development of the Employment Equity Act.

The Employment Equity Act (1995) requires employers and Crown corporations that have 100 employees or more and that are regulated under the Canada Labour Code to implement employment equity and report on their results. Under the act, the employer must:

- Distribute to employees a questionnaire that allows them to indicate whether they belong to one of the four designated groups.
- Identify jobs in which the percentage of members of designated groups is below their relative representation in the labour market.
- Disseminate information on employment equity to employees, and consult with employee representatives.
- Scrutinize the current employment system in order to assess whether any barriers exist which may limit the employment opportunities of members of designated groups.
- Generate an employment equity plan directed at promoting an equitable workplace.

FIGURE 17–6

History of Employment Equity

1950s–1960s

- New employment statutes in most Canadian jurisdictions prohibited racial and religious discrimination and prescribed equal pay for men and women.
- 1960: The first Canadian Bill of Rights was introduced.
- Equal Opportunity: One of the first concepts commonly used to define equality in employment for all Canadians. However, Equal Opportunity programs did not result in any significant redistribution in the employment of disadvantaged group members in the Canadian work force.

1970s

- Increased pressure from women and minority groups led federal, provincial, and municipal governments to establish special programs to improve the employment situation of these groups. Human Rights Commissions were established in all provinces by the mid-1970s.
- 1977: Parliament enacted the Canadian Human Rights Act.
- 1978: The federal government launched a voluntary Affirmative Action Program aimed at private industry.

1980s

- 1983: The Royal Commission on Equality in Employment was established to address the lack of progress experienced through voluntary affirmative action programs.
- 1984: Judge Rosalie Abella released the Commission's report and coined the term *employment equity* to describe the Canadian approach to dealing with employment disadvantage.
- 1985: The federal government responded to the Commission's report by introducing Bill 62: a Bill with respect to Employment Equity. Section 15 of the Charter of Rights and Freedoms came into effect, further strengthening the idea of workplace equality.
- 1986: The Employment Equity Act was passed.

1990s

- 1995: The second Employment Equity Act received royal assent in 1995 and came into force on October 24, 1996.

Source: Human Resources Canada, http://www.sdc.gc.ca/en/lp/lo/lswe/we/information/history.shtml. Reproduced with the permission of the Minister of Public Works and Government Services Canada, 2004.

- Endeavour to implement the employment equity plan.
- Monitor, assess, and revise the plan in a timely fashion.
- Complete an annual report on the company's employment equity status and activities.

Employment Equity Planning in the Organization

The Employment Equity Act requires all federally regulated employers to prepare an employment equity plan. The successful implementation of employment equity in an organization requires that it be integrated into the overall business strategy. The Federal Contractors Program offers an overview of what a plan should include.[58] As succinctly summarized by Belcourt and colleagues,[59] the implementation of employment equity involves six steps: (1) senior management support, (2) data collection and analysis, (3) an employment system review, (4) establishment of a work plan, (5) implementation, and (6) a follow-up process that includes monitoring, reviewing, and revision.

Step 1: Senior Management Commitment Commitment to an employment equity plan requires top management support. Ideally, the business leader will publicly introduce a written policy describing the organization's commitment to employment equity. The contents of such a policy should be disseminated throughout the organization.

The policy statement requires ample detail and explanation. Supplemental communication therefore should include an explanation of what employment equity is, the reason for the program, and its implications for current and future employees. Such communication should also identify the persons responsible for administering the program, and any planned activities necessary to establish the program (e.g., assessment of the work force or of policies and procedures). Methods of communication may also include information sessions, workplace posters, departmental or group meetings, orientation and training programs, newsletters, employee handbooks, and memos from the union. The commitment to employment equity must cover all aspects of the employment relationship, including recruitment, work assignment, training opportunities, compensation, promotions, transfers, and terminations.

Responsibility for employment equity should be assigned to a senior manager, a joint labour–management committee, and an employment equity advisory committee (or, in nonunion contexts, for consultation with designated employee representatives). Those assigned such duties should have sufficient knowledge regarding the problems and concerns of designated groups, and they should be capable of gaining the cooperation of employees at all levels in the organization. Such individuals should also be prepared to assess and report on the results of employment equity measures in such areas as employment practices, training and recruitment policies, the organization of work schedules and facilities, and systems for promotion.

Step 2: Data Collection and Analysis Assessment of employment practices and policies requires the development of an internal work force profile. This includes a "snapshot" of the current nature of the organization—such as how many members of designated groups are employed in the organization, and what are their positions, salaries, and status? Other critical information includes the distribution of designated groups in applications, interviews, hiring decisions, training and promotion opportunities, and terminations.

Much of the data required for equity planning (e.g., salary, sex, access to benefits, seniority status, occupational and career history within the organization) is contained in personnel files. On the other hand, information regarding the distribution of members of designated groups in the employer's organization must be obtained through a self-identification process. The Employment Equity Act permits employers to gather data on members of designated groups with the voluntary consent of employees and solely for the purpose of employment equity planning or reporting.

Step 3: Employment Systems Review "Employment systems" and "employment practices" refer to such personnel activities as recruitment, hiring, training and development, promotion, job classification, discipline, and termination. The review of these practices may require an assessment of personnel manuals, or collective agreements. In addition, certain practices may lack formal documentation and have simply become accepted practice. These too must be scrutinized.

Step 4: Establishment of a Work Plan The workplace review and assessment is aimed at assisting the employer in developing a plan to address the equity issue. The analysis forms part of the employment equity work plan. The plan is aimed at identifying how intended actions will yield desirable results. This plan should be a central part of the organization's overall operational plans, and typically would include:

- An estimate of concrete goals including numerical goals with time frames (e.g., 45 percent of our personnel should be women).
- An identification of programs or activities aimed at achieving the estimated goals.
- A description of the planned changes in hiring, training, and promotion of the four designated groups in order to improve their representation and distribution throughout the organization.
- An indication of the methods of monitoring and evaluating the program implementation.

It is important for the organization to keep in mind the ultimate aim of its equity work plan. As human resource expert Monica Belcourt observed:

> *The overall goal for an organization is to achieve a representative workforce. An organization's workforce is representative when it reflects the demographic composition of the external workforce. A nonrepresentative workforce is an indicator of the need for evaluation and action to remove the barriers that block or discourage certain groups from employment and advancement. Workplan initiatives in conjunction with special measures and reasonable accommodation should contribute to the overall success of this goal.*[60]

Step 5: Implementation In addition to the need for senior management commitment, the success of plan implementation depends upon clear definitions of roles and responsibilities, adequate training and resources, an effective communications strategy, and acceptance of plan initiatives and objectives by organizational members. Throughout the implementation period, it may be necessary to adapt the plan as contingencies arise. Consequently, plan strategies may be altered or eliminated when results are not achieved or if resource constraints or economic conditions dictate changes. It is critical that the implementation is consistently monitored by those responsible for its outcomes.

Step 6: Evaluation, Monitoring, and Revision Obviously, it is necessary to monitor and assess the outcomes of the equity initiatives used to achieve a representative work force, as well as to adapt to organizational and environmental changes. Progress reports provided to all members should communicate plan initiatives and outcomes. Monitoring and evaluation may determine whether a plan is successful or whether additional actions need to be taken. Consequently, such activity can help assess whether revisions need to be made to the plans and build on past experience.

Advocates and Opponents of Employment Equity

Both employment equity in Canada and affirmative action in the U.S. share the notion that certain groups may receive preferential treatment in order to redress historical inequities faced by these groups in the work force. Let us briefly consider some of the arguments that have been set forth both for and against the concept of **preferential treatment**.

The underlying rationale for preferential treatment is the principle of *compensatory justice*, which holds that whenever an injustice is done, just compensation or reparation is owed to the injured party or parties.[61] Many people believe that groups discriminated against in the past (e.g., women, blacks, Aboriginals) should be recompensed for these injustices by positive employment equity. Over the years, deliberate barriers were placed on opportunities for minorities. These groups were prevented from participating in business, law, universities, and other desirable professions and institutions. Additionally, when official barriers were finally dropped, matters frequently did not improve. Inequalities became built into the system, and although mechanisms for screening and promotion did not intentionally discriminate against certain groups, they did favour other groups. Thus, the view that we can and should restore the balance of justice by showing preferential treatment became established as a viable option for moving more quickly toward economic equality in the workplace and in our society.[62]

Those opposed to employment equity have argued that it can lead to **reverse discrimination**. This concept holds that when any sort of preference is given to minorities, women, or other groups, discrimination may occur against those in the majority—often, but not always, white males. For well over a decade, lawsuits have been filed in the U.S. by individuals who have argued that they have been the victims of reverse discrimination where women or minorities have been given preference.[63] These individuals argue that the law prohibits discrimination based on race, colour, or sex and that this includes reverse discrimination as well.

Search the web

Employment Equity Resources on the Web

1. *HRDC Workplace Equity.* The HRDC Workplace Equity Web site (**http://info.load-otea.hrdc-drhc. gc. ca/workplace_equity/home.shtml**) is a national clearinghouse of employment equity technical expertise. Through the site, you can obtain general information on equal pay and employment equity, or access tools and resources for the implementation of employment equity as well as information on legislation and programs.

2. *The Department of Social Development.* This department is mandated with breaking down barriers to equality of opportunity for Canadians. Responsibilities include helping families with children, supporting people with disabilities, and ensuring that seniors can fully participate in their communities. The department provides policies, services, and programs for Canadians who need assistance in overcoming challenges they encounter in their lives and their communities. Check out their site at **http://www.hrdc-drhc.gc.ca/dept/ dept_social.shtml**.

3. *The Department of Human Resources and Skills Development (HRSD).* HRSD supports human capital development and labour market development. Among their clients are employees, employers, individuals receiving Employment Insurance benefits, students, and those who need focused support to participate in the workplace. HRSD provides federal-level management of labour and homelessness issues, and supports students and communities through the Canada Student Loans Program and Community Economic Development initiatives. Visit their site at **http://www.hrdc-drhc.gc.ca/ dept/dept_hrsd.shtml**.

In Canada, the issue has not been as controversial. Section 15 of the Charter of Rights and Freedoms came into effect in 1985, and it further strengthened the drive toward workplace equality. In addition, subsection 15(2) acknowledges that equality requires that the conditions of disadvantage be addressed. This means that the argument that employment equity is "reverse discrimination" is not considered to be legally valid in Canada. In contrast to discrimination, employment equity does not target individuals or groups for exclusion. Its aim, as described above, is to ensure the inclusion of groups that were excluded in the past.[64]

It is not easy to generalize on how the corporate community feels about employment equity and affirmative action. Initially, business was opposed to the idea. As time passed, however, and as business leaders gained experience with equity programs, their views changed. The Canadian corporate sector largely does not appear to be opposed to employment equity (nor to affirmative action in the U.S.). However, it is also clear that business would prefer to be free of government mandates.

The business community seems to have accepted employment equity programs as good business policy. Some executives see goals and timetables simply as good ways of measuring progress, and others see them as ways to stave off expensive discrimination suits. For some employers, employment equity has practical business value in customer relations, especially for makers of consumer goods and providers of consumer services. Companies are increasingly recognizing that their diversity programs may constitute a competitive advantage or may be used as competitive weapons and that this strategic incentive is an added reason for them to stay on track.

More and more businesses have begun to recognize that employment equity is "good for business," and Canada continues to strengthen its programs in order to exploit the strength of an increasingly diverse work force. Among the numerous organizations that focus on employee equity is the Bank of Montreal Group of Companies (BMO). BMO recently received accolades from the Conference Board of Canada for its employment equity and diversity initiatives, including its employee-led diversity action teams, internal employee assistance program, and its recently launched project to help identify workplace barriers among persons with disabilities.

Many businesses have also stepped up their efforts to assist the Aboriginal community in gaining greater self-sufficiency and participation in the work force. There are a number of companies that have been actively involved in boosting the presence of Aboriginals in the workplace. Many businesses have proven that they can work with Aboriginal communities, educational institutions, and government to enhance employment prospects for Aboriginals. A typical recruitment method for companies is to offer support for educational institutions, training initiatives, and scholarships for Aboriginal students. For example, 3M Canada contributes to bursaries given through the Department of Indian and Northern Affairs Canada for Aboriginal students who are pursuing careers in fields related to health care. In addition, recruitment strategies that reach out to Aboriginal communities and organizations are also employed.[65]

Dating back to 1990, the federal government formally recognizes federally regulated companies for achievements in implementing employment equity and addressing the needs of a diverse work force. Employment Equity Awards have been given to those organizations deemed as models in the establishment and implementation of equity practices. The Vision Award is presented to those organizations that exhibited outstanding approaches to the implementation of equity, diversity, and inclusiveness in the workplace. The Certificate of Merit is presented to organizations for their sustained efforts toward attaining a representative work force.

Recent awards have been presented to such high achievers in equity and diversity as Pelmorex Inc., the company that runs the Weather Network. Employee surveys conducted at Pelmorex indicated that more than 90 percent of employees feel the company highly values equity. This company also offers training on nondiscriminatory interviewing techniques, integrating new employees into the workplace, and accommodation strategies. Interestingly, the company rewards managers for their support of the company's efforts—annual bonuses for managers are linked to promoting equity.

The Saskatoon-based trucking company Yanke Group was another recent award winner. It was recognized for its involvement with community organizations in order to facilitate the hiring of people with disabilities and Aboriginals. In addition, Yanke Group was applauded for its practice of generating employment equity benchmarks, which are reviewed quarterly. Figure 17–7 lists other recipients of these government awards.

Pay Equity

Pay equity refers to two different issues—the legislation and the principles behind it. On the one hand, pay equity is entrenched in legislation and can be referred to in its legal sense. Pay equity came into law as the result of an amendment to the Canadian Human Rights Act in 1978 that made it illegal for employers to discriminate against individuals on the basis of job content. There are legislated programs that attempt to

---

FIGURE 17–7

Employment Equity Awards

Vision Awards: IBM Canada, Markham, Ontario

- Diversity presentations are given to all new employees with an emphasis on the importance of equity and a discrimination-free workplace. Additional training opportunities are available focusing on cultural differences, misconceptions, and stereotypes.

- In 2003, IBM launched the Canadian Women's Leadership Council, involving the participation of women executives and senior leaders to become active in the development of high-potential women in IBM Canada. This program mirrors the goals of a similar body created in 2002 to increase development of visible minorities.

- For the past five years, IBM Canada's visually impaired employees have mentored students at the Canadian National Institute for the Blind's Summer Camp to acquaint them with technology.

- The company's Black Network Group delivers technology workshops at community-based organizations with donated equipment to assist with program delivery and training. Members of the Aboriginal work force and Native students also participate in company-sponsored workshops and outreach programs.

Certificates of Merit: Shell Canada Limited, Calgary, Alberta

- Shell Canada provides diversity awareness training to all employees, including management, and has implemented an Ombuds office to facilitate fair and equitable resolution of workplace issues.

- In 2001, the company completed a review of their progress related to diversity and implemented various initiatives, including hiring a full-time diversity advisor and developing a diversity gap analysis to help identify priority areas of action.

- The company offers a disability management program to assist ill or injured employees.

- Shell Canada supports the recruitment and retention of Aboriginal employees through participation in Aboriginal community outreach programs, funding of educational initiatives, and offering scholarships through the National Aboriginal Achievement Foundation.

Source: Government of Canada, http://www.sdc.gc.ca/en/lp/lo/lswe/we/merit_awards/2003/index-we.shtml.

achieve equity in pay. The objective of pay equity legislation is to eliminate the historical wage gap that has existed between men and women and to ensure that salary ranges reflect the value of the work performed.

Three kinds of laws offer provisions governing equal pay: human rights legislation, employment standards legislation, and pay equity legislation. Human rights laws and employment standards laws typically target the more blatant kinds of discrimination—the wage gap between men and women who hold the same, or similar, job. Some of these laws apply to both government and private sectors, while in some jurisdictions they apply only to the government sector.

Aside from its legal meaning, the notion of pay equity refers to two important principles: (1) equal pay for equal work and (2) equal pay for work of equal value or comparable worth.[66] That is, pay equity can be approached from two directions: equal pay and comparable worth. Each of these principles has a different implication with regard to how comparisons are made in the wage gaps between men and women.

Equal pay argues that workers doing the same job should receive the same pay, irrespective of gender. All else being equal, men and women should receive the same pay for the same job. Implementing this principle involves a direct comparison of jobs filled by men and women where the job is the same or essentially the same. Violations of the principle of "equal pay for equal work" potentially constitute blatant wage discrimination on the basis of gender.

Although many believe that the gap between men's and women's incomes has closed since the human rights activism of the 1960s, a recent study by the Economic Policy Institute says otherwise. The report shows that, in recent times, women continue to earn only about three-fourths of the income earned by men.[67] This is relatively unchanged from the wage differentials throughout the 1990s.[68] In 2002, women aged 15 and over who had employment income made 79.3 cents for every dollar earned by their male counterparts (however, the gap was smaller for younger women).[69] Some have tried to explain the discrepancy by arguing that these statistics include women who lost both time and experience through extended maternity leave. A recent study from the Economic Policy Institute evaluated this issue by studying highly accomplished new media workers. They found that female Internet workers were earning, on average, $10 000 less per year than comparable male workers. According to Rosemary Batt, a co-author of the study, "Along gender lines, the new economy doesn't seem to be very different from the old economy."[70]

The second principle behind pay equity, equal pay for work of equal value, underscores the need to eliminate wage gaps between men and women that may exist in jobs of a different nature that are considered "male" or "female" jobs. In other words, male and female workers must be paid the same wage rate for jobs of a similar nature even though they may have different titles (e.g., "nurse's aide" and "orderly"). This principle of comparable worth presents a more controversial solution: Workers doing different jobs should receive the same pay if those different jobs have equal inherent worth (i.e., contribute equally to the firm's performance). While pay equity legislation requires that people holding equal positions receive equal compensation, the pay of men and women remains disparate, due largely to the wage effects of labour market segregation, whereby jobs traditionally held by women pay less than their requirements or contributions might indicate. The persistent disparity between men's and women's median incomes has led some legal scholars and women's advocates to recommend comparable worth.[71] Opponents counter that it is not pragmatic to apply comparable worth[72] given that inherent job worth is a subject that is difficult to measure reliably and accurately.[73]

Advocates of comparable worth argue that differences in seniority and education cannot explain the fact that women generally earn only about three-fourths of what men do. They argue that certain jobs are paid less just because they are traditionally held by women. Consider the case of clerical work. Clerical work was a male-dominated occupation for most of the nineteenth century. However, subsequent to the invention of the typewriter, clerical work became routinized, and it no longer provided entry into the organization's internal labour market. Consequently, clerical work was *re-gendered* as female work, given that women could be hired to perform it for less pay, while men were able to obtain higher-paying work with greater opportunities for advancement.[74]

Achieving the directives of pay equity first requires a comparison of the work of female-dominated job classes with the value of work performed by males. Such comparisons require the use of a gender-neutral, unbiased comparison system to evaluate the jobs in an organization.[75] Comparisons are based on the amount and type of skill, effort, and responsibility needed to perform the job as well as on the working conditions. The comparison may include a fair valuation of job characteristics that have traditionally been associated with male and female work. For example, the valuation must be conducted in a manner that is equitable in its valuation of the characteristics of "male" jobs, such as heavy lifting and "dirty" working conditions, in comparison to the characteristics of "female" jobs, such as manual dexterity and caring for others.[76] Figure 17–8 presents information regarding the Government of Canada's Equal Pay Program.

FIGURE 17–8

Equal Pay Program

Program Objective
The Labour Program's objective is to eliminate sex-based wage discrimination in the federal jurisdiction.

Program Overview
Employers are responsible for implementing equal pay. The Labour Program believes that employers should be given an opportunity to understand the legislation. They should also be given sufficient time to implement pay equity plans prior to being inspected for compliance. The Labour Program has identified the following three-step process in order to determine employer compliance and to respond to non-compliance.

Step 1: Education
The first step is an educational visit. It is intended to inform federal jurisdiction employers of their obligations with respect to the equal pay legislation and to advise them of the means to fulfill these obligations.

Step 2: Monitoring
The second step is a monitoring visit to these same employers to answer technical questions, to verify the employer's progress on implementation, and to obtain general information. Monitoring visits will be conducted throughout the implementation process.

Step 3: Audit or Inspection
The final step is an on-site inspection. On-site audits are arranged with employers who report that they have fully implemented an equal pay program. When employers have not taken any action to review their compensation system for gender discrimination, the Labour Program can schedule an inspection. If the inspector identifies reasonable grounds for believing that gender-based wage discrimination exists, then the case may be referred to the Canadian Human Rights Commission for investigation and resolution.

Source: Government of Canada, http://www.sdc.gc.ca/en/lp/lo/lswe/we/programs/epp/index-we.shtml.

Among the most prominent companies embroiled in pay equity disputes in recent years has been Bell Canada. Its battle over pay equity started when seven human rights complaints were filed against Bell Canada between 1990 and 1994, alleging that female employees were being paid lower wages than male employees for performing work of equal value. In addition, a complaint was filed with the Canadian Human Rights Commission in 1995. The Bell workers had claimed that they were owed raises of as much as 20 percent going back to 1992. The demand for salary adjustments was based on a study of the work performed in such positions as telephone operators, clerical staff, and sales associates, most of these employees being women. Their salaries were compared with other job functions that were dominated by men. In 2002, Bell Canada tentatively settled the pay equity dispute with thousands of its largely female staff for $178 million. More than two-thirds of the settlement, $128 million, was set aside as a cash payout. The other $50 million was allocated for pension improvements. The agreement was reached between representatives of Bell Canada and the Canadian Telecommunications Employees' Association (CTEA), the union representing 96 percent of the employees involved in the dispute.[77]

Summary

This chapter addresses several subgroups of employee stakeholders whose job rights are protected by law. Organizations need to take a closer look at their policies and practices in order to combat and prevent both direct and indirect discrimination. Employment equity was one of the government's answers to the problem of systemic discrimination. While some controversy has surrounded the question of how far employment equity should go, it seems clear that corporate Canada cannot ignore the needs of an increasingly diverse labour force. Corporations have undertaken employment equity by building their human resource management policies on employment equity principles, and they will likely continue these practices in the future. Sound stakeholder management requires that companies continue to be fair in their employment practices.

Key Terms

designated groups (page 524)
disparate treatment (page 530)
employment equity (page 540)
pay equity (page 547)

preferential treatment (page 545)
reasonable accommodation (page 539)
reverse discrimination (page 545)

Discussion Questions

1. List the major legislation protecting against discrimination and indicate what they prohibit. Which agency is primarily responsible for enforcing these laws?

2. Give two different definitions of discrimination, and provide an example of each.

3. What effect do you think employee equity programs have in the Canadian workplace? Explain your answer.

4. Explain the dilemma of employment equity versus reverse discrimination. Is it an issue? Explain.

5. To whom do you think preferential treatment should be given in university admissions? Explain your answer.

Endnotes

1. Statistics Canada, http://www.statcan.ca/.
2. Human Resources Development Canada, "Annual Report, Analysis of Employers' Reports," http://www.hrdc-drhc.gc.ca/LEEP/Annual _Reports/03.
3. Statistics Canada, http://www.statcan.ca/; Canadian Labour Congress, http://clc-ctc.ca/web/workplace_works/en/realities.htm.
4. Human Resources Development Canada, *Annual Report, Employment Equity Act, 2003*, Labour Standards and Workplace Equity, Cat. No. MP31-5/2002; Human Resources Development Canada, "Workplace Equity," http://info.load-otea.hrdc-drhc.gc.ca/workplace_equity/leep/annual/2002/.
5. A. Tomlinson, "Wall Street Rougher than Bay Street," *Canadian HR Reporter* (Vol. 15, No. 5, March 11, 2002), 1, 14.
6. Women's Executive Network, http://www.wxnetwork.com/images/externalrpt_2002.pdf; Asha Tomlinson, "Is There a War of the Sexes? It Depends on Who You Ask," *Canadian HR Reporter* (Vol. 15, No. 18, October 21, 2002), 2–3.
7. Stelios Loizides, "Aboriginal Baby Boom a Challenge for Employment Prospects," *Canadian HR Reporter* (Vol. 16, No. 22, December 15, 2003), 10.
8. David Brown, "Overcoming Sense of Exclusion Is Key to Making Inroads in Mainstream Jobs," *Canadian HR Reporter* (Vol. 16, No. 22, December 15, 2003), 9.
9. Loizides, *op cit.*
10. Brown, *op cit.*
11. Canadian Health Network, http://www.canadian-health-network.ca/servlet/ContentServer?cid=1045848110489&pagename=CHN-RCS%2FPage%2FGTPageTemplate&c=Page&lang=En.
12. *Ibid.*
13. Statistics Canada, http://www.statcan.ca/start.html.
14. Statistics Canada, "Designated Minority Representation," http://www.statcan.ca/english/IPS/Data/ 96F0030XIE2001 008.htm; Human Resources Development Canada, "Workplace Equity," http:// www.statcan.ca/Daily/ English/ 030311/d030311a.htm; http://info.loadotea. hrdcdrhc.gc.ca/workplace_equity/ leep/annual/2002/2002annual rep08.shtml.
15. Canadian Council on Social Development, http://www.ccsd.ca/; Canadian Race Relations Foundation, http://www.crr.ca/en/MediaCentre/NewsReleases/eMedCen_NewsRe20010110.htm.
16. Department of Justice, http://canada.justice.gc.ca/en/dept/pub/guide/appendix_C.htm.
17. *Ibid.*
18. Canadian Human Rights Commission, http://www.chrc-ccdp.ca/.
19. Natalie C MacDonald, "Training Staff on Human Rights," *Canadian HR Reporter* (Vol. 16, No. 20, November 17, 2003), G5.
20. Department of Justice, http://canada.justice.gc.ca/en/dept/pub/guide/appendix_C.htm.
21. James Ledvinka, *Federal Regulation of Personnel and Human Resource Management* (Boston: Kent, 1982), 37. Also see W. N. Outten, R. J. Rabin, and L. R. Lipman, *The Rights of Employees and Union Members* (Carbondale, IL: Southern Illinois University Press, 1994), Chapter VIII, 154–156.
22. Roy S. Johnson, "The New Black Power," *Fortune* (August 4, 1997), 47.
23. Eileen P. Gunn, "The Money Men," *Fortune* (August 4, 1997), 75.
24. William F. Glueck and James Ledvinka, "Equal Employment Opportunity Programs," in William F. Glueck, *Personnel: A Diagnostic Approach*, rev. ed. (Dallas, TX: Business Publications, 1978), 304.
25. Ledvinka, 37–38.
26. Department of Justice, http://canada.justice.gc.ca/en/dept/pub/guide/appendix_C.htm.
27. *Griggs v. Duke Power Company*, 401 U.S. 424, 1971.
28. Theodore Purcell, "Minorities, Management of and Equal Employment Opportunity," in L. R. Bittel (ed.), *Encyclopedia of Professional Management* (New York: McGraw-Hill, 1978), 744–745.
29. A. P. Aggarwal, *Sex Discrimination: Employment Law and Practices* (Toronto: Butterworths Canada, 1994).
30. Lesley Young, "Employers Need to Scrutinize All Job Testing for Human Rights Violations, Supreme Court Rules," *Canadian HR Reporter* (Vol. 12, No. 17, October 4, 1999), 3.
31. Department of Justice, http://canada.justice.gc.ca/en/dept/pub/guide/appendix_C.htm.
32. David Brown, "Employers Ignoring Systemic Discrimination," *Canadian HR Reporter* (Vol. 13, No. 22, December 18, 2000), 1, 3.
33. Employment and Immigration Canada, *Employment Equity: A Guide for Employers*, Cat. No. LM-143-5-91 (May 1991), 9.
34. Christine L. Taylor, "Dimensions of Diversity in Canadian Business: Building a Business Case for Valuing Ethnocultural Diversity," *Conference Board of Canada Report 143-95* (April 1995), 1.
35. Employment and Immigration Canada.
36. Catalyst, http://www.catalystwomen.org/2004fin perf.htm.
37. Janet McFarland, "Women Still Find Slow Rise to Power," *The Globe and Mail, Report on Business* (March 13, 2003); Catalyst, 2002 Catalyst Census of Women

Corporate Officers and Top Earners of Canada, http://www.catalystwomen.org/press_room/factsheets/2002_cote_canada_factsheet.pdf.

38. Regina Fazio Maruca, "Says Who?" *Harvard Business Review* (November/December 1997), 15–17.

39. Louisa Wah, "Workplace Conscience Needs a Boost," *American Management Association International* (July/August 1998), 6.

40. Canadian Advisory Council on the Status of Women, "Sexual Harassment," *CACSW Fact Sheet* (March 1993).

41. "Ending Sexual Harassment: Business Is Getting the Message," *Business Week* (March 18, 1991), 98–99.

42. John D. Rapoport and Brian L. P. Zevnik, *The Employee Strikes Back* (New York: Collier Books, 1994), 86–87.

43. Marilyn Machlowitz and David Machlowitz, "Hug by the Boss Could Lead to a Slap from the Judge," *The Wall Street Journal* (September 25, 1986), 20.

44. "Mitsubishi Harassment Settlement Approved," *The New York Times* (June 26, 1998), D20.

45. Dan Lonkevich, "Demand Growing for Harassment Coverage," *National Underwriter (Property and Casualty/Risk and Benefits Management)* (August 10, 1998), 26.

46. John Cloud, "Sex and the Law," *Time* (March 23, 1998), 48–54.

47. Sheldon Steinhauser, "Age Bias: Is Your Corporate Culture in Need of an Overhaul?" *HR Magazine* (July 1998), 86–88.

48. George J. Church, "Unmasking Age Bias," *Time* (September 7, 1998), H3.

49. Steinhauser, 86–88.

50. *Rowbotham v. Addison* [2000] B.C.J. No. 250; *Galbraith v. Acres International Limited*, [2001] O.J. No. 1036 (Ont. C.A.); Natalie C. MacDonald, "Training Staff on Human Rights," *Canadian HR Reporter* (Vol. 16, No. 20, November 17, 2003), G5.

51. *Ontario (Human Rights Commission) v. Roosma*, [2002] O.J. 3688, released Sept. 19, 2002.

52. Mark Hansen, "Suing Bosses over Beliefs," *ABA Journal* (April 1998), 30–32.

53. Department of Justice, http://canada.justice.gc.ca/en/dept/pub/guide/appendix_C.htm.

54. Human Resources Development Canada, http://info.load-otea.hrdc-drhc.gc.ca/workplace_equity/information/what.shtml.

55. *Employment Equity: A Guide for Employers*, Employment and Immigration Canada, Cat. No. LM-143-5-91 (May 1991), 9.

56. *Ibid.*

57. *Ibid.*

58. Human Resources Development Canada, http://info.load-otea.hrdc-drhc.gc.ca/workplace_equity/fcp/suppliers/criteria.shtml.

59. Monica Belcourt, George W. Bohlander, Scott A. Snell, and Arthur W. Sherman, *Managing Human Resources*, 4th Canadian ed. (Toronto: Nelson, 2004).

60. *Ibid.*

61. Tom L. Beauchamp and Norman E. Bowie (eds.), *Ethical Theory and Business*, 2d ed. (Englewood Cliffs, NJ: Prentice Hall, 1983), 477–478.

62. *Ibid.*, 478.

63. "White, Male and Worried," *Business Week* (January 31, 1994), 50–55.

64. Human Resources Development Canada, http://info.load-otea.hrdc-drhc.gc.ca/workplace_equity/information/history.shtml.

65. Loizides, *op cit.*

66. Russel J. G. Juriansz, *Equal Pay Legislation and Ontario's New Pay Equity Act* (Toronto: Blake, Cassels & Graydon, 1995), 3–5.

67. Victor D. Infante, "Why Woman Still Earn Less Than Men," *WorkForce* (April 2001), 31.

68. Rochelle Sharpe, "Women Make Strides, But Men Stay Firmly in Top Company Jobs," *The Wall Street Journal* (March 29, 1994), A1.

69. Human Resources Development Canada, *Annual Report, Employment Equity Act, 2001,* Labour Standards and Workplace Equity, Cat. No. LT-020-12-01.

70. Rosemary Batt, Susan Christopherson, Ned Rightor, and Danielle Van Jaarsveld, "Net Working: Work Patterns and Workforce Policies for the New Media Industry," *Economic Policy Institute* (February 2001), 1–57. Quoted in Infante.

71. Laura Pincus and Bill Shaw, "Comparable Worth: An Economic and Ethical Analysis," *Journal of Business Ethics* (April 1998), 455–470.

72. Cathy Trost, "Pay Equity, Born in Public Sector, Emerges as an Issue in Private Firms," *The Wall Street Journal* (July 8, 1985), 15.

73. E. Jane Arnault, Louis Gordon, Douglas H. Jones, and G. Michael Phillips, "An Experimental Study of Job Evaluation and Comparable Worth," *Industrial and Labor Relations Review* (July 2001), 806–815.

74. S. Cohn, *The Process of Occupational Sex-Typing: The Feminization of Clerical Labor in Great Britain* (Philadelphia: Temple University Press, 1985).

75. Susan Riggs, "Comparing Apples and Oranges: Job Evaluations," *Worklife* (Vol. 8, No. 1, 1991), 7–10.

76. "Achieving Pay Equity First Goal, But through Co-operation: Commissioner," *Pay Equity Commission Report* (Vol. 1, No. 1, March 1988), 6.

77. *CBC Online*, http://cbc.ca/storyview/CBC/2002/09/04/bell020904.

Chapter 18

Owner Stakeholders and Corporate Governance

Chapter Objectives

After studying this chapter, you should be able to:

1 Link the issue of legitimacy to corporate governance.

2 Discuss the components of corporate governance and the challenges to "good governance."

3 Describe the general obstacles to achieving properly functioning boards of directors.

4 Identify controversies associated with CEOs and boards of directors, such as compensation, mergers and acquisitions, and insider trading.

5 Explain the major changes in boards of directors required to improve corporate governance.

6 Discuss the principal ways in which shareholder activism exerts pressure on corporate management groups to improve governance.

Throughout the 1980s and 1990s, there was rampant shareholder unrest. This unrest became an all-out revolution by the beginning of the twenty-first century with a sudden onslaught of corporate scandals. In 2002, U.S. telecommunications giant WorldCom admitted to perpetrating one of the largest accounting frauds in history. The company had inflated its profits by US$3.8 billion between January 2001 and March 2002. Adelphia Communications Corp. founder John Rigas, along with his two sons, were arrested in 2002 and faced charges of improperly taking US$1 billion from the cable-television giant.[1] Tyco, Parmalat, Merrill Lynch, and Global Crossing were among the other high-profile cases of corporate misdeeds and fraudulent acts in recent years. And, of course, among the most prominent corporate scandals in recent memory was Enron. This energy and trading company was once the U.S.'s seventh largest corporation, with 21 000 employees, and the largest marketer of electricity and natural gas. Enron's downward spiral in 2001 began when the company revealed that it falsified accounting records, including keeping hundreds of millions of dollars of losses off the accounting records. In the third quarter of 2001 alone, Enron had incurred a US$600 million loss, and its bankruptcy (declared on December 2, 2001) was among the largest in U.S. corporate history. In addition to the massive layoffs, employees lost much of their retirement money since their pension accounts were built around Enron stock—stock that once sold for US$85 a share became worthless.

Like their U.S. counterparts, many Canadian corporate scandals, including Hollinger Inc., Bre-X Minerals Ltd., YBM Magnex International, Livent Inc., and Cinar Corporation "violated the basic tenets of good governance by staffing their boards with insiders, rubber-stamping rich compensation packages and interest-free loans for executives and failing to disclose company financial dealings to investors."[2]

In 2004, Nortel Networks, the Canadian telecom equipment giant, fired its chief executive officer for "just cause," in the wake of an accounting scandal that forced the company to restate its finances over the last three years. That same year, the Canadian software company Descartes Systems Group Inc. terminated its chief executive officer amid a furor over its financial reporting irregularities.

News of the latest unfolding debacles seems to only confirm the lack of credibility of the governance of many businesses. These scandals have caused shareholder groups to become increasingly critical of how management groups and boards of directors run their firms. There is outrage over management's lack of accountability, ineffective and complacent boards, excessive managerial compensation, and a general lack of focus on the importance of shareholders relative to management.

In this chapter, we will explore corporate governance and the ways in which it has evolved. First, we will examine the concept of legitimacy and the part that corporate governance plays in establishing the legitimacy of the firm. We will explore how good corporate governance can mitigate the problems created by the separation of ownership and control and examine some of the specific challenges facing board members today.

Legitimacy and Corporate Governance

To understand corporate governance, it is useful to understand the idea of **legitimacy**. Legitimacy is a somewhat abstract concept, but it is vital in that it helps explain the importance of the relative roles of a corporation's charter, shareholders, board of directors, management, and employees—all of which are components of the modern corporate governance system.

Let us start with a slightly modified version of Talcott Parsons's definition of legitimacy. He argued that "organizations are legitimate to the extent that their activities are congruent with the goals and values of the social system within which they function."[3] From this definition, we may see legitimacy as a condition that prevails when there is a congruence between the organization's activities and society's expectations. Thus, whereas legitimacy is a condition, **legitimation** is a dynamic process by which business seeks to perpetuate its acceptance. The dynamic process aspect should be emphasized, because society's norms and values change, and business must change if its legitimacy is to continue. It is also useful to consider legitimacy at both the micro, or company, level and the macro, or business institution, level.

At the *micro level of legitimacy*, we refer to individual business firms achieving and maintaining legitimacy by conforming with societal expectations. According to Epstein and Votaw, companies seek legitimacy in several ways. First, a company may adapt its methods of operating to conform to what it perceives to be the prevailing standard. For example, a company may discontinue door-to-door selling if that marketing approach comes to be viewed in the public mind as a shoddy sales technique,[4] or a pharmaceutical company may discontinue offering free drug samples to medical students if this practice begins to take on the aura of a bribe. Second, a company may try to change the public's values and norms to conform to its own practices by advertising and other techniques.[5] Amazon.com was successful at this when it began marketing over the Internet.

Finally, an organization may seek to enhance its legitimacy by identifying itself with other organizations, people, values, or symbols that have a powerful legitimate base in society.[6] This occurs at several levels. At the national level, companies proudly announce appointments of celebrities, former politicians, or other famous people to managerial positions or board directorships. At the community level, the winning local football coach may be asked to endorse a company by sitting on its board or promoting its products.[7]

The *macro level of legitimacy* is the level with which we are most concerned in this chapter. The macro level refers to the corporate system—the totality of business enterprises. It is difficult to talk about the legitimacy of business in pragmatic terms at this level. North American business is such a potpourri of institutions of different shapes, sizes, and industries that saying anything conclusive about it is difficult. Yet this is an important level at which business needs to be concerned about its legitimacy. What is at stake is the existence, acceptance, and form of business as an institution in our society. William Dill has suggested that business's social (or societal) legitimacy is a fragile thing:

> *Business has evolved by initiative and experiment*. It never had an overwhelmingly clear endorsement as a social institution *[emphasis added]*. *The idea of allowing individuals to joust with one another in pursuit of personal profit was an exciting and romantic one when it was first proposed as a way of correcting other problems in society; but over time, its ugly side and potential for abuse became apparent.*[8]

Quite a bit of the excitement and romanticism has long since worn off; business must accept that it has a fragile mandate.[9] It must realize that its legitimacy is constantly subject to ratification. And it must realize that it has no inherent right to exist—It exists solely because society has given it that right.[10]

In comparing the micro view of legitimacy with the macro view, one may observe that, although specific business organizations try to perpetuate their own legitimacy, the corporate or business system as a whole rarely addresses the issue at all. This is unfortunate because the spectrum of powerful issues regarding business conduct clearly indicates that such institutional introspection is needed if business is to survive and prosper. If business is to continue to justify its right to exist, the question of legitimacy and its operational ramifications must be remembered.

The Issue of Corporate Governance

The issue of corporate governance is a direct outgrowth of the question of legitimacy. For business to be legitimate and to maintain its legitimacy in the eyes of the public, its governance must correspond to the will of the people.

Corporate governance refers to the method by which a firm is being governed, directed, administered, or controlled and to the goals for which it is being governed. Corporate governance is concerned with the relative roles, rights, and accountability of such stakeholder groups as owners, boards of directors, managers, employees, and others who assert to be stakeholders.

Components of Corporate Governance

To appreciate fully the legitimacy and corporate governance issues, it is important that we understand the major groups that make up the corporate form of business organization, because it is only by so doing that we can appreciate how the system has failed to work according to its intended design.

Roles of Four Major Groups The four major groups we need to mention in setting the stage are the shareholders (owners/stakeholders), the board of directors, the managers, and the employees. Overarching these groups is the legal **charter**, giving the corporation the right to exist and stipulating the basic terms of its existence. Figure 18–1 presents these four groups, along with the charter, in a hierarchy of corporate governance authority.

Under corporate law, **shareholders** are the owners of a corporation. As owners, they should have ultimate control over the corporation. This control is manifested primarily in the right to select the board of directors of the company. Generally, the degree of each shareholder's right is determined by the number of shares of stock owned. The individual who owns 100 shares of Apple Computer, for example, has 100 "votes" when electing the board of directors. By contrast, the large public pension fund that owns 10 million shares has 10 million "votes."

Because large organizations may have hundreds of thousands of shareholders, they elect a smaller group, known as the **board of directors**, to govern and oversee the management of the business. The board is responsible for ascertaining that the manager puts the interests of the owners (i.e., shareholders) first. The third major group in the authority hierarchy is **management**—the group of individuals hired by the board to run the company and manage it on a daily basis. Along with the board, top management establishes overall policy. Middle- and lower-level managers carry out this policy and conduct the daily supervision of the operative employees. **Employees** are those hired by the company to perform the actual operational work. Managers are employees, too, but in this discussion we use the term *employees* to refer to nonmanagerial employees.

Separation of Ownership from Control The social and ethical issues that have evolved in recent years focus on the *intended* versus *actual* roles, rights, responsibili-

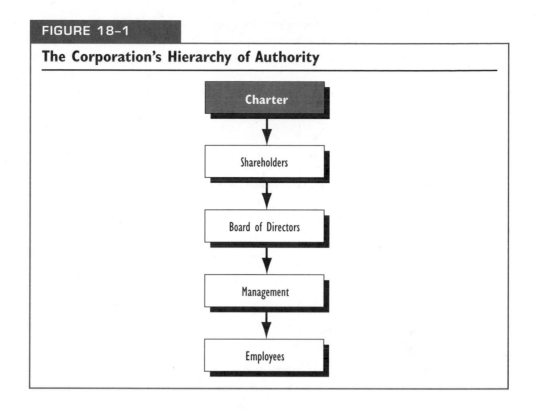

FIGURE 18-1

The Corporation's Hierarchy of Authority

ties, and accountability of these four major groups. The major condition embedded in the structure of modern corporations that has contributed to the corporate governance problem has been the **separation of ownership from control**. In the precorporate period, owners were typically the managers themselves. Thus, the system worked the way it was intended; the owners also controlled the business. Even when firms grew larger and managers were hired, the owners often were on the scene to hold the management group accountable. For example, if a company got in trouble, the Carnegies or Mellons or Morgans were always there to fire the president.[11]

As the public corporation grew and stock ownership became widely dispersed, a separation of ownership from control became the prevalent condition. Figure 18–2 illustrates the precorporate and corporate periods. The dispersion of ownership into hundreds of thousands or millions of shares meant that essentially no one or no one group owned enough shares to exercise control. This being the case, the most effective control that owners could exercise was the election of the board of directors to serve as their representative and watch over management.

The problem with this evolution was that authority, power, and control rested with the group that had the most concentrated interest at stake—management. The corporation did not function according to its designed plan with effective authority, power, and control flowing downward from the owners. The shareholders were owners in a technical sense, but most of them perceived themselves as investors rather than owners. If you owned 100 shares of Walt Disney Co. and there were 10 million shares outstanding, you likely would see yourself as an investor rather than an owner. With just a telephone call issuing a sell order to your stockbroker, your "ownership" stake could be gone. Furthermore, with stock ownership so dispersed, no conscious, intended supervision of corporate boards was possible.

FIGURE 18-2

Precorporate Versus Corporate Ownership and Control

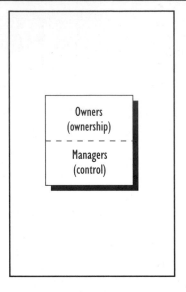

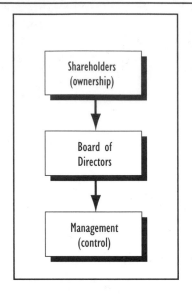

[a] In the precorporate period, the owners were also the managers, and therefore ownership and control were combined. Later, large companies hired managers, but the owners were always there to exercise control.

[b] In the corporate period, ownership was separated from control by the intervention of a board of directors. Theoretically, the board should have kept control on behalf of owners, but it did not always turn out that way.

The other factors that added to management's power were the corporate laws and traditions that gave the management group control over the **proxy process**—the method by which the shareholders elected boards of directors. Over time, it was not difficult for management groups to create boards of directors of like-minded executives who would simply collect their fees and defer to management on whatever it wanted. The result of this process was that power, authority, and control began to flow upward from management rather than downward from the shareholders (owners). **Agency problems** developed when the interests of the shareholders were not aligned with the interests of the manager, and the manager (who is simply a hired *agent* with the responsibility of representing the owner's best interest) began to pursue self-interest instead.

The Role of the Board of Directors

All democratic societies endeavour to develop legal frameworks for safeguarding the operations of corporations. Legal statutes require that boards be appointed by the owners of corporations to hold corporations accountable. Boards are intended to connect owners' interests with the operation of the corporation, and consequently should provide for corporate legitimacy, accountability, and responsible ownership.[12] As indicated earlier, a potential governance problem is built into the corporate system because of the separation of ownership from control. It is equally clear that the board of directors is intended to oversee management on behalf of the shareholders. However, this is where the system has broken down. For corporate governance to function as it was originally intended, the board of directors must be an effective, potent body carrying out its roles and responsibilities in ascertaining that management pursue the shareholders' best interests.

Are boards doing what they are supposed to be doing? Many observers suggest that boards have been largely irrelevant to the operations of many organizations. In an article for *Corporate Knights*, Caroline Oliver made the following comments:

> *Given that boards are so essential to the operation of corporations within a citizen-democracy and essential to the operation of owner-democracy within a corporation, how do they come to be so irrelevant in practice? Why do boards only cross our screens when there is a crisis—is democracy merely an insurance policy for when things go awry or is it a permanent commitment to making all human endeavors work? I believe that a large part of the reason why boards are considered irrelevant is not that this democracy does not matter but that their job, as currently constructed, is impossible. Boards may sound important in theory but if in practice they can't deliver it is not surprising that they are ignored.*[13]

Enron's demise was closely linked not just to management but also to its board of directors. The agency problem is traditionally viewed as a consequence of the separation of the management of the company from the owners of the company. That is, top managers cannot be trusted to necessarily act in the best interest of the owners—the shareholders. Boards of directors were initially viewed as offering an answer to the agency problem because they have a legal responsibility to protect and serve the shareholders. However, the case of such scandals as Enron illustrates that boards may also have incentives not to act in the best interest of shareholders.[14] Enron and the other corporate wrongdoers that followed all share one common characteristic—they represent business failures that were a consequence of failures in corporate governance.

Board deficiencies have been painfully evident in many other recent corporate scandals. In 2002, the U.S. Security and Exchange Commission (SEC) filed a civil suit against Xerox for misstating four years' worth of profits, resulting in an overstatement of close to US$3 billion. In the settlement of the lawsuit, Xerox agreed to pay a US$10 million fine and restate four years' worth of financial statements. *Business Week* characterized Xerox as possessing a board that was "asleep at the wheel" with a "host of governance problems."[15] In the case of Xerox, the board was flawed in such ways as having too many members with ties to the firm, having board members who sat on too many other boards, and having directors who owned little equity in the firm.[16] Many of the firms recently embroiled in legal battles share much in common with these board characteristics.

A recent KPMG survey of 116 board directors in 75 large Canadian companies found that almost half of these directors believed that they may be sitting on a board that could likely fall prey to financial manipulation and corporate misconduct in the near future. These findings were viewed as a "stunning admission about the state of corporate governance in Canada and one that will do very little to boost investor confidence," according to J. Richard Finlay, chairman of the Centre for Corporate and Public Governance. Interestingly, only 28 percent of the respondents viewed the board of directors as ultimately responsible for ensuring against financial manipulation and fraud. In addition, 72 percent of the respondents indicated that they largely rely on the company's external auditor to inform them of attempts at manipulation. Ironically, representatives of major auditing firms suggest that this is a misguided belief—external auditors cannot compensate for a lack of internal controls that would bring to light any financial wrongdoing, since external auditors don't look for fraud, and they have signed agreements that defer those responsibilities to the company's management or directors.[17]

The Need for Board Independence   Board independence from management is a crucial aspect of good governance. It is here that the difference between **inside directors** and **outside directors** becomes most pronounced. Outside directors are independent from the firm and its top managers. In contrast, inside directors have some sort of ties to the firm. Sometimes they are top managers in the firm; other times, insiders are family members or others with close ties to the CEO. To varying degrees, each of these parties is "beholden" to the CEO and, therefore, might be hesitant to speak out when necessary. As Professor Bujaki of the University of Ottawa comments:

> *Boards of directors need to adhere to, or exceed, principles of good governance, and need to represent the interests of all shareholders. To do this effectively, boards need to be able to function independently from management and be sufficiently well-versed in accounting and finance to be able to effectively challenge management's accounting and reporting practices.*[18]

The importance of board independence was starkly addressed in the recent scandal involving Canadian media baron Conrad Black. In 2003 Conrad Black was forced to step down as chief executive of Hollinger International, the newspaper publisher. The resignation followed accusations that he and other senior Hollinger executives and parent company Hollinger Inc. received millions in unauthorized payments. Allegedly, $32.15 million in payments were made that were not authorized by either the audit committee or the full board of directors of Hollinger. According to many observers, a salient feature of this case was the complicity of the company's board of directors in all this activity and its lack of independence from the CEO.[19]

Lack of board independence also played a central role in the downfall of Parmalat Finanziaria, the Italian dairy and food giant. This company filed for bankruptcy protection in Italy on December 27, 2003, following discovery that huge assets, estimated from US$8–$12 billion were unaccounted for. The alleged financial fraud at Parmalat spans more than a decade. Founder, chairman, and chief executive Calisto Tanzi was fired from the company and board and placed under arrest in 2003. Interestingly, at the time the scandal broke, Parmalat had a particularly poor rating on Institutional Shareholder Service's Global Corporate Governance Quotient, which measures corporations' governance practices against a set of 61 criteria. Parmalat ranked at the bottom of all 69 Italian companies that were rated. Why did Parmalat receive such poor corporate governance scores? As Michael Gray observed, Parmalat shared many of the same weaknesses in corporate governance structure and practices as those found in other family-controlled companies. However, the combination of shortcomings across numerous areas drove Parmalat's poor rating, including the following deficiencies:

- *Lack of board independence.* The board was composed of nine insiders, one affiliated outsider, and just three independent directors. The company was family-owned and went public in 1990.

- *Deficiencies in key board committees*. Insiders sat on each key board committee. Members of the audit and remuneration committee also served on the executive committee with founder and boss Tanzi. The executive committee, which consists of company executives, proposes actions for board approval and then implements them.
- *Deficiencies in disclosure*. There was a lack of timely disclosure of executive and director compensation and directors' stock ownership.[20]

Courtney Brown, an experienced director who served on many boards, said that he never saw a subordinate officer serving on a board dissent from the position taken by the CEO.[21] Insiders might also be professionals such as lawyers under contract to the firm or bankers whose bank does business with the firm: This can create conflict-of-interest situations.[22] For example, a commercial banker/director may expect the company on whose board she or he is serving to restrict itself to using the services of her or his own firm and be willing to support the CEO in return for the business provided.

Another problem is managerial control of the board processes. CEOs often can control board perks such as director compensation and committee assignments. Board members who rock the boat may find they are left out in the cold. As one corporate board member told *Fortune*, under conditions of anonymity, "This stuff is wrong.... What people understand they have to do is go along with management, because if they don't they won't be part of the club.... What it comes down to is that directors aren't really independent. CEOs don't want independent directors."[23] Shortly following the announcements of a workers' severance-pay agreement, it was disclosed that Enron had paid more than US$800 million in the previous year to 152 executives and senior managers.

Unfortunately, a recent glimpse into the composition of many Canadian companies presents a disturbing picture of board independence. *The Globe and Mail*'s Report on Business 2002 Study assessed the quality of boards and the governance practices of 270 companies that comprised Canada's benchmark Standard and Poor's/Toronto Exchange Index. The results indicated that many of Canada's largest corporations did not score well with regard to board member independence.

In the study, boards considered to be "independent" typically would separate the roles of the chairman and CEO, and the board's audit, compensation, and nominating committees would have complete autonomy from management. In addition, the study's standards defined as "related" any directors who are immediate family members of management, who provide professional services to the company (typically lawyers, accountants, bankers, and consultants), who are former executives of the company, or who are executives of a parent company. The results indicated that 29 percent of companies scored lower than 10 out of 26 possible marks for independence of boards and key committees, meaning they lack most of the features of independent boards.[24]

For example, though grocery store chain Sobeys Inc. claims its board is composed of a majority of independent directors, "the Sobeys board of directors includes five people with the surname 'Sobey,' plus two lawyers whose firm acts as the company's primary external legal counsel, as well as the head of a frozen food company that sells to Sobeys, and a partner in a consulting firm that also does work for Sobeys.... DuPont Canada Inc. and Sears Canada Inc., for example, say representatives from their parent companies are unrelated directors.... Barrick Gold Corp., for example, admits that it does not have an independent board, noting that it only has five unrelated directors out of 13."[25]

There are many additional challenges to achieving board independence. For example, another question raised in the post-Enron environment is the issue of share ownership among board members. Is it better or worse for board members to own shares of a company? While one popular view is that board members should own shares if they are to represent the shareholders, the implication of the Enron-type debacles is that when board members own shares, there may also be a disincentive to fully scrutinize corporate behaviour for fear that such scrutiny and criticism could reduce share values.[26] Figure 18–3 lists some of the best and worst boards according to a recent *Business Week* survey.

Issues Surrounding Compensation

CEO Compensation   The issue of executive pay was a lightning rod for the concern that managers place their own interests over those of their shareholders. Two issues

---

FIGURE 18–3

Business Week's Winners and Losers: The Best and Worst Boards

The Best Boards	The Worst Boards

The Best Boards

3M

With just one insider on its nine-member board, the company gets high marks for independence. Outside directors include the CEOs of Lockheed-Martin, Allstate, and Amgen. Audit-committee chairman is the former CFO at Sears. No directors have business ties to the company.

General Electric

This talent-packed board, with an unrivalled record of creating shareholder value, remains a favourite with governance experts, although there have been recent revelations of lavish retirement perks for former CEO Jack Welch. The company is improving board independence; it recently added Ralph Larsen, former CEO of Johnson & Johnson and a long-time champion of good governance.

Home Depot

With the departure of co-founder Bernard Marcus, the 12-member board now has only two insiders. Independent directors meet regularly without management. Directors are required to visit 20 stores a year.

Intel

One of the few boards that has a lead director. No insiders sit on the audit, compensation, or nominating committees. The board conducts an annual self-evaluation. Directors have big stakes in the company.

Pfizer

The board was second only to GE in overall approval by governance experts. Independent directors meet without the CEO. No Pfizer executives sit on the audit, nominating, or compensation committees. Stock transactions for directors and executives are posted on the company Web site.

The Worst Boards

Apple

Founder Steve Jobs owns just two shares in the company. Recently departed director Larry Ellison had none and had missed more than 25 percent of meetings in the past five years. The CEO of Micro Warehouse, which accounted for nearly 2.9 percent of Apple's net sales in 2001, sits on the compensation committee. Since 2000, the board has awarded Jobs 27.5 million stock options and a US$90 million jet. There is an interlocking directorship—with Gap CEO Mickey Drexler and Jobs sitting on each other's boards.

Gap

Self-dealing includes contracts with the chairman's brother to build and remodel stores and a consulting deal with the chairman's wife. Slow to replace outgoing CEO Mickey Drexler as performance declined. Interlocking directorship with Drexler sitting on the Apple board, while Apple's Steve Jobs sits on Gap's. Two other directors sit on the Charles Schwab board, while Chuck Schwab sits on Gap's.

Tyson Foods

Out of 15 board members, 10 have ties to the company, including seven who have extensive business dealings. CEO John Tyson got a US$2.1 million bonus for negotiating the acquisition of meatpacker IBP—which Tyson Foods tried unsuccessfully to back out of—in a year when net income fell 42 percent.

Xerox

The bungled succession of Paul Allaire, accusations of funny accounting, billions in shareholder wealth up in smoke, and a decades-long failure to keep up with changing technology add up to an ineffectual board. With departures of Allaire and CFO Barry Romeril, the board is far more independent. But too many directors sit on too many boards. Director Vernon Jordan's law firm provides legal services. Two audit committee members had attendance problems in 2001.

Source: "The Best and Worst Boards," *Business Week* (cover story, October 7, 2002), http://www.businessweek.com/magazine/content/02_40/b3802001.htm.

are at the heart of the CEO pay controversy: (1) the extent to which CEO pay is tied to firm performance, and (2) the overall level of CEO pay.

The move to tie CEO pay more closely to firm performance grew in momentum when shareholders observed CEO pay rising as firm performance fell. Many executives had gotten staggering salaries, even while profits were falling, workers were being laid off, and shareholder return was dropping. Shareholders were assisted in their effort to monitor CEO pay by stricter disclosure requirements from the U.S. Securities and Exchange Commission (SEC) in 1992. Similar rules were adopted by regulators in Canada (like the Ontario Securities Commission) shortly thereafter, and they require publicly listed companies to disclose to shareholders: (1) all types of compensation, including salaries, bonuses, and stock options, for each of the five most highly paid individuals in the company; (2) a comparison of the company's performance relative to its peer group and a broad-based stock index; and (3) a report by the compensation committee that provides the rationale for the compensation packages.

The revised compensation disclosure rule was designed to provide shareholders with more information about the relationship between firm performance and CEO compensation.[27] According to the results of one study, it seems to have worked. Since the rule's implementation, compensation committees have met more frequently, lessened the number of insiders as members, and become more moderate in size. More importantly, largely through the use of stock options, CEO pay has become more closely aligned with accounting and market performance measures than it was before the rule's implementation.[28] There is some evidence that boards of directors are becoming the watchdogs they are always supposed to be.[29] On the other hand, public trust in boards is currently not high, and shareholders have been advised to assess the legitimacy of compensation packages, as indicated in Figure 18–4.

During the 1990s, in the midst of a growing economy, CEO pay mushroomed. Pay was tied more closely to the firm's market performance and firms were performing very well—so the pay went up as market performance went up. However, as the market went down, so did the value of CEO stock options. After almost five years of double-digit increases, CEO compensation fell by about 5 percent in 2000. Salaries and cash bonuses went up by about 10 percent, but they comprise only about 6 percent of the average CEO's compensation package.[30] This decline in total compensation notwithstanding, the typical CEO still makes a very good living. In the words of Louis Lavelle of *Business Week*, "The gravy train is slowing but it hasn't jumped the rails."[31]

In 2002, CEO Pierre Lessard of the grocery retailer Metro Inc. cashed in his stock options when the company changed its option plan, for a gain of $27 million. Intrawest CEO Joe Houssian also gained from cashing in his stock options, taking home $2 million in fiscal 2003, $10.5 million in 2002, and more than $5 million in 2001.[32]

Although stock options are an effective way of tying CEO pay to firm performance, some analysts question their true value. A recent study has shown that the extensive use of stock options in CEO salary may be unwise, whether the market be bull or bear. Options are much more expensive for firms than cash salaries and bonuses because options entail a risk. The expectation is that the potential reward will be

FIGURE 18–4

What's Behind the Big Pay Packages?

Investigate these issues to assess legitimacy of board approval of big pay packages:

1. *Find Out Who They Are*: The board of directors and the directors that serve on the compensation committee are listed on the proxy statement.

2. *Start Finding the Facts*: A careful reading of the proxy statement can give you an inside peek at how decisions are made at a company and why directors are approving these big pay packages. Here are some things to look for:

   - *Board Interlocks:* By looking at the biography of each director and the CEO listed in the proxy, determine if your CEO sits on the board of any of the director's companies. For example, you might find that your CEO approved a big pay plan for an executive or CEO who sits on your board and approves your CEO's compensation.

   - *Conflict of Interest:* The proxy will list any substantial business relationships a director may have with the company. If a director has a big contract with the company, he or she may not want to oppose a CEO's big pay package.

   - *Director Perks:* How much are directors getting paid? The proxy lists the retainers, pension funds, stock awards, and other perks a director may receive.

   - *Attendance Records:* The proxy usually lists the attendance records of directors at board meetings. A low attendance record may indicate that a director isn't taking the time to adequately review the CEO's compensation plan.

   - *Family Relationships:* Are any of the members of the board of directors related to the CEO? That might explain why a CEO is getting approval for a big compensation package.

   - *Independence:* Check to see how many directors are independent—i.e., have no business ties to the company, are not related to the CEO or top executives, and are not employed by the company.

   - *Pattern of Overpay:* Directors often sit on more than one company's board. See if the director has a pattern of overpaying CEOs at those additional companies. Use the compensation data at this site or the proxy statement from those companies.

Source: AFL-CIO, http://www.aflcio.org/corporateamerica/paywatch/what2do/w_bdspot.cfm.

higher than it would be if the return were certain. CEOs tend to not value options as highly as cash, yet options are much more expensive for firms to offer. Therefore, firms are getting less for their dollars in executive motivation. Furthermore, CEOs tend to be largely undiversified and so stock options can make the executive risk averse: Risk aversion can be a detriment in high-velocity and hypercompetitive industries. Clearly, the design of CEO compensation is a complex decision in which many factors must be weighed.[33]

Tying firm pay to performance is only one issue surrounding CEO pay. The other is the level of pay that CEOs receive. Gordon Nixon, the CEO of the Royal Bank of Canada, was paid a salary of $1.15 million in 2003, as well as a bonus of $2.2 million. At Molson Inc., CEO Dan O'Neill earned a total of $18.8 million in 2003, including a salary and bonus of $4.9 million and a $13.9 million gain from options.[34]

This issue has taken on increasing meaning as CEO salaries have skyrocketed. Josef Fridman, in his article for *CA Magazine*, noted:

> *Executive compensation is arguably the most conspicuous component of corporate governance, and has been one of the main examples of abusive practices cited by critics. Respondents agreed with the widely held view that compensation is out of control.*[35]

Executive Excess 2003, the annual CEO compensation survey by the Institute for Policy Studies and United for a Fair Economy, offers interesting insight into the pattern of CEO pay. According to the report, between 1990 and 2002, average CEO pay rose 279 percent, far above the 46 percent increase in worker pay, which was just 8 percent above inflation. CEO pay outpaced the performance of the S&P 500, which rose 166 percent in the same period, as well as the 93 percent rise in corporate profits. In addition, the CEO–worker pay gap was 281-to-1 in 2002, nearly seven times greater than the 1982 ratio of 42-to-1. The report lists a number of "ironies" in terms of the pay for CEOs who recently engaged in major downsizings:

- CEO Carly S. Fiorina of Hewlett-Packard fired 25 700 workers in 2001, and saw her pay jump 231 percent, from US$1.2 million in 2001 to US$4.1 million in 2002.
- AOL Time Warner CEO Gerald M. Levin, whose company laid off 4380 employees in 2001, achieved a pay increase of 1612 percent, from US$1.2 million in 2001 to US$21.2 million in 2002.
- Tyco's former CEO, Dennis Kozlowski, earned over US$71 million in 2002, a US$34.7 million raise, even though he was forced out amid the Tyco scandal in that year.[36]

Consequences of the Merger, Acquisition, and Takeover Craze

Mergers and acquisitions are another form of corporate governance, one that comes from outside the corporation. The expectation is that the threat of a possible takeover will motivate top managers to pursue shareholder, rather than self, interest. The merger, acquisition, and hostile takeover craze of the 1980s brought out many new issues related to corporate governance. The economic prosperity of the 1980s, coupled with the rise of junk bonds and other creative methods of financing, made it possible for small firms and individuals to buy large corporations. Many corporate CEOs and boards went to great lengths to protect themselves from these takeovers. A major criticism of CEOs and boards during this period was that they were overly obsessed with self-preservation rather than making optimal decisions on behalf of their owners/ stakeholders. Three of the most questionable top management practices to emerge from the hostile takeover wave were greenmail, poison pills, and golden parachutes. We will briefly consider each of these and see how they fit into the corporate governance problem we have been discussing. Then, we will examine the issue of insider trading.

Greenmail   Named after blackmail, **greenmail** is the repurchase of stock from an unwanted suitor at a higher-than-market price. Companies pay the greenmail to end the threat of a takeover.[37] For example, assume that Corporate Raider A quietly purchases a 5 percent stake in the ABC Corporation. It threatens to launch an all-out hostile takeover of ABC. ABC's management sees this as a threat to their jobs and agrees to pay greenmail for (buy back) the shares from Corporate Raider A at a premium price. This example is somewhat simplified, but it basically describes the process. With greenmail, the potential acquirer wins big, and management gets to keep its jobs and perks. The losers are the shareholders of the target company who are left sitting with shares whose underlying value has been eroded.[38]

Poison Pill   A **poison pill** is a shareholder rights plan aimed at discouraging or preventing a hostile takeover. Typically, the poison pill provides that when a hostile suitor acquires more than a certain percentage of a company's stock, other shareholders receive share purchase rights designed to dilute the suitor's holdings and make the acquisition prohibitively expensive. While controversial, efforts to adopt poison pills continue. In 2001, Yahoo!'s board of directors adopted a poison pill that would make a hostile takeover prohibitively expensive. The plan gives Yahoo! shareholders the right to buy one unit of a share of preferred stock for US$250 if a person or group acquires at least 15 percent of Yahoo!'s stock. According to the company, the poison pill was not instituted in response to any specific acquisition threat but instead to "deter coercive takeover tactics."[39]

In January of 2004, amid the Conrad Black scandal, Hollinger International Inc. announced a poison pill defence and launched a court action aimed at preventing its controlling shareholder, Conrad Black, from "manipulating the company's corporate machinery for his own selfish financial purposes." In this case, the move was intended to thwart Black's then-pending sale of Hollinger Inc. The poison pill would provide holders of Hollinger International shares with rights to buy new shares at a 50-percent discount, in the event that anyone attempts to obtain more than 20 percent voting control of the company. The poison pill would make any purchaser's bid for Hollinger Inc. far less attractive because it would dilute their holdings.[40]

In Canada, securities commissions and stock exchanges require that corporations submit their plans for implementing a poison pill strategy to shareholders within six months of adopting the plan. Plans are only valid if they receive shareholder approval. On the other hand, in the U.S., a shareholder vote on the implementation of a poison pill plan is not required, though it is increasingly common to seek shareholder resolutions in support of such decisions.[41] Poison pill plans are relatively new in corporate Canada and there remains much controversy regarding whom poison pills are designed to protect.

Golden Parachutes   A **golden parachute** is a contract in which a corporation agrees to make payments to key officers in the event of a change in the control of the corporation.[42] The original intent of golden parachutes was to prevent top executives involved in takeover battles from putting themselves before their shareholders. However, in a study of over 400 tender offers (i.e., takeover attempts in which the acquirers offered shareholders premiums to sell their shares), golden parachutes showed no effect on takeover resistance. Neither the existence of the parachute, nor the magnitude of the potential parachute payout, influenced CEO reactions to takeover attempts.[43]

Cochran and Wartick offer several arguments against golden parachutes. They argue that executives are already being paid well to represent their companies and that getting additional rewards constitutes "double dipping." They also argue that these executives are, in essence, being rewarded for failure. The logic here is that if the executives have managed their companies in such a way that the companies' stock prices are low enough to make the firms attractive to takeover specialists, the executives are being rewarded for failure. Another argument is that executives, to the extent that they control their own boards, are giving themselves the golden parachutes. This represents a conflict of interest.[44]

Insider Trading Scandals   **Insider trading** is the practice of obtaining critical information from inside a company and then using that information for one's own personal financial gain. Specifically, according to the Ontario Securities Commission (OSC):

> *Illegal insider trading involves the buying or selling of a security while in the possession of undisclosed material information about the issuer of the*

security, and includes related violations such as "tipping" information and securities trading by the person "tipped." Trading on inside information, especially illegal insider trading, can cause significant harm to the fairness and efficiency of Canadian capital markets. Even the perception that illegal insider trading is prevalent can cause harm. This is so because it undermines investor confidence in the fairness and integrity of capital markets.[45]

The SEC uses a similar definition. Examples of insider trading cases include:

- Corporate officers, directors, and employees who trade the corporation's securities after learning of significant, confidential corporate developments.
- Friends, business associates, family members, and other "tippees" of such officers, directors, and employees, who trade the securities after receiving such information.
- Other persons who misappropriate, and take advantage of, confidential information from their employers.[46]

Unfortunately, examples of insider trading abound in both Canada and the U.S. In 2003, Corel Corp. founder Michael Cowpland paid $575 000 to settle insider trading charges levelled at him by the OSC. Cowpland was also barred from serving as a director on any publicly traded company for two years. The charges stemmed from his 1997 sale of 2.4 million shares in Corel, worth more than $20 million, four weeks before the company issued an earnings warning which sent the stock into a major decline. The OSC alleged that Cowpland sold the shares with knowledge of significant facts that were not widely known—that Corel would fall short of quarterly sales figures.[47]

Allegations of insider trading were also recently directed at six employees and the chairman of ATI Technologies, one of the world's largest makers of computer graphics chips. The OSC asserted that this illegal activity resulted in more than $7.9 million in profits or avoided losses.[48]

The largest insider trading scandal in Canadian history occurred in 2004 and involved illicit gains totalling nearly $2 million. The OSC charged Andrew Rankin, a former investment banker at RBC, with ten counts of illegal insider trading and ten counts of "tipping" (leaking inside information) to his friend Daniel Duic about pending mergers and acquisitions deals involving the firm's clients. Rankin was managing director of the brokerage's mergers and acquisitions group and he was fired following the firm's investigation of "suspicious" trading practices.[49]

Perhaps the highest-profile insider trading case to hit the press in recent years was the scandal involving Martha Stewart. Stewart was charged by the SEC with insider trading and accused of lying to investigators regarding her sale of 3928 shares (worth US$227 000) in a biotechnology firm. The accusations levelled at Stewart specifically pertained to her sale of shares in ImClone on December 27, 2001, the day before the stock's value plummeted as a result of negative news about the company—the U.S. Food and Drug Administration's refusal to approve ImClone's anti-cancer drug that it had been developing. According to the SEC, Stewart received this inside information from the former CEO of ImClone, Sam Waksal, a close friend of Stewart's, who was also charged with insider trading and perjury.

Not only are shareholders suspicious of what has been going on unbeknownst to them, but small investors and the general public have lost faith in what they once thought was the stable and secure financial industry. Starting in 2001, the SEC instituted new disclosure rules designed to aid the small investor who historically has not had access to the information large investors hold. Regulation FD (fair disclosure) set limits on the common company practice of selective disclosure. When companies disclose meaningful information to shareholders and securities professionals, they must now do so publicly so that small investors can enjoy a more level playing field.[50] Securities regulators in Canada have been following suit with similar disclosure rules.

Improving Corporate Governance

In light of the long string of corporate scandals and the increased public and government scrutiny, organizations need to take a much more serious approach to the role and functions of their boards of directors. In a recent annual report on the "Best and Worst Corporate Boards in America," *Business Week* suggested that boards are becoming much more accountable than in the past and "in the face of shareholder dissatisfaction they are more likely to demand change."[51] However, the corporate governance war is far from over. In addition to the need for significant improvements in the large corporations, mid-size and smaller companies, and overseas boards, also have a long way to go in terms of adopting strict guidelines for good governance. Dot-coms in particular have tended to have boards dominated by insiders, a combination of current management and others with connections to the company.[52] Europe too is just entering the corporate governance battle. Mass stock ownership is a new phenomenon but investors who feel stung by steep price drops are taking action. European shareholders are going to court and showing up en masse at annual meetings.[53]

The Sarbanes-Oxley Act

Credit for the improvements in corporate governance goes to several sources. Information on executive and director compensation is much more clearly presented than it was in the 1980s and early 1990s.[54] However, the aftermath of the scandals in the early twenty-first century were the biggest impetus for change, which led to the enactment of such legislation as the 2002 Sarbanes-Oxley Act in the U.S. and the initiation of similar legislation in Canada.

The Sarbanes-Oxley Act was introduced in the United States following the flood of accounting scandals at companies such as Enron and WorldCom. The act was aimed at re-establishing corporate accountability and investor confidence. The central purpose of the act is to make public companies more accountable by increasing transparency in their financial reporting. This required additional regulations governing public company accounting, corporate responsibility, and investor protection. In order to accomplish this, increased requirements were also placed on CEOs, chief financial officers (CFOs), and the functions that they oversee.

The significant impact of the Sarbanes-Oxley Act is evident to many observers, such as Megan Barnett, who made the following comments:

> *More than just a buzzword born in the depths of the corporate scandals, good governance has turned into a new way of life for some company gatekeepers.... Under the new rule regime, boards find themselves under intense scrutiny. They have fired members who have conflicts of interest, possess thin credentials, or are past their prime. They have hired new directors they believe are beyond reproach, with no skeletons and talents more suited to the job. They have more meetings, more conference calls,*

and more questions to ask of senior management. They face the challenge of simultaneously beefing up controls to meet new regulatory requirements while remaining active in shaping the company's strategy. They consult more with their lawyers…. Boards must now comprise mostly independent directors, which means the individuals must not have any material ties (à la Enron) to the company or its management.[55]

While the Sarbanes-Oxley Act itself is not directed at Canadian jurisdictions, it does affect Canadian companies that trade on U.S. stock exchanges, and it has served as an impetus for similar Canadian legislation. In 2004, the OSC presented 18 new corporate governance standards for boards of publicly traded companies that replaced the guidelines drafted by the Toronto Stock Exchange in 1994. The redeveloped guidelines add new, more stringent standards for Canadian boards. The OSC's new corporate governance standards for boards of publicly traded companies included the following:

- Boards should be a majority of independent directors.
- Chairperson must be an independent director.
- Board satisfied as to integrity of CEO.
- Develop clear position descriptions for directors.
- Adopt a written code of conduct and ethics.
- Independent directors on compensation committees.[56]

Efforts to improve corporate governance may be classified into two major categories for discussion purposes. First, changes could be made in the composition, structure, and functioning of boards of directors. Second, shareholders—on their own initiative or on the initiative of management or the board—could assume a more active role in governance. Each of these possibilities deserves closer examination.

Composition, Structure, and Functioning of Boards

In the past decade or so, changes have begun to be made in boards of directors. These changes have occurred because of the growing belief that CEOs and executive teams need to be made more accountable to shareholders and other stakeholders. Here we will discuss several of these changes and some other recommendations that have been set forth for improving board functioning.

Composition of the Board The 2003 Canadian Spencer Stuart Board Index (CSSBI) is the eighth annual survey of board trends and practices of leading Canadian companies, conducted by Spencer Stuart in partnership with the University of Toronto's Rotman School of Management.[57] The CSSBI analysis is conducted from 100 leading public Canadian companies. Among the interesting findings are the following outlined below.

The average board size among the CSSBI 100 firms was about 12 members, which is about 17 percent larger than comparable U.S. firms. The presence of women in Canadian boards continues to rise. In addition, the survey suggests that that the gender gap between Canadian and U.S. boards has largely closed. Overall, 79 percent of Canadian firms report at least one women director, compared to 83.2 percent in the U.S. However, women still only represent 11.7 percent of all directors (12.8 percent in the U.S.).

While Canadian boards have traditionally trailed their U.S. counterparts in the representation of women as directors, these findings indicate that for Canadian public boards (of firms with revenues over $1 billion), the gender balance is close to those in similar-sized U.S. firms. On the other hand, the survey indicates that Canada still significantly lags behind the U.S. in the representation of visible minorities on boards. Directors who are also visible minorities account for only 1.7 percent of board directorships among the surveyed companies, compared to 13 percent in the U.S. In addition, only 19 percent of the firms had at least one minority director, while 76 percent of comparable U.S. firms had at least one minority director.

Canadian boards do make use of international directors—with 86 percent of the firms surveyed having at least one international director, while only 28 percent of comparable U.S. firms make use of international directors. In addition, over two-thirds of those international directors on Canadian boards are United States citizens. On the other hand, Canadian citizens account for only about 18 percent of international directors who sit on U.S. company boards.

The survey indicates that, for the most part, board independence is relatively high. One key indicator of board independence is the separation of the chair and CEO functions. Among the companies surveyed, 77 percent separated the role of the chair from that of the CEO. This reflects an increase of 15 percent over the past five years. On the other hand, only about 25 percent of comparable U.S. firms split the functions of the chair and the CEO. Among the 41 largest of the Canadian firms surveyed, almost 80 percent of the directors are unrelated. Figure 18–5 reports the average numbers of directors and related directors for the CSSBI 100 firms and their comparable U.S. counterparts.

Finally, the CSSBI survey noted that it is becoming increasingly difficult to find qualified individuals to serve on boards. It is estimated that up to 75 percent of direc-

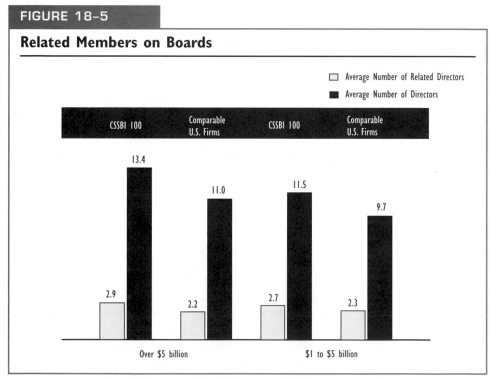

FIGURE 18–5

Related Members on Boards

☐ Average Number of Related Directors
■ Average Number of Directors

	CSSBI 100	Comparable U.S. Firms	CSSBI 100	Comparable U.S. Firms

13.4
11.0
11.5
9.7
2.9
2.2
2.7
2.3

Over $5 billion $1 to $5 billion

Source: The 2003 Canadian Spencer Stuart Board Index (CSSBI), conducted by Spencer Stuart in partnership with the University of Toronto's Rotman School of Management, http://www.rotman.utoronto.ca/news/boardindex.pdf.

tors will be retiring in the next decade, given that the average age of a director is 60, and most of these boards impose mandatory retirement between the ages of 65 and 72.[58] Among the companies surveyed, the other most common reasons for looking to add new directors in the coming year are to increase board diversity, to add directors with financial expertise, and to add more independent members.

Another part of the problem is an increase in demand for good independent directors. Institutional investors value good corporate governance so highly that they are willing to pay a premium for firms with outside directors. This increase in demand for outside directors is part of the reason they are in increasingly short supply. In 2004, the Ontario Securities Commission released new draft guidelines that force corporate boards to include a majority of independent directors. These rules also require a company's chairperson to be an independent director. Boards must be satisfied with the integrity of the CEO, and independent directors must sit on compensation committees.[59]

Another factor limiting the supply of directors is the greater level of expectations placed on board members. Board committees and subcommittees are now given more to do than ever before. Furthermore, the globalization of business has placed new demands on board members for travel. Last, firms realize the time demands placed on outside directors and so they limit the number of outside boards on which their own executives may sit. For example, former General Electric CEO Jack Welch would not allow his senior managers to sit on the boards of other companies.[60]

The difficulty in finding outside board members is exacerbated when searching for members of minority groups or women to bring diversity to the board. In the past, many candidates were excluded because they never had the title of CEO. A new trend in board recruitment, focusing more on experience than title, is helping to bring more independence and diversity to the boardroom. This broadens the pool of candidates available.[61]

Today, advocates of strong, independent, and diverse boards have largely succeeded in convincing corporations of the importance of board composition. The difficulty now is in putting those recommendations into effect.

Use of Board Committees   Boards often have to make use of a variety of committees in order to keep them properly apprised of the company's situation. The committee structure of many Canadian boards differs from their U.S. counterparts. According to the CSSBI survey, 43 percent of Canadian boards have an environmental or health and safety committee, compared to only 5 percent of U.S. boards. The survey also revealed that 18 percent of Canadian boards have a risk committee, compared to only 2 percent of their U.S. counterparts. Figure 18–6 offers more information on the variety of committees employed by boards in Canada versus the U.S.

The **audit committee** is typically responsible for assessing the adequacy of internal control systems and the integrity of financial statements. Recent scandals underscore the importance of a strong audit committee. Commenting on such scandals, *The Wall Street Journal* recently opined, "Too many audit committees are turning out to be toothless tigers."[62] To lessen the occurrence of such scandals, the SEC and the OSC have placed much emphasis on audit committees. Recent legislation in Canada requires public companies to hire auditors who are members of the Canadian Public Accountability Board. Companies must also have "an independent and financially literate" audit committee.

Charles Anderson and Robert Anthony, authors of *The New Corporate Directors: Insights for Board Members and Executives*,[63] argue that the principal responsibilities of an audit committee are as follows:

FIGURE 18-6

Board Committees

Committee	Percent of CSSBI 100 Firms with Committee	Percent of Comparable U.S. Firms with Committee
Audit	100%	100%
Compensation/Human Resources	95%	100%
Nominating Governance	92%	95%
Environment, Health and Safety	43%	5%
Investment/Pension	32%	7%
Executive	27%	46%
Risk	18%	2%
Finance	10%	30%
Conduct Review	8%	1%
Public Policy and Social Responsibility	7%	12%
Strategy and Planning	3%	3%
Stock Options and Retraction Price	2%	4%

Source: The 2003 Canadian Spencer Stuart Board Index (CSSBI), conducted by Spencer Stuart in partnership with the University of Toronto's Rotman School of Management, http://www.rotman.utoronto.ca/news/boardindex.pdf.

1. To ensure that published financial statements are not misleading.
2. To ensure that internal controls are adequate.
3. To follow up on allegations of material, financial, ethical, and legal irregularities.
4. To ratify the selection of the external auditor.

According to Arjay Miller, a board member and former president of Ford Motor Company, there should be at least one meeting per year between the audit committee and the firm's internal auditor.[64] The internal auditor should be scheduled to meet alone with the committee and always be instructed to speak out whenever she or he believes something should be brought to the committee's attention. The committee should also meet with the outside auditor in a setting in which members of management are not present. Three major questions should be asked of the outside auditor by the audit committee:

1. Is there anything more that you think we should know?
2. What is your biggest area of concern?
3. In what area did you have the largest difference of opinion with company accounting personnel?

The **nominating committee,** which should be composed of outside directors, or at least a majority of outside directors, has the responsibility of ensuring that competent, objective board members are selected. Many observers have recommended that this committee be composed entirely of independent outside directors. The function of the nominating committee is to nominate candidates for the board and for senior management positions. In spite of the suggested role and responsibility of this committee, in most companies the CEO continues to exercise a powerful role in the selection of board members. As one observer commented:

> *In the pre-Sarbox [Sarbanes-Oxley] world, new directors frequently materialized from a spin of the CEO's Rolodex and a handshake over lunch. Now nominating committees, mandated under the new rules, are playing a much more active role in attracting talent.*[65]

The **compensation committee** has the responsibility of evaluating executive performance and recommending terms and conditions of employment. This committee should be composed of outside directors. Although most large companies have compensation committees, one might ask how objective these board members are when the CEO has played a significant role in their being elected to the board.

The CSSBI survey indicates that about 20 percent of Canadian firms still have related directors on their compensation committees, while only about 6 percent of U.S. boards reported related directors on their compensation committees. In light of the onslaught of recent corporate scandals, there is a concern over this presence of boards with related directors in compensation/human resources committees, given that "this is the group that is supposed to be evaluating the performance and pay of the senior executives with an unbiased perspective," as Professor David Beatty of the University of Toronto observed.[66]

Finally, each board has a **public issues committee**, or **public policy committee**. Although it is recognized that most management structures have some sort of formal mechanism for responding to public or social issues, this area is important enough to warrant a board committee that would become sensitive to these issues, provide policy leadership, and monitor management's performance on these issues. Most major companies today have public issues committees that typically deal with such issues as employment equity, environmental affairs, employee health and safety, consumer affairs, political action, and other areas in which public or ethical issues are present. Debate continues over the extent to which large firms really use such committees, but the fact that they have institutionalized such concerns by way of formal corporate committees is encouraging. It has been recommended that firms develop evaluation systems to help them monitor the social performance of their corporate executives, but the evidence does not show that companies are doing this.[67]

Getting Tough with CEOs   The agency problem at Enron and other companies has been viewed as partly a consequence of the CEO also serving as chairperson of the company's board of directors. Critics assert that when the CEO also serves as chairperson, the nature of information that goes to the board is often distorted. Moreover, the CEO can also have the power to staff the board largely with supporters. This essentially destroys the objective oversight role of the board, as was the case with Enron.[68]

It has always been a major responsibility of board directors to monitor CEO performance and to get tough if the situation dictates. Historically, chief executives were protected from the axe that hit other employees when times got rough. Changes are now occurring that are resulting in CEOs being taken to task, or even fired, for reasons that heretofore did not create a stir in the boardroom. These changes include the tough, competitive economic times, the rising vigilance of outside directors, and the increasing power of large institutional investors.

w w w

Search the web

Share: Shareholder Association for Research and Education

SHARE (**http://www.share.ca/index.cfm**) is a national not-for-profit organization helping pension funds to build sound investment practices, to protect the interest of plan beneficiaries, and to contribute to a just and healthy society. SHARE facilitates shareholder–corporate dialogue on issues of concern to investors, including corporate governance, corporate social responsibility, and other measures to improve long-term corporate performance.

Shareholder democracy is challenged in Canada by complex legal rules governing shareholder proposals and shareholder dialogue. SHARE's expertise in coordinating shareholder activism helps make this process more effective and efficient for institutional investors. SHARE assists its affiliate organizations in:

- facilitating institutional shareholder dialogue and action
- drafting and filing shareholder proposals
- presenting proposals at corporate annual general meetings
- coordinating internationally with other institutional shareholders

Business Week observed that in recent times CEOs are "dropping like flies."[69] Some analysts see the increasing turnover in CEOs as a positive thing. "I take it as a good sign, because it says boards of directors are tougher on CEOs than they used to be," says Donald P. Jacobs, former dean of the Kellogg School of Business at Northwestern University. Still others express their concern. Rakhesh Kurana of Harvard Business School opines, "We've made this a superhero job. Boards look at the CEO as a panacea and get fixated on the idea that one single individual will solve all the company's problems." One thing is clear: Boards in general cannot now be accused of giving CEOs a free ride.[70] Among the new national rules unveiled in 2004 by securities regulators across Canada (except for British Columbia) was the requirement that chief executives and chief financial officers certify their financial statements.[71]

Other suggestions have been proposed for creating effective boards of directors and for improving board members' abilities to monitor executive teams to ensure that crises do not occur undetected. Figure 18–7 summarizes some of these recommendations.

Increased Role of Shareholders

Prior to the 1980s, human rights activists, consumer groups, and other social activist pressure groups insisted that companies join their causes. Today, companies are increasingly understanding the stakeholder perspective. However, it has created a new dilemma for companies as they deal with two broad types of shareholders. First, there are the traditional shareholder groups that are primarily interested in the firm's financial performance. Examples of such groups include the large institutional investors, such as pension funds. Second, there are growing numbers of social activist shareholders. These groups are typically pressuring firms to adopt their desired postures on social causes, such as Third World employment practices, animal testing, affirmative action, and environmental protection.

A major problem seems to be that both groups of shareholders feel like neglected constituencies, particularly in light of recent corporate abuses. Shareholders are attempting to rectify this condition through a variety of means. They are demanding effective power. They want to hold management groups accountable. They want to make changes, including changes in management if necessary. Like companies' earlier responses to other stakeholder activist groups, many managements are resisting. The result is a battle between managers and shareholders for corporate control.[72]

A recent example of this battle between managers and shareholders is the effort by the Living Wage, an anti-sweatshop group, to use shareholder resolutions to raise wages for workers in Indonesia. A shareholder must own US$2000 of Nike stock for a minimum of one year to propose a resolution that would change company policy. Jim Keady and Leslie Kredu, directors of the group, are travelling the United States, speaking at colleges in an effort to find individuals and organizations to donate to their cause. Among other demands, the group wants Nike to disclose all factory locations, remove language that prohibits athletes who wear Nike gear from criticizing

---

FIGURE 18-7

Improving Boards and Board Members

Building a Better Board[a]

- Don't overload it with too many members.
- Don't think you need high-profile CEOs or famous academics.
- Keep directors on for at least five years.
- Encourage directors to buy large quantities of stock.

Sharpening the Board's Sensors[b]

- Insist that board members become educated about their company.
- Insist that information-gathering systems deliver quickly the right information from the bottom to the top.
- Insist that board members understand board decision-making processes and not operate by consensus.
- Insist that the company undergo periodic audits of corporate activities and results.

Board Actions[c]

- Directors should evaluate regularly the CEO's performance against established goals and strategies.
- Evaluations of the CEO should be done by "outside directors."
- Outside directors should meet alone at least once a year.
- Directors should set qualifications for board members and communicate these expectations to shareholders.
- Outside directors should screen and recommend board candidates who meet the established qualifications.

Keep Directors' Eyes on CEO[d]

- CEOs need written job descriptions and annual report cards.
- Boards should measure their own performance as well as assess individual members.
- Board nominating committees should exclude the company's major suppliers, officials of non-profit organizations that receive substantial donations from the corporation, and the CEO's close friends.
- A chief executive should hold only one outside board seat.

Sources: [a]Graef S. Crystal, "Do Directors Earn Their Keep?" *Fortune* (May 6, 1991), 79. [b]Richard O. Jacobs, "Why Boards Miss Black Holes," *Across the Board* (June 1991), 54. [c]The Working Group on Corporate Governance, "A New Compact for Owners and Directors," *Harvard Business Review* (July–August 1991), 142–143. [d]Joann S. Lublin, "How to Keep Directors' Eyes on the CEO," *The Wall Street Journal* (July 20, 1994), B1.

Nike, allow monitoring of factories by a worker rights consortium, and only work with factories that pay a wage sufficient to support a small family and still allow savings. Nike spokeswoman Vada Manager questions the group's claims and states that Nike has strict wage, labour, and environmental codes in its factories that are monitored and enforced.[73]

Our discussion of an increased role for shareholders centres around two perspectives: (1) the perspective of shareholders themselves asserting their rights on their own initiative, and (2) initiatives being taken by companies to make shareholders a true constituency. The shareholder initiatives will dominate our discussion, because they clearly constitute the bulk of the activity underway.

Shareholder Initiatives   These initiatives may be classified into two major, overlapping areas: (1) the rise of shareholder activist groups and (2) the filing of shareholder resolutions and activism at annual meetings.

Rise of Shareholder Activist Groups. One major reason that relations between management groups and shareholders have heated up is that shareholders have discovered the benefits of organizing and wielding power. **Shareholder activism** in North America is not a new phenomenon. In the U.S., it arguably goes back over 60 years to 1932, when Lewis Gilbert, then a young owner of ten shares, was appalled by the absence of communication between New York–based Consolidated Gas Company's management and its owners. Supported by a family inheritance, Gilbert decided to quit his job as a newspaper reporter and "fight this silent dictatorship over other people's money." He resolved to devote himself "to the cause of the public shareholder."[74]

In both Canada and the U.S., the major impetus for the movement came in the 1960s and early 1970s. The early shareholder activists were an unlikely conglomeration—corporate gadflies, political radicals, young lawyers, an assortment of church groups, and a group of physicians.[75] The movement grew out of a period of political and social upheaval—human rights, pollution, and consumerism.

The watershed event for shareholder activism in the U.S. was Campaign GM in the early 1970s, also known as the Campaign to Make General Motors Responsible. Among those involved with this effort was, not surprisingly, Ralph Nader. The shareholder group did not achieve all its objectives, but it won enough to demonstrate that shareholder groups could wield power if they worked hard enough at it. Two of Campaign GM's most notable early accomplishments were that (1) the company created a public policy committee of the board, composed of five outside directors, to monitor social performance, and (2) GM appointed the Reverend Leon Sullivan as its first black director.[76]

One direct consequence of the success of Campaign GM was the growth of church activism in North America. Church groups were the early mainstay of the corporate social responsibility movement and were among the first shareholder groups to adopt Campaign GM's strategy of raising social issues with corporations. Church groups began examining the relationship between their portfolios and corporate practices, such as minority hiring and companies' presence in South Africa. Church groups remain among the largest groups of institutional shareholders willing to take on management and press for what they think is right. Many churches' activist efforts are coordinated by the Interfaith Center on Corporate Responsibility (ICCR), which coordinates the shareholder advocacy of about 275 religious orders with about US$90 billion in investments. The ICCR was instrumental in convincing Kimberly-Clark to divest the cigarette paper business and pressuring PepsiCo to move out of Burma. It is now taking on such issues as global warming, environmental pollution, and the practice of using sweatshops to manufacture garments and shoes.[77]

In December 1972, the Investor Responsibility Research Center (IRRC) was formed "to provide timely and impartial analysis concerning corporate social responsibility issues."[78] The IRRC (http://www.irrc.org) became a central organization that served as a resource centre for shareholder activism. Institutional investors (pension funds, church groups, foundations) now dominate the marketplace and thus wield considerable power because of their enormous stock holdings. A similar situation now exists in Canada, as Professor Don Tapscott of the University of Toronto observes:

> *Twenty-five years ago, 80 percent of stock in Canada was owned by wealthy Canadians. Today, two-thirds of stock is owned by institutions such as pension funds—and they're just getting started. This is a reflection of a fundamental trend that's underway. It's like a train that's left*

Search the web WWW

The Ethical Funds Company

The Ethical Funds Company (**http://www.ethical funds.com/Do_the_right_thing/**) describes itself as the first mutual fund company in Canada to file shareholder resolutions on socially responsible business policies and practices. Their stance on shareholder activism is clearly reflected in their Web site comments: "Ownership of common stock confers certain rights. These include the right to propose corporate policies through the shareholder resolution process.... Shareholder resolutions are an important opportunity to influence corporations on significant issues.... The shareholder resolution process allows us to use our influence as a large shareholder, based on the collective voice and values of our unitholders."

There are many useful resources and links contained at this site, including links to the most recent shareholder resolutions submitted to a variety of companies (Canadian and international) by the Ethical Funds Company.

Source: The Ethical Funds Company, http://www.ethicalfunds.com/do_the_right_thing/sri/shareholder_action/shareholder_resolutions.asp.

the station. There will be countless other ... examples of large institutional shareholders getting involved and getting active. It's an historical change that's underway.[79]

Duff Conacher, head of Ottawa-based Democracy Watch and a long-time shareholders' rights advocate, views the recent corporate scandals as underscoring the need for greater shareholder unity. Conacher asserts that the current system is flawed and what is needed is "systemic change to end the scandals that the system produces.... The systemic change that will best do that is to give individual investors an easy way to band together." According to Conacher, associations that would allow individual investors to band together give them more power to effect change within a company.[80]

Indeed, shareholder activists are no longer viewed as a fringe element. They are increasingly being taken seriously by corporations that recognize that their image in the community can impact the bottom line. Certainly, this is the message that recent corporate scandals in the U.S. are driving home.[81]

Shareholder activism motivated by a concern for social and environmental issues gained momentum during the mid-1970s and '80s in Canada. Collections of churches and religious groups united to form the Taskforce on Churches and Corporate Responsibility (TCCR). The initial aim was to pressure Canadian banks to stop making loans to the apartheid regime in South Africa. Later, this group attempted to persuade forest companies to adopt environmental codes of practice. This culminated in the creation of the Forest Stewardship Council. Other issues included convincing Noranda to improve its environmental reporting to shareholders.

More recently, a major success for the task force involved pressuring Calgary's Talisman Energy to divest its 25 percent ownership in an oil facility in Sudan, where a violent civil war had already accounted for millions of civilians deaths. The activists were outraged that money flowing from the project to the Sudanese government was used to build new factories for manufacturing ammunition and thereby fuelling continued war in the region.

A shareholder resolution filed in January 2000 outlined the risk of sanctions by investors and government if Talisman refused to cooperate. The resolution also demanded that the company file an independently verified report on its compliance with human rights standards and the International Code of Ethics for Canadian Business, ensuring that revenue from the Greater Nile Petroleum Operating Company wasn't being used to finance the government's war requirements. Failing these conditions, the resolution urged Talisman to leave the region. Following investor pressure, Talisman finally agreed to sell its interest in the Sudan facility to an Indian firm for $1.2 billion, citing public pressure. Following this news, Talisman shares rose almost 9 percent.[82]

While these examples sound encouraging for shareholders, Josef Fridman makes the following skeptical observations:

Some successes of shareholder activists and the ability of shareholders to dominate or even disrupt annual meetings has created the belief that shareholders are winning back some control of a company from management. However, other than the expanding role of the institutional investor, with both the benefits and the challenges it brings, the notion that shareholder capitalism is gaining ground is mostly an illusion. Real power, for the most part, still rests in the hands of executives, a view a majority of those interviewed held and wished to perpetuate. In fact, for what they see as very practical reasons, most would not like to see shareholders given greater control as they believed it could lead to mismanagement.[83]

This skepticism might be somewhat tempered by recent additions to the shareholder movement in Canada—including the establishment of such relatively new institutions as the Canadian Coalition for Good Governance (CCGG). This organization represents a coalition among such institutional investors as the Ontario Teachers Pension Plan Board, the CPP Investment Board, Mackenzie Financial Corp., and UBS Global Asset Management. Together, they possess approximately $600 billion in assets under management. The mission of the CCGG is "to represent Canadian institutional shareholders through the promotion of best corporate governance practices and to align the interests of boards and management with those of the shareholder."[84] According to a recent *Globe and Mail* report, the CCGG reflects "a new form of shareholder activism. Institutional investors had long pursued issues on an individual basis but the coalition represented the first time they had banded together with the purpose of raising governance standards in Canada."[85]

Among CCGG's central objectives are to encourage the following corporate governance practices:

- All public corporations have highly qualified boards of directors who understand that they are accountable only to the shareholders in carrying out their fiduciary duties.
- Boards of directors insist on excellent and ethical management.
- Boards of directors supervise management proactively.
- All committees of the board of directors are independent from management and highly qualified.
- External auditors follow policies of transparent accounting, reporting directly to the audit committee, thereby ensuring independence from the management of the company.
- Compensation schemes reward employees for superior performance.[86]

CCGG aims to assess organizations using a set of 12 governance guidelines that it has developed. The guidelines delineate how companies should deal with issues such as appointing a majority of independent directors, separating the roles of CEO and chairperson, evaluating the performance of boards and committees, and so on. Figure 18–8 outlines the 12 guidelines.

Filing of Shareholder Resolutions and Activism at Annual Meetings One of the major vehicles by which shareholder activists communicate their concerns to management groups is through the filing of **shareholder resolutions**, or shareholder proposals. An example of such a resolution is, "The company should name women and minorities to the board of directors." To file a resolution, a shareholder or a shareholder group must obtain a stated number of signatures to require management to

FIGURE 18-8

Criteria for Good Governance: CCGG's 12 Guidelines

Individual Directors

1. Ensure quality motivation of board members
2. Require director share ownership
3. Appoint majority independent directors

Board Structure

4. Separate chairperson and CEO
5. Establish independence and mandates of board committees
6. Follow new audit committee requirements

Board Processes

7. Evaluate performance of boards and committees
8. Review performance of individual board members
9. Assess CEO and plan succession
10. Provide management oversight and strategic planning
11. Oversee management evaluation and compensation
12. Report governance policies and initiatives to shareholders

Source: Canadian Coalition for Good Governance, "Corporate Governance Guidelines for Building High-Performing Boards" (January 2004), http://www.ccgg.ca/web/website.nsf/web/CCGG_Guidelines/$FILE/CCGG_Guidelines_v1_Jan04.pdf

place the resolution on the proxy statement so that it can be voted on by all the shareholders. In the U.S., resolutions that are defeated (fail to get majority votes) may be resubmitted provided that they meet certain SEC requirements for such resubmission.

The legislative environment in Canada has traditionally been less favourable for social and environmental shareholder resolutions. Historically, the Canada Business Corporations Act (CBCA) granted management the power to exclude shareholder resolutions that they regard as undesirable. This includes resolutions aimed at promoting general economic, political, racial, or social causes. Consequently, it has been easier for large corporations to restrict shareholder activism in Canada. When shareholder resolutions were excluded (under the CBCA), shareholders could only turn to the court to potentially gain inclusion. In the U.S., on the other hand, the burden of proof rested with the company to demonstrate to the SEC why a resolution should be excluded.[87]

However, the environment for shareholder activism in Canada recently became more favourable, fuelled in part by a change in federal legislation. In 2001, the CBCA was amended to remove the clause banning shareholder resolutions aimed at promoting "economic, political, racial, religious or social" causes. This change made it much more difficult for companies to refuse to circulate shareholder proposals. In other words, it has become easier for shareholders of a corporation, who meet certain eligibility criteria, to submit a resolution to a company, have it circulated to other shareholders, and have it voted on at the company's annual general meeting. Consequently, there has been a significant increase in the number of shareholder proposals filed with Canadian companies starting in 2002.[88]

The shareholder groups behind these shareholder proposals are usually socially oriented—that is, they want to exert pressure to make the companies in which they own stock more socially responsive. Although an individual could initiate a shareholder resolution, she or he probably would not have the resources or means to obtain the required signatures to have the resolution placed on the proxy. Thus, most resolutions are initiated by large institutional investors that own large blocks of stock or by other activist groups that own few shares of stock but have financial backing. Foundations, religious groups, universities, and other such large shareholders are in an ideal position to initiate resolutions.

Shareholder proposals permit investors to present issues of concern to corporate management, and to other shareholders who can then vote in order to support or reject the proposals. Recent proposals were submitted to Hudson's Bay Co. and Sears Canada on the issue of sweatshop labour. Both Sears and the Bay have faced allegations that they purchase apparel from sweatshop factories in Lesotho, where child labour, unsafe conditions, and sexual harassment have been reported. Shareholder initiatives have been led by such organizations as SHARE (Shareholder Association for Research and Education), Working Enterprises (a union-owned organization in Vancouver), and Ethical Funds (a socially conscious fund manager).[89] The Ethical Funds company filed a shareholder resolution in 2004 with Merck & Co. in order to draw attention to the need for easier access to drugs among countries suffering from epidemics of AIDS and malaria. These shareholder resolutions are outlined in Figure 18–9.

The issues on which shareholder resolutions are filed vary widely, but they typically concern some aspect of a firm's social performance. For example, Mobil, Pfizer, and Union Camp were asked to study the safety of tobacco additives produced and sold by them and combusted and inhaled by humans. Several firms, including American Brands, Kimberly-Clark, Philip Morris, and RJR Nabisco, were asked to spin off their tobacco units from the rest of their operations. Wendy's and PepsiCo (Kentucky Fried Chicken, Taco Bell, Pizza Hut) were asked again to make all their restaurants smoke-free. Other popular resolutions have dealt with environmental issues, and board diversity (naming more women and minorities to corporate boards).[90]

Because most shareholder resolutions never pass, one might ask why groups pursue them. The main reason is that they gain publicity, which is part of what protesting groups are out to achieve. Increasingly, companies are negotiating with groups to settle issues before resolutions ever come up for a vote. Several years ago, in a rare reversal of attitude, Exxon Corporation's management recommended that shareholders vote in favour of a resolution calling for the company to provide reams of data on its strip-mining operations. Exxon had agreed ahead of time to the request of the United Presbyterian Church and several Catholic groups, which sponsored the resolution, but the groups wanted the resolution to go all the way to a vote, and the company acquiesced. What happened at Exxon reflects subtle changes as management groups, increasingly sensitive to public criticism, are more willing to sit down before annual meetings and work out agreements on shareholder resolutions. In other instances, resolution requests were withdrawn from Pfizer, Inc., and Union Camp after Pfizer agreed to draft a written policy banning sales of its products to tobacco makers, and Union Camp agreed to cease promoting flavours it generates for tobacco products.[91]

Closely related to the surge in shareholder resolutions has been the increased activism at corporate annual meetings in the past decade. Professional "corporate gadflies" purchase small numbers of shares of a company's stock and then attend its annual meetings to put pressure on managers to explain themselves. An example of the kind of social activism that can occur during an annual meeting was the case in which GM shareholders sought explanations for a series of embarrassing controversies surrounding the automaker. Some shareholders wanted to know why the company substituted

---

FIGURE 18-9

Shareholder Resolutions

Call for Improved Corporate Governance at Sears

Forty-six percent of Sears Canada's minority shareholders supported a shareholder proposal calling on the company's board of directors to employ an independent director as chair of the board. At present, Sears Canada's CEO also serves as chair of the board. Two shareholder proposals, filed by Working Enterprises, Real Assets Investment Management Inc., and the Ontario Public Service Employees' Union staff pension plan, were voted on at the company's annual general meeting on April 22, 2003.

Call for Boycott of Sweatshops at the Bay

A 2002 resolution calling on Hudson's Bay Company to put in place a process to end alleged sweatshop abuses in its supply chain was supported by more than 36 percent of the shares voting at the annual shareholders' meeting. The resolution put forward at the meeting urged the board of directors to adhere to the International Labor Organization's Declaration on Fundamental Principles and Rights at Work and report to shareholders annually on compliance.

Call for Policy on Drug Access at Merck & Co.

There are more than 42 million people worldwide currently living with HIV/AIDS, over 95% of whom live in the developing world; effective treatments for HIV/AIDS exist, but only 4% of those who need treatment have access to it; MALARIA kills between one and two million people each year and 300–500 million new cases occur every year; malaria is often treated in developing countries with drugs that are no longer effective, and people with resistant malaria cannot access the treatment that could save their lives. It has been reported that "Merck does not disclose its position on patent flexibility or give examples of where it has relaxed patents to improve access in developing countries." Shareholders request that our Board review the economic effects of the HIV/AIDS, tuberculosis and malaria pandemics on the company's business strategy, and its initiatives to date, and report to shareholders within six months following the 2004 annual meeting.

Sources: SHARE, http://www.share.ca/index.cfm/fuseaction/page.inside/pageID/75FFDFB7-B0D0-157F-F4671 FC552F14374/index.cfm; Ethical Funds, http://www.ethicalfunds.com/do_the_right_thing/sri/shareholder_action/shareholder_resolutions.asp.

Chevrolet engines in cars sold by some of its other divisions, a move that infuriated many consumers who were not notified of the changes.[92] More recently, corporate executives have been asked to explain high executive compensation packages, positions on hostile takeover attempts, plant closings, greenmail, golden parachutes, and environmental issues.

The motives for bringing up these issues at annual meetings are similar to those for filing shareholder resolutions: to put management on the spot and publicly demand some explanation or corrective action. Activism at annual meetings is one of the few methods shareholders have of demanding explanations and obtaining accountability from top management.

Defending a company at annual meetings has become such an important task of top management that several consulting firms now publish annual booklets of shareholder questions that are likely to be asked. These booklets are intended to help management and directors anticipate and plan for what they might be quizzed on at annual meetings.

Company Initiatives   The need for companies to re-establish a relationship with their owners/stakeholders is somewhat akin to parents having to re-establish relations with their children once the children have grown up. Over the years, the evidence suggests that corporate managements have neglected their owners rather than making them a genuine part of the family. As share ownership has dispersed, there are several legitimate reasons why this separation has taken place. But there is also evidence that management groups have been too preoccupied with their own self-interests. In either case, corporations are beginning to realize that they have a responsibility to their shareholders that cannot be further neglected. Owners are demanding accountability, and it appears that they will be tenacious until they get it.

Public corporations have obligations to their shareholders and to potential shareholders. **Full disclosure** is one of these responsibilities. Disclosure should be made at regular and frequent intervals and should contain information that might affect the investment decisions of shareholders. This information might include the nature and activities of the business, financial and policy matters, tender offers, and special problems and opportunities in the near future and in the longer term.[93] Of paramount importance are the interests of the investing public, not the interests of the incumbent management team. Board members should avoid conflicts between personal interests and the interests of shareholders. Company executives and directors have an obligation to avoid taking personal advantage of information that is not disclosed to the investing public and to avoid any personal use of corporation assets and influence.

With regard to corporate takeovers, fair treatment of shareholders necessitates special safeguards, including (1) candour in public statements on the offer made, (2) full disclosure of all information, (3) absence of undue pressure, and (4) sufficient time for shareholders to make considered decisions. A constructive purpose, not a predatory one, should be served by takeovers. The firm's major stakeholders are its owners. They are interdependent with other stakeholders, and, therefore, management should carry out its obligations to other constituency groups within the context of shareholder concern.[94]

Berkshire Hathaway Inc. is a company known for attending to its shareholders. They have set up a program whereby shareholders are allowed to determine the recipients of the several million dollars in charitable contributions the firm gives each year. For each share owned, a shareholder can instruct the firm to send $3 to a designated charity. Warren E. Buffett, chairman, told shareholders: "Your charitable preferences are as good as mine." Shareholders have sent Mr. Buffett many letters praising this idea. Buffett hopes that the shareholder designation program will foster what he calls "an owner mentality" in the shareholders and that it will strengthen shareholder loyalty.[95] Another indication of Berkshire Hathaway's relationship with shareholders is the annual meeting. Buffett calls the annual shareholders' meeting "Woodstock weekend for capitalists." It's not unusual for shareholders to attend a minor league baseball game decked out in their forest green Berkshire Hathaway t-shirts and caps. Many wait in line to have a picture taken with Buffett or get his autograph.[96]

Shareholder programs are not a substitute for keeping shareholders foremost in the minds of managements and boards when economic decisions are being made. However, they do demonstrate an attempt by managements to give serious consideration to corporate/shareholder relations. These types of programs help the corporate governance problem because they show the shareholders that they matter and that they are important to the firm.

The Conference Board of Canada recently acknowledged organizations that made great effort in managing their governance and thereby in respecting the rights of all stakeholders. Some of the winners of the Conference Board Awards are listed in Figure 18–10.

> ### FIGURE 18–10
>
> ### The 2003 Conference Board/Spencer Stuart National Awards in Governance
>
> #### BC Gas Inc. (Private Sector)
>
> BC Gas Inc. is the private sector and overall winner. Its board has demonstrated a long-term commitment to its enterprise risk management program, and provided leadership and resources in this area. The board of this energy and water distribution and transportation company works closely with management to enhance financial, shareholder, and stakeholder returns in a volatile industry and market.
>
> #### Canada Mortgage and Housing Corporation (Public Sector)
>
> Canada Mortgage and Housing Corporation (CMHC) is the public sector winner. As a federal Crown corporation, Canada's national housing agency defines its success through achieving public policy objectives, while remaining commercially successful in an increasingly competitive environment. Building on past corporate governance commitments, the board of directors has most recently focused on integrating enterprise risk management and performance measurement into its governance framework. The initiative has enhanced the quality of CMHC's strategic leadership and capacity to achieve corporate goals.
>
> #### Canadian Institute for Health Information (Nonprofit Sector)
>
> The not-for-profit winner, the Canadian Institute for Health Information (CIHI), provides a unique example of a governance model and board that successfully integrated multiple stakeholder needs into a new, unified organizational culture, and achieved respected results in a critical sector that is facing enormous challenges. Established in 1994 by Canada's Health Ministers, CIHI's balanced and diverse board provides a firm guiding hand to an organization whose role in the country continues to grow.

Source: Conference Board of Canada, http://www.conferenceboard.ca/GCSR/awards/2003winners/.

Summary

To remain legitimate, corporations must be governed according to the intended and legal pattern. Corporations are not always being governed the way they were intended to be, and the governance challenge has yet to be adequately addressed across the entire business sector. Runaway CEO compensation remains a concern, as is finding qualified and independent candidates to fill vacant board seats. While the corporate governance picture may be slowing improving, it appears, in light of recent scandals, that continual vigilance must be maintained if corporate governance is to fully realize its promise—being responsive to the needs of the range of individuals and groups who have a stake in the firm.

Key Terms

agency problems (page 558)

audit committee (page 571)

board of directors (page 556)

charter (page 556)

compensation committee (page 573)

corporate governance (page 556)

employees (page 556)

full disclosure (page 582)

golden parachute (page 566)

greenmail (page 565)

inside directors (page 560)

insider trading (page 566)

legitimacy (page 554)

legitimation (page 555)

management (page 556)

nominating committee (page 572)

outside directors (page 560)

poison pill (page 565)

proxy process (page 558)

public issues committee (page 573)

public policy committee (page 573)

separation of ownership from control (page 557)

shareholder activism (page 576)

shareholder resolutions (page 578)

shareholders (page 556)

Discussion Questions

1. Explain the evolution of corporate governance. What problems developed? What are the current trends?

2. What are the major criticisms of boards of directors? Which single criticism do you find to be the most important? Why?

3. Explain how mergers, acquisitions, takeovers, greenmail, golden parachutes, and insider trading are related to the corporate governance issue.

4. Outline the major suggestions that have been set forth for improving corporate governance. In your opinion, which suggestions are most important? Why?

5. In what ways have companies taken the initiative in becoming more responsive to owners/stakeholders? Where would you like to see more improvement? Discuss.

Endnotes

1. Joseph McCafferty, "Adelphia Comes Clean," *CFO Magazine* (December 1, 2003).

2. Nadine Winter, "Fair Pay for Fair Play," *CA Magazine* (Vol. 136, No. 10, December 2003), 34.

3. Cited in Edwin M. Epstein and Dow Votaw (eds.), *Rationality, Legitimacy, Responsibility: Search for New Directions in Business and Society* (Santa Monica, CA: Goodyear Publishing Co., 1978), 72.

4. *Ibid.*, 73.

5. *Ibid.*

6. *Ibid.*

7. *Ibid.*

8. William R. Dill (ed.), *Running the American Corporation* (Englewood Cliffs, NJ: Prentice-Hall, 1978), 11.

9. *Ibid.*

10. *Ibid.*

11. Carl Icahn, "What Ails Corporate America—And What Should Be Done," *Business Week* (October 17, 1986), 101.

12. Caroline Oliver, "Democracy in the Boardroom," *Corporate Knights*, http://www.corporateknights.ca/stories/democracy_in_the_boardroom.asp.

13. *Ibid.*

14. John Della Contrada, "Faculty Comment on Enron Debacle," *University of Buffalo Reporter* (Vol. 33, No. 15, January 31, 2002).

15. Louis Lavelle, "Shhh, You'll Wake the Board," *Business Week* (March 5, 2001), 92.

16. *Ibid.*

17. David Paddon, "Canadian Corporate Directors Bracing for More Scandals in 2004: KPMG," *Canadian Press* (February 10, 2004), http://www.canada.com/national/; KPMG, http://www.kpmg.ca/english/.

18. Christopher Guly, "Greed Will Trigger Capitalist Reformation: Professor," *The Ottawa Citizen* (June 29, 2002), http://www.crgq.com/press/06_29_2002/.

19. Seth Sutel, "Lawyers for Hollinger Lay Out Case Against Conrad Black in Delaware Court," *Canadian Press* (February 18, 2004), http://www.canada.com/search/story.html?id=d9ac2f5d-8e7c-48f7-a2e8-018c07cd6451.

20. Michael Gray, Carlotta Amaduzzi, and Stephen Deane, "Governance Lessons from Europe's Enron," http://www.issproxy.com/articles/2004archived/001.asp.

21. Murray L. Weidenbaum, *Strengthening the Corporate Board: A Constructive Response to Hostile Takeovers* (St. Louis: Washington University, Center for the Study of American Business, September 1985), 4–5.

22. Linda Himelstein, "Boardrooms: The Ties That Blind," *Business Week* (May 2, 1994), 112–114.

23. Carol J. Loomis, "This Stuff Is Wrong," *Fortune* (June 25, 2001), 72–84.

24. Janet McFarland, "Related Boards a Matter of Opinion," *Globe and Mail, Report on Business* (October 8, 2002), B1, http://www.globeandmail.com/series/boardgames/stories/20021008related.html.

25. *Ibid.*

26. Della Contrada, *op cit.*

27. John A. Byrne, "Executive Pay: Deliver—Or Else," *Business Week* (March 27, 1995), 36–38.

28. Nikos Vafeas and Zaharoulla Afxentiou, "The Association Between the SEC's 1992 Compensation Disclosure Rule and Executive Compensation Policy Changes," *Journal of Accounting and Public Policy* (Spring 1998), 27–54.

29. Ann Buchholtz, Michael Young, and Gary Powell, "Are Board Members Pawns or Watchdogs? The Link Between CEO Pay and Firm Performance," *Group and Organization Management* (March 1998), 6–26.

30. Louis Lavelle, "The Gravy Train Is Slowing," *Business Week* (April 2, 2001), 44.

31. Louis Lavelle, "Executive Pay," *Business Week* (April 16, 2001), 76–80.

32. Janet McFarland, "Some CEO Pay Below the Radar Screen," *Globe and Mail* (January 28, 2004), http://www.globeinvestor.com/servlet/ArticleNews/story/GAM/20040128/RMCFARLAND28.

33. Peter Coy, "Funny Money or Real Incentive," *Business Week* (January 15, 2001), 71–72.

34. Janet McFarland, "Some CEO Pay Below the Radar Screen."

35. Josef Fridman, "Compensation, Boardroom Evaluation," *CA Magazine* (Vol. 136, No. 10, December 2003), 39.

36. United for a Fair Economy, http://www.ufenet.org/press/2003/EE2003_pr.html.

37. Ed Leefeldt, "Greenmail, Far from Disappearing, Is Doing Quite Well in Disguised Forms," *The Wall Street Journal* (December 4, 1984), 15.

38. Ruth Simon, "Needed: A Generic Remedy," *Forbes* (November 5, 1984), 40.

39. Verne Kopytoff, "Yahoo's Not an Attractive Target for a Takeover, Analysts Say," *San Francisco Chronicle* (March 3, 2001), D1.

40. Richard Blackwell, "Hollinger International Employs Poison Pill to Fight Black," *Globe and Mail, Report on Business* (January 27, 2004), B1.

41. OMERS, http://www.omers.com/investments/proxy voting_guidelines/C-1.htm.

42. Philip L. Cochran and Steven L. Wartick, "Golden Parachutes: Good for Management and Society?" in S. Prakash Sethi and Cecilia M. Falbe (eds.), *Business and Society: Dimensions of Conflict and Cooperation* (Lexington, MA: Lexington Books, 1987), 321.

43. Ann K. Buchholtz and Barbara A. Ribbens, "Role of Chief Executive Officers in Takeover Resistance: Effects of CEO Incentives and Individual Characteristics," *Academy of Management Journal* (June 1994), 554–579.

44. Cochran and Wartick, 325–326.

45. Ontario Securities Commission, http://www.osc.gov.on.ca/en/HotTopics/currentinfo/intr_20031112_taskforce-report.htm; U.S. Securities and Exchange Commission, http://www.sec.gov/answers/insider.htm.

46. U.S. Securities and Exchange Commission, http://www.sec.gov/answers/insider.htm.

47. "Cowpland Settles Insider Trading Case for $575,000," *CBC Online* (December 4, 2003), http://www.cbc.ca/stories/2003/10/20/cowpland201003.

48. "OSC Freezes Accounts Amid ATI Technologies Insider Trading Probe" (December 22, 2003), http://money.canoe.ca/News/Sectors/Technology/2003/12/22/pf-294894.html.

49. Karen Howlett, "OSC Lays Charges in Trading Scandal," *Globe and Mail* (February 5, 2004), B1.

50. Christopher H. Schmitt, "The SEC Lifts the Curtain on Company Info," *Business Week* (August 11, 2000).

51. John A. Byrne, "The Best and Worst Boards," *Business Week* (January 24, 2000), 142.

52. "The Fading Appeal of the Boardroom," *The Economist* (February 10, 2001), 67–69.

53. "Europe's Shareholders to the Barricades," *Business Week* (March 19, 2001).

54. Robert W. Lear and Boris Yavitz, "Boards on Trial," *Chief Executive* (October 2000), 40–48.

55. Megan Barnett, Margaret Mannix, and Tim Smart, "The New Regime; Corporate Reform Measures Are Forcing Boards of Directors to Clean Up Their Act," *U.S. News & World Report* (Vol. 136, No. 6, February 16, 2004), E-2.

56. Janet McFarland, "Guidelines Urge Ethics Codes: New Standards Being Unveiled Today Get Tougher with Boards of Directors," *Globe and Mail* (January 16, 2004), http://ctv2.theglobeandmail.com/servlet/story/LAC.20040116.ROSCRULES16/business/Business/Business/&id=LAC_20040116_ROSCRULES16.

57. Rotman School of Management, http://www.rotman.utoronto.ca/news/boardindex.pdf.

58. Rotman School of Management, http://www.rotman.utoronto.ca/news/newsrelease_021003.htm.

59. "CEOs, CFOs Will Have to Sign Off on Financial Statements," *CBC Online* (January 16, 2004), http://www.cbc.ca/storyview/CBC/2004/01/16/securitiesrules_040116.

60. "The Fading Appeal of the Boardroom," *The Economist* (February 10, 2001), 67.

61. Toddi Gutner, "Wanted: More Diverse Directors," *Business Week* (April 30, 2001), 134.

62. Joann S. Lublin and Elizabeth MacDonald, "Scandals Signal Laxity of Audit Panels," *The Wall Street Journal* (July 17, 1998), B1.

63. Charles A. Anderson and Robert N. Anthony, *The New Corporate Directors: Insights for Board Members and Executives* (New York: John Wiley & Sons, 1986), 141.

64. Arjay Miller, "A Director's Questions," *The Wall Street Journal* (August 18, 1980), 10.

65. Barnett et al., *op cit.*

66. Rotman School of Management, http://www.rotman. utoronto.ca/news/newsrelease_021003.htm; http://www. rotman.utoronto.ca/news/boardindex.pdf.

67. Donald E. Schwartz, "Corporate Governance," in Thorton Bradshaw and David Vogel (eds.), *Corporations and Their Critics* (New York: McGraw-Hill, 1981), 227–228.

68. Della Contrada, *op cit.*

69. Anthony Bianco and Louis Lavelle, "The CEO Trap," *Business Week* (December 11, 2000), 86–92.

70. *Ibid.*

71. "CEOs, CFOs Will Have to Sign Off on Financial Statements."

72. Bruce Nussbaum and Judith Dobrzynski, "The Battle for Corporate Control," *Business Week* (May 18, 1987), 102–109.

73. Andy Dworkin, "Critic Aims to Change Nike from Within," *The Oregonian* (March 9, 2001).

74. Lauren Tainer, *The Origins of Shareholder Activism* (Washington, DC: Investor Responsibility Research Center, July 1983), 2.

75. *Ibid*, 1.

76. *Ibid*, 12–22.

77. "Religious Activists Raise Cain with Corporations," *Chicago Tribune* (June 7, 1998), business section, 8.

78. *Ibid*, 28–44. Also see the IRRC Web site at http://www.irrc.org.

79. James McCarten, "Growing Shareholder Power in Canada Has a Long Way to Go, Experts Say" (November 23, 2003), http://money.canoe.ca/News/MoversShakers/ ConradBlack/2003/11/23/pf-266393.html.

80. *Ibid.*

81. Patricia Coppard, "Share and Share Alike," http://www. vancourier.com/021203/news/021203nn1.html.

82. *Ibid.*

83. Fridman, *op cit.*

84. Canadian Coalition for Good Governance, http://www. ccgg.ca/web/website.nsf/web/ccgghome.

85. Michael Ryval, "CCGG: Much Done, Much More Remains," *Globe and Mail* (October 9, 2003), http:// www.globeinvestor.com/servlet/ArticleNews/story/GAM/ 20031009/CGCCGG09.

86. Canadian Coalition for Good Governance, http:// www.ccgg.ca/web/website.nsf/web/ccggmandate.

87. Douglas Coldwell Foundation, http://www.dcf.ca/discussion/ investing.asp?pg=4; Social Funds, http://www.social funds.com/index.cgi.

88. KAIROS, http://www.kairoscanada.org/e/ecology/climate Change/backgrounder.asp.

89. Paul Pellizzari, "New Muscle for Conscientious Capital Changes to Law Would Give Activist Shareholders New Power in the Boardroom" (2001), http://www.straight goods.com/Pellizzari/010618.shtml.

90. Dale Kurschner, "Tobacco Taboo: How Affirmative Action Are You?" *Business Ethics* (March/April 1995), 14–15. Also see Robert C. Pozen, "Institutional Investors: The Reluctant Activists," *Harvard Business Review* (January–February 1994), 140–149.

91. John A. Byrne, "How Much Should It Take to Keep the Board on Board?" *Business Week* (April 17, 1995), 41.

92. Leonard Apcar and Terry Brown, "GM Reputation Is Defended by Chairman Under Barrage of Shareholder Questions," *The Wall Street Journal* (May 23, 1977), 17.

93. "The Responsibility of a Corporation to Its Shareholders," *Criteria for Decision Making* (C. W. Post Center, Long Island University, 1979), 14.

94. *Ibid*, 14–15.

95. Bill Richards, "Berkshire Hathaway Pleases Shareholders by Letting Them Earmark Corporate Gifts," *The Wall Street Journal* (April 26, 1983), 26.

96. Amy Kover, "Warren Buffett: Revivalist," *Fortune* (May 29, 2000), 58–60.

Cases

Cases

Case Analysis Guidelines

The guidelines presented below have been designed to help the student analyze the cases. They are not intended to be a rigid format. Each question is intended to bring out information that will be helpful in analyzing and resolving the case. Each case is different, and some parts of the guidelines may not apply in every case. Also, the student should be attentive to the questions for discussion at the end of each case. These questions should be answered in any complete case analysis. The heart of any case analysis is the recommendations that are made. The Problem/Issue Identification and Analysis/Evaluation steps should be focused on generating and defending the most effective set of recommendations possible. In all stages of the case analysis, the stakeholder, ethics, and CSR concepts presented in the text should be used. The guidelines are presented in three stages:

Problem/Issue Identification

1. What are the *central facts* of the case and the *assumptions* you are making on the basis of these facts?
2. What are the *major overriding issues* in this case? (What major questions/issues does this case address that merit(s) their/its study in this course and in connection with the chapter/material you are now covering?)
3. What *subissues or related issues* are present in the case that merit consideration, discussion, and action?

Analysis/Evaluation

4. Who are the *stakeholders* in this case, and what are their *stakes*? (Create a stakeholder map to depict relationships.) What *challenges/threats/opportunities* are posed by these stakeholders? What stakeholder characteristics are at work (legitimacy, power, urgency)?
5. What *economic/legal/ethical/philanthropic responsibilities* does the company have, and what exactly are the *nature* and *extent* of these responsibilities to the various stakeholders?
6. If the case involves a company's or manager's actions, evaluate what the company or manager did or did not do correctly in handling the issue affecting it.

Recommendations

7. What *recommendations* would you make in this case? If a company's or a manager's strategies or actions are involved, should they have acted the way they did? What actions *should* they have taken? What actions should the company or manager take now, and why? Be specific and include a discussion of alternatives (*short-term* and *long-term*). Identify and discuss any important *implementation considerations*.

Martha Stewart and the Insider Trading Scandal

One of the highest-profile insider trading cases to hit the press in recent years was the scandal involving Martha Stewart. In 2003, Stewart was charged by the U.S. Securities and Exchange Commission (SEC) with insider trading and accused of lying to investigators regarding her sale of 3928 shares (worth US$227 000) in a biotechnology firm. The accusations levelled at Stewart specifically pertained to her sale of shares in ImClone on December 27, 2001, the day before the stock's value plummeted as a result of negative news about the company—the U.S. Food and Drug Administration (FDA)'s refusal to approve ImClone's anti-cancer drug that it had been developing. According to the SEC, Stewart received this inside information from the former CEO of ImClone, Sam Waksal, a close friend of Stewart's, who was also charged with insider trading and perjury. In 2004 Stewart was found guilty on four counts of obstructing justice and lying to investigators about the timing of her share sale. However, public opinions, such as those stated below, varied with regard to the nature of Stewart's guilt or innocence.

Chasing Martha Stewart[1]

Just days after selling her ImClone Systems stock, Martha Stewart said she knew that ImClone CEO Sam Waksal had been trying to dump his shares in the company, a close friend of the domestic style maven testified.

The revelation by Mariana Pasternak, a friend of Stewart for more than 20 years, was perhaps the most damaging testimony yet against Stewart, who claims she sold the stock for an entirely different reason.

Pasternak said Stewart told her about the Waksal sale on December 30, 2001, just three days after Stewart sold her 3928 shares of ImClone. They were on a terrace at a Mexican resort where they were vacationing.

Pasternak said Stewart recalled Waksal "was selling or trying to sell his stock, that his daughter was selling or trying to sell his stock."

From "A Comedy of Injustice," by Paul Craig Roberts, July 16, 2003, townhall.com. Copyright © 2003 Creators Syndicate, Inc.

She said Stewart added, "Isn't it nice to have brokers who tell you those things?"

What Stewart knew about Waksal when she sold her stock goes to the heart of the U.S. government's case that the homemaking mogul repeatedly lied to investigators in the ImClone probe.

Stewart told investigators she never recalled being tipped that Waksal was selling, and that she sold instead because she and her stockbroker had a pre-arranged agreement to sell Stewart's ImClone shares at a certain price.

Defending Martha Stewart[2]

Martha Stewart was indicted because in December 2001 she sold her shares of ImClone stock the day before the company announced that its cancer drug, Erbitux, was not approved by the FDA. Martha's indictment originated in speculation that Sam Waksal, the CEO of ImClone, gave her "inside information" that the FDA had turned down the company's application.

The investigation established that neither Martha nor her broker had any inside information. Martha's broker noticed that Waksal was selling his shares and that the price was declining. He relayed the information to Martha.

A CEO might sell shares in a company he heads for a variety of reasons, but it is usually regarded as a sign that management has lost confidence in the company's prospects—a good reason for investors to sell the stock.

If Martha had made a large speculative investment in ImClone based on Erbitux, she might have been following the FDA process. She could have concluded that Waksal's sale of ImClone shares meant the drug had failed to gain approval. But this would not be a crime. Moreover, her investment was too modest to have any material effect on her wealth or to occupy her time in following the stock.

Martha and her broker had good reason not to suspect that Waksal's sale indicated FDA disapproval of Erbitux. Insider trading applies to persons with a fiduciary relationship with the firm—a relationship that a

CEO clearly has. As Waksal had inside information, his sale of shares prior to the public announcement is a red flag. Neither Martha nor her broker had any reason to believe that Waksal had gone off his head and decided to get himself indicted.

As neither Martha nor her broker had a fiduciary relationship with ImClone and as neither knew of the FDA decision, no felony charge of insider trading could be brought against her. An ambitious prosecutor might bring a civil action, arguing that knowledge that Waksal was selling is a form of inside information. But that should be the extent of the charge.

The story gets worse. The prosecutor owes his indictments to FDA incompetence. It turns out that Erbitux is just as effective as ImClone said and should have been approved.

Questions for Discussion

1. Was Martha Stewart's behaviour unethical? What was her crime?
2. Who are the stakeholders in this case and how are they affected by Martha Stewart's actions?
3. If you had been in Martha Stewart's position, what would you have done regarding your ownership of the shares?

Case Endnotes

1. Erin McClam, "Close Friend: Martha Stewart Knew ImClone CEO Was Dumping Stock," *Canadian Press* (February 20, 2004), http://www.canada.com/search/story.html?id=5196124f-63c9-4b60-9fcb-8fa211b5eed8.
2. Paul Craig Roberts, "A Comedy of Injustice" (July 16, 2003), http://www.townhall.com/columnists/paulcraig roberts/pcr20030716.shtml.

Case 2

The Enron Debacle

Enron, the energy and trading company, was once the U.S.'s seventh largest corporations, with 21 000 employees, and was the largest marketer of electricity and natural gas. Enron's downward spiral in 2001 began when the company revealed that it falsified accounting records, including keeping hundreds of millions of dollars of losses off the accounting records. In the third quarter of 2001 alone, Enron had incurred a US$600 million loss, and its bankruptcy (declared on December 2, 2001) was among the largest in U.S. corporate history. In addition to the massive layoffs, employees lost much of their retirement money since their pension accounts were built around Enron stock—stock that once sold for US$85 a share became worthless.

The Sins of Enron[1]

Enron's board of directors contributed to the energy trader's collapse because they were aware of the accounting gimmicks, risky business practices, and conflicts of interest but did nothing to stop it, says a highly critical report released Sunday by a U.S. Senate panel. "Enron's directors protest that they can't be held accountable for misconduct that was concealed from them, but much that was wrong with Enron was known to the board," the 61-page report by the Permanent Subcommittee on Investigations concluded.

The Houston-based energy company filed for bankruptcy protection on December 2, 2001, after its stock collapsed amid allegations that its officers hid debt to boost overall profits. The report cited more than a dozen "red flags" that lawmakers said should have resulted in board members challenging management and asking tough questions. They included from a February 1999 Enron audit committee meeting where the board was

From "Corporate Ethics: Right Makes Might," by Heesun Wee, *Business Week*, April 11, 2002.

told Enron's accounting practices are "at the edge" of generally accepted accounting principles to a March 2001 article in *Fortune* questioning Enron's "opaque" bookkeeping.

W. Neil Eggleston, attorney for 13 of Enron's former outside directors, branded the report "unfairly critical." The board, he contends, was misled by top Enron executives and Enron's auditor, Arthur Andersen. Andersen was found guilty of obstruction of justice in federal court last month for the destruction of documents related to the Enron case.

The Senate panel said the board "knowingly allowed" Enron to engage in "high-risk" accounting and failed to ensure auditor independence. It also criticized the board for allowing Enron executives to reap huge pay packages and to park billions of dollars off the books to "make its financial condition appear better than it was."

Shifting part of the blame for Enron's demise from its top executives and accountants to its board members—who were paid US$350 000 a year—will intensify the already heated debate over what reforms are needed to clean up shoddy corporate governance.

The Ethics of Enron[2]

After the dust from the Enron collapse settles, one positive outcome may arise. CEOs, take note: The energy trader's demise provides an important lesson in the value—the necessity, really—of having a corporate conscience and a culture built around knowing the difference between right and wrong.

It's tempting to brush aside business ethics as a nebulous, well-intentioned subject suitable for Business School 101 but of little practical value in the real world. Big mistake. Now we know the heavy toll that ignoring ethics can exact.

Former top Enron executives Jeffrey Skilling and Kenneth Lay insist they were too preoccupied running the global company to know the details of murky, off-the-books partnerships used to hide debt or to question auditor Arthur Andersen's willingness to allow such transactions.

Textbook Case

With Enron the subject of a grand-jury investigation, scrutiny of top execs' behaviour is about to intensify. So far, the details that have emerged about the Houston-based energy giant paint a picture of a Wild West culture that sublimated everything to the goal of driving up the stock price. "In this competitive, capitalistic system of ours, of course you have to have financial targets and goals that keep you pointed in the right economic and competitive direction," says W. Michael Hoffman, executive director of the Center for Business Ethics at Bentley College in Waltham, Massachusetts. "But you've also got to tell employees you can only meet those goals with the framework of our ethical values."

Indeed, the story of Enron is fast becoming a textbook case for how not to lead a business. While Lay was busy exercising his stock options and pocketing profits, he was promoting Enron shares as a bargain to employees. Some Enron executives pressed UBS PaineWebber to take action against a broker who advised some Enron workers to sell their shares. The brokerage firm fired the broker within hours of the complaint, e-mail messages released by congressional investigators show.

Enron was "a swagger place," recalls Doug Schuler, associate professor of management at the Jones Graduate School of Management at Rice University, who worked for Enron's government affairs department for six months. While Schuler conducted research on political activities and corporations and wasn't schmoozing with gung-ho traders, he said the profits *uber alles* work culture was evident.

Enron hired top graduates from top schools, and the perennial question among colleagues seemed to be, "Can you make the deal?" Schuler recalls. "If you're really a clever person, you make the deal. If you're not clever, you're going to work for [rival] Reliant or Duke because you're not going to last long," he added.

Inadequate Defence

Lay and Skilling both vehemently insist that they encouraged employees to work with integrity. Enron had an ethics code. But "at Enron, ethics was simply a piece of paper with three Ps—print, post [in the company lunch room], and then pray that something is actually going to happen," says Stuart Gilman, president of the Ethics Resource Center in Washington, D.C.

Perhaps Skilling and Lay couldn't know all the goings-on at Enron, as they claim. However, "people at the top tend to set the target, the climate, the ethos, the expectations that fuel behaviour," says Thomas Donaldson, a business ethics professor at the Wharton School at the University of Pennsylvania. Adds Steven Currall, associate professor of management, psychology, and statistics at Rice: "I don't think it's an adequate defence for a CEO to say, 'How could I know everything that's going on?' It doesn't absolve them of responsibility."

Practising good business ethics creates dividends that go beyond avoiding legal disaster. A host of studies have shown that employees who perceive their companies to have a conscience possess a higher level of job satisfaction and feel more valued as workers. The 2000 Ethics Resource Center study canvassed corporations and non-profits across the country. Among its findings: Managers' efforts to instill good business ethics were welcomed overwhelmingly by workers.

Positive Environments

"We found a strong connection between employees' perception of their leaders and their own ethical behaviour," says Josh Joseph, top researcher of the ethics center. Workers also said their own behaviour was influenced by the perceived ethics of direct supervisors and co-workers.

So, how do you create a positive work environment in which standards for behaviour are clear and employees serve as role models for one another? Some businesses promote an ethical work atmosphere, along with salary, as a way to woo top talent. At Illinois-based health-care giant Baxter, employees are encouraged to chat up the company's ethics program as a recruiting tool.

Sometimes, fostering ethics can mean crossing national borders. Motorola, also based in Illinois, published a global ethics guide in 1998 to help managers who work abroad. A sample question: What do you do if you're in a country where payments are expected in business dealings? Motorola's code says no. The upshot of the ethics guide: Just because you're not at headquarters doesn't mean you throw your company's standards out the window.

Window Dressing?

How not to instill an ethos in the workplace? Enron also provides a textbook example, say experts. It required employees to sign a code of conduct statement before joining. However, emerging details suggest that any efforts related to a meaningful ethics program may have been window dressing at best. For example, the Enron board twice suspended the company's ethics code in 1999 to allow two outside partnerships to be led by a top Enron executive who stood to gain financially from them, according to a report Houston law firm Vinson & Elkins prepared for Enron.

Companies should instead take a page from health-care giant Johnson & Johnson, where core values have long held centre stage. J&J employees periodically sur-vey and evaluate how well the company is adhering to its code of ethics, called "Credo" responsibilities. Their opinions are relayed to senior managers, and any possible shortcomings in the Credo are promptly addressed.

Small wonder that, when the Tylenol scare hit in the '80s and seven Chicago residents died after ingesting cyanide-laced capsules, J&J managers knew what they had to do—even without consulting with then-CEO James Burke, who was on a plane as the news broke. By the time Burke landed and caught up with his top managers, they already had called for all Tylenol products to be pulled off shelves and for production of all Tylenol items to be halted.

Values in Action

The J&J managers ignored advice from consultants and attorneys who had argued such dramatic steps might harm the Tylenol brand and imply the contamination was the work of a J&J employee. "In the end, it was a joint consensus agreement around the company's values, the No. 1 value being that the health of our customers comes first before anything else, including stockholder value," says Donaldson of Wharton. "This is a story about a company that really lived its values."

Bentley College's Hoffman points out that the decision to do right was a gut reaction. "Ethics is a matter of developing good habits, and it doesn't happen overnight," he says. "It happens through repetition and a long process of development."

You'll find the roots of a companywide commitment to ethics in the top suite. In 1991, a bid-rigging scandal surrounding senior Salomon Brothers officials in connection with U.S. Treasury securities pushed the Wall Street trading house close to bankruptcy. Enter billionaire Warren Buffett.

"Give Me a Call"

As one of his first actions as interim CEO, Buffett wrote a letter to his managers. "It basically said, 'Here's my home phone number in Omaha. If you see anything unethical, give me a call,'" recalls Donaldson. Managers indeed called Buffett, and they collectively came up with a plan to rehabilitate Salomon's tattered reputation. CEOs also can send a clear message about conduct by making business ethics part of performance reviews—along with meeting transparent financial targets, experts say.

"The vast majority of CEOs are ethical and diligent in watching over these issues," says Rice's Currall. "But many of them have got so much on their plates it takes something like Enron to really get their attention, to get them to reevaluate their policies and procedures, and to ensure they're not guilty of some of these same things."

The implication is clear: Business ethics aren't just the province of the Ivy Tower. After Enron, smart CEOs will realize that an honest, transparent, and trustworthy culture can also bolster employee morale and ultimately guard shareholder value.

Questions for Discussion

1. How important are corporate codes of conduct?
2. Why were codes irrelevant to Enron?
3. How can an organization enforce its code of conduct?

4. In your opinion, how different is Enron's "ethics" from other large corporations? Is it an anomaly?

Case Endnotes

1. Adapted from Adam Shell, "Enron Directors Ignored Warnings, Report Finds," *USA Today* (July 8, 2002), http://www.usatoday.com/money/energy/enron/2002-07-07-enron-report.htm#more.
2. Adapted from Heesun Wee, "Corporate Ethics: Right Makes Might," *Business Week* (April 11, 2002), http://www.businessweek.com/bwdaily/dnflash/apr2002/nf20020411_6350.htm.

Case 3

Acres in Oakville and Bribery in Lesotho

Acres International Ltd., an engineering consulting firm based in Oakville, Ontario, isn't a household name—unless you happen to work in the engineering and construction business. The privately held parent company—with 1,100 employees and offices across Canada, in the US, Iran and elsewhere—is a significant player. Since Henry Acres started the firm in 1924, it has worked on power stations, water treatment facilities, steam plants and airports in more than 100 countries. In 2002, it posted revenue of $132.5 million.

Acres' global ambitions brought it to Lesotho in the early 1980s to work on the Moshoeshoe Airport in Maseru. It was therefore well positioned to participate in the immense Lesotho Highlands Water Project, one of the world's largest dam constructions. In 1986, Lesotho and neighboring South Africa agreed to divert Lesotho's Orange River for their mutual benefit. The idea was to deliver water to Johannesburg and generate electricity and income for Lesotho.

Adapted from Matthew McClearn, *Canadian Business Journal* (cover date Sept. 2, 2003), http://www.halifaxinitiative.org/index.php/PressResponses_WorldBank/443/?submit=print.

The Lesotho Highlands Development Authority (LHDA) was formed to oversee the Lesotho component; Masupha Sole, a veteran civil servant, was appointed as its chief executive. Technically, Sole answered to an oversight board. According to critics, however, he acted with considerable autonomy, particularly when awarding contracts. That alleged behavior eventually touched off a series of legal battles. *Canadian Business* used court documents, supplemented with interviews and news reports, to assemble the following account of what happened.

Acres set its sights on providing employees for key technical jobs within the LHDA, under the so-called Contract 19. To help win the deal, Acres hired a local agent, Zaliswonga Mini Bam, to keep it apprised of the political situation and developments in Lesotho and to introduce Acres to local officials. Bam, a civil engineer, had previously worked alongside Acres on the airport contract; he and his wife were close friends of Sole.

Acres won Contract 19 in the spring of 1987. In early 1989, Sole visited Acres' management in Canada and invited the firm to submit another proposal, for a $22 million assignment dubbed Contract 65. Again, Acres contacted Bam and signed him to a representative agreement. And again, Acres emerged victorious, winning Contract 65 in 1990.

Prosecutors would later claim that there were irregularities in Bam's relationship with Acres, however. Bam appears to have issued no invoices, and the representative agreement itself was between Acres and an unregistered firm whose address corresponded to a banker in Geneva. In retrospect, prosecutors claimed, Bam was ill-positioned to carry out his duties for Contract 65: he took a job in Botswana in late 1988 and made only brief visits to Lesotho until his return in February 1991. Still, Bam was to be paid 3.6% of Contract 65's net value—about US$700 000.

At the same time, with Acres employees occupying key positions within the LHDA, alleged conflicts of interest were emerging. For example, one senior Acres employee signed invoices on the company's behalf and then authorized payment of those same invoices for the LHDA as its assistant chief executive. Also, Acres received advance payments before Sole's board had formally approved Contract 65.

Still, those alleged irregularities went largely unchallenged—and things might have remained that way, had Sole not fallen out with the governing board. It had become increasingly dissatisfied with his autocratic management style and was concerned he was misusing his travel budget. Eventually, there was an audit; Sole was suspended in late 1994 and fired a year later.

When Sole launched a wrongful dismissal suit against the LHDA, he was required to disclose his foreign bank accounts. He denied having any. His Maseru accounts told another story, however, uncovering a trail to South Africa that in turn revealed his Swiss accounts. In 1999, Swiss authorities—who in recent years have become more co-operative with transborder investigations—turned over 14 boxes of records.

They were revealing. From 1991 to 1997, Bam's Swiss accounts received dozens of payments, totaling $493 000, from Acres. Of that, he transferred $320 000 to Sole's Swiss accounts. A forensic accountant with PricewaterhouseCoopers saw a pattern: Bam forwarded roughly 60% of Acres' payments to Sole and kept the rest. In May 1997—around the same time Sole's legal machinations to regain his position at LHDA collapsed—Acres' payments to Bam decreased to about 40% of the original amount. Almost simultaneously, Bam ceased money transfers to Sole.

Bam, it turned out, had also forwarded to Sole portions of payments he received from other multinational clients: Zurich-based giant Asea Brown Bovari (ABB),

Germany's Lahmeyer and Nigeria's Dumez. Two other local representatives also made payments to Sole, under the employ of seven other contractors. All told, between 1988 and 1997, Sole received millions of dollars. Each of the 11 companies—including Acres—won one or more contracts on the Lesotho Highlands Water Project.

Lesotho declared war on bribery with its Prevention of Corruption and Economic Offenses Act, enacted in 1999. Sole was first to go down. Facing 18 counts of bribery before the High Court, he at first denied any responsibility; later, he deemed the bribery insignificant and expressed little remorse. But acting judge B.P. Cullinan determined that Sole and the contractors "entered into a corrupt agreement" in which Sole agreed to further their interests in return for money. Accordingly, he convicted Sole of 13 counts and sentenced him to 18 years in prison.

To understand the uproar Sole's conviction touched off, one must first understand the changes in international bribery laws and the shifting attitudes behind them. Until recently, only American companies and other firms listed on US stock exchanges had reason to be cautious when paying graft: the US Foreign Corrupt Practices Act, introduced in 1977, threatens serious sanctions to companies caught bribing foreign officials. US businesses complained that the act undermined their competitiveness against bribe-paying rivals on international projects because other developed countries lacked similar legislation.

Under US pressure, the Organization for Economic Cooperation and Development introduced an anti-bribery convention in late 1997, since ratified by 35 signatories. Those countries promised to adopt national legislation making it a crime to bribe foreign officials. In 1999, Canada introduced the Corruption of Foreign Public Officials Act, under which persons found guilty of bribing such officials can be imprisoned for up to five years.

As a result, certain government bodies, including Export Development Canada, have introduced rigorous anti-bribery policies, according to corporate governance lawyer P.K. Pal, with Flavell Kubrick LLP in Ottawa. (It's too early to say how well such policies are enforced, he notes.) Internationally, further efforts are afoot: member states of the United Nations, for example, are negotiating the terms of its Convention Against Corruption, which is scheduled to be signed in December of 2002.

The allegations in the Lesotho bribery scandal predate 1999, the year of Canada's anti-corruption act. Were similar allegations to arise today, the accused could wind up in a Canadian courtroom—closer to shareholders, customers and the media. "A criminal conviction under the new Canadian law would be a calamity of unthinkable proportions for any company," says Pal. Nevertheless, the Acres case speaks volumes about the progress of international anti-corruption efforts. "Five or 10 years ago," Pal observes, "the Acres matter wouldn't have gone this far."

The tribunal ruled in February 2002 that there was insufficient evidence to debar Acres. The Bank's sanctions committee refuses to reveal its reasoning, but it likely came down to a failure to demonstrate that Acres knew Bam paid Sole.

Undeterred, Lesotho pursued the case. Guido Penzhorn, a Durban-based lawyer, represented the Crown against Acres on two counts of bribery before High Court judge Mahapela Lehohla. Once again, the key question was whether Acres knew about Bam's illicit payments. Penzhorn's case relied entirely on circumstantial evidence. The representative agreement, he argued, was a smoke screen. "By 1990, Acres had been involved in Lesotho for some eight years," he pointed out in court. "The services of a representative would clearly not have been necessary." Had Bam been Acres' legitimate agent in Lesotho, he said, key people within the LHDA would have known—but witnesses testified that they didn't. Most compellingly, Penzhorn contended, in 1997 Acres decreased its payments to Bam by approximately the same amount Bam had been paying Sole, suggesting that Acres knew all along.

Acres' lawyers claimed Bam's representative agreement, role and salary were within industry norms and legitimate. One Acres vice-president said he received continuous reports by phone from Bam, and the company was satisfied with his services. As Acres earlier explained to the World Bank, there was little paperwork detailing Bam's services because "this intelligence function, clearly a sensitive task, was carried out largely without documentation." Also, Acres argued that the contract with Bam was a sort of insurance policy—his services might have become indispensable in "crises, such as political turmoil and civil unrest necessitating for instance the evacuation of personnel." Acres said it reduced Bam's pay in 1997 because he'd been overpaid.

Acres was the first of 11 multinationals to stand trial on bribery charges relating to a corruption scandal. Lesotho's High Court found Acres guilty and fined it US$2.2 million—its estimated profit from Contract 65.

Acres issued statements saying it was "disturbed and dismayed" with the "unjustified decision," which the company said "means that Canadian and other developed country firms can be found guilty of crimes without any clear evidence."

Multinational corporations have often viewed bribery as a distasteful but necessary part of doing business in certain countries—particularly underdeveloped ones. Money under the table can help win contracts, cut through red tape and reduce taxes and other expenses. In the past, various nations, among them France, Germany, Switzerland and Japan, have even allowed companies to deduct bribes to foreign public officials as legitimate expenses. (Japan classified them as "entertainment and social expenses.") As near as anyone can figure, bribery is widespread: between 1994 and 2001, "the US government learned of significant allegations of bribery by foreign firms in over 400 competitions for international contracts valued at US$200 billion," claims the US Department of Justice. "The practice is global in scope, with firms from over 50 countries implicated in offering bribes for contracts in over 100 buyer countries during the seven-year period." In all likelihood, far more goes undetected.

As trade becomes increasingly global, however, multinationals, international financial organizations, and Western governments are starting to address the problem. And Lesotho raised eyebrows by aggressively pursuing this corruption case in court. Companies both in Canada and other Western countries have been put on notice: the world has changed.

Questions for Discussion

1. Who are the stakeholders in this case?
2. Is this action unethical according to various models of ethical decision making?
3. Does the law dictate what is ethical here?
4. Is bribery in business ever considered acceptable? Why or why not?

Case 4

Nova Scotia's Westray Mine Tragedy

From the start, the mandate of the Westray operation was clear: get the mine running, get the coal out, sell it quickly.

Toronto-based Curragh Resources Inc. announced the creation of the Westray mine in the village of Plymouth in Pictou County on September 1, 1988, five days before the provincial election in Nova Scotia. The coal mine was described as a $127 million operation, which would create 300 new jobs in the area. The next day the Nova Scotia government promised to contribute a $12 million loan to the mine.

A week later, Nova Scotia Power Corp. announced a deal to buy 700,000 tons of coal a year for 15 years at a price of $60 to $74 a ton. The reserves of coal at the Westray mine were estimated at 45 million tons. Another week later, the Bank of Nova Scotia kicked in a $100 million loan to the mine operation, with the federal government guaranteeing 85 per cent of it.

The facilities at Westray were supposed to be state of the art. The coal was there in abundance, the buyers were waiting for it, big loans were guaranteed by governments—everything was in place except some nagging concerns from workers that it was a dangerous mine and safety precautions were lax.

In July 1991, Liberal MLA Bernie Boudreau sent a letter to Nova Scotia Labour Minister Leroy Legere warning that the new Westray coal mine scheduled to open in two months near Stellarton in Pictou County "is potentially one of the most dangerous in the world."

On September 11, 1991, 500 guests attended the official opening of the Westray mine. The local member of Parliament, Revenue Minister Elmer MacKay, arrived from Ottawa to cut the ribbon, opening the new coal mine that promised 300 badly needed jobs that would last at least 15 years.

On March 9, 1992, Mike Piché, an organizer for the United Steelworkers of America, said in a report on safety in the mine: "I strongly feel there will be someone killed in the near future."

Adapted from Martin O'Malley, *CBC News Online* (May 9, 2002), http://cbc.ca/news/features/westray.html.

Two months later, on May 9, 1992, at 5:18 A.M., a spark deep in the southeast section of the mine ignited an invisible cloud of methane gas, triggering a massive explosion that trapped and killed 26 miners. The force of the blast shattered windows and shook homes in nearby Stellarton and New Glasgow.

The Westray story is a complex mosaic of "actions, omissions, mistakes, incompetence, apathy, cynicism, stupidity and neglect," said Mr. Justice Peter Richard in his report on the explosion and fire at the coal mine in Pictou County, Nova Scotia, that killed 26 miners. The title of Mr. Justice Richard's report on the tragedy—the inquiry took five years and cost nearly $5 million—says it all: *The Westray Story: A Predictable Path to Disaster.* According to the report, the tragedy of Westray goes far beyond a simple, ghastly accident. It involved corporate greed, bureaucratic bungling and government incompetence of the highest order.

Richard's report zeroed in on Curragh Resources Inc., the private company that managed the coal mine, and various government inspectors who ignored glaring safety abuses, among them:

- Inadequate ventilation design and maintenance that failed to keep methane and coal dust at safe levels;
- Unauthorized mine layout, forcing miners to work risky tunnels to get the coal out faster;
- Methane detectors were disconnected because frequent alarms, signalling dangerous concentrations of methane, interrupted coal production;
- Procedures to "stonedust" coal to render it non-explosive were done only sporadically, usually before inspections;
- An "appalling lack of safety training and indoctrination" of miners.

Looking back on the tragedy, Judge Richard commented: "A safe workplace demands a responsible and conscientious commitment from management—from the Chief Executive Officer down." Such a commitment was sadly lacking at the Westray mine. "Since there was no discernible safety ethic, including a training program and a management safety mentality, there could be no continuum of responsible safety practice within that workplace." Complacency seemed to be the prevailing attitude at Westray—which at times regressed to a heedless disregard for the most fundamental safety imperatives. According to Richard:

> As I stated in the report, compliance with safety regulations was the clear duty of Westray management. To insure that this duty was undertaken and fulfilled by management was the legislated duty of the inspectorate. Management failed, the inspectorate failed, and the mine blew up.

The Westray miners not killed in the blast, 117 of them, were awarded severance pay for 12 weeks, which came to $1.2 million. Individual cheques to the miners ranged from $6,626 to $12,367. A $30 million lawsuit was launched against the province of Nova Scotia by families of the dead miners, but Nova Scotia's Supreme Court threw it out, ruling that the province was protected from lawsuits under the Workers Compensation Act.

Curragh Resources Inc. initially was charged with 52 non-criminal counts of operating an unsafe mine. The company went bankrupt in 1993. The charges then were dropped after a Nova Scotia judge criticized the way in which they were laid. The case went back to trial, was dismissed again, then the Supreme Court of Canada ordered a new trial.

Charges of criminal negligence and manslaughter had been laid against mine managers Gerald Phillips and Roger Parry, but these came to nothing when the Crown stayed proceeding, saying there was not enough evidence to ensure a conviction.

Clifford Frame, founder and chief executive officer of Curragh Resources Inc., refused to testify at the Richard Inquiry, as did Marvin Pelley, former president of Westray. The inquiry had no federal powers, which meant subpoenas could not be enforced outside of Nova Scotia, leaving company officials safe in their Toronto headquarters.

Ten years later, the province is selling off what's left of the Westray operation, hoping to raise money for the families of the miners. The remains of Westray have been knocked down, and soon will be covered and seeded to grass, entombing the 11 miners whose bodies never made it up from the doomed mine.

Coal mining has always been dangerous work. Between 1838 and 1950, the peak years of coal mining in Pictou County, 246 miners were killed in similar methane-and-coal-dust explosions, many of them working the rich Foord seam that became part of the Westray operation. Between 1866 and 1972, another 330 miners were killed in other accidents—mangled in machinery, buried under stone, squashed in coal-car collisions.

Questions for Discussion

1. How could an organization permit such "actions, omissions, mistakes, incompetence, apathy, cynicism, stupidity and neglect" to occur here?

2. What level of accountability should the government accept for this disaster?

3. What lessons do we learn from Westray with regard to holding organizations accountable for their actions?

4. Who should be punished? What type of punishment should be exacted?

Case 5

The Whistle-blower at Canadian Marconi Co.

Russell Hayes, bearing only a high-school education, had accumulated years of experience in sales, marketing, contracts and program management. By the early 1990s he was working as project manager for Montreal-based CMC—Canadian Marconi Co. (now CMC Electronics Inc.), a company largely servicing military needs. The company earned $358 million in revenue during fiscal 2002. Recently, the company won contracts to supply satellite communications systems to upgrade avionics equipment on the U.S. navy's fleet of F-14B fighters and a US$110 million contract to supply flight systems for 1,200 U.S. army Black Hawk helicopters.

Among other products, CMC's military communications division manufactured and sold the AN/GRC-103(V)1, a tactical radio developed in the 1960s that found extensive military application, particularly among members of the North Atlantic Treaty Organization. A combination of five portable components, it provides secure, line-of-sight communications—essentially serving as a sort of wireless telephone—within a range of up to 80 kilometres. During its heyday, the popular 103 radio was a "cash cow" for CMC. However, this device eventually became the source of a major battle between Hayes and his employer.

In the 1990's, U.S. military bases and depots were closing, and gear deployed in the Middle East during the first Persian Gulf War of 1990–91 was repatriated. Consequently, hundreds of 103 radios appeared on the surplus market. To prevent surplus gear from competing with newly manufactured units, Hayes alleges, CMC quietly began buying the more intact units from surplus dealers in late 1991. In fact, Hayes claims he did much of the buying himself.

Assembling radios using surplus and used parts would cost 80% less than manufacturing new ones, Hayes estimates. However, most contracts specifically prohibited this—and where permissible, doing so would significantly reduce the amount CMC could charge. Nevertheless, in documents filed at the U.S. district court

Adapted from Matthew McClearn, "A Snitch in Time," *Canadian Business*, Dec. 28, 2003.

of New Jersey, Hayes alleges that CMC used the old gear to fill contracts, without informing customers. He says he learned about the practice early on. "I warned them in writing to be careful who they sold [used gear] to—that was my initial thought," Hayes claims. "I was more or less told, 'Get with the program, or else.' So I did."

The 103 radio is a critical component of the American Patriot air defence system. Patriot missiles are used to shoot down ballistic missiles and other aerial threats. The 103s allow communications between the various vehicles, radar stations and other mobile units that comprise the Patriot system. The U.S. government sometimes provides Patriot systems to allies under its foreign military sales program; in 1993, it awarded CMC a contract to supply 97 radio sets for Saudi Arabia's Patriot program.

It wasn't until 1995 that Hayes raised his allegations a second time. According to him, CMC's marketer in Saudi Arabia wrote letters to company executives complaining that the 103 radios supplied to the Saudi Patriot program were malfunctioning. This raised concerns that CMC would lose a follow-up contract for about 200 more units. In fact, Hayes says, the failures originated from newly manufactured meters, not surplus parts—but the internal wrangling worried him. "I didn't want to get blamed," he explains.

Hayes knew nothing about whistle-blowing, and it's unclear what processes CMC had in place to handle internal complaints. Hayes, however, says he collected two boxes of documents. And then on June 14, 1995, he penned a letter to J. E. Soos, then CEO of CMC. That letter ended Hayes's career.

The letter, addressed to Soos, laid out allegations of how and why his company defrauded its customers, among them the U.S. government. Hayes wrote of falsified invoices and of changed serial numbers—in short, the stuff of potentially great embarrassment to any military contractor. Hayes's fateful letter to his boss was not a product of outrage, an epiphany or a sudden shocking discovery. In fact, Hayes says he knew all along what his company was doing and, indeed, actively participated. Subsequent to writing this letter, he went on paid leave and vowed he wouldn't return until the problem was rectified.

Hayes's action was rooted in a costly miscalculation: in his words, "I thought they'd fix things." Instead, it precipitated his departure from CMC. According to Hayes, after many months and several discussions, CMC offered him an arrangement under which he would leave on permanent disability provided by Sun Life Insurance Co. It gave him a lump-sum payment of $22,723, plus undisclosed monthly payments until 2011. Oddly, Hayes says nothing more than a 15-minute consultation with a psychiatrist was required—and he insists he's in good health now, as he was then. "It's pretty much hush money," Hayes asserts. Hayes had a lawyer review the agreement. She wasn't pleased, nor was he. "But I was getting into my 50s," Hayes says. "I'm not an engineer. To go and find a job with the money I was making was almost impossible. He signed the agreement in February 1996—and hasn't worked since.

Hayes, 58, now retired and living in suburban Montreal, recently became embroiled in a court battle in which he's helping the U.S. Department of Justice sue his former employer. Hayes alleges in court documents that, contrary to specific contractual provisions, CMC built radios from used, reconditioned and overhauled components. He further alleges that serial numbers were changed, and that the radios in question were shipped with new packaging and documentation. What's more, Hayes claims CMC overbilled by charging for support, integration, training and other costs that it never actually incurred. "They took a US$20,000 radio and sold it for US$122,000—that's the bottom line," Hayes maintains. "The executives all knew it was going on and were thrilled that they were making money."

Paul Keys, a surplus dealer in Somis, California, largely agrees with Hayes: "I'm not sure why they sold them, but the U.S. army disposed of quite a few sets." Keys, who bought hundreds of old 103s at the time, says it's standard industry practice for surplus dealers to notify manufacturers after—and sometimes even before—buying surplus gear to line up potential buyers. "That's the first thing most savvy surplus dealers do," he says.

None of these allegations have been proven in court, and CMC's version of events, also spelled out in court filings, is entirely different. Though the company admits to "a small percentage of new and unused surplus parts and components" in the units it supplied to the Saudis, it says this was permitted by the terms of its contract. Costs were not inflated, CMC asserts, nor were false invoices issued.

The CMC of today is much changed from what it was in Hayes's day. The company was bought by Gerry Schwartz's ONCAP LP, the Onex small-cap fund, in 2001, which sold the military communications division to Britain's Ultra Electronics Holdings PLC for US$33.7 million in August 2002. As for Hayes, he now regrets raising his concerns with management. If he had it to do over again, he "would have stayed with the company," he says. "I would have done it for selfish reasons. I would have had that nice paycheque...."

Hayes's version of events supports several well-established observations about whistle-blowing. One: whistle-blowers seldom anticipate the consequences of their actions. Two: organizations typically respond poorly to criticism from within. And three: many lack a system that protects complainants from retaliation. These observations hold particular relevance in Canada, where policies that help whistle-blowers raise concerns and protect them from abuse have largely been absent. The result, all too frequently, is that whistle-blowers are intimidated, alienated and drummed out of the organizations they work for. However, apart from new laws and public pressure, organizations have other compelling motives to allow employees to raise concerns internally. Hayes's case demonstrates one: if an employer won't listen to complaints, maybe somebody else will.

Questions for Discussion

1. Who are the stakeholders in this situation and what are their stakes?

2. What are the ethical issues in this case?

3. What company policies might have prevented this situation?

4. What should Hayes have done differently in terms of whistle-blowing?

Case 6

The Ethics of Drug Patents

Here are some numbers to consider: 14 million, 35.9 billion, and one.

The first figure is an estimate of the number of people who will die of AIDS and other treatable diseases over the course of the coming year, most of them in the poor countries of the developing world.

The second figure represents the combined 2002 profits, in dollars, of the ten biggest pharmaceutical companies, according to *Fortune* magazine's annual analysis of America's largest businesses.

The third figure corresponds to the number of countries that, Wednesday, November 19, 2003, voted against a U.N. resolution on access to drugs in global epidemics such as HIV/AIDS, tuberculosis and malaria. The resolution emphasized that the failure to deliver lifesaving drugs to millions of people who are living with HIV/AIDS constitutes a global health emergency. One hundred sixty-seven countries voted in favor of the resolution. The single vote against it was cast by the United States.

Sadly, these numbers are closely related. To protect their exorbitant profits, drug companies are fighting the production and distribution of cheap generic versions of patented drugs. Unable to afford the medicines necessary to save their lives, millions of poor people die of treatable illnesses every year.

And, as the recent U.N. vote exemplifies, the drug companies have a reliable ally. Not only does the U.S. government use its considerable economic power to bully developing countries into restricting access to low-cost generics, it continues to try to change the international rules that allow such generics to be produced in the first place.

Unnecessary Deaths

In their vulnerability to treatable diseases, the rich and the poor live in different worlds. Every year, millions of people in developing countries die of illnesses that they

Adapted from Joanne Mariner, "Profit Margins, Death Rates, Drug Patents and HIV/AIDS" (Monday, November 24, 2003), http://writ.news.findlaw.com/mariner/20031124.html; and "Canada's Vital Role in the AIDS War, *CBC News Online* (February 6, 2004).

would likely have survived had they lived in Europe or the United States. A key factor in the enormous global disparities in death rates is poor people's lack of access to needed drugs.

Consider the case of HIV/AIDS. An estimated 42 million people are living with HIV/AIDS worldwide, 39 million of them in the developing world. India alone has at least 4.5 million people who are HIV-positive, and possibly many more. China, a country that has yet to act decisively to address the epidemic, has at least another 1.5 million people living with HIV. In sub-Saharan Africa, as is well known, the rate of HIV infection has reached crisis proportions.

In Africa, 20 years after the appearance of AIDS, 20 million people have AIDS/HIV, 17 million have died of the disease, and only 70,000 are receiving treatment. About 67 per cent of AIDS sufferers between the ages of 15 and 24 are female. As a result of AIDS, there are 11 million orphans in Africa, a number that is expected to rise to 20 million by 2010.

In the United States and other rich countries, since the advent of effective anti-retroviral drug treatment, AIDS has become a manageable disease, not a death sentence. But for the millions living with HIV in the developing world, prospects for effective treatment remain dim.

At present, only a tiny minority of HIV-positive people in poor countries have access to anti-retroviral drugs. For most people in the developing world, as well as some marginalized populations in rich countries, the cost of treatment remains prohibitively high.

Patent Protections and Profits

Nothing in the ingredients of anti-retroviral drug treatment makes it inherently expensive. Indeed, when a combination of generic drugs is used, treatment costs are about $600 per patient per year.

But low drug costs do not appeal to those who profit from drug sales. Unsurprisingly, therefore, the pharmaceutical companies that own the patents for anti-retroviral drugs bear an enormous share of the responsibility for keeping them beyond the reach of so many people with HIV. In the United States, the cost of anti-retroviral drugs is generally in the range of $10,000 to $15,000 per patient annually, and people with advanced cases of AIDS may pay far more. Relying on international patent protections, drug companies have been trying to maintain drug prices artificially high by restricting the production and distribution of low-cost generic substitutes.

Global protections on intellectual property are tied to global rules on trade, specifically, the rules of the World Trade Organization. Under the WTO's intellectual property rules—known as the Agreement on Trade Related Aspects of Intellectual Property, or TRIPS—countries belonging to the WTO must give pharmaceutical companies twenty years of protection for drug patents filed after 1995. Although the rules carve out exceptions for national health emergencies, they still go a long way toward limiting poor people's access to life-saving medicines.

And as Oxfam has shown in a paper titled "Patent Injustice," the problem extends beyond HIV/AIDS. Brand name drugs for a number of major diseases cost several times more than their generic equivalents. The increasing drug resistance of endemic diseases such as tuberculosis and malaria—and the resulting need for access to new drugs—mean that the WTO's monopolistic pricing rules threaten many millions of the world's poor.

The Brazil Model

Despite the WTO's restrictions, some developing countries have made important steps in meeting their people's drug treatment needs.

In Brazil, notably, extensive prevention efforts combined with state-funded anti-retroviral treatment have reduced AIDS-related deaths by more than half since 1996. The cornerstone of Brazil's treatment program has been the local production of generic equivalents of brand-name anti-retroviral drugs, which has driven down the cost of treatment enormously.

But Brazil's successes, and those of countries like it, have been hard fought. The TRIPS rules have been a battleground on which Brazil and others have fought a series of high-stakes skirmishes with drug companies.

Canada's Role

The 2004 government throne speech said Canada will push ahead with legislation to provide the drugs to assist victims of the AIDS pandemic. "There is a moral imperative to do all we can to make medical treatment accessible to the untold millions suffering from deadly infectious diseases, notably HIV/AIDS, particularly in the poorest countries of Africa. The Government of Canada will therefore proceed with legislation to enable the provision of generic drugs to developing countries," the throne speech said.

In October 2003, when Canada's Stephen Lewis heard of the government's decision to support affordable drugs for AIDS victims in Africa, he called it "a stunning breakthrough." Lewis is the U.N.'s special envoy for AIDS in Africa. Before Canada's announcement in October, Lewis had called rich nations' indifference to the AIDS crisis in Africa "mass murder by complacency."

When the AIDS legislation was introduced in Ottawa in October 2003, Canada became the first country to follow up an agreement by the World Trade Organization in August 2003 urging member countries to provide cheap drugs to developing countries to assist victims of AIDS.

The new legislation, still to be approved, allows Canadian companies to sign contracts with developing countries to supply cheaper, generic drugs in the war against AIDS. Under the legislation, companies supplying generic versions of brand-name patented drugs would pay the patent-holder a royalty of 2 per cent.

The savings would be enormous. In North America, brand-name AIDS drugs—also drugs for victims of tuberculosis and malaria—cost between $8,000 and $15,000 a person. Generic drugs cost about $250 a person. Lewis said Canada's decision to rewrite its patent laws so as to supply generic drugs to developing countries is a global breakthrough.

Questions for Discussion

1. Who are the stakeholders in this context and how are they affected by drug patents?

2. What is the social responsibility of drug companies in this case?

3. Are generic drug producers the best solution to this issue?

4. Is the argument presented above fair to drug companies?

Nancy Olivieri: Corporate Funding of Medical Research

Thalassemia

Thalassemia is fatal genetic disease that affects millions of people around the world. It is estimated that 180 million people carry the thalassemia gene. If both parents carry the disease, there is a one in four chance in a pregnancy that the child will inherit the fatal form of the disorder. The most severe form, alpha thalassemia mostly strikes people from Southeast Asia, China and the Philippines and often results in the death of the newborn child. Others have milder forms of the disease.

Children affected with thalassemia cannot make enough hemoglobin, the substance that carries oxygen in the blood. For centuries, most children born with the disease did not survive past their 10th birthday.

Children who have the disease appear healthy at first but by one or two lose their appetite and energy, become pale and eventually develop jaundice, or a yellowing of the skin. If the disease is not treated, the heart, spleen and liver become enlarged. Bones can become thin. The children can die from heart failure or infection.

There are two types of hemoglobin, hemoglobin A and hemoglobin F. Either will do the job of carrying oxygen in the blood. Babies are born with hemoglobin F, but after a few months, the body shuts off and starts making hemoglobin A. That's called the hemoglobin switch. Thalassemia patients don't make enough hemoglobin A.

Most patients are treated with a monthly transfusion of red blood cells. The transfusions help the child feel better, and can prevent heart failure and bone deformity. But, the frequent blood transfusions also build up iron in the body and that can damage the heart and the liver.

The most common method of ridding the body of iron is to use a drug called deferoxamine. But it means a painful and time-confusing process, where the patient is

Adapted from "Thalassemia," http://www.tv.cbc.ca/national/pgminfo/ thal/; and Anne McIlroy, "Toronto Doctor Loses Round in Drug Battle," *Globe and Mail* (December 19, 2003), http://www.globeand mail.com/servlet/ArticleNews/TPStory/LAC/20031219/OLIVIERI19/ TPHealth/.

hooked up to a pump over a 12-hour period. Younger patients quite often want to stop taking the drug.

Deferiprone, Nancy Olivieri and Apotex

Dr. Nancy Olivieri, Professor of Pediatrics and Medicine at the University of Toronto, and Director of the Hospital for Sick Children (HSC) Program in Haemoglobinopathy, was an early proponent of deferiprone—an experimental drug (also referred to as L-1) that held promise in treating thalessemia. What made deferiprone so attractive was that it could be given in pill form instead of the daily 12-hour injection of the drug, which is so cumbersome that many patients stop.

An expert on inherited blood disorders, Olivieri ran trials on L-1 in the early 1990s at HSC. Her pilot study showed the drug was worth investigating further. This further investigation was facilitated through the financial support of a commercial drug company, Apotex Inc.

Apotex Inc. acquired the commercial rights for the drug and in 1993 became the corporate sponsor for the research. Apotex helped fund a clinical trial comparing the drug to the existing treatment. It also funded the continuation of the pilot study to monitor long-term effects.

In 1996, Dr. Olivieri found that the drug wasn't working for some patients and she identified an unexpected medical risk of the drug to long-term patients. Her 1997 research findings suggested that L-1 could cause liver damage. Although she relayed her findings to Apotex, the company's scientists disagreed with her interpretation of the data.

In addition to informing her patients of the negative effects of the drug, Olivieri wanted to make her findings known to the public. However, there was a problem. She'd signed a contract giving Apotex control over communications about the research. Medical scientists are commonly requested to maintain data confidentiality for longer than the 30 to 60 days considered necessary to file a patent. However, Olivieri's contract with Apotex was unusual in that it required her to keep the data confidential for three years.[1] She was warned by the company that a breach of the confidentiality agreement would result in legal action.

In the spring of 1996, Apotex revoked Olivieri's research funding and terminated her clinical trial.

Dr. Olivieri defied the agreement with Apotex and wrote an article, published on August 13, 1998 in the prestigious *New England Journal of Medicine,* which indicated, among the findings, that five of 14 patients taking deferiprone showed evidence of liver damage.

In January 1999 Olivieri was dismissed (though later reinstated) as Director of the HSC Program in Haemoglobinopathy and was sued by Apotex. Neither the Hospital for Sick Children in Toronto nor the University of Toronto, where Dr. Olivieri held joint appointments, backed her in the dispute with the drug company. At the time, Apotex was negotiating a $30 million donation to the university and its affiliated teaching hospitals. However, university and hospital officials asserted that their actions were not influenced by the possible donation.

Shortly thereafter, Olivieri "went public" with her allegations regarding the company, the hospital, and the university. The lawsuit against Olivieri was dropped and she was reinstated. The case of Nancy Olivieri attracted worldwide attention and prompted debate at medical schools on how to protect the public interest in drug trials financed by pharmaceutical companies.

Postscript: Whose Research Can You Trust?

To Dr. Olivieri, having her study published meant long-sought vindication. But questions are being asked about her research. An editorial in the same issue of the journal raises some important concerns and finds her study inconclusive. The editorial pointed out that the study had a "limited number of patients," that some researchers would consider Olivieri's method of sampling the liver as "unacceptable." Their biggest objection was that the patients studied weren't comparable. The findings, wrote the editors, "weakened their conclusion."

For Dr. Jerome Kassirer, the editor-in-chief of the *New England Journal of Medicine,* the study is intriguing, but hardly the last word. "It is some evidence— I wouldn't be willing to describe it as weak, it is some evidence that adds to our current knowledge about the efficacy and perhaps even the toxicity of the drug," Kassirer said. Officials at Apotex have called the editorial a vindication of their position that deferiprone is safe.

More recently, in 2003, a European court justice ruled against Olivieri's objections and upheld a European drug approval agency's decision to allow the sale of a controversial drug used to treat an inherited blood disorder.

Apotex, the drug's manufacturer, welcomed the court's ruling, and moved ahead with plans to expand sales in Europe and get the drug approved in Canada and the United States. Michael Spino, Apotex's senior vice-president for scientific affairs, said the decision will benefit patients who were worried about the safety of the drug because of Dr. Olivieri's court challenge.

As of 2003, the drug was being now sold in 29 countries, although not in Canada or the United States. Apotex has asserted that several subsequent studies have found that the drug is safe and effective, but Dr. Olivieri continues to argue that those studies were flawed.

In the end, what looked like a battle between David and Goliath is turning into a scientific debate as to whose research you can trust.

Questions for Discussion

1. In what ways does this case reflect the dynamics of whistle-blowers' scenarios? Is this a case of whistle-blowing?

2. Does corporate sponsorship necessarily compromise the objectivity of researchers?

3. What alternatives exist to corporate sponsorship?

4. What lessons can we take from this case?

Case Endnote

1. "For Profit or for Patients?" CBC Radio, *Quirks & Quarks* (September 12, 1998).

Case 8

IBM and the Final Solution

A recent book by Edwin Black, entitled *IBM and the Holocaust*, offers compelling evidence that IBM played an important role in some of the most horrific events of the 1930s and 1940s in Europe. Specifically, IBM's production of hundreds of Hollerith machines, the precursor to the computer, played a central role in the first racial censuses conducted by the Nazis. Beginning in 1933, the Hollerith machine was used by the German government to identify its intended targets.

As Black comments in his book:

Nearly every Nazi concentration camp operated a Hollerith Department ... in some camps ... as many as two dozen IBM sorters, tabulators and printers were installed.... [I]t did not matter whether IBM did or did not know exactly which machine was used at which death camp. All that mattered was that the money would be waiting—once the smoke cleared.[1]

The author suggests that IBM's involvement with Nazi Germany helps explain one mystery of the Holocaust—how so many people were killed in so little time. With the knowledge of top IBM management in the United States, IBM's European subsidiaries actually perfected the means for the Nazis to quickly collect census data for its murderous plans. Hitler awarded IBM chairman Thomas Watson a medal for his company's work.

IBM's Role in the Holocaust[2]

In the upside-down world of the Holocaust, dignified professionals were Hitler's advance troops. Police officials disregarded their duty in favor of protecting villains and persecuting victims. Lawyers perverted concepts of justice to create anti-Jewish laws. Doctors defiled the art of medicine to perpetrate ghastly experiments and even choose who was healthy enough to be worked to death—and who could be cost-effectively sent to the gas chamber. Scientists and engineers debased their higher

Excerpted from *IBM and the Holocaust: The Strategic Alliance between Nazi Germany and America's Most Powerful Corporation*, by Edwin Black (New York: Crown Publishers, 2001), p. 375. Used by permission of Crown Publishers, a division of Random House, Inc.

calling to devise the instruments and rationales of destruction. And statisticians used their little known but powerful discipline to identify the victims, project and rationalize the benefits of their destruction, organize their persecution, and even audit the efficiency of genocide. Enter IBM and its overseas subsidiaries.

Solipsistic and dazzled by its own swirling universe of technical possibilities, IBM was self-gripped by a special amoral corporate mantra: if it can be done, it should be done. To the blind technocrat, the means were more important than the ends. The destruction of the Jewish people became even less important because the invigorating nature of IBM's technical achievement was only heightened by the fantastical profits to be made at a time when bread lines stretched across the world.

So how did it work?

When Hitler came to power, a central Nazi goal was to identify and destroy Germany's 600,000 Jews. To Nazis, Jews were not just those who practiced Judaism, but those of Jewish blood, regardless of their assimilation, intermarriage, religious activity, or even conversion to Christianity. Only after Jews were identified could they be targeted for asset confiscation, ghettoization, deportation, and ultimately extermination. To search generations of communal, church, and governmental records all across Germany—and later throughout Europe—was a cross-indexing task so monumental, it called for a computer. But in 1933, no computer existed.

When the Reich needed to mount a systematic campaign of Jewish economic disenfranchisement and later began the massive movement of European Jews out of their homes and into ghettos, once again, the task was so prodigious it called for a computer. But in 1933, no computer existed.

When the Final Solution sought to efficiently transport Jews out of European ghettos along railroad lines and into death camps, with timing so precise the victims were able to walk right out of the boxcar and into a waiting gas chamber, the coordination was so complex a task, this too called for a computer. But in 1933, no computer existed.

However, another invention did exist: the IBM punch card and card sorting system—a precursor to the computer. IBM, primarily through its German subsidiary, made Hitler's program of Jewish destruction a technologic mission the company pursued with chilling success. IBM Germany, using its own staff and equipment, designed, executed, and supplied the indispensable technologic assistance Hitler's Third Reich needed to accomplish what had never been done before—the automation of human destruction. More than 2,000 such multi-machine sets were dispatched throughout Germany, and thousands more throughout German-dominated Europe. Card sorting operations were established in every major concentration camp. People were moved from place to place, systematically worked to death, and their remains cataloged with icy automation.

IBM Germany, known in those days as Deutsche Hollerith Maschinen Gesellschaft, or Dehomag, did not simply sell the Reich machines and then walk away. IBM's subsidiary, with the knowledge of its New York headquarters, enthusiastically custom-designed the complex devices and specialized applications as an official corporate undertaking. Dehomag's top management was comprised of openly rabid Nazis who were arrested after the war for their party affiliation. IBM NY always understood—from the outset in 1933—that it was courting and doing business with the upper echelon of the Nazi Party. The company leveraged its Nazi Party connections to continuously enhance its business relationship with Hitler's Reich, in Germany and throughout Nazi-dominated Europe.

Dehomag and other IBM subsidiaries custom-designed the applications. Its technicians sent mock-ups of punch cards back and forth to Reich offices until the data columns were acceptable, much as any software designer would today. Punch cards could only be designed, printed, and purchased from one source: IBM. The machines were not sold, they were leased, and regularly maintained and upgraded by only one source: IBM. IBM subsidiaries trained the Nazi officers and their surrogates throughout Europe, set up branch offices and local dealerships throughout Nazi Europe staffed by a revolving door of IBM employees, and scoured paper mills to produce as many as 1.5 billion punch cards a year in Germany alone. Moreover, the fragile machines were serviced on site about once per month, even when that site was in or near a concentration camp. IBM Germany's headquarters in Berlin maintained duplicates of many code books, much as any IBM service bureau today would maintain data backups for computers.

I was haunted by a question whose answer has long eluded historians. The Germans always had the lists of Jewish names. Suddenly, a squadron of grim-faced SS would burst into a city square and post a notice demanding those listed assemble the next day at the train station for deportation to the East. But how did the Nazis get the lists? For decades, no one has known. Few have asked.

The answer: IBM Germany's census operations and similar advanced people counting and registration technologies. IBM was founded in 1898 by German inventor Herman Hollerith as a census tabulating company. Census was its business. But when IBM Germany formed its philosophical and technologic alliance with Nazi Germany, census and registration took on a new mission. IBM Germany invented the racial census—listing not just religious affiliation, but bloodline going back generations. This was the Nazi data lust. Not just to count the Jews—but to identify them.

People and asset registration was only one of the many uses Nazi Germany found for high-speed data sorters. Food allocation was organized around databases, allowing Germany to starve the Jews. Slave labor was identified, tracked, and managed largely through punch cards. Punch cards even made the trains run on time and cataloged their human cargo. German Railway, the Reichsbahn, Dehomag's biggest customer, dealt directly with senior management in Berlin. Dehomag maintained punch card installations at train depots across Germany, and eventually across all Europe.

How much did IBM know? Some of it IBM knew on a daily basis throughout the 12-year Reich. The worst of it IBM preferred not to know—"don't ask, don't tell" was the order of the day. Yet IBM NY officials, and frequently Watson's personal representatives, Harrison Chauncey and Werner Lier, were almost constantly in Berlin or Geneva, monitoring activities, ensuring that the parent company in New York was not cut out of any of the profits or business opportunities Nazism presented. When U.S. law made such direct contact illegal, IBM's Swiss office became the nexus, providing the New York office continuous information and credible deniability.

Questions for Discussion

1. How responsible is IBM for the atrocities that the Nazis committed?
2. Should IBM have been held accountable for its involvement?
3. If IBM is guilty of assisting the Nazis, how do you "punish" an "organization"? Who do you punish?
4. Can or should the present-day IBM attempt to "make amends"? If so, how?

Case Endnotes

1. Edwin Black, *IBM and the Holocaust: The Strategic Alliance between Nazi Germany and America's Most* *Powerful Corporation* (New York: Crown Publishers, 2001), 375.

2. http://www.ibmandtheholocaust.com/excerpts.php.

Case 9

Bombardier and the Socially Responsible Ski-Doo

Jacques Ruelland has had just about enough of the ever-present whining of distant snowmobiles cutting through the crisp winter air in the once-idyllic cottage and wilderness country known as the Laurentides, north of Montreal. According to Ruelland, who used to be the president of the Regional Environmental Council of the Laurentides (CRELA), "the growth of recreational vehicles and their unbridled use make it impossible for the people of this region to make use its very real resources in a way that increases the quality of life and ensures local prosperity."[1]

The conflict between those who derive a tremendous thrill from riding their snowmobiles, and those who are supremely annoyed by them, is now commonplace in rural areas of Canada and the northern United States. Sometimes the snowmobilists have the upper hand, but occasionally the anti-snowmobile lobby scores successes. One of the last acts of U.S. President Clinton, in January 2001, was to ban the use of snowmobiles in Yellowstone National Park, in Wyoming. (This order has since been contested by the pro-snowmobile lobby in the courts.) In Quebec the situation is complicated by the fact that it was a Quebec firm, Bombardier, that invented the modern snowmobile and still dominates the local market. Bombardier is in many ways a "national icon" in Quebec. Founded by a French-Canadian inventor, Joseph-Armand Bombardier, in the 1930s, it has grown into an industrial giant with 80 000 employees in 24 countries (and 20 000 in Quebec alone). The company made its mark internationally by riding the first boom in snowmobiling with its signature brand, the Ski-Doo, in the 1960s. In 1972, the last year before the energy crisis that would cut deeply into sales, it produced a staggering 200 000 of these vehicles. Since 1974 Bombardier has diversified. By the early years of the twenty-first century, it had become the world's number-one producer of regional commuter jets and the number-two producer of trains, while still holding on to 27 percent of the North American market for snowmobiles. For many in Quebec, Bombardier is the symbol of the possibility for Quebecers to compete and win on the world stage. To be against the Ski-Doo would seem to be almost unpatriotic!

In 2001 it was estimated that some 150 000 snowmobiles were "off the road" in Quebec. The production, sales, and maintenance of these vehicles amounted to a billion-dollar industry in the province. Most of these machines are used for purely recreational purposes, although in a territory largely covered in snow and ice for a substantial part of the year, there are also a not insignificant number of snowmobiles used by industry (e.g., mining- and forestry-related activities), by members of isolated communities as an essential means of transportation, by government departments, police, park rangers, and so on. (According to the director of communications for Bombardier's recreational-products division, Marc R. Lacroix, Bombardier is the only company that makes vehicles specifically designed for rural police forces.[2]) Ski-Doo remains the most popular brand in Quebec, even though it now trails rivals like Arctic Cat and Polaris in the U.S. market.

But again, not everybody is happy about the popularity of recreational snowmobiling. A typical snowmobile uses as much fuel and produces as much greenhouse gasses in three months as a family car uses in one year—as many as twenty 20 litres of gasoline per hundred kilo-

This case was written by Charles Bilodeau, Marie-Claude Couturier, Alexis Lapointe, and Wayne Norman, at the Centre de Recherche en Éthique de l'Université de Montréal (CRÉUM).

metres. Recreational snowmobiles often do hundreds of kilometres on a weekend. Relatively few snowmobiles possess the catalytic converters that reduce toxic emissions in cars.

And they are dangerous. According to Quebec's government automobile insurance board (the SAAQ), 10 people were killed in snowmobile accidents in 2001, with another 28 seriously injured. This compares to 363 fatal accidents and 3085 serious injuries involving cars (of which more than 2.5 million were on the roads in Quebec in 2001), and 34 deaths and 334 serious injuries caused by the roughly 93 000 motorcycles on the road. Of course, it should be remembered that the snowmobile season is relatively short, typically less than three months, with most of the activity happening on weekends only. The accident rate per-hour-of-use must be many times higher than for automobiles or even motorcycles.

In Quebec (and elsewhere) there are relatively few laws and regulations governing snowmobilists' activities, especially when they are off-road. There is a speed limit of 90 km/h on specially marked paths, and 70 km/h elsewhere. There seem to be no current regulations governing the emission of toxic and greenhouse gasses. The law for off-road vehicles (L.R.Q. V-1.2) and the rules for snowmobiles (R.R. Q. V-1.2, r. 1) have one pollution-related provision, namely the requirement that snowmobiles must not exceed 82 decibels of noise—a volume similar to that of a heavy truck used in the construction industry. The Oregon-based NGO Dangerous Decibels estimates that just eight hours of exposure to this kind of "noise pollution" can lead to permanent hearing loss.

Who should be held responsible for the damage caused by recreational snowmobiling? One could imagine spokespeople for the snowmobile manufacturers arguing that "snowmobiles do not cause problems, people cause problems." In other words, they could argue that they have little control over how the buyers of snowmobiles use them: as long as they are used safely, at moderate speeds, in areas where they will not bother local residents or outdoors people, then snowmobiles are relatively benign.

This is not, however, the approach that Bombardier has taken. Since the mid-1960s, long before there was evidence of any kind of backlash against snowmobile use, Bombardier has taken three different steps to reduce the potential hazards of their products.

First, Bombardier actively promotes safety. In 1968 it began its first publicity campaign to promote "safe snowmobiling." Working with the Canada Safety Council they produced and distributed pamphlets urging snowmobilers to "Be safe and make the most of winter fun!" Similar campaigns have continued ever since, and these days Bombardier's Web site places a much greater emphasis on safety and the environment than do those of its principal competitors. Bombardier gives all buyers of its products a video and booklet promoting safety and proper conduct. The company sponsors safety teams in Alberta, Ontario, New Brunswick, Quebec, and elsewhere that visit schools, snowmobile clubs, and events to promote safety. And it has donated a fleet of 20 snowmobiles to patrol popular off-road trails in Quebec.

Secondly, Bombardier was instrumental in the creation, in 1965, of the International Snowmobiles Industry Association (ISIA), which would become, in 1995, International Snowmobiles Manufacturers Association (ISMA). Within this group it helped to launch the Snowmobile Safety Council Committee (SSCC), which established standards governing the manufacture of products, and promoted safety for users through the ongoing "Safe Rider" program. Although the manufacturers claim to be paying particular attention to the problems of noise and air pollution, the group has so far resisted establishing strict environmental standards. Many critics charge that industry associations like this one exist not to promote social responsibility on behalf of the manufacturers, but rather to fend off or soften government regulations, in part by serving as a lobby group. Bombardier, however, continues to take a leadership role within the association and believes that the association raises the standards of all of the manufacturers.

Thirdly, outside of its efforts as a member of the ISMA, Bombardier has sought to be an industry leader in introducing technological solutions to problems of safety, noise pollution, and toxic emissions. It has recently launched the first four-stroke engine in the industry, the "Rotax V-1000 4-TEC," which is supposed to reduce hydrocarbon emissions by 80 percent and fuel consumption by 30 percent, compared to conventional two-stroke engines. To date, Bombardier is also the only manufacturer to offer the option of less-polluting semi-direct injection systems. They have been working for years on the development of an electric snowmobile, but have yet to put one into production. Bombardier's operations, from its factories to its dealerships and service centres, have earned the rigorous ISO 14000 environmental certification.

By the early years of the twenty-first century the snowmobile market in North America was "mature," with little room for growth, tight competition, and much lower profit-margins than in previous decades. In April 2003, the new CEO of Bombardier, Paul Tellier, decided to spin off the Recreational Products division of the firm which produces the Ski-Doo, and it was bought in December 2003 for $960 million by a consortium that included members of the Bombardier family. The new corporation continues to operate under the name "Bombardier Recreational Products," and the chairman of the board is Laurent Beaudoin, the son-in-law of Joseph-Armand Bombardier, and the former long-time CEO of Bombardier.

Bombardier and the Bombardier family pride themselves on their sense of social responsibility. Long before "corporate social responsibility" became a buzzword and a popular movement, Bombardier had made serious and enduring commitments to the communities it operated in, to its employees, and to philanthropy more generally (3 percent of profits are given to the Bombardier charitable foundation). Still, the question remains whether they should be doing more to reduce the pollution and safety hazards of their most famous product, the Ski-Doo. Some might say that it is inherently impossible to produce some products in a socially responsible way. Could it be that the "safe cigarette" or the "socially responsible snowmobile" are oxymorons?

Questions for Discussion

1. Who is responsible for the dangers and disturbances caused by recreational snowmobiling—governments (local, provincial, federal), the manufacturers, or the owners? Or put another way, what responsibilities do each of these three groups have to reduce the hazards of this recreational activity? What *could* each of these parties do to reduce the hazards, and what *should* they be doing?

2. Some might argue that recreational snowmobiling causes more harm than good. What would we need to know in order to evaluate this claim? Does it seem plausible?

3. Is it possible to be a socially responsible snowmobile manufacturer? Is Bombardier?

Case Endnotes

1. Louis-Gilles Francoeur, "Les pétaradeurs de toutes sortes soulèvent du mécontentement dans les Laurentides," *Le Devoir* (January 6, 1998), A4.

2. Lacroix was interviewed for this case study by Alexis Lapointe. Many of the details about Bombardier's efforts to reduce the "negative externalities" of snowmobiling come from this interview.

Case 10

Child Sponsorship and the "Future of Basketball"

On February 4, 2003, Mark Walker shot 18 baskets in a row. The feat was captured on video, and would soon appear in a television advertisement throughout the U.S. Mark was decked out in the latest gear from the athletic shoe giant, Reebok: shoes, socks, cargo pants, a sweatshirt and headband—all sporting Reebok's logo. Mark was three-and-a-half years old at the time. He is Reebok's latest, and youngest, spokesman.

This case was written by Martin Leblanc, Pierre-Yves Néron, and Wayne Norman, at the Centre de Recherche en Éthique de l'Université de Montréal (CRÉUM).

He may not be the youngest for long, though. On the Web site that bears Mark's name and shows four short videos of him in action and interview (http://markwalker.reebok.com/), Reebok invites parents to share their son's or daughter's "special skills with the rest of us. Describe your child's superior abilities in an email or capture the action and send in a tape." The Web site also directs parents to the Reebok Kids online store.

Neither Reebok nor Mark and LaShawn Walker, Mark Jr.'s parents, have disclosed how much Mark was paid for his sponsorship. His parents note that it is certainly enough to ensure that Mark will be able to attend the college of his choice when he graduates from high school, around 2018. Of course if Mark really is "the future of basketball," as he proclaims in an interview on Reebok's Web site (he pronounces it "backetball"), then he will probably be given a full scholarship by the college of his choice. Or better yet, he could go directly from high school to professional basketball, like the current "future of basketball," LeBron James, who in 2003 began playing for the Cleveland Cavaliers, and signed a sponsorship contract worth US$138 million with Reebok's rival Nike. LeBron was 17 when he signed this contract.

There is nothing new about the sponsorship of athletes by the big sporting-goods companies. It is well known that this has been the most important component in the marketing strategy that made Nike number-one in the world, thanks to its long-term relationships with international stars like Michael Jordan and Tiger Woods. Nor is the sponsorship of minors a particularly recent phenomenon, especially in individual sports like tennis and track and field, where future stars are often identified and signed up in their teenage years. It does, however, appear to be the case that sponsorship contracts are going to younger and younger athletes, in a wider variety of sports, and for much greater sums. Mark Walker is the poster child, literally, for this trend.

The reaction to this new trend is also on the rise. Rob Walker (no relation to Mark), writing in the online magazine, *Slate*, sums up some of the raw emotion on both sides of the issue: "A 3-year-old saying 'I am Reebok' strikes me as just about the creepiest and most disheartening image that a company could possibly offer to society. But I suspect that many viewers will have a different reaction—more along the lines of, 'I want in on that. *My* boy can be Reebok, too.'"[1]

What specifically is there to worry about with this kind of youth sponsorship? Many people will be concerned about the welfare of the child who is sponsored. How many hours—or dozens or hundreds of hours—might Mark have been made to shoot baskets under his mother's watchful camcorder before he hit the streak of 18? It is reported (on the site Africana.com) that LaShawn Walker, a former high school athlete, had put young Mark through 90-minute training sessions from about the time he was 18 months old. Similarly, there is the question of how the early fame affects the emotional state and development of a young child. Before Wayne Gretzky was 10 years old he was already attracting national press coverage in Canada, but in that era there were no significant sponsorships to speak of. The young

future "Great One" continued to practise with his father on a humble backyard sheet of ice in Branford, Ontario. If the family had been given millions of dollars at that point, would Wayne have matured in the same way?

Many will also worry about the welfare not simply of the children lucky (or talented) enough to receive these endorsement contracts, but also all of the many thousands more kids whose parents push them to achieve greatness early but who "fail." Are companies like Reebok behaving responsibly when they appeal directly to these parents with the call: "Young Sensations Wanted. Does your son or daughter have super talent?" The shoe companies might plausibly reply that there have always been incentives for overly zealous parents to exploit their children's talents, be they in sports, the arts, or other kinds of performance that could lead to exposure in television or movies. But do these new sponsorships increase the damage caused by misplaced dreams of stardom, or do they simply open up the possibility of child stardom to a greater pool of families?

A very different kind of worry about the phenomenon of child sponsorship concerns the more general issue of marketing to children. At least some advertising campaigns using child sports stars will surely be used to appeal directly to other children. A study from researchers at Texas A&M University estimates that four- to 12-year-olds in the U.S. spend US$30 billion out of their own pockets, and influence the spending of some US$600 billion by their parents. A Belgian study found that 84 percent of family purchases at grocery stores were determined by the tastes or demands of children. According to Claude Cossette, a professor of advertising at the Université Laval, and founder of one of the largest marketing agencies in Canada, "It is clear that children are now a priority target for a good many companies." The aim, he notes, is not merely to sell to them now, but rather to create a bond of loyalty with a brand that will endure throughout their lives. "A kid who drinks Coke will not suddenly switch to Pepsi at 18."[2] The basic fear of critics of advertising to children is that it manipulates them before they have sufficient critical faculties to make up their own minds freely.

A final danger of the "Mark Walker" phenomenon is for companies like Reebok themselves. As many of the hundreds of bloggers who have commented on the issue have enjoyed pointing out, there is a potential irony in such advertising campaigns. Athletic shoe companies like Nike, Reebok, and Adidas have long faced accusations—sometimes well founded[3]—of using child labour in their manufacturing facilities in the developing world.

The Mark Walker campaign could remind consumers something that the shoe companies have worked hard to make them forget, namely that (as a columnist at Africana.com puts it) "for every Mark Walker, Jr. who is exploited by Reebok, well, there are ten thousand more laboring for chump change stitching [shoes] in Asian sweatshops."[4] There is some precedent for this kind of "ironic backlash." In the late 1990s, Nike delayed the launch of a campaign emphasizing the empowerment of women athletes when certain nongovernmental organizations threatened a countercampaign emphasizing the working conditions of women in Nike's factories. Even for the hippest of companies, it seems, irony is not always good for sales.

Questions for Discussion

1. What, if anything, is wrong with companies like Reebok offering sponsorships to children like Mark Walker and their families? Do you think that Mark or his parents are being exploited?

2. Reebok is a company that has, since 1992, been at the vanguard of progressive change in its industry. For example, it has very detailed codes and practices to promote human rights and to improve the conditions of workers in the factories that make its products, including a commitment not to use child labour.

If they are going to continue the practice of sponsoring children and teenagers, are there any policies or principles they could use to minimize the chance of doing harm to young athletes and their families?

3. Should governments be regulating the sponsorship of children and teenagers? If so, how? If not, why not?

Case Endnotes

1. Rob Walker, "The Littlest Endorser: Reebok Robs the Cradle," *Slate* (June 9, 2003).

2. Quoted in Alec Castonguay, "Enfant de pub: la nouvelle cible, les 4 à 12 ans," *Le Devoir* (December 20–21, 2003).

3. Before the early 1990s, the big shoe firms paid little attention to the working conditions in the factories of the firms to which they subcontracted their shoe manufacturing. The workers in these factories were not literally employees of the big name-brand firms. Reebok introduced its first human-rights standards for all of its sourcing firms—which, among other things, prohibited use of child labour—in 1992.

4. Staff columnist, *Africana.com* (June 13, 2003). If this remark is charging that companies like Nike and Reebok have children making their shoes in 2003, it is probably in error. These firms do not permit child labour and have their sourcing factories monitored by third parties, including human rights NGOs. Nevertheless, the popular impression of the continued use of child labour surely persists.

Case 11

Assurance Magnum of Quebec

There are many things that Justine Winstod loves about being the manager of one of the very successful and award-winning call centres at Assurance Magnum, but having to discipline employees for "ethics violations" is not one of them. The principal activity of the call centre is selling Magnum's insurance products; primarily automobile insurance, which is often bundled with various other products, such as roadside assistance, and the pro-

This case was written by Olivier Larouche, Patrick Deschênes, and Wayne Norman, at the Centre de Recherche en Éthique de l'Université de Montréal (CRÉUM).

vision of rental cars during repair periods. Winstod oversees about 40 agents (known as "associates"), most of whom are university or college graduates, and all of whom are certified as "damage insurance representatives" by the *Bureau des Services Financiers*,[1] an agency of the government of Quebec. (In order to obtain their licences, most of the agents were trained in a four-month-long program at full pay when they joined the staff at Magnum.)

On Monday afternoon, Winstod scheduled a meeting with one of the associates, Benjamin Ryan, for the following morning. During the previous week, as part of a routine internal audit, a quality-control manager at the call centre listened to recorded conversations between Ryan and a number of prospective clients. Winstod was alerted on Friday afternoon that Ryan's aggressive selling techniques may possibly have violated some of Magnum's ethical standards, and perhaps even one or more of the articles of the profession's code of ethics as regulated by the *Chambre de l'assurance de dommages*. Winstod downloaded these audio files onto her laptop and listened to them over the weekend.

Magnum is a small and young firm, by industry standards in Quebec. They specialize in automobile insurance, whereas most of their competitors sell a broad range of insurance products and financial services. Nevertheless, in its relatively short existence Magnum has built up an impressive and loyal customer base, largely because of its effective use of the Internet and the most advanced call centres in the industry. The biggest players in the province, such as Desjardins (a huge credit union, and the auto-insurance market leader in Quebec), Bélair, Assurances Banque Nationale, Capitale, and Wawanesa, have in fact tried to imitate the more nimble newcomer, Magnum, in its effective and efficient use of call centres. The industry used to rely on face-to-face contact in branch offices, where clients might typically work with the same agent for many years. The relative anonymity of the call centre approach challenges many of the old norms of these kinds of relationships.

Magnum has also been innovative in its commitment to ethical business practices. The founder, David Duquette, had worked for many years in a Dutch financial-services giant, and right from the start attempted to create a culture at Magnum founded on ethics, integrity, and social responsibility. Senior and middle managers, like Winstod, were expected to ensure that their units operated within the spirit of Magnum's credo. Every year Magnum published a so-called "Triple Bottom Line" report detailing not just financial performance, but also social and environmental performance. Included in "social performance" was a detailed account that included, among many other things, measures of customer and employee satisfaction, progress on the status of women and visible minorities within the firm, charitable contributions, and details of legal and regulatory violations by the firm or its employees. As part of its commitment to "all three bottom lines," Magnum promised to include data about social and environmental performance into its calculations and decisions for bonuses and promotions.

Winstod's call centre had done well on the two previous social audits. She knew that this year's social audit was still a couple of months off when Ryan opened her door and took a seat. He knew that they were going to discuss the "quality" of his dealings with clients, since this was a routine way that Magnum worked with employees to improve their performance. But he was not aware that he was also going to be questioned on his ethics. Winstod confronted Ryan with two "selling techniques" he had used on more than one occasion. First of all, he had sold customers special roadside assistance and "loaner" rental car insurance without first asking whether they were already covered for these things by their dealers. (Some new cars are sold with such coverage over the first five years or 100 000 km.) A quick perusal of the provincial code of ethics—of which selected articles are reprinted in Appendix 1, below—would suggest that agents are not allowed to knowingly sell insurance products that customers do not need; although the code does not quite say this in black and white.

Many potential clients are ignorant or unsure of the terms of their dealership guarantees, and will sometimes purchase unnecessary coverage. Of course, the agents know well that if the potential customer ends a call in order to investigate his or her current coverage, then the agent may lose the sale not only for the supplementary coverage (roadside assistance or a "loaner" car during repairs), but also for the primary auto insurance policy that was usually the product that the customer was calling about in the first place.

Ryan looked embarrassed when he was confronted with this first issue. He said he did not remember the precise details of the calls in question, though he did not doubt the accuracy of the computer-generated transcript of the calls. He claimed that he was satisfied from the customers' tones of voice and other subtle clues that they were well informed about the extent of their current coverage, and if they were willing to purchase new plans from Magnum it was because they felt this was a good deal. It was certainly not his intention to deceive them, he pleaded. Winstod knew, as perhaps Ryan did not, that these "redundant insurance" sales do occasionally cause problems for the company. Sometimes they are discovered by the customer or the customer's partner or even children (in the case of older people) after the policy has arrived in the mail. This can result in unpleasant phone calls for Winstod and other managers, as well as cancelled policies and even complaints to the *Chambre de l'assurance de dommages*.

The second issue with Ryan's phone "etiquette" concerned the wording he used with several potential customers when attempting to sell them a package that included comprehensive accident insurance, roadside assistance, and "loaner" rental car insurance. Magnum calls this coverage its "No Problemo!" package. When purchased in combination like this, each of the insurance products is cheaper. The invoice that is sent to the customers lists all three products with a reduced price. In fact, the price of the package is the same as the price of the first two products, if they were purchased individually. So in *some sense*, the third product—the rental car in case of repairs—is "free" when you purchase the "No Problemo!" combo. Or at least this is how Ryan was presenting it to some customers. Winstod asked Ryan whether he thought this was tantamount to lying to customers, and hence a clear violation of the provincial code of ethics.

"No, it's definitely not lying," Ryan replied. "It's literally true. If they bought these two products separately they would pay the same price as they would for the package that includes the rental car coverage."

"Yes, but that coverage is not *free*," Winstod insisted. "When they receive their invoice in the mail they will see in black and white that they are being charged for it. Some of them are then going to call me back and ask me to take another $50 off their package (since the 'No Problemo!' invoice puts a price tag of $50 beside the rental car coverage); and if we did that we'd be losing our shirts on this package. And that's if we're lucky. They could just go right ahead and call the *Chambre de l'assurance de dommages*, or worse yet, some consumer-affairs TV show! Either way, your little white lie could cost us dearly."

As Winstod's tone became more insistent, Ryan's sheepish embarrassment turned into frustration and even anger. "Look, Justine, you used to be on the phones, and now you're supervising us. You know what goes on out there," he said, as he pointed to the calling floor. "And you know what it took to get promoted up here. People call in for car insurance and it's our job to sell them as many other products as we can. You and I both know that Magnum would go broke in no time if we sold nothing but that cut-rate car insurance."

By now it was Winstod who felt pangs of embarrassment, because she knew that what Ryan was saying was largely true. And he wasn't through. "You also know the pressure on us to sell this 'No Problemo!' package this month—you wouldn't be offering a free trip to Disney World for the associate who sells the most of them if you didn't want us to be aggressive out there." These month-long competitions were a routine event at Magnum. Sometimes there were as many as six a year, featuring various product bundles, but often linked to the "No Problemo!" package. Agents knew that doing well in these competitions led not only to prizes but also to raises and promotions. Everyone knew, for example, that Justine Winstod had won five such contests when she was an agent. Since agents are not paid commissions, these prizes and chances for promotion are the only financial incentives they have. "When you get right down to it, Justine," Ryan concluded, "the only ethics violation going on here is the conflict of interest that the company is placing the agents in. We all have personal interests to sell products that are not necessarily in the clients' interest."

Winstod wasn't sure what to do with Ryan, since she respected his candour. "Look, Ben, of course I know what it's like out there. But you have to appreciate the risks some of these tactics can expose for us all. The last thing we need are more official complaints as we head into this year's 'ethics audit.' Listen, I'm going to have to give you a warning at this stage. And if I receive word of any legitimate complaints from any of your clients over the next couple of months, I'll be forced to take this further. In the meantime, please, please tell your buddies out there that we don't want to be hearing the words 'No Problemo!' and 'free' in the same sentence when we listen to your calls."

As Benjamin Ryan left her office, Justine Winstod felt the conflicting imperatives of her position more acutely than ever before. She wanted to balance profitability and integrity not just because it was the company's credo, but because she really believed in it. It made her feel much more positive about the value of her career as a manager. She also knew—given Magnum's price strategy, where basic car insurance is sold almost as a loss-leader—that her call centre could not be successful if the associates did not encourage the clients to consider buying products they had not thought they needed before they phoned. It was also clear that her agents sold significantly more products during the competitions, perhaps as much as 40 percent more. She didn't think this was unethical in itself, because she believed that Magnum offered good insurance products that were competitively priced. But she was certainly not comfortable with exploiting clients' ignorance, trust, or naïveté.

What could she do to make her agents work diligently and skillfully at their phones? Was there some way they could be convinced to work as hard as possible, to serve the clients' best interests, and to maintain the strictest standards of professional ethics? She would be happy if they could be motivated without competitions, but how? Should she consider different incentives? Perhaps a more thorough regime of monitoring would help. Should they hire more auditors to listen to more hours of each agent's conversations? Should there be stricter punishments, along with more precise rules about what is and is not allowed? Perhaps what the agents need is more training on the importance of ethics for their profession, as well as better inculcation into the ethical culture of Magnum. Is there anything she should be doing as the immediate supervisor of 40 associates to ensure that her call centre distinguishes itself in terms of both revenue-generation and professionalism? Or must one of these goals necessarily be sacrificed for the sake of the other?

Appendix 1: Selected Articles from the Code of Ethics of the Chambre de la Sécurité Financière (Quebec)

An Act Respecting the Distribution of Financial Products and Services (1998, c. 37, s. 313, 1st par., subpar. (1))

11. A representative must practise with integrity.

12. A representative must act towards his client or any potential client with integrity and as a conscientious adviser, giving him all the information that may be necessary or useful. He must take reasonable steps so as to advise his client properly.

13. A representative must fully and objectively explain to his client or any potential client the type, advantages and disadvantages of the product or service that he is proposing to him and must refrain from giving information that may be inaccurate or incomplete.

14. A representative must provide his client or any potential client with the explanations the client needs to understand and evaluate the product or services that he is proposing or that he provides to the client.

15. Before providing information or making a recommendation to his client or to any potential client, a representative must seek to have a complete understanding of the facts.

16. No representative may, by whatever means, make statements that are incomplete, false, deceptive or liable to mislead.

18. A representative must, in the practice of his profession, always remain independent and avoid any conflict of interest.

19. A representative must subordinate his personal interests to those of his client or any potential client....

20. A representative must be objective when his client or any potential client asks him for information. He must express opinions and make recommendations objectively and impartially, without considering his personal interest.

21. A representative must ignore any intervention by a third party that could influence the way in which he performs the duties related to his practice to the detriment of his client or any potential client.

23. A representative must demonstrate availability and diligence with respect to his client or any potential client.

25. In the practice of his profession, a representative must not, through dishonesty, fraud, trickery or other deceitful means, avoid or attempt to avoid his professional civil liability or that of the firm or independent partnership in which he practises.

28. A representative must not dissuade his client or any potential client from consulting another representative or another person of his choosing.

Questions for Discussion

1. What, if anything, is unethical about Benjamin Ryan's selling techniques? Which of the articles in the code of ethics (in Appendix 1) seem most relevant?

2. Are the incentives given to agents consistent with the espoused values of the company? Are they consistent with the provincial code of ethics?

3. What do you think about the way Winstod dealt with Ryan's case?

4. Is Justine Winstod asking the right questions at the end of this case? What other questions should she be posing? How should she answer these questions?

Case Endnote

1. The names of the official bodies cited in this case are not officially translated into English in Quebec. The *Bureau*

Case 12

McDonald's on Krakow's Market Square

Krakow (English spelling Cracow) is the third largest city in Poland with a population of approximately 800 000. Located in the southern part of the country, it was first settled about 1000 years ago. The cathedral was built in 1020 and Krakow served as the nation's capital from then to 1596. Krakow was granted city rights in 1257 and became an important commercial centre. The city grew because of its location on trade routes from Europe to Byzantium and from the southeast to the Baltic Sea.

The city was devastated by the Tatar invasion during the thirteenth century but was rebuilt. Fortunately the city was saved during World War II by the Soviet army, which encircled the city in June 1945, forcing the occupying Germans to evacuate and quickly minimizing damage to property. This situation is quite different from other Polish cities, which were largely destroyed in the fighting; for example, in Warsaw 86 percent of the buildings were destroyed or damaged.

As a result of the quick liberation, Krakow's old town, the stare miastro, is well preserved and contains many historical structures including museums, an opera house, many churches, and a university. The old town serves as a city centre and is a thriving commercial area containing retail outlets, offices, theatres, restaurants, bars, and hotels. Numerous street vendors sell food, flowers, books, and other wares.

The old town area was included in a UNESCO list of twelve World Cultural Heritage sites identified in 1978. The World Heritage List identifies cultural and natural properties of outstanding universal value, and, by virtue of this quality, especially worth safeguarding

for future generations. The purpose of the list is to make the sites known throughout the world and to create an awareness among the public of their responsibility in respecting and safeguarding that universal heritage. A World Heritage Fund assists in providing resources for the safeguarding of the sites.

Krakow's old town was considered to be an historically valuable site and much of the area's buildings have been restored. In particular, nearly all the buildings located on the town square, or rynek, have been restored. Exhibit 12–1 is a map of the town centre, or old town. Note that the park or shaded areas were formerly the location of the city's walls which were nearly all removed in the 1800s.

The Market Square

The Market Square is the centre of the old town and is referred to as the Rynek Glowny (rynek meaning market place and glowny meaning main or central). The shape of the Square comes from the thirteenth century and it was included on a city plan drawn at that time. Each side of the Square is 200 metres in length. As shown in Exhibit 12–1, several streets enter the Square. The Market Square forms part of the royal way once used by the king's retinue through the city via Florianska and Grodzka Streets to the castle, or Wawel. The Market Square has been the site of commercial activity and a place where important ceremonies were held.

There are several historically prominent buildings on the Square. St. Mary's Basilica (at the corner of Mikolajska and Florianska Streets) was erected in the fourteenth century. The church is famous for its high alter and the pentaptych, a work of art consisting of five panels, carved in limewood in 1477–1489 to the order of the city's burghers or citizens. At the entrance of

This case was prepared by Dr. Robert W. Sexty, Memorial University of Newfoundland, as a basis for classroom discussion and is not meant to illustrate either effective or ineffective management. Copyright © 1994, Robert W. Sexty.

EXHIBIT 12-1

Krakow Town Centre

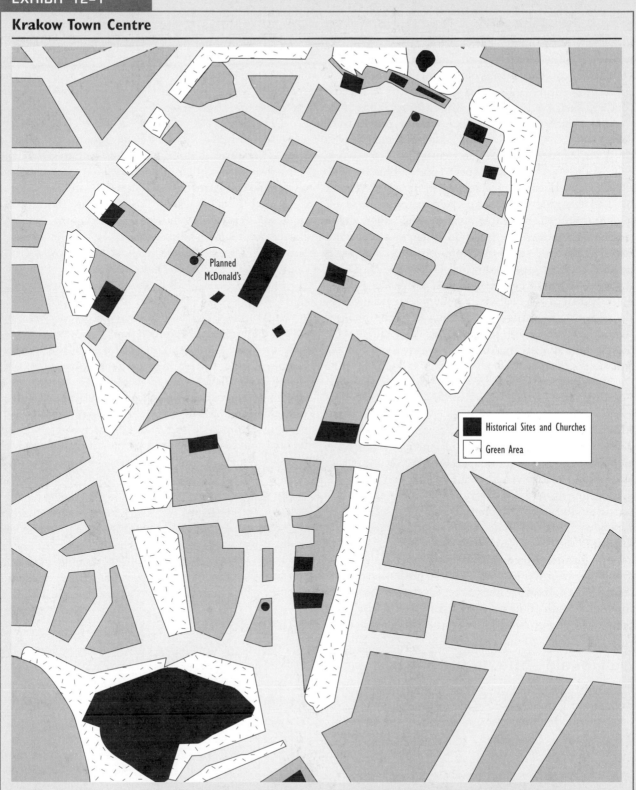

Planned
McDonald's

Historical Sites and Churches

Green Area

Grodzka Street stands St. Adalbert's Church, one of the oldest churches in Krakow. Some fragments of pre-Romanesque architecture have been preserved in the lower part of the building.

At the corner of Wislna and Anny Streets is the Town Hall Tower, all that remains of the Town Hall built in the thirteenth century and pulled down in the nineteenth century. The sixteenth century brick Cloth Hall is in the middle of the Square. It was the centre of ancient trade and commerce of Krakow and today is a main tourist shopping centre for souvenirs, crafts, and art work. Several cafés and bars also operate in the building with tables placed outside in the Square during good weather.

Private vendors sell a variety of merchandise in the Square from carts and tables, with several selling a wide selection of cut flowers. Each side of the Square contains many retail and restaurant/café business enterprises including stores prominently displaying Kodak, Puma, Athlete's World, Marlboro, Adidas, Nike, Coca-Cola, and Pepsi signs. The newest building is one occupied by the Orbis travel agency and is obviously more modern than other buildings on the square. It was built after the Second World War and created a controversy between traditionalists who wished to retain old architectural styles, and progressives, who approved of a modern style.

Restaurants in the Town Centre

There are dozens of eating establishments in the Town Centre ranging from the expensive and very exclusive Wierzynck to street vendors. The large number of eating establishments may be a function of the large numbers of tourists in the area. Also, 10 percent of the city's population is comprised of students, with one university being located in the Town Centre.

American fast-food outlets are already located in the Town Centre. Wendy's, Pizza Hut, and McDonald's operate restaurants but not on the Square. The success of the McDonald's outlet on Florianska Street led the company to seek a second location in the city.

McDonald's Site on the Square

The site of the second McDonald's outlet is indicated on the map in Exhibit 12–1. McDonald's Polish operators have applied for permission to open the restaurant, but the application is waiting approval from the local government's department responsible for the preservation of historic monuments. The department has received dozens of letters and petitions protesting the opening of the fast-food outlet. Many citizens see the outlet on the historical market square as an undesirable symbol of the American way of life, and feel that one McDonald's in the Town Centre is enough.

Those in opposition to the second McDonald's feel that it is a threat to Krakow's cultural identity and is a form of cultural infiltration. They want to avoid the "Americanization" that has occurred in other European cities, and in particular, to prevent capitalism from destroying the historical nature of the city. The Square outlet is opposed by historical associations and the Polish Ecological Club, which is affiliated with Solidarity, a social, political, and labour movement at one time headed by Lech Walesa.

McDonald's responds by saying that they understand that some people don't want change. As far as Americanization is concerned, there are many other symbols of this already, for example, cars, footwear, clothing, and soft drinks. They point out that the McDonald's philosophy is to fit in with the community as their first outlet did on Florianska Street. The outlet is located in a building that was renovated to restore its historical features and large yellow arches are not displayed prominently. McDonald's feels that it did a beautiful job on the building and that the outlet does not stand out as an eyesore. The same approach would be taken with the outlet on the square. As further evidence of the company's attempts to fit in with the surroundings, McDonald's points to its outlets in famous historical locations around the world, including on the Champs-Elysées in Paris and at the Spanish Steps in Rome.

The controversy has left McDonald's officials wondering whether or not it is worthwhile to continue with the new outlet.

Questions for Discussion

1. What is the issue involved with the opening of the McDonald's on the Market Square?

2. Who are the stakeholders involved and what are their positions?

3. What should McDonald's do now?

Case 13

Direct-to-Home Satellite TV: Protectionism and Personal Freedoms

Bill Kay, owner of SaTeks Satellite in Windsor, Ontario, sat anxiously contemplating the future of his store. For the past seven years, he had been selling American Direct-to-Home (DTH) satellite systems as well as providing the means to obtain U.S. DTH subscriptions. These systems were extremely popular and quite profitable. He was able to buy the American DTH satellite systems for $125 and resell them for $400 and last summer he couldn't keep up with the demand. Bill noted that there were two types of people who purchased the system and the American DTH subscription: those who found the Canadian programming too expensive, and those who disliked Canadian programming (the CRTC requires a significant percentage of content to be Canadian). The latter wanted to watch the SciFi channel, action, history, international soccer, golf, education (a range of channels provide instruction in wood working, gardening, distance learning, e.g., University of Washington), and many other forms of content not available through Canadian distributors.

On May 22, 2002, the Supreme Court of Canada, based on the Radio Telecommunications Act (and political pressure), ruled against Canadians being able to receive U.S. satellite programming. Currently, that ruling and more specifically the section of the act pertaining to lawful distributors (s. 9(1)(c)) are being challenged as unconstitutional based on section 1 of the Canadian Charter of Rights and Freedoms. The constitutional challenge is fuelled in part by several special-interest groups such as "Congres Iberoamerican du Canada," who intend to defend the rights of the Spanish-speaking community in Canada. (That is, DTH provides programming in languages other than English and French, not available in Canada.)

Despite the possible consequences of selling an American DTH satellite system in Canada (one person had recently been fined $25 000 and faces two years in jail), Bill Kay was concerned about ethical issues. Now

This case was prepared by Dr. David Hemsworth, Ph.D., Assistant Professor, School of Business and Economics, Nipissing University, and Dr. Bruce Bidgood, Assistant Professor, Faculty of Social Work, University of Windsor.

that American DTH subscriptions were not available to Canadians, was this morally wrong? What about the freedom given to Canadians to watch whatever programming they wish? Furthermore, what about the companies that produced the shows—did they have rights? While Bill was pondering these issues, the phone rang: another eager customer was calling to purchase a satellite system. As Bill hung up, he knew he had to make a decision. The fall season was fast approaching and it was the peak buying period for DTH satellite systems. Bill had to decide quickly.

The Canadian Radio-television and Telecommunications Commission (CRTC)

The CRTC is an independent agency which reports to Parliament through the Minister of Canadian Heritage and is responsible for regulating Canada's broadcasting and telecommunications systems. It regulates over 5900 Canadian broadcasters, including television, cable distribution, AM and FM radio, direct-to-home satellite systems, subscription television, and pay audio.

In order to become a DTH satellite television provider in Canada, the provider is required to comply with the Canadian Broadcasting Act, which includes regulations that require a company to be owned and controlled by Canadians. Furthermore, the company has to contribute to Canadian culture by providing predominantly Canadian programming. Currently, the CRTC has licensed only two DTH satellite providers in Canada, BEV and Star Choice. Although American-owned DIRECTV and DISH Network satellite signals can be received in Canada, they are not licensed by the CRTC as distributors of DTH satellite programming since they fail to meet the necessary Canadian content requirements. By the end of 2000, DIRECTV and DISH Networks had over 9 million and 5 million U.S. subscribers respectively and together can be found in over 700 000 Canadian homes. In Canada, BEV had approximately 722 000 subscribers, and Star Choice had 509 000.

How DTH Satellite Programming Is Received

DTH satellite systems use digital broadcast satellites (DBS) to send audio and video images to a geosynchronous satellite. The satellite then retransmits the signal toward Earth, covering virtually all of North America. A small satellite dish is mounted on the outside of a building (for example, a house) and pointed toward the satellite. The signal is fed to a satellite receiver/decoder (the size of a small VCR) located indoors and connected to the TV. An access card containing the authorization to decode the satellite broadcasts based on the customer's subscription is located inside the satellite receiver.

For a Canadian to receive U.S.-based programming there are three choices. The first option is for Canadians to subscribe to DIRECTV or DISH Networks using an American address, which is necessary since DIRECTV and DISH Networks are not authorized to sell their subscriptions in Canada. Bill, for example, provides "fictional" American addresses for his customers. The second option, mostly run from people's homes, is to have someone program the access card for a fee using either an illegitimate programming code available on the Internet or privately purchased. This allows the consumer to have unlimited access to the U.S. DTH satellite programming, including pay-per-views. Bill, like many others, has ethical concerns about this method and therefore will not program people's cards. The final option requires the consumer to purchase a $125 card programmer that allows them to use the Internet, either to subscribe to a service that provides code, or download code readily available on hundreds of Web sites (e.g., www.dssfilexchange.com or www.sattech.net). This allows the consumer to program the access card themselves in order to receive all available channels, including pay-per-view.

The high piracy rate of both Canadian and U.S. DTH satellite programming caused distributors to take action. Recently, in order to reduce unauthorized reception, distributors required that a subscription be activated within 30 days of purchasing a DTH satellite system or a fee of up to $200 (to recover some of the subsidized receiver cost) would be charged to the person's credit card. Another method used to prevent unauthorized reception of the DTH satellite programming is

the use of electronic countermeasures (ECMs) distributed by the satellite, designed to disable unauthorized access cards. ECMs can be designed to physically damage the access card (which may accidentally harm legitimate customers' access cards), by looping (sending programming code that causes the card to cycle repetitively through a set of instructions), or "hashing" the card. Hashing disrupts a viewer's service, either by blocking a section of channels by freezing the video every few seconds, or by putting a "call customer service" message on the screen. Once the card becomes hashed or looped, it needs to be reprogrammed with a new code. Reprogramming can be required as often as every few days, which benefits dealers that charge for their service. However, the hassle of reprogramming the card on a regular basis is the reason some U.S. viewers decide to subscribe, or for Canadian viewers of U.S. satellite to go through people like Bill to obtain a subscription.

Canadian Criminal Cases Involving U.S. DTH Satellite Systems

Canadian satellite providers who sell American DTH satellite systems have been facing ongoing criminal and civil court battles. These businesses are being taken to court in an attempt to prevent the sale of U.S. DTH satellite systems, the programming of access cards, and the provision of U.S. addresses to Canadian customers.

One of the most recent cases that pertains to the decoding of U.S. satellite television signals was held before the Quebec Provincial Court. The decision was handed down on October 16, 2000. This case reflects the majority of the criminal cases going to trial on this issue. Gregory Electronique was charged with possessing and selling DTH satellite equipment, which allowed their customers to receive and decode DIRECTV's signal. They were charged under the Radiocommunication Act (RCA), which explains that:

9. (1) No person shall

*(c) decode an encrypted subscription programming signal or encrypted network feed otherwise than under and in accordance with an authorization from the **lawful distributor** of the signal or feed.*

The act defines "lawful distributor," in relation to an encrypted subscription programming signal or encrypted network feed, as a person who has the lawful right in Canada to transmit it and authorize its decoding. Gregory Electronique argued that since DIRECTV is not authorized by the CRTC to distribute their signal in Canada, they are not a lawful distributor and thus cannot charge Canadians for a subscription or criminally charge Canadians for receiving their signal without subscribing.

Canadian Parliament had the option to change the Radiocommunication Act of Canada to prohibit the reception of satellite signals without a subscription from any distributor, instead of just lawful distributors (*R v. Gregory Electronique*, 2000). However, Parliament has chosen not to modify the statute. The judge in this case decided that only the decoding of signals from lawful distributors was against the Radiocommunication Act. Since Gregory Electronique was charged with decoding U.S. DTH satellite programming, and U.S. DTH satellite providers are not lawful distributors in Canada, Gregory Electronique was found not guilty.

Court Cases

BEV v. Can-Am was an appeal to the Supreme Court of British Columbia. The decision was handed down on December 10, 1999. BEV had charged Can-Am with selling U.S. DTH satellite systems to Canadians, programming access cards, and providing U.S. addresses for subscription purposes. Although Can-Am agreed to stop programming access cards, a decision still had to be made on the legality of supplying U.S. addresses to Canadians for subscribing to DTH satellite programming. Based on the courts' interpretations of the Radiocommunication Act, BEV was unable to stop Can-Am's activities. The court of appeals dismissed the motion to appeal, along with this case. BEV appealed to the Supreme Court of Canada on December 4, 2001.

The following statement by Judge Leblanc of Nova Scotia summarizes the majority of the courts' thinking:

> *I agree with Kennedy J. In addition, I am of the view that for a programming signal to qualify as a "subscription programming signal" under ss. 9(l) and 10(l)(b) of the RCA, it must be lawfully intended for reception by the public in Canada and the public must also be entitled to lawfully subscribe for it in Canada. Mere production of "pirate" or "grey market" programming signals is insufficient to constitute an offence under s. 10(l)(b). (See http://www.legal-rights.org/ for more information.)*

The British Columbia Court of Appeal (2000) had a similar ruling:

> *Section 9(1)(c) enjoins the decoding of encrypted signals without the authorization of the "lawful distrib-*

utor of the signal or feed" *[emphasis added]. The majority interpreted the legislator's choice of the definite article "the," underlined in the above phrase, to mean that the prohibition applies only "to signals broadcast by lawful distributors who are licensed to authorize decoding of that signal" (para. 36). In other words, "[i]f there is no lawful distributor for an encrypted subscription program signal in Canada, there can be no one licensed to authorize its decoding." Consequently, according to the majority, there is no contravention of s. 9(1)(c) when a person decodes unregulated signals such as those broadcast by the U.S. DTH companies.*

Supreme Court Ruling

On December 4, 2001, the BEV appeal of the British Columbia Court of Appeal ruling reached the Supreme Court of Canada. On April 26, 2002, they made the following ruling:

> *(68) In the result, we would allow the appeal with costs throughout, set aside the judgment of the Court of Appeal for British Columbia, and declare that s. 9(1)(c) of the Radiocommunication Act creates a prohibition against all decoding of encrypted programming signals, followed by an exception where authorization is received from the person holding the lawful right in Canada to transmit and authorize decoding of the signal. No answer is given to the constitutional questions stated by order of the Chief Justice. Appeal allowed with costs.* [BEV won.]

Other Considerations

Previous to the Supreme Court ruling, 17 judges had ruled, including provincial Supreme Courts, and were virtually unanimous in their rulings. Many of the lower and provincial Supreme Courts were outraged at the Canadian Supreme Court overturning their decisions. The ruling made several inferences that the judgment was made in light of the political climate and intent. Many critics say that judgment was unduly influenced by this climate, which included statements by the Minister indicating opposition, as well as major lobbying by BEV employing strategies such as buying Jean Chrétien a private golf game with Tiger Woods (for an estimated $25 000).

In the Supreme Court ruling, the judges commented that the section 9(1)(c) may be unconstitutional and is currently being appealed based on the Canadian Charter of Rights and Freedoms:

Canadian Charter of Rights and Freedoms Section 2. Everyone has the following fundamental freedoms:

… (b) Freedom of thought, belief, opinion and expression, including freedom of the press and other means of communication …

This appeal may take years for the courts to decide. Although the RCMP seems to be taking a hands-off approach while awaiting the outcome of the Charter challenge, many suppliers of satellite equipment have shut down, gone underground, or moved offshore (e.g., Russia where foreign signal reception is legal).

In addition, since the Supreme Court ruling, the CBC News (http://cbc.ca/national/sasa/gms_bell.html) reported that BEV sold 3800 "illegal" "repatriated" U.S. satellite systems (i.e., U.S. systems that customers traded in exchange for Bell systems) to a Canadian company to be redistributed. The massive quantity potentially makes them the single largest distributor of "illegal" systems in Canada. One spokesman for the company that purchased the U.S. systems, which were resold in Canada, said that he had seen the same system (i.e., serial number) four times! Some critics question whether the Supreme Court would have ruled against Can-Am Satellites in favour of BEV if they had known that BEV was also selling U.S. satellite systems in Canada (http://www.legal-rights.org/bell/bellwitdrawinjunc.html). Another confusing action is that Canada Customs has not been told to bar the import of systems as long as applicable taxes have been paid. To further complicate the situation, the Canadian government continues to auction off U.S. systems received from "assets obtained through criminal proceeds" or which were surrendered at the border (rather than pay taxes).

The Canadian DTH satellite providers were not the only threat to cable companies; American DTH satellite television viewers were also decreasing the number of cable subscribers. A recent BEV survey reported that hundreds of thousands of Canadians already subscribe to U.S. satellite services. An estimated additional 600 000–800 000 Canadians would prefer to pay an American satellite provider rather than pay Rogers or Shaw for their cable, or get their satellite service from BEV or Star Choice. The same study claims that U.S. subscriptions take $400 million in revenues from the indigenous cable television business.

Is the restriction imposed on the viewing of U.S. DTH satellite programming infringing on Canadians' freedom or rights? A well-known lawyer, Ian Angus, who has argued various DTH satellite television cases, believes that "satellite broadcasting is, like the Internet, a barrier-free medium…. The CRTC is going to find itself unable to continue with its present policy of setting out what it is that Canadians may watch and listen to. Under the current regulatory environment, we are only allowed, in their minds, to watch what they approve. That is going to have to change."

In an interview in 2001 with the CBC, the CRTC chairman suggested that Canadians should do what they think is right. "The western world has spent 40 years telling the Russians it was immoral to block broadcasts, the CRTC is not going to turn around and say that Canadians cannot watch American television." When the issue of U.S. DTH satellite signals was discussed in Parliament, this was the major reason the laws were not changed. Laws governing what we watch can infringe on our freedom of choice.

Many Canadians believe they have the right, under the "freedom of expression" section 2B in the Canadian Charter of Rights and Freedoms, to purchase subscriptions of their choice and to *choose* the TV they watch. They do not want to be forced by the Liberal government to buy the system that some Ottawa bureaucrat thinks best for them. These bureaucrats act like the "thought police" and the Liberals want to choose what TV we can watch. Big Brother has *truly arrived*. International soccer is not shown on ExpressVu. If I want to watch it, I need an American satellite system. Why should I let ExpressVu dictate what I want to watch?

Are Canadian viewers infringing on copyright laws when they receive U.S. DTH satellite signals and don't pay for them? Greg Walling, president of Star Choice, in 2001 claimed that "Canadian broadcasters and programmers have spent millions of dollars acquiring the rights to programs." Is it fair to view DTH satellite programming without paying for a subscription, which includes copyright costs?

Back to Bill's Dilemma

Bill remains perplexed. He contemplated the ethical impact and ramifications of his actions on all the stakeholders involved. Should he shut down his business or continue in violation of the Supreme Court ruling? Should he continue to provide access to U.S. programming for his customers? He has an ongoing revenue stream from existing customers to maintain their subscriptions. And satellite customers tend to be quite loyal—does he want to lose his market share? He recalls that the BEV victory caused an initial celebration for their company, but that quickly turned into a big headache when their lawyers read the Supreme Court judgment. The judgment suggested that section 9(1)(c) may be unconstitutional and the justices expect to see the case return for a challenge based on the Charter of Rights and Freedoms. This and related sections provide the protection from foreign competition. If the act is successfully challenged and thereby struck down, the Canadian market could be opened up to foreign competition.

Bill feels frustrated by the Supreme Court's ruling and the position taken by the Canadian government because he feels he should have the right to view whatever television he chooses to pay for. And many of Bill's customers have similar opinions. For example, one customer is a Canadian truck driver who spends 90 percent of his time driving in the U.S. He had purchased a U.S. DTH system and subscription from Bill so that he could watch TV at truck stops. Although it is perfectly legal for him to watch TV while he is in the U.S.A., it becomes illegal for him to drive back into Canada and watch the same programs, even though he is paying for a subscription!

The controversies surrounding the sale of U.S. DTH satellite systems and subscriptions are numerous. Are the profits worth the risks? If a business like Bill's is charged but fights and wins, there would still be legal costs. Based on everything he has just learned, Bill has a tough decision to make.

Questions for Discussion

1. Should Bill stay in business and if so what services/hardware should he provide?

2. What impacts will the Supreme Court decision have on all stakeholders?

3. Is the Supreme Court ruling constitutional and in the best interest of Canada, Canadians, and corporations? Should Canadians be free to subscribe to any satellite service (domestic or foreign) they choose?

Case 14

Ethics and Legalities of MP3 File Sharing in Canada

Introduction

Prior to the influential and well-publicized court case that led to Napster's eventual shutdown, online music around the world was shared primarily through its software. Since this landmark American court case, it has been widely debated whether or not Napster would have suffered a similar fate had the central server been located in Canada because of distinct differences in the copyright laws. Would users still have been able to download their favourite songs for free through Napster's network today if the company had been tried in Canadian courts with Canadian laws being applied? Let's proceed with the case and you be the judge!

This case was prepared by Dr. David Hemsworth, Ph.D., School of Business and Economics, Nipissing University, and Dr. Cristobal Sanchez-Rodriguez, York University.

Napster Inc. Background

Napster's name is derived from a high-school nickname based on the "nappy" hairstyle of the 18-year-old software creator and founder and was incorporated in 1999. As a freshman at Northeastern University, Sean Fanning became very frustrated with the lack of digital music available online. This motivated him to develop software that would facilitate the transfer and sharing of MP3 songs over the Internet. After only one semester at university, he dropped out and committed himself to developing the source code for the Internet file-sharing software. Napster facilitates file sharing over the Internet and provides users with the ability to search for and share MP3 and other file types. While the Napster server must be in place to permit the direct file transfer between users, the server itself never actually processes the file. However, though valued by users, this service transfers songs without the permission of record companies, songwriters, or musicians, so it has raised numerous copyright concerns.

Napster uses a hybrid network architecture, which combines aspects of both a client-server and peer-to-peer architecture. This combination of server architectures is a result of centrally located servers stationed at the company's California headquarters. These central servers facilitate two uses. First, they hold the master list of files (compiled from users connected), and second, they connect these users in a peer-to-peer fashion (i.e., it directly connects together two users on the Internet). Users can query the master list for specific files by title or artist in order to have the central server reply to the query with the IP address of the user holding the queried file. These users are connected in a peer-to-peer fashion, so the file is then transferred between the users privately, without ever passing through Napster servers.

Legal Issues

Original music, like art, is considered intellectual property: that is, basically any idea or innovation that has been expressed, and does not have to be published, is protected by copyright laws. These laws are designed to protect the rights of individuals and businesses pertaining to their intellectual property, which includes ideas that are written, designed, invented, coded (software), sung, spoken, drawn, and so on. It is important to keep in mind that protection exists only for the expression of the idea (original work) as soon as it is created and fixed in a medium (whether published or not) and that there is no protection for the idea itself. Musical works and MP3s are considered to be intellectual property and are protected by copyright statute, which ensures that specific rights remain in the property of the creator or owner (such as selling or manipulating this property for gain). Copyright statute exists internationally thanks to the Berne Convention—more than 150 countries have signed and committed to the protection of copyright around the world.

The reason for the creation of the Canadian and American Copyright Acts was to protect intellectual property owners' rights of ownership. The acts were in place long before the Internet and, except for minor revisions, have not changed significantly since its creation. Consequently, this has led to conflicts in court cases involving Internet-related issues because the laws must be interpreted in order to make decisions concerning these new areas. It is important to understand that laws do not exist for every unique situation, but instead it is the court's responsibility to translate, interpret, and apply the law to these new situations. Some of the basic rights to the copyright owner, which are outlined in both Canada and the U.S., include (a) the right to produce or reproduce the work in question, or any substantial part, in any material form; (b) the right to make a recording of the work; (c) the right to convert or manipulate the work; (d) the right to authorize any of the previous; and (e) the right to restrict another from using the property without authorization. Once infringement is proven, any profits an infringer may make from another's intellectual property may be blocked by court order and illegal copies confiscated may be impounded and destroyed. The owner may be awarded the infringer's resulting profits plus full compensation for his or her lost sales, or the owner may choose a court-determined award as well as receiving full compensation for litigation costs and lawyers' fees.

United States Laws

In the U.S., the three degrees of copyright infringement include:

- *Direct infringement.* "Anyone who violates any of the exclusive rights of the copyright owner [reproduction, adaptation, distribution to the public, public performance, public display, rental for commercial advantage or importation] is an infringer of the copyright or the right of the author" (Section 501(a) of the U.S. Copyright Act).
- *Vicarious liability.* A person will be liable for vicarious infringement if he or she has the right and ability to supervise infringing activity and also has a direct financial interest in such activities.
- *Contributory infringement.* Contributory infringement is similar to "aiding and abetting" liability: one who knowingly contributes to another's infringement can be held accountable.

The prosecution in the Napster case sought to prove that Napster was guilty of vicarious and contributory infringement. They were able to show that there were acts of direct infringement by the end users and that Napster knew that these were occurring and had the ability to stop them (e.g., filter these files or shut down the server). Since it was proven that Napster had plans for a subscription-based service in the future, it was apparent that they had a significant financial interest in these transactions. The prosecution demonstrated that

Napster had "induced, caused, or materially contributed to the infringing conduct" by showing that music sales to the college and university student market segment had significantly dropped (even though overall music CD sales had increased).

Napster's Defences

Napster's first argument was "Fair Use" and that their file sharing was legitimate because users had "fair or legitimate uses" (section 107 of the American Copyright Act) of the copyrighted material. This doctrine attempts to balance the rights of copyright owners with society's interest in allowing copying in certain limited circumstances. Napster argued that users were sampling the works, which would presumably lead them to then buy the CD. Also, that a high percentage of songs had the artists' permission to distribute them (e.g., new artists use Napster to promote their work). However, the court rejected the "fair use" defence due to the commercial nature of the network (future commercial potential). The judge found that the harm caused to the music industry outweighed the fact that some individuals may purchase the CD after sampling or that some artists permitted the file sharing of their songs. Record companies also argued that they had already invested considerable funds to sell their own recordings through digital means using the Internet. The judge agreed that although the Napster system had legitimate uses, Napster apparently reduced audio CD sales among university and college users, and it also raised barriers to the record companies' entry into the legitimate digital music market.

Napster's second defence was "Safe Harbour." In an attempt to provide Internet service providers (ISPs) with a safe harbour from liability for acts of infringement by their users, the U.S. Congress passed the Digital Millennium Copyright Act. An ISP was determined to be a company that provides the transmission, routing, or providing connections for users online. Napster claimed that they were an Internet service provider and were therefore under the protection of the Safe Harbour statute. Napster argued that MP3s were never transmitted or held directly by the central server; it acted only as a search engine and facilitated the user's search by creating a master list of available songs. However, during the case it was brought out that "any company using the safe harbour defence must first show that it provides online services and has adopted and implemented a policy providing for termination of users who violate copyright laws." The American court found that Napster did not qualify as an Internet service provider and therefore was not protected by the statute.

The Result

Judge Patel found that Napster had prior knowledge of its infringing activities and had the ability to police the system, yet had failed to do so effectively; Napster was also found to have a proven commercial interest in future services. This meant that they were vicariously liable for the copyright infringements that took place. Judge Patel claimed that the defendants had failed to prove the software had substantial, noninfringing uses. The judge also stated that "the significant use of this service is obviously trading copyrighted material without obtaining copyright holders' permission." As a result of the evidence put forth and legal interpretation of the copyrights laws, Napster was ordered to stop the file sharing and shut down their central server. Various members of the music industry brought numerous cases to court; however, no charges were laid because Napster sided with record giants and settled the issues out of court.

Alternatives to Napster

During Napster's market domination, competing Internet file-sharing programs were largely unrecognized by the public so they could not attract the critical mass of users necessary to be successful. However, since Napster's shutdown, the use of alternative networks has increased significantly. Sites such as KaZaA, MusicCity, and Gnutella quickly filled the gap left by Napster and, combined, these alternatives now have higher traffic than Napster ever did. Napster's popularity peaked at 1.57 million simultaneous users in February 2001. In this month, a total of 2.79 billion songs were downloaded, which is about 220 files available per user. To date, over 3 billion files have been transferred using the top four networks. Napigator, a file-sharing alternative that used a hybrid peer-to-peer network (using a central server) similar to Napster's, has also been shut down by the courts because Napigator had a central server. In January 2002, KaZaA stopped distribution of its software in the Netherlands because of a Dutch court decision. In California, in the spring of 2003, Morpheus and Grokster faced American federal prosecution for their Napster-like copyright violations and, since it was shown that there are legal uses for their service, they were not convicted.

The music industry and the courts have been unable to successfully prosecute some of the alternative Internet file-sharing programs in the same manner as they prosecuted Napster because there is no central server that can be located and shut down. This architectural defence has made it difficult for courts to shut down these peer-to-peer architectures. Proponents of Internet file sharing have argued that the distributed nature of P2P renders these networks virtually impossible to police, shut down, or control without shutting down all the users' computers running the software and connected to the Internet. Initially Morpheus, KaZaA, and Grokster (three popular peer-to-peer file-sharing programs) shared the FastTrack peer-to-peer network platform but, due to a software revision to the FastTrack software kernel (the core of a software program), which caused incompatibilities, the file-sharing network Morpheus ground to a halt, demonstrating that it would be possible to terminate these P2P networks.

Canadian Law

However, since Canadian law is independent from the U.S., the legal issues surrounding peer-to-peer MP3 file sharing are different. Vicarious and contributory liability charges are replaced in Canadian law with two degrees of copyright infringement, which are:

- *Direct infringement.* According to the Canadian Copyright Act, direct infringement describes a party that has committed an affirmative act against legislated law. Without an affirmative action, direct infringement cannot be proven. In this case, affirmative action would be the actual copyright infringement.
- *Secondary infringement.* In contrast, if a user is not directly responsible for copyright infringement, as mentioned above, they may be secondarily liable if they commit the following infringements:

  (2) It is an infringement of copyright for any person to

  (a) sell or rent out, (b) distribute to such an extent as to affect prejudicially the owner of the copyright, (c) by way of trade distribute, expose or offer for sale or rental, or exhibit in public, (d) possess for the purpose of doing anything referred to in section …

  … a copy of a work, sound recording or fixation of a performer's performance or of a communication signal that the person knows or should have known infringes copyright or would infringe copyright if it had been made in Canada by the person who made it.

P2P Possible Canadian Defences

Canadian copyright law does not include the concept of "fair use." However, Section 80 of the Copyright Act states that:

> *the act of reproducing all or any substantial part of a musical work embodied in a sound recording … onto an audio recording medium for the private use of the person who makes the copy does not constitute an infringement of the copyright.*

On March 19, 1998, Part VIII of the Copyright Act dealing with private copying came into force. The amendment to the act legalized in Canada copying of sound recordings of musical works onto audio recording media for the private use of the person who makes the copy (referred to as "private copying"). In addition, the amendment made provision for the imposition of a levy on blank audio recording media to compensate authors, performers, and makers who own copyright in eligible sound recordings being copied for private use (e.g., $0.51 per audio cassette and $1.15 per CD-R or CD-RW). The copyright board ruled that the source of the recording does not matter (pre-owned CD, borrowed CD, or downloaded from the Internet), only the destination (must be for private use and stored on an audio recording medium as defined in the act).

Recently the Recording Industry of Canada has been threatening end-users that upload files with prosecution, as has been done in the U.S. A U.S. survey found that the number of people willing to download music using P2P networks had dropped, due to prosecutions, from 29 percent in the previous year to 14 percent. At the same time as the Recording Industry of America's U.S. subpoena campaign, the sales of albums sharply declined (762 million in 2001 to 681 million in 2002). The Canadian copyright board maintains that uploading a copy of music without permission is a violation of copyright law; however, downloading of the music file for recording to an audio medium for private use is permissible under Section 80. The recording industry disagrees and is threatening to charge users that download and upload files and has begun an advertising campaign that promotes that "Buying music makes more music." In April 2004, the Recording Industry attempted to have the Canadian Federal Court force five of the major ISPs (including Bell, Rogers, and Shaw) turn over the identities of 29 P2P file-sharing users for copyright infringement prosecution. However, the court ruled that the users were placing MP3s in a shared directory that was accessible to other computers and that there was insufficient evidence to conclude that any infringement on current Canadian copyright laws was occurring that did not fall under the act's legitimate "private copying" section.

The Users

People who would never consider stealing seem to have no problem with downloading and uploading copyrighted music from the Internet. Yet many musicians, including Metallica and Creed, insist that each time a song is downloaded the user is stealing from them. "When my music is given away, as taboo as it is for me to say, it is stealing…. My music is like my home. Napster is sneaking in the back door of my house and robbing me blind," says Scott Stapp of Creed. Record companies echo the sentiments of their artists, asserting that Internet file sharing is cutting into their profits. But many users suggest that the cost of music is too high and possibly should be free. Others imply that file sharing allows them to "try before they buy" as well as experience the works of artists that never would have been promoted by record companies.

Many critics have pointed to the music industry itself as being the major source of their own problems due to its resistance to implement current technology to update its distribution and supply chains. Many people state that the current supply chain is inefficient and that end users have to pay for this with higher music prices. The P2P networks have emerged to address these inefficiencies and simultaneously increased the availability and user exposure to many more works and artists and demonstrated the viability of a new distribution model. These critics are vocal in denouncing the use of litigation by the recording industry to bolster outdated business models rather than re-engineer them. The frequently heard statement is "turn users into customers rather than criminals." The recording industry insists that since they have the legal title to the music copyrights, they can distribute music using any methods they deem suitable. Recently, third-party companies such as Apple Computer Corp. (I-Tunes) have signed contracts to distribute music of the major record labels, using an Internet-based distribution model.

There are currently no internationally accepted copyright laws that govern the use and actions of P2P file-sharing networks, and in some countries they are, in fact, legal. Therefore, we need to look to ethical principles and an analysis of the stakeholders as a guide to considering the issues that must be taken into account for the development of future Internet copyright laws.

Conclusion

Whether an individual agrees or disagrees with P2P file sharing and the surrounding issues, Napster has changed the perception of music and MP3 sharing forever. With an understanding of the legal and ethical issues surrounding the software, it becomes clear why Napster's actions are considered by record companies to be "the greatest crime of the century." This precedent-setting case will have significant influence for many related cases for years to come. Would Napster and other file-sharing programmers have suffered the same fate in the Canadian court? Which ethical issues should be considered in new Internet laws for the future? What new laws should be legislated? "The Honourable Judge [*insert your last name here*] is now presiding."

Appendix: Stakeholders' Perceptions of Internet MP3 Sharing

Napster and Internet file sharing have changed the face of the music-recording industry forever. There is a growing opinion since Napster's conception that MP3s should be free. Many users feel that, just as listening to radio is free, listening to music via a computer should also be free. Since it is unrealistic to enforce regulations upon the millions of Napster users, it is the individual user's ethical conscience that should regulate behaviour. The following are examples of typical statements that could be made by the various parties in order to rationalize their actions (users, singers, and the music industry).

1. If Listeners Feel That Record Companies Are Exploiting Listeners, Does It Mean That It Is Ethical for Them to Violate Copyright?

- "The prices that record companies charge for CDs are unreasonably high. Through exploiting us, the music companies are in effect forcing us to steal music by giving us no other legitimate alternative."
- "Why is downloading MP3s wrong if I can legally record songs from the radio for my own private use?"
- "Artists spend a lot time and energy creating and making their music. Who gave you the right to decide if an artist has made too much money and who are you to say how much my effort and creativity is worth? If you feel that music is overpriced, then don't buy it. Your opinion of record companies does not justify stealing my music."

2. Since Napster Is Perceived as Socially Acceptable, Doesn't That Make It Ethical?

- "We should ensure the greatest good for the greatest number of people, and millions enjoy and support the idea of sharing free music. Surely there is a net benefit."
- "I don't see how that justifies sharing copyrighted music without the permission from the artists who created the music—it should be the artists' choice."

3. Muddy Thinking and the Music Biz (an Excerpt)

> *During the Napster era, music sales were up 4%. Since the death of Napster, music sales are down 40%. The music industry seems to be ignoring this obvious relationship. Napster was a promotional tool. Promotion sells music. No promotion, no sale. Hello! Blaming the downturn on piracy is ridiculous when the major conduits are shut off, underground, or scattered. And yes, those dwellers in the underground are pirates. But they never buy anything anyway. Remember that the music industry once decried radio as the death of the industry, claiming that nobody would buy a record if it were played on the radio. Once the industry understood promotion, it paid stations to play the music, and the payola scandal emerged. Can't these guys get it straight after all these years? It's the promotion, stupid.[1]*

4. Should Music Eventually Become Public Domain and Part of the Fabric of Society?

Many current thinkers feel that copyright protection is being abused, and frequently. We are concentrating the power and control of the works (music) in the hands of a few corporations. They argue that after a period of time (initial protection or when the monetary value is negligible), music and other works should become part of the fabric of a culture and should be released to the public domain (similar to Grimm's fairytales and Santa Claus). It is then "right" to return to the culture what is society's, as generations before us have done. By putting reasonable limits on copyright, we would limit "milking the monopoly" and cause additional creations/creativity to be born, in order to generate profits and continue revenue streams. Society also has claims on produced works because it has provided the infrastructure to enable the creation of such works and that right should also be recognized. Is the Internet a medium that society can use to speak out against copyright protection abuse? We have to balance the rights of society with that of creators: for those who follow the news, "free Mickey Mouse."

Questions for Discussion

Review the different points of view in the appendix to aid formulating answers to the following questions:

1. What do you think the Canadian verdict would have been for Napster had it been located in Canada? Defend your arguments. Would the same judgment also apply to P2P alternatives?

2. Should users be held accountable for downloading and listening to MP3s, and should users be punished for copyright violation? What should be done?

3. Imagine you are legislating new international Internet copyright laws. How would the ethical frameworks apply to the different stakeholders (i.e., apply a stakeholder and ethical analysis) and their viewpoints?

4. How should international Internet copyright laws deal with the issue of Internet file sharing? If P2P file sharing is legal in Canada, how would the laws apply if someone from the U.S. downloaded an MP3?

Case Endnote

1. John C. Dvorak, "Muddy Thinking and the Music Biz," *PC Magazine, Ziff Davis* (Vol. 21, No. 10, May 21, 2002), 27.

Wal-Mart: The Main Street Merchant of Doom

The small town was in need of a hired gun. The people were tired of dealing with the local price-fixing merchant scum who ran the town like a company store. This low-life bunch held the people of the town in a death grip and were perceived by the townspeople to overcharge on every purchase. In spite of what appeared to be a case of collusion, the law was powerless to do anything. What competition there was had been effectively eliminated.

Suddenly, coming over the rise and wearing white, their hired man came riding. The women and children buzzed with excitement. The men were happy. Although his methods of getting the job done turned some people's stomachs, the local watering hole buzzed with tales of how this hired gun would change their world for the better, how someday soon they would have the benefits long afforded the big city. But, others asked, at what price?

The Modern Version of the "Hired Gun"

In his final days, the man appeared to be somewhat too frail to handle the enormous job. Yet, the courage and self-confidence that he instilled in his associates radiated a belief in low prices and good value for all to see. As his associates rode into town, that radiance put to rest the people's fears that things had changed. Sam's spirit, the Wal-Mart Way, had come to town.

Sam Walton, founder, owner, and mastermind of Wal-Mart, passed away on April 5, 1992, leaving behind his spirit to ride herd on the massive Wal-Mart organization. To the consumer in the small community, his store, Wal-Mart, was seen as a friend. On the flip side, many a small-town merchant had been the victim of Sam's blazing merchandising tactics. So what is Wal-Mart to the communities it serves? Is Wal-Mart the consumer's best friend, the purveyor of the free-enterprise system, the "Mother of All Discount Stores," or, conversely, is it really "The Main Street Merchant of Doom"?

This case was prepared by William T. Rupp, College of Management, Robert Morris University. It was revised by Archie B. Carroll, University of Georgia.

The Man Named Sam

Samuel Moore Walton was born March 29, 1918, near Kingfisher, Kansas. His father was a salesman in the insurance, real estate, and mortgage businesses. The family moved often. Sam was a strong, lean boy who learned to work hard in order to help the family. He attended the University of Missouri starting in the fall of 1936 and graduated with a degree in business administration. During his time there, he was a member of the Beta Theta Phi fraternity, was president of the senior class, played various sports, and taught what was believed to be the largest Sunday school class in the world, numbering over 1,200 Missouri students.[1]

At age 22, Sam joined J. C. Penney. One of his first tasks was to memorize and practice the "Penney Idea." Adopted in 1913, this credo exhorts the associate to serve the public; not to demand all the profit the traffic will bear; to pack the customer's dollar full of value, quality, and satisfaction; to continue to be trained; to reward men and women in the organization through participation in what the business produces; and to test every policy, method, and act against the question: "Does it square with what is right and just?"[2]

In 1962, at age 44, Sam Walton opened his first Wal-Mart store. He took all the money and expertise he could gather and applied the J. C. Penney Idea to Middle America. Sam first targeted small, underserved rural towns with populations of no more than 10,000 people. The people responded, and Wal-Mart soon developed a core of loyal customers who loved the fast, friendly service coupled with consistently low prices. Later, Sam grew his company into the large cities, often with numerous Wal-Marts spread throughout every part of the city.

The Store That Sam Built

By 1981, Wal-Mart's rapid growth was evident to all and especially disturbing to Sears, J. C. Penney, Target, and Kmart, because Wal-Mart had become America's largest retailer. The most telling figures are those of overhead expenses and sales per employee. The overhead expenses of Sears and Kmart ran 29 and 23 percent of sales, respectively, whereas Wal-Mart's overhead expenses ran 16 percent of sales. At this time, the average Sears employee generated $85,000 in sales per year, whereas the average Wal-Mart employee generated $95,000.[3]

By 2001, Wal-Mart Stores, Inc., was the world's largest retailer with $191 billion in sales. The company employed 1 million associates worldwide through nearly 3,500 facilities in the United States and more than 1,000 stores throughout nine other countries. Wal-Mart claimed that more than 100 million customers per week visited Wal-Mart stores. The company had four major retail divisions—Wal-Mart Supercenters, Discount Stores, Neighborhood Markets, and Sam's Club warehouses. As it entered the 2000s, Wal-Mart had been named "Retailer of the Century" by *Discount Store News*, made *Fortune* magazine's lists of the "Most Admired Companies in America" and the "100 Best Companies to Work For," and was ranked on *Financial Times*' "Most Respected in the World" list.[4]

Sam was a motivational genius. He promoted the associate—the hourly employee—to a new level of participation within the organization. He offered profit sharing, incentive bonuses, and stock options in an effort to have his Wal-Mart associates share in the wealth. Sam, as the head cheerleader, saw his job as the chief proponent of the "Wal-Mart Way." The Wal-Mart Way reflected Sam's idea of the essential Wal-Mart culture that was needed for success. Sam felt that when a customer entered Wal-Mart in any part of the country, he or she should feel at home. Examples of the culture included "exceeding customer expectations" and "helping people make a difference." He was a proponent of the "Ten-Foot Rule," which held that if a customer came within 10 feet of an associate, the associate would look the customer in the eye, greet him or her, and ask if the customer needed help.

As he was growing the business, Sam, the courageous, borrowed and borrowed, sometimes just to pay other creditors. Arkansas banks that at one time had turned him down later competed with banks that Sam himself owned. Sam, the CEO, hired the best managers he could find. He let them talk him into buying an extensive computer network system. This network corporate satellite system enabled Sam to use round-the-clock inventory control and credit card sales control and provided him with information on total sales of which products where and when. This computer control center was about the size of a football field and used a Hughes satellite for uplinking and downlinking to each store.

In 1992, Sam, the mortal, died of incurable bone cancer. At age 73, Sam Walton said that if he had to do it over again he would not change a thing. He said, "This is still the most important thing I do, going around to the stores, and I'd rather do it than anything I know of. I know I'm helping our folks when I get out to the stores. I learn a lot about who's doing good things in the office, and I also see things that need fixing, and I help fix them. Any good management person in retail has got to do what I do in order to keep his finger on what's going on. You've got to have the right chemistry and the right attitude on the part of the folks who deal with the customers."[5]

Sam, the innovator, developed the "store within a store" concept of training people to be merchants, not just employees. These "store within a store" managers have all the numbers for their departments—breakdowns of how they are doing in relation to the store and the company as a whole. This concept provides big opportunities by providing big responsibilities. Sam set the goal of visiting every Wal-Mart store every year. To do this, he flew his own twin-prop Cessna and visited up to five or six stores per day. Two early social responsibility innovations were Wal-Mart's "Buy American" plan and its "Environmental Awareness" campaign.

Sam and Social Awareness: The "Buy American" Plan

The "Buy American" program was a result of a 1984 telephone conversation with then Arkansas Governor Bill Clinton. The program was a response to Sam's own enlightenment: He learned that Wal-Mart was adding to the loss of American jobs by buying cheaper foreign goods. Everything Sam stood for came out of his heartfelt obligation to supply the customer with low-cost quality goods, but running counter to this inner driving force was the realization that he was responsible for the loss of American jobs. This contradiction and dilemma drove him to find a solution. The conversation with Governor Clinton inspired Sam to do something about the problem.

The goal of the Buy American plan was to support American-based manufacturers by doing business with them so that they would not go out of business. His primary method for doing this was to give the manufacturers large orders or contracts so that they could stay in business.[6]

Sam wanted other manufacturers to join him in the Buy American plan. He wrote to 3,000 American manufacturers and solicited them to sell to Wal-Mart items that Wal-Mart was currently buying from overseas suppliers. Wal-Mart's competitors did not meet the challenge to "Buy American." Kmart stated that it would rather buy American-made goods but that it was looking for the best deal for the customer. Target said it was for free trade and that as the customer's representative it just wanted the best deal for the customer. Wall Street analysts responded positively, saying that Wal-Mart's plan was possibly the beginning of a change of direction for American retailers.[7]

In February 1986, about 12 months after the Buy American plan had begun, Sam held a press conference. He showed off all the merchandise Wal-Mart was now buying domestically. He estimated that Wal-Mart's Buy American plan had restored 4,538 jobs to the American economy and its people.[8]

Sam and Social Concerns: The "Environmental Awareness" Campaign

As awareness of the environment was on the rise, Sam looked for a way to involve Wal-Mart in the environmental movement. In August 1989, an ad in *The Wall Street Journal* proclaimed Wal-Mart's "commitment to our land, air and water." Sam envisioned Wal-Mart as a leader among American companies in the struggle to clean up the environment. John Lowne, corporate vice president and division manager for Reynolds Metals Company, stated, "Wal-Mart's move will indeed set a precedent for the entire retail industry. I'm surprised it has taken other retailers this long to follow suit."[9]

Wal-Mart wanted to use its tremendous buying power to aid in the implementation of the campaign. Wal-Mart sent a booklet to manufacturers stating the following:

> At Wal-Mart we're committed to help improve our environment. Our customers are concerned about the quality of our land, air and water, and want the opportunity to do something positive. We believe it is our responsibility to step up to their challenge.[10]

In the stores, shelf tags made from 100 percent recycled paper informed customers as to the environmental friendliness of the highlighted product. As a result of these shelf tags and Wal-Mart's advertising, customer awareness has increased, and some environmentally safe product manufacturers are reaping the rewards of increased Wal-Mart orders. Linda Downs, administra-

tive manager of Duraflame/California, said that Duraflame logs have been proven to burn cleaner than wood and that Wal-Mart's campaign has helped Duraflame to deliver this message. She went on to say, "Wal-Mart has helped drive home the message we have been trying to promote for years. They have really given us great publicity."[11]

In the *Wal-Mart Associates Handbook*, new associates were indoctrinated with the "Wal-Mart spirit." The section on the environment said:

> As a responsible member of the community, Wal-Mart's commitments go beyond simply selling merchandise. With environmental concerns mounting world-wide, Wal-Mart has taken action. Home office and store associates are taking decisive steps to help the environment by making community recycling bins available on our facility parking lots. Other action plans include "Adopt-a-Highway" and "Adopt-a-Beach" programs, tree planting and community clean up and beautification. By forming a partnership with our associates, our manufacturers and our customers, we're convinced we can make the world a better place to live.[12, 13]

Sam and the Merchants of Main Street

Not everyone has been excited to see Sam and his mechanized Wal-Mart army succeed. Small merchants across America shudder when the winds of the "Wal-Mart Way" begin to blow. Kennedy Smith of the National Main Street Center in Washington, DC, says, "The first thing towns usually do is panic." Once Wal-Mart comes to town, Smith says, "Downtowns will never again be the providers of basic consumer goods and services they once were."[14]

Some towns have learned to "just say 'no'" to Wal-Mart's overtures. Steamboat Springs, Colorado, is one such city. Colorado newspapers called it the "Shootout at Steamboat Springs." Wal-Mart was denied permission to build on a 9-acre parcel along U.S. Route 40. Owners of upscale shops and condos were very concerned with the image of their resort community, and Wal-Mart, with its low-cost reputation, just did not fit. The shootout lasted for 2 years, and finally Wal-Mart filed a damage suit against the city. Countersuits followed. A petition was circulated to hold a referendum on the matter. This was the shot that made Wal-Mart blink and back down. Just before the vote, Don Shinkle, corporate affairs vice president, said, "A vote would not be good for Steamboat Springs, and it would not be good for Wal-Mart. I truly believe Wal-Mart is a kinder, gentler company, and, while we have the votes to win, an election would only split the town more."[15]

In Iowa City, Iowa (population 50,000+), Wal-Mart was planning an 87,000-square-foot store on the outskirts of town. A group of citizens gathered enough signatures during a petition drive to put a referendum on the ballot to block Wal-Mart and the city council from building the new store (the city council had approved the rezoning of the land Wal-Mart wanted). Jim Clayton, a downtown merchant, said, "Wal-Mart is a freight train going full steam in the opposite direction of this town's philosophy." If businesses wind up going down, Clayton says, "you lose their involvement in the community, involvement I promise you won't get with some assistant manager over at Wal-Mart."[16] Wal-Mart spokesperson Brenda Lockhart commented that downtown merchants can only benefit from the increase in customer traffic provided "they offer superior service and aren't gouging their customers."[17] Efforts to stop Wal-Mart and the Iowa City Council were not successful. Wal-Mart opened its Iowa City store on November 5, 1991.

Meanwhile, in Pawhuska, Oklahoma, as a result of Wal-Mart's entry in 1983 and other local factors, the local "five-and-dime," J. C. Penney, Western Auto, and a whole block of other stores closed their doors. Four years later, Dave Story, general manager of the local *Pawhuska Daily Journal Capital*, wrote that Wal-Mart was a "billion-dollar parasite" and a "national retail ogre."[18]

Wal-Mart managers have become very active in Pawhuska and surrounding communities since that time. A conversation with the editor of the Pawhuska paper, Jody Smith, and her advertising editor, Suzy Burns, revealed that Wal-Mart sponsored the local rodeo, gave gloves to the local coat drive, and was involved with the local cerebral palsy and multiple sclerosis fund-raisers. On the other hand, Fred Wright, former owner of a TV and record store, said, "Wal-Mart really craters a little town's downtown."[19]

Shift to Kinder, Louisiana (population 2,608). Wal-Mart moved into this small Louisiana town in 1981. On December 31, 1990, the store was closed. During the time Wal-Mart operated in Kinder, one-third of the downtown stores closed. The downtown became three blocks of mostly run-down, red-brick buildings. The closest place to buy shoes or sewing thread was 30 miles away in Oakdale, Louisiana—at another Wal-Mart. Moreover, Kinder lost $5,500 in annual tax revenues, which represented 10 percent of the total revenues for the city.

The tactics Wal-Mart employed during its 10 years in Kinder left a bad taste in the mouths of some small retailers. Soon after Wal-Mart's arrival, a price war broke out between Wal-Mart and the downtown retailers. The retailers told *The Atlanta Journal-Constitution* in November 1990, "Wal-Mart sent employees, wearing name tags and smocks, into their stores to scribble down prices and list merchandise." Lou Pearl, owner of Kinder Jewelry and Gifts, stated that Wal-Mart associates came to her store and noted the type of art supplies she was carrying. Shortly thereafter, Wal-Mart began carrying the same merchandise at discount prices. Sales at Kinder Jewelry and Gifts dropped drastically, and Pearl dropped the merchandise line. Within several weeks, so did Wal-Mart.[20] Perhaps Troy Marcantel, a 29-year-old downtown clothing merchant, said it best: "What really rankled me was that they used people we have known all our lives. I still don't understand how our own people could do that to us."[21]

The Main Street Merchants Organize Welcoming Committees

By the 1990s, there were dozens of organized groups actively opposing Wal-Mart's expansion.[22] Some of these groups were and are run by activists left over from the 1960s and 1970s. Instead of protesting the Vietnam War, nuclear proliferation, or the destruction of the environment, they have turned their efforts to Wal-Mart specifically and capitalism in general. One of these activists, Paul Glover, who was an antiwar organizer, has defined Wal-Mart as the epitome of capitalism, which he despises. For Mr. Glover and others, Wal-Mart stands for "everything they dislike about American society— mindless consumerism, paved landscapes, and homogenization of community identity."[23]

In Boulder, Colorado, Wal-Mart tried to counter these allegations by proposing a "green" store. Steven Lane, Wal-Mart's real estate manager, said that a "green store" would be built that would be environmentally friendly, with a solar-powered sign out front and everything. His efforts were trumped by Spencer Havlick, an organizer of the first Earth Day in 1970, suggesting that the entire store be powered by solar energy. Mr. Lane did not respond.[24]

Protest organizers united against the spread of the "Wal-Mart Way" differ from the downtown merchants in that these protesters have no financial stake. Hence, these activists are attacking on a higher plane, a philosophical plane. The accusations ring with a tone of argument that was made by other activists protesting polluting industries (e.g., the coal, nuclear, and chemical industries). These activists accuse Wal-Mart of "strip-mining" towns and communities of their culture and values.

One possible root of this culture clash may be attributed to the unique facets of the internal corporate culture at Wal-Mart's headquarters. This is a place where competition for the reputation as the "cheapest" is practiced. An example is the competition among employees in procuring the cheapest haircut, shoes, or necktie. Wal-Mart is a place where playacting as a backwoods "hick" has been an acceptable behavior within the organization. Consequently, as a result of the internal culture of Wal-Mart and the external environment, some analysts believe that a clash of priorities was inevitable as Wal-Mart moved into larger, more urban settings.

Some of the greatest opposition to Wal-Mart's growth has come from the New England area. This area holds great promise for Wal-Mart because of the large population and the many underserved towns. These towns are typically underserved in three ways: in variety of product choices, in value, and in convenience. The opposition to Wal-Mart entering these New England markets includes some high-profile names, such as Jerry Greenfield, cofounder of Ben & Jerry's Homemade ice cream, and Arthur Frommer, a well-known travel writer.[25] In addition to New England, other areas, such as resort areas, oppose Wal-Marts because they want to insulate their unique cultures from what they consider to be the offensive consumerism that is generated by Wal-Mart's presence.

Al Norman, a lobbyist and media consultant, has turned opposition to Wal-Mart into a cottage industry. Mr. Norman publishes a monthly newsletter called *Sprawl-Busters Alert*. He has also developed a Web site (http://www.sprawl-busters.com) that has vast information for citizens who are fighting to prevent Wal-Mart or other "big box" stores from locating in their cities or neighborhoods. Norman achieved national attention in 1993, when he stopped Wal-Mart from locating in his hometown of Greenfield, Massachusetts. Since then, he has appeared on "60 Minutes," which called him "the guru of the anti–Wal-Mart movement," and has gained widespread media attention. Today Norman continues to serve as a consultant and travels throughout the United States helping dozens of coalitions fight Wal-Mart. One of Norman's recent projects was the publication of his book, *Slam-Dunking Wal-Mart: How You Can Stop Superstore Sprawl in Your Hometown* (1999).

In this book, he lays out the arguments against urban "sprawl."

On the Sprawl-Busters Web page, consumers around the country are given the opportunity to write in the details of their fights with Wal-Mart. Examples in 2001 included Clemson, South Carolina, pulling the plug on Wal-Mart; Overland Park, Kansas, fighting the fact that "Wal-Mart is back"; and growing concern in Atascocita, Texas, with Wal-Mart's "concrete jungle."[26]

Sprawl-Busters is not alone in its focused criticism of Wal-Mart's presence in communities. Another organization, Wal-Mart Watch, has an active Web page (http://www.walmartwatch.com) that details what it believes to be Wal-Mart's threat to America. Its "Bad Neighbor Fact Sheet" outlines how the company is a threat to and is destroying workers and communities.

Recent Developments

For its part, Wal-Mart has continued its aggressive diversification and growth pattern. In 2001, Wal-Mart announced plans for 50 new discount stores and approximately 185 new Supercenters by their fiscal year beginning February 2002. When Wal-Mart replaces regular stores with Supercenters, communities face a new problem: what to do with the vacant Wal-Mart locations, which leave empty buildings as well as other merchants who built near them to capitalize on Wal-Mart's heavy traffic. The company plans the expansion of its Neighborhood Markets (grocery stores) by adding 15 to 20 new units in the coming fiscal year. The company hopes that its new grocery stores will be able to beat conventional grocery stores with lower prices and more conveniences than its Supercenters. Many grocery store industry executives continue to shudder at the prospects of Wal-Mart growing into their industry, where margins are already razor thin. The Sam's Club division plans to open 50 to 55 domestic clubs and will aggressively remodel its existing stores.

In addition to domestic growth, Wal-Mart plans to continue growing internationally. It plans to develop approximately 130 new retail units outside the United States. New stores are planned for Argentina, Brazil, Canada, China, Korea, Mexico, and Puerto Rico.[27] Though Wal-Mart has had some early missteps in selling overseas, there is evidence that the company is finally getting the hang of operating in foreign cultures. From Wal-Mart's perspective, it has no choice but to expand rapidly abroad because its culture and stock price seem to be built on the expectation of double-digit sales and profits gains year after year. Already, Wal-Mart is the biggest retailer in both Canada and Mexico. In 2001, its $32 billion in international business equaled 17 percent of its total sales.[28] Given the challenges Wal-Mart has had moving into communities in the United States, one can only imagine the issues that might arise as Wal-Mart expands around the world, crossing cultural lines defined by separate nationalities.

Wal-Mart has millions of supporters, 100 million of them weekly customers. Many consider the company to be socially responsible in addition to a provider of thousands of jobs, low prices, and high value and service. As we progress through the first years of the new millennium, Wal-Mart has numerous corporate citizenship initiatives at the local and national levels. Locally, Wal-Mart stores underwrite college scholarships for high school seniors, raise funds for children's hospitals through The Children's Miracle Network Telethon, provide local fund-raisers money and manpower, and educate the public about recycling and other environmental topics with the help of "Green Coordinators."[29] On October 6, 1998, the Walton Family Charitable Support Foundation, the charitable program created by Sam Walton's family, announced the largest ever single gift made to an American business school: $50 million to the College of Business Administration of the University of Arkansas. Helen R. Walton, the "first lady" of Wal-Mart, said that she and her husband established the Foundation to support specific charities, including the University.[30]

Nationally, Wal-Mart provides industrial development grants to cities and towns trying to bolster their economic bases; encourages American companies to bring offshore manufacturing operations "back home" through its Buy American program; underwrites Support American Manufacturing (SAM), a program administered by Southwest Missouri State University that shows small companies how to improve their operations; and sponsors the American Hometown Leadership Award, which salutes small-town government leaders who are mapping long-term goals for their communities.[31]

On its own Web page, Wal-Mart touts in detail its "Commitment to our Communities," its "Commitment to People," and its "Commitment to Energy Conservation." In September 2001, right after the terrorist attacks in New York and Washington, DC, Wal-Mart pledged $2 million for national relief efforts. In addition, Wal-Mart trucks delivered much-needed supplies requested by the Salvation Army. This included trucks with medical supplies, clothing, blankets and other essential supplies. According to Cone, Inc., a market survey company, in 2001 Wal-Mart was named for the second consecutive year as the company Americans think of first in terms of supporting local causes and issues.[32]

Epilogue

Sam, the hired gun, learned his lessons well. The people who bought at his stores were well satisfied. The downtown merchants who survived learned to coexist with the hired gun's associates. But things would never be the same. The changes had come rapidly. The social fabric of the small town was changed forever. The larger cities continued to fight.

The hired gun rode on, searching for that next town that needed to be liberated from the downtown price-fixing bad guys. The search has become more complicated as the opposition has risen, but the spirit of Sam rides on.

Questions for Discussion

1. What are the major issues in this case? Assess Wal-Mart's corporate social responsibility using the four-part CSR model. Is Wal-Mart socially responsible for its devastating impact on small merchants? What about its impact on communities in terms of sprawl, traffic congestion, and impact on the appearance of the environment? What responsibility, if any, does the company have to these merchants or to the communities it enters?

2. Most of Wal-Mart's success has come at the expense of the small merchant. What should Wal-Mart do, if anything, to help other vital businesses in the community survive? Why?

3. Sam Walton has been called a motivational genius. After reading this case and with what you have observed at your local Wal-Mart store, explain how this motivational genius empowered the employee. What is the "Wal-Mart Way"? Explain its impact on the associate and on the community. What will happen now that Sam is no longer the motivational leader?

4. Some regard Wal-Mart as a leader in the area of corporate social responsibility. How do the "Buy American" program and the "Environmental Awareness" campaign illustrate this? Are these programs really examples of corporate social responsibility or are they gimmicks to entice customers into the stores? Are the benefits of these programs offset by the company's devastating impact on merchants?

5. Wal-Mart has closed five stores in its short history. What responsibility, if any, does Wal-Mart have to the employees who are let go? What about its loyal customers and the community?

6. In the case of Kinder, Louisiana, Wal-Mart left town without any type of reciprocity. Given Wal-Mart's commitment statements, did the company owe a debt to the city of Kinder? Why or why not?

7. Wal-Mart is finding severe resistance to its expansion into New England. From Wal-Mart's perspective, draw the stakeholder map. Define the true goals of the opponents of Wal-Mart. Include a consideration of the following: (a) stopping Wal-Mart's expansion, (b) preserving the status quo (e.g., downtown community, social fabric), (c) developing a cause that will pay their bills, (d) fighting for an ideology, or (e) something else. What should Wal-Mart do?

8. As Wal-Mart expands into the international arena, what problems or issues do you anticipate it will face? In general, what should Wal-Mart's approach be in these other countries?

Case Endnotes

1. Vance H. Trimble, *Sam Walton: The Inside Story of America's Richest Man* (New York: Penguin Books, 1990), 30. Also see Bob Ortega, *In Sam We Trust* (New York: Times Business, 1998).
2. *Ibid.*, 34.
3. Janice Castro, "Mr. Sam Stuns Goliath," *Time* (February 25, 1991), 62.
4. Wal-Mart's Web page (http://www.walmartstores.com), "Wall Mart at a Glance."
5. John Huey, "America's Most Successful Merchant," *Fortune* (September 23, 1991), 50.
6. Wal-Mart's Web page, *ibid*.
7. Trimble, 260.
8. *Ibid.*, 261.
9. Richard Turcsik, "A New Environment Evolves at Wal-Mart," *Supermarket News* (January 15, 1990), 10.
10. *Ibid.*, 10.
11. *Ibid.*, 11.
12. Wal-Mart Corporation, *Wal-Mart Associates Handbook* (July 1991), 14.
13. *Ibid.*, 14.
14. Dan Koeppel, "Wal-Mart Finds New Rivals on Main Street," *Adweek's Marketing Week* (November 10, 1990), 5.
15. Trimble, 255.
16. "Just Saying No to Wal-Mart," *Newsweek* (November 13, 1989), 65.
17. *Ibid.*, 65.
18. Karen Blumenthal, "Arrival of Discounter Tears the Civic Fabric of Small-Town Life," *The Wall Street Journal* (April 14, 1987), 1, 23.
19. *Ibid.*, 23.
20. Charles Haddad, "Wal-Mart Leaves Town 'High, Dry,'" *The Atlanta Journal-Constitution* (November 26, 1990), A4.
21. *Ibid.*, A4.
22. Bob Ortega, "Aging Activists Turn, Turn, Turn Attention to Wal-Mart Protests," *The Wall Street Journal* (October 11, 1994), A1, A8.
23. *Ibid.*, A1.
24. *Ibid.*, A8.
25. Joseph Pereira and Bob Ortega, "Once Easily Turned Away by Local Foes, Wal-Mart Gets Tough in New England," *The Wall Street Journal* (September 7, 1994), B1.
26. "Sprawl-Busters," http://www.sprawl-busters.com.
27. Wal-Mart Web page, "Wal-Mart Announces Expansion Plans for FYI 2003."
28. Wendy Zellner, "How Well Does Wal-Mart Travel?" *Business Week* (September 3, 2001), 82–84. Also see Emily Nelson, "Why Wal-Mart Sings, 'Yes, We Have Bananas!'" *The Wall Street Journal* (October 6, 1998), B1; and Wendy Zellner, "Look Out, Supermarkets—Wal-Mart Is Hungry," *Business Week* (September 14, 1998), 98–100.
29. Wal-Mart Web page, www.walmartstores.com.
30. University of Arkansas Web page, www.uark.edu (October 6, 1998), press release.
31. Wal-Mart Web page, http://www.walmartstores.com.
32. *Ibid.*

Case 16

The Body Shop International PLC: A Different Philosophy

When North American consumers have been asked to describe the cosmetics industry, they often respond with words such as "glamour" and "beauty." Beginning in 1976, The Body Shop provided a contrast to this image by selling a range of 400 products designed to "cleanse and polish the skin and hair." The product line included such items as "Honeyed Beeswax, Almond, and Jojoba Oil Cleanser" and "Carrot Facial Oil." Women's cosmetics and men's toiletries were also available. They were all produced without the use of animal testing and were packaged in plain-looking, recyclable packages.[1] The primary channel of distribution was a network of over 600 franchised retail outlets in Europe, Australia, Asia, and North America.[2] The company enjoyed annual growth rates of approximately 50 percent until 1990, when net income began to level off. Few questions were raised in the media about this decline in performance, because the firm's social agenda and exotic product line captured most of the public's interest. Indeed, at this point in time, The Body Shop was the poster-child company for the burgeoning corporate social responsibility movement.

Managing director and founder Anita Roddick was responsible for creating and maintaining much of the company's marketing strategy and product development.[3] Roddick believed that The Body Shop was fundamentally different from other firms in the cosmetics industry because "we don't claim that our products will make you look younger, we say they will only help you look your best."[4] She regularly assailed her competitors: "We loathe the cosmetics industry with a passion. It's run by men who create needs that don't exist."[5] During the 1980s, Anita Roddick became one of the richest women in the United Kingdom by challenging the well-established firms and rewriting the rules of the cosmetics industry.

Anita Roddick became admired within the business community for the conviction of her beliefs and the success of her company. She received many honors and awards, including U.K. Businesswoman of the Year in 1985, British Retailer of the Year in 1989, and the Order of the British Empire.[6] The firm's customers included several celebrities, including Diana, Princess of Wales, Sting, and Bob Weir of the Grateful Dead. Ben Cohen, cofounder and chairman of Ben and Jerry's, described her as an incredibly dynamic, passionate, humorous and intelligent individual who believes it's the responsibility of a business to give back to the community ... she understands that a business has the power to influence the world in a positive way.[7]

Mrs. Roddick opened the first Body Shop store in Brighton, England, as a means of supporting her family while her husband was taking a year-long sabbatical in America. Her husband, Gordon Roddick, a chartered accountant by trade, was using much of their savings to finance his trip. Anita Roddick had little money to open a store, much less to develop products or purchase packaging materials.[8]

She called upon her previous experience as a resource. Having been a United Nations researcher for several years in the 1960s, she had had many opportunities during field expeditions to see how men and women in Africa, Asia, and Australia used locally grown plants and extracts, such as beeswax, rice grains, almonds, bananas, and jojoba, as grooming products. Roddick knew that these materials were inexpensive and readily obtainable. With some library research, she found several recipes, some of which were centuries old, that used these same ingredients to make cosmetics and skin cleansers. With the addition of inexpensive bottles and handwritten labels, Roddick quickly developed a line of products for sale in her first Body Shop. She soon opened a second store in a nearby town. When Gordon Roddick returned to the United Kingdom in 1977, The Body Shop was recording sizable profits. At Anita's request, he joined the company as its chief executive officer.[9]

The Body Shop's strategy grew out of the company's early reliance on cost containment. Roddick was able to afford only 600 bottles when she opened her first store. Customers were offered a small discount to encourage the return of empty bottles for product refills. This offer was extended to both retail and mail-order customers.[10]

This case was prepared by William A. Sodeman using publicly available information.

The Body Shop could not afford advertising, so Roddick resolved to succeed without it.[11]

The Body Shop's retail stores were somewhat different from the cosmetic salons and counters familiar to shoppers in highly industrialized nations. The typical retail sales counter relied on high-pressure tactics that included promotions, makeovers, and an unspoken contract with the customer that virtually required a purchase in order for the customer to receive any advice or consultation from a sales counter employee.[12] Body Shop employees were taught to wait for the customer to ask questions, be forthright and helpful, and not to press for sales.[13]

Store employees were paid a half-day's wages every week to perform community service activities. At the company headquarters in Littlchampton, England, The Body Shop employed an anthropologist, six herbalists, and a variety of others in similar fields. There was nothing that resembled a marketing department. Husbands and wives frequently worked together and could visit their children during the workday at the on-site day-care center.[14] The company's hiring procedures included questions about the applicant's personal heroes and literary tastes, as well as their individual beliefs on certain social issues. At one time, Roddick was ready to hire a retail director, but refused to do so when he professed his fondness for hunting, a sport that Roddick despised because of her support for animal rights.[15]

As the company prospered, Anita Roddick used her enthusiasm and growing influence on her suppliers and customers. The Body Shop began to produce products in the country of origin when it was feasible and paid the workers wages that were comparable to those in the European Community.[16] Customers were asked to sign petitions and join activist groups that The Body Shop endorsed, mostly in the areas of animal rights and environmental causes. The Body Shop contributed significant portions of its earnings to these groups, including Amnesty International and People for the Ethical Treatment of Animals (PETA). Roddick was careful to choose causes that were "easy to understand"[17] and could be communicated quickly to a customer during a visit to a Body Shop store.

An example of this corporate activism was The Body Shop's opposition to a practice that had become common in the cosmetics industry. Cosmetics firms were not required to perform animal testing of their products to comply with product safety and health regulations. Rather, companies voluntarily adopted animal-based testing procedures to guard against product liability lawsuits.[18]

The Body Shop was not worried about such lawsuits, because the product ingredients Roddick chose had been used safely for centuries. In addition, the older recipes had been used for many decades without incident. These circumstances led to the company's rejection of animal-based product testing. Any supplier wishing to do business with The Body Shop had to sign a statement guaranteeing that it had done no animal testing for the previous 5 years and would never do such testing in the future. The Body Shop used human volunteers from its own staff and the University Hospital of Wales to test new and current products under normal use. The Body Shop also volunteered to share the results of its tests on individual ingredients with other cosmetics manufacturers.[19]

Most other cosmetics firms used a variety of procedures to determine the safety of cosmetics products, with two animal-based tests becoming the standard procedures. The Draize test involved dripping the substance in question, such as shampoo or a detergent paste, into the eyes of conscious, restrained rabbits and measuring the resultant damage over the course of several days. Rabbits cannot cry, which allowed researchers to complete the tests quickly. Another test required researchers to force-feed large quantities of a substance to a sample of laboratory animals. The substance could be a solid (such as lipstick or shaving cream), a paste, or a liquid. The lethal dose of a substance was determined by the amount that had been ingested by an individual surviving animal when 50 percent of the sample had died, hence the name of the test, LD50.[20] Beginning in the 1970s, animal rights groups such as the Humane Society and PETA began protesting the use of these tests by the cosmetics industry. The Body Shop lent its support to these groups' efforts, labeling all animal testing as "cruel and unnecessary." By 1991, alternative procedures that involved far less cruelty to animals had already been developed but were yet to be approved for industry use.[21]

In the United States, The Body Shop's market share was limited by two factors. First, its prices were significantly higher than those charged for mass-marketed products in drugstores, although they were generally comparable to the prices charged for cosmetics and cleansers at department store sales counters. Second, The Body Shop was constrained by the number of stores it had opened in the United States. By 1991, only 40 stores had been opened in a dozen metropolitan areas across the country. A mail-order catalog and a telephone order line were used to supplement the American retail stores, but they were inadequate substitutes for the product sampling and advice that were readily available at The Body Shop's stores. Roddick maintained that those consumers who sampled Body Shop products became loyal customers: "Once they walk into one of our stores or buy from our catalogue, they're hooked."[22]

The Body Shop was taken public in 1984, with the Roddicks owning a combined 30 percent of the outstanding stock. The firm's subsequent sales and net income figures grew during 1985 to 1990 from sales revenue of $15.3 and net income of $1.4 million to $137.7 and $14.7 million.[23] Without The Body Shop's monetary donations to various social causes, all of these net income figures would be higher than reported in the financial statements. Estimates of the company's annual contributions to outside organizations varied from several hundred thousand to several million dollars.

Industry analysts considered The Body Shop to be a strong performer with the potential to prosper even in an economic downturn. The exotic nature of its products, such as hair conditioner made with 10 percent real bananas and a peppermint foot lotion, would attract consumers who desired affordable luxuries. Analysts regarded the public's desire for personal care products as "insatiable," especially in North America.[24] The addition of the strong emotional appeal of social issues formed the basis for one of the most successful marketing and promotional concepts in the cosmetics industry in decades.

The twentieth anniversary of Earth Day, celebrated in 1990, focused media attention on many of the environmental issues that Roddick and The Body Shop regularly addressed. Further, it spurred interest in environmental issues in the commercial sector.

Several new entrants and existing competitors challenged The Body Shop in the United States and Europe. Among the largest of these firms were Estee Lauder and Revlon. The Limited had opened 50 Bath & Body Works stores, patterned after The Body Shop's outlets and located in shopping malls across the United States. In addition, an English competitor, Crabtree & Evelyn, had held a significant presence in North America and Europe since the mid-1970s.

By 1991, The Body Shop was a successful and profitable firm that had attracted a variety of well-financed competitors. The company faced a real threat from these firms because they were all well financed and had a broad range of experience in marketing cosmetics. Each of these firms was well established in the United States, yet no one firm dominated the new product segment that The Body Shop had helped create.

In addition, there were indications that the environmental concerns that attracted customers to The Body Shop might not have permanent drawing power. Roddick had vowed never to sell anything but environmentally friendly cosmetics and grooming products in her stores, but the industry was growing and changing faster than anyone had anticipated. It seemed that The Body Shop needed to take action to ensure its long-term survival.

When asked about her role in the company, Anita Roddick stated:

The purpose of a business isn't just to generate profits to create an ever-larger empire. It's to have the power to affect social change, to make the world a better place. I have always been an activist, I have always been incredibly impassioned about human rights and environmental issues. The Body Shop is simply my stage.[25]

Questions for Discussion

1. How does The Body Shop address the four components of corporate social responsibility? In The Body Shop, what tensions among these components are at work?

2. Anita Roddick claims that her firm does not advertise, yet it receives free media exposure and publicity through the social causes it champions and her personal appearances. Is this an appropriate approach for a business to follow?

3. Analyze The Body Shop's power using both levels and spheres of power discussed in Chapter 1.

4. What is your assessment of Anita Roddick's philosophy regarding the "purpose of a business"?

5. What are Anita Roddick's strengths and weaknesses as a leader? Should she stay on in a managing role or step aside and allow a more experienced person to run the marketing operations?

6. The Body Shop asks potential employees questions about "personal heroes" and individual beliefs. Is it ethical to ask such questions of applicants? Are these questions legitimate ones to ask in the first place? Are such questions fair to the applicants?

Case Endnotes

1. Catalog, The Body Shop (Fall 1990).
2. Laura Zinn, "Whales, Human Rights, Rain Forests—and the Heady Smell of Profits," *Business Week* (July 15, 1991), 114.

3. *Ibid.*, 114.
4. Samuel Greengard, "Face Values," *USAir Magazine* (November 1990), 89.
5. Zinn, 114.
6. Greengard, 93.
7. Greengard, 97.
8. Zinn, 115.
9. Greengard, 94.
10. Greengard, 94.
11. Zinn, 114.
12. Greengard, 90.
13. Maria Koklanaris, "Trio of Retailers Finds Soap and Social Concern an Easy Sell," *The Washington Post* (April 27, 1991).
14. Greengard, 90.
15. Zinn, 115.
16. The Body Shop promotional literature, 1991.
17. Zinn, 115.
18. The Body Shop promotional literature, 1991.
19. The Body Shop promotional literature, 1991.
20. Peter Singer, *Animal Liberation: A New Ethics for Treatment of Animals* (New York: Avon Books, 1975), 48.
21. The Body Shop promotional literature, 1991.
22. Greengard, 89.
23. Compact Disclosure database, 1991.
24. Koklanaris.
25. Greengard, 97.

Case 17

The Body Shop International PLC: Growing Pains

Between 1991 and 1995, The Body Shop continued to expand its operations. The Body Shop had opened 1,200 stores by early 1995.[1] Over 100 company-owned and franchised stores were operating in U.S. shopping malls and downtown shopping districts. During the period 1991 to 1994, sales and net income grew from $231 million and $41 million to $330 million and $47 million, respectively.

The Body Shop had moved its U.S. headquarters from Cedar Knolls, New Jersey, to a less expensive and more central location—Raleigh, North Carolina. The original location worked well when The Body Shop opened its first U.S. stores in New York City and Washington, DC, but soon proved to be a logistical problem. Roddick was frustrated that the New Jersey hires did not seem as creative or impulsive as her English staff. In retrospect, she realized that having some of her U.K. staff help train the first U.S. managers and employees or even setting up her headquarters in a college town such as Boulder, Colorado, or a city such as San Francisco would have been a better choice than starting from scratch in New Jersey.[2]

This case was prepared by William A. Sodeman using publicly available information.

Limitations

The Body Shop had bigger problems to deal with than the location of its national headquarters. The Limited continued to open its chain of Bath & Body Works stores on a nationwide scale. Placement of a Bath & Body Works store in a mall usually precluded The Body Shop from entering the same mall. (There were some exceptions, most notably very large shopping malls such as the Mall of America in Bloomington, Minnesota.) All of The Limited's stores, from Express and Victoria's Secret to Structure and Lerner's, were company owned. This allowed a greater degree of flexibility and speed than The Body Shop's franchising system. Further, The Limited had started grouping its stores in malls to create its own version of the department store. During the holidays, Express and Structure stores carried special selections of Bath & Body Works products to induce customer trial and develop brand awareness. The Limited's size and power as one of the major retailers in the United States made the company a strong threat to The Body Shop's continued presence in the U.S. retail market. In an alarming move, The Limited began opening Bath & Body Works stores in the United Kingdom, which presented a direct threat to The Body Shop on the company's home soil.

The similarities between The Body Shop and Bath & Body Works stores also created some confusion. Some less-observant customers of The Body Shop were bringing empty Bath & Body Works bottles to The Body Shop to be refilled because Bath & Body Works did not have its own refill policy and the products often seemed similar. The Body Shop protected its slogans, territory, and franchises with an aggressive legal strategy that included an out-of-court settlement with The Limited in 1993.[3]

Other companies had successfully introduced organic or natural beauty products in discount and drugstores, a market segment that The Body Shop had completely ignored in its global operations. Traditional retailers including Woolworth's and Kmart had also entered what had come to be known as the minimalist segment of the personal care products industry. Woolworth's entry was an expanded selection of organic bath and body care products in its deep discount R_x Place chain. Kmart's line of Naturalistic cosmetics was sold in over 1,800 stores.[4] Other new companies included H_2O Plus, which sold its products in its own retail stores but did not make claims about animal testing as had The Body Shop and Bath & Body Works.

Good Press

The Body Shop continued to receive new accolades and to hit new heights of prosperity. Anita Roddick published her autobiography, *Body and Soul*, in late 1991. Roddick donated her portion of the royalties to several groups, including the Unrepresented Nations and Peoples Organization, a self-governing group that spoke for Kurds, Tibetans, and Native Americans; the Medical Foundation, which treated victims of torture; and a variety of individual political prisoners. The 256-page book, which was written and designed by Roddick, Body Shop staff, and an outside group, resembled a mixture of catalog and personal memoir. Hundreds of pictures and headlines were used throughout to emphasize and clarify particular points of interest. On the final page of the book, where one would expect to see the last page of the index, is the coda of the final chapter. The last line of text, printed in large boldface letters, reads "Make no mistake about it—I'm doing this for me."[5]

Partly as a result of the book's publication, The Body Shop received a great deal of flattering media attention. *Inc.*[6] and *Working Woman*[7] ran cover stories featuring Anita Roddick. *Fortune*[8] and *Business Week*[9] published shorter articles that focused on Anita Roddick and the company's performance. *Time* began its article with a

story on Anita's fact-finding mission to Oman, where she obtained a perfume recipe from a local tribe only after dropping her pants and showing the Bedouin women her pubic hair. Bedouin women pluck theirs every day.[10]

Bad Press

In 1992, some members of the media began to criticize The Body Shop and the Roddicks. The *Financial Times* gave The Body Shop the dubious honor of headlining its 1992 list of top 10 corporate losers after the price of Body Shop stock dipped from $5.20 to $2.70 during September.[11] Stock analysts had reacted to a disappointing earnings report, and the news set some minds to wondering if the company could indeed grow quickly enough to capture a leadership position in the minimalist market, or if there was a minimalist market at all.

Around this time, The Body Shop invested $5 million in a 10-part documentary series called *Millennium*. This series, which was shown around the world on television networks including PBS and the BBC, was meant to celebrate the wisdom and history of native cultures. The director quit the project during filming, accusing the Roddicks of distorting the tribal rituals depicted in the film to suit various new-age ideals.[12] The Body Shop sold a book version of *Millennium* in its stores to help promote the series and raise funds for donations.

In 1993, a British television news magazine telecast a report on The Body Shop. The show alleged that The Body Shop knowingly sourced materials from suppliers that had recently performed animal testing. The Body Shop sued the TV station and the production company for libel and won a significant financial award after a 6-week court battle. Anita Roddick sat in the courtroom every day and compared the experience to confinement in a "mahogany coffin." The Body Shop won the suit and a £276,000 settlement by proving to the British court that the company had never intentionally misled consumers about the animal-testing policy, which encouraged manufacturers to give up animal testing but did not claim that ingredients had never been tested on animals.[13]

In 1994, *Business Ethics* magazine, a well-respected U.S. publication, published a cover story on The Body Shop that built upon many of the allegations that others had presented over the years. The resulting controversy engulfed the journalist, the magazine, and The Body Shop in a new wave of controversy that threatened The Body Shop's already slow expansion into the U.S. market.

In June 1993, journalist Jon Entine had first been approached by disgruntled current and former Body Shop staffers about several of the company's practices. After overcoming his initial skepticism and doing some preliminary investigations in Littlehampton, The Body Shop's headquarters, Entine was convinced he had a sound basis on which to develop a story for his current employer, the ABC news magazine "Primetime Live." When ABC decided not to renew the contract and to drop The Body Shop story, Entine began his own investigation, which eventually resulted in the *Business Ethics* article.[14] In the preface to the article, magazine editor and publisher Marjorie Kelly wrote:

> *Long-time readers will note that the following article represents a distinct departure from our typical editorial style. It has not been part of our mission to publish the exploits of companies that fall short of their stated social goals. But we believe the story of The Body Shop must be told, chiefly for the lessons it provides those of us who seek to promote ethical business practices. Still, we bring this story to you with mixed emotions. We have been ardent admirers of Anita Roddick and her company for many years; two years ago this month [September 1992] we featured her on our cover. But, after weeks of debate, including several conversations with Body Shop representatives, we concluded the greater good would be served by raising these issues in print. We earnestly hope this dialogue will be a constructive one.*

In the article, Entine made several claims:

- Anita Roddick had stolen the concept of The Body Shop, including the store name, recycling of bottles, store design, catalogs, and products, from a similar store she had visited in Berkeley, California, in 1971, several years before she opened her first Body Shop in Brighton in 1976.
- Roddick had not discovered exotic recipes for some of her products as she had previously claimed: Some were outdated, off-the-shelf formulas that had been used by other manufacturers, whereas others featured unusual ingredients, around which Roddick and company employees had woven fanciful tales of her travels of discovery.
- Many Body Shop products were full of petrochemicals, artificial colors and fragrances, and synthetic preservatives and contained only small amounts of naturally sourced ingredients.
- Quality control was a continuing problem with instances of mold, formaldehyde, and E. coli contamination reported around the world, thus requiring the use of large amounts of preservatives to give the products stable shelf lives.
- The U.S. Federal Trade Commission had launched a probe into The Body Shop's franchising practices, including deceptive financial data, unfair competition, and misleading company representation. One husband-and-wife franchising team compared the company to the Gambino crime family.
- The Body Shop's "Trade Not Aid" program was a sham, providing only a small portion of The Body Shop's raw materials while failing to fulfill the company's promises to suppliers.
- Between 1986 and 1993, The Body Shop contributed far less than the average annual pretax charitable donations for U.S. companies, according to the Council on Economic Priorities.

Entine published a similar article in a trade magazine, *Drug and Cosmetic Industry*, in February 1995.[15] In this article, he discussed The Body Shop's policies regarding animal testing, citing an internal memo from May 1992. At that time, 46.5 percent of The Body Shop's ingredients had been tested on animals by the ingredients' manufacturers, which was an increase from 34 percent the previous year. This and other practices raised new concerns about the company's slogan "Against Animal Testing" and tainted the company's 1993 victory in its libel suit against the TV program.[16]

The response to Entine's *Business Ethics* article was swift and furious. In June, well before the article's publication, Franklin Development and Consulting, a leading U.S.-based provider of social investment services, had sold 50,000 shares of The Body Shop because of "financial concerns."[17] With rumors spreading about the article in early August, the stock fell from $3.75 to $3.33 per share. Ben Cohen, cofounder of Ben & Jerry's and a *Business Ethics* advisory board member, severed his ties with the magazine. The U.S. and British press ran numerous pieces on the article and its allegations. These articles appeared in newspapers and magazines such as *USA Today,*[18] *The Economist,*[19] *The New York Post,*[20] and *The San Francisco Chronicle.*[21] *The London Daily Mail* secured an exclusive interview with one of the founders of the California Body Shop, who described the company's early years and how they eventually came to legal terms with the Roddicks over the rights to The Body Shop trademark.[22]

Entine was interviewed by a small newsletter, the *Corporate Crime Reporter*, in which he defended and explained his research and the article.[23] One point of interest was Entine's claim that Body Shop products were of "drugstore quality," which he based on the company's use of obsolete ingredients and formulas and a *Consumer Reports* ranking that placed Body Shop Dewberry perfume last out of 66 tested.[24] Dewberry is The Body Shop's trademark scent and is used in all of its stores as part of the "atmosphere." *Corporate Crime Reporter* also noted that another reporter, David Moberg, had brought similar allegations against The Body Shop in a separate article published the same month as Entine's.[25]

In January 1995, *Utne Reader* published a forum including commentaries by Anita Roddick, Entine, Moberg, and Franklin Research founder Joan Bavaria. The forum was remarkable in the sense that it presented a structured set of responses to the charges. Editor Eric Utne noted the rift that the article had caused in the progressive business community and described how the Roddicks, Marjorie Kelly, and other parties had begun holding face-to-face meetings to mend their relationships.[26] Entine described the same meetings as "a family gathering a few days after everyone's favorite uncle was found molesting a neighbor's child. The scandal was on everyone's mind, few would openly talk about it, and most hoped that ignoring it would make it fade away. It didn't."[27] Moberg encouraged consumer watchdog groups to do their jobs more carefully, citing the case of the British group New Consumer, which had previously given The Body Shop high ratings.[28] Roddick maintained that the truth had been sacrificed in a rush to judgment but that she had managed to cope with and learn from the experience.[29]

Gordon Roddick: Defender of the Realm

Anita Roddick has been known to ask her employees what irritates them about their store.[30] Gordon, Anita's husband, is a bit more philosophical in his approach, yet he also speaks out on issues that concern him. After their entry into the U.S. market, the Roddicks became frustrated with the regulatory barriers they encountered. Most of the problems that The Body Shop encountered were small. However, The Body Shop had two full-time employees and one lawyer devoted exclusively to regulatory compliance in the United States. Gordon Roddick estimated that it cost The Body Shop an additional 5 percent of its revenues to do business in the United States,

thus supporting his claim that the American free market economy was anything but free.[31]

Entine's *Business Ethics* article aroused Gordon to new heights of anger according to those who knew him. Body Shop lawyers had successfully persuaded *Vanity Fair* to refrain from publishing a different version of the article earlier in the year. *Vanity Fair* compensated Entine for his work, paying him $15,000 plus an additional $18,000 to cover his expenses in writing and researching the article. Entine was paid only $750 by *Business Ethics* magazine for the article.[32]

Early in Entine's investigation, The Body Shop had hired the international public relations firm of Hill & Knowlton (H&K) to launch a counterattack on Entine's credibility and motives. H&K vice president Frank Mankiewicz, who was a former president of National Public Radio (NPR), sent letters to ABC requesting that it drop its Body Shop story.[33] He also used his contacts at NPR to place an interview with Entine and a follow-up story that included comments from Body Shop supporters on NPR news programs such as "All Things Considered." Further attempts to intimidate *Business Ethics* magazine failed. The editor and publisher, Marjorie Kelly, knew that publishing the article was a risk, but she had checked and rechecked Entine's sources and was satisfied that his charges were sound. However, if The Body Shop chose to sue the magazine, she also knew that the cost of getting to the summary/judgment phase of the trial could put the small magazine out of business.[34]

Gordon Roddick responded to the *Business Ethics* article within a month of its publication by sending a 10-page letter on Body Shop letterhead to all *Business Ethics* subscribers. In this letter, he denied many of the charges made in the article. The letter offered statements by several people that appeared to contradict their own quotations in the article.

Several staff members at *Business Ethics* magazine were not pleased with the letter, which they had received in the mail because they were included as decoys on the subscriber mailing list. This is a common practice in the mailing-list industry to help prevent the misuse of subscriber addresses. The publisher of *Business Ethics* magazine could not recall authorizing the magazine's mailing-list service to rent the list to The Body Shop. It did not take long for the mailing-list company to discover that The Body Shop had obtained the magazine's subscriber list through a third party. Said Ralph Stevens, president of the mailing-list firm, "The Body Shop duped a prominent and legitimate list-brokerage company, a respected magazine, and they duped us…. If this is any indication of the way [The Body Stop does] business, of their regard for honesty and integrity, I give them a failing mark on all counts."[35] In late 1994, The Body Shop hired a business ethics expert to lead a social audit of the company.[36]

The Aftermath and the Future of The Body Shop

By July 1995, Anita Roddick was already considering the possibility of opening Body Shop stores in Cuba, hoping to beat her competitors to that market and at the same time convert the Cubans' social revolution into a profitable yet honorable business revolution.[37] The company was also considering opening retail stores in Eastern European countries. At the same time, the media attention on the company had raised serious concerns among customers, among Body Shop supporters, and within the financial community. Since August 1994, the company's stock price had plummeted by almost 50 percent to 120p, an all-time low. The Roddicks took millions of dollars in paper losses on their holdings, despite having sold a portion of their stock in July 1994.[38] The company faced increased competition from several larger firms, including Procter & Gamble, Avon, Kmart, The Limited, L'Oreal, Crabtree & Evelyn, and Marks & Spencer. Other companies, such as H_2O Plus, were making progress in their efforts to open retail stores that featured products similar to those of The Body Shop. The company had hired Chiat/Day to develop advertising campaigns for worldwide use and conduct a marketing study in the United States.[39] There was at least one report that the company was looking for a U.S. advertising agency.[40] The questions that had been raised as a result of media investigations and The Body Shop's responses left some observers wondering what principles the company espoused and if the company could regain its earlier level of success.

Questions for Discussion

1. How has The Body Shop continued to address the four components of corporate social responsibility?

2. What is your assessment of The Body Shop's response to the *Business Ethics* article? Has The Body Shop misrepresented itself to stakeholders, and if so, how?

3. Jon Entine and others have accused The Body Shop of using intimidation to stifle critics. Does this appear to be a valid criticism? Was The Body Shop justified in hiring Hill & Knowlton to conduct a public relations campaign?

4. Has The Body Shop's reputation been damaged by the incidents in this case? How might the company improve its reputation? Do you believe the steps described in this case, including the hiring of an advertising agency, will help or hinder these efforts?

5. Describe the roles you believe Gordon and Anita Roddick should play in The Body Shop's operations. How might a stockholder, a customer, a supplier, and an employee assess the roles that the Roddicks should play?

Case Endnotes

1. *Body Language—The Body Shop*, World Wide Web site http://www.the-body-shop.com (May 1995).
2. Anita Roddick, *Body and Soul: Profits with Principles, The Amazing Success Story of Anita Roddick & The Body Shop* (New York: Crown, 1991), 135–136.
3. Jennifer Conlin, "Survival of the Fittest," *Working Woman* (February 1994).
4. Faye Brookman, "Prototypes Debut," *Stores* (April 1994), 20–22.
5. Roddick, 1991.
6. Bo Burlingame, "This Woman Has Changed Business Forever," *Inc.* (June 1990).
7. Conlin, 29.
8. Andrew Erdman, "Body Shop Gets into Ink," *Fortune* (October 7, 1991), 166.
9. Laura Zinn, "Whales, Human Rights, Rain Forests—And the Heady Smell of Profits," *Business Week* (July 15, 1991), 114–115.
10. Philip Elmer-Dewitt, "Anita the Agitator," *Time* (January 25, 1993), 52–54.
11. *Ibid.*, 54.
12. *Ibid.*, 54.
13. Conlin, 30–31.
14. Jon Entine, "Shattered Image," *Business Ethics* (October 1994), 23–28.
15. Jon Entine, "The Body Shop: Truth & Consequences," *Drug and Cosmetic Industry* (February 1995), 54–64.
16. Entine, 1995, 62.
17. Judith Valente, "Body Shop Shares Plunge on Reports of Sales by Funds and FTC Inquiry," *The Wall Street Journal* (August 24, 1994).
18. Ellen Neuborne, "Body Shop in a Lather over Ethics Criticism," *USA Today* (August 29, 1995), B1.
19. "Storm in a Bubble Bath," *The Economist* (September 3, 1994), 56.
20. Martin Peers, "Journalist's Probe Hits Body Shop," *New York Post* (August 25, 1994), 33.

21. Dirk Beveridge, "Uproar Threatens Body Shop Stock," *The San Francisco Chronicle* (August 25, 1994), D1.
22. Rebecca Hardy, "American Woman Recalls the Heady Days of Her Hippy Perfume Store … And a £2.3m Deal with the Roddicks," *London Daily Mail* (August 28, 1994).
23. "Interview with Jon Entine," *Corporate Crime Reporter* (September 19, 1994), 13–18.
24. "Interview with Jon Entine," 17.
25. David Moberg, "The Beauty Myth," *In These Times* (September 19–October 2, 1994).
26. Eric Utne, "Beyond the Body Shop Brouhaha," *Utne Reader* (January–February 1995), 101–102.
27. Jon Entine, "Exploiting Idealism," *Utne Reader* (January–February 1995), 108–109.
28. David Moberg, "Call in the Watchdogs!" *Utne Reader* (January–February 1995), 101–102.
29. Anita Roddick, "Who Judges the Judges?" *Utne Reader* (January–February 1995), 104.
30. Elmer-Dewitt, 52.
31. "Regulation Time: 60 Seconds with … Gordon Roddick," *Inc.* (June, 1993), 16.
32. Ruth G. Davis, "The Body Shop Plays Hardball," *New York Magazine* (September 19, 1994), 16.
33. *Ibid.*
34. Maureen Clark, "Socially Responsible Business Brawl," *The Progressive* (March 1995), 14.
35. *Ibid.*
36. "Ethics Study for Body Shop," *The New York Times* (October 31, 1994), C7.
37. Conlin, 73.
38. "Stake Reduced in Body Shop," *The New York Times* (July 11, 1994), C7.
39. James Fallon, "Body Shop Regroups to Meet Competition in Crowded U.S. Arena," *Women's Wear Daily* (October 21, 1994), 1.
40. Anthony Ramirez, "Body Shop Seeks Its First U.S. Agency," *The New York Times* (June 27, 1995), D7.

Case 18

The Body Shop International PLC: Toward the Future

By 1998, The Body Shop International had grown into a multinational enterprise with almost 1,600 stores and 5,000 employees in 47 countries.[1] That year, after several years of lackluster financial performance, Anita Roddick gave the company's CEO post to a professional manager and became executive cochairman with her husband, Gordon. Anita maintained that job titles were meaningless, anyway.[2]

Despite the change, the company's financial performance between 1995 and 1997 continued to be unimpressive:[3] Worldwide sales revenue and operating profits grew from $303 million and $21 million in 1995 to $377 million and $19 million, respectively, in 1997.

In 1995 to 1996, The Body Shop began to experiment with advertising in North American markets. According to one observer, The Body Shop originally

This case was prepared by Archie B. Carroll, University of Georgia, using publicly available information.

thought that its brands and human-rights agenda would create valuable word-of-mouth promotion among socially conscious consumers and that advertising would not be needed. The Body Shop's antiadvertising strategy largely paid off in the United Kingdom and other European nations, where human rights activism and commerce blended more seamlessly and consumers had fewer brands and retailers than in the United States. The strategy did not work effectively in the United States, where brand differentiation was crucial. In 1997, for example, The Body Shop's samestores sales in the United States dropped 6 percent, the company's worst performance since entering the U.S. market 10 years earlier.[4]

Since it has begun, U.S. advertising has been piecemeal, often targeted toward the Christmastime holiday sales push. In addition, it has been quirky. For example, Anita Roddick taped a radio spot that slammed the cosmetics industry. In the radio spot, Roddick said, "If more men and more women understood what really makes people beautiful, most cosmetic companies would be out of business."[5]

The Body Shop has seemed to be trying hard to get its act together in the U.S. market. It hired a new CEO in fall 1998 and created the position of vice president for promotions. These are significant moves for the company, but it may take more than advertising to turn things around. The Body Shop typically plays down product efficacy in favor of hyping product ethicality. A case in point is its Mango Body Butter, whose ingredients the company promotes as from a "woman's cooperative in Ghana." Sean Mehegan, a writer for *Brandweek*, summarized the company's dilemma this way: "How much American consumers care about such claims lies at the heart of whether The Body Shop can turn itself around here."[6]

The Body Shop's Social Audits

In 1994, perhaps in response to the *Business Ethics* magazine article by Jon Entine calling its integrity into question and perhaps on its own initiative, The Body Shop began an elaborate program of annual social audits examining, in particular, its environmental, social, and animal protection initiatives. Through the social audit program, which the company based on mission statements and goals in numerous social performance categories, the company established detailed social and ecological milestones for 1995–1997. In its 218-page *Values Report 1997*, the company reported its progress.[7]

The Body Shop set policies in three areas: human and civil rights, environmental sustainability, and animal protection. In each category, the company set forth a conceptual framework for the auditing process. The auditing process in each category depended heavily on stakeholder interviews. The stakeholders who were interviewed included employees, international franchisees, customers, suppliers, shareholders, and local community/campaigning groups. The company identified the media as a potential stakeholder group for inclusion in future social auditing cycles.[8]

Allegations Continue

In 1998, The Body Shop continued to face charges that could threaten its future. The company faced a possible flood of allegations and lawsuits by franchisees charging fraudulent presentations by the company when they bought their franchises. Many U.S. franchisees have been angry at what they see as unfair buyback terms if they want to get out of the business. There is talk of group

action that could involve claims in the hundreds of millions of dollars.[9]

An example of the kind of lawsuit being filed is that of Jim White, who was asking for $32 million in damages. He was suing The Body Shop for fraud, fraudulent inducement, and inequitable treatment of franchisees. White claims that the company offered rock-bottom buyback prices to franchisees caught in a 5-year spiral of declining U.S. sales. White claimed he was offered only 20 cents on the dollar and that others were offered as low as 5 cents on the dollar.[10]

The Early 2000s

The early 2000s have continued to be tumultuous for The Body Shop. The company has continued to grow, but sales and profits have not been good. As a result of poor Christmas sales in 2000, its annual profits were down 55 percent as it entered 2001. In the United Kingdom, the company finds itself operating in a much more competitive marketplace than its beginnings 25 years ago. Most high street retail chains now are fielding their own "natural" cosmetics and toiletries, and price and promotional battles have left the company's products more expensive than its rivals'.[11] In 2001 The Body Shop began reviewing its communications strategies and was considering the appointment of an advertising agency. According to one observer, the company has come under increasing pressure to move beyond its traditional antipathy to advertising as it loses ground to rivals.[12] Also, in 2001, The Body Shop has stated that it is planning to soften its campaigning image after admitting that its strategy of fighting for social and environmental causes has produced mixed results. Steve McIvor, head of communications, said that the mixture of politics and marketing has not always worked for the company and that the brand will become "less soap-boxy, patronizing, and lecturing." In addition, the company admitted that many of its new products have not been successful and that the retailer would return to "heritage" products to restore customers' faith in the brand.[13]

In September 2001, a major *Fortune* magazine article featured some of the legal difficulties The Body Shop was facing because of conflicts with franchisees. It was reported that eight U.S. Body Shop franchisees, who owned 13 locations, were accusing the parent company of impeding their business. In December 2000, this group filed a lawsuit against the company asking for damages in the neighborhood of $2 million. One major complaint was that the company-owned stores were getting much better treatment than the franchisee-owned stores. Franchisee owners complained of the company failing to deliver them products while the company-owned stores had no problem getting products. Some franchisee owners have seen this chronic out-of-stock problem as a ploy to force them to sell their franchises back for a fraction on the dollar.[14]

What about Anita Roddick now? She published her second book, *Business As Unusual: The Triumph of Anita Roddick and the Body Shop*, in 2001. She is still the cochair of The Body Shop, but says her first priority is now writing. She is already working on another manuscript. She explained, "I'm at the point in my life where I want to be heard." She adds, "I have knowledge and I want to pass it on."[15] In an interview with *Across the Board* magazine published in 2001, Anita commented on her experiences with professional consultants and executives who are not as concerned as she is about preserving The Body Shop's values. She stated: "The hardest thing for me are the marketing people, because they focus on us as a brand and our customers as consumers. We've never called it a brand; we call it The Body Shop. In 20 years, we've never, ever, ever called a customer a consumer. Customers aren't there to consume. They're there to live, love, die, get married, have friendships—they're not put on this planet to bloody consume."[16]

The future is uncertain for The Body Shop. Journalists like Jon Entine continue to write articles that are critical of The Body Shop.[17] Despite the criticism, the company continues to make management and strategic changes and to pursue social programs and social audits. In the hard, cold world of global competition, founder Anita Roddick has experienced some tough lessons in the past decade. Although she may still believe that the purpose of a business is not just to generate profits, it is becoming increasingly apparent that the tension between financial and social performance requires delicate balancing of, and careful attention to, both. At stake is nothing less than the firm's survival and Roddick's stage for bringing about social change.

Questions for Discussion

1. Has Anita Roddick betrayed her philosophy about advertising by beginning to advertise in U.S. markets? Does this decision have ethical implications? Or, is it just a business decision?

2. Does it seem like The Body Shop will make it in North America? Why or why not?

3. Will The Body Shop's social auditing program save the firm's reputation? Has the firm "snapped back" from the damage done to its reputation in the mid-1990s?

4. Do the low buyback prices offered to U.S. franchisees reflect poor Body Shop ethics or just the economic reality of risky investments?

5. Is The Body Shop regarded today as a socially responsible and ethical firm? Research the answer to this question and be prepared to report your findings.

6. At the end of these cases, what is your impression of Anita Roddick? Comment on her strengths and weaknesses as a businessperson and leader.

Case Endnotes

1. "Capitalism and Cocoa Butter," *The Economist* (May 16, 1998), 66–67.
2. *Ibid*. Also see Ernest Beck, "Body Shop Founder Roddick Steps Aside as CEO," *The Wall Street Journal* (May 13, 1998), B14.
3. *Values Report 1997*, The Body Shop (October 1997), 150.
4. Sean Mehegan, "Not Tested on Humans," *Brandweek* (May 19, 1997), 54.
5. *Ibid*.
6. *Ibid*.
7. *Values Report 1997*, 7–12.
8. *Ibid*., 10–12.
9. Jan Spooner, "Body Shop Faces U.S. Legal Fights," *Financial Mail* (London) (February 22, 1998).
10. *Ibid*.
11. Harriet Marsh, "Has the Body Shop Lost Its Direction for Good?" *Marketing* (London) (May 10, 2001), 19.
12. Matthew Cowen, "Body Shop Overhauls Ad Strategy," *Campaign* (July 27, 2001), 1. Also see Mairi Clark, "Live Issue/The Body Shop," *Campaign* (August 3, 2001), 19.
13. James Curtis, "Body Shop Plans to Scale Down Its Political Activity," *Marketing* (London) (July 26, 2001), 3.
14. Carlye Adler, "The Disenfranchised," *Fortune* (September 2001), 66–72.
15. Mike Hofman, "Anita Roddick: The Body Shop International, Established in 1976," *Inc.* (April 30, 2001), 61.
16. Matthew Budman, "Questioning Authority," *Across the Board* (January 2001), 15–16.
17. Jon Entine, "Vivisecting the Anti-Vivisectionist Movement," *Drug & Cosmetic Industry* (January 1997), 38–41.

Toxic Tacos? The Case of Genetically Modified Foods

In September 2000, the Genetically Engineered Food Alert Coalition, a coalition of environmental and consumer groups, accused Taco Bell of using StarLink genetically modified (GM) corn in their taco shells. The FDA [U.S. Food and Drug Administration] had approved the StarLink gene for animal (but not human) consumption. The incident prompted the recall of 300 corn-based foods and alarmed the public about the possible dangers of genetically modified foods.[1]

The debates surrounding genetically modified food have continued to grow since the StarLink incident. According to David Roy of the Centre for Bioethics at the Clinical Research Institute of Montreal, the debates often produce "more heat than light." They are more emotional in nature than they are intellectual. One of the main dangers of the GM food debate is that neither side is listening to the other: Involved parties "tend to let debates become excessively polarized."[2]

Some of the Current Arguments

Proponents for GM foods argue that their potential risks should be judged once scientific consensus has been reached. In the meantime, they say these GM crops will feed a hungry world by multiplying per-acre yields and at the same time reduce the need for herbicides and pesticides. GMs detractors, on the other hand, claim that possible future benefits of the technology should not outweigh present dangers. They recommend a slowdown in order that society may digest innovations of past years. They want long-term outcomes to be "clearer" before anything else is done.

Science-based arguments contrast for both parties as well. Governments, often citing company studies, make the claim that GM crops are similar to non-GM ones and, therefore, do not pose a threat to consumers. Environmental watchdog groups, like the U.S. Public Interest Research Group, a member of the Genetically Engineered Food Alert Coalition, disagree. Studies

This case was prepared by Joseph G. Gerard and Ann K. Buchholtz, University of Georgia.

claiming similarity between GM and non-GM crops, they say, are flawed and conclude nontoxicity without sufficient evidence.[3]

Going to Extremes?

Neither pole is exempt from accusations of extremist thinking. Anti-"GMers" believe that researchers and developers of new technology promise too much. In recent years, a variety of plants that produce their own pesticide—as well as herbicide-resistant seed and plants, and others with more "exotic" features—have made it to the marketplace where their benefits are lauded and their deficits seem nonexistent. But, ask GM food opponents, has testing been sufficiently long term to really test environmental impact? Have possible dangers for wildlife and plants that consume or ingest GM food been tested? What is the effect of that food as it moves through the food chain? Has gene flow been controlled? Some say that new reports provide evidence that studies are often too limited in both space and time to reach a conclusion.[4]

GM proponents respond that their detractors often exaggerate environmental hazards, do not substantiate their claims with scientific evidence, and are simply reacting out of fear. Those who stand by GM technology then point to examinations by government agencies "so long and rigorous that many standard foods wouldn't pass." Their field research never uncovers even a slight headache. Some even say it would be wrong to try to replicate the research.[5]

Questions for Discussion

1. What are the ethical issues in this case?

2. Do you think that either group, pro-GM or anti-GM foods, is correct while the other group is wrong? If so, what reasoning do you give for supporting the position of one group over the other? Is it possible for both to be right? What ethical concepts help you decide?

3. Is there any way to bridge the gap between these groups? If so, what would the advantages and disadvantages be?

4. If you were crafting GMO (genetically modified organism) public policy, what would you recommend?

Case Endnotes

1. "The StarLink Fallout," *Successful Farming* (January 2001), 33–39.
2. "Biotechnology and Bioethics," *Maclean's* (November 5, 2001), 38.
3. Geoffrey Lean, "Ask No Questions, Hear No Truths; Geoffrey Lean on the Scandalous Treatment of a Scientist Who Dared to Cast Doubt on the Safety of GM Foods," *The New Statesman* (September 24, 2001).
4. *Ibid.*
5. "Biotechnology and Bioethics."

Case 20

Nike Inc.

In January 2001, Jonah Peretti decided to customize his Nike shoes and visited the Nike iD Web site. The company allows customers to personalize their Nikes with the colors of their choice and their own personal 16-character message. Peretti chose the word "sweatshop" for his Nikes.

After receiving his order, Nike informed Peretti via e-mail that the term "sweatshop" represents "inappropriate slang" and is not considered viable for print on a Nike shoe. Thus, his order was summarily rejected. Peretti e-mailed Nike, arguing that the term "sweatshop" is present in Webster's dictionary and could not possibly be considered inappropriate slang. Nike responded by quoting the company's rules, which state that the company can refuse to print anything on its shoes that it does not deem appropriate. Peretti replied that he was changing his previous order and would instead like to order a pair of shoes with a "color snapshot of the 10-year-old Vietnamese girl who makes my shoes." He never received a response.[1]

Before Nike could blink an eye, the situation turned into a public relations nightmare. Peretti forwarded the e-mail exchange to a few friends, who forwarded it to a few friends, and so forth. Within 6 weeks of his initial order, the story appeared in *The Wall Street Journal*,

This case was written by Bryan Dennis, University of Georgia.

USA Today, and *The Village Voice*. Peretti himself appeared on "The Today Show" and he estimates that 2 million people have seen the e-mail. At the height of the incident, Peretti was receiving 500 e-mails a day from people who had read the e-mail from as far away as Asia, Australia, Europe, and South America.[2,3]

Nike refused to admit any wrongdoing in the incident and stated that they reserve the right to refuse any order for whatever reason. Beth Gourney, a spokesperson for Nike, had the following to say regarding the incident:

Clearly, he [Peretti] was attempting to stir up trouble; he has admitted it. He's not an activist. Mr. Peretti does not understand our labor policy. If he did, he would know that we do not hire children; our minimum age for hiring is 18 ... and we don't apologize for not putting the word "sweatshop" because our policy clearly states: "We reserve the right to cancel any order up to 24 hours after it has been submitted."[4]

Nike Inc. is no stranger to sweatshop allegations. Ever since the mid-1990s, the company has been subject to negative press, lawsuits, and demonstrations on college campuses alleging that firm's overseas contractors subject employees to work in inhumane conditions for low wages. As Philip Knight, the CEO and founder of Nike, once lamented, "The Nike product has become synonymous with slave wages, forced overtime, and arbitrary abuse."[5]

History of Nike Inc.

Philip Knight started his own athletic shoe distribution company in 1964. Using his Plymouth Reliant as a warehouse, he began importing and distributing track shoes from Onitsuka Company, Ltd., a Japanese manufacturer. First-year sales of $8,000 resulted in a profit of $254. After 8 years, annual sales reached $2 million, and the firm employed 45 people. However, Onitsuka saw the huge potential of the American shoe market and dropped Knight's relatively small company in favor of larger, more experienced distributors. Knight was forced to start anew. However, instead of importing and distributing another firm's track shoes, he decided to design his own shoes and create his own company. The name he chose for his new company was "Nike."[6]

When the company began operations, Knight contracted the manufacture of Nike's shoes to two firms in Japan. Shortly thereafter, Nike began to contract with firms in Taiwan and Korea. In 1977, Nike purchased two shoe manufacturing facilities in the United States—one in Maine, the other in New Hampshire. Eventually, the two plants became so unprofitable that the firm was forced to close them. The loss due to the write-off of the plants was approximately $10 million in a year in which the firm's total profit was $15 million. The firm had a successful IPO in 1980, 8 years after the company was founded. Currently, Nike is the largest athletic shoe company in the world.[7]

Nike does not own a single shoe or apparel factory. Instead, the firm contracts the production of its products to independently owned manufacturers. Today, practically all Nike subcontracted factories are in countries such as Indonesia, Vietnam, China, and Thailand, where the labor costs are significantly less than those in the United States. Worldwide, roughly 53,000 people are employed in factories that manufacture Nike products. The company gives the following as a rough breakdown of the costs per shoe:

Consumer pays: $65
Retailer pays: $32.50 to Nike, and then doubles the price for retail
Nike pays: $16.25 and then doubles the price to retailers for shipping, insurance, duties, R&D, marketing, sales, administration, and profits

The $16.25 price paid the factory includes:
Materials: $10.75
Labor: $2.43
Overhead + Depreciation: $2.10
Factory Profit: $0.97
Total Costs: $16.25[8]

Even in today's hi-tech environment, the production of athletic shoes is still a labor-intensive process. For example, for practically all athletic shoes, the upper portion of the shoe must be sewn together with the lower portion by hand. The soles must be manually glued together. Although most leaders in the industry are confident that practically the entire production process will someday be automated, it will still be many years before the industry will not have to rely upon human labor.

Nike's use of overseas contractors is not unique in the athletic shoe and apparel industry. All other major athletic shoe manufacturers also contract with overseas manufacturers, albeit to various degrees. However, one athletic shoe firm, New Balance Inc., is somewhat of an anomaly and operates six factories in the United States.[9]

Nike spends heavily on endorsements and advertising and pays several top athletes well over a million dollars a year in endorsement contracts. In 2000, golfer Tiger Woods entered into a reported 5-year contract worth $100 million. That same year, Vince Carter, a basketball player for the Toronto Raptors, signed a reported $30 million endorsement contract.[10] Nike has a policy of not officially divulging the financial details of its endorsement contracts. The firm spent $978.2 million dollars in advertising and promotion during fiscal year 2000. This figure includes all endorsement contracts as well as media advertising and advertising production costs.[11] Almost all of Nike's competitors also rely on endorsement contracts as a marketing tool.

Interestingly, New Balance Inc. has developed a different strategy. They do not use professional athletes to market their products. According to their "Endorsed by No One" policy, New Balance instead chooses to invest in product research and development and forgoes expensive endorsement contracts.[12]

The Sweatshop Movement Versus Nike

There is one pivotal event that is largely responsible for introducing the term "sweatshop" to the American public. In 1996, Kathie Lee Gifford, cohost of the nationally syndicated talk show "Live with Regis and Kathie Lee," endorsed her own line of clothing for Wal-Mart. During that same year, labor rights activists disclosed that her "Kathie Lee Collection" was made in Honduras by seamstresses who earn 31 cents an hour and are sometimes required to work 20 hour days. Traditionally known for her pleasant, jovial demeanor and her love of children, Kathie Lee was outraged. She tearfully informed the public that she was unaware that her clothes were being made in so-called "sweatshops" and vowed to do whatever she could to promote the antisweatshop cause.[13]

In a national press conference, Gifford named Michael Jordan as another celebrity who, like herself, endorses products without knowing under what conditions the products are made. At the time, Michael Jordan was Nike's premier endorser and was reportedly under a $20 million per year contract with the firm.[14] Nike, the number-one athletic shoe brand in the world, soon found itself under attack by the rapidly growing antisweatshop movement.

Shortly after the Gifford story broke, Joel Joseph, chairman of the Made in the USA Foundation, accused Nike of paying underage Indonesian workers 14 cents an hour to make the company's line of Air Jordan Shoes. He also claimed that the total payroll of Nike's six Indonesian subcontracted factories is less that the reported $20 million per year that Jordan receives from his endorsement contract with Nike. The Made in the USA Foundation is one of the organizations that ignited the Gifford controversy and is largely financed by labor unions and U.S. apparel manufacturers that are against free trade with low-wage countries.[15]

Nike quickly pointed out that Air Jordan shoes are made in Taiwan, not Indonesia. Additionally, the company maintained that employee wages are fair and higher than the government-mandated minimum wage in all of the countries where the firm has contracted factories. The company released the following data as proof of its wages:

Country	Minimum Monthly Wage	Average Monthly Wage at Nike Factories
Taiwan	14,124 NT$	25,609 NT$
South Korea	Won 306,030	Won 640,000
Indonesia	115,000 rupiah	239,800 rupiah
China	RMB 276	RMB 636
Thailand	2,950–3,150 baht	4,435 baht
Vietnam	331.050 VND$	640.030 VND$

Nike asserted that the entry-level income of an Indonesian factory is five times that of a farmer. The firm also claimed that an assistant line supervisor in a Chinese subcontracted factory earns more than a surgeon with 20 years of experience.[16] In response to the allegations regarding Michael Jordan's endorsement contract, Nike

stated that the total wages in Indonesia are $50 million a year, which is well over what the firm pays Jordan.[17]

Nike soon faced more negative publicity. Michael Moore, the movie director whose 1989 documentary *Roger and Me* shed light on the plight of laid-off auto workers in Flint, Michigan, and damaged the reputation of General Motors chairman Roger Smith, interviewed Philip Knight for his 1997 movie *The Big One*. On camera, Knight referred to some employees at subcontracted factories as "poor little Indonesian workers." Moore's cameras also recorded the following exchange between Moore and Knight:

Moore: Twelve-year-olds working in [Indonesian] factories? That's OK with you?

Knight: They're not 12-year-olds working in factories ... the minimum age is 14.

Moore: How about 14, then? Doesn't that bother you?

Knight: No.[18]

Knight, the only CEO interviewed in the movie, received harsh criticism for his comments. Nike alleged that the comments were taken out of context and were deceitful because Moore failed to include Knight's pledge to make a transition from a 14- to a 16-year-old minimum age labor force. Nike prepared its own video that includes the entire interview.[19]

In early 1998, Thomas Nguyen, founder of Vietnam Labor Watch, inspected several of Nike's plants in Vietnam and reported cases of worker abuse. At one factory that manufactures Nike products, a supervisor punished 56 women for wearing inappropriate work shoes by forcing them to run around the factory in the hot sun. Twelve workers fainted and were taken to the hospital. Nguyen also reported that workers were only allowed one bathroom break and two drinks of water during each 8-hour shift. Nike responded that the supervisor who was involved in the fainting incident has been suspended and that the firm had hired an independent accounting firm to look into the matters further.[20]

In early 1997, Nike hired former Atlanta mayor Andrew Young, a vocal opponent of sweatshops and child labor, to review the firm's overseas labor practices. Neither party has disclosed the fee that Young received for his services. Young toured 12 factories in Vietnam, Indonesia, and China and was reportedly given unlimited access. However, he was constantly accompanied by Nike representatives during all factory tours. Furthermore, Young relied upon Nike translators when communicating with factory workers.[21]

In his 75-page report, Young concluded that "Nike is doing a good job, but it can do better." He provided Nike with six recommendations for improving the working conditions at subcontracted factories. Nike immediately responded to the report and agreed to implement all six recommendations. Young did not address the issue of wages and standards of living because he felt he lacks the "academic credentials" for such a judgment.[22]

Public reaction to Young's report is mixed. Some praise Nike. However, many of Nike's opponents disregarded Young's report as biased and incomplete. One went so far as to state the report could not have been better if Nike had written it themselves and questioned Young's independence.[23,24]

In 1998, Nike hired Maria Eitel to the newly created position of vice president for corporate and social responsibility. Eitel was formerly a public relations executive for Microsoft. Her responsibilities are to oversee Nike's labor practices, environmental affairs, and involvement in the global community. Although this move is applauded by some, others are skeptical and claim that Nike's move is nothing more than a publicity stunt.[25]

Later that same year, Philip Knight gave a speech at the National Press Club in Washington, DC, and announced six initiatives that are intended to improve the working conditions in its overseas factories. The firm chose to raise the minimum hiring age from 16 to 18 years of age. Nike also decided to expand its worker education program so that all workers in Nike factories will have the option to take middle and high school equivalency tests.[26] The director of Global Exchange, one of Nike's staunchest opponents, called the initiatives "significant and very positive." He also added that "we feel that the measures—if implemented—could be exciting."[27]

College Students, Organized Labor, and Nike

Colleges and universities have direct ties to the many athletic shoe and apparel companies (such as Nike, Champion, and Reebok) that contract with overseas manufacturers. Most universities receive money from athletic shoe and apparel corporations in return for outfitting the university's sports teams with the firm's products. In 1997, Nike gave $7.1 million to the University of North Carolina for the right to outfit all of UNC's sports teams with products bearing the Nike Swoosh logo.[28] Additionally, academic institutions allow firms to manufacture apparel bearing the university's official name, colors, and insignias in return for a fee. In 1998, the University of Michigan received $5.7 million dollars in licensing fees.[29] Most of these contract and licensing fees are allocated toward scholarships and other academic programs.

In 1995, the Union of Needletrades, Industrial and Textile Employees (UNITE) was founded. The union, a member of the AFL-CIO [American Federation of Labor—Congress of Industrial Organizations], is formed by the merger of the International Ladies' Garment Workers' Union and the Amalgamated Clothing and Textile Workers Union and represents 250,000 workers in North America and Puerto Rico. Most of the union members work in the textile and apparel industry. In 1996, UNITE launched a "Stop Sweatshops" campaign after the Kathie Lee Gifford story broke to "link union, consumers, student, civil rights and women's groups in the fight against sweatshops at home and abroad."[30]

In 1997, UNITE, along with the AFL-CIO, recruited dozens of college students for summer internships. Many of the students referred to that summer as "Union Summer and it had a similar impact as Freedom Summer did for students during the civil rights movement."[31] The United Students Against Sweatshops (USAS) organization was formed the following year. The USAS was founded and is led by former UNITE summer interns.[32]

The USAS has chapters at over 50 universities across the United States. Since its inception, the organization has staged a large number of campus demonstrations that are reminiscent of the 1960s. One notable demonstration occurred on the campus of UNC in 1997. Students of the Nike Awareness Campaign protested against the university's contract with Nike due to the firm's alleged sweatshop abuses. More than 100 students demanded that the university not renew its contract with Nike and rallied outside the office of the university's chancellor. More than 50 other universities, such as the University of Wisconsin and Duke, staged similar protests and sit-ins.[33]

In response to the protests at UNC, Nike invited the editor of the university's student newspaper to tour Nike's overseas contractors to examine the working conditions firsthand. Nike offered to fund the trip by pledging $15,000 toward the students' travel and accommodations costs. Ironically, Michael Jordan is an alumnus of UNC.[34]

Critics of the USAS contend that the student organization is merely a puppet of UNITE and organized labor. They cite the fact that the AFL-CIO has spent more than

$3 million dollars on internships and outreach programs with the alleged intent of interesting students in careers as union activists. The founders of the USAS are former UNITE interns. The USAS admits that UNITE has tipped off the student movement as to the whereabouts of alleged sweatshop factories. Also, in an attempt to spur campus interest in the sweatshop cause, UNITE sent two sweatshop workers on a five-campus tour. They have also coached students via phone during sit-ins and paid for regularly scheduled teleconferences between antisweatshop student leaders on different campuses. According to Allan Ryan, a Harvard University lawyer who has negotiated with the USAS, "[T]he students are vocal, but it's hard to get a viewpoint from them that does not reflect that of UNITE."[35]

Many students have denied allegations that they are being manipulated by organized labor and claim that they discovered the sweatshop issues on their own. Others acknowledge the assistance of organized labor but claim it is "no different from [student] civil rights activists using the NAACP in the 1960s."[36] John Sweeney, president of the AFL-CIO, claims the role of organized labor is not one of manipulation but of motivation. Others assert that the union merely provides moral support.[37]

Regardless of the AFL-CIO's intentions, the students have had a positive impact upon the promotion of organized labor's antisweatshop agenda. According to the director of one of the several human rights groups that are providing assistance to the students:

> At this moment, the sweatshop protest is definitely being carried on the backs of university students. If a hundred students hold a protest, they get a page in The New York Times. If a hundred union people did that, they'd be locked up.[38]

The Fair Labor Association and the Worker Rights Consortium

In 1996, a presidential task force of industry and human rights representatives was given the job of addressing the sweatshop issue. The key purpose of this task force was to develop a workplace code of conduct and a system for monitoring factories to ensure compliance. In 1998, the task force created the Fair Labor Association (FLA) to accomplish these goals. This organization is made up of consumer and human rights groups as well as footwear and apparel manufacturers. Nike is one of the first companies to join the FLA. As

of July 2001, many other major manufacturers (Levi Strauss & Co., Liz Claiborne, Patagonia, Polo Ralph Lauren, Reebok, Eddie Bauer, and Phillips-Van Heusen) along with 157 colleges and universities have also joined the FLA.[39]

Members of the FLA must follow the principles set forth in the organization's Workplace Code of Conduct. Member organizations that license or contract with overseas manufacturers or suppliers are responsible for ensuring that factory employees are paid either the minimum wage as required by law or the average industry wage, whichever is higher. Additionally, the code of conduct sets limits on the number of hours employees can work, allows workers the right to collective bargaining, and forbids discrimination.[40]

Each member firm must conduct an internal audit of every manufacturing facility on a yearly basis. Furthermore, members of the FLA must disclose to the FLA the location of all subcontracted factories. This information will not be made public. The FLA uses a team of external auditors to monitor the compliance of these factories with the FLA's code of conduct. For the first year of a firm's membership, 30 percent of the total number of factories will be examined by the FLA. After the first year, 5 to 15 percent will be monitored. These monitoring activities consist of a combination of announced and unannounced factory visits, and results are made available to the public.[41]

The USAS opposed several of the FLA's key components and created the Worker Rights Consortium (WRC) as an alternative to the FLA. The WRC asserts that the prevailing industry or legal minimum wage in some countries is too low and does not provide employees with the basic human needs they require. They propose that factories should instead pay a higher "living wage" that takes into account the wage required to provide factory employees with enough income to afford housing, energy, nutrition, clothing, health care, education, potable water, child care, transportation, and savings. Additionally, the WRC supports public disclosure of all factory locations and the right to monitor any factory at any time. As of July 2001, 80 colleges and universities have joined the WRC and agreed to adhere to its policies. UNITE and the AFL-CIO support the WRC and are opposed to the FLA.[42]

Nike, a member and supporter of the FLA, opposes the Worker Rights Consortium. The firm states that a concept of a living wage is impractical as "there is no common, agreed-upon definition of the living wage. Definitions range from complex mathematical formulas to vague philosophical notions." Additionally, Nike is opposed to the WRC's proposal that the location of all factories be publicly disclosed. The firm states that this is classified information that may divulge trade secrets to its competitors. Nike also claims that the monitoring provisions set out by the WRC are unrealistic and biased towards organized labor.[43]

In 2000, the University of Oregon joined the WRC. Philip Knight, an alumnus of the university, had previously contributed over $50 million to the university—$30 million for academics and $20 million for athletics. Upon hearing that his alma mater had joined the WRC, Knight was shocked. He withdrew a proposed $30 million donation and stated that the "the bonds of trust, which allowed me to give at a high level, have been shredded" and "there will be no further donations of any kind to the University of Oregon."[44,45]

Epilogue

In May 2001, Harsh Saini, Nike's corporate and social responsibility manager, acknowledged that the firm may not have handled the sweatshop issue as well as they could have and stated that Nike had not been adequately monitoring its subcontractors in overseas operations until the media and other organizations revealed the presence of sweatshops.

> We were a bunch of shoe geeks who expanded so much without thinking of being socially responsible that we went from being a very big sexy brand name to suddenly becoming the poster boy for everything bad in manufacturing.

She added, "We realized that if we still want to be the brand of choice in 20 years, we had certain responsibilities to fulfill."[46]

In early 2001, Oregon's state board of higher education cast doubt on the legality of the University of Oregon's WRC membership, and the university dissolved its ties with the labor organization.[47] In September of the same year, Phil Knight renewed his financial support. Although the exact amount of Knight's donation was kept confidential, it is sufficient enough to ensure that the $85 million expansion of the university's football stadium will go through as originally planned. In 2000, the stadium expansion plans suffered a significant setback when Knight withdrew his funding. Many of the proposed additions, such as a 12,000-seat capacity increase and 32 brand new skyboxes, are now guaranteed to happen, largely due to Knight's pledge of financial support.[48,49]

Nike released its first corporate social responsibility report in October 2001. According to Phil Knight, "[I]n this report, Nike for the first time has assembled a comprehensive public review of our corporate responsibility practices."[50] The report cites several areas in which the firm could do better, such as worker conditions in Indonesia and Mexico. The report, compiled by both internal auditors and outside monitors, also notes that Nike is one of only four companies that has joined a World Wildlife Fund program to reduce greenhouse admissions. Jason Mark, a spokesman for Global Exchange, one of Nike's chief critics, praised the report and stated that Nike is "obviously responding to consumer concerns."[51]

Questions for Discussion

1. What are the ethical and social issues in this case?
2. Why should Nike be held responsible for what happens in factories that it does not own? Does Nike have a responsibility to ensure that factory workers receive a "living wage"?
3. Is it ethical for Nike to pay endorsers millions while its factory employees receive a few dollars a day?
4. Is Nike's responsibility to monitor its subcontracted factories a legal, economic, social, or philanthropic responsibility? What was it 15 years ago? What will it be 15 years from now?
5. What could Nike have done, if anything, to prevent the damage to its corporate reputation? What steps should Nike take in the future? Is it "good business" for Nike to acknowledge its past errors and become more socially responsible?

Case Endnotes

1. Copy of e-mail exchange found at Department of Personal Freedom Web site, http://www.shey.net/niked.html.
2. Ibid.
3. ABC News Web site, http://abcnews.go.com/sections/business/DailyNews/nike010402.html.
4. Ibid.
5. Bien Hoa, "Job Opportunity or Exploitation," Los Angeles Times (April 18, 1999).
6. Philip Knight, "Global Manufacturing: The Nike Story Is Just Good Business," Vital Speeches of the Day, 64(20): 637–640.
7. Ibid, 637–640.
8. Nike Web site, http://www.nikebiz.com/labor/faq.shtml.
9. New Balance Web site, http://www.newbalance.com/.

10. Louise Lee, "Nike Tries Getting in Touch with Its Feminine Side," *Business Week* (October 30, 2000), 139.
11. *Nike Inc. 2000 Annual Report.*
12. New Balance Web site, http://www.newbalance.com/.
13. David Bauman, "After the Tears, Gifford Testifies on Sweatshops—She Turns Lights, Cameras on Issue," *Seattle Times* (July 16, 1996), A3.
14. Del Jones, "Critics Tie Sweatshop Sneakers to 'Air' Jordan," *USA Today* (June 6, 1996), 1B.
15. *Ibid.*
16. Nike Press Release (June 6, 1996).
17. Del Jones, 1B.
18. Garry Trudeau, "Sneakers in Tinseltown," *Time* (April 20, 1998), 84.
19. William J. Holstein, "Casting Nike as the Bad Guy," *U.S. News & World Report* (September 22, 1997), 49.
20. Verena Dobnik, "Nike Shoe Contractor Abuses Alleged," *The Atlanta Journal-Constitution* (March 18, 1997), A14.
21. Simon Beck, "Nike in Sweat over Heat Raised by Claims of Biases Assessment," *South China Morning Post* (July 6, 1997), 2.
22. Matthew C. Quinn, "Footwear Maker's Labor Pledge Unlikely to Stamp Out Criticism," *The Atlanta Journal-Constitution* (June 25, 1997), F8.
23. G. Pascal Zachary, "Nike Tries to Quell Exploitation Charges," *The Wall Street Journal* (June 15, 1997).
24. Simon Beck, 2.
25. Bill Richards, "Nike Hires an Executive from Microsoft for New Post Focusing on Labor Policies," *The Wall Street Journal* (January 15, 1998), B14.
26. Philip Knight, 640.
27. Patti Bond, "Nike Promises to Improve Factory Worker Conditions," *The Atlanta Journal-Constitution* (May 13, 1998), 3B.
28. Allan Wolper, "Nike's Newspaper Temptation," *Editor & Publisher* (January 10, 1998), 8–10.
29. Gregg Krupa, "Antisweatshop Activists Score in Campaign Targeting Athletic Retailers," *Boston Globe* (April 18, 1999), F1.
30. UNITE Web page, http://www.uniteunion.org/research/history/unionisborn.html.
31. Krupa, F1.
32. UNITE Web page.
33. Wolper, 8–10.
34. Wolper, 8.
35. Jodie Morse, "Campus Awakening," *Time* (April 12, 1999), 77–78.
36. Krupa, F1.
37. Morse, 77–78.
38. *Ibid.*
39. Fair Labor Association Web site, http://www.fairlabor.org.
40. *Ibid.*
41. *Ibid.*
42. Worker Rights Consortium Web site, http://www.workers rights.org/.
43. Nike Web site, http://www.nikebiz.com/labor/index.shtml.
44. Philip Knight Press Release (April 24, 1000) found at: http://www.nikebiz.com/media/n_uofo.shtml.
45. Louise Lee and Aaron Bernstein, "Who Says Student Protests Don't Matter?" *Business Week* (June 12, 1000), 96.
46. Ravina Shamdasani, "Soul Searching by 'Shoe Geeks' Led to Social Responsibility," *South China Morning Post* (May 17, 2001), 2.
47. Greg Bolt, "University of Oregon Ends Relationship with Antisweatshop Group," *The Register Guard* (March 6, 2001).
48. Hank Hager, "Frohnmayer: It's a Very Happy Day for Us," *Oregon Daily Emerald* (September 27, 2001).
49. Ron Bellamy, "Nike CEO to Resume Donations to University of Oregon," *The Register Guard* (September 26, 2001).
50. William McCall, "Nike Releases First Corporate Responsibility Report," *Associated Press State & Local Wire* (October 9, 2001).
51. *Ibid.*

Name Index

Subject Index